# HYGRADE®

## CATALOG & PRICE GUIDE OF TOPPS, DONRUSS, FLEER AND SPORTFLICS

# BASEBALL CARDS

## Features card values of virtually every baseball card issued by these manufacturers:

- **TOPPS—years 1951 to 1989**
- **DONRUSS—years 1981 to 1989**
- **FLEER—years 1981 to 1989**
- **SCORE—years 1988 to 1989**
- **SPORTFLICS—years 1986 to 1989**

Published annually in March—
every year since 1986.

Fourth Edition

**Publisher: HYGRADE SPORTS CARD CO., 5 East 17th Street, New York, N.Y. 10003**

## General Information

Card values in this catalog represent approximate retail values as of **Jan., 1989.** Due to high demand, the values of popular cards (especially rookie cards of star players from the past five years) have been fluctuating every few weeks. Keep up-to-date on the latest market values with a monthly price guide.

Information on card values was compiled from various sources including dealer ads in card magazines, dealer catalogs, card auctions, offers at card conventions, etc. **The card values in this catalog do not represent an offer to buy or sell by the publisher. We are not responsible for typographical errors.**

## What Makes a Card Valuable?

The value of a baseball card is determined by *supply* (how many cards are offered for sale at a certain price), and *demand* (how many cards buyers are willing and able to purchase at a certain price). When the demand is greater than the supply, the card's value *increases*; when supply exceeds demand, the card's value *decreases*. However, as with stamps and coins, the *condition* of a card also affects its value. Cards which have been preserved in *mint* condition are much more in demand by collectors, and therefore worth more than the same cards in worn condition. If the card shows *very light wear*, its value is usually about 65% to 80% of the price for the same card in mint condition. The more wear or damage the card shows, the less it is worth. So if you eventually hope to sell your collection for a profit, try to buy cards in the best possible condition.

## Rookie Cards

A *rookie* card is a player's first card from the *main* card set of a major card manufacturer. Today, the major card manufacturers are Topps, Donruss, Fleer, Score and Sportflics. Sometimes several players are shown on one rookie card. For example, Pete Rose is pictured with three other players on his 1963 rookie card. Occasionally a rookie card is issued one or more years after the player's actual rookie season. Each of the major manufacturers issues a main card set each year, as well as several special card sets. But in order for a card to qualify as the *rookie* card it must appear in the main card set, which is universally distributed. Sometimes special card sets, like the Topps *Traded Update*, include a player's first card, but this card is not generally considered to be a rookie card. Traded cards are only distributed though card hobby dealers, unlike cards from the main set which are sold everywhere. From 1956 to 1980 Topps was the only major card manufacturer, so each player had only one rookie card. Today there are five major card sets—so each player can have up to five rookie cards.

## Complete Sets

The total cost of the individual cards in a set is always much greater than the complete set price—which makes the complete set an economical purchase. This is because a complete set includes many common cards, and minor-star cards which a dealer will sell at a reduced price when sold as a group. The complete set value does not include any error or variety cards. Donruss factory-sealed sets issued from 1983 to date sell at a premium over hand-collated sets.

## Double-Printed Cards

Baseball cards are not printed individually, but are printed on big sheets that have space for up to 132 cards. Once printed, these sheets are cut apart, and the cards are sorted and packaged. If the number of cards on a sheet is the same as the number of cards in a set, or divides evenly into that set number, then each of the cards on the sheet shows a different player. From 1973 to 1977, Topps issued baseball sets of 660 cards. These were printed on five sheets, each with 132 different cards. But beginning in 1978 and continuing until 1981, Topps changed the number of cards in its sets from 660 to 726, an increase of 66 cards. Rather than print a sixth sheet only half filled, Topps decided to *double-print* (print twice the quantity) 66 cards in each set.

## Common Cards

*Common* cards are the lowest valued cards in a set. They are cards that feature ordinary players, not stars or popular personalities. There is very little demand by collectors for individual common cards. They are often sold in lots and used primarily to assemble card sets. A typical Topps card set includes about 60% *common* cards, 25% *minor star* cards and 15% *star* cards.

## High-Numbers

During the period from 1952 to 1973 Topps released their annual card sets in series, rather than issuing the complete set at one time as they do now. Most Topps sets consisted of six or seven card series, each released a few weeks or months apart. For example, the first series of the 1970 Topps card set had 132 cards, numbers 1 to 132; the second series contained numbers 133 to 263, etc. Since sales of the cards tended to become less and less as the season progressed, Topps usually printed fewer of the later card series, which contained the high number cards. Because the high number cards are scarcer today, they are generally more valuable as a group, than the low number cards of the same set. If the last series is not scarce, compared to other series in the same set, it is not a high number series. Every Topps set issued from 1952 to 1973 has a high number series except years 1954, 1956, 1957, 1958 and 1969.

Several Topps card sets from 1952 to 1973 also have a *semi-high-number* series. This is the next to the last series of a card set in which there is also a high number series, and the semi-high number cards are scarce. Semi-high number cards as a group are generally worth less than high numbers, but more than low numbers. Beginning in 1974 and continuing until today, Topps changed their policy and distributed their card sets all at one time, thus eliminating high numbers.

# SPECIAL CARD SETS

Beginning in 1982, major card manufacturers began issuing special card sets for exclusive distribution through specially selected retail chain stores. Many of the card sets were coated with a high gloss finish and packaged in a printed box.

## TOPPS® CHAIN STORE SETS

| Year | Exclusive Distributor | Description | Cards in Set | Value Mint |
|------|----------------------|-------------|--------------|------------|
| 1988 | Kaybee | Superstars | 33 | $4.00 |
| 1988 | Toys R Us | Rookies | 33 | 4.00 |
| 1988 | Woolworth | BB Highlights | 33 | 4.00 |
| 1988 | Rite Aid | MVP's | 33 | 4.00 |
| 1988 | Revco | League Leaders | 33 | 4.00 |
| 1987 | Boardwalk & BB | Run Makers | 33 | 4.00 |
| 1987 | K-Mart | Stars of Decade | 33 | 4.00 |
| 1987 | Kay Bee | Young Superstars | 33 | 4.00 |
| 1987 | Toys R Us | Rookies | 33 | 4.00 |
| 1987 | Woolworth | BB Highlights | 33 | 4.00 |
| 1986 | Kaybee | Superstars | 33 | 4.00 |
| 1986 | Woolworth | Champion Superstars | 33 | 5.00 |
| 1985 | Circle K | All-Time Home Run Kings | 33 | 4.00 |
| 1985 | Woolworth | All-Time Record Holders | 44 | 4.00 |
| 1982 | K-Mart | MVP's | 44 | 2.50 |

## FLEER® CHAIN STORE SETS

| Year | Exclusive Distributor | Description | Cards in Set | Value Mint |
|------|----------------------|-------------|--------------|------------|
| 1988 | Ben Franklin | All Stars | 44 | $4.00 |
| 1988 | Cumberland | Exciting Stars | 44 | 4.00 |
| 1988 | Eckerd Drug | Record Setters | 44 | 4.00 |
| 1988 | McCrory Group | Sluggers vs. Pitchers | 44 | 4.00 |
| 1988 | McCrory Group | Lim. Ed. Superstars | 44 | 4.00 |
| 1988 | Revco Drug | Hottest Stars | 44 | 4.00 |
| 1988 | Walgreen | Lim. Ed. League Leaders | 44 | 4.00 |
| 1988 | Kaybee | Team Leaders | 44 | 4.00 |
| 1988 | Toys R Us | MVP's | 44 | 4.00 |
| 1987 | 7-Eleven | Award Winners | 44 | 4.00 |
| 1987 | Ben Franklin | All-Stars | 44 | 4.00 |
| 1987 | Cumberland | Exciting Stars | 44 | 4.00 |
| 1987 | Eckerd Drug | Record Setters | 44 | 4.00 |
| 1987 | McCrory Group | Sluggers vs. Pitchers | 44 | 4.00 |
| 1987 | McCrory Group | Lim. Ed. Super Stars | 44 | 4.00 |
| 1987 | Pay 'n Save | Game Winners | 44 | 4.00 |
| 1987 | Revco Drug | Hottest Stars | 44 | 4.00 |
| 1987 | Walgreen | Lim. Ed. League Leaders | 44 | 4.00 |
| 1986 | McCrory Group | Lim. Ed. Super Stars | 44 | 4.00 |
| 1986 | McCrory Group | Sluggers vs. Pitchers | 44 | 4.00 |
| 1986 | Walgreen | Lim. Ed. League Leaders | 44 | 4.00 |
| 1985 | McCrory Group | Lim. Ed. Super Stars | 44 | 4.00 |

# RARE & FAMOUS BASEBALL CARDS

1910 Honus Wagner

1933 Goudey Gum

1933 Goudey Gum

1911 Sherry "Magie"

| Year | Manufacturer | Player | Value Near Mint |
|------|-------------|--------|-----------------|
| 1910 | T-206 Tobacco | Honus Wagner (Pitt) | $100,000.00 |
| 1910 | T-206 Tobacco | Eddie Plank (Phil) | 8,500.00 |
| 1910 | T-206 Tobacco | Ray Demmitt (St. L) | 2,000.00 |
| 1911 | T-206 Tobacco | Sherry "Magie" (misspelled) | 6,000.00 |
| 1911 | T-3 Tobacco | Ty Cobb | 2,500.00 |
| 1911 | T-3 Tobacco | Walter Johnson | 1,500.00 |
| 1911 | T-3 Tobacco | Christy Mathewson | 1,500.00 |
| 1911 | T-205 Tobacco | Ty Cobb | 1,000.00 |
| 1912 | T-207 Tobacco | Duffy Lewis (Boston N.) | 1,800.00 |
| 1914 | Cracker Jack | Ty Cobb | 1,500.00 |
| 1933 | Goudey Gum | Napoleon Lajoie | 9,500.00 |
| 1933 | Goudey Gum | Babe Ruth (4 diff. cards) | 3,000.00 each |
| 1933 | De Long Gum | Lou Gegrig | 1,500.00 |
| 1934 | Goudey Gum | Lou Gehrig (2 diff. cards) | 2,000.00 each |
| 1938 | Goudey Gum | Joe DiMaggio (2 diff. cards) | 900.00 each |
| 1940 | Play Ball (Gum, Inc.) | Joe DiMaggio | 1,000.00 |
| 1941 | Play Ball (Gum, Inc.) | Joe DiMaggio | 900.00 |
| 1948 | Leaf Gum | Satchel Paige | 1,000.00 |
| 1951 | Topps All-Stars | Jim Konstanty | 5,000.00 |
| 1951 | Topps All-Stars | Robin Roberts | 5,000.00 |
| 1951 | Topps All-Stars | Eddie Stanky | 5,000.00 |
| 1951 | Bowman Gum | Mickey Mantle | 4,500.00 |
| 1951 | Bowman Gum | Willie Mays | 1,000.00 |
| 1952 | Topps | Mickey Mantle | 6,750.00 |
| 1954 | Bowman Gum | Ted Williams | 1,500.00 |
| 1963 | Topps : | Pete Rose | 550.00 |
| 1968 | Topps 3-D | Roberto Clemente | 1,500.00 |

1910 Eddie Plank

1934 Goudey Gum

1938 Goudey Gum

1912 Duffy Lewis

# BASEBALL CARDS & SUPPLIES CATALOG & ORDER FORM

Enjoy the convenience of shopping by mail from one of America's largest card dealers—Hygrade Sports Co. You're backed by our guarantee that you must be satisfied with your purchase, or return it within 10 days for a refund.

We sell *genuine*, original Topps, Donruss, and Fleer cards in complete sets and assortments at *big* savings over individual card prices. Most orders shipped within two weeks by UPS. Select what you need and order today!

## New! 1989 Baseball Complete Card Sets...Super Special Offer!

Five major baseball card sets were issued in 1989—Topps, Donruss, Fleer, Score and Sportflics. Each card set has its own beautiful design and features all of your favorite players—Brett, Gooden, Mattingly, Henderson, Rice, Boggs, Strawberry, Clemens . . . and more! You can buy each complete card set at a much lower price than you would pay if you bought all the cards individually. And each card set is shipped in its own storage box.

### 1989 TOPPS Complete Set 792 Cards

**FREE BONUS!**
25 Card Holders (Poly)

**$34⁹⁵**

### 1989 DONRUSS Complete Set 660 Cards

**FREE BONUS!**
Hall of Fame Puzzle

**$39⁹⁵**

### 1989 FLEER Complete Set 660 Cards

**FREE BONUS!**
Team Logo Stickers

**$42⁹⁵**

## ORDER ALL 3 1989 BASEBALL CARD SETS ABOVE AND SAVE $7.90

*Special Price!*

- Complete 1989 Set of 792 Topps Baseball Cards
- Complete 1989 Set of 660 Donruss Baseball Cards
- Complete 1989 Set of 660 Fleer Baseball Cards
- All 3 Free Bonuses . . . card holders, puzzle, and team stickers

**$109⁹⁵**

## "ALL-TIME GREATS" CARD SETS

**45 ALL-TIME GREATEST HITTERS** - Joe DiMaggio, Lou Brock, Roberto Clemente, Jackie Robinson, Stan Musial, Al Kaline, Honus Wagner, Richie Ashburn . . . and more! Includes career highlights. . . . . . . . . . . . . .

**45 ALL-TIME GREATEST SLUGGERS** - Babe Ruth, Willie Mays, Hank Aaron, Ted Williams, Mickey Mantle, Lou Gehrig, Joe DiMaggio, Mel Ott, Jimmy Fox . . . and more! Includes career highlights. . . . . . . . . . . . . . . . . . .

**45 ALL-TIME GREATEST PITCHERS** - Jim "Catfish" Hunter, Whitey Ford, Satchell Paige, Bob Gibson, Cy Young, Sandy Koufax . . . more! . . . . . . . . . . . . . .

**ALL 3 SETS . . . Only $12.95 (save $1.90)**

## ASSORTMENTS OF "STAR" CARDS

Each assortment saves you money over individual card prices. Includes: Reggie Jackson, Pete Rose, Dale Murphy, George Brett, Mike Schmidt . . . and many more stars! All cards are *genuine* originals—no duplicates!

| | |
|---|---|
| 50 Topps (1978-up) . . . . . . . . . . . | $14.95 |
| 50 Donruss & Fleer (1981-up) . . | $12.95 |
| 100 Topps (1976-up) . . . . . . . . . . | $29.95 |
| 100 Donruss & Fleer (1981-up) . . | $25.95 |
| 200 Topps (1973-up) . . . . . . . . . . | $59.95 |

## HYGRADE SPORTS CARD CO.
5 East 17th Street, New York, N.Y. 10003

Credit Card
Phone Orders
(212) 807-7935

# LEGEND

**R**—the player's rookie card. Only rookie cards of "star" players are noted.

**RR**—the manufacturer's first card for that player, which is in the Traded Update or Rookie set.

**\***—there is a special feature of this card, which can be determined by referring to the headline for the set.

**AS**—a card featuring a player who was on the previous year's all-star team.

**DK**—abbreviation for Diamond King, which is a Donruss card with artwork by the Perez-Steele Gallery.

**Mgr.**—a card featuring the manager of a baseball team.

**MVP**—Most Valuable Player award

## 1951 Topps "Red Backs"...Complete Set of 52 Cards—Value $225.00 (Exc.); $350.00 (Mint)

This set, as well as the 1951 "Blue Backs", was Topps' first baseball card issue. The backs of the 2" x 2⅝" cards can be used to play a baseball card game. Card 36 was issued as either White Sox or Athletics. Card 52 was issued as either Hartford or Braves.

| NO. PLAYER | MINT |
|---|---|
| 1 Yogi Berra | 45.00 |
| 2 Sid Gordon | 4.00 |
| 3 Ferris Fain | 4.00 |
| 4 Verne Stephens | 4.00 |
| 5 Phil Rizzuto | 15.00 |
| 6 Allie Reynolds | 7.50 |
| 7 Howie Pollet | 4.00 |
| 8 Early Wynn | 12.00 |
| 9 Roy Sievers | 4.00 |
| 10 Mel Parnell | 4.00 |
| 11 Gene Hermanski | 4.00 |
| 12 Jim Hegan | 4.00 |
| 13 Dale Mitchell | 4.00 |
| 14 Wayne Terwilliger | 4.00 |
| 15 Ralph Kiner | 14.00 |
| 16 Preacher Roe | 6.00 |
| 17 Dave Bell | 4.00 |
| 18 Gerry Coleman | 4.00 |
| 19 Dick Kokos | 4.00 |
| 20 Dominick DiMaggio | 7.00 |
| 21 Larry Jansen | 4.00 |
| 22 Bob Feller | 17.00 |
| 23 Ray Boone | 4.00 |
| 24 Hank Bauer | 8.00 |
| 25 Cliffe Chambers | 4.00 |
| 26 Luke Easter | 4.00 |
| 27 Wally Westlake | 4.00 |
| 28 Elmer Valo | 4.00 |
| 29 Bob Kennedy | 4.00 |
| 30 Warren Spahn | 15.00 |
| 31 Gil Hodges | 15.00 |
| 32 Henry Thompson | 4.00 |
| 33 William Werle | 4.00 |
| 34 Grady Hatton | 4.00 |
| 35 Al Rosen* | 7.50 |
| 36 Gus Zernial* | 12.00 |
| 37 Wes Westrum | 4.00 |
| 38 Duke Snider | 35.00 |
| 39 Ted Kluszewski | 6.00 |
| 40 Mike Garcia | 4.00 |
| 41 Whitey Lockman | 4.00 |
| 42 Ray Scarborough | 4.00 |
| 43 Maurice McDermott | 4.00 |
| 44 Sid Hudson | 4.00 |
| 45 Andy Seminick | 4.00 |
| 46 Billy Goodman | 4.00 |
| 47 Tom Glaviano | 4.00 |
| 48 Ed Stanky | 4.00 |
| 49 Al Zarilla | 4.00 |
| 50 M. Irvin | 15.00 |
| 51 Eddie Robinson | 4.00 |
| 52 Tommy Holmes* | 15.00 |

## 1951 Topps "Blue Backs"....Complete Set of 52 Cards— Value $700.00 (Exc.); $1200.00 (Mint)

Similar in format to the 1951 "Red Backs." The backs of the 2" x 2⅝" cards can be used to play a baseball card game.

| NO. PLAYER | MINT |
|---|---|
| 1 Eddie Yost | 18.00 |
| 2 Hank Majeski | 17.00 |
| 3 Richie Ashburn | 35.00 |
| 4 Del Ennis | 18.00 |
| 5 Johnny Pesky | 18.00 |
| 6 Al Schoendienst | 24.00 |
| 7 Gerald Staley | 18.00 |
| 8 Dick Sisler | 18.00 |
| 9 Johnny Sain | 30.00 |
| 10 Joe Page | 25.00 |
| 11 Johnny Groth | 18.00 |
| 12 Sam Jethroe | 18.00 |
| 13 Mickey Vernon | 18.00 |
| 14 George Munger | 18.00 |
| 15 Eddie Joost | 18.00 |
| 16 Murry Dickson | 18.00 |
| 17 Roy Smalley | 18.00 |
| 18 Ned Garver | 18.00 |
| 19 Phil Masi | 18.00 |
| 20 Ralph Branca | 18.00 |
| 21 Bill Johnson | 18.00 |
| 22 Bob Kuzava | 18.00 |
| 23 Dizzy Trout | 18.00 |
| 24 Sherman Lollar | 18.00 |
| 25 Sam A. Mele | 18.00 |
| 26 Chico Carrasquel | 18.00 |
| 27 Andy Pafko | 18.00 |
| 28 Harry Brecheen | 18.00 |
| 29 Granville Hamner | 18.00 |
| 30 Enos Slaughter | 45.00 |
| 31 Lou Brissie | 18.00 |
| 32 Bob Elliott | 18.00 |
| 33 Don Lenhardt | 18.00 |
| 34 Earl Torgeson | 18.00 |
| 35 Tom Byrne (R) | 18.00 |
| 36 Cliff Fannin | 18.00 |
| 37 Bobby Doerr | 40.00 |
| 38 Irv Noren | 18.00 |
| 39 Ed Lopat | 25.00 |
| 40 Vic Wertz | 18.00 |
| 41 Johnny Schmitz | 18.00 |
| 42 Bruce Edwards | 18.00 |
| 43 Willie Jones | 18.00 |
| 44 Johnny Wyrostek | 18.00 |
| 45 Bill Pierce (R) | 25.00 |
| 46 Gerry Priddy | 18.00 |
| 47 Herman Wehmeier | 18.00 |
| 48 Billy Cox | 18.00 |
| 49 Hank Sauer | 18.00 |
| 50 John Mize | 50.00 |
| 51 Ed Waitkus | 18.00 |
| 52 Sam Chapman | 18.00 |

**Prices for the 1951 set are for cards in *Mint* condition. *Excellent* copies sell for 40% to 50% of prices shown; *Very Good*—25% to 30%.**

# 1952 Topps . . . Complete Set of 407 Cards—Value $15,000.00 (Exc.); $35,000.00 (Mint)

Features the rookie cards of Hoyt Wilhelm, Billy Martin and Eddie Mathews. This is Topps' first *major* baseball card set. Cards 1 to 80 were printed with *black* or *red* backs. The high number series is 311 to 407. Semi-high numbers are 251 to 310. Topps introduced a new card size—2⅝″ x 3¾″, used until 1956. Cards 48 and 49 exist with each other's backs transposed—worth $200.00 each.

| NO. | PLAYER | MINT | NO. | PLAYER | MINT | NO. | PLAYER | MINT | NO. | PLAYER | MINT |
|---|---|---|---|---|---|---|---|---|---|---|---|
| 1 | Andy Pafko (Exc. $20.00) | .550.00 | 69 | Virgil Stallcup | .50.00 | 137 | Roy McMillan | .20.00 | 205 | Clyde King | .20.00 |
| 2 | James Runnels | .70.00 | 70 | Al Zarilla | .50.00 | 138 | Bill MacDonald | .20.00 | 206 | Joe Ostrowski | .20.00 |
| 3 | Hank Thompson | .50.00 | 71 | Tom Upton | .50.00 | 139 | Ken Wood | .20.00 | 207 | Mickey Harris | .20.00 |
| 4 | Donald Lenhardt | .50.00 | 72 | Karl Olson | .50.00 | 140 | John Antonelli | .20.00 | 208 | Marlin Stuart | .20.00 |
| 5 | Larry Jansen | .50.00 | 73 | William Werle | .50.00 | 141 | Clint Hartung | .20.00 | 209 | Howie Fox | .20.00 |
| 6 | Grady Hatton | .50.00 | 74 | Andy Hansen | .50.00 | 142 | Harry Perkowski | .20.00 | 210 | Dick Fowler | .20.00 |
| 7 | Wayne Terwilliger | .50.00 | 75 | Wes Westrum | .50.00 | 143 | Les Moss | .20.00 | 211 | Ray Coleman | .20.00 |
| 8 | Fred Marsh | .50.00 | 76 | Eddie Stanky | .50.00 | 144 | Edward Blake | .20.00 | 212 | Ned Garver | .20.00 |
| 9 | Bob Hogue | .50.00 | 77 | Bob Kennedy | .50.00 | 145 | Joe Haynes | .20.00 | 213 | Nippy Jones | .20.00 |
| 10 | Al Rosen | .60.00 | 78 | Ellis Kinder | .50.00 | 146 | Frank House | .20.00 | 214 | Johnny Hopp | .20.00 |
| 11 | Phil Rizzuto | .120.00 | 79 | Gerald Staley | .50.00 | 147 | Bob Young | .20.00 | 215 | Hank Bauer | .35.00 |
| 12 | Monty Basgall | .50.00 | 80 | Herman Wehmeier | .50.00 | 148 | John Klippstein | .20.00 | 216 | Richie Ashburn | .40.00 |
| 13 | Johnny Wyrostek | .50.00 | 81 | Vernon Law | .20.00 | 149 | Dick Kryhoski | .20.00 | 217 | George Stirnweiss | .20.00 |
| 14 | Bob Elliott | .50.00 | 82 | Duane Pillette | .20.00 | 150 | Ted Beard | .20.00 | 218 | Clyde McCullough | .20.00 |
| 15 | Johnny Pesky | .50.00 | 83 | Billy Johnson | .20.00 | 151 | Wally Post | .20.00 | 219 | Bobby Shantz | .20.00 |
| 16 | Gene Hermanski | .50.00 | 84 | Vern Stephens | .20.00 | 152 | Al Evans | .20.00 | 220 | Joe Presko | .20.00 |
| 17 | Jim Hegan | .50.00 | 85 | Bob Kuzava | .20.00 | 153 | Bob Rush | .20.00 | 221 | Granny Hamner | .20.00 |
| 18 | Merrill Combs | .50.00 | 86 | Teddy Gray | .20.00 | 154 | Joe Muir | .20.00 | 222 | Walter Evers | .20.00 |
| 19 | John Bucha | .50.00 | 87 | Dale Coogan | .20.00 | 155 | Frank Overmire | .20.00 | 223 | Del Ennis | .20.00 |
| 20 | Billy Loes | .70.00 | 88 | Bob Feller | .95.00 | 156 | Frank Hiller | .20.00 | 224 | Bruce Edwards | .20.00 |
| 21 | Ferris Fain | .50.00 | 89 | Johnny Lipon | .20.00 | 157 | Bob Usher | .20.00 | 225 | Frank Baumholtz | .20.00 |
| 22 | Dom DiMaggio | .60.00 | 90 | Mickey Grasso | .20.00 | 158 | Eddie Waitkus | .20.00 | 226 | Dave Philley | .20.00 |
| 23 | Billy Goodman | .50.00 | 91 | Al Schoendienst | .30.00 | 159 | Saul Rogovin | .20.00 | 227 | Joe Garagiola | .55.00 |
| 24 | Luke Easter | .50.00 | 92 | Dale Mitchell | .20.00 | 160 | Owen Friend | .20.00 | 228 | Al Brazle | .20.00 |
| 25 | Johnny Grothe | .50.00 | 93 | Al Sima | .20.00 | 161 | Bud Byerly | .20.00 | 229 | Gene Bearden | .20.00 |
| 26 | Monte Irvin | .80.00 | 94 | Sam Mele | .20.00 | 162 | Del Crandall | .20.00 | 230 | Matt Batts | .20.00 |
| 27 | Sam Jethroe | .50.00 | 95 | Ken Holcombe | .20.00 | 163 | Stan Rojek | .20.00 | 231 | Sam Zoldak | .20.00 |
| 28 | Jerry Priddy | .50.00 | 96 | Willard Marshall | .20.00 | 164 | Walt Dubiel | .20.00 | 232 | Billy Cox | .20.00 |
| 29 | Ted Kluszewski | .70.00 | 97 | Earl Torgeson | .20.00 | 165 | Ed Kazak | .20.00 | 233 | Bob Friend | .20.00 |
| 30 | Mel Parnell | .50.00 | 98 | Bill Pierce | .20.00 | 166 | Paul LaPalme | .20.00 | 234 | Steve Souchock | .20.00 |
| 31 | Gus Zernial | .50.00 | 99 | Gene Woodling | .35.00 | 167 | Bill Howerton | .20.00 | 235 | Walt Dropo | .20.00 |
| 32 | Eddie Robinson | .50.00 | 100 | Del Rice | .20.00 | 168 | Charlie Silvera | .20.00 | 236 | Ed Fitzgerald | .20.00 |
| 33 | Warren Spahn | .135.00 | 101 | Max Lanier | .20.00 | 169 | Howie Judson | .20.00 | 237 | Jerry Coleman | .20.00 |
| 34 | Elmer Valo | .50.00 | 102 | Bill Kennedy | .20.00 | 170 | Gus Bell | .20.00 | 238 | Art Houtteman | .20.00 |
| 35 | Hank Sauer | .50.00 | 103 | Cliff Mapes | .20.00 | 171 | Ed Erautt | .20.00 | 239 | Rocky Bridges | .20.00 |
| 36 | Gil Hodges | .100.00 | 104 | Don Kolloway | .20.00 | 172 | Eddie Miksis | .20.00 | 240 | Jack Phillips | .20.00 |
| 37 | Duke Snider | .200.00 | 105 | John Pramesa | .20.00 | 173 | Roy Smalley | .20.00 | 241 | Tommy Byrne | .20.00 |
| 38 | Wally Westlake | .50.00 | 106 | Mickey Vernon | .20.00 | 174 | Clarence Marshall | .20.00 | 242 | Tom Poholsky | .20.00 |
| 39 | Dizzy Trout | .50.00 | 107 | Connie Ryan | .20.00 | 175 | Billy Martin (R) | .180.00 | 243 | Larry Doby | .35.00 |
| 40 | Irv Noren | .50.00 | 108 | Jimmy Konstanty | .20.00 | 176 | Hank Edwards | .20.00 | 244 | Vic Wertz | .20.00 |
| 41 | Bob Wellman | .50.00 | 109 | Ted Wilks | .20.00 | 177 | Bill Wight | .20.00 | 245 | Sherry Robertson | .20.00 |
| 42 | Lou Kretlow | .50.00 | 110 | Dutch Leonard | .20.00 | 178 | Cass Michaels | .20.00 | 246 | George Kell | .50.00 |
| 43 | Ray Scarborough | .50.00 | 111 | Harry Lowrey | .20.00 | 179 | Frank Smith | .20.00 | 247 | Randy Gumpert | .20.00 |
| 44 | Con Dempsey | .50.00 | 112 | Henry Majeski | .20.00 | 180 | Charley Maxwell | .20.00 | 248 | Frank Shea | .20.00 |
| 45 | Ed Joost | .50.00 | 113 | Dick Sisler | .20.00 | 181 | Bob Swift | .20.00 | 249 | Bobby Adams | .20.00 |
| 46 | Gordon Goldsberry | .50.00 | 114 | Willard Ramsdell | .20.00 | 182 | Bill Hitchcock | .20.00 | 250 | Carl Erskine | .35.00 |
| 47 | Willie Jones | .50.00 | 115 | George Munger | .20.00 | 183 | Erv Dusak | .20.00 | 251 | Chico Carrasquel | .35.00 |
| 48 | Joe Page* | .75.00 | 116 | Carl Scheib | .20.00 | 184 | Bob Ramazzotti | .20.00 | 252 | Vern Bickford | .35.00 |
| 49 | Johnny Sain* | .75.00 | 117 | Sherman Lollar | .20.00 | 185 | Bill Nicholson | .20.00 | 253 | Johnny Berardino | .35.00 |
| 50 | Marv Rickertt | .50.00 | 118 | Ken Raffensberger | .20.00 | 186 | Walt Masterson | .20.00 | 254 | Joe Dobson | .35.00 |
| 51 | Jim Russell | .50.00 | 119 | Maurice McDermott | .20.00 | 187 | Bob Miller | .20.00 | 255 | Clyde Vollmer | .35.00 |
| 52 | Don Mueller | .50.00 | 120 | Bob Chakales | .20.00 | 188 | Clarence Podbielan | .20.00 | 256 | Pete Suder | .35.00 |
| 53 | Chris Van Cuyk | .50.00 | 121 | Gus Niarhos | .20.00 | 189 | Harold Reiser | .20.00 | 257 | Bob Avila | .35.00 |
| 54 | Leo Kiely | .50.00 | 122 | Jack Jensen | .35.00 | 190 | Don Johnson | .20.00 | 258 | Steve Gromek | .35.00 |
| 55 | Ray Boone | .50.00 | 123 | Eddie Yost | .20.00 | 191 | Yogi Berra | .200.00 | 259 | Bob Addis | .35.00 |
| 56 | Tom Glaviano | .50.00 | 124 | Monte Kennedy | .20.00 | 192 | Myron Ginsberg | .20.00 | 260 | Pete Castiglione | .35.00 |
| 57 | Eddie Lopat | .70.00 | 125 | Bill Rigney | .20.00 | 193 | Harry Simpson | .20.00 | 261 | Willie Mays | .900.00 |
| 58 | Bob Mahoney | .50.00 | 126 | Fred Hutchinson | .20.00 | 194 | Joe Hatten | .20.00 | 262 | Virgil Trucks | .35.00 |
| 59 | Robin Roberts | .100.00 | 127 | Paul Minner | .20.00 | 195 | Orestes Minoso (R) | .25.00 | 263 | Harry Brecheen | .35.00 |
| 60 | Sid Hudson | .50.00 | 128 | Don Bollweg | .20.00 | 196 | Solly Hemus | .20.00 | 264 | Roy Hartsfield | .35.00 |
| 61 | Tookie Gilbert | .50.00 | 129 | Johnny Mize | .60.00 | 197 | George Strickland | .20.00 | 265 | Chuck Diering | .35.00 |
| 62 | Chuck Stobbs | .50.00 | 130 | Sheldon Jones | .20.00 | 198 | Phil Haugstad | .20.00 | 266 | Murry Dickson | .35.00 |
| 63 | Howie Pollett | .50.00 | 131 | Morris Martin | .20.00 | 199 | George Zuverink | .20.00 | 267 | Sid Gordon | .35.00 |
| 64 | Roy Sievers | .50.00 | 132 | Clyde Klutz | .20.00 | 200 | Ralph Houk (R) | .50.00 | 268 | Bob Lemon | .125.00 |
| 65 | Enos Slaughter | .90.00 | 133 | Al Widmar | .20.00 | 201 | Alex Kellner | .20.00 | 269 | Willard Nixon | .35.00 |
| 66 | Preacher Roe | .60.00 | 134 | Joe Tipton | .20.00 | 202 | Joe Collins | .20.00 | 270 | Lou Brissie | .35.00 |
| 67 | Allie Reynolds | .65.00 | 135 | Dixie Howell | .20.00 | 203 | Curt Simmons | .20.00 | 271 | Jim Delsing | .35.00 |
| 68 | Cliff Chambers | .50.00 | 136 | Johnny Schmitz | .20.00 | 204 | Ron Northey | .20.00 | 272 | Mike Garcia | .35.00 |

# 1952 Topps (Continued)

| NO. | PLAYER | MINT | NO. | PLAYER | MINT | NO. | PLAYER | MINT | NO. | PLAYER | MINT |
|---|---|---|---|---|---|---|---|---|---|---|---|
| 273 | Erv Palica | 35.00 | 307 | Frank Campos | 35.00 | 341 | Hal Jeffcoat | 125.00 | 375 | Jack Merson | 125.00 |
| 274 | Ralph Branca | 35.00 | 308 | Luis Aloma | 35.00 | 342 | Clem Labine | 125.00 | 376 | Faye Throneberry | 125.00 |
| 275 | Pat Mullin | 35.00 | 309 | Jim Busby | 35.00 | 343 | Dick Gernert | 125.00 | 377 | Chuck Dressen | 150.00 |
| 276 | Jim Wilson | 35.00 | 310 | George Metkovich | 35.00 | 344 | Ewell Blackwell | 125.00 | 378 | Les Fusselman | 125.00 |
| 277 | Early Wynn | 150.00 | 311 | M. Mantle (Exc. $3000.00) | 6750.00 | 345 | Sammy White | 125.00 | 379 | Joe Rossi | 125.00 |
| 278 | Al Clark | 35.00 | 312 | Jackie Robinson | 700.00 | 346 | George Spencer | 125.00 | 380 | Clem Koshorek | 125.00 |
| 279 | Ed Stewart | 35.00 | 313 | Bobby Thomson | 150.00 | 347 | Joe Adcock | 125.00 | 381 | Milton Stock | 125.00 |
| 280 | Cloyd Boyer | 35.00 | 314 | Roy Campanella | 1200.00 | 348 | Bob Kelly | 125.00 | 382 | Samuel Jones | 125.00 |
| 281 | Tom Brown | 45.00 | 315 | Leo Durocher (Mgr) | 225.00 | 349 | Bob Cain | 125.00 | 383 | Del Wilber | 125.00 |
| 282 | Birdie Tebbetts | 45.00 | 316 | Dave Williams | 125.00 | 350 | Cal Abrams | 125.00 | 384 | Frank Crosetti | 225.00 |
| 283 | Phil Masi | 45.00 | 317 | Connie Marrerro | 125.00 | 351 | Alvin Dark | 165.00 | 385 | Herman Franks | 125.00 |
| 284 | Hank Arft | 45.00 | 318 | Hal Gregg | 125.00 | 352 | Karl Drews | 125.00 | 386 | Eddie Yuhas | 125.00 |
| 285 | Cliff Fannin | 45.00 | 319 | Al Walker | 125.00 | 353 | Robert Del Greco | 125.00 | 387 | Bill Meyer | 125.00 |
| 286 | Joe DeMaestri | 45.00 | 320 | John Rutherford | 125.00 | 354 | Fred Hatfield | 125.00 | 388 | Bob Chipman | 125.00 |
| 287 | Steve Bilko | 45.00 | 321 | Joe Black (R) | 125.00 | 355 | Bobby Morgan | 125.00 | 389 | Ben Wade | 125.00 |
| 288 | Chet Nichols | 45.00 | 322 | Randy Jackson | 125.00 | 356 | Toby Atwell | 125.00 | 390 | Glenn Nelson | 125.00 |
| 289 | Tommy Holmes | 45.00 | 323 | Bubba Church | 125.00 | 357 | Smokey Burgess | 150.00 | 391 | Ben Chapman | 125.00 |
| 290 | Joe Astroth | 45.00 | 324 | Warren Hacker | 125.00 | 358 | John Kucab | 125.00 | | (photo of Sam Chapman) | |
| 291 | Gil Coan | 45.00 | 325 | Bill Serena | 125.00 | 359 | Dee Fondy | 125.00 | 392 | Hoyt Wilhelm (R) | 400.00 |
| 292 | Floyd Baker | 45.00 | 326 | George Shuba | 125.00 | 360 | George Crowe | 125.00 | 393 | Ebba St. Claire | 125.00 |
| 293 | Sibby Sisti | 45.00 | 327 | Archie Wilson | 125.00 | 361 | Bill Posedel | 125.00 | 394 | Billy Herman | 165.00 |
| 294 | Walker Cooper | 45.00 | 328 | Bob Borkowski | 125.00 | 362 | Kenny Heintzelman | 125.00 | 395 | Jake Pitler | 125.00 |
| 295 | Phil Cavarretta | 45.00 | 329 | Ivan Delock | 125.00 | 363 | Dick Rozek | 125.00 | 396 | Dick Williams (R) | 150.00 |
| 296 | Red Rolfe | 45.00 | 330 | Turk Lown | 125.00 | 364 | Clyde Sukeforth | 125.00 | 397 | Forrest Main | 125.00 |
| 297 | Andy Seminick | 45.00 | 331 | Tom Morgan | 125.00 | 365 | Cookie Lavagetto | 125.00 | 398 | Hal Rice | 125.00 |
| 298 | Bob Ross | 45.00 | 332 | Anthony Bartirome | 125.00 | 366 | Dave Madison | 125.00 | 399 | Jim Fridley | 125.00 |
| 299 | Ray Murray | 45.00 | 333 | Pee Wee Reese | 500.00 | 367 | Bob Thorpe | 125.00 | 400 | Bill Dickey | 450.00 |
| 300 | Barney McCosky | 45.00 | 334 | Wilmer Mizell | 125.00 | 368 | Ed Wright | 125.00 | 401 | Bob Schultz | 125.00 |
| 301 | Bob Porterfield | 35.00 | 335 | Ted Lepcio | 125.00 | 369 | Dick Groat (R) | 225.00 | 402 | Earl Harrist | 125.00 |
| 302 | Max Surkont | 35.00 | 336 | Dave Koslo | 125.00 | 370 | Bill Hoeft | 125.00 | 403 | Bill Miller | 125.00 |
| 303 | Harry Dorish | 35.00 | 337 | Jim Hearn | 125.00 | 371 | Bob Hofman | 125.00 | 404 | Dick Brodowski | 125.00 |
| 304 | Sam Dente | 35.00 | 338 | Sal Yvars | 125.00 | 372 | Gil McDougald (R) | 225.00 | 405 | Eddie Pellagrini | 125.00 |
| 305 | Paul Richards | 35.00 | 339 | Russ Meyer | 125.00 | 373 | Jim Turner | 125.00 | 406 | Joseph Nuxhall (R) | 160.00 |
| 306 | Lou Sleater | 35.00 | 340 | Bob Hooper | 125.00 | 374 | Al Benton | 125.00 | 407 | E. Mathews (R) | 1500.00 |
| | | | | | | | | | | (Exc. $300.00) | |

Prices for the 1952 set are for cards in *Mint* condition. Cards no's. 2 to 80: *Excellent*—20%; *Very Good*—10%.
Cards no's. 81 to 310: *Excellent*—30%; *Very Good*—15%. Cards no's. 311 to 406: *Excellent*—50%; *Very Good*—30%.

# 1953 Topps. . . .Complete Set of 274 Cards—Value $3250.00 (Exc.); $8500.00 (Mint)

Features the rookie cards of Johnny Padres and Jim Gilliam. Although the cards are numbered up to 280, there are only 274 cards in the set. Six cards were not issued—numbers 253, 261, 267, 268, 271 and 275. The high number series is 221 to 280. Card size 2⅝″ x 3¾″.

| NO. | PLAYER | MINT | NO. | PLAYER | MINT | NO. | PLAYER | MINT | NO. | PLAYER | MINT |
|---|---|---|---|---|---|---|---|---|---|---|---|
| 1 | J. Robinson (Exc. $100.00) | 375.00 | 23 | Toby Atwell | 13.00 | 45 | Grady Hatton | 13.00 | 67 | Roy Sievers | 13.00 |
| 2 | Luke Easter | 13.00 | 24 | Ferris Fain | 13.00 | 46 | John Klippstein | 13.00 | 68 | Del Rice | 13.00 |
| 3 | George Crowe | 13.00 | 25 | R. Boone | 13.00 | 47 | Bubba Church | 13.00 | 69 | Dick Brodowski | 13.00 |
| 4 | Benjamin Wade | 13.00 | 26 | Dale Mitchell | 13.00 | 48 | Bob Del Greco | 13.00 | 70 | Eddie Yuhas | 13.00 |
| 5 | Joe Dobson | 13.00 | 27 | Roy Campanella | 125.00 | 49 | Faye Throneberry | 13.00 | 71 | Tony Bartirome | 13.00 |
| 6 | Sam Jones | 13.00 | 28 | Eddie Pellagrini | 13.00 | 50 | Chuck Dressenn | 13.00 | 72 | Fred Hutchison | 13.00 |
| 7 | Bob Borkowski | 12.00 | 29 | Hal Jeffcoat | 13.00 | 51 | Frank Campos | 13.00 | 73 | Eddie Robinson | 13.00 |
| 8 | Clem Koshorek | 12.00 | 30 | Willard Nixon | 13.00 | 52 | Ted Gray | 13.00 | 74 | Joe Rossi | 13.00 |
| 9 | Joe Collins | 12.00 | 31 | Ewell Blackwell | 25.00 | 53 | Sherman Lollar | 13.00 | 75 | Mike Garcia | 13.00 |
| 10 | Smokey Burgess | 18.00 | 32 | Clyde Vollmer | 13.00 | 54 | Bob Feller | 65.00 | 76 | Pee Wee Reese | 75.00 |
| 11 | Sal Yvars | 13.00 | 33 | Bob Kennedy | 13.00 | 55 | Maurice McDermott | 13.00 | 77 | John Mize | 40.00 |
| 12 | Howie Judson | 12.00 | 34 | George Shuba | 13.00 | 56 | Gerald Staley | 13.00 | 78 | Al Schoendienst | 20.00 |
| 13 | Connie Marrero | 13.00 | 35 | Irv Noren | 13.00 | 57 | Carl Scheib | 13.00 | 79 | Johnny Wyrostek | 13.00 |
| 14 | Clem Labine | 12.00 | 36 | Johnny Groth | 13.00 | 58 | George Metkovich | 13.00 | 80 | Jim Hegan | 13.00 |
| 15 | Bobo Newsom | 12.00 | 37 | Ed Mathews | 65.00 | 59 | Karl Drews | 13.00 | 81 | Joe Black | 20.00 |
| 16 | Harry Lowrey | 11.00 | 38 | Jim Hearn | 13.00 | 60 | Cloyd Boyer | 13.00 | 82 | Mickey Mantle | 1650.00 |
| 17 | Billy Hitchcock | 13.00 | 39 | Eddie Miksis | 13.00 | 61 | Early Wynn | 50.00 | 83 | Howie Pollett | 13.00 |
| 18 | Ted Lepcio | 12.00 | 40 | Johnny Lipon | 13.00 | 62 | Monte Irvin | 25.00 | 84 | Bob Hooper | 13.00 |
| 19 | Melvin Parnell | 13.00 | 41 | Enos Slaughter | 45.00 | 63 | Gus Niarhos | 12.00 | 85 | Bobby Morgan | 13.00 |
| 20 | Hank Thompson | 13.00 | 42 | Gus Zernial | 13.00 | 64 | David Philley | 13.00 | 86 | Billy Martin | 50.00 |
| 21 | Billy Johnson | 13.00 | 43 | Gil McDougald | 25.00 | 65 | Earl Harrist | 13.00 | 87 | Ed Lopat | 17.00 |
| 22 | Howie Fox | 13.00 | 44 | Ellis Kinder | 13.00 | 66 | Orestes Minoso | 20.00 | 88 | Willie Jones | 11.00 |

9

# 1953 Topps (Continued)

| NO. PLAYER | MINT | NO. PLAYER | MINT | NO. PLAYER | MINT | NO. PLAYER | MINT |
|---|---|---|---|---|---|---|---|
| 89 Chuck Stobbs | 12.00 | 136 Ken Heintzelman | 13.00 | 183 Stuart Miller | 10.00 | 229 Rocky Krsnich | 40.00 |
| 90 Hank Edwards | 12.00 | 137 John Rutherford | 13.00 | 184 Hal Brown | 10.00 | 230 Johnny Lindell | 40.00 |
| 91 Ebba St. Claire | 12.00 | 138 George Kell | 32.00 | 185 Jim Pendleton | 10.00 | 231 Solly Hemus | 40.00 |
| 92 Paul Minner | 12.00 | 139 Sammy White | 12.00 | 186 Charles Bishop | 10.00 | 232 Dick Kokos | 40.00 |
| 93 Hal Rice | 12.00 | 140 Tommy Glaviano | 12.00 | 187 Jim Fridley | 10.00 | 233 Al Aber | 40.00 |
| 94 William Kennedy | 12.00 | 141 Allie Reynolds | 20.00 | 188 Andy Carey | 10.00 | 234 Ray Murray | 40.00 |
| 95 Willard Marshall | 12.00 | 142 Vic Wertz | 12.00 | 189 Ray Jablonski | 10.00 | 235 John Hetki | 40.00 |
| 96 Virgil Trucks | 12.00 | 143 Billy Pierce | 12.00 | 190 Dixie Walker | 10.00 | 236 Harold Perkowski | 40.00 |
| 97 Don Kolloway | 12.00 | 144 Bob Schultz | 12.00 | 191 Ralph Kiner | 35.00 | 237 Clarence Podbielan | 40.00 |
| 98 Cal Abrams | 12.00 | 145 Harry Dorish | 12.00 | 192 Wally Westlake | 10.00 | 238 Cal Hogue | 40.00 |
| 99 Dave Madison | 12.00 | 146 Granville Hamner | 12.00 | 193 Mike Clark | 10.00 | 239 Jim Delsing | 40.00 |
| 100 Bill Miller | 12.00 | 147 Warren Spahn | 65.00 | 194 Eddie Kazak | 10.00 | 240 Fred Marsh | 40.00 |
| 101 Ted Wilks | 12.00 | 148 Mickey Grasso | 12.00 | 195 Eddie McGhee | 10.00 | 241 Al Sima | 40.00 |
| 102 Connie Ryan | 12.00 | 149 Dom DiMaggio | 18.00 | 196 Bob Keegan | 10.00 | 242 Charlie Silvera | 40.00 |
| 103 Joe Astroth | 12.00 | 150 Harry Simpson | 12.00 | 197 Del Crandall | 10.00 | 243 Carlos Bernier | 40.00 |
| 104 Yogi Berra | 120.00 | 151 Hoyt Wilhelm | 35.00 | 198 Forrest Main | 10.00 | 244 Willie Mays | 1200.00 |
| 105 Joe Nuxhall | 13.00 | 152 Bob Adams | 12.00 | 199 Marion Fricano | 10.00 | 245 Bill Norman | 40.00 |
| 106 John Antonelli | 13.00 | 153 Andy Seminick | 12.00 | 200 Gordon Goldsberry | 10.00 | 246 Roy Face (R) | 60.00 |
| 107 Danny O'Connell | 13.00 | 154 Dick Groat | 15.00 | 201 Paul LaPalme | 10.00 | 247 Mike Sandlock | 40.00 |
| 108 Bob Porterfield | 13.00 | 155 Dutch Leonard | 12.00 | 202 Carl Sawatski | 10.00 | 248 Gene Stephens | 40.00 |
| 109 Alvin Dark | 18.00 | 156 Jim Rivera | 12.00 | 203 Cliff Fannin | 10.00 | 249 Ed O'Brien | 40.00 |
| 110 Herman Wehmeier | 12.00 | 157 Bob Addis | 12.00 | 204 Dick Bokelmann | 10.00 | 250 Bob Wilson | 40.00 |
| 111 Hank Sauer | 12.00 | 158 Jim Logan | 12.00 | 205 Vern Benson | 10.00 | 251 Sid Hudson | 40.00 |
| 112 Ned Garver | 12.00 | 159 Wayne Terwilliger | 12.00 | 206 Ed Bailey | 10.00 | 252 Henry Foiles | 40.00 |
| 113 Jerry Priddy | 12.00 | 160 Bob Young | 12.00 | 207 Whitey Ford | 65.00 | 254 Preacher Roe | 70.00 |
| 114 Phil Rizzuto | 50.00 | 161 Vern Bickford | 12.00 | 208 Jim Wilson | 10.00 | 255 Dixie Howell | 40.00 |
| 115 George Spencer | 13.00 | 162 Ted Kluszewski | 22.00 | 209 Jim Greengrass | 10.00 | 256 Les Peden | 40.00 |
| 116 Frank Smith | 13.00 | 163 Fred Hatfield | 12.00 | 210 Bob Cerv | 10.00 | 257 Bob Boyd | 40.00 |
| 117 Sidney Gordon | 13.00 | 164 Frank Shea | 12.00 | 211 J.W. Porter | 10.00 | 258 Jim Gilliam (R) | 200.00 |
| 118 Gus Bell | 13.00 | 165 Billy Hoeft | 12.00 | 212 Jack Dittmer | 10.00 | 259 Roy McMillan | 40.00 |
| 119 Johnny Sain | 20.00 | 166 Bill Hunter | 10.00 | 213 Ray Scarborough | 10.00 | 260 Sam Calderone | 40.00 |
| 120 Davey Williams | 13.00 | 167 Art Schult | 10.00 | 214 Bill Bruton | 10.00 | 262 Bob Oldis | 40.00 |
| 121 Walt Dropo | 13.00 | 168 Willard Schmidt | 10.00 | 215 Gene Conley | 10.00 | 263 John Podres (R) | 225.00 |
| 122 Elmer Valo | 13.00 | 169 Dizzy Trout | 10.00 | 216 Jim Hughes | 10.00 | 264 Gene Woodling | 60.00 |
| 123 Tommy Byrne | 13.00 | 170 Bill Werle | 10.00 | 217 Murray Wall | 10.00 | 265 Jackie Jensen | 70.00 |
| 124 Sibby Sisti | 13.00 | 171 Bill Glynn | 10.00 | 218 Les Fusselman | 10.00 | 266 Bob Cain | 40.00 |
| 125 Dick Williams | 15.00 | 172 Rip Repulski | 10.00 | 219 Pete Runnels | 10.00 | 269 Duane Pillette | 40.00 |
| 126 Billy Connelly | 12.00 | 173 Preston Ward | 10.00 | (Photo of Don Johnson) | | 270 Vern Stephens | 40.00 |
| 127 Clint Courtney | 12.00 | 174 Billy Loes | 10.00 | 220 Satchell Paige | 200.00 | 272 Bill Antonello | 40.00 |
| 128 Wilmer Mizell | 12.00 | 175 Ronald Kline | 10.00 | 221 Bob Milliken | 40.00 | 273 Harvey Haddix (R) | 50.00 |
| 129 Keith Thomas | 12.00 | 176 Don Hoak | 10.00 | 222 Vic Janowicz | 40.00 | 274 John Riddle | 40.00 |
| 130 Turk Lown | 12.00 | 177 Jim Dyck | 10.00 | 223 John O'Brien | 40.00 | 276 Ken Raffensberger | 40.00 |
| 131 Harry Byrd | 12.00 | 178 Jim Waugh | 10.00 | 224 Lou Sleater | 40.00 | 277 Don Lund | 40.00 |
| 132 Tom Morgan | 12.00 | 179 Gene Hermanski | 10.00 | 225 Bobby Shantz | 50.00 | 278 Willie Miranda | 40.00 |
| 133 Gil Coan | 12.00 | 180 Virgil Stallcup | 10.00 | 226 Edward Erautt | 40.00 | 279 Joe Coleman | 40.00 |
| 134 Rube Walker | 12.00 | 181 Al Zarilla | 10.00 | 227 Morris Martin | 40.00 | 280 M. Boling (R) (Exc. $30.00) | 200.00 |
| 135 Al Rosen | 20.00 | 182 Robert Hofman | 10.00 | 228 Hal Newhouser | 65.00 | | |

**Prices for the 1953 set are for cards in *Mint* condition. *Excellent* copies sell for 40% to 50% of prices shown; *Very Good*—25% to 30%.**

## 1954 Topps....Complete Set of 250 Cards—Value $2000.00 (Exc.); $5250.00 (Mint)

Features the rookie cards of Hank Aaron, Al Kaline and Ernie Banks. Card size 2⅝" x 3¾". Topps' signed Ted Williams to a special contract for this set, and he appears on two cards.

| NO. PLAYER | MINT | NO. PLAYER | MINT | NO. PLAYER | MINT | NO. PLAYER | MINT |
|---|---|---|---|---|---|---|---|
| 1 Ted Williams (Exc. $70.00) | 350.00 | 6 Pete Runnels | 7.00 | 11 Paul Smith | 7.00 | 16 Vic Janowicz | 7.00 |
| 2 Gus Zernial | 8.00 | 7 Ted Kluszewski | 12.00 | 12 Del Crandall | 7.00 | 17 Phil Rizzuto | 35.00 |
| 3 Monte Irvin | 20.00 | 8 Bobby Young | 7.00 | 13 Billy Martin | 35.00 | 18 Walt Dropo | 7.00 |
| 4 Hank Sauer | 7.00 | 9 Harvey Haddix | 7.00 | 14 Preacher Roe | 10.00 | 19 Johnny Lipon | 7.00 |
| 5 Ed Lopat | 12.00 | 10 Jackie Robinson | 150.00 | 15 Al Rosen | 10.00 | 20 Warren Spahn | 45.00 |

| NO. | PLAYER | MINT |
|---|---|---|
| 21 | Bobby Shantz | 8.00 |
| 22 | Jim Greengrass | 7.00 |
| 23 | Luke Easter | 7.00 |
| 24 | Granny Hamner | 7.00 |
| 25 | Harv. Kuenn (R) | 15.00 |
| 26 | Ray Jablonski | 7.00 |
| 27 | Ferris Fain | 7.00 |
| 28 | Paul Minner | 7.00 |
| 29 | Jim Hegan | 7.00 |
| 30 | Ed Mathews | 35.00 |
| 31 | John Klippstein | 7.00 |
| 32 | Duke Snider | 85.00 |
| 33 | Johnny Schmitz | 7.00 |
| 34 | Jim Rivera | 7.00 |
| 35 | Junior Gilliam | 12.00 |
| 36 | Hoyt Wilhelm | 18.00 |
| 37 | Whitey Ford | 45.00 |
| 38 | Eddie Stanky | 7.00 |
| 39 | Sherm Lollar | 7.00 |
| 40 | Mel Parnell | 7.00 |
| 41 | Willie Jones | 7.00 |
| 42 | Don Mueller | 7.00 |
| 43 | Dick Groat | 9.00 |
| 44 | Ned Garver | 7.00 |
| 45 | Richie Ashburn | 15.00 |
| 46 | Ken Raffensberger | 7.00 |
| 47 | Ellis Kinder | 7.00 |
| 48 | Bill Hunter | 7.00 |
| 49 | Ray Murray | 7.00 |
| 50 | Y. Berra | 95.00 |
| 51 | Johnny Lindell | 12.00 |
| 52 | Vic Power | 12.00 |
| 53 | Jack Dittmer | 12.00 |
| 54 | Vern Stephens | 12.00 |
| 55 | Phil Cavarretta | 12.00 |
| 56 | Willie Miranda | 12.00 |
| 57 | Luis Aloma | 12.00 |
| 58 | Bob Wilson | 12.00 |
| 59 | Gene Conley | 12.00 |
| 60 | Frank Baumholtz | 12.00 |
| 61 | Bob Cain | 12.00 |
| 62 | Eddie Robinson | 12.00 |
| 63 | Johnny Pesky | 12.00 |
| 64 | Hank Thompson | 12.00 |
| 65 | Bob Swift | 12.00 |
| 66 | Thad Lepcio | 12.00 |
| 67 | Jim Willis | 12.00 |
| 68 | Sammy Calderone | 12.00 |
| 69 | Bud Podbielan | 12.00 |
| 70 | Larry Doby | 25.00 |
| 71 | Frank Smith | 12.00 |
| 72 | Preston Ward | 12.00 |
| 73 | Wayne Terwilliger | 12.00 |
| 74 | Bill Taylor | 12.00 |
| 75 | Fred Haney | 12.00 |
| 76 | Bob Scheffing | 8.00 |
| 77 | Ray Boone | 8.00 |
| 78 | Ted Kazanski | 8.00 |
| 79 | Andy Pafko | 8.00 |
| 80 | Jackie Jensen | 9.00 |
| 81 | Dave Hoskins | 8.00 |
| 82 | Milt Bolling | 8.00 |
| 83 | Joe Collins | 8.00 |
| 84 | Dick Cole | 8.00 |
| 85 | Bob Turley (R) | 13.00 |
| 86 | Billy Herman | 12.00 |
| 87 | Roy Face | 8.00 |
| 88 | Matt Batts | 8.00 |
| 89 | Howie Pollet | 8.00 |
| 90 | Willie Mays | 200.00 |
| 91 | Bob Oldis | 8.00 |
| 92 | Wally Westlake | 8.00 |
| 93 | Sid Hudson | 8.00 |
| 94 | Ernie Banks (R) | 400.00 |
| 95 | Hal Rice | 9.00 |
| 96 | Charlie Silvera | 9.00 |
| 97 | Jerry Lane | 9.00 |
| 98 | Joe Black | 10.00 |
| 99 | Bob Hofman | 9.00 |
| 100 | Bob Keegan | 9.00 |
| 101 | Gene Woodling | 11.00 |
| 102 | Gil Hodges | 40.00 |
| 103 | Jim Lemon | 9.00 |
| 104 | Mike Sandlock | 9.00 |
| 105 | Andy Carey | 9.00 |
| 106 | Dick Kokos | 9.00 |
| 107 | Duane Pillette | 9.00 |
| 108 | Thornton Kipper | 9.00 |
| 109 | Bill Bruton | 9.00 |
| 110 | Harry Dorish | 9.00 |
| 111 | Jim Delsing | 9.00 |
| 112 | Bill Renna | 9.00 |
| 113 | Bob Boyd | 9.00 |
| 114 | Dean Stone | 9.00 |
| 115 | Rip Repulski | 9.00 |
| 116 | Steve Bilko | 9.00 |
| 117 | Solly Hemus | 9.00 |
| 118 | Carl Scheib | 9.00 |
| 119 | John Antonelli | 9.00 |
| 120 | Roy McMillan | 9.00 |
| 121 | Clem Labine | 9.00 |
| 122 | Johnny Logan | 9.00 |
| 123 | Bobby Adams | 9.00 |
| 124 | Marion Fricano | 9.00 |
| 125 | Harry Perkowski | 9.00 |
| 126 | Ben Wade | 9.00 |
| 127 | Steve O'Neill | 9.00 |
| 128 | Hank Aaron (R) | 750.00 |
| 129 | Forrest Jacobs | 9.00 |
| 130 | Hank Bauer | 15.00 |
| 131 | Reno Bertoia | 9.00 |
| 132 | Tommy Lasorda (R) | 105.00 |
| 133 | Del Baker | 9.00 |
| 134 | Cal Hogue | 9.00 |
| 135 | Joe Presko | 9.00 |
| 136 | Connie Ryan | 9.00 |
| 137 | Wally Moon | 11.00 |
| 138 | Bob Borkowski | 9.00 |
| 139 | The O'Brien's: Johnny O'Brien, Eddie O'Brien | 13.00 |
| 140 | Tom Wright | 8.00 |
| 141 | Joe Jay | 8.00 |
| 142 | Tom Poholsky | 8.00 |
| 143 | Rollie Hemsley | 8.00 |
| 144 | Bill Werle | 8.00 |
| 145 | Elmer Valo | 8.00 |
| 146 | Don Johnson | 8.00 |
| 147 | John Riddle | 8.00 |
| 148 | Bob Trice | 8.00 |
| 149 | Jim Robertson | 8.00 |
| 150 | Dick Kryhoski | 8.00 |
| 151 | Alex Grammas | 8.00 |
| 152 | Mike Blyzka | 8.00 |
| 153 | Albert Walker | 8.00 |
| 154 | Mike Fornieles | 8.00 |
| 155 | Bob Kennedy | 8.00 |
| 156 | Joe Coleman | 8.00 |
| 157 | Don Lenhardt | 8.00 |
| 158 | Peanuts Lowrey | 8.00 |
| 159 | Dave Philley | 8.00 |
| 160 | Red Kress | 8.00 |
| 161 | John Hetki | 8.00 |
| 162 | Herman Wehmeier | 8.00 |
| 163 | Frank House | 8.00 |
| 164 | Stuart Miller | 8.00 |
| 165 | Jim Pendleton | 8.00 |
| 166 | Johnny Podres | 15.00 |
| 167 | Don Lund | 8.00 |
| 168 | Morrie Martin | 8.00 |
| 169 | Jim Hughes | 8.00 |
| 170 | Jim Rhodes | 8.00 |
| 171 | Leo Kiely | 8.00 |
| 172 | Hal Brown | 8.00 |
| 173 | Jack Harshman | 8.00 |
| 174 | Tom Qualters | 8.00 |
| 175 | Frank Leja | 8.00 |
| 176 | Robert Kelley | 8.00 |
| 177 | Bob Milliken | 8.00 |
| 178 | Bill Glynn | 8.00 |
| 179 | Gair Allie | 8.00 |
| 180 | Wes Westrum | 8.00 |
| 181 | Mel Roach | 8.00 |
| 182 | Chuck Harmon | 8.00 |
| 183 | Earle Combs | 11.00 |
| 184 | Ed Bailey | 8.00 |
| 185 | Chuck Stobbs | 8.00 |
| 186 | Karl Olson | 8.00 |
| 187 | Heinie Manush | 10.00 |
| 188 | Dave Jolly | 8.00 |
| 189 | Bob Ross | 8.00 |
| 190 | Ray Herbert | 8.00 |
| 191 | Dick Schofield | 8.00 |
| 192 | Ellis Deal | 8.00 |
| 193 | Johnny Hopp | 8.00 |
| 194 | Bill Sarni | 8.00 |
| 195 | Bill Consolo | 8.00 |
| 196 | Stan Jok | 8.00 |
| 197 | L. Rowe | 8.00 |
| 198 | Carl Sawatski | 8.00 |
| 199 | Glenn Nelson | 8.00 |
| 200 | Larry Jansen | 8.00 |
| 201 | Al Kaline (R) | 450.00 |
| 202 | Bob Purkey | 8.00 |
| 203 | Harry Brecheen | 8.00 |
| 204 | Angel Scull | 8.00 |
| 205 | Johnny Sain | 15.00 |
| 206 | Ray Crone | 8.00 |
| 207 | Tom Oliver | 8.00 |
| 208 | Grady Hatton | 8.00 |
| 209 | Charlie Thompson | 8.00 |
| 210 | Bob Buhl | 8.00 |
| 211 | Don Hoak | 8.00 |
| 212 | Bob Micelotta | 8.00 |
| 213 | John Fitzpatrick | 8.00 |
| 214 | A. Portocarrero | 8.00 |
| 215 | Ed McGhee | 8.00 |
| 216 | Al Sima | 8.00 |
| 217 | Paul Schreiber | 8.00 |
| 218 | Fred Marsh | 8.00 |
| 219 | Charles Kress | 8.00 |
| 220 | Ruben Gomez | 8.00 |
| 221 | Dick Brodowski | 8.00 |
| 222 | Bill Wilson | 8.00 |
| 223 | Joe Haynes | 8.00 |
| 224 | Dick Weik | 8.00 |
| 225 | Don Liddle | 8.00 |
| 226 | Jehosie Heard | 8.00 |
| 227 | Buster Mills | 8.00 |
| 228 | Gene Hermanski | 8.00 |
| 229 | Bob Talbot | 8.00 |
| 230 | Bob Kuzava | 8.00 |
| 231 | Roy Smalley | 8.00 |
| 232 | Lou Limmer | 8.00 |
| 233 | Augie Galan | 8.00 |
| 234 | Jerry Lynch | 8.00 |
| 235 | Vernon Law | 8.00 |
| 236 | Paul Penson | 8.00 |
| 237 | Mike Ryba | 8.00 |
| 238 | Al Aber | 8.00 |
| 239 | Bill Skowron (R) | 22.00 |
| 240 | Sam Mele | 8.00 |
| 241 | Bob Miller | 8.00 |
| 242 | Curt Roberts | 8.00 |
| 243 | Ray Blades | 8.00 |
| 244 | Leroy Wheat | 8.00 |
| 245 | Roy Sievers | 10.00 |
| 246 | Howie Fox | 8.00 |
| 247 | Ed Mayo | 8.00 |
| 248 | Al Smith | 8.00 |
| 249 | Wilmer Mizell | 8.00 |
| 250 | Ted Williams (Exc. $70.00) | 350.00 |

**Prices for the 1954 set are for cards in *Mint* condition. *Excellent* copies sell for 40% to 50% of prices shown; *Very Good*—25% to 30%.**

## 1955 Topps....Complete Set of 206 Cards—Value $1600.00 (Exc.); $4000.00 (Mint)

Features the rookie cards of Roberto Clemente, Sandy Koufax and Harmon Killebrew. Topps' switched to a horizontal format in 1955. Card size 2⅝" x 3¾". Four cards originally intended to be issued—175, 186, 203 and 209 were withdrawn. The high number series is 161 to 210.

| NO. PLAYER | MINT | NO. PLAYER | MINT | NO. PLAYER | MINT | NO. PLAYER | MINT |
|---|---|---|---|---|---|---|---|
| 1 Dusty Rhodes (Exc. $5.00) | 20.00 | 53 Bill Taylor | 5.00 | 104 Jack Harshman | 5.00 | 155 Eddie Mathews | 50.00 |
| 2 Ted Williams | 160.00 | 54 Lou Limmer | 5.00 | 105 Chuck Diering | 5.00 | 156 Joe Black | 15.00 |
| 3 Art Fowler | 5.00 | 55 Eldon Repulski | 5.00 | 106 Frank Sullivan | 5.00 | 157 Bob Miller | 8.00 |
| 4 Al Kaline | 150.00 | 56 Ray Jablonski | 5.00 | 107 Curt Roberts | 5.00 | 158 Tommy Carroll | 8.00 |
| 5 Jim Gilliam | 7.50 | 57 Bill O'Dell | 5.00 | 108 Rube Walker | 5.00 | 159 Johnny Schmitz | 8.00 |
| 6 Stan Hack | 5.00 | 58 Manuel Rivera | 5.00 | 109 Ed Lopat | 10.00 | 160 Raymond Narleski | 8.00 |
| 7 Jim Hegan | 5.00 | 59 Gair Allie | 5.00 | 110 Gus Zernial | 5.00 | 161 Chuck Tanner (R) | 15.00 |
| 8 Hal Smith | 5.00 | 60 Dean Stone | 5.00 | 111 Bob Milliken | 5.00 | 162 Joe Coleman | 10.00 |
| 9 Bob Miller | 5.00 | 61 Forrest Jacobs | 5.00 | 112 Nelson King | 5.00 | 163 Faye Throneberry | 10.00 |
| 10 Bob Keegan | 5.00 | 62 Thornton Kipper | 5.00 | 113 Harry Brecheen | 5.00 | 164 Roberto Clemente (R) | 550.00 |
| 11 Ferris Fain | 5.00 | 63 Joe Collins | 6.00 | 114 Louie Ortiz | 5.00 | 165 Don Johnson | 10.00 |
| 12 Vernon Thies | 5.00 | 64 Gus Triandos | 6.00 | 115 Ellis Kinder | 5.00 | 166 Hank Bauer | 20.00 |
| 13 Fred Marsh | 5.00 | 65 Ray Boone | 5.00 | 116 Tom Hurd | 5.00 | 167 Tom Casagrande | 10.00 |
| 14 Jim Finigan | 5.00 | 66 Ron Jackson | 5.00 | 117 Mel Roach | 5.00 | 168 Duane Pillette | 10.00 |
| 15 Jim Pendleton | 5.00 | 67 Wally Moon | 5.00 | 118 Bob Purkey | 5.00 | 169 Bob Oldis | 10.00 |
| 16 Roy Sievers | 5.00 | 68 Jim Davis | 5.00 | 119 Bob Lennon | 5.00 | 170 Jim Pearce | 10.00 |
| 17 Bobby Hofman | 5.00 | 69 Ed Bailey | 5.00 | 120 Ted Kluszewski | 9.00 | 171 Dick Brodowski | 10.00 |
| 18 Russ Kemmerer | 5.00 | 70 Al Rosen | 7.00 | 121 Bill Renna | 4.00 | 172 Frank Baumholtz | 10.00 |
| 19 Billy Herman | 7.00 | 71 Ruben Gomez | 5.00 | 122 Carl Sawatski | 4.00 | 173 Bob Kline | 10.00 |
| 20 Andy Carey | 5.00 | 72 Karl Olson | 5.00 | 123 Sandy Koufax (R) | 300.00 | 174 Rudy Minarcin | 10.00 |
| 21 Alex Grammas | 5.00 | 73 Jack Shepard | 5.00 | 124 Harmon Killebrew (R) | 150.00 | 176 Norm Zauchin | 10.00 |
| 22 Bill Skowron | 9.00 | 74 Bob Borkowski | 5.00 | 125 Ken Boyer (R) | 20.00 | 177 Jim Robertson | 10.00 |
| 23 Jack Parks | 5.00 | 75 Sandy Amoros (R) | 7.00 | 126 Dick Hall | 5.00 | 178 Bobby Adams | 10.00 |
| 24 Hal Newhouser | 6.00 | 76 Howie Pollet | 5.00 | 127 Dale Long | 5.00 | 179 Jim Bolger | 10.00 |
| 25 Johnnie Podres | 8.00 | 77 Arnold Portocarrero | 5.00 | 128 Ted Lepcio | 5.00 | 180 Clem Labine | 10.00 |
| 26 Dick Groat | 5.00 | 78 Gordon Jones | 5.00 | 129 Elvin Tappe | 5.00 | 181 Roy McMillan | 10.00 |
| 27 Billy Gardner | 5.00 | 79 Clyde Schell | 5.00 | 130 Mayo Smith | 5.00 | 182 Humberto Robinson | 10.00 |
| 28 Ernie Banks | 55.00 | 80 Bob Grim (R) | 6.00 | 131 Grady Hatton | 5.00 | 183 Anthony Jacobs | 10.00 |
| 29 Herman Wehmeier | 5.00 | 81 Gene Conley | 5.00 | 132 Bob Trice | 5.00 | 184 Harry Perkowski | 10.00 |
| 30 Vic Power | 5.00 | 82 Chuck Harmon | 5.00 | 133 Dave Hoskins | 5.00 | 185 Don Ferrarese | 10.00 |
| 31 Warren Spahn | 30.00 | 83 Thomas Brewer | 5.00 | 134 Joe Jay | 5.00 | 187 Gil Hodges | 85.00 |
| 32 Ed McGhee | 5.00 | 84 Camilo Pascual (R) | 6.00 | 135 Johnny O'Brien | 5.00 | 188 Charlie Silvera | 10.00 |
| 33 Tom Qualters | 5.00 | 85 Don Mossi (R) | 6.00 | 136 Bunky Stewart | 5.00 | 189 Phil Rizzuto | 95.00 |
| 34 Wayne Terwilliger | 5.00 | 86 Bill Wilson | 5.00 | 137 Harry Elliott | 5.00 | 190 Gene Woodling | 10.00 |
| 35 Dave Jolly | 5.00 | 87 Frank House | 5.00 | 138 Ray Herbert | 5.00 | 191 Eddie Stanky | 10.00 |
| 36 Leo Kiely | 5.00 | 88 Bob Skinner | 5.00 | 139 Steve Kraly | 5.00 | 192 Jim Delsing | 10.00 |
| 37 Joe Cunningham | 5.00 | 89 Joe Frazier | 5.00 | 140 Mel Parnell | 5.00 | 193 Johnny Sain | 15.00 |
| 38 Bob Turley | 7.00 | 90 Karl Spooner | 5.00 | 141 Tom Wright | 5.00 | 194 Willie Mays | 300.00 |
| 39 Billy Glynn | 5.00 | 91 Milton Bolling | 5.00 | 142 Jerry Lynch | 5.00 | 195 Eddie Roebuck | 10.00 |
| 40 Don Hoak | 5.00 | 92 Don Zimmer (R) | 11.00 | 143 Dick Schofield | 5.00 | 196 Gale Wade | 10.00 |
| 41 Chuck Stobbs | 5.00 | 93 Steve Bilko | 5.00 | 144 Joe Amalfitano | 5.00 | 197 Al Smith | 10.00 |
| 42 John McCall | 5.00 | 94 Reno Bertoia | 5.00 | 145 Elmer Valo | 5.00 | 198 Yogi Berra | 125.00 |
| 43 Harvey Haddix | 6.00 | 95 Preston Ward | 5.00 | 146 Dick Donovan | 5.00 | 199 Bert Hamrick | 10.00 |
| 44 Harold Valentine | 5.00 | 96 Charlie Bishop | 5.00 | 147 Laurin Pepper | 5.00 | 200 Jack Jensen | 22.00 |
| 45 Hank Sauer | 5.00 | 97 Carlos Paula | 5.00 | 148 Hal Brown | 5.00 | 201 Sherman Lollar | 10.00 |
| 46 Ted Kazanski | 5.00 | 98 Johnny Riddle | 5.00 | 149 Ray Crone | 5.00 | 202 Jim Owens | 10.00 |
| 47 Hank Aaron | 150.00 | 99 Frank Leja | 5.00 | 150 Michael Higgins | 5.00 | 204 Frank Smith | 10.00 |
| 48 Bob Kennedy | 5.00 | 100 Monte Irvin | 15.00 | 151 Ralph Kress | 8.00 | 205 Gene Freese | 10.00 |
| 49 J.W. Porter | 5.00 | 101 Johnny Gray | 5.00 | 152 Harry Agganis (R) | 30.00 | 206 Pete Daley | 10.00 |
| 50 Jack Robinson | 100.00 | 102 Wally Westlake | 5.00 | 153 Bud Podbielan | 8.00 | 207 Bill Consolo | 10.00 |
| 51 Jim Hughes | 5.00 | 103 Charlie White | 5.00 | 154 Willie Miranda | 8.00 | 208 Ray Moore | 10.00 |
| 52 Bill Tremel | 5.00 | | | | | 210 Duke Snider (Exc. $85.00) | 375.00 |

Prices for the 1955 set are for cards in *Mint* condition. *Excellent* copies sell for 40% to 50% of prices shown; *Very Good*—25% to 30%.

## 1956 Topps....Complete Set of 340 Cards—Value $1750.00 (Exc.); $4000.00 (Mint)

In 1956 Topps bought its competitor—Bowman Card Co., including all of its player contracts. Topps card sets would now be larger and more complete. Card size 2⅝" x 3¾". Features the rookie card of Luis Aparicio. Card numbers 1 to 180 were printed with *gray* or *white* backs. The six team cards indicated by an *asterisk* were issued with three different *face* designs. The team card dated *1955* is worth about four times the value of the other team cards. The two checklists are not included in the complete set price.

| NO. PLAYER | MINT | NO. PLAYER | MINT | NO. PLAYER | MINT | NO. PLAYER | MINT |
|---|---|---|---|---|---|---|---|
| 1 W. Harridge (Exc. $5.00) | 50.00 | 3 Elmer Valo | 3.00 | 7 Ron Negray | 3.00 | 11 Chicago Cubs* | 7.00 |
| (AL President) | | 4 Carlos Paula | 3.00 | 8 Walter Alston (Mgr) | 15.00 | 12 Andy Carey | 3.00 |
| 2 Warren Giles | 7.50 | 5 Ted Williams | 125.00 | 9 Ruben Gomez | 3.00 | 13 Roy Face | 3.00 |
| (NL President) | | 6 Ray Boone | 3.00 | 10 Warren Spahn | 24.00 | 14 Ken Boyer | 7.00 |

# 1956 Topps (Continued)

| NO. PLAYER | MINT | NO. PLAYER | MINT | NO. PLAYER | MINT | NO. PLAYER | MINT |
|---|---|---|---|---|---|---|---|
| 15 Ernie Banks | 45.00 | 97 Jerry Lynch | 3.00 | 179 Harry Chiti | 4.00 | 261 Bobby Shantz | 5.00 |
| 16 Hector Lopez | 3.00 | 98 Camilo Pascual | 3.00 | 180 Robin Roberts | 20.00 | 262 Howie Pollett | 5.00 |
| 17 Gene Conley | 3.00 | 99 Don Zimmer | 4.00 | 181 Billy Martin | 30.00 | 263 Bob Miller | 5.00 |
| 18 Dick Donovan | 3.00 | 100 Baltimore Orioles* | 6.00 | 182 Paul Minner | 6.00 | 264 Ray Monzant | 5.00 |
| 19 Chuck Diering | 3.00 | 101 Roy Campanella | 80.00 | 183 Stan Lopata | 6.00 | 265 Sandy Consuegra | 5.00 |
| 20 Al Kaline | 35.00 | 102 Jim Davis | 4.00 | 184 Don Bessent | 6.00 | 266 Don Ferrarese | 5.00 |
| 21 Joe Collins | 4.00 | 103 Willie Miranda | 4.00 | 185 Bill Bruton | 6.00 | 267 Bob Nieman | 5.00 |
| 22 Jim Finigan | 3.00 | 104 Bob Lennon | 4.00 | 186 Ron Jackson | 6.00 | 268 Dale Mitchell | 5.00 |
| 23 Freddie Marsh | 3.00 | 105 Al Smith | 4.00 | 187 Early Wynn | 20.00 | 269 Jack Meyer | 5.00 |
| 24 Dick Groat | 4.00 | 106 Joe Astroth | 4.00 | 188 Chicago White Sox | 15.00 | 270 Billy Loes | 5.00 |
| 25 Ted Kluszeski | 8.00 | 107 Ed Mathews | 25.00 | 189 Ned Garver | 6.00 | 271 Foster Castleman | 5.00 |
| 26 Grady Hatton | 3.00 | 108 Laurin Pepper | 4.00 | 190 Carl Furillo | 10.00 | 272 Danny O'Connell | 5.00 |
| 27 Nelson Burbrink | 3.00 | 109 Enos Slaughter | 15.00 | 191 Frank Lary | 7.00 | 273 Walker Cooper | 5.00 |
| 28 Bobby Hofman | 3.00 | 110 Yogi Berra | 60.00 | 192 Smokey Burgess | 6.00 | 274 Frank Baumholtz | 5.00 |
| 29 Jack Harshman | 3.00 | 111 Boston Red Sox | 10.00 | 193 Wilmer Mizell | 6.00 | 275 Jim Greengrass | 5.00 |
| 30 Jackie Robinson | 105.00 | 112 Dee Fondy | 4.00 | 194 Monte Irvin | 15.00 | 276 George Zuverink | 5.00 |
| 31 Hank Aaron | 135.00 | 113 Phil Rizzuto | 20.00 | 195 George Kell | 16.00 | 277 Daryl Spencer | 5.00 |
| 32 Frank House | 3.00 | 114 Jim Owens | 4.00 | 196 Tom Poholsky | 6.00 | 278 Chet Nichols | 5.00 |
| 33 Roberto Clemente | 125.00 | 115 Jackie Jensen | 6.00 | 197 Granny Hamner | 6.00 | 279 Johnny Groth | 5.00 |
| 34 Tom Brewer | 3.00 | 116 Eddie O'Brien | 4.00 | 198 Ed Fitzgerald | 6.00 | 280 Jim Gilliam | 7.00 |
| 35 Al Rosen | 6.00 | 117 Virgil Trucks | 4.00 | 199 Hank Thompson | 6.00 | 281 Art Houtteman | 5.00 |
| 36 Rudy Minarcin | 3.00 | 118 Nellie Fox | 11.00 | 200 Bob Feller | 45.00 | 282 Warren Hacker | 5.00 |
| 37 Alex Grammas | 3.00 | 119 Larry Jackson | 4.00 | 201 Rip Repulski | 6.00 | 283 Hal Smith | 5.00 |
| 38 Bob Kennedy | 3.00 | 120 Richie Ashburn | 10.00 | 202 Jim Hearn | 6.00 | 284 Ike Delock | 5.00 |
| 39 Don Mossi | 4.00 | 121 Pittsburgh Pirates | 6.00 | 203 Bill Tuttle | 6.00 | 285 Eddie Miksis | 5.00 |
| 40 Bob Turley | 5.00 | 122 Willard Nixon | 4.00 | 204 Arthur Swanson | 6.00 | 286 Bill Wight | 5.00 |
| 41 Hank Sauer | 3.00 | 123 Roy McMillan | 4.00 | 205 Whitey Lockman | 6.00 | 287 Bobby Adams | 5.00 |
| 42 Sandy Amoros | 4.00 | 124 Don Kaiser | 4.00 | 206 Erv Palica | 6.00 | 288 Bob Cerv | 5.00 |
| 43 Ray Moore | 3.00 | 125 Minnie Minoso | 7.00 | 207 Jim Small | 6.00 | 289 Hal Jeffcoat | 5.00 |
| 44 Windy McCall | 3.00 | 126 Jim Brady | 4.00 | 208 Elston Howard | 15.00 | 290 Curt Simmons | 5.00 |
| 45 Gus Zernial | 3.00 | 127 Willie Jones | 4.00 | 209 Max Surkont | 6.00 | 291 Frank Kellert | 5.00 |
| 46 Gene Freese | 3.00 | 128 Eddie Yost | 4.00 | 210 Mike Garcia | 6.00 | 292 Luis Aparicio (R) | 40.00 |
| 47 Art Fowler | 3.00 | 129 Jake Martin | 4.00 | 211 Murry Dickson | 6.00 | 293 Stu Miller | 5.00 |
| 48 Jim Hegan | 3.00 | 130 Willie Mays | 135.00 | 212 Johnny Temple | 6.00 | 294 Ernie Johnson | 5.00 |
| 49 Pedro Ramos | 3.00 | 131 Bob Roselli | 4.00 | 213 Detroit Tigers | 15.00 | 295 Clem Labine | 5.00 |
| 50 Dusty Rhode | 3.00 | 132 Bobby Avila | 4.00 | 214 Bob Rush | 6.00 | 296 Andy Seminick | 5.00 |
| 51 Ernie Oravetz | 3.00 | 133 Ray Narleski | 4.00 | 215 Tommy Byrne | 6.00 | 297 Bob Skinner | 5.00 |
| 52 Bob Grim | 3.00 | 134 St. Louis Cardinals | 6.00 | 216 Jerry Schoonmaker | 6.00 | 298 Johnny Schmitz | 5.00 |
| 53 Arnold Portocarrero | 3.00 | 135 Mickey Mantle | 600.00 | 217 Billy Klaus | 6.00 | 299 Charley Neal | 5.00 |
| 54 Bob Keegan | 3.00 | 136 Johnny Logan | 4.00 | 218 Joe Nuxhall | 6.00 | 300 Vic Wertz | 5.00 |
| 55 Wally Moon | 3.00 | 137 Al Silvera | 4.00 | 219 Lew Burdette | 10.00 | 301 Marv Grissom | 5.00 |
| 56 Dale Long | 3.00 | 138 Johnny Antonelli | 4.00 | 220 Del Ennis | 6.00 | 302 Eddie Robinson | 5.00 |
| 57 Duke Maas | 3.00 | 139 Tommy Carroll | 4.00 | 221 Bob Friend | 6.00 | 303 Jim Dyck | 5.00 |
| 58 Ed Roebuck | 3.00 | 140 Herb Score (R) | 8.00 | 222 Dave Philley | 6.00 | 304 Frank Malzone | 6.00 |
| 59 Jose Santiago | 3.00 | 141 Joe Frazier | 4.00 | 223 Randy Jackson | 6.00 | 305 Brooks Lawrence | 5.00 |
| 60 Mayo Smith | 3.00 | 142 Gene Baker | 4.00 | 224 Bud Podbielan | 6.00 | 306 Curt Roberts | 5.00 |
| 61 Bill Skowron | 7.50 | 143 Jimmy Piersall | 6.00 | 225 Gil McDougald | 12.00 | 307 Hoyt Wilhelm | 20.00 |
| 62 Hal Smith | 3.00 | 144 Leroy Powell | 4.00 | 226 New York Giants | 30.00 | 308 Charles Harmon | 5.00 |
| 63 Roger Craig (R) | 8.00 | 145 Gil Hodges | 22.00 | 227 Russ Meyer | 6.00 | 309 Don Blasingame | 5.00 |
| 64 Luis Arroyo | 3.00 | 146 Washington Nat'l | 6.00 | 228 Mickey Vernon | 6.00 | 310 Steve Gromek | 5.00 |
| 65 Johnny O'Brien | 3.00 | 147 Earl Torgeson | 4.00 | 229 Harry Brecheen | 6.00 | 311 Hal Naragon | 5.00 |
| 66 Bob Speake | 3.00 | 148 Alvin Dark | 4.00 | 230 Chico Carrasquel | 6.00 | 312 Andy Pafko | 5.00 |
| 67 Vic Power | 3.00 | 149 Dixie Howell | 4.00 | 231 Bob Hale | 6.00 | 313 Gene Stephens | 5.00 |
| 68 Chuck Stobbs | 3.00 | 150 Duke Snider | 75.00 | 232 Toby Atwell | 6.00 | 314 Hobie Landrith | 5.00 |
| 69 Chuck Tanner | 3.00 | 151 Spook Jacobs | 4.00 | 233 Carl Erskine | 12.00 | 315 Milt Bolling | 5.00 |
| 70 Jim Rivera | 3.00 | 152 Billy Hoeft | 4.00 | 234 Pete Runnels | 6.00 | 316 Jerry Coleman | 5.00 |
| 71 Frank Sullivan | 3.00 | 153 Frank Thomas | 4.00 | 235 Don Newcombe | 20.00 | 317 Al Aber | 5.00 |
| 72 Philadelphia Phillies* | 6.00 | 154 David Pope | 4.00 | 236 Kansas C. Athletics | 8.00 | 318 Fred Hatfield | 5.00 |
| 73 Wayne Terwilliger | 3.00 | 155 Harvey Kuenn | 5.00 | 237 Jose Valdivielso | 6.00 | 319 Jack Crimian | 5.00 |
| 74 Jim King | 3.00 | 156 Wes Westrum | 4.00 | 238 Walt Dropo | 6.00 | 320 Joe Adcock | 5.00 |
| 75 Roy Sievers | 4.00 | 157 Dick Brodowski | 4.00 | 239 Harry Simpson | 6.00 | 321 Jim Konstanty | 5.00 |
| 76 Ray Crone | 3.00 | 158 Wally Post | 4.00 | 240 Whitey Ford | 45.00 | 322 Karl Olson | 5.00 |
| 77 Harvey Haddix | 4.00 | 159 Clint Courtney | 4.00 | 241 Don Mueller | 6.00 | 323 Willard Schmidt | 5.00 |
| 78 Herman Wehmeier | 3.00 | 160 Billy Pierce | 5.00 | 242 Hershell Freeman | 6.00 | 324 Rocky Bridges | 5.00 |
| 79 Sandy Koufax | 120.00 | 161 Joe DeMaestri | 4.00 | 243 Sherm Lollar | 6.00 | 325 Don Liddle | 5.00 |
| 80 Gus Triandos | 3.00 | 162 Gus Bell | 4.00 | 244 Bob Buhl | 6.00 | 236 Connie Johnson | 5.00 |
| 81 Wally Westlake | 3.00 | 163 Gene Woodling | 4.00 | 245 Billy Goodman | 6.00 | 327 Bob Wiesler | 5.00 |
| 82 Bill Renna | 3.00 | 164 Harmon Killebrew | 50.00 | 246 Tom Gorman | 6.00 | 328 Preston Ward | 5.00 |
| 83 Karl Spooner | 3.00 | 165 Red Schoendienst | 6.00 | 247 Bill Sarni | 6.00 | 329 Lou Berberet | 5.00 |
| 84 Babe Birrer | 3.00 | 166 Brooklyn Dodgers | 75.00 | 248 Bob Porterfield | 6.00 | 330 Jim Busby | 5.00 |
| 85 Cleveland Indians* | 6.00 | 167 Harry Dorish | 4.00 | 249 Johnny Klippstein | 6.00 | 331 Dick Hall | 5.00 |
| 86 Ray Jablonski | 3.00 | 168 Sammy White | 4.00 | 250 Larry Doby | 9.00 | 332 Don Larsen | 9.00 |
| 87 Dean Stone | 3.00 | 169 Bob Nelson | 4.00 | 251 New York Yankees | 75.00 | 333 Rube Walker | 5.00 |
| 88 Johnny Kucks | 3.00 | 170 Bill Virdon | 5.00 | 252 Vernon Law | 6.00 | 334 Bob Miller | 5.00 |
| 89 Norm Zauchin | 3.00 | 171 Jim Wilson | 4.00 | 253 Irv Noren | 6.00 | 335 Don Hoak | 5.00 |
| 90 Cincinnati Redlegs* | 6.00 | 172 Frank Torre | 4.00 | 254 George Crowe | 6.00 | 336 Ellis Kinder | 5.00 |
| 91 Gail Harris | 3.00 | 173 Johnny Podres | 8.00 | 255 Bob Lemon | 20.00 | 337 Bobby Morgan | 5.00 |
| 92 Red Wilson | 3.00 | 174 Glen Gorbous | 4.00 | 256 Tom Hurd | 6.00 | 338 Jim Delsing | 5.00 |
| 93 George Susce Jr. | 3.00 | 175 Del Crandall | 4.00 | 257 Bobby Thomson | 10.00 | 339 Rance Pless | 5.00 |
| 94 Ronald Kline | 3.00 | 176 Alex Kellner | 4.00 | 258 Art Ditmar | 6.00 | 340 M. McDermott (Exc. $4.00) | 15.00 |
| 95 Milwaukee Braves* | 6.00 | 177 Hank Bauer | 8.00 | 259 Sam Jones | 6.00 | — Checklist 1/3 | 150.00 |
| 96 Bill Tremel | 3.00 | 178 Joe Black | 4.00 | 260 Pee Wee Reese | 80.00 | — Checklist 2/4 | 150.00 |

**Prices for the 1956 set are for cards in *Mint* condition. *Excellent* copies sell for 40% to 50% of prices shown; *Very Good*—25% to 30%.**

# 1957 Topps . . . . Complete Set of 407 Cards—Value $1750.00 (Exc.); $4750.00 (Mint)

Topps' switched to a 2½" x 3½" card size. The 1957 set features the rookie cards of Don Drysdale, Frank Robinson, Tony Kubek and Brooks Robinson. The four checklists are not included in the complete set price.

| NO. PLAYER | MINT |
|---|---|
| 1 Ted Williams (Exc. $50.00) | 250.00 |
| 2 Yogi Berra | 65.00 |
| 3 Dale Long | 2.50 |
| 4 Johnny Logan | 2.50 |
| 5 Sal Maglie | 4.00 |
| 6 Hector Lopez | 2.50 |
| 7 Luis Aparicio | 11.00 |
| 8 Don Mossi | 2.50 |
| 9 Johnny Temple | 2.50 |
| 10 Willie Mays | 110.00 |
| 11 George Zuverink | 2.50 |
| 12 Dick Groat | 4.00 |
| 13 Wally Burnette | 2.50 |
| 14 Bob Nieman | 2.50 |
| 15 Robin Roberts | 11.00 |
| 16 Walt Moryn | 2.50 |
| 17 Billy Gardner | 2.50 |
| 18 Don Drysdale (R) | 90.00 |
| 19 Bob Wilson | 2.50 |
| 20 Hank Aaron | 120.00 |
| (negative reversed) | |
| 21 Frank Sullivan | 2.50 |
| 22 Jerry Snyder | 2.50 |
| (photo of Ed Fitzgerald) | |
| 23 Sherm Lollar | 2.50 |
| 24 Bill Mazeroski (R) | 12.50 |
| 25 W. Ford | 30.00 |
| 26 Bob Boyd | 2.50 |
| 27 Ted Kazanski | 2.50 |
| 28 Gene Conley | 2.50 |
| 29 Whitey Herzog | 10.00 |
| 30 Pee Wee Reese | 30.00 |
| 31 Ron Northey | 2.50 |
| 32 Hersh Freeman | 2.50 |
| 33 Jim Small | 2.50 |
| 34 Tom Sturdivant | 2.50 |
| 35 Frank Robinson (R) | 120.00 |
| 36 Bob Grim | 2.50 |
| 37 Frank Torre | 2.50 |
| 38 Nellie Fox | 7.00 |
| 39 Al Worthington | 2.50 |
| 40 Early Wynn | 12.00 |
| 41 Hal Smith | 2.50 |
| 42 Dee Fondy | 2.50 |
| 43 Connie Johnson | 2.50 |
| 44 Joe DeMaestri | 2.50 |
| 45 Carl Furillo | 6.00 |
| 46 Bob Miller | 2.50 |
| 47 Don Blasingame | 2.50 |
| 48 Bill Bruton | 2.50 |
| 49 Daryl Spencer | 2.50 |
| 50 Herb A. Score | 4.00 |
| 51 Clint Courtney | 2.50 |
| 52 Lee Walls | 2.50 |
| 53 Clem Labine | 2.50 |
| 54 Elmer Valo | 2.50 |
| 55 Ernie Banks | 35.00 |
| 56 Dave Sisler | 2.50 |
| 57 Jim Lemon | 2.50 |
| 58 Ruben Gomez | 2.50 |
| 59 Dick Williams | 2.50 |
| 60 Billy Hoeft | 2.50 |
| 61 Dusty Rhodes | 2.50 |
| 62 Billy Martin | 24.00 |
| 63 Ike Delock | 2.50 |
| 64 Pete Runnels | 2.50 |

| NO. PLAYER | MINT |
|---|---|
| 65 Wally Moon | 2.50 |
| 66 Brooks Lawrence | 2.50 |
| 67 Chico Carrasquel | 2.50 |
| 68 Ray Crone | 2.50 |
| 69 Roy McMillan | 2.50 |
| 70 Richie Ashburn | 7.00 |
| 71 Murry Dickson | 2.50 |
| 72 Bill Tuttle | 2.50 |
| 73 George Crowe | 2.50 |
| 74 Vito Valentinetti | 2.50 |
| 75 Jim Piersall | 4.00 |
| 76 Roberto Clemente | 75.00 |
| 77 Paul Foytack | 2.50 |
| 78 Vic Wertz | 2.50 |
| 79 Lindy McDaniel | 2.50 |
| 80 Gil Hodges | 20.00 |
| 81 Herman Wehmeier | 2.50 |
| 82 Elston Howard | 7.00 |
| 83 Lou Skizas | 2.50 |
| 84 Moe Drabowsky | 2.50 |
| 85 Larry Doby | 5.00 |
| 86 Bill Sarni | 2.50 |
| 87 Tom Gorman | 2.50 |
| 88 Harvey Kuenn | 5.00 |
| 89 Roy Sievers | 3.00 |
| 90 Warren Spahn | 25.00 |
| 91 Mack Burk | 2.50 |
| 92 Mickey Vernon | 2.50 |
| 93 Hal Jeffcoat | 2.50 |
| 94 Bobby Del Greco | 2.50 |
| 95 Mickey Mantle | 600.00 |
| 96 Hank Aguirre | 2.50 |
| 97 New York Yankees | 22.00 |
| 98 Alvin Dark | 5.00 |
| 99 Bob Keegan | 2.50 |
| 100 Giles and Harridge | 5.00 |
| (League Presidents) | |
| 101 Chuck Stobbs | 2.50 |
| 102 Ray Boone | 2.50 |
| 103 Joe Nuxhall | 2.50 |
| 104 Hank Foiles | 2.50 |
| 105 Johnny Antonelli | 2.50 |
| 106 Ray Moore | 2.50 |
| 107 Jim Rivera | 2.50 |
| 108 Tommy Byrne | 2.50 |
| 109 Hank Thompson | 2.50 |
| 110 Bill Virdon | 4.00 |
| 111 Hal Smith | 2.50 |
| 112 Tom Brewer | 2.50 |
| 113 Wilmer Mizell | 2.50 |
| 114 Milwaukee Braves | 6.00 |
| 115 Jim Gilliam | 6.00 |
| 116 Mike Fornieles | 2.50 |
| 117 Joe Adcock | 5.00 |
| 118 Bob Porterfield | 2.50 |
| 119 Stan Lopata | 2.50 |
| 120 Bob Lemon | 11.00 |
| 121 Cletis Boyer | 5.00 |
| 122 Ken Boyer | 5.00 |
| 123 Steve Ridzik | 2.50 |
| 124 Dave Philley | 2.50 |
| 125 Al Kaline | 30.00 |
| 126 Bob Wiesler | 2.50 |
| 127 Bob Buhl | 2.50 |
| 128 Ed Bailey | 2.50 |
| 129 Saul Rogovin | 2.50 |

| NO. PLAYER | MINT |
|---|---|
| 130 Don Newcombe | 6.00 |
| 131 Milt Bolling | 2.50 |
| 132 Art Ditmar | 2.50 |
| 133 Del Crandall | 2.50 |
| 134 Don Kaiser | 2.50 |
| 135 Bill Skowron | 8.00 |
| 136 Jim Hegan | 2.50 |
| 137 Bob Rush | 2.50 |
| 138 Minnie Minoso | 5.00 |
| 139 Lou Kretlow | 2.50 |
| 140 Frank Thomas | 2.50 |
| 141 Al Aber | 2.50 |
| 142 Charley Thompson | 2.50 |
| 143 Andy Pafko | 2.50 |
| 144 Ray Narleski | 2.50 |
| 145 Al Smith | 2.50 |
| 146 Don Ferrarese | 2.50 |
| 147 Al Walker | 2.50 |
| 148 Don Mueller | 2.50 |
| 149 Bob Kennedy | 2.50 |
| 150 Bob Friend | 2.50 |
| 151 Willie Miranda | 2.50 |
| 152 Jack Harshman | 2.50 |
| 153 Karl Olson | 2.50 |
| 154 Red Schoendienst | 5.00 |
| 155 Jim Brosnan | 2.50 |
| 156 Gus Triandos | 2.50 |
| 157 Wally Post | 2.50 |
| 158 Curt Simmons | 2.50 |
| 159 Solly Drake | 2.50 |
| 160 Billy Pierce | 5.00 |
| 161 Pittsburgh Pirates | 6.00 |
| 162 Jack Meyer | 2.50 |
| 163 Sammy White | 2.50 |
| 164 Tommy Carroll | 2.50 |
| 165 Ted Kluszewski | 8.00 |
| 166 Roy Face | 3.50 |
| 167 Vic Power | 2.50 |
| 168 Frank Lary | 2.50 |
| 169 Herb Plews | 2.50 |
| 170 Duke Snider | 60.00 |
| 171 Boston Red Sox | 8.00 |
| 172 Gene Woodling | 3.00 |
| 173 Roger Craig | 5.00 |
| 174 Willie Jones | 2.50 |
| 175 Don Larsen | 6.00 |
| 176 Gene Baker | 2.50 |
| 177 Eddie Yost | 2.50 |
| 178 Don Bessent | 2.50 |
| 179 Ernie Oravetz | 2.50 |
| 180 Dave Bell | 2.50 |
| 181 Dick Donovan | 2.50 |
| 182 Hobie Landrith | 2.50 |
| 183 Chicago Cubs | 6.00 |
| 184 Tito Francona | 2.50 |
| 185 Johnny Kucks | 2.50 |
| 186 Jim King | 2.50 |
| 187 Virgil Trucks | 2.50 |
| 188 Felix Mantilla | 2.50 |
| 189 Willard Nixon | 2.50 |
| 190 Randy Jackson | 2.50 |
| 191 Joe Margoneri | 2.50 |
| 192 Gerry Coleman | 2.50 |
| 193 Del Rice | 2.50 |
| 194 Hal Brown | 2.50 |
| 195 Bobby Avila | 2.50 |

| NO. PLAYER | MINT |
|---|---|
| 196 Larry Jackson | 2.50 |
| 197 Hank Sauer | 2.50 |
| 198 Detroit Tigers | 10.00 |
| 199 Vernon Law | 2.50 |
| 200 Gil McDougald | 7.00 |
| 201 Sandy Amoros | 2.50 |
| 202 Dick Gernert | 2.50 |
| 203 Hoyt Wilhelm | 12.00 |
| 204 Kansas C. Athletics | 5.00 |
| 205 Charlie Maxwell | 2.50 |
| 206 Willard Schmidt | 2.50 |
| 207 Bill Hunter | 2.50 |
| 208 Lew Burdette | 6.00 |
| 209 Bob Skinner | 2.50 |
| 210 Roy Campanella | 50.00 |
| 211 Camilo Pascual | 2.50 |
| 212 Rocco Colavito (R) | 18.00 |
| 213 Les Moss | 2.50 |
| 214 Philadelphia Phillies | 5.00 |
| 215 Enos Slaughter | 12.00 |
| 216 Marv Grissom | 2.50 |
| 217 Gene Stephens | 2.50 |
| 218 Ray Jablonski | 2.50 |
| 219 Tom Acker | 2.50 |
| 220 Jackie Jensen | 5.00 |
| 221 Dixie Howell | 2.50 |
| 222 Alex Grammas | 2.50 |
| 223 Frank House | 2.50 |
| 224 Marv Blaylock | 2.50 |
| 225 Harry Simpson | 2.50 |
| 226 Preston Ward | 2.50 |
| 227 Jerry Staley | 2.50 |
| 228 Smokey Burgess | 2.50 |
| 229 George Susce | 2.50 |
| 230 George Kell | 12.00 |
| 231 Solly Hemus | 2.50 |
| 232 Whitey Lockman | 2.50 |
| 233 Art Fowler | 2.50 |
| 234 Dick Cole | 2.50 |
| 235 Tom Poholsky | 2.50 |
| 236 Joe Ginsberg | 2.50 |
| 237 Foster Catleman | 2.50 |
| 238 Eddie Robinson | 2.50 |
| 239 Tom Morgan | 2.50 |
| 240 Hank Bauer | 6.00 |
| 241 Joe Lonnett | 2.50 |
| 242 Charlie Neal | 2.50 |
| 243 St. Louis Cardinals | 7.00 |
| 244 Billy Loes | 2.50 |
| 245 Rip Repulski | 2.50 |
| 246 Jose Valdivielso | 2.50 |
| 247 Turk Lown | 2.50 |
| 248 Jim Finigan | 2.50 |
| 249 Dave Pope | 2.50 |
| 250 Ed Mathews | 16.00 |
| 251 Baltimore Orioles | 16.00 |
| 252 Carl Erskine | 6.00 |
| 253 Gus Zernial | 2.50 |
| 254 Ron Negray | 2.50 |
| 255 Charlie Silvera | 2.50 |
| 256 Ronnie Kline | 2.50 |
| 257 Walt Dropo | 2.50 |
| 258 Steve Gromek | 2.50 |
| 259 Eddie O'Brien | 2.50 |
| 260 Del Ennis | 2.50 |
| 261 Bob Chakales | 2.50 |

| NO. PLAYER | MINT | NO. PLAYER | MINT | NO. PLAYER | MINT | NO. PLAYER | MINT |
|---|---|---|---|---|---|---|---|
| 262 Bobby Thomson | 4.00 | 301 Sam Esposito | 10.00 | 339 Bob Speake | 10.00 | 377 Andre Rodgers | 3.00 |
| 263 George Strickland | 2.50 | 302 Sandy Koufax | 250.00 | 340 Bill Wight | 10.00 | 378 Elmer Singleton | 3.00 |
| 264 Bob Turley | 4.00 | 303 Billy Goodman | 10.00 | 341 Don Gross | 10.00 | 379 Don Lee | 3.00 |
| 265 Harvey Haddix | 12.00 | 304 Joe Cunningham | 10.00 | 342 Gene Mauch | 15.00 | 380 Walker Cooper | 3.00 |
| 266 Kenny Kuhn | 10.00 | 305 Chico Fernandez | 10.00 | 343 Taylor Phillips | 10.00 | 381 Dean Stone | 3.00 |
| 267 Danny Kravitz | 10.00 | 306 Darrell Johnson | 10.00 | 344 Paul LaPalme | 10.00 | 382 Jim Brideweser | 3.00 |
| 268 Jackie Collum | 10.00 | 307 Jack Phillips | 10.00 | 345 Paul Smith | 10.00 | 383 Juan Pizarro | 3.00 |
| 269 Bob Cerv | 10.00 | 308 Dick Hall | 10.00 | 346 Dick Littlefield | 10.00 | 384 Bobby Smith | 3.00 |
| 270 Washington Senators | 15.00 | 309 Jim Busby | 10.00 | 347 Hal Naragon | 10.00 | 385 Art Houtteman | 3.00 |
| 271 Danny O'Connell | 10.00 | 310 Max Surkont | 10.00 | 348 Jim Hearn | 10.00 | 386 Lyle Luttrell | 3.00 |
| 272 Bobby Shantz | 20.00 | 311 Al Pilarcik | 10.00 | 349 Nelson King | 10.00 | 387 Jack Sanford (R) | 4.00 |
| 273 Jim Davis | 10.00 | 312 Tony Kubek (R) | 70.00 | 350 Eddie Miksis | 10.00 | 388 Pete Daley | 3.00 |
| 274 Don Hoak | 10.00 | 313 Mel Parnell | 10.00 | 351 Dave Hillman | 10.00 | 389 Dave Jolly | 3.00 |
| 275 Cleveland Indians | 15.00 | 314 Ed Bouchee | 10.00 | 352 Ellis Kinder | 10.00 | 390 Reno Bertoia | 3.00 |
| 276 Jim Pyburn | 10.00 | 315 Lou Berberet | 10.00 | 353 Cal Neeman | 3.00 | 391 Ralph Terry (R) | 6.00 |
| 277 Johnny Podres | 40.00 | 316 Billy O'Dell | 10.00 | 354 Rip Coleman | 3.00 | 392 Chuck Tanner | 3.00 |
| 278 Fred Hatfield | 10.00 | 317 New York Giants | 30.00 | 355 Frank Malzone | 3.00 | 393 Raul Sanchez | 3.00 |
| 279 Bob Thurman | 10.00 | 318 Mickey McDermott | 10.00 | 356 Faye Throneberry | 3.00 | 394 Luis Aroyo | 3.00 |
| 280 Alex Kellner | 10.00 | 319 Gino Cimoli | 10.00 | 357 Earl Torgeson | 3.00 | 395 Bubba Phillips | 3.00 |
| 281 Gail Harris | 10.00 | 320 Neil Chrisley | 10.00 | 358 Jerry Lynch | 3.00 | 396 Casey Wise | 3.00 |
| 282 Jack Dittmer | 10.00 | 321 Red Murff | 10.00 | 359 Tom Cheney | 3.00 | 397 Roy Smalley | 3.00 |
| 283 Wes Covington | 10.00 | 322 Cincinnati Redlegs | 30.00 | 360 Johnny Groth | 3.00 | 398 Al Cicotte | 3.00 |
| 284 Don Zimmer | 15.00 | 323 Wes Westrum | 10.00 | 361 Curt Barclay | 3.00 | 399 Billy Consolo | 3.00 |
| 285 Ned Garver | 10.00 | 324 Brooklyn Dodgers | 60.00 | 362 Roman Mejias | 3.00 | 400 Dodgers' Sluggers: | 120.00 |
| 286 Bobby Richardson (R) | 60.00 | 325 Frank Bolling | 10.00 | 363 Eddie Kasko | 3.00 | Carl Furillo, Gil Hodges | |
| 287 Sam Jones | 10.00 | 326 Pedro Ramos | 10.00 | 364 Cal McLish | 3.00 | Duke Snider, | |
| 288 Ted Lepcio | 10.00 | 327 Jim Pendleton | 10.00 | 365 Ossie Virgil | 3.00 | Roy Campanella | |
| 289 Jim Bolger | 10.00 | 328 Brooks Robinson | 250.00 | 366 Ken Lehman | 3.00 | 401 Earl Battey | 3.00 |
| 290 Andy Carey | 10.00 | 329 Chicago White Sox | 16.00 | 367 Ed Fitzgerald | 3.00 | 402 Jim Pisani | 3.00 |
| 291 Windy McCall | 10.00 | 330 Jim Wilson | 10.00 | 368 Bob Purkey | 3.00 | 403 Dick Hyde | 3.00 |
| 292 Bill Klaus | 10.00 | 331 Ray Katt | 10.00 | 369 Milt Graff | 3.00 | 404 Harry Anderson | 3.00 |
| 293 Ted Abernathy | 10.00 | 332 Bob Bowman | 10.00 | 370 Warren Hacker | 3.00 | 405 Duke Maas | 3.00 |
| 294 Rocky Bridges | 10.00 | 333 Ernie Johnson | 10.00 | 371 Bob Lennon | 3.00 | 406 Bob Hale | 3.00 |
| 295 Joe Collins | 10.00 | 334 Jerry Schoonmaker | 10.00 | 372 Norm Zauchin | 3.00 | 407 Yanks' Power Hitters: | 200.00 |
| 296 Johnny Klippstein | 10.00 | 335 Granny Hamner | 10.00 | 373 Pete Whisenant | 3.00 | M. Mantle, Y. Berra (Exc. $50.00) | |
| 297 Jack Crimian | 10.00 | 336 Haywood Sullivan | 10.00 | 374 Don Cardwell | 3.00 | — Checklist 1/2 | 75.00 |
| 298 Irv Noren | 10.00 | 337 Rene Valdes | 10.00 | 375 Jim Landis | 3.00 | — Checklist 2/3 | 100.00 |
| 299 Chuck Harmon | 10.00 | 338 Jim Bunning (R) | 65.00 | 376 Don Elston | 3.00 | — Checklist 3/4 | 200.00 |
| 300 Mike Garcia | 10.00 | | | | | — Checklist 4/5 | 275.00 |

Prices for the 1957 set are for cards in *Mint* condition. *Excellent* copies sell for 40% to 50% of prices shown; *Very Good*—25% to 30%.

## 1958 Topps. . . .Complete Set of 494 Cards—Value $1200.00 (Exc.); $3000.00 (Mint)

Features the rookie cards of Roger Maris and Orlando Cepeda. 33 cards exist with the player's name or team in *yellow* type. These cards are worth more than the cards with *white* type. Card 145 was not issued. Prices for team checklists (377, 397, 408 and 428) are with the teams listed in alphabetical order. Team checklists with the teams in numerical order are worth about $12.00 each.

| NO. PLAYER | MINT | NO. PLAYER | MINT | NO. PLAYER | MINT | NO. PLAYER | MINT |
|---|---|---|---|---|---|---|---|
| 1 Ted Williams (Exc. $35.00) | 200.00 | 11 Jim Rivera | 15.00 | 21 Curt Barclay | 2.50 | 31 Tex Clevenger | 2.50 |
| 2 Bob Lemon | 13.00 | (yellow type) | | 22 Hal Naragon | 2.50 | 32 J.W. Porter | 2.50 |
| 2 Bob Lemon | 26.00 | 12 George Crowe | 2.50 | 23 Bill Tuttle | 2.50 | 32 J.W. Porter | 18.00 |
| (yellow type) | | 13 Billy Hoeft | 2.50 | 23 Bill Tuttle | 18.00 | (yellow letters) | |
| 3 Alex Kellner | 2.00 | 13 Billy Hoeft | 18.00 | (yellow type) | | 33 Cal Neeman | 2.50 |
| 4 Hank Foiles | 2.00 | (yellow type) | | 24 Hobie Landrith | 2.50 | 33 Cal Neeman | 15.00 |
| 5 Willie Mays | 75.00 | 14 Rip Repulski | 2.50 | 24 Hobie Landrith | 18.00 | (yellow letters) | |
| 6 George Zuverink | 2.00 | 15 Jim Lemon | 2.50 | (yellow type) | | 34 Bob Thurman | 2.50 |
| 7 Dale Long | 2.50 | 16 Charley Neal | 2.50 | 25 Don Drysdal | 20.00 | 35 Don Mossi | 2.50 |
| 8 Eddie Kasko | 2.50 | 17 Felix Mantilla | 2.50 | 26 Ron Jackson | 2.50 | 35 Don Mossi | 15.00 |
| 8 Eddie Kasko | 18.00 | 18 Frank Sullivan | 2.50 | 27 Bud Freeman | 2.50 | (yellow letters) | |
| (yellow type) | | 19 New York Giants | 10.00 | 28 Jim Busby | 2.50 | 36 Ted Kazanski | 2.50 |
| 9 Hank Bauer | 5.00 | 20 Gil McDougald | 6.00 | 29 Ted Lepcio | 2.50 | 37 Mike McCormick | 3.50 |
| 10 Lou Burdette | 4.00 | 20 Gil McDougald | 20.00 | 30 Hank Aaron | 80.00 | (photo of Ray Monzant) | |
| 11 Jim Rivera | 2.50 | (yellow type) | | 30 Hank Aaron | 160.00 | 38 Dick Gernert | 2.50 |
| | | | | (yellow letters) | | | |

| NO. PLAYER | MINT |
|---|---|
| 39 Bob Martyn | 2.50 |
| 40 George Kell | 10.00 |
| 41 Dave Hillman | 2.50 |
| 42 John Roseboro (R) | 4.00 |
| 43 Sal Maglie | 4.00 |
| 44 Wash Senators | 5.00 |
| 45 Dick Groat | 4.00 |
| 46 Lou Sleater | 2.50 |
| 46 Lou Sleater | 18.00 |
| (yellow letters) | |
| 47 Roger Maris (R) | 220.00 |
| 48 Chuck Harmon | 2.50 |
| 49 Smokey Burgess | 2.50 |
| 50 Billy Pierc | 2.50 |
| 50 Billy Pierc | 15.00 |
| (yellow letters) | |
| 51 Del Rice | 2.50 |
| 52 Bob Clemente | 45.00 |
| 52 Bob Clemente | 90.00 |
| (yellow letters) | |
| 53 Morrie Martin | 2.50 |
| 53 Morrie Martin | 18.00 |
| (yellow letters) | |
| 54 Norm Siebern | 2.50 |
| 55 Chico Carrasquel | 2.50 |
| 56 Bill Fischer | 2.50 |
| 57 Tim Thompson | 2.50 |
| 57 Tim Thompson | 18.00 |
| (yellow letters) | |
| 58 Art Schult | 2.50 |
| 58 Art Schult | 15.00 |
| (yellow letters) | |
| 59 Dave Sisler | 2.50 |
| 60 Del Ennis | 2.50 |
| 60 Del Ennis | 18.00 |
| (yellow letters) | |
| 61 Darrell Johnson | 2.50 |
| 61 Darrell Johnson | 18.00 |
| (yellow letters) | |
| 62 Joe DeMaestri | 2.50 |
| 63 Joe Nuxhall | 2.50 |
| 64 Joe Lonnett | 2.50 |
| 65 Von McDaniel | 2.50 |
| 65 Von McDaniel | 18.00 |
| (yellow letters) | |
| 66 Lee Walls | 2.50 |
| 67 Joe Ginsberg | 2.50 |
| 68 Daryl Spencer | 2.50 |
| 69 Wally Burnette | 2.50 |
| 70 Al Kaline | 25.00 |
| 70 Al Kaline | 70.00 |
| (yellow letters) | |
| 71 Brooklyn Dodgers | 10.00 |
| 72 Bud Byerly | 2.50 |
| 73 Pete Daley | 2.50 |
| 74 Roy Face | 2.50 |
| 75 Gus Bell | 2.50 |
| 76 Dick Farrell | 2.50 |
| 76 Dick Farrell | 15.00 |
| (yellow letters) | |
| 77 Don Zimmer | 2.50 |
| 77 Don Zimmer | 15.00 |
| (yellow letters) | |
| 78 Ernie Johnson | 2.50 |
| 78 Ernie Johnson | 18.00 |
| (yellow letters) | |
| 79 Dick Williams | 2.50 |
| 79 Dick Williams | 15.00 |
| (yellow letters) | |
| 80 Dick Drott | 2.50 |
| 81 Steve Boros | 2.50 |
| 81 Steve Boros | 15.00 |
| (yellow letters) | |
| 82 Ronnie Kline | 2.50 |
| 83 Bob Hazle | 2.50 |
| 84 Billy O'Dell | 2.50 |
| 85 Luis Aparicio | 10.00 |
| 85 Luis Aparicio | 20.00 |
| (yellow letters) | |
| 86 Valmy Thomas | 2.50 |
| 87 Johnny Kucks | 2.50 |
| 88 Duke Snider | 35.00 |

| NO. PLAYER | MINT |
|---|---|
| 89 Bill Klaus | 2.50 |
| 90 Robin Roberts | 12.00 |
| 91 Chuck Tanner | 2.50 |
| 92 Clint Courtney | 2.50 |
| 92 Clint Courtney | 18.00 |
| (yellow letters) | |
| 93 Sandy Amoros | 2.50 |
| 94 Bob Skinner | 2.50 |
| 95 Frank Bolling | 2.50 |
| 96 Joseph Durham | 2.50 |
| 97 Larry Jackson | 2.50 |
| 97 Larry Jackson | 18.00 |
| (yellow letters) | |
| 98 Bill Hunter | 2.50 |
| 98 Bill Hunter | 18.00 |
| (yellow letters) | |
| 99 Bobby Adams | 2.50 |
| 100 Early Wynn | 12.50 |
| 100 Early Wynn | 25.00 |
| (yellow letters) | |
| 101 Bob Richardson | 7.50 |
| 101 Bob Richardson | 27.00 |
| (yellow letters) | |
| 102 George Strickland | 2.50 |
| 103 Jerry Lynch | 2.50 |
| 104 Jim Pendleton | 2.50 |
| 105 Billy Gardner | 2.50 |
| 106 Dick Schofield | 2.50 |
| 107 Ossie Virgil | 2.50 |
| 108 Jim Landis | 2.50 |
| 108 Jim Landis | 15.00 |
| (yellow letters) | |
| 109 Herb Plews | 2.50 |
| 110 Johnny Logan | 2.50 |
| 111 Stu Miller | 2.00 |
| 112 Gus Zernial | 2.00 |
| 113 Jerry Walker | 2.00 |
| 114 Irv Noren | 2.00 |
| 115 Jim Bunning | 6.00 |
| 116 Dave Philley | 2.00 |
| 117 Frank Torre | 2.00 |
| 118 Harvey Haddix | 2.00 |
| 119 Harry Chiti | 2.00 |
| 120 Johnny Podres | 4.00 |
| 121 Ed Miksis | 2.00 |
| 122 Walter Moryn | 2.00 |
| 123 Dick Tomanek | 2.00 |
| 124 Bobby Usher | 2.00 |
| 125 Al Dark | 3.00 |
| 126 Stan Palys | 2.00 |
| 127 Tom Sturdivant | 2.00 |
| 128 Willie Kirkland | 2.00 |
| 129 Jim Derrington | 2.00 |
| 130 Jackie Jensen | 5.00 |
| 131 Bob Henrich | 2.00 |
| 132 Vernon Law | 2.00 |
| 133 Russ Nixon | 2.00 |
| 134 Philadelphia Phillies | 5.00 |
| 135 Mike Drabowsky | 2.00 |
| 136 Jim Finigan | 2.00 |
| 137 Russ Kemmerer | 2.00 |
| 138 Earl Torgeson | 2.00 |
| 139 George Brunet | 2.00 |
| 140 Wes Covington | 2.00 |
| 141 Ken Lehman | 2.00 |
| 142 Enos Slaughter | 10.00 |
| 143 Billy Muffett | 2.00 |
| 144 Bobby Morgan | 2.00 |
| 146 Dick Gray | 2.00 |
| 147 Don McMahon | 2.00 |
| 148 Billy Consolo | 2.00 |
| 149 Tom Acker | 2.00 |
| 150 Mickey Mantle | 400.00 |
| 151 Buddy Pritchard | 2.00 |
| 152 Johnny Antonelli | 2.00 |
| 153 Les Moss | 2.00 |
| 154 Harry Byrd | 2.00 |
| 155 Hector Lopez | 2.00 |
| 156 Dick Hyde | 2.00 |
| 157 Dee Fondy | 2.00 |
| 158 Cleveland Indians | 5.00 |
| 159 Taylor Phillips | 2.50 |

| NO. PLAYER | MINT |
|---|---|
| 160 Don Hoak | 2.50 |
| 161 Don Larsen | 5.00 |
| 162 Gil Hodges | 16.00 |
| 163 Jim Wilson | 2.00 |
| 164 Bob Taylor | 2.00 |
| 165 Bob Nieman | 2.00 |
| 166 Danny O'Connell | 2.00 |
| 167 Frank Baumann | 2.00 |
| 168 Joe Cunningham | 2.00 |
| 169 Ralph Terry | 2.00 |
| 170 Vic Wertz | 2.00 |
| 171 Harry Anderson | 2.00 |
| 172 Don Gross | 2.00 |
| 173 Eddie Yost | 2.00 |
| 174 Kansas C. Athletics | 5.00 |
| 175 Marv Throneberry (R) | 6.00 |
| 176 Bob Buhl | 2.00 |
| 177 Al Smith | 2.00 |
| 178 Ted Kluszewski | 5.00 |
| 179 Willy Miranda | 2.00 |
| 180 Lindy McDaniel | 2.00 |
| 181 Willie Jones | 2.00 |
| 182 Joe Caffie | 2.00 |
| 183 Dave Jolly | 2.00 |
| 184 Elvin Tappe | 2.00 |
| 185 Ray Boone | 2.00 |
| 186 Jack Meyer | 2.00 |
| 187 Sandy Koufax | 75.00 |
| 188 Milt Bolling | 2.00 |
| (photo of Lou Berberet) | |
| 189 George Susce | 2.00 |
| 190 Red Schoendienst | 4.00 |
| 191 Art Ceccarelli | 2.00 |
| 192 Milt Graff | 2.00 |
| 193 Jerry Lumpe | 2.00 |
| 194 Roger Craig | 3.00 |
| 195 Whitey Lockman | 2.00 |
| 196 Mike Garcia | 2.00 |
| 197 Haywood Sullivan | 2.00 |
| 198 Bill Virdon | 2.50 |
| 199 Don Blasingame | 1.50 |
| 200 Bob Keegan | 1.50 |
| 201 Jim Bolger | 1.50 |
| 202 Woody Held | 1.50 |
| 203 Al Walker | 1.50 |
| 204 Leo Kiely | 1.50 |
| 205 Johnny Temple | 1.50 |
| 206 Bob Shaw | 1.50 |
| 207 Solly Hemus | 1.50 |
| 208 Cal McLish | 1.50 |
| 209 Bob Anderson | 1.50 |
| 210 Wally Moon | 1.50 |
| 211 Pete Burnside | 1.50 |
| 212 Bubba Phillips | 1.50 |
| 213 Red Wilson | 1.50 |
| 214 Willard Schmidt | 1.50 |
| 215 Jim Gilliam | 5.00 |
| 216 St. Louis Cardinals | 5.00 |
| 217 Jack Harshman | 1.50 |
| 218 Dick Rand | 1.50 |
| 219 Camilo Pascual | 1.50 |
| 220 Tom Brewer | 1.50 |
| 221 Jerry Kindall | 1.50 |
| 222 Bud Daley | 1.50 |
| 223 Andy Pafko | 1.50 |
| 224 Bob Grim | 1.50 |
| 225 Billy Goodman | 1.50 |
| 226 Bob Smith | 1.50 |
| 227 Gene Stephens | 1.50 |
| 228 Duke Maas | 1.50 |
| 229 Frank Zupo | 1.50 |
| 230 Richie Ashburn | 7.00 |
| 231 Lloyd Merritt | 1.50 |
| 232 Reno Bertoia | 1.50 |
| 233 Mickey Vernon | 1.50 |
| 234 Carl Sawatski | 1.50 |
| 235 Tom Gorman | 1.50 |
| 236 Ed Fitzgerald | 1.50 |
| 237 Bill Wight | 1.50 |
| 238 Bill Mazeroski | 6.00 |
| 239 Chuck Stobbs | 1.50 |
| 240 Moose Skowron | 6.00 |

| NO. PLAYER | MINT |
|---|---|
| 241 Dick Littlefield | 1.50 |
| 242 Johnny Klippstein | 1.50 |
| 243 Larry Raines | 1.50 |
| 244 Don Demeter | 1.50 |
| 245 Frank Lary | 1.50 |
| 246 New York Yankees | 17.00 |
| 247 Casey Wise | 1.50 |
| 248 Herm Wehmeier | 1.50 |
| 249 Ray Moore | 1.50 |
| 250 Roy Sievers | 1.50 |
| 251 Warren Hacker | 1.50 |
| 252 Bob Trowbridge | 1.50 |
| 253 Don Mueller | 1.50 |
| 254 Alex Grammas | 1.50 |
| 255 Bob Turley | 5.00 |
| 256 Chicago White Sox | 5.00 |
| 257 Hal Smith | 1.50 |
| 258 Carl Erskine | 4.00 |
| 259 Alan Pilarcik | 1.50 |
| 260 Frank Malzone | 1.50 |
| 261 Turk Lown | 1.50 |
| 262 John Groth | 1.50 |
| 263 Ed Bressoud | 1.50 |
| 264 Jack Sanford | 1.50 |
| 265 Pete Runnels | 1.50 |
| 266 Connie Johnson | 1.50 |
| 267 Sherm Lollar | 1.50 |
| 268 Granny Hamner | 1.50 |
| 269 Paul Smith | 1.50 |
| 270 Warren Spahn | 18.00 |
| 271 Billy Martin | 7.00 |
| 272 Ray Crone | 1.50 |
| 273 Hal Smith | 1.50 |
| 274 Rocky Bridges | 1.50 |
| 275 Elston Howard | 5.00 |
| 276 Bobby Avila | 1.50 |
| 277 Virgil Trucks | 1.50 |
| 278 Mack Burk | 1.50 |
| 279 Bob Boyd | 1.50 |
| 280 Jim Piersall | 4.00 |
| 281 Sam Taylor | 1.50 |
| 282 Paul Foytack | 1.50 |
| 283 Ray Shearer | 1.50 |
| 284 Ray Katt | 1.50 |
| 285 Frank Robinson | 27.00 |
| 286 Gino Cimoli | 1.50 |
| 287 Sam Jones | 1.50 |
| 288 Harmon Killebrew | 22.00 |
| 289 Hurling Rivals: | 4.00 |
| Lou Burdette, Bobby Shantz | |
| 290 Dick Donovan | 1.50 |
| 291 Don Landrum | 1.50 |
| 292 Ned Garver | 1.50 |
| 293 Gene Freese | 1.50 |
| 294 Hal Jeffcoat | 1.50 |
| 295 Minnie Minoso | 4.00 |
| 296 Ryne Duren | 4.00 |
| 297 Don Buddin | 1.50 |
| 298 Jim Hearn | 1.50 |
| 299 Harry Simpson | 1.50 |
| 300 Harridge and Giles | 4.00 |
| League Presidents | |
| 301 Randy Jackson | 1.50 |
| 302 Mike Baxes | 1.50 |
| 303 Neil Chrisley | 1.50 |
| 304 Tigers' Big Bats: | 6.00 |
| Harvey Kuenn, Al Kaline | |
| 305 Clem Labine | 2.00 |
| 306 Whammy Douglas | 1.50 |
| 307 Brooks Robinson | 35.00 |
| 308 Paul Giel | 1.50 |
| 309 Gail Harris | 1.50 |
| 310 Ernie Banks | 30.00 |
| 311 Bob Purkey | 1.50 |
| 312 Boston Red Sox | 6.00 |
| 313 Bob Rush | 1.50 |
| 314 Boss and Power | 12.00 |
| Duke Snider, Walt Alston | |
| 315 Bob Friend | 1.50 |
| 316 Tito Francona | 1.50 |
| 317 Albie Pearson | 2.00 |
| 318 Frank House | 1.50 |

| NO. PLAYER | MINT | NO. PLAYER | MINT | NO. PLAYER | MINT | NO. PLAYER | MINT |
|---|---|---|---|---|---|---|---|
| 319 Lou Skizas | 1.50 | 362 Ray Jablonski | 1.50 | 407 Carlton Willey | 1.50 | 450 Preston Ward | 4.00 |
| 320 Whitey Ford | 20.00 | 363 Don Elston | 1.50 | 408 Baltimore Orioles* | 6.00 | 451 Joe Taylor | 1.25 |
| 321 Sluggers Supreme: | 12.00 | 364 Earl Battey | 1.50 | 409 Frank Thomas | 1.50 | 452 Roman Mejias | 1.25 |
| Ted Kluszewski, | | 365 Tom Morgan | 1.50 | 410 Murray Wall | 1.50 | 453 Tom Qualters | 1.25 |
| Ted Williams | | 366 Gene Green | 1.50 | 411 Tony Taylor | 1.50 | 454 Harry Hanebrink | 1.25 |
| 322 Harding Peterson | 1.50 | 367 Jack Urban | 1.50 | 412 Jerry Staley | 1.50 | 455 Hal Griggs | 1.25 |
| 323 Elmer Valo | 1.50 | 368 Rocky Colavito | 6.00 | 413 Jim Davenport | 1.50 | 456 Dick Brown | 1.25 |
| 324 Hoyt Wilhelm | 10.00 | 369 Ralph Lumenti | 1.50 | 414 Sammy White | 1.50 | 457 Milt Pappas (R) | 4.00 |
| 325 Joe Adcock | 2.00 | 370 Yogi Berra | 35.00 | 415 Bob Bowman | 1.50 | 458 Julio Becquer | 1.25 |
| 326 Bob Miller | 1.50 | 371 Marty Keough | 1.50 | 416 Foster Castleman | 1.50 | 459 Ron Blackburn | 1.25 |
| 327 Chicago Cubs | 5.00 | 372 Don Cardwell | 1.50 | 417 Carl Furillo | 5.00 | 460 Chuck Essegian | 1.25 |
| 328 Ike Delock | 1.50 | 373 Joe Pignatano | 1.50 | 418 W. Series Batting Foes: | 100.00 | 461 Ed Mayer | 1.25 |
| 329 Bob Cerv | 1.50 | 374 Brooks Lawrence | 1.50 | Mickey Mantle, Hank Aaron | | 462 Gary Geiger | 4.00 |
| 330 Ed Bailey | 1.50 | 375 Pee Wee Reese | 25.00 | 419 Bobby Shantz | 2.50 | 463 Vito Valentinetti | 1.25 |
| 331 Pedro Ramos | 1.50 | 376 Charley Rabe | 1.50 | 420 Vada Pinson | 8.00 | 464 Curt Flood (R) | 6.00 |
| 332 Jim King | 1.50 | 377 Milwaukee Braves* | 6.00 | 421 Dixie Howell | 1.50 | 465 Arnie Portocarrero | 1.25 |
| 333 Andy Carey | 1.50 | 378 Hank Sauer | 1.50 | 422 Norm Zauchin | 1.50 | 466 Pete Whisenant | 1.25 |
| 334 Mound Aces: | 2.50 | 379 Ray Herbert | 1.50 | 423 Phil Clark | 1.50 | 467 Glen Hobbie | 1.25 |
| Bob Friend, Billy Pierce | | 380 Charley Maxwell | 1.50 | 424 Larry Doby | 3.00 | 468 Bob Schmidt | 1.25 |
| 335 Ruben Gomez | 2.50 | 381 Hal Brown | 1.50 | 425 Sam Esposito | 1.50 | 469 Don Ferrarese | 1.25 |
| 336 Bert Hamric | 2.50 | 382 Al Cicotte | 1.50 | 426 Johnny O'Brien | 1.50 | 470 R.C. Stevens | 1.25 |
| 337 Hank Aguirre | 2.50 | 383 Lou Berberet | 1.50 | 427 Al Worthington | 1.50 | 471 Lenny Green | 1.25 |
| 338 Walter Dropo | 2.50 | 384 John Goryl | 1.50 | 428 Cincinnati Redlegs* | 6.00 | 472 Joe Jay | 1.25 |
| 339 Fred Hatfield | 2.50 | 385 Wilmer Mizell | 1.50 | 429 Gus Triandos | 1.50 | 473 Bill Renna | 1.25 |
| 340 Don Newcombe | 4.00 | 386 Young Sluggers: | 5.00 | 430 Bobby Thomson | 3.00 | 474 Roman Semproch | 1.25 |
| 341 Pittsburgh Pirates | 5.00 | Ed Bailey, Birdie Tebbetts, | | 431 Gene Conley | 1.50 | 475 All-Star Managers: | 10.00 |
| 342 Jim Brosnan | 1.50 | Frank Robinson | | 432 John Powers | 1.50 | Stengel, Haney |
| 343 Orlando Cepeda (R) | 20.00 | 387 Wally Post | 1.50 | 433 Pancho Herrera | 3.00 | 476 Stan Musial (AS) | 13.00 |
| 344 Bob Porterfield | 1.50 | 388 Billy Moran | 1.50 | 433 Pancho Herrer | 200.00 | 477 Bill Skowron (AS) | 3.00 |
| 345 Jim Hegan | 1.50 | 389 Bill Taylor | 1.50 | (name spelled wrong) | | 478 Johnny Temple (AS) | 2.00 |
| 346 Steve Bilko | 1.50 | 390 Del Crandall | 1.50 | 434 Harvey Kuenn | 4.00 | 479 Nellie Fox (AS) | 3.00 |
| 347 Don Rudolph | 1.50 | 391 Dave Melton | 1.50 | 435 Ed Roebuck | 1.50 | 480 Eddie Mathews (AS) | 8.00 |
| 348 Chico Fernandez | 1.50 | 392 Bennie Daniels | 1.50 | 436 Rival Fence Busters: | 30.00 | 481 Frank Malzone (AS) | 2.00 |
| 349 Murry Dickson | 1.50 | 393 Tony Kubek | 7.00 | Willie Mays, Duke Snider | | 482 Ernie Banks (AS) | 10.00 |
| 350 Ken Boyer | 4.00 | 394 Jim Grant | 1.50 | 437 Bob Speake | 1.50 | 483 Luis Aparicio (AS) | 6.00 |
| 351 Braves Fence Busters: | 15.00 | 395 Willard Nixon | 1.50 | 438 Whitey Herzog | 1.50 | 484 Frank Robinson (AS) | 8.00 |
| Del Crandall, Eddie Mathews, | | 396 Dutch Dotterer | 1.50 | 439 Ray Narleski | 1.50 | 485 Ted Williams (AS) | 20.00 |
| Hank Aaron, Joe Adcock | | 397 Detroit Tigers* | 6.00 | 440 Eddie Mathews | 15.00 | 486 Willie Mays (AS) | 18.00 |
| 352 Herb Score | 3.00 | 398 Gene Woodling | 1.50 | 441 Jim Marshall | 1.25 | 487 Mickey Mantle (AS) | 35.00 |
| 353 Stan Lopata | 1.50 | 399 Marv Grissom | 1.50 | 442 Phil Paine | 1.25 | 488 Hank Aaron (AS) | 16.00 |
| 354 Art Ditmar | 1.50 | 400 Nellie Fox | 6.00 | 443 Billy Harrell | 4.00 | 489 Jackie Jensen (AS) | 3.00 |
| 355 Billy Bruton | 1.50 | 401 Don Bessent | 1.50 | 444 Danny Kravitz | 1.25 | 490 Ed Bailey (AS) | 2.00 |
| 356 Bob Malkmus | 1.50 | 402 Bobby Gene Smith | 1.50 | 445 Bob Smith | 1.25 | 491 Sherm Lollar (AS) | 2.00 |
| 357 Danny McDevitt | 1.50 | 403 Steve Korcheck | 1.50 | 446 Carroll Hardy | 4.00 | 492 Bob Friend (AS) | 2.00 |
| 358 Gene Baker | 1.50 | 404 Curt Simmons | 1.50 | 447 Ray Monzant | 1.25 | 493 Bob Turley (AS) | 2.50 |
| 359 Billy Loes | 1.50 | 405 Ken Aspromonte | 1.50 | 448 Charlie Lau | 3.00 | 494 Warren Spahn (AS) | 7.00 |
| 360 Roy McMillan | 1.50 | 406 Vic Power | 1.50 | 449 Gene Fodge | 1.25 | 495 H. Score (AS) (Exc. $1.50) | 5.00 |
| 361 Mike Fornieles | 1.50 | | | | | | |

Prices for the 1958 set are for cards in *Mint* condition. *Excellent* copies sell for 40% to 50% of prices shown; *Very Good*—25% to 30%.

# 1959 Topps. . . .Complete Set of 572 Cards—Value $1200.00 (Exc.); $3000.00 (Mint)

Includes Bob Gibson's rookie card. The high numbers are 507 to 572. Cards 199 to 286 were issued with *white* or *gray* backs. Cards 316, 321, 322, 336 and 362 exist without the *option* or *traded* line—worth $50.00 each.

| NO. PLAYER | MINT | NO. PLAYER | MINT | NO. PLAYER | MINT | NO. PLAYER | MINT |
|---|---|---|---|---|---|---|---|
| 1 BB Commissioner | 15.00 | 10 Mickey Mantle | 300.00 | 18 Jack Urban | 1.50 | 28 Red Worthington | 1.50 |
| Ford Frick (Exc. $3.00) | | 11 Billy Hunter | 1.50 | 19 Ed Bressoud | 1.50 | 29 Jim Bolger | 1.50 |
| 2 Eddie Yost | 1.50 | 12 Vern Law | 2.50 | 20 Duke Snider | 30.00 | 30 Nellie Fox | 5.00 |
| 3 Don McMahon | 1.50 | 13 Dick Gernert | 1.50 | 21 Connie Johnson | 1.50 | 31 Ken Lehman | 1.50 |
| 4 Albie Pearson | 1.50 | 14 Pete Whisenant | 1.50 | 22 Al Smith | 1.50 | 32 Don Buddin | 1.50 |
| 5 Dick Donovan | 1.50 | 15 Dick Drott | 1.50 | 23 Murry Dickson | 1.50 | 33 Ed Fizgerald | 1.50 |
| 6 Alex Grammas | 1.50 | 16 Joe Pignatano | 1.50 | 24 Red Wilson | 1.50 | 34 Pitchers Beware: | 6.00 |
| 7 Al Pilarcik | 1.50 | 17 Danny's All-Stars: | 3.00 | 25 Dan Hoak | 1.50 | Al Kaline, Charley Maxwell |
| 8 Philadelphia Phillies | 4.00 | Frank Thomas, Danny | | 26 Chuck Stobbs | 1.50 | 35 Ted Kluszewski | 4.00 |
| 9 Paul Giel | 1.50 | Murtaugh, Ted Kluszewski | | 27 Andy Pafko | 1.50 | 36 Hank Aguirre | 1.50 |

| NO. | PLAYER | MINT |
|---|---|---|
| 37 | Gene Green | 1.50 |
| 38 | Morrie Martin | 1.50 |
| 39 | Ed Bouchee | 1.50 |
| 40 | Warren Spahn | 17.00 |
| 41 | Bob Martyn | 1.50 |
| 42 | Murray Wall | 1.50 |
| 43 | Steven Bilko | 1.50 |
| 44 | Vito Valentinetti | 1.50 |
| 45 | Andy Carey | 1.50 |
| 46 | Bill Henry | 1.50 |
| 47 | Jim Finigan | 1.50 |
| 48 | Baltimore Orioles | 3.00 |
| 49 | Bill Hall | 1.50 |
| 50 | Willie May | 75.00 |
| 51 | Rip Coleman | 1.50 |
| 52 | Coot Veal | 1.50 |
| 53 | Stan Williams | 1.50 |
| 54 | Mel Roach | 1.50 |
| 55 | Tom Brewer | 1.50 |
| 56 | Carl Sawatski | 1.50 |
| 57 | Al Cicotte | 1.50 |
| 58 | Eddie Miksis | 1.50 |
| 59 | Irv Noren | 1.50 |
| 60 | Bob Turley | 3.00 |
| 61 | Dick Brown | 1.50 |
| 62 | Tony Taylor | 1.50 |
| 63 | Jim Hearn | 1.50 |
| 64 | Joe DeMaestri | 1.50 |
| 65 | Frank Torre | 1.50 |
| 66 | Joe Ginsberg | 1.50 |
| 67 | Brooks Lawrence | 1.50 |
| 68 | Dick Schofield | 1.50 |
| 69 | San F. Giants | 3.50 |
| 70 | Harvey Kuenn | 3.50 |
| 71 | Don Bessent | 1.50 |
| 72 | Bill Renna | 1.50 |
| 73 | Ron Jackson | 1.50 |
| 74 | Directing the Power: | 2.50 |
|  | Jim Lemon, Cookie Lavagetto, Roy Sievers | |
| 75 | Sam Jones | 1.50 |
| 76 | Bobby Richardson | 5.00 |
| 77 | John Goryl | 1.50 |
| 78 | Pedro Ramos | 1.50 |
| 79 | Harry Chiti | 1.50 |
| 80 | Minnie Minoso | 3.00 |
| 81 | Hal Jeffcoat | 1.50 |
| 82 | Bob Boyd | 1.50 |
| 83 | Bob Smith | 1.50 |
| 84 | Reno Bertoia | 1.50 |
| 85 | Harry Anderson | 1.50 |
| 86 | Bob Keegan | 1.50 |
| 87 | Danny O'Connell | 1.50 |
| 88 | Herb Score | 2.00 |
| 89 | Billy Gardner | 1.50 |
| 90 | Bill Skowron | 6.00 |
| 91 | Herb Moford | 1.50 |
| 92 | David Philley | 1.50 |
| 93 | Julio Becquer | 1.50 |
| 94 | Chicago White Sox | 3.50 |
| 95 | Carl Willey | 1.50 |
| 96 | Lou Berberet | 1.50 |
| 97 | Jerry Lynch | 1.50 |
| 98 | Arnie Portocarrero | 1.50 |
| 99 | Ted Kazanski | 1.50 |
| 100 | Bob Cerv | 1.50 |
| 101 | Alex Kellner | 1.50 |
| 102 | Felipe Alou (R) | 5.00 |
| 103 | Billy Goodman | 1.50 |
| 104 | Del Rice | 1.50 |
| 105 | Lee Walls | 1.50 |
| 106 | Hal Woodeshick | 1.50 |
| 107 | Norm Larker | 1.50 |
| 108 | Zack Monroe | 1.50 |
| 109 | Bob Schmidt | 1.50 |
| 110 | George Witt | 1.50 |
| 111 | Cincinnati Redlegs | 4.00 |
| 112 | Billy Consolo | 1.50 |
| 113 | Taylor Phillips | 1.50 |
| 114 | Earl Battey | 1.50 |
| 115 | Mickey Vernon | 1.50 |

**No. 116 to 146 Rookie Stars**

| NO. | PLAYER | MINT |
|---|---|---|
| 116 | Bob Allison | 5.00 |
| 117 | John Blanchard | 1.25 |
| 118 | John Buzhardt | 1.25 |
| 119 | John Callison | 3.00 |
| 120 | Chuck Coles | 1.25 |
| 121 | Bob Conley | 1.25 |
| 122 | Bennie Daniels | 1.25 |
| 123 | Donald Dillard | 1.25 |
| 124 | Dan Dobbek | 1.25 |
| 125 | Ron Fairly | 3.00 |
| 126 | Eddie Haas | 1.25 |
| 127 | Kent Hadley | 1.25 |
| 128 | Bob Hartman | 1.25 |
| 129 | Frank Herrera | 1.25 |
| 130 | Lou Jackson | 1.25 |
| 131 | Deron Johnson | 1.25 |
| 132 | Don Lee | 1.25 |
| 133 | Bob Lillis | 1.25 |
| 134 | Jim McDaniel | 1.25 |
| 135 | Gene Oliver | 1.25 |
| 136 | Jim O'Toole | 1.25 |
| 137 | Dick Ricketts | 1.25 |
| 138 | John Romano | 1.25 |
| 139 | Ed Sadowski | 1.25 |
| 140 | Charlie Secrest | 1.25 |
| 141 | Joe Shipley | 1.25 |
| 142 | Dick Stigman | 1.25 |
| 143 | Willie Tasby | 1.25 |
| 144 | Jerry Walker | 1.25 |
| 145 | Dom Zanni | 1.25 |
| 146 | Jerry Zimmerman | 1.25 |
| 147 | Cubs' Clubbers: | 6.00 |
|  | Dale Long, Ernie Banks, Walt Moryn | |
| 148 | Mike McCormick | 1.25 |
| 149 | Jim Bunning | 6.00 |
| 150 | Stan Musial | 65.00 |
| 151 | Bob Malkmus | 1.25 |
| 152 | Johnny Klippstein | 1.25 |
| 153 | Jim Marshall | 1.25 |
| 154 | Ray Herbert | 1.25 |
| 155 | Enos Slaughter | 9.00 |
| 156 | Ace Hurlers: | 4.00 |
|  | Billy Pierce, Robin Roberts | |
| 157 | Felix Mantilla | 1.25 |
| 158 | Walt Dropo | 1.25 |
| 159 | Bob Shaw | 1.25 |
| 160 | Dick Groat | 3.00 |
| 161 | Frank Baumann | 1.25 |
| 162 | Bobby Smith | 1.25 |
| 163 | Sandy Koufax | 55.00 |
| 164 | Johnny Groth | 1.25 |
| 165 | Bill Bruton | 1.25 |
| 166 | Destruction Crew: | 2.50 |
|  | Minnie Minoso, Rocky Colavito, Larry Doby | |
| 167 | Duke Maas | 1.25 |
| 168 | Carroll Hardy | 1.25 |
| 169 | Ted Abernathy | 1.25 |
| 170 | Gene Woodling | 1.25 |
| 171 | Willard Schmidt | 1.25 |
| 172 | Kansas C. Athletics | 3.00 |
| 173 | Bill Monbouquette | 1.25 |
| 174 | Jim Pendleton | 1.25 |
| 175 | Dick Farrell | 1.25 |
| 176 | Preston Ward | 1.25 |
| 177 | John Briggs | 1.25 |
| 178 | Ruben Amaro | 1.25 |
| 179 | Don Rudolph | 1.25 |
| 180 | Yogi Berra | 25.00 |
| 181 | Bob Porterfield | 1.25 |
| 182 | Milt Graff | 1.25 |
| 183 | Stu Miller | 1.25 |
| 184 | Harvey Haddix | 1.75 |
| 185 | Jim Busby | 1.25 |
| 186 | Mudcat Grant | 1.25 |
| 187 | Bubba Phillips | 1.25 |
| 188 | Juan Pizarro | 1.25 |
| 189 | Neil Chrisley | 1.25 |
| 190 | Bill Virdon | 3.00 |

| NO. | PLAYER | MINT |
|---|---|---|
| 191 | Russ Kemmerer | 1.25 |
| 192 | Charley Beamon | 1.25 |
| 193 | Sammy Taylor | 1.25 |
| 194 | Jim Brosnan | 1.25 |
| 195 | Rip Repulski | 1.25 |
| 196 | Billy Moran | 1.25 |
| 197 | Ray Semproch | 1.25 |
| 198 | Jim Davenport | 1.25 |
| 199 | Leo Kiely | 1.25 |
| 200 | NL President: Warren Giles | 3.00 |
| 201 | Tom Acker | 1.25 |
| 202 | Roger Maris | 60.00 |
| 203 | Ozzie Virgil | 1.25 |
| 204 | Casey Wise | 1.25 |
| 205 | Don Larsen | 3.50 |
| 206 | Carl Furillo | 4.00 |
| 207 | George Strickland | 1.25 |
| 208 | Willie Jones | 1.25 |
| 209 | Lenny Green | 1.25 |
| 210 | Ed Bailey | 1.25 |
| 211 | Bob Blaylock | 1.25 |
| 212 | Fence Busters: | 16.00 |
|  | Hank Aaron, Eddie Mathews | |
| 213 | Jim Rivera | 1.25 |
| 214 | Marcelino Solis | 1.25 |
| 215 | Jim Lemon | 1.25 |
| 216 | Andre Rodgers | 1.25 |
| 217 | Carl Erskine | 3.00 |
| 218 | Roman Mejias | 1.25 |
| 219 | George Zuverink | 1.25 |
| 220 | Frank Malzone | 1.25 |
| 221 | Bob Bowman | 1.25 |
| 222 | Bobby Shantz | 1.25 |
| 223 | St. Louis Cardinals | 4.00 |
| 224 | Claude Osteen (R) | 3.00 |
| 225 | Johnny Logan | 1.25 |
| 226 | Art Ceccarelli | 1.25 |
| 227 | Hal Smith | 1.25 |
| 228 | Don Gross | 1.25 |
| 229 | Vic Power | 1.25 |
| 230 | Bill Fischer | 1.25 |
| 231 | Ellis Burton | 1.25 |
| 232 | Eddie Kasko | 1.25 |
| 233 | Paul Foytack | 1.25 |
| 234 | Chuck Tanner | 1.75 |
| 235 | Valmy Thomas | 1.25 |
| 236 | Ted Bowsfield | 1.25 |
| 237 | Run Preventers: | 2.00 |
|  | Gil McDougald, Bob Turley, Bobby Richardson | |
| 238 | Gene Baker | 1.25 |
| 239 | Bob Trowbridge | 1.25 |
| 240 | Hank Bauer | 4.00 |
| 241 | Billy Muffett | 1.25 |
| 242 | Ron Samford | 1.25 |
| 243 | Marv Grissom | 1.25 |
| 244 | Dick Gray | 1.25 |
| 245 | Ned Garver | 1.25 |
| 246 | J.W. Porter | 1.25 |
| 247 | Don Ferrarese | 1.25 |
| 248 | Boston Red Sox | 5.00 |
| 249 | Bobby Adams | 1.25 |
| 250 | Billy O'Dell | 1.25 |
| 251 | Cletis Boyer | 3.00 |
| 252 | Ray Boone | 1.25 |
| 253 | Seth Morehead | 1.25 |
| 254 | Zeke Bella | 1.25 |
| 255 | Del Ennis | 1.25 |
| 256 | Jerry Davie | 1.25 |
| 257 | Leon Wagner | 1.25 |
| 258 | Fred Kipp | 1.25 |
| 259 | Jim Pisoni | 1.25 |
| 260 | Early Wynn | 12.00 |
| 261 | Gene Stephens | 1.25 |
| 262 | Hitters' Foes: | 4.00 |
|  | Johnny Podres, Clem Labine, Don Drysdale | |
| 263 | Buddy Daley | 1.25 |
| 264 | Chico Carrasquel | 1.25 |
| 265 | Ron Kline | 1.25 |

| NO. | PLAYER | MINT |
|---|---|---|
| 266 | Woody Held | 1.25 |
| 267 | John Romonosky | 1.25 |
| 268 | Tito Francona | 1.25 |
| 269 | Jack Mayer | 1.25 |
| 270 | Gil Hodges | 12.00 |
| 271 | Orlando Pena | 1.25 |
| 272 | Jerry Lumpe | 1.25 |
| 273 | Joey Jay | 1.25 |
| 274 | Jerry Kindall | 1.25 |
| 275 | Jack Sanford | 1.25 |
| 276 | Pete Daley | 1.25 |
| 277 | Turk Lown | 1.25 |
| 278 | Chuck Essegian | 1.25 |
| 279 | Ernie Johnson | 1.25 |
| 280 | Frank Bolling | 1.25 |
| 281 | Walt Craddock | 1.25 |
| 282 | R.C. Stevens | 1.25 |
| 283 | Russ Heman | 1.25 |
| 284 | Steve Korcheck | 1.25 |
| 285 | Joe Cunningham | 1.25 |
| 286 | Dean Stone | 1.25 |
| 287 | Don Zimmer | 1.50 |
| 288 | Dutch Dotterer | 1.25 |
| 289 | Johnny Kucks | 1.25 |
| 290 | Wes Covington | 1.25 |
| 291 | Pitching Partners: | 2.00 |
|  | Pedro Ramos, Camilo Pascual | |
| 292 | Dick Williams | 1.25 |
| 293 | Ray Moore | 1.25 |
| 294 | Hank Foiles | 1.25 |
| 295 | Billy Martin | 5.00 |
| 296 | Ernie Broglio | 1.25 |
| 297 | Jackie Brandt | 1.25 |
| 298 | Tex Clevenger | 1.25 |
| 299 | Billy Klaus | 1.25 |
| 300 | Richie Ashburn | 6.00 |
| 301 | Earl Averill | 1.25 |
| 302 | Don Mossi | 1.25 |
| 303 | Marty Keough | 1.25 |
| 304 | Chicago Cubs | 4.00 |
| 305 | Curt Raydon | 1.25 |
| 306 | Jim Gilliam | 4.00 |
| 307 | Curt Barclay | 1.25 |
| 308 | Norm Siebern | 1.25 |
| 309 | Sal Maglie | 3.00 |
| 310 | Luis Aparicio | 9.00 |
| 311 | Norm Zauchin | 1.25 |
| 312 | Don Newcombe | 3.00 |
| 313 | Frank House | 1.25 |
| 314 | Don Cardwell | 1.25 |
| 315 | Joe Adcock | 2.00 |
| 316 | Ralph Lumenti* | 1.25 |
|  | (photo of Camilo Pascual) | |
| 317 | Hitting Kings: | 15.00 |
|  | Willie Mays, Richie Ashburn | |
| 318 | Rocky Bridges | 1.25 |
| 319 | Dave Hillmann | 1.25 |
| 320 | Bob Skinner | 1.25 |
| 321 | Bob Giallombardo* | 1.25 |
| 322 | Harry Hanebrink* | 1.25 |
| 323 | Frank Sullivan | 1.25 |
| 324 | Donald Demeter | 1.25 |
| 325 | Ken Boyer | 3.00 |
| 326 | Marv Throneberry | 1.25 |
| 327 | Gary Bell | 1.25 |
| 328 | Lou Skizas | 1.25 |
| 329 | Detroit Tigers | 5.00 |
| 330 | Gus Triandos | 1.25 |
| 331 | Steve Boros | 1.25 |
| 332 | Ray Monzant | 1.25 |
| 333 | Harry Simpson | 1.25 |
| 334 | Glen Hobbie | 1.25 |
| 335 | Johnny Temple | 1.25 |
| 336 | Billy Loes* | 1.25 |
| 337 | George Crowe | 1.25 |
| 338 | Sparky Anderson (R) | 8.00 |
| 339 | Roy Face | 2.50 |
| 340 | Roy Sievers | 2.00 |
| 341 | Tom Qualters | 1.25 |
| 342 | Ray Jablonski | 1.25 |

| NO. PLAYER | MINT | NO. PLAYER | MINT | NO. PLAYER | MINT | NO. PLAYER | MINT |
|---|---|---|---|---|---|---|---|
| 343 Billy Hoeft | 1.25 | 401 Ron Blackburn | 1.25 | 458 Gordon Jones | 1.25 | 518 Mike Cueller (R) | 8.00 |
| 344 Russ Nixon | 1.25 | 402 Hector Lopez | 1.25 | 459 Bill Tuttle | 1.25 | 519 Infield Power: | 5.00 |
| 345 Gil McDougald | 4.00 | 403 Clem Labine | 1.25 | 460 Bob Friend | 1.25 | Pete Runnels, Dick |  |
| 346 Batter Bafflers: | 1.25 | 404 Hank Sauer | 1.25 | 461 Mantle Hits 42nd HR | 25.00 | Gernert, Frank Malzone |  |
| Tom Brewer, Dave Sisler |  | 405 Roy McMillan | 1.25 | 462 Colavito's Catch | 2.50 | 520 Don Elston | 5.00 |
| 347 Bob Buhl | 1.25 | 406 Solly Drake | 1.25 | 463 Kaline Bat Champ | 6.00 | 521 Gary Geiger | 5.00 |
| 348 Ted Lepcio | 1.25 | 407 Moe Drabowsky | 1.25 | 464 Mays' Series Catch | 12.00 | 522 Gene Snyder | 5.00 |
| 349 Hoyt Wilhelm | 8.00 | 408 Keystone Combo: | 5.00 | 465 Sievers HR Mark | 2.00 | 523 Harry Bright | 5.00 |
| 350 Ernie Banks | 25.00 | Nellie Fox, Luis Aparicio |  | 466 Pierce All-Star | 2.00 | 524 Larry Osborne | 5.00 |
| 351 Earl Torgeson | 1.25 | 409 Gus Zernial | 1.25 | 467 Aaron Clubs Homer | 12.00 | 525 Jim Coates | 5.00 |
| 352 Robin Roberts | 10.00 | 410 Billy Pierce | 1.25 | 468 Snider's Play | 9.00 | 526 Bob Speake | 5.00 |
| 353 Curt Flood | 3.00 | 411 Whitey Lockman | 1.25 | 469 Banks MVP | 8.00 | 527 Solly Hemus | 5.00 |
| 354 Pete Burnside | 1.25 | 412 Stan Lopata | 1.25 | 470 Musial's 3000 Hits | 8.00 | 528 Pittsburgh Pirates | 12.00 |
| 355 Jim Piersall | 2.00 | 413 Camillo Pascual | 1.25 | 471 Tom Sturdivant | 1.25 | 529 George Bamberger (R) | 8.00 |
| 356 Bob Mabe | 1.25 | 414 Dale Long | 1.25 | 472 Gene Freese | 1.25 | 530 Wally Moon | 5.00 |
| 357 Dick Stuart (R) | 2.00 | 415 Bill Mazeroski | 4.00 | 473 Mike Fornieles | 1.25 | 531 Ray Webster | 5.00 |
| 358 Ralph Terry | 1.25 | 416 Haywood Sullivan | 1.25 | 474 Moe Thacker | 1.25 | 532 Mark Freeman | 5.00 |
| 359 Bill White (R) | 4.00 | 417 Virgil Trucks | 1.25 | 475 Jack Harshman | 1.25 | 533 Darrell Johnson | 5.00 |
| 360 Al Kaline | 21.00 | 418 Gino Cimoli | 1.25 | 476 Cleveland Indians | 3.00 | 534 Faye Throneberry | 5.00 |
| 361 Willard Nixon | 1.25 | 419 Milwaukee Braves | 4.00 | 477 Barry Latman | 1.25 | 535 Ruben Gomez | 5.00 |
| 362 Dolan Nichols* | 1.25 | 420 Rocky Colavito | 4.00 | 478 Bob Clemente | 40.00 | 536 Dan Kravitz | 5.00 |
| 363 Bobby Avila | 1.25 | 421 Herm Wehmeier | 1.25 | 479 Lindy McDaniel | 1.25 | 537 Rudolph Arias | 5.00 |
| 364 Danny McDevitt | 1.25 | 422 Hobie Landrith | 1.25 | 480 Red Schoendienst | 3.00 | 538 Chick King | 5.00 |
| 365 Gus Bell | 1.25 | 423 Bob Grim | 1.25 | 481 Charlie Maxwell | 1.25 | 539 Gary Blaylock | 5.00 |
| 366 Humberto Robinson | 1.25 | 424 Ken Aspromonte | 1.25 | 482 Russ Meyer | 1.25 | 540 Willie Miranda | 5.00 |
| 367 Cal Neeman | 1.25 | 425 Del Crandall | 1.25 | 483 Clint Courtney | 1.25 | 541 Bob Thurman | 5.00 |
| 368 Don Mueller | 1.25 | 426 Jerry Staley | 1.25 | 484 Willie Kirkland | 1.25 | 542 Jim Perry (R) | 8.00 |
| 369 Dick Tomanek | 1.25 | 427 Charlie Neal | 1.25 | 485 Ryne Duren | 2.50 | 543 Corsair Outfield Trio: | 22.00 |
| 370 Pete Runnels | 1.25 | 428 Buc Hill Aces: | 2.50 | 486 Sammy White | 1.25 | Bob Skinner, Bll Virdon, |  |
| 371 Dick Brodowski | 1.25 | Ron Kline, Bob Friend, |  | 487 Hal Brown | 1.25 | Roberto Clemente |  |
| 372 Jim Hegan | 1.25 | Vernon Law, Roy Face |  | 488 Walt Moryn | 1.25 | 544 Lee Tate | 5.00 |
| 373 Herb Plews | 1.25 | 429 Bobby Thomson | 1.50 | 489 John Powers | 1.25 | 545 Tom Morgan | 5.00 |
| 374 Art Ditmar | 1.25 | 430 Whitey Ford | 20.00 | 490 Frank Thomas | 1.25 | 546 Al Schroll | 5.00 |
| 375 Bob Nieman | 1.25 | 431 Whammy Douglas | 1.25 | 491 Don Blasingame | 1.25 | 547 Jim Baxes | 5.00 |
| 376 Hal Naragon | 1.25 | 432 Smokey Burgess | 1.25 | 492 Gene Conley | 1.25 | 548 Elmer Singleton | 5.00 |
| 377 Johnny Antonelli | 1.25 | 433 Billy Harrell | 1.25 | 493 Jim Landis | 1.25 | 549 Howie Nunn | 5.00 |
| 378 Gail Harris | 1.25 | 434 Hal Griggs | 1.25 | 494 Don Pavletich | 1.25 | 550 Symbol of Courage: | 65.00 |
| 379 Bob Miller | 1.25 | 435 Frank Robinson | 20.00 | 495 Johnny Podres | 3.00 | Roy Campanella |  |
| 380 Hank Aaron | 60.00 | 436 Granny Hamner | 1.25 | 496 Wayne Terwilliger | 1.25 | 551 F. Haney—Mgr.(AS) | 6.00 |
| 381 Mike Baxes | 1.25 | 437 Ike Delock | 1.25 | 497 Hal R. Smith | 1.25 | 552 C. Stengel—Mgr. (AS) | 15.00 |
| 382 Curt Simmons | 1.25 | 438 Sam Esposito | 1.25 | 498 Dick Hyde | 1.25 | 553 Orlando Cepeda (AS) | 7.00 |
| 383 Words of Wisdom: | 5.00 | 439 Brooks Robinson | 22.00 | 499 Johnny O'Brien | 1.25 | 554 Bll Skowron (AS) | 6.00 |
| Don Larsen, Casey Stengel |  | 440 Lou Burdette | 3.50 | 500 Vic Wertz | 1.25 | 555 Bill Mazeroski (AS) | 6.00 |
| 384 Dave Sisler | 1.25 | 441 John Roseboro | 1.25 | 501 Bobby Tiefenauer | 1.25 | 556 Nellie Fox (AS) | 8.00 |
| 385 Sherm Lollar | 1.25 | 442 Ray Narleski | 1.25 | 502 Al Dark | 1.50 | 557 Ken Boyer (AS) | 6.00 |
| 386 Jim Delsing | 1.25 | 443 Daryl Spencer | 1.25 | 503 Jim Owens | 1.25 | 558 Frank Malzone (AS) | 6.00 |
| 387 Don Drysdale | 15.00 | 444 Ronnie Hansen | 1.25 | 504 Ossie Alvarez | 1.25 | 559 Ernie Banks (AS) | 20.00 |
| 388 Bob Will | 1.25 | 445 Cal McLish | 1.25 | 505 Tony Kubek | 5.00 | 560 Luis Aparicio (AS) | 11.00 |
| 389 Joe Nuxhall | 1.25 | 446 Rocky Nelson | 1.25 | 506 Bob Purkey | 1.25 | 561 Hank Aaron (AS) | 40.00 |
| 390 Orlando Cepeda | 6.00 | 447 Bob Anderson | 1.25 | 507 Bob Hale | 5.00 | 562 Al Kaline (AS) | 20.00 |
| 391 Milt Pappas | 1.25 | 448 Vada Pinson | 3.50 | 508 Art Fowler | 5.00 | 563 Willie Mays (AS) | 40.00 |
| 392 Whitey Herzog | 2.50 | 449 Tom Gorman | 1.25 | 509 Norm Cash (R) | 15.00 | 564 Mickey Mantle (AS) | 135.00 |
| 393 Frank Lary | 1.25 | 450 Ed Mathews | 15.00 | 510 New York Yankees | 25.00 | 565 Wes Covington (AS) | 6.00 |
| 394 Randy Jackson | 1.25 | 451 Jimmy Constable | 1.25 | 511 George Susce | 5.00 | 566 Roy Sievers (AS) | 6.00 |
| 395 Elston Howard | 5.00 | 452 Chico Fernandez | 1.25 | 512 George Altman | 5.00 | 567 Del Crandall (AS) | 6.00 |
| 396 Bob Rush | 1.25 | 453 Les Moss | 1.25 | 513 Tommy Carroll | 5.00 | 568 Gus Triandos (AS) | 6.00 |
| 397 Washington Senators | 3.00 | 454 Phil Clark | 1.25 | 514 Bob Gibson (R) | 175.00 | 569 Bob Friend (AS) | 6.00 |
| 398 Wally Post | 1.25 | 455 Larry Doby | 3.00 | 515 Harmon Killebrew | 50.00 | 570 Bob Turley (AS) | 6.00 |
| 399 Larry Jackson | 1.25 | 456 Jerry Casale | 1.25 | 516 Mike Garcia | 5.00 | 571 Warren Spahn (AS) | 18.00 |
| 400 Jackie Jensen | 2.00 | 457 Los Angeles Dodgers | 11.00 | 517 Joe Koppe | 5.00 | 572 B. Pierce (AS) (Exc. $3.00) | 15.00 |

Prices for the 1959 set are for cards in *Mint* condition. *Excellent* copies sell for 40% to 50% of prices shown; *Very Good*—25% to 30%.

## 1960 Topps....Complete Set of 572 Cards—Value $1150.00 (Exc.); $2700.00 (Mint)

This set features the rookie cards of Willie McCovey and Carl Yastrzemski. The high numbers are 507 to 572. Semi-high numbers are 441 to 506. Topps' switched to a predominately horizontal format, and used it for the last time. Cards 375 to 440 exist with *gray* or *white* backs.

| NO. PLAYER | MINT |
|---|---|
| 1 E. Wynn (Exc. $4.00) | 18.00 |
| 2 Roman Mejias | 1.00 |
| 3 Joe Adcock | 2.00 |
| 4 Bob Purkey | 1.00 |
| 5 Wally Moon | 1.00 |
| 6 Lou Berberet | 1.00 |
| 7 Master & Mentor: | 8.00 |
| Willie Mays, Bill Rigney | |
| 8 Bud Daley | 1.00 |
| 9 Faye Throneberry | 1.00 |
| 10 Ernie Banks | 16.00 |
| 11 Norm Siebern | 1.00 |
| 12 Milt Pappas | 1.00 |
| 13 Wally Post | 1.00 |
| 14 Jim Grant | 1.00 |
| 15 Pete Runnels | 1.00 |
| 16 Ernie Broglio | 1.00 |
| 17 John Callison | 1.00 |
| 18 Los Angeles Dodgers | 8.00 |
| 19 Felix Mantilla | 1.00 |
| 20 Roy Face | 1.50 |
| 21 Dutch Dotterer | 1.00 |
| 22 Rocky Bridges | 1.00 |
| 23 Eddie Fisher | 1.00 |
| 24 Dick Gray | 1.00 |
| 25 Ray Sievers | 1.00 |
| 26 Wayne Terwilliger | 1.00 |
| 27 Dick Drott | 1.00 |
| 28 Brooks Robinson | 22.00 |
| 29 Clem Labine | 1.00 |
| 30 Tito Francona | 1.00 |
| 31 Sammy Esposito | 1.00 |
| 32 Sophomore Stalwarts: | 1.50 |
| Jim O'Toole, Vada Pinson | |
| 33 Tom Morgan | 1.00 |
| 34 Sparky Anderson | 2.50 |
| 35 Whitey Ford | 16.00 |
| 36 Russ Nixon | 1.00 |
| 37 Bill Bruton | 1.00 |
| 38 Jerry Casale | 1.00 |
| 39 Earl Averill | 1.00 |
| 40 Joe Cunningham | 1.00 |
| 41 Barry Latman | 1.00 |
| 42 Hobie Landrith | 1.00 |
| 43 Washington Senators | 2.00 |
| 44 Bobby Locke | 1.00 |
| 45 Roy McMillan | 1.00 |
| 46 Jack Fisher | 1.00 |
| 47 Don Zimmer | 2.00 |
| 48 Hal Smith | 1.00 |
| 49 Curt Raydon | 1.00 |
| 50 Al Kaline | 16.00 |
| 51 Jim Coates | 1.00 |
| 52 Dave Philley | 1.00 |
| 53 Jackie Brandt | 1.00 |
| 54 Mike Fornieles | 1.00 |
| 55 Bill Mazeroski | 2.50 |
| 56 Steve Korcheck | 1.00 |
| 57 Win Savers: | 1.25 |
| Turk Lown, Jerry Staley | |
| 58 Gino Cimoli | 1.00 |
| 59 Juan Pizarro | 1.00 |
| 60 Gus Triandos | 1.00 |
| 61 Eddie Kasko | 1.00 |
| 62 Roger Craig | 1.25 |
| 63 George Strickland | 1.00 |
| 64 Jack Meyer | 1.00 |
| 65 Elston Howard | 3.00 |
| 66 Bob Trowbridge | 1.00 |
| 67 Jose Pagan | 1.00 |
| 68 Dave Hillman | 1.00 |
| 69 Billy Goodman | 1.00 |
| 70 Lou Burdette | 2.50 |
| 71 Marty Keough | 1.00 |
| 72 Detroit Tigers | 4.00 |
| 73 Bob Gibson | 17.00 |
| 74 Walt Moryn | 1.00 |
| 75 Vic Power | 1.00 |
| 76 Bill Fischer | 1.00 |
| 77 Hank Foiles | 1.00 |
| 78 Bob Grim | 1.00 |
| 79 Walt Dropo | 1.00 |

| NO. PLAYER | MINT |
|---|---|
| 80 Johnny Antonelli | 1.00 |
| 81 Russ Snyder | 1.00 |
| 82 Ruben Gomez | 1.00 |
| 83 Tony Kubek | 4.00 |
| 84 Hal Smith | 1.00 |
| 85 Frank Lary | 1.00 |
| 86 Dick Gernert | 1.00 |
| 87 John Romonosky | 1.00 |
| 88 John Roseboro | 1.00 |
| 89 Hal Brown | 1.00 |
| 90 Bobby Avila | 1.00 |
| 91 Bennie Daniels | 1.00 |
| 92 Whitey Herzog | 2.00 |
| 93 Art Schult | 1.00 |
| 94 Leo Kiely | 1.00 |
| 95 Frank Thomas | 1.00 |
| 96 Ralph Terry | 1.00 |
| 97 Ted Lepcio | 1.00 |
| 98 Gordon Jones | 1.00 |
| 99 Lenny Green | 1.00 |
| 100 Nellie Fox | 4.00 |
| 101 Bob Miller | 1.00 |
| 102 Kent Hadley | 1.00 |
| 103 Dick Farrell | 1.00 |
| 104 Dick Schofield | 1.00 |
| 105 Larry Sherry (R) | 1.50 |
| 106 Billy Gardner | 1.00 |
| 107 Carl Willey | 1.00 |
| 108 Pete Daley | 1.00 |
| 109 Cletis Boyer | 1.25 |
| 110 Cal McLish | 1.00 |
| 111 Vic Wertz | 1.00 |
| 112 Jack Harshman | 1.00 |
| 113 Bob Skinner | 1.00 |
| 114 Ken Aspromonte | 1.00 |
| 115 Fork & Knuckler: | 3.50 |
| Roy Face, Hoyt Wilhelm | |
| 116 Jim Rivera | 1.00 |

**No. 117 to 148—ROOKIE STARS**

| NO. PLAYER | MINT |
|---|---|
| 117 Tom Borland | 1.00 |
| 118 Bob Bruce | 1.00 |
| 119 Chico Cardenas | 1.00 |
| 120 Duke Carmel | 1.00 |
| 121 Camilo Carreon | 1.00 |
| 122 Don Dillard | 1.00 |
| 123 Dan Dobbek | 1.00 |
| 124 Jim Donohue | 1.00 |
| 125 Dick Ellsworth | 1.00 |
| 126 Chuck Estrada (R) | 1.50 |
| 127 Ronnie Hansen | 1.00 |
| 128 Bill Harris | 1.00 |
| 129 Bob Hartman | 1.00 |
| 130 Frank Herrera | 1.00 |
| 131 Ed Hobaugh | 1.00 |
| 132 Frank Howard (R) | 7.00 |
| 133 Manuel Javier | 1.00 |
| 134 Deron Johnson | 1.00 |
| 135 Ken Johnson | 1.00 |
| 136 Jim Kaat (R) | 20.00 |
| 137 Lou Klimchock | 1.00 |
| 138 Art Mahaffey | 1.00 |
| 139 Carl Mathias | 1.00 |
| 140 Julio Navarro | 1.00 |
| 141 Jim Proctor | 1.00 |
| 142 Bill Short | 1.00 |
| 143 Al Spangler | 1.00 |
| 144 Al Stieglitz | 1.00 |
| 145 Jim Umbricht | 1.00 |
| 146 Ted Wieand | 1.00 |
| 147 Bob Will | 1.00 |
| 148 Carl Yastrzemski (R) | 175.00 |
| 149 Bob Nieman | 1.00 |
| 150 Billy Pierce | 1.50 |
| 151 San F. Giants | 4.00 |
| 152 Gail Harris | 1.00 |
| 153 Bobby Thomson | 1.50 |
| 154 Jim Davenport | 1.00 |
| 155 Charlie Neal | 1.00 |
| 156 Art Ceccarelli | 1.00 |
| 157 Rocky Nelson | 1.00 |
| 158 Wes Covington | 1.00 |

| NO. PLAYER | MINT |
|---|---|
| 159 Jim Piersall | 2.00 |
| 160 Rival All-Stars: | 22.00 |
| Mickey Mantle, Ken Boyer | |
| 161 Ray Narleski | 1.00 |
| 162 Sammy Taylor | 1.00 |
| 163 Hector Lopez | 1.00 |
| 164 Cincinnati Reds | 4.00 |
| 165 Jack Sanford | 1.00 |
| 166 Chuck Essegian | 1.00 |
| 167 Valmy Thomas | 1.00 |
| 168 Alex Grammas | 1.00 |
| 169 Jake Striker | 1.00 |
| 170 Del Crandall | 1.00 |
| 171 Johnny Groth | 1.00 |
| 172 Willie Kirkland | 1.00 |
| 173 Billy Martin | 4.00 |
| 174 Cleveland Indians | 3.00 |
| 175 Pedro Ramos | 1.00 |
| 176 Vada Pinson | 3.00 |
| 177 Johnny Kucks | 1.00 |
| 178 Woody Held | 1.00 |
| 179 Rip Coleman | 1.00 |
| 180 Harry Simpson | 1.00 |
| 181 Billy Loes | 1.00 |
| 182 Glen Hobbie | 1.00 |
| 183 Eli Grba | 1.00 |
| 184 Gary Geiger | 1.00 |
| 185 Jim Owens | 1.00 |
| 186 Dave Sisler | 1.00 |
| 187 Jay Hook | 1.00 |
| 188 Dick Williams | 1.00 |
| 189 Don McMahon | 1.00 |
| 190 Gene Woodling | 1.00 |
| 191 Johnny Klippstein | 1.00 |
| 192 Danny O'Connell | 1.00 |
| 193 Dick Hyde | 1.00 |
| 194 Bobby Gene Smith | 1.00 |
| 195 Lindy McDaniel | 1.00 |
| 196 Andy Carey | 1.00 |
| 197 Ron Kline | 1.00 |
| 198 Jerry Lynch | 1.00 |
| 199 Dick Donovan | 1.00 |
| 200 Willie Mays | 55.00 |
| 201 Larry Osborne | 1.00 |
| 202 Fred Kipp | 1.00 |
| 203 Sammy White | 1.00 |
| 204 Ryne Duren | 1.00 |
| 205 Johnny Logan | 1.00 |
| 206 Claude Osteen | 1.00 |
| 207 Bob Boyd | 1.00 |
| 208 Chicago White Sox | 3.00 |
| 209 Ron Blackburn | 1.00 |
| 210 Hamon Killebrew | 15.00 |
| 211 Taylor Phillips | 1.00 |
| 212 Walt Alston (Mgr.) | 5.00 |
| 213 Chuck Dressen (Mgr.) | 1.00 |
| 214 Jim Dykes (Mgr.) | 1.00 |
| 215 Bob Elliott (Mgr.) | 1.00 |
| 216 Joe Gordon (Mgr.) | 1.00 |
| 217 Charley Grimm (Mgr.) | 1.00 |
| 218 Solly Hemus (Mgr.) | 1.00 |
| 219 Fred Hutchinson (Mgr.) | 1.00 |
| 220 Billy Jurges (Mgr.) | 1.00 |
| 221 Cookie Lavagetto (Mgr.) | 1.00 |
| 222 Al Lopez (Mgr.) | 3.00 |
| 223 Danny Murtaugh (Mgr.) | 1.00 |
| 224 Paul Richards (Mgr.) | 1.00 |
| 225 Bill Rigney (Mgr.) | 1.00 |
| 226 Eddie Sawyer (Mgr.) | 1.00 |
| 227 Casey Stengel (Mgr.) | 8.00 |
| 228 Ernie Johnson | 1.00 |
| 229 Joe Morgan | 2.00 |
| 230 Mound Magicians: | 5.00 |
| Lou Burdette, Warren Spahn, Bob Buhl | |
| 231 Hal Naragon | 1.00 |
| 232 Jim Busby | 1.00 |
| 233 Don Elston | 1.00 |
| 234 Don Demeter | 1.00 |
| 235 Gus Bell | 1.00 |
| 236 Dick Ricketts | 1.00 |
| 237 Elmer Valo | 1.00 |

| NO. PLAYER | MINT |
|---|---|
| 238 Danny Kravitz | 1.00 |
| 239 Joe Shipley | 1.00 |
| 240 Luis Aparicio | 9.00 |
| 241 Albie Pearson | 1.00 |
| 242 St. Louis Cardinals | 3.00 |
| 243 Bubba Phillips | 1.00 |
| 244 Hal Griggs | 1.00 |
| 245 Eddie Yost | 1.00 |
| 246 Lee Maye | 1.00 |
| 247 Gil McDougald | 3.00 |
| 248 Del Rice | 1.00 |
| 249 Earl Wilson | 1.00 |
| 250 Stan Musial | 45.00 |
| 251 Bobby Malkmus | 1.00 |
| 252 Ray Herbert | 1.00 |
| 253 Eddie Bressoud | 1.00 |
| 254 Arnie Portocarrero | 1.00 |
| 255 Jim Gilliam | 3.00 |
| 256 Dick Brown | 1.00 |
| 257 Gordy Coleman | 1.00 |
| 258 Dick Groat | 3.00 |
| 259 George Altman | 1.00 |
| 260 Power Plus: | 1.50 |
| Rocky Colavito, Tito Francona | |
| 261 Pete Burnside | 1.00 |
| 262 Hank Bauer | 1.00 |
| 263 Darrell Johnson | 1.00 |
| 264 Robin Roberts | 8.00 |
| 265 Rip Repulski | 1.00 |
| 266 Joe Jay | 1.00 |
| 267 Jim Marshall | 1.00 |
| 268 Al Worthington | 1.00 |
| 269 Gene Green | 1.00 |
| 270 Bob Turley | 2.00 |
| 271 Julio Bequer | 1.00 |
| 272 Fred Green | 1.00 |
| 273 Neil Chrisley | 1.00 |
| 274 Tom Acker | 1.00 |
| 275 Curt Flood | 2.00 |
| 276 Ken McBride | 1.00 |
| 277 Harry Bright | 1.00 |
| 278 Stan Williams | 1.00 |
| 279 Chuck Tanner | 1.00 |
| 280 Frank Sullivan | 1.00 |
| 281 Ray Boone | 1.00 |
| 282 Joe Nuxhall | 1.00 |
| 283 John Blanchard | 1.00 |
| 284 Don Gross | 1.00 |
| 285 Harry Anderson | 1.00 |
| 286 Ray Semproch | 1.00 |
| 287 Felipe Alou | 2.00 |
| 288 Bob Mabe | 1.00 |
| 289 Willie Jones | 1.00 |
| 290 Jerry Lumpe | 1.00 |
| 291 Bob Keegan | 1.00 |
| 292 Dodger Backstops: | 1.50 |
| Joe Pignatano, John Roseboro | |
| 293 Gene Conley | 1.00 |
| 294 Tony Taylor | 1.00 |
| 295 Gil Hodges | 10.00 |
| 296 Nelson Chittum | 1.00 |
| 297 Reno Bertoia | 1.00 |
| 298 George Witt | 1.00 |
| 299 Earl Torgeson | 1.00 |
| 300 Hank Aaron | 50.00 |
| 301 Jerry Davie | 1.00 |
| 302 Philadelphia Phillies | 3.50 |
| 303 Billy O'Dell | 1.00 |
| 304 Joe Ginsberg | 1.00 |
| 305 Richie Ashburn | 5.00 |
| 306 Frank Baumann | 1.00 |
| 307 Gene Oliver | 1.00 |
| 308 Dick Hall | 1.00 |
| 309 Bob Hale | 1.00 |
| 310 Frank Malzone | 1.00 |
| 311 Raul Sanchez | 1.00 |
| 312 Charlie Lau | 1.00 |
| 313 Turk Lown | 1.00 |
| 314 Chico Fernandez | 1.00 |
| 315 Bobby Shantz | 2.00 |

| NO. PLAYER | MINT | NO. PLAYER | MINT | NO. PLAYER | MINT | NO. PLAYER | MINT |
|---|---|---|---|---|---|---|---|
| 316 Willie McCovey (R) | 75.00 | 386 World Series Game 2 | 3.00 | 449 Jim Brosnan | 1.50 | 499 Johnny James | 1.50 |
| 317 Pumpsie Green | 1.00 | Neal Belts 2nd Homer | | 450 Orlando Cepeda | 5.00 | 500 Johnny Temple | 1.50 |
| 318 Jim Baxes | 1.00 | 387 World Series Game 3 | 3.00 | 451 Curt Simmons | 2.00 | 501 Bob Schmidt | 1.50 |
| 319 Joe Koppe | 1.00 | Furillo Breaks Up Game | | 452 Ray Webster | 2.00 | 502 Jim Bunning | 5.00 |
| 320 Bob Allison | 1.00 | 388 World Series Game 4 | 3.00 | 453 Vern Law | 3.00 | 503 Don Lee | 1.50 |
| 321 Ron Fairly | 1.00 | Hodges' Winning Homer | | 454 Hal Woodeshick | 1.50 | 504 Seth Morehead | 1.50 |
| 322 Willie Tasby | 1.00 | 389 World Series Game 5 | 3.00 | 455 Orioles Coaches: | 2.00 | 505 Ted Kluszewski | 4.00 |
| 323 Johnny Romano | 1.00 | Luis Swipes Base | | Robinson, Brecheen, Harris | | 506 Lee Walls | 1.50 |
| 324 Jim Perry | 2.00 | 390 World Series Game 6 | 3.00 | 456 Red Sox Coaches: | 3.00 | 507 Dick Stigman | 4.00 |
| 325 Jim O'Toole | 1.00 | Scrambling After Ball | | York, Herman, Maglie, Baker | | 508 Billy Consolo | 4.00 |
| 326 Bob Clemente | 55.00 | 391 World Series | 3.00 | 457 Cubs Coaches: | 2.50 | 509 Tommy Davis (R) | 8.00 |
| 327 Ray Sadecki | 1.00 | The Champs Celebrate | | Klein, Tappe, Root | | 510 Jerry Staley | 5.00 |
| 328 Earl Battey | 1.00 | 392 Tex Clevenger | 1.00 | 458 White Sox Coaches: | 2.50 | 511 Ken Walters | 5.00 |
| 329 Zack Monroe | 1.00 | 393 Smokey Burgess | 1.25 | Cooney, Gutteridge, | | 512 Joe Gibbon | 5.00 |
| 330 Harvey Kuenn | 2.00 | 394 Norm Larker | 1.00 | Cuccinello, Berres | | 513 Chicago Cubs | 12.00 |
| 331 Henry Mason | 1.00 | 395 Hoyt Wilhelm | 9.00 | 459 Reds Coaches: | 2.50 | 514 Steve Barber | 5.00 |
| 332 New York Yankees | 12.00 | 396 Steve Bilko | 1.00 | Deal, Moses, Otero | | 515 Stan Lopata | 5.00 |
| 333 Danny McDevitt | 1.00 | 397 Don Blasingame | 1.00 | 460 Indians Coaches: | 2.50 | 516 Marty Kutyna | 5.00 |
| 334 Ted Abernathy | 1.00 | 398 Mike Cuellar | 1.00 | White, Lemon, Harder, Kress | | 517 Charley James | 5.00 |
| 335 Red Schoendienst | 2.50 | 399 Young Hill Stars: | 1.00 | 461 Tigers Coaches: | 2.50 | 518 Tony Gonzalez | 5.00 |
| 336 Ike Delock | 1.00 | Milt Pappas, Jack Fisher, | | Ferrick, Appling, Hitchcock | | 519 Ed Roebuck | 5.00 |
| 337 Cal Neeman | 1.00 | Jerry Walker | | 462 Athletics Coaches: | 2.50 | 520 Don Buddin | 5.00 |
| 338 Ray Monzant | 1.00 | 400 Rocky Colavito | 2.50 | Cooper, Fitzsimmons, | | 521 Mike Lee | 5.00 |
| 339 Harry Chiti | 1.00 | 401 Bob Duliba | 1.00 | Heffner | | 522 Ken Hunt | 5.00 |
| 340 Harvey Haddix | 1.75 | 402 Dick Stuart | 1.00 | 463 Dodgers Coaches: | 2.50 | 523 Clay Dalrymple | 5.00 |
| 341 Carroll Hardy | 1.00 | 403 Ed Sadowski | 1.00 | Bragan, Reiser, | | 524 Bill Henry | 5.00 |
| 342 Casey Wise | 1.00 | 404 Bob Rush | 1.00 | Becker, Mulleavy | | 525 Marv Breeding | 5.00 |
| 343 Sandy Kofax | 55.00 | 405 Bobby Richardson | 4.00 | 464 Braves Coaches: | 2.50 | 526 Paul Giel | 5.00 |
| 344 Clint Courtney | 1.00 | 406 Billy Klaus | 1.00 | Scheffing, Myatt, | | 527 Jose Valdivielso | 5.00 |
| 345 Don Newcombe | 1.25 | 407 Gary Peters | 1.00 | Wyatt, Pafko | | 528 Ben Johnson | 5.00 |
| 346 J.C. Martin | 1.00 | (photo of J.C. Martin) | | 465 Yankees Coaches: | 6.00 | 529 Norm Sherry (R) | 5.00 |
| (photo of Gary Peters) | | 408 Carl Furillo | 3.00 | Dickey, Houk, | | 530 Mike McCormick | 5.00 |
| 347 Ed Bouchee | 1.00 | 409 Ron Samford | 1.00 | Lopat, Crosetti | | 531 Sandy Amoros | 5.00 |
| 348 Barry Shetrone | 1.00 | 410 Sam Jones | 1.00 | 466 Phillies Coaches: | 2.50 | 532 Mike Garcia | 5.00 |
| 349 Moe Drabowsky | 1.00 | 411 Ed Bailey | 1.00 | Silvestri, Cohen, Carter | | 533 L. Clinton | 5.00 |
| 350 Mickey Mantle | 275.00 | 412 Bob Anderson | 1.00 | 467 Pirates Coaches: | 2.50 | 534 Ken Mackenzie | 5.00 |
| 351 Don Nottebart | 1.00 | 413 Kansas C. Athletics | 3.00 | Vernon, Oceak, | | 535 Whitey Lockman | 5.00 |
| 352 Cincy Clouters: | 3.00 | 414 Don Williams | 1.00 | Narron, Burwell | | 536 Wynn Hawkins | 5.00 |
| Gus Bell, Frank | | 415 Bob Cerv | 1.00 | 468 Cardinals Coaches: | 2.50 | 537 Boston Red Sox | 12.00 |
| Robinson, Jerry Lynch | | 416 Humberto Robinson | 1.00 | Keane, Pollet, | | 538 Frank Barnes | 5.00 |
| 353 Don Larsen | 1.50 | 417 Chuck Cottier (R) | 1.25 | Katt, Walker | | 539 Gene Baker | 5.00 |
| 354 Bob Lillis | 1.25 | 418 Don Mossi | 1.00 | 469 Giants Coaches: | 2.50 | 540 Jerry Walker | 5.00 |
| 355 Bill White | 2.00 | 419 George Crowe | 1.00 | Westrum, Parker, Posedel | | 541 Tony Curry | 5.00 |
| 356 Joe Amalfitano | 1.00 | 420 Ed Mathews | 12.00 | 470 Senators Coaches: | 2.50 | 542 Ken Hamlin | 5.00 |
| 357 Al Schroll | 1.00 | 421 Duke Maas | 1.00 | Swift, Mele, Clary | | 543 Elio Chacon | 5.00 |
| 358 Joe DeMaestri | 1.00 | 422 Johnny Powers | 1.00 | 471 Ned Garver | 1.50 | 544 Bill Monbouquette | 5.00 |
| 359 Buddy Gilbert | 1.00 | 423 Ed Fitzgerald | 1.00 | 472 Al Dark | 2.00 | 545 Carl Sawatski | 5.00 |
| 360 Herb Score | 1.50 | 424 Pete Whisenant | 1.00 | 473 Al Cicotte | 1.50 | 546 Hank Aguirre | 5.00 |
| 361 Bob Oldis | 1.00 | 425 Johnny Podres | 2.50 | 474 Haywood Sullivan | 1.50 | 547 Bob Aspromonte | 5.00 |
| 362 Russ Kemmerer | 1.00 | 426 Ron Jackson | 1.00 | 475 Don Drysdale | 15.00 | 548 Don Mincher | 5.00 |
| 363 Gene Stephens | 1.00 | 427 Al Grunwald | 1.00 | 476 Lou Johnson | 1.50 | 549 John Buzhardt | 5.00 |
| 364 Paul Foytack | 1.00 | 428 Al Smith | 1.00 | 477 Don Ferrarese | 1.50 | 550 Jim Landis | 5.00 |
| 365 Minnie Minoso | 3.00 | 429 Amer. League Kings: | 2.50 | 478 Frank Torre | 1.50 | 551 Ed Rakow | 5.00 |
| 366 Dallas Green (R) | 2.50 | Nellie Fox, Harvey Kuenn | | 479 Georges Maranda | 1.50 | 552 Walt Bond | 5.00 |
| 367 Bill Tuttle | 1.00 | 430 Art Ditmar | 1.00 | 480 Yogi Berra | 30.00 | 553 Bill Skowron (AS) | 6.00 |
| 368 Daryl Spencer | 1.00 | 431 Andre Rodgers | 1.00 | 481 Wes Stock | 2.00 | 554 Willie McCovey (AS) | 28.00 |
| 369 Billy Hoeft | 1.00 | 432 Chuck Stobbs | 1.00 | 482 Frank Bolling | 1.50 | 555 Nellie Fox (AS) | 8.00 |
| 370 Bill Skowron | 3.50 | 433 Irv Noren | 1.00 | 483 Camilo Pascual | 1.50 | 556 Charlie Neal (AS) | 5.00 |
| 371 Bud Byerly | 1.00 | 434 Brooks Lawrence | 1.00 | 484 Pittsburgh Pirates | 8.00 | 557 Frank Malzone (AS) | 5.00 |
| 372 Frank House | 1.00 | 435 Gene Freese | 1.00 | 485 Ken Boyer | 4.00 | 558 Eddie Mathews (AS) | 16.00 |
| 373 Don Hoak | 1.00 | 436 Marv Throneberry | 2.50 | 486 Bobby Del Greco | 1.50 | 559 Luis Aparicio (AS) | 12.00 |
| 374 Bob Buhl | 1.00 | 437 Bob Friend | 1.00 | 487 Tom Sturdivant | 1.50 | 560 Ernie Banks (AS) | 20.00 |
| 375 Dale Long | 1.00 | 438 Jim Coker | 1.00 | 488 Norm Cash | 4.00 | 561 Al Kaline (AS) | 18.00 |
| 376 Johnny Briggs | 1.00 | 439 Tom Brewer | 1.00 | 489 Steve Ridzik | 1.50 | 562 Joe Cunningham (AS) | 5.00 |
| 377 Roger Maris | 65.00 | 440 Jim Lemon | 1.00 | 490 Frank Robinson | 20.00 | 563 Mickey Mantle (AS) | 160.00 |
| 378 Stu Miller | 1.00 | 441 Gary Bell | 1.50 | 491 Mel Roach | 1.50 | 564 Willie Mays (AS) | 50.00 |
| 379 Red Wilson | 1.00 | 442 Joe Pignatano | 1.50 | 492 Larry Jackson | 1.50 | 565 Roger Maris (AS) | 36.00 |
| 380 Bob Shaw | 1.00 | 443 Charlie Maxwell | 1.50 | 493 Duke Snider | 25.00 | 566 Hank Aaron (AS) | 45.00 |
| 381 Milwakee Braves | 3.00 | 444 Jerry Kindall | 1.50 | 494 Baltimore Orioles | 6.00 | 567 Sherm Lollar (AS) | 5.00 |
| 382 Ted Bowsfield | 1.00 | 445 Warren Spahn | 17.00 | 495 Sherm Lollar | 1.50 | 568 Del Crandall (AS) | 5.00 |
| 383 Leon Wagner | 1.00 | 446 Ellis Burton | 1.50 | 496 Bill Virdon | 2.50 | 569 Camilo Pascual (AS) | 5.00 |
| 384 Don Cardwell | 1.00 | 447 Ray Moore | 1.50 | 497 John Tsitouris | 1.50 | 570 Don Drysdale (AS) | 15.00 |
| 385 World Series Game 1 | 3.00 | 448 Jim Gentile | 2.00 | 498 Al Pilarcik | 1.50 | 571 Billy Pierce (AS) | 5.00 |
| Neal Steals Second | | | | | | 572 J. Antonelli (AS) | 12.00 |
| | | | | | | (Exc. $4.00) | |

**Prices for the 1960 set are for cards in *Mint* condition. *Excellent* copies sell for 40% to 50% of prices shown; *Very Good*—25% to 30%.**

# 1961 Topps. . . .Complete Set of 587 Cards—Value $1400.00 (Exc.); $3800.00 (Mint)

Juan Marichal and Billy Williams' rookie cards are in this set. The high numbers are 523 to 589. Cards 587 and 588 were not issued. Card 426 (Braves team) was mistakenly numbered 463.

| NO. | PLAYER | MINT |
|---|---|---|
| 1 | Dick Groat (Exc. $1.50) | 12.00 |
| 2 | Roger Maris | 55.00 |
| 3 | John Buzhardt | .90 |
| 4 | Lenny Green | .90 |
| 5 | Johnny Romano | .90 |
| 6 | Ed Roebuck | .90 |
| 7 | Chicago White Sox | 2.00 |
| 8 | Dick Williams | .90 |
| 9 | Bob Purkey | .90 |
| 10 | Brooks Robinson | 16.00 |
| 11 | Curt Simmons | 1.25 |
| 12 | Moe Thacker | .90 |
| 13 | Chuck Cottier | .90 |
| 14 | Don Mossi | .90 |
| 15 | Willie Kirkland | .90 |
| 16 | Billy Muffett | .90 |
| 17 | Checklist No. 1 | 4.00 |
| 18 | Jim Grant | .90 |
| 19 | Cletis Boyer | 2.00 |
| 20 | Robin Roberts | 8.00 |
| 21 | Zorro Versalles | 1.25 |
| 22 | Clem Labine | 1.00 |
| 23 | Don Demeter | .90 |
| 24 | Ken Johnson | .90 |
| 25 | Reds' Heavy Artillery: Vada Pinson, Gus Bell, Frank Robinson | 4.00 |
| 26 | Wes Stock | .90 |
| 27 | Jerry Kindall | .90 |
| 28 | Hector Lopez | .90 |
| 29 | Don Nottebart | .90 |
| 30 | Nellie Fox | 4.00 |
| 31 | Bob Schmidt | .90 |
| 32 | Ray Sadecki | .90 |
| 33 | Gary Geiger | .90 |
| 34 | Wynn Hawkins | .90 |
| 35 | Ron Santo (R) | 5.00 |
| 36 | Jack Kralick | .90 |
| 37 | Charlie Maxwell | .90 |
| 38 | Bob Lillis | .90 |
| 39 | Leo Posada | .90 |
| 40 | Bob Turley | 1.25 |
| 41 | NL Batting Leaders: Willie Mays, Dick Gorat, Norm Larker, Roberto Clemente | 3.00 |
| 42 | AL Batting Leaders: Pete Runnels, Minnie Minoso, Al Smith, Bill Skowron | 2.00 |
| 43 | NL Home Run Leaders: Ernie Banks, Ed Mathews, Hank Aaron, Ken Boyer | 3.00 |
| 44 | AL Home Run Leaders: Mickey Mantle, Roger Maris, Jim Lemon, Rocky Colavito | 10.00 |
| 45 | NL ERA Leaders: Mike McCormick, Ernie Broglio, Don Drysdale, Bob Friend, Stan Williams | 3.00 |
| 46 | AL ERA Leaders: Frank Baumann, Jim Bunning, Art Ditmar, Hal Brown | 3.00 |
| 47 | NL Pitching Leaders: E. Broglio, W. Spahn, Vern Law, Lou Burdette | 3.00 |

| NO. | PLAYER | MINT |
|---|---|---|
| 48 | AL Pitching Leaders: Chuck Estrada, Jim Perry, Bud Daley, Art Ditmar, Frank Lary, Milt Pappas | 2.50 |
| 49 | NL Strikeout Leaders: Don Drysdale, Sandy Koufax, Sam Jones, Ernie Broglio | 4.00 |
| 50 | AL Strikeout Leaders: Jim Bunning, Pedro Ramos, Early Wynn, Frank Lary | 2.50 |
| 51 | Detroit Tigers | 3.00 |
| 52 | George Crowe | .90 |
| 53 | Russ Nixon | .90 |
| 54 | Earl Francis | .90 |
| 55 | Jim Davenport | .90 |
| 56 | Russ Kemmerer | .90 |
| 57 | Marv Throneberry | 1.50 |
| 58 | Joe Schaffernoth | .90 |
| 59 | Jim Woods | .90 |
| 60 | Woodie Held | .90 |
| 61 | Ron Piche | .90 |
| 62 | Al Pilarcik | .90 |
| 63 | Jim Kaat | 5.00 |
| 64 | Alex Grammas | .90 |
| 65 | Ted Kluszewski | 3.00 |
| 66 | Bill Henry | .90 |
| 67 | Ossie Virgil | .90 |
| 68 | Deron Johnson | 1.25 |
| 69 | Earl Wilson | .90 |
| 70 | Bill Virdon | 1.50 |
| 71 | Jerry Adair | .90 |
| 72 | Stu Miller | .90 |
| 73 | Al Spangler | .90 |
| 74 | Joe Pignatano | .90 |
| 75 | Lindy Shows Larry: Lindy McDaniel, Larry Jackson | 1.50 |
| 76 | Harry Anderson | .90 |
| 77 | Dick Stigman | .90 |
| 78 | Lee Walls | .90 |
| 79 | Joe Ginsberg | .90 |
| 80 | Harmon Killebrew | 15.00 |
| 81 | Tracy Stallard | .90 |
| 82 | Joe Christopher | .90 |
| 83 | Bob Bruce | .90 |
| 84 | Lee Maye | .90 |
| 85 | Jerry Walker | .90 |
| 86 | Los Angeles Dodgers | 3.00 |
| 87 | Joe Amalfitano | .90 |
| 88 | Richie Ashburn | 4.00 |
| 89 | Billy Martin | 4.00 |
| 90 | Jerry Staley | .90 |
| 91 | Walt Moryn | .90 |
| 92 | Hal Naragon | .90 |
| 93 | Tony Gonzalez | .90 |
| 94 | John Kucks | .90 |
| 95 | Norm Cash | 2.50 |
| 96 | Bill O'Dell | .90 |
| 97 | Jerry Lynch | .90 |
| 98 | Checklist No. 2 | 4.00 |
| 99 | Don Buddin | .90 |
| 100 | Harvey Haddix | 2.00 |
| 101 | Bubba Phillips | .90 |
| 102 | Gene Stephens | .90 |
| 103 | Ruben Amaro | .90 |
| 104 | John Blanchard | 1.25 |

| NO. | PLAYER | MINT |
|---|---|---|
| 105 | Carl Willey | .90 |
| 106 | Whitey Herzog | 2.00 |
| 107 | Seth Morehead | .90 |
| 108 | Dan Dobbek | .90 |
| 109 | Johnny Podres | 2.50 |
| 110 | Vada Pinson | 2.50 |
| 111 | Jack Meyer | .90 |
| 112 | Chico Fernandez | .90 |
| 113 | Mike Fornieles | .90 |
| 114 | Hobie Landrith | .90 |
| 115 | Johnny Antonelli | 1.25 |
| 116 | Joe DeMaestri | .90 |
| 117 | Dale Long | .90 |
| 118 | Chris Cannizzaro | .90 |
| 119 | A's Big Armor: Norm Siebern, Hank Bauer, Jerry Lumpe | 1.50 |
| 120 | Ed Mathews | 10.00 |
| 121 | Eli Grba | .90 |
| 122 | Chicago Cubs | 2.00 |
| 123 | Billy Gardner | .90 |
| 124 | J.C. Martin | .90 |
| 125 | Steve Barber | .90 |
| 126 | Dick Stuart | .90 |
| 127 | Ron Kline | .90 |
| 128 | Rip Repulski | .90 |
| 129 | Ed Hobaugh | .90 |
| 130 | Norm Larker | .90 |
| 131 | Paul Richards (Mgr.) | 1.25 |
| 132 | Al Lopez (Mgr.) | 3.00 |
| 133 | Ralph Houk (Mgr.) | 2.50 |
| 134 | Mickey Vernon (Mgr.) | 1.25 |
| 135 | Fred Hutchinson (Mgr.) | 1.25 |
| 136 | Walt Alston (Mgr.) | 3.00 |
| 137 | Chuck Dressen (Mgr.) | .90 |
| 138 | Danny Murtaugh (Mgr.) | .90 |
| 139 | Solly Hemus (Mgr.) | .90 |
| 140 | Gus Triandos | .90 |
| 141 | Billy Williams (R) | 40.00 |
| 142 | Luis Arroyo | .90 |
| 143 | Russ Snyder | .90 |
| 144 | Jim Coker | .90 |
| 145 | Bob Buhl | .90 |
| 146 | Marty Keough | .90 |
| 147 | Ed Rakow | .90 |
| 148 | Julian Javier | .90 |
| 149 | Bob Oldis | .90 |
| 150 | Willie Mays | 45.00 |
| 151 | Jim Donohue | .90 |
| 152 | Earl Torgeson | .90 |
| 153 | Don Lee | .90 |
| 154 | Bobby Del Greco | .90 |
| 155 | Johnny Temple | .90 |
| 156 | Ken Hunt | .90 |
| 157 | Cal McLish | .90 |
| 158 | Pete Daley | .90 |
| 159 | Baltimore Orioles | 2.00 |
| 160 | Whitey Ford | 16.00 |
| 161 | Sherman Jones | .90 |
| 162 | Jay Hook | .90 |
| 163 | Ed Sadowski | .90 |
| 164 | Felix Mantilla | .90 |
| 165 | Gino Cimoli | .90 |
| 166 | Danny Kravitz | .90 |
| 167 | San F. Giants | 2.50 |
| 168 | Tommy Davis | 2.00 |
| 169 | Don Elston | .90 |

| NO. | PLAYER | MINT |
|---|---|---|
| 170 | Al Smith | .90 |
| 171 | Paul Foytack | .90 |
| 172 | Don Dillard | .90 |
| 173 | Beantown Bombers: Frank Malzone, Vic Wertz, Jackie Jensen | 1.25 |
| 174 | Ray Semproch | .90 |
| 175 | Gene Freese | .90 |
| 176 | Ken Aspromonte | .90 |
| 177 | Don Larsen | 1.25 |
| 178 | Bob Nieman | .90 |
| 179 | Joe Koppe | .90 |
| 180 | Bobby Richardson | 3.00 |
| 181 | Fred Green | .90 |
| 182 | Dave Nicholson | .90 |
| 183 | Andre Rodgers | .90 |
| 184 | Steve Bilko | .90 |
| 185 | Herb Score | 1.25 |
| 186 | Elmer Valo | .90 |
| 187 | Billy Klaus | .90 |
| 188 | Jim Marshall | .90 |
| 189 | Checklist No. 3 | 4.00 |
| 190 | Stan Williams | .90 |
| 191 | Mike De La Hoz | .90 |
| 192 | Dick Brown | .90 |
| 193 | Gene Conley | .90 |
| 194 | Gordy Coleman | .90 |
| 195 | Jerry Casale | .90 |
| 196 | Ed Bouchee | .90 |
| 197 | Dick Hall | .90 |
| 198 | Carl Sawatski | .90 |
| 199 | Bob Boyd | .90 |
| 200 | Warren Spahn | 12.00 |
| 201 | Pete Whisenant | .90 |
| 202 | Al Neiger | .90 |
| 203 | Eddie Bressoud | .90 |
| 204 | Bob Skinner | .90 |
| 205 | Bill Pierce | 1.25 |
| 206 | Gene Green | .90 |
| 207 | Dodger Southpaws: Sandy Koufax, J. Podres | 8.00 |
| 208 | Larry Osborne | .90 |
| 209 | Ken McBride | .90 |
| 210 | Pete Runnels | .90 |
| 211 | Bob Gibson | 12.00 |
| 212 | Haywood Sullivan | .90 |
| 213 | Bill Stafford | .90 |
| 214 | Danny Murphy | .90 |
| 215 | Gus Bell | .90 |
| 216 | Ted Bowsfield | .90 |
| 217 | Mel Roach | .90 |
| 218 | Hal Brown | .90 |
| 219 | Gene Mauch (Mgr.) | 1.50 |
| 220 | Al Dark (Mgr.) | 1.25 |
| 221 | Mike Higgins (Mgr.) | 1.25 |
| 222 | Jimmie Dykes (Mgr.) | 1.25 |
| 223 | Bob Scheffing (Mgr.) | 1.25 |
| 224 | Joe Gordon (Mgr.) | 1.25 |
| 225 | Bill Rigney (Mgr.) | 1.25 |
| 226 | Harry Lavagetto (Mgr.) | 1.25 |
| 227 | Juan Pizarro | .90 |
| 228 | New York Yankees | 12.00 |
| 229 | Rudy Hernandez | .90 |
| 230 | Don Hoak | .90 |
| 231 | Dick Drott | .90 |
| 232 | Bill White | 1.25 |
| 233 | Joe Jay | .90 |

| NO. PLAYER | MINT |
|---|---|
| 234 Ted Lepcio | .90 |
| 235 Camilo Pascual | .90 |
| 236 Don Gile | .90 |
| 237 Billy Loes | .90 |
| 238 Jim Gilliam | 3.00 |
| 239 Dave Sisler | .90 |
| 240 Ron Hansen | .90 |
| 241 Al Cicotte | .90 |
| 242 Hal Smith | .90 |
| 243 Frank Lary | .90 |
| 244 Chico Cardenas | .90 |
| 245 Joe Adcock | 1.25 |
| 246 Bob Davis | .90 |
| 247 Billy Goodman | .90 |
| 248 Ed Keegan | .90 |
| 249 Cincinnati Reds | 3.00 |
| 250 Buc Hill Aces: | 1.25 |
| Vern Law, Roy Face | |
| 251 Bill Bruton | .90 |
| 252 Bill Short | .90 |
| 253 Sammy Taylor | .90 |
| 254 Ted Sadowski | .90 |
| 255 Vic Power | .90 |
| 256 Billy Hoeft | .90 |
| 257 Carroll Hardy | .90 |
| 258 Jack Sanford | .90 |
| 259 John Schaive | .90 |
| 260 Don Drysdale | 10.00 |
| 261 Charlie Lau | .90 |
| 262 Tony Curry | .90 |
| 263 Ken Hamlin | .90 |
| 264 Glen Hobbie | .90 |
| 265 Tony Kubek | 4.00 |
| 266 Lindy McDaniel | .90 |
| 267 Norm Siebern | .90 |
| 268 Ike Delock | .90 |
| 269 Harry Chiti | .90 |
| 270 Bob Friend | .90 |
| 271 Jim Landis | .90 |
| 272 Tom Morgan | .90 |
| 273 Checklist No. 4 | 4.00 |
| 274 Gary Bell | .90 |
| 275 Gene Woodling | .90 |
| 276 Ray Rippelmeyer | .90 |
| 277 Hank Foiles | .90 |
| 278 Don McMahon | .90 |
| 279 Jose Pagan | .90 |
| 280 Frank Howard | 2.00 |
| 281 Frank Sullivan | .90 |
| 282 Faye Throneberry | .90 |
| 283 Bob Anderson | .90 |
| 284 Dick Gernert | .90 |
| 285 Sherm Lollar | .90 |
| 286 George Witt | .90 |
| 287 Carl Yastrzemski | 80.00 |
| 288 Albie Pearson | .90 |
| 289 Ray Moore | .90 |
| 290 Stan Musial | 40.00 |
| 291 Tex Clevenger | .90 |
| 292 Jim Baumer | .90 |
| 293 Tom Sturdivant | .90 |
| 294 Don Blasingame | .90 |
| 295 Milt Pappas | .90 |
| 296 Wes Covington | .90 |
| 297 Kansas C. Athletics | 2.00 |
| 298 Jim Golden | .90 |
| 299 Clay Dalrymple | .90 |
| 300 Mickey Mantle | 250.00 |
| 301 Chet Nichols | .90 |
| 302 Al Heist | .90 |
| 303 Gary Peters | .90 |
| 304 Rocky Nelson | .90 |
| 305 Mike McCormick | .90 |
| 306 World Series Game 1 | 3.00 |
| Virdon Saves Game | |
| 307 World Series Game 2 | 18.00 |
| Mantle Slams 2 Homers | |
| 308 World Series Game 3 | 3.00 |
| Richardson is Hero | |
| 309 World Series Game 4 | 3.00 |
| Cimoli Safe | |

| NO. PLAYER | MINT |
|---|---|
| 310 World Series Game 5 | 3.00 |
| Face Saves the Day | |
| 311 World Series Game 6 | 3.00 |
| Ford Shutout | |
| 312 World Series Game 7 | 3.00 |
| Mazeroski's Homer | |
| 313 W.S. Celebration | 2.50 |
| 314 Bob Miller | .90 |
| 315 Earl Battey | .90 |
| 316 Bobby Gene Smith | .90 |
| 317 Jim Brewer | .90 |
| 318 Danny O'Connell | .90 |
| 319 Valmy Thomas | .90 |
| 320 Lou Burdette | 2.50 |
| 321 Marv Breeding | .90 |
| 322 Bill Kunkel | .90 |
| 323 Sammy Esposito | .90 |
| 324 Hank Aguirre | .90 |
| 325 Wally Moon | .90 |
| 326 Dave Hillman | .90 |
| 327 Matty Alou (R) | 2.00 |
| 328 Jim O'Toole | .90 |
| 329 Julio Becquer | .90 |
| 330 Rocky Colavito | 3.00 |
| 331 Ned Garver | .90 |
| 332 Dutch Dotterer | .90 |
| (photo of Tommy Dotterer) | |
| 333 Fritz Brickell | .90 |
| 334 Walt Bond | .90 |
| 335 Frank Bolling | .90 |
| 336 Don Mincher | .90 |
| 337 Al's Aces: | 2.50 |
| Herb Score, Early Wynn, | |
| Al Lopez | |
| 338 Don Landrum | .90 |
| 339 Gene Baker | .90 |
| 340 Vic Wertz | .90 |
| 341 Jim Owens | .90 |
| 342 Clint Courtney | .90 |
| 343 Earl Robinson | .90 |
| 344 Sandy Koufax | 37.00 |
| 345 Jim Piersall | 1.50 |
| 346 Howie Nunn | .90 |
| 347 St. Louis Cardinals | 2.00 |
| 348 Steve Boros | .90 |
| 349 Danny McDevitt | .90 |
| 350 Ernie Banks | 15.00 |
| 351 Jim King | .90 |
| 352 Bob Shaw | .90 |
| 353 Howie Bedell | .90 |
| 354 Billy Harrell | .90 |
| 355 Bob Allison | .90 |
| 356 Ryne Duren | .90 |
| 357 Daryl Spencer | .90 |
| 358 Earl Averill | .90 |
| 359 Dallas Green | 1.25 |
| 360 Frank Robinson | 18.00 |
| 361 Checklist No. 5 | 6.00 |
| 362 Frank Funk | .90 |
| 363 John Roseboro | .90 |
| 364 Moe Drabowski | .90 |
| 365 Jerry Lumpe | .90 |
| 366 Eddie Fisher | .90 |
| 367 Jim Rivera | .90 |
| 368 Bennie Daniels | .90 |
| 369 Dave Philley | .90 |
| 370 Roy Face | 1.50 |
| 371 Bill Skowron | 6.00 |
| 372 Ben Hendley | .90 |
| 373 Boston Red Sox | 3.00 |
| 374 Paul Giel | 1.25 |
| 375 Ken Boyer | 3.50 |
| 376 Mike Roarke | 1.25 |
| 377 Ruben Gomez | 1.25 |
| 378 Wally Post | 1.25 |
| 379 Bobby Shantz | 2.00 |
| 380 Minnie Minoso | 3.00 |
| 381 Dave Wickersham | 1.25 |
| 382 Frank Thomas | 1.25 |
| 383 Frisco First Liners: | 1.50 |
| Mike McCormick, Jack | |
| Sanford, Billy O'Dell | |

| NO. PLAYER | MINT |
|---|---|
| 384 Chuck Essegian | 1.25 |
| 385 Jim Perry | 1.50 |
| 386 Joe Hicks | 1.25 |
| 387 Duke Maas | 1.25 |
| 388 Bob Clemente | 40.00 |
| 389 Ralph Terry | 1.50 |
| 390 Del Crandall | 1.50 |
| 391 Winston Brown | 1.25 |
| 392 Reno Bertoia | 1.25 |
| 393 Batter Bafflers: | 1.25 |
| Don Cardwell, Glen Hobbie | |
| 394 Ken Walters | 1.25 |
| 395 Chuck Estrada | 1.25 |
| 396 Bob Aspromonte | 1.25 |
| 397 Hal Woodeshick | 1.25 |
| 398 Hank Bauer | 1.50 |
| 399 Cliff Cook | 1.25 |
| 400 Vern Law | 1.75 |
| 401 Ruth 60th Homer | 10.00 |
| 402 Larsen—Perfect Game | 4.00 |
| 403 26 Inning Tie | 2.00 |
| 404 Honsby .424 Average | 3.00 |
| 405 Gehrig—2,130 Games | 6.00 |
| 406 Mantle 565 Ft. HR | 16.00 |
| 407 Chesbro Wins 41 | 2.00 |
| 408 Mathewson 267 SO's | 3.00 |
| 409 Johnson Shutouts | 3.00 |
| 410 Haddix Perfect Game | 2.00 |
| 411 Tony Taylor | 1.25 |
| 412 Larry Sherry | 1.25 |
| 413 Eddie Yost | 1.25 |
| 414 Dick Donovan | 1.25 |
| 415 Hank Aaron | 60.00 |
| 416 Dick Howser (R) | 5.00 |
| 417 Juan Marichal (R) | 60.00 |
| 418 Ed Bailey | 1.25 |
| 419 Tom Borland | 1.25 |
| 420 Ernie Broglio | 1.25 |
| 421 Ty Cline | 1.25 |
| 422 Bud Daley | 1.25 |
| 423 Charlie Neal | 1.25 |
| 424 Turk Lown | 1.25 |
| 425 Yogi Berra | 30.00 |
| 426 Milwaukee Braves | 6.00 |
| (error—numbered 463) | |
| 427 Dick Ellsworth | 1.25 |
| 428 Ray Barker | 1.25 |
| 429 Al Kaline | 20.00 |
| 430 Bill Mazeroski | 4.00 |
| 431 Chuck Stobbs | 1.25 |
| 432 Coot Veal | 1.25 |
| 433 Art Mahaffey | 1.25 |
| 434 Tom Brewer | 1.25 |
| 435 Orlando Cepeda | 5.00 |
| 436 Jim Maloney (R) | 3.00 |
| 437 Checklist No. 6 | 4.00 |
| 438 Curt Flood | 2.00 |
| 439 Phil Regan | 1.25 |
| 440 Luis Aparicio | 8.00 |
| 441 Dick Bertell | 1.25 |
| 442 Gordon Jones | 1.25 |
| 443 Duke Snider | 20.00 |
| 444 Joe Nuxhall | 1.25 |
| 445 Frank Malzone | 1.25 |
| 446 Bob Taylor | 1.25 |
| 447 Harry Bright | 1.25 |
| 448 Del Rice | 1.25 |
| 449 Bobby Bolin | 1.25 |
| 450 Jim Lemon | 1.25 |
| 451 Power for Ernie: | 1.25 |
| Daryl Spencer, Bill White, | |
| Ernie Broglio | |
| 452 Bob Allen | 1.25 |
| 453 Dick Schofield | 1.25 |
| 454 Pumpsie Green | 1.25 |
| 455 Early Wynn | 8.00 |
| 456 Hal Bevan | 1.25 |
| 457 Johnny James | 1.25 |
| 458 Willie Tasby | 1.25 |
| 459 Terry Fox | 1.25 |
| 460 Gil Hodges | 9.00 |
| 461 Smoky Burgess | 1.25 |

| NO. PLAYER | MINT |
|---|---|
| 462 Lou Klimchock | 1.25 |
| 463 Jack Fisher (see #426) | 1.25 |
| 464 Leroy Thomas | 1.25 |
| 465 Roy McMillan | 1.25 |
| 466 Ron Moeller | 1.25 |
| 467 Cleveland Indians | 3.00 |
| 468 John Callison | 1.25 |
| 469 Ralph Lumenti | 1.25 |
| 470 Roy Sievers | 1.25 |
| 471 Phil Rizzuto (MVP) | 8.00 |
| 472 Yogi Berra (MVP) | 16.00 |
| 473 Bobby Shantz (MVP) | 2.00 |
| 474 Al Rosen (MVP) | 2.00 |
| 475 Mickey Mantle (MVP) | 55.00 |
| 476 Jackie Jensen (MVP) | 2.00 |
| 477 Nellie Fox (MVP) | 2.00 |
| 478 Roger Maris (MVP) | 20.00 |
| 479 Jim Konstanty (MVP) | 2.00 |
| 480 R. Campanella (MVP) | 16.00 |
| 481 Hank Sauer (MVP) | 2.00 |
| 482 Willie Mays (MVP) | 16.00 |
| 483 Don Newcombe (MVP) | 2.00 |
| 484 Hank Aaron (MVP) | 20.00 |
| 485 Ernie Banks (MVP) | 10.00 |
| 486 Dick Groat (MVP) | 1.50 |
| 487 Gene Oliver | 1.25 |
| 488 Joe McClain | 1.25 |
| 489 Walt Dropo | 1.25 |
| 490 Jim Bunning | 4.00 |
| 491 Philadelphia Phillies | 3.00 |
| 492 Ron Fairly | 1.25 |
| 493 Don Zimmer | 2.00 |
| 494 Tom Cheney | 1.25 |
| 495 Elston Howard | 4.00 |
| 496 Ken MacKenzie | 1.25 |
| 497 Willie Jones | 1.25 |
| 498 Ray Herbert | 1.25 |
| 499 Chuck Schilling | 1.25 |
| 500 Harvey Kuenn | 3.00 |
| 501 John DeMerit | 1.25 |
| 502 Clarence Coleman | 1.25 |
| 503 Tito Francona | 1.25 |
| 504 Billy Consolo | 1.25 |
| 505 Red Schoendienst | 3.00 |
| 506 Willie Davis (R) | 4.00 |
| 507 Pete Burnside | 1.25 |
| 508 Rocky Bridges | 1.25 |
| 509 Camilo Carreon | 1.25 |
| 510 Art Ditmar | 1.25 |
| 511 Joe Morgan | 1.25 |
| 512 Bob Will | 1.25 |
| 513 Jim Brosnan | 1.25 |
| 514 Jake Wood | 1.25 |
| 515 Jackie Brandt | 1.25 |
| 516 Checklist No. 7 | 4.00 |
| 517 Willie McCovey | 30.00 |
| 518 Andy Carey | 1.25 |
| 519 Jim Pagliaroni | 1.25 |
| 520 Joe Cunningham | 1.25 |
| 521 Brother Battery: | 1.25 |
| Norm Sherry, Larry Sherry | |
| 522 Dick Farrell | 1.25 |
| 523 Joe Gibbon | 15.00 |
| 524 Johnny Logan | 15.00 |
| 525 Ron Perranoski | 15.00 |
| 526 R.C. Stevens | 15.00 |
| 527 Gene Leek | 15.00 |
| 528 Pedro Ramos | 15.00 |
| 529 Bob Roselli | 15.00 |
| 530 Bobby Malkmus | 15.00 |
| 531 Jim Coates | 15.00 |
| 532 Bob Hale | 15.00 |
| 533 Jack Curtis | 15.00 |
| 534 Eddie Kasko | 15.00 |
| 535 Larry Jackson | 15.00 |
| 536 Bill Tuttle | 15.00 |
| 537 Bobby Locke | 15.00 |
| 538 Chuck Hiller | 15.00 |
| 539 John Klippstein | 15.00 |
| 540 Jackie Jensen | 18.00 |
| 541 Roland Sheldon | 15.00 |
| 542 Minnesota Twins | 22.00 |

| NO. | PLAYER | MINT |
|---|---|---|
| 543 | Roger Craig | 20.00 |
| 544 | George Thomas | 15.00 |
| 545 | Hoyt Wilhelm | 35.00 |
| 546 | Marty Kutyna | 15.00 |
| 547 | Leon Wagner | 15.00 |
| 548 | Ted Wills | 15.00 |
| 549 | Hal R. Smith | 15.00 |
| 550 | Frank Baumann | 15.00 |
| 551 | George Altman | 15.00 |
| 552 | Jim Archer | 15.00 |
| 553 | Bill Fischer | 15.00 |
| 554 | Pittsburgh Pirates | 25.00 |

| NO. | PLAYER | MINT |
|---|---|---|
| 555 | Sam Jones | 15.00 |
| 556 | Ken R. Hunt | 15.00 |
| 557 | Jose Valdivielso | 15.00 |
| 558 | Don Ferrarese | 15.00 |
| 559 | Jim Gentile | 15.00 |
| 560 | Barry Latman | 15.00 |
| 561 | Charley James | 15.00 |
| 562 | Bill Monbouquette | 15.00 |
| 563 | Bob Cerv | 15.00 |
| 564 | Don Cardwell | 15.00 |
| 565 | Felipe Alou | 15.00 |

| NO. | PLAYER | MINT |
|---|---|---|
| 566 | P. Richards—Mgr. (AS) | 15.00 |
| 567 | D. Murtaugh—Mgr. (AS) | 15.00 |
| 568 | Bill Skowron (AS) | 15.00 |
| 569 | Frank Herrera (AS) | 15.00 |
| 570 | Nellie Fox (AS) | 22.00 |
| 571 | Bill Mazeroski (AS) | 15.00 |
| 572 | Brooks Robinson (AS) | 45.00 |
| 573 | Ken Boyer (AS) | 15.00 |
| 574 | Luis Aparicio (AS) | 25.00 |
| 575 | Ernie Banks (AS) | 50.00 |
| 576 | Roger Maris (AS) | 55.00 |

| NO. | PLAYER | MINT |
|---|---|---|
| 577 | Hank Aaron (AS) | 120.00 |
| 578 | Mickey Mantle (AS) | 300.00 |
| 579 | Willie Mays (AS) | 115.00 |
| 580 | Al Kaline (AS) | 50.00 |
| 581 | Frank Robinson (AS) | 50.00 |
| 582 | Earl Battey (AS) | 15.00 |
| 583 | Del Crandall (AS) | 15.00 |
| 584 | Jim Perry (AS) | 15.00 |
| 585 | Bob Friend (AS) | 15.00 |
| 586 | Whitey Ford (AS) | 50.00 |
| 589 | W. Spahn (AS) (Exc. $25.00) | 75.00 |

**Prices for the 1961 set are for cards in *Mint* condition. *Excellent* copies sell for 40% to 50% of prices shown; *Very Good*—25% to 30%.**

## 1962 Topps....Complete Set of 598 Cards—Value $1100.00 (Exc.); $3300.00 (Mint)

The rookie cards of Lou Brock, Gaylord Perry and Bob Uecker are in this set. The high numbers are 523 to 598. Nine cards were reprinted with different photos. These are worth a premium. The value of the complete set does not include the *variety* cards.

| NO. | PLAYER | MINT |
|---|---|---|
| 1 | Roger Maris (Exc. $16.00) | 125.00 |
| 2 | Jim Brosnan | .90 |
| 3 | Pete Runnels | .90 |
| 4 | John DeMerit | .90 |
| 5 | Sandy Koufax | 40.00 |
| 6 | Marv Breeding | .90 |
| 7 | Frank Thomas | .90 |
| 8 | Ray Herbert | .90 |
| 9 | Jim Davenport | .90 |
| 10 | Bob Clemente | 40.00 |
| 11 | Tom Morgan | .90 |
| 12 | Harry Craft (Mgr.) | .90 |
| 13 | Dick Howser | 1.50 |
| 14 | Bill White | 1.25 |
| 15 | Dick Donovan | .90 |
| 16 | Darrell Johnson | .90 |
| 17 | Johnny Callison | .90 |
| 18 | Managers' Dream: | 55.00 |
|  | Mickey Mantle, Willie Mays | |
| 19 | Ray Washburn | .90 |
| 20 | Rocky Colavito | 2.00 |
| 21 | Jim Kaat | 3.00 |
| 22 | Checklist No. 1 | 3.50 |
| 23 | Norm Larker | .90 |
| 24 | Detroit Tigers | 3.00 |
| 25 | Ernie Bank | 12.00 |
| 26 | Chris Cannizzaro | .90 |
| 27 | Chuck Cottier | .90 |
| 28 | Minnie Minoso | 2.00 |
| 29 | Casey Stengel (Mgr.) | 9.00 |
| 30 | Ed Mathews | 9.00 |
| 31 | Tom Tresh (R) | 6.00 |
| 32 | John Roseboro | .90 |
| 33 | Don Larsen | .90 |
| 34 | Johnny Temple | .90 |
| 35 | Don Schwall | .90 |
| 36 | Don Leppert | .90 |
| 37 | Tribe Hill Trio: | .90 |
|  | Barry Latman, Dick Stigman, Jim Perry | |
| 38 | Gene Stephens | .90 |
| 39 | Joe Koppe | .90 |
| 40 | Orlando Cepeda | 4.00 |
| 41 | Cliff Cook | .90 |

| NO. | PLAYER | MINT |
|---|---|---|
| 42 | Jim King | .90 |
| 43 | Los Angeles Dodgers | 3.00 |
| 44 | Don Taussig | .90 |
| 45 | Brooks Robinson | 13.00 |
| 46 | Jack Baldschun | .90 |
| 47 | Bob Will | .90 |
| 48 | Ralph Terry | .90 |
| 49 | Hal Jones | .90 |
| 50 | Stan Musal | 35.00 |
| 51 | AL Batting Leaders: | 1.50 |
|  | Al Kaline, Norm Cash, Jim Piersall, Elston Howard | |
| 52 | NL Batting Leaders: | 1.50 |
|  | Wally Moon, Bob Clemente, Vada Pinson, Ken Boyer | |
| 53 | AL Home Run Leaders: | 10.00 |
|  | Jim Gentile, Roger Maris, Mickey Mantle, Harmon Killebrew | |
| 54 | NL Home Run Leaders: | 2.00 |
|  | Orlando Cepeda, Willie Mays, Frank Robinson | |
| 55 | AL ERA Leaders: | 1.50 |
|  | Dick Donovan, Bill Stafford, Don Mossi, Milt Pappas | |
| 56 | NL ERA Leaders: | 1.50 |
|  | Warren Spahn, Jim O'Toole, Curt Simmons, Mike McCormick | |
| 57 | AL Win Leaders: | 1.50 |
|  | Frank Lary, Whitey Ford, Steve Barber, Jim Bunning | |
| 58 | NL Win Leaders: | 1.50 |
|  | Warren Spahn, Joe Jay, Jim O'Toole | |
| 59 | AL Strikeout Leaders: | 1.50 |
|  | Camilo Pascual, Whitey Ford, Jim Bunning, Juan Pizzaro | |
| 60 | NL Strikeout Leaders: | 1.50 |
|  | Sandy Koufax, Stan Williams, Don Drysdale, Jim O'Toole | |
| 61 | St. Louis Cardinals | 1.50 |

| NO. | PLAYER | MINT |
|---|---|---|
| 62 | Steve Boros | .90 |
| 63 | Tony Cloninger | .90 |
| 64 | Russ Snyder | .90 |
| 65 | Bobby Richardson | 3.00 |
| 66 | Cuno Barragon | .90 |
| 67 | Harvey Haddix | .90 |
| 68 | Ken Hunt | .90 |
| 69 | Phil Ortega | .90 |
| 70 | Harmon Killebrew | 12.00 |
| 71 | Dick Le May | .90 |
| 72 | Bob's Pupils: | .90 |
|  | Steve Boros, Bob Scheffing, Jake Wood | |
| 73 | Nellie Fox | 3.00 |
| 74 | Bob Lillis | .90 |
| 75 | Milt Pappas | .90 |
| 76 | Howie Bedell | .90 |
| 77 | Tony Taylor | .90 |
| 78 | Gene Green | .90 |
| 79 | Ed Hobaugh | .90 |
| 80 | Vada Pinson | 2.50 |
| 81 | Jim Pagliaroni | .90 |
| 82 | Deron Johnson | .90 |
| 83 | Larry Jackson | .90 |
| 84 | Lenny Green | .90 |
| 85 | Gil Hodges | 9.00 |
| 86 | Donn Clendenon | .90 |
| 87 | Mike Roarke | .90 |
| 88 | Ralph Houk | 1.50 |
| 89 | Barney Schultz | .90 |
| 90 | Jim Piersall | 1.25 |
| 91 | J.C. Martin | .90 |
| 92 | Sam Jones | .90 |
| 93 | John Blanchard | .90 |
| 94 | Jay Hook | .90 |
| 95 | Don Hoak | .90 |
| 96 | Eli Grba | .90 |
| 97 | Tito Francona | .90 |
| 98 | Checklist No. 2 | 3.50 |
| 99 | John Powell (R) | 6.00 |
| 100 | Warren Spahn | 12.00 |
| 101 | Carroll Hardy | .90 |
| 102 | Al Schroll | .90 |
| 103 | Don Blasingame | .90 |

| NO. | PLAYER | MINT |
|---|---|---|
| 104 | Ted Savage | .90 |
| 105 | Don Mossi | .90 |
| 106 | Carl Sawatski | .90 |
| 107 | Mike McCormick | .90 |
| 108 | Willie Davis | .90 |
| 109 | Bob Shaw | .90 |
| 110 | Bill Skowron | 3.00 |
| 111 | Dallas Green | .90 |
| 112 | Hank Foiles | .90 |
| 113 | Chicago White Sox | 2.00 |
| 114 | Howie Koplitz | .90 |
| 115 | Bob Skinner | .90 |
| 116 | Herb Score | 1.50 |
| 117 | Gary Geiger | .90 |
| 118 | Julian Javier | .90 |
| 119 | Danny Murphy | .90 |
| 120 | Bob Purkey | .90 |
| 121 | Billy Hitchcock | .90 |
| 122 | Norm Bass | .90 |
| 123 | Mike De La Hoz | .90 |
| 124 | Bill Pleis | .90 |
| 125 | Gene Woodling | .90 |
| 126 | Al Cicotte | .90 |
| 127 | Pride of A's: | .90 |
|  | Norm Siebern, Hank Bauer, Jerry Lumpe | |
| 128 | Art Fowler | .90 |
| 129 | Lee Walls (faces right) | 1.00 |
| 129 | Lee Walls (faces left) | 8.00 |
| 130 | Frank Bolling | .90 |
| 131 | Pete Richert | .90 |
| 132 | Los Angeles Angels* | 1.50 |
| 133 | Felipe Alou | .90 |
| 134 | Billy Hoeft (faces right) | 1.00 |
| 134 | Billy Hoeft (faces front) | 8.00 |
| 135 | Babe Ruth Special: | 6.00 |
|  | Babe as a Boy | |
| 136 | Babe Ruth Special: | 6.00 |
|  | Babe Joins Yanks | |
| 137 | Babe Ruth Special: | 6.00 |
|  | Babe and Mgr. Huggins | |
| 138 | Babe Ruth Special: | 6.00 |
|  | Famous Slugger | |

| NO. PLAYER | MINT | NO. PLAYER | MINT | NO. PLAYER | MINT | NO. PLAYER | MINT |
|---|---|---|---|---|---|---|---|
| 139 Babe Ruth Special.......6.00<br>Babe Hits 60<br>See Card no. 159 | | 205 Gene Freese..............90 | | 278 Ken Johnson.............90 | | 357 Jerry Walker.............90 | |
| 140 Babe Ruth Special:.......6.00<br>Gehrig and Ruth | | 206 Washington Senators....2.00 | | 279 Hobie Landrith..........90 | | 358 Tommy Davis..........1.50 | |
| 141 Babe Ruth Special:.......6.00<br>Twilight Years | | 207 Pete Burnside............90 | | 280 Johnny Podres..........2.00 | | 359 Bobby Locke............90 | |
| 142 Babe Ruth Special:.......6.00<br>Coaching for Dodgers | | 208 Billy Martin.............4.00 | | 281 Jake Gibbs.............1.25 | | 360 Yogi Berra.........20.00 | |
| 143 Babe Ruth Special:.......6.00<br>Greatest Sports Hero | | 209 Jim Fregosi (R).........3.50 | | 282 Dave Hillman...........90 | | 361 Bob Hendley...........90 | |
| 144 Babe Ruth Special:.......6.00<br>Farewell Speech | | 210 Roy Face...............1.25 | | 283 Charlie Smith..........90 | | 362 Ty Cline..............90 | |
| 145 Barry Latman............90 | | 211 Midway Masters........1.00<br>Frank Bolling, Roy McMillan | | 284 Ruben Amaro...........90 | | 363 Bob Roselli...........90 | |
| 146 Don Demeter............90 | | 212 Jim Owens.............90 | | 285 Curt Simmons..........90 | | 364 Ken Hunt.............90 | |
| 147 Bill Kunkel (head shot)...1.00 | | 213 Richie Ashburn.........4.00 | | 286 Al Lopez (Mgr.).......2.50 | | 365 Charley Neal..........90 | |
| 147 Bill Kunkel (pitching)...8.00 | | 214 Dom Zanni.............90 | | 287 George Witt...........90 | | 366 Phil Regan...........90 | |
| 148 Wally Post.............90 | | 215 Woody Held............90 | | 288 Billy Williams.........10.00 | | 367 Checklist No. 5........3.50 | |
| 149 Bob Duliba............90 | | 216 Ron Kline.............90 | | 289 Mike Krsnich..........90 | | 368 Bob Tillman...........90 | |
| 150 Al Kaline.............11.00 | | 217 Walt Alston (Mgr.).....3.00 | | 290 Jim Gentile...........1.25 | | 369 Ted Bowsfield.........90 | |
| 151 Johnny Klippstein.......90 | | 218 Joe Torre (R)..........9.00 | | 291 Hal Stowe............90 | | 370 Ken Boyer............3.00 | |
| 152 Mickey Vernon (Mgr.)...1.25 | | 219 Al Downing (R).........2.00 | | 292 Jerry Kindall..........90 | | 371 Earl Battey...........1.50 | |
| 153 Pumpsie Green..........90 | | 220 Roy Sievers...........1.25 | | 293 Bob Miller............90 | | 372 Jack Curtis...........1.50 | |
| 154 Lee Thomas............90 | | 221 Bill Short.............90 | | 294 Philadelphia Phillies....2.00 | | 373 Al Heist.............1.50 | |
| 155 Stu Miller.............90 | | 222 Jerry Zimmerman.......90 | | 295 Vern Law.............1.50 | | 374 Gene Mauch (Mgr.).....1.50 | |
| 156 Merritt Ranew..........90 | | 223 Alex Grammas.........90 | | 296 Ken Hamlin...........90 | | 375 Ron Fairly...........1.50 | |
| 157 Wes Covington.........90 | | 224 Don Rudolph..........90 | | 297 Ron Perranoski........90 | | 376 Bud Daley...........1.50 | |
| 158 Milwaukee Braves.......2.00 | | 225 Frank Malzone.........90 | | 298 Bill Tuttle............90 | | 377 Johnny Orsino........1.50 | |
| 159 Hal Reniff............1.25 | | 226 San F. Giants.........2.50 | | 299 Don Wert.............90 | | 378 Bennie Daniels........1.50 | |
| 159 Hal Reniff (head shot)..10.00<br>Error—reads no. 139 | | 227 Bobby Tiefenauer.......90 | | 300 Willie Mays..........60.00 | | 379 Chuck Essegian.......1.50 | |
| 159 Hal Reniff (pitching)...35.00<br>Error—reads no. 139 | | 228 Dale Long.............90 | | 301 Galen Cisco..........90 | | 380 Lou Burdette.........2.00 | |
| 160 Dick Stuart............1.25 | | 229 Jesus McFarlane........90 | | 302 John Edwards.........90 | | 381 Chico Cardenas.......1.50 | |
| 161 Frank Baumann.........90 | | 230 Camilo Pascual........90 | | 303 Frank Torre...........90 | | 382 Dick Williams........3.00 | |
| 162 Sammy Drake..........90 | | 231 Ernie Bowman.........90 | | 304 Dick Farrell..........90 | | 383 Ray Sadecki.........1.50 | |
| 163 Hot Corner Guardians:...1.50<br>Billy Gardner, Cletis Boyer | | 232 World Series Game 1:...2.50<br>Yanks Win Opener | | 305 Jerry Lumpe..........90 | | 384 K.C. Athletics........3.00 | |
| 164 Hal Naragon...........90 | | 233 World Series Game 2:...2.50<br>Jay Ties It Up | | 306 Redbird Rippers:......90<br>Lindy McDaniel,<br>Larry Jackson | | 385 Early Wynn..........8.00 | |
| 165 Jackie Brandt..........90 | | 234 World Series Game 3:...4.00<br>Maris Wins In 9th | | 307 Jim Grant............90 | | 386 Don Mincher.........1.50 | |
| 166 Don Lee..............90 | | 235 World Series Game 4:...4.00<br>Ford Sets New Mark | | 308 Neil Chrisley..........90 | | 387 Lou Brock (R)........75.00 | |
| 167 Tim McCarver (R)......8.00 | | 236 World Series Game 5:...2.50<br>Yanks Crush Reds | | 309 Moe Morhardt.........90 | | 388 Ryne Duren..........1.50 | |
| 168 Leo Posada...........90 | | 237 World Series..........2.50<br>Winners Celebrate | | 310 Whitey Ford.........15.00 | | 389 Smoky Burgess.......1.50 | |
| 169 Bob Cerv.............90 | | 238 Norm Sherry..........1.25 | | 311 Kubek Double Play....2.50 | | 390 Orlando Cepeda (AS)...3.00 | |
| 170 Ron Santo............2.00 | | 239 Cecil Butler...........90 | | 312 Spahn No-Hit.........6.00 | | 391 Bill Mazeroski (AS)....2.50 | |
| 171 Dave Sisler...........90 | | 240 George Altman.........90 | | 313 Maris Blasts 61 HR..8.00 | | 392 Ken Boyer (AS).......1.50 | |
| 172 Fred Hutchinson (Mgr.)...90 | | 241 Johnny Kucks..........90 | | 314 Colavito's Power.....2.50 | | 393 Roy McMillan (AS)....1.50 | |
| 173 Chico Fernandez........90 | | 242 Mel McGaha (Mgr.)....90 | | 315 Ford Curveball.......6.00 | | 394 Hank Aaron (AS).....16.00 | |
| 174 Carl Willey (no hat)....1.00 | | 243 Robin Roberts.........7.00 | | 316 Killebrew's Orbit.....5.00 | | 395 Willie Mays (AS).....16.00 | |
| 174 Carl Willey (with hat)...8.00 | | 244 Don Gile.............90 | | 317 Musial's 21st Season...90 | | 396 Frank Robinson (AS)...9.00 | |
| 175 Frank Howard..........2.00 | | 245 Ron Hansen...........90 | | 318 Switch Hitter Mantle...30.00 | | 397 John Roseboro (AS)....1.50 | |
| 176 Eddie Yost (head shot)...1.00 | | 246 Art Ditmar............90 | | 319 McCormick in Action...2.00 | | 398 Don Drysdale (AS).....7.00 | |
| 176 Eddie Yost (with bat)...8.00 | | 247 Joe Pignatano.........90 | | 320 Hank Aaron.........65.00 | | 399 Warren Spahn (AS)....7.00 | |
| 177 Bobby Shantz..........1.25 | | 248 Bob Aspromonte........90 | | 321 Lee Stange...........90 | | 400 Elston Howard........4.00 | |
| 178 Camilo Carreon.........90 | | 249 Ed Keegan............90 | | 322 Al Dark (Mgr.).......1.50 | | 401 AL & NL Homer Kings:..14.00<br>Roger Maris, O. Cepeda | |
| 179 Tom Sturdivant.........90 | | 250 Norm Cash...........2.00 | | 323 Don Landrum.........90 | | 402 Gino Cimoli..........1.25 | |
| 180 Bob Allison...........1.25 | | 251 New York Yankees....8.00 | | 324 Joe McClain..........90 | | 403 Chet Nichols.........1.25 | |
| 181 Paul Brown...........90 | | 252 Earl Francis...........90 | | 325 Luis Aparicio.........9.00 | | 404 Tim Harkness........1.25 | |
| 182 Bob Nieman...........90 | | 253 Harry Chiti...........90 | | 326 Tom Parsons..........90 | | 405 Jim Perry............1.50 | |
| 183 Roger Craig...........1.25 | | 254 Gordon Windhorn......90 | | 327 Ozzie Virgil..........90 | | 406 Bob Taylor...........1.50 | |
| 184 Haywood Sullivan.......90 | | 255 Joan Pizarro..........90 | | 328 Ken Walters..........90 | | 407 Hank Aguirre........1.50 | |
| 185 Roland Sheldon.........90 | | 256 Elio Chacon...........90 | | 329 Bob Bolin............90 | | 408 Gus Bell............1.50 | |
| 186 Mack Jones...........90 | | 257 Jack Spring...........90 | | 330 Johnny Romano........90 | | 409 Pittsburgh Pirates.....2.50 | |
| 187 Gene Conley...........90 | | 258 Marty Keough..........90 | | 331 Moe Drabowsky........90 | | 410 Al Smith............1.50 | |
| 188 Chuck Hiller...........90 | | 259 Lou Klimchock.........90 | | 332 Don Buddin...........90 | | 411 Danny O'Connell......1.50 | |
| 189 Dick Hall.............90 | | 260 Bill Pierce............1.25 | | 333 Frank Cipriani.........90 | | 412 Charlie James........1.50 | |
| 190 Wally Moon (head shot)..1.00 | | 261 George Alusik..........75 | | 334 Boston Red Sox.......3.00 | | 413 Matty Alou..........2.00 | |
| 190 Wally Moon (with bat)...8.00 | | 262 Bob Schmidt..........75 | | 335 Bill Bruton...........1.50 | | 414 Joe Gaines...........1.50 | |
| 191 Jim Brewer............90 | | 263 The Right Pitch:.......75<br>Bob Purkey, Jim Turner,<br>Joe Jay | | 336 Billy Muffett..........90 | | 415 Bill Virdon...........2.00 | |
| 192 Checklist No. 3.........4.00 | | 264 Dick Ellsworth.........90 | | 337 Jim Marshall..........1.25 | | 416 Bob Scheffing (Mgr.)...1.50 | |
| 193 Eddie Kasko...........90 | | 265 Joe Adcock...........1.50 | | 338 Billy Gardner.........1.25 | | 417 Joe Azcue...........1.50 | |
| 194 Dean Chance..........1.50 | | 266 John Anderson.........90 | | 339 Jose Valdivielso.......90 | | 418 Andy Carey..........1.50 | |
| 195 Joe Cunningham........90 | | 267 Dan Dobbek...........90 | | 340 Don Drysdale........12.00 | | 419 Bob Bruce...........1.50 | |
| 196 Terry Fox.............90 | | 268 Ken McBride..........90 | | 341 Mike Hershberger......90 | | 420 Gus Triandos.........1.50 | |
| 197 Daryl Spencer..........90 | | 269 Bob Oldis............90 | | 342 Ed Rakow............90 | | 421 Ken MacKenzie.......1.50 | |
| 198 Johnny Keane (Mgr.).....90 | | 270 Dick Groat...........2.00 | | 343 Albie Pearson.........90 | | 422 Steve Bilko..........1.50 | |
| 199 Gaylord Perry (R).....50.00 | | 271 Ray Rippelmeyer.......90 | | 344 Ed Bauta............90 | | 423 Rival Relief Aces:......4.00<br>Roy Face, Hoyt Wilhelm | |
| 200 Mickey Mantle........350.00 | | 272 Earl Robinson.........90 | | 345 Chuck Schilling.......90 | | 424 Al McBean..........1.50 | |
| 201 Ike Delock............90 | | 273 Gary Bell............90 | | 346 Jack Kralick..........90 | | 425 Carl Yastrzemski....120.00 | |
| 202 Carl Warwick..........90 | | 274 Sammy Taylor.........90 | | 347 Chuck Hinton.........90 | | 426 Bob Farley..........1.50 | |
| 203 Jack Fisher...........90 | | 275 Norm Siebern.........90 | | 348 Larry Burright........90 | | 427 Jake Wood..........1.50 | |
| 204 Johnny Weekly.........90 | | 276 Hal Kolstad...........90 | | 349 Paul Foytack.........90 | | 428 Joe Hicks...........1.50 | |
| | | 277 Checklist No. 4.........4.00 | | 350 Frank Robinson......12.50 | | 429 Billy O'Dell.........1.50 | |
| | | | | 351 Braves' Backstops:.....2.00<br>Joe Torre, Del Crandall | | 430 Tony Kubek.........5.00 | |
| | | | | 352 Frank Sullivan.........90 | | 431 Bob Rodgers.........2.00 | |
| | | | | 353 Bill Mazeroski........2.00 | | 432 Jim Pendleton.......1.50 | |
| | | | | 354 Roman Mejias........90 | | 433 Jim Archer..........1.50 | |
| | | | | 355 Steve Barber.........90 | | 434 Clay Dalrymple......1.50 | |
| | | | | 356 Tom Haller...........1.25 | | 435 Larry Sherry.........1.50 | |
| | | | | | | 436 Felix Mantilla........1.50 | |

**Prices for the 1962 set are for cards in *Mint* condition. *Excellent* copies sell for 40% to 50% of prices shown; *Very Good*—25% to 30%.**

| NO. PLAYER | MINT | NO. PLAYER | MINT | NO. PLAYER | MINT | NO. PLAYER | MINT |
|---|---|---|---|---|---|---|---|
| 437 Ray Moore | 1.50 | 480 Harvey Kuenn | 2.00 | 527 Dick McAuliffe | 5.00 | 574 Dean Stone | 5.00 |
| 438 Dick Brown | 1.50 | 481 Vic Wertz | 1.50 | 528 Turk Lown | 5.00 | 575 Red Schoendienst | 8.00 |
| 439 Jerry Buchek | 1.50 | 482 Sam Mele | 1.50 | 529 John Schaive | 5.00 | 576 Russ Kemmerer | 5.00 |
| 440 Joe Jay | 1.50 | 483 Don McMahon | 1.50 | 530 Bob Gibson | .65.00 | 577 Dave Nicholson | 5.00 |
| 441 Checklist No. 6 | 3.50 | 484 Dick Schofield | 1.50 | 531 Bobby G. Smith | 5.00 | 578 Jim Duffalo | 5.00 |
| 442 Wes Stock | 1.50 | 485 Pedro Ramos | 1.50 | 532 Dick Stigman | 5.00 | 579 Jim Schaffer | 5.00 |
| 443 Del Crandall | 2.50 | 486 Jim Gilliam | 4.00 | 533 Charley Lau | 5.00 | 580 Bill Monbouquette | 5.00 |
| 444 Ted Wills | 1.50 | 487 Jerry Lynch | 1.50 | 534 Tony Gonzalez | 5.00 | 581 Mel Roach | 5.00 |
| 445 Vic Power | 1.50 | 488 Hal Brown | 1.50 | 535 Ed Roebuck | 5.00 | 582 Ron Piche | 5.00 |
| 446 Don Elston | 1.50 | 489 Julio Gotay | 1.50 | 536 Dick Gernert | 5.00 | 583 Larry Osborne | 5.00 |
| 447 Willie Kirland | 1.50 | 490 Clete Boyer | 3.00 | 537 Cleveland Indians | 8.00 | 584 Minnesota Twins | 8.00 |
| 448 Joe Gibbon | 1.50 | 491 Leon Wagner | 1.50 | 538 Jack Sanford | 5.00 | 585 Glen Hobbie | 5.00 |
| 449 Jerry Adair | 1.50 | 492 Hal Smith | 1.50 | 539 Billy Moran | 5.00 | 586 Sammy Esposito | 5.00 |
| 450 Jim O'Toole | 1.50 | 493 Danny McDevitt | 1.50 | 540 Jim Landis | 5.00 | 587 Frank Funk | 5.00 |
| 451 Jose Tartabull | 1.50 | 494 Sammy White | 1.50 | 541 Don Nottebart | 5.00 | 588 Birdie Tebbetts (Mgr.) | 5.00 |
| 452 Earl Averill | 1.50 | 495 Don Cardwell | 1.50 | 542 Dave Philley | 5.00 | 589 Bob Turley | 10.00 |
| 453 Cal McLish | 1.50 | 496 Wayne Causey | 1.50 | 543 Bob Allen | 5.00 | 590 Curt Flood | 10.00 |
| 454 Floyd Robinson | 1.50 | 497 Ed Bouchee | 1.50 | 544 Willie McCovey | .75.00 | 591 Rookie Pitchers: | 22.00 |
| 455 Luis Arroyo | 1.50 | 498 Jim Donohue | 1.50 | 545 Hoyt Wilhelm | .30.00 |    Sam McDowell, D. Radatz, | |
| 456 Joe Amalfitano | 1.50 | 499 Zoilo Versalles | 1.50 | 546 Moe Thacker | 5.00 |    Ron Taylor, Ron Nischwitz, | |
| 457 Lou Clinton | 1.50 | 500 Duke Snider | 25.00 | 547 Don Ferrarese | 5.00 |    Art Quirk | |
| 458 Bob Buhl ("M" on hat) | 2.00 | 501 Claude Osteen | 1.50 | 548 Bobby Del Greco | 5.00 | 592 Rookie Pitchers: | 25.00 |
| 458 Bob Buhl | 25.00 | 502 Hector Lopez | 1.50 | 549 Bill Rigney (Mgr.) | 5.00 |    D. Stenhouse, Dan Pfister, | |
|    (without "M" on hat) | | 503 Danny Murtaugh (Mgr.) | 1.50 | 550 Art Mahaffey | 5.00 |    Bo Belinsky, Jim Bouton, | |
| 459 Ed Bailey | 1.50 | 504 Eddie Bressoud | 1.50 | 551 Harry Bright | 5.00 |    Joe Bonikowski | |
| 460 Jim Bunning | 6.00 | 505 Juan Marichal | 20.00 | 552 Chicago Cubs | 10.00 | 593 Rookie Pitchers: | 12.00 |
| 461 Ken Hubbs (R) | 6.00 | 506 Charley Maxwell | 1.50 | 553 Jim Coates | 6.00 |    Bob Moorhead, Jack | |
| 462 Willie Tasby | 2.00 | 507 Ernie Broglio | 1.50 | 554 Bubba Morton | 5.00 |    Lamabe, Jack Hamilton, | |
|    ("W" on hat) | | 508 Gordy Coleman | 1.50 | 555 John Buzhardt | 5.00 |    Bob Veale, Craig Anderson | |
| 462 Willie Tasby | 25.00 | 509 Dave Giusti | 1.50 | 556 Al Spangler | 5.00 | 594 Rookie Catchers: | 90.00 |
|    (without "W" on hat) | | 510 Jim Lemon | 1.50 | 557 Bob Anderson | 5.00 |    Bob Uecker, Doc Edwards, | |
| 463 Hank Bauer (Mgr.) | 2.50 | 511 Bubba Phillips | 1.50 | 558 John Goryl | 5.00 |    Ken Retzer, Doug Camilli, | |
| 464 Al Jackson | 1.50 | 512 Mike Fornieles | 1.50 | 559 Mike Higgins (Mgr.) | 5.00 |    Don Pavletich | |
| 465 Cincinnati Reds | 5.00 | 513 Whitey Herzog | 3.00 | 560 Chuck Estrada | 5.00 | 595 Rookie Infielders: | 12.00 |
| 466 Norm Cash (AS) | 4.00 | 514 Sherm Lollar | 1.50 | 561 Gene Oliver | 5.00 |    Bob Sadowski, Marlan | |
| 467 Chuck Schilling (AS) | 2.50 | 515 Stan Williams | 1.50 | 562 Bill Henry | 5.00 |    Coughtry, Ed Charles, | |
| 468 Brooks Robinson (AS) | 10.00 | 516 Checklist No. 7 | 6.00 | 563 Ken Aspromonte | 5.00 |    Felix Torres | |
| 469 Luis Aparicio (AS) | 6.00 | 517 Dave Wickersham | 1.50 | 564 Bob Grim | 5.00 | 596 Rookie Infielders: | 20.00 |
| 470 Al Kaline (AS) | 12.00 | 518 Lee Maye | 1.50 | 565 Jose Pagan | 5.00 |    Bernie Allen, Phil Linz, | |
| 471 Mickey Mantle (AS) | .55.00 | 519 Bob Johnson | 1.50 | 566 Marty Kutyna | 5.00 |    Rich Rollins, Joe Pepitone | |
| 472 Rocky Colavito (AS) | 3.00 | 520 Bob Friend | 1.50 | 567 Tracy Stallard | 5.00 | 597 Rookie Infielders: | 12.00 |
| 473 Elston Howard (AS) | 3.00 | 521 Jacke Davis | 1.50 | 568 Jim Golden | 5.00 |    Denis Menke, Jim | |
| 474 Frank Lary (AS) | 2.00 | 522 Lindy McDaniel | 1.50 | 569 Ed Sadowski | 5.00 |    McKnight, Rod Kanehl, | |
| 475 Whitey Ford (AS) | 10.00 | 523 Russ Nixon | 5.00 | 570 Bill Stafford | 5.00 |    Amado Samuel | |
| 476 Baltimore Orioles | 3.00 | 524 Howie Nunn | 5.00 | 571 Billy Klaus | 5.00 | 598 Rookie Outfielders: | 20.00 |
| 477 Andre Rodgers | 1.50 | 525 George Thomas | 5.00 | 572 Bob Miller | 5.00 |    Al Luplow, Danny Jimenez, | |
| 478 Don Zimmer | 2.50 | 526 Hal Woodeschick | 5.00 | 573 Johnny Logan | 5.00 |    Ed Olivares, Howie Gross, | |
| 479 Joel Horlen | 1.50 | | | | |    Jim Hickman | |

## 1963 Topps. . . .Complete Set of 576 Cards—Value $1200.00 (Exc.); $3100.00 (Mint)

Pete Rose's rookie card is in this set. Cards 507 to 576 are the high numbers. Also includes the rookie cards of Willie Stargell, Tony Oliva, and Rusty Staub. Cards 29 and 54 exist with the error "1962 Rookie Stars" instead of "1963 Rookie Stars"—worth $5.00 each.

| NO. PLAYER | MINT | NO. PLAYER | MINT | NO. PLAYER | MINT | NO. PLAYER | MINT |
|---|---|---|---|---|---|---|---|
| 1 NL Bat Ldrs.: (Exc. $2.50) | 10.00 | 3 NL Home Run Leaders: | 4.00 | 5 NL ERA Leaders: | 1.75 | 7 NL Pitching Leaders: | 1.25 |
|    Frank Robinson, Stan | |    O. Cepeda, Hank Aaron, | |    Bob Purkey, Bob Shaw, | |    Don Drysdale, Billy O'Dell, | |
|    Musial, Tommy Davis, Bill | |    Ernie Banks, Frank | |    Sandy Koufax, Bob Gibson, | |    Jack Sanford, Bob Purkey, | |
|    White, Hank Aaron | |    Robinson, Willie Mays | |    Don Drysdale | |    Art Mahaffey, Joe Jay | |
| 2 AL Batting Leaders: | 6.00 | 4 AL Home Run Leaders: | 1.50 | 6 AL ERA Leaders: | 1.50 | 8 AL Pitching Leaders: | 1.25 |
|    Norm Siebern, Pete | |    Roger Maris, R. Colavito, | |    Whitey Ford, Robin Roberts, | |    Dick Donovan, Ray Herbert, | |
|    Runnels, Floyd Robinson, | |    Harmon Killebrew, Norm | |    Eddie Fisher, Hank Aguirre, | |    Ralph Terry, Jim Bunning, | |
|    C. Hinton, Mickey Mantle | |    Cash, J. Gentile, L. Wagner | |    Dean Chance | |    Camilo Pascual | |

| NO. | PLAYER | MINT |
|---|---|---|
| 9 | NL Strikeout Leaders: ... | 1.50 |
| | Sandy Koufax, Bob Gibson, | |
| | Don Drysdale, Billy O'Dell, | |
| | Dick Farrell | |
| 10 | AL Strikeout Leaders: ... | 1.25 |
| | Ralph Terry, Juan Pizarro, | |
| | Camilo Pascual, Jim | |
| | Bunning, Jim Kaat | |
| 11 | Lee Walls | .40 |
| 12 | Steve Barber | .40 |
| 13 | Philadelphia Phillies | .75 |
| 14 | Pedro Ramos | .40 |
| 15 | Ken Hubbs | 1.00 |
| 16 | Al Smith | .40 |
| 17 | Ryne Duren | .40 |
| 18 | Buc Blasters: | 5.00 |
| | Smoky Burgess, Dick Stuart, | |
| | Bob Clemente, Bob Skinner | |
| 19 | Pete Burnside | .40 |
| 20 | Tony Kubek | 3.00 |
| 21 | Marty Keough | .40 |
| 22 | Curt Simmons | .40 |
| 23 | Ed Lopat (Mgr.) | .50 |
| 24 | Bob Bruce | .40 |
| 25 | A. Kaline | 11.00 |
| 26 | Ray Moore | .40 |
| 27 | Choo Choo Coleman | .40 |
| 28 | Mike Fornieles | .40 |
| 29 | Rookie Stars:* | 1.25 |
| | Sammy Ellis, Jesse Gonder, | |
| | Ray Culp, John Boozer | |
| 30 | Harvey Kuenn | .75 |
| 31 | Cal Koonce | .40 |
| 32 | Tony Gonzalez | .40 |
| 33 | Bo Belinsky | .40 |
| 34 | Dick Schofield | .40 |
| 35 | John Buzhardt | .40 |
| 36 | Jerry Kindall | .40 |
| 37 | Jerry Lynch | .40 |
| 38 | Bud Daley | .40 |
| 39 | Los Angeles Angels | .75 |
| 40 | Vic Power | .40 |
| 41 | Charlie Lau | .40 |
| 42 | Stan Williams | .40 |
| 43 | Veteran Masters: | 3.00 |
| | C. Stengel, G. Woodling | |
| 44 | Terry Fox | .40 |
| 45 | Bob Aspromonte | .40 |
| 46 | Tommie Aaron | .40 |
| 47 | Don Lock | .40 |
| 48 | Birdie Tebbetts (Mgr.) | .40 |
| 49 | Dal Maxvill | .40 |
| 50 | Bill Pierc | .45 |
| 51 | George Alusik | .40 |
| 52 | Chuck Schilling | .40 |
| 53 | Joe Moeller:* | .40 |
| 54 | Rookie Stars:* | 3.50 |
| | N. Mathews, D. DeBusschere, | |
| | Harry Fanok, J. Cullen | |
| 55 | Bill Virdon | .75 |
| 56 | Dennis Bennett | .40 |
| 57 | Billy Moran | .40 |
| 58 | Bob Will | .40 |
| 59 | Craig Anderson | .40 |
| 60 | Elston Howard | 3.00 |
| 61 | Ernie Bowman | .40 |
| 62 | Bob Hendley | .40 |
| 63 | Cincinnati Reds | 1.00 |
| 64 | Dick McAuliffe | .40 |
| 65 | Jackie Brandt | .40 |
| 66 | Mike Joyce | .40 |
| 67 | Ed Charles | .40 |
| 68 | Friendly Foes: | 6.00 |
| | Duke Snider, Gil Hodges | |
| 69 | Bud Zipfel | .40 |
| 70 | Jim O'Toole | .40 |
| 71 | Bobby Wine | .40 |
| 72 | Johnny Romano | .40 |
| 73 | Bob Bragan (Mgr.) | .40 |
| 74 | Denver Lemaster | .40 |
| 75 | Bobby Allison | .40 |
| 76 | Earl Wilson | .40 |
| 77 | Al Spangler | .40 |
| 78 | Marv Throneberry | 1.00 |
| 79 | Checklist No. 1 | 3.00 |
| 80 | Jim Gilliam | 2.00 |
| 81 | Jim Schaffer | .40 |
| 82 | Ed Rakow | .40 |
| 83 | Charley James | .40 |
| 84 | Ron Kline | .40 |
| 85 | Tom Haller | .40 |
| 86 | Charley Maxwell | .40 |
| 87 | Bob Veale | .40 |
| 88 | Ron Hansen | .40 |
| 89 | Dick Stigman | .40 |
| 90 | Gordy Coleman | .40 |
| 91 | Dallas Green | .60 |
| 92 | Hector Lopez | .40 |
| 93 | Galen Cisco | .40 |
| 94 | Bob Schmidt | .40 |
| 95 | Larry Jackson | .40 |
| 96 | Lou Clinton | .40 |
| 97 | Bob Duliba | .40 |
| 98 | George Thomas | .40 |
| 99 | Jim Umbricht | .40 |
| 100 | Joe Cunningham | .40 |
| 101 | Joe Gibbon | .40 |
| 102 | Checklist No. 2 | 3.00 |
| 103 | Chuck Essegian | .40 |
| 104 | Lew Krausse | .40 |
| 105 | Ron Fairly | .40 |
| 106 | Bob Bolin | .40 |
| 107 | Jim Hickman | .40 |
| 108 | Hoyt Wilhelm | 6.00 |
| 109 | Lee Maye | .40 |
| 110 | Rich Rollins | .40 |
| 111 | Al Jackson | .40 |
| 112 | Dick Brown | .40 |
| 113 | Don Landrum | .40 |
| | (photo of Ron Santo) | |
| 114 | Dan Osinski | .40 |
| 115 | Carl Yastrzemski | .50.00 |
| 116 | Jim Brosnan | .40 |
| 117 | Jacke Davis | .40 |
| 118 | Sherm Lollar | .40 |
| 119 | Bob Lillis | .40 |
| 120 | Roger Maris | 25.00 |
| 121 | Jim Hannan | .40 |
| 122 | Julio Gotay | .40 |
| 123 | Frank Howard | 1.50 |
| 124 | Dick Howser | .40 |
| 125 | Robin Roberts | 7.00 |
| 126 | Bob Uecker | 20.00 |
| 127 | Bill Tuttle | .40 |
| 128 | Matty Alou | .40 |
| 129 | Gary Bell | .40 |
| 130 | Dick Groat | .60 |
| 131 | Washington Senators | 1.00 |
| 132 | Jack Hamilton | .40 |
| 133 | Gene Freese | .40 |
| 134 | Bob Scheffing (Mgr.) | .40 |
| 135 | Richie Ashburn | 4.00 |
| 136 | Ike Delock | .40 |
| 137 | Mack Jones | .40 |
| 138 | Pride Of N.L.: | .12.00 |
| | Willie Mays, Stan Musial | |
| 139 | Earl Averill | .40 |
| 140 | Frank Lary | .40 |
| 141 | Manny Mota (R) | 3.00 |
| 142 | World Series Game 1 | 3.00 |
| | Ford Wins Opener | |
| 143 | World Series Game 2 | 2.00 |
| | Sanford Shutout | |
| 144 | World Series Game 3 | 4.00 |
| | Maris Sparks Rally | |
| 145 | World Series Game 4 | 2.00 |
| | Hiller Grand Slam | |
| 146 | World Series Game 5 | 2.00 |
| | Tresh's Homer | |
| 147 | World Series Game 6 | 2.00 |
| | Pierce Victory | |
| 148 | World Series Game 7 | 2.00 |
| | Yanks Celebrate | |
| 149 | Marv Breeding | .40 |
| 150 | Johnny Podres | 1.50 |
| 151 | Pittsburgh Pirates | 1.50 |
| 152 | Ron Nischwitz | .40 |
| 153 | Hal Smith | .40 |
| 154 | Walt Alston (Mgr.) | 2.50 |
| 155 | Bill Stafford | .40 |
| 156 | Roy McMillan | .40 |
| 157 | Diego Segui | .40 |
| 158 | Rookie Stars: | .60 |
| | Bob Saverine, Rogelio | |
| | Alvarez, Dave Roberts, | |
| | Tommy Harper | |
| 159 | Jim Pagliaroni | .40 |
| 160 | Juan Pizarro | .40 |
| 161 | Frank Torre | .40 |
| 162 | Minnesota Twins | 1.00 |
| 163 | Don Larsen | .60 |
| 164 | Bubba Morton | .40 |
| 165 | Jim Kaat | 3.00 |
| 166 | Johnny Keane (Mgr.) | .40 |
| 167 | Jim Fregosi | 1.00 |
| 168 | Russ Nixon | .40 |
| 169 | Rookie Stars: | 15.00 |
| | Gaylord Perry, Dick Egan, | |
| | Julio Navarro, Tommie Sisk | |
| 170 | Joe Adcock | .40 |
| 171 | Steve Hamilton | .40 |
| 172 | Gene Oliver | .40 |
| 173 | Bombers' Best: | 22.00 |
| | Tom Tresh, Mickey Mantle, | |
| | Bobby Richardson | |
| 174 | Larry Burright | .40 |
| 175 | Bob Buhl | .40 |
| 176 | Jim King | .40 |
| 177 | Bubba Phillips | .40 |
| 178 | Johnny Edwards | .40 |
| 179 | Ron Pich | .40 |
| 180 | Bill Skowron | 1.50 |
| 181 | Sammy Esposito | .40 |
| 182 | Albie Pearson | .40 |
| 183 | Joe Pepitone | 2.00 |
| 184 | Vern Law | .40 |
| 185 | Chuck Hiller | .40 |
| 186 | Jerry Zimmerman | .40 |
| 187 | Willie Kirkland | .40 |
| 188 | Eddie Bressoud | .40 |
| 189 | Dave Giusti | .40 |
| 190 | Minnie Minoso | 1.50 |
| 191 | Checklist No. 3 | 3.00 |
| 192 | Clay Dalrymple | .40 |
| 193 | Andre Rodgers | .40 |
| 194 | Joe Nuxhall | .40 |
| 195 | Manny Jimenez | .40 |
| 196 | Doug Camilli | .40 |
| 197 | Roger Craig | .60 |
| 198 | Lenny Green | .60 |
| 199 | Joe Amalfitano | .60 |
| 200 | Mickey Mantle | 250.00 |
| 201 | Cecil Butler | .60 |
| 202 | Boston Red Sox | 2.50 |
| 203 | Chico Cardenas | .60 |
| 204 | Don Nottebart | .60 |
| 205 | Luis Aparicio | 7.00 |
| 206 | Ray Washburn | .60 |
| 207 | Ken Hunt | .60 |
| 208 | Rookie Stars: | .60 |
| | Ron Herbel, John Miller, | |
| | Ron Taylor, Wally Wolf | |
| 209 | Hobie Landrith | .60 |
| 210 | Sandy Koufax | 65.00 |
| 211 | Fred Whitfield | .60 |
| 212 | Glen Hobbie | .60 |
| 213 | Billy Hitchcock (Mgr.) | .60 |
| 214 | Orlando Pena | .60 |
| 215 | Bob Skinner | .60 |
| 216 | Gene Conley | .60 |
| 217 | Joe Christopher | .60 |
| 218 | Tiger Twirlers: | 1.50 |
| | Frank Lary, Don Mossi, | |
| | Jim Bunning | |
| 219 | Chuck Cottier | .60 |
| 220 | Camilo Pascual | .60 |
| 221 | Cookie Rojas | 1.25 |
| 222 | Chicago Cubs | 1.00 |
| 223 | Eddie Fisher | .60 |
| 224 | Mike Roarke | .60 |
| 225 | Joe Jay | .60 |
| 226 | Julian Javier | .60 |
| 227 | Jim Grant | .60 |
| 228 | Rookie Stars: | .15.00 |
| | Max Alvis, Bob Bailey, | |
| | Pedro Oliva, Ed Kranepool | |
| 229 | Willie Davis | .60 |
| 230 | Pete Runnels | .60 |
| 231 | Eli Grba | .60 |
| | (photo of Ryne Duren) | |
| 232 | Frank Malzone | .60 |
| 233 | Casey Stengel (Mgr.) | .9.00 |
| 234 | Dave Nicholson | .60 |
| 235 | Bill O'Dell | .60 |
| 236 | Bill Bryan | .60 |
| 237 | Jim Coates | .60 |
| 238 | Lou Johnson | .60 |
| 239 | Harvey Haddix | .60 |
| 240 | Rocky Colavito | 2.00 |
| 241 | Billy Smith | .60 |
| 242 | Power Plus: | 12.00 |
| | Ernie Banks, Hank Aaron | |
| 243 | Don Leppert | .60 |
| 244 | John Tsitouris | .60 |
| 245 | Gil Hodges | .8.00 |
| 246 | Lee Stange | .60 |
| 247 | New York Yankees | .8.00 |
| 248 | Tito Francona | .60 |
| 249 | Leo Burke | .60 |
| 250 | Stan Musial | .50.00 |
| 251 | Jack Lamabe | .60 |
| 252 | Ron Santo | 2.00 |
| 253 | Rookie Stars; | .60 |
| | Len Gabrielson, Pete | |
| | Jernigan, Deacon Jones, | |
| | John Wojcik | |
| 254 | Mike Hershberger | .60 |
| 255 | Bob Shaw | .60 |
| 256 | Jerry Lumpe | .60 |
| 257 | Hank Aguirre | .60 |
| 258 | Alvin Dark (Mgr.) | .60 |
| 259 | Johnny Logan | .60 |
| 260 | Jim Gentile | .60 |
| 261 | Bob Miller | .60 |
| 262 | Ellis Burton | .60 |
| 263 | Dave Stenhouse | .60 |
| 264 | Phil Linz | .60 |
| 265 | Vada Pinson | 2.00 |
| 266 | Bob Allen | .60 |
| 267 | Carl Sawatski | .60 |
| 268 | Don Demter | .60 |
| 269 | Don Mincher | .60 |
| 270 | Felipe Alou | .60 |
| 271 | Dean Stone | .60 |
| 272 | Danny Murphy | .60 |
| 273 | Sammy Taylor | .60 |
| 274 | Checklist No. 4 | 3.00 |
| 275 | Ed Mathews | .8.00 |
| 276 | Barry Shetrone | .60 |
| 277 | Dick Farrell | .60 |
| 278 | Chico Fernandez | .60 |
| 279 | Wally Moon | .60 |
| 280 | Bob Rodgers | .60 |
| 281 | Tom Sturdivant | .60 |
| 282 | Bob Del Greco | .60 |
| 283 | Roy Sievers | .60 |
| 284 | Dave Sisler | 1.00 |
| 285 | Dick Stuart | 1.00 |
| 286 | Stu Miller | 1.00 |
| 287 | Dick Bertell | 1.00 |
| 288 | Chicago White Sox | 2.00 |
| 289 | Hal Brown | 1.00 |
| 290 | Bill White | 1.00 |
| 291 | Don Rudolph | 1.00 |
| 292 | Pumpsie Green | 1.00 |
| 293 | Bill Pleis | 1.00 |
| 294 | Bill Rigney (Mgr.) | 1.00 |
| 295 | Ed Roebuck | 1.00 |

| NO. | PLAYER | MINT |
|---|---|---|
| 296 | Doc Edwards | 1.00 |
| 297 | Jim Golden | 1.00 |
| 298 | Don Dillard | 1.00 |
| 299 | Rookie Stars: | 1.00 |
| | Dave Morehead, Bob Dustal, | |
| | Dan Schenider, Tom Butters | |
| 300 | Willie Mays | 70.00 |
| 301 | Bill Fischer | 1.00 |
| 302 | Whitey Herzog | 1.50 |
| 303 | Earl Francis | 1.00 |
| 304 | Harry Bright | 1.00 |
| 305 | Don Hoak | 1.00 |
| 306 | Star Receivers: | 1.50 |
| | Earl Battey, Elston Howard | |
| 307 | Chet Nichols | 1.00 |
| 308 | Camilo Carreon | 1.00 |
| 309 | Jim Brewer | 1.00 |
| 310 | Tommy Davis | 2.00 |
| 311 | Joe McClain | 1.00 |
| 312 | Houston Colts | 6.00 |
| 313 | Ernie Broglio | 1.00 |
| 314 | John Goryl | 1.00 |
| 315 | Ralph Terry | 1.00 |
| 316 | Norm Sherry | 1.00 |
| 317 | Sam McDowell | 1.25 |
| 318 | Gene Mauch (Mgr.) | 1.25 |
| 319 | Joe Gaines | 1.00 |
| 320 | Warren Spahn | 12.00 |
| 321 | Gino Cimoli | 1.00 |
| 322 | Bob Turley | 1.25 |
| 323 | Bill Mazeroski | 1.50 |
| 324 | Rookie Stars: | 1.50 |
| | G. Williams, Vic Davalillo, | |
| | P. Ward, Phil Roof | |
| 325 | Jack Sanford | 1.00 |
| 326 | Hank Foiles | 1.00 |
| 327 | Paul Foytack | 1.00 |
| 328 | Dick Williams | 1.25 |
| 329 | Lindy McDaniel | 1.00 |
| 330 | Chuck Hinton | 1.00 |
| 331 | Series Foes: | 1.25 |
| | Bill Stafford, Bill Pierce | |
| 332 | Joel Horlen | 1.00 |
| 333 | Carl Warwick | 1.00 |
| 334 | Wynn Hawkins | 1.00 |
| 335 | Leon Wagner | 1.00 |
| 336 | Ed Bauta | 1.00 |
| 337 | Los Angeles Dodgers | 6.00 |
| 338 | Russ Kemmerer | 1.00 |
| 339 | Ted Bowsfield | 1.00 |
| 340 | Yogi Berra | 28.00 |
| 341 | Jack Baldschun | 1.00 |
| 342 | Gene Woodling | 1.00 |
| 343 | Johnny Pesky (Mgr.) | 1.00 |
| 344 | Don Schwall | 1.00 |
| 345 | Brooks Robinson | 22.00 |
| 346 | Billy Hoeft | 1.00 |
| 347 | Joe Torre | 3.00 |
| 348 | Vic Wertz | 1.00 |
| 349 | Zoilo Versalles | 1.00 |
| 350 | Bob Purkey | 1.00 |
| 351 | Al Luplow | 1.00 |
| 352 | Ken Johnson | 1.00 |
| 353 | Billy Williams | 8.00 |
| 354 | Dom Zanni | 1.00 |
| 355 | Dean Chance | 1.00 |
| 356 | John Schaive | 1.00 |
| 357 | George Altman | 1.00 |
| 358 | Milt Pappas | 1.00 |
| 359 | Haywood Sullivan | 1.00 |
| 360 | Don Drysdale | 12.00 |
| 361 | Clete Boyer | 1.25 |
| 362 | Checklist No. 5 | 4.00 |
| 363 | Dick Radatz | 1.00 |
| 364 | Howie Goss | 1.00 |
| 365 | Jim Bunning | 5.00 |
| 366 | Tony Taylor | 1.00 |
| 367 | Tony Cloninger | 1.00 |
| 368 | Ed Bailey | 1.00 |

| NO. | PLAYER | MINT |
|---|---|---|
| 369 | Jim Lemon | 1.00 |
| 370 | Dick Donovan | 1.00 |
| 371 | Rod Kanehl | 1.00 |
| 372 | Don Lee | 1.00 |
| 373 | Jim Campbell | 1.00 |
| 374 | Claude Osteen | 1.00 |
| 375 | Ken Boyer | 2.50 |
| 376 | John Wyatt | 1.00 |
| 377 | Baltimore Orioles | 3.00 |
| 378 | Bill Henry | 1.00 |
| 379 | Bob Anderson | 1.00 |
| 380 | Ernie Banks | 25.00 |
| 381 | Frank Baumann | 1.00 |
| 382 | Ralph Houk (Mgr.) | 1.25 |
| 383 | Pete Richert | 1.00 |
| 384 | Bob Tillman | 1.00 |
| 385 | Art Mahaffey | 1.00 |
| 386 | Rookie Stars: | 1.25 |
| | Ed Kirkpatrick, J. Bateman, | |
| | G. Roggenburk, L. Bearnarth | |
| 387 | Al McBean | 1.00 |
| 388 | Jim Davenport | 1.00 |
| 389 | Frank Sullivan | 1.00 |
| 390 | Hank Aaron | 70.00 |
| 391 | Bill Dailey | 1.00 |
| 392 | Tribe Thumpers: | 1.00 |
| | Johnny Romano, | |
| | Tito Francona | |
| 393 | Ken MacKenzie | 1.00 |
| 394 | Tim McCarver | 2.00 |
| 395 | Don McMahon | 1.00 |
| 396 | Joe Koppe | 1.00 |
| 397 | Kansas C. Athletics | 2.50 |
| 398 | Boog Powell | 4.00 |
| 399 | Dick Ellsworth | 1.00 |
| 400 | Frank Robinson | 20.00 |
| 401 | Jim Bouton | 3.00 |
| 402 | Mickey Vernon (Mgr.) | 1.00 |
| 403 | Ron Perranoski | 1.00 |
| 404 | Bob Oldis | 1.00 |
| 405 | Floyd Robinson | 1.00 |
| 406 | Howie Koplitz | 1.00 |
| 407 | Rookie Stars: | 1.00 |
| | Dick Simpson, Frank Kostro, | |
| | Chico Ruiz, Larry Elliot | |
| 408 | Billy Gardner | 1.00 |
| 409 | Roy Face | 1.00 |
| 410 | Earl Battey | 1.00 |
| 411 | Jim Constable | 1.00 |
| 412 | Dodger Big Three: | 15.00 |
| | Sandy Koufax, Johnny | |
| | Podres, Don Drysdale | |
| 413 | Jerry Walker | 1.00 |
| 414 | Ty Cline | 1.00 |
| 415 | Bob Gibson | 20.00 |
| 416 | Alex Grammas | 1.00 |
| 417 | San F. Giants | 2.50 |
| 418 | Johnny Orsino | 1.00 |
| 419 | Tracy Stallard | 1.00 |
| 420 | Bobby Richardson | 4.00 |
| 421 | Tom Morgan | 1.00 |
| 422 | Fred Hutchinson (Mgr.) | 1.25 |
| 423 | Ed Hobaugh | 1.00 |
| 424 | Charley Smith | 1.00 |
| 425 | Smokey Burgess | 1.00 |
| 426 | Barry Latman | 1.00 |
| 427 | Bernie Allen | 1.00 |
| 428 | Carl Boles | 1.00 |
| 429 | Lou Burdette | 1.50 |
| 430 | Norm Siebern | 1.00 |
| 431 | Checklist No. 6 | 4.00 |
| 432 | Roman Mejias | 1.00 |
| 433 | Denis Menke | 1.00 |
| 434 | Johnny Callison | 1.00 |
| 435 | Woody Held | 1.00 |
| 436 | Tim Harkness | 1.00 |
| 437 | Bill Bruton | 1.00 |
| 438 | Wes Stock | 1.00 |
| 439 | Don Zimmer | 1.50 |

| NO. | PLAYER | MINT |
|---|---|---|
| 440 | Juan Marichal | 13.00 |
| 441 | Lee Thomas | 1.00 |
| 442 | J.C. Hartman | 1.00 |
| 443 | Jim Piersall | 1.50 |
| 444 | Jim Maloney | 1.00 |
| 445 | Norm Cash | 2.00 |
| 446 | Whitey Ford | 22.00 |
| 447 | Felix Mantilla | 5.00 |
| 448 | Jack Kralick | 5.00 |
| 449 | Jose Tartabull | 5.00 |
| 450 | Bob Friend | 5.00 |
| 451 | Cleveland Indians | 6.00 |
| 452 | Barney Schultz | 5.00 |
| 453 | Jake Wood | 5.00 |
| 454 | Art Fowler | 5.00 |
| 455 | Ruben Amaro | 5.00 |
| 456 | Jim Coker | 5.00 |
| 457 | Tex Clevenger | 5.00 |
| 458 | Al Lopez (Mgr.) | 8.00 |
| 459 | Dick LeMay | 5.00 |
| 460 | Del Crandall | 5.00 |
| 461 | Norm Bass | 5.00 |
| 462 | Wally Post | 5.00 |
| 463 | Joe Schaffernoth | 5.00 |
| 464 | Ken Aspromonte | 5.00 |
| 465 | Chuck Estrada | 5.00 |
| 466 | Rookie Stars: | 12.00 |
| | Tony Martinez, Bill Freehan, | |
| | Jerry Robinson, Nate Oliver | |
| 467 | Phil Ortega | 5.00 |
| 468 | Carroll Hardy | 5.00 |
| 469 | Jay Hook | 5.00 |
| 470 | Tom Tresh | 20.00 |
| 471 | Ken Retzer | 5.00 |
| 472 | Lou Brock | 70.00 |
| 473 | New York Mets | 15.00 |
| 474 | Jack Fisher | 5.00 |
| 475 | Gus Triandos | 5.00 |
| 476 | Frank Funk | 5.00 |
| 477 | Donn Clendenon | 5.00 |
| 478 | Paul Brown | 5.00 |
| 479 | Ed Brinkman | 5.00 |
| 480 | Bill Monbouquette | 5.00 |
| 481 | Bob Taylor | 5.00 |
| 482 | Felix Torres | 5.00 |
| 483 | Jim Owens | 5.00 |
| 484 | Dale Long | 5.00 |
| 485 | Jim Landis | 5.00 |
| 486 | Ray Sadecki | 5.00 |
| 487 | John Roseboro | 5.00 |
| 488 | Jerry Adair | 5.00 |
| 489 | Paul Toth | 5.00 |
| 490 | Willie McCovey | 60.00 |
| 491 | Harry Craft (Mgr.) | 5.00 |
| 492 | Dave Wickersham | 5.00 |
| 493 | Walt Bond | 5.00 |
| 494 | Phil Regan | 5.00 |
| 495 | Frank Thomas | 5.00 |
| 496 | Rookie Stars: | 5.00 |
| | Steve Dalkowski, Carl | |
| | Bouldin, Fred Newman, | |
| | Jack Smith | |
| 497 | Bennie Daniels | 5.00 |
| 498 | Eddie Kasko | 5.00 |
| 499 | J.C. Martin | 5.00 |
| 500 | Harmon Killebrew | 40.00 |
| 501 | Joe Azcue | 5.00 |
| 502 | Daryl Spencer | 5.00 |
| 503 | Milwaukee Braves | 8.00 |
| 504 | Bob Johnson | 5.00 |
| 505 | Curt Flood | 8.00 |
| 506 | Gene Green | 5.00 |
| 507 | Roland Sheldon | 4.00 |
| 508 | Ted Savage | 4.00 |
| 509 | Checklist No. 7 | 13.00 |
| 510 | Ken McBride | 4.00 |
| 511 | Charlie Neal | 4.00 |
| 512 | Cal McLish | 4.00 |
| 513 | Gary Geiger | 4.00 |

| NO. | PLAYER | MINT |
|---|---|---|
| 514 | Larry Osborne | 4.00 |
| 515 | Don Elston | 4.00 |
| 516 | Purnal Goldy | 4.00 |
| 517 | Hal Woodeschick | 4.00 |
| 518 | Don Blasingame | 4.00 |
| 519 | Claude Raymond | 4.00 |
| 520 | Orlando Cepeda | 10.00 |
| 521 | Dan Pfister | 4.00 |
| 522 | Rookie Stars: | 4.00 |
| | Mel Nelson, Gary Peters, | |
| | Art Quirk, Jim Roland | |
| 523 | Bill Kunkel | 4.00 |
| 524 | St. Louis Cards | 6.00 |
| 525 | Nellie Fox | 8.00 |
| 526 | Dick Hall | 4.00 |
| 527 | Ed Sadowski | 4.00 |
| 528 | Carl Willey | 4.00 |
| 529 | Wes Covington | 4.00 |
| 530 | Don Mossi | 4.00 |
| 531 | Sam Mele (Mgr.) | 4.00 |
| 532 | Steve Boros | 4.00 |
| 533 | Bobby Shantz | 4.00 |
| 534 | Ken Walters | 4.00 |
| 535 | Jim Perry | 4.00 |
| 536 | Norm Larker | 4.00 |
| 537 | Rookie Stars: | 550.00 |
| | Pedro Gonzalez, Pete Rose, | |
| | Ken McMullen, Al Weis | |
| 538 | George Brunet | 4.00 |
| 539 | Wayne Causey | 4.00 |
| 540 | Bob Clemente | 90.00 |
| 541 | Ron Moeller | 4.00 |
| 542 | Lou Klimchock | 4.00 |
| 543 | Russ Snyder | 4.00 |
| 544 | Rookie Stars: | 25.00 |
| | Rusty Staub, Duke Carmel, | |
| | Bill Haas, Dick Phillips | |
| 545 | Jose Pagan | 4.00 |
| 546 | Hal Reniff | 4.00 |
| 547 | Gus Bell | 4.00 |
| 548 | Tom Satriano | 4.00 |
| 549 | Rookie Stars: | 4.00 |
| | Paul Ratliff, Marcelino | |
| | Lopez, Pete Lovrich, | |
| | Elmo Plaskett | |
| 550 | Duke Snider | 50.00 |
| 551 | Billy Klaus | 4.00 |
| 552 | Detroit Tigers | 15.00 |
| 553 | Rookie Stars: | 135.00 |
| | Brock Davis, Jim Gosger, | |
| | W. Stargell, J. Herrnstein | |
| 554 | Hank Fischer | 4.00 |
| 555 | John Blanchard | 4.00 |
| 556 | Al Worthington | 4.00 |
| 557 | Cuno Barragan | 4.00 |
| 558 | Rookie Stars: | 4.00 |
| | Bill Faul, Ron Hunt, | |
| | Bob Lipski, Al Moran | |
| 559 | Danny Murtaugh (Mgr.) | 4.00 |
| 560 | Ray Herbert | 4.00 |
| 561 | Mike De La Hoz | 4.00 |
| 562 | Rookie Stars: | 6.00 |
| | Don Rowe, Randy Cardinal, | |
| | Dave McNally, Ken Rowe | |
| 563 | Mike McCormick | 4.00 |
| 564 | George Banks | 4.00 |
| 565 | Larry Sherry | 4.00 |
| 566 | Clif Cook | 4.00 |
| 567 | Jim Duffalo | 4.00 |
| 568 | Bob Sadowski | 4.00 |
| 569 | Luis Arroyo | 4.00 |
| 570 | Frank Bolling | 4.00 |
| 571 | Johnny Klippstein | 4.00 |
| 572 | Jack Spring | 4.00 |
| 573 | Coot Veal | 4.00 |
| 574 | Hal Kolstad | 4.00 |
| 575 | Don Cardwell | 4.00 |
| 576 | Johnny Temple | 4.00 |

Prices for the 1963 set are for cards in *Mint* condition. *Excellent* copies sell for 50% of prices shown; *Very Good*—30%.

# 1964 Topps. . . .Complete Set of 587 Cards—Value $700.00 (Exc.); $1850.00 (Mint)

Phil Niekro's rookie card is in this set. The high numbers are 523 to 587. For the first time a card was issued for a deceased player—Ken Hubbs.

    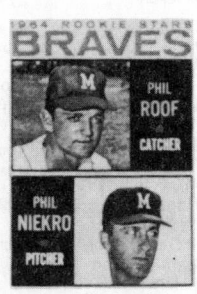

| NO. PLAYER | MINT |
|---|---|
| 1 NL ERA Ldrs.: (Exc. $1.50)..7.00 | |
| Sandy Koufax, Dick | |
| Ellsworth, Bob Friend | |
| 2 AL ERA Leaders: .......1.00 | |
| Gary Peters, Juan Pizarro, | |
| Camilo Pascual | |
| 3 NL Pitching Leaders: ....2.50 | |
| S. Koufax, Juan Marichal, | |
| W. Spahn, Jim Maloney | |
| 4 AL Pitching Leaders: ....1.50 | |
| Whitey Ford, Camilo | |
| Pascual, Jim Bouton | |
| 5 NL Strikeout Leaders: ...2.50 | |
| Sandy Koufax, Jim | |
| Maloney, Don Drysdale | |
| 6 AL Strikeout Leaders:....1.50 | |
| Camilo Pascual, Jim | |
| Bunning, Dick Stigman | |
| 7 NL Batting Leaders: .....1.50 | |
| T. Davis, Bob Clemente, | |
| D. Groat, Hank Aaron | |
| 8 AL Batting Leaders: .....1.50 | |
| Carl Yastrzemski, Al Kaline, | |
| Rich Rollins | |
| 9 NL Home Run Leaders: ..6.00 | |
| Hank Aaron, W. McCovey, | |
| W. Mays, Orlando Cepeda | |
| 10 AL Home Run Leaders: ..1.50 | |
| Harmon Killebrew, Dick | |
| Stuart, Bob Allison | |
| 11 NL RBI Leaders:........1.50 | |
| Hank Aaron, Ken Boyer, | |
| Bill White | |
| 12 AL RBI Leaders:........1.50 | |
| Dick Stuart, Al Kaline, | |
| Harmon Killebrew | |
| 13 Hoyt Wilhelm ..........5.00 | |
| 14 Dodgers Rookies: ........40 | |
| Dick Nen, Nick Willhite | |
| 15 Zoilo Versalles ...........40 | |
| 16 John Boozer .............40 | |
| 17 Willie Kirkland ...........40 | |
| 18 Bill O'Dell..............40 | |
| 19 Don Wert ...............40 | |
| 20 Bob Friend...............40 | |
| 21 Yogi Berra (Mgr.).......18.00 | |
| 22 Jerry Adair.............40 | |
| 23 Chris Zachary...........40 | |
| 24 Carl Sawatski ............40 | |
| 25 Bill Monbouquett.........40 | |
| 26 Gino Cimoli .............40 | |
| 27 New York Mets ..........2.00 | |
| 28 Claude Osteen ...........40 | |
| 29 Lou Brock .............22.00 | |
| 30 Ron Perranoski ...........40 | |
| 31 Dave Nicholson ...........40 | |
| 32 Dean Chance ............1.00 | |
| 33 Reds Rookies:............40 | |
| Sammy Ellis, Mel Queen | |
| 34 Jim Perry ...............40 | |
| 35 Ed Mathews .............8.00 | |
| 36 Hal Reniff..............40 | |
| 37 Smoky Burgess ...........40 | |
| 38 Jim Wynn (R) ...........1.50 | |
| 39 Hank Aguirre............40 | |
| 40 Dick Groat..............75 | |

| NO. PLAYER | MINT |
|---|---|
| 41 Friendly Foes:...........3.00 | |
| W. McCovey, Leon Wagner | |
| 42 Moe Drabowski ..........40 | |
| 43 Roy Sievers .............50 | |
| 44 Duke Carmel .............40 | |
| 45 Milt Pappas .............40 | |
| 46 Ed Brinkman .............40 | |
| 47 Giants Rookies:..........1.00 | |
| Jesus Alou, Ron Herbel | |
| 48 Bob Perry ...............40 | |
| 49 Bill Henry ...............40 | |
| 50 M. Mantle .............200.00 | |
| 51 Pete Richert ............40 | |
| 52 Chuck Hinton ...........40 | |
| 53 Denis Menke ............40 | |
| 54 Sam Mele ...............40 | |
| 55 Ernie Banks ...........12.00 | |
| 56 Hal Brown ..............40 | |
| 57 Tim Harkness ...........40 | |
| 58 Don Demeter ............40 | |
| 59 Ernie Broglio ............40 | |
| 60 Frank Malzone ...........40 | |
| 61 Angel Backstops:.........40 | |
| Bob Rodgers, Ed Sadowski | |
| 62 Ted Savage .............40 | |
| 63 Johnny Orsino ...........40 | |
| 64 Ted Abernathy ...........40 | |
| 65 Felipe Alou .............40 | |
| 66 Eddie Fisher ............40 | |
| 67 Detroit Tigers ...........1.50 | |
| 68 Willie Davis .............60 | |
| 69 Clete Boyer .............40 | |
| 70 Joe Torre ..............1.50 | |
| 71 Jack Spring .............40 | |
| 72 Chico Cardenas ..........40 | |
| 73 Jimmie Hall .............40 | |
| 74 Pirates Rookies: .........40 | |
| Bob Priddy, Tom Butters | |
| 75 Wayne Causey ...........40 | |
| 76 Checklist No. 1 ..........2.00 | |
| 77 Jerry Walker .............40 | |
| 78 Merritt Ranew ...........40 | |
| 79 Bob Heffner .............40 | |
| 80 Vada Pinson .............1.50 | |
| 81 All-Star Vets:............3.00 | |
| Nellie Fox, H. Killebrew | |
| 82 Jim Davenport ...........40 | |
| 83 Gus Triandos ............40 | |
| 84 Carl Willey ..............40 | |
| 85 Pete Ward ..............40 | |
| 86 Al Doning ...............40 | |
| 87 St. Louis Cardinals ......1.00 | |
| 88 John Roseboro ...........40 | |
| 89 Boog Powell ............1.50 | |
| 90 Earl Battey ..............40 | |
| 91 Bob Bailey ..............40 | |
| 92 Steve Ridzik .............40 | |
| 93 Gary Geiger .............40 | |
| 94 Braves Rookies: ..........40 | |
| Jim Britton, Larry Maxie | |
| 95 George Altman ...........40 | |
| 96 Bob Buhl ...............40 | |
| 97 Jim Fregosi .............40 | |
| 98 Bill Bruton ..............40 | |
| 99 Al Stanek ...............40 | |
| 100 Elston Howard ..........2.00 | |

| NO. PLAYER | MINT |
|---|---|
| 101 Walt Alston (Mgr.) .......2.00 | |
| 102 Checklist No. 2 ..........2.00 | |
| 103 Curt Flood .............1.00 | |
| 104 Art Mahaffey ............40 | |
| 105 Woody Held .............40 | |
| 106 Joe Nuxhall .............40 | |
| 107 White Sox Rookies:.......40 | |
| B. Howard, F. Kreutzer | |
| 108 John Wyatt ..............40 | |
| 109 Rusty Staub.............4.00 | |
| 110 Albie Pearson ...........40 | |
| 111 Don Elston ..............40 | |
| 112 Bob Tillman .............40 | |
| 113 Grover Powell ...........40 | |
| 114 Don Lock ...............40 | |
| 115 Frank Bolling ............40 | |
| 116 Twins Rookies: ..........5.00 | |
| Jay Ward, Tony Oliva | |
| 117 Earl Francis ..............40 | |
| 118 John Blanchard ..........40 | |
| 119 Gary Kolb ...............40 | |
| 120 Don Drysdale ...........7.00 | |
| 121 Pete Runnels ............40 | |
| 122 Don McMahon ...........40 | |
| 123 Jose Pagan .............40 | |
| 124 Orlando Pena ............40 | |
| 125 Pete Rose ............140.00 | |
| 126 Russ Snyder .............40 | |
| 127 Angels Rookies:...........40 | |
| Dick Simpson, | |
| Aubrey Gatewood | |
| 128 Mickey Lolich (R) .......5.00 | |
| 129 Amado Samuel..........40 | |
| 130 Gary Peters .............40 | |
| 131 Steve Boros .............40 | |
| 132 Milwaukee Braves .......1.00 | |
| 133 Jim Grant ...............40 | |
| 134 Don Zimmer .............75 | |
| 135 Johnny Callison ..........40 | |
| 136 World Series Game 1 ....5.00 | |
| Koufax Strikes Out 15 | |
| 137 World Series Game 2 ....2.00 | |
| Davis Sparks Rally | |
| 138 World Series Game 3 ....2.00 | |
| LA Takes 3 Straight | |
| 139 World Series Game 4 ....2.00 | |
| Sealing Yanks' Doom | |
| 140 World Series ............2.00 | |
| Dodgers Celebrate | |
| 141 Danny Murtaugh (Mgr......40 | |
| 142 John Bateman ............40 | |
| 143 Bubba Phillips ...........40 | |
| 144 Al Worthington ...........40 | |
| 145 Norm Siebern ............40 | |
| 146 Indians Rookies: .......20.00 | |
| Tommy John, Bob Chance | |
| 147 Ray Sadecki .............40 | |
| 148 J.C. Martin ..............40 | |
| 149 Paul Foytack .............40 | |
| 150 Willie Mays .............35.00 | |
| 151 K.C. Athletics ...........1.00 | |
| 152 Denver LeMaster .........40 | |
| 153 Dick Williams ............40 | |
| 154 Dick Tracewski ...........40 | |
| 155 Duke Snider ............12.00 | |
| 156 Bill Dailey ...............40 | |

| NO. PLAYER | MINT |
|---|---|
| 157 Gene Mauch .............40 | |
| 158 Ken Johnson ............40 | |
| 159 Charlie Dees ............40 | |
| 160 Ken Boyer ..............4.00 | |
| 161 Dave McNally ...........40 | |
| 162 Hitting Area: .............40 | |
| Dick Sisler, Vada Pinson | |
| 163 Donn Clendenon .........40 | |
| 164 Bud Daley ..............40 | |
| 165 Jerry Lumpe ............40 | |
| 166 Marty Keough ...........40 | |
| 167 Senators Rookies: .......75.00 | |
| Mike Brumley, Lou Piniella | |
| 168 Al Weis .................40 | |
| 169 Del Crandall ............40 | |
| 170 Dick Radatz .............40 | |
| 171 Ty Cline ................40 | |
| 172 Cleveland Indians ........1.00 | |
| 173 Ryne Duren .............40 | |
| 174 Doc Edwards ............40 | |
| 175 Billy Williams ...........6.00 | |
| 176 Tracy Stallard ...........40 | |
| 177 Harmon Killebrew .......8.00 | |
| 178 Hank Bauer (Mgr.) ........40 | |
| 179 Carl Warwick ............40 | |
| 180 Tommy Davis .............60 | |
| 181 Dave Wickersham .........40 | |
| 182 Sox Sockers:...........7.00 | |
| C. Schilling, C. Yastrzemski | |
| 183 Ron Taylor ..............40 | |
| 184 Al Luplow ..............40 | |
| 185 Jim O'Toole .............40 | |
| 186 Roman Mejias ...........40 | |
| 187 Ed Roebuck .............40 | |
| 188 Checklist No. 3 .........2.00 | |
| 189 Bob Hendley ............40 | |
| 190 Bobby Richardson .......3.00 | |
| 191 Clay Dalrymple ..........40 | |
| 192 Cubs Rookies: ...........40 | |
| J. Boccabella, B. Cowan | |
| 193 Jerry Lynch ..............40 | |
| 194 John Goryl ..............40 | |
| 195 Floyd Robinson ..........40 | |
| 196 Jim Gentile ..............40 | |
| 197 Frank Lary ..............40 | |
| 198 Len Gabrielson ..........40 | |
| 199 Joe Azcue ...............40 | |
| 200 Sandy Koufax ...........35.00 | |
| 201 Orioles Rookies: .........40 | |
| Wally Bunker, Sam Bowens | |
| 202 Galen Cisco .............40 | |
| 203 John Kennedy ...........40 | |
| 204 Matty Alou ..............40 | |
| 205 Nellie Fox ..............3.00 | |
| 206 Steve Hamilton ..........40 | |
| 207 Fred Hutchinson (Mgr.) ...40 | |
| 208 Wes Covington ..........40 | |
| 209 Bob Allen ...............40 | |
| 210 Carl Yastrzemski .......45.00 | |
| 211 Jim Coker ..............40 | |
| 212 Pete Lovrich ............40 | |
| 213 L.A. Angels .............1.00 | |
| 214 Ken McMullen ...........40 | |
| 215 Ray Herbert .............40 | |
| 216 Mike De La Hoz .........40 | |
| 217 Jim King ................40 | |

| NO. | PLAYER | MINT |
|---|---|---|
| 218 | Hank Fischer | .40 |
| 219 | Young Aces: | 1.00 |
| | Al Downing, Jim Bouton | |
| 220 | Dick Ellsworth | .40 |
| 221 | Bob Saverine | .40 |
| 222 | Bill Pierce | .60 |
| 223 | George Banks | .40 |
| 224 | Tommie Sisk | .40 |
| 225 | Roger Maris | 25.00 |
| 226 | Colts Rookies: | .40 |
| | Gerald Grote, Larry Yellen | |
| 227 | Barry Latman | .40 |
| 228 | Felix Mantilla | .40 |
| 229 | Charley Lau | .40 |
| 230 | Brooks Robinson | 16.00 |
| 231 | Dick Calmus | .40 |
| 232 | Al Lopez (Mgr.) | 2.00 |
| 233 | Hal Smith | .40 |
| 234 | Gary Bell | .40 |
| 235 | Ron Hunt | .40 |
| 236 | Bill Faul | .40 |
| 237 | Chicago Cubs | 2.00 |
| 238 | Roy McMillan | .40 |
| 239 | Herm Starrette | .40 |
| 240 | Bill White | .40 |
| 241 | Jim Owens | .40 |
| 242 | Harvey Kuenn | .75 |
| 243 | Phillies Rookies (R) | 8.00 |
| | Richie Allen, J. Herrnstein | |
| 244 | Tony LaRussa (R) | 3.00 |
| 245 | Dick Stigman | .40 |
| 246 | Manny Mota | 1.00 |
| 247 | Dave DeBusschere | 1.50 |
| 248 | Johnny Pesky | .40 |
| 249 | Doug Camlli | .40 |
| 250 | Al Kaline | 10.00 |
| 251 | Choo Choo Coleman | .40 |
| 252 | Ken Aspromonte | .40 |
| 253 | Wally Post | .40 |
| 254 | Don Hoak | .40 |
| 255 | Lee Thomas | .40 |
| 256 | Johnny Weekly | .40 |
| 257 | San F. Giants | 1.50 |
| 258 | Garry Roggenburk | .40 |
| 259 | Harry Bright | .40 |
| 260 | Frank Robinson | 10.00 |
| 261 | Jim Hannan | .40 |
| 262 | Cardinals Rookies: | 2.00 |
| | Harry Fanok, Mike Shannon | |
| 263 | Chuck Estrada | .40 |
| 264 | Jim Landis | .40 |
| 265 | Jim Bunning | 3.00 |
| 266 | Gene Freese | .40 |
| 267 | Wilbur Wood | 1.00 |
| 268 | Bill's Got It: | .40 |
| | Bill Virdon, D. Murtaugh | |
| 269 | Ellis Burton | .40 |
| 270 | Rich Rollins | .40 |
| 271 | Bob Sadowski | .40 |
| 272 | Jake Wood | .40 |
| 273 | Mel Nelson | .40 |
| 274 | Checklist No. 4 | 3.00 |
| 275 | John Tsitouris | .40 |
| 276 | Jose Tartabull | .40 |
| 277 | Ken Retzer | .40 |
| 278 | Bobby Shantz | .40 |
| 279 | Joe Koppe | .40 |
| 280 | Juan Marichal | 8.00 |
| 281 | Yankees Rookies: | .65 |
| | Jake Gibbs, Tom Metcalf | |
| 282 | Bob Bruce | .40 |
| 283 | Tommy McCraw | .40 |
| 284 | Dick Schofield | .40 |
| 285 | Robin Roberts | 6.00 |
| 286 | Don Landrum | .40 |
| 287 | Red Sox Rookies: | 4.00 |
| | T. Conigliaro, B. Spanswick | |
| 288 | Al Moran | .40 |
| 289 | Frank Funk | .40 |
| 290 | Bob Allison | .40 |
| 291 | Phil Ortega | .40 |

| NO. | PLAYER | MINT |
|---|---|---|
| 292 | Mike Roarke | .40 |
| 293 | Philadelphia Phillies | 1.00 |
| 294 | Ken Hunt | .40 |
| 295 | Roger Craig | .40 |
| 296 | Ed Kirkpatrick | .40 |
| 297 | Ken MacKenzie | .40 |
| 298 | Harry Craft (Mgr.) | .40 |
| 299 | Bill Stafford | .40 |
| 300 | Hank Aaron | 40.00 |
| 301 | Larry Brown | .40 |
| 302 | Dan Pfister | .40 |
| 303 | Jim Campbell | .40 |
| 304 | Bob Johnson | .40 |
| 305 | Jack Lamabe | .40 |
| 306 | Giant Gunners: | 10.00 |
| | Willie Mays, O. Cepeda | |
| 307 | Joe Gibbon | .40 |
| 308 | Gene Stephens | .40 |
| 309 | Paul Toth | .40 |
| 310 | Jim Gilliam | 2.00 |
| 311 | Tom Brown | .40 |
| 312 | Tigers Rookies: | .40 |
| | Fred Gladding, Fritz Fisher | |
| 313 | Chuck Hiller | .40 |
| 314 | Jerry Buchek | .40 |
| 315 | Bo Belinsky | .40 |
| 316 | Gene Oliver | .40 |
| 317 | Al Smith | .40 |
| 318 | Minnesota Twins | 1.50 |
| 319 | Paul Brown | .40 |
| 320 | Rocky Colavito | 2.00 |
| 321 | Bob Lillis | .40 |
| 322 | George Brunet | .40 |
| 323 | John Buzhardt | .40 |
| 324 | Casey Stengel (Mgr.) | 8.00 |
| 325 | Hector Lopez | .40 |
| 326 | Ron Brand | .40 |
| 327 | Don Blasingame | .40 |
| 328 | Bob Shaw | .40 |
| 329 | Russ Nixon | .40 |
| 330 | Tommy Harper | .40 |
| 331 | AL Bombers: | 50.00 |
| | Mickey Mantle, R. Maris, | |
| | Norm Cash, Al Kaline | |
| 332 | Ray Washburn | .40 |
| 333 | Billy Moran | .40 |
| 334 | Lew Krausse | .40 |
| 335 | Don Mossi | .40 |
| 336 | Andre Rodgers | .40 |
| 337 | Dodgers Rookies: | 1.00 |
| | Al Ferrara, Jeff Torborg | |
| 338 | Jack Kralick | .40 |
| 339 | Walt Bond | .40 |
| 340 | Joe Cunningham | .40 |
| 341 | Jim Roland | .40 |
| 342 | Willie Stargell | 20.00 |
| 343 | Washington Senators | 1.25 |
| 344 | Phil Linz | .40 |
| 345 | Frank Thomas | .40 |
| 346 | Joe Jay | .40 |
| 347 | Bobby Wine | .40 |
| 348 | Ed Lopat | 1.00 |
| 349 | Art Fowler | .40 |
| 350 | Willie McCovey | 10.00 |
| 351 | Dan Schneider | .40 |
| 352 | Eddie Bressoud | .40 |
| 353 | Wally Moon | .40 |
| 354 | Dave Giusti | .40 |
| 355 | Vic Power | .40 |
| 356 | Reds Rookies: | .40 |
| | Bill McCool, Chico Ruiz | |
| 357 | Charley James | .40 |
| 358 | Ron Kline | .40 |
| 359 | Jim Schaffer | .40 |
| 360 | Joe Pepitone | 1.25 |
| 361 | Jay Hook | .40 |
| 362 | Checklist No. 5 | 3.00 |
| 363 | Dick McAuliffe | .40 |
| 364 | Joe Gaines | .40 |
| 365 | Cal McLish | .40 |
| 366 | Nelson Mathews | .40 |

| NO. | PLAYER | MINT |
|---|---|---|
| 367 | Fred Whitfield | .40 |
| 368 | White Sox Rookies: | .40 |
| | Fritz Ackley, Don Buford | |
| 369 | Jerry Zimmerman | .40 |
| 370 | Hal Woodeschick | .40 |
| 371 | Frank Howard | 2.00 |
| 372 | Howie Koplitz | .60 |
| 373 | Pittsburgh Pirates | 1.50 |
| 374 | Bobby Bolin | .60 |
| 375 | Ron Santo | 2.00 |
| 376 | Dave Morehead | .75 |
| 377 | Bob Skinner | .75 |
| 378 | Braves Rookies: | .75 |
| | W. Woodward, Jack Smith | |
| 379 | Tony Gonzalez | .75 |
| 380 | Whitey Ford | 12.00 |
| 381 | Bob Taylor | .75 |
| 382 | Wes Stock | .75 |
| 383 | Bill Rigney (Mgr.) | .75 |
| 384 | Ron Hansen | .75 |
| 385 | Curt Simmons | .90 |
| 386 | Lenny Green | .75 |
| 387 | Terry Fox | .75 |
| 388 | A's Rookies: | .75 |
| | G. Williams, J. O'Donoghue | |
| 389 | Jim Umbricht | .75 |
| 390 | Orlando Cepeda | 5.00 |
| 391 | Sam McDowell | 1.00 |
| 392 | Jim Pagliaroni | .75 |
| 393 | Casey Teaches: | 4.00 |
| | C. Stengel, Ed Kranepool | |
| 394 | Bob Miller | .75 |
| 395 | Tom Tresh | 1.25 |
| 396 | Dennis Bennett | .75 |
| 397 | Chuck Cottier | .75 |
| 398 | Mets Rookies: | .75 |
| | Bill Haas, Dick Smith | |
| 399 | Jackie Brandt | .75 |
| 400 | Warren Spahn | 10.00 |
| 401 | Charlie Maxwell | .75 |
| 402 | Tom Sturdivant | .75 |
| 403 | Cincinnati Reds | 2.50 |
| 404 | Tony Martinez | .75 |
| 405 | Ken McBride | .75 |
| 406 | Al Spangler | .75 |
| 407 | Bill Freehan | 2.50 |
| 408 | Cubs Rookies: | .75 |
| | Jim Stewart, Fred Burdette | |
| 409 | Bill Fischer | .75 |
| 410 | Dick Stuart | 1.00 |
| 411 | Lee Walls | .75 |
| 412 | Ray Culp | .75 |
| 413 | Johnny Keane (Mgr.) | .75 |
| 414 | Jack Sanford | .75 |
| 415 | Tony Kubek | 4.00 |
| 416 | Lee Maye | .75 |
| 417 | Don Cardwell | .75 |
| 418 | Orioles Rookies: | 1.50 |
| | Les Narum, D. Knowles | |
| 419 | Ken Harrelson (R) | 5.00 |
| 420 | Jim Maloney | .75 |
| 421 | Camilo Carreon | .75 |
| 422 | Jack Fisher | .75 |
| 423 | Tops in N.L.: | 25.00 |
| | Hank Aaron, Willie Mays | |
| 424 | Dick Bertell | .75 |
| 425 | Norm Cash | 2.00 |
| 426 | Bob Rodgers | .75 |
| 427 | Don Rudolph | .75 |
| 428 | Red Sox Rookies: | .75 |
| | Archie Skeen, Pete Smith | |
| 429 | Tim McCarver | 2.00 |
| 430 | Juan Pizarro | .75 |
| 431 | George Alusik | .75 |
| 432 | Ruben Amaro | .75 |
| 433 | New York Yankees | 8.00 |
| 434 | Don Nottebart | .75 |
| 435 | Vic Davalillo | .75 |
| 436 | Charlie Neal | .75 |
| 437 | Ed Bailey | .75 |
| 438 | Checklist No. 6 | 3.00 |

| NO. | PLAYER | MINT |
|---|---|---|
| 439 | Harvey Haddix | 1.25 |
| 440 | Bob Clemente | 35.00 |
| 441 | Bob Duliba | .75 |
| 442 | Pumpsie Green | .75 |
| 443 | Chuck Dressen (Mgr.) | .75 |
| 444 | Larry Jackson | .75 |
| 445 | Bill Skowron | 1.25 |
| 446 | Julian Javier | .75 |
| 447 | Ted Bowsfield | .75 |
| 448 | Cookie Rojas | .75 |
| 449 | Deron Johnson | .75 |
| 450 | Steve Barber | .75 |
| 451 | Joe Amalfitano | .75 |
| 452 | Giants Rookies: | 1.25 |
| | Gil Garrido, Jim Hart | |
| 453 | Frank Baumann | .75 |
| 454 | Tommie Aaron | .75 |
| 455 | Bernie Allen | .75 |
| 456 | Dodgers Rookies: | 2.00 |
| | John Werhas, Wes Parker | |
| 457 | Jesse Gonder | .75 |
| 458 | Ralph Terry | .75 |
| 459 | Red Sox Rookies: | .75 |
| | Pete Charton, D. Jones | |
| 460 | Bob Gibson | 13.00 |
| 461 | George Thomas | .75 |
| 462 | Birdie Tebbetts | .75 |
| 463 | Don Leppert | .75 |
| 464 | Dallas Green | 1.00 |
| 465 | Mike Hershberger | .75 |
| 466 | A's Rookies: | .75 |
| | D. Green, A. Monteagudo | |
| 467 | Bob Aspromonte | .75 |
| 468 | Gaylord Perry | 15.00 |
| 469 | Cubs Rookies: | 1.25 |
| | S. Slaughter, Fred Norman | |
| 470 | Jim Bouton | 2.00 |
| 471 | Gates Brown (R) | 1.50 |
| 472 | Vern Law | 1.00 |
| 473 | Baltimore Orioles | 1.50 |
| 474 | Larry Sherry | .75 |
| 475 | Ed Charles | .75 |
| 476 | Braves Rookies: | 3.00 |
| | Rico Carty, Dick Kelley | |
| 477 | Mike Joyce | .75 |
| 478 | Dick Howser | 1.25 |
| 479 | Cardinals Rookies: | .75 |
| | D. Bakenhaster, J. Lewis | |
| 480 | Bob Purkey | .75 |
| 481 | Chuck Schilling | .75 |
| 482 | Phillies Rookies: | .75 |
| | John Briggs, Danny Cater | |
| 483 | Fred Valentine | .75 |
| 484 | Bill Pleis | .75 |
| 485 | Tom Haller | .75 |
| 486 | Bob Kennedy | .75 |
| 487 | Mike McCormick | .75 |
| 488 | Yankees Rookies: | .75 |
| | Pete Mikkelsen, Bob Meyer | |
| 489 | Julio Navarro | .75 |
| 490 | Ron Fairly | .75 |
| 491 | Ed Rakow | .75 |
| 492 | Colts Rookies: | .75 |
| | Jim Beauchamp, M. White | |
| 493 | Don Lee | .75 |
| 494 | Al Jackson | .75 |
| 495 | Bill Virdon | 1.50 |
| 496 | Chicago White Sox | 1.50 |
| 497 | Jeoff Long | .75 |
| 498 | Dave Stenhouse | .75 |
| 499 | Indians Rookies: | .75 |
| | Chico Salmon, G. Seyfried | |
| 500 | Camilo Pascual | .75 |
| 501 | Bob Veale | .75 |
| 502 | Angels Rookies: | .75 |
| | Bobby Knoop, Bob Lee | |
| 503 | Earl Wilson | .75 |
| 504 | Claude Raymond | .75 |
| 505 | Stan Williams | .75 |
| 506 | Bobby Bragan (Mgr.) | .75 |
| 507 | John Edwards | .75 |

**Prices for the 1964 set are for cards in *Mint* condition. *Excellent* copies sell for 50% of prices shown; *Very Good*—30%.**

| NO. PLAYER | MINT |
|---|---|
| 508 Diego Segui | .75 |
| 509 Pirates Rookies: | 1.50 |
| Gene Alley, O. McFarlane | |
| 510 Lindy McDaniel | .75 |
| 511 Lou Jackson | .75 |
| 512 Tigers Rookies: | 4.00 |
| Joe Sparma, Willie Horton | |
| 513 Don Larsen | 1.00 |
| 514 Jim Hickman | .75 |
| 515 Johnny Romano | .75 |
| 516 Twins Rookies: | .75 |
| Dwight Siebler, Jerry Arrigo | |
| 517 Checklist No. 7 | 4.00 |
| 518 Carl Bouldin | .75 |
| 519 Charlie Smith | .75 |
| 520 Jack Baldschun | .75 |
| 521 Tom Satriano | .75 |
| 522 Bobby Tiefenauer | .75 |
| 523 Lou Burdette | 4.00 |
| 524 Reds Rookies: | 2.50 |
| Jim Dickson, Bobby Klaus | |
| 525 Al McBean | 2.50 |
| 526 Lou Clinton | 2.50 |
| 527 Larry Bearnarth | 2.50 |
| 528 A's Rookies: | 2.50 |
| D. Duncan, Tom Reynolds | |
| 529 Al Dark | 2.50 |
| 530 Leon Wagner | 2.50 |
| 531 L.A. Dodgers | 6.00 |
| 532 Twins Rookies: | 2.50 |
| Bud Bloomfield (wrong photo), Joe Nossek | |
| 533 John Klippstein | 2.50 |
| 534 Gus Bell | 2.50 |
| 535 Phil Regan | 2.50 |
| 536 Mets Rookies: | 2.50 |
| Larry Elliot, J. Stephenson | |
| 537 Dan Osinski | 2.50 |
| 538 Minnie Minoso | 4.00 |
| 539 Roy Face | 3.00 |
| 540 Luis Aparicio | 12.00 |
| 541 Braves Rookies: | 65.00 |
| Phil Niekro, Phil Roof | |
| 542 Don Mincher | 2.50 |
| 543 Bob Uecker | 35.00 |
| 544 Colts Rookies: | 2.50 |
| Steve Hertz, Joe Hoerner | |
| 545 Max Alvis | 2.50 |
| 546 Joe Christopher | 2.50 |
| 547 Gil Hodges (Mgr.) | 8.00 |
| 548 NL Rookies: | 2.50 |
| W. Schurr, P. Speckenbach | |
| 549 Joe Moeller | 2.50 |
| 550 Ken Hubbs | 7.00 |
| (In Memoriam) | |
| 551 Billy Hoeft | 2.50 |
| 552 Indians Rookies: | 2.50 |
| Tom Kelley, Sonny Siebert | |
| 553 Jim Brewer | 2.50 |
| 554 Hank Foiles | 2.50 |
| 555 Lee Stange | 2.50 |
| 556 Mets Rookies: | 2.50 |
| Steve Dillon, Ron Locke | |
| 557 Leo Burke | 2.50 |
| 558 Don Schwall | 2.50 |
| 559 Dick Phillips | 2.50 |
| 560 Dick Farrell | 2.50 |
| 561 Phillies Rookies: | 4.00 |
| Dave Bennett, Rick Wise | |
| 562 Pedro Ramos | 2.50 |
| 563 Dal Maxvill | 2.50 |
| 564 AL Rookies: | 2.50 |
| Joe McCabe, J. McNertney | |
| 565 Stu Miller | 2.50 |
| 566 Ed Kranepool | 2.50 |
| 567 Jim Kaat | 6.00 |
| 568 NL Rookies: | 2.50 |
| Phil Gagliano, Cap Peterson | |
| 569 Fred Newman | 2.50 |
| 570 Bill Mazeroski | 4.00 |
| 571 Gene Conley | 2.50 |
| 572 AL Rookies: | 2.50 |
| Dave Gray, Dick Egan | |
| 573 Jim Duffalo | 2.50 |
| 574 Manny Jimenez | 2.50 |
| 575 Tony Cloninger | 2.50 |
| 576 Mets Rookies: | 2.50 |
| J. Hinsley, Bill Wakefield | |
| 577 Gordy Coleman | 2.50 |
| 578 Glen Hobbie | 2.50 |
| 579 Boston Red Sox | 6.00 |
| 580 Johnny Podres | 4.00 |
| 581 Yankees Rookies: | 2.50 |
| P. Gonzalez, Archie Moore | |
| 582 Rod Kanehl | 2.50 |
| 583 Tito Francona | 2.50 |
| 584 Joel Horlen | 2.50 |
| 585 Tony Taylor | 2.50 |
| 586 Jim Piersall | 4.00 |
| 587 Bennie Daniels (Exc. $1.00) | 4.00 |

# 1965 Topps. . . .Complete Set of 598 Cards—Value $850.00 (Exc.); $2000.00 (Mint)

This set includes the rookie cards of Steve Carlton, Joe Morgan, Tony Perez and "Catfish" Hunter. Cards 523 to 598 are the high numbers. Semi-high numbers are 447 to 522.

  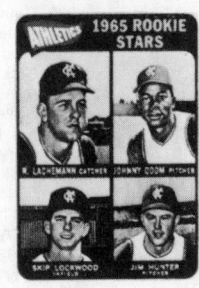  

| NO. PLAYER | MINT |
|---|---|
| 1 AL Bat Ldrs.: (Exc. $.75) | 6.00 |
| Elston Howard, Tony Oliva, Brooks Robinson | |
| 2 NL Batting Leaders: | 4.00 |
| Hank Aaron, Bob Clemente, Rico Carty | |
| 3 AL Home Run Leaders: | 7.50 |
| Boog Powell, Harmon Killebrew, Mickey Mantle | |
| 4 NL Home Run Leaders: | 4.00 |
| Willie Mays, Billy Williams, Johnny Callison, Jim Hart, Orlando Cepeda | |
| 5 AL RBI Leaders: | 6.00 |
| Brooks Robinson, Dick Stuart, Harmon Killebrew, Mickey Mantle | |
| 6 NL RBI Leaders: | 2.50 |
| Ken Boyer, Willie Mays, Ron Santo | |
| 7 AL ERA Leaders: | 1.50 |
| Dean Chance, Joel Horlen | |
| 8 NL ERA Leaders: | 4.00 |
| S. Koufax, Don Drysdale | |
| 9 AL Pitching Leaders: | 1.50 |
| D. Chance, G. Peters, J. Pizarro, W. Bunker, D. Wickersham | |
| 10 NL Pitching Leaders: | 2.00 |
| L. Jackson, Juan Marichal, Ray Sadecki | |
| 11 AL Strikeout Leaders: | 1.50 |
| A. Downing, D. Chance, C. Pascual | |
| 12 NL Strikeout Leaders: | 2.00 |
| Bob Gibson, B. Veale, Don Drysdale | |
| 13 Pedro Ramos | .50 |
| 14 Len Gabrielson | .50 |
| 15 Robin Roberts | 6.00 |
| 16 Houston Rookies: | 40.00 |
| Joe Morgan, Sonny Jackson | |
| 17 John Romano | .50 |
| 18 Bill McCool | .50 |
| 19 Gates Brown | .50 |
| 20 Jim Bunning | 3.00 |
| 21 Don Blasingame | .50 |
| 22 Charlie Smith | .50 |
| 23 Bob Tiefenauer | .50 |
| 24 Twins—6th Place | 2.00 |
| 25 Al McBean | .50 |
| 26 Bob Knoop | .50 |
| 27 Dick Bertell | .50 |
| 28 Barney Schultz | .50 |
| 29 Felix Mantilla | .50 |
| 30 Jim Bouton | 1.50 |
| 31 Mike White | .50 |
| 32 Herman Franks | .50 |
| 33 Jackie Brandt | .50 |
| 34 Cal Koonce | .50 |
| 35 Ed Charles | .50 |
| 36 Bobby Wine | .50 |
| 37 Fred Gladding | .50 |
| 38 Jim King | .50 |
| 39 Gerry Arrigo | .50 |
| 40 Frank Howard | 1.50 |
| 41 White Sox Rookies: | .50 |
| Bruce Howard, Marv Staehle | |
| 42 Earl Wilson | .50 |
| 43 Mike Shannon | .60 |
| 44 Wade Blasingame | .50 |
| 45 Roy McMillan | .50 |
| 46 Bob Lee | .50 |
| 47 Tommy Harper | .50 |
| 48 Claude Raymond | .50 |
| 49 Orioles Rookies: | 1.00 |
| John Miller, Curt Blefary | |
| 50 Juan Marical | 8.00 |
| 51 Billy Bryan | .50 |
| 52 Ed Roebuck | .50 |
| 53 Dick McAuliffe | .50 |
| 54 Joe Gibbon | .50 |
| 55 Tony Conigliaro | 2.00 |
| 56 Ron Kline | .50 |
| 57 Cardinals—1st Place | 1.25 |
| 58 Fred Talbot | .50 |
| 59 Nate Oiver | .50 |
| 60 Jim O'Toole | .50 |
| 61 Chris Cannizzaro | .50 |
| 62 Jim Kaat | 4.00 |
| 63 Ty Cline | .50 |
| 64 Lou Burdette | 1.25 |
| 65 Tony Kubek | 3.00 |
| 66 Bill Rigney | .50 |
| 67 Harvey Haddix | .50 |
| 68 Del Crandall | .50 |
| 69 Bill Virdon | 1.00 |
| 70 Bill Skowron | 1.25 |
| 71 John O'Donoghue | .50 |
| 72 Tony Gonzalez | .50 |
| 73 Dennis Ribant | .50 |
| 74 Red Sox Rookies: | 3.00 |
| R. Petrocelli, J. Stephenson | |
| 75 Deron Johnson | .50 |
| 76 Sam McDowell | .75 |
| 77 Doug Camilli | .50 |
| 78 Dal Maxvill | .50 |
| 79 Checklist No. 1 | 2.50 |
| 80 Turk Farrell | .50 |
| 81 Don Buford | .50 |
| 82 Braves Rookies: | .50 |
| Santos Alomar, John Braun | |
| 83 George Thomas | .50 |
| 84 Ron Herbel | .50 |
| 85 Willie Smith | .50 |
| 86 Les Narum | .50 |
| 87 Nelson Mathews | .50 |
| 88 Jack Lamabe | .50 |
| 89 Mike Hershberger | .50 |
| 90 Rich Rollins | .50 |
| 91 Cubs—8th Place | 1.25 |
| 92 Dick Howser | 1.00 |
| 93 Jack Fisher | .50 |
| 94 Charlie Lau | .50 |

| NO. PLAYER | MINT | NO. PLAYER | MINT | NO. PLAYER | MINT | NO. PLAYER | MINT |
|---|---|---|---|---|---|---|---|
| 95 Bill Mazeroski | 1.50 | 168 Dick Green | .50 | 248 Gus Triandos | .75 | 329 Hawk Taylor | .75 |
| 96 Sonny Siebert | .50 | 169 Dave Vineyard | .50 | 249 Dave McNally | 1.25 | 330 Whitey Ford | 12.00 |
| 97 Pedro Gonzalez | .50 | 170 Hank Aaron | 40.00 | 250 Willie Mays | 50.00 | 331 Dodgers Rookies: | 1.00 |
| 98 Bob Miller | .50 | 171 Jim Roland | .50 | 251 Billy Herman (Mgr.) | 1.50 | Al Ferrara, John Purdin | |
| 99 Gil Hodges | 5.00 | 172 Jim Piersall | 1.00 | 252 Pete Richert | .75 | 332 Ted Abernathy | .75 |
| 100 Ken Boyer | 2.50 | 173 Tigers—4th Place | 2.00 | 253 Danny Cater | .75 | 333 Tommie Reynolds | .75 |
| 101 Fred Newman | .50 | 174 Joe Jay | .50 | 254 Roland Sheldon | .75 | 334 Vic Roznovsky | .75 |
| 102 Steve Boros | .50 | 175 Bob Aspromonte | .50 | 255 Camilo Pascual | .75 | 335 Mickey Lolich | 2.00 |
| 103 Harvey Kuenn | .75 | 176 Willie McCovey | 10.00 | 256 Tito Francona | .75 | 336 Woody Held | .75 |
| 104 Checklist No. 2 | 2.50 | 177 Pete Mikkelsen | .50 | 257 Jim Wynn | 1.00 | 337 Mike Cuellar | 1.00 |
| 105 Chico Salmon | .50 | 178 Dalton Jones | .50 | 258 Larry Bearnarth | .75 | 338 Phillies—2nd Place | 1.50 |
| 106 Gene Oliver | .50 | 179 Hal Woodeschick | .50 | 259 Tigers Rookies: | 1.50 | 339 Ryne Duren | .75 |
| 107 Phillies Rookies: | 1.50 | 180 Bob Allison | .75 | Jim Northrup, Ray Oyler | | 340 Tony Oliva | 4.00 |
| C. Shockley, Pat Corrales | | 181 Senators Rookies: | .50 | 260 Don Drysdale | 9.00 | 341 Bobby Bolin | .75 |
| 108 Don Mincher | .50 | Don Loun, Joe McCabe | | 261 Duke Carmel | .75 | 342 Bob Rodgers | .75 |
| 109 Walt Bond | .50 | 182 Mike De La Hoz | .50 | 262 Bud Daley | .75 | 343 Mike McCormick | .75 |
| 110 Ron Santo | 1.50 | 183 Dave Nicholson | .50 | 263 Marty Keough | .75 | 344 Wes Parker | .75 |
| 111 Lee Thomas | .50 | 184 John Boozer | .50 | 264 Bob Buhl | .75 | 345 Floyd Robinson | .75 |
| 112 Derrell Griffith | .50 | 185 Max Alvis | .50 | 265 Jim Pagliaroni | .75 | 346 Bob Bragan (Mgr.) | .75 |
| 113 Steve Barber | .50 | 186 Bill Cowan | .50 | 266 Bert Campaneris | 2.50 | 347 Roy Face | 1.00 |
| 114 Jim Hickman | .50 | 187 Casey Stengel (Mgr.) | 7.50 | 267 Senators—9th Place | 1.25 | 348 George Banks | .75 |
| 115 Bob Richardson | 2.50 | 188 Sam Bowens | .50 | 268 Ken McBride | .75 | 349 Larry Miller | .75 |
| 116 Cardinals Rookies: | 1.00 | 189 Checklist No. 3 | 2.50 | 269 Frank Bolling | .75 | 350 Mickey Mantle | 300.00 |
| Dave Dowling, Bob Tolan | | 190 Bill White | .75 | 270 Milt Pappas | .75 | 351 Jim Perry | 1.00 |
| 117 Wes Stock | .50 | 191 Phil Regan | .50 | 271 Don Wert | .75 | 352 Alex Johnson | .75 |
| 118 Hal Lanier (R) | 1.25 | 192 Jim Coker | .50 | 272 Chuck Schilling | .75 | 353 Jerry Lumpe | .75 |
| 119 John Kennedy | .50 | 193 Gaylord Perry | 8.00 | 273 Checklist No. 4 | 2.50 | 354 Cubs Rookies: | .75 |
| 120 Frank Robinson | 9.00 | 194 Angels Rookies: | .50 | 274 Lum Harris (Mgr.) | .75 | Billy Ott, Jack Warner | |
| 121 Gene Alley | .50 | Rick Reichardt, Bill Kelso | | 275 Dick Groat | 1.00 | 355 Vada Pinson | 1.50 |
| 122 Bill Pleis | .50 | 195 Bob Veale | .50 | 276 Hoyt Wilhelm | 6.00 | 356 Bill Spanswick | .75 |
| 123 Frank Thomas | .50 | 196 Ron Fairly | .50 | 277 Johnny Lewis | .75 | 357 Carl Warwick | .75 |
| 124 Tom Satriano | .50 | 197 Diego Segui | .50 | 278 Ken Retzer | .75 | 358 Albie Pearson | .75 |
| 125 Juan Pizarro | .50 | 198 Smoky Burgess | .50 | 279 Dick Tracewski | .75 | 359 Ken Johnson | .75 |
| 126 Dodgers—6th Place | 2.50 | 199 Bob Heffner | .75 | 280 Dick Stuart | .75 | 360 Orlando Cepeda | 4.00 |
| 127 Frank Lary | .50 | 200 Joe Torre | 1.50 | 281 Bill Stafford | .75 | 361 Checklist No. 5 | 2.50 |
| 128 Vic Davalillo | .50 | 201 Twins Rookies: | 1.25 | 282 Giants Rookies: | 1.50 | 362 Don Schwall | .75 |
| 129 Bennie Daniels | .50 | S. Valdespino, Cesar Tovar | | Dick Estelle, M. Murakami | | 363 Bob Johnson | .75 |
| 130 Al Kaline | 12.00 | 202 Leo Burke | .75 | 283 Fred Whitfield | .75 | 364 Galen Cisco | .75 |
| 131 Johnny Keane (Mgr.) | .50 | 203 Dallas Green | .75 | 284 Nick Willhite | .75 | 365 Jim Gentile | .75 |
| 132 World Series Game 1 | 2.00 | 204 Russ Snyder | .75 | 285 Ron Hunt | .75 | 366 Dan Schneider | .75 |
| Cards Take Opener | | 205 Warren Spahn | 10.00 | 286 Athletics Rookies: | .75 | 367 Leon Wagner | .75 |
| 133 World Series Game 2 | 2.00 | 206 Willie Horton | 1.25 | J. Dickson, A. Monteagudo | | 368 White Sox Rookies: | 1.00 |
| Stottlemyre Wins | | 207 Pete Rose | 140.00 | 287 Gary Kolb | .75 | Ken Berry, Joel Gibson | |
| 134 World Series Game 3 | 15.00 | 208 Tommy John | 6.00 | 288 Jack Hamilton | .75 | 369 Phil Linz | .75 |
| Mantle's Clutch Homer | | 209 Pirates—6th Place | 1.50 | 289 Gordy Coleman | .75 | 370 Tommy Davis | 1.25 |
| 135 World Series Game 4 | 2.00 | 210 Jim Fregosi | 1.25 | 290 Wally Bunker | .75 | 371 Frank Kreutzer | .75 |
| Boyer's Grand-Slam | | 211 Steve Ridzik | .75 | 291 Jerry Lynch | .75 | 372 Clay Dalrymple | .75 |
| 136 World Series Game 5 | 2.00 | 212 Ron Brand | .75 | 292 Larry Yellen | .75 | 373 Curt Simmons | .75 |
| 10th Inning Triumph | | 213 Jim Davenport | .75 | 293 Angels—5th Place | 1.50 | 374 Angels Rookies: | 1.00 |
| 137 World Series Game 6 | 2.00 | 214 Bob Purkey | .75 | 294 Tim McCarver | 1.50 | J. Cardenal, D. Simpson | |
| Bouton Wins Again | | 215 Pete Ward | .75 | 295 Dick Radatz | .75 | 375 Dave Wickersham | .75 |
| 138 World Series Game 7 | 3.00 | 216 Al Worthington | .75 | 296 Tony Taylor | .75 | 376 Jim Landis | .75 |
| Gibson Wins Finale | | 217 Walt Alston (Mgr.) | 2.50 | 297 Dave Debusschere | 2.50 | 377 Willie Stargell | 15.00 |
| 139 World Series | 2.00 | 218 Dick Schofield | .75 | 298 Jim Stewart | .75 | 378 Chuck Estrada | .75 |
| The Cards Celebrate | | 219 Bob Meyer | .75 | 299 Jerry Zimmerman | .75 | 379 Giants—4th Place | 1.50 |
| 140 Dean Chance | .50 | 220 Billy Williams | 6.00 | 300 Sandy Koufax | 50.00 | 380 Rocky Colavito | 2.50 |
| 141 Charlie James | .50 | 221 John Tsitouris | .75 | 301 Birdie Tebbetts | .75 | 381 Al Jackson | .75 |
| 142 Bill Monbouquette | .50 | 222 Bob Tillman | .75 | 302 Al Stanek | .75 | 382 J.C. Martin | .75 |
| 143 Pirates Rookies: | .50 | 223 Dan Osinski | .75 | 303 John Orsino | .75 | 383 Felipe Alou | 1.00 |
| John Gelnar, Jerry May | | 224 Bob Chance | .75 | 304 Dave Stenhouse | .75 | 384 Johnny Klippstein | .75 |
| 144 Ed Kranepool | .50 | 225 Bo Belinsky | .75 | 305 Rico Carty | 1.25 | 385 Carl Yastrzemski | 45.00 |
| 145 Luis Tiant (R) | 6.00 | 226 Yankees Rookies: | 1.50 | 306 Bubba Phillips | .75 | 386 Cubs Rookies: | 1.00 |
| 146 Ron Hansen | .50 | Elvio Jimenez, Jake Gibbs | | 307 Barry Latman | .75 | Paul Jaeckl, Fred Norman | |
| 147 Dennis Bennett | .50 | 227 Bobby Klaus | .75 | 308 Mets Rookies: | .75 | 387 Johnny Podres | 1.25 |
| 148 Willie Kirkland | .50 | 228 Jack Sanford | .75 | Tom Parsons, Cleon Jones | | 388 John Blanchard | .75 |
| 149 Wayne Schurr | .50 | 229 Lou Clinton | .75 | 309 Steve Hamilton | .75 | 389 Don Larsen | 1.25 |
| 150 Brooks Robinson | 12.00 | 230 Ray Sadecki | .75 | 310 Johnny Callison | .75 | 390 Bill Freehan | 1.00 |
| 151 Athletics—10th Place | 1.25 | 231 Jerry Adair | .75 | 311 Orlando Pena | .75 | 391 Mel McGaha | .75 |
| 152 Phil Ortega | .50 | 232 Steve Blass (R) | 1.25 | 312 Joe Nuxhall | .75 | 392 Bob Friend | .75 |
| 153 Norm Cash | 1.25 | 233 Don Zimmer | 1.25 | 313 Jim Schaffer | .75 | 393 Ed Kirkpatrck | .75 |
| 154 Bob Humphreys | .50 | 234 White Sox—2nd Place | 1.25 | 314 Sterling Slaughter | .75 | 394 Jim Hannan | .75 |
| 155 Roger Maris | 25.00 | 235 Chuck Hinton | .75 | 315 Frank Malzone | .75 | 395 Jim Hart | 1.00 |
| 156 Bob Sadowski | .50 | 236 Dennis McLain (R) | 7.00 | 316 Reds—2nd Place | 1.50 | 396 Frank Bertaina | .75 |
| 157 Zoilo Versalles | 1.00 | 237 Bernie Allen | .75 | 317 Don McMahon | .75 | 397 Jerry Buchek | .75 |
| 158 Dick Sisler (Mgr.) | .50 | 238 Joe Moeller | .75 | 318 Matty Alou | .75 | 398 Reds Rookies: | .75 |
| 159 Jim Duffalo | .50 | 239 Doc Edwards | 1.00 | 319 Ken McMullen | .75 | Art Shamsky, Dan Neville | |
| 160 Bob Clemente | 25.00 | 240 Bob Bruce | .75 | 320 Bob Gibson | 10.00 | 399 Ray Herbert | .75 |
| 161 Frank Baumann | .50 | 241 Mack Jones | .75 | 321 Rusty Staub | 3.50 | 400 Harmon Killebrew | 11.00 |
| 162 Russ Nixon | .50 | 242 George Brunet | .75 | 322 Rick Wise | .75 | 401 Carl Willey | .75 |
| 163 John Briggs | .50 | 243 Reds Rookies: | 1.50 | 323 Hank Bauer (Mgr.) | .75 | 402 Joe Amalfitano | .75 |
| 164 Al Spangler | .50 | T. Helms, Ted Davidson | | 324 Bobby Locke | .75 | 403 Red Sox—8th Place | 1.50 |
| 165 Dick Ellsworth | .50 | 244 Lindy McDaniel | .75 | 325 Donn Clendenon | .75 | 404 Stan Williams | .75 |
| 166 Indians Rookies: | 1.25 | 245 Joe Pepitone | 1.25 | 326 Dwight Siebler | .75 | 405 John Roseboro | .75 |
| G. Culver, Tommie Agee | | 246 Tom Butters | .75 | 327 Dennis Menke | .75 | 406 Ralph Terry | .75 |
| 167 Bill Wakefield | .50 | 247 Wally Moon | .75 | 328 Eddie Fisher | .75 | 407 Lee Maye | .75 |

| NO. PLAYER | MINT | NO. PLAYER | MINT | NO. PLAYER | MINT | NO. PLAYER | MINT |
|---|---|---|---|---|---|---|---|
| 408 Larry Sherry | .75 | 461 Braves Rookies: | 25.00 | 510 Ernie Banks | 25.00 | 554 Chico Ruiz | 2.50 |
| 409 Astros Rookies: | 1.00 | Clay Carroll, Phil Niekro | | 511 Ron Locke | 1.25 | 555 Jack Baldschun | 2.50 |
| Jim Beauchamp, L. Dierker | | 462 Lew Krausse | 1.25 | 512 Cap Peterson | 1.25 | 556 Red Schoendienst | 3.00 |
| 410 Luis Aparicio | 7.00 | (photo of Pete Lovrich) | | 513 Yankees—1st Place | 6.00 | 557 Jose Santiago | 2.50 |
| 411 Roger Craig | .75 | 463 Manny Mota | 1.50 | 514 Joe Azcue | 1.25 | 558 Tommie Sisk | 2.50 |
| 412 Bob Bailey | .75 | 464 Ron Piche | 1.25 | 515 Vern Law | 1.25 | 559 Ed Bailey | 2.50 |
| 413 Hal Reniff | .75 | 465 Tom Haller | 1.25 | 516 Al Weis | 1.25 | 560 Boog Powell | 4.00 |
| 414 Al Lopez | 2.00 | 466 Senators Rookies: | 1.25 | 517 Angels Rookies: | 1.25 | 561 Dodgers Rookies: | 4.00 |
| 415 Curt Flood | 1.25 | Pete Craig, Dick Nen | | Paul Schaal, Jack Warner | | D. Daboll, Mike Kekich, | |
| 416 Jim Brewer | .75 | 467 Ray Washburn | 1.25 | 518 Ken Rowe | 1.25 | H. Valle, Jim Lefebvre | |
| 417 Ed Brinkman | .75 | 468 Larry Brown | 1.25 | 519 Bob Uecker | 30.00 | 562 Billy Moran | 2.50 |
| 418 Johnny Edwards | .75 | 469 Don Nottebart | 1.25 | 520 Tony Cloninger | 1.25 | 563 Julio Navarro | 2.50 |
| 419 Ruben Amaro | .75 | 470 Yogi Berra | 24.00 | 521 Phillies Rookies: | 1.25 | 564 Mel Nelson | 2.50 |
| 420 Larry Jackson | .75 | 471 Billy Hoeft | 1.25 | Dave Bennett, M. Steevens | | 565 Ernie Broglio | 2.50 |
| 421 Twins Rookies: | .75 | 472 Don Pavletich | 1.25 | 522 Hank Aguirre | 1.25 | 566 Yankees Rookies: | 2.50 |
| Gary Dotter, Jay Ward | | 473 Orioles Rookies: | 7.00 | 523 Mike Brumley | 2.50 | Art Lopez, Gil Blanco, | |
| 422 Aubrey Gatewood | .75 | Paul Blair, Dave Johnson | | 524 Dave Giusti | 2.50 | Ross Moschitto | |
| 423 Jesse Gonder | .75 | 474 Cookie Rojas | 1.25 | 525 Ed Bressoud | 2.50 | 567 Tommie Aaron | 2.50 |
| 424 Gary Bell | .75 | 475 Clete Boyer | 2.00 | 526 Athletics Rookies: | .50 | 568 Ron Taylor | 2.50 |
| 425 Wayne Causey | .75 | 476 Billy O'Dell | 1.25 | S. Lockwood, R. Lachemann, | | 569 Gino Cimoli | 2.50 |
| 426 Braves—5th Place | 1.25 | 477 Cards Rookies: | 120.00 | Johnny Odom, Jim Hunter | | 570 Claude Osteen | 2.50 |
| 427 Bob Saverine | .75 | Fritz Ackley, Steve Carlton | | 527 Jeff Torborg | 2.50 | 571 Ossie Virgil | 2.50 |
| 428 Bob Shaw | .75 | 478 Wilbur Wood | 1.25 | 528 George Altman | 2.50 | 572 Orioles—3rd Place | 3.50 |
| 429 Don Demeter | .75 | 479 Ken Harrelson | 2.50 | 529 Jerry Fosnow | 2.50 | 573 Red Sox Rookies: | 5.00 |
| 430 Gary Peters | .75 | 480 Joel Horlen | 1.25 | 530 Jim Maloney | 2.50 | Jim Lonborg, Mike Ryan, | |
| 431 Cards Rookies: | 1.00 | 481 Indians—7th Place | 2.50 | 531 Chuck Hiller | 2.50 | G. Moses, Bill Schlesinger | |
| Nelson Briles, W. Spiezio | | 482 Bob Priddy | 1.25 | 532 Hector Lopez | 2.50 | 574 Roy Sievers | 3.00 |
| 432 Jim Grant | .75 | 483 George Smith | 1.25 | 533 Mets Rookies: | 10.00 | 575 Jose Pagan | 2.50 |
| 433 John Bateman | .75 | 484 Ron Perranoski | 1.50 | Dan Napoleon, Ron | | 576 Terry Fox | 2.50 |
| 434 Dave Morehead | .75 | 485 Nellie Fox | 4.00 | Swoboda, Jim Bethke, | | 577 AL Rookie Stars: | 2.50 |
| 435 Willie Davis | 1.00 | 486 Angels Rookies: | 1.25 | Tug McGraw | | D. Knowles, R. Schein | |
| 436 Don Elston | .75 | Pat Rogan Tom Egan | | 534 John Herrnstein | 2.50 | Don Buschhorn | |
| 437 Chico Cardenas | .75 | 487 Woody Woodward | 1.25 | 535 Jack Kralick | 2.50 | 578 Camilo Carreon | 2.50 |
| 438 Harry Walker (Mgr.) | .75 | 488 Ted Wills | 1.25 | 536 Andre Rodgers | 2.50 | 579 Dick Smith | 2.50 |
| 439 Moe Drabowsky | .75 | 489 Gene Mauch (Mgr.) | 1.25 | 537 Angels Rookies: | 2.50 | 580 Jimmie Hall | 2.50 |
| 440 Tom Tresh | 1.25 | 490 Earl Battey | 1.25 | Marcelino Lopez, Rudy | | 581 NL Rookie Stars: | 40.00 |
| 441 Denver LeMaster | .75 | 491 Tracy Stallard | 1.25 | May, Phil Roof | | Tony Perez, Dave Ricketts, | |
| 442 Vic Power | .75 | 492 Gene Freese | 1.25 | 538 Chuck Dressen (Mgr.) | 2.50 | Kevin Collins | |
| 443 Checklist No. 6 | 2.50 | 493 Tigers Rookies: | 1.25 | 539 Herm Starrette | 2.50 | 582 Bob Schmidt | 2.50 |
| 444 Bob Hendley | .75 | Bill Roman, Bruce Brubaker | | 540 Lou Brock | 25.00 | 583 Wes Covington | 2.50 |
| 445 Don Lock | .75 | 494 Jay Ritchie | 1.25 | 541 White Sox Rookies: | 2.50 | 584 Harry Bright | 2.50 |
| 446 Art Mahaffey | .75 | 495 Joe Christopher | 1.25 | Bob Locker, Greg Bollo | | 585 Hank Fischer | 2.50 |
| 447 Julian Javier | 1.25 | 496 Joe Cunningham | 1.25 | 542 Lou Klimchock | 2.50 | 586 Tommy McCraw | 2.50 |
| 448 Lee Stange | 1.25 | 497 Giants Rookies: | 1.25 | 543 Ed Connolly | 2.50 | 587 Joe Sparma | 2.50 |
| 449 Mets Rookies: | 1.25 | Ken Henderson, Jack Hiatt | | 544 Howie Reed | 2.50 | 588 Lenny Green | 2.50 |
| Jerry Hinsley, Gary Kroll | | 498 Gene Stephens | 1.25 | 545 Jesus Alou | 2.50 | 589 Giants Rookies: | 2.50 |
| 450 Elston Howard | 3.00 | 499 Stu Miller | 1.25 | 546 Indians Rookies: | 2.50 | Frank Linzy, B. Schroder | |
| 451 Jim Owens | 1.25 | 500 Ed Mathews | 15.00 | Floyd Weaver, Bill Davis, | | 590 Johnnie Wyatt | 2.50 |
| 452 Gary Geiger | 1.25 | 501 Indians Rookies: | 1.25 | Mike Hedlund, Ray Barker | | 591 Bob Skinner | 2.50 |
| 453 Dodgers Rookies: | 2.00 | Jim Rittwage, R. Gagliano | | 547 Jake Wood | 2.50 | 592 Frank Bork | 2.50 |
| W. Crawford, J. Werhas | | 502 Don Cardwell | 1.25 | 548 Dick Stigman | 2.50 | 593 Tigers Rookies: | 2.50 |
| 454 Ed Rakow | 1.25 | 503 Phil Gagliano | 1.25 | 549 Cubs Rookies: | 4.00 | Jackie Moore, John Sullivan | |
| 455 Norm Siebern | 1.25 | 504 Jerry Grote | 1.25 | R. Pena, Glenn Beckert | | 594 Joe Gaines | 2.50 |
| 456 Bill Henry | 1.25 | 505 Ray Culp | 1.25 | 550 Mel Stottlemyre (R) | 10.00 | 595 Don Lee | 2.50 |
| 457 Bob Kennedy—Coach | 1.25 | 506 Sam Mele | 1.25 | 551 Mets—10th Place | 6.00 | 596 Don Landrum | 2.50 |
| 458 John Buzhardt | 1.25 | 507 Sammy Ellis | 1.25 | 552 Julio Gotay | 2.50 | 597 Twins Rookies: | 2.50 |
| 459 Frank Kostro | 1.25 | 508 Checklist No. 7 | 4.00 | 553 Astros Rookies: | 2.50 | Dick Reese, Joe Nossek, | |
| 460 Richie Allen | 4.00 | 509 Red Sox Rookies: | 1.25 | Gene Ratliff, Dan Coombs, | | John Sevcik | |
| | | Bob Guindon, G. Vezendy | | Jack McClure | | 598 Al Downing (Exc. $1.25) | 4.00 |

**Prices for the 1965 set are for cards in *Mint* condition. *Excellent* copies sell for 50% of prices shown; *Very Good*—30%.**

## 1966 Topps . . . Complete Set of 598 Cards—Value $900.00 (Exc.); $2400.00 (Mint)

Features the rookie cards of Jim Palmer, and Don Sutton. The high numbers are 523 to 598. Cards 62, 103 and 104 (worth $20.00) and card 91 (worth $50.00) exist without a *traded* or *sold* line. Card 101 (checklist) exists identifying card 115 as either Bill Henry—worth $3.00 or Warren Spahn—worth $7.50.

| NO. PLAYER | MINT |
|---|---|
| 1 Willie Mays (Exc. $20.00) | 90.00 |
| 2 Ted Abernathy | 30 |
| 3 Sam Mele (Mgr.) | 30 |
| 4 Ray Culp | 30 |
| 5 Jim Fregosi | 75 |
| 6 Chuck Schilling | 30 |
| 7 Tracy Stallard | 30 |
| 8 Floyd Robinson | 30 |
| 9 Clete Boyer | 1.00 |
| 10 Tony Cloninger | 30 |
| 11 Senators Rookies: | 30 |
| Brant Alyea, Pete Craig | |
| 12 John Tsitouris | 30 |
| 13 Lou Johnson | 30 |
| 14 Norm Siebern | 30 |
| 15 Vern Law | 75 |
| 16 Larry Brown | 30 |
| 17 John Stephenson | 30 |
| 18 Roland Sheldon | 30 |
| 19 Giants—2nd Place | 1.00 |
| 20 Willie Horton | 1.00 |
| 21 Don Nottebart | 30 |
| 22 Joe Nossek | 30 |
| 23 Jack Sanford | 30 |
| 24 Don Kessinger (R) | 1.00 |
| 25 Joe Ward | 30 |
| 26 Ray Sadecki | 30 |
| 27 Orioles Rookies: | 75 |
| D. Knowles, A. Etchebarren | |
| 28 Phil Niekro | 10.00 |
| 29 Mike Brumley | 75 |
| 30 Pete Rose | 55.00 |
| 31 Jack Cullen | 30 |
| 32 Adolfo Phillips | 30 |
| 33 Jim Pagliaroni | 30 |
| 34 Checklist No. 1 | 2.00 |
| 35 Ron Swoboda | 75 |
| 36 Jim Hunter | 12.00 |
| 37 Billy Herman | 1.25 |
| 38 Ron Nischwitz | 30 |
| 39 Ken Henderson | 30 |
| 40 Jim Grant | 30 |
| 41 Don LeJohn | 30 |
| 42 Aubrey Gatewood | 30 |
| 43 Don Landrum | 30 |
| 44 Indians Rookies: | 30 |
| Bill Davis, Tom Kelley | |
| 45 Jim Gentile | 40 |
| 46 Howie Koplitz | 30 |
| 47 J.C. Martin | 30 |
| 48 Paul Blair | 75 |
| 49 Woody Woodward | 30 |
| 50 Mick Mantle | 175.00 |
| 51 Gordon Richardson | 30 |
| 52 Power Plus: | 50 |
| W. Covington, J. Callison | |
| 53 Bob Duliba | 30 |
| 54 Jose Pagan | 30 |
| 55 Ken Harrelson | 1.00 |
| 56 Sandy Valdespino | 30 |
| 57 Jim Lefebvre | 30 |
| 58 Dave Wickersham | 30 |
| 59 Reds—4th Place | 1.25 |
| 60 Curt Flood | 1.00 |
| 61 Bob Bolin | 30 |
| 62 Merritt Ranew* | 30 |
| 63 Jim Stewart | 30 |
| 64 Bob Bruce | 30 |
| 65 Leon Wagner | 30 |
| 66 Al Weis | 30 |
| 67 Mets Rookies: | 75 |
| Cleon Jones, Dick Selma | |
| 68 Hal Reniff | 30 |
| 69 Ken Hamlin | 30 |
| 70 Carl Yastrzemski | 35.00 |
| 71 Frank Carpin | 30 |
| 72 Tony Perez | 7.50 |
| 73 Jerry Zimmerman | 30 |
| 74 Don Mossi | 60 |
| 75 Tommy Davis | 1.00 |
| 76 R. Schoendienst (Mgr.) | 1.00 |
| 77 Johnny Orsino | 30 |
| 78 Frank Linzy | 30 |
| 79 Joe Pepitone | 1.25 |
| 80 Richie Allen | 1.50 |

| NO. PLAYER | MINT |
|---|---|
| 81 Ray Oyler | 30 |
| 82 Bob Hendley | 30 |
| 83 Albie Pearson | 30 |
| 84 Braves Rookies: | 30 |
| J. Beauchamp, D. Kelley | |
| 85 Eddie Fisher | 30 |
| 86 John Bateman | 30 |
| 87 Dan Napoleon | 30 |
| 88 Fred Whitfield | 30 |
| 89 Ted Davidson | 30 |
| 90 Luis Aparicio | 5.00 |
| 91 Bob Uecker* | 12.00 |
| 92 Yankees—6th Place | 3.00 |
| 93 Jim Lonborg | 75 |
| 94 Matty Alou | 75 |
| 95 Pete Richert | 30 |
| 96 Felipe Alou | 75 |
| 97 Jim Merritt | 30 |
| 98 Don Demeter | 30 |
| 99 Buc Belters: | 3.00 |
| W. Stargell, D. Clendenon | |
| 100 Sandy Koufax | 32.00 |
| 101 Checklist No. 2* | 3.00 |
| 102 Ed Kirkpatrick | 30 |
| 103 Dick Groat* | 1.00 |
| 104 Alex Johnson* | 75 |
| 105 Milt Pappas | 50 |
| 106 Rusty Staub | 1.50 |
| 107 A's Rookies: | 30 |
| L. Stahl, Ron Tompkins | |
| 108 Bobby Klaus | 30 |
| 109 Ralph Terry | 30 |
| 110 Ernie Banks | 11.00 |
| 111 Gary Peters | 50 |
| 112 Manny Mota | 75 |
| 113 Hank Aguirre | 50 |
| 114 Jim Gosger | 50 |
| 115 Bill Henry* | 50 |
| 116 Walt Alston (Mgr.) | 2.50 |
| 117 Jake Gibbs | 50 |
| 118 Mike McCormick | 50 |
| 119 Art Shamsky | 50 |
| 120 Harmon Killebrew | 9.00 |
| 121 Ray Herbert | 50 |
| 122 Joe Gaines | 50 |
| 123 Pirates Rookies: | 50 |
| Frank Bork, Jerry May | |
| 124 Tug McGraw | 2.50 |
| 125 Lou Brock | 10.00 |
| 126 Jim Palmer (R) | 60.00 |
| 127 Ken Berry | 50 |
| 128 Jim Landis | 50 |
| 129 Jack Kralick | 50 |
| 130 Joe Torre | 1.25 |
| 131 Angels—7th Place | 1.00 |
| 132 Orlando Cepeda | 3.00 |
| 133 Don McMahon | 50 |
| 134 Wes Parker | 50 |
| 135 Dave Morehead | 50 |
| 136 Woody Held | 50 |
| 137 Pat Corrales | 75 |
| 138 Roger Repoz | 50 |
| 139 Cubs Rookies: | 50 |
| Byron Browne, Don Young | |
| 140 Jim Maloney | 75 |
| 141 Tom McCraw | 50 |
| 142 Don Dennis | 50 |
| 143 Jose Tartabull | 50 |
| 144 Don Schwall | 50 |
| 145 Bill Freehan | 75 |
| 146 George Altman | 50 |
| 147 Lum Harris (Mgr.) | 50 |
| 148 Bob Johnson | 50 |
| 149 Dick Nen | 50 |
| 150 Rocky Colavito | 1.25 |
| 151 Gary Wagner | 50 |
| 152 Frank Malzone | 50 |
| 153 Rico Carty | 1.00 |
| 154 Chuck Hiller | 50 |
| 155 Marcelino Lopez | 50 |
| 156 Double Play Combo: | 75 |
| Dick Schofield, Hal Lanier | |
| 157 Rene Lachemann | 50 |
| 158 Jim Brewer | 50 |
| 159 Chico Ruiz | 50 |

| NO. PLAYER | MINT |
|---|---|
| 160 Whitey Ford | 10.00 |
| 161 Jerry Lumpe | 50 |
| 162 Lee Maye | 50 |
| 163 Tito Francona | 50 |
| 164 White Sox Rookies: | 75 |
| Tommie Agee, M. Staehle | |
| 165 Don Lock | 50 |
| 166 Chris Krug | 50 |
| 167 Boog Powell | 1.50 |
| 168 Dan Osinski | 50 |
| 169 Duke Sims | 50 |
| 170 Cookie Rojas | 50 |
| 171 Nick Willhite | 50 |
| 172 Mets—10th Place | 1.50 |
| 173 Al Spangler | 50 |
| 174 Ron Taylor | 50 |
| 175 Bert Campaneris | 1.00 |
| 176 Jim Davenport | 50 |
| 177 Hector Lopez | 50 |
| 178 Bob Tillman | 50 |
| 179 Cards Rookies: | 75 |
| Dennis Aust, Bob Tolan | |
| 180 Vada Pinson | 1.25 |
| 181 Al Worthington | 50 |
| 182 Jerry Lynch | 50 |
| 183 Checklist No. 3 | 2.00 |
| 184 Denis Menke | 50 |
| 185 Bob Buhl | 50 |
| 186 Ruben Amaro | 50 |
| 187 Chuck Dressen (Mgr.) | 75 |
| 188 Al Luplow | 50 |
| 189 John Roseboro | 50 |
| 190 Jimmie Hall | 50 |
| 191 Darrell Sutherland | 50 |
| 192 Vic Power | 50 |
| 193 Dave McNally | 75 |
| 194 Senators—8th Place | 1.00 |
| 195 Joe Morgan | 12.00 |
| 196 Don Pavletich | 50 |
| 197 Sonny Siebert | 50 |
| 198 Mickey Stanley | 75 |
| 199 Chisox Clubbers: | 75 |
| Bill Skowron, Johnny | |
| Romano, Floyd Robinson | |
| 200 Ed Mathews | 8.00 |
| 201 Jim Dickson | 50 |
| 202 Clay Dalrymple | 50 |
| 203 Jose Santiago | 50 |
| 204 Cubs—8th Place | 1.25 |
| 205 Tom Tresh | 1.00 |
| 206 Alvin Jackson | 75 |
| 207 Frank Quilici | 75 |
| 208 Bob Miller | 75 |
| 209 Tigers Rookies: | 1.25 |
| Fritz Fisher, John Hiller | |
| 210 Bill Mazeroski | 1.00 |
| 211 Frank Kreutzer | 50 |
| 212 Ed Kranepool | 75 |
| 213 Fred Newman | 50 |
| 214 Tommy Harper | 50 |
| 215 NL Batting Leaders: | 8.00 |
| Willie Mays, Bob | |
| Clemente, Hank Aaron | |
| 216 AL Batting Leaders: | 3.00 |
| Tony Oliva, Carl | |
| Yastrzemski, Vic Davalillo | |
| 217 NL Home Run Leaders: | 3.00 |
| Willie McCovey, Willie | |
| Mays, Billy Williams | |
| 218 AL Home Run Leaders: | 1.50 |
| Norm Cash, Willie | |
| Horton, Tony Conigliaro | |
| 219 NL RBI Leaders: | 1.50 |
| Frank Robinson, Deron | |
| Johnson, Willie Mays | |
| 220 AL RBI Leaders: | 1.25 |
| Rocky Colavito, Willie | |
| Horton, Tony Oliva | |
| 221 NL ERA Leaders: | 2.50 |
| Sandy Koufax, Vern | |
| Law, Juan Marichal | |
| 222 AL ERA Leaders: | 1.25 |
| Sam McDowell, Sonny | |
| Siebert, Eddie Fisher | |
| 223 NL Pitching Leaders: | 2.50 |
| Sandy Koufax, Tony | |
| Cloninger, Don Drysdale | |

| NO. PLAYER | MINT |
|---|---|
| 224 AL Pitching Leaders: | 1.25 |
| Mel Stottlemyre, | |
| Jim Grant, Jim Kaat | |
| 225 NL Strikeout Leaders: | 2.50 |
| Bob Gibson, Sandy Koufax, | |
| Bob Veale | |
| 226 AL Strikeout Leaders: | 1.25 |
| Sam McDowell, Mickey | |
| Lolich, Denny McLain, | |
| Sonny Siebert | |
| 227 Russ Nixon | 50 |
| 228 Larry Dierker | 50 |
| 229 Hank Bauer | 75 |
| 230 Johnny Callison | 75 |
| 231 F. Weaver | 50 |
| 232 Glenn Beckert | 75 |
| 233 Dom Zanni | 50 |
| 234 Yankees Rookies: | 3.00 |
| Roy White, Rich Beck | |
| 235 Don Cardwell | 50 |
| 236 Mike Hershberger | 50 |
| 237 Billy O'Dell | 50 |
| 238 Dodgers—1st Place | 2.00 |
| 239 Orlando Pena | 50 |
| 240 Earl Battey | 50 |
| 241 Dennis Ribant | 50 |
| 242 Jesus Alou | 50 |
| 243 Nelson Briles | 50 |
| 244 Astros Rookies: | 50 |
| C. Harrison, S. Jackson | |
| 245 John Buzhardt | 50 |
| 246 Ed Bailey | 50 |
| 247 Carl Warwick | 50 |
| 248 Pete Mikkelsen | 50 |
| 249 Bill Rigney (Mgr.) | 50 |
| 250 Sam Ellis | 50 |
| 251 Ed Brinkman | 50 |
| 252 Denver Lemaster | 50 |
| 253 Don Wert | 50 |
| 254 Phillies Rookies: | 15.00 |
| Ferguson Jenkins, | |
| Bill Sorrell | |
| 255 Willie Stargell | 12.00 |
| 256 Lew Krausse | 50 |
| 257 Jeff Torborg | 50 |
| 258 Dave Giusti | 50 |
| 259 Red Sox—9th Place | 1.50 |
| 260 Bob Shaw | 50 |
| 261 Ron Hansen | 50 |
| 262 Jack Hamilton | 50 |
| 263 Tom Egan | 50 |
| 264 Twins Rookies: | 50 |
| Ted Uhlaender, Andy Kosco | |
| 265 Stu Miller | 50 |
| 266 Pedro Gonzalez | 50 |
| 267 Joe Sparma | 50 |
| 268 John Blanchard | 50 |
| 269 Don Heffner (Mgr.) | 50 |
| 270 Claude Osteen | 75 |
| 271 Hal Lanier | 75 |
| 272 Jack Baldschun | 50 |
| 273 Astro Aces: | 1.00 |
| Bob Aspromonte, | |
| Rusty Staub | |
| 274 Buster Narum | 50 |
| 275 Tim McCarver | 2.00 |
| 276 Jim Bouton | 1.00 |
| 277 George Thomas | 50 |
| 278 Calvin Koonce | 50 |
| 279 Checklist No. 4 | 2.00 |
| 280 Bobby Knoop | 50 |
| 281 Bruce Howard | 50 |
| 282 Johnny Lewis | 50 |
| 283 Jim Perry | 1.00 |
| 284 Bobby Wine | 50 |
| 285 Luis Tiant | 2.00 |
| 286 Gary Geiger | 50 |
| 287 Jack Aker | 50 |
| 288 Dodgers Rookies: | 50.00 |
| Bill Singer, Don Sutton | |
| 289 Larry Sherry | 60 |
| 290 Ron Santo | 1.00 |
| 291 Moe Drabowsky | 50 |
| 292 Jim Coker | 50 |

| NO. PLAYER | MINT | NO. PLAYER | MINT | NO. PLAYER | MINT | NO. PLAYER | MINT |
|---|---|---|---|---|---|---|---|
| 293 Mike Shannon | .50 | 374 Bob Locker | .50 | 455 Mickey Lolich | 1.50 | 531 Joe Cunningham | 10.00 |
| 294 Steve Ridzik | .50 | 375 Donn Clendenon | .60 | 456 Red Sox Rookies: | 1.50 | 532 Aurelio Monteagudo | 10.00 |
| 295 Jim Hart | .50 | 376 Paul Schaal | .50 | Darrell Brandon, Joe Foy | | 533 Jerry Adair | 10.00 |
| 296 Johnny Keane (Mgr.) | .50 | 377 Turk Farrell | .50 | 457 Joe Gibbon | 1.50 | 534 Mets Rookies: | 10.00 |
| 297 Jim Owens | .50 | 378 Dick Tracewski | .50 | 458 Manny Jiminez | 1.50 | Dave Eilers, Rob Gardner |  |
| 298 Rico Petrocelli | 1.00 | 379 Cardinal—7th Place | 1.00 | 459 Bill McCool | 1.50 | 535 Willie Davis | 12.00 |
| 299 Lou Burdette | 1.25 | 380 Tony Conigliaro | 2.00 | 460 Curt Blefary | 1.50 | 536 Dick Egan | 10.00 |
| 300 Bob Clemente | 36.00 | 381 Hank Fischer | .50 | 461 Roy Face | 2.00 | 537 Herman Franks (Mgr.) | 10.00 |
| 301 Greg Bollo | .50 | 382 Phil Roof | .50 | 462 Bob Rodgers | 2.00 | 538 Bob Allen | 10.00 |
| 302 Ernie Bowman | .50 | 383 Jack Brandt | .50 | 463 Phillies—6th Place | 3.00 | 539 Astros Rookies: | 10.00 |
| 303 Indians—5th Place | 1.00 | 384 Al Downing | 1.00 | 464 Larry Bearnarth | 1.50 | Bill Heath, Carroll Sembera |  |
| 304 John Herrnstein | .50 | 385 Ken Boyer | 2.00 | 465 Don Buford | 1.50 | 540 Denny McLain | 20.00 |
| 305 Camilo Pascual | .75 | 386 Gil Hodges (Mgr.) | 4.00 | 466 Ken Johnson | 1.50 | 541 Gene Oliver | 10.00 |
| 306 Ty Cline | .50 | 387 Howie Reed | .50 | 467 Vic Roznovsky | 1.50 | 542 George Smith | 10.00 |
| 307 Clay Carroll | .50 | 388 Don Mincher | .50 | 468 Johnny Podres | 2.50 | 543 Roger Craig | 13.00 |
| 308 Tom Haller | .50 | 389 Jim O'Toole | .50 | 469 Yankees Rookies: | 8.00 | 544 Cardinals Rookies: | 10.00 |
| 309 Diego Segui | .50 | 390 Brooks Robinson | 12.00 | Bobby Murcer, | | J. Williams, J. Hoerner, |  |
| 310 Frank Robinson | 16.00 | 391 Chuck Hinton | .50 | Dooley Womack | | George Kernek |  |
| 311 Reds Rookies: | .60 | 392 Cubs Rookies: | .50 | 470 Sam McDowell | 2.00 | 545 Dick Green | 10.00 |
| D. Simpson, T. Helms | | Bill Hands, Randy Hundley | | 471 Bob Skinner | 1.50 | 546 Dwight Siebler | 10.00 |
| 312 Bob Saverine | .50 | 393 George Brunet | .50 | 472 Terry Fox | 1.50 | 547 Horace Clarke (R) | 10.00 |
| 313 Chris Zachary | .50 | 394 Ron Brand | .50 | 473 Rich Rollins | 1.50 | 548 Gary Kroll | 10.00 |
| 314 Hector Valle | .50 | 395 Len Gabrielson | .50 | 474 Dick Schofield | 1.50 | 549 Senators Rookies: | 10.00 |
| 315 Norm Cash | 1.25 | 396 Jerry Stephenson | .50 | 475 Dick Radatz | 1.50 | Al Closter, Casey Cox |  |
| 316 Jack Fisher | .50 | 397 Bill White | 1.00 | 476 Bobby Bragan | 1.50 | 550 Willie McCovey | 90.00 |
| 317 Dalton Jones | .50 | 398 Danny Cater | .50 | 477 Steve Barber | 1.50 | 551 Bob Purkey | 10.00 |
| 318 Harry Walker | .50 | 399 Ray Washburn | .50 | 478 Tony Gonzalez | 1.50 | 552 Birdie Tebbetts | 10.00 |
| 319 Gene Freese | .50 | 400 Zoilo Versalles | .50 | 479 Jim Hannan | 1.50 | 553 Rookie Stars: | 10.00 |
| 320 Bob Gibson | 11.00 | 401 Ken McMullen | .50 | 480 Dick Stuart | 1.50 | Pat Garrett, Jackie Warner |  |
| 321 Rick Reichardt | .50 | 402 Jim Hickman | .50 | 481 Bob Lee | 1.50 | 554 Jim Northrup | 10.00 |
| 322 Bill Faul | .50 | 403 Fred Talbot | .50 | 482 Cubs Rookies: | 1.50 | 555 Ron Perranoski | 10.00 |
| 323 Ray Barker | .50 | 404 Pirates—3rd Place | 1.00 | J. Boccabella, D. Dowling | | 556 Mel Queen | 10.00 |
| 324 John Boozer | .50 | 405 Elston Howard | 2.00 | 483 Joe Nuxhall | 2.00 | 557 Felix Mantilla | 10.00 |
| 325 Vic Davalillo | .75 | 406 Joe Jay | .50 | 484 Wes Covington | 1.50 | 558 Red Sox Rookies: | 15.00 |
| 326 Braves—5th Place | 1.00 | 407 John Kennedy | .50 | 485 Bob Bailey | 1.50 | Pete Magrini, Guido Grilli, |  |
| 327 Bernie Allen | .50 | 408 Lee Thomas | .50 | 486 Tommy John | 6.00 | George Scott |  |
| 328 Jerry Grote | .50 | 409 Billy Hoeft | .50 | 487 Al Ferrara | 1.50 | 559 Roberto Pena | 10.00 |
| 329 Pete Charton | .50 | 410 Al Kaline | 10.00 | 488 George Banks | 1.50 | 560 Joel Horlen | 10.00 |
| 330 Ron Fairly | .75 | 411 Gene Mauch (Mgr.) | .75 | 489 Curt Simmons | 1.50 | 561 Choo Choo Coleman | 10.00 |
| 331 Ron Herbel | .50 | 412 Sam Bowens | .50 | 490 Bobby Richardson | 6.00 | 562 Russ Snyder | 10.00 |
| 332 Billy Bryan | .50 | 413 John Romano | .50 | 491 Dennis Bennett | 1.50 | 563 Twins Rookies: | 10.00 |
| 333 Senators Rookies: | .50 | 414 Dan Coombs | .50 | 492 Athletics—10th Place | 2.50 | Pete Cimino, Cesar Tovar |  |
| Joe Coleman, Jim French | | 415 Max Alvis | .50 | 493 John Klippstein | 1.50 | 564 Bob Chance | 10.00 |
| 334 Marty Keough | .50 | 416 Phil Ortega | .50 | 494 Gordon Coleman | 1.50 | 565 Jimmy Piersall | 15.00 |
| 335 Juan Pizarro | .50 | 417 Angels Rookies: | .50 | 495 Dick McAuliffe | 1.50 | 566 Mike Cuellar | 11.00 |
| 336 Gene Alley | .50 | Jim McGlothlin, Ed Sukla | | 496 Lindy McDaniel | 1.50 | 567 Dick Howser | 12.00 |
| 337 Fred Gladding | .50 | 418 Phil Gagliano | .50 | 497 Chris Cannizzaro | 1.50 | 568 Athletics Rookies: | 10.00 |
| 338 Dal Maxvill | .50 | 419 Mike Ryan | .50 | 498 Pirates Rookies: | 1.50 | Paul Lindblad, Ron Stone |  |
| 339 Del Crandall | .75 | 420 Juan Marichal | 7.00 | Luke Walker, W. Fryman | | 569 Orlando McFarlane | 10.00 |
| 340 Dean Chance | .60 | 421 Roy McMillan | .50 | 499 Wally Bunker | 1.50 | 570 Art Mahaffey | 10.00 |
| 341 Wes Westrum | .50 | 422 Ed Charles | .50 | 500 Hank Aaron | 45.00 | 571 Dave Roberts | 10.00 |
| 342 Bob Humphreys | .50 | 423 Ernie Broglio | .50 | 501 John O'Donoghue | 1.50 | 572 Bob Priddy | 10.00 |
| 343 Joe Christopher | .50 | 424 Reds Rookies: | 2.00 | 502 Lenny Green | 1.50 | 573 Derrell Griffith | 10.00 |
| 344 Steve Blass | .60 | Lee May, Darrell Osteen | | 503 Steve Hamilton | 1.50 | 574 Mets Rookies: | 10.00 |
| 345 Bob Allison | .75 | 425 Bob Veale | .50 | 504 Grady Hatton | 1.50 | Billy Hepler, Bill Murphy |  |
| 346 Mike De La Hoz | .50 | 426 White Sox—2nd Place | 1.00 | 505 Jose Cardenal | 1.50 | 575 Earl Wilson | 10.00 |
| 347 Phil Regan | .50 | 427 John Miller | .50 | 506 Bo Belinsky | 1.50 | 576 Dave Nicholson | 10.00 |
| 348 Orioles—3rd Place | 1.00 | 428 Sandy Alomar | .50 | 507 John Edwards | 1.50 | 577 Jack Lamabe | 10.00 |
| 349 Cap Peterson | .50 | 429 Bill Monbouquette | .50 | 508 Steve Hargan | 1.50 | 578 Chi Chi Olivo | 10.00 |
| 350 Mel Stottlemyre | 1.25 | 430 Don Drysdale | 8.00 | 509 Jake Wood | 1.50 | 579 Orioles Rookies: | 10.00 |
| 351 Fred Valentine | .50 | 431 Walt Bond | .50 | 510 Hoyt Wilhelm | 8.00 | F. Bertaina, G. Brabender, |  |
| 352 Bob Aspromonte | .50 | 432 Bob Heffner | .50 | 511 Giants Rookies: | 1.50 | Dave Johnson |  |
| 353 Al McBean | .50 | 433 Alvin Dark (Mgr.) | .75 | Bob Barton, Tito Fuentes | | 580 Billy Williams | 45.00 |
| 354 Smoky Burgess | .50 | 434 Willie Kirkland | .50 | 512 Dick Stigman | 1.50 | 581 Tony Martinez | 10.00 |
| 355 Wade Blasingame | .50 | 435 Jim Bunning | 3.00 | 513 Camilo Carreon | 1.50 | 582 Garry Roggenburk | 10.00 |
| 356 Red Sox Rookies: | .50 | 436 Julian Javier | .50 | 514 Hal Woodeschick | 1.50 | 583 Tigers—3rd Place | 45.00 |
| Owen Johnson, | | 437 Al Stanek | .50 | 515 Frank Howard | 2.50 | 584 Yankees Rookies: | 10.00 |
| Ken Sanders | | 438 Willie Smith | .50 | 516 Eddie Bressoud | 1.50 | F. Fernandez, F. Peterson |  |
| 357 Gerry Arrigo | .50 | 439 Pedro Ramos | .50 | 517 Checklist No. 7 | 8.00 | 585 Tony Taylor | 10.00 |
| 358 Charlie Smith | .50 | 440 Deron Johnson | .50 | 518 Braves Rookies: | 1.50 | 586 Claude Raymond | 10.00 |
| 359 Johnny Briggs | .50 | 441 Tommie Sisk | .50 | Arnie Umbach, H. Hippauf | | 587 Dick Bertell | 10.00 |
| 360 Ron Hunt | .50 | 442 Orioles Rookies: | .50 | 519 Bob Friend | 1.50 | 588 Athletics Rookies: | 10.00 |
| 361 Tom Satriano | .50 | Ed Barnowski, Eddie Watt | | 520 Jim Wynn | 1.50 | Ken Suarez, Chuck Dobson |  |
| 362 Gates Brown | .50 | 443 Bill Wakefield | .50 | 521 John Wyatt | 1.50 | 589 Lou Klimchock | 10.00 |
| 363 Checklist No. 5 | 3.00 | 444 Checklist No. 6 | 3.00 | 522 Phil Linz | 1.50 | 590 Bill Skowron | 20.00 |
| 364 Nate Oliver | .50 | 445 Jim Kaat | 4.00 | 523 Bob Sadowski | 10.00 | 591 NL Rookie Stars: | 10.00 |
| 365 Roger Maris | 25.00 | 446 Mack Jones | .50 | 524 Giants Rookies: | 10.00 | Bart Shirley, Grant Jackson |  |
| 366 Wayne Causey | .50 | 447 Dick Ellsworth | 2.00 | Ollie Brown, Don Mason | | 592 Andre Rodgers | 10.00 |
| 367 Mel Nelson | .50 | (photo of Ken Hubbs) | | 525 Gary Bell | 10.00 | 593 Doug Camilli | 10.00 |
| 368 Charlie Lau | .50 | 448 Eddie Stanky | 2.00 | 526 Twins—1st Place | 25.00 | 594 Chico Salmon | 10.00 |
| 369 Jim King | .50 | 449 Joe Moeller | 2.00 | 527 Julio Navarro | 10.00 | 595 Larry Jackson | 10.00 |
| 370 Chico Cardenas | .50 | 450 Tony Oliva | 4.00 | 528 Jesse Gonder | 10.00 | 596 John Sullivan | 10.00 |
| 371 Lee Stange | .50 | 451 Barry Latman | 1.50 | 529 White Sox Rookies: | 10.00 | 597 Astros Rookies: | 10.00 |
| 372 Harvey Kuenn | .75 | 452 Joe Azcue | 1.50 | Dennis Higgins, Lee Elia, | | Nate Colbert, Greg Sims |  |
| 373 Giants Rookies: | .60 | 453 Ron Kline | 1.50 | Bill Voss | | 598 G. Perry (Exc. $35.00) | 160.00 |
| Jack Hiatt, Dick Estelle | | 454 Jerry Buchek | 1.50 | 530 Robin Roberts | 30.00 |  |  |

**Prices for the 1966 set are for cards in *Mint* condition. *Excellent* copies sell for 50% of prices shown; *Very Good*—30%.**

# 1967 Topps . . . Complete Set of 609 Cards—Value $950.00 (Exc.); $2700.00 (Mint)

Features the rookie cards of Tom Seaver and Rod Carew. Cards 534 to 609 are high numbers. Cards 458 to 533 are semi-high numbers. Cards 26 and 86 exist without the *traded* line—worth $12.00 each. Card 191 exists identifying card 214 as either Dick Kelley—worth $5.00 or Tom Kelley—worth $1.50.

| NO. PLAYER | MINT |
|---|---|
| 1 The Champs: (Exc. $1.50) ..8.00 | |
| Frank Robinson, Hank | |
| Bauer, Brooks Robinson | |
| 2 Jack Hamilton | .35 |
| 3 Duke Sims | .35 |
| 4 Hal Lanier | .60 |
| 5 Whitey Ford | 8.00 |
| 6 Dick Simpson | .35 |
| 7 Don McMahon | .35 |
| 8 Chuck Harrison | .35 |
| 9 Ron Hansen | .35 |
| 10 Matty Alou | .60 |
| 11 Barry Moore | .35 |
| 12 Dodgers Rookies: | .60 |
| J. Campanis, Bill Singer | |
| 13 Joe Sparma | .35 |
| 14 Phil Linz | .35 |
| 15 Earl Battey | .60 |
| 16 Bill Hands | .35 |
| 17 Jim Gosger | .35 |
| 18 Gene Oliver | .35 |
| 19 Jim McGlothlin | .35 |
| 20 Orlando Cepeda | 4.00 |
| 21 Dave Bristol (Mgr.) | .35 |
| 22 Gene Brabender | .35 |
| 23 Larry Elliot | .35 |
| 24 Bob Allen | .35 |
| 25 Elstan Howard | 2.00 |
| 26 Bob Priddy* | .35 |
| 27 Bob Saverine | .35 |
| 28 Barry Latman | .35 |
| 29 Tom McCraw | .35 |
| 30 Al Kaline | 8.00 |
| 31 Jim Brewer | .35 |
| 32 Bob Bailey | .35 |
| 33 Athletic Rookies: | 1.50 |
| Sal Bando, R. Schwartz | |
| 34 Pete Cimino | .40 |
| 35 Rico Carty | .75 |
| 36 Bob Tillman | .35 |
| 37 Rick Wise | .60 |
| 38 Bob Johnson | .35 |
| 39 Curt Simmons | .60 |
| 40 Rick Reichardt | .35 |
| 41 Joe Hoerner | .35 |
| 42 Mets Team | 1.50 |
| 43 Chico Salmon | .35 |
| 44 Joe Nuxhall | .75 |
| 45 Roger Maris | 18.00 |
| 46 Lindy McDaniel | .35 |
| 47 Ken McMullen | .35 |
| 48 Bill Freehan | .75 |
| 49 Roy Face | 1.00 |
| 50 Tony Olava | 2.50 |
| 51 Astros Rookies: | .35 |
| Dave Adlesh, W. Bales | |
| 52 Dennis Higgins | .35 |
| 53 Clay Dalrymple | .35 |
| 54 Dick Green | .35 |
| 55 Don Drysdale | 6.00 |
| 56 Jose Tartabull | .35 |
| 57 Pat Jarvis | .35 |
| 58 Paul Schaal | .35 |
| 59 Ralph Terry | .35 |
| 60 Luis Aparicio | 4.00 |
| 61 Gordy Coleman | .35 |

| NO. PLAYER | MINT |
|---|---|
| 62 Checklist No. 1 | .2.50 |
| 63 Cards Clubbers | 4.00 |
| Lou Brock, Curt Flood | |
| 64 Fred Valentine | .35 |
| 65 Tom Haller | .35 |
| 66 Manny Mota | .75 |
| 67 Ken Berry | .35 |
| 68 Bob Buhl | .35 |
| 69 Vic Davalillo | .50 |
| 70 Ron Santo | 1.00 |
| 71 Camilo Pascual | .35 |
| 72 Tigers Rookies: | .60 |
| George Korince (Photo of | |
| John Brown), J. Matchick | |
| 73 Rusty Staub | 1.50 |
| 74 Wes Stock | .35 |
| 75 George Scott | .75 |
| 76 Jim Barbieri | .35 |
| 77 Dooley Womack | .35 |
| 78 Pat Corrales | .60 |
| 79 Bubba Morton | .35 |
| 80 Jim Maloney | .35 |
| 81 Eddie Stanky (Mgr.) | .60 |
| 82 Steve Barber | .35 |
| 83 Ollie Brown | .35 |
| 84 Tommie Sisk | .35 |
| 85 Johnny Callison | .60 |
| 86 Mike McCormick* | .75 |
| 87 George Altman | .35 |
| 88 Mickey Lolich | 1.25 |
| 89 Felix Millan | .35 |
| 90 Jim Nash | .35 |
| 91 Johnny Lewis | .35 |
| 92 Ray Washburn | .35 |
| 93 Yankees Rookies: | 2.50 |
| Stan Bahnsen, B. Murcer | |
| 94 Ron Fairly | .60 |
| 95 Sonny Siebert | .50 |
| 96 Art Shamsky | .35 |
| 97 Mike Cuellar | .65 |
| 98 Rich Rollins | .35 |
| 99 Lee Stange | .35 |
| 100 Frank Robinson | 7.50 |
| 101 Ken Johnson | .35 |
| 102 Phillies Team | 1.50 |
| 103 Checklist No. 2 | .6.00 |
| 104 Minnie Rojas | .35 |
| 105 Ken Boyer | 1.25 |
| 106 Randy Hundley | .35 |
| 107 Joel Horlen | .35 |
| 108 Alex Johnson | .35 |
| 109 Tribe Thumpers: | .80 |
| R. Colavito, Leon Wagner | |
| 110 Jack Aker | .35 |
| 111 John Kennedy | .50 |
| 112 Dave Wickersham | .50 |
| 113 Dave Nicholson | .50 |
| 114 Jack Baldschun | .50 |
| 115 Paul Casanova | .50 |
| 116 Herman Franks | .50 |
| 117 Darrell Brandon | .50 |
| 118 Bernie Allen | .50 |
| 119 Wade Blasingame | .50 |
| 120 Floyd Robinson | .50 |
| 121 Ed Bressoud | .50 |
| 122 George Brunet | .50 |

| NO. PLAYER | MINT |
|---|---|
| 123 Pirates Rookies: | .50 |
| Jim Price, L. Walker | |
| 124 Jim Stewart | .50 |
| 125 Moe Drabowsky | .50 |
| 126 Tony Taylor | .50 |
| 127 John O'Donoghue | .50 |
| 128 Ed Spiezio | .50 |
| 129 Phil Roof | .50 |
| 130 Phil Regan | .50 |
| 131 Yankees Team | 3.00 |
| 132 Ozzie Virgil | .50 |
| 133 Ron Kline | .50 |
| 134 Gates Brown | .50 |
| 135 Deron Johnson | .50 |
| 136 Carroll Sembera | .50 |
| 137 Twins Rookies: | .50 |
| Ron Clark, Jim Ollum | |
| 138 Dick Kelley | .50 |
| 139 Dalton Jones | .50 |
| 140 Willie Stargell | .10.00 |
| 141 John Miller | .50 |
| 142 Jackie Brandt | .50 |
| 143 Sox Sockers: | .50 |
| Don Buford, Pete Ward | |
| 144 Bill Hepler | .50 |
| 145 Larry Brown | .50 |
| 146 Steve Carlton | .55.00 |
| 147 Tom Egan | .50 |
| 148 Adolfo Phillips | .50 |
| 149 Joe Moeller | .50 |
| 150 Mickey Mantle | 210.00 |
| 151 World Series Game 1: | .2.00 |
| Moe Mows Down 11 | |
| 152 World Series Game 2: | .2.50 |
| Palmer Blanks Dodgers | |
| 153 World Series Game 3: | .2.00 |
| Blair's Homer Defeats L.A. | |
| 154 World Series Game 4: | .2.00 |
| Orioles Win 4 Straight | |
| 155 World Series: | 2.00 |
| The Winners Celebrate | |
| 156 Ron Herbel | .50 |
| 157 Danny Cater | .50 |
| 158 Jimmy Coker | .50 |
| 159 Bruce Howard | .50 |
| 160 Willie Davis | .75 |
| 161 Dick Williams (Mgr.) | .75 |
| 162 Billy O'Dell | .50 |
| 163 Vic Roznovsky | .50 |
| 164 Dwight Siebler | .50 |
| 165 Cleon Jones | .50 |
| 166 Ed Mathews | 7.00 |
| 167 Senators Rookies: | .50 |
| Joe Coleman, Tim Cullen | |
| 168 Ray Culp | .50 |
| 169 Horace Clarke | .50 |
| 170 Dick McAuliffe | .50 |
| 171 Calvin Koonce | .50 |
| 172 Bill Heath | .50 |
| 173 Cardinals Team | 1.25 |
| 174 Dick Radatz | .50 |
| 175 Bobby Knoop | .50 |
| 176 Sammy Ellis | .50 |
| 177 Tito Fuentes | .50 |
| 178 John Buzhardt | .50 |
| 179 Braves Rookies: | .50 |
| C. Vaughan, Cecil Upshaw | |

| NO. PLAYER | MINT |
|---|---|
| 180 Curt Blefary | .50 |
| 181 Terry Fox | .50 |
| 182 Ed Charles | .50 |
| 183 Jim Pagliaroni | .50 |
| 184 George Thomas | .50 |
| 185 Ken Holtzman (R) | 1.00 |
| 186 Mets Maulers | .80 |
| Ed Kranepool, R. Swoboda | |
| 187 Pedro Ramos | .50 |
| 188 Ken Harrelson | 1.25 |
| 189 Chuck Hinton | .50 |
| 190 Turk Farrell | .50 |
| 191 Checklist No. 3* | .3.00 |
| 192 Fred Gladding | .50 |
| 193 Jose Cardenal | .50 |
| 194 Bob Allison | .50 |
| 195 Al Jackson | .50 |
| 196 Johnny Romano | .50 |
| 197 Ron Perranoski | .50 |
| 198 Chuck Hiller | .50 |
| 199 Billy Hitchcock | .50 |
| 200 Willie Mays | .35.00 |
| 201 Hal Reniff | .5C |
| 202 Johnny Edwards | .50 |
| 203 Al McBean | .50 |
| 204 Orioles Rookies: | .75 |
| Mike Epstein, Tom Phoebus | |
| 205 Dick Groat | .75 |
| 206 Dennis Bennett | .50 |
| 207 John Orsino | .50 |
| 208 Jack Lamabe | .50 |
| 209 Joe Nossek | .50 |
| 210 Bob Gibson | .7.00 |
| 211 Twins Team | 1.50 |
| 212 Chris Zachary | .50 |
| 213 Jay Johnstone | 1.00 |
| 214 Tom Kelley | .50 |
| 215 Ernie Banks | 8.00 |
| 216 Bengal Belters: | .3.00 |
| Norm Cash, Al Kaline | |
| 217 Rob Gardner | .50 |
| 218 Wes Parker | .50 |
| 219 Clay Carroll | .50 |
| 220 Jim Hart | .50 |
| 221 Woody Fryman | .50 |
| 222 Reds Rookies: | .50 |
| Darrell Osteen, Lee May | |
| 223 Mike Ryan | .50 |
| 224 Walt Bond | .50 |
| 225 Mel Stottlemyre | 1.00 |
| 226 Julian Javier | .50 |
| 227 Paul Lindblad | .50 |
| 228 Gil Hodges (Mgr.) | 4.00 |
| 229 Larry Jackson | .50 |
| 230 Boog Powell | 1.50 |
| 231 John Bateman | .50 |
| 232 Don Buford | .50 |
| 233 AL ERA Leaders: | 1.50 |
| Joel Horlen, Gary Peters, | |
| Steve Hargan | |
| 234 NL ERA Leaders: | 4.00 |
| Sandy Koufax, Mike | |
| Cuellar, Juan Marichal | |
| 235 AL Pitching Leaders: | .2.00 |
| Earl Wilson, Jim Kaat, | |
| Denny McLain | |

# 1967 Topps (Continued)

| NO. | PLAYER | MINT |
|---|---|---|
| 236 | NL Pitching Leaders: | 5.00 |
| | Sandy Koufax, Juan Marichal, Gaylord Perry, Bob Gibson | |
| 237 | AL Strikeout Leaders: | 1.50 |
| | Jim Kaat, Earl Wilson, Sam McDowell | |
| 238 | NL Strikeout Leaders: | 2.00 |
| | Sandy Koufax, Jim Bunning, Bob Veale | |
| 239 | AL Batting Leaders: | 2.00 |
| | Al Kaline, Frank Robinson, Tony Oliva | |
| 240 | NL Batting Leaders: | 1.25 |
| | Matty Alou, Felipe Alou, Rico Carty | |
| 241 | AL RBI Leaders | 2.00 |
| | Frank Robinson, Boog Powell, Harmon Killebrew | |
| 242 | NL RBI Leaders: | 2.50 |
| | Bob Clemente, Richie Allen, Hank Aaron | |
| 243 | AL Home Run Leaders: | 2.00 |
| | Frank Robinson, Harmon Killebrew, Boog Powell | |
| 244 | NL Home Run Leaders: | 3.00 |
| | Hank Aaron, Richie Allen, Willie Mays | |
| 245 | Curt Flood | .75 |
| 246 | Jim Perry | .75 |
| 247 | Jerry Lumpe | .50 |
| 248 | Gene Mauch (Mgr.) | .75 |
| 249 | Nick Willhite | .50 |
| 250 | Hank Aaron | 40.00 |
| 251 | Woody Held | .50 |
| 252 | Bob Bolin | .50 |
| 253 | Indians Rookies: | .50 |
| | Bill Davis, Gus Gil | |
| 254 | Milt Pappas | .50 |
| 255 | Frank Howard | 1.00 |
| 256 | Bob Hendley | .50 |
| 257 | Charley Smith | .50 |
| 258 | Lee Maye | .50 |
| 259 | Don Dennis | .50 |
| 260 | Jim Lefebvre | .75 |
| 261 | John Wyatt | .50 |
| 262 | Athletics Team | 1.00 |
| 263 | Hank Aguirre | .50 |
| 264 | Ron Swoboda | .60 |
| 265 | Lou Burdette | .75 |
| 266 | Pitt Power: | 3.00 |
| | W. Stargell, D. Clendenon | |
| 267 | Don Schwall | .50 |
| 268 | John Briggs | .50 |
| 269 | Don Nottebart | .50 |
| 270 | Zoilo Versalles | .50 |
| 271 | Eddie Watt | .50 |
| 272 | Cubs Rookies: | .50 |
| | Bill Connors, Dave Dowling | |
| 273 | Dick Lines | .50 |
| 274 | Bob Aspromonte | .50 |
| 275 | Fred Whitfield | .50 |
| 276 | Bruce Brubaker | .50 |
| 277 | Steve Whitaker | .50 |
| 278 | Checklist No. 4 | 2.00 |
| 279 | Frank Linzy | .50 |
| 280 | Tony Conigliaro | 2.00 |
| 281 | Bob Rodgers | .50 |
| 282 | Johnny Odom | .50 |
| 283 | Gene Alley | .50 |
| 284 | Johnny Podres | .75 |
| 285 | Lou Brock | 10.00 |
| 286 | Wayne Causey | .50 |
| 287 | Mets Rookies: | .50 |
| | Greg Goossen, Bart Shirley | |
| 288 | Denver Lemaster | .50 |
| 289 | Tom Tresh | .75 |
| 290 | Bill White | .75 |
| 291 | Jim Hannan | .50 |
| 292 | Don Pavletich | .50 |
| 293 | Ed Kirkpatrick | .50 |
| 294 | Walt Alston (Mgr.) | 2.00 |
| 295 | Sam McDowell | .75 |
| 296 | Glenn Beckert | .50 |
| 297 | Dave Morehead | .50 |
| 298 | Ron Davis | .50 |
| 299 | Norm Siebern | .50 |
| 300 | Jim Kaat | 2.00 |
| 301 | Jesse Gonder | .50 |
| 302 | Orioles Team | 1.00 |
| 303 | Gil Blanco | .50 |
| 304 | Phil Gagliano | .50 |
| 305 | Earl Wilson | .50 |
| 306 | Bud Harrelson | .75 |
| 307 | Jim Beauchamp | .50 |
| 308 | Al Downing | .60 |
| 309 | Hurlers Beware: | .75 |
| | J. Callison, Richie Allen | |
| 310 | Gary Peters | .50 |
| 311 | Ed Brinkman | .50 |
| 312 | Don Mincher | .50 |
| 313 | Bob Lee | .50 |
| 314 | Red Sox Rookies: | 2.50 |
| | Mike Andrews, R. Smith | |
| 315 | Billy Williams | 5.00 |
| 316 | Jack Kralick | .50 |
| 317 | Cesar Tovar | .50 |
| 318 | Dave Giusti | .50 |
| 319 | Paul Blair | .50 |
| 320 | Gaylord Perry | 5.00 |
| 321 | Mayo Smith (Mgr.) | .50 |
| 322 | Jose Pagan | .50 |
| 323 | Mike Hershberger | .50 |
| 324 | Hal Woodeschick | .50 |
| 325 | Chico Cardenas | .50 |
| 326 | Bob Uecker | 11.00 |
| 327 | Angels Team | 1.00 |
| 328 | Clete Boyer | .60 |
| 329 | Charlie Lau | .60 |
| 330 | Claude Osteen | .50 |
| 331 | Joe Foy | .50 |
| 332 | Jesus Alou | .50 |
| 333 | Ferguson Jenkins | 4.00 |
| 334 | Twin Terrors: | 3.00 |
| | Bob Allison, H. Killebrew | |
| 335 | Bob Veale | .50 |
| 336 | Joe Azcue | .50 |
| 337 | Joe Morgan | 5.00 |
| 338 | Bob Locker | .50 |
| 339 | Chico Ruiz | .50 |
| 340 | Joe Pepitone | .75 |
| 341 | Giants Rookies: | .75 |
| | Dick Dietz, Bill Sorrell | |
| 342 | Hank Fischer | .50 |
| 343 | Tom Satriano | .50 |
| 344 | Ossie Chavarria | .50 |
| 345 | Stu Miller | .50 |
| 346 | Jim Hickman | .50 |
| 347 | Grady Hatton (Mgr.) | .50 |
| 348 | Tug McGraw | 1.00 |
| 349 | Bob Chance | .50 |
| 350 | Joe Torre | 1.00 |
| 351 | Vern Law | .50 |
| 352 | Ray Oyler | .50 |
| 353 | Bill McCool | .50 |
| 354 | Cubs Team | 1.00 |
| 355 | Carl Yastrzemski | 70.00 |
| 356 | Larry Jaster | .50 |
| 357 | Bill Skowron | .75 |
| 358 | Ruben Amaro | .50 |
| 359 | Dick Ellsworth | .50 |
| 360 | Leon Wagner | .50 |
| 361 | Checklist No. 5 | 1.50 |
| 362 | Darold Knowles | .50 |
| 363 | Dave Johnson | 1.00 |
| 364 | Claude Raymond | .50 |
| 365 | John Roseboro | .50 |
| 366 | Andy Kosco | .50 |
| 367 | Angels Rookies: | .50 |
| | Bill Kelso, Don Wallace | |
| 368 | Jack Hiatt | .50 |
| 369 | Jim Hunter | 6.00 |
| 370 | Tommy Davis | .60 |
| 371 | Jim Lonborg | 1.00 |
| 372 | Mike De La Hoz | .75 |
| 373 | White Sox Rookies: | .75 |
| | D. Josephson, F. Klages | |
| 374 | Mel Queen | .75 |
| 375 | Jake Gibbs | .75 |
| 376 | Don Lock | .75 |
| 377 | Luis Tiant | 1.50 |
| 378 | Tigers Team | 1.50 |
| 379 | Jerry May | .75 |
| 380 | Dean Chance | .75 |
| 381 | Dick Schofield | .75 |
| 382 | Dave McNally | 1.00 |
| 383 | Ken Henderson | .75 |
| 384 | Cardinals Rookies: | .75 |
| | Dick Hughes, Jim Cosman | |
| 385 | Jim Fregosi | 1.00 |
| 386 | Dick Selma | .75 |
| 387 | Cap Peterson | .75 |
| 388 | Arnold Earley | .75 |
| 389 | Al Dark (Mgr.) | 1.00 |
| 390 | Jim Wynn | .75 |
| 391 | Wilbur Wood | .75 |
| 392 | Tommy Harper | .75 |
| 393 | Jim Bouton | 1.50 |
| 394 | Jake Wood | .75 |
| 395 | Chris Short | .75 |
| 396 | Atlanta Aces: | .75 |
| | D. Meke, T. Cloninge | |
| 397 | Willie Smith | .75 |
| 398 | Jeff Torborg | 1.00 |
| 399 | Al Worthington | .75 |
| 400 | Bob Clemente | 30.00 |
| 401 | Jim Coates | .75 |
| 402 | Phillies Rookies: | 1.00 |
| | Grant Jackson, Billy Wilson | |
| 403 | Dick Nen | .75 |
| 404 | Nelson Briles | .75 |
| 405 | Russ Snyder | .75 |
| 406 | Lee Elia | .75 |
| 407 | Reds Team | 1.25 |
| 408 | Jim Northrup | .75 |
| 409 | Ray Sadecki | .75 |
| 410 | Lou Johnson | .75 |
| 411 | Dick Howser | 1.25 |
| 412 | Astros Rookies: | 1.00 |
| | Norm Miller, Doug Rader | |
| 413 | Jerry Grote | .75 |
| 414 | Casey Cox | .75 |
| 415 | Sonny Jackson | .75 |
| 416 | Roger Repoz | .75 |
| 417 | Bob Bruce | .75 |
| 418 | Sam Mele (Mgr.) | .75 |
| 419 | Don Kessinger | .75 |
| 420 | Denny McLain | 2.00 |
| 421 | Dal Maxvill | .75 |
| 422 | Hoyt Wilhelm | 5.00 |
| 423 | Fence Busters | 8.00 |
| | Willie Mays, Willie McCovey | |
| 424 | Pedro Gonzalez | .75 |
| 425 | Pete Mikkelsen | .75 |
| 426 | Lou Clinton | .75 |
| 427 | Ruben Gomez | .75 |
| 428 | Dodgers Rookies: | 1.00 |
| | Tom Hutton, Gene Michael | |
| 429 | Garry Roggenburk | .75 |
| 430 | Pete Rose | 70.00 |
| 431 | Ted Uhlaender | .75 |
| 432 | Jimmie Hall | .75 |
| 433 | Al Luplow | .75 |
| 434 | Eddie Fisher | .75 |
| 435 | Mack Jones | .75 |
| 436 | Pete Ward | .75 |
| 437 | Senators Team | 1.00 |
| 438 | Chuck Dobson | .75 |
| 439 | Byron Browne | .75 |
| 440 | Steve Hargan | .75 |
| 441 | Jim Davenport | .75 |
| 442 | Yankees Rookies: | 1.00 |
| | Bill Robinson, Joe Verbanic | |
| 443 | Tito Francona | .75 |
| 444 | George Smith | .75 |
| 445 | Don Sutton | 10.00 |
| 446 | Russ Nixon | .75 |
| 447 | Bo Belinsky | .75 |
| 448 | Harry Walker (Mgr.) | .75 |
| 449 | Orlando Pena | .75 |
| 450 | Richie Allen | 2.00 |
| 451 | Fred Newman | .75 |
| 452 | Ed Kranepool | 1.00 |
| 453 | Aurelio Monteagudo | .75 |
| 454 | Checklist No. 6 | 2.50 |
| 455 | Tommy Agee | .75 |
| 456 | Phil Niekro | 6.00 |
| 457 | Andy Etchebarren | .75 |
| 458 | Lee Thomas | 1.50 |
| 459 | Senators Rookies: | 1.50 |
| | Dick Bosman, Pete Craig | |
| 460 | Harmon Killebrew | 18.00 |
| 461 | Bob Miller | 1.50 |
| 462 | Bob Barton | 1.50 |
| 463 | Hill Aces: | 1.50 |
| | Sam McDowell, S. Siebert | |
| 464 | Dan Coombs | 1.50 |
| 465 | Willie Horton | 1.50 |
| 466 | Bobby Wine | 1.50 |
| 467 | Jim O'Toole | 1.50 |
| 468 | Ralph Houk (Mgr.) | 2.00 |
| 469 | Len Gabrielson | 1.50 |
| 470 | Bob Shaw | 1.50 |
| 471 | Rene Lachemann | 1.50 |
| 472 | Rookies Pirates: | 1.50 |
| | John Gelnar, G. Spriggs | |
| 473 | Jose Santiago | 1.50 |
| 474 | Bob Tolan | 1.50 |
| 475 | Jim Palmer | 25.00 |
| 476 | Tony Perez | 30.00 |
| 477 | Braves Team | 2.50 |
| 478 | Bob Humphreys | 1.50 |
| 479 | Gary Bell | 1.50 |
| 480 | Willie McCovey | 13.00 |
| 481 | Leo Durocher (Mgr.) | 2.00 |
| 482 | Bill Monbouquette | 1.50 |
| 483 | Jim Landis | 1.50 |
| 484 | Jerry Adair | 1.50 |
| 485 | Tim McCarver | 2.00 |
| 486 | Twins Rookies: | 1.50 |
| | Rich Reese, Bill Whitby | |
| 487 | Tom Reynolds | 1.50 |
| 488 | Gerry Arrigo | 1.50 |
| 489 | Doug Clemens | 1.50 |
| 490 | Tony Cloninger | 1.50 |
| 491 | Sam Bowens | 1.50 |
| 492 | Pirates Team | 2.50 |
| 493 | Phil Ortega | 1.50 |
| 494 | Bill Rigney (Mgr.) | 1.50 |
| 495 | Fritz Peterson | 1.50 |
| 496 | Orlando McFarlane | 1.50 |
| 497 | Ron Campbell | 1.50 |
| 498 | Larry Dierker | 1.50 |
| 499 | Indians Rookies: | 1.50 |
| | George Culver, Jose Vidal | |
| 500 | Juan Marichal | 10.00 |
| 501 | Jerry Zimmerman | 1.50 |
| 502 | Derrell Griffith | 1.50 |
| 503 | Dodgers Team | 3.00 |
| 504 | Orlando Martinez | 1.50 |
| 505 | Tommy Helms | 1.50 |
| 506 | Smoky Burgess | 1.50 |
| 507 | Orioles Rookies: | 1.50 |
| | Ed Barnowski, Larry Haney | |
| 508 | Dick Hall | 1.50 |
| 509 | Jim King | 1.50 |
| 510 | Bill Mazeroski | 2.00 |
| 511 | Don Wert | 1.50 |
| 512 | R. Schoendienst (Mgr.) | 2.00 |
| 513 | Marcelino Lopez | 1.50 |
| 514 | John Werhas | 1.50 |
| 515 | Bert Campaneris | 2.00 |
| 516 | Giants Team | 2.50 |
| 517 | Fred Talbot | 1.50 |
| 518 | Denis Menke | 1.50 |
| 519 | Ted Davidson | 1.50 |
| 520 | Max Alvis | 1.50 |
| 521 | Bird Bombers: | 2.00 |
| | Boog Powell, Curt Blefary | |
| 522 | John Stephenson | 1.50 |
| 523 | Jim Merritt | 1.50 |
| 524 | Felix Mantilla | 1.50 |
| 525 | Ron Hunt | 1.50 |
| 526 | Tigers Rookies: | 2.50 |
| | Pat Dobson, G. Korince | |
| 527 | Dennis Ribant | 1.50 |
| 528 | Rico Petrocelli | 2.00 |
| 529 | Gary Wagner | 1.50 |
| 530 | Felipe Alou | 2.00 |
| 531 | Checklist No. 7 | 4.00 |

**Prices for the 1967 set are for cards in *Mint* condition. *Excellent* copies sell for 50% of prices shown; *Very Good*—30%.**

| NO. PLAYER | MINT | NO. PLAYER | MINT | NO. PLAYER | MINT | NO. PLAYER | MINT |
|---|---|---|---|---|---|---|---|
| 532 Jim Hicks | 1.50 | 552 Ted Savage | 4.00 | 571 Larry Sherry | 4.00 | 591 Ty Cline | 4.00 |
| 533 Jack Fisher | 1.50 | 553 Yankees Rookies: | 8.00 | 572 Don Demeter | 4.00 | 592 NL Rookies: | 4.00 |
| 534 Hank Bauer (Mgr.) | 5.00 | Mike Hegan, Thad Tillotson | | 573 White Sox Team | 9.00 | Jim Shellenback, Ron Willis | |
| 535 Donn Clendenon | 5.00 | 554 Andre Rodgers | 4.00 | 574 Jerry Buchek | 4.00 | 593 Wes Westrum (Mgr.) | 4.00 |
| 536 Cubs Rookies: | 11.00 | 555 Don Cardwell | 4.00 | 575 Dave Boswell | 4.00 | 594 Dan Osinski | 4.00 |
| Joe Niekro, Paul Popovich | | 556 Al Weis | 4.00 | 576 NL Rookies: | 4.00 | 595 Cookie Rojas | 4.00 |
| 537 Chuck Estrada | 5.00 | 557 Al Ferrara | 4.00 | R. Hernandez, Norm Gigon | | 596 Galen Cisco | 4.00 |
| 538 J.C. Martin | 5.00 | 558 Orioles Rookies: | 10.00 | 577 Bill Short | 4.00 | 597 Ted Abernathy | 4.00 |
| 539 Dick Egan | 5.00 | Mark Belanger, Bill Dillman | | 578 John Boccabella | 4.00 | 598 White Sox Rookies: | 4.00 |
| 540 Norm Cash | 14.00 | 559 Dick Tracewski | 4.00 | 579 Bill Henry | 4.00 | Ed Stroud, Walt Williams | |
| 541 Joe Gibbon | 4.00 | 560 Jim Bunning | 27.00 | 580 Rocky Colavito | 18.00 | 599 Bob Duliba (Mgr.) | 4.00 |
| 542 Athletics Rookies: | 5.00 | 561 Sandy Alomar | 4.00 | 581 Mets Rookies: | 400.00 | 600 Brooks Robinson | 160.00 |
| Tony Pierce, Rick Monday | | 562 Steve Blass | 4.00 | Bill Denehy, Tom Seaver | | 601 Bill Bryan | 4.00 |
| 543 Dan Schneider | 4.00 | 563 Joe Adcock (Mgr.) | 10.00 | 582 Jim Owens | 4.00 | 602 Juan Pizarro | 4.00 |
| 544 Indians Team | 8.00 | 564 Astros Rookies: | 4.00 | 583 Ray Barker | 4.00 | 603 Athletics Rookies: | 4.00 |
| 545 Jim Grant | 4.00 | Alonzo Harris, A. Pointer | | 584 Jim Piersall | 15.00 | Tim Talton, Ramon Webster | |
| 546 Woody Woodward | 4.00 | 565 Lew Krausse | 4.00 | 585 Wally Bunker | 4.00 | 604 Red Sox Team | 25.00 |
| 547 Red Sox Rookies: | 4.00 | 566 Gary Geiger | 4.00 | 586 Manny Jimenez | 4.00 | 605 Mike Shannon | 10.00 |
| Russ Gibson, Bill Rohr | | 567 Steve Hamilton | 4.00 | 587 NL Rookies: | 4.00 | 606 Ron Taylor | 4.00 |
| 548 Tony Gonzalez | 4.00 | 568 John Sullivan | 4.00 | Don Shaw, Gary Sutherland | | 607 Mickey Stanley | 4.00 |
| 549 Jack Sanford | 4.00 | 569 AL Rookies: | 160.00 | 588 Johnny Klippstein | 4.00 | 608 Cubs Rookies: | 4.00 |
| 550 Vada Pinson | 5.00 | Rod Carew, Hank Allen | | 589 Dave Ricketts | 4.00 | John Upham, Rich Nye | |
| 551 Doug Camilli | 4.00 | 570 Maury Wills | 70.00 | 590 Pete Richert | 4.00 | 609 Tommy John (Exc. $15.00) | 65.00 |

# 1968 Topps . . . Complete Set of 598 Cards—Value $550.00 (Exc.); $1400.00 (Mint)

Features the rookie cards of Johnny Bench and Nolan Ryan. High numbers are 534 to 598. Card 66 exists with "Senators" in *white*—worth $.35 and "Senators" in *yellow*—worth $30.00. Card 518 (checklist) exists identifying card 539 as "Maj. L. Rookies"—worth $2.00 or "Am. L. Rookies"—worth $6.00.

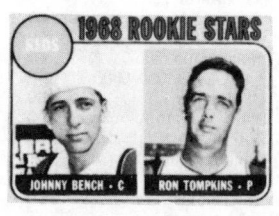

| NO. PLAYER | MINT | NO. PLAYER | MINT | NO. PLAYER | MINT | NO. PLAYER | MINT |
|---|---|---|---|---|---|---|---|
| 1 NL Ldrs. (Exc. $1.25) | 5.00 | 13 Chuck Hartenstein | .35 | 47 Ralph Houk (Mgr.) | .60 | 81 Larry Jackson | .35 |
| Bob Clemente, Matty Alou, Tony Gonzalez | | 14 Jerry McNertney | .35 | 48 Ted Davidson | .35 | 82 Sam Bowens | .35 |
| 2 AL Batting Leaders: | 2.50 | 15 Ron Hunt | .35 | 49 Ed Brinkman | .35 | 83 John Stephenson | .35 |
| Frank Robinson, Al Kaline, Carl Yastrzemski | | 16 Indians Rookies: | 2.00 | 50 Willy Mays | 25.00 | 84 Bob Tolan | .35 |
| 3 NL RBI Leaders: | 2.50 | Lou Piniella, R. Schienblum | | 51 Bob Locker | .35 | 85 Gaylord Perry | 4.00 |
| Hank Aaron, O. Cepeda, Bob Clemente | | 17 Dick Hall | .35 | 52 Hawk Taylor | .35 | 86 Willie Stargell | 6.00 |
| 4 AL RBI Leaders: | 2.50 | 18 Mike Hershberger | .35 | 53 Gene Alley | .35 | 87 Dick Williams (Mgr.) | .50 |
| C. Yastrzemski, H. Killebrew, F. Robinson | | 19 Juan Pizzaro | .35 | 54 Stan Williams | .35 | 88 Phil Regan | .35 |
| 5 NL Home Run Leaders: | 2.50 | 20 Brooks Robinson | 8.00 | 55 Felipe Alou | .50 | 89 Jake Gibbs | .35 |
| Ron Santo, Hank Aaron, Jim Wynn, Willie McCovey | | 21 Ron Davis | .35 | 56 Orioles Rookies: | .45 | 90 Vada Pinson | .75 |
| 6 AL Home Run Leaders: | 2.50 | 22 Pat Dobson | .45 | Dave May, Dave Leonhard | | 91 Jim Ollom | .35 |
| C. Yastrzemski, H. Killebrew, F. Howard | | 23 Chico Cardenas | .35 | 57 Dan Schneider | .35 | 92 Ed Kranepool | .35 |
| 7 NL ERA Leaders: | 1.25 | 24 Bobby Locke | .35 | 58 Ed Mathews | 5.00 | 93 Tony Cloninger | .35 |
| Jim Bunning, Chris Short, Phil Niekro | | 25 Jan Javier | .35 | 59 Don Lock | .35 | 94 Lee Maye | .35 |
| 8 AL ERA Leaders: | 1.25 | 26 Darrell Brandon | .35 | 60 Ken Holtzman | .40 | 95 Bob Aspromonte | .35 |
| Joe Horlen, Sonny Siebert, Gary Peters | | 27 Gil Hodges (Mgr.) | 3.00 | 61 Reggie Smith | 1.00 | 96 Senator Rookies: | .35 |
| 9 NL Pitching Leaders: | 1.25 | 28 Ted Uhlaender | .35 | 62 Chuck Dobson | .35 | Frank Coggins, Dick Nold | |
| C. Osteen, M. McCormick, F. Jenkins, J. Bunning | | 29 Joe Verbanic | .35 | 63 Dick Kenworthy | .35 | 97 Tom Phoebus | .35 |
| 10 AL Pitching Leaders: | 1.25 | 30 Joe Torre | 1.00 | 64 Jim Merritt | .35 | 98 Gary Sutherland | .35 |
| Jim Lonborg, Earl Wilson, Dean Chance | | 31 Ed Stroud | .35 | 65 John Roseboro | .35 | 99 Rocky Colavito | 1.00 |
| 11 NL Strikeout Leaders: | 1.25 | 32 Joe Gibbon | .35 | 66 Casey Cox* | .35 | 100 Bob Gibson | 7.50 |
| Ferguson Jenkins, Gaylord Perry, Jim Bunning | | 33 Pete Ward | .35 | 67 Checklist No. 1 | 2.50 | 101 Glenn Beckert | .35 |
| 12 AL Strikeout Leaders: | 1.25 | 34 Al Ferrara | .35 | 68 Ron Willis | .35 | 102 Jose Cardenal | .35 |
| Jim Lonborg, Dean Chance, Sam McDowell | | 35 Steve Hargan | .35 | 69 Tom Tresh | .60 | 103 Don Sutton | 4.00 |
| | | 36 Pirates Rookies: | .50 | 70 Bob Veale | .50 | 104 Dick Dietz | .35 |
| | | Bob Moose, B. Robertson | | 71 Vern Fuller | .35 | 105 Al Downing | .50 |
| | | 37 Billy Williams | 5.00 | 72 Tommy John | 3.00 | 106 Dalton Jones | .35 |
| | | 38 Tony Pierce | .35 | 73 Jim Hart | .35 | 107 Checklist No. 2 | 2.50 |
| | | 39 Cookie Rojas | .35 | 74 Milt Pappas | .50 | 108 Don Pavletich | .35 |
| | | 40 Denny McLain | 2.50 | 75 Don Mincher | .35 | 109 Bert Campaneris | .35 |
| | | 41 Julio Gotay | .35 | 76 Braves Rookies: | .50 | 110 Hank Aaron | 25.00 |
| | | 42 Larry Haney | .35 | Jim Britton, Ron Reed | | 111 Rich Reese | .35 |
| | | 43 Gary Bell | .35 | 77 Don Wilson | .35 | 112 Woody Fryman | .35 |
| | | 44 Frank Kostro | .35 | 78 Jim Northrup | .50 | 113 Tigers Rookies: | .35 |
| | | 45 Tom Seaver | 65.00 | 79 Ted Kubiak | .35 | T. Matchick, D. Patterson | |
| | | 46 Dave Ricketts | .35 | 80 Rod Carew | 30.00 | 114 Ron Swoboda | .60 |

| NO. | PLAYER | MINT |
|---|---|---|
| 115 | Sam McDowell | .60 |
| 116 | Ken McMullen | .35 |
| 117 | Larry Jaster | .35 |
| 118 | Mark Belanger | .75 |
| 119 | Ted Savage | .35 |
| 120 | Mel Stottlemyre | 1.00 |
| 121 | Jimmie Hall | .35 |
| 122 | Gene Mauch (Mgr.) | .50 |
| 123 | Jose Santiago | .35 |
| 124 | Nate Oliver | .35 |
| 125 | Joe Horlen | .35 |
| 126 | Bobby Etheridge | .35 |
| 127 | Paul Lindblad | .35 |
| 128 | Astros Rookies: | .35 |
| | Alonzo Harris, Tom Dukes | |
| 129 | Mickey Stanley | .35 |
| 130 | Tony Perez | 3.50 |
| 131 | Frank Bertaina | .35 |
| 132 | Bud Harrelson | .35 |
| 133 | Fred Whitfield | .35 |
| 134 | Pat Jarvis | .35 |
| 135 | Paul Blair | .35 |
| 136 | Randy Hundley | .35 |
| 137 | Minnesota Twins | 1.00 |
| 138 | Ruben Amaro | .35 |
| 139 | Chris Short | .35 |
| 140 | Tony Conigliaro | 1.00 |
| 141 | Dal Maxvill | .35 |
| 142 | White Sox Rookies: | .35 |
| | Bill Voss, B. Bradford | |
| 143 | Pete Cimino | .35 |
| 144 | Joe Morgan | 4.00 |
| 145 | Don Drysdale | 5.00 |
| 146 | Sal Bando | 1.00 |
| 147 | Frank Linzy | .35 |
| 148 | Dave Bristol (Mgr.) | .35 |
| 149 | Bob Saverine | .35 |
| 150 | Bob Clemente | 20.00 |
| 151 | World Series Game 1: | 3.00 |
| | Brock Socks 4 Hits | |
| 152 | World Series Game 2: | 3.00 |
| | Yaz Smashes 2 Homers | |
| 153 | World Series Game 3: | 1.50 |
| | Briles Cools Off Boston | |
| 154 | World Series Game 4: | 3.00 |
| | Gibson Hurls Shutout | |
| 155 | World Series Game 5: | 1.50 |
| | Lonborg Wins Again | |
| 156 | World Series Game 6: | 1.50 |
| | Petrocelli 2 Homers | |
| 157 | World Series Game 7: | 1.50 |
| | St. Louis Wins It | |
| 158 | World Series: | 1.50 |
| | The Cardinal Celebrate | |
| 159 | Don Kessinger | .60 |
| 160 | Earl Wilson | .35 |
| 161 | Norm Miller | .35 |
| 162 | Cardinals Rookies: | 1.00 |
| | Hal Gilson, Mike Torrez | |
| 163 | Gene Brabender | .35 |
| 164 | Ramon Webster | .35 |
| 165 | Tony Oliva | 2.00 |
| 166 | Claude Raymond | .35 |
| 167 | Elston Howard | 1.50 |
| 168 | Los Angeles Dodgers | 1.50 |
| 169 | Bob Bolin | .35 |
| 170 | Jim Fregosi | .75 |
| 171 | Don Nottebart | .35 |
| 172 | Walt Williams | .35 |
| 173 | John Boozer | .35 |
| 174 | Bob Tillman | .35 |
| 175 | Maury Wills | 2.00 |
| 176 | Bob Allen | .35 |
| 177 | Mets Rookies: | 160.00 |
| | J. Koosman, Nolan Ryan | |
| 178 | Don Wert | .35 |
| 179 | Bill Stoneman | .35 |
| 180 | Curt Flood | 1.00 |
| 181 | Jerry Zimmerman | .35 |
| 182 | Dave Guisti | .35 |
| 183 | Bob Kennedy | .35 |
| 184 | Lou Johnson | .35 |
| 185 | Tom Haller | .35 |
| 186 | Eddie Watt | .35 |
| 187 | Sonny Jackson | .35 |
| 188 | Cap Peterson | .35 |
| 189 | Bill Landis | .35 |
| 190 | Bill White | .75 |
| 191 | Dan Frisella | .35 |
| 192 | Checklist No. 3 | 2.50 |
| 193 | Jack Hamilton | .35 |
| 194 | Don Buford | .35 |
| 195 | Joe Pepitone | 1.00 |
| 196 | Gary Nolan | .35 |
| 197 | Larry Brown | .35 |
| 198 | Roy Face | .75 |
| 199 | A's Rookies: | .40 |
| | R. Rodriguez, D. Osteen | |
| 200 | Orlando Cepeda | 2.50 |
| 201 | Mike Marshall (R) | 1.00 |
| 202 | Adolfo Phillips | .35 |
| 203 | Dick Kelley | .35 |
| 204 | Andy Etchebarren | .35 |
| 205 | Juan Marichal | 4.00 |
| 206 | Cal Ermer | .35 |
| 207 | Carroll Sembera | .35 |
| 208 | Willie Davis | .75 |
| 209 | Tim Cullen | .35 |
| 210 | Gary Peters | .35 |
| 211 | J.C. Martin | .35 |
| 212 | Dave Morehead | .35 |
| 213 | Chico Ruiz | .35 |
| 214 | Yankees Rookies: | 1.00 |
| | S. Bahnsen, F. Fernandez | |
| 215 | Jim Bunning | 2.50 |
| 216 | Bubba Morton | .35 |
| 217 | Turk Farrell | .35 |
| 218 | Ken Suarez | .35 |
| 219 | Rob Gardner | .35 |
| 220 | Harmon Killebrew | 6.00 |
| 221 | Atlanta Braves | .75 |
| 222 | Jim Hardin | .35 |
| 223 | Ollie Brown | .35 |
| 224 | Jack Aker | .35 |
| 225 | Richie Allen | 1.50 |
| 226 | Jimmie Price | .35 |
| 227 | Joe Hoerner | .35 |
| 228 | Dodgers Rookies: | .50 |
| | Jack Billingham, Jim Fairey | |
| 229 | Fred Klages | .35 |
| 230 | Pete Rose | 45.00 |
| 231 | Dave Baldwin | .35 |
| 232 | Denis Menke | .35 |
| 233 | George Scott | .60 |
| 234 | Bill Monbouquette | .35 |
| 235 | Ron Santo | .75 |
| 236 | Tug McGraw | 1.00 |
| 237 | Alvin Dark (Mgr.) | .50 |
| 238 | Tom Satriano | .35 |
| 239 | Bill Henry | .35 |
| 240 | Al Kaline | 10.00 |
| 241 | Felix Millan | .35 |
| 242 | Moe Drabowsky | .35 |
| 243 | Rich Rollins | .35 |
| 244 | John Donaldson | .35 |
| 245 | Tony Gonzalez | .35 |
| 246 | Fritz Peterson | .35 |
| 247 | Reds Rookies: | 150.00 |
| | Johnny Bench, R. Tompkins | |
| 248 | Fred Valentine | .35 |
| 249 | Bill Singer | .35 |
| 250 | Carl Yastrzemski | 20.00 |
| 251 | Manny Sanguillen (R) | 1.25 |
| 252 | Angels Team | .75 |
| 253 | Dick Hughes | .35 |
| 254 | Cleon Jones | .35 |
| 255 | Dean Chance | .35 |
| 256 | Norm Cash | 1.00 |
| 257 | Phil Niekro | 4.00 |
| 258 | Cubs Rookies: | .50 |
| | J. Arcia, B. Schlesinger | |
| 259 | Ken Boyer | 1.00 |
| 260 | Jim Wynn | .75 |
| 261 | Dave Duncan | .35 |
| 262 | Rick Wise | .35 |
| 263 | Horace Clarke | .60 |
| 264 | Ted Abernathy | .35 |
| 265 | Tommy Davis | .75 |
| 266 | Paul Popovich | .35 |
| 267 | Herman Franks (Mgr.) | .35 |
| 268 | Bob Humphreys | .35 |
| 269 | Bob Tiefenauer | .35 |
| 270 | Matty Alou | .75 |
| 271 | Bobby Knoop | .35 |
| 272 | Ray Culp | .35 |
| 273 | Dave Johnson | 1.00 |
| 274 | Mike Cuellar | .60 |
| 275 | Tim McCarver | 1.00 |
| 276 | Jim Roland | .35 |
| 277 | Jerry Buchek | .35 |
| 278 | Checklist No. 4 | 2.50 |
| 279 | Bill Hands | .35 |
| 280 | Mickey Mantle | 160.00 |
| 281 | Jim Campanis | .35 |
| 282 | Rick Monday | 1.00 |
| 283 | Mel Queen | .35 |
| 284 | John Briggs | .35 |
| 285 | Dick McAuliffe | .35 |
| 286 | Cecil Upshaw | .35 |
| 287 | White Sox Rookies: | .50 |
| | Mickey Abarbanel, Cisco Carlos | |
| 288 | Dave Wickersham | .35 |
| 289 | Woody Held | .35 |
| 290 | Willie McCovey | 7.50 |
| 291 | Dick Lines | .35 |
| 292 | Art Shamsky | .35 |
| 293 | Bruce Howard | .35 |
| 294 | Red Schoendienst | 1.00 |
| 295 | Sonny Siebert | .35 |
| 296 | Byron Browne | .35 |
| 297 | Russ Gibson | .35 |
| 298 | Jim Brewer | .35 |
| 299 | Gene Michael | .75 |
| 300 | Rusty Staub | 1.00 |
| 301 | Twins Rookies: | .50 |
| | G. Mitterwald, R. Renick | |
| 302 | Gerry Arrigo | .35 |
| 303 | Dick Green | .35 |
| 304 | Sandy Valdespino | .35 |
| 305 | Minnie Rojas | .35 |
| 306 | Mike Ryan | .35 |
| 307 | John Hiller | .50 |
| 308 | Pittsburgh Pirates | 1.00 |
| 309 | Ken Henderson | .35 |
| 310 | Luis Aparicio | 4.00 |
| 311 | Jack Lamabe | .35 |
| 312 | Curt Blefary | .35 |
| 313 | Al Weis | .35 |
| 314 | Red Sox Rookies: | .35 |
| | Bill Rohr, George Spriggs | |
| 315 | Zoilo Versalles | .35 |
| 316 | Steve Barber | .35 |
| 317 | Ron Brand | .35 |
| 318 | Chico Salmon | .35 |
| 319 | George Culver | .35 |
| 320 | Frank Howard | 1.00 |
| 321 | Leo Durocher (Mgr.) | 1.25 |
| 322 | Dave Boswell | .35 |
| 323 | Deron Johnson | .35 |
| 324 | Jim Nash | .35 |
| 325 | Manny Mota | .75 |
| 326 | Denny Ribant | .35 |
| 327 | Tony Taylor | .35 |
| 328 | Angels Rookies: | .35 |
| | Chuck Vinson, Jim Weaver | |
| 329 | Duane Josephson | .35 |
| 330 | Roger Maris | 12.00 |
| 331 | Dan Osinski | .35 |
| 332 | Doug Rader | .35 |
| 333 | Ron Herbel | .35 |
| 334 | Baltimore Orioles | 1.00 |
| 335 | Bob Allison | .35 |
| 336 | John Purdin | .35 |
| 337 | Bill Robinson | .35 |
| 338 | Bob Johnson | .35 |
| 339 | Rich Nye | .35 |
| 340 | Max Alvis | .35 |
| 341 | Jim Lemon (Mgr.) | .35 |
| 342 | Ken Johnson | .35 |
| 343 | Jim Gosger | .35 |
| 344 | Don Clendenon | .50 |
| 345 | Bob Hendley | .35 |
| 346 | Jerry Adair | .35 |
| 347 | George Brunet | .35 |
| 348 | Phillies Rookies: | .35 |
| | Larry Colton, Dick Thoenen | |
| 349 | Ed Spiezio | .35 |
| 350 | Hoyt Wilhelm | 4.00 |
| 351 | Bob Barton | .35 |
| 352 | Jackie Hernandez | .35 |
| 353 | Mack Jones | .35 |
| 354 | Pete Richert | .35 |
| 355 | Ernie Banks | 7.50 |
| 356 | Checklist No. 5 | 2.50 |
| 357 | Len Gabrielson | .35 |
| 358 | Mike Epstein | .35 |
| 359 | Joe Moeller | .35 |
| 360 | Willie Horton | .75 |
| 361 | Harmon Killebrew (AS) | 3.50 |
| 362 | Orlando Cepeda (AS) | 2.00 |
| 363 | Rod Carew (AS) | 6.00 |
| 364 | Joe Morgan (AS) | 3.00 |
| 365 | Brooks Robinson (AS) | 4.00 |
| 366 | Ron Santo (AS) | 1.25 |
| 367 | Jim Fregosi (AS) | .75 |
| 368 | Gene Alley (AS) | .75 |
| 369 | Carl Yastrzemski (AS) | 6.00 |
| 370 | Hank Aaron (AS) | 7.00 |
| 371 | Tony Oliva (AS) | 1.50 |
| 372 | Lou Brock (AS) | 4.00 |
| 373 | Frank Robinson (AS) | 4.00 |
| 374 | Bob Clemente (AS) | 6.00 |
| 375 | Bill Freehan (AS) | .75 |
| 376 | Tim McCarver (AS) | 1.50 |
| 377 | Joe Horlen (AS) | .75 |
| 378 | Bob Gibson (AS) | 5.00 |
| 379 | Gary Peters (AS) | .75 |
| 380 | Ken Holtzman (AS) | .75 |
| 381 | Boog Powell | 1.50 |
| 382 | Ramon Hernandez | .50 |
| 383 | Steve Whitaker | .50 |
| 384 | Reds Rookies: | 3.00 |
| | Bill Henry, Hal McRae | |
| 385 | Jim Hunter | 4.00 |
| 386 | Greg Goossen | .35 |
| 387 | Joe Foy | .35 |
| 388 | Ray Washburn | .35 |
| 389 | Jay Johnstone | .50 |
| 390 | Bill Mazeroski | 1.25 |
| 391 | Bob Priddy | .35 |
| 392 | Grady Hatton (Mgr.) | .35 |
| 393 | Jim Perry | .75 |
| 394 | Tommie Aaron | .60 |
| 395 | Camilo Pascual | .60 |
| 396 | Bobby Wine | .35 |
| 397 | Vic Davalillo | .50 |
| 398 | Jim Grant | .35 |
| 399 | Ray Oyler | .35 |
| 400 | Mike McCormick | .35 |
| 401 | New York Mets | 1.50 |
| 402 | Mike Hegan | .35 |
| 403 | John Buzhardt | .35 |
| 404 | Floyd Robinson | .35 |
| 405 | Tommy Helms | .35 |
| 406 | Dick Ellsworth | .35 |
| 407 | Gary Kolb | .35 |
| 408 | Steve Carlton | .30.00 |
| 409 | Orioles Rookies: | .50 |
| | Frank Peters, Don Stone | |
| 410 | Ferguson Jenkins | 3.00 |
| 411 | Ron Hansen | .35 |
| 412 | Clay Carroll | .35 |
| 413 | Tommy McCraw | .35 |
| 414 | Mickey Lolich | 1.50 |
| 415 | Johnny Callison | .35 |
| 416 | Bill Rigney (Mgr.) | .35 |
| 417 | Willie Crawford | .35 |
| 418 | Eddie Fisher | .35 |
| 419 | Jack Hiatt | .35 |
| 420 | Cesar Tovar | .35 |
| 421 | Ron Taylor | .35 |
| 422 | Rene Lachemann | .35 |
| 423 | Fred Gladding | .35 |
| 424 | Chicago White Sox | 1.25 |
| 425 | Jim Maloney | .35 |
| 426 | Hank Allen | .35 |
| 427 | Dick Calmus | .35 |
| 428 | Vic Roznovsky | .35 |
| 429 | Tommie Sisk | .35 |

**Prices for the 1968 set are for cards in *Mint* condition. *Excellent* copies sell for 50% of prices shown; *Very Good*—30%.**

| NO. PLAYER | MINT | NO. PLAYER | MINT | NO. PLAYER | MINT | NO. PLAYER | MINT |
|---|---|---|---|---|---|---|---|
| 430 Rico Petrocelli | .75 | 474 Paul Schaal | .50 | 516 Pete Mikkelsen | .50 | 558 John Edwards | .50 |
| 431 Dooley Womack | .35 | 475 Joe Niekro | 1.25 | 517 Diego Segui | .50 | 559 Pirates Rookies: | .75 |
| 432 Indians Rookies: | .35 | 476 Woody Woodward | .50 | 518 Checklist No. 7* | 2.50 | Carl Taylor, Luke Walker | |
| Bill Davis, Jose Vidal | .50 | 477 Philadelphia Phillies | 1.00 | 519 Jerry Stephenson | .50 | 560 Paul Casanova | .50 |
| 433 Bob Rodgers | .35 | 478 Dave McNally | 1.00 | 520 Lou Brock | 8.00 | 561 Lee Elia | .50 |
| 434 Ricardo Joseph | .50 | 479 Phil Gagliano | .50 | 521 Don Shaw | .50 | 562 Jim Bouton | 1.00 |
| 435 Ron Perranoski | .60 | 480 Manager's Dream: | 7.50 | 522 Wayne Causey | .50 | 563 Ed Charles | .50 |
| 436 Hal Lanier | .35 | Tony Oliva, Chico | | 523 John Tsitouris | .50 | 564 Eddie Stanky | .50 |
| 437 Don Cardwell | .35 | Cardenas, Bob Clemente | | 524 Andy Kosco | .50 | 565 Larry Dierker | .50 |
| 438 Lee Thomas | .35 | 481 John Wyatt | .50 | 525 Jim Davenport | .50 | 566 Ken Harrelson | 1.25 |
| 439 Luman Harris (Mgr.) | .50 | 482 Jose Pagan | .50 | 526 Bill Denehy | .50 | 567 Clay Dalrymple | .50 |
| 440 Claude Osteen | .35 | 483 Darold Knowles | .50 | 527 Tito Francona | .50 | 568 Willie Smith | .50 |
| 441 Alex Johnson | .35 | 484 Phil Roof | .50 | 528 Detroit Tigers | 4.00 | 569 NL Rookies: | .50 |
| 442 Dick Bosman | .35 | 485 Ken Berry | .50 | 529 Bruce Von Hoff | .50 | Ivan Murrell, Les Rohr | |
| 443 Joe Azcue | .35 | 486 Cal Koonce | .50 | 530 Bird Belters: | 4.00 | 570 Rick Reichardt | .50 |
| 444 Jack Fisher | .50 | 487 Lee May | .75 | Frank Robinson, | | 571 Tony LaRussa | .75 |
| 445 Mike Shannon | .35 | 488 Dick Tracewski | .50 | Brooks Robinson | | 572 Don Bosch | .50 |
| 446 Ron Kline | .35 | 489 Wally Bunker | .50 | 531 Chuck Hinton | .50 | 573 Joe Coleman | .50 |
| 447 Tigers Rookies: | .35 | 490 Super Stars: | .30.00 | 532 Luis Tiant | 1.00 | 574 Cincinnati Reds | 1.50 |
| G. Korince, F. Lasher | | Harmon Killebrew, Willie | | 533 Wes Parker | .50 | 575 Jim Palmer | 11.00 |
| 448 Gary Wagner | .35 | Mays, Mickey Mantle | | 534 Bob Miller | .50 | 576 Dave Adlesh | .50 |
| 449 Gene Oliver | .35 | 491 Denny LeMaster | .50 | 535 Danny Cater | .50 | 577 Fred Talbot | .50 |
| 450 Jim Kaat | 2.50 | 492 Jeff Torborg | .50 | 536 Bill Short | .50 | 578 Orlando Martinez | .50 |
| 451 Al Spangler | .35 | 493 Jim McGlothlin | .50 | 537 Norm Siebern | .50 | 579 NL Rookies: | 1.00 |
| 452 Jesus Alou | .35 | 494 Ray Sadecki | .50 | 538 Manny Jimenez | .50 | Larry Hisle, Mike Lum | |
| 453 Sammy Ellis | .35 | 495 Leon Wagner | .50 | 539 Major League Rookies: | .65 | 580 Bob Bailey | .50 |
| 454 Checklist No. 6 | 2.50 | 496 Steve Hamilton | .50 | Jim Ray, Mike Ferraro | | 581 Garry Roggenburk | .50 |
| 455 Rico Carty | 1.00 | 497 St. Louis Cardinals | 2.00 | 540 Nelson Briles | .50 | 582 Jerry Grote | .50 |
| 456 John O'Donoghue | .35 | 498 Bill Bryan | .50 | 541 Sandy Alomar | .50 | 583 Gates Brown | .50 |
| 457 Jim Lefebvre | .50 | 499 Steve Blass | .50 | 542 John Boccabella | .50 | 584 Larry Shepard | .50 |
| 458 Lew Krausse | .50 | 500 Frank Robinson | 7.50 | 543 Bob Lee | .50 | 585 Wilbur Wood | .50 |
| 459 Dick Simpson | .50 | 501 John Odom | .50 | 544 Mayo Smith (Mgr.) | .50 | 586 Jim Pagliaroni | .50 |
| 460 Jim Lonborg | .75 | 502 Mike Andrews | .50 | 545 Lindy McDaniel | .50 | 587 Roger Repoz | .50 |
| 461 Chuck Hiller | .50 | 503 Al Jackson | .50 | 546 Roy White | 1.25 | 588 Dick Schofield | .50 |
| 462 Barry Moore | .50 | 504 Russ Snyder | .50 | 547 Dan Coombs | .50 | 589 Twins Rookies: | .50 |
| 463 Jimmie Schaffer | .50 | 505 Joe Sparma | .50 | 548 Bernie Allen | .50 | Ron Clark, Moe Ogier | |
| 464 Don McMahon | .50 | 506 Clarence Jones | .50 | 549 Orioles Rookies: | .50 | 590 Tommy Harper | .50 |
| 465 Tommie Agee | .50 | 507 Wade Blasingame | .50 | Curt Motton, Roger Nelson | | 591 Dick Nen | .50 |
| 466 Bill Dillman | .50 | 508 Duke Sims | .50 | 550 Clete Boyer | .75 | 592 John Bateman | .50 |
| 467 Dick Howser | .75 | 509 Dennis Higgins | .50 | 551 Darrell Sutherland | .50 | 593 Lee Stange | .50 |
| 468 Larry Sherry | .50 | 510 Ron Fairly | .50 | 552 Ed Kirkpatrick | .50 | 594 Phil Linz | .50 |
| 469 Ty Cline | .50 | 511 Bill Kelso | .50 | 553 Hank Aguirre | .50 | 595 Phil Ortega | .50 |
| 470 Bill Freehan | .60 | 512 Grant Jackson | .50 | 554 Oakland A's | 1.50 | 596 Charlie Smith | .50 |
| 471 Orlando Pena | 1.00 | 513 Hank Bauer (Mgr.) | .50 | 555 Jose Tartabull | .50 | 597 Bill McCool | .50 |
| 472 Walt Alston (Mgr.) | 1.50 | 514 Al McBean | .50 | 556 Dick Selma | .50 | 598 Jerry May (Exc. $.50) | 2.00 |
| 473 Al Worthington | .50 | 515 Russ Nixon | .50 | 557 Frank Quilici | .50 | | |

## 1969 Topps . . . Complete Set of 664 Cards—Value $550.00 (Exc.); $1250.00 (Mint)

Includes the rookie cards of Reggie Jackson, Al Oliver and Rollie Fingers. The high numbers are 513 to 664. The values listed for the 23 cards with an *asterisk* are with the player's entire name in *yellow* letters. These cards also exist with the player's name in *white* letters—worth $8.00 each, except card no. 440—$50.00, no. 485—$30.00 and no. 500—$350.00.

| NO. PLAYER | MINT | NO. PLAYER | MINT | NO. PLAYER | MINT | NO. PLAYER | MINT |
|---|---|---|---|---|---|---|---|
| 1 AL Bat Ldrs. (Exc. $1.50) | 5.00 | 4 NL RBI Leaders: | 1.00 | 7 AL ERA Leaders: | .75 | 10 NL Pitching Leaders: | 1.75 |
| Carl Yastrzemski, Tony | | Willie McCovey, Ron | | Luis Tiant, Sam | | Juan Marichal, Bob | |
| Oliva, Danny Cater | | Santo, Billy Williams | | McDowell, Dave McNally | | Gibson, Fergie Jenkins | |
| 2 NL Batting Leaders: | 2.00 | 5 AL Home Run Leaders: | 1.00 | 8 NL ERA Leaders: | 1.00 | 11 AL Strikeout Leaders: | .75 |
| Matty Alou, Felipe Alou, | | Frank Howard, Willie | | Bobby Bolin, Bob Gibson, | | Sam McDowell, Denny | |
| Pete Rose | | Horton, Ken Harrelson | | Bob Veale | | McLain, Luis Tiant | |
| 3 AL RBI Leaders: | 1.00 | 6 NL Home Run Leaders: | 1.75 | 9 AL Pitching Leaders: | .75 | 12 NL Strikeout Leaders: | 1.00 |
| Frank Howard, Ken | | Willie McCovey, Richie | | Mel Stottlemyre, Denny | | Bob Gibson, Fergie | |
| Harrelson, Jim Northrup | | Allen, Ernie Banks | | McLain, Dave McNally, | | Jenkins, Bill Singer | |
| | | | | Luis Tiant | | | |

| NO. PLAYER | MINT |
|---|---|
| 13 Mickey Stanley | .50 |
| 14 Al McBean | .35 |
| 15 Boog Powell | 1.50 |
| 16 Giants Rookies: | .50 |
| C. Gutierrez, R. Robertson | |
| 17 Mike Marshall | .75 |
| 18 Dick Schofield | .35 |
| 19 Ken Suarez | .35 |
| 20 Ernie Banks | 7.50 |
| 21 Jose Santiago | .35 |
| 22 Jesus Alou | .35 |
| 23 Lew Krause | .35 |
| 24 Walt Alston (Mgr.) | 1.25 |
| 25 Ray White | .75 |
| 26 Clay Carroll | .35 |
| 27 Bernie Allen | .35 |
| 28 Mike Ryan | .35 |
| 29 Dave Morehead | .35 |
| 30 Bob Allison | .35 |
| 31 Mets Rookies: | 1.50 |
| Gary Gentry, Amos Otis | |
| 32 Sammy Ellis | .35 |
| 33 Wayne Causey | .35 |
| 34 Gary Peters | .35 |
| 35 Joe Morgan | 3.50 |
| 36 Luke Walker | .35 |
| 37 Curt Motton | .35 |
| 38 Zoilo Versalles | .35 |
| 39 Dick Hughes | .35 |
| 40 Mayo Smith (Mgr.) | .35 |
| 41 Bob Barton | .35 |
| 42 Tommy Harper | .35 |
| 43 Joe Niekro | .75 |
| 44 Danny Cater | .35 |
| 45 Maury Wills | 1.50 |
| 46 Fritz Peterson | .35 |
| 47 Paul Popovich | .35 |
| (without "C" on helmet) | |
| 47 Paul Popovich | 8.00 |
| (with "C" on helmet) | |
| 48 Brant Alyea | .35 |
| 49 Royals Rookies | .35 |
| Steve Jones, E. Rodriguez | |
| 49 Royals Rookies | 8.00 |
| Error—name misspelled | |
| "Rodriquez" | |
| 50 Bob Clement | 18.00 |
| 51 Woody Fryman | .35 |
| 52 Mike Andrews | .35 |
| 53 Sonny Jackson | .35 |
| 54 Cisco Carlos | .35 |
| 55 Jerry Grote | .35 |
| 56 Rich Reese | .35 |
| 57 Checklist No. 1 | 2.00 |
| 58 Fred Gladding | .35 |
| 59 Jay Johnstone | .35 |
| 60 Nelson Briles | .35 |
| 61 Jimmie Hall | .35 |
| 62 Chico Salmon | .35 |
| 63 Jim Hickman | .35 |
| 64 Bill Monbouquette | .35 |
| 65 Willie Davis | .60 |
| 66 Orioles Rookies: | .50 |
| M. Adamson, M. Rettenmund | |
| 67 Bill Stoneman | .35 |
| 68 Dave Duncan | .35 |
| 69 Steve Hamilton | .35 |
| 70 Tommy Helms | .35 |
| 71 Steve Whitaker | .35 |
| 72 Ron Taylor | .35 |
| 73 Johnny Briggs | .35 |
| 74 Preston Gomez (Mgr.) | .35 |
| 75 Luis Aparicio | 4.00 |
| 76 Norm Miller | .35 |
| 77 Ron Perranoski | .35 |
| (no team logo on hat) | |
| 77 Ron Perranoski | 8.00 |
| (with team logo on hat) | |
| 78 Tom Satriano | .35 |
| 79 Milt Pappas | .35 |
| 80 Norm Cash | 1.00 |
| 81 Mel Queen | .35 |
| 82 Pirates Rookies: | 7.00 |
| Rich Hebner, Al Oliver | |
| 83 Mike Ferraro | .35 |

| NO. PLAYER | MINT |
|---|---|
| 84 Bob Humphreys | .35 |
| 85 Lou Brock | 7.00 |
| 86 Pete Richert | .35 |
| 87 Horace Clarke | .35 |
| 88 Rich Nye | .35 |
| 89 Russ Gibson | .35 |
| 90 Jerry Koosman | 1.00 |
| 91 Al Dark (Mgr.) | .50 |
| 92 Jack Billingham | .35 |
| 93 Joe Foy | .35 |
| 94 Hank Aguirre | .35 |
| 95 Johnny Bench | 45.00 |
| 96 Denver LeMaster | .35 |
| 97 Buddy Bradford | .35 |
| 98 Dave Giusti | .35 |
| 99 Twins Rookies: | 12.00 |
| Danny Morris, Graig Nettles | |
| 100 Hank Aaron | 24.00 |
| 101 Daryl Patterson | .35 |
| 102 Jim Davenport | .35 |
| 103 Roger Repoz | .35 |
| 104 Steve Blass | .35 |
| 105 Rick Monday | .35 |
| 106 Jim Hannan | .35 |
| 107 Checklist No.2 | 1.50 |
| (error—#161 Jim Purdin) | |
| 107 Checklist No.2 | 5.00 |
| (correct—#161 John Purdin) | |
| 108 Tony Taylor | .35 |
| 109 Jim Lonborg | .35 |
| 110 Mike Shannon | .35 |
| 111 Johnny Morris | .35 |
| 112 J.C. Martin | .35 |
| 113 Dave May | .35 |
| 114 Yankees Rookies: | .35 |
| A. Closter, J. Cumberland | |
| 115 Bill Hands | .35 |
| 116 Chuck Harrison | .35 |
| 117 Jim Fairey | .35 |
| 118 Stan Williams (Mgr.) | .35 |
| 119 Doug Rader | .35 |
| 120 Pete Rose | 30.00 |
| 121 Joe Grzenda | .35 |
| 122 Ron Fairly | .35 |
| 123 Wilbur Wood | .35 |
| 124 Hank Bauer (Mgr.) | .35 |
| 125 Ray Sadecki | .35 |
| 126 Dick Tracewski | .35 |
| 127 Kevin Collins | .35 |
| 128 Tommie Aaron | .35 |
| 129 Bill McCool | .35 |
| 130 Carl Yastrzemski | 20.00 |
| 131 Chris Cannizzaro | .35 |
| 132 Dave Baldwin | .35 |
| 133 Johnny Callison | .35 |
| 134 Jim Weaver | .35 |
| 135 Tommy Davis | .50 |
| 136 Cards Rookies: | .50 |
| Steve Huntz, Mike Torrez | |
| 137 Wally Bunker | .35 |
| 138 John Bateman | .35 |
| 139 Andy Kosco | .35 |
| 140 Jim Lefebvre | .35 |
| 141 Bill Dillman | .35 |
| 142 Woody Woodward | .35 |
| 143 Joe Nossek | .35 |
| 144 Bob Hendley | .35 |
| 145 Max Alvis | .35 |
| 146 Jim Perry | .60 |
| 147 Leo Durocher (Mgr.) | 1.00 |
| 148 Lee Stange | .35 |
| 149 Ollie Brown | .35 |
| 150 Denny McLain | 1.25 |
| 151 Clay Dalrymple | .35 |
| (Orioles Team) | |
| 151 Clay Dalrymple | 6.00 |
| (Phillies Team) | |
| 152 Tommie Sisk | .35 |
| 153 Ed Brinkman | .35 |
| 154 Jim Britton | .35 |
| 155 Pete Ward | .35 |
| 156 Houston Rookies: | .35 |
| Hal Gilson, Leon McFadden | |
| 157 Bob Rodgers | .35 |
| 158 Joe Gibbon | .35 |

| NO. PLAYER | MINT |
|---|---|
| 159 Jerry Adair | .35 |
| 160 Vada Pinson | .75 |
| 161 John Purdin | .35 |
| 162 World Series Game 1: | 2.50 |
| Gibson Fans 17 | |
| 163 World Series Game 2: | 1.50 |
| Tigers Deck Cards | |
| 164 World Series Game 3: | 1.50 |
| McCarver's Homer | |
| 165 World Series Game 4: | 2.50 |
| Brock Lead-Off HR | |
| 166 World Series Game 5: | 3.00 |
| Kaline's Key Hit | |
| 167 World Series Game 6: | 1.50 |
| Tigers 10-Run Inning | |
| 168 World Series Game 7: | 2.50 |
| Lolich Outduels Gibson | |
| 169 World Series: | 1.50 |
| Tigers Celebrate Victory | |
| 170 Frank Howard | 1.00 |
| 171 Glenn Beckert | .35 |
| 172 Jerry Stephenson | .35 |
| 173 White Sox Rookies: | .35 |
| B. Christian, G. Nyman | |
| 174 Grant Jackson | .35 |
| 175 Jim Bunning | 1.25 |
| 176 Joe Azcue | .35 |
| 177 Ron Reed | .35 |
| 178 Ray Oyler | .35 |
| 179 Don Pavletich | .35 |
| 180 Willie Horton | .50 |
| 181 Mel Nelson | .35 |
| 182 Bill Rigney (Mgr.) | .35 |
| 183 Don Shaw | .35 |
| 184 Roberto Pena | .35 |
| 185 Tom Phoebus | .35 |
| 186 John Edwards | .35 |
| 187 Leon Wagner | .35 |
| 188 Rick Wise | .35 |
| 189 Red Sox Rookies: | .35 |
| J. Lahoud, J. Thibadeau | |
| 190 Willie Mays | 18.00 |
| 191 Lindy McDaniel | .35 |
| 192 Jose Pagan | .35 |
| 193 Don Cardwell | .35 |
| 194 Ted Uhlaender | .35 |
| 195 John Odom | .35 |
| 196 Lum Harris (Mgr.) | .35 |
| 197 Dick Selma | .35 |
| 198 Willie Smith | .35 |
| 199 Jim French | .35 |
| 200 Bob Gibson | 4.00 |
| 201 Russ Snyder | .35 |
| 202 Don Wilson | .35 |
| 203 Dave Johnson | .75 |
| 204 Jack Hiatt | .35 |
| 205 Rick Reichardt | .35 |
| 206 Phillies Rookies: | .50 |
| Larry Hisle, Barry Lersch | |
| 207 Roy Face | .50 |
| 208 Donn Clendenon | .35 |
| (Astros Team) | |
| 208 Donn Clendenon | 9.00 |
| (Expos Team) | |
| 209 Larry Haney | .35 |
| (negative reversed) | |
| 210 Felix Millan | .35 |
| 211 Galen Cisco | .35 |
| 212 Tom Tresh | .50 |
| 213 Gerry Arrigo | .35 |
| 214 Checklist No. 3 | 2.00 |
| 215 Rico Petrocelli | .35 |
| 216 Don Sutton | 4.00 |
| 217 John Donaldson | .35 |
| 218 John Roseboro | .35 |
| 219 Freddie Patek | .60 |
| 220 Sam McDowell | .60 |
| 221 Art Shamsky | .35 |
| 222 Duane Josephson | .60 |
| 223 Tom Dukes | .60 |
| 224 Angels Rookies: | .60 |
| B. Harrelson, S. Kealey | |
| 225 Don Kessinger | 1.00 |
| 226 Bruce Howard | .60 |
| 227 Frank Johnson | .60 |

| NO. PLAYER | MINT |
|---|---|
| 228 Dave Leonhard | .60 |
| 229 Don Lock | .60 |
| 230 Rusty Staub | 1.00 |
| 231 Pat Dobson | .60 |
| 232 Dave Ricketts | .60 |
| 233 Steve Barber | .60 |
| 234 Dave Bristol (Mgr.) | .60 |
| 235 Jim Hunter | 4.00 |
| 236 Manny Mota | .60 |
| 237 Bobby Cox | 1.00 |
| 238 Ken Johnson | .60 |
| 239 Bob Taylor | .60 |
| 240 Ken Harrelson | 1.00 |
| 241 Jim Brewer | .60 |
| 242 Frank Kostro | .60 |
| 243 Ron Kline | .60 |
| 244 Indians Rookies: | .75 |
| R. Fosse, G. Woodson | |
| 245 Ed Charles | .60 |
| 246 Joe Coleman | .60 |
| 247 Gene Oliver | .60 |
| 248 Bob Priddy | .60 |
| 249 Ed Spiezio | .60 |
| 250 Frank Robinson | 8.00 |
| 251 Ron Herbel | .60 |
| 252 Chuck Cottier | .60 |
| 253 Jerry Johnson | .60 |
| 254 Joe Schultz (Mgr.) | .60 |
| 255 Steve Carlton | 25.00 |
| 256 Gates Brown | .60 |
| 257 Jim Ray | .60 |
| 258 Jackie Hernandez | .60 |
| 259 Bill Short | .60 |
| 260 Reggie Jackson (R) | 180.00 |
| 261 Bob Johnson | .60 |
| 262 Mike Kekich | .60 |
| 263 Jerry May | .60 |
| 264 Bill Landis | .60 |
| 265 Chico Cardenas | .60 |
| 266 Dodger Rookies: | .75 |
| Tom Hutton, Alan Foster | |
| 267 Vicente Romo | .60 |
| 268 Al Spangler | .60 |
| 269 Al Weis | .60 |
| 270 Mickey Lolich | 1.25 |
| 271 Larry Stahl | .60 |
| 272 Ed Stroud | .60 |
| 273 Ron Willis | .60 |
| 274 Clyde King (Mgr.) | .60 |
| 275 Vic Davalillo | .60 |
| 276 Gary Wagner | .60 |
| 277 Ron Hendricks | .60 |
| 278 Gary Geiger | .60 |
| 279 Roger Nelson | .60 |
| 280 Alex Johnson | .60 |
| 281 Ted Kubiak | .60 |
| 282 Pat Jarvis | .60 |
| 283 Sandy Alomar | .60 |
| 284 Expos Rookies: | .60 |
| M. Wegener, J. Robertson | |
| 285 Don Mincher | .60 |
| 286 Dock Ellis | .60 |
| 287 Jose Tartabull | .60 |
| 288 Ken Holtzman | 1.00 |
| 289 Bart Shirley | .60 |
| 290 Jim Kaat | 2.50 |
| 291 Vern Fuller | .60 |
| 292 Al Downing | .75 |
| 293 Dick Dietz | .60 |
| 294 Jim Lemon | .60 |
| 295 Tony Perez | 3.00 |
| 296 Andy Messersmith (R) | 1.00 |
| 297 Deron Johnson | .60 |
| 298 Dave Nicholson | .60 |
| 299 Mark Belanger | 1.00 |
| 300 Felipe Alou | 1.00 |
| 301 Darrell Brandon | .60 |
| 302 Jim Pagliaroni | .60 |
| 303 Cal Koonce | .60 |
| 304 Padres Rookies: | .60 |
| Bill Davis, Clarence Gaston | |
| 305 Dick McAuliffe | .60 |
| 306 Jim Grant | .60 |
| 307 Gary Kolb | .60 |
| 308 Wade Blasingame | .60 |

| NO. PLAYER | MINT |
|---|---|
| 309 Walt Williams | .60 |
| 310 Tom Haller | .60 |
| 311 Sparky Lyle (R) | 1.50 |
| 312 Lee Elia | .60 |
| 313 Bill Robinson | .75 |
| 314 Checklist No. 4 | 2.00 |
| 315 Eddie Fisher | .60 |
| 316 Hal Lanier | .75 |
| 317 Bruce Look | .60 |
| 318 Jack Fisher | .60 |
| 319 Ken McMullen | .60 |
| 320 Dal Maxvill | .60 |
| 321 Jim McAndrew | .60 |
| 322 Jose Vidal | .60 |
| 323 Larry Miller | .60 |
| 324 Tiger Rookies: | .75 |
| Les Cain, Dave Campbell | |
| 325 Jose Cardenal | .60 |
| 326 Gary Sutherland | .60 |
| 327 Willie Crawford | .60 |
| 328 Joe Horlen | .35 |
| 329 Rick Joseph | .35 |
| 330 Tony Conigliaro | .75 |
| 331 Braves Rookies: | .50 |
| Tom House, Gil Garrido | |
| 332 Fred Talbot | .35 |
| 333 Ivan Murrell | .35 |
| 334 Phil Roof | .35 |
| 335 Bill Mazeroski | 1.00 |
| 336 Jim Roland | .35 |
| 337 Marty Martinez | .35 |
| 338 Del Unser | .35 |
| 339 Reds Rookies: | .50 |
| Steve Mingori, Jose Pena | |
| 340 Dave McNally | .60 |
| 341 Dave Adlesh | .35 |
| 342 Bubba Morton | .35 |
| 343 Dan Frisella | .35 |
| 344 Tom Matchick | .35 |
| 345 Frank Linzy | .35 |
| 346 Wayne Comer | .35 |
| 347 Randy Hundley | .35 |
| 348 Steve Hargan | .35 |
| 349 Dick Williams (Mgr.) | .35 |
| 350 Richie Allen | 1.00 |
| 351 Carroll Sembera | .35 |
| 352 Paul Schaal | .35 |
| 353 Jeff Torborg | .35 |
| 354 Nate Oliver | .35 |
| 355 Phil Niekro | 3.00 |
| 356 Frank Quilici | .35 |
| 357 Carl Taylor | .35 |
| 358 Athletics Rookies: | .35 |
| George Lauzerique, Roberto Rodriguez | |
| 359 Dick Kelley | .35 |
| 360 Jim Wynn | .50 |
| 361 Gary Holman | .35 |
| 362 Jim Maloney | .35 |
| 363 Russ Nixon | .35 |
| 364 Tommie Agee | .35 |
| 365 Jim Fregosi | .75 |
| 366 Bo Belinsky | .35 |
| 367 Lou Johnson | .35 |
| 368 Vic Roznovsky | .35 |
| 369 Bob Skinner (Mgr.) | .35 |
| 370 Juan Marichal | 4.00 |
| 371 Sal Bando | .75 |
| 372 Adolfo Phillips | .35 |
| 373 Fred Lasher | .35 |
| 374 Bob Tillman | .35 |
| 375 Harmon Killebrew | 8.00 |
| 376 Royals Rookies: | .45 |
| Mike Fiore, Jim Rooker | |
| 377 Gary Bell | .35 |
| 378 Jose Herrera | .35 |
| 379 Ken Boyer | 1.00 |
| 380 Stan Bahnsen | .35 |
| 381 Ed Kranepool | .35 |
| 382 Pat Corrales | .35 |
| 383 Casey Cox | .35 |
| 384 Larry Shepard | .35 |
| 385 Orlando Cepeda | 1.75 |
| 386 Jim McGlothlin | .35 |

| NO. PLAYER | MINT |
|---|---|
| 387 Bobby Klaus | .35 |
| 388 Tom McCraw | .35 |
| 389 Dan Coombs | .35 |
| 390 Bill Freehan | .50 |
| 391 Ray Culp | .35 |
| 392 Bob Burda | .35 |
| 393 Gene Brabender | .35 |
| 394 Pilots Rookies: | 2.00 |
| Lou Piniella, M. Staehle | |
| 395 Chris Short | .35 |
| 396 Jim Campanis | .35 |
| 397 Chuck Dobson | .35 |
| 398 Tito Francona | .35 |
| 399 Bob Bailey | .35 |
| 400 Don Drysdale | 5.00 |
| 401 Jake Gibbs | .35 |
| 402 Ken Boswell | .35 |
| 403 Bob Miller | .35 |
| 404 Cubs Rookies: | .50 |
| Vic LaRose, Gary Ross | |
| 405 Lee May | .50 |
| 406 Phil Ortega | .35 |
| 407 Tom Egan | .35 |
| 408 Nate Colbert | .35 |
| 409 Bob Moose | .35 |
| 410 Al Kaline | 6.00 |
| 411 Larry Dierker | .35 |
| 412 Checklist No. 5 | 5.00 |
| 413 Roland Sheldon | .35 |
| 414 Duke Sims | .35 |
| 415 Ray Washburn | .35 |
| 416 Willie McCovey (AS) | 3.00 |
| 417 Ken Harrelson (AS) | .50 |
| 418 Tommy Helms (AS) | .50 |
| 419 Rod Carew (AS) | 4.00 |
| 420 Ron Santo (AS) | .50 |
| 421 Brooks Robinson (AS) | 3.00 |
| 422 Don Kessinger (AS) | .50 |
| 423 Bert Campaneris (AS) | .50 |
| 424 Pete Rose (AS) | 7.00 |
| 425 Carl Yastrzemski (AS) | 4.00 |
| 426 Curt Flood (AS) | .50 |
| 427 Tony Oliva (AS) | .75 |
| 428 Lou Brock (AS) | 3.00 |
| 429 Willie Horton (AS) | .50 |
| 430 Johnny Bench (AS) | 5.00 |
| 431 Bill Freehan (AS) | .50 |
| 432 Bob Gibson (AS) | 2.00 |
| 433 Denny McLain (AS) | .60 |
| 434 Jerry Koosman (AS) | .50 |
| 435 Sam McDowell (AS) | .50 |
| 436 Gene Alley | .35 |
| 437 Luis Alcaraz | .35 |
| 438 Gary Waslewski | .35 |
| 439 White Sox Rookies: | .50 |
| Ed Herrmann, Dan Lazar | |
| 440 Willie McCovey* | 10.00 |
| 441 Dennis Higgins* | .35 |
| 442 Ty Cline | .35 |
| 443 Don Wert | .35 |
| 444 Joe Moeller* | .35 |
| 445 Bobby Knoop | .35 |
| 446 Claude Raymond | .35 |
| 447 Ralph Houk (Mgr.)* | .65 |
| 448 Bob Tolan | .35 |
| 449 Paul Lindblad | .35 |
| 450 Billy Williams | 3.00 |
| 451 Rich Rollins* | .35 |
| 452 Al Ferrara* | .35 |
| 453 Mike Cuellar | .65 |
| 454 Phillies Rookies:* | .50 |
| Larry Colton, Don Money | |
| 455 Sonny Siebert | .35 |
| 456 Bud Harrelson | .35 |
| 457 Dalton Jones | .35 |
| 458 Curt Blefary | .35 |
| 459 Dave Boswell | .35 |
| 460 Joe Torre | .75 |
| 461 Mike Epstein* | .35 |
| 462 Red Schoendienst | .65 |
| 463 Dennis Ribant | .35 |
| 464 Dave Marshall* | .35 |
| 465 Tommy John | 1.50 |
| 466 John Boccabella | .35 |

| NO. PLAYER | MINT |
|---|---|
| 467 Tom Reynolds | .35 |
| 468 Pirates Rookies:* | .50 |
| Bruce Del Canton, Bob Robertson | |
| 469 Chico Ruiz | .35 |
| 470 Mel Stottlemyre* | .65 |
| 471 Ted Savage* | .35 |
| 472 Jim Price | .35 |
| 473 Jose Arcia* | .35 |
| 474 Tom Murphy | .35 |
| 475 Tim McCarver | 1.00 |
| 476 Boston Rookies:* | .50 |
| Ken Brett, Gerry Moses | |
| 477 Jeff James | .35 |
| 478 Don Buford | .35 |
| 479 Richie Scheinblum | .35 |
| 480 Tom Seaver | 40.00 |
| 481 Bill Melton | .35 |
| 482 Jim Gosger* | .35 |
| 483 Ted Abernathy | .35 |
| 484 Joe Gordon | .35 |
| 485 Gaylord Perry* | 4.00 |
| 486 Paul Casanova* | .35 |
| 487 Denis Menke | .35 |
| 488 Joe Sparma | .35 |
| 489 Clete Boyer | .50 |
| 490 Matty Alou | .50 |
| 491 Twins Rookies:* | .50 |
| Jerry Crider, George Mitterwald | |
| 492 Tony Cloninger | .35 |
| 493 Wes Parker* | .35 |
| 494 Ken Berry | .35 |
| 495 Bert Campaneris | .50 |
| 496 Larry Jaster | .35 |
| 497 Julian Javier | .35 |
| 498 Juan Pizarro | .35 |
| 499 Astro Rookies: | .50 |
| Don Bryant, Steve Shea | |
| 500 Mickey Mantle* | 160.00 |
| 501 Tony Gonzalez* | .35 |
| 502 Minnie Rojas | .35 |
| 503 Larry Brown | .35 |
| 504 Checklist No. 6 | 2.00 |
| 505 Bobby Bolin* | .35 |
| 506 Paul Blair | .35 |
| 507 Cookie Rojas | .35 |
| 508 Moe Drabowsky | .35 |
| 509 Manny Sanguillen | .50 |
| 510 Rod Carew | 22.00 |
| 511 Diego Segui* | .35 |
| 512 Cleon Jones | .35 |
| 513 Camilo Pascual | .60 |
| 514 Mike Lum | .50 |
| 515 Dick Green | .50 |
| 516 Earl Weaver (Mgr.) | 3.00 |
| 517 Mike McCormick | .50 |
| 518 Fred Whitfield | .50 |
| 519 Yankees Rookies: | .75 |
| G. Kenney, Len Boehmer | |
| 520 Bob Veale | .65 |
| 521 George Thomas | .50 |
| 522 Joe Hoerner | .50 |
| 523 Bob Chance | .50 |
| 524 Expos Rookies: | .50 |
| Jose Laboy, Floyd Wicker | |
| 525 Earl Wilson | .50 |
| 526 Hector Torres | .50 |
| 527 Al Lopez (Mgr.) | 1.50 |
| 528 Claude Osteen | .50 |
| 529 Ed Kirkpatrick | .50 |
| 530 Cesar Tovar | .50 |
| 531 Dick Farrell | .50 |
| 532 Bird Hill Aces: | .65 |
| D. McNally, T. Phoebus, J. Hardin, M. Cuellar | |
| 533 Nolan Ryan | 45.00 |
| 534 Jerry McNertney | .50 |
| 535 Phil Regan | .50 |
| 536 Padres Rookies: | .60 |
| D. Breeden, Dave Roberts | |
| 537 Mike Paul | .50 |
| 538 Charlie Smith | .50 |
| 539 Ted Shows How: | 2.50 |
| Mike Epstein, Ted Williams | |

| NO. PLAYER | MINT |
|---|---|
| 540 Curt Flood | .75 |
| 541 Joe Verbanic | .50 |
| 542 Bob Aspromonte | .50 |
| 543 Fred Newman | .50 |
| 544 Tigers Rookies: | .75 |
| Mike Kilkenny, Ron Woods | |
| 545 Willie Stargell | 8.00 |
| 546 Jim Nash | .50 |
| 547 Billy Martin (Mgr.) | 2.00 |
| 548 Bob Locker | .50 |
| 549 Ron Brand | .50 |
| 550 Brooks Robinson | 9.00 |
| 551 Wayne Granger | .50 |
| 552 Dodgers Rookies: | .75 |
| Ted Sizemore, Bill Sudakis | |
| 553 Ron Davis | .50 |
| 554 Frank Bertaina | .50 |
| 555 Jim Hart | .50 |
| 556 A's Stars: | .75 |
| Bert Campaneris, Sal Bando, Danny Cater | |
| 557 Frank Fernandez | .50 |
| 558 Tom Burgmeier | .50 |
| 559 Cardinals Rookies: | .60 |
| Joe Hague, Jim Hicks | |
| 560 Luis Tiant | 1.00 |
| 561 Ron Clark | .50 |
| 562 Bob Watson (R) | 1.25 |
| 563 Marty Pattin | .50 |
| 564 Gil Hodges (Mgr.) | 4.00 |
| 565 Hoyt Wilhelm | 4.00 |
| 566 Ron Hansen | .50 |
| 567 Pirates Rookies: | .60 |
| Elvio Jimenez, Jim Shellenback | |
| 568 Cecil Upshaw | .50 |
| 569 Billy Harris | .50 |
| 570 Ron Santo | .75 |
| 571 Cap Peterson | .50 |
| 572 Giants Heroes: | 5.00 |
| Willie McCovey, Juan Marichal | |
| 573 Jim Palmer | 9.00 |
| 574 George Scott | .50 |
| 575 Bill Singer | .50 |
| 576 Phillies Rookies: | .50 |
| Ron Stone, Bill Wilson | |
| 577 Mike Hegan | .50 |
| 578 Don Bosch | .50 |
| 579 Dave Nelson | .50 |
| 580 Jim Northrup | .50 |
| 581 Gary Nolan | .50 |
| 582 Checklist No. 7 | 2.00 |
| 583 Clyde Wright | .50 |
| 584 Don Mason | .50 |
| 585 Ron Swoboda | .50 |
| 586 Tim Cullen | .50 |
| 587 Joe Rudi (R) | 1.00 |
| 588 Bill White | .50 |
| 589 Joe Pepitone | .75 |
| 590 Rico Carty | .50 |
| 591 Mike Hedlund | .50 |
| 592 Padres Rookies: | .50 |
| R. Robles, Al Santorini | |
| 593 Don Nottebart | .50 |
| 594 Dooley Womack | .50 |
| 595 Lee Maye | .50 |
| 596 Chuck Hartenstein | .50 |
| 597 AL Rookies: | .15.00 |
| Bob Floyd, Larry Burchart, Rollie Fingers | |
| 598 Ruben Amaro | .50 |
| 599 John Boozer | .50 |
| 600 Tony Oliva | 1.50 |
| 601 Tug McGraw | 1.00 |
| 602 Cubs Rookies: | .50 |
| Alec Distaso, Jim Qualls, Don Young | |
| 603 Joe Keough | .50 |
| 604 Bobby Etheridge | .50 |
| 605 Dick Ellsworth | .50 |
| 606 Gene Mauch (Mgr.) | .50 |
| 607 Dick Bosman | .50 |
| 608 Dick Simpson | .50 |

**Prices for the 1969 set are for cards in *Mint* condition. *Excellent* copies sell for 50% of prices shown; *Very Good*—30%.**

| NO. PLAYER | MINT |
|---|---|
| 609 Phil Gagliano | .50 |
| 610 Jim Hardin | .50 |
| 611 Braves Rookies: | .50 |
| Bob Didier, Walt Hriniak, | |
| Gary Neibauer | |
| 612 Jack Aker | .50 |
| 613 Jim Beauchamp | .50 |
| 614 Houston Rookies: | .50 |
| Tom Griffin, Skip Guinn | |
| 615 Len Gabrielson | .50 |
| 616 Don McMahon | .50 |
| 617 Jesse Gonder | .50 |
| 618 Ramon Webster | .50 |
| 619 Royals Rookies: | .65 |
| Pat Kelly, Juan Rios, | |
| Bill Butler | |
| 620 Dean Chance | .50 |
| 621 Bill Voss | .50 |
| 622 Dan Osinski | .50 |
| 623 Hank Allen | .50 |

| NO. PLAYER | MINT |
|---|---|
| 624 NL Rookies: | .50 |
| Darrel Chaney, Duffy Dyer, | |
| Terry Harmon | |
| 625 Mack Jones | .50 |
| 626 Gene Michael | .50 |
| 627 George Stone | .50 |
| 628 Red Sox Rookies: | .75 |
| Bill Conigliaro, Syd | |
| O'Brien, Fred Wenz | |
| 629 Jack Hamilton | .50 |
| 630 Bobby Bonds (R) | 5.00 |
| 631 John Kennedy | .50 |
| 632 Jon Warden | .50 |
| 633 Harry Walker (Mgr.) | .50 |
| 634 Andy Etchebarren | .50 |
| 635 George Culver | .50 |
| 636 Woodie Held | .50 |
| 637 Padres Rookies: | .50 |
| Jerry DaVanon, Frank | |
| Reberger, Clay Kirby | |

| NO. PLAYER | MINT |
|---|---|
| 638 Ed Sprague | .50 |
| 639 Barry Moore | .50 |
| 640 Fergie Jenkins | 2.50 |
| 641 NL Rookies: | .50 |
| Bobby Darwin, John Miller, | |
| Tommy Dean | |
| 642 John Hiller | .50 |
| 643 Billy Cowan | .50 |
| 644 Chuck Hinton | .50 |
| 645 George Brunet | .50 |
| 646 Expos Rookies: | .50 |
| Carl Morton, Dan McGinn | |
| 647 Dave Wickersham | .50 |
| 648 Bobby Wine | .50 |
| 649 Al Jackson | .50 |
| 650 Ted Williams (Mgr.) | 4.00 |
| 651 Gus Gil | .50 |
| 652 Eddie Watt | .50 |
| 653 Aurelio Rodriguez | 1.50 |
| (Photo of Angels Batboy) | |

| NO. PLAYER | MINT |
|---|---|
| 654 White Sox Rookies: | .60 |
| Carlos May, Don Secrist, | |
| Rich Morales | |
| 655 Mike Hershberger | .50 |
| 656 Dan Schneider | .50 |
| 657 Bobby Murcer | 1.00 |
| 658 AL Rookies: | .50 |
| Tom Hall, Bill Burbach, | |
| Jim Miles | |
| 659 Johnny Podres | .75 |
| 660 Reggie Smith | 1.00 |
| 661 Jim Merritt | .50 |
| 662 Royals Rookies: | .75 |
| Dick Drago, Bob Oliver, | |
| George Spriggs | |
| 663 Dick Radatz | .50 |
| 664 Ron Hunt (Exc. $.35) | 1.50 |

## 1970 Topps . . . Complete Set of 720 Cards—Value $600.00 (Exc.); $1100.00 (Mint)

Features the rookie cards of Thurman Munson, Darrell Evans, Vida Blue, and Bill Buckner. The high numbers are 634 to 720. Card 588 (checklist) exists with *Adolpho* misspelled *Adolfo*—worth $5.00.

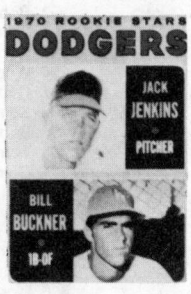

| NO. PLAYER | MINT |
|---|---|
| 1 Champ Mets (Exc $1.25) | 5.00 |
| 2 Diego Segui | .25 |
| 3 Darrel Chaney | .25 |
| 4 Tom Egan | .25 |
| 5 Wes Parker | .25 |
| 6 Grant Jackson | .25 |
| 7 Indians Rookies: | .25 |
| Gary Boyd, Russ Nagelson | |
| 8 Jose Martinez | .25 |
| 9 Checklist No. 1 | 1.50 |
| 10 Carl Yastrzemski | 18.00 |
| 11 Nate Colbert | .25 |
| 12 John Hiller | .25 |
| 13 Jack Hiatt | .25 |
| 14 Hank Allen | .25 |
| 15 Larry Dierker | .25 |
| 16 Charlie Metro | .25 |
| 17 Hoyt Wilhelm | 3.00 |
| 18 Carlos May | .25 |
| 19 John Boccabella | .25 |
| 20 Dave McNally | .40 |
| 21 A's Rookies: | 2.00 |
| Gene Tenace, Vida Blue | |
| 22 Ray Washburn | .25 |
| 23 Bill Robinson | .40 |
| 24 Dick Selma | .25 |
| 25 Cesaer Tovar | .25 |
| 26 Tug McGraw | .75 |
| 27 Chuck Hinton | .25 |
| 28 Billy Wilson | .25 |
| 29 Sandy Alomar | .25 |
| 30 Matty Alou | .50 |
| 31 Marty Pattin | .25 |
| 32 Harry Walker | .25 |
| 33 Don Wert | .25 |
| 34 Willie Crawford | .25 |
| 35 Joe Horlen | .25 |

| NO. PLAYER | MINT |
|---|---|
| 36 Red Rookies: | .25 |
| D. Breeden, B. Carbo | |
| 37 Dick Drago | .25 |
| 38 Mack Jones | .25 |
| 39 Mike Nagy | .25 |
| 40 Rich Allen | .60 |
| 41 George Lauzerique | .25 |
| 42 Tito Fuentes | .25 |
| 43 Jack Aker | .25 |
| 44 Roberto Pena | .25 |
| 45 Dave Johnson | .75 |
| 46 Ken Rudolph | .25 |
| 47 Bob Miller | .25 |
| 48 Gil Garrido | .25 |
| 49 Tim Cullen | .25 |
| 50 Tommy Agee | .40 |
| 51 Bob Christian | .25 |
| 52 Bruce Dal Canton | .25 |
| 53 John Kennedy | .25 |
| 54 Jeff Torborg | .35 |
| 55 John Odom | .25 |
| 56 Phillies Rookies: | .25 |
| Joe Lis, Scott Reid | |
| 57 Pat Kelly | .25 |
| 58 Dave Marshall | .25 |
| 59 Dick Ellsworth | .25 |
| 60 Jim Wynn | .45 |
| 61 NL Batting Leaders: | 3.00 |
| Cleon Jones, Pete Rose, | |
| Bob Clemente | |
| 62 AL Batting Leaders: | 1.25 |
| Rod Carew, Reggie Smith, | |
| Tony Oliva | |
| 63 NL RBI Leaders: | 1.25 |
| Ron Santo, Tony Perez, | |
| Willie McCovey | |

| NO. PLAYER | MINT |
|---|---|
| 64 AL RBI Leaders: | 1.25 |
| Harmon Killebrew, Boog | |
| Powell, Reggie Jackson | |
| 65 NL Home Run Leaders: | 1.50 |
| Hank Aaron, Willie | |
| McCovey, Lee May | |
| 66 AL Home Run Leaders: | 1.50 |
| Harmon Killebrew, Frank | |
| Howard, Reggie Jackson | |
| 67 NL ERA Leaders: | 3.00 |
| Bob Gibson, Juan | |
| Marichal, Steve Carlton | |
| 68 AL ERA Leaders: | 1.00 |
| Dick Bosman, Jim Palmer, | |
| Mike Cuellar | |
| 69 NL Pitching Leaders: | 3.00 |
| Phil Niekro, Tom Seaver, | |
| F. Jenkins, Juan Marichal | |
| 70 AL Pitching Leaders: | .75 |
| Dennis McLain, Mike | |
| Cuellar, Dave McNally, | |
| Jim Perry, Dave Boswell, | |
| Mel Stottlemyre | |
| 71 NL Strikeout Leaders: | 1.00 |
| Fergie Jenkins, Bob | |
| Gibson, Bill Singer | |
| 72 AL Strikeout Leaders: | .75 |
| Andy Messersmith, Sam | |
| McDowell, Mickey Lolich | |
| 73 Wayne Granger | .25 |
| 74 Angels Rookies: | .40 |
| Greg Washburn, Wally Wolf | |
| 75 Jim Kaat | 2.00 |
| 76 Carl Taylor | .25 |
| 77 Frank Linzy | .25 |
| 78 Joe Lahoud | .25 |
| 79 Clay Kirby | .25 |

| NO. PLAYER | MINT |
|---|---|
| 80 Don Kessinger | .25 |
| 81 Dave May | .25 |
| 82 Frank Fernandez | .25 |
| 83 Don Cardwell | .25 |
| 84 Paul Casanova | .25 |
| 85 Max Alvis | .25 |
| 86 Lum Harris (Mgr.) | .25 |
| 87 Steve Renko | .25 |
| 88 Pilots Rookies: | .25 |
| Miguel Fuentes, Dick Baney | |
| 89 Juan Rios | .25 |
| 90 Tim McCarver | 1.00 |
| 91 Rich Morales | .25 |
| 92 George Culver | .25 |
| 93 Rick Renick | .25 |
| 94 Fred Patek | .25 |
| 95 Earl Wilson | .25 |
| 96 Cardinals Rookies: | 2.00 |
| Leron Lee, Jerry Reuss | |
| 97 Joe Moeller | .25 |
| 98 Gates Brown | .25 |
| 99 Bobby Pfeil | .25 |
| 100 Mel Stottlemyre | .50 |
| 101 Bobby Floyd | .25 |
| 102 Joe Rudi | .50 |
| 103 Frank Reberger | .25 |
| 104 Gerry Moses | .25 |
| 105 Tony Gonzalez | .25 |
| 106 Darold Knowles | .25 |
| 107 Bobby Etheridge | .25 |
| 108 Tom Burgmeier | .25 |
| 109 Expos Rookies: | .35 |
| Garry Jestadt, Carl Morton | |
| 110 Bob Moose | .25 |
| 111 Mike Hegan | .25 |
| 112 Dave Nelson | .25 |
| 113 Jim Ray | .25 |

| NO. PLAYER | MINT |
|---|---|
| 114 Gene Michael | .25 |
| 115 Alex Johnson | .25 |
| 116 Sparky Lyle | .50 |
| 117 Don Young | .25 |
| 118 George Mitterwald | .25 |
| 119 Chuck Taylor | .25 |
| 120 Sal Bando | .45 |
| 121 Orioles Rookies: | .40 |
|     Fred Beene, Terry Crowley | |
| 122 George Stone | .25 |
| 123 Don Gutteridge (Mgr.) | .25 |
| 124 Larry Jaster | .25 |
| 125 Deron Johnson | .25 |
| 126 Marty Martinez | .25 |
| 127 Joe Coleman | .25 |
| 128 Checklist No. 2 | 1.50 |
| 129 Jimmie Price | .25 |
| 130 Ollie Brown | .25 |
| 131 Dodgers Rookies: | .40 |
|     Ray Lamb, Bob Stinson | |
| 132 Jim McGlothlin | .25 |
| 133 Clay Carroll | .25 |
| 134 Danny Walton | .25 |
| 135 Dick Dietz | .25 |
| 136 Steve Hargan | .25 |
| 137 Art Shamsky | .25 |
| 138 Joe Foy | .25 |
| 139 Rich Nye | .25 |
| 140 Reggie Jackson | 40.00 |
| 141 Pirates Rookies: | .40 |
|     Dave Cash, Johnny Jeter | |
| 142 Fritz Peterson | .25 |
| 143 Phil Gagliano | .25 |
| 144 Ray Culp | .25 |
| 145 Rico Carty | .50 |
| 146 Danny Murphy | .25 |
| 147 Angel Hermoso | .25 |
| 148 Earl Weaver (Mgr.) | 1.00 |
| 149 Billy Champion | .30 |
| 150 Harmon Killebrew | 4.00 |
| 151 Dave Roberts | .25 |
| 152 Ike Brown | .25 |
| 153 Gary Gentry | .25 |
| 154 Senators Rookies: | .35 |
|     Jim Miles, Jan Dukes | |
| 155 Denis Menke | .25 |
| 156 Eddie Fisher | .25 |
| 157 Manny Mota | .40 |
| 158 Jerry McNertney | .25 |
| 159 Tommy Helms | .35 |
| 160 Phil Niekro | 3.00 |
| 161 Richie Scheinblum | .25 |
| 162 Jerry Johnson | .25 |
| 163 Syd O'Brien | .25 |
| 164 Ty Cline | .25 |
| 165 Ed Kirkpatrick | .25 |
| 166 Al Oliver | 2.50 |
| 167 Bill Burbach | .25 |
| 168 Dave Watkins | .25 |
| 169 Tom Hall | .25 |
| 170 Billy Williams | 4.00 |
| 171 Jim Nash | .25 |
| 172 Braves Rookies: | .75 |
|     Garry Hill, Ralph Garr | |
| 173 Jim Hicks | .25 |
| 174 Ted Sizemore | .25 |
| 175 Dick Bosman | .25 |
| 176 Jim Hart | .35 |
| 177 Jim Northrup | .25 |
| 178 Denny Lemaster | .25 |
| 179 Ivan Murrell | .25 |
| 180 Tommy John | 2.00 |
| 181 Sparky Anderson | .50 |
| 182 Dick Hall | .25 |
| 183 Jerry Grote | .25 |
| 184 Ray Fosse | .25 |
| 185 Don Mincher | .25 |
| 186 Rick Joseph | .25 |
| 187 Mike Hedlund | .25 |
| 188 Manny Sanguillen | .40 |
| 189 Yankees Rookies: | 25.00 |
|     Thurman Munson, | |
|     Dave McDonald | |
| 190 Joe Torre | .75 |
| 191 Vicente Romo | .25 |

| NO. PLAYER | MINT |
|---|---|
| 192 Jim Qualls | .25 |
| 193 Mike Wegener | .25 |
| 194 Chuck Manuel | .25 |
| 195 NL Playoff Game 1: | 1.50 |
|     Seaver Wins Opener | |
| 196 NL Playoff Game 2: | 1.00 |
|     Mets Show Muscle | |
| 197 NL Playoff Game 3: | 1.50 |
|     Ryan Saves the Day | |
| 198 We're Number One | 1.00 |
|     Mets Celebrate | |
| 199 AL Playoff Game 1: | 1.00 |
|     Orioles Win Squeaker | |
| 200 AL Playoff Game 2: | 1.00 |
|     Powell Scores Winning Run | |
| 201 AL Playoff Game 3: | 1.00 |
|     Birds Wrap it Up | |
| 202 Sweep Twins in Three! | 1.00 |
|     Orioles Celebrate | |
| 203 Rudy May | .25 |
| 204 Len Gabrielson | .25 |
| 205 Bert Campaneris | .40 |
| 206 Clete Boyer | .25 |
| 207 Tigers Rookies: | .50 |
|     Norman McRae, Bob Reed | |
| 208 Fred Gladding | .25 |
| 209 Ken Suarez | .25 |
| 210 Juan Marichal | 4.00 |
| 211 Ted Williams (Mgr.) | 5.00 |
| 212 Al Santorini | .25 |
| 213 Andy Etchebarren | .25 |
| 214 Ken Boswell | .25 |
| 215 Reggie Smith | .75 |
| 216 Chuck Hartenstein | .25 |
| 217 Ron Hansen | .25 |
| 218 Ron Stone | .25 |
| 219 Jerry Kenney | .25 |
| 220 Steve Carlton | 12.00 |
| 221 Ron Brand | .25 |
| 222 Jim Rooker | .25 |
| 223 Nate Oliver | .25 |
| 224 Steve Barber | .25 |
| 225 Lee May | .40 |
| 226 Ron Perranoski | .35 |
| 227 Astros Rookies: | .75 |
|     J. Mayberry, B. Watkins | |
| 228 Aurelio Rodriguez | .25 |
| 229 Rich Robertson | .25 |
| 230 Brooks Robinson | 5.00 |
| 231 Luis Tiant | .50 |
| 232 Bob Didier | .25 |
| 233 Lew Krausse | .25 |
| 234 Tommy Dean | .25 |
| 235 Mike Epstein | .25 |
| 236 Bob Veale | .25 |
| 237 Russ Gibson | .25 |
| 238 Jose Laboy | .25 |
| 239 Ken Berry | .25 |
| 240 Fergie Jenkins | 2.00 |
| 241 Royals Rookies: | .40 |
|     A. Fitzmorris, S. Northey | |
| 242 Walter Alston (Mgr.) | 1.00 |
| 243 Joe Sparma | .25 |
| 244 Checklist No. 4 | 1.00 |
| 245 Leo Cardenas | .25 |
| 246 Jim McAndrew | .25 |
| 247 Lou Klimchock | .25 |
| 248 Jesus Alou | .25 |
| 249 Bob Locker | .25 |
| 250 Willie McCovey | 5.00 |
| 251 Dick Schofield | .25 |
| 252 Lowell Palmer | .25 |
| 253 Ron Woods | .25 |
| 254 Camilo Pascual | .25 |
| 255 Jim Spencer | .25 |
| 256 Vic Davalillo | .25 |
| 257 Dennis Higgins | .25 |
| 258 Paul Popovich | .25 |
| 259 Tommie Reynolds | .25 |
| 260 Claude Osteen | .25 |
| 261 Curt Motton | .25 |
| 262 Twins Rookies: | .35 |
|     Jerry Morales, Jim Williams | |
| 263 Duane Josephson | .25 |
| 264 Rich Hebner | .50 |

| NO. PLAYER | MINT |
|---|---|
| 265 Randy Hundley | .25 |
| 266 Wally Bunker | .25 |
| 267 Twins Rookies: | .35 |
|     Paul Ratliff, Herman Hill | |
| 268 Claude Raymond | .25 |
| 269 Cesar Gutierrez | .25 |
| 270 Chris Short | .25 |
| 271 Greg Goossen | .25 |
| 272 Hector Torres | .25 |
| 273 Ralph Houk (Mgr.) | .40 |
| 274 Gerry Arrigo | .25 |
| 275 Duke Sims | .25 |
| 276 Ron Hunt | .25 |
| 277 Paul Doyle | .25 |
| 278 Tommie Aaron | .50 |
| 279 Bill Lee | .50 |
| 280 Donn Clendenon | .50 |
| 281 Casey Cox | .25 |
| 282 Steve Huntz | .25 |
| 283 Angel Bravo | .25 |
| 284 Jack Baldschun | .25 |
| 285 Paul Blair | .25 |
| 286 Dodgers Rookies: | 5.00 |
|     Bill Buckner, Jack Jenkins | |
| 287 Fred Talbot | .25 |
| 288 Larry Hisle | .40 |
| 289 Gene Brabender | .25 |
| 290 Rod Carew | 12.00 |
| 291 Leo Durocher (Mgr.) | 1.00 |
| 292 Eddie Leon | .25 |
| 293 Bob Bailey | .25 |
| 294 Jose Azcue | .25 |
| 295 Cecil Upshaw | .25 |
| 296 Woody Woodward | .25 |
| 297 Curt Blefary | .25 |
| 298 Ken Henderson | .25 |
| 299 Buddy Bradford | .25 |
| 300 Tom Seaver | 25.00 |
| 301 Chico Salmon | .25 |
| 302 Jeff James | .25 |
| 303 Brant Alyea | .25 |
| 304 Bill Russell (R) | 1.25 |
| 305 World Series Game 1 | 1.00 |
|     Buford's Leadoff Hom | |
| 306 World Series Game 2 | 1.00 |
|     Clendenon's Homer | |
| 307 World Series Game 3 | 1.00 |
|     Agee's Catch | |
| 308 World Series Game 4 | 1.00 |
|     Martin's Bunt | |
| 309 World Series Game 5 | 1.00 |
|     Koosman Shuts Door | |
| 310 World Series Celebratio | 1.00 |
|     Mets Whoop it Up | |
| 311 Dick Green | .25 |
| 312 Mike Torrez | .40 |
| 313 Mayo Smith (Mgr.) | .25 |
| 314 Bill McCool | .25 |
| 315 Luis Aparicio | 3.00 |
| 316 Skip Guinn | .25 |
| 317 Red Sox Rookies: | .50 |
|     B. Conigliaro, L. Alvarado | |
| 318 Willie Smith | .25 |
| 319 Clay Dalrymple | .25 |
| 320 Jim Maloney | .25 |
| 321 Lou Piniella | 1.00 |
| 322 Luke Walker | .25 |
| 323 Wayne Comer | .25 |
| 324 Tony Taylor | .25 |
| 325 Dave Boswell | .25 |
| 326 Bill Voss | .25 |
| 327 Hal King | .25 |
| 328 George Brunet | .25 |
| 329 Chris Cannizzaro | .25 |
| 330 Lou Brock | 4.00 |
| 331 Chuck Dobson | .25 |
| 332 Bobby Wine | .25 |
| 333 Bobby Murcer | .60 |
| 334 Phil Regan | .25 |
| 335 Bill Freehan | .50 |
| 336 Del Unser | .25 |
| 337 Mike McCormick | .25 |
| 338 Paul Schaal | .25 |
| 339 Johnny Edwards | .25 |
| 340 Tony Conigliaro | .60 |

| NO. PLAYER | MINT |
|---|---|
| 341 Bill Sudakis | .25 |
| 342 Wilbur Wood | .25 |
| 343 Checklist No. 4 | 1.50 |
| 344 Marcelino Lopez | .25 |
| 345 Al Ferrara | .25 |
| 346 Red Schoendienst | .75 |
| 347 Russ Snyder | .25 |
| 348 Mets Rookies: | .45 |
|     M. Jorgensen, J. Hudson | |
| 349 Steve Hamilton | .25 |
| 350 Roberto Clemente | 20.00 |
| 351 Tom Murphy | .25 |
| 352 Bob Barton | .25 |
| 353 Stan Williams | .25 |
| 354 Amos Otis | .40 |
| 355 Doug Rader | .25 |
| 356 Fred Lasher | .25 |
| 357 Bob Burda | .25 |
| 358 Pedro Borbon | .25 |
| 359 Phil Roof | .25 |
| 360 Curt Flood | .50 |
| 361 Ray Jarvis | .25 |
| 362 Joe Hague | .25 |
| 363 Tom Shopay | .25 |
| 364 Dan McGinn | .25 |
| 365 Zoilo Versalles | .25 |
| 366 Barry Moore | .25 |
| 367 Mike Lum | .25 |
| 368 Ed Herrmann | .25 |
| 369 Alan Foster | .25 |
| 370 Tommy Harper | .25 |
| 371 Rod Gaspar | .25 |
| 372 Dave Guisti | .25 |
| 373 Roy White | .40 |
| 374 Tommie Sisk | .25 |
| 375 Johnny Callison | .25 |
| 376 Lefty Phillips (Mgr.) | .25 |
| 377 Bill Butler | .25 |
| 378 Jim Davenport | .25 |
| 379 Tom Tischinski | .25 |
| 380 Tony Perez | 2.00 |
| 381 Athletics Rookies: | .35 |
|     Bobby Brooks, Mike Olivo | |
| 382 Jack DiLauro | .25 |
| 383 Mickey Stanley | .35 |
| 384 Gary Neibauer | .25 |
| 385 George Scott | .35 |
| 386 Bill Dillman | .25 |
| 387 Baltimore Orioles | .75 |
| 388 Byron Browne | .25 |
| 389 Jim Shellenback | .25 |
| 390 Willie Davis | .60 |
| 391 Larry Brown | .25 |
| 392 Walt Hriniak | .25 |
| 393 John Gelnar | .25 |
| 394 Gil Hodges (Mgr.) | 2.50 |
| 395 Walt Williams | .25 |
| 396 Steve Blass | .25 |
| 397 Roger Repoz | .25 |
| 398 Bill Stoneman | .25 |
| 399 New York Yankees | 1.00 |
| 400 Denny McLain | .75 |
| 401 Giants Rookies: | .40 |
|     John Harrell, B. Williams | |
| 402 Ellie Rodriguez | .25 |
| 403 Jim Bunning | 2.00 |
| 404 Rich Reese | .25 |
| 405 Bill Hands | .25 |
| 406 Mike Andrews | .25 |
| 407 Bob Watson | .40 |
| 408 Paul Lindblad | .25 |
| 409 Bob Tolan | .25 |
| 410 Boog Powell | 1.50 |
| 411 L.A. Dodgers | 1.25 |
| 412 Larry Burchart | .25 |
| 413 Sonny Jackson | .25 |
| 414 Paul Edmondson | .25 |
| 415 Julian Javier | .25 |
| 416 Joe Verbanic | .25 |
| 417 John Bateman | .25 |
| 418 John Donaldson | .25 |
| 419 Ron Taylor | .25 |
| 420 Ken McMullen | .25 |
| 421 Pat Dobson | .25 |
| 422 Kansas City Royals | .60 |

| NO. | PLAYER | MINT |
|---|---|---|
| 423 | Jerry May | .25 |
| 424 | Mike Kilkenny | .25 |
| 425 | Bobby Bonds | 2.00 |
| 426 | Bill Rigney (Mgr.) | .25 |
| 427 | Fred Norman | .25 |
| 428 | Don Buford | .25 |
| 429 | Cubs Rookies: | .40 |
| | Randy Bobb, Jim Cosman | |
| 430 | Andy Messersmith | .50 |
| 431 | Ron Swoboda | .50 |
| 432 | Checklist No. 5 | 1.00 |
| 433 | Ron Bryant | .25 |
| 434 | Felipe Alou | .40 |
| 435 | Nelson Briles | .25 |
| 436 | Philadelphia Phillies | 1.00 |
| 437 | Danny Cater | .25 |
| 438 | Pat Jarvis | .25 |
| 439 | Lee Maye | .25 |
| 440 | Bill Mazeroski | .50 |
| 441 | John O'Donoghue | .25 |
| 442 | Gene Mauch (Mgr.) | .40 |
| 443 | Al Jackson | .25 |
| 444 | White Sox Rookies: | .35 |
| | Billy Farmer, John Matias | |
| 445 | Vada Pinson | .75 |
| 446 | B. Grabarkewitz | .25 |
| 447 | Lee Stange | .25 |
| 448 | Houston Astros | .75 |
| 449 | Jim Palmer | 6.50 |
| 450 | Willie McCovey (AS) | 3.00 |
| 451 | Boog Powell (AS) | .60 |
| 452 | Felix Millan (AS) | .45 |
| 453 | Rod Carew (AS) | 4.00 |
| 454 | Ron Santo (AS) | .45 |
| 455 | Brooks Robinson (AS) | 3.00 |
| 456 | Don Kessinger (AS) | .45 |
| 457 | Rico Petrocelli (AS) | .45 |
| 458 | Pete Rose (AS) | 8.00 |
| 459 | Reggie Jackson (AS) | 6.00 |
| 460 | Matty Alou (AS) | .40 |
| 461 | Carl Yastrzemski (AS) | 5.00 |
| 462 | Hank Aaron (AS) | 5.00 |
| 463 | Frank Robinson (AS) | 3.00 |
| 464 | Johnny Bench (AS) | 4.00 |
| 465 | Bill Freehan (AS) | .40 |
| 466 | Juan Marichal (AS) | 3.00 |
| 467 | Denny McLain (AS) | .60 |
| 468 | Jerry Koosman (AS) | .50 |
| 469 | Sam McDowell (AS) | .50 |
| 470 | Willie Stargell | 5.00 |
| 471 | Chris Zachary | .35 |
| 472 | Atlanta Braves | .75 |
| 473 | Don Bryant | .35 |
| 474 | Dick Kelley | .35 |
| 475 | Dick McAuliffe | .35 |
| 476 | Don Shaw | .35 |
| 477 | Orioles Rookies: | .40 |
| | Roger Freed, Al Severins | |
| 478 | Bob Heise | .35 |
| 479 | Dick Woodson | .35 |
| 480 | Glen Beckert | .35 |
| 481 | Jose Tartabull | .35 |
| 482 | Tom Hilgendorf | .35 |
| 483 | Gail Hopkins | .35 |
| 484 | Gary Nolan | .35 |
| 485 | Jay Johnstone | .45 |
| 486 | Terry Harmon | .35 |
| 487 | Cisco Carlos | .35 |
| 488 | J.C. Martin | .35 |
| 489 | Eddie Kasko (Mgr.) | .35 |
| 490 | Bill Singer | .35 |
| 491 | Graig Nettles | 3.00 |
| 492 | Astros Rookies: | .40 |
| | K. Lampard, S. Spinks | |
| 493 | Lindy McDaniel | .35 |
| 494 | Larry Stahl | .35 |
| 495 | Dave Morehead | .35 |
| 496 | Steve Whitaker | .35 |
| 497 | Eddie Watt | .35 |
| 498 | Al Weis | .35 |
| 499 | Skip Lockwood | .35 |

| NO. | PLAYER | MINT |
|---|---|---|
| 500 | Hank Aaron | 18.00 |
| 501 | Chicago White Sox | .75 |
| 502 | Rollie Fingers | 3.50 |
| 503 | Dal Maxvill | .35 |
| 504 | Don Pavletich | .35 |
| 505 | Ken Holtzman | .35 |
| 506 | Ed Stroud | .35 |
| 507 | Pat Corrales | .35 |
| 508 | Joe Niekro | .75 |
| 509 | Montreal Expos | .60 |
| 510 | Tony Oliva | 1.50 |
| 511 | Joe Hoerner | .35 |
| 512 | Billy Harris | .35 |
| 513 | Preston Gomez (Mgr.) | .35 |
| 514 | Steve Hovley | .35 |
| 515 | Don Wilson | .35 |
| 516 | Yankees Rookies: | .50 |
| | John Ellis, Jim Lyttle | |
| 517 | Joe Gibbon | .35 |
| 518 | Bill Melton | .35 |
| 519 | Don McMahon | .35 |
| 520 | Willie Horton | .50 |
| 521 | Cal Koonce | .35 |
| 522 | California Angels | .75 |
| 523 | Jose Pena | .35 |
| 524 | Alvin Dark (Mgr.) | .50 |
| 525 | Jerry Adair | .35 |
| 526 | Ron Herbel | .35 |
| 527 | Don Bosch | .35 |
| 528 | Elrod Hendricks | .35 |
| 529 | Bob Aspromonte | .35 |
| 530 | Bob Gibson | 5.00 |
| 531 | Ron Clark | .35 |
| 532 | Danny Murtaugh (Mgr.) | .35 |
| 533 | Buzz Stephen | .35 |
| 534 | Minnesota Twins | .75 |
| 535 | Andy Kosco | .35 |
| 536 | Mike Kekich | .35 |
| 537 | Joe Morgan | 4.00 |
| 538 | Bob Humphreys | .35 |
| 539 | Phillies Rookies: | .35 |
| | Larry Bowa, Dennis Doyle | |
| 540 | Gary Peters | .35 |
| 541 | Bill Heath | .35 |
| 542 | Checklist No. 6 | 1.50 |
| 543 | Clyde Wright | .35 |
| 544 | Cincinnati Reds | 1.00 |
| 545 | Ken Harrelson | .75 |
| 546 | Ron Reed | .35 |
| 547 | Rick Monday | 1.00 |
| 548 | Howie Reed | .60 |
| 549 | St. Louis Cardinals | 1.00 |
| 550 | Frank Howard | .75 |
| 551 | Dock Ellis | .60 |
| 552 | Royals Rookies: | .60 |
| | Dennis Paepke, Fred Rico, | |
| | Don O'Riley | |
| 553 | Jim LeFebvre | .60 |
| 554 | Tom Timmermann | .60 |
| 555 | Orlando Cepeda | 3.00 |
| 556 | Dave Bristol | .60 |
| 557 | Ed Kranepool | .60 |
| 558 | Vern Fuller | .60 |
| 559 | Tommy Davis | .60 |
| 560 | Gaylord Perry | 4.00 |
| 561 | Tom McCraw | .60 |
| 562 | Ted Abernathy | .60 |
| 563 | Boston Red Sox | 1.25 |
| 564 | Johnny Briggs | .60 |
| 565 | Jim Hunter | 4.00 |
| 566 | Gene Alley | .60 |
| 567 | Bob Oliver | .60 |
| 568 | Stan Bahnsen | .60 |
| 569 | Cookie Rojas | .60 |
| 570 | Jim Fregosi | .75 |
| 571 | Jim Brewer | .60 |
| 572 | Frank Quilici | .60 |
| 573 | Padres Rookies: | .60 |
| | Mike Corkins, Rafael | |
| | Robles, Ron Slocum | |
| 574 | Bobby Bolin | .60 |

| NO. | PLAYER | MINT |
|---|---|---|
| 575 | Cleon Jones | .60 |
| 576 | Milt Pappas | .60 |
| 577 | Bernie Allen | .60 |
| 578 | Tom Griffin | .60 |
| 579 | Detroit Tigers | 1.50 |
| 580 | Pete Rose | 70.00 |
| 581 | Tom Satriano | .60 |
| 582 | Mike Paul | .60 |
| 583 | Hal Lanier | .60 |
| 584 | Al Downing | .60 |
| 585 | Rusty Staub | 1.50 |
| 586 | Rickey Clark | .60 |
| 587 | Jose Arcia | .60 |
| 588 | Checklist No. 7* | 3.00 |
| 589 | Joe Keough | .60 |
| 590 | Mike Cuellar | .75 |
| 591 | Mike Ryan | .60 |
| 592 | Daryl Patterson | .60 |
| 593 | Chicago Cubs | 1.25 |
| 594 | Jake Gibbs | .60 |
| 595 | Maury Wills | 2.00 |
| 596 | Mike Hershberger | .60 |
| 597 | Sonny Siebert | .60 |
| 598 | Joe Pepitone | 1.00 |
| 599 | Senators Rookies: | .60 |
| | Dick Such, Gene Martin, | |
| | Dick Stelmaszek, | |
| 600 | Willie Mays | 20.00 |
| 601 | Pete Richert | .60 |
| 602 | Ted Savage | .60 |
| 603 | Ray Oyler | .60 |
| 604 | Clarence Gaston | .60 |
| 605 | Rick Wise | .60 |
| 606 | Chico Ruiz | .60 |
| 607 | Gary Waslewski | .60 |
| 608 | Pittsburgh Pirates | 1.00 |
| 609 | Buck Martinez | .60 |
| 610 | Jerry Koosman | 1.25 |
| 611 | Norm Cash | .75 |
| 612 | Jim Hickman | .60 |
| 613 | Dave Baldwin | .60 |
| 614 | Mike Shannon | .60 |
| 615 | Mark Belanger | .60 |
| 616 | Jim Merritt | .60 |
| 617 | Jim French | .60 |
| 618 | Billy Wynne | .60 |
| 619 | Norm Miller | .60 |
| 620 | Jim Perry | 1.00 |
| 621 | Braves Rookies: | 10.00 |
| | Darrell Evans, Mike | |
| | McQueen, Rick Kester | |
| 622 | Don Sutton | 5.00 |
| 623 | Horace Clarke | .60 |
| 624 | Clyde King | .60 |
| 625 | Dean Chance | .60 |
| 626 | Dave Ricketts | .60 |
| 627 | Gary Wagner | .60 |
| 628 | Wayne Garrett | .60 |
| 629 | Merv Rettenmund | .60 |
| 630 | Ernie Banks | 12.00 |
| 631 | Oakland Athletics | 1.00 |
| 632 | Gary Sutherland | .60 |
| 633 | Roger Nelson | .60 |
| 634 | Bud Harrelson | 2.00 |
| 635 | Bob Allison | 1.50 |
| 636 | Jim Stewart | .60 |
| 637 | Cleveland Indians | 2.50 |
| 638 | Frank Bertaina | 1.50 |
| 639 | Dave Campbell | 1.50 |
| 640 | Al Kaline | 20.00 |
| 641 | Al McBean | 1.50 |
| 642 | Angels Rookies: | 1.50 |
| | Greg Garrett, Jarvis Tatum, | |
| | Gordon Lund | |
| 643 | Jose Pagan | 1.50 |
| 644 | Gerry Nyman | 1.50 |
| 645 | Don Money | 1.50 |
| 646 | Jim Britton | 1.50 |
| 647 | Tom Matchick | 1.50 |
| 648 | Larry Haney | 1.50 |
| 649 | Jimmie Hall | 1.50 |

| NO. | PLAYER | MINT |
|---|---|---|
| 650 | Sam McDowell | 1.50 |
| 651 | Jim Gosger | 1.50 |
| 652 | Rich Rollins | 1.50 |
| 653 | Moe Drabowsky | 1.50 |
| 654 | NL Rookies: | 2.00 |
| | Oscar Gamble, Boots Day, | |
| | Angel Mangual | |
| 655 | John Roseboro | 1.50 |
| 656 | Jim Hardin | 1.50 |
| 657 | San Diego Padres | 3.00 |
| 658 | Ken Tatum | 1.50 |
| 659 | Pete Ward | 1.50 |
| 660 | Johnny Bench | 75.00 |
| 661 | Jerry Robertson | 1.50 |
| 662 | Frank Lucchesi | 1.50 |
| 663 | Tito Francona | 1.50 |
| 664 | Bob Robertson | 1.50 |
| 665 | Jim Lonborg | 1.50 |
| 666 | Adolfo Phillips | 1.50 |
| 667 | Bob Meyer | 1.50 |
| 668 | Bob Tillman | 1.50 |
| 669 | White Sox Rookies: | 1.50 |
| | Bart Johnson, Dan Lazar, | |
| | Mickey Scott | |
| 670 | Ron Santo | 3.00 |
| 671 | Jim Campanis | 1.50 |
| 672 | Leon McFadden | 1.50 |
| 673 | Ted Uhlaender | 1.50 |
| 674 | Dave Leonhard | 1.50 |
| 675 | Jose Cardenal | 1.50 |
| 676 | Washington Senators | 2.50 |
| 677 | Woodie Fryman | 1.50 |
| 678 | Dave Duncan | 1.50 |
| 679 | Ray Sadecki | 1.50 |
| 680 | Rico Petrocelli | 2.00 |
| 681 | Bob Garibaldi | 1.50 |
| 682 | Dalton Jones | 1.50 |
| 683 | Reds Rookies: | 2.50 |
| | Wayne Simpson, Vern | |
| | Geishert, Hal McRae | |
| 684 | Jack Fisher | 1.50 |
| 685 | Tom Haller | 1.50 |
| 686 | Jackie Hernandez | 1.50 |
| 687 | Bob Priddy | 1.50 |
| 688 | Ted Kubiak | 1.50 |
| 689 | Frank Tepedino | 1.50 |
| 690 | Ron Fairly | 1.50 |
| 691 | Joe Grzenda | 1.50 |
| 692 | Duffy Dyer | 1.50 |
| 693 | Bob Johnson | 1.50 |
| 694 | Gary Ross | 1.50 |
| 695 | Bobby Knoop | 1.50 |
| 696 | S.F. Giants | 2.50 |
| 697 | Jim Hannan | 1.50 |
| 698 | Tom Tresh | 2.00 |
| 699 | Hank Aguirre | 1.50 |
| 700 | Frank Robinson | 18.00 |
| 701 | Jack Billingham | 1.50 |
| 702 | AL Rookies: | 1.50 |
| | Bob Johnson, Ron | |
| | Klimkowski, Bill Zepp | |
| 703 | Lou Marone | 1.50 |
| 704 | Frank Baker | 1.50 |
| 705 | Tony Cloninger | 1.50 |
| 706 | John McNamara (R) | 2.50 |
| 707 | Kevin Collins | 1.50 |
| 708 | Jose Santiago | 1.50 |
| 709 | Mike Fiore | 1.50 |
| 710 | Felix Millan | 1.50 |
| 711 | Ed Brinkman | 1.50 |
| 712 | Nolan Ryan | 45.00 |
| 713 | Seattle Pilots | 7.00 |
| 714 | Al Spangler | 1.50 |
| 715 | Mickey Lolich | 3.00 |
| 716 | Cardinals Rookies: | 1.50 |
| | Sal Campisi, R. Cleveland, | |
| | Santiago Guzman | |
| 717 | Tom Phoebus | 1.50 |
| 718 | Ed Spiezio | 1.50 |
| 719 | Jim Roland | 1.50 |
| 720 | R. Reichardt (Exc. $.75) | 4.00 |

**Prices for the 1970 set are for cards in *Mint* condition. *Excellent* copies sell for 50% of prices shown; *Very Good*—30%.**

# 1971 Topps....Complete Set of 752 Cards—Value $450.00 (Exc.); $1050.00 (Mint)

Features the rookie cards of Steve Garvey, Don Baylor and George Foster. The high numbers are 644 to 752. Semi-high numbers are 524 to 643. The cards in this set are more difficult to find in *mint* condition because the black border scratches easily.

| NO. PLAYER | MINT |
|---|---|
| 1 World Champs (Exc. $1.50) | 5.00 |
| 2 Dock Ellis | .25 |
| 3 Dick McAuliffe | .25 |
| 4 Vic Davalillo | .25 |
| 5 Thurman Munson | 12.00 |
| 6 Ed Spiezio | .25 |
| 7 Jim Holt | .25 |
| 8 Mike McQueen | .25 |
| 9 George Scott | .25 |
| 10 Claude Osteen | .25 |
| 11 Elliott Maddox | .25 |
| 12 Johnny Callison | .25 |
| 13 White Sox Rookies: | .30 |
|    C. Brinkman, D. Moloney | |
| 14 Dave Concepcion (R) | 3.50 |
| 15 Andy Messersmith | .25 |
| 16 Ken Singleton (R) | 2.00 |
| 17 Billy Sorrell | .25 |
| 18 Norm Miller | .25 |
| 19 Skip Pitlock | .25 |
| 20 Reggie Jackson | 17.50 |
| 21 Dan McGinn | .25 |
| 22 Phil Roof | .25 |
| 23 Oscar Gamble | .35 |
| 24 Rich Hand | .25 |
| 25 Clarence Caston | .25 |
| 26 Bert Blyleven (R) | 9.00 |
| 27 Pirates Rookies | .30 |
|    Fred Cambria, Gene Clines | |
| 28 Ron Klimkowski | .25 |
| 29 Don Buford | .25 |
| 30 Phil Niekro | 3.00 |
| 31 Eddie Kasko | .25 |
| 32 Jerry Da Vanon | .25 |
| 33 Del Unser | .25 |
| 34 Sandy Vance | .25 |
| 35 Lou Piniella | .75 |
| 36 Dean Chance | .25 |
| 37 Rich McKinney | .25 |
| 38 Jim Colborn | .25 |
| 39 Tiger Rookies: | .40 |
|    L. LaGrow, Gene Lamont | |
| 40 Lee May | .25 |
| 41 Rick Austin | .25 |
| 42 Boots Day | .25 |
| 43 Steve Kealey | .25 |
| 44 Johnny Edwards | .25 |
| 45 Jim Hunter | 3.00 |
| 46 Dave Campbell | .25 |
| 47 Johnny Jeter | .25 |
| 48 Dave Baldwin | .25 |
| 49 Don Money | .25 |
| 50 Willy McCovey | 5.00 |
| 51 Steve Kline | .25 |
| 52 Braves Rookies: | .35 |
|    Oscar Brown, Earl Williams | |
| 53 Paul Blair | .25 |
| 54 Checklist No. 1 | 1.50 |
| 55 Steve Carlton | 10.00 |
| 56 Duane Josephson | .25 |
| 57 Von Joshua | .25 |
| 58 Bill Lee | .25 |
| 59 Gene Mauch (Mgr.) | .25 |
| 60 Dick Bosman | .25 |
| 61 AL Batting Leaders: | 1.00 |
|    Alex Johnson, Carl Yastrzemski, Tony Oliva | |

| NO. PLAYER | MINT |
|---|---|
| 62 NL Batting Leaders: | .60 |
|    Joe Torre, Rico Carty, Manny Sanguillen | |
| 63 AL RBI Leaders: | .75 |
|    Boog Powell, Frank Robinson, Tony Conigliaro | |
| 64 NL RBI Leaders: | .75 |
|    Johnny Bench, Billy Williams, Tony Perez | |
| 65 AL HR Leaders | .75 |
|    Frank Howard, Harmon Killewbrew, C. Yastrzemski | |
| 66 NL HR Leaders: | .75 |
|    Johnny Bench, Billy Williams, Tony Perez | |
| 67 AL ERA Leaders: | .60 |
|    Clyde Wright, Diego Segui, Jim Palmer | |
| 68 NL ERA Leaders: | .75 |
|    Wayne Simpson, Luke Walker, Tom Seaver | |
| 69 AL Pitching Leaders: | .60 |
|    Mike Cuellar, Dave McNally, Jim Perry | |
| 70 NL Pitching Leaders: | 1.00 |
|    Gaylord Perry, Bob Gibson, Fergie Jenkins | |
| 71 AL Strikeout Leaders: | .60 |
|    Sam McDowell, Mickey Lolich, Bob Johnson | |
| 72 NL Strikeout Leaders. | 1.00 |
|    Bob Gibson, Tom Seaver, Fergie Jenkins | |
| 73 George Brunet | .25 |
| 74 Twins Rookies: | .30 |
|    Pete Hamm, Jim Nettles | |
| 75 Gary Nolan | .25 |
| 76 Ted Savage | .25 |
| 77 Mike Compton | .25 |
| 78 Jim Spencer | .25 |
| 79 Wade Blasingame | .25 |
| 80 Bill Melton | .25 |
| 81 Felix Millan | .25 |
| 82 Casey Cox | .25 |
| 83 Met Rookies: | .35 |
|    Tim Foli, Randy Bobb | |
| 84 Marcel Lachemann | .25 |
| 85 Bill Grabarkewitz | .25 |
| 86 Mike Kilkenny | .25 |
| 87 Jack Heidemann | .25 |
| 88 Hal King | .25 |
| 89 Ken Brett | .25 |
| 90 Joe Pepitone | .35 |
| 91 Bob Lemon (Mgr.) | .75 |
| 92 Fred Wenz | .25 |
| 93 Senators Rookies: | .25 |
|    Norm McRae, Denny Riddleberger | |
| 94 Don Hahn | .25 |
| 95 Luis Tiant | .50 |
| 96 Joe Hague | .25 |
| 97 Floyd Wicker | .25 |
| 98 Joe Decker | .25 |
| 99 Mark Belanger | .40 |
| 100 Pete Rose | 42.00 |
| 101 Les Cain | .25 |

| NO. PLAYER | MINT |
|---|---|
| 102 Astros Rookies: | .50 |
|    Ken Forsch, Larry Howard | |
| 103 Rich Severson | .25 |
| 104 Dan Frisella | .25 |
| 105 Tony Conigliaro | 1.00 |
| 106 Tom Dukes | .25 |
| 107 Roy Foster | .25 |
| 108 John Cumberland | .25 |
| 109 Steve Hovley | .25 |
| 110 Bill Mazeroski | .75 |
| 111 Yankee Rookies: | .35 |
|    L. Colson, B. Mitchell | |
| 112 Manny Mota | .50 |
| 113 Jerry Crider | .25 |
| 114 Billy Conigliaro | .25 |
| 115 Donn Clendenon | .25 |
| 116 Ken Sanders | .25 |
| 117 Ted Simmons (R) | 6.00 |
| 118 Cookie Rojas | .25 |
| 119 Frank Lucchesi (Mgr.) | .25 |
| 120 Willie Horton | .30 |
| 121 Cubs Rookies: | .35 |
|    J. Dunegan, R. Skidmore | |
| 122 Eddie Watt | .25 |
| 123 Checklist No. 2 | 1.50 |
| 124 Don Gullett | .25 |
| 125 Ray Fosse | .25 |
| 126 Danny Coombs | .25 |
| 127 Danny Thompson | .25 |
| 128 Frank Johnson | .25 |
| 129 Aurelio Monteagudo | .25 |
| 130 Denis Menke | .25 |
| 131 Curt Blefary | .25 |
| 132 Jose Laboy | .25 |
| 133 Mickey Lolich | .60 |
| 134 Jose Arcia | .25 |
| 135 Rick Monday | .50 |
| 136 Duffy Dyer | .25 |
| 137 Marcelino Lopez | .25 |
| 138 Phillies Rookies: | .35 |
|    Joe Lis, W. Montanez | |
| 139 Paul Casanova | .35 |
| 140 Gaylord Perry | 2.50 |
| 141 Frank Quilici | .25 |
| 142 Mack Jones | .25 |
| 143 Steve Blass | .25 |
| 144 Jackie Hernandez | .25 |
| 145 Bill Singer | .25 |
| 146 Ralph Houk (Mgr.) | .30 |
| 147 Bob Priddy | .25 |
| 148 John Mayberry | .25 |
| 149 Mike Hershberger | .25 |
| 150 Sam McDowell | .50 |
| 151 Tommy Davis | .30 |
| 152 Angels Rookies: | .30 |
|    Lloyd Allen, Winston Llenas | |
| 153 Gary Ross | .25 |
| 154 Cesar Gutierrez | .25 |
| 155 Ken Henderson | .25 |
| 156 Bart Johnson | .25 |
| 157 Bob Bailey | .25 |
| 158 Jerry Reuss | .45 |
| 159 Jarvis Tatum | .25 |
| 160 Tom Seaver | 14.00 |
| 161 Coins Checklist | 1.25 |
| 162 Jack Billingham | .25 |

| NO. PLAYER | MINT |
|---|---|
| 163 Buck Martinez | .25 |
| 164 Reds Rookies: | .60 |
|    Frank Duffy, Milt Wilcox | |
| 165 Cesar Tovar | .25 |
| 166 Joe Hoerner | .25 |
| 167 Tom Grieve | .25 |
| 168 Bruce Dal Canton | .25 |
| 169 Ed Herrmann | .25 |
| 170 Mike Cuellar | .50 |
| 171 Bobby Wine | .25 |
| 172 Duke Sims | .25 |
| 173 Gil Garrido | .25 |
| 174 Dave LaRoche | .25 |
| 175 Jim Hickman | .25 |
| 176 Red Sox Rookies: | .35 |
|    Bob Montgomery, Doug Griffin | |
| 177 Hal McRae | .50 |
| 178 Dave Duncan | .25 |
| 179 Mike Corkins | .25 |
| 180 Al Kaline | 5.00 |
| 181 Hal Lanier | .50 |
| 182 Al Downing | .25 |
| 183 Gil Hodges (Mgr.) | 2.00 |
| 184 Stan Bahnsen | .25 |
| 185 Julian Javier | .25 |
| 186 Bob Spence | .25 |
| 187 Ted Abernathy | .25 |
| 188 Dodgers Rookies: | 2.00 |
|    Mike Strahler, Bob Valentine | |
| 189 George Mitterwald | .25 |
| 190 Bob Tolan | .25 |
| 191 Mike Andrews | .25 |
| 192 Billy Wilson | .25 |
| 193 Bob Grich (R) | 1.50 |
| 194 Mike Lum | .25 |
| 195 AL Playoff Game 1 | .75 |
|    Powell Muscles Twins | |
| 196 AL Playoff Game 2 | .75 |
|    McNally's Two Straight | |
| 197 AL Playoff Game 3 | 1.50 |
|    Palmer Mows 'Em Down | |
| 198 Orioles Celebrate | .75 |
|    A Team Effort | |
| 199 NL Playoff Game 1 | .75 |
|    Cline Pinch-Triple | |
| 200 NL Playoff Game 2 | .75 |
|    Tolan Scores Third Time | |
| 201 NL Playoff Game 3 | .75 |
|    Cline Scores Winning Run | |
| 202 Reds Celebrate | .75 |
|    World Series Bound | |
| 203 Larry Gura (R) | 1.00 |
| 204 Brewers Rookies: | .30 |
|    B. Smith, G. Kopacz | |
| 205 Gerry Moses | .25 |
| 206 Checklist No. 3 | 1.50 |
| 207 Alan Foster | .25 |
| 208 Billy Martin | 1.50 |
| 209 Steve Renko | .25 |
| 210 Rod Carew | 10.00 |
| 211 Phil Hennigan | .25 |
| 212 Rich Hebner | .25 |
| 213 Frank Baker | .25 |
| 214 Al Ferrara | .25 |
| 215 Diego Segui | .25 |

| NO. PLAYER | MINT |
|---|---|
| 216 Cards Rookies: | .30 |
| Reggie Cleveland, | |
| Luis Melendez | |
| 217 Ed Stroud | .25 |
| 218 Tony Cloninger | .25 |
| 219 Elrod Hendricks | .25 |
| 220 Ron Santo | .60 |
| 221 Dave Morehead | .25 |
| 222 Bob Watson | .40 |
| 223 Cecil Upshaw | .25 |
| 224 Alan Gallagher | .25 |
| 225 Gary Peters | .25 |
| 226 Bill Russell | .40 |
| 227 Floyd Weaver | .25 |
| 228 Wayne Garrett | .25 |
| 229 Jim Hannan | .25 |
| 230 Willie Stargell | 5.00 |
| 231 Indians Rookies: | .35 |
| Vince Colbert, | |
| John Lowenstein | |
| 232 John Strohmayer | .25 |
| 233 Larry Bowa | 1.50 |
| 234 Jim Lyttle | .25 |
| 235 Nate Colbert | .25 |
| 236 Bob Humphreys | .25 |
| 237 Cesar Cedeno (R) | 1.50 |
| 238 Chuck Dobson | .25 |
| 239 R. Schoendienst (Mgr.) | .40 |
| 240 Clyde Wright | .25 |
| 241 Dave Nelson | .25 |
| 242 Jim Ray | .25 |
| 243 Carlos May | .25 |
| 244 Bob Tillman | .25 |
| 245 Jim Kaat | 1.50 |
| 246 Tony Taylor | .25 |
| 247 Royals Rookies: | .50 |
| Jerry Cram, Paul Splittorff | |
| 248 Hoyt Wilhelm | 2.50 |
| 249 Chico Salmon | .25 |
| 250 Johnny Bench | 15.00 |
| 251 Frank Reberger | .25 |
| 252 Eddie Leon | .25 |
| 253 Bill Sudakis | .25 |
| 254 Cal Koonce | .25 |
| 255 Bob Robertson | .25 |
| 256 Tony Gonzalez | .25 |
| 257 Nelson Briles | .25 |
| 258 Dick Green | .25 |
| 259 Dave Marshall | .25 |
| 260 Tommy Harper | .25 |
| 261 Darold Knowles | .25 |
| 262 Padres Rookies: | .30 |
| D. Robinson, J. Williams | |
| 263 John Ellis | .25 |
| 264 Joe Morgan | 2.50 |
| 265 Jim Northrup | .25 |
| 266 Bill Stoneman | .25 |
| 267 Rich Morales | .25 |
| 268 Philadelphia Phillies | .60 |
| 269 Gail Hopkins | .25 |
| 270 Rico Carty | .50 |
| 271 Bill Zepp | .25 |
| 272 Tommy Helms | .25 |
| 273 Pete Richert | .25 |
| 274 Ron Slocum | .25 |
| 275 Vada Pinson | .60 |
| 276 Giants Rookies: | 5.00 |
| M. Davison, George Foster | |
| 277 Gary Waslewski | .25 |
| 278 Jerry Grote | .25 |
| 279 Lefty Phillips (Mgr.) | .25 |
| 280 Fergie Jenkins | 2.50 |
| 281 Danny Walton | .25 |
| 282 Jose Pagan | .25 |
| 283 Dick Such | .25 |
| 284 Jim Gosger | .25 |
| 285 Sal Bando | .50 |
| 286 Jerry McNertney | .25 |
| 287 Mike Fiore | .25 |
| 288 Joe Moeller | .25 |
| 289 Chicago White Sox | .40 |
| 290 Tony Oliva | 1.50 |
| 291 George Culver | .25 |
| 292 Jay Johnstone | .25 |
| 293 Pat Corrales | .40 |

| NO. PLAYER | MINT |
|---|---|
| 294 Steve Dunning | .25 |
| 295 Bobby Bonds | 1.25 |
| 296 Tom Timmermann | .25 |
| 297 Johnny Briggs | .25 |
| 298 Jim Nelson | .25 |
| 299 Ed Kirkpatrick | .25 |
| 300 Brooks Robinson | 6.00 |
| 301 Earl Wilson | .25 |
| 302 Phil Gagliano | .25 |
| 303 Lindy McDaniel | .25 |
| 304 Ron Brand | .25 |
| 305 Reggie Smith | .75 |
| 306 Jim Nash | .25 |
| 307 Don Wert | .25 |
| 308 St. Louis Cardinals | .50 |
| 309 Dick Ellsworth | .25 |
| 310 Tommie Agee | .40 |
| 311 Lee Stange | .25 |
| 312 Harry Walker | .25 |
| 313 Tom Hall | .25 |
| 314 Jeff Torborg | .25 |
| 315 Ron Fairly | .40 |
| 316 Fred Scherman | .25 |
| 317 Athletic Rookies: | .25 |
| Angel Mangual, Jim Driscoll | |
| 318 Rudy May | .25 |
| 319 Ty Cline | .25 |
| 320 Dave McNally | .40 |
| 321 Tom Matchick | .25 |
| 322 Jim Beauchamp | .25 |
| 323 Billy Champion | .25 |
| 324 Graig Nettles | 2.00 |
| 325 Juan Marichal | 4.00 |
| 326 Richie Scheinblum | .25 |
| 327 World Series Game 1 | 1.00 |
| Powell Homers | |
| 328 World Series Game 2 | 1.00 |
| Buford Goes 2 For 4 | |
| 329 World Series Game 3 | 1.50 |
| F. Robinson Shows Muscle | |
| 330 World Series Game 4 | 1.00 |
| Reds Stay Alive | |
| 331 World Series Game 5 | 1.50 |
| B. Robinson Robbery | |
| 332 World Series Celebratio | 1.00 |
| Convincing Performance | |
| 333 Clay Kirby | .25 |
| 334 Roberto Pena | .25 |
| 335 Jerry Koosman | .75 |
| 336 Detroit Tigers | .60 |
| 337 Jesus Alou | .25 |
| 338 Gene Tenace | .40 |
| 339 Wayne Simpson | .25 |
| 340 Rico Petrocelli | .40 |
| 341 Steve Garvey (R) | 70.00 |
| 342 Frank Tepedino | .25 |
| 343 Pirates Rookies: | .30 |
| Ed Acosta, M. May | |
| 344 Ellie Rodriguez | .25 |
| 345 Joe Horlen | .25 |
| 346 Lum Harris | .25 |
| 347 Ted Uhlaender | .25 |
| 348 Fred Norman | .25 |
| 349 Rich Reese | .25 |
| 350 Billy Williams | 4.00 |
| 351 Jim Shellenback | .25 |
| 352 Denny Doyle | .25 |
| 353 Carl Taylor | .25 |
| 354 Don McMahon | .25 |
| 355 Bud Harrelson | .40 |
| 356 Bob Locker | .25 |
| 357 Cincinnati Reds | .75 |
| 358 Danny Cater | .25 |
| 359 Ron Reed | .25 |
| 360 Jim Fregosi | .50 |
| 361 Don Sutton | 3.00 |
| 362 Orioles Rookies: | .35 |
| Mike Adamson, R. Freed | |
| 363 Mike Nagy | .25 |
| 364 Tommy Dean | .25 |
| 365 Bob Johnson | .25 |
| 366 Ron Stone | .25 |
| 367 Dalton Jones | .25 |
| 368 Bob Veale | .25 |
| 369 Checklist No. 4 | 1.50 |

| NO. PLAYER | MINT |
|---|---|
| 370 Joe Torre | 2.00 |
| 371 Jack Hiatt | .25 |
| 372 Lew Krausse | .25 |
| 373 Tom McCraw | .25 |
| 374 Clete Boyer | .50 |
| 375 Steve Hargan | .25 |
| 376 Expos Rookies: | .25 |
| C. Mashore, E. McAnally | |
| 377 Greg Garrett | .25 |
| 378 Tito Fuentes | .25 |
| 379 Wayne Granger | .25 |
| 380 Ted Williams (Mgr.) | 3.00 |
| 381 Fred Gladding | .25 |
| 382 Jake Gibbs | .25 |
| 383 Rod Gaspar | .25 |
| 384 Rollie Fingers | 2.00 |
| 385 Maury Wills | 1.00 |
| 386 Boston Red Sox | 1.00 |
| 387 Ron Herbel | .25 |
| 388 Al Oliver | 2.00 |
| 389 Ed Brinkman | .25 |
| 390 Glenn Beckert | .25 |
| 391 Twins Rookies: | .25 |
| Steve Brye, Cotton Nash | |
| 392 Grant Jackson | .25 |
| 393 Merv Rettenmund | .25 |
| 394 Clay Carroll | .25 |
| 395 Roy White | .40 |
| 396 Dick Schofield | .25 |
| 397 Alvin Dark (Mgr.) | .40 |
| 398 Howie Reed | .25 |
| 399 Jim French | .25 |
| 400 Hank Aaron | 15.00 |
| 401 Tom Murphy | .25 |
| 402 Los Angeles Dodgers | 1.00 |
| 403 Joe Coleman | .25 |
| 404 Astros Rookies: | .25 |
| B. Harris, R. Metzger | |
| 405 Leo Cardenas | .25 |
| 406 Ray Sadecki | .25 |
| 407 Joe Rudi | .50 |
| 408 Rafael Robles | .25 |
| 409 Don Pavletich | .25 |
| 410 Ken Holtzman | .40 |
| 411 George Spriggs | .25 |
| 412 Jerry Johnson | .25 |
| 413 Pat Kelly | .25 |
| 414 Woodie Fryman | .25 |
| 415 Mike Hegan | .25 |
| 416 Gene Alley | .25 |
| 417 Dick Hall | .25 |
| 418 Adolfo Phillips | .25 |
| 419 Ron Hansen | .25 |
| 420 Jim Merritt | .25 |
| 421 John Stephenson | .25 |
| 422 Frank Bertaina | .25 |
| 423 Tigers Rookies: | .45 |
| T. Marting, D. Saunders | |
| 424 Roberto Rodriguez | .25 |
| 425 Doug Rader | .40 |
| 426 Chris Cannizzaro | .25 |
| 427 Bernie Allen | .25 |
| 428 Jim McAndrew | .25 |
| 429 Chuck Hinton | .25 |
| 430 Wes Parker | .40 |
| 431 Tom Burgmeier | .25 |
| 432 Bob Didier | .25 |
| 433 Skip Lockwood | .25 |
| 434 Gary Sutherland | .25 |
| 435 Jose Cardenal | .25 |
| 436 Wilbur Wood | .25 |
| 437 Danny Murtaugh (Mgr.) | .25 |
| 438 Mike McCormick | .25 |
| 439 Phillies Rookies: | 2.00 |
| Greg Luzinski, Scott Reid | |
| 440 Bert Campaneris | .50 |
| 441 Milt Pappas | .25 |
| 442 California Angels | .75 |
| 443 Rich Robertson | .25 |
| 444 Jimmie Price | .25 |
| 445 Art Shamsky | .25 |
| 446 Bobby Bolin | .25 |
| 447 Cesar Geronimo | .25 |
| 448 Dave Roberts | .25 |
| 449 Brant Alyea | .25 |

| NO. PLAYER | MINT |
|---|---|
| 450 Bob Gibson | 4.50 |
| 451 Joe Keough | .25 |
| 452 John Boccabella | .25 |
| 453 Terry Crowley | .25 |
| 454 Mike Paul | .25 |
| 455 Don Kessinger | .40 |
| 456 Bob Meyer | .25 |
| 457 Willie Smith | .25 |
| 458 White Sox Rookies: | .30 |
| Ron Lolich, Dave Lemonds | |
| 459 Jim LeFebvre | .25 |
| 460 Fritz Peterson | .25 |
| 461 Jim Hart | .40 |
| 462 Senators Team | .75 |
| 463 Tom Kelley | .25 |
| 464 Aurelio Rodriguez | .25 |
| 465 Tim McCarver | .75 |
| 466 Ken Berry | .25 |
| 467 Al Santorini | .25 |
| 468 Frank Fernandez | .25 |
| 469 Bob Aspromonte | .25 |
| 470 Bob Oliver | .25 |
| 471 Tom Griffin | .25 |
| 472 Ken Rudolph | .25 |
| 473 Gary Wagner | .25 |
| 474 Jim Fairey | .25 |
| 475 Ron Perranoski | .40 |
| 476 Dal Maxvill | .35 |
| 477 Earl Weaver (Mgr.) | .75 |
| 478 Bernie Carbo | .25 |
| 479 Dennis Higgins | .25 |
| 480 Manny Sanguillen | .40 |
| 481 Daryl Patterson | .25 |
| 482 San Diego Padres | .50 |
| 483 Gene Michael | .40 |
| 484 Don Wilson | .25 |
| 485 Ken McMullen | .25 |
| 486 Steve Huntz | .25 |
| 487 Paul Schaal | .25 |
| 488 Jerry Stephenson | .25 |
| 489 Luis Alvardao | .25 |
| 490 Deron Johnson | .25 |
| 491 Jim Hardin | .25 |
| 492 Ken Boswell | .25 |
| 493 Dave May | .25 |
| 494 Braves Rookies: | .50 |
| Ralph Garr, Rick Kester | |
| 495 Felipe Alou | .50 |
| 496 Woody Woodward | .40 |
| 497 Horacio Pina | .25 |
| 498 John Kennedy | .25 |
| 499 Checklist No. 5 | 1.50 |
| 500 Jim Perry | .50 |
| 501 Andy Etchebarren | .25 |
| 502 Chicago Cubs | .60 |
| 503 Gates Brown | .25 |
| 504 Ken Wright | .25 |
| 505 Ollie Brown | .25 |
| 506 Bobby Knoop | .25 |
| 507 George Stone | .25 |
| 508 Roger Repoz | .25 |
| 509 Jim Grant | .25 |
| 510 Ken Harrelson | .75 |
| 511 Chris Short | .25 |
| 512 Red Sox Rookies: | .35 |
| Dick Mills, Mike Garman | |
| 513 Nolan Ryan | 15.00 |
| 514 Ron Woods | .25 |
| 515 Carl Morton | .25 |
| 516 Ted Kubiak | .25 |
| 517 Charlie Fox (Mgr.) | .25 |
| 518 Joe Grzenda | .25 |
| 519 Willie Crawford | .25 |
| 520 Tommy John | 2.00 |
| 521 Leron Lee | .25 |
| 522 Minnesota Twins | .60 |
| 523 John Odom | .25 |
| 524 Mickey Stanley | .75 |
| 525 Ernie Banks | 9.00 |
| 526 Ray Jarvis | .75 |
| 527 Cleon Jones | .75 |
| 528 Wally Bunker | .25 |
| 529 NL Rookies: | 2.50 |
| Enzo, Hernandez, Bill | |
| Buckner, Marty Perez | |

**Prices for the 1971 set are for cards in *Mint* condition. *Excellent* copies sell for 50% of prices shown; *Very Good*—30%.**

# 1971 Topps (Continued)

| NO. PLAYER | MINT |
|---|---|
| 530 Carl Yastrzemski | 22.00 |
| 531 Mike Torrez | .75 |
| 532 Bill Rigney (Mgr.) | .75 |
| 533 Mike Ryan | .75 |
| 534 Luke Walker | .75 |
| 535 Curt Flood | 1.00 |
| 536 Claude Raymond | .75 |
| 537 Tom Egan | .75 |
| 538 Angel Bravo | .75 |
| 539 Larry Brown | .75 |
| 540 Larry Dierker | .75 |
| 541 Bob Burda | .75 |
| 542 Bob Miller | .75 |
| 543 New York Yankees | 2.00 |
| 544 Vida Blue | 2.00 |
| 545 Dick Dietz | .75 |
| 546 John Matias | .75 |
| 547 Pat Dobson | .75 |
| 548 Don Mason | .75 |
| 549 Jim Brewer | .75 |
| 550 Harmon Killebrew | 9.00 |
| 551 Frank Linzy | .75 |
| 552 Buddy Bradford | .75 |
| 553 Kevin Collins | .75 |
| 554 Lowell Palmer | .75 |
| 555 Walt Williams | .75 |
| 556 Jim McGlothlin | .75 |
| 557 Tom Satriano | .75 |
| 558 Hector Torres | .75 |
| 559 AL Rookies: | .75 |
| Gary Jones, Terry Cox, Bill Gogolewski | |
| 560 Rusty Staub | 1.50 |
| 561 Syd O'Brien | .75 |
| 562 Dave Giusti | .75 |
| 563 Giants Team | 1.50 |
| 564 Al Fitzmorris | .75 |
| 565 Jim Wynn | .75 |
| 566 Tim Cullen | .75 |
| 567 Walt Alston (Mgr.) | 1.50 |
| 568 Sal Campisi | .75 |
| 569 Ivan Murrell | .75 |
| 570 Jim Palmer | 8.00 |
| 571 Ted Sizemore | .75 |
| 572 Jerry Kenney | .75 |
| 573 Ed Kranepool | .75 |
| 574 Jim Bunning | 2.00 |
| 575 Bill Freehan | 1.00 |
| 576 Cubs Rookies: | .75 |
| Brock Davis, Adrian Garrett, Garry Jestadt | |
| 577 Jim Lonborg | 1.00 |
| 578 Ron Hunt | .75 |
| 579 Marty Pattin | .75 |
| 580 Tony Perez | 2.50 |
| 581 Roger Nelson | .75 |
| 582 Dave Cash | .75 |
| 583 Ron Cook | .75 |
| 584 Cleveland Indians | 1.25 |
| 585 Willie Davis | .75 |
| 586 Dick Woodson | .75 |

| NO. PLAYER | MINT |
|---|---|
| 587 Sonny Jackson | .75 |
| 588 Tom Bradley | .75 |
| 589 Bob Barton | .75 |
| 590 Alex Johnson | .75 |
| 591 Jackie Brown | .75 |
| 592 Randy Hundley | .75 |
| 593 Jack Aker | .75 |
| 594 Cardinals Rookies: | 1.00 |
| Bob Chlupsa, Bob Stinson, Al Hrabosky | |
| 595 Dave Johnson | 1.50 |
| 596 Mike Jorgensen | .75 |
| 597 Ken Suarez | .75 |
| 598 Rick Wise | .75 |
| 599 Norm Cash | 1.00 |
| 600 Willie Mays | 27.00 |
| 601 Ken Tatum | .75 |
| 602 Marty Martinez | .75 |
| 603 Pittsburgh Pirates | 1.50 |
| 604 John Gelnar | .75 |
| 605 Orlando Cepeda | 2.50 |
| 606 Chuck Taylor | .75 |
| 607 Paul Ratliff | .75 |
| 608 Mike Wegener | .75 |
| 609 Leo Durocher (Mgr.) | 1.25 |
| 610 Amos Otis | 1.00 |
| 611 Tom Phoebus | .75 |
| 612 Indians Rookies: | .75 |
| Ted Ford, Steve Mingori, Lou Camilli | |
| 613 Pedro Borbon | .75 |
| 614 Billy Cowan | .75 |
| 615 Mel Stottlemyre | 1.25 |
| 616 Larry Hisle | .75 |
| 617 Clay Dalrymple | .75 |
| 618 Tug McGraw | 1.00 |
| 619 Checklist No. 6 | 2.00 |
| 620 Frank Howard | 1.00 |
| 621 Ron Bryant | .75 |
| 622 Joe LaHoud | .75 |
| 623 Pat Jarvis | .75 |
| 624 Oakland Athletics | 1.25 |
| 625 Lou Brock | 9.00 |
| 626 Freddie Patek | .75 |
| 627 Steve Hamilton | .75 |
| 628 John Bateman | .75 |
| 629 John Hiller | .75 |
| 630 Roberto Clemente | 18.00 |
| 631 Eddie Fisher | .75 |
| 632 Darrel Chaney | .75 |
| 633 AL Rookies: | .75 |
| Pete Koegel, Bobby Brooks, Scott Northey | |
| 634 Phil Regan | .75 |
| 635 Bobby Murcer | 1.50 |
| 636 Denny LeMaster | .75 |
| 637 Dave Bristol (Mgr.) | .75 |
| 638 Stan Williams | .75 |
| 639 Tom Haller | .75 |
| 640 Frank Robinson | 10.00 |
| 641 New York Mets | 2.00 |

| NO. PLAYER | MINT |
|---|---|
| 642 Jim Roland | .75 |
| 643 Rick Reichardt | .75 |
| 644 Jim Stewart | 1.35 |
| 645 Jim Maloney | 1.50 |
| 646 Bobby Floyd | 1.35 |
| 647 Juan Pizarro | 1.35 |
| 648 Mets Rookies: | 2.50 |
| Rich Folkers, Ted Martinez, John Matlack | |
| 649 Sparky Lyle | 2.00 |
| 650 Rich Allen | 5.00 |
| 651 Jerry Robertson | 1.35 |
| 652 Atlanta Braves | 2.50 |
| 653 Russ Snyder | 1.25 |
| 654 Don Shaw | 1.25 |
| 655 Mike Epstein | 1.25 |
| 656 Gerry Nyman | 1.25 |
| 657 Jose Azcue | 1.25 |
| 658 Paul Lindblad | 1.25 |
| 659 Byron Browne | 1.25 |
| 660 Ray Culp | 1.25 |
| 661 Chuck Tanner (Mgr.) | 2.00 |
| 662 Mike Hedlund | 1.25 |
| 663 Marv Staehle | 1.25 |
| 664 Rookies Pitchers: | 1.25 |
| Archie Reynolds, Bob Reynolds, K. Reynolds | |
| 665 Ron Swoboda | 1.25 |
| 666 Gene Brabender | 1.25 |
| 667 Pete Ward | 1.25 |
| 668 Gary Neibauer | 1.25 |
| 669 Ike Brown | 1.25 |
| 670 Bill Hands | 1.25 |
| 671 Bill Voss | 1.25 |
| 672 Ed Crosby | 1.25 |
| 673 Gerry Janeski | 1.25 |
| 674 Montreal Expos | 3.00 |
| 675 Dave Boswell | 1.25 |
| 676 Tommie Reynolds | 1.25 |
| 677 Jack DiLauro | 1.25 |
| 678 George Thomas | 1.25 |
| 679 Don O'Riley | 1.25 |
| 680 Don Mincher | 1.25 |
| 681 Bill Butler | 1.25 |
| 682 Terry Harmon | 1.25 |
| 683 Bill Burbach | 1.25 |
| 684 Curt Motton | 1.25 |
| 685 Moe Drabowsky | 1.25 |
| 686 Chico Ruiz | 1.25 |
| 687 Ron Taylor | 1.25 |
| 688 S. Anderson (Mgr.) | 2.50 |
| 689 Frank Baker | 1.25 |
| 690 Bob Moose | 1.25 |
| 691 Bob Heise | 1.25 |
| 692 AL Rookies Pitchers: | 1.25 |
| Hal Haydel, Rogelio Moret, Wayne Twitchell | |
| 693 Jose Pena | 1.25 |
| 694 Rick Renick | 1.25 |
| 695 Joe Niekro | 2.00 |
| 696 Jerry Morales | 1.25 |

| NO. PLAYER | MINT |
|---|---|
| 697 Rickey Clark | 1.25 |
| 698 Milwaukee Brewers | 3.00 |
| 699 Jim Britton | 1.25 |
| 700 Boog Powell | 3.50 |
| 701 Bob Garibaldi | 1.25 |
| 702 Milt Ramirez | 1.25 |
| 703 Mike Kekich | 1.25 |
| 704 J.C. Martin | 1.25 |
| 705 Dick Selma | 1.25 |
| 706 Joe Foy | 1.25 |
| 707 Fred Lasher | 1.25 |
| 708 Russ Nagelson | 1.25 |
| 709 Rookie Outfielders: | 20.00 |
| Don Baylor, Tom Paciorek, Dusty Baker | |
| 710 Sonny Siebert | 1.25 |
| 711 Larry Stahl | 1.25 |
| 712 Jose Martinez | 1.25 |
| 713 Mike Marshall | 2.00 |
| 714 Dick Williams (Mgr.) | 1.75 |
| 715 Horace Clarke | 1.25 |
| 716 Dave Leonhard | 1.25 |
| 717 Tommie Aaron | 1.25 |
| 718 Billy Wynne | 1.25 |
| 719 Jerry May | 1.25 |
| 720 Matty Alou | 1.25 |
| 721 John Morris | 1.25 |
| 722 Houston Astros | 2.00 |
| 723 Vicente Romo | 1.25 |
| 724 Tom Tischinski | 1.25 |
| 725 Gary Gentry | 1.25 |
| 726 Paul Popovich | 1.25 |
| 727 Ray Lamb | 1.25 |
| 728 NL Rookie Outfielders: | 1.25 |
| Wayne Redmond, Keith Lampard, Bernie Williams | |
| 729 Dick Billings | 1.25 |
| 730 Jim Rooker | 1.25 |
| 731 Jim Qualls | 1.25 |
| 732 Bob Reed | 1.25 |
| 733 Lee Maye | 1.25 |
| 734 Rob Gardner | 1.25 |
| 735 Mike Shannon | 1.25 |
| 736 Mel Queen | 1.25 |
| 737 Preston Gomez (Mgr.) | 1.25 |
| 738 Russ Gibson | 1.25 |
| 739 Barry Lersch | 1.25 |
| 740 Luis Aparicio | 8.00 |
| 741 Skip Guinn | 1.25 |
| 742 Kansas City Royals | 2.50 |
| 743 John O'Donoghue | 1.25 |
| 744 Chuck Manuel | 1.25 |
| 745 Sandy Alomar | 1.25 |
| 746 Andy Kosco | 1.25 |
| 747 NL Rookie Pitchers: | 1.25 |
| Al Severinsen, Scipio Spinks, Balor Moore | |
| 748 John Purdin | 1.25 |
| 749 Ken Szotkiewicz | 1.25 |
| 750 Denny McLain | 3.50 |
| 751 Al Weis | 1.25 |
| 752 Dick Drago (Exc. $.75) | 3.50 |

## 1972 Topps....Complete Set of 787 Cards—Value $450.00 (Exc.); $1100.00 (Mint)

Features the rookie cards of Carlton Fisk and Ben Oglivie. The high numbers are 657 to 787. Semi-high numbers are 526 to 656.

| NO. PLAYER | MINT |
|---|---|
| 1 Pirates-Champs (Exc. $1.00) | 5.00 |
| 2 Ray Culp | .25 |
| 3 Bob Tolan | .25 |
| 4 Checklist No. 1 | 1.00 |
| 5 John Bateman | .25 |
| 6 Fred Scherman | .25 |
| 7 Enzo Hernandez | .25 |
| 8 Ron Swoboda | .25 |
| 9 Stan Williams | .25 |
| 10 Amos Otis | .35 |
| 11 Bobby Valentine | .50 |
| 12 Jose Cardenal | .25 |
| 13 Joe Grzenda | .25 |
| 14 Phillies Rookies: | .30 |
| Pete Koegel, Mike | |
| Anderson, W. Twitchell | |
| 15 Walt Williams | .25 |
| 16 Mike Jorgensen | .25 |
| 17 Dave Duncan | .25 |
| 18 Juan Pizarro | .25 |
| 19 Billy Cowan | .25 |
| 20 Don Wilson | .25 |
| 21 Atlanta Braves | .50 |
| 22 Rob Gardner | .25 |
| 23 Ted Kubiak | .25 |
| 24 Ted Ford | .25 |
| 25 Will Singer | .25 |
| 26 Andy Etchebarren | .25 |
| 27 Bob Johnson | .25 |
| 28 Twins Rookies: | .30 |
| Steve Brye, Bob Gebhard, | |
| Hal Haydel | |
| 29 Bill Bonham | .25 |
| 30 Rico Petrocelli | .30 |
| 31 Cleon Jones | .25 |
| 32 C. Jones (In Action) | .25 |
| 33 Billy Martin | 1.00 |
| 34 B. Martin (In Action) | .60 |
| 35 Jerry Johnson | .25 |
| 36 J. Johnson (In Action) | .25 |
| 37 Carl Yastrzemski | 10.00 |
| 38 Yastrzemski (In Action) | 5.00 |
| 39 Bob Barton | .25 |
| 40 B. Barton (In Action) | .25 |
| 41 Tommy Davis | .60 |
| 42 T. Davis (In Action) | .30 |
| 43 Rick Wise | .35 |
| 44 R. Wise (In Action) | .35 |
| 45 Glenn Beckert | .35 |
| 46 G. Beckert (In Action) | .35 |
| 47 John Ellis | .25 |
| 48 J. Ellis (In Action) | .25 |
| 49 Willie Mays | 10.00 |
| 50 W. Mays (All Action) | 5.00 |
| 51 Harmon Killebrew | 4.00 |
| 52 H. Killebrew (In Action) | 2.00 |
| 53 Bud Harrelson | .50 |
| 54 B. Harrelson (In Action) | .30 |
| 55 Clyde Wright | .25 |
| 56 Rich Chiles | .25 |
| 57 Bob Oliver | .25 |
| 58 Ernie McAnally | .25 |
| 59 Fred Stanley | .25 |
| 60 Manny Sanguillen | .35 |
| 61 Cubs Rookies: | .75 |
| Burt Hooton, Gene Hiser, | |
| Earl Stephenson | |
| 62 Angel Mangual | .25 |
| 63 Duke Sims | .25 |
| 64 Pete Broberg | .25 |
| 65 Cesar Cedeno | .75 |
| 66 Ray Corbin | .25 |
| 67 Red Schoendienst | .40 |
| 68 Jim York | .25 |
| 69 Roger Freed | .25 |
| 70 Mike Cuellar | .40 |
| 71 Angels Team | .50 |
| 72 Bruce Kison (R) | .50 |
| 73 Steve Huntz | .25 |
| 74 Cecil Upshaw | .25 |
| 75 Bert Campaneris | .50 |
| 76 Don Carrithers | .25 |
| 77 Ron Theobald | .25 |
| 78 Steve Arlin | .25 |

| NO. PLAYER | MINT |
|---|---|
| 79 Red Sox Rookies: | 17.50 |
| Carlton Fisk, Mike Garman, | |
| Cecil Cooper | |
| 80 Tony Perez | 1.75 |
| 81 Mike Hedlund | .25 |
| 82 Ron Woods | .25 |
| 83 Dalton Jones | .25 |
| 84 Vince Colbert | .25 |
| 85 NL Batting Leaders: | 1.00 |
| Ralph Garr, Glenn Beckert, | |
| Joe Torre | |
| 86 AL Batting Leaders: | 1.00 |
| Tony Oliva, Bobby Murcer, | |
| Merv Rettenmund | |
| 87 NL RBI Leaders: | 1.25 |
| Joe Torre, Willie Stargell, | |
| Hank Aaron | |
| 88 AL RBI Leaders: | 1.00 |
| Harmon Killebrew, Frank | |
| Robinson, Reggie Smith | |
| 89 NL Home Run Leaders: | 1.25 |
| Willie Stargell, Lee May, | |
| Hank Aaron | |
| 90 AL Home Run Leaders: | 1.25 |
| Reggie Jackson, Bill | |
| Melton, Norm Cash | |
| 91 NL ERA Leaders: | 1.00 |
| Tom Seaver, Dave Roberts | |
| (wrong photo), D. Wilson | |
| 92 AL ERA Leaders: | .75 |
| Vida Blue, Wilbur Wood, | |
| Jim Palmer | |
| 93 NL Pitching Leaders: | 1.25 |
| Tom Seaver, Fergie | |
| Jenkins, Steve Carlton, | |
| Al Downing | |
| 94 AL Pitching Leaders: | .60 |
| Mickey Lolich, Vida Blue, | |
| Wilbur Wood | |
| 95 NL Strikeout Leaders: | 1.00 |
| Bill Stoneman, Tom Seaver, | |
| Fergie Jenkins | |
| 96 AL Strikeout Leaders: | .60 |
| Mickey Lolich, Vida Blue, | |
| Joe Coleman | |
| 97 Tom Kelley | .25 |
| 98 Chuck Tanner | .35 |
| 99 Ross Grimsley | .25 |
| 100 Frank Robinson | 3.50 |
| 101 Astros Rookies: | 1.00 |
| B. Greif, J.R. Richard, | |
| Ray Busse | |
| 102 Lloyd Allen | .25 |
| 103 Checklist No. 2 | 1.00 |
| 104 Toby Harrah (R) | 1.50 |
| 105 Gary Gentry | .25 |
| 106 Milwaukee Brewers | .50 |
| 107 Jose Cruz (R) | 2.50 |
| 108 Gary Waslewski | .25 |
| 109 Jerry May | .25 |
| 110 Ron Hunt | .25 |
| 111 Jim Grant | .25 |
| 112 Greg Luzinski | 1.00 |
| 113 Rogelio Moret | .25 |
| 114 Bill Buckner | 1.25 |
| 115 Jim Fregosi | .35 |
| 116 Ed Farmer | .25 |
| 117 Cleo James | .25 |
| 118 Skip Lockwood | .25 |
| 119 Marty Perez | .25 |
| 120 Bill Freehan | .35 |
| 121 Ed Sprague | .25 |
| 122 Larry Biittner | .25 |
| 123 Ed Acosta | .25 |
| 124 Yankees Rookies: | .45 |
| Alan Closter, Rusty | |
| Torres, R. Hambright | |
| 125 Dave Cash | .25 |
| 126 Bart Johnson | .25 |
| 127 Duffy Dyer | .25 |
| 128 Eddie Watt | .25 |
| 129 Charlie Fox | .25 |
| 130 Bob Gibson | 3.50 |
| 131 Jim Nettles | .25 |

| NO. PLAYER | MINT |
|---|---|
| 132 Joe Morgan | 2.50 |
| 133 Joe Keough | .25 |
| 134 Carl Morton | .25 |
| 135 Vada Pinson | .50 |
| 136 Darrel Chaney | .25 |
| 137 Dick Williams | .35 |
| 138 Mike Kekich | .25 |
| 139 Tim McCarver | .50 |
| 140 Pat Dobson | .35 |
| 141 Mets Rookies: | .60 |
| Buzz Capra, Leroy Stanton, | |
| Jon Matlack | |
| 142 Chris Chambliss (R) | 2.00 |
| 143 Garry Jestadt | .25 |
| 144 Marty Pattin | .25 |
| 145 Don Kessinger | .30 |
| 146 Steve Kealey | .25 |
| 147 Dave Kingman (R) | 3.50 |
| 148 Dick Billings | .25 |
| 149 Gary Neibauer | .25 |
| 150 Norm Cash | .35 |
| 151 Jim Brewer | .25 |
| 152 Gene Clines | .25 |
| 153 Rick Auerbach | .25 |
| 154 Ted Simmons | 1.25 |
| 155 Larry Dierker | .30 |
| 156 Minnesota Twins | .50 |
| 157 Don Gullett | .35 |
| 158 Jerry Kenney | .25 |
| 159 John Boccabella | .25 |
| 160 Andy Messersmith | .35 |
| 161 Brock Davis | .25 |
| 162 Brewers Rookies: | 1.00 |
| Darrell Porter, Jerry Bell, | |
| Bob Reynolds (Bell and | |
| Porter photos switched) | |
| 163 Tug McGraw | .60 |
| 164 T. McGraw (In Action) | .30 |
| 165 Chris Speier | .50 |
| 166 C. Speier (In Action) | .25 |
| 167 Deron Johnson | .25 |
| 168 D. Johnson (In Action) | .25 |
| 169 Vida Blue | .60 |
| 170 V. Blue (In Action) | .30 |
| 171 Darrell Evans | 1.00 |
| 172 D. Evans (In Action) | .50 |
| 173 Clay Kirby | .25 |
| 174 C. Kirby (In Action) | .25 |
| 175 Tom Haller | .25 |
| 176 T. Haller (In Action) | .25 |
| 177 Paul Schaal | .25 |
| 178 P. Schaal (In Action) | .25 |
| 179 Dock Ellis | .25 |
| 180 D. Ellis (In Action) | .25 |
| 181 Ed Kranepool | .30 |
| 182 E. Kranepool (In Action) | .20 |
| 183 Bill Melton | .25 |
| 184 B. Melton (In Action) | .25 |
| 185 Ron Bryant | .25 |
| 186 R. Bryant (In Action) | .25 |
| 187 Gates Brown | .25 |
| 188 Frank Lucchesi | .25 |
| 189 Gene Tenace | .30 |
| 190 Dave Giusti | .25 |
| 191 Jeff Burroughs | .60 |
| 192 Chicago Cubs | .60 |
| 193 Kurt Bevacqua | .25 |
| 194 Fred Norman | .25 |
| 195 Orlando Cepeda | 1.50 |
| 196 Mel Queen | .25 |
| 197 Johnny Briggs | .25 |
| 198 Dodgers Rookies: | 1.50 |
| Charlie Hough, Bob | |
| O'Brien, Mike Strahler | |
| 199 Mike Fiore | .25 |
| 200 Lou Brock | 3.50 |
| 201 Phil Roof | .25 |
| 202 Scipio Spinks | .25 |
| 203 Ron Blomberg | .25 |
| 204 Tommy Helms | .25 |
| 205 Dick Drago | .25 |
| 206 Dal Maxvill | .25 |
| 207 Tom Egan | .25 |
| 208 Milt Pappas | .35 |

| NO. PLAYER | MINT |
|---|---|
| 209 Joe Rudi | .30 |
| 210 Denny McLain | .75 |
| 211 Gary Sutherland | .25 |
| 212 Grant Jackson | .25 |
| 213 Angels Rookies: | .30 |
| Tom Silverio, Billy Parker, | |
| Art Kusnyer | |
| 214 Mike McQueen | .25 |
| 215 Alex Johnson | .25 |
| 216 Joe Niekro | .50 |
| 217 Roger Metzger | .25 |
| 218 Eddie Kasko | .25 |
| 219 Rennie Stennett | .30 |
| 220 Jim Perry | .30 |
| 221 NL Playoffs: | 1.00 |
| Bucs Champs | |
| 222 AL Playoffs: | 1.50 |
| Orioles Champs | |
| 223 World Series Game 1 | .75 |
| 224 World Series Game 2 | .75 |
| 225 World Series Game 3 | .75 |
| 226 World Series Game 4 | 1.50 |
| 227 World Series Game 5 | .75 |
| 228 World Series Game 6 | .75 |
| 229 World Series Game 7 | .75 |
| 230 World S. Celebration | .75 |
| 231 Casey Cox | .25 |
| 232 Giants Rookies: | .30 |
| Chris Arnold, Jim Barr, | |
| Dave Rader | |
| 233 Jay Johnstone | .30 |
| 234 Ron Taylor | .25 |
| 235 Merv Rettenmund | .25 |
| 236 Jim McGlothlin | .25 |
| 237 New York Yankees | 1.00 |
| 238 Leron Lee | .25 |
| 239 Tom Timmermann | .25 |
| 240 Rich Allen | 1.50 |
| 241 Rollie Fingers | 2.00 |
| 242 Don Mincher | .25 |
| 243 Frank Linzy | .25 |
| 244 Steve Braun | .25 |
| 245 Tommie Agee | .40 |
| 246 Tom Burgmeier | .25 |
| 247 Milt May | .25 |
| 248 Tom Bradley | .25 |
| 249 Garry Walker | .25 |
| 250 Boog Powell | .75 |
| 251 Checklist No. 3 | 1.00 |
| 252 Ken Reynolds | .25 |
| 253 Sandy Alomar | .25 |
| 254 Boots Day | .25 |
| 255 Jim Lonborg | .30 |
| 256 George Foster | 1.50 |
| 257 Tigers Rookies: | .30 |
| Paul Jata, Jim Foor, | |
| Tim Hosley | |
| 258 Randy Hundley | .25 |
| 259 Sparky Lyle | .35 |
| 260 Ralph Garr | .25 |
| 261 Steve Mingori | .25 |
| 262 San Diego Padres | .50 |
| 263 Felipe Alou | .30 |
| 264 Tommy John | 1.50 |
| 265 Wes Parker | .25 |
| 266 Bobby Bolin | .25 |
| 267 Dave Concepcion | 1.25 |
| 268 A's Rookies: | .35 |
| Dwain Anderson, C. Floethe | |
| 269 Don Hahn | .25 |
| 270 Jim Palmer | 3.00 |
| 271 Ken Rudolph | .25 |
| 272 Mickey Rivers | 1.00 |
| 273 Bobby Floyd | .25 |
| 274 Al Severinsen | .25 |
| 275 Cesar Tovar | .25 |
| 276 Gene Mauch | .25 |
| 277 Eliott Maddox | .25 |
| 278 Dennis Higgins | .25 |
| 279 Larry Brown | .25 |
| 280 Willie McCovey | 3.50 |
| 281 Bill Parsons | .25 |
| 282 Houston Astros | .60 |
| 283 Darrell Brandon | .25 |

| NO. PLAYER | MINT |
|---|---|
| 284 Ike Brown | .25 |
| 285 Gaylord Perry | 3.50 |
| 286 Gene Alley | .25 |
| 287 Jim Hardin | .25 |
| 288 Johnny Jeter | .25 |
| 289 Syd O'Brien | .25 |
| 290 Sonny Siebert | .25 |
| 291 Hal McRae | .50 |
| 292 H. McRae (In Action) | .25 |
| 293 Danny Frisella | .25 |
| 294 D. Frisella (In Action) | .25 |
| 295 Dick Dietz | .25 |
| 296 D. Dietz (In Action) | .25 |
| 297 Claude Osteen | .25 |
| 298 C. Osteen (In Action) | .25 |
| 299 Hank Aaron | 11.00 |
| 300 H. Aaron (In Action) | 6.00 |
| 301 George Mitterwald | .25 |
| 302 Mitterwald (In Action) | .25 |
| 303 Joe Pepitone | .50 |
| 304 J. Pepitone (In Action) | .25 |
| 305 Ken Boswell | .25 |
| 306 K. Boswell (In Action) | .25 |
| 307 Steve Renko | .25 |
| 308 S. Renko (In Action) | .25 |
| 309 Roberto Clemente | 11.00 |
| 310 Clemente (In Action) | 6.00 |
| 311 Clay Carroll | .25 |
| 312 C. Carroll (In Action) | .25 |
| 313 Luis Aparicio | 2.50 |
| 314 L. Aparicio (In Action) | 1.25 |
| 315 Paul Splittorff | .30 |
| 316 Cardinals Rookies: | .50 |
| Jim Bibby, Jorge Roque, Santiago Guzman | |
| 317 Rich Hand | .25 |
| 318 Sonny Jackson | .25 |
| 319 Aurelio Rodriguez | .25 |
| 320 Steve Blass | .25 |
| 321 Joe LaHoud | .25 |
| 322 Jose Pena | .25 |
| 323 Earl Weaver | .60 |
| 324 Mike Ryan | .25 |
| 325 Mel Stottlemyre | .40 |
| 326 Pat Kelly | .25 |
| 327 Steve Stone (R) | .50 |
| 328 Boston Red Sox | .60 |
| 329 Roy Foster | .25 |
| 330 Jim Hunter | 2.50 |
| 331 Stan Swanson | .25 |
| 332 Buck Martinez | .25 |
| 333 Steve Barber | .25 |
| 334 Rangers Rookies: | .30 |
| Bill Fahey, Jim Mason, Tom Ragland | |
| 335 Bill Hands | .25 |
| 336 Marty Martinez | .25 |
| 337 Mike Kilkenny | .25 |
| 338 Bob Grich | .65 |
| 339 Ron Cook | .25 |
| 340 Roy White | .50 |
| 341 Joe Torre (Boyhood) | .35 |
| 342 Wilbur Wood (Boyhood) | .35 |
| 343 W. Stargell (Boyhood) | .75 |
| 344 D. McNally (Boyhood) | .35 |
| 345 Rick Wise (Boyhood) | .35 |
| 346 Jim Fregosi (Boyhood) | .35 |
| 347 Tom Seaver (Boyhood) | 1.25 |
| 348 Sal Bando (Boyhood) | .35 |
| 349 Al Fitzmorris | .25 |
| 350 Frank Howard | .50 |
| 351 Braves Rookies: | .30 |
| Tom House, Rick Kester, Jimmy Britton | |
| 352 Dave LaRoche | .25 |
| 353 Art Shamsky | .25 |
| 354 Tom Murphy | .25 |
| 355 Bob Watson | .40 |
| 356 Gerry Moses | .25 |
| 357 Woodie Fryman | .25 |
| 358 Sparky Anderson | .40 |
| 359 Don Pavletich | .25 |
| 360 Dave Roberts | .25 |
| 361 Mike Andrews | .25 |
| 362 New York Mets | 1.00 |
| 363 Ron Klimkowski | .25 |
| 364 Johnny Callison | .40 |
| 365 Dick Bosman | .25 |
| 366 Jimmy Rosario | .25 |
| 367 Ron Perranoski | .35 |
| 368 Danny Thompson | .25 |
| 369 Jim LeFebvre | .25 |
| 370 Don Buford | .25 |
| 371 Denny LeMaster | .25 |
| 372 Royals Rookies: | .25 |
| Lance Clemons, Monty Montgomery | |
| 373 John Mayberry | .35 |
| 374 Jack Heidemann | .25 |
| 375 Reggie Cleveland | .25 |
| 376 Andy Kosco | .25 |
| 377 Terry Harmon | .25 |
| 378 Checklist No. 4 | 1.00 |
| 379 Ken Berry | .25 |
| 380 Earl Williams | .25 |
| 381 Chicago White Sox | .50 |
| 382 Joe Gibbon | .25 |
| 383 Brant Alyea | .25 |
| 384 Dave Campbell | .25 |
| 385 Mickey Stanley | .25 |
| 386 Jim Colborn | .25 |
| 387 Horace Clarke | .25 |
| 388 Charlie Williams | .25 |
| 389 Bill Rigney | .25 |
| 390 Willie Davis | .35 |
| 391 Kan Sanders | .25 |
| 392 Pirates Rookies: | .75 |
| Fred Cambria, Richie Zisk | |
| 393 Curt Motton | .25 |
| 394 Ken Forsch | .35 |
| 395 Matty Alou | .50 |
| 396 Paul Lindblad | .35 |
| 397 Philadelphia Phillies | .75 |
| 398 Larry Hisle | .35 |
| 399 Milt Wilcox | .35 |
| 400 Tony Oliva | 1.50 |
| 401 Jim Nash | .30 |
| 402 Bobby Heise | .30 |
| 403 John Cumberland | .30 |
| 404 Jeff Torborg | .30 |
| 405 Ron Fairly | .30 |
| 406 George Hendrick (R) | 1.25 |
| 407 Chuck Taylor | .30 |
| 408 Jim Northrup | .30 |
| 409 Frank Baker | .30 |
| 410 Fergie Jenkins | 1.50 |
| 411 Bob Montgomery | .30 |
| 412 Dick Kelley | .30 |
| 413 White Sox Rookies: | .40 |
| Don Eddy, Dave Lemonds | |
| 414 Bob Miller | .30 |
| 415 Cookie Rojas | .30 |
| 416 Johnny Edwards | .30 |
| 417 Tom Hall | .30 |
| 418 Tom Shopay | .30 |
| 419 Jim Spencer | .30 |
| 420 Steve Carlton | 10.00 |
| 421 Ellie Rodriguez | .30 |
| 422 Ray Lamb | .30 |
| 423 Oscar Gamble | .35 |
| 424 Bill Gogolewski | .30 |
| 425 Ken Singleton | .60 |
| 426 K. Singleton (In Action) | .30 |
| 427 Tito Fuentes | .30 |
| 428 T. Fuentes (In Action) | .30 |
| 429 Bob Robertson | .30 |
| 430 B. Robertson (In Action) | .30 |
| 431 Clarence Gaston | .30 |
| 432 C. Gaston (In Action) | .30 |
| 433 Johnny Bench | 15.00 |
| 434 J. Bench (In Action) | 8.00 |
| 435 Reggie Jackson | 15.00 |
| 436 R. Jackson (In Action) | 8.00 |
| 437 Maury Wills | 1.00 |
| 438 M. Wills (In Action) | .50 |
| 439 Billy Williams | 3.00 |
| 440 B. Williams (In Action) | .75 |
| 441 Thurman Munson | 8.00 |
| 442 T. Munson (In Action) | 4.00 |
| 443 Ken Henderson | .30 |
| 444 Henderson (In Action) | .30 |
| 445 Tom Seaver | 13.00 |
| 446 T. Seaver (In Action) | 5.00 |
| 447 Willie Stargell | 3.50 |
| 448 W. Stargell (In Action) | 2.00 |
| 449 Bob Lemon | .75 |
| 450 Mickey Lolich | .50 |
| 451 Tony LaRussa | .40 |
| 452 Ed Herrmann | .30 |
| 453 Barry Lersch | .30 |
| 454 Oakland A's | 1.00 |
| 455 Tommy Harper | .30 |
| 456 Mark Belanger | .40 |
| 457 Padres Rookies: | .40 |
| Darcy Fast, Derrel Thomas, Mike Ivie | |
| 458 Aurelio Monteagudo | .30 |
| 459 Rick Renick | .30 |
| 460 Al Downing | .30 |
| 461 Tim Cullen | .30 |
| 462 Rickey Clark | .30 |
| 463 Bernie Carbo | .30 |
| 464 Jim Roland | .30 |
| 465 Gil Hodges | 2.00 |
| 466 Norm Miller | .30 |
| 467 Steve Kline | .30 |
| 468 Richie Scheinblum | .30 |
| 469 Ron Herbel | .30 |
| 470 Ray Fosse | .30 |
| 471 Luke Walker | .30 |
| 472 Phil Gagliano | .30 |
| 473 Dan McGinn | .30 |
| 474 Orioles Rookies: | 2.00 |
| Johnny Oates, Don Baylor, Roric Harrison | |
| 475 Gary Nolan | .30 |
| 476 Lee Richard | .30 |
| 477 Tom Phoebus | .30 |
| 478 Checklist No. 5 | 1.00 |
| 479 Don Shaw | .30 |
| 480 Lee May | .50 |
| 481 Billy Conigliaro | .30 |
| 482 Joe Hoerner | .30 |
| 483 Ken Suarez | .30 |
| 484 Lum Harris | .30 |
| 485 Phil Regan | .30 |
| 486 John Lowenstein | .30 |
| 487 Detroit Tigers | .75 |
| 488 Mike Nagy | .30 |
| 489 Expos Rookies: | .30 |
| T. Humphrey, K. Lampard | |
| 490 Dave McNally | .30 |
| 491 Lou Piniella (Boyhood) | .40 |
| 492 M. Stottlemyre (Boyhood) | .40 |
| 493 Bob Bailey (Boyhood) | .40 |
| 494 Willie Horton (Boyhood) | .40 |
| 495 Bill Melton (Boyhood) | .40 |
| 496 B. Harrelson (Boyhood) | .40 |
| 497 Jim Perry (Boyhood) | .40 |
| 498 B. Robinson (Boyhood) | 1.25 |
| 499 Vicente Romo | .30 |
| 500 Joe Torre | .60 |
| 501 Pete Hamm | .30 |
| 502 Jackie Hernandez | .30 |
| 503 Gary Peters | .30 |
| 504 Ed Spiezio | .30 |
| 505 Mike Marshall | .35 |
| 506 Indians Rookies: | .35 |
| Terry Ley, Dick Tidrow, Jim Moyer | |
| 507 Fred Gladding | .30 |
| 508 Ellie Hendricks | .30 |
| 509 Don McMahon | .30 |
| 510 Ted Williams (Mgr.) | 4.00 |
| 511 Tony Taylor | .30 |
| 512 Paul Popovich | .30 |
| 513 Lindy McDaniel | .30 |
| 514 Ted Sizemore | .30 |
| 515 Bert Blyleven | 3.00 |
| 516 Oscar Brown | .30 |
| 517 Ken Brett | .30 |
| 518 Wayne Garrett | .30 |
| 519 Ted Abernathy | .30 |
| 520 Larry Bowa | 1.00 |
| 521 Alan Foster | .30 |
| 522 Los Angeles Dodgers | 1.00 |
| 523 Chuck Dobson | .30 |
| 524 Reds Rookies: | .45 |
| Ed Armbrister, Mel Behney | |
| 525 Carlos May | .30 |
| 526 Bob Bailey | .60 |
| 527 Dave Leonhard | .60 |
| 528 Ron Stone | .60 |
| 529 Dave Nelson | .60 |
| 530 Don Sutton | 3.00 |
| 531 Freddie Patek | .60 |
| 532 Fred Kendall | .60 |
| 533 Ralph Houk (Mgr.) | .60 |
| 534 Jim Hickman | .60 |
| 535 Ed Brinkman | .60 |
| 536 Doug Rader | .60 |
| 537 Bob Locker | .60 |
| 538 Charlie Sands | .60 |
| 539 Terry Forster (R) | 1.00 |
| 540 Felix Milan | .60 |
| 541 Roger Repoz | .60 |
| 542 Jack Billingham | .60 |
| 543 Duane Josephson | .60 |
| 544 Ted Martinez | .60 |
| 545 Wayne Granger | .60 |
| 546 Joe Hague | .60 |
| 547 Cleveland Indians | 1.00 |
| 548 Frank Reberger | .60 |
| 549 Dave May | .60 |
| 550 Brooks Robinson | 9.00 |
| 551 Ollie Brown | .60 |
| 552 O. Brown (In Action) | .60 |
| 553 Wilbur Wood | .75 |
| 554 W. Wood (In Action) | .60 |
| 555 Ron Santo | .75 |
| 556 R. Santo (In Action) | .60 |
| 557 John Odom | .60 |
| 558 J. Odom (In Action) | .60 |
| 559 Pete Rose | 55.00 |
| 560 P. Rose (In Action) | 30.00 |
| 561 Leo Cardenas | .60 |
| 562 L. Cardenas (In Action) | .60 |
| 563 Ray Sadecki | .60 |
| 564 R. Sadecki (In Action) | .60 |
| 565 Reggie Smith | .75 |
| 566 R. Smith (In Action) | .60 |
| 567 Juan Marichal | 4.00 |
| 568 J. Marichal (In Action) | 1.50 |
| 569 Ed Kirkpatrick | .60 |
| 570 Kirkpatrick (In Action) | .60 |
| 571 Nate Colbert | .60 |
| 572 N. Colbert (In Action) | .60 |
| 573 Fritz Peterson | .60 |
| 574 F. Peterson (In Action) | .60 |
| 575 Al Oliver | 2.00 |
| 576 Leo Durocher | 1.00 |
| 577 Mike Paul | .60 |
| 578 Billy Grabarkewitz | .60 |
| 579 Doyle Alexander (R) | 3.00 |
| 580 Lou Piniella | 1.50 |
| 581 Wade Blasingame | .60 |
| 582 Montreal Expos | 1.25 |
| 583 Darold Knowles | .60 |
| 584 Jerry McNertney | .60 |
| 585 George Scott | .60 |
| 586 Denis Menke | .60 |
| 587 Billy Wilson | .60 |
| 588 Jim Holt | .60 |
| 589 Hal Lanier | 1.00 |
| 590 Graig Nettles | 1.75 |
| 591 Paul Casanova | .60 |
| 592 Lew Krausse | .60 |
| 593 Rich Morales | .60 |
| 594 Jim Beauchamp | .60 |
| 595 Nolan Ryan | 15.00 |
| 596 Manny Mota | .75 |
| 597 Jim Magnuson | .60 |
| 598 Hal King | .60 |
| 599 Billy Champion | .60 |
| 600 Al Kaline | 10.00 |
| 601 George Stone | .60 |
| 602 Dave Bristol | .60 |
| 603 Jim Ray | .60 |
| 604 Checklist No. 6 | 3.00 |
| 605 Nelson Briles | .60 |

**Prices for the 1972 set are for cards in *Mint* condition. *Excellent* copies sell for 50% of prices shown; *Very Good*—30%.**

| NO. PLAYER | MINT | NO. PLAYER | MINT | NO. PLAYER | MINT | NO. PLAYER | MINT |
|---|---|---|---|---|---|---|---|
| 606 Luis Melendez | .60 | 653 Jim Fairey | .60 | 700 B. Murcer (In Action) | 2.00 | 744 Jim Slaton | 1.35 |
| 607 Frank Duffy | .60 | 654 Horacio Pina | .60 | 701 Jose Pagan | 1.35 | 745 Julian Javier | 1.35 |
| 608 Mike Corkins | .60 | 655 Jerry Grote | .60 | 702 J. Pagan (In Action) | 1.35 | 746 Lowell Palmer | 1.35 |
| 609 Tom Grieve | .60 | 656 Rudy May | .60 | 703 Doug Griffin | 1.35 | 747 Jim Stewart | 1.35 |
| 610 Bill Stoneman | .60 | 657 Bobby Wine | 1.35 | 704 D. Griffin (In Action) | 1.35 | 748 Phil Hennigan | 1.35 |
| 611 Rich Reese | .60 | 658 Steve Dunning | 1.35 | 705 Pat Corrales | 1.35 | 749 Walter Alston (Mgr.) | 3.00 |
| 612 Joe Decker | .60 | 659 Bob Aspromonte | 1.35 | 706 P. Corrales (In Action) | 1.35 | 750 Willie Horton | 2.00 |
| 613 Mike Ferraro | .60 | 660 Paul Blair | 1.75 | 707 Tim Foli | 1.35 | 751 S. Carlton (Traded) | 30.00 |
| 614 Ted Uhlaender | .60 | 661 Bill Virdon | 2.00 | 708 T. Foli (In Action) | 1.35 | 752 Joe Morgan (Traded) | 11.00 |
| 615 Steve Hargan | .60 | 662 Stan Bahnsen | 1.35 | 709 Jim Kaat | 5.00 | 753 D. McLain (Traded) | 3.50 |
| 616 Joe Ferguson (R) | .60 | 663 Fran Healy | 1.35 | 710 J. Kaat (In Action) | 2.50 | 754 F. Robinson (Traded) | 10.00 |
| 617 Kansas City Royals | 1.25 | 664 Bobby Knoop | 1.35 | 711 Bobby Bonds | 4.00 | 755 Jim Fregosi (Traded) | 2.00 |
| 618 Rich Robertson | .60 | 665 Chris Short | 1.35 | 712 B. Bonds (In Action) | 2.00 | 756 Rick Wise (Traded) | 2.00 |
| 619 Rich McKinney | .60 | 666 Hector Torres | 1.35 | 713 Gene Michael | 1.35 | 757 J. Cardenal (Traded) | 2.00 |
| 620 Phil Niekro | 4.00 | 667 Ray Newman | 1.35 | 714 G. Michael (In Action) | 1.35 | 758 Gil Garrido | 1.50 |
| 621 Commissioners Award | 1.00 | 668 Texas Rangers | 3.00 | 715 Mike Epstein | 1.35 | 759 Chris Cannizzaro | 1.50 |
| 622 MVP Award | 1.00 | 669 Willie Crawford | 1.35 | 716 Jesus Alou | 1.35 | 760 Bill Mazeroski | 2.50 |
| 623 Cy Young Award | 1.00 | 670 Ken Holtzman | 1.50 | 717 Bruce Dal Canton | 1.35 | 761 Rookie Stars: | 12.50 |
| 624 Minor League Player of the Year | 1.00 | 671 Donn Clendenon | 1.75 | 718 Del Rice | 1.35 | Bernie Williams, Ben Oglivie, Ron Cey | |
| 625 Rookie of the Year | 1.00 | 672 Archie Reynolds | 1.35 | 719 Cesar Geronimo | 1.35 | 762 Wayne Simpson | 1.35 |
| 626 Babe Ruth Award | 1.00 | 673 Dave Marshall | 1.35 | 720 Sam McDowell | 1.35 | 763 Ron Hansen | 1.35 |
| 627 Moe Drabowsky | .60 | 674 John Kennedy | 1.35 | 721 Eddie Leon | 1.35 | 764 Dusty Baker | 3.00 |
| 628 Terry Crowley | .60 | 675 Pat Jarvis | 1.35 | 722 Bill Sudakis | 1.35 | 765 Ken McMullen | 1.35 |
| 629 Paul Doyle | .60 | 676 Danny Cater | 1.35 | 723 Al Santorini | 1.35 | 766 Steve Hamilton | 1.35 |
| 630 Rich Hebner | .60 | 677 Ivan Murrell | 1.35 | 724 AL Rookie Pitchers: | 1.25 | 767 Tom McCraw | 1.35 |
| 631 John Strohmayer | .60 | 678 Steve Luebber | 1.35 | John Curtis, Rich Hinton, Mickey Scott | | 768 Denny Doyle | 1.35 |
| 632 Mike Hegan | .60 | 679 Astros Rookies: | 1.25 | 725 Dick McAuliffe | 1.35 | 769 Jack Aker | 1.35 |
| 633 Jack Hiatt | .60 | Bob Fenwick, Bob Stinson | | 726 Dick Selma | 1.35 | 770 Jim Wynn | 1.50 |
| 634 Dick Woodson | .60 | 680 Dave Johnson | 2.50 | 727 Jose LaBoy | 1.35 | 771 San Francisco Giants | 2.50 |
| 635 Don Money | .75 | 681 Bobby Pfeil | 1.35 | 728 Gail Hopkins | 1.35 | 772 Ken Tatum | 1.35 |
| 636 Bill Lee | .75 | 682 Mike McCormick | 1.35 | 729 Bob Veale | 1.35 | 773 Ron Brand | 1.35 |
| 637 Preston Gomez | .60 | 683 Steve Hovley | 1.35 | 730 Rick Monday | 2.00 | 774 Luis Alvarado | 1.35 |
| 638 Ken Wright | .60 | 684 Hal Breeden | 1.35 | 731 Baltimore Orioles | 2.00 | 775 Jerry Reuss | 3.00 |
| 639 J.C. Martin | .60 | 685 Joe Horlen | 1.35 | 732 George Culver | 1.35 | 776 Bill Voss | 1.35 |
| 640 Joe Coleman | .60 | 686 Steve Garvey | 75.00 | 733 Jim Hart | 1.75 | 777 Hoyt Wilhelm | 8.00 |
| 641 Mike Lum | .60 | 687 Del Unser | 1.35 | 734 Bob Burda | 1.35 | 778 Twins Rookies: | 1.50 |
| 642 Dennis Riddleberger | .60 | 688 St. Louis Cardinals | 2.50 | 735 Diego Segui | 1.35 | Vic Albury, Rick Dempsey, Jim Strickland | |
| 643 Russ Gibson | .60 | 689 Eddie Fisher | 1.35 | 736 Bill Russell | 2.50 | 779 Tony Cloninger | 1.35 |
| 644 Bernie Allen | .60 | 690 Willie Montanez | 1.35 | 737 Lenny Randle | 1.35 | 780 Dick Green | 1.35 |
| 645 Jim Maloney | .75 | 691 Curt Blefary | 1.35 | 738 Jim Merritt | 1.35 | 781 Jim McAndrew | 1.35 |
| 646 Chico Salmon | .60 | 692 C. Blefary (In Action) | 1.35 | 739 Don Mason | 1.35 | 792 Larry Stahl | 1.35 |
| 647 Bob Moose | .60 | 693 Alan Gallagher | 1.35 | 740 Rico Carty | 2.00 | 783 Les Cain | 1.35 |
| 648 Jim Lyttle | .60 | 694 Gallagher (In Action) | 1.35 | 741 Rookie Stars: | 2.00 | 784 Ken Aspromonte | 1.35 |
| 649 Pete Richert | .60 | 695 Rod Carew | 60.00 | Tom Hutton, John Milner, Rick Miller | | 785 Vic Davalillo | 1.35 |
| 650 Sal Bando | 1.00 | 696 R. Carew (In Action) | 30.00 | 742 Jim Rooker | 1.35 | 786 Chuck Brinkman | 1.35 |
| 651 Cincinnati Reds | 1.50 | 697 Jerry Koosman | 4.00 | 743 Cesar Gutierrez | 1.35 | 787 Ron Reed (Exc. .80) | 3.00 |
| 652 Marcelino Lopez | .60 | 698 J. Koosman (In Action) | 2.00 | | | | |
| | | 699 Bobby Murcer | 4.00 | | | | |

## 1973 Topps. . . .Complete Set of 660 Cards—Value $250.00 (Exc.); $600.00 (Mint)

Includes the rookie cards of Mike Schmidt, Darrell Evans and Davey Lopes. The high numbers are 529 to 660. This was the last Topps' set to be issued in *series*. Starting in 1974 the entire set was issued at one time.

| NO. PLAYER | MINT | NO. PLAYER | MINT | NO. PLAYER | MINT | NO. PLAYER | MINT |
|---|---|---|---|---|---|---|---|
| 1 All-Time HR Leaders | 9.00 | 10 Don Sutton | 2.00 | 21 Randy Hundley | .20 | 32 Fred Norman | .20 |
| Babe Ruth, Hank Aaron, Willie Mays (Exc. $3.00) | | 11 Chris Chambliss | .40 | 22 Ted Abernathy | .20 | 33 Jim Breazeale | .20 |
| 2 Rich Hebner | .20 | 12 Don Zimmer (Mgr.) | .35 | 23 Dave Kingman | 1.00 | 34 Pat Dobson | .20 |
| 3 Jim Lonborg | .20 | 13 George Hendrick | .60 | 24 Al Santorini | .20 | 35 Willie Davis | .35 |
| 4 John Milner | .20 | 14 Sonny Siebert | .20 | 25 Ray White | .30 | 36 Steve Barber | .20 |
| 5 Ed Brinkman | .20 | 15 Ralph Garr | .20 | 26 Pittsburgh Pirates | .50 | 37 Bill Robinson | .20 |
| 6 Mac Scarce | .20 | 16 Steve Braun | .20 | 27 Bill Gogolewski | .20 | 38 Mike Epstein | .20 |
| 7 Texas Rangers | .30 | 17 Fred Gladding | .20 | 28 Hal McRae | .40 | 39 Dave Roberts | .20 |
| 8 Tom Hall | .20 | 18 Leroy Stanton | .20 | 29 Tony Taylor | .20 | 40 Reggie Smith | .60 |
| 9 Johnny Oates | .20 | 19 Tim Foli | .20 | 30 Tug McGraw | .60 | 41 Tom Walker | .20 |
| | | 20 Stan Bahnsen | .20 | 31 Buddy Bell (R) | 3.00 | 42 Mike Andrews | .20 |

| NO. | PLAYER | MINT |
|---|---|---|
| 43 | Randy Moffitt | .20 |
| 44 | Rick Monday | .30 |
| 45 | Ellie Rodriguez (wrong photo) | .20 |
| 46 | Lindy McDaniel | .20 |
| 47 | Luis Melendez | .20 |
| 48 | Paul Splittorff | .35 |
| 49 | Frank Quilici (Mgr.) | .30 |
| 50 | Roberto Clemente | 10.00 |
| 51 | Chuck Seelbach | .20 |
| 52 | Denis Menke | .20 |
| 53 | Steve Dunning | .20 |
| 54 | Checklist No. 1 | 1.25 |
| 55 | Jon Matlack | .30 |
| 56 | Merv Rettenmund | .20 |
| 57 | Derrel Thomas | .20 |
| 58 | Mike Paul | .20 |
| 59 | Steve Yeager (R) | .50 |
| 60 | Ken Holtzman | .30 |
| 61 | Batting Leaders: Billy Williams, Rod Carew | 1.00 |
| 62 | Home Run Leaders: Johnny Bench, Dick Allen | 1.00 |
| 63 | RBI Leaders: Johnny Bench, Dick Allen | 1.00 |
| 64 | Stolen Base Leaders: B. Campaneris, L. Brock | .60 |
| 65 | ERA Leaders: Steve Carlton, Luis Tiant | .75 |
| 66 | Victory Leaders: Wilbur Wood, Steve Carlton, Gaylord Perry | 1.00 |
| 67 | Strikeout Leaders: Steve Carlton, Nolan Ryan | 2.25 |
| 68 | Leading Firemen: Clay Carroll, Sparky Lyle | .35 |
| 69 | Phil Gagliano | .20 |
| 70 | Milt Pappas | .20 |
| 71 | Johnny Briggs | .20 |
| 72 | Ron Reed | .20 |
| 73 | Ed Herrmann | .20 |
| 74 | Billy Champion | .20 |
| 75 | Vada Pinson | .40 |
| 76 | Doug Rader | .20 |
| 77 | Mike Torrez | .30 |
| 78 | Richie Scheinblum | .20 |
| 79 | Jim Willoughby | .20 |
| 80 | Tony Oliva | .75 |
| 81 | Whitey Lockman (Mgr.) | .45 |
| 82 | Fritz Peterson | .20 |
| 83 | Leron Lee | .20 |
| 84 | Rollie Fingers | 1.50 |
| 85 | Ted Simmons | 1.25 |
| 86 | Tom McCraw | .20 |
| 87 | Ken Boswell | .20 |
| 88 | Mickey Stanley | .20 |
| 89 | Jack Billingham | .20 |
| 90 | Brooks Robinson | 3.50 |
| 91 | Los Angeles Dodgers | .75 |
| 92 | Jerry Bell | .20 |
| 93 | Jesus Alou | .20 |
| 94 | Dick Billings | .20 |
| 95 | Steve Blass | .20 |
| 96 | Doug Griffin | .20 |
| 97 | Willie Montanez | .20 |
| 98 | Dick Woodson | .20 |
| 99 | Carl Taylor | .20 |
| 100 | Hank Aaron | 11.00 |
| 101 | Ken Henderson | .20 |
| 102 | Rudy May | .20 |
| 103 | Celerino Sanchez | .20 |
| 104 | Reggie Cleveland | .20 |
| 105 | Carlos May | .20 |
| 106 | Terry Humphrey | .20 |
| 107 | Phil Hennigan | .20 |
| 108 | Bill Russell | .20 |
| 109 | Doyle Alexander | .50 |
| 110 | Bob Watson | .30 |
| 111 | Dave Nelson | .20 |
| 112 | Gary Ross | .20 |
| 113 | Jerry Grote | .20 |
| 114 | Lynn McGlothen | .20 |
| 115 | Ron Santo | .50 |
| 116 | Ralph Houk (Mgr.) | .60 |
| 117 | Ramon Hernandez | .20 |
| 118 | John Mayberry | .30 |
| 119 | Larry Bowa | .60 |
| 120 | Joe Coleman | .20 |
| 121 | Dave Rader | .20 |
| 122 | Jim Strickland | .20 |
| 123 | Sandy Alomar | .20 |
| 124 | Jim Hardin | .20 |
| 125 | Ron Fairly | .20 |
| 126 | Jim Brewer | .20 |
| 127 | Milwaukee Brewers | .50 |
| 128 | Ted Sizemore | .20 |
| 129 | Terry Forster | .35 |
| 130 | Pete Rose | 16.00 |
| 131 | Eddie Kasko (Mgr.) | .40 |
| 132 | Matty Alou | .40 |
| 133 | Dave Roberts | .20 |
| 134 | Milt Wilcox | .30 |
| 135 | Lee May | .30 |
| 136 | Earl Weaver (Mgr.) | .60 |
| 137 | Jim Beauchamp | .20 |
| 138 | Horacio Pina | .20 |
| 139 | Carmen Fanzone | .20 |
| 140 | Lou Piniella | .60 |
| 141 | Bruce Kison | .30 |
| 142 | Thurman Munson | 4.00 |
| 143 | John Curtis | .20 |
| 144 | Marty Perez | .20 |
| 145 | Bobby Bonds | .50 |
| 146 | Woodie Fryman | .20 |
| 147 | Mike Anderson | .20 |
| 148 | Dave Goltz | .20 |
| 149 | Ron Hunt | .20 |
| 150 | Wilbur Wood | .20 |
| 151 | Wes Parker | .20 |
| 152 | Dave May | .20 |
| 153 | Al Hrabosky | .30 |
| 154 | Jeff Torborg | .20 |
| 155 | Sal Bando | .35 |
| 156 | Cesar Geronimo | .20 |
| 157 | Denny Riddleberger | .20 |
| 158 | Houston Astros | .50 |
| 159 | Clarence Gaston | .20 |
| 160 | Jim Palmer | 3.00 |
| 161 | Ted Martinez | .20 |
| 162 | Pete Broberg | .20 |
| 163 | Vic Davalillo | .20 |
| 164 | Monty Montgomery | .20 |
| 165 | Luis Aparicio | 2.00 |
| 166 | Terry Harmon | .20 |
| 167 | Steve Stone | .25 |
| 168 | Jim Northrup | .20 |
| 169 | Ron Schueler | .20 |
| 170 | Harmon Killebrew | 3.00 |
| 171 | Bernie Carbo | .20 |
| 172 | Steve Kline | .20 |
| 173 | Hal Breeden | .20 |
| 174 | Rich Gossage (R) | 6.50 |
| 175 | Frank Robinson | 3.00 |
| 176 | Chuck Taylor | .20 |
| 177 | Bill Plummer | .20 |
| 178 | Don Rose | .20 |
| 179 | Dick Williams (Mgr.) | .50 |
| 180 | Fergie Jenkins | .75 |
| 181 | Jack Brohamer | .20 |
| 182 | Mike Caldwell (R) | .40 |
| 183 | Don Buford | .20 |
| 184 | Jerry Koosman | .40 |
| 185 | Jim Wynn | .30 |
| 186 | Bill Fahey | .20 |
| 187 | Luke Walker | .20 |
| 188 | Cookie Rojas | .20 |
| 189 | Greg Luzinski | .75 |
| 190 | Bob Gibson | 2.50 |
| 191 | Detroit Tigers | .75 |
| 192 | Pat Jarvis | .20 |
| 193 | Carlton Fisk | 2.50 |
| 194 | Jorge Orta | .20 |
| 195 | Clay Carroll | .20 |
| 196 | Ken McMullen | .20 |
| 197 | Ed Goodson | .20 |
| 198 | Horace Clarke | .20 |
| 199 | Bert Blyleven | 1.00 |
| 200 | Billy Williams | 2.50 |
| 201 | AL Playoffs: Hendrick Scores | .75 |
| 202 | NL Playoffs: Foster's Run Decides It | .75 |
| 203 | World Series Game 1 Tenace the Menace | .75 |
| 204 | World Series Game 2 A's Make It Two Straight | .75 |
| 205 | World Series Game 3 Reds Win Squeaker | .75 |
| 206 | World Series Game 4 Tenace Singles In Ninth | .75 |
| 207 | World Series Game 5 Odom Out at Plate | .75 |
| 208 | World Series Game 6 Red's Ties Series | .75 |
| 209 | World Series Game 7 Campy Stars Rally | .75 |
| 210 | World Series A's— World Champions | .75 |
| 211 | Balor Moore | .20 |
| 212 | Joe LaHoud | .20 |
| 213 | Steve Garvey | 9.00 |
| 214 | Steve Hamilton | .20 |
| 215 | Dusty Baker | .75 |
| 216 | Toby Harrah | .35 |
| 217 | Don Wilson | .20 |
| 218 | Aurelio Rodriguez | .20 |
| 219 | St. Louis Cardinals | .50 |
| 220 | Nolan Ryan | 7.50 |
| 221 | Fred Kendall | .20 |
| 222 | Rob Gardner | .20 |
| 223 | Bud Harrelson | .20 |
| 224 | Bill Lee | .20 |
| 225 | Al Oliver | 1.25 |
| 226 | Ray Fosse | .20 |
| 227 | Wayne Twitchell | .20 |
| 228 | Bobby Darwin | .20 |
| 229 | Roric Harrison | .20 |
| 230 | Joe Morgan | 2.00 |
| 231 | Bill Parsons | .20 |
| 232 | Ken Singleton | .50 |
| 233 | Ed Kirkpatrick | .20 |
| 234 | Bill North | .20 |
| 235 | Jim Hunter | 2.50 |
| 236 | Tito Fuentes | .20 |
| 237 | Eddie Mathews (Mgr.) | .75 |
| 238 | Tony Muser | .20 |
| 239 | Pete Richert | .20 |
| 240 | Bobby Murcer | .50 |
| 241 | Dwain Anderson | .20 |
| 242 | George Culver | .20 |
| 243 | California Angels | .75 |
| 244 | Ed Acosta | .20 |
| 245 | Carl Yastrzemski | 10.00 |
| 246 | Ken Sanders | .20 |
| 247 | Del Unser | .20 |
| 248 | Jerry Johnson | .20 |
| 249 | Larry Biittner | .20 |
| 250 | Manny Sanguillen | .30 |
| 251 | Roger Nelson | .20 |
| 252 | Charlie Fox (Mgr.) | .35 |
| 253 | Mark Belanger | .25 |
| 254 | Bill Stoneman | .20 |
| 255 | Reggie Jackson | 12.00 |
| 256 | Chris Zachary | .20 |
| 257 | Yogi Berra (Mgr.) | 1.25 |
| 258 | Tommy John | 1.25 |
| 259 | Jim Holt | .20 |
| 260 | Gary Nolan | .20 |
| 261 | Pat Kelly | .20 |
| 262 | Jack Aker | .20 |
| 263 | George Scott | .20 |
| 264 | Checklist No. 2 | 1.00 |
| 265 | Gene Michael | .40 |
| 266 | Mike Lum | .20 |
| 267 | Lloyd Allen | .20 |
| 268 | Jerry Morales | .20 |
| 269 | Tim McCarver | .50 |
| 270 | Luis Tiant | .40 |
| 271 | Tom Hutton | .20 |
| 272 | Ed Farmer | .20 |
| 273 | Chris Speier | .35 |
| 274 | Darold Knowles | .20 |
| 275 | Tony Perez | 1.00 |
| 276 | Joe Lovitto | .20 |
| 277 | Bob Miller | .20 |
| 278 | Baltimore Orioles | .50 |
| 279 | Mike Strahler | .20 |
| 280 | Al Kaline | 3.50 |
| 281 | Mike Jorgensen | .20 |
| 282 | Steve Hovley | .20 |
| 283 | Ray Sadecki | .20 |
| 284 | Glenn Borgmann | .20 |
| 285 | Don Kessinger | .35 |
| 286 | Frank Linzy | .20 |
| 287 | Eddie Leon | .20 |
| 288 | Gary Gentry | .20 |
| 289 | Bob Oliver | .20 |
| 290 | Cesar Cedeno | .50 |
| 291 | Rogelio Moret | .20 |
| 292 | Jose Cruz | .75 |
| 293 | Bernie Allen | .20 |
| 294 | Steve Arlin | .20 |
| 295 | Bert Campaneris | .35 |
| 296 | Sparky Anderson (Mgr.) | .50 |
| 297 | Walt Williams | .20 |
| 298 | Ron Bryant | .20 |
| 299 | Ted Ford | .20 |
| 300 | Steve Carlton | 6.00 |
| 301 | Billy Grabarkewitz | .20 |
| 302 | Terry Crowley | .20 |
| 303 | Nelson Briles | .20 |
| 304 | Duke Sims | .20 |
| 305 | Willie Mays | 11.00 |
| 306 | Tom Burgmeier | .20 |
| 307 | Boots Day | .20 |
| 308 | Skip Lockwood | .20 |
| 309 | Paul Popovich | .20 |
| 310 | Dick Allen | .60 |
| 311 | Joe Decker | .20 |
| 312 | Oscar Brown | .20 |
| 313 | Jim Ray | .20 |
| 314 | Ron Swoboda | .20 |
| 315 | John Odom | .20 |
| 316 | San Diego Padres | .50 |
| 317 | Danny Cater | .20 |
| 318 | Jim McGlothlin | .20 |
| 319 | Jim Spencer | .20 |
| 320 | Lou Brock | 3.00 |
| 321 | Rich Hinton | .20 |
| 322 | Garry Maddox (R) | .75 |
| 323 | Billy Martin (Mgr.) | .60 |
| 324 | Al Downing | .40 |
| 325 | Boog Powell | .60 |
| 326 | Darrell Brandon | .20 |
| 327 | John Lowenstein | .20 |
| 328 | Bill Bonham | .20 |
| 329 | Ed Kranepool | .40 |
| 330 | Rod Carew | 6.50 |
| 331 | Carl Morton | .20 |
| 332 | John Felske | .20 |
| 333 | Gene Clines | .20 |
| 334 | Freddie Patek | .20 |
| 335 | Bob Tolan | .20 |
| 336 | Tom Bradley | .20 |
| 337 | Dave Duncan | .20 |
| 338 | Checklist No. 3 | 1.25 |
| 339 | Dick Tidrow | .20 |
| 340 | Nate Colbert | .20 |
| 341 | Jim Palmer (Boyhood) | 1.00 |
| 342 | S. McDowell (Boyhood) | .35 |
| 343 | B. Murcer (Boyhood) | .35 |
| 344 | Jim Hunter (Boyhood) | 1.00 |
| 345 | Chris Speier (Boyhood) | .35 |
| 346 | G. Perry (Boyhood) | 1.00 |
| 347 | Kansas City Royals | .75 |
| 348 | Rennie Stennett | .20 |
| 349 | Dick McAuliffe | .20 |
| 350 | Tom Seaver | 8.00 |
| 351 | Jimmy Stewart | .20 |
| 352 | Don Stanhouse | .20 |
| 353 | Steve Brye | .20 |
| 354 | Billy Parker | .20 |
| 355 | Mike Marshall | .35 |
| 356 | Chuck Tanner (Mgr.) | .45 |
| 357 | Ross Grimsley | .20 |
| 358 | Jim Nettles | .20 |
| 359 | Cecil Upshaw | .20 |
| 360 | Joe Rudi (photo of Gene Tenace) | .50 |
| 361 | Fran Healy | .20 |

| NO. PLAYER | MINT | NO. PLAYER | MINT | NO. PLAYER | MINT | NO. PLAYER | MINT |
|---|---|---|---|---|---|---|---|
| 362 Eddie Watt | .20 | 447 Joe Hague | .40 | 523 Wayne Granger | .40 | 603 Rookie 3rd Basemen: | 1.25 |
| 363 Jackie Hernandez | .20 | 448 John Hiller | .40 | 524 Gene Tenace | .50 | Billy McNulty, Ken Reitz, | |
| 364 Rick Wise | .20 | 449 Ken Aspromonte (Mgr.) | .50 | 525 Jim Fregosi | .60 | Terry Hughes | |
| 365 Rico Petrocelli | .40 | 450 Joe Torre | .75 | 526 Ollie Brown | .40 | 604 Rookie Pitchers: | 1.25 |
| 366 Brock Davis | .20 | 451 John Vuckovich | .40 | 527 Dan McGinn | .40 | Jesse Jefferson, Dennis | |
| 367 Burt Hooton | .20 | 452 Paul Casanova | .40 | 528 Paul Blair | .40 | O'Toole, Bob Strampe | |
| 368 Bill Buckner | .75 | 453 Checklist No. 4 | 1.25 | 529 Milt May | 1.00 | 605 Rookie 1st Basemen: | 1.25 |
| 369 Lerrin LaGrow | .20 | 454 Tom Haller | .40 | 530 Jim Kaat | 2.50 | Pat Bourque, Enos Cabell, | |
| 370 Willie Stargell | 3.00 | 455 Bill Melton | .40 | 531 Ron Woods | 1.00 | Gonzalo Marquez | |
| 371 Mike Kekich | .20 | 456 Dick Green | .40 | 532 Steve Mingori | 1.00 | 606 Rookie Outfielders: | 2.50 |
| 372 Oscar Gamble | .30 | 457 John Strohmayer | .40 | 533 Larry Stahl | 1.00 | Jorge Roque, Gary | |
| 373 Clyde Wright | .20 | 458 Jim Mason | .40 | 534 Dave Lemonds | 1.00 | Matthews, T. Paciorek | |
| 374 Darrell Evans | .60 | 459 Jimmy Howarth | .40 | 535 John Callison | 1.00 | 607 Rookie Shortstops: | 1.25 |
| 375 Larry Dierker | .30 | 460 Bill Freehan | .50 | 536 Philadelphia Phillies | 1.50 | Pepe Frias, Ray Busse, | |
| 376 Frank Duffy | .20 | 461 Mike Corkins | .40 | 537 Bill Slayback | 1.00 | Mario Guerrero | |
| 377 Gene Mauch (Mgr.) | .35 | 462 Ron Blomberg | .40 | 538 Jim Hart | 1.00 | 608 Rookie Pitchers: | 1.25 |
| 378 Lenny Randle | .20 | 463 Ken Tatum | .40 | 539 Tom Murphy | 1.00 | S. Busby, G. Medich, | |
| 379 Cy Acosta | .20 | 464 Chicago Cubs | 1.00 | 540 Cleon Jones | 1.25 | Dick Colpaert | |
| 380 Johnny Bench | 9.00 | 465 Dave Giusti | .40 | 541 Bob Bolin | 1.00 | 609 Rookie 2nd Basemen: | 3.00 |
| 381 Vicente Romo | .20 | 466 Jose Arcia | .40 | 542 Pat Corrales | 1.25 | Larvell Blanks, P. Garcia, | |
| 382 Mike Hegan | .20 | 467 Mike Ryan | .40 | 543 Alan Foster | 1.00 | Dave Lopes | |
| 383 Diego Segui | .20 | 468 Tom Griffin | .40 | 544 Von Joshua | 1.00 | 610 Rookie Pitchers: | 2.00 |
| 384 Don Baylor | 1.00 | 469 Dan Monzon | .40 | 545 Orlando Cepeda | 3.00 | Hank Webb, J. Freeman, | |
| 385 Jim Perry | .35 | 470 Mike Cuellar | .50 | 546 Jim York | 1.00 | Charlie Hough | |
| 386 Don Money | .20 | 471 All-Time Hits | 2.00 | 547 Bobby Heise | 1.00 | 611 Rookie Outfielders: | 1.50 |
| 387 Jim Barr | .20 | Ty Cobb (4,191) | | 548 Don Durham | 1.00 | Richie Zisk, Rich Coggins, | |
| 388 Ben Oglivie | .50 | 472 All-Time Grand Slams: | 2.00 | 549 Whitey Herzog (Mgr.) | 1.50 | J. Wohlford | |
| 389 New York Mets | 1.50 | Lou Gehrig (23) | | 550 Dave Johnson | 2.50 | 612 Rookie Pitchers: | 1.25 |
| 390 Mickey Lolich | .60 | 473 All-Time Total Bases | 2.00 | 551 Mike Kilkenny | 1.00 | Steve Lawson, Bob | |
| 391 Lee Lacy (R) | .75 | hank Aaron (6,172) | | 552 J.C. Martin | 1.00 | Reynolds, Brent Strom | |
| 392 Dick Drago | .20 | 474 All-Time RBI's | 5.00 | 553 Mickey Scott | 1.00 | 613 Rookie Catchers: | 4.00 |
| 393 Jose Cardenal | .20 | Babe Ruth (2,209) | | 554 Dave Concepcion | 2.00 | Bob Boone, S. Jutze, | |
| 394 Sparky Lyle | .50 | 475 All-Time Batting: | 2.00 | 555 Bill Hands | 1.00 | Mike Ivie | |
| 395 Roger Metzger | .20 | Ty Cobb (.367) | | 556 New York Yankees | 3.00 | 614 Rookie Outfielders: | 30.00 |
| 396 Grant Jackson | .20 | 476 All-Time Shutouts: | 1.50 | 557 Bernie Williams | 1.00 | A. Bumbry, Dwight Evans, | |
| 397 Dave Cash | .40 | Walter Johnson (113) | | 558 Jerry May | 1.00 | Charlie Spikes | |
| 398 Rich Hand | .40 | 477 All-Time Victory Ldrs. | 1.50 | 559 Barry Lersch | 1.00 | 615 Rookie 3rd Basemen: | 160.00 |
| 399 George Foster | 1.50 | Cy Young (511) | | 560 Frank Howard | 2.00 | Ron Cey, Mike Schmidt, | |
| 400 Gaylord Perry | 2.25 | 478 All-Time Strikeouts: | 1.50 | 561 Jim Geddes | 1.00 | John Hilton | |
| 401 Clyde Mashore | .40 | Walter Johnson (3,508) | | 562 Wayne Garrett | 1.00 | 616 Rookie Pitchers: | 1.25 |
| 402 Jack Hiatt | .40 | 479 Hal Lanier | .50 | 563 Larry Haney | 1.00 | S. Blateric, Norm Angelini, | |
| 403 Sonny Jackson | .40 | 480 Juan Marichal | 3.00 | 564 Mike Thompson | 1.00 | Mike Garman | |
| 404 Chuck Brinkman | .40 | 481 Chicago White Sox | .75 | 565 Jim Hickman | 1.00 | 617 Rich Chiles | 1.25 |
| 405 Cesar Tovar | .40 | 482 Rick Reuschel (R) | 3.00 | 566 Lew Krausse | 1.00 | 618 Andy Etchebarren | 1.25 |
| 406 Paul Lindblad | .40 | 483 Dal Maxvill | .40 | 567 Bob Fenwick | 1.00 | 619 Billy Wilson | 1.25 |
| 407 Felix Millan | .40 | 484 Ernie McAnally | .40 | 568 Ray Newman | 1.00 | 620 Tommy Harper | 1.25 |
| 408 Jim Colborn | .40 | 485 Norm Cash | .50 | 569 Walt Alston (Mgr.) | 3.00 | 621 Joe Ferguson | 1.25 |
| 409 Ivan Murrell | .40 | 486 Danny Ozark (Mgr.) | .60 | 570 Bill Singer | 1.00 | 622 Larry Hisle | 1.25 |
| 410 Willie McCovey | 3.50 | 487 Bruce Dal Canton | .40 | 571 Rusty Torres | 1.00 | 623 Steve Renko | 1.25 |
| 411 Ray Corbin | .40 | 488 Dave Campbell | .40 | 572 Gary Sutherland | 1.00 | 624 Leo Durocher (Mgr.) | 2.00 |
| 412 Manny Mota | .60 | 489 Jeff Burroughs | .40 | 573 Fred Beene | 1.00 | 625 Angel Mangual | 1.25 |
| 413 Tom Timmerman | .40 | 490 Claude Osteen | .50 | 574 Bob Didier | 1.00 | 626 Bob Barton | 1.25 |
| 414 Ken Rudolph | .40 | 491 Bob Montgomery | .40 | 575 Dock Ellis | 1.00 | 627 Luis Alvarado | 1.25 |
| 415 Marty Pattin | .40 | 492 Pedro Borbon | .40 | 576 Montreal Expos | 1.75 | 628 Jim Slaton | 1.25 |
| 416 Paul Schaal | .40 | 493 Duffy Dyer | .40 | 577 Eric Soderholm | 1.00 | 629 Cleveland Indians | 1.50 |
| 417 Scipio Spinks | .40 | 494 Rich Morales | .40 | 578 Ken Wright | 1.00 | 630 Denny McLain | 2.00 |
| 418 Bobby Grich | .50 | 495 Tommy Helms | .40 | 579 Tom Grieve | 1.00 | 631 Tom Matchick | 1.25 |
| 419 Casey Cox | .40 | 496 Ray Lamb | .40 | 580 Joe Pepitone | 1.25 | 632 Dick Selma | 1.25 |
| 420 Tommie Agee | .60 | 497 R. Schoendienst (Mgr.) | .60 | 581 Steve Kealey | 1.00 | 633 Ike Brown | 1.25 |
| 421 Bobby Winkles (Mgr.) | .50 | 498 Graig Nettles | 2.00 | 582 Darrell Porter | 1.25 | 634 Alan Closter | 1.25 |
| 422 Bob Robertson | .40 | 499 Bob Moose | .40 | 583 Bill Grief | 1.00 | 635 Gene Alley | 1.25 |
| 423 Johnny Jeter | .40 | 500 Oakland A's | 1.25 | 584 Chris Arnold | 1.00 | 636 Rick Clark | 1.25 |
| 424 Denny Doyle | .40 | 501 Larry Gura | .40 | 585 Joe Niekro | 2.50 | 637 Norm Miller | 1.25 |
| 425 Alex Johnson | .40 | 502 Bobby Valentine | .60 | 586 Bill Sudakis | 1.00 | 638 Ken Reynolds | 1.25 |
| 426 Dave LaRoche | .40 | 503 Phil Niekro | 2.50 | 587 Rich McKinney | 1.00 | 639 Willie Crawford | 1.25 |
| 427 Rick Auerbach | .40 | 504 Earl Williams | .40 | 588 Checklist No. 5 | 9.00 | 640 Dick Bosman | 1.25 |
| 428 Wayne Simpson | .40 | 505 Bob Bailey | .40 | 589 Ken Forsch | 1.25 | 641 Cincinnati Reds | 2.00 |
| 429 Jim Fairey | .40 | 506 Bart Johnson | .40 | 590 Deron Johnson | 1.00 | 642 Jose LaBoy | 1.25 |
| 430 Vida Blue | .60 | 507 Darrel Chaney | .40 | 591 Mike Hedlund | 1.00 | 643 Al Fitzmorris | 1.25 |
| 431 Gerry Moses | .40 | 508 Gates Brown | .40 | 592 John Boccabella | 1.00 | 644 Jack Heidemann | 1.25 |
| 432 Dan Frisella | .40 | 509 Jim Nash | .40 | 593 Jack McKeon (Mgr.) | 1.00 | 645 Bob Locker | 1.25 |
| 433 Willie Horton | .50 | 510 Amos Otis | .60 | 594 Vic Harris | 1.00 | 646 Del Crandall (Mgr.) | 1.50 |
| 434 San F. Giants | .60 | 511 Sam McDowell | .50 | 595 Don Gullett | 1.25 | 647 George Stone | 1.25 |
| 435 Rico Carty | .50 | 512 Dalton Jones | .40 | 596 Boston Red Sox | 2.00 | 648 Tom Egan | 1.25 |
| 436 Jim McAndrew | .40 | 513 Dave Marshall | .40 | 597 Mickey Rivers | 1.50 | 649 Rich Folkers | 1.25 |
| 437 John Kennedy | .40 | 514 Jerry Kenney | .40 | 598 Phil Roof | 1.00 | 650 Felipe Alou | 1.50 |
| 438 Enzo Hernandez | .40 | 515 Andy Messersmith | .50 | 599 Ed Crosby | 1.00 | 651 Don Carrithers | 1.25 |
| 439 Eddie Fisher | .40 | 516 Danny Walton | .40 | 600 Dave McNally | 1.00 | 652 Ted Kubiak | 1.25 |
| 440 Glenn Beckert | .40 | 517 Bill Virdon (Mgr.) | .50 | 601 Rookie Catchers: | 1.25 | 653 Joe Hoerner | 1.25 |
| 441 Gail Hopkins | .40 | 518 Bob Veale | .40 | George Pena, Sergio | | 654 Minnesota Twins | 1.50 |
| 442 Dick Dietz | .40 | 519 John Edwards | .40 | Robles, R. Stelmaszek | | 655 Clay Kirby | 1.25 |
| 443 Danny Thompson | .40 | 520 Mel Stottlemyre | .40 | 602 Rookie Pitchers: | 1.25 | 656 John Ellis | 1.25 |
| 444 Ken Brett | .40 | 521 Atlanta Braves | .60 | Doug Rau, Mel Behney, | | 657 Bob Johnson | 1.25 |
| 445 Ken Berry | .40 | 522 Leo Cardenas | .40 | Ralph Garcia | | 658 Elliott Maddox | 1.25 |
| 446 Jerry Reuss | .50 | | | | | 659 Jose Pagan | 1.25 |
| | | | | | | 660 F. Scherman (Exc. .50) | 2.50 |

**Prices for the 1973 set are for cards in *Mint* condition. *Excellent* copies sell for 50% of prices shown; *Very Good*—30%.**

Features the rookie cards of Dave Parker and Dave Winfield. This was Topps' first card set to be released all at one time. Previous card sets were released in series, several weeks or months apart. Fifteen Padres cards were printed either "San Diego" or "Washington". Because of a false rumor that the Padres were moving, Topps printed "Washington" on the cards, but it was quickly corrected.

   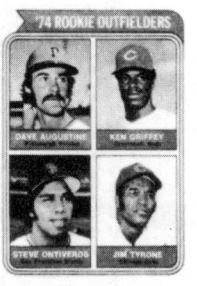 

| NO. PLAYER | MINT | NO. PLAYER | MINT | NO. PLAYER | MINT | NO. PLAYER | MINT |
|---|---|---|---|---|---|---|---|
| 1 Hank Aaron (Exc. $4.00) Home Run King | 12.00 | 64 Doug Rau | .25 | 127 Tom Paciorek | .25 | 191 Al Fitzmorris | .25 |
| 2 Aaron Special (1954-57) | 2.50 | 65 Amos Otis | .35 | 128 John Ellis | .25 | 192 Mario Guerrero | .25 |
| 3 Aaron Special (1958-61) | 2.50 | 66 Sparky Lyle | .50 | 129 Chris Speier | .25 | 193 Tom Walker | .25 |
| 4 Aaron Special (1962-65) | 2.50 | 67 Tommy Helms | .25 | 130 Reggie Jackson | 8.00 | 194 Darrell Porter | .25 |
| 5 Aaron Special (1966-69) | 2.50 | 68 Grant Jackson | .25 | 131 Bob Boone | .40 | 195 Carlos May | .25 |
| 6 Aaron Special (1970-73) | 2.50 | 69 Del Unser | .25 | 132 Felix Milan | .25 | 196 Jim Fregosi | .35 |
| 7 Jim Hunter | 2.25 | 70 Dick Allen | .50 | 133 David Clyde | .25 | 197 Vicente Romo (SD) | .30 |
| 8 George Theodore | .25 | 71 Dan Frisella | .25 | 134 Denis Menke | .25 | 197 Vicente Romo (Wash.) | 3.00 |
| 9 Mickey Lolich | .50 | 72 Aurelio Rodriguez | .25 | 135 Roy White | .30 | 198 Dave Cash | .25 |
| 10 Johnny Bench | 7.00 | 73 Mike Marshall | .60 | 136 Rick Reuschel | .50 | 199 Mike Kekich | .25 |
| 11 Jim Bibby | .25 | 74 Minnesota Twins | .50 | 137 Al Bumbry | .25 | 200 Cesar Cedeno | .50 |
| 12 Dave May | .25 | 75 Jim Colborn | .25 | 138 Ed Brinkman | .25 | 201 Batting Leaders: Rod Carew, Pete Rose | 2.50 |
| 13 Tom Hilgendorf | .25 | 76 Mickey Rivers | .25 | 139 Aurelio Monteagudo | .25 | 202 Home Run Leaders: R. Jackson, Willie Starge | 1.25 |
| 14 Paul Popovich | .25 | 77 Rich Troedson (SD) | .25 | 140 Darrell Evans | .50 | 203 RBI Leaders: R. Jackson, Willie Starge | 1.25 |
| 15 Joe Torre | .60 | 77 Rich Troedson (Wash.) | 3.00 | 141 Pat Bourque | .25 | 204 Stolen Base Leaders: Tommy Harper, Lou Broc | .75 |
| 16 Baltimore Orioles | .50 | 78 Charlie Fox (Mgr.) | .25 | 142 Pedro Garcia | .25 | 205 Victory Leaders: Wilbur Wood, Ron Bryan | .60 |
| 17 Doug Bird | .25 | 79 Gene Tenace | .25 | 143 Dick Woodson | .25 | 206 ERA Leaders: Jim Palmer, T. Seaver | 1.50 |
| 18 Gary Thomasson | .25 | 80 Tom Seaver | 6.00 | 144 Walter Alston (Mgr.) | .75 | 207 Strikeout Leaders: Nolan Ryan, Tom Seaver | 1.50 |
| 19 Gerry Moses | .25 | 81 Frank Duffy | .25 | 145 Dock Ellis | .25 | 208 Leading Firemen: John Hiller, M. Marshall | .50 |
| 20 Nolan Ryan | 5.00 | 82 Dave Giusti | .25 | 146 Ron Fairly | .25 | 209 Ted Sizemore | .25 |
| 21 Bob Gallagher | .25 | 83 Orlando Cepeda | 1.00 | 147 Bart Johnson | .25 | 210 Bill Singer | .25 |
| 22 Cy Acosta | .25 | 84 Rick Wise | .25 | 148 Dave Hilton (SD) | .30 | 211 Chicago Cubs | .50 |
| 23 Craig Robinson | .25 | 85 Joe Morgan | 2.00 | 148 Dave Hilton (Wash.) | 3.00 | 212 Rollie Fingers | 1.25 |
| 24 John Hiller | .25 | 86 Joe Ferguson | .25 | 149 Mac Scarce | .25 | 213 Dave Rader | .25 |
| 25 Len Singleton | .40 | 87 Fergie Jenkins | 1.00 | 150 John Mayberry | .30 | 214 Bill Grabarkewitz | .25 |
| 26 Bill Campbell (R) | .35 | 88 Freddie Patek | .25 | 151 Diego Segui | .25 | 215 Al Kaline | 3.00 |
| 27 George Scott | .25 | 89 Jackie Brown | .25 | 152 Oscar Gamble | .30 | 216 Ray Sadecki | .25 |
| 28 Manny Sanguillen | .25 | 90 Bobby Murcer | .50 | 153 Jon Matlack | .25 | 217 Tim Foli | .25 |
| 29 Phil Niekro | 2.00 | 91 Ken Forsch | .25 | 154 Houston Astros | .40 | 218 Johnny Briggs | .25 |
| 30 Bobby Bonds | .50 | 92 Paul Blair | .25 | 155 Bert Campaneris | .35 | 219 Doug Griffin | .25 |
| 31 Preston Gomez (Mgr.) | .25 | 93 Rod Gilbreath | .25 | 156 Randy Moffitt | .25 | 220 Don Sutton | 1.50 |
| 32 John Grubb (SD) | .30 | 94 Detroit Tigers | .75 | 157 Vic Harris | .25 | 221 Chuck Tanner (Mgr.) | .35 |
| 32 John Grubb (Wash) | 3.00 | 95 Steve Carlton | 5.00 | 158 Jack Billingham | .25 | 222 Ramon Hernandez | .25 |
| 33 Don Newhauser | .25 | 96 Jerry Hairston | .25 | 159 Jim Hart | .25 | 223 Jeff Burroughs | .50 |
| 34 Andy Kosco | .25 | 97 Bob Bailey | .25 | 160 Brooks Robinson | 3.00 | 224 Roger Metzger | .25 |
| 35 Gaylord Perry | 2.00 | 98 Bert Blyleven | .60 | 161 Ray Burris (R) | .60 | 225 Paul Splittorff | .30 |
| 36 St. Louis Cardinals | .45 | 99 Del Crandall (Mgr.) | .35 | 162 Bill Freehan | .40 | 226 Padres Team (SD) | .75 |
| 37 Dave Sells | .25 | 100 Willie Stargell | 3.00 | 163 Ken Berry | .25 | 226 Padres Team (Wash.) | 4.00 |
| 38 Don Kessinger | .25 | 101 Bobby Valentine | .35 | 164 Tom House | .25 | 227 Mike Lum | .25 |
| 39 Ken Suarez | .25 | 102 Bill Greif (SD) | .30 | 165 Willie Davis | .25 | 228 Ted Kubiak | .25 |
| 40 Jim Palmer | 3.00 | 102 Bill Greif (Wash.) | 3.00 | 166 Jack McKeon (Mgr.) | .25 | 229 Fritz Peterson | .25 |
| 41 Bobby Floyd | .25 | 103 Sal Bando | .50 | 167 Luis Tiant | .40 | 230 Tony Perez | 1.00 |
| 42 Claude Osteen | .25 | 104 Ron Bryant | .25 | 168 Danny Thompson | .25 | 231 Dick Tidrow | .25 |
| 43 Jim Wynn | .25 | 105 Carlton Fisk | 1.50 | 169 Steve Rogers (R) | .75 | 232 Steve Brye | .25 |
| 44 Mel Stottlemyre | .35 | 106 Harry Parker | .25 | 170 Bill Melton | .25 | 233 Jim Barr | .25 |
| 45 Dave Johnson | .60 | 107 Alex Johnson | .25 | 171 Eduardo Rodriguez | .25 | 234 John Milner | .25 |
| 46 Pat Kelly | .25 | 108 Al Hrabosky | .35 | 172 Gene Clines | .25 | 235 Dave McNally | .25 |
| 47 Dick Ruthven | .25 | 109 Bob Grich | .35 | 173 Randy Jones (SD) | .50 | 236 R. Schoendienst (Mgr.) | .40 |
| 48 Dick Sharon | .25 | 110 Billy Williams | 2.50 | 173 Randy Jones (Wash.) | 3.50 | 237 Ken Brett | .25 |
| 49 Steve Renko | .25 | 111 Clay Carroll | .25 | 174 Bill Robinson | .25 | 238 Fran Healy | .25 |
| 50 R. Carew | 5.50 | 112 Dave Lopes | .50 | 175 Reggie Cleveland | .25 | 239 Bill Russell | .25 |
| 51 Bob Heise | .25 | 113 Dick Drago | .25 | 176 John Lowenstein | .25 | 240 Joe Coleman | .25 |
| 52 Al Oliver | 1.00 | 114 California Angels | .50 | 177 Dave Roberts | .25 | 241 Glenn Beckert (SD) | .25 |
| 53 Fred Kendall (SD) | .25 | 115 Willie Horton | .40 | 178 Garry Maddox | .25 | 241 Glenn Beckert (Wash.) | 3.00 |
| 53 Fred Kendall (Wash.) | 3.00 | 116 Jerry Reuss | .35 | 179 Yogi Berra (Mgr.) | 1.00 | 242 Bill Gogolewski | .25 |
| 54 Elias Sosa | .25 | 117 Ron Blomberg | .25 | 180 Ken Holtzman | .25 | 243 Bob Oliver | .25 |
| 55 Frank Robinson | 3.00 | 118 Bill Lee | .30 | 181 Cesar Geronimo | .25 | 244 Carl Morton | .25 |
| 56 New York Mets | 1.00 | 119 Danny Ozark (Mgr.) | .30 | 182 Lindy McDaniel | .25 | 245 Cleon Jones | .25 |
| 57 Darold Knowles | .25 | 120 Wilbur Wood | .25 | 183 Johnny Oates | .25 | | |
| 58 Charlie Spikes | .25 | 121 Larry Lintz | .25 | 184 Texas Rangers | .60 | | |
| 59 Ross Grimsley | .25 | 122 Jim Holt | .25 | 185 Jose Cardenal | .25 | | |
| 60 Lou Brock | 3.00 | 123 Nellie Briles | .25 | 186 Fred Scherman | .25 | | |
| 61 Luis Aparicio | 2.00 | 124 Bobby Coluccio | .25 | 187 Don Baylor | 1.00 | | |
| 62 Bob Locker | .25 | 125 Nate Colbert (SD) | .30 | 188 Rudy Meoli | .25 | | |
| 63 Bill Sudakis | .25 | 125 Nate Colbert (Wash.) | 3.00 | 189 Jim Brewer | .25 | | |
| | | 126 Checklist No. 1 | 1.00 | 190 Tony Oliva | .75 | | |

| NO. PLAYER | MINT |
|---|---|
| 246 Oakland Athletics | .40 |
| 247 Rick Miller | .25 |
| 248 Tom Hall | .25 |
| 249 George Mitterwald | .25 |
| 250 W. McCovey (SD) | 3.50 |
| 250 W. McCovey (Wash.) | 15.00 |
| 251 Graig Nettles | 1.25 |
| 252 Dave Parker (R) | 20.00 |
| 253 John Boccabella | .25 |
| 254 Stan Bahnsen | .25 |
| 255 Larry Bowa | .60 |
| 256 Tom Griffin | .25 |
| 257 Buddy Bell | 1.00 |
| 258 Jerry Morales | .25 |
| 259 Bob Reynolds | .25 |
| 260 Ted Simmons | 1.00 |
| 261 Jerry Bell | .25 |
| 262 Ed Kirkpatrick | .25 |
| 263 Checklist No. 2 | 1.00 |
| 264 Joe Rudi | .25 |
| 265 Tug McGraw | .50 |
| 266 Jim Northrup | .25 |
| 267 Andy Messersmith | .35 |
| 268 Tom Grieve | .25 |
| 269 Bob Johnson | .25 |
| 270 Ron Santo | .40 |
| 271 Bill Hands | .25 |
| 272 Paul Casanova | .25 |
| 273 Checklist No. 3 | 1.00 |
| 274 Fred Beene | .25 |
| 275 Ron Hunt | .25 |
| 276 Bobby Winkles (Mgr.) | .35 |
| 277 Gary Nolan | .25 |
| 278 Cookie Rojas | .25 |
| 279 Jim Crawford | .25 |
| 280 Carl Yastrzemski | 7.00 |
| 281 San F. Giants | .40 |
| 282 Doyle Alexander | .25 |
| 283 Mike Schmidt | 40.00 |
| 284 Dave Duncan | .25 |
| 285 Reggie Smith | .40 |
| 286 Tony Muser | .25 |
| 287 Clay Kirby | .25 |
| 288 Gorman Thomas (R) | 2.00 |
| 289 Rick Auerback | .25 |
| 290 Vida Blue | .40 |
| 291 Don Hahn | .25 |
| 292 Chuck Seelbach | .25 |
| 293 Milt May | .25 |
| 294 Steve Foucault | .25 |
| 295 Rick Monday | .35 |
| 296 Ray Corbin | .25 |
| 297 Hal Breeden | .25 |
| 298 Roric Harrison | .25 |
| 299 Gene Michael | .30 |
| 300 Pete Rose | 15.00 |
| 301 Bob Montgomery | .25 |
| 302 Rudy May | .25 |
| 303 George Hendrick | .50 |
| 304 Don Wilson | .25 |
| 305 Tito Fuentes | .25 |
| 306 Earl Weaver (Mgr.) | .60 |
| 307 Luis Melendez | .25 |
| 308 Bruce Dal Canton | .25 |
| 309 Dave Roberts (SD) | .30 |
| 309 Dave Roberts (Wash.) | 4.00 |
| 310 Terry Forster | .25 |
| 311 Jerry Grote | .25 |
| 312 Deron Johnson | .25 |
| 313 Barry Lersch | .25 |
| 314 Milwaukee Brewers | .40 |
| 315 Ron Cey | 1.00 |
| 316 Jim Perry | .25 |
| 317 Richie Zisk | .25 |
| 318 Jim Merritt | .25 |
| 319 Randy Hundley | .25 |
| 320 Dusty Baker | .50 |
| 321 Steve Braun | .25 |
| 322 Ernie McAnally | .25 |
| 323 Richie Scheinblum | .25 |
| 324 Steve Kline | .25 |
| 325 Tommy Harper | .25 |
| 326 Sparky Anderson (Mgr.) | .50 |
| 327 Tom Timmermann | .25 |
| 328 Skip Jutze | .25 |

| NO. PLAYER | MINT |
|---|---|
| 329 Mark Belanger | .25 |
| 330 Juan Marichal | 2.00 |
| 331 All-Star Catchers: Carlton Fisk, Johnny Bench | 1.25 |
| 332 AS 1st Baseman: Dick Allen, Hank Aaron | 1.25 |
| 333 AS 2nd Baseman: Rod Carew, Joe Morgan | 1.50 |
| 334 AS 3rd Baseman: B. Robinson, Ron Santo | 1.00 |
| 335 AS Shortstops: B. Campaneris, C. Speier | .35 |
| 336 AS Left Fielders: Pete Rose, Bobby Mercer | 2.50 |
| 337 AS Center Fielders: Amos Otis, Cesar Cedeno | .35 |
| 338 AS Right Fielders: R. Jackson, B. Williams | 1.75 |
| 339 AS Pitchers: Jim Hunter, Rick Wise | .75 |
| 340 Thurman Munson | 4.00 |
| 341 Dan Driessen | .75 |
| 342 Jim Lonborg | .25 |
| 343 Kansas City Royals | .50 |
| 344 Mike Caldwell | .25 |
| 345 Bill North | .25 |
| 346 Ron Reed | .25 |
| 347 Sandy Alomar | .25 |
| 348 Pete Richert | .25 |
| 349 John Vukovich | .25 |
| 350 Bob Gibson | 2.50 |
| 351 Dwight Evans | 3.50 |
| 352 Bill Stoneman | .25 |
| 353 Rich Coggins | .25 |
| 354 Whitey Lockman (Mgr.) | .35 |
| 355 Dave Nelson | .25 |
| 356 Jerry Koosman | .50 |
| 357 Buddy Bradford | .25 |
| 358 Dal Maxvill | .25 |
| 359 Brent Strom | .25 |
| 360 Greg Luzinski | .75 |
| 361 Don Carrithers | .25 |
| 362 Hal King | .25 |
| 363 New York Yankees | 1.00 |
| 364 C. Gaston (SD) | .30 |
| 364 C. Gaston (Wash.) | 3.00 |
| 365 Steve Busby | .25 |
| 366 Larry Hisle | .25 |
| 367 Norm Cash | .40 |
| 368 Manny Mota | .40 |
| 369 Paul Lindblad | .25 |
| 370 Bob Watson | .35 |
| 371 Jim Slaton | .25 |
| 372 Ken Reitz | .25 |
| 373 John Curtis | .25 |
| 374 Marty Perez | .25 |
| 375 Earl Williams | .25 |
| 376 Jorge Orta | .25 |
| 377 Ron Woods | .25 |
| 378 Burt Hooton | .25 |
| 379 Billy Martin (Mgr.) | .60 |
| 380 Bud Harrelson | .60 |
| 381 Charlies Sands | .25 |
| 382 Bob Moose | .25 |
| 383 Phil. Phillies | .50 |
| 384 Chris Chambliss | .35 |
| 385 Don Gullett | .35 |
| 386 Gary Matthews | .50 |
| 387 Rich Morales (SD) | .30 |
| 387 Rich Morales (Wash.) | 3.00 |
| 388 Phil Roof | .25 |
| 389 Gates Brown | .25 |
| 390 Lou Piniella | .50 |
| 391 Billy Champion | .25 |
| 392 Dick Green | .25 |
| 393 Orlando Pena | .25 |
| 394 Ken Henderson | .25 |
| 395 Doug Rader | .25 |
| 396 Tommy Davis | .35 |
| 397 George Stone | .25 |
| 398 Duke Sims | .25 |
| 399 Mike Paul | .25 |
| 400 Harmon Killebrew | 3.00 |
| 401 Elliott Maddox | .25 |
| 402 Jim Rooker | .25 |

| NO. PLAYER | MINT |
|---|---|
| 403 Darrell Johnson (Mgr.) | .30 |
| 404 Jim Howarth | .25 |
| 405 Ellie Rodriguez | .25 |
| 406 Steve Arlin | .25 |
| 407 Jim Wohlford | .25 |
| 408 Charlie Hough | .35 |
| 409 Ike Brown | .25 |
| 410 Pedro Borbon | .25 |
| 411 Frank Baker | .25 |
| 412 Chuck Taylor | .25 |
| 413 Don Money | .35 |
| 414 Checklist No. 4 | 1.00 |
| 415 Gary Gentry | .25 |
| 416 Chicago White Sox | .60 |
| 417 Rich Folkers | .25 |
| 418 Walt Williams | .25 |
| 419 Wayne Twitchell | .25 |
| 420 Ray Fosse | .25 |
| 421 Dan Fife | .25 |
| 422 Gonzalo Marquez | .25 |
| 423 Fred Stanley | .25 |
| 424 Jim Beauchamp | .25 |
| 425 Pete Broberg | .25 |
| 426 Rennie Stennett | .25 |
| 427 Bobby Bolin | .25 |
| 428 Gary Sutherland | .25 |
| 429 Dick Lange | .25 |
| 430 Matty Alou | .40 |
| 431 Gene Garber | .25 |
| 432 Chris Arnold | .25 |
| 433 Lerrin LaGrow | .25 |
| 434 Ken McMullen | .25 |
| 435 Dave Concepcion | .60 |
| 436 Don Hood | .25 |
| 437 Jim Lyttle | .25 |
| 438 Ed Herrmann | .25 |
| 439 Norm Miller | .25 |
| 440 Jim Kaat | .75 |
| 441 Tom Ragland | .25 |
| 442 Alan Foster | .25 |
| 443 Tom Hutton | .25 |
| 444 Vic Davalillo | .25 |
| 445 George Medich | .25 |
| 446 Len Randle | .25 |
| 447 Frank Quilici (Mgr.) | .30 |
| 448 Ron Hodges | .25 |
| 449 Tom McCraw | .25 |
| 450 Rich Hebner | .25 |
| 451 Tommy John | 1.25 |
| 452 Gene Hiser | .25 |
| 453 Balor Moore | .25 |
| 454 Kurt Bevacqua | .25 |
| 455 Tom Bradley | .25 |
| 456 Dave Winfield (R) | 35.00 |
| 457 Chuck Goggin | .25 |
| 458 Jim Ray | .25 |
| 459 Cincinnati Reds | .50 |
| 460 Boog Powell | .50 |
| 461 John Odom | .25 |
| 462 Luis Alvarado | .25 |
| 463 Pat Dobson | .25 |
| 464 Jose Cruz | .50 |
| 465 Dick Bosman | .25 |
| 466 Dick Billings | .25 |
| 467 Winston Llenas | .25 |
| 468 Pepe Frias | .25 |
| 469 Joe Decker | .25 |
| 470 A.L. Playoffs: A's Beat Orioles | 1.50 |
| 471 N.L. Playoffs: Mets Beat Reds | .50 |
| 472 World Series Game 1: Oakland 2, N.Y. 1 | .50 |
| 473 World Series Game 2: N.Y. 10, Oakland 7 | 1.50 |
| 474 World Series Game 3: Oakland 3, N.Y. 2 | .50 |
| 475 World Series Game 4: N.Y. 6, Oakland 1 | .50 |
| 476 World Series Game 5: N.Y. 2, Oakland 0 | .50 |
| 477 World Series Game 6: Oakland 3, N.Y. 1 | 1.50 |
| 478 World Series Game 7: Oakland 5, N.Y. 2 | .50 |

| NO. PLAYER | MINT |
|---|---|
| 479 World Series: A's Win | .50 |
| 480 Willie Crawford | .25 |
| 481 Jerry Terrell | .25 |
| 482 Bob Didier | .25 |
| 483 Atlanta Braves | .50 |
| 484 Carmen Fanzone | .25 |
| 485 Felipe Alou | .40 |
| 486 Steve Stone | .30 |
| 487 Ted Martinez | .25 |
| 488 Andy Etchebarren | .25 |
| 489 Danny Murtaugh (Mgr.) | .25 |
| 490 Vada Pinson | .50 |
| 491 Roger Nelson | .25 |
| 492 Mike Rogodzinski | .25 |
| 493 Joe Hoerner | .25 |
| 494 Ed Goodson | .25 |
| 495 Dick McAuliffe | .25 |
| 496 Tom Murphy | .25 |
| 497 Bobby Mitchell | .25 |
| 498 Pat Corrales | .35 |
| 499 Rusty Torres | .25 |
| 500 Lee May | .30 |
| 501 Eddie Leon | .25 |
| 502 Dave LaRoche | .25 |
| 503 Eric Soderholm | .25 |
| 504 Joe Niekro | .50 |
| 505 Bill Buckner | .40 |
| 506 Ed Farmer | .25 |
| 507 Larry Stahl | .25 |
| 508 Montreal Expos | .40 |
| 509 Jesse Jefferson | .30 |
| 510 Wayne Garrett | .30 |
| 511 Toby Harrah | .35 |
| 512 Joe Lahoud | .25 |
| 513 Jim Campanis | .25 |
| 514 Paul Schaal | .25 |
| 515 Willie Montanez | .25 |
| 516 Horacio Pina | .25 |
| 517 Mike Hegan | .25 |
| 518 Derrel Thomas | .25 |
| 519 Bill Sharp | .25 |
| 520 Tim McCarver | .50 |
| 521 Ken Aspromonte (Mgr.) | .30 |
| 522 J.R. Richard | .40 |
| 523 Cecil Cooper | 2.00 |
| 524 Bill Plummer | .25 |
| 525 Clyde Wright | .25 |
| 526 Frank Tepedino | .25 |
| 527 Bobby Darwin | .25 |
| 528 Bill Bonham | .25 |
| 529 Horace Clarke | .25 |
| 530 Mickey Stanley | .25 |
| 531 Gene Mauch (Mgr.) | .35 |
| 532 Skip Lockwood | .25 |
| 533 Mike Phillips | .25 |
| 534 Eddie Watt | .25 |
| 535 Bob Tolan | .25 |
| 536 Duffy Dyer | .25 |
| 537 Steve Mingori | .25 |
| 538 Cesar Tovar | .25 |
| 539 Lloyd Allen | .25 |
| 540 Bob Robertson | .25 |
| 541 Cleveland Indians | .60 |
| 542 Rich Gossage | 2.00 |
| 543 Danny Cater | .25 |
| 544 Ron Schueler | .25 |
| 545 Billy Conigliaro | .25 |
| 546 Mike Corkins | .25 |
| 547 Glenn Borgmann | .25 |
| 548 Sonny Siebert | .25 |
| 549 Mike Jorgensen | .25 |
| 550 Sam McDowell | .35 |
| 551 Von Joshua | .25 |
| 552 Denny Doyle | .25 |
| 553 Jim Willoughby | .25 |
| 554 Tim Johnson | .25 |
| 555 Woodie Fryman | .25 |
| 556 Dave Campbell | .25 |
| 557 Jim McGlothlin | .25 |
| 558 Bill Fahey | .25 |
| 559 Darrell Chaney | .25 |
| 560 Mike Cuellar | .35 |
| 561 Ed Kranepool | .35 |
| 562 Jack Aker | .25 |

| NO. PLAYER | MINT |
|---|---|
| 563 Hal McRae | .35 |
| 564 Mike Ryan | .25 |
| 565 Milt Wilcox | .25 |
| 566 Jackie Hernandez | .25 |
| 567 Boston Red Sox | .50 |
| 568 Mike Torrez | .35 |
| 569 Rick Dempsey | .25 |
| 570 Ralph Garr | .25 |
| 571 Rich Hand | .25 |
| 572 Enzo Hernandez | .25 |
| 573 Mike Adams | .25 |
| 574 Bill Parsons | .25 |
| 575 Steve Garvey | 7.00 |
| 576 Scipio Spinks | .25 |
| 577 Mike Sadek | .25 |
| 578 Ralph Houk (Mgr.) | .35 |
| 579 Cecil Upshaw | .25 |
| 580 Jim Spencer | .25 |
| 581 Fred Norman | .25 |
| 582 Bucky Dent (R) | 1.00 |
| 583 Marty Pattin | .25 |
| 584 Ken Rudolph | .25 |
| 585 Merv Rettenmund | .25 |
| 586 Jack Brohamer | .25 |
| 587 Larry Christenson | .25 |
| 588 Hal Lanier | .35 |
| 589 Boots Day | .25 |
| 590 Roger Moret | .25 |
| 591 Sonny Jackson | .25 |
| 592 Ed Bane | .25 |
| 593 Steve Yeager | .25 |
| 594 Leroy Stanton | .25 |
| 595 Steve Blass | .25 |
| 596 Rookie Pitchers: | .40 |
| Wayne Garland, Fred Holdsworth, Dick Pole, Mark Littell | |

| NO. PLAYER | MINT |
|---|---|
| 597 Rookie Shortstops: | .75 |
| John Gamble, Pete MacKanin, Dave Chalk, Manny Trillo | |
| 598 Rookie Outfielders: | 2.00 |
| Steve Ontiveros, Dave Augustine, Ken Griffey, Jim Tyrone | |
| 599 Rookie Pitchers | 5.00 |
| "San Diego"—small type Ron Diorio, D. Freisleben, F. Riccelli, G. Shanahan | |
| 599 Rookie Pitchers | 2.50 |
| "San Diego"—large type | |
| 599 Rookie Pitchers | 1.00 |
| "Washington" Ron Diorio, D. Freisleben, F. Riccelli, G. Shanahan | |
| 600 Rookie Infielders: | 5.00 |
| Ron Cash, Jim Cox, Bill Madlock, Reggie Sanders | |
| 601 Rookie Outfielders: | 2.00 |
| Ed Armbrister, Rich Bladt, B. Downing, B. McBride | |
| 602 Rookie Pitchers | .50 |
| Glenn Abbott, Craig Swan, R. Henninger, D. Vossler | |
| 603 Rookie Catchers: | .50 |
| B. Foote, T. Lundstedt, C. Moore, S. Robles | |
| 604 Rookie Infielders: | 2.50 |
| Terry Hughes, John Knox, A. Thornton, F. White | |

| NO. PLAYER | MINT |
|---|---|
| 605 Rookie Pitchers: | 1.50 |
| Vic Albury, Ken Frailing, Kevin Kobel, Frank Tanana | |
| 606 Rookie Outfielders: | .50 |
| Jim Fuller, Wilbur Howard, Tommy Smith, Otto Velez | |
| 607 Rookie Shortstops: | .50 |
| Leo Foster, Dave Rosello, T. Heintzelman, F. Taveras | |
| 608 Rookie Pitchers: | .50 |
| Bob Apodaca, Mike Wallace, D. Baney, J. D'Acquisto | |
| 608 "Apodaca"—error | 2.00 |
| misspelled "Apodoco" | |
| 609 Rico Petrocelli | .25 |
| 610 Dave Kingman | .75 |
| 611 Rich Stelmaszek | .25 |
| 612 Luke Walker | .25 |
| 613 Dan Monzon | .25 |
| 614 Adrian Devine | .25 |
| 615 John Jeter | .25 |
| 616 Larry Gura | .35 |
| 617 Ted Ford | .25 |
| 618 Jim Mason | .25 |
| 619 Mike Anderson | .25 |
| 620 Al Downing | .35 |
| 621 Bernie Carbo | .25 |
| 622 Phil Gagliano | .25 |
| 623 Celerino Sanchez | .25 |
| 624 Bob Miller | .25 |
| 625 Ollie Brown | .25 |
| 626 Pittsburgh Pirates | .40 |
| 627 Carl Taylor | .25 |
| 628 Ivan Murrell | .25 |

| NO. PLAYER | MINT |
|---|---|
| 629 Rusty Staub | .50 |
| 630 Tommie Agee | .40 |
| 631 Steve Barber | .25 |
| 632 George Culver | .25 |
| 633 Dave Hamilton | .25 |
| 634 Eddie Mathews (Mgr.) | .75 |
| 635 John Edwards | .25 |
| 636 Dave Goltz | .25 |
| 637 Checklist No. 5 | 1.00 |
| 638 Ken Sanders | .25 |
| 639 Joe Lovitto | .25 |
| 640 Milt Pappas | .40 |
| 641 Chuck Brinkman | .25 |
| 642 Terry Harmon | .25 |
| 643 Los Angeles Dodgers | .75 |
| 644 Wayne Granger | .25 |
| 645 Ken Boswell | .25 |
| 646 George Foster | 1.50 |
| 647 Juan Beniquez | .60 |
| 648 Terry Crowley | .25 |
| 649 Fernando Gonzalez | .25 |
| 650 Mike Epstein | .25 |
| 651 Leron Lee | .25 |
| 652 Gail Hopkins | .25 |
| 653 Bob Stinson | .25 |
| 654 Jesus Alou | .40 |
| 654 Jesus Alou | 5.00 |
| "outfield" deleted on front | |
| 655 Mike Tyson | .25 |
| 656 Adrian Garrett | .25 |
| 657 Jim Shellenback | .25 |
| 658 Lee Lacy | .25 |
| 659 Joe Lis | .25 |
| 660 Larry Dierker (Exc. .15) | .50 |

**Prices for the 1974 set are for cards in *Mint* condition. *Excellent* copies sell for 50% of prices shown; *Very Good*—30%.**

## 1974 Topps Traded.... Complete Set of 44 Cards—Value $6.00

Topps' first Traded set. Topps issued another in 1976, and beginning in 1981 issued a Traded set every year. The traded set features players who were traded after the main set was printed. This set uses the same numbers as the regular set, followed by a "T".

| NO. PLAYER | MINT |
|---|---|
| 23 T Craig Robinson | .10 |
| 42 T Claude Osteen | .12 |
| 43 T Jim Wynn | .15 |
| 51 T Bobby Heise | .10 |
| 59 T Ross Grimsley | .10 |
| 62 T Bob Locker | .10 |
| 63 T Bill Sudakis | .10 |
| 73 T Mike Marshall | .15 |
| 123 T Nelson Briles | .10 |
| 139 T Aurelio Monteagudo | .10 |
| 151 T Diego Segui | .10 |

| NO. PLAYER | MINT |
|---|---|
| 165 T Willie Davis | .25 |
| 175 T Reggie Cleveland | .10 |
| 182 T Lindy McDaniel | .10 |
| 186 T Fred Scherman | .10 |
| 249 T George Mitterwald | .10 |
| 262 T Ed Kirkpatrick | .10 |
| 269 T Bob Johnson | .10 |
| 270 T Ron Santo | .25 |
| 313 T Barry Lersch | .10 |
| 319 T Randy Hundley | .10 |
| 330 T Juan Marichal | 1.00 |

| NO. PLAYER | MINT |
|---|---|
| 348 T Pete Richert | .10 |
| 373 T John Curtis | .10 |
| 390 T Lou Piniella | .40 |
| 428 T Gary Sutherland | .10 |
| 454 T Kurt Bevacqua | .10 |
| 458 T Jim Ray | .10 |
| 485 T Felipe Alou | .15 |
| 486 T Steve Stone | .12 |
| 496 T Tom Murphy | .10 |
| 516 T Horacio Pina | .10 |
| 534 T Eddie Watt | .10 |

| NO. PLAYER | MINT |
|---|---|
| 538 T Cesar Tovar | .10 |
| 544 T Ron Schueler | .10 |
| 579 T Cecil Upshaw | .10 |
| 585 T Merv Rettenmund | .10 |
| 612 T Luke Walker | .10 |
| 616 T Larry Gura | .20 |
| 618 T Jim Mason | .10 |
| 630 T Tommie Agee | .10 |
| 648 T Terry Crowley | .10 |
| 649 T Fernando Gonzalez | .10 |
| — Traded Checklist | .60 |

# 1975 Topps. . . .Complete Set of 660 Cards—Value $500.00

Features the rookie cards of Robin Yount, George Brett, Jim Rice, Gary Carter, Fred Lynn and Keith Hernandez. The set was also issued in a mini-size (2¼" x 3⅛") which was tested in a section of the country. The mini-size cards are worth 2 to 2½ times more than the regular size cards.

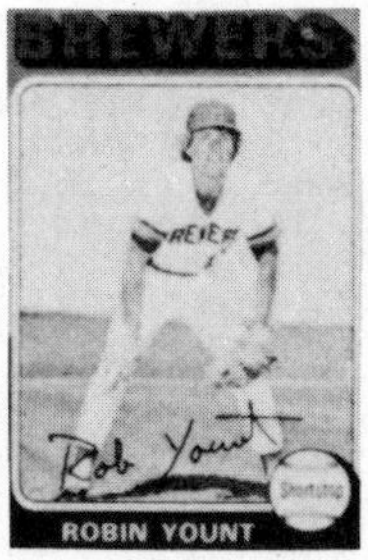

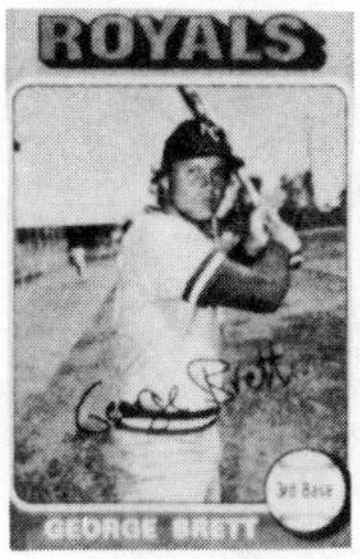

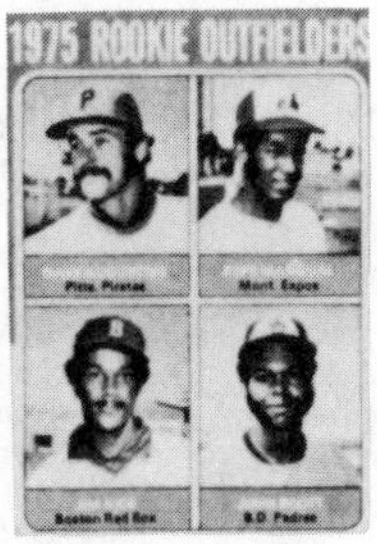

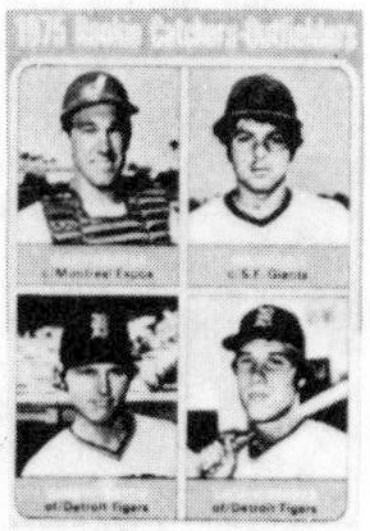
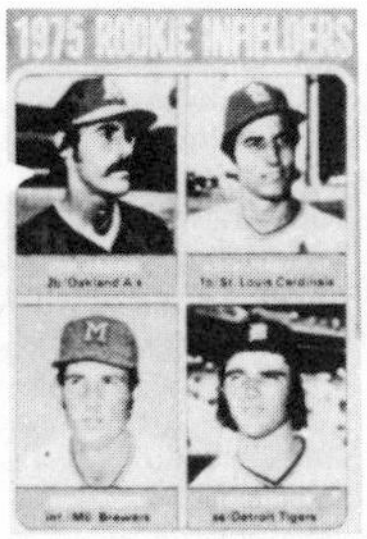


| NO. | PLAYER | MINT |
|---|---|---|
| 1 | Highlights: (Exc. $2.00) Aaron Sets Homer Mark | 8.00 |
| 2 | Highlights: Brock Steals 118 Bases | 1.50 |
| 3 | Highlights: Gibson's 3000th Strikeout | 1.25 |
| 4 | Highlights: Kaline's 3000th Hit | 1.25 |
| 5 | Highlights: Ryan Fans 300—3rd Year | 1.50 |
| 6 | Highlights: Marshall Hurls 106 Games | .50 |
| 7 | Highlights: No Hitters: Nolan Ryan, Dick Bosman, Steve Busby | .75 |
| 8 | Rogelio Moret | .20 |
| 9 | Frank Tepedino | .20 |
| 10 | Willie Davis | .35 |
| 11 | Bill Melton | .20 |
| 12 | David Clyde | .20 |
| 13 | Gene Locklear | .20 |
| 14 | Milt Wilcox | .20 |
| 15 | Jose Cardenal | .20 |
| 16 | Frank Tanana | .40 |
| 17 | Dave Concepcion | .50 |
| 18 | Tigers/R. Houk (Mgr.) | .50 |
| 19 | Jerry Koosman | .40 |
| 20 | Thurman Munson | 3.50 |
| 21 | Rollie Fingers | 1.00 |
| 22 | Dave Cash | .20 |
| 23 | Bill Russell | .30 |
| 24 | Al Fitzmorris | .20 |
| 25 | Lea May | .40 |
| 26 | Dave McNally | .35 |
| 27 | Ken Reitz | .20 |
| 28 | Tom Murphy | .20 |
| 29 | Dave Parker | 5.00 |
| 30 | Bert Blyleven | .75 |
| 31 | Dave Rader | .20 |
| 32 | Reggie Cleveland | .20 |
| 33 | Dusty Baker | .50 |
| 34 | Steve Renko | .20 |
| 35 | Ron Santo | .40 |
| 36 | Joe Lovitto | .20 |
| 37 | Dave Freisleben | .20 |
| 38 | Buddy Bell | .75 |
| 39 | Andy Thornton | .75 |
| 40 | Bill Singer | .20 |
| 41 | Cesar Geronimo | .20 |
| 42 | Joe Coleman | .20 |
| 43 | Cleon Jones | .20 |
| 44 | Pat Dobson | .20 |
| 45 | Joe Rudi | .35 |
| 46 | Phillies/D. Ozark (Mgr.) | .50 |
| 47 | Tommy John | 1.00 |
| 48 | Freddie Patek | .20 |
| 49 | Larry Dierker | .20 |
| 50 | Brook Robinson | 3.00 |
| 51 | Bob Forsch | .75 |
| 52 | Darrell Porter | .35 |
| 53 | Dave Giusti | .20 |
| 54 | Eric Soderholm | .20 |
| 55 | Bobby Bonds | .50 |
| 56 | Rick Wise | .20 |
| 57 | Dave Johnson | .60 |
| 58 | Chuck Taylor | .20 |
| 59 | Ken Henderson | .20 |
| 60 | Fergie Jenkins | .75 |
| 61 | Dave Winfield | 10.00 |
| 62 | Fritz Peterson | .20 |
| 63 | Steve Swisher | .20 |
| 64 | Dave Chalk | .20 |
| 65 | Don Gullett | .20 |
| 66 | Willie Horton | .35 |
| 67 | Tug McGraw | .40 |
| 68 | Ron Blomberg | .20 |
| 69 | John Odom | .20 |
| 70 | Mike Schmidt | 18.00 |
| 71 | Charlie Hough | .30 |
| 72 | Royals/J. McKeon (Mgr. | .40 |
| 73 | J.R. Richard | .35 |
| 74 | Mark Belanger | .35 |
| 75 | Ted Simmons | .75 |
| 76 | Ed Sprague | .20 |
| 77 | Richie Zisk | .35 |
| 78 | Ray Corbin | .20 |
| 79 | Gary Matthews | .40 |
| 80 | Carlton Fisk | 1.25 |
| 81 | Ron Reed | .20 |
| 82 | Pat Kelly | .20 |
| 83 | Jim Merritt | .20 |
| 84 | Enzo Hernandez | .20 |
| 85 | Bill Bonham | .20 |
| 86 | Joe Lis | .20 |
| 87 | George Foster | 1.00 |
| 88 | Tom Egan | .20 |
| 89 | Jim Ray | .20 |
| 90 | Rusty Staub | .50 |
| 91 | Dick Green | .20 |
| 92 | Cecil Upshaw | .20 |
| 93 | Dave Lopes | .35 |
| 94 | Jim Lonborg | .20 |
| 95 | John Mayberry | .35 |
| 96 | Mike Cosgrove | .20 |
| 97 | Earl Williams | .20 |
| 98 | Rich Folkers | .20 |
| 99 | Mike Hegan | .20 |
| 100 | Willie Stargell | 2.50 |
| 101 | Expos/G. Mauch (Mgr.) | .60 |
| 102 | Joe Decker | .20 |
| 103 | Rick Miller | .20 |
| 104 | Bill Madlock | 1.50 |
| 105 | Buzz Capra | .20 |
| 106 | Mike Hargrove (R) | .60 |
| 107 | Jim Barr | .20 |
| 108 | Tom Hall | .20 |
| 109 | George Hendrick | .40 |
| 110 | Wilbur Wood | .30 |
| 111 | Wayne Garrett | .20 |
| 112 | Larry Hardy | .20 |
| 113 | Elliot Maddox | .20 |
| 114 | Dick Lange | .20 |
| 115 | Joe Ferguson | .20 |
| 116 | Lerrin LaGrow | .20 |
| 117 | Orioles/E. Weaver (Mgr.) | .60 |
| 118 | Mike Anderson | .20 |
| 119 | Tommy Helms | .20 |
| 120 | Steve Busby (photo of Fran Healy) | .35 |
| 121 | Bill North | .20 |
| 122 | Al Hrabosky | .30 |
| 123 | Johnny Briggs | .20 |
| 124 | Jerry Reuss | .35 |
| 125 | Ken Singleton | .35 |
| 126 | Checklist No.1 | .75 |
| 127 | Glenn Borgmann | .20 |
| 128 | Bill Lee | .25 |
| 129 | Rick Monday | .35 |
| 130 | Phil Niekro | 1.50 |
| 131 | Toby Harrah | .25 |
| 132 | Randy Moffitt | .20 |
| 133 | Dan Driessen | .35 |
| 134 | Ron Hodges | .20 |
| 135 | Charlie Spikes | .20 |
| 136 | Jim Mason | .20 |
| 137 | Terry Forster | .35 |
| 138 | Del Unser | .20 |
| 139 | Horacio Pina | .20 |
| 140 | Steve Garvey | 5.50 |
| 141 | Mickey Stanley | .35 |
| 142 | Bob Reynolds | .20 |
| 143 | Cliff Johnson | .20 |
| 144 | Jim Wohlford | .20 |
| 145 | Ken Holtzman | .30 |
| 146 | San Diego Padres J. McNamara (Mgr.) | .60 |
| 147 | Pedro Garcia | .20 |
| 148 | Jim Rooker | .20 |
| 149 | Tim Foli | .20 |
| 150 | Bob Gibson | 2.00 |
| 151 | Steve Brye | .20 |
| 152 | Mario Guerrero | .20 |
| 153 | Rick Reuschel | .50 |
| 154 | Mike Lum | .20 |
| 155 | Jim Bibby | .20 |
| 156 | Dave Kingman | .75 |
| 157 | Pedro Borbon | .20 |
| 158 | Jerry Grote | .20 |
| 159 | Steve Arlin | .20 |
| 160 | Graig Nettles | 1.00 |
| 161 | Stan Bahnsen | .20 |
| 162 | Willie Montanez | .20 |
| 163 | Jim Brewer | .20 |
| 164 | Mickey Rivers | .30 |
| 165 | Doug Rader | .20 |
| 166 | Woodie Fryman | .20 |
| 167 | Rich Coggins | .20 |
| 168 | Bill Greif | .20 |
| 169 | Cookie Rojas | .20 |
| 170 | Bert Campaneris | .40 |
| 171 | Ed Kirkpatrick | .20 |
| 172 | Boston Red Sox D. Johnson (Mgr.) | .75 |
| 173 | Steve Rogers | .30 |
| 174 | Bake McBride | .20 |
| 175 | Don Money | .20 |
| 176 | Burt Hooton | .30 |
| 177 | Vic Correll | .20 |
| 178 | Cesar Tovar | .20 |
| 179 | Tom Bradley | .20 |
| 180 | Joe Morgan | 2.50 |
| 181 | Fred Beene | .20 |
| 182 | Don Hahn | .20 |
| 183 | Mel Stottlemyre | .35 |
| 184 | Jorge Orta | .20 |
| 185 | Steve Carlton | 5.00 |
| 186 | Willie Crawford | .20 |
| 187 | Denny Doyle | .20 |
| 188 | Tom Griffin | .20 |
| 189 | 1951 MVP's: Y. Berra, R. Campanella | 1.00 |
| 190 | 1952 MVP': B. Shantz, Hank Bauer | .35 |
| 191 | 1953 MVP's: Al Rosen, R. Campanella | .60 |
| 192 | 1954 MVP's: Yogi Berra, Willie Mays | 1.00 |
| 193 | 1955 MVP's: Y. Berra, R. Campanella | 1.00 |
| 194 | 1956 MVP's: M. Mantle, D. Newcombe | 2.00 |
| 195 | 1957 MVP's: Hank Aaron, M. Mantle | 4.00 |
| 196 | 1958 MVP's: J. Jensen, Ernie Banks | .60 |
| 197 | 1959 MVP's: Nellie Fox, Ernie Banks | .75 |
| 198 | 1960 MVP's: Roger Maris, Dick Groat | .60 |
| 199 | 1961 MVP's: F. Robinson, Roger Maris | 1.00 |
| 200 | 1962 MVP's: M. Mantle, Maury Wills | 2.50 |
| 201 | 1963 MVP's: Elston Howard, S. Koufax | .50 |
| 202 | 1964 MVP's: Ken Boyer, B. Robinson | .60 |
| 203 | 1965 MVP's: Zoilo Versalles, W. Mays | .75 |
| 204 | 1966 MVP's: F. Robinson, Bob Clemente | .75 |
| 205 | 1967 MVP's: C. Yastrzemski, O. Cepeda | .75 |
| 206 | 1968 MVP's: D. McLain, Bob Gibson | .75 |
| 207 | 1969 MVP's: W. McCovey, H. Killebrew | .75 |
| 208 | 1970 MVP's: Bopg Powell, J. Bench | .65 |
| 209 | 1971 MVP's; Vida Blue, Joe Torre | .50 |
| 210 | 1972 MVP's: Richie Allen, J. Bench | .50 |
| 211 | 1973 MVP's: Pete Rose, R. Jackson | 2.50 |
| 212 | 1974 MVP's: J. Burroughs, S. Garvey | .60 |
| 213 | Oscar Gamble | .25 |
| 214 | Harry Parker | |
| 215 | Bobby Valentine | .35 |
| 216 | San Francisco Giants Wes Westrum (Mgr.) | .35 |
| 217 | Lou Piniella | .45 |
| 218 | Jerry Johnson | .20 |
| 219 | Ed Herrmann | .20 |
| 220 | Don Sutton | 1.00 |
| 221 | Aurelio Rodriguez | .20 |
| 222 | Dan Spillner | .20 |
| 223 | Robin Yount (R) | 27.50 |
| 224 | Ramon Hernandez | .20 |
| 225 | Bob Grich | .35 |
| 226 | Bill Campbell | .20 |
| 227 | Bob Watson | .25 |
| 228 | George Brett (R) | 45.00 |

| NO. PLAYER | MINT |
|---|---|
| 229 Barry Foote | .20 |
| 230 Jim Hunter | 1.50 |
| 231 Mike Tyson | .20 |
| 232 Diego Segui | .20 |
| 233 Billy Grabarkewitz | .20 |
| 234 Tom Grieve | .20 |
| 235 Jack Billingham | .20 |
| 236 Angels/D. Williams (Mgr.) | .50 |
| 237 Carl Morton | .20 |
| 238 Dave Duncan | .20 |
| 239 George Stone | .20 |
| 240 Garry Maddox | .35 |
| 241 Dick Tidrow | .20 |
| 242 Jay Johnstone | .20 |
| 243 Jim Kaat | .75 |
| 244 Bill Buckner | .50 |
| 245 Mickey Lolich | .35 |
| 246 St. Louis Cardinals | .50 |
| Red Schoendienst (Mgr.) | |
| 247 Enos Cabell | .20 |
| 248 Randy Jones | .20 |
| 249 Danny Thompson | .20 |
| 250 Ken Brett | .20 |
| 251 Fran Healy | .20 |
| 252 Fred Scherman | .20 |
| 253 Jesus Alou | .20 |
| 254 Mike Torrez | .30 |
| 255 Dwight Evans | 1.50 |
| 256 Billy Champion | .20 |
| 257 Checklist No. 2 | .75 |
| 258 Dave LaRoche | .20 |
| 259 Len Randle | .20 |
| 260 Johnny Bench | 6.00 |
| 261 Andy Hassler | .20 |
| 262 Rowland Office | .20 |
| 263 Jim Perry | .20 |
| 264 John Milner | .20 |
| 265 Ron Bryant | .20 |
| 266 Sandy Alomar | .20 |
| 267 Dick Ruthven | .20 |
| 268 Hal McRae | .35 |
| 269 Doug Rau | .20 |
| 270 Ron Fairly | .20 |
| 271 Jerry Moses | .20 |
| 272 Lynn McGlothen | .20 |
| 273 Steve Braun | .20 |
| 274 Vincente Romo | .20 |
| 275 Paul Blair | .20 |
| 276 Chicago White Sox | .50 |
| Chuck Tanner (Mgr.) | |
| 277 Frank Taveras | .35 |
| 278 Paul Lindblad | .20 |
| 279 Milt May | .20 |
| 280 Carl Yastrzemski | 7.00 |
| 281 Jim Slaton | .20 |
| 282 Jerry Morales | .20 |
| 283 Steve Foucault | .20 |
| 284 Ken Griffey | .75 |
| 285 Ellie Rodriguez | .20 |
| 286 Mike Jorgensen | .20 |
| 287 Roric Harrison | .20 |
| 288 Bruce Ellingsen | .20 |
| 289 Ken Rudolph | .20 |
| 290 Jon Matlack | .30 |
| 291 Bill Sudakis | .20 |
| 292 Ron Schueler | .20 |
| 293 Dick Sharon | .20 |
| 294 Geoff Zahn | .20 |
| 295 Vada Pinson | .40 |
| 296 Alan Foster | .20 |
| 297 Craig Kusick | .20 |
| 298 Johnny Grubb | .20 |
| 299 Bucky Dent | .35 |
| 300 Reggie Jackson | 7.50 |
| 301 Dave Roberts | .20 |
| 302 Rick Burleson (R) | .50 |
| 303 Grant Jackson | .20 |
| 304 Pittsburgh Pirates | .40 |
| Danny Murtaugh (Mgr.) | |
| 305 Jim Colborn | .20 |
| 306 Batting Leaders: | .50 |
| Rod Carew, Ralph Garr | |
| 307 Home Run Leaders: | .75 |
| Dick Allen, Mike Schmidt | |

| NO. PLAYER | MINT |
|---|---|
| 308 RBI Leaders: | .60 |
| J. Burroughs, J. Bench | |
| 309 Stolen Base Leaders: | .50 |
| Bill North, Lou Brock | |
| 310 Victory Leaders: | .50 |
| Andy Messersmith, | |
| Jim Hunter, Fergie | |
| Jenkins, Phil Niekro | |
| 311 ERA Leaders: | .40 |
| Jim Hunter, Buzz Capra | |
| 312 Strikeout Leaders: | 1.50 |
| Nolan Ryan, Steve Ca | |
| 313 Leading Firemen: | .30 |
| Mike Marshall, | |
| Terry Forster | |
| 314 Buck Martinez | .20 |
| 315 Don Kessinger | .35 |
| 316 Jackie Brown | .20 |
| 317 Joe LaHoud | .20 |
| 318 Ernie McAnally | .20 |
| 319 Johnny Oates | .20 |
| 320 Pete Rose | 17.50 |
| 321 Rudy May | .20 |
| 322 Ed Goodson | .20 |
| 323 Fred Holdsworth | .20 |
| 324 Ed Kranepool | .35 |
| 325 Tony Oliva | .75 |
| 326 Wayne Twitchell | .20 |
| 327 Jerry Hairston | .20 |
| 328 Sonny Siebert | .20 |
| 329 Ted Kubiak | .20 |
| 330 Mike Marshall | .30 |
| 331 Cleveland Indians | .50 |
| Frank Robinson (Mgr. | |
| 332 Fred Kendall | .20 |
| 333 Dick Drago | .20 |
| 334 Greg Gross | .20 |
| 335 Jim Palmer | 3.00 |
| 336 Rennie Stennett | .20 |
| 337 Kevin Kobel | .20 |
| 338 Rick Stelmaszek | .20 |
| 339 Jim Fregosi | .30 |
| 340 Paul Splittorff | .20 |
| 341 Hal Breeden | .20 |
| 342 Leroy Stanton | .20 |
| 343 Danny Frisella | .20 |
| 344 Ben Oglivie | .30 |
| 345 Clay Carroll | .20 |
| 346 Bobby Darwin | .20 |
| 347 Mike Caldwell | .20 |
| 348 Tony Muser | .20 |
| 349 Ray Sadecki | .20 |
| 350 Bobby Murcer | .50 |
| 351 Bob Boone | .25 |
| 352 Darold Knowles | .20 |
| 353 Luis Melendez | .20 |
| 354 Dick Bosman | .20 |
| 355 Chris Cannizzaro | .20 |
| 356 Rico Petrocelli | .30 |
| 357 Ken Frosch | .20 |
| 358 Al Bumbry | .20 |
| 359 Paul Popovich | .20 |
| 360 George Scott | .20 |
| 361 Los Angeles Dodgers | .60 |
| Walter Alston (Mgr.) | |
| 362 Steve Hargan | .20 |
| 363 Carmen Fanzone | .20 |
| 364 Doug Bird | .20 |
| 365 Bob Bailey | .20 |
| 366 Ken Sanders | .20 |
| 367 Craig Robinson | .20 |
| 368 Vic Albury | .20 |
| 369 Merv Rettenmund | .20 |
| 370 Tom Seaver | 6.00 |
| 371 Gates Brown | .20 |
| 372 John D'Acquisto | .20 |
| 373 Bill Sharp | .20 |
| 374 Eddie Watt | .20 |
| 375 Roy White | .35 |
| 376 Steve Yeager | .20 |
| 377 Tom Hilgendorf | .20 |
| 378 Derrel Thomas | .20 |
| 379 Bernie Carbo | .20 |
| 380 Sal Bando | .35 |

| NO. PLAYER | MINT |
|---|---|
| 381 John Curtis | .20 |
| 382 Don Baylor | .75 |
| 383 Jim York | .20 |
| 384 Milwaukee Brewers | .40 |
| Del Crandall (Mgr.) | |
| 385 Dock Ellis | .20 |
| 386 Checklist: No. 3 | .75 |
| 387 Jim Spencer | .20 |
| 388 Steve Stone | .20 |
| 389 Tony Solaita | .20 |
| 390 Ron Cey | .75 |
| 391 Don DeMola | .20 |
| 392 Bruce Bochte (R) | .50 |
| 393 Gary Gentry | .20 |
| 394 Larvell Blanks | .20 |
| 395 Bud Harrelson | .40 |
| 396 Fred Norman | .20 |
| 397 Bill Freehan | .30 |
| 398 Elias Sosa | .20 |
| 399 Terry Harmon | .20 |
| 400 Dick Allen | .35 |
| 401 Mike Wallace | .20 |
| 402 Bob Tolan | .20 |
| 403 Tom Buskey | .20 |
| 404 Ted Sizemore | .20 |
| 405 John Montague | .20 |
| 406 Bob Gallagher | .20 |
| 407 Herb Washington | .20 |
| 408 Clyde Wright | .20 |
| 409 Bob Robertson | .20 |
| 410 Mike Cueller | .30 |
| 411 George Mitterwald | .20 |
| 412 Bill Hands | .20 |
| 413 Marty Pattin | .20 |
| 414 Manny Mota | .35 |
| 415 John Hiller | .20 |
| 416 Larry Lintz | .20 |
| 417 Skip Lockwood | .20 |
| 418 Leo Foster | .20 |
| 419 Dave Goltz | .20 |
| 420 Larry Bowa | .50 |
| 421 Mets/Y. Berra (Mgr.) | .60 |
| 422 Brian Downing | .40 |
| 423 Clay Kirby | .20 |
| 424 John Lowenstein | .20 |
| 425 Tito Fuentes | .20 |
| 426 Geroge Medich | .20 |
| 427 Clarence Gaston | .20 |
| 428 Dave Hamilton | .20 |
| 429 Jim Dwyer | .20 |
| 430 Luis Tiant | .30 |
| 431 Rod Gilbreath | .20 |
| 432 Ken Berry | .20 |
| 433 Larry Demery | .20 |
| 434 Bob Locker | .20 |
| 435 Dave Nelson | .20 |
| 436 Ken Frailing | .20 |
| 437 Al Cowens (R) | .50 |
| 438 Don Carrithers | .20 |
| 439 Ed Brinkman | .20 |
| 440 Andy Messersmith | .30 |
| 441 Bobby Heise | .20 |
| 442 Maximino Leon | .20 |
| 443 Twins/F. Quilici (Mgr.) | .40 |
| 444 Gene Garber | .20 |
| 445 Felix Millan | .20 |
| 446 Bart Johnson | .20 |
| 447 Terry Crowley | .20 |
| 448 Frank Duffy | .20 |
| 449 Charlie Williams | .20 |
| 450 Willie McCovey | 2.50 |
| 451 Rick Dempsey | .30 |
| 452 Angel Mangual | .20 |
| 453 Claude Osteen | .20 |
| 454 Doug Griffin | .20 |
| 455 Don Wilson | .20 |
| 456 Bob Coluccio | .20 |
| 457 Mario Mendoza | .20 |
| 458 Ross Grimsley | .20 |
| 459 1974 AL Champs: | .40 |
| A's over Orioles | |
| 460 1974 NL Champs: | .60 |
| Dodgers over Pirates | |
| 461 World Series Game 1: | 1.25 |
| Oakland 3, Los Angeles 2 | |

| NO. PLAYER | MINT |
|---|---|
| 462 World Series Game 2: | .40 |
| Los Angeles 3, Oakland 2 | |
| 463 World Series Game 3: | .65 |
| Oakland 3, Los Angeles 2 | |
| 464 World Series Game 4: | .35 |
| Oakland 5, Los Angeles 2 | |
| 465 World Series Game 5 | .35 |
| Oakland 3, Los Angeles 2 | |
| 466 A's Win 3rd World Series | .40 |
| 467 Ed Halicki | .20 |
| 468 Bobby Mitchell | .20 |
| 469 Tom Dettore | .20 |
| 470 Jeff Burroughs | .30 |
| 471 Bob Stinson | .20 |
| 472 Bruce Dal Canton | .20 |
| 473 Ken McMullen | .20 |
| 474 Luke Walker | .20 |
| 475 Darrell Evans | .50 |
| 476 Eduardo Figueroa | .20 |
| 477 Tom Hutton | .20 |
| 478 Tom Burgmeier | .20 |
| 479 Ken Boswell | .20 |
| 480 Carlos May | .20 |
| 481 Will McEnaney | .20 |
| 482 Tom McCraw | .20 |
| 483 Steve Ontiveros | .20 |
| 484 Glenn Beckert | .20 |
| 485 Sparky Lyle | .35 |
| 486 Ray Fosse | .20 |
| 487 Astros/P. Gomez (Mgr.) | .40 |
| 488 Bill Travers | .20 |
| 489 Cecil Cooper | 1.25 |
| 490 Reggie Smith | .30 |
| 491 Doyle Alexander | .20 |
| 492 Rich Hebner | .20 |
| 493 Don Stanhouse | .20 |
| 494 Pete LaCock | .20 |
| 495 Nelson Briles | .20 |
| 496 Pepe Frias | .20 |
| 497 Jim Nettles | .20 |
| 498 Al Downing | .20 |
| 499 Marty Perez | .20 |
| 500 Nolan Ryan | 5.00 |
| 501 Bill Robinson | .20 |
| 502 Pat Bourque | .20 |
| 503 Fred Stanley | .20 |
| 504 Buddy Bradford | .20 |
| 505 Chris Speier | .20 |
| 506 Leron Lee | .20 |
| 507 Tom Carroll | .20 |
| 508 Bob Hansen | .20 |
| 509 Dave Hilton | .20 |
| 510 Vida Blue | .35 |
| 511 Rangers/B. Martin (Mgr.) | .60 |
| 512 Larry Milbourne | .20 |
| 513 Dick Pole | .20 |
| 514 Jose Cruz | .50 |
| 515 Manny Sanguillen | .25 |
| 516 Don Hood | .20 |
| 517 Checklist: No. 4 | .75 |
| 518 Leo Cardenas | .20 |
| 519 Jim Todd | .20 |
| 520 Amos Otis | .40 |
| 521 Dennis Blair | .20 |
| 522 Gary Sutherland | .20 |
| 523 Tom Paciorek | .20 |
| 524 John Doherty | .20 |
| 525 Tom House | .20 |
| 526 Larry Hisle | .20 |
| 527 Mac Scarce | .20 |
| 528 Eddie Leon | .20 |
| 529 Gary Thomasson | .20 |
| 530 Gaylord Perry | 1.50 |
| 531 Cincinnati Reds | .60 |
| Sparky Anderson (Mgr.) | |
| 532 Gorman Thomas | .75 |
| 533 Rudy Meoli | .20 |
| 534 Alex Johnson | .20 |
| 535 Gene Tenace | .20 |
| 536 Bob Moose | .20 |
| 537 Tommy Harper | .20 |
| 538 Duffy Dyer | .20 |
| 539 Jesse Jefferson | .20 |
| 540 Lou Brock | 2.50 |

**Prices for the 1975 set are for cards in *Mint* condition. *Excellent* copies sell for 50% of prices shown; *Very Good*—30%.**

| NO. PLAYER | MINT | NO. PLAYER | MINT | NO. PLAYER | MINT | NO. PLAYER | MINT |
|---|---|---|---|---|---|---|---|
| 541 Roger Metzger | .20 | 579 Skip Pitlock | .20 | 615 Rookie Pitchers: | 1.00 | 627 Tom Walker | .20 |
| 542 Pete Broberg | .20 | 580 Frank Robinson | 2.50 | Dennis Leonard, Tom | | 628 Ron LeFlore (R) | .60 |
| 543 Larry Biittner | .20 | 581 Darrel Chaney | .20 | Underwood, Hank Webb, | | 629 Joe Hoerner | .20 |
| 544 Steve Mingori | .20 | 582 Eduardo Rodriguez | .20 | Pat Darcy | | 630 Greg Luzinski | .75 |
| 545 Billy Williams | 1.75 | 583 Andy Etchebarren | .20 | 616 Rookie Outfielders | .35.00 | 631 Lee Lacy | .20 |
| 546 John Knox | .20 | 584 Mike Garman | .20 | Jim Rice, D. Augustine, | | 632 Morris Nettles | .20 |
| 547 Von Joshua | .20 | 585 Chris Chambliss | .40 | Pepe Mangual, J. Scott | | 633 Paul Casanova | .20 |
| 548 Charlie Sands | .20 | 586 Tim McCarver | .50 | 617 Rookie Infielders: | 2.00 | 634 Cy Acosta | .20 |
| 549 Bill Butler | .20 | 587 Chris Ward | .20 | Mike Cubbage, Reggie | | 635 Chuck Dobson | .20 |
| 550 Ralph Garr | .20 | 588 Rick Auerbach | .20 | Sanders, Manny Trillo, | | 636 Charlie Moore | .20 |
| 551 Larry Christenson | .20 | 589 Braves/C. King (Mgr.) | .75 | Doug DeCinces | | 637 Ted Martinez | .20 |
| 552 Jack Brohamer | .20 | 590 Cesar Cedeno | .50 | 618 Rookie Pitchers: | 3.00 | 638 Cubs/J. Marshall (Mgr.) | .40 |
| 553 John Boccabella | .20 | 591 Glenn Abbott | .20 | Tom Johnson, Jamie | | 639 Steve Kline | .20 |
| 554 Rich Gossage | 1.25 | 592 Balor Moore | .20 | Easterly, Scott McGregor, | | 640 Harmon Killebrew | 2.25 |
| 555 Al Oliver | .75 | 593 Gene Lamont | .20 | Rick Rhoden | | 641 Jim Northrup | .20 |
| 556 Tim Johnson | .20 | 594 Jim Fuller | .20 | 619 Rookie Outfielders: | .30 | 642 Mike Phillips | .20 |
| 557 Larry Gura | .20 | 595 Joe Niekro | .50 | Benny Ayala, Nyls Nyman, | | 643 Brent Strom | .20 |
| 558 Dave Roberts | .20 | 596 Ollie Brown | .20 | Tommy Smith, Jerry Turner | | 644 Bill Fahey | .20 |
| 559 Bob Montgomery | .20 | 597 Winston Llenas | .20 | 620 Rookie Catchers/OF's | .35.00 | 645 Danny Cater | .20 |
| 560 Tony Perez | 1.00 | 598 Bruce Kison | .20 | Gary Carter, Marc Hill, | | 646 Checklist No. 5 | .75 |
| 561 A's/Alvin Dark (Mgr.) | .60 | 599 Nate Colbert | .20 | Danny Meyer, Leon Roberts | | 647 Claudell Washington | 1.50 |
| 562 Gary Nolan | .20 | 600 Rod Carew | 5.00 | 621 Rookie Pitchers: | .75 | 648 Dave Pagan | .20 |
| 563 Wilbur Howard | .20 | 601 Juan Beniquez | .20 | John Denny, Rawly | | 649 Jack Heidemann | .20 |
| 564 Tommy Davis | .40 | 602 John Vukovich | .20 | Eastwick, Jim Kern, | | 650 Dave May | .20 |
| 565 Joe Torre | .50 | 603 Lew Krausse | .20 | Juan Veintidos | | 651 John Morlan | .20 |
| 566 Ray Burris | .20 | 604 Oscar Zamora | .20 | 622 Rookie Outfielders: | 12.00 | 652 Lindy McDaniel | .20 |
| 567 Jim Sundberg (R) | .75 | 605 John Ellis | .20 | Ed Armbrister, Fred Lynn, | | 653 Lee Richards | .20 |
| 568 Dale Murray | .20 | 606 Bruce Miller | .20 | T. Whitfield, Tom Poquette | | 654 Jerry Terrell | .20 |
| 569 Frank White | .50 | 607 Jim Holt | .20 | 623 Rookie Infielders: | 24.00 | 655 Rico Carty | .40 |
| 570 Jim Wynn | .35 | 608 Gene Michael | .20 | Phil Garner, Bob Sheldon, | | 656 Bill Plummer | .20 |
| 571 Dave Lemanczyk | .20 | 609 Ellie Hendricks | .20 | K. Hernandez, T. Veryzer | | 657 Bob Oliver | .20 |
| 572 Roger Nelson | .20 | 610 Ron Hunt | .20 | 624 Rookie Pitchers: | .40 | 658 Vic Harris | .20 |
| 573 Orlando Pena | .20 | 611 Yankees/B. Virdon (Mgr.) | .75 | Doug Konieczny, Gary | | 659 Bob Apodaca | .20 |
| 574 Tony Taylor | .20 | 612 Terry Hughes | .20 | Lavelle, Jim Otten, | | 660 Hank Aaron | 10.00 |
| 575 Gene Clines | .20 | 613 Bill Parsons | .20 | Eddie Solomon | | | |
| 576 Phil Roof | .20 | 614 Rookie Pitchers: | .35 | 625 Boog Powell | .50 | | |
| 577 John Morris | .20 | Jack Kucek, Dyar Miller, | | 626 Larry Haney | .20 | | |
| 578 Dave Tomlin | .20 | Paul Siebert, Vern Ruhle | | (Photo of Dave Duncan) | | | |

# 1976 Topps.... Complete Set of 660 Cards—Value $250.00

Features the rookie card of Ron Guidry. This set includes the only card ever issued for the Joe Garagiola and Bazooka "Bubble Gum Blowing Champ". Topps added a 44-card Traded set later in the season.

| NO. PLAYER | MINT | NO. PLAYER | MINT | NO. PLAYER | MINT | NO. PLAYER | MINT |
|---|---|---|---|---|---|---|---|
| 1 Record—Aaron (Exc. $2.00) | .8.00 | 9 Paul Lindblad | .15 | 29 Rick Burleson | .25 | 49 Dave Duncan | .15 |
| Most RBI's—2,262 | | 10 Lou Brock | 2.00 | 30 John Montefusco (R) | .35 | 50 F. Lynn | 2.00 |
| 2 Record—Bonds | .30 | 11 Jim Hughes | .15 | 31 Len Randle | .15 | 51 Ray Buris | .15 |
| Most Lead-Off Homers—32; | | 12 Richie Zisk | .25 | 32 Danny Frisella | .15 | 52 Dave Chalk | .15 |
| Most Seasons of 30 HR's; | | 13 Johnny Wockenfuss | .15 | 33 Bill North | .15 | 53 Mike Beard | .15 |
| and 30 Stolen Bases | | 14 Gene Garber | .15 | 34 Mike Garman | .15 | 54 Dave Rader | .15 |
| 3 Record—Lolich | .30 | 15 George Scott | .20 | 35 Tony Oliva | .50 | 55 Gaylord Perry | 1.50 |
| Most Strikeouts | | 16 Bob Apodaca | .15 | 36 Frank Taveras | .15 | 56 Bob Toaln | .15 |
| Lefthander—2,679 | | 17 New York Yankees | 1.00 | 37 John Hiller | .15 | 57 Phil Garner | .20 |
| 4 Record—Lopes | .30 | 18 Dale Murray | .15 | 38 Garry Maddox | .15 | 58 Ron Reed | .15 |
| Most Consecutive Steal | | 19 George Brett | 13.50 | 39 Pete Broberg | .15 | 59 Larry Hisle | .15 |
| Attempts—38 | | 20 Bob Watson | .15 | 40 Dave Kingman | .60 | 60 Jerry Reuss | .20 |
| 5 Record—Seaver | 1.75 | 21 Dave LaRoche | .15 | 41 Tippy Martinez (R) | .35 | 61 Ron LeFlore | .20 |
| Most Consecutive Seasons | | 22 Bill Russell | .15 | 42 Barry Foote | .15 | 62 Johnny Oates | .15 |
| of 200 Strikeouts—8 | | 23 Brian Downing | .25 | 43 Paul Splittorff | .25 | 63 Bobby Darwin | .15 |
| 6 Record—Stennett | .30 | 24 Cesar Geronimo | .15 | 44 Doug Rader | .15 | 64 Jerry Koosman | .30 |
| Most Hits in a Nine | | 25 Mick Torrez | .15 | 45 Boog Powell | .40 | 65 Chris Chambliss | .30 |
| Inning Game—7 | | 26 Andy Thornton | .25 | 46 Los Angeles Dodgers | .65 | 66 Father & Son: | .40 |
| 7 Jim Umbarger | .15 | 27 Ed Figueroa | .15 | 47 Jesse Jefferson | .15 | Gus Bell, |
| 8 Tito Fuentes | .15 | 28 Dusty Baker | .30 | 48 Dave Concepcion | .40 | Buddy Bell |

| NO. | PLAYER | MINT |
|---|---|---|
| 67 | Father & Son: Ray Boone, Bob Boone | .20 |
| 68 | Father & Son: Joe Coleman, Joe Coleman, Jr. | .20 |
| 69 | Father & Son: Jim Hegan, Mike Hegan | .20 |
| 70 | Father & Son: Roy Smalley, Roy Smalley Jr. | .20 |
| 71 | Steve Rogers | .30 |
| 72 | Hal McRae | .25 |
| 73 | Baltimore Orioles | .50 |
| 74 | Oscar Gamble | .20 |
| 75 | Larry Dierker | .15 |
| 76 | Willie Crawford | .15 |
| 77 | Pedro Borbon | .15 |
| 78 | Cecil Cooper | 1.00 |
| 79 | Jerry Morales | .15 |
| 80 | Jim Kaat | .50 |
| 81 | Darrell Evans | .50 |
| 82 | Von Joshua | .15 |
| 83 | Jim Spencer | .15 |
| 84 | Brent Strom | .15 |
| 85 | Mickey Rivers | .25 |
| 86 | Mike Tyson | .15 |
| 87 | Tom Burgmeier | .15 |
| 88 | Duffy Dyer | .15 |
| 89 | Vern Ruhle | .15 |
| 90 | Sal Bando | .30 |
| 91 | Tom Hutton | .15 |
| 92 | Eduardo Rodriguez | .15 |
| 93 | Mike Phillips | .15 |
| 94 | Jim Dwyer | .15 |
| 95 | Brooks Robinson | 2.50 |
| 96 | Doug Bird | .15 |
| 97 | Wilbur Howard | .15 |
| 98 | Dennis Eckersley (R) | 3.00 |
| 99 | Lee Lacy | .20 |
| 100 | Jim Hunter | 1.50 |
| 101 | Pete LaCock | .15 |
| 102 | Jim Willoughby | .15 |
| 103 | Biff Pocoroba | .15 |
| 104 | Cincinnati Reds | .60 |
| 105 | Gary Lavelle | .15 |
| 106 | Tom Grieve | .15 |
| 107 | Dave Roberts | .15 |
| 108 | Don Kirkwood | .15 |
| 109 | Larry Lintz | .15 |
| 110 | Carlos May | .15 |
| 111 | Danny Thompson | .15 |
| 112 | Kent Tekulve (R) | .75 |
| 113 | Gary Sutherland | .15 |
| 114 | Jay Johstone | .15 |
| 115 | Ken Holtzman | .15 |
| 116 | Charlie Moore | .15 |
| 117 | Mike Jorgensen | .15 |
| 118 | Boston Red Sox | .65 |
| 119 | Checklist No. 1 | .75 |
| 120 | Rusty Staub | .35 |
| 121 | Tony Solaita | .15 |
| 122 | Mike Cosgrove | .15 |
| 123 | Walt Williams | .15 |
| 124 | Doug Rau | .15 |
| 125 | Don Baylor | .50 |
| 126 | Tom Dettore | .15 |
| 127 | Larvell Blanks | .15 |
| 128 | Ken Griffey | .40 |
| 129 | Andy Etchebarren | .15 |
| 130 | Luis Tiant | .35 |
| 131 | Bill Stein | .15 |
| 132 | Don Hood | .15 |
| 133 | Gary Matthews | .30 |
| 134 | Mike Ivie | .15 |
| 135 | Bake McBride | .15 |
| 136 | Dave Goltz | .15 |
| 137 | Bill Robinson | .15 |
| 138 | Lerrin LaGrow | .15 |
| 139 | Gorman Thomas | .50 |
| 140 | Vida Blue | .30 |
| 141 | Larry Parrish (R) | 2.00 |
| 142 | Dick Drago | .15 |
| 143 | Jerry Grote | .15 |
| 144 | Al Fitzmorris | .15 |
| 145 | Larry Bowa | .50 |
| 146 | George Medich | .15 |
| 147 | Houston Astros | .40 |
| 148 | Stan Thomas | .15 |
| 149 | Tommy Davis | .30 |
| 150 | Steve Garvey | 4.00 |
| 151 | Bill Bonham | .15 |
| 152 | Leroy Stanton | .15 |
| 153 | Buzz Capra | .15 |
| 154 | Bucky Dent | .30 |
| 155 | Jack Billingham | .15 |
| 156 | Rico Carty | .30 |
| 157 | Mike Caldwell | .15 |
| 158 | Ken Reitz | .15 |
| 159 | Jerry Terrell | .15 |
| 160 | Dave Winfield | 6.00 |
| 161 | Bruce Kison | .15 |
| 162 | Jack Pierce | .15 |
| 163 | Jim Staton | .15 |
| 164 | Pepe Mangual | .15 |
| 165 | Gene Tenace | .15 |
| 166 | Skip Lockwood | .15 |
| 167 | Freddie Patek | .15 |
| 168 | Tom Hilgendorf | .15 |
| 169 | Graig Nettles | 1.00 |
| 170 | Rick Wise | .25 |
| 171 | Greg Gross | .15 |
| 172 | Texas Rangers | .50 |
| 173 | Steve Swisher | .15 |
| 174 | Charlie Hough | .30 |
| 175 | Ken Singleton | .30 |
| 176 | Dick Lange | .15 |
| 177 | Marty Perez | .15 |
| 178 | Tom Buskey | .15 |
| 179 | George Foster | 1.00 |
| 180 | Rich Gossage | 1.00 |
| 181 | Willie Montanez | .15 |
| 182 | Harry Rasmussen | .15 |
| 183 | Steve Braun | .15 |
| 184 | Bill Greif | .15 |
| 185 | Dave Parker | 3.00 |
| 186 | Tom Walker | .15 |
| 187 | Pedro Garcia | .15 |
| 188 | Fred Scherman | .15 |
| 189 | Claudell Washington | .50 |
| 190 | Jon Matlack | .20 |
| 191 | NL Batting Leaders: Ted Simmons, Bill Madlock, Manny Sanguillen | .50 |
| 192 | AL Batting Leaders: Fred Lynn, Rod Carew, Thurman Munson | 1.00 |
| 193 | NL Home Run Leaders: Mike Schmidt, Greg Luzinski, Dave Kingman | .60 |
| 194 | AL Home Run Leaders: John Mayberry, Reggie Jackson, George Scott | .60 |
| 195 | NL RBI Leaders: Greg Luzinski, Johnny Bench, Tony Perez | .50 |
| 196 | AL RBI Leaders: John Mayberry, George Scott, Fred Lynn | .40 |
| 197 | NL Stolen Base Leaders: Dave Lopes, Lou Brock, Joe Morgan | .60 |
| 198 | AL Stolen Base Leaders: Mickey Rivers, Claudell Washington, Amos Otis | .30 |
| 199 | NL Victory Leaders: Tom Seaver, Randy Jones, Andy Messersmith | .50 |
| 200 | AL Victory Leaders: Jim Palmer, Jim Hunter, Vida Blue | .60 |
| 201 | NL ERA Leaders: Randy Jones, Andy Messersmith, Tom Seaver | .50 |
| 202 | AL ERA Leaders: Jim Hunter, Dennis Eckersley, Jim Palmer | .50 |
| 203 | NL Strikeout Leaders: John Montefusco, Andy Messersmith, Tom Seaver | .50 |
| 204 | AL Strikeout Leaders: Frank Tanana, Gaylord Perry, Bert Blyleven | .50 |
| 205 | Leading Firemen: Al Hrabosky, Rich Gossage | .35 |
| 206 | Manny Trillo | .25 |
| 207 | Andy Hassler | .15 |
| 208 | Mike Lum | .15 |
| 209 | Alan Ashby | .30 |
| 210 | Lee May | .30 |
| 211 | Clay Carroll | .15 |
| 212 | Pat Kelly | .15 |
| 213 | Dave Heaverlo | .15 |
| 214 | Eric Soderholm | .15 |
| 215 | Reggie Smith | .35 |
| 216 | Montreal Expos | .60 |
| 217 | Dave Freisleben | .15 |
| 218 | John Knox | .15 |
| 219 | Tom Murphy | .15 |
| 220 | Manny Sanguillen | .30 |
| 221 | Jim Todd | .15 |
| 222 | Wayne Garrett | .15 |
| 223 | Ollie Brown | .15 |
| 224 | Jim York | .15 |
| 225 | Roy White | .30 |
| 226 | Jim Sundberg | .20 |
| 227 | Oscar Zamora | .15 |
| 228 | John Hale | .15 |
| 229 | Jerry Remy (R) | .30 |
| 230 | Carl Yastrzemski | 6.00 |
| 231 | Tom House | .15 |
| 232 | Frank Duffy | .15 |
| 233 | Grant Jackson | .15 |
| 234 | Mike Sadek | .15 |
| 235 | Bert Blyleven | .50 |
| 236 | Kansas City Royals | .40 |
| 237 | Dave Hamilton | .15 |
| 238 | Larry Biittner | .15 |
| 239 | John Curtis | .15 |
| 240 | Pete Rose | 15.00 |
| 241 | Hector Torres | .15 |
| 242 | Dan Meyer | .15 |
| 243 | Jim Rooker | .15 |
| 244 | Bill Sharp | .15 |
| 245 | Felix Millan | .15 |
| 246 | Cesar Tovar | .15 |
| 247 | Terry Harmon | .15 |
| 248 | Dick Tidrow | .15 |
| 249 | Cliff Johnson | .15 |
| 250 | Fergie Jenkins | .60 |
| 251 | Rick Monday | .30 |
| 252 | Tim Nordbrook | .15 |
| 253 | Bill Buckner | .40 |
| 254 | Rudy Meoli | .15 |
| 255 | Fritz Peterson | .15 |
| 256 | Rowland Office | .15 |
| 257 | Ross Grimsley | .15 |
| 258 | Nyls Nyman | .15 |
| 259 | Darrel Chaney | .15 |
| 260 | Steve Busby | .25 |
| 261 | Gary Thomasson | .15 |
| 262 | Checklist No. 2 | .75 |
| 263 | Lyman Bostock (R) | .50 |
| 264 | Steve Renko | .15 |
| 265 | Willie Davis | .30 |
| 266 | Alan Foster | .15 |
| 267 | Aurelio Rodriguez | .15 |
| 268 | Del Unser | .15 |
| 269 | Rick Austin | .15 |
| 270 | Willie Stargell | 2.00 |
| 271 | Jim Lonborg | .15 |
| 272 | Rick Dempsey | .20 |
| 273 | Joe Niekro | .30 |
| 274 | Tommy Harper | .15 |
| 275 | Rick Manning (R) | .30 |
| 276 | Mickey Scott | .15 |
| 277 | Chicago Cubs | .50 |
| 278 | Bernie Carbo | .15 |
| 279 | Roy Howell | .15 |
| 280 | Burt Hooton | .30 |
| 281 | Dave May | .15 |
| 282 | Dan Osborn | .15 |
| 283 | Merv Rettenmund | .15 |
| 284 | Steve Ontiveros | .15 |
| 285 | Mike Cuellar | .25 |
| 286 | Jim Wohlford | .15 |
| 287 | Pete Mackanin | .15 |
| 288 | Bill Campbell | .15 |
| 289 | Enzo Hernandez | .15 |
| 290 | Ted Simmons | .50 |
| 291 | Ken Sanders | .15 |
| 292 | Leon Roberts | .15 |
| 293 | Bill Castro | .15 |
| 294 | Ed Kirkpatrick | .15 |
| 295 | Dave Cash | .15 |
| 296 | Pat Dobson | .15 |
| 297 | Roger Metzger | .15 |
| 298 | Dick Bosman | .15 |
| 299 | Champ Summers | .15 |
| 300 | Johnny Bench | 5.00 |
| 301 | Jackie Brown | .15 |
| 302 | Rick Miller | .15 |
| 303 | Steve Foucault | .15 |
| 304 | California Angels | .50 |
| 305 | Andy Messersmith | .25 |
| 306 | Rod Gilbreath | .15 |
| 307 | Al Bumbry | .15 |
| 308 | Jim Barr | .15 |
| 309 | Bill Melton | .15 |
| 310 | Randy Jones | .30 |
| 311 | Cookie Rojas | .15 |
| 312 | Don Carrithers | .15 |
| 313 | Dan Ford (R) | .35 |
| 314 | Ed Kranepool | .30 |
| 315 | Al Hrabosky | .15 |
| 316 | Robin Yount | 5.50 |
| 317 | John Candelaria (R) | 3.00 |
| 318 | Bob Boone | .35 |
| 319 | Larry Gura | .15 |
| 320 | Willie Horton | .25 |
| 321 | Jose Cruz | .40 |
| 322 | Glenn Abbott | .15 |
| 323 | Rob Sperring | .15 |
| 324 | Jim Bibby | .15 |
| 325 | Tony Perez | .75 |
| 326 | Dick Pole | .15 |
| 327 | Dave Moates | .15 |
| 328 | Carl Morton | .15 |
| 329 | Joe Ferguson | .15 |
| 330 | Nolan Ryan | 4.00 |
| 331 | San Diego Padres | .40 |
| 332 | Charlie Williams | .15 |
| 333 | Bob Coluccio | .15 |
| 334 | Dennis Leonard | .20 |
| 335 | Bob Grich | .20 |
| 336 | Vic Albury | .15 |
| 337 | Bud Harrelson | .15 |
| 338 | Bob Bailey | .15 |
| 339 | John Denny | .35 |
| 340 | Jim Rice | 8.00 |
| 341 | All-Time 1B: Lou Gehrig | 2.00 |
| 342 | All-Time 2B: Rogers Hornsby | 1.00 |
| 343 | All-Time 3B: Pie Traynor | .75 |
| 344 | All-Time SS: Honus Wagner | 1.00 |
| 345 | All-Time OF: Babe Ruth | 3.50 |
| 346 | All-Time OF: Ty Cobb | 2.00 |
| 347 | All-Time OF: Ted Williams | 2.00 |
| 348 | All-Time Catcher: Mickey Cochrane | .75 |
| 349 | All-Time Pitcher (Right) Walter Johnson | 1.00 |
| 350 | All-Time Pitcher (Left) Lefty Grove | .75 |
| 351 | Randy Hundley | .15 |
| 352 | Dave Giusti | .15 |
| 353 | Sixto Lezcano (R) | .40 |
| 354 | Ron Blomberg | .15 |
| 355 | Steve Carlton | 4.00 |
| 356 | Ted Martinez | .15 |
| 357 | Ken Forsch | .15 |
| 358 | Buddy Bell | .50 |
| 359 | Rick Reuschel | .20 |
| 360 | Jeff Burroughs | .15 |

| NO. | PLAYER | MINT |
|---|---|---|
| 361 | Detroit Tigers | .60 |
| 362 | Will McEnaney | .15 |
| 363 | Dave Collins (R) | .75 |
| 364 | Elias Sosa | .15 |
| 365 | Carlton Fisk | 1.00 |
| 366 | Bobby Valentine | .25 |
| 367 | Bruce Miller | .15 |
| 368 | Wilbur Wood | .15 |
| 369 | Frank White | .35 |
| 370 | Ron Cey | .50 |
| 371 | Ellie Hendricks | .15 |
| 372 | Rick Baldwin | .15 |
| 373 | Johnny Briggs | .15 |
| 374 | Dan Warthen | .15 |
| 375 | Ron Fairly | .15 |
| 376 | Rich Hebner | .15 |
| 377 | Mike Hegan | .15 |
| 378 | Steve Stone | .15 |
| 379 | Ken Boswell | .15 |
| 380 | Bobby Bonds | .25 |
| 381 | Denny Doyle | .15 |
| 382 | Matt Alexander | .15 |
| 383 | John Ellis | .15 |
| 384 | Philadelphia Phillies | .60 |
| 385 | Mickey Lolich | .35 |
| 386 | Ed Goodson | .15 |
| 387 | Mike Miley | .15 |
| 388 | Stan Perzanowski | .15 |
| 389 | Glenn Adams | .15 |
| 390 | Don Gullett | .15 |
| 391 | Jerry Hariston | .15 |
| 392 | Checklist No. 3 | .75 |
| 393 | Paul Mitchell | .15 |
| 394 | Fran Healy | .15 |
| 395 | Jim Wynn | .25 |
| 396 | Bill Lee | .15 |
| 397 | Tim Foli | .15 |
| 398 | Dave Tomlin | .15 |
| 399 | Luis Melendez | .15 |
| 400 | Rod Carew | 3.50 |
| 401 | Ken Brett | .15 |
| 402 | Don Money | .15 |
| 403 | Geoff Zahn | .15 |
| 404 | Enos Cabell | .15 |
| 405 | Rollie Fingers | .75 |
| 406 | Ed Herrmann | .15 |
| 407 | Tom Underwood | .15 |
| 408 | Charlie Spikes | .15 |
| 409 | Dave Lemanczyk | .15 |
| 410 | Ralph Garr | .15 |
| 411 | Bill Singer | .15 |
| 412 | Toby Harrah | .25 |
| 413 | Pete Varney | .15 |
| 414 | Wayne Garland | .15 |
| 415 | Vada Pinson | .30 |
| 416 | Tommy John | .75 |
| 417 | Gene Clines | .15 |
| 418 | Jose Morales | .15 |
| 419 | Reggie Cleveland | .15 |
| 420 | Joe Morgan | 2.50 |
| 421 | Oakland A's | .40 |
| 422 | Johnny Grubb | .15 |
| 423 | Ed Halicki | .15 |
| 424 | Phil Roof | .15 |
| 425 | Rennie Stennett | .15 |
| 426 | Bob Forsch | .25 |
| 427 | Kurt Bevacqua | .15 |
| 428 | Jim Crawford | .15 |
| 429 | Fred Stanley | .15 |
| 430 | Jose Cardenal | .15 |
| 431 | Dick Ruthven | .15 |
| 432 | Tom Veryzer | .15 |
| 433 | Rick Waits | .15 |
| 434 | Morris Nettles | .15 |
| 435 | Phil Niekro | 1.50 |
| 436 | Bill Fahey | .15 |
| 437 | Terry Forster | .15 |
| 438 | Doug DeCinces | .60 |
| 439 | Rick Rhoden | .50 |
| 440 | John Mayberry | .25 |
| 441 | Gary Carter | 12.00 |
| 442 | Hank Webb | .15 |
| 443 | S.F. Giants | .40 |
| 444 | Gary Nolan | .15 |
| 445 | Rico Petrocelli | .15 |
| 446 | Larry Haney | .15 |
| 447 | Gene Locklear | .15 |
| 448 | Tom Johnson | .15 |
| 449 | Bob Robertson | .15 |
| 450 | Jim Palmer | 2.50 |
| 451 | Buddy Bradford | .15 |
| 452 | Tom Hausman | .15 |
| 453 | Lou Piniella | .35 |
| 454 | Tom Griffin | .15 |
| 455 | Dick Allen | .25 |
| 456 | Joe Coleman | .15 |
| 457 | Ed Crosby | .15 |
| 458 | Earl Williams | .15 |
| 459 | Jim Brewer | .15 |
| 460 | Cesar Cedeno | .25 |
| 461 | Championships: | .50 |
| | Reds Sweep Bucs, | |
| | Bosox Surprise A's | |
| 462 | World Series: | .50 |
| | Reds Champs! | |
| 463 | Steve Hargan | .15 |
| 464 | Ken Henderson | .15 |
| 465 | Mike Marshall | .25 |
| 466 | Bob Stinson | .15 |
| 467 | Woodie Fryman | .15 |
| 468 | Jesus Alou | .15 |
| 469 | Rawly Eastwick | .15 |
| 470 | Bobby Murcer | .40 |
| 471 | Jim Burton | .15 |
| 472 | Bob Davis | .15 |
| 473 | Paul Blair | .15 |
| 474 | Ray Corbin | .15 |
| 475 | Joe Rudi | .25 |
| 476 | Bob Moose | .15 |
| 477 | Cleveland Indians | .40 |
| 478 | Lynn McGlothen | .15 |
| 479 | Bobby Mitchell | .15 |
| 480 | Mike Schmidt | 11.00 |
| 481 | Rudy May | .15 |
| 482 | Tim Hosley | .15 |
| 483 | Mickey Stanley | .15 |
| 484 | Eric Raich | .15 |
| 485 | Mike Hargrove | .15 |
| 486 | Bruce Dal Canton | .15 |
| 487 | Leron Lee | .15 |
| 488 | Claude Osteen | .15 |
| 489 | Skip Jutze | .15 |
| 490 | Frank Tanana | .30 |
| 491 | Terry Crowley | .15 |
| 492 | Marty Pattin | .15 |
| 493 | Derrel Thomas | .15 |
| 494 | Craig Swan | .15 |
| 495 | Nate Colbert | .15 |
| 496 | Juan Beniquez | .15 |
| 497 | Joe McIntosh | .15 |
| 498 | Glenn Borgmann | .15 |
| 499 | Mario Guerrero | .15 |
| 500 | Reggie Jackson | 7.00 |
| 501 | Billy Champion | .15 |
| 502 | Tim McCarver | .30 |
| 503 | Elliott Maddox | .15 |
| 504 | Pittsburgh Pirates | .40 |
| 505 | Mark Belanger | .25 |
| 506 | George Mitterwald | .15 |
| 507 | Ray Bare | .15 |
| 508 | Duane Kuiper | .15 |
| 509 | Bill Hands | .15 |
| 510 | Amos Otis | .25 |
| 511 | Jamie Easterley | .15 |
| 512 | Ellie Rodriguez | .15 |
| 513 | Bart Johnson | .15 |
| 514 | Dan Driessen | .20 |
| 515 | Steve Yeager | .15 |
| 516 | Wayne Granger | .15 |
| 517 | John Milner | .15 |
| 518 | Doug Flynn | .15 |
| 519 | Steve Brye | .15 |
| 520 | Willie McCovey | 2.00 |
| 521 | Jim Colborn | .15 |
| 522 | Ted Sizemore | .15 |
| 523 | Bob Montgomery | .15 |
| 524 | Pete Falcone | .15 |
| 525 | Billy Williams | 1.50 |
| 526 | Checklist No. 4 | .75 |
| 527 | Mike Anderson | .15 |
| 528 | Dock Ellis | .15 |
| 529 | Deron Johnson | .15 |
| 530 | Don Sutton | 1.25 |
| 531 | New York Mets | .75 |
| 532 | Milt May | .15 |
| 533 | Lee Richard | .15 |
| 534 | Stan Bahnsen | .15 |
| 535 | Dave Nelson | .15 |
| 536 | Mike Thompson | .15 |
| 537 | Tony Muser | .15 |
| 538 | Pat Darcy | .15 |
| 539 | John Balaz | .15 |
| 540 | Bill Freehan | .25 |
| 541 | Steve Mingori | .15 |
| 542 | Keith Hernandez | 5.00 |
| 543 | Wayne Twitchell | .15 |
| 544 | Pepe Frias | .15 |
| 545 | Sparky Lyle | .25 |
| 546 | Dave Rosello | .15 |
| 547 | Roric Harrison | .15 |
| 548 | Manny Mota | .25 |
| 549 | Randy Tate | .15 |
| 550 | Hank Aaron | 6.00 |
| 551 | Jerry DaVanon | .15 |
| 552 | Terry Humphrey | .15 |
| 553 | Randy Moffitt | .15 |
| 554 | Ray Fosse | .15 |
| 555 | Dyar Miller | .15 |
| 556 | Minnesota Twins | .50 |
| 557 | Dan Spillner | .15 |
| 558 | Clarence Gaston | .15 |
| 559 | Clyde Wright | .15 |
| 560 | Jorge Orta | .15 |
| 561 | Tom Carroll | .15 |
| 562 | Adrian Garrett | .15 |
| 563 | Larry Demery | .15 |
| 564 | Gum Blowing Champ: | .25 |
| | Kurt Bevacqua | |
| 565 | Tug McGraw | .35 |
| 566 | Ken McMullen | .15 |
| 567 | George Stone | .15 |
| 568 | Rob Andrews | .15 |
| 569 | Nelson Briles | .15 |
| 570 | George Hendrick | .30 |
| 571 | Don DeMola | .15 |
| 572 | Rich Coggins | .15 |
| 573 | Bill Travers | .15 |
| 574 | Don Kessinger | .15 |
| 575 | Dwight Evans | 1.25 |
| 576 | Maximino Leon | .15 |
| 577 | Marc Hill | .15 |
| 578 | Ted Kubiak | .15 |
| 579 | Clay Kirby | .15 |
| 580 | Bert Campaneris | .30 |
| 581 | St. Louis Cardinals | .60 |
| 582 | Mike Kekich | .15 |
| 583 | Tommy Helms | .15 |
| 584 | Stan Wall | .15 |
| 585 | Joe Torre | .35 |
| 586 | Ron Schueler | .15 |
| 587 | Leo Cardenas | .15 |
| 588 | Kevin Kobel | .15 |
| 589 | Rookie Pitchers: | 2.00 |
| | Joe Pactwa, Santo Alcala, | |
| | Mike Flanagan, P. Torrealba | |
| 590 | Rookie Outfielders: | 1.50 |
| | Henry Cruz, Ellis Valentine, | |
| | Chet Lemon, T. Whitfield | |
| 591 | Rookie Pitchers: | .30 |
| | Steve Grilli, C. Mitchell, | |
| | Jose Sosa, George Throop | |
| 592 | Rookie Infielders: | 3.50 |
| | W. Randolph, D. McKay, | |
| | J. Royster, R. Staiger | |
| 593 | Rookie Pitchers: | .40 |
| | Larry Anderson, M. Littell, | |
| | Butch Metzger, Ken Crosby | |
| 594 | Rookie Catchers & OF's | .40 |
| | Andy Merchant, Ed Ott, | |
| | R. Stillman, Jerry White | |
| 595 | Rookie Pitchers: | .40 |
| | Art DeFillipis, R. Lerch, | |
| | Sid Monge, Steve Barr | |
| 596 | Rookie Infielders: | .50 |
| | C. Reynolds, L. Johnson, | |
| | J. LeMaster, J. Manuel | |
| 597 | Rookie Pitchers: | .60 |
| | D. Aase, Jack Kucek, | |
| | Frank LaCorte, Mike Pazik | |
| 598 | Rookie Outfielders: | .40 |
| | Hector Cruz, J. Quirk, | |
| | Jerry Turner, Joe Wallis | |
| 599 | Rookie Pitchers: | 13.00 |
| | Rob Dressler, Ron Guidry, | |
| | Bob McClure, Pat Zachry | |
| 600 | Tom Seaver | 4.00 |
| 601 | Ken Rudolph | .15 |
| 602 | Doug Konieczny | .15 |
| 603 | Jim Holt | .15 |
| 604 | Joe Lovitto | .15 |
| 605 | Al Downing | .25 |
| 606 | Milwaukee Brewers | .40 |
| 607 | Rich Hinton | .15 |
| 608 | Vic Correll | .15 |
| 609 | Fred Norman | .15 |
| 610 | Greg Luzinski | .50 |
| 611 | Rich Folkers | .15 |
| 612 | Joe Lahoud | .15 |
| 613 | Tim Johnson | .15 |
| 614 | Fernando Arroyo | .15 |
| 615 | Mike Cubbage | .15 |
| 616 | Buck Martinez | .15 |
| 617 | Darold Knowles | .15 |
| 618 | Jack Brohamer | .15 |
| 619 | Bill Butler | .15 |
| 620 | Al Oliver | .50 |
| 621 | Tom Hall | .15 |
| 622 | Rick Auerbach | .15 |
| 623 | Bob Allietta | .15 |
| 624 | Tony Taylor | .15 |
| 625 | J.R. Richard | .20 |
| 626 | Bob Sheldon | .15 |
| 627 | Bill Plummer | .15 |
| 628 | John D'Acquisto | .15 |
| 629 | Sandy Alomar | .15 |
| 630 | Chris Speier | .15 |
| 631 | Atlanta Braves | .40 |
| 632 | Rogelio Moret | .15 |
| 633 | John Stearns (R) | .25 |
| 634 | Larry Christenson | .15 |
| 635 | Jim Fregosi | .25 |
| 636 | Joe Decker | .15 |
| 637 | Bruce Bochte | .15 |
| 638 | Doyle Alexander | .15 |
| 639 | Fred Kendall | .15 |
| 640 | Bill Madlock | 1.00 |
| 641 | Tom Paciorek | .15 |
| 642 | Dennis Blair | .15 |
| 643 | Checklist No. 5 | .75 |
| 644 | Tom Bradley | .15 |
| 645 | Darrell Porter | .15 |
| 646 | John Lowenstein | .15 |
| 647 | Ramon Hernandez | .15 |
| 648 | Al Cowens | .15 |
| 649 | Dave Roberts | .15 |
| 650 | Thurman Munson | 3.50 |
| 651 | John Odom | .15 |
| 652 | Ed Armbrister | .15 |
| 653 | Mike Norris (R) | .25 |
| 654 | Doug Griffin | .15 |
| 655 | Mike Vail | .15 |
| 656 | Chicago White Sox | .40 |
| 657 | Roy Smalley (R) | .40 |
| 658 | Jerry Johnson | .15 |
| 659 | Ben Oglivie | .30 |
| 660 | D. Lopes (Exc. .15) | .75 |

**Prices for the 1976 set are for cards in *Mint* condition. *Excellent* copies sell for 50% of prices shown; *Very Good*—30%.**

# 1976 Topps....Complete Set of 44 Cards—Value $6.50

This set features players who were traded after the regular 1976 set was printed. The card numbers are the same as the main set, with the addition of "T" after the number.

| NO. | PLAYER | MINT | NO. | PLAYER | MINT | NO. | PLAYER | MINT | NO. | PLAYER | MINT |
|---|---|---|---|---|---|---|---|---|---|---|---|
| 27 T | Ed Figueroa | .15 | 146 T | George Medich | .15 | 380 T | Bobby Bonds | .25 | 527 T | Mike Anderson | .15 |
| 28 T | Dusty Baker | .35 | 158 T | Ken Reitz | .15 | 383 T | John Ellis | .15 | 528 T | Dock Ellis | .15 |
| 44 T | Doug Rader | .20 | 208 T | Mike Lum | .15 | 385 T | Mickey Lolich | .35 | 532 T | Milt May | .15 |
| 58 T | Ron Reed | .20 | 211 T | Clay Carroll | .15 | 401 T | Ken Brett | .20 | 554 T | Ray Fosse | .15 |
| 74 T | Oscar Gamble | .25 | 231 T | Tom House | .15 | 410 T | Ken Brett | .20 | 579 T | Clay Kirby | .15 |
| 80 T | Jim Kaat | .50 | 250 T | Fergie Jenkins | .60 | 411 T | Bill Singer | .15 | 583 T | Tommy Helms | .15 |
| 83 T | Jim Spencer | .15 | 259 T | Darrel Chaney | .15 | 428 T | Jim Crawford | .15 | 592 T | Willie Randolph | .75 |
| 85 T | Mickey Rivers | .25 | 292 T | Leon Roberts | .15 | 434 T | Morris Nettles | .15 | 618 T | Jack Brohamer | .15 |
| 99 T | Lee Lacy | .25 | 296 T | Pat Dobson | .15 | 464 T | Ken Henderson | .15 | 632 T | Rogelio Moret | .15 |
| 120 T | Rusty Staub | .75 | 309 T | Bill Melton | .15 | 497 T | Joe McIntosh | .15 | 649 T | Dave Roberts | .15 |
| 127 T | Larvell Blanks | .15 | 338 T | Bob Bailey | .15 | 524 T | Pete Falcone | .15 | — | Checklist | .60 |

# 1977 Topps....Complete Set of 660 Cards—Value $250.00

Dale Murphy, Tony Armas, and Andre Dawson's rookie cards are in this set. There is an error on card 634—the photos are switched.

  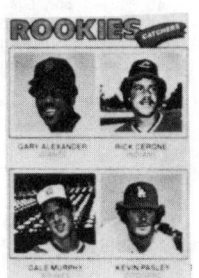  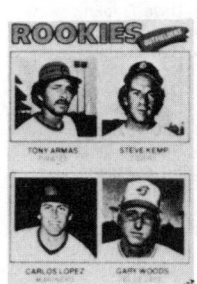

| NO. | PLAYER | MINT | NO. | PLAYER | MINT | NO. | PLAYER | MINT | NO. | PLAYER | MINT |
|---|---|---|---|---|---|---|---|---|---|---|---|
| 1 | Batting Leaders: George Brett, Bill Madlock | 2.00 | 21 | Ken Frosch | .12 | 50 | R. Cey | .50 | 78 | Bob Davis | .12 |
| 2 | Home Run Leaders: Graig Nettles, Mike Schmidt | .75 | 22 | Bill Freehan | .12 | 51 | Milwaukee Brewers/ Alex Grammas (Mgr.) | .50 | 79 | Don Money | .12 |
| 3 | RBI Leaders: Lee May, George Foster | .40 | 23 | Dan Driessen | .12 | 52 | Ellis Valentine | .12 | 80 | Andy Messersmith | .20 |
| 4 | Stolen Base Leaders: B. North, Dave Lopes | .30 | 24 | Carl Morton | .12 | 53 | Paul Mitchell | .12 | 81 | Juan Beniquez | .15 |
| 5 | Victory Leaders: Jim Palmer, Randy Jones | .50 | 25 | Dwight Evans | .65 | 54 | Sandy Alomar | .12 | 82 | Jim Rooker | .12 |
| 6 | Strikeout Leaders: Nolan Ryan, Tom Seaver | 1.25 | 26 | Ray Sadeki | .12 | 55 | Jeff Burroughs | .20 | 83 | Kevin Bell | .12 |
| 7 | ERA Leaders: Mark Fidrych, J. Denny | .30 | 27 | Bill Buckner | .35 | 56 | Rudy May | .12 | 84 | Ollie Brown | .12 |
| 8 | Leading Firemen: B. Campbell, R. Eastwick | .25 | 28 | Woodie Fryman | .12 | 57 | Marc Hill | .12 | 85 | Duane Kuiper | .12 |
| 9 | Doug Rader | .12 | 29 | Bucky Dent | .20 | 58 | Chet Lemon | .35 | 86 | Pat Zachry | .12 |
| 10 | Reggie Jackson | 7.00 | 30 | Greg Luzinski | .30 | 59 | Larry Christenson | .12 | 87 | Glenn Borgmann | .12 |
| 11 | Rob Dressler | .12 | 31 | Jim Todd | .12 | 60 | Jim Rice | 6.00 | 88 | Stan Wall | .12 |
| 12 | Larry Haney | .12 | 32 | Checklist No. 1 | .75 | 61 | Manny Sanguillen | .12 | 89 | Butch Hobson | .12 |
| 13 | Luis Gomez | .12 | 33 | Wayne Garland | .12 | 62 | Eric Raich | .12 | 90 | Cesar Cedeno | .25 |
| 14 | Tommy Smith | .12 | 34 | Angels/Norm Sherry (Mgr.) | .40 | 63 | Tito Fuentes | .12 | 91 | John Verhoeven | .12 |
| 15 | Don Gullett | .12 | 35 | Rennie Stennett | .12 | 64 | Larry Biittner | .12 | 92 | Dave Rosello | .12 |
| 16 | Bob Jones | .12 | 36 | John Ellis | .12 | 65 | Skip Lockwood | .12 | 93 | Tom Poquette | .12 |
| 17 | Steve Stone | .12 | 37 | Steve Hargan | .12 | 66 | Roy Smalley | .12 | 94 | Craig Swan | .12 |
| 18 | Cleveland Indians/ Frank Robinson (Mgr.) | .40 | 38 | Craig Kusick | .12 | 67 | Joaquin Andujar (R) | 1.25 | 95 | Keith Hernandez | 3.00 |
| 19 | John D'Acquisto | .12 | 39 | Tom Griffin | .12 | 68 | Bruce Bochte | .12 | 96 | Lou Piniella | .35 |
| 20 | Graig Nettles | .75 | 40 | Bobby Murcer | .40 | 69 | Jim Crawford | .12 | 97 | Dave Heaverlo | .12 |
| | | | 41 | Jim Kern | .12 | 70 | Johnny Bench | 3.00 | 98 | Milt May | .12 |
| | | | 42 | Jose Cruz | .35 | 71 | Dock Ellis | .12 | 99 | Tom Hausman | .12 |
| | | | 43 | Ray Bare | .12 | 72 | Mike Anderson | .12 | 100 | Joe Morgan | 1.25 |
| | | | 44 | Bud Harrelson | .12 | 73 | Charlie Williams | .12 | 101 | Dick Bosman | .12 |
| | | | 45 | Rawly Eastwick | .12 | 74 | A's/J. McKeon (Mgr.) | .40 | 102 | Jose Morales | .12 |
| | | | 46 | Buck Martinez | .12 | 75 | Dennis Leonard | .12 | 103 | Mike Bacsik | .12 |
| | | | 47 | Lynn McGlothen | .12 | 76 | Tim Foli | .12 | 104 | Omar Moreno (R) | .35 |
| | | | 48 | Tom Paciorek | .12 | 77 | Dyar Miller | .12 | 105 | Steve Yeager | .15 |
| | | | 49 | Grant Jackson | .12 | | | | 106 | Mike Flanagan | .30 |

| NO. | PLAYER | MINT |
|-----|--------|------|
| 107 | Bill Melton | .12 |
| 108 | Alan Foster | .12 |
| 109 | Jorge Orta | .12 |
| 110 | Steve Carlton | 4.00 |
| 111 | Rico Petrocelli | .20 |
| 112 | Bill Greif | .12 |
| 113 | Toronto Blue Jays/ Roy Hartsfield (Mgr.) | .35 |
| 114 | Bruce Dal Canton | .12 |
| 115 | Rick Manning | .12 |
| 116 | Joe Niekro | .35 |
| 117 | Frank White | .35 |
| 118 | Rick Jone | .12 |
| 119 | John Stearns | .12 |
| 120 | Rod Carew | 3.50 |
| 121 | Gary Nolan | .12 |
| 122 | Ben Oglivie | .20 |
| 123 | Fred Stanley | .12 |
| 124 | George Mitterwald | .12 |
| 125 | Bill Travers | .12 |
| 126 | Rod Gilbreath | .12 |
| 127 | Ron Fairly | .12 |
| 128 | Tommy John | .75 |
| 129 | Mike Sadek | .12 |
| 130 | Al Oliver | .40 |
| 131 | Orlando Ramirez | .12 |
| 132 | Chip Lang | .12 |
| 133 | Ralph Garr | .12 |
| 134 | San Diego Padres/ John McNamara (Mgr.) | .40 |
| 135 | Mark Belanger | .20 |
| 136 | Jerry Mumphrey (R) | .50 |
| 137 | Jeff Terpko | .12 |
| 138 | Bob Stinson | .12 |
| 139 | Fred Norman | .12 |
| 140 | Mike Schmidt | 9.00 |
| 141 | Mark Littell | .12 |
| 142 | Steve Dillard | .12 |
| 143 | Ed Herrmann | .12 |
| 144 | Bruce Sutter (R) | 3.50 |
| 145 | Tom Veryzer | .12 |
| 146 | Dusty Baker | .30 |
| 147 | Jackie Brown | .12 |
| 148 | Fran Healy | .12 |
| 149 | Mike Cubbage | .12 |
| 150 | Tom Seaver | 4.00 |
| 151 | Johnnie LeMaster | .12 |
| 152 | Gaylord Perry | 1.50 |
| 153 | Ron Jackson | .12 |
| 154 | Dave Guisti | .12 |
| 155 | Joe Rudi | .20 |
| 156 | Pete Mackanin | .12 |
| 157 | Ken Brett | .12 |
| 158 | Ted Kubiak | .12 |
| 159 | Bernie Carbo | .12 |
| 160 | Will McEnaney | .12 |
| 161 | Garry Templeton (R) | 1.25 |
| 162 | Mike Cuellar | .20 |
| 163 | Dave Hilton | .12 |
| 164 | Tug McGraw | .25 |
| 165 | Jim Wynn | .12 |
| 166 | Bill Campbell | .12 |
| 167 | Rich Hebner | .12 |
| 168 | Charlie Spikes | .12 |
| 169 | Darold Knowles | .12 |
| 170 | Thurman Munson | 2.50 |
| 171 | Ken Sanders | .12 |
| 172 | John Milner | .12 |
| 173 | Chuck Scrivener | .12 |
| 174 | Nelson Briles | .12 |
| 175 | Butch Wynegar (R) | .75 |
| 176 | Bob Robertson | .12 |
| 177 | Bart Johnson | .12 |
| 178 | Bombo Rivera | .12 |
| 179 | Paul Hartzell | .12 |
| 180 | Dave Lopes | .25 |
| 181 | Ken McMullen | .12 |
| 182 | Dan Spillner | .12 |
| 183 | Cardinals/V. Rapp (Mgr.) | .50 |
| 184 | Bo McLaughlin | .12 |
| 185 | Sixto Lezcano | .12 |
| 186 | Doug Flynn | .12 |
| 187 | Dick Pole | .12 |
| 188 | Bob Tolan | .12 |
| 189 | Rick Dempsey | .15 |

| NO. | PLAYER | MINT |
|-----|--------|------|
| 190 | Ray Burris | .12 |
| 191 | Doug Griffin | .12 |
| 192 | Clarence Gaston | .12 |
| 193 | Larry Gura | .12 |
| 194 | Gary Matthews | .30 |
| 195 | Ed Figueroa | .12 |
| 196 | Len Randle | .12 |
| 197 | Ed Ott | .12 |
| 198 | Wilbur Wood | .12 |
| 199 | Pepe Frias | .12 |
| 200 | Frank Tanana | .20 |
| 201 | Ed Kranepool | .25 |
| 202 | Tom Johnson | .12 |
| 203 | Ed Armbrister | .12 |
| 204 | Jeff Newman | .12 |
| 205 | Pete Falcone | .12 |
| 206 | Boog Powell | .30 |
| 207 | Glenn Abbott | .12 |
| 208 | Checklist No. 2 | .75 |
| 209 | Rob Andrews | .12 |
| 210 | Fred Lynn | 1.50 |
| 211 | San Francisco Giants/ Joe Altobelli (Mgr.) | .40 |
| 212 | Jim Mason | .12 |
| 213 | Maximino Leon | .12 |
| 214 | Darrell Porter | .20 |
| 215 | Butch Metzger | .20 |
| 216 | Doug DeCinces | .40 |
| 217 | Tom Underwood | .12 |
| 218 | John Wathan | .75 |
| 219 | Joe Coleman | .12 |
| 220 | Chris Chambliss | .20 |
| 221 | Bob Bailey | .12 |
| 222 | Francisco Barrios | .12 |
| 223 | Earl Williams | .12 |
| 224 | Rusty Torres | .12 |
| 225 | Bob Apodaca | .12 |
| 226 | Leroy Stanton | .12 |
| 227 | Joe Sambito | .30 |
| 228 | Minnesota Twins/ Gene Mauch (Mgr.) | .50 |
| 229 | Don Kessinger | .12 |
| 230 | Vida Blue | .25 |
| 231 | Record—Brett Most Consecutive Games with 3 or More Hits | 1.50 |
| 232 | Record—Minoso Oldest Player to Hit Safely | .25 |
| 233 | Record—Morales Most Pinch-Hits for Season | .20 |
| 234 | Record—Ryan Most Seasons 300 SO's | 1.00 |
| 235 | Cecil Cooper | .50 |
| 236 | Tom Buskey | .12 |
| 237 | Gene Clines | .12 |
| 238 | Tippy Martinez | .12 |
| 239 | Bill Plummer | .12 |
| 240 | Ron LeFlore | .15 |
| 241 | Dave Tomlin | .12 |
| 242 | Ken Henderson | .12 |
| 243 | Ron Reed | .12 |
| 244 | John Mayberry | .25 |
| 245 | Rick Rhoden | .25 |
| 246 | Mike Vail | .12 |
| 247 | Chris Knapp | .12 |
| 248 | Wilbur Howard | .12 |
| 249 | Pete Redfern | .12 |
| 250 | Bill Madlock | .50 |
| 251 | Tony Muser | .12 |
| 252 | Dale Murray | .12 |
| 253 | John Hale | .12 |
| 254 | Doyle Alexander | .12 |
| 255 | George Scott | .12 |
| 256 | Joe Hoerner | .12 |
| 257 | Mike Miley | .12 |
| 258 | Luis Tiant | .15 |
| 259 | Mets/J. Frazier (Mgr.) | .60 |
| 260 | J.R. Richard | .20 |
| 261 | Phil Garner | .20 |
| 262 | Al Cowens | .20 |
| 263 | Mike Marshall | .20 |
| 264 | Tom Hutton | .12 |
| 265 | Mark Fidrych (R) | .50 |
| 266 | Derrel Thomas | .12 |
| 267 | Ray Fosse | .12 |

| NO. | PLAYER | MINT |
|-----|--------|------|
| 268 | Rick Sawyer | .12 |
| 269 | Joe Lis | .12 |
| 270 | Dave Parker | 2.00 |
| 271 | Terry Forster | .20 |
| 272 | Lee Lacy | .15 |
| 273 | Eric Soderholm | .12 |
| 274 | Don Stanhouse | .12 |
| 275 | Mike Hargrove | .12 |
| 276 | A.L. Championship: Chambliss' Homer | .40 |
| 277 | N.L. Championship: Reds Sweep Phillies in 3 | .45 |
| 278 | Danny Frisella | .12 |
| 279 | Joe Wallis | .12 |
| 280 | Jim Hunter | 1.50 |
| 281 | Roy Staiger | .12 |
| 282 | Sid Monge | .12 |
| 283 | Jerry DaVanon | .12 |
| 284 | Mike Norris | .12 |
| 285 | Brooks Robinson | 2.50 |
| 286 | Johnny Grubb | .12 |
| 287 | Cincinnati Reds/ Sparky Anderson (Mgr.) | .50 |
| 288 | Bob Montgomery | .12 |
| 289 | Gene Garber | .12 |
| 290 | Amos Otis | .30 |
| 291 | Jason Thompson (R) | .75 |
| 292 | Rogelio Moret | .12 |
| 293 | Jack Brohamer | .12 |
| 294 | George Medich | .12 |
| 295 | Gary Carter | 6.50 |
| 296 | Don Hood | .12 |
| 297 | Ken Reitz | .12 |
| 298 | Charlie Hough | .12 |
| 299 | Otto Velez | .12 |
| 300 | Jerry Koosman | .30 |
| 301 | Toby Harrah | .15 |
| 302 | Mike Garman | .12 |
| 303 | Gene Tenace | .12 |
| 304 | Jim Hughes | .12 |
| 305 | Mickey Rivers | .20 |
| 306 | Rick Waits | .12 |
| 307 | Gary Sutherland | .12 |
| 308 | Gene Pentz | .12 |
| 309 | Boston Red Sox/ Don Zimmer (Mgr.) | .50 |
| 310 | Larry Bowa | .30 |
| 311 | Vern Ruhle | .12 |
| 312 | Rob Belloir | .12 |
| 313 | Paul Blair | .12 |
| 314 | Steve Mingori | .12 |
| 315 | Dave Chalk | .12 |
| 316 | Steve Rogers | .20 |
| 317 | Kurt Bevacqua | .12 |
| 318 | Duffy Dyer | .12 |
| 319 | Rich Gossage | .75 |
| 320 | Ken Griffey | .25 |
| 321 | Dave Goltz | .12 |
| 322 | Bill Russell | .12 |
| 323 | Larry Lintz | .12 |
| 324 | John Curtis | .12 |
| 325 | Mike Ivie | .12 |
| 326 | Jesse Jefferson | .12 |
| 327 | Astros/B. Virdon (Mgr.) | .50 |
| 328 | Tommy Boggs | .12 |
| 329 | Ron Hodges | .12 |
| 330 | George Hendrick | .25 |
| 331 | Jim Colborn | .12 |
| 332 | Elliott Maddox | .12 |
| 333 | Paul Reuschel | .12 |
| 334 | Bill Stein | .12 |
| 335 | Bill Robinson | .12 |
| 336 | Denny Doyle | .12 |
| 337 | Ron Schueler | .12 |
| 338 | Dave Duncan | .12 |
| 339 | Adrian Devine | .12 |
| 340 | Hal McRae | .15 |
| 341 | Joe Kerrigan | .12 |
| 342 | Jerry Remy | .12 |
| 343 | Ed Halicki | .12 |
| 344 | Brian Downing | .12 |
| 345 | Reggie Smith | .25 |
| 346 | Bill Singer | .12 |
| 347 | George Foster | 1.25 |
| 348 | Brent Strom | .12 |

| NO. | PLAYER | MINT |
|-----|--------|------|
| 349 | Jim Holt | .12 |
| 350 | Larry Dierker | .12 |
| 351 | Jim Sundberg | .12 |
| 352 | Mike Phillips | .12 |
| 353 | Stan Thomas | .12 |
| 354 | Pirates/C. Tanner (Mgr.) | .40 |
| 355 | Lou Brock | 1.50 |
| 356 | Checklist No. 3 | .75 |
| 357 | Tim McCarver | .35 |
| 358 | Tom House | .12 |
| 359 | Willie Randolph | .50 |
| 360 | Rick Monday | .20 |
| 361 | Eduardo Rodriguez | .12 |
| 362 | Tommy Davis | .12 |
| 363 | Dave Roberts | .12 |
| 364 | Vic Correll | .12 |
| 365 | Mike Torrez | .12 |
| 366 | Ted Sizemore | .12 |
| 367 | Dave Hamilton | .12 |
| 368 | Mike Jorgensen | .12 |
| 369 | Terry Humphrey | .12 |
| 370 | John Montefusco | .12 |
| 371 | Royals/W. Herzog (Mgr.) | .50 |
| 372 | Rich Folkers | .12 |
| 373 | Bert Campaneris | .20 |
| 374 | Kent Tekulve | .15 |
| 375 | Larry Hisle | .15 |
| 376 | Nino Espinosa | .12 |
| 377 | Dave McKay | .12 |
| 378 | Jim Umbarger | .12 |
| 379 | Larry Cox | .12 |
| 380 | Lee May | .20 |
| 381 | Bob Forsch | .20 |
| 382 | Charlie Moore | .12 |
| 383 | Stan Bahnsen | .12 |
| 384 | Darrel Chaney | .12 |
| 385 | Dave LaRoche | .12 |
| 386 | Manny Mota | .25 |
| 387 | New York Yankees/ Billy Martin (Mgr.) | .75 |
| 388 | Terry Harmon | .12 |
| 389 | Ken Kravec | .12 |
| 390 | Dave Winfield | 4.00 |
| 391 | Dan Warthen | .12 |
| 392 | Phil Roof | .12 |
| 393 | John Lowenstein | .12 |
| 394 | Bill Laxton | .12 |
| 395 | Manny Trillo | .20 |
| 396 | Tom Murphy | .12 |
| 397 | Larry Herndon (R) | .50 |
| 398 | Tom Burgmeier | .12 |
| 399 | Bruce Boisclair | .12 |
| 400 | Steve Garvey | 3.00 |
| 401 | Mickey Scott | .12 |
| 402 | Tommy Helms | .12 |
| 403 | Tom Grieve | .12 |
| 404 | Eric Rasmussen | .12 |
| 405 | Claudell Washington | .20 |
| 406 | Tim Johnson | .12 |
| 407 | Dave Freisleben | .12 |
| 408 | Cesar Tovar | .12 |
| 409 | Pete Broberg | .12 |
| 410 | Willie Montanez | .12 |
| 411 | World Series Morgan Homers, Bench Stars for Reds | .60 |
| 412 | World Series # 1 & 2 Reds' Defense, Bench's Two Homers | .60 |
| 413 | World Series # 3 & 4 Cincy Wins | .60 |
| 414 | Tommy Harper | .12 |
| 415 | Jay Johnstone | .12 |
| 416 | Chuck Hartenstein | .12 |
| 417 | Wayne Garrett | .12 |
| 418 | Chicago White Sox/ Bob Lemon (Mgr.) | .40 |
| 419 | Steve Swisher | .12 |
| 420 | Rusty Staub | .30 |
| 421 | Doug Rau | .12 |
| 422 | Freddie Patek | .12 |
| 423 | Gary Lavelle | .12 |
| 424 | Steve Brye | .12 |
| 425 | Joe Torre | .30 |
| 426 | Dick Drago | .12 |

| NO. PLAYER | MINT |
|---|---|
| 427 Dave Rader | .12 |
| 428 Texas Rangers/ | .40 |
| Frank Lucchesi (Mgr.) | |
| 429 Ken Boswell | .12 |
| 430 Fergie Jenkins | .50 |
| 431 Dave Collins | .20 |
| (photo of Bobby Jones) | |
| 432 Buzz Capra | .12 |
| 433 Turn Back Clock (1972) | .20 |
| Colbert Hits 5 Homers | |
| 434 Turn Back Clock (1967) | 1.50 |
| Yaz Wins Triple Crown | |
| 435 Turn Back Clock (1962) | .50 |
| Wills 104 Steals | |
| 436 Turn Back Clock (1957) | .20 |
| Keegan No-Hitter | |
| 437 Turn Back Clock (1952) | .50 |
| Kiner Leads NL | |
| 438 Marty Perez | .12 |
| 439 Gorman Thomas | .40 |
| 440 Jon Matlack | .12 |
| 441 Larvell Blanks | .12 |
| 442 Atlanta Braves/ | .40 |
| Dave Bristol (Mgr.) | |
| 443 Lamar Johnson | .12 |
| 444 Wayne Twitchell | .12 |
| 445 Ken Singleton | .30 |
| 446 Bill Bonham | .12 |
| 447 Jerry Turner | .12 |
| 448 Ellie Rodriguez | .12 |
| 449 Al Fitzmorris | .12 |
| 450 Pete Rose | 7.50 |
| 451 Checklist No. 4 | .75 |
| 452 Mike Caldwell | .12 |
| 453 Pedro Garcia | .12 |
| 454 Andy Etchebarren | .12 |
| 455 Rick Wise | .12 |
| 456 Leon Roberts | .12 |
| 457 Steve Luebber | .12 |
| 458 Leo Foster | .12 |
| 459 Steve Foucault | .12 |
| 460 Willie Stargell | 2.00 |
| 461 Dick Tidrow | .12 |
| 462 Don Baylor | .50 |
| 463 Jamie Quirk | .12 |
| 464 Randy Moffitt | .12 |
| 465 Rico Carty | .25 |
| 466 Fred Holdsworth | .12 |
| 467 Philadelphia Phillies/ | .45 |
| Danny Ozark (Mgr.) | |
| 468 Ramon Hernandez | .12 |
| 469 Pat Kelly | .12 |
| 470 Ted Simmons | .50 |
| 471 Del Unser | .12 |
| 472 Rookie Pitchers: | .40 |
| Bob McClure, Don Aase, | |
| Gil Patterson, Dave | |
| Wehrmeister | |
| 473 Rookie Outfielders: | 30.00 |
| Gene Richards, John Scott, | |
| D. Walling, A. Dawson | |
| 474 Rookie Shortstops: | .40 |
| Bob Bailor, Kiko Garcia, | |
| C. Reynolds, A. Taveras | |
| 475 Rookie Pitchers: | .60 |
| Chris Batton, Rick Camp | |
| S. McGregor, M. Sarmiento | |
| 476 Rookie Catchers: | 55.00 |
| Dale Murphy, Rick Cerone, | |
| G. Alexander, K. Pasley | |
| 477 Rookie Infielders: | .40 |
| R. Dauer, O. Gonzalez, | |
| D. Ault, P. Mankowski | |

| NO. PLAYER | MINT |
|---|---|
| 478 Rookie Pitchers: | .40 |
| Leon Hooten, Jim Gideon, | |
| Mark Lemongello, | |
| Dave Johnson. | |
| 479 Rookie Outfielders: | .40 |
| A. Woods, Wayne Gross, | |
| B. Asselstine, S. Mejias | |
| 480 Carl Yastrzemski | 3.50 |
| 481 Roger Metzger | .12 |
| 482 Tony Solaita | .12 |
| 483 Richie Zisk | .20 |
| 484 Burt Hooton | .20 |
| 485 Roy White | .20 |
| 486 Ed Bane | .12 |
| 487 Rookie Pitchers: | .30 |
| Joe Henderson, Ed Glynn, | |
| L. Anderson, G. Terlecky | |
| 488 Rookie Outfielders: | 20.00 |
| Lee Mazzilli, Jack Clark, | |
| R. Jones, D. Thomas | |
| 489 Rookie Pitchers: | .50 |
| Len Barker, Randy Lerch, | |
| Greg Minton, Mike Overy | |
| 490 Rookie Shortstops: | .40 |
| T. McMillan, B. Almon, | |
| M. Klutts, M. Wagner | |
| 491 Rookie Pitchers: | .75 |
| Mike Dupree, Bob Sykes, | |
| D. Martinez, C. Mitchell | |
| 492 Rookie Outfielders: | 1.50 |
| Tony Armas, Steve Kemp, | |
| C. Lopez, Gary Woods | |
| 493 Rookie Pitchers: | 1.00 |
| G. Wheelock, M. Krukow, | |
| Jim Otten, Mike Willis | |
| 494 Rookie Infielders: | .60 |
| Juan Bernhardt, J. Gantner, | |
| M. Champion, B. Wills | |
| 495 Al Hrabosky | .12 |
| 496 Gary Thomasson | .12 |
| 497 Clay Carroll | .12 |
| 498 Sal Bando | .20 |
| 499 Pablo Torealba | .12 |
| 500 Dave Kingman | .50 |
| 501 Jim Bibby | .12 |
| 502 Randy Hundley | .12 |
| 503 Bill Lee | .12 |
| 504 Los Angeles Dodgers/ | .60 |
| Tom Lasorda (Mgr.) | |
| 505 Oscar Gamble | .20 |
| 506 Steve Grilli | .12 |
| 507 Mike Hegan | .12 |
| 508 Dave Pagan | .12 |
| 509 Cookie Rojas | .12 |
| 510 John Candelaria | .50 |
| 511 Bill Fahey | .12 |
| 512 Jack Billingham | .12 |
| 513 Jerry Terrell | .12 |
| 514 Cliff Johnson | .12 |
| 515 Chris Speier | .12 |
| 516 Bake McBride | .15 |
| 517 Pete Vuckovich (R) | .50 |
| 518 Chicago Cubs/ | .45 |
| Herman Franks (Mgr.) | |
| 519 Don Kirkwood | .12 |
| 520 Garry Maddox | .15 |
| 521 Bob Grich | .20 |
| 522 Enzo Hernandez | .12 |
| 523 Rollie Fingers | .60 |
| 524 Rowland Office | .12 |
| 525 Dennis Eckersley | .25 |
| 526 Larry Parrish | .25 |

| NO. PLAYER | MINT |
|---|---|
| 527 Dan Meyer | .12 |
| 528 Bill Castro | .12 |
| 529 Jim Essian | .12 |
| 530 Rick Reuschel | .25 |
| 531 Lyman Bostock | .25 |
| 532 Jim Willoughby | .12 |
| 533 Mickey Stanley | .12 |
| 534 Paul Splittorff | .12 |
| 535 Cesar Geronimo | .12 |
| 536 Vic Albury | .12 |
| 537 Dave Roberts | .12 |
| 538 Frank Taveras | .12 |
| 539 Mike Wallace | .12 |
| 540 Bob Watson | .20 |
| 541 John Denny | .25 |
| 542 Frank Duffy | .12 |
| 543 Ron Blomberg | .12 |
| 544 Gary Ross | .12 |
| 545 Bob Boone | .15 |
| 546 Baltimore Orioles/ | .50 |
| Earl Weaver (Mgr.) | |
| 547 Willie McCovey | 2.00 |
| 548 Joel Youngblood | .12 |
| 549 Jerry Royster | .12 |
| 550 Randy Jones | .12 |
| 551 Bill North | .12 |
| 552 Pepe Mangual | .12 |
| 553 Jack Heidemann | .12 |
| 554 Bruce Kimm | .12 |
| 555 Dan Ford | .12 |
| 556 Doug Bird | .12 |
| 557 Jerry White | .12 |
| 558 Elias Sosa | .12 |
| 559 Alan Bannister | .12 |
| 560 Dave Concepcion | .40 |
| 561 Pete LaCock | .12 |
| 562 Checklist No. 5 | .75 |
| 563 Bruce Kison | .12 |
| 564 Alan Ashby | .15 |
| 565 Mickey Lolich | .20 |
| 566 Rick Miller | .12 |
| 567 Enos Cabell | .12 |
| 568 Carlos May | .12 |
| 569 Jim Lonborg | .12 |
| 570 Bobby Bonds | .25 |
| 571 Darrell Evans | .35 |
| 572 Ross Grimsley | .12 |
| 573 Joe Ferguson | .12 |
| 574 Aurelio Rodriguez | .12 |
| 575 Dick Ruthven | .12 |
| 576 Fred Kendall | .12 |
| 577 Jerry Augustine | .12 |
| 578 Bob Randall | .12 |
| 579 Don Carrithers | .12 |
| 580 George Brett | 7.50 |
| 581 Pedro Borbon | .12 |
| 582 Ed Kirkpatrick | .12 |
| 583 Paul Lindblad | .12 |
| 584 Ed Goodson | .12 |
| 585 Rick Burleson | .12 |
| 586 Steve Renko | .12 |
| 587 Rick Baldwin | .12 |
| 588 Dave Moates | .12 |
| 589 Mike Cosgrove | .12 |
| 590 Buddy Bell | .40 |
| 591 Chris Arnold | .12 |
| 592 Dan Briggs | .12 |
| 593 Dennis Blair | .12 |
| 594 Biff Pocoroba | .12 |
| 595 John Hiller | .12 |
| 596 Jerry Martin | .12 |

| NO. PLAYER | MINT |
|---|---|
| 597 Seattle Mariners/ | .35 |
| Darrell Johnson (Mgr.) | |
| 598 Sparky Lyle | .30 |
| 599 Mike Tyson | .12 |
| 600 Jim Palmer | 1.50 |
| 601 Mike Lum | .12 |
| 602 Andy Hassler | .12 |
| 603 Willie Davis | .12 |
| 604 Jim Slaton | .12 |
| 605 Felix Millan | .12 |
| 606 Steve Braun | .12 |
| 607 Larry Demery | .12 |
| 608 Roy Howell | .12 |
| 609 Jim Barr | .12 |
| 610 Jose Cardenal | .12 |
| 611 Dave Lemanczyk | .12 |
| 612 Barry Foote | .12 |
| 613 Reggie Cleveland | .12 |
| 614 Greg Gross | .12 |
| 615 Phil Niekro | 1.25 |
| 616 Tommy Sandt | .12 |
| 617 Bobby Darwin | .12 |
| 618 Pat Dobson | .12 |
| 619 Johnny Oates | .12 |
| 620 Don Sutton | 1.25 |
| 621 Detroit Tigers/ | .50 |
| Ralph Houk (Mgr.) | |
| 622 Jim Wohlford | .12 |
| 623 Jack Kucek | .12 |
| 624 Hector Cruz | .12 |
| 625 Ken Holtzman | .12 |
| 626 Al Bumbry | .12 |
| 627 Bob Myrick | .12 |
| 628 Mario Guerrero | .12 |
| 629 Bobby Valentine | .25 |
| 630 Bert Blyleven | .40 |
| 631 Big League Brothers: | 1.25 |
| George Brett, Ken Brett | |
| 632 Big League Brothers: | .30 |
| Ken Forsch, Bob Forsch | |
| 633 Big League Brothers: | .30 |
| Lee May, Carlos May | |
| 634 Big League Brothers: | .30 |
| Paul Reuschel, Rick | |
| Reuschel (photos switched) | |
| 635 Robin Yount | 3.00 |
| 636 Santo Alcala | .12 |
| 637 Alex Johnson | .12 |
| 638 Jim Kaat | .45 |
| 639 Jerry Morales | .12 |
| 640 Carlton Fisk | .65 |
| 641 Dan Larson | .12 |
| 642 Willie Crawford | .12 |
| 643 Mike Pazik | .12 |
| 644 Matt Alexander | .12 |
| 645 Jerry Reuss | .15 |
| 646 Andres Mora | .12 |
| 647 Montreal Expos/ | .40 |
| Dick Williams (Mgr.) | |
| 648 Jim Spencer | .12 |
| 649 Dave Cash | .12 |
| 650 Nolan Ryan | 3.00 |
| 651 Von Joshua | .12 |
| 652 Tom Walker | .12 |
| 653 Diego Segui | .12 |
| 654 Ron Pruitt | .12 |
| 655 Tony Perez | .75 |
| 656 Ron Guidry | 2.00 |
| 657 Mick Kelleher | .12 |
| 658 Marty Pattin | .12 |
| 659 Merv Rettenmund | .12 |
| 660 W. Horton (Exc. .12) | .50 |

**Prices for the 1977 set are for cards in *Mint* condition. *Excellent* copies sell for 50% of prices shown; *Very Good*—30%.**

# 1978 Topps....Complete Set of 726 Cards—Value $200.00

After five consecutive years of issuing sets of 660 cards, Topps increased the size of its main set to 726 cards. 66 cards were double printed. Eddie Murray, Paul Molitor, and Lou Whitaker's rookie cards are in this set.

| NO. PLAYER | MINT |
|---|---|
| 1 Record — L. Brock | 2.00 |
| Most Career Steals | |
| 2 Record — S. Lyle | .25 |
| Most Career Relief | |
| 3 Record — W. McCovey | .60 |
| Most 2 HR's in Inning | |
| 4 Record — B. Robinson | .75 |
| Most Seasons — Same Club | |
| 5 Record — P. Rose | 1.75 |
| Most Hits — Switch Hitter | |
| 6 Record — N. Ryan | 1.00 |
| Games 10 or More SO's | |
| 7 Record — R. Jackson | 1.50 |
| Most Homers — W. Series | |
| 8 Mike Sadek | .10 |
| 9 Doug DeCinces | .25 |
| 10 Phil Niekro | 1.00 |
| 11 Rick Manning | .10 |
| 12 Don Aase | .20 |
| 13 Art Howe | .10 |
| 14 Lerrin LaGrow | .10 |
| 15 Tony Perez | .20 |
| 16 Roy White | .20 |
| 17 Mike Krukow | .25 |
| 18 Bob Grich | .20 |
| 19 Darrell Porter | .10 |
| 20 Pete Rose | 3.50 |
| 21 Steve Kemp | .30 |
| 22 Charlie Hough | .10 |
| 23 Bump Wills | .10 |
| 24 Don Money | .10 |
| 25 Jon Motlack | .10 |
| 26 Rich Hebner | .10 |
| 27 Geoff Zahn | .10 |
| 28 Ed Ott | .10 |
| 29 Bob Lacey | .10 |
| 30 George Hendrick | .20 |
| 31 Glenn Abbott | .10 |
| 32 Garry Templeton | .30 |
| 33 Dave Lemanczyk | .10 |
| 34 Willie McCovey | 1.50 |
| 35 Sparky Lyle | .20 |
| 36 Eddie Murray (R) | 30.00 |
| 37 Rick Waits | .10 |
| 38 Willie Montanez | .10 |
| 39 Floyd Bannister (R) | 1.00 |
| 40 Carl Yastrzemski | 2.50 |
| 41 Burt Hooton | .10 |
| 42 Jorge Orta | .10 |
| 43 Bill Atkinson | .10 |
| 44 Toby Harrah | .10 |
| 45 Mark Fidrych | .20 |
| 46 Al Cowens | .15 |
| 47 Jack Billingham | .10 |
| 48 Don Baylor | .40 |
| 49 Ed Kranepool | .20 |
| 50 Rick Reushel | .25 |
| 51 Charlie Moore | .10 |
| 52 Jim Lonborg | .10 |
| 53 Phil Garner | .10 |
| 54 Tom Johnson | .10 |
| 55 Mitchell Page | .10 |
| 56 Randy Jones | .10 |
| 57 Dan Meyer | .10 |
| 58 Bob Forsch | .15 |
| 59 Otto Velez | .10 |
| 60 Thurman Munson | 2.00 |
| 61 Larvell Blanks | .10 |
| 62 Jim Barr | .10 |
| 63 Don Zimmer (Mgr.) | .10 |
| 64 Gene Pentz | .10 |
| 65 Ken Singleton | .20 |
| 66 Chicago White Sox | .35 |
| 67 Claudell Washington | .15 |
| 68 Steve Foucault | .10 |
| 69 Mike Vail | .10 |
| 70 Rich Gossage | .50 |
| 71 Terry Humphrey | .10 |
| 72 Andre Dawson | 5.00 |
| 73 Andy Hassler | .10 |
| 74 Checklist No. 1 | .50 |
| 75 Dick Ruthven | .10 |
| 76 Steve Ontiveros | .10 |
| 77 Ed Kirpatrick | .10 |
| 78 Pablo Torrealba | .10 |
| 79 Darrell Johnson (Mgr.) | .10 |
| 80 Ken Griffey | .25 |
| 81 Pete Redfern | .10 |
| 82 San Fran. Giants | .35 |
| 83 Bob Montgomery | .10 |
| 84 Kent Tekulve | .15 |
| 85 Ron Fairly | .10 |
| 86 Dave Tomlin | .10 |
| 87 John Lowenstein | .10 |
| 88 Mike Phillips | .10 |
| 89 Ken Clay | .10 |
| 90 Larry Bowa | .20 |
| 91 Oscar Zamora | .10 |
| 92 Adrian Devine | .10 |
| 93 Bobby Cox (Mgr.) | .10 |
| 94 Chuck Scrivener | .10 |
| 95 Jamie Quirk | .10 |
| 96 Baltimore Orioles | .40 |
| 97 Stan Bahnsen | .10 |
| 98 Jim Essian | .10 |
| 99 Willie Hernandez (R) | 1.25 |
| 100 George Brett | 4.00 |
| 101 Sid Monge | .10 |
| 102 Matt Alexander | .10 |
| 103 Tom Murphy | .10 |
| 104 Lee Lacy | .10 |
| 105 Reggie Cleveland | .10 |
| 106 Bill Plummer | .10 |
| 107 Ed Halicki | .10 |
| 108 Von Joshua | .10 |
| 109 Joe Torre (Mgr.) | .20 |
| 110 Richie Zisk | .20 |
| 111 Mike Tyson | .10 |
| 112 Houston Astros | .30 |
| 113 Don Carrithers | .10 |
| 114 Paul Blair | .10 |
| 115 Gary Nolan | .10 |
| 116 Tucker Ashford | .10 |
| 117 John Montague | .10 |
| 118 Terry Harmon | .10 |
| 119 Denny Martinez | .10 |
| 120 Gary Carter | 3.00 |
| 121 Alvis Woods | .10 |
| 122 Dennis Eckersley | .15 |
| 123 Manny Trillo | .15 |
| 124 Dave Rozema | .10 |
| 125 George Scott | .10 |
| 126 Paul Moskau | .10 |
| 127 Chet Lemon | .15 |
| 128 Bill Russell | .10 |
| 129 Jim Colborn | .10 |
| 130 Jeff Burroughs | .20 |
| 131 Bert Blyleven | .30 |
| 132 Enos Cabell | .10 |
| 133 Jerry Augustine | .10 |
| 134 Steve Henderson | .10 |
| 135 Ron Guidry | .60 |
| 136 Ted Sizemore | .10 |
| 137 Craig Kusick | .10 |
| 138 Larry Demery | .10 |
| 139 Wayne Gross | .10 |
| 140 Rollie Fingers | .50 |
| 141 Ruppert Jones | .10 |
| 142 John Montefusco | .10 |
| 143 Keith Hernandez | 2.00 |
| 144 Jesse Jefferson | .10 |
| 145 Rick Monday | .10 |
| 146 Doyle Alexander | .10 |
| 147 Lee Mazzilli | .15 |
| 148 Andre Thornton | .20 |
| 149 Dale Murray | .10 |
| 150 Bobby Bonds | .25 |
| 151 Milt Wilcox | .10 |
| 152 Ivan DeJesus | .10 |
| 153 Steve Stone | .10 |
| 154 Cecil Cooper | .30 |
| 155 Butch Hobson | .10 |
| 156 Andy Messersmith | .10 |
| 157 Pete LaCock | .10 |
| 158 Joaquin Andujar | .25 |
| 159 Lou Piniella | .40 |
| 160 Jim Palmer | 1.50 |
| 161 Bob Boone | .25 |
| 162 Paul Thormodsgard | .10 |
| 163 Bill North | .10 |
| 164 Bob Owchinko | .10 |
| 165 Rennie Stennett | .10 |
| 166 Carlos Lopez | .10 |
| 167 Tim Foli | .10 |
| 168 Reggie Smith | .25 |
| 169 Jerry Johnson | .10 |
| 170 Lou Brock | 1.50 |
| 171 Pat Zachry | .10 |
| 172 Mike Hargrove | .10 |
| 173 Robin Yount | 2.00 |
| 174 Wayne Garland | .10 |
| 175 Jerry Morales | .10 |
| 176 Milt May | .10 |
| 177 Gene Garber | .10 |
| 178 Dave Chalk | .10 |
| 179 Dick Tidrow | .10 |
| 180 Dave Concepcion | .25 |
| 181 Ken Forsch | .10 |
| 182 Jim Spencer | .10 |
| 183 Doug Bird | .10 |
| 184 Checklist No. 2 | .50 |
| 185 Ellis Valentine | .10 |
| 186 Bob Stanley (R) | .35 |
| 187 Jerry Royster | .10 |
| 188 Al Bumbry | .10 |
| 189 Tom Lasorda (Mgr.) | .20 |
| 190 John Candelaria | .15 |
| 191 Rodney Scott | .10 |
| 192 San Diego Padres | .30 |
| 193 Rich Chiles | .10 |
| 194 Derrel Thomas | .10 |
| 195 Larry Dierker | .10 |
| 196 Bob Bailor | .10 |
| 197 Nino Espinosa | .10 |
| 198 Ron Pruitt | .10 |
| 199 Craig Reynolds | .10 |
| 200 Reggie Jackson | 3.50 |
| 201 Batting Leaders: | .60 |
| Dave Parker, Rod Carew | |
| 202 Home Run Leaders: | .25 |
| George Foster, Jim Rice | |
| 203 RBI Leaders: | .25 |
| George Foster, Larry Hisle | |
| 204 Stolen Base Leaders: | .20 |
| F. Taveras, Freddie Patek | |
| 205 Victory Leaders: | .60 |
| Steve Carlton, D. Goltz, | |
| D. Leonard, J. Palmer | |
| 206 Strikeout Leaders: | .25 |
| Phil Niekro, Nolan Ryan | |
| 207 ERA Leaders: | .20 |
| J. Candelaria, F. Tanana | |
| 208 Leading Firemen: | .30 |
| R. Fingers, B. Campbell | |
| 209 Dock Ellis | .10 |
| 210 Jose Cardenal | .10 |
| 211 Earl Weaver (Mgr.) | .10 |
| 212 Mike Caldwell | .10 |
| 213 Alan Bannister | .10 |
| 214 California Angels | .35 |
| 215 Darrell Evans | .35 |
| 216 Mike Paxton | .10 |
| 217 Rod Gilbreath | .10 |
| 218 Marty Pattin | .10 |
| 219 Mike Cubbage | .10 |
| 220 Pedro Borbon | .10 |
| 221 Chris Speier | .10 |
| 222 Jerry Martin | .10 |
| 223 Bruce Kison | .10 |
| 224 Jerry Tabb | .10 |
| 225 Don Gullett | .10 |
| 226 Joe Ferguson | .10 |
| 227 Al Fitzmorris | .10 |
| 228 Manny Mota | .10 |
| 229 Leo Foster | .10 |
| 230 Al Hrabosky | .10 |
| 231 Wayne Nordhagen | .10 |
| 232 Mickey Stanley | .10 |
| 233 Dick Pole | .10 |
| 234 Herman Franks (Mgr.) | .10 |
| 235 Tim McCarver | .25 |
| 236 Terry Whitfield | .10 |
| 237 Rich Dauer | .10 |
| 238 Juan Beniquez | .10 |
| 239 Dyar Miller | .10 |
| 240 Gene Tenace | .10 |
| 241 Pete Vuckovich | .15 |
| 242 Barry Bonnell | .10 |
| 243 Bob McClure | .10 |
| 244 Montreal Expos | .25 |
| 245 Rick Burleson | .10 |
| 246 Dan Driessen | .10 |
| 247 Larry Christenson | .10 |
| 248 Frank White | .10 |

| NO. | PLAYER | MINT | NO. | PLAYER | MINT | NO. | PLAYER | MINT | NO. | PLAYER | MINT |
|---|---|---|---|---|---|---|---|---|---|---|---|
| 249 | Dave Goltz | .10 | 334 | John Stearns | .10 | 416 | Jack Brohamer | .10 | 501 | Dave Roberts | .10 |
| 250 | Graig Nettles | .20 | 335 | Bucky Dent | .15 | 417 | Mike Garman | .10 | 502 | Pat Rockett | .10 |
| 251 | Don Kirkwood | .10 | 336 | Steve Busby | .10 | 418 | Tony Muser | .10 | 503 | Ike Hampton | .10 |
| 252 | Steve Swisher | .10 | 337 | Tom Grieve | .10 | 419 | Jerry Garvin | .10 | 504 | Roger Freed | .10 |
| 253 | Jim Kern | .10 | 338 | Dave Heaverlo | .10 | 420 | Greg Luzinski | .30 | 505 | Felix Millan | .10 |
| 254 | Dave Collins | .15 | 339 | Mario Guerrero | .10 | 421 | Junior Moore | .10 | 506 | Ron Blomberg | .10 |
| 255 | Jerry Reuss | .15 | 340 | Bake McBride | .10 | 422 | Steve Braun | .10 | 507 | Willie Crawford | .10 |
| 256 | Joe Altobelli (Mgr.) | .10 | 341 | Mike Flanagan | .20 | 423 | Dave Rosello | .10 | 508 | Johnny Oates | .10 |
| 257 | Hector Cruz | .10 | 342 | Aurelio Rodriguez | .10 | 424 | Boston Red Sox | .40 | 509 | Brent Strom | .10 |
| 258 | John Hiller | .10 | 343 | John Wathan | .10 | 425 | Steve Rogers | .10 | 510 | Willie Stargell | 2.00 |
| 259 | Los Angeles Dodgers | .50 | 344 | Sam Ewing | .10 | 426 | Fred Kendall | .10 | 511 | Frank Duffy | .10 |
| 260 | Bert Campaneris | .15 | 345 | Luis Tiant | .20 | 427 | Mario Soto (R) | 1.00 | 512 | Larry Herndon | .15 |
| 261 | Tim Hosely | .10 | 346 | Larry Biittner | .10 | 428 | Joel Youngblood | .10 | 513 | Barry Foote | .10 |
| 262 | Rudy May | .10 | 347 | Terry Forster | .15 | 429 | Mike Barlow | .10 | 514 | Rob Sperring | .10 |
| 263 | Danny Walton | .10 | 348 | Del Unser | .10 | 430 | Al Oliver | .50 | 515 | Tim Corcoran | .10 |
| 264 | Jamie Easterly | .10 | 349 | Rick Camp | .10 | 431 | Butch Metzger | .10 | 516 | Gary Beare | .10 |
| 265 | Sal Bando | .10 | 350 | Steve Garvey | 2.50 | 432 | Terry Bulling | .10 | 517 | Andres Mora | .10 |
| 266 | Bob Shirley | .10 | 351 | Jeff Torborg (Mgr.) | .10 | 433 | Fernando Gonzalez | .10 | 518 | Tommy Boggs | .10 |
| 267 | Doug Ault | .10 | 352 | Tony Scott | .10 | 434 | Mike Norris | .10 | 519 | Brian Downing | .10 |
| 268 | Gil Flores | .10 | 353 | Doug Bair | .10 | 435 | Checklist No. 4 | .50 | 520 | Larry Hisle | .10 |
| 269 | Wayne Twitchell | .10 | 354 | Cesar Geronimo | .10 | 436 | Vic Harris | .10 | 521 | Steve Staggs | .10 |
| 270 | Carlton Fisk | .60 | 355 | Bill Travers | .10 | 437 | Bo McLaughlin | .10 | 522 | Dick Williams (Mgr.) | .15 |
| 271 | Randy Lerch | .10 | 356 | New York Mets | .50 | 438 | John Ellis | .10 | 523 | Donnie Moore (R) | .40 |
| 272 | Royle Stillman | .10 | 357 | Tom Poquette | .10 | 439 | Ken Kravec | .10 | 524 | Bernie Carbo | .10 |
| 273 | Fred Norman | .10 | 358 | Mark Lemongello | .10 | 440 | Dave Lopes | .25 | 525 | Jerry Terrell | .10 |
| 274 | Freddie Patek | .10 | 359 | Marc Hill | .10 | 441 | Larry Gura | .15 | 526 | Cincinnati Reds | .45 |
| 275 | Dan Ford | .10 | 360 | Mike Schmidt | 4.50 | 442 | Elliott Maddox | .10 | 527 | Vic Correll | .10 |
| 276 | Bill Bonham | .10 | 361 | Chris Knapp | .10 | 443 | Darrell Chaney | .10 | 528 | Rob Picciolo | .10 |
| 277 | Bruce Boisclair | .10 | 362 | Dave May | .10 | 444 | Roy Hartsfield (Mgr.) | .10 | 529 | Paul Hartzell | .10 |
| 278 | Enrique Romo | .10 | 363 | Bob Randall | .10 | 445 | Mike Ivie | .10 | 530 | Dave Winfield | 2.00 |
| 279 | Bill Virdon (Mgr.) | .15 | 364 | Jerry Turner | .10 | 446 | Tug McGraw | .20 | 531 | Tom Underwood | .10 |
| 280 | Buddy Bell | .30 | 365 | Ed Figueroa | .10 | 447 | Leroy Stanton | .10 | 532 | Skip Jutze | .10 |
| 281 | Eric Rasmussen | .10 | 366 | Larry Milbourne | .10 | 448 | Bill Castro | .10 | 533 | Sandy Alomar | .10 |
| 282 | New York Yankees | .60 | 367 | Rick Dempsey | .15 | 449 | Tim Blackwell | .10 | 534 | Wilbur Howard | .10 |
| 283 | Omar Moreno | .15 | 368 | Balor Moore | .10 | 450 | Tom Seaver | 2.00 | 535 | Checklist No. 5 | .50 |
| 284 | Randy Moffitt | .10 | 369 | Tim Nordbrook | .10 | 451 | Minnesota Twins | .35 | 536 | Roric Harrison | .10 |
| 285 | Steve Yeager | .10 | 370 | Rusty Staub | .20 | 452 | Jerry Mumphrey | .10 | 537 | Bruce Bochte | .10 |
| 286 | Ben Oglivie | .15 | 371 | Ray Burris | .10 | 453 | Doug Flynn | .10 | 538 | Johnnie LeMaster | .10 |
| 287 | Kiko Garcia | .10 | 372 | Brian Asselstine | .10 | 454 | Dave LaRoche | .10 | 539 | Vic Davalillo | .10 |
| 288 | Dave Hamilton | .10 | 373 | Jim Willoughby | .10 | 455 | Bill Robinson | .10 | 540 | Steve Carlton | 2.00 |
| 289 | Checklist No. 3 | .50 | 374 | Jose Morales | .10 | 456 | Vern Ruhle | .10 | 541 | Larry Cox | .10 |
| 290 | Willie Horton | .15 | 375 | Tommy John | .50 | 457 | Bob Bailey | .10 | 542 | Tim Johnson | .10 |
| 291 | Gary Ross | .10 | 376 | Jim Wohlford | .10 | 458 | Jeff Newman | .10 | 543 | Larry Harlow | .10 |
| 292 | Gene Richards | .10 | 377 | Manny Sarmiento | .10 | 459 | Charlie Spikes | .10 | 544 | Len Randle | .10 |
| 293 | Mike Willis | .10 | 378 | Bobby Winkles (Mgr.) | .10 | 460 | Jim Hunter | 1.00 | 545 | Bill Campbell | .10 |
| 294 | Larry Parrish | .20 | 379 | Skip Lockwood | .10 | 461 | Rob Andrews | .10 | 546 | Ted Martinez | .10 |
| 295 | Bill Lee | .10 | 380 | Ted Simmons | .40 | 462 | Rogelio Moret | .10 | 547 | John Scott | .10 |
| 296 | Biff Pocoroba | .10 | 381 | Philadelphia Phillies | .35 | 463 | Kevin Bell | .10 | 548 | Billy Hunter (Mgr.) | .10 |
| 297 | Warren Brusstar | .10 | 382 | Joe Lahoud | .10 | 464 | Jerry Grote | .10 | 549 | Joe Kerrigan | .10 |
| 298 | Tony Armas | .50 | 383 | Mario Mendoza | .10 | 465 | Hal McRae | .15 | 550 | John Mayberry | .15 |
| 299 | Whitey Herzog (Mgr.) | .15 | 384 | Jack Clark | 3.00 | 466 | Dennis Blair | .10 | 551 | Atlanta Braves | .35 |
| 300 | Joe Morgan | 1.25 | 385 | Tito Fuentes | .10 | 467 | Alvin Dark (Mgr.) | .10 | 552 | Francisco Barrios | .10 |
| 301 | Buddy Schultz | .10 | 386 | Bob Gorinski | .10 | 468 | Warren Cromartie | .10 | 553 | Terry Puhl (R) | .45 |
| 302 | Chicago Cubs | .45 | 387 | Ken Holtzman | .10 | 469 | Rick Cerone | .10 | 554 | Joe Coleman | .10 |
| 303 | Sam Hinds | .10 | 388 | Bill Fahey | .10 | 470 | J.R. Richard | .15 | 555 | Butch Wynegar | .15 |
| 304 | John Milner | .10 | 389 | Julio Gonzalez | .10 | 471 | Roy Smalley | .10 | 556 | Ed Armbrister | .10 |
| 305 | Rico Carty | .20 | 390 | Oscar Gamble | .10 | 472 | Ron Reed | .10 | 557 | Tony Solaita | .10 |
| 306 | Joe Niekro | .20 | 391 | Larry Haney | .10 | 473 | Bill Buckner | .25 | 558 | Paul Mitchell | .10 |
| 307 | Glenn Borgmann | .10 | 392 | Billy Almon | .10 | 474 | Jim Slaton | .10 | 559 | Phil Mankowski | .10 |
| 308 | Jim Rooker | .10 | 393 | Tippy Martinez | .10 | 475 | Gary Matthews | .20 | 560 | Dave Parker | 1.50 |
| 309 | Cliff Johnson | .10 | 394 | Roy Howell | .10 | 476 | Bill Stein | .10 | 561 | Charlie Williams | .10 |
| 310 | Don Sutton | 1.00 | 395 | Jim Hughes | .10 | 477 | Doug Capilla | .10 | 562 | Glenn Burke | .10 |
| 311 | Jose Baez | .10 | 396 | Bob Stinson | .10 | 478 | Jerry Remy | .10 | 563 | Dave Rader | .10 |
| 312 | Greg Minton | .10 | 397 | Greg Gross | .10 | 479 | St. Louis Cardinals | .40 | 564 | Mick Kelleher | .10 |
| 313 | Andy Etchebarren | .10 | 398 | Don Hood | .10 | 480 | Ron LeFlore | .15 | 565 | Jerry Koosman | .25 |
| 314 | Paul Lindblad | .10 | 399 | Pete Mackanin | .10 | 481 | Jackson Todd | .10 | 566 | Merv Rettenmund | .10 |
| 315 | Mark Belanger | .10 | 400 | Nolan Ryan | 2.50 | 482 | Rick Miller | .10 | 567 | Dick Drago | .10 |
| 316 | Henry Cruz | .10 | 401 | Sparky Anderson (Mgr.) | .15 | 483 | Ken Macha | .10 | 568 | Tom Hutton | .10 |
| 317 | Dave Johnson | .30 | 402 | Dave Campbell | .10 | 484 | Jim Norris | .10 | 569 | Lary Sorensen | .10 |
| 318 | Tom Griffin | .10 | 403 | Bud Harrelson | .10 | 485 | Chris Chambliss | .15 | 570 | Dave Kingman | .50 |
| 319 | Alan Ashby | .10 | 404 | Detroit Tigers | .60 | 486 | John Curtis | .10 | 571 | Buck Martinez | .10 |
| 320 | Fred Lynn | 1.00 | 405 | Rawly Eastwick | .10 | 487 | Jim Tyrone | .10 | 572 | Rick Wise | .10 |
| 321 | Santo Alcala | .10 | 406 | Mike Jorgensen | .10 | 488 | Dan Spillner | .10 | 573 | Luis Gomez | .10 |
| 322 | Tom Paciorek | .10 | 407 | Odell Jones | .10 | 489 | Rudy Meoli | .10 | 574 | Bob Lemon (Mgr.) | .25 |
| 323 | Jim Fregosi | .10 | 408 | Joe Zdeb | .10 | 490 | Amos Otis | .15 | 575 | Pat Dobson | .10 |
| 324 | Vern Rapp (Mgr.) | .10 | 409 | Ron Schueler | .10 | 491 | Scott McGregor | .15 | 576 | Sam Mejias | .10 |
| 325 | Bruce Sutter | .75 | 410 | Bill Madlock | .50 | 492 | Jim Sundberg | .10 | 577 | Oakland A's | .30 |
| 326 | Mike Lum | .10 | 411 | Al Championships: Yankees Defeat Royals | .75 | 493 | Steve Renko | .10 | 578 | Buzz Capra | .10 |
| 327 | Rick Langford | .10 | 412 | NL Championships: Dodgers Defeat Phillies | .75 | 494 | Chuck Tanner (Mgr.) | .10 | 579 | Rance Mulliniks | .10 |
| 328 | Milwaukee Brewers | .40 | | | | 495 | Dave Cash | .10 | 580 | Rod Carew | 2.00 |
| 329 | John Verhoeven | .10 | 413 | World Series: Yankees Reign Supreme | 1.50 | 496 | Jim Clancy | .10 | 581 | Lynn McGlothen | .10 |
| 330 | Bob Watson | .10 | | | | 497 | Glenn Adams | .10 | 582 | Fran Healy | .10 |
| 331 | Mark Littell | .10 | 414 | Darold Knowles | .10 | 498 | Joe Sambito | .10 | 583 | George Medich | .10 |
| 332 | Duane Kuiper | .10 | 415 | Ray Fosse | .10 | 499 | Seattle Mariners | .40 | 584 | John Hale | .10 |
| 333 | Jim Todd | .10 | | | | 500 | George Foster | .75 | 585 | Woodie Fryman | .10 |

**Prices for the 1978 set are for cards in *Mint* condition. *Excellent* copies sell for 50% of prices shown; *Very Good*—30%.**

| NO. PLAYER | MINT | NO. PLAYER | MINT | NO. PLAYER | MINT | NO. PLAYER | MINT |
|---|---|---|---|---|---|---|---|
| 586 Ed Goodson | .10 | 628 Ralph Garr | .10 | 669 Pete Falcone | .10 | 704 Rookie 2nd Basemen: | 7.50 |
| 587 John Urrea | .10 | 629 Don Stanhouse | .10 | 670 Jim Rice | 3.50 | Garth Iorg, Sam Perlozzo, | |
| 588 Jim Mason | .10 | 630 Ron Cey | .40 | 671 Gary Lavelle | .10 | Dave Oliver, Lou Whitaker | |
| 589 Bob Knepper (R) | 1.50 | 631 Danny Ozark (Mgr.) | .15 | 672 Don Kessinger | .10 | 705 Rookie Outfielders: | .50 |
| 590 Bobby Murcer | .25 | 632 Rowland Office | .10 | 673 Steve Brye | .10 | D. Bergman, W. Norwood, | |
| 591 George Zeber | .10 | 633 Tom Veryzer | .10 | 674 Ray Knight (R) | 1.00 | M. Dilone, C. Hurdle | |
| 592 Bob Apodaca | .10 | 634 Len Barker | .10 | 675 Jay Johnstone | .10 | 706 Rookie 1st Basemen: | .40 |
| 593 Dave Skaggs | .10 | 635 Joe Rudi | .10 | 676 Bob Myrick | .10 | Wayne Cage, Ted Cox, | |
| 594 Dave Freisleben | .10 | 636 Jim Bibby | .10 | 677 Ed Herrmann | .10 | P. Putnam, D. Revering | |
| 595 Sixto Lezcano | .10 | 637 Duffy Dyer | .10 | 678 Tom Burgmeier | .10 | 707 Rookie Shortstops: | 30.00 |
| 596 Gary Wheelock | .10 | 638 Paul Splittorff | .10 | 679 Wayne Garrett | .10 | Mickey Klutts, Paul Molitor, | |
| 597 Steve Dillard | .10 | 639 Gene Clines | .10 | 680 Vida Blue | .15 | Alan Trammell, | |
| 598 Eddie Solomon | .10 | 640 Lee May | .10 | 681 Bob Belloir | .10 | U.L. Washington | |
| 599 Gary Woods | .10 | 641 Doug Rau | .10 | 682 Ken Brett | .10 | 708 Rookie Catchers: | 28.00 |
| 600 Frank Tanana | .20 | 642 Denny Doyle | .10 | 683 Mike Champion | .10 | Bo Diaz, Dale Murphy, | |
| 601 Gene Mauch (Mgr.) | .15 | 643 Tom House | .10 | 684 Ralph Houk (Mgr.) | .15 | Ernie Whitt, Lance Parrish | |
| 602 Eric Soderholm | .10 | 644 Jim Dwyer | .10 | 685 Frank Taveras | .10 | 709 Rookie Pitchers: | .40 |
| 603 Will McEnaney | .10 | 645 Mike Torrez | .10 | 686 Gaylord Perry | 1.25 | Steve Burke, Lance | |
| 604 Earl Williams | .10 | 646 Rick Auerbach | .10 | 687 Julio Cruz (R) | .40 | Rautzhan, Matt Keough, | |
| 605 Rick Rhoden | .20 | 647 Steve Dunning | .10 | 688 George Mitterwald | .10 | Dan Schatzeder | |
| 606 Pittsburgh Pirates | .35 | 648 Gary Thomasson | .10 | 689 Cleveland Indians | .35 | 710 Rookie Outfielders: | 1.00 |
| 607 Fernando Arroyo | .10 | 649 Moose Haas (R) | .30 | 690 Mickey Rivers | .15 | Dell Alston, Rick Bosetti, | |
| 608 Johnny Grubb | .10 | 650 Cesar Cedeno | .20 | 691 Ross Grimsley | .10 | Mike Easler, Keith Smith | |
| 609 John Denny | .25 | 651 Doug Rader | .10 | 692 Ken Reitz | .10 | 711 Rookie Pitchers: | .35 |
| 610 Garry Maddox | .15 | 652 Checklist No. 6 | .50 | 693 Lamar Johnson | .10 | C. Camper, D. Lamp, | |
| 611 Pat Scanlon | .10 | 653 Ron Hodges | .10 | 694 Elias Sosa | .10 | R. Thomas, C. Mitchell | |
| 612 Ken Henderson | .10 | 654 Pepe Frias | .10 | 695 Dwight Evans | 1.00 | 712 Bobby Valentine | .25 |
| 613 Marty Perez | .10 | 655 Lyman Bostock | .15 | 696 Steve Mingori | .10 | 713 Bob Davis | .10 |
| 614 Joe Wallis | .10 | 656 Dave Garcia (Mgr.) | .10 | 697 Roger Metzger | .10 | 714 Mike Anderson | .10 |
| 615 Clay Carroll | .10 | 657 Bombo Rivera | .10 | 698 Juan Bernhardt | .10 | 715 Jim Kaat | .40 |
| 616 Pat Kelly | .10 | 658 Manny Sanguillen | .10 | 699 Jackie Brown | .10 | 716 Clarence Gaston | .10 |
| 617 Joe Nolan | .10 | 659 Texas Rangers | .35 | 700 Johnny Bench | 2.50 | 717 Nelson Briles | .10 |
| 618 Tommy Helms | .10 | 660 Jason Thompson | .25 | 701 Rookie Pitchers: | .40 | 718 Ron Jackson | .10 |
| 619 Thad Bosley | .10 | 661 Grant Jackson | .10 | Larry Landreth, Tom Hume, | | 719 Randy Elliott | .10 |
| 620 Willie Randolph | .30 | 662 Paul Dade | .10 | Steve McCatty, B. Taylor | | 720 Fergie Jenkins | .40 |
| 621 Craig Swan | .10 | 663 Paul Reuschel | .10 | 702 Rookie Catchers: | .20 | 721 Billy Martin (Mgr.) | .35 |
| 622 Champ Summers | .10 | 664 Fred Stanley | .10 | Rick Sweet, Bill Nahordony | | 722 Pete Broberg | .10 |
| 623 Eduardo Rodriquez | .10 | 665 Dennis Leonard | .15 | Kevin Pasley, Don Werner | | 723 John Wockenfuss | .10 |
| 624 Gary Alexander | .10 | 666 Billy Smith | .10 | 703 Rookie Pitchers: | 6.00 | 724 K.C. Royals | .40 |
| 625 Jose Cruz | .35 | 667 Jeff Byrd | .10 | Jack Morris, L. Andersen, | | 725 Kurt Bevacqua | .10 |
| 626 Toronto Blue Jays | .20 | 668 Dusty Baker | .20 | Tim Jones, M. Mahler | | 726 W. Wood (Exc. .10) | .40 |
| 627 Dave Johnson | .10 | | | | | | |

# 1979 Topps....Complete Set of 726 Cards—Value $125.00

Features the rookie cards of Pedro Guerrero and Bob Horner. 66 cards were double printed. Card 369 (Bump Wills) was originally issued in error as a "Blue Jay". A corrected card was issued showing Wills as a "Ranger".

| NO. PLAYER | MINT | NO. PLAYER | MINT | NO. PLAYER | MINT | NO. PLAYER | MINT |
|---|---|---|---|---|---|---|---|
| 1 Batting Leaders: | 1.25 | 9 Dave Campbell | .10 | 25 Steve Carlton | 1.50 | 41 Minnesota Twins/ | .40 |
| Rod Carew, Dave Parker | | 10 Lee May | .10 | 26 Jamie Quirk | .10 | Gene Mauch (Mgr.) | |
| 2 Home Run Leaders: | .50 | 11 Marc Hill | .10 | 27 Dave Goltz | .10 | 42 Ron Blomberg | .10 |
| Jim Rice, George Foster | | 12 Dick Drago | .10 | 28 Steve Brye | .10 | 43 Wayne Twitchell | .10 |
| 3 RBI Leaders: | .50 | 13 Paul Dade | .10 | 29 Rick Langford | .10 | 44 Kurt Bevacqua | .10 |
| Jim Rice, George Foster | | 14 Rafael Landestoy | .10 | 30 Dave Winfield | 2.50 | 45 Al Hrabosky | .10 |
| 4 Stolen Base Leaders: | .25 | 15 Ross Grimsley | .10 | 31 Tom House | .10 | 46 Ron Hodges | .10 |
| Ron LeFlore, Omar Moreno | | 16 Fred Stanley | .10 | 32 Jerry Mumphrey | .15 | 47 Fred Norman | .10 |
| 5 Victory Leaders: | .40 | 17 Donnie Moore | .15 | 33 Dave Rozema | .10 | 48 Merv Rettenmund | .10 |
| Ron Guidry, Gaylord Perry | | 18 Tony Solaita | .10 | 34 Rob Andrews | .10 | 49 Vern Ruhle | .10 |
| 6 Stikeout Leaders: | .40 | 19 Larry Gura | .10 | 35 Ed Figueroa | .10 | 50 Steve Garvey | 1.25 |
| Nolan Ryan, J.R. Richard | | 20 Joe Morgan | .40 | 36 Alan Ashby | .10 | 51 Ray Fosse | .10 |
| 7 ERA Leaders: | .25 | 21 Kevin Kobel | .10 | 37 Joe Kerrigan | .10 | 52 Randy Lerch | .10 |
| Ron Guidry, Craig Swan | | 22 Mike Jorgensen | .10 | 38 Bernie Carbo | .10 | 53 Mick Kelleher | .10 |
| 8 Leading Firemen: | .35 | 23 Terry Forster | .15 | 39 Dale Murphy | 8.00 | 54 Del Alston | .10 |
| R. Gossage, R. Fingers | | 24 Paul Molitor | 3.00 | 40 Dennis Eckersley | .25 | 55 Wllie Stargell | 2.00 |

| NO. PLAYER | MINT |
|---|---|
| 56 John Hale | .10 |
| 57 Eric Rasmussen | .10 |
| 58 Bob Randall | .10 |
| 59 John Denny | .10 |
| 60 Mickey Rivers | .15 |
| 61 Bo Diaz | .25 |
| 62 Randy Moffitt | .10 |
| 63 Jack Brohamer | .10 |
| 64 Tom Underwood | .10 |
| 65 Mark Belanger | .10 |
| 66 Tigers/L. Moss (Mgr.) | .50 |
| 67 Jim Mason | .10 |
| 68 Joe Niekro | .10 |
| 69 Elliott Maddox | .10 |
| 70 John Candelaria | .15 |
| 71 Brian Downing | .15 |
| 72 Steve Mingori | .10 |
| 73 Ken Henderson | .10 |
| 74 Shane Rawley (R) | 1.00 |
| 75 Steve Yeager | .10 |
| 76 Warren Cromartie | .10 |
| 77 Dan Briggs | .10 |
| 78 Elias Sosa | .10 |
| 79 Ted Cox | .10 |
| 80 Jason Thompson | .15 |
| 81 Roger Erickson | .10 |
| 82 Mets/J. Torre (Mgr.) | .40 |
| 83 Fred Kendall | .10 |
| 84 Greg Minton | .10 |
| 85 Gary Matthews | .20 |
| 86 Rodney Scott | .10 |
| 87 Pete Falcone | .10 |
| 88 Bob Molinaro | .10 |
| 89 Dick Tidrow | .10 |
| 90 Bob Boone | .10 |
| 91 Terry Crowley | .10 |
| 92 Jim Bibby | .10 |
| 93 Phil Mankowski | .10 |
| 94 Len Barker | .15 |
| 95 Robin Yount | 2.00 |
| 96 Cleveland Indians/ | .25 |
| Jeff Torborg (Mgr.) | |
| 97 Sam Mejias | .10 |
| 98 Ray Burris | .10 |
| 99 John Wathan | .10 |
| 100 Tom Seaver | 1.00 |
| 101 Roy Howell | .10 |
| 102 Mike Anderson | .10 |
| 103 Jim Todd | .10 |
| 104 Johnny Oates | .10 |
| 105 Rick Camp | .10 |
| 106 Frank Duffy | .10 |
| 107 Jesus Alou | .10 |
| 108 Eduardo Rodriguez | .10 |
| 109 Joel Youngblood | .10 |
| 110 Vida Blue | .15 |
| 111 Roger Freed | .10 |
| 112 Philadelphia Phillies/ | .35 |
| Danny Ozark (Mgr.) | |
| 113 Pete Redfern | .10 |
| 114 Cliff Johnson | .10 |
| 115 Nolan Ryan | 2.00 |
| 116 Ozzie Smith (R) | 16.00 |
| 117 Grant Jackson | .10 |
| 118 Bud Harrelson | .10 |
| 119 Don Stanhouse | .10 |
| 120 Jim Sundberg | .10 |
| 121 Checklist No. 1 | .20 |
| 122 Mike Paxton | .10 |
| 123 Lou Whitaker | 1.50 |
| 124 Dan Schatzeder | .10 |
| 125 Rick Burleson | .10 |
| 126 Doug Bair | .10 |
| 127 Thad Bosley | .10 |
| 128 Ted Martinez | .10 |
| 129 Marty Pattin | .10 |
| 130 Bob Watson | .10 |
| 131 Jim Clancy | .10 |
| 132 Rowland Office | .10 |
| 133 Bill Castro | .10 |
| 134 Alan Bannister | .10 |
| 135 Bobby Murcer | .25 |
| 136 Jim Kaat | .35 |
| 137 Larry Wolfe | .10 |
| 138 Mark Lee | .10 |

| NO. PLAYER | MINT |
|---|---|
| 139 Luis Pujols | .10 |
| 140 Don Gullett | .10 |
| 141 Tom Paciorek | .10 |
| 142 Charlie Williams | .10 |
| 143 Tony Scott | .10 |
| 144 Sandy Alomar | .10 |
| 145 Rick Rhoden | .20 |
| 146 Duane Kuiper | .10 |
| 147 Dave Hamilton | .10 |
| 148 Bruce Boisclair | .10 |
| 149 Manny Sarmiento | .10 |
| 150 Wayne Cage | .10 |
| 151 John Hiller | .10 |
| 152 Rick Cerone | .10 |
| 153 Dennis Lamp | .10 |
| 154 Jim Gantner | .10 |
| 155 Dwight Evans | .60 |
| 156 Buddy Solomon | .10 |
| 157 U.L. Washington | .10 |
| 158 Joe Sambito | .10 |
| 159 Roy White | .10 |
| 160 Mike Flanagan | .25 |
| 161 Barry Foote | .10 |
| 162 Tom Johnson | .10 |
| 163 Glenn Burke | .10 |
| 164 Mickey Lolich | .15 |
| 165 Frank Taveras | .10 |
| 166 Leon Roberts | .10 |
| 167 Roger Metzger | .10 |
| 168 Dave Freisleben | .10 |
| 169 Bill Nahorodny | .10 |
| 170 Don Sutton | 1.00 |
| 171 Gene Clines | .10 |
| 172 Mike Bruhert | .10 |
| 173 John Lowenstein | .10 |
| 174 Rick Auerbach | .10 |
| 175 George Hendrick | .15 |
| 176 Aurelio Rodriguez | .10 |
| 177 Ron Reed | .10 |
| 178 Alvis Woods | .10 |
| 179 Jim Beattie | .10 |
| 180 Larry Hisle | .10 |
| 181 Mike Garman | .10 |
| 182 Tim Johnson | .10 |
| 183 Paul Splittorff | .10 |
| 184 Darrel Chaney | .10 |
| 185 Mike Torrez | .10 |
| 186 Eric Soderholm | .10 |
| 187 Mark Lemongello | .10 |
| 188 Pat Kelly | .10 |
| 189 Eddie Whitson (R) | .40 |
| 190 Ron Cey | .40 |
| 191 Mike Norris | .10 |
| 192 St. Louis Cardinals/ | .35 |
| Ken Boyer (Mgr.) | |
| 193 Glenn Adams | .10 |
| 194 Randy Jones | .10 |
| 195 Bill Madlock | .40 |
| 196 Steve Kemp | .10 |
| 197 Bob Apodaca | .10 |
| 198 Johnny Grubb | .10 |
| 199 Larry Milbourne | .10 |
| 200 Johnny Bench | 1.00 |
| 201 Record — M. Edwards | .15 |
| Most Unassisted DP's | |
| by 2nd Baseman | |
| 202 Record — R. Guidry | .25 |
| Most Strikeouts, | |
| Lefthander, 9 Inning Game | |
| 203 Record — J.R. Richard | .25 |
| Most Season Stikeouts, | |
| Righthander | |
| 204 Record — P. Rose | 1.25 |
| Most Consecutive Games | |
| Batting Safely | |
| 205 Record — J. Stearns | .20 |
| Most Steals by Catcher, | |
| Season | |
| 206 Record — S. Stewart | .20 |
| 7 Straight Stikeouts, | |
| First Major League Game | |
| 207 Dave Lemanczyk | .10 |
| 208 Clarence Gaston | .10 |
| 209 Reggie Cleveland | .10 |
| 210 Larry Bowa | .20 |

| NO. PLAYER | MINT |
|---|---|
| 211 Denny Martinez | .10 |
| 212 Carney Lansford (R) | 2.00 |
| 213 Bill Travers | .10 |
| 214 Boston Red Sox/ | .45 |
| Don Zimmer (Mgr.) | |
| 215 Willie McCovey | 1.25 |
| 216 Wilbur Wood | .10 |
| 217 Steve Dillard | .10 |
| 218 Dennis Leonard | .15 |
| 219 Roy Smalley | .10 |
| 220 Cesar Geronimo | .10 |
| 221 Jesse Jefferson | .10 |
| 222 Bob Beall | .10 |
| 223 Kent Tekulve | .15 |
| 224 Dave Revering | .10 |
| 225 Rich Gossage | .50 |
| 226 Ron Pruitt | .10 |
| 227 Steve Stone | .10 |
| 228 Vic Davalillo | .10 |
| 229 Doug Flynn | .10 |
| 230 Bob Forsch | .10 |
| 231 Johnny Wockenfuss | .10 |
| 232 Jimmy Sexton | .10 |
| 233 Paul Mitchell | .10 |
| 234 Toby Harrah | .10 |
| 235 Steve Rogers | .15 |
| 236 Jim Dwyer | .10 |
| 237 Billy Smith | .10 |
| 238 Balor Moore | .10 |
| 239 Willie Horton | .10 |
| 240 Rick Reuschel | .20 |
| 241 Checklist No. 2 | .20 |
| 242 Pablo Torrealba | .10 |
| 243 Buck Martinez | .10 |
| 244 Pittsburgh Pirates/ | .35 |
| Chuck Tanner (Mgr.) | |
| 245 Jeff Burroughs | .10 |
| 246 Darrell Jackson | .10 |
| 247 Tucker Ashford | .10 |
| 248 Pete LaCock | .10 |
| 249 Paul Thormodsgard | .10 |
| 250 Willie Randolph | .25 |
| 251 Jack Morris | 2.50 |
| 252 Bob Stinson | .10 |
| 253 Rick Wise | .10 |
| 254 Luis Gomez | .10 |
| 255 Tommy John | .40 |
| 256 Mike Sadek | .10 |
| 257 Adrian Devine | .10 |
| 258 Mike Phillips | .10 |
| 259 Cincinnati Reds/ | .40 |
| Sparky Anderson (Mgr.) | |
| 260 Richie Zisk | .10 |
| 261 Mario Guerrero | .10 |
| 262 Nelson Briles | .10 |
| 263 Oscar Gamble | .10 |
| 264 Don Robinson (R) | .50 |
| 265 Don Money | .10 |
| 266 Jim Willoughby | .10 |
| 267 Joe Rudi | .10 |
| 268 Julio Gonzalez | .10 |
| 269 Woodie Fryman | .10 |
| 270 Butch Hobson | .10 |
| 271 Rawly Eastwick | .10 |
| 272 Tim Corcoran | .10 |
| 273 Jerry Terrell | .10 |
| 274 Willie Norwood | .10 |
| 275 Junior Moore | .10 |
| 276 Jim Colborn | .10 |
| 277 Tom Grieve | .10 |
| 278 Andy Messersmith | .20 |
| 279 Jerry Grote | .10 |
| 280 Andre Thornton | .15 |
| 281 Vic Correll | .10 |
| 282 Toronto Blue Jays/ | .20 |
| Roy Hartsfield (Mgr.) | |
| 283 Ken Kravec | .10 |
| 284 Johnnie LeMaster | .10 |
| 285 Bobby Bonds | .20 |
| 286 Duffy Dyer | .10 |
| 287 Andres Mora | .10 |
| 288 Milt Wilcox | .10 |
| 289 Jose Cruz | .25 |
| 290 Dave Lopes | .20 |
| 291 Tom Griffin | .10 |

| NO. PLAYER | MINT |
|---|---|
| 292 Don Reynolds | .10 |
| 293 Jerry Garvin | .10 |
| 294 Pepe Frias | .10 |
| 295 Mitchell Page | .10 |
| 296 Preston Hanna | .10 |
| 297 Ted Sizemore | .10 |
| 298 Rich Gale | .10 |
| 299 Steve Ontiveros | .10 |
| 300 Rod Carew | 2.00 |
| 301 Tom Hume | .10 |
| 302 Atlanta Braves/ | .35 |
| Bobby Cox (Mgr.) | |
| 303 Lary Sorensen | .10 |
| 304 Steve Swisher | .10 |
| 305 Willie Montanez | .10 |
| 306 Floyd Bannister | .15 |
| 307 Larvell Blanks | .10 |
| 308 Bert Blyleven | .30 |
| 309 Ralph Garr | .10 |
| 310 Thurman Munson | 1.50 |
| 311 Gary Lavelle | .10 |
| 312 Bob Robertson | .10 |
| 313 Dyar Miller | .10 |
| 314 Larry Harlow | .10 |
| 315 John Matlack | .10 |
| 316 Milt May | .10 |
| 317 Jose Cardenal | .10 |
| 318 Bob Welch (R) | 2.00 |
| 319 Wayne Garrett | .10 |
| 320 Carl Yastrzemski | 2.00 |
| 321 Gaylord Perry | 1.00 |
| 322 Danny Goodwin | .10 |
| 323 Lynn McGlothen | .10 |
| 324 Mike Tyson | .10 |
| 325 Cecil Cooper | .60 |
| 326 Pedro Borbon | .10 |
| 327 Art Howe | .10 |
| 328 Oakland A's/ | .20 |
| Jack McKeon (Mgr.) | |
| 329 Joe Coleman | .10 |
| 330 George Brett | 2.50 |
| 331 Mickey Mahler | .10 |
| 332 Gary Alexander | .10 |
| 333 Chet Lemon | .35 |
| 334 Craig Swan | .10 |
| 335 Chris Chambliss | .15 |
| 336 Bobby Thompson | .10 |
| 337 John Montague | .10 |
| 338 Vic Harris | .10 |
| 339 Ron Jackson | .10 |
| 340 Jim Palmer | 1.00 |
| 341 Willie Upshaw (R) | 1.00 |
| 342 Dave Roberts | .10 |
| 343 Ed Glynn | .10 |
| 344 Jerry Royster | .10 |
| 345 Tug McGraw | .20 |
| 346 Bill Buckner | .20 |
| 347 Doug Rau | .10 |
| 348 Andre Dawson | 4.00 |
| 349 Jim Wright | .10 |
| 350 Garry Templeton | .30 |
| 351 Wayne Nordhagen | .10 |
| 352 Steve Renko | .10 |
| 353 Checklist No. 3 | .20 |
| 354 Bill Bonham | .10 |
| 355 Lee Mazzilli | .15 |
| 356 San Francisco Giants/ | .40 |
| Joe Altobelli (Mgr.) | |
| 357 Jerry Augustine | .10 |
| 358 Alan Trammell | 4.50 |
| 359 Dan Spillner | .10 |
| 360 Amos Otis | .15 |
| 361 Tom Dixon | .10 |
| 362 Mike Cubbage | .10 |
| 363 Craig Skok | .10 |
| 364 Gene Richards | .10 |
| 365 Sparky Lyle | .15 |
| 366 Juan Bernhardt | .10 |
| 367 Dave Skaggs | .10 |
| 368 Don Aase | .10 |
| 369 Bump Wills (error) | 3.00 |
| (Blue Jays) | |
| 369 Bump Wills (correct) | 4.00 |
| (Rangers) | |
| 370 Dave Kingman | .40 |

| NO. PLAYER | MINT | NO. PLAYER | MINT | NO. PLAYER | MINT | NO. PLAYER | MINT |
|---|---|---|---|---|---|---|---|
| 371 Jeff Holly | .10 | 437 Rick Williams | .10 | 519 Ben Oglivie | .15 | 601 Dave LaRoche | .10 |
| 372 Lamar Johnson | .10 | 438 Horace Speed | .10 | 520 Gary Carter | 2.50 | 602 Checklist No. 5 | .20 |
| 373 Lance Rautzhan | .10 | 439 Frank White | .15 | 521 Sam Ewing | .10 | 603 Rudy May | .10 |
| 374 Ed Herrmann | .10 | 440 Rusty Staub | .20 | 522 Ken Holtzman | .10 | 604 Jeff Newman | .10 |
| 375 Bill Campbell | .10 | 441 Lee Lacy | .15 | 523 John Milner | .10 | 605 Rick Monday | .10 |
| 376 Gorman Thomas | .35 | 442 Doyle Alexander | .10 | 524 Tom Burgmeier | .10 | 606 Montreal Expos/ | .25 |
| 377 Paul Moskau | .10 | 443 Bruce Bochte | .10 | 525 Freddie Patek | .10 | Dick Williams (Mgr.) | |
| 378 Rob Picciolo | .10 | 444 Aurelio Lopez (R) | .35 | 526 Los Angeles Dodgers/ | .50 | 607 Omar Moreno | .10 |
| 379 Dale Murray | .10 | 445 Steve Henderson | .10 | Tom Lasorda (Mgr.) | | 608 Dave McKay | .10 |
| 380 John Mayberry | .15 | 446 Jim Lonborg | .10 | 527 Lerrin LaGrow | .10 | 609 Silvio Martinez | .10 |
| 381 Houston Astros/ | .25 | 447 Manny Sanguillen | .10 | 528 Wayne Gross | .10 | 610 Mike Schmidt | 4.50 |
| Bill Virdon (Mgr.) | | 448 Moose Haas | .10 | 529 Brian Asselstine | .10 | 611 Jim Norris | .10 |
| 382 Jerry Martin | .10 | 449 Bombo Rivera | .10 | 530 Frank Tanana | .15 | 612 Rick Honeycutt (R) | .60 |
| 383 Phil Garner | .10 | 450 Dave Concepcion | .25 | 531 Fernando Gonazalez | .10 | 613 Mike Edwards | .10 |
| 384 Tommy Boggs | .10 | 451 Kansas City Royals/ | .25 | 532 Buddy Schultz | .10 | 614 Willie Hernandez | .50 |
| 385 Dan Ford | .10 | Whitey Herzog (Mgr.) | | 533 Leroy Stanton | .10 | 615 Ken Singleton | .15 |
| 386 Francisco Barrios | .10 | 452 Jerry Morales | .10 | 534 Ken Forsch | .10 | 616 Billy Almon | .10 |
| 387 Gary Thomasson | .10 | 453 Chris Knapp | .10 | 535 Ellis Valentine | .10 | 617 Terry Puhl | .10 |
| 388 Jack Billingham | .10 | 454 Len Randle | .10 | 536 Jerry Reuss | .15 | 618 Jerry Remy | .10 |
| 389 Joe Zdeb | .10 | 455 Bill Lee | .10 | 537 Tom Veryzer | .10 | 619 Ken Landreaux | .30 |
| 390 Rollie Fingers | .35 | 456 Chuck Baker | .10 | 538 Mike Ivie | .10 | 620 Bert Campaneris | .15 |
| 391 Al Oliver | .35 | 457 Bruce Sutter | .75 | 539 John Ellis | .10 | 621 Pat Zachry | .10 |
| 392 Doug Ault | .10 | 458 Jim Essian | .10 | 540 Greg Luzinski | .25 | 622 Dave Collins | .15 |
| 393 Scott McGregor | .15 | 459 Sid Monge | .10 | 541 Jim Slaton | .10 | 623 Bob McClure | .10 |
| 394 Randy Stein | .10 | 460 Graig Nettles | .30 | 542 Rick Bosetti | .10 | 624 Larry Herndon | .10 |
| 395 Dave Cash | .10 | 461 Jim Barr | .10 | 543 Kiko Garcia | .10 | 625 Mark Fidrych | .15 |
| 396 Bill Plummer | .10 | 462 Otto Velez | .10 | 544 Fergie Jenkins | .25 | 626 New York Yankees/ | .40 |
| 397 Sergio Ferrer | .10 | 463 Steve Comer | .10 | 545 John Stearns | .10 | Bob Lemon (Mgr.) | |
| 398 Ivan DeJesus | .10 | 464 Joe Nolan | .10 | 546 Bill Russell | .10 | 627 Gary Serum | .10 |
| 399 David Clyde | .10 | 465 Reggie Smith | .20 | 547 Clint Hurdle | .10 | 628 Del Unser | .10 |
| 400 Jim Rice | 2.50 | 466 Mark Littell | .10 | 548 Enrique Romo | .10 | 629 Gene Garber | .10 |
| 401 Ray Knight | .15 | 467 Don Kessinger | .10 | 549 Bob Bailey | .10 | 630 Bake McBride | .10 |
| 402 Paul Hartzell | .10 | 468 Stan Bahnsen | .10 | 550 Sal Bando | .10 | 631 Jorge Orta | .10 |
| 403 Tim Foli | .10 | 469 Lance Parrish | 4.00 | 551 Chicago Cubs/ | .35 | 632 Don Kirkwood | .10 |
| 404 Chicago White Sox/ | .25 | 470 Garry Maddox | .10 | Herman Franks (Mgr.) | | 633 Rob Wilfong | .10 |
| Don Kessinger (Mgr.) | | 471 Joaquin Andujar | .35 | 552 Jose Morales | .10 | 634 Paul Lindblad | .10 |
| 405 Butch Wynegar | .10 | 472 Craig Kusick | .10 | 553 Denny Walling | .10 | 635 Don Baylor | .75 |
| 406 Joe Wallis | .10 | 473 Dave Roberts | .10 | 554 Matt Keough | .10 | 636 Wayne Garland | .10 |
| 407 Pete Vuckovich | .10 | 474 Dick Davis | .10 | 555 Biff Pocoroba | .10 | 637 Bill Robinson | .10 |
| 408 Charlie Moore | .10 | 475 Dan Driessen | .10 | 556 Mike Lum | .10 | 638 Al Fitzmorris | .10 |
| 409 Willie Wilson (R) | 1.75 | 476 Tom Poquette | .10 | 557 Ken Brett | .10 | 639 Manny Trillo | .10 |
| 410 Darrell Evans | .30 | 477 Bob Grich | .15 | 558 Jay Johnstone | .10 | 640 Eddie Murray | 4.00 |
| 411 All-Time Hits: | .50 | 478 Juan Beniquez | .10 | 559 Greg Pryor | .10 | 641 Bobby Castillo | .10 |
| Season — George Sisler, | | 479 San Diego Padres/ | .25 | 560 John Montefusco | .10 | 642 Wilbur Howard | .10 |
| Career — Ty Cobb | | Roger Craig (Mgr.) | | 561 Ed Ott | .10 | 643 Tom Hausman | .10 |
| 412 All-Time RBI's: | .50 | 480 Fred Lynn | .75 | 562 Dusty Baker | .20 | 644 Manny Mota | .10 |
| Season — Hack Wilson | | 481 Skip Lockwood | .10 | 563 Roy Thomas | .10 | 645 George Scott | .10 |
| Career — Hank Aaron | | 482 Craig Reynolds | .10 | 564 Jerry Turner | .10 | 646 Rick Sweet | .10 |
| 413 All-Time Home Runs: | .50 | 483 Checklist No. 4 | .20 | 565 Rico Carty | .10 | 647 Bob Lacey | .10 |
| Season — Roger Maris | | 484 Rick Waits | .10 | 566 Nino Espinosa | .10 | 648 Lou Piniella | .30 |
| Career — Hank Aaron | | 485 Bucky Dent | .15 | 567 Rich Hebner | .10 | 649 John Curtis | .10 |
| 414 All-Time Batting Avg.: | .50 | 486 Bob Knepper | .25 | 568 Carlos Lopez | .10 | 650 Pete Rose | 4.00 |
| Career — Ty Cobb | | 487 Miguel Dilone | .10 | 569 Bob Sykes | .10 | 651 Mike Caldwell | .10 |
| Season — R. Hornsby | | 488 Bob Owchinko | .10 | 570 Cesar Cedeno | .20 | 652 Stan Papi | .10 |
| 415 All-Time Stolen Bases: | .50 | 489 Larry Cox | .10 | 571 Darrell Porter | .15 | 653 Warren Brusstar | .10 |
| Career — Lou Brock | | (photo of Dave Rader) | | 572 Rod Gilbreath | .10 | 654 Rick Miller | .10 |
| Season — Lou Brock | | 490 Al Cowens | .10 | 573 Jim Kern | .10 | 655 Jerry Koosman | .20 |
| 416 All-Time Wins: | .25 | 491 Tippy Martinez | .10 | 574 Claudell Washington | .15 | 656 Hosken Powell | .10 |
| Career: Cy Young | | 492 Bob Bailor | .10 | 575 Luis Tiant | .20 | 657 George Medich | .10 |
| Season: J. Chesbro | | 493 Larry Christenson | .10 | 576 Mike Parrott | .10 | 658 Taylor Duncan | .10 |
| 417 All-Time Strikeouts: | .25 | 494 Jerry White | .10 | 577 Milwaukee Brewers/ | .30 | 659 Seattle Mariners/ | .20 |
| Career: Walter Johnson | | 495 Tony Perez | .50 | George Bamberger (Mgr.) | | Darrell Johnson (Mgr.) | |
| Season: Nolan Ryan | | 496 Barry Bonnell | .10 | 578 Pete Broberg | .10 | 660 Ron LeFlore | .10 |
| 418 All-Time ERA: | .25 | 497 Glenn Abbott | .10 | 579 Greg Gross | .10 | 661 Bruce Kison | .10 |
| Career: W. Johnson | | 498 Rich Chiles | .10 | 580 Ron Fairly | .10 | 662 Kevin Bell | .10 |
| Season: Dutch Leonard | | 499 Texas Rangers/ | .25 | 581 Darold Knowles | .10 | 663 Mike Vail | .10 |
| 419 Dick Ruthven | .10 | Pat Corrales (Mgr.) | | 582 Paul Blair | .10 | 664 Doug Bird | .10 |
| 420 Ken Griffey | .15 | 500 Ron Guidry | .75 | 583 Julio Cruz | .10 | 665 Lou Brock | 1.25 |
| 421 Doug DeCinces | .20 | 501 Junior Kennedy | .10 | 584 Jim Rooker | .10 | 666 Rich Dauer | .10 |
| 422 Ruppert Jones | .15 | 502 Steve Braun | .10 | 585 Hal McRae | .15 | 667 Don Hood | .10 |
| 423 Bob Montgomery | .10 | 503 Terry Humphrey | .10 | 586 Bob Horner (R) | 3.00 | 668 Bill North | .10 |
| 424 California Angels/ | .30 | 504 Larry McWilliams (R) | .40 | 587 Ken Reitz | .10 | 669 Checklist No. 6 | .20 |
| Jim Fregosi (Mgr.) | | 505 Ed Kranepool | .10 | 588 Tom Murphy | .10 | 670 Jim Hunter | .50 |
| 425 Rick Manning | .10 | 506 John D'Acquisto | .10 | 589 Terry Whitfield | .10 | 671 Joe Ferguson | .10 |
| 426 Chris Speier | .10 | 507 Tony Armas | .35 | 590 J.R. Richard | .15 | 672 Ed Halicki | .10 |
| 427 Andy Replogle | .10 | 508 Charlie Hough | .10 | 591 Mike Hargrove | .10 | 673 Tom Hutton | .10 |
| 428 Bobby Valentine | .10 | 509 Mario Mendoza | .10 | 592 Mike Krukow | .10 | 674 Dave Tomlin | .10 |
| 429 John Urrea | .10 | 510 Ted Simmons | .35 | 593 Rick Dempsey | .10 | 675 Tim McCarver | .25 |
| 430 Dave Parker | 1.00 | 511 Paul Reuschel | .10 | 594 Bob Shirley | .10 | 676 Johnny Sutton | .10 |
| 431 Glenn Borgmann | .10 | 512 Jack Clark | 2.00 | 595 Phil Niekro | .75 | 677 Larry Parrish | .10 |
| 432 Dave Heaverlo | .10 | 513 Dave Johnson | .25 | 596 Jim Wohlford | .10 | 678 Geoff Zahn | .10 |
| 433 Larry Biittner | .10 | 514 Mike Proly | .10 | 597 Bob Stanley | .15 | 679 Derrel Thomas | .10 |
| 434 Ken Clay | .10 | 515 Enos Cabell | .10 | 598 Mark Wagner | .10 | 680 Carlton Fisk | .50 |
| 435 Gene Tenace | .10 | 516 Champ Summers | .10 | 599 Jim Spencer | .10 | 681 John Johnson | .10 |
| 436 Hector Cruz | .10 | 517 Al Bumbry | .10 | 600 George Foster | .50 | 682 Dave Chalk | .10 |
| | | 518 Jim Umbarger | .10 | | | | |

| NO. | PLAYER | MINT |
|---|---|---|
| 683 | Dan Meyer | .10 |
| 684 | Jamie Easterly | .10 |
| 685 | Sixto Lezcano | .10 |
| 686 | Ron Schueler | .10 |
| 687 | Rennie Stennett | .10 |
| 688 | Mike Willis | .10 |
| 689 | Baltimore Orioles/ | .35 |
| | Earl Weaver (Mgr.) | |
| 690 | Buddy Bell | .10 |
| 691 | Dock Ellis | .10 |
| 692 | Mickey Stanley | .10 |
| 693 | Dave Rader | .10 |
| 694 | Burt Hooton | .10 |
| 695 | Keith Hernandez | 2.00 |
| 696 | Andy Hassler | .10 |
| 697 | Dave Bergman | .10 |
| 698 | Bill Stein | .10 |
| 699 | Hal Dues | .10 |
| 700 | Reggie Jackson | 1.25 |
| 701 | Orioles Prospects: | .35 |
| | Mark Corey, John Flinn, | |
| | Sammy Stewart | |
| 702 | Red Sox Prospects: | .20 |
| | Garry Hancock, Joel Finch, | |
| | Allen Ripley | |
| 703 | Angels Prospects: | .15 |
| | Bob Slater, J. Anderson, | |
| | Dave Frost | |
| 704 | White Sox Prospects: | .15 |
| | Ross Baumgarten, Mike | |
| | Colbern, Mike Squires | |
| 705 | Indians Prospects: | .60 |
| | Tim Norrid, D. Oliver, | |
| | Alfredo Griffin | |
| 706 | Tigers Prospects: | .20 |
| | Dave Stegman, Dave Tobik, | |
| | Kip Young | |
| 707 | Royals Prospects: | .15 |
| | Randy Bass, Jim Gaudet, | |
| | R. McGilberry | |
| 708 | Brewers Prospects: | 2.00 |
| | Kevin Bass, Ned Yost, | |
| | Eddie Romero | |
| 709 | Twins Prospects: | .15 |
| | R. Sofield, Kevin Stanfield, | |
| | Sam Perlozzo | |
| 710 | Yankees Prospects: | .40 |
| | Mike Heath, D. Rajsich, | |
| | Brian Doyle | |
| 711 | A's Prospects: | .65 |
| | Dwayne Murphy, Bruce | |
| | Robinson, Alan Wirth | |
| 712 | Mariners Prospects: | .15 |
| | Greg Biercevicz, | |
| | B. McLaughlin, B. Anderson | |
| 713 | Rangers Prospects: | .40 |
| | Danny Darwin, Pat Putnam, | |
| | Billy Sample | |
| 714 | Blue Jays Prospects: | .15 |
| | Victor Cruz, Pat Kelly, | |
| | Ernie Whitt | |
| 715 | Braves Prospects: | .50 |
| | Larry Whisenton, Bruce | |
| | Benedict, Glenn Hubbard | |
| 716 | Cubs Prospects | .20 |
| | S. Thompson, Dave Geisel, | |
| | Karl Pagel | |
| 717 | Reds Prospects: | .50 |
| | M. LaCoss, Ron Oester, | |
| | Harry Spilman | |
| 718 | Astros Prospects: | .15 |
| | Mike Fischlin, Bruce Bochy, | |
| | Don Pisker | |
| 719 | Dodgers Prospects: | 6.00 |
| | Pedro Guerrero, Rudy Law, | |
| | Joe Simpson | |
| 720 | Expos Prospects: | .30 |
| | Jerry Fry, Jerry Pirtle, | |
| | Scott Sanderson | |
| 721 | Mets Prospects: | .25 |
| | Dwight Bernard, Juan | |
| | Berenguer, Dan Norman | |
| 722 | Phillies Prospects: | .60 |
| | Jim Morrison, Lonnie | |
| | Smith, Jim Wright | |
| 723 | Pirates Prospects: | .35 |
| | Eugenio Cotes, | |
| | B. Wiltbank, Dale Berra | |
| 724 | Cardinals Prospects: | .75 |
| | Tom Bruno, George | |
| | Frazier, Terry Kennedy | |
| 725 | Padres Prospects: | .15 |
| | Jim Beswick, Broderick | |
| | Perkins, Steve Mura | |
| 726 | Giants Prospects: | .20 |
| | J. Tamargo, Greg | |
| | Johnston, Joe Strain | |

## 1980 Topps....Complete Set of 726 Cards—Value $140.00

Features the rookie cards of Rickey Henderson, Dan Quisenberry, Mike Scott and Dave Stieb. 66 cards were double printed.

| NO. | PLAYER | MINT |
|---|---|---|
| 1 | Highlights: Brock and | 1.50 |
| | Yaz Get 3000 Hits (Exc. .30) | |
| 2 | Highlights: McCovey | .50 |
| | 512 Home Runs | |
| 3 | Highlights: Manny Mota | .15 |
| | 145 Pinch Hits | |
| 4 | Highlights: Pete Rose | 1.50 |
| | 10th 200 Hit Season | |
| 5 | Highlights: G. Templeton | .25 |
| | 100 Lefty and Righty Hits | |
| 6 | Highlights: Del Unser | .15 |
| | 3rd Consec. Pinch Homer | |
| 7 | Mike Lum | .08 |
| 8 | Craig Swan | .08 |
| 9 | Steve Braun | .08 |
| 10 | Denny Martinez | .12 |
| 11 | Jimmy Sexton | .08 |
| 12 | John Curtis | .08 |
| 13 | Ron Pruitt | .08 |
| 14 | Dave Cash | .08 |
| 15 | Bill Campbell | .08 |
| 16 | Jerry Narron | .08 |
| 17 | Bruce Sutter | .50 |
| 18 | Ron Jackson | .08 |
| 19 | Balor Moore | .08 |
| 20 | Dan Ford | .08 |
| 21 | Manny Sarmiento | .08 |
| 22 | Pat Putnam | .08 |
| 23 | Derrel Thomas | .08 |
| 24 | Jim Slaton | .08 |
| 25 | Lee Mazzilli | .12 |
| 26 | Marty Pattin | .08 |
| 27 | Del Unser | .08 |
| 28 | Bruce Kison | .08 |
| 29 | Mark Wagner | .08 |
| 30 | Vida Blue | .15 |
| 31 | Jay Johnstone | .08 |
| 32 | Julio Cruz | .08 |
| 33 | Tony Scott | .08 |
| 34 | Jeff Newman | .08 |
| 35 | Luis Tiant | .12 |
| 36 | Rusty Torres | .08 |
| 37 | Kiko Garcia | .08 |
| 38 | Dan Spillner | .08 |
| 39 | Rowland Office | .08 |
| 40 | Carlton Fisk | .40 |
| 41 | Texas Rangers/ | .30 |
| | Pat Corrales (Mgr.) | |
| 42 | Dave Palmer (R) | .40 |
| 43 | Bombo Rivera | .08 |
| 44 | Bill Fahey | .08 |
| 45 | Frank White | .15 |
| 46 | Rico Carty | .15 |
| 47 | Bill Bonham | .08 |
| 48 | Rick Miller | .08 |
| 49 | Mario Guerrero | .08 |
| 50 | J. Richard | .12 |
| 51 | Joe Ferguson | .08 |
| 52 | Warren Brusstar | .08 |
| 53 | Ben Oglivie | .12 |
| 54 | Dennis Lamp | .08 |
| 55 | Bill Madlock | .40 |
| 56 | Bobby Valentine | .12 |
| 57 | Pete Vuckovich | .12 |
| 58 | Doug Flynn | .08 |
| 59 | Eddy Putman | .08 |
| 60 | Bucky Dent | .12 |
| 61 | Gary Serum | .08 |
| 62 | Mike Ivie | .08 |
| 63 | Bob Stanley | .12 |
| 64 | Joe Nolan | .08 |
| 65 | Al Bumbry | .08 |
| 66 | Kansas City Royals/ | .35 |
| | Jim Frey (Mgr.) | |
| 67 | Doyle Alexander | .08 |
| 68 | Larry Harlow | .08 |
| 69 | Rick Williams | .08 |
| 70 | Gary Carter | 2.00 |
| 71 | John Milner | .08 |
| 72 | Fred Howard | .08 |
| 73 | Dave Collins | .08 |
| 74 | Sid Monge | .08 |
| 75 | Bill Russell | .08 |
| 76 | John Stearns | .08 |
| 77 | Dave Stieb (R) | 2.50 |
| 78 | Ruppert Jones | .08 |
| 79 | Bob Owchinko | .08 |
| 80 | Ron LeFlore | .12 |
| 81 | Ted Sizemore | .08 |
| 82 | Houston Astros/ | .35 |
| | Bill Virdon (Mgr.) | |
| 83 | Steve Trout (R) | .40 |
| 84 | Gary Lavelle | .08 |
| 85 | Ted Simmons | .30 |
| 86 | Dave Hamilton | .08 |
| 87 | Pepe Frias | .08 |
| 88 | Ken Landreaux | .12 |
| 89 | Don Hood | .08 |
| 90 | Manny Trillo | .08 |
| 91 | Rick Dempsey | .08 |
| 92 | Rick Rhoden | .12 |
| 93 | Dave Roberts | .08 |
| 94 | Neil Allen (R) | .40 |
| 95 | Cecil Cooper | .40 |
| 96 | Oakland A's/ | .35 |
| | Jim Marshall (Mgr.) | |
| 97 | Bill Lee | .15 |
| 98 | Jerry Terrell | .08 |
| 99 | Victor Cruz | .08 |
| 100 | Johnny Bench | 2.00 |
| 101 | Aurelio Lopez | .08 |
| 102 | Rich Dauer | .08 |
| 103 | Bill Caudill (R) | .40 |
| 104 | Manny Mota | .15 |
| 105 | Frank Tanana | .15 |
| 106 | Jeff Leonard (R) | 1.50 |
| 107 | Francisco Barrios | .08 |
| 108 | Bob Horner | .80 |
| 109 | Bill Travers | .08 |
| 110 | Fred Lynn | .35 |
| 111 | Bob Knepper | .20 |
| 112 | Chicago White Sox/ | .35 |
| | Tony LaRussa (Mgr.) | |
| 113 | Geoff Zahn | .08 |
| 114 | Juan Beniquez | .12 |
| 115 | Sparky Lyle | .15 |
| 116 | Larry Cox | .08 |
| 117 | Dock Ellis | .08 |
| 118 | Phil Garner | .08 |
| 119 | Sammy Stewart | .08 |
| 120 | Greg Luzinski | .25 |
| 121 | Checklist No. 1 | .25 |
| 122 | Dave Rosello | .08 |
| 123 | Lynn Jones | .08 |
| 124 | Dave Lemanczyk | .08 |
| 125 | Tony Perez | .40 |
| 126 | Dave Tomlin | .08 |
| 127 | Gary Thomasson | .08 |
| 128 | Tom Burgmeier | .08 |

| NO. | PLAYER | MINT |
|---|---|---|
| 129 | Craig Reynolds | .08 |
| 130 | Amos Otis | .15 |
| 131 | Paul Mitchell | .08 |
| 132 | Biff Pocoroba | .08 |
| 133 | Jerry Turner | .08 |
| 134 | Matt Keough | .08 |
| 135 | Bill Buckner | .20 |
| 136 | Dick Ruthven | .08 |
| 137 | John Castino | .20 |
| 138 | Ross Baumgarten | .08 |
| 139 | Dane Iorg | .20 |
| 140 | Rich Gossage | .50 |
| 141 | Gary Alexander | .08 |
| 142 | Phil Huffman | .08 |
| 143 | Bruce Bochte | .08 |
| 144 | Steve Comer | .08 |
| 145 | Darrell Evans | .30 |
| 146 | Bob Welch | .30 |
| 147 | Terry Puhl | .08 |
| 148 | Manny Sanguillen | .15 |
| 149 | Tom Hume | .08 |
| 150 | Jason Thompson | .15 |
| 151 | Tom Hausman | .12 |
| 152 | John Fulgham | .08 |
| 153 | Tim Blackwell | .08 |
| 154 | Lary Sorensen | .08 |
| 155 | Jerry Remy | .08 |
| 156 | Tony Brizzolara | .08 |
| 157 | Willie Wilson | .25 |
| 158 | Rob Picciolo | .08 |
| 159 | Ken Clay | .08 |
| 160 | Eddie Murray | 2.50 |
| 161 | Larry Christenson | .08 |
| 162 | Bob Randall | .08 |
| 163 | Steve Swisher | .08 |
| 164 | Greg Pryor | .08 |
| 165 | Omar Moreno | .08 |
| 166 | Glenn Abbott | .08 |
| 167 | Jack Clark | 1.50 |
| 168 | Rick Waits | .08 |
| 169 | Luis Gomez | .08 |
| 170 | Burt Hooton | .08 |
| 171 | Fernando Gonzalez | .08 |
| 172 | Ron Hodges | .08 |
| 173 | John Henry Johnson | .08 |
| 174 | Ray Knight | .20 |
| 175 | Rick Reuschel | .12 |
| 176 | Champ Summers | .08 |
| 177 | Dave Heaverlo | .08 |
| 178 | Tim McCarver | .20 |
| 179 | Ron Davis (R) | .25 |
| 180 | Warren Cromartie | .08 |
| 181 | Moose Haas | .08 |
| 182 | Ken Reitz | .08 |
| 183 | Jim Anderson | .08 |
| 184 | Steve Renko | .08 |
| 185 | Hal McRae | .12 |
| 186 | Junior Moore | .08 |
| 187 | Alan Ashby | .08 |
| 188 | Terry Crowley | .08 |
| 189 | Kevin Kobel | .08 |
| 190 | Buddy Bell | .20 |
| 191 | Ted Martinez | .08 |
| 192 | Atlanta Braves/<br>Bobby Cox (Mgr.) | .35 |
| 193 | Dave Goltz | .08 |
| 194 | Mike Easler | .25 |
| 195 | John Montefusco | .15 |
| 196 | Lance Parrish | 1.00 |
| 197 | Byron McLaughlin | .08 |
| 198 | Dell Alston | .08 |
| 199 | Mike LaCoss | .15 |
| 200 | Jim Rice | 1.50 |
| 201 | Batting Leaders:<br>K. Hernandez, Fred Lynn | .30 |
| 202 | Home Run Leaders:<br>Dave Kingman, G. Thomas | .30 |
| 203 | RBI Leaders:<br>Don Baylor, Dave Winfield | .30 |
| 204 | Stolen Base Leaders:<br>Omar Moreno, Willie Wilson | .15 |
| 205 | Victory Leaders:<br>Phil Niekro, Joe Niekro,<br>Mike Flanagan | .25 |

| NO. | PLAYER | MINT |
|---|---|---|
| 206 | Strikeout Leaders:<br>J.R. Richard, Nolan Ryan | .25 |
| 207 | ERA Leaders:<br>J.R. Richard, Ron Guidry | .20 |
| 208 | Wayne Cage | .08 |
| 209 | Von Joshua | .08 |
| 210 | Steve Carlton | 1.50 |
| 211 | Dave Skaggs | .08 |
| 212 | Dave Roberts | .08 |
| 213 | Mike Jorgensen | .08 |
| 214 | California Angels/<br>Jim Fregosi (Mgr.) | .35 |
| 215 | Sixto Lezcano | .08 |
| 216 | Phil Mankowski | .08 |
| 217 | Ed Halicki | .08 |
| 218 | Jose Morales | .08 |
| 219 | Steve Mingori | .08 |
| 220 | Dave Concepcion | .25 |
| 221 | Joe Cannon | .08 |
| 222 | Ron Hassey | .08 |
| 223 | Bob Sykes | .08 |
| 224 | Willie Montanez | .08 |
| 225 | Lou Piniella | .25 |
| 226 | Bill Stein | .08 |
| 227 | Len Barker | .08 |
| 228 | Johnny Oates | .08 |
| 229 | Jim Bibby | .08 |
| 230 | Dave Winfield | 1.50 |
| 231 | Steve McCatty | .08 |
| 232 | Alan Trammell | 2.00 |
| 233 | LaRue Washington | .08 |
| 234 | Vern Ruhle | .08 |
| 235 | Andre Dawson | 2.00 |
| 236 | Marc Hill | .08 |
| 237 | Scott McGregor | .12 |
| 238 | Rob Wilfong | .08 |
| 239 | Don Aase | .08 |
| 240 | Dave Kingman | .35 |
| 241 | Checklist No. 2 | .25 |
| 242 | Lamar Johnson | .08 |
| 243 | Jerry Augustine | .08 |
| 244 | St. Louis Cardinals/<br>Ken Boyer (Mgr.) | .40 |
| 245 | Phil Niekro | .75 |
| 246 | Tim Foli | .08 |
| 247 | Frank Riccelli | .08 |
| 248 | Jamie Quirk | .08 |
| 249 | Jim Clancy | .08 |
| 250 | Jim Kaat | .40 |
| 251 | Kip Young | .08 |
| 252 | Ted Cox | .08 |
| 253 | John Montague | .08 |
| 254 | Paul Dade | .08 |
| 255 | Dusty Baker | .08 |
| 256 | Roger Erickson | .08 |
| 257 | Larry Herndon | .08 |
| 258 | Paul Moskau | .08 |
| 259 | New York Mets/<br>Joe Torre (Mgr.) | .50 |
| 260 | Al Oliver | .35 |
| 261 | Dave Chalk | .08 |
| 262 | Benny Ayala | .08 |
| 263 | Dave LaRoche | .08 |
| 264 | Bill Robinson | .08 |
| 265 | Robin Yount | 1.50 |
| 266 | Bernie Carbo | .08 |
| 267 | Dan Schatzeder | .08 |
| 268 | Rafael Landestoy | .08 |
| 269 | Dave Tobik | .08 |
| 270 | Mike Schmidt | 1.50 |
| 271 | Dick Drago | .08 |
| 272 | Ralph Garr | .08 |
| 273 | Eduardo Rodriguez | .08 |
| 274 | Dale Murphy | 5.00 |
| 275 | Jerry Koosman | .20 |
| 276 | Tom Veryzer | .08 |
| 277 | Rick Bosetti | .08 |
| 278 | Jim Spencer | .08 |
| 279 | Rob Andrews | .08 |
| 280 | Gaylord Perry | .75 |
| 281 | Paul Blair | .08 |
| 282 | Seattle Mariners/<br>Darrell Johnson (Mgr.) | .35 |
| 283 | John Ellis | .08 |

| NO. | PLAYER | MINT |
|---|---|---|
| 284 | Larry Murray | .08 |
| 285 | Don Baylor | .35 |
| 286 | Darold Knowles | .08 |
| 287 | John Lowenstein | .08 |
| 288 | Dave Rozema | .08 |
| 289 | Bruce Bochy | .08 |
| 290 | Steve Garvey | 1.50 |
| 291 | Randy Scarberry | .08 |
| 292 | Dale Berra | .08 |
| 293 | Elias Sosa | .08 |
| 294 | Charlie Spikes | .08 |
| 295 | Larry Gura | .08 |
| 296 | Dave Rader | .08 |
| 297 | Tim Johnson | .08 |
| 298 | Ken Holtzman | .08 |
| 299 | Steve Henderson | .08 |
| 300 | Ron Guidry | .60 |
| 301 | Mike Edwards | .08 |
| 302 | Los Angeles Dodgers/<br>Tom Lasorda (Mgr.) | .50 |
| 303 | Bill Castro | .08 |
| 304 | Butch Wynegar | .08 |
| 305 | Randy Jones | .08 |
| 306 | Denny Walling | .08 |
| 307 | Rick Honeycutt | .12 |
| 308 | Mike Hargrove | .08 |
| 309 | Larry McWilliams | .12 |
| 310 | Dave Parker | 1.00 |
| 311 | Roger Metzger | .08 |
| 312 | Mike Barlow | .08 |
| 313 | Johnny Grubb | .08 |
| 314 | Tim Stoddard | .20 |
| 315 | Steve Kemp | .15 |
| 316 | Bob Lacey | .08 |
| 317 | Mike Anderson | .08 |
| 318 | Jerry Reuss | .12 |
| 319 | Chris Speier | .08 |
| 320 | Dennis Eckersley | .35 |
| 321 | Keith Hernandez | 1.25 |
| 322 | Claudell Washington | .15 |
| 323 | Mick Kelleher | .08 |
| 324 | Tom Underwood | .08 |
| 325 | Dan Driessen | .08 |
| 326 | Bo McLaughlin | .08 |
| 327 | Ray Fosse | .08 |
| 328 | Minnesota Twins/<br>Gene Mauch (Mgr.) | .35 |
| 329 | Bert Roberge | .08 |
| 330 | Al Cowens | .08 |
| 331 | Rich Hebner | .08 |
| 332 | Enrique Romo | .08 |
| 333 | Jim Norris | .08 |
| 334 | Jim Beattie | .08 |
| 335 | Willie McCovey | 1.25 |
| 336 | George Medich | .08 |
| 337 | Carney Lansford | .35 |
| 338 | Johnny Wockenfuss | .08 |
| 339 | John D'Acquisto | .08 |
| 340 | Ken Singleton | .15 |
| 341 | Jim Essian | .08 |
| 342 | Odell Jones | .08 |
| 343 | Mike Vail | .08 |
| 344 | Randy Lerch | .08 |
| 345 | Larry Parrish | .12 |
| 346 | Buddy Solomon | .08 |
| 347 | Harry Chappas | .08 |
| 348 | Checklist No. 3 | .25 |
| 349 | Jack Brohamer | .08 |
| 350 | George Hendrick | .15 |
| 351 | Bob Davis | .08 |
| 352 | Dan Briggs | .08 |
| 353 | Andy Hassler | .08 |
| 354 | Rick Auerbach | .08 |
| 355 | Gary Matthews | .15 |
| 356 | San Diego Padres/<br>Jerry Coleman (Mgr.) | .35 |
| 357 | Bob McClure | .08 |
| 358 | Lou Whitaker | .75 |
| 359 | Randy Moffitt | .08 |
| 360 | Darrell Porter | .08 |
| 361 | Wayne Garland | .08 |
| 362 | Danny Goodwin | .08 |
| 363 | Wayne Gross | .08 |
| 364 | Ray Burris | .08 |

| NO. | PLAYER | MINT |
|---|---|---|
| 365 | Bobby Murcer | .20 |
| 366 | Rob Dressler | .08 |
| 367 | Billy Smith | .08 |
| 368 | Willie Aikens (R) | .25 |
| 369 | Jim Kern | .08 |
| 370 | Cesar Cedeno | .15 |
| 371 | Jack Morris | 1.25 |
| 372 | Joel Youngblood | .08 |
| 373 | Dan Petry (R) | .75 |
| 374 | Jim Gantner | .08 |
| 375 | Ross Grimsley | .08 |
| 376 | Gary Allenson | .15 |
| 377 | Junior Kennedy | .08 |
| 378 | Jerry Mumphrey | .08 |
| 379 | Kevin Bell | .08 |
| 380 | Garry Maddox | .09 |
| 381 | Chicago Cubs/<br>Preston Gomez (Mgr.) | .35 |
| 382 | Dave Freisleben | .08 |
| 383 | Ed Ott | .08 |
| 384 | Joey McLaughlin | .08 |
| 385 | Enos Cabell | .08 |
| 386 | Darrell Jackson | .08 |
| 387 | Fred Stanley | .08 |
| 388 | Mike Paxton | .08 |
| 389 | Pete LaCock | .08 |
| 390 | Fergie Jenkins | .25 |
| 391 | Tony Armas | .12 |
| 392 | Milt Wilcox | .08 |
| 393 | Ozzie Smith | 2.50 |
| 394 | Reggie Cleveland | .08 |
| 395 | Ellis Valentine | .08 |
| 396 | Dan Meyer | .08 |
| 397 | Roy Thomas | .08 |
| 398 | Barry Foote | .08 |
| 399 | Mike Proly | .08 |
| 400 | George Foster | .50 |
| 401 | Pete Falcone | .08 |
| 402 | Merv Rettenmund | .08 |
| 403 | Pete Redfern | .08 |
| 404 | Baltimore Orioles/<br>Earl Weaver (Mgr.) | .45 |
| 405 | Dwight Evans | .75 |
| 406 | Paul Molitor | 1.25 |
| 407 | Tony Solaita | .08 |
| 408 | Bill North | .08 |
| 409 | Paul Splittorff | .08 |
| 410 | Bobby Bonds | .12 |
| 411 | Frank LaCorte | .08 |
| 412 | Thad Bosley | .08 |
| 413 | Allen Ripley | .08 |
| 414 | George Scott | .12 |
| 415 | Bill Atkinson | .08 |
| 416 | Tom Brookens | .08 |
| 417 | Carig Chamberlain | .08 |
| 418 | Roger Freed | .08 |
| 419 | Vic Correll | .08 |
| 420 | Butch Hobson | .08 |
| 421 | Doug Bird | .08 |
| 422 | Larry Milbourne | .08 |
| 423 | Dave Frost | .08 |
| 424 | New York Yankees/<br>Dick Howser (Mgr.) | .60 |
| 425 | Mark Belanger | .15 |
| 426 | Grant Jackson | .08 |
| 427 | Tom Hutton | .08 |
| 428 | Pat Zachry | .08 |
| 429 | Duane Kuiper | .08 |
| 430 | Larry Hisle | .08 |
| 431 | Mike Krukow | .12 |
| 432 | Willie Norwood | .08 |
| 433 | Rich Gale | .08 |
| 434 | Johnnie LeMaster | .08 |
| 435 | Don Gullett | .08 |
| 436 | Billy Almon | .08 |
| 437 | Joe Niekro | .15 |
| 438 | Dave Revering | .08 |
| 439 | Mike Phillips | .08 |
| 440 | Don Sutton | .60 |
| 441 | Eric Soderholm | .08 |
| 442 | Jorge Orta | .08 |
| 443 | Mike Parrott | .08 |
| 444 | Alvis Woods | .08 |
| 445 | Mark Fidrych | .15 |

| NO. PLAYER | MINT |
|---|---|
| 446 Duffy Dyer | .08 |
| 447 Nino Espinosa | .08 |
| 448 Jim Wohlford | .08 |
| 449 Doug Bair | .08 |
| 450 George Brett | 3.50 |
| 451 Cleveland Indians/ Dave Garcia (Mgr.) | .35 |
| 452 Steve Dillard | .08 |
| 453 Mike Bacsik | .08 |
| 454 Tom Donohue | .08 |
| 455 Mike Torrez | .08 |
| 456 Frank Taveras | .08 |
| 457 Bert Blyleven | .30 |
| 458 Billy Sample | .08 |
| 459 Mickey Lolich | .08 |
| 460 Willie Randolph | .20 |
| 461 Dwayne Murphy | .15 |
| 462 Mike Sadek | .08 |
| 463 Jerry Royster | .08 |
| 464 John Denny | .15 |
| 465 Rick Monday | .15 |
| 466 Mike Squires | .08 |
| 467 Jesse Jefferson | .08 |
| 468 Aurelio Rodriquez | .08 |
| 469 Randy Niemann | .08 |
| 470 Bob Boone | .12 |
| 471 Hosken Powell | .08 |
| 472 Willie Hernandez | .25 |
| 473 Bump Wills | .08 |
| 474 Steve Busby | .08 |
| 475 Cesar Geronimo | .08 |
| 476 Bob Shirley | .08 |
| 477 Buck Martinez | .08 |
| 478 Gil Flores | .08 |
| 479 Montreal Expos/ Dick Williams (Mgr.) | .35 |
| 480 Bob Watson | .08 |
| 481 Tom Paciorek | .08 |
| 482 R. Henderson (R) | 30.00 |
| 483 Bo Diaz | .08 |
| 484 Checklist No. 4 | .25 |
| 485 Mickey Rivers | .15 |
| 486 Mike Tyson | .08 |
| 487 Wayne Nordhagen | .08 |
| 488 Roy Howell | .08 |
| 489 Preston Hanna | .08 |
| 490 Lee May | .15 |
| 491 Steve Mura | .08 |
| 492 Todd Cruz | .08 |
| 493 Jerry Martin | .08 |
| 494 Craig Minetto | .08 |
| 495 Bake McBride | .08 |
| 496 Silvio Martinez | .08 |
| 497 Jim Mason | .08 |
| 498 Danny Darwin | .08 |
| 499 San Francisco Giants/ Dave Bristol (Mgr.) | .35 |
| 500 Tom Seaver | 1.50 |
| 501 Rennie Stennett | .08 |
| 502 Rich Wortham | .08 |
| 503 Mike Cubbage | .08 |
| 504 Gene Garber | .08 |
| 505 Bert Campaneris | .15 |
| 506 Tom Buskey | .08 |
| 507 Leon Roberts | .08 |
| 508 U.L. Washington | .08 |
| 509 Ed Glynn | .08 |
| 510 Ron Cey | .40 |
| 511 Eric Wilkins | .08 |
| 512 Jose Cardenal | .08 |
| 513 Tom Dixon | .08 |
| 514 Steve Ontiveros | .08 |
| 515 Mike Caldwell | .08 |
| 516 Hector Cruz | .08 |
| 517 Don Stanhouse | .08 |
| 518 Nelson Norman | .08 |
| 519 Steve Nicosia | .08 |
| 520 Steve Rogers | .15 |
| 521 Ken Brett | .08 |
| 522 Jim Morrison | .08 |
| 523 Ken Henderson | .08 |
| 524 Jim Wright | .08 |
| 525 Clint Hurdle | .08 |
| 526 Philadelphia Phillies/ Dallas Green (Mgr.) | .35 |
| 527 Doug Rau | .08 |

| NO. PLAYER | MINT |
|---|---|
| 528 Adrian Devine | .08 |
| 529 Jim Barr | .08 |
| 530 Jim Sundberg | .08 |
| 531 Eric Rasmussen | .08 |
| 532 Willie Horton | .12 |
| 533 Checklist No. 5 | .25 |
| 534 Andre Thornton | .15 |
| 535 Bob Forsch | .12 |
| 536 Lee Lacy | .12 |
| 537 Alex Trevino | .12 |
| 538 Joe Strain | .08 |
| 539 Rudy May | .08 |
| 540 Pete Rose | 3.00 |
| 541 Miguel Dilone | .08 |
| 542 Joe Coleman | .08 |
| 543 Pat Kelly | .08 |
| 544 Rick Sutcliffe (R) | 3.50 |
| 545 Jeff Burroughs | .08 |
| 546 Rick Langford | .08 |
| 547 John Wathan | .08 |
| 548 Dave Rajsich | .08 |
| 549 Larry Wolfe | .08 |
| 550 Ken Griffey | .12 |
| 551 Pittsburgh Pirates/ Chuck Tanner (Mgr.) | .35 |
| 552 Bill Nahorodny | .08 |
| 553 Dick Davis | .08 |
| 554 Art Howe | .08 |
| 555 Ed Figueroa | .08 |
| 556 Joe Rudi | .15 |
| 557 Mark Lee | .08 |
| 558 Alfredo Griffin | .15 |
| 559 Dale Murray | .08 |
| 560 Dave Lopes | .15 |
| 561 Eddie Whitson | .12 |
| 562 Joe Wallis | .08 |
| 563 Will McEnaney | .08 |
| 564 Rick Manning | .08 |
| 565 Dennis Leonard | .12 |
| 566 Bud Harrelson | .08 |
| 567 Skip Lockwood | .08 |
| 568 Gary Roenicke (R) | .30 |
| 569 Terry Kennedy | .30 |
| 570 Roy Smalley | .08 |
| 571 Joe Sambito | .08 |
| 572 Jerry Morales | .08 |
| 573 Kent Tekulve | .12 |
| 574 Scot Thompson | .08 |
| 575 Ken Kravec | .08 |
| 576 Jim Dwyer | .08 |
| 577 Toronto Blue Jays/ Bobby Mattick (Mgr.) | .30 |
| 578 Scott Sanderson | .08 |
| 579 Charlie Moore | .08 |
| 580 Nolan Ryan | 1.50 |
| 581 Bob Bailor | .08 |
| 582 Brian Doyle | .08 |
| 583 Bob Stinson | .08 |
| 584 Kurt Bevacqua | .08 |
| 585 Al Hrabosky | .08 |
| 586 Mitchell Page | .08 |
| 587 Garry Templeton | .25 |
| 588 Greg Minton | .08 |
| 589 Chet Lemon | .15 |
| 590 Jim Palmer | 1.00 |
| 591 Rick Cerone | .08 |
| 592 Jon Matlack | .08 |
| 593 Jesus Alou | .08 |
| 594 Dick Tidrow | .08 |
| 595 Don Money | .08 |
| 596 Rick Matula | .08 |
| 597 Tom Poquette | .08 |
| 598 Fred Kendall | .08 |
| 599 Mike Norris | .08 |
| 600 Reggie Jackson | 2.00 |
| 601 Buddy Schultz | .08 |
| 602 Brian Downing | .08 |
| 603 Jack Billingham | .08 |
| 604 Glenn Adams | .08 |
| 605 Terry Forster | .12 |
| 606 Cincinnati Reds/ John McNamara (Mgr.) | .30 |
| 607 Woodie Fryman | .08 |
| 608 Alan Bannister | .08 |
| 609 Ron Reed | .08 |
| 610 Willie Stargell | 1.25 |

| NO. PLAYER | MINT |
|---|---|
| 611 Jerry Garvin | .08 |
| 612 Cliff Johnson | .08 |
| 613 Randy Stein | .08 |
| 614 John Hiller | .08 |
| 615 Doug DeCinces | .20 |
| 616 Gene Richards | .08 |
| 617 Joaquin Andujar | .30 |
| 618 Bob Montgomery | .08 |
| 619 Sergio Ferrer | .08 |
| 620 Richie Zisk | .15 |
| 621 Bob Grich | .12 |
| 622 Mario Soto | .20 |
| 623 Gorman Thomas | .25 |
| 624 Lerrin LaGrow | .08 |
| 625 Chris Chambliss | .12 |
| 626 Detroit Tigers/ S. Anderson (Mgr.) | .50 |
| 627 Pedro Borbon | .08 |
| 628 Doug Capilla | .08 |
| 629 Jim Todd | .08 |
| 630 Larry Bowa | .15 |
| 631 Mark Littell | .08 |
| 632 Barry Bonnell | .08 |
| 633 Bob Apodaca | .08 |
| 634 Glenn Borgmann | .08 |
| 635 John Candelaria | .12 |
| 636 Toby Harrah | .08 |
| 637 Joe Simpson | .08 |
| 638 Mark Clear (R) | .30 |
| 639 Larry Biittner | .08 |
| 640 Mike Flanagan | .12 |
| 641 Ed Kranepool | .15 |
| 642 Ken Forsch | .08 |
| 643 John Mayberry | .15 |
| 644 Charlie Hough | .12 |
| 645 Rick Burleson | .12 |
| 646 Checklist No. 6 | .25 |
| 647 Milt May | .08 |
| 648 Roy White | .12 |
| 649 Tom Griffin | .08 |
| 650 Joe Morgan | .75 |
| 651 Rollie Fingers | .40 |
| 652 Mario Mendoza | .08 |
| 653 Stan Bahnsen | .08 |
| 654 Bruce Boisclair | .08 |
| 655 Tug McGraw | .15 |
| 656 Larvell Blanks | .08 |
| 657 Dave Edwards | .08 |
| 658 Chris Knapp | .08 |
| 659 Milwaukee Brewers/ George Bamberger (Mgr.) | .25 |
| 660 Rusty Staub | .25 |
| 661 Orioles Rookies: Wayne Krenchicki, Mark Corey, D. Ford | .15 |
| 662 Red Sox Rookies: J. Finch, Mike O'Berry, Chuck Rainey | .15 |
| 663 Angels Rookies: Ralph Botting, Bob Clark, Dickey Thon | .50 |
| 664 White Sox Rookies: Guy Hoffman, M. Colbern, Dewey Robinson | .15 |
| 665 Indians Rookies: Larry Anderson, Bobby Cuellar, Randy Wihtol | .15 |
| 666 Tigers Rookies: M. Chris, Bruce Robbins, Al Greene | .25 |
| 667 Royals Rookies: R. Martin, Bill Paschall, Dan Quisenberry | 2.00 |
| 668 Brewers Rookies: Danny Boitano, W. Mueller, Lenn Sakata | .15 |
| 669 Twin Rookies: Rick Sofield, Dan Graham, Gary Ward | .50 |
| 670 Yankee Rookies: B. Brown, Brad Gulden, Darryl Jones | .25 |
| 671 A's Rookies: Derek Bryant, B. Kingman, Mike Morgan | .25 |

| NO. PLAYER | MINT |
|---|---|
| 672 Mariners Rookies: Rodney Craig, Charlie Beamon, Rafael Vasquez | .15 |
| 673 Rangers Rookies: Brian Allard, Jerry Don Gleaton, Greg Mahlberg | .15 |
| 674 Blue Jays Rookies: Butch Edge, Pat Kelly, Ted Wilborn | .15 |
| 675 Braves Rookies: Bruce Benedict, Eddie Miller, Larry Bradford | .20 |
| 676 Cubs Rookies: Steve Macko, Dave Geisel, Karl Pagel | .20 |
| 677 Reds Rookies: Art DeFreites, Harry Spilman, Frank Pastore | .15 |
| 678 Astros Rookies: Reggie Baldwin, A. Knicely, Pete Ladd | .20 |
| 679 Dodgers Rookies: Joe Beckwith, Mickey Hatcher, Dave Patterson | .40 |
| 680 Expos Rookies: Randy Miller, Tony Bernazard, John Tamargo | .40 |
| 681 Mets Rookies: Dan Norman, J. Orosco, Mike Scott | 7.00 |
| 682 Phillies Rookies: Kevin Saucier, Ramon Aviles, Dickie Noles | .25 |
| 683 Pirates Rookies: D. Boyland, Alberto Lois, Harry Saferight | .15 |
| 684 Cardinals Rookies: George Frazier, Tom Herr, Dan O'Brien | .60 |
| 685 Padres Rookies: Brian Greer, Tim Flannery, Jim Wilhelm | .15 |
| 686 Giants Rookies: Greg Johnston, D. Littlejohn, Phil Nastu | .15 |
| 687 Mike Heath | .08 |
| 688 Steve Stone | .12 |
| 689 Boston Red Sox/ Don Zimmer (Mgr.) | .40 |
| 690 Tommy John | .40 |
| 691 Ivan DeJesus | .08 |
| 692 Rawly Eastwick | .08 |
| 693 Craig Kusick | .08 |
| 694 Jim Rooker | .08 |
| 695 Reggie Smith | .15 |
| 696 Julio Gonzalez | .08 |
| 697 David Clyde | .08 |
| 698 Oscar Gamble | .15 |
| 699 Floyd Bannister | .15 |
| 700 Rod Carew | .75 |
| 701 Ken Oberkfell | .30 |
| 702 Ed Farmer | .08 |
| 703 Otto Velez | .08 |
| 704 Gene Tenace | .08 |
| 705 Freddie Patek | .08 |
| 706 Tippy Martinez | .08 |
| 707 Elliott Maddox | .08 |
| 708 Bob Tolan | .08 |
| 709 Pat Underwood | .08 |
| 710 Graig Nettles | .25 |
| 711 Bob Galasso | .08 |
| 712 Rodney Scott | .08 |
| 713 Terry Whitfield | .08 |
| 714 Fred Norman | .08 |
| 715 Sal Bando | .15 |
| 716 Lynn McGlothen | .08 |
| 717 Mickey Klutts | .08 |
| 718 Greg Gross | .08 |
| 719 Don Robinson | .12 |
| 720 Carl Yastrzemski | 1.00 |
| 721 Paul Hartzell | .08 |
| 722 Jose Cruz | .25 |
| 723 Shane Rawley | .12 |
| 724 Jerry White | .08 |
| 725 Rick Wise | .12 |
| 726 Steve Yeager | .12 |

Features the rookie cards of Fernando Valenzuela, Kirk Gibson, Harold Baines and Tim Raines. 66 cards were double printed. In 1981 Topps began getting competition from two other card manufacturers—Donruss and Fleer.

| NO. | PLAYER | MINT |
|---|---|---|
| 1 | Batting Leaders: Bill Buckner, George Brett | .50 |
| 2 | Home Run Leaders: Reggie Jackson, Ben Oglivie, M. Schmidt | .25 |
| 3 | RBI Leaders: Cecil Cooper, Mike Schmidt | .25 |
| 4 | Stolen Base Leaders: Rickey Henderson, Ron LeFlore | .20 |
| 5 | Victory Leaders: Steve Carlton, Steve Stone | .15 |
| 6 | Strikeout Leaders: Len Barker, Steve Carlton | .15 |
| 7 | ERA Leaders: Don Sutton, Rudy May | .10 |
| 8 | Leading Firemen: Dan Quisenberry, Tom Hume, Rollie Fingers | .15 |
| 9 | Pete LaCock | .07 |
| 10 | Mike Flanagan | .12 |
| 11 | Jim Wohlford | .07 |
| 12 | Mark Clear | .07 |
| 13 | Joe Charboneau | .12 |
| 14 | John Tudor (R) | 1.50 |
| 15 | Larry Parrish | .10 |
| 16 | Ron Davis | .10 |
| 17 | Cliff Johnson | .07 |
| 18 | Glenn Adams | .07 |
| 19 | Jim Clancy | .07 |
| 20 | Jeff Burroughs | .07 |
| 21 | Ron Oester | .07 |
| 22 | Danny Darwin | .07 |
| 23 | Alex Trevino | .07 |
| 24 | Don Stanhouse | .07 |
| 25 | Sicto Lezcano | .07 |
| 26 | U.L. Washington | .07 |
| 27 | Champ Summers | .07 |
| 28 | Enrique Romo | .07 |
| 29 | Gene Tenace | .07 |
| 30 | Jack Clark | .60 |
| 31 | Checklist No. 1 | .15 |
| 32 | Ken Oberkfell | .07 |
| 33 | Rick Honeycutt | .07 |
| 34 | Aurelio Rodriquez | .07 |
| 35 | Mitchell Page | .07 |
| 36 | Ed Farmer | .07 |
| 37 | Gary Roenicke | .07 |
| 38 | Win Remmerswaal | .07 |
| 39 | Tom Veryzer | .07 |
| 40 | Tug McGraw | .12 |
| 41 | Ranger Rookies: Bob Babcock, J. Butcher, Jerry Don Gleaton | .20 |
| 42 | Jerry White | .07 |
| 43 | Jose Morales | .07 |
| 44 | Larry McWilliams | .07 |
| 45 | Enos Cabell | .07 |
| 46 | Rick Bosetti | .07 |
| 47 | Ken Brett | .07 |
| 48 | Dave Skaggs | .07 |
| 49 | Bob Shirley | .07 |
| 50 | Dave Lope | .12 |
| 51 | Bill Robinson | .07 |
| 52 | Hector Cruz | .07 |
| 53 | Kevin Saucler | .07 |
| 54 | Ivan DeJesus | .07 |
| 55 | Mike Norris | .07 |
| 56 | Buck Martinez | .07 |
| 57 | Dave Roberts | .07 |
| 58 | Joel Youngblood | .07 |
| 59 | Dan Petry | .25 |
| 60 | Willie Randolph | .12 |
| 61 | Butch Wynegar | .10 |
| 62 | Joe Pettini | .07 |
| 63 | Steve Renko | .07 |
| 64 | Brian Asselstine | .07 |
| 65 | Scott McGregor | .10 |
| 66 | Royals Rookies: Tim Ireland, Manny Castillo, Mike Jones | .15 |
| 67 | Ken Kravec | .07 |
| 68 | Matt Alexander | .07 |
| 69 | Ed Halicki | .07 |
| 70 | Al Oliver | .12 |
| 71 | Hal Dues | .07 |
| 72 | Barry Evans | .07 |
| 73 | Doug Bair | .07 |
| 74 | Mike Hargrove | .07 |
| 75 | Reggie Smith | .12 |
| 76 | Mario Mendoza | .07 |
| 77 | Mike Barlow | .07 |
| 78 | Steve Dillard | .07 |
| 79 | Bruce Robbins | .07 |
| 80 | Rusty Staub | .15 |
| 81 | Dave Stapleton | .15 |
| 82 | Astros Rookies: Bobby Sprowl, Danny Heep, Alan Knicely | .10 |
| 83 | Mike Proly | .07 |
| 84 | Johnnie LeMaster | .07 |
| 85 | Mike Caldwell | .07 |
| 86 | Wayne Gross | .07 |
| 87 | Rick Camp | .07 |
| 88 | Joe LeFebvre | .15 |
| 89 | Darrell Jackson | .07 |
| 90 | Bake McBride | .07 |
| 91 | Tim Stoddard | .07 |
| 92 | Mike Easler | .12 |
| 93 | Ed Glynn | .07 |
| 94 | Harry Spilman | .07 |
| 95 | Jim Sundberg | .07 |
| 96 | A's Rookies: Dave Beard, Pat Dempsey, E. Camacho | .12 |
| 97 | Chris Speier | .07 |
| 98 | Clint Hurdle | .07 |
| 99 | Eric Wilkins | .07 |
| 100 | Rod Carew | 1.00 |
| 101 | Benny Ayala | .07 |
| 102 | Dave Tobik | .07 |
| 103 | Jerry Martin | .07 |
| 104 | Terry Forster | .12 |
| 105 | Jose Cruz | .20 |
| 106 | Don Money | .07 |
| 107 | Rich Wortham | .07 |
| 108 | Bruce Benedict | .07 |
| 109 | Mike Scott | 1.00 |
| 110 | Carl Yastrzemski | 1.00 |
| 111 | Greg Minton | .07 |
| 112 | White Sox Rookies: Rusty Kuntz, F. Mullin, Leo Sutherland | .15 |
| 113 | Mike Phillips | .07 |
| 114 | Tom Underwood | .07 |
| 115 | Roy Smalley | .07 |
| 116 | Joe Simpson | .07 |
| 117 | Pete Falcone | .07 |
| 118 | Kurt Bevacqua | .07 |
| 119 | Tippy Martinez | .07 |
| 120 | Larry Bowa | .12 |
| 121 | Larry Harlow | .07 |
| 122 | John Denny | .15 |
| 123 | Al Cowens | .07 |
| 124 | Jerry Garvin | .07 |
| 125 | Andre Dawson | 1.00 |
| 126 | Charlie Leibrandt (R) | .50 |
| 127 | Rudy Law | .07 |
| 128 | Garry Allenson | .07 |
| 129 | Art Howe | .07 |
| 130 | Larry Gura | .07 |
| 131 | Keith Moreland (R) | .60 |
| 132 | Tommy Boggs | .07 |
| 133 | Jeff Cox | .07 |
| 134 | Steve Mura | .07 |
| 135 | Gorman Thomas | .20 |
| 136 | Doug Capilla | .07 |
| 137 | Hosken Powell | .07 |
| 138 | Rich Dotson (R) | .40 |
| 139 | Oscar Gamble | .07 |
| 140 | Bob Forsch | .07 |
| 141 | Miguel Dilone | .07 |
| 142 | Jackson Todd | .07 |
| 143 | Dan Meyer | .07 |
| 144 | Allen Ripley | .07 |
| 145 | Mickey Rivers | .10 |
| 146 | Bobby Castillo | .07 |
| 147 | Dale Berra | .07 |
| 148 | Randy Niemann | .07 |
| 149 | Joe Nolan | .07 |
| 150 | Mark Fidrych | .10 |
| 151 | Claudell Washington | .10 |
| 152 | John Urrea | .07 |
| 153 | Tom Poquette | .07 |
| 154 | Rick Langford | .07 |
| 155 | Chris Chambliss | .10 |
| 156 | Bob McClure | .07 |
| 157 | John Wathan | .07 |
| 158 | Fergie Jenkins | .20 |
| 159 | Brian Doyle | .07 |
| 160 | Garry Maddox | .07 |
| 161 | Dan Graham | .07 |
| 162 | Doug Corbett | .12 |
| 163 | Billy Almon | .07 |
| 164 | LaMarr Hoyt (R) | .30 |
| 165 | Tony Scott | .07 |
| 166 | Floyd Bannister | .07 |
| 167 | Terry Whitfield | .07 |
| 168 | Don Robinson | .07 |
| 169 | John Mayberry | .07 |
| 170 | Ross Grimsley | .07 |
| 171 | Gene Richards | .07 |
| 172 | Gary Woods | .07 |
| 173 | Bump Wills | .07 |
| 174 | Doug Rau | .07 |
| 175 | Dave Collins | .07 |
| 176 | Mike Krukow | .07 |
| 177 | Rick Peters | .12 |
| 178 | Jim Essian | .07 |
| 179 | Rudy May | .07 |
| 180 | Pete Rose | 3.00 |
| 181 | Elias Sosa | .07 |
| 182 | Bob Grich | .12 |
| 183 | Dick Davis | .07 |
| 184 | Jim Dwyer | .07 |
| 185 | Dennis Leonard | .07 |
| 186 | Wayne Nordhagen | .07 |
| 187 | Mike Parrott | .07 |
| 188 | Doug DeCinces | .15 |
| 189 | Craig Swan | .07 |
| 190 | Cesar Cedeno | .15 |
| 191 | Rick Sutcliffe | .50 |
| 192 | Braves Rookies: Terry Harper, Rafael Ramirez, Ed Miller | .35 |
| 193 | Pete Vuckovich | .12 |
| 194 | Rod Scurry | .10 |
| 195 | Rich Murray | .07 |
| 196 | Duffy Dyer | .07 |
| 197 | Jim Kern | .07 |
| 198 | Jerry Dybzinski | .07 |
| 199 | Chuck Rainey | .07 |
| 200 | George Foster | .30 |
| 201 | Record—J. Bench Most HR's, Catcher, Career | .45 |
| 202 | Record—S. Carlton Strikeouts, Lefty, Career | .35 |
| 203 | Record—B. Gullickson Strikeouts, Game, Rookie | .12 |
| 204 | Rec.—LeFlore, Scott SB's, Teammates, Season | .12 |
| 205 | Record—P. Rose Most Consecutive Seasons, 600 or More At-Bats | .75 |
| 206 | Record—M. Schmidt Homers, 3B, Season | .45 |
| 207 | Record—O. Smith Assists, SS, Season | .15 |
| 208 | Record—W. Wilson Most At-Bats, Season | .15 |
| 209 | Dickie Thon | .07 |
| 210 | Jim Palmer | .75 |
| 211 | Derrel Thomas | .07 |
| 212 | Steve Nicosia | .07 |
| 213 | Al Holland (R) | .25 |
| 214 | Angels Rookies: John Harris, Ralph Botting, Jim Dorsey | .15 |
| 215 | Larry Hisle | .07 |
| 216 | John Henry Johnson | .07 |
| 217 | Rich Hebner | .07 |
| 218 | Paul Splittorff | .07 |
| 219 | Ken Landreaux | .07 |
| 220 | Tom Seaver | 1.00 |
| 221 | Bob Davis | .07 |
| 222 | Jorge Orta | .07 |
| 223 | Roy Lee Jackson | .10 |
| 224 | Pat Zachry | .07 |
| 225 | Ruppert Jones | .07 |
| 226 | Manny Sanguillen | .07 |
| 227 | Fred Martinez | .07 |
| 228 | Tom Paciorek | .07 |

| NO. PLAYER | MINT |
|---|---|
| 229 Rollie Fingers | .50 |
| 230 George Hendrick | .12 |
| 231 Joe Beckwith | .07 |
| 232 Mickey Klutts | .07 |
| 233 Skip Lockwood | .07 |
| 234 Lou Whitaker | .40 |
| 235 Scott Sanderson | .07 |
| 236 Mike Ivie | .07 |
| 237 Charlie Moore | .07 |
| 238 Willie Hernandez | .20 |
| 239 Rick Miller | .07 |
| 240 Nolan Ryan | 1.00 |
| 241 Checklist No. 2 | .15 |
| 242 Chet Lemon | .12 |
| 243 Sal Butera | .07 |
| 244 Cardinals Rookies: | .20 |
|     Andy Rincon, T. Landrum, Al Olmsted | |
| 245 Ed Figueroa | .07 |
| 246 Ed Ott | .07 |
| 247 Glenn Hubbard | .07 |
| 248 Joey McLaughlin | .07 |
| 249 Larry Cox | .07 |
| 250 Ron Guidry | .40 |
| 251 Tom Brookens | .07 |
| 252 Victor Cruz | .07 |
| 253 Dave Bergman | .07 |
| 254 Ozzie Smith | .75 |
| 255 Mark Littell | .07 |
| 256 Bombo Rivera | .07 |
| 257 Rennie Stennett | .07 |
| 258 Joe Price | .07 |
| 259 Mets Rookies: | 2.00 |
|     Juan Berenguer, H. Brooks, Mookie Wilson | |
| 260 Ron Cey | .30 |
| 261 Ricky Henderson | 4.00 |
| 262 Sammy Stewart | .07 |
| 263 Brian Downing | .07 |
| 264 Jim Norris | .07 |
| 265 John Candelaria | .10 |
| 266 Tom Herr | .20 |
| 267 Stan Bahnsen | .07 |
| 268 Jerry Royster | .07 |
| 269 Ken Forsch | .07 |
| 270 Greg Luzinski | .15 |
| 271 Bill Castro | .07 |
| 272 Bruce Kimm | .07 |
| 273 Stan Papi | .07 |
| 274 Craig Chamberlain | .07 |
| 275 Dwight Evans | .35 |
| 276 Dan Spillner | .07 |
| 277 Alfredo Griffin | .10 |
| 278 Rick Sofield | .07 |
| 279 Bob Knepper | .12 |
| 280 Ken Griffey | .12 |
| 281 Fred Stanley | .07 |
| 282 Mariners Rookies: | .15 |
|     Rick Anderson, Rodney Craig, Greg Biercevicz | |
| 283 Billy Sample | .07 |
| 284 Brian Kingman | .07 |
| 285 Jerry Turner | .07 |
| 286 Dave Frost | .07 |
| 287 Lenn Sakata | .07 |
| 288 Bob Clark | .07 |
| 289 Mickey Hatcher | .07 |
| 290 Bob Boone | .07 |
| 291 Aurelio Lopez | .07 |
| 292 Mike Squires | .07 |
| 293 Charlie Lea (R) | .20 |
| 294 Mike Tyson | .07 |
| 295 Hal McRae | .10 |
| 296 Bill Nahorodny | .07 |
| 297 Bob Bailor | .07 |
| 298 Buddy Solomon | .07 |
| 299 Elliott Maddox | .07 |
| 300 Paul Molitor | .40 |
| 301 Matt Keough | .07 |
| 302 Dodgers Rookies: | 6.00 |
|     Mike Scioscia, Jack Perconte, F. Valenzuela | |
| 303 Johnny Oates | .07 |
| 304 John Castino | .07 |
| 305 Ken Clay | .07 |

| NO. PLAYER | MINT |
|---|---|
| 306 Juan Beniquez | .07 |
| 307 Gene Garber | .07 |
| 308 Rick Manning | .07 |
| 309 Luis Salazar | .15 |
| 310 Vida Blue | .07 |
| 311 Freddie Patek | .07 |
| 312 Rick Rhoden | .12 |
| 313 Luis Pujols | .07 |
| 314 Rich Dauer | .07 |
| 315 Kirk Gibson (R) | 6.00 |
| 316 Craig Minetto | .07 |
| 317 Lonnie Smith | .15 |
| 318 Steve Yeager | .07 |
| 319 Rowland Office | .07 |
| 320 Tom Burgmeier | .07 |
| 321 Leon Durham (R) | 1.00 |
| 322 Neil Allen | .07 |
| 323 Jim Morrison | .07 |
| 324 Mike Willis | .07 |
| 325 Ray Knight | .15 |
| 326 Biff Pocoroba | .07 |
| 327 Moose Haas | .07 |
| 328 Twins Rookies: | .35 |
|     Dave Engle, G. Johnston, Gary Ward | |
| 329 Joaquin Andujar | .15 |
| 330 Frank White | .12 |
| 331 Dennis Lamp | .07 |
| 332 Lee Lacy | .07 |
| 333 Sid Monge | .07 |
| 334 Dane Iorg | .07 |
| 335 Rick Cerone | .07 |
| 336 Eddie Whitson | .10 |
| 337 Lynn Jones | .05 |
| 338 Checklist No.3 | .15 |
| 339 John Ellis | .07 |
| 340 Bruce Kison | .07 |
| 341 Dwayne Murphy | .12 |
| 342 Eric Rasmussen | .07 |
| 343 Frank Taveras | .07 |
| 344 Byron McLaughlin | .07 |
| 345 Warren Cromartie | .07 |
| 346 Larry Christenson | .07 |
| 347 Harold Baines (R) | 4.00 |
| 348 Bob Sykes | .12 |
| 349 Glenn Hoffman | .15 |
| 350 J.R. Richard | .12 |
| 351 Otto Velez | .07 |
| 352 Dick Tidrow | .07 |
| 353 Terry Kennedy | .15 |
| 354 Mario Soto | .15 |
| 355 Bob Horner | .40 |
| 356 Padres Rookies: | .15 |
|     George Stablein, C. Stimac, Tom Tellmann | |
| 357 Jim Slaton | .07 |
| 358 Mark Wagner | .07 |
| 359 Tom Hausman | .07 |
| 360 Willie Wilson | .25 |
| 361 Joe Strain | .07 |
| 362 Bo Diaz | .07 |
| 363 Geoff Zahn | .07 |
| 364 Mike Davis (R) | .40 |
| 365 Graig Nettles | .15 |
| 366 Mike Ramsey | .07 |
| 367 Denny Martinez | .07 |
| 368 Leon Roberts | .07 |
| 369 Frank Tanana | .15 |
| 370 Dave Winfield | 1.25 |
| 371 Charlie Hough | .07 |
| 372 Jay Johnstone | .07 |
| 373 Pat Underwood | .07 |
| 374 Tom Hutton | .07 |
| 375 Dave Concepcion | .15 |
| 376 Ron Reed | .07 |
| 377 Jerry Morales | .07 |
| 378 Dave Rader | .07 |
| 379 Lary Sorensen | .07 |
| 380 Willie Stargell | 1.00 |
| 381 Cubs Rookies: | .20 |
|     Carlos Lezcano, Steve Macko, Randy Martz | |
| 382 Paul Mirabella | .07 |
| 383 Eric Soderholm | .07 |
| 384 Mike Sadek | .07 |

| NO. PLAYER | MINT |
|---|---|
| 385 Joe Sambito | .07 |
| 386 Dave Edwards | .07 |
| 387 Phil Niekro | .50 |
| 388 Andre Thornton | .15 |
| 389 Marty Pattin | .07 |
| 390 Cesar Geronimo | .07 |
| 391 Dave Lemanczyk | .07 |
| 392 Lance Parrish | .60 |
| 393 Broderick Perkins | .07 |
| 394 Woodie Fryman | .07 |
| 395 Scot Thompson | .07 |
| 396 Bill Campbell | .07 |
| 397 Julio Cruz | .07 |
| 398 Ross Baumgarten | .07 |
| 399 Orioles Rookies: | 1.50 |
|     Mike Boddicker, Mark Corey, Floyd Rayford | |
| 400 Reggie Jackson | 1.50 |
| 401 A.L. Championships: | .40 |
|     Royals Sweep Yanks | |
| 402 N.L. Championships: | .25 |
|     Phillies Beat Astros | |
| 403 1980 World Series: | .25 |
|     Phillies Beat Royals | |
| 404 1980 World Series: | .25 |
|     Phillies Win | |
| 405 Nino Espinosa | .07 |
| 406 Dickie Noles | .07 |
| 407 Ernie Whitt | .07 |
| 408 Fernando Arroyo | .07 |
| 409 Larry Herndon | .07 |
| 410 Bert Campaneris | .07 |
| 411 Terry Puhl | .07 |
| 412 Britt Burns (R) | .20 |
| 413 Tony Bernazard | .07 |
| 414 John Pacella | .07 |
| 415 Ben Oglivie | .12 |
| 416 Gary Alexander | .07 |
| 417 Dan Schatzeder | .07 |
| 418 Bobby Brown | .07 |
| 419 Tom Hume | .07 |
| 420 Keith Hernandez | .75 |
| 421 Bob Stanley | .07 |
| 422 Dan Ford | .07 |
| 423 Shane Rawley | .12 |
| 424 Yankees Rookies: | .20 |
|     Tim Lollar, Bruce Robinson, Dennis Werth | |
| 425 Al Bumbry | .07 |
| 426 Warren Brusstar | .07 |
| 427 Jonn D'Acquisto | .07 |
| 428 John Stearns | .07 |
| 429 Mick Kelleher | .07 |
| 430 Jim Bibby | .07 |
| 431 Dave Roberts | .07 |
| 432 Len Barker | .12 |
| 433 Rance Mulliniks | .07 |
| 434 Roger Erickson | .07 |
| 435 Jim Spencer | .07 |
| 436 Gary Lucas | .12 |
| 437 Mike Heath | .07 |
| 438 John Montefusco | .07 |
| 439 Denny Walling | .07 |
| 440 Jerry Reuss | .12 |
| 441 Ken Reitz | .07 |
| 442 Ron Pruitt | .07 |
| 443 Jim Beattie | .07 |
| 444 Garth Iorg | .07 |
| 445 Ellis Valentine | .07 |
| 446 Checklist No. 4 | .15 |
| 447 Junior Kennedy | .07 |
| 448 Tim Corcoran | .07 |
| 449 Paul Mitchell | .07 |
| 450 Dave Kingman | .15 |
| 451 Indians Rookies: | .20 |
|     Chris Bando, Tom Brennan, Sandy Wihtol | |
| 452 Renie Martin | .07 |
| 453 Rob Wilfong | .07 |
| 454 Andy Hassler | .07 |
| 455 Rick Burleson | .12 |
| 456 Jeff Reardon (R) | .75 |
| 457 Mike Lum | .07 |
| 458 Randy Jones | .07 |
| 459 Greg Gross | .07 |

| NO. PLAYER | MINT |
|---|---|
| 460 Rich Gossage | .35 |
| 461 Dave McKay | .07 |
| 462 Jack Brohamer | .07 |
| 463 Milt May | .07 |
| 464 Adrian Devine | .07 |
| 465 Bill Russell | .07 |
| 466 Bob Molinaro | .07 |
| 467 Dave Stieb | .45 |
| 468 Johnny Wockenfuss | .07 |
| 469 Jeff Leonard | .30 |
| 470 Manny Trillo | .07 |
| 471 Mike Vail | .07 |
| 472 Dyar Miller | .07 |
| 473 Jose Cardenal | .07 |
| 474 Mike LaCoss | .07 |
| 475 Buddy Bell | .20 |
| 476 Jerry Koosman | .15 |
| 477 Luis Gomez | .07 |
| 478 Juan Eichelberger | .07 |
| 479 Expos Rookies: | 8.00 |
|     B. Pate, Tim Raines, Roberto Ramos | |
| 480 Carlton Fisk | .40 |
| 481 Bob Lacey | .07 |
| 482 Jim Gantner | .07 |
| 483 Mike Griffin | .07 |
| 484 Max Venable | .07 |
| 485 Garry Templeton | .20 |
| 486 Marc Hill | .07 |
| 487 Dewey Robinson | .07 |
| 488 Damaso Garcia (R) | .30 |
| 489 John Littlefield | .07 |
| 490 Eddie Murray | 1.25 |
| 491 Gordy Pladson | .07 |
| 492 Barry Foote | .07 |
| 493 Dan Quisenberry | .30 |
| 494 Bob Walk | .15 |
| 495 Dusty Baker | .12 |
| 496 Paul Dade | .07 |
| 497 Fred Norman | .07 |
| 498 Pat Putnam | .07 |
| 499 Frank Pastore | .07 |
| 500 Jim Rice | .75 |
| 501 Tim Foli | .07 |
| 502 Giants Rookies: | .15 |
|     Chris Bourjos, Mike Rowland, A. Hargesheimer | |
| 503 Steve McCatty | .07 |
| 504 Dale Murphy | 2.50 |
| 505 Jason Thompson | .12 |
| 506 Phil Huffman | .07 |
| 507 Jamie Quirk | .07 |
| 508 Rob Dressler | .07 |
| 509 Pete Mackanin | .07 |
| 510 Lee Mazzilli | .07 |
| 511 Wayne Garland | .07 |
| 512 Gary Thomasson | .07 |
| 513 Frank LaCorte | .07 |
| 514 George Riley | .07 |
| 515 Robin Yount | .75 |
| 516 Doug Bird | .07 |
| 517 Richie Zisk | .07 |
| 518 Grant Jackson | .07 |
| 519 John Tamargo | .07 |
| 520 Steve Stone | .07 |
| 521 Sam Mejias | .07 |
| 522 Mike Colbern | .07 |
| 523 John Fulgham | .07 |
| 524 Willie Aikens | .10 |
| 525 Mike Torrez | .07 |
| 526 Phillies Rookies: | .25 |
|     Marty Bystrom, Jay Loviglio, J. Wright | |
| 527 Danny Goodwin | .07 |
| 528 Gary Matthews | .12 |
| 529 Dave LaRoche | .07 |
| 530 Steve Garvey | 1.00 |
| 531 John Curtis | .07 |
| 532 Bill Stein | .07 |
| 533 Jesus Figueroa | .07 |
| 534 Dave Smith | .35 |
| 535 Omar Moreno | .12 |
| 536 Bob Owchinko | .07 |
| 537 Ron Hodges | .07 |
| 538 Tom Griffin | .07 |

| NO. PLAYER | MINT |
|---|---|
| 539 Rodney Scott | .07 |
| 540 Mike Schmidt | 1.00 |
| 541 Steve Swisher | .07 |
| 542 Larry Bradford | .07 |
| 543 Terry Crowley | .07 |
| 544 Rich Gale | .07 |
| 545 Johnny Grubb | .07 |
| 546 Paul Moskau | .07 |
| 547 Mario Guerrero | .07 |
| 548 Dave Goltz | .07 |
| 549 Jerry Remy | .07 |
| 550 Tommy John | .30 |
| 551 Pirates Rookies: | 2.00 |
| Vance Law, Pascual Perez | |
| Tony Pena | |
| 552 Steve Trout | .07 |
| 553 Tim Blackwell | .07 |
| 554 Bert Blyleven | .25 |
| 555 Cecil Cooper | .30 |
| 556 Jerry Mumphrey | .07 |
| 557 Chris Knapp | .07 |
| 558 Barry Bonnell | .07 |
| 559 Willie Montanez | .07 |
| 560 Joe Morgan | .75 |
| 561 Dennis Littlejohn | .07 |
| 562 Checklist No. 5 | .15 |
| 563 Jim Kaat | .25 |
| 564 Ron Hassey | .07 |
| 565 Burt Hooton | .07 |
| 566 Del Unser | .07 |
| 567 Mark Bomback | .07 |
| 568 Dave Revering | .07 |
| 569 Al Williams | .07 |
| 570 Ken Singleton | .12 |
| 571 Todd Cruz | .07 |
| 572 Jack Morris | .60 |
| 573 Phil Garner | .07 |
| 574 Bill Caudill | .15 |
| 575 Tony Perez | .25 |
| 576 Reggie Cleveland | .07 |
| 577 Blue Jays Rookies: | .25 |
| Luis Leal, Brian Miller, | |
| Ken Schrom | |
| 578 Bill Gullickson (R) | .40 |
| 579 Tim Flannery | .07 |
| 580 Don Baylor | .30 |
| 581 Roy Howell | .07 |
| 582 Gaylord Perry | .50 |
| 583 Larry Milbourne | .07 |
| 584 Randy Lerch | .07 |

| NO. PLAYER | MINT |
|---|---|
| 585 Amos Otis | .12 |
| 586 Silvio Martinez | .07 |
| 587 Jeff Newman | .07 |
| 588 Gary Lavelle | .07 |
| 589 Lamar Johnson | .07 |
| 590 Bruce Sutter | .30 |
| 591 John Lowenstein | .07 |
| 592 Steve Comer | .07 |
| 593 Steve Kemp | .15 |
| 594 Preston Hanna | .07 |
| 595 Butch Hobson | .07 |
| 596 Jerry Augustine | .07 |
| 597 Rafael Landestoy | .07 |
| 598 George Vukovich | .07 |
| 599 Dennis Kinney | .07 |
| 600 Johnny Bench | 1.00 |
| 601 Don Aase | .07 |
| 602 Bobby Murcer | .15 |
| 603 John Verhoeven | .07 |
| 604 Rob Picciolo | .07 |
| 605 Don Sutton | .40 |
| 606 Reds Rookies: | .15 |
| Bruce Berenyi, Geoff | |
| Combe, P. Householder | |
| 607 Dave Palmer | .07 |
| 608 Greg Pryor | .07 |
| 609 Lynn McGlothen | .07 |
| 610 Darrell Porter | .07 |
| 611 Rick Matula | .07 |
| 612 Duane Kuiper | .07 |
| 613 Jim Anderson | .07 |
| 614 Dave Rozema | .07 |
| 615 Rick Dempsey | .07 |
| 616 Rick Wise | .07 |
| 617 Craig Reynolds | .07 |
| 618 John Milner | .07 |
| 619 Steve Henderson | .07 |
| 620 Dennis Eckersley | .07 |
| 621 Tom Donohue | .07 |
| 622 Randy Moffitt | .07 |
| 623 Sal Bando | .07 |
| 624 Bob Welch | .12 |
| 625 Bill Buckner | .15 |
| 626 Tigers Rookies: | .20 |
| D. Steffen, Jerry Ujdur, | |
| Roger Weaver | |
| 627 Luis Tiant | .12 |
| 628 Vic Correll | .07 |
| 629 Tony Armas | .20 |
| 630 Steve Carlton | .75 |

| NO. PLAYER | MINT |
|---|---|
| 631 Ron Jackson | .07 |
| 632 Alan Bannister | .07 |
| 633 Bill Lee | .07 |
| 634 Doug Flynn | .07 |
| 635 Bobby Bonds | .12 |
| 636 Al Hrabosky | .07 |
| 637 Jerry Narron | .07 |
| 638 Checklist No. 6 | .15 |
| 639 Carney Lansford | .30 |
| 640 Dave Parker | .50 |
| 641 Mark Belanger | .07 |
| 642 Vern Ruhle | .07 |
| 643 Lloyd Moseby (R) | 2.00 |
| 644 Ramon Aviles | .07 |
| 645 Rick Reuschel | .15 |
| 646 Marvis Foley | .07 |
| 647 Dick Drago | .07 |
| 648 Darrell Evans | .20 |
| 649 Manny Sarmiento | .07 |
| 650 Bucky Dent | .12 |
| 651 Pedro Guerrero | 1.25 |
| 652 John Montague | .07 |
| 653 Bill Fahey | .07 |
| 654 Ray Burris | .07 |
| 655 Dan Driessen | .07 |
| 656 Jon Matlack | .07 |
| 657 Mike Cubbage | .07 |
| 658 Milt Wilcox | .07 |
| 659 Brewers Rookies: | .07 |
| Ned Yost, J. Flinn, | |
| Ed Romero | |
| 660 Gary Carter | 1.25 |
| 661 Orioles Team | .20 |
| 662 Red Sox Team | .20 |
| 663 Angels Team | .20 |
| 664 White Sox Team | .20 |
| 665 Indians Team | .20 |
| 666 Tigers Team | .25 |
| 667 Royals Team | .20 |
| 668 Brewers Team | .20 |
| 669 Twins Team | .20 |
| 670 Yankees Team | .25 |
| 671 A's Team | .20 |
| 672 Mariners Team | .15 |
| 673 Rangers Team | .20 |
| 674 Blue Jays Team | .20 |
| 675 Braves Team | .20 |
| 676 Cubs Team | .20 |
| 677 Reds Team | .20 |
| 678 Astros Team | .20 |

| NO. PLAYER | MINT |
|---|---|
| 679 Dodgers Team | .25 |
| 680 Expos Team | .15 |
| 681 Mets Team | .20 |
| 682 Phillies Team | .20 |
| 683 Pirates Team | .20 |
| 684 Cardinals Team | .20 |
| 685 Padres Team | .20 |
| 686 Giants Team | .20 |
| 687 Jeff Jones | .10 |
| 688 Kiko Garcia | .07 |
| 689 Red Sox Rookies: | 2.00 |
| Bruce Hurst, Reid Nichols, | |
| Keith MacWhorter | |
| 690 Bob Watson | .07 |
| 691 Dick Ruthven | .07 |
| 692 Lenny Randle | .07 |
| 693 Steve Howe (R) | .20 |
| 694 Bud Harrelson | .07 |
| 695 Kent Tekulve | .07 |
| 696 Alan Ashby | .07 |
| 697 Rick Waits | .07 |
| 698 Mike Jorgensen | .07 |
| 699 Glenn Abbott | .07 |
| 700 George Brett | 2.00 |
| 701 Joe Rudi | .07 |
| 702 George Medich | .07 |
| 703 Alvis Woods | .07 |
| 704 Bill Travers | .07 |
| 705 Ted Simmons | .25 |
| 706 Dave Ford | .07 |
| 707 Dave Cash | .07 |
| 708 Doyle Alexander | .07 |
| 709 Alan Trammell | .20 |
| 710 Ron LeFlore | .07 |
| 711 Joe Ferguson | .07 |
| 712 Bill Bonham | .07 |
| 713 Bill North | .07 |
| 714 Pete Redfern | .07 |
| 715 Bill Madlock | .25 |
| 716 Glenn Borgmann | .07 |
| 717 Jim Barr | .07 |
| 718 Larry Biittner | .07 |
| 719 Sparky Lyle | .12 |
| 720 Fred Lynn | .35 |
| 721 Toby Harrah | .07 |
| 722 Joe Niekro | .12 |
| 723 Bruce Bochte | .07 |
| 724 Lou Piniella | .15 |
| 725 Steve Rogers | .12 |
| 726 Rick Monday | .15 |

## 1981 Topps Traded....Complete Set of 132 Cards—Value $25.00

This was the first Topps "traded" set issued since 1976. It updates the main 1981 card set with players who had changed teams during the season and rookies who joined their teams early in the season. The first card in the traded set is numbered 727. It begins where the main set ends. The complete set was packaged in a printed box and only distributed through card hobby dealers.

| NO. PLAYER | MINT |
|---|---|
| 727 Danny Ainge (RR) | .40 |
| 728 Doyle Alexander | .15 |
| 729 Gary Alexander | .08 |
| 730 Billy Almon | .08 |
| 731 Joaquin Andujar | .20 |
| 732 Bob Bailor | .08 |
| 733 Juan Beniquez | .12 |

| NO. PLAYER | MINT |
|---|---|
| 734 Dave Bergman | .08 |
| 735 Tony Bernazard | .08 |
| 736 Larry Biittner | .08 |
| 737 Doug Bird | .08 |
| 738 Bert Blyleven | .40 |
| 739 Mark Bomback | .08 |
| 740 Bobby Bonds | .12 |

| NO. PLAYER | MINT |
|---|---|
| 741 Rick Bosetti | .08 |
| 742 Hubie Brooks | 1.25 |
| 743 Rick Burleson | .10 |
| 744 Ray Burris | .08 |
| 745 Jeff Burroughs | .10 |
| 746 Enos Cabell | .08 |
| 747 Ken Clay | .08 |

| NO. PLAYER | MINT |
|---|---|
| 748 Mark Clear | .08 |
| 749 Larry Cox | .08 |
| 750 Hector Cruz | .08 |
| 751 Victor Cruz | .08 |
| 752 Mike Cubbage | .08 |
| 753 Dick Davis | .08 |
| 754 Brian Doyle | .08 |

| NO. PLAYER | MINT | NO. PLAYER | MINT | NO. PLAYER | MINT | NO. PLAYER | MINT |
|---|---|---|---|---|---|---|---|
| 755 Dick Drago | .08 | 781 Dave Kingman | .30 | 807 Joe Morgan | 1.25 | 833 Harry Spilman | .08 |
| 756 Leon Durham | .60 | 782 Bob Knepper | .12 | 808 Jerry Mumphrey | .12 | 834 Fred Stanley | .08 |
| 757 Jim Dwyer | .08 | 783 Ken Kravec | .08 | 809 Gene Nelson (RR) | .25 | 835 Rusty Staub | .25 |
| 758 Dave Edwards | .08 | 784 Bob Lacey | .08 | 810 Ed Ott | .08 | 836 Bill Stein | .08 |
| 759 Jim Essian | .08 | 785 Dennis Lamp | .08 | 811 Bob Owchinko | .08 | 837 Joe Strain | .08 |
| 760 Bill Fahey | .08 | 786 Rafael Landestoy | .08 | 812 Gaylord Perry | 1.00 | 838 Bruce Sutter | .50 |
| 761 Rollie Ringers | .75 | 787 Ken Landreaux | .12 | 813 Mike Phillips | .08 | 839 Don Sutton | .75 |
| 762 Carlton Fisk | .60 | 788 Carney Lansford | .40 | 814 Darrell Porter | .12 | 840 Steve Swisher | .08 |
| 763 Barry Foote | .08 | 789 Dave LaRoche | .08 | 815 Mike Proly | .08 | 841 Frank Tanana | .08 |
| 764 Ken Forsch | .12 | 790 Joe LeFebvre | .08 | 816 Tim Raines | 6.00 | 842 Gene Tenace | .08 |
| 765 Kiko Garcia | .08 | 791 Ron LeFlore | .12 | 817 Lenny Randle | .08 | 843 Jason Thompson | .15 |
| 766 Cesar Geronimo | .08 | 792 Randy Lerch | .08 | 818 Doug Rau | .08 | 844 Dickie Thon | .25 |
| 767 Gary Gray | .08 | 793 Sixto Lezcano | .12 | 819 Jeff Reardon | .50 | 845 Bill Travers | .08 |
| 768 Mickey Hatcher | .08 | 794 John Littlefield | .08 | 820 Ken Reitz | .08 | 846 Tom Underwood | .08 |
| 769 Steve Henderson | .12 | 795 Mike Lum | .08 | 821 Steve Renko | .08 | 847 John Urrea | .08 |
| 770 Marc Hill | .08 | 796 Greg Luzinski | .30 | 822 Rick Reuschel | .20 | 848 Mike Vail | .08 |
| 771 Butch Hobson | .08 | 797 Fred Lynn | .65 | 823 Dave Revering | .08 | 849 Ellis Valentine | .12 |
| 772 Rick Honeycutt | .12 | 798 Jerry Martin | .08 | 824 Dave Roberts | .08 | 850 Fernando Valenzuela | 5.00 |
| 773 Roy Howell | .08 | 799 Buck Martinez | .08 | 825 Leon Roberts | .08 | 851 Pete Vuckovich | .12 |
| 774 Mike Ivie | .08 | 800 Gary Matthews | .12 | 826 Joe Rudi | .12 | 852 Mark Wagner | .08 |
| 775 Roy Lee Jackson | .08 | 801 Mario Mendoza | .08 | 827 Kevin Saucier | .08 | 853 Bob Walk | .08 |
| 776 Cliff Johnson | .08 | 802 Larry Milbourne | .08 | 828 Tony Scott | .08 | 854 Claudell Washington | .12 |
| 777 Randy Jones | .10 | 803 Rick Miller | .08 | 829 Bob Shirley | .08 | 855 Dave Winfield | 2.00 |
| 778 Ruppert Jones | .08 | 804 John Montefusco | .12 | 830 Ted Simmons | .40 | 856 Geoff Zahn | .08 |
| 779 Mick Kelleher | .08 | 805 Jerry Morales | .08 | 831 Lary Sorensen | .08 | 857 Richie Zisk | .12 |
| 780 Terry Kennedy | .30 | 806 Jose Morales | .08 | 832 Jim Spencer | .08 | 858 Traded Checklist | .20 |

# 1982 Topps....Complete Set of 792 Cards—Value $85.00

The complete set was increased to 792 cards. Double printed cards were eliminated (66 double prints were in each set from 1978 to 1981). Includes the rookie cards of Cal Ripken, Jesse Barfield, Kent Hrbek and Steve Sax. Card 342 exists with the *autograph* deleted.

| NO. PLAYER | MINT | NO. PLAYER | MINT | NO. PLAYER | MINT | NO. PLAYER | MINT |
|---|---|---|---|---|---|---|---|
| 1 Highlights—Carlton | .40 | 27 Tom Herr | .15 | 58 John D'Acquisto | .07 | 89 Steve Henderson | .07 |
| Sets NL Strikeout Record | | 28 John Urrea | .07 | 59 Rich Gedman (R) | .60 | 90 Nolan Ryan | .75 |
| 2 Highlights—Davis | .10 | 29 Dwayne Murphy | .07 | 60 Tony Armas | .20 | 91 Carney Lansford | .15 |
| Fans 8 Straight | | 30 Tom Seaver | .75 | 61 Tommy Boggs | .07 | 92 Brad Havens | .10 |
| 3 Highlights—Raines | .15 | 31 Seaver (Action) | .25 | 62 Mike Tyson | .07 | 93 Larry Hisle | .07 |
| Swipes 71 Bases, Rookie | | 32 Gene Garber | .07 | 63 Mario Soto | .15 | 94 Andy Hassler | .07 |
| 4 Highlights—Rose | .60 | 33 Jerry Morales | .07 | 64 Lynn Jones | .07 | 95 Ozzie Smith | .50 |
| Sets NL Career Hit Mark | | 34 Joe Sambito | .07 | 65 Terry Kennedy | .15 | 96 Royals Leaders: | .20 |
| 5 Highlights—Ryan | .25 | 35 Willie Aikens | .10 | 66 Astros Leaders: | .15 | G. Brett, L. Gura | |
| 5th Career No-Hitter | | 36 Rangers Leaders: | .15 | Art Howe, Nolan Ryan | | 97 Paul Moskau | .07 |
| 6 Highlights—Valenzuela | .25 | Al Oliver, George Medich | | 67 Rich Gale | .07 | 98 Terry Bulling | .07 |
| 8 Rookie Shutouts | | 37 Dan Graham | .07 | 68 Roy Howell | .07 | 99 Barry Bonnell | .07 |
| 7 Scott Sanderson | .07 | 38 Charlie Lea | .07 | 69 Al Williams | .07 | 100 Mike Schmidt | 1.25 |
| 8 Rich Dauer | .07 | 39 Lou Whitaker | .35 | 70 Tim Raines | 1.50 | 101 Schmidt (Action) | .60 |
| 9 Ron Guidry | .30 | 40 Dave Parker | .40 | 71 Roy Lee Jackson | .07 | 102 Dan Briggs | .07 |
| 10 Guidry (Action) | .15 | 41 Parker (Action) | .20 | 72 Rick Auerbach | .07 | 103 Bob Lacey | .07 |
| 11 Gary Alexander | .07 | 42 Rick Sofield | .07 | 73 Buddy Solomon | .07 | 104 Rance Mulliniks | .07 |
| 12 Moose Haas | .07 | 43 Mike Cubbage | .07 | 74 Bob Clark | .07 | 105 Kirk Gibson | 1.25 |
| 13 Lamar Johnson | .07 | 44 Britt Burns | .10 | 75 Tommy John | .25 | 106 Enrique Romo | .07 |
| 14 Steve Howe | .07 | 45 Rick Cerone | .07 | 76 Greg Pryor | .07 | 107 Wayne Krenchicki | .07 |
| 15 Ellis Valentine | .07 | 46 Jerry Augustine | .07 | 77 Miguel Dilone | .07 | 108 Bob Sykes | .07 |
| 16 Steve Comer | .07 | 47 Jeff Leonard | .15 | 78 George Medich | .07 | 109 Dave Revering | .07 |
| 17 Darrell Evans | .15 | 48 Bobby Castillo | .07 | 79 Bob Bailor | .07 | 110 Carlton Fisk | .30 |
| 18 Fernando Arroyo | .07 | 49 Alvis Woods | .07 | 80 Jim Palmer | .50 | 111 Fisk (Action) | .15 |
| 19 Ernie Whitt | .07 | 50 Buddy Bell | .15 | 81 Palmer (Action) | .15 | 112 Billy Sample | .07 |
| 20 Garry Maddox | .07 | 51 Cubs Rookies: | .30 | 82 Bob Welch | .10 | 113 Steve McCatty | .07 |
| 21 Orioles Rookies: | 13.00 | Jay Howell, C. Lezcano, | | 83 Yankees Rookies: | .50 | 114 Ken Landreaux | .07 |
| Bob Bonner, Cal Ripken, | | Ty Waler | | S. Balboni, A. Robertson, | | 115 Gaylord Perry | .40 |
| Jeff Schneider | | 52 Larry Andersen | .07 | A. McGaffigan | | 116 Jim Wohlford | .07 |
| 22 Jim Beattie | .07 | 53 Greg Gross | .07 | 84 Rennie Stennett | .07 | 117 Rawly Eastwick | .07 |
| 23 Willie Hernandez | .20 | 54 Ron Hassey | .07 | 85 Lynn McGlothen | .07 | 118 Expos Rookies: | .30 |
| 24 Dave Frost | .07 | 55 Rick Burleson | .07 | 86 Dane Iorg | .07 | Brad Mills, Terry Francona, |
| 25 Jerry Remy | .07 | 56 Mark Littell | .07 | 87 Matt Keough | .07 | Bryn Smith | |
| 26 George Orta | .07 | 57 Craig Reynolds | .07 | 88 Biff Pocoroba | .07 | 119 Joe Pittman | .07 |

| NO. | PLAYER | MINT |
|---|---|---|
| 120 | Gary Lucas | .07 |
| 121 | Ed Lynch | .12 |
| 122 | Jamie Easterly | .07 |
| 123 | Danny Goodwin | .07 |
| 124 | Reid Nichols | .07 |
| 125 | Danny Ainge | .07 |
| 126 | Braves Leaders: C. Washington, Rick Mahler | .15 |
| 127 | Lonnie Smith | .12 |
| 128 | Frank Pastore | .07 |
| 129 | Checklist No. 1 | .15 |
| 130 | Julio Cruz | .07 |
| 131 | Stan Bahnsen | .07 |
| 132 | Lee May | .07 |
| 133 | Pat Underwood | .07 |
| 134 | Dan Ford | .07 |
| 135 | Adny Rincon | .07 |
| 136 | Lenn Sakata | .07 |
| 137 | George Cappuzzello | .07 |
| 138 | Tony Pena | .25 |
| 139 | Jeff Jones | .07 |
| 140 | Ron Leflore | .07 |
| 141 | Indians Rookies: Chris Bando, Von Hayes, Tom Brennan | 1.50 |
| 142 | Dave LaRoche | .07 |
| 143 | Mookie Wilson | .15 |
| 144 | Fred Breining | .12 |
| 145 | Bob Horner | .35 |
| 146 | Mike Griffin | .07 |
| 147 | Denny Walling | .07 |
| 148 | Mickey Klutts | .07 |
| 149 | Pat Putnam | .07 |
| 150 | Ted Simmons | .15 |
| 151 | Dave Edwards | .07 |
| 152 | Ramon Aviles | .07 |
| 153 | Roger Erickson | .07 |
| 154 | Dennis Werth | .07 |
| 155 | Otto Velez | .07 |
| 156 | A's Leaders: Rickey Henderson, Steve McCatty | .15 |
| 157 | Steve Crawford | .10 |
| 158 | Brian Downing | .07 |
| 159 | Larry Biittner | .07 |
| 160 | Luis Tiant | .10 |
| 161 | Batting Leaders: B. Madlock, C. Lansford | .15 |
| 162 | Home Run Leaders: Bobby Grich, Mike Schmidt, T. Armas, Dwight Evans, Eddie Murray | .25 |
| 163 | RBI Leaders: M. Schmidt, E. Murray | .25 |
| 164 | Stolen Base Leaders: R. Henderson, T. Raines | .25 |
| 165 | Victory Leaders: Tom Seaver, D. Martinez, Steve McCatty, Pete Vuckovich, Jack Morris | .25 |
| 166 | Strikeout Leaders: F. Valenzuela, L. Barker | .20 |
| 167 | ERA Leaders: Steve McCatty, Nolan Ryan | .20 |
| 168 | Leading Relievers: Bruce Sutter, Rollie Fingers | .25 |
| 169 | Charlie Leibrandt | .10 |
| 170 | Jim Bibby | .07 |
| 171 | Giants Rookies: Bob Tufts, Bob Brenly, Chili Davis | 1.00 |
| 172 | Bill Gullickson | .07 |
| 173 | Jamie Quirk | .07 |
| 174 | Dave Ford | .07 |
| 175 | Jerry Mumphrey | .07 |
| 176 | Dewey Robinson | .07 |
| 177 | John Ellis | .07 |
| 178 | Dyar Miller | .07 |
| 179 | Steve Garvey | .75 |
| 180 | Garvey (Action) | .35 |
| 181 | Silvio Martinez | .07 |
| 182 | Larry Herndon | .07 |
| 183 | Mike Proly | .07 |
| 184 | Mick Kelleher | .07 |
| 185 | Phil Niekro | .35 |
| 186 | Cardinals Leaders: K. Hernandez, B. Forsch | .15 |
| 187 | Jeff Newman | .07 |
| 188 | Randy Martz | .07 |
| 189 | Glenn Hoffman | .07 |
| 190 | J.R. Richard | .10 |
| 191 | Tim Wallach (R) | 1.50 |
| 192 | Broderick Perkins | .07 |
| 193 | Darrell Jackson | .07 |
| 194 | Mike Vail | .07 |
| 195 | Paul Molitor | .35 |
| 196 | Willie Upshaw | .25 |
| 197 | Shane Rawley | .07 |
| 198 | Chris Speier | .07 |
| 199 | Don Aase | .07 |
| 200 | George Brett | 1.50 |
| 201 | Brett (Action) | .60 |
| 202 | Rick Manning | .07 |
| 203 | Blue Jays Rookies: Jesse Barfield, Brian Milner, Boomer Wells | 5.00 |
| 204 | Gray Roenicke | .07 |
| 205 | Neil Allen | .07 |
| 206 | Tony Bernazard | .07 |
| 207 | Rod Scurry | .07 |
| 208 | Bobby Murcer | .15 |
| 209 | Gary Lavelle | .07 |
| 210 | Keith Hernandez | .50 |
| 211 | Dan Petry | .25 |
| 212 | Mario Mendoza | .07 |
| 213 | Dave Stewart | 1.50 |
| 214 | Brian Asselstine | .07 |
| 215 | Mike Krukow | .07 |
| 216 | White Sox Leaders: Chet Lemon, Dennis Lamp | .15 |
| 217 | Bo McLaughlin | .07 |
| 218 | Dave Roberts | .07 |
| 219 | John Curtis | .07 |
| 220 | Manny Trillo | .07 |
| 221 | Jim Slaton | .07 |
| 222 | Butch Wynegar | .07 |
| 223 | Lloyd Moseby | .25 |
| 224 | Bruce Bochte | .07 |
| 225 | Mike Torrez | .07 |
| 226 | Checklist No. 2 | .15 |
| 227 | Ray Burris | .07 |
| 228 | Sam Mejias | .07 |
| 229 | Geoff Zahn | .07 |
| 230 | Willie Wilson | .25 |
| 231 | Phillies Rookies: Ozzie Virgil, Bob Dernier, Mark Davis | .45 |
| 232 | Terry Crowley | .07 |
| 233 | Duane Kuiper | .07 |
| 234 | Ron Hodges | .07 |
| 235 | Mike Easler | .10 |
| 236 | John Martin | .07 |
| 237 | Rusty Kuntz | .07 |
| 238 | Kevin Saucier | .07 |
| 239 | Jon Matlack | .07 |
| 240 | Bucky Dent | .10 |
| 241 | Dent (Action) | .07 |
| 242 | Milt May | .07 |
| 243 | Bob Owchinko | .07 |
| 244 | Rufino Linares | .07 |
| 245 | Ken Reitz | .07 |
| 246 | Mets Leaders: Hubie Brooks, Mike Scott | .20 |
| 247 | Pedro Guerrero | .75 |
| 248 | Frank LaCorte | .07 |
| 249 | Tim Flannery | .07 |
| 250 | Tug McGraw | .10 |
| 251 | Fred Lynn | .35 |
| 252 | Lynn (Action) | .20 |
| 253 | Chuck Baker | .07 |
| 254 | Jorge Bell (R) | 10.00 |
| 255 | Tony Perez | .20 |
| 256 | Perez (Action) | .12 |
| 257 | Larry Harlow | .07 |
| 258 | Bo Diaz | .10 |
| 259 | Rodney Scott | .07 |
| 260 | Bruce Sutter | .25 |
| 261 | Tigers Rookies: Howard Bailey, M. Castillo, Dave Rucker | .20 |
| 262 | Doug Bair | .07 |
| 263 | Victor Cruz | .07 |
| 264 | Dan Quisenberry | .20 |
| 265 | Al Bumbry | .07 |
| 266 | Rick Leach | .12 |
| 267 | Kurt Bevacqua | .07 |
| 268 | Rickey Keeton | .07 |
| 269 | Jim Essian | .07 |
| 270 | Rusty Staub | .20 |
| 271 | Larry Bradford | .07 |
| 272 | Bump Wills | .07 |
| 273 | Doug Bird | .07 |
| 274 | Bob Ojeda (R) | .75 |
| 275 | Bob Watson | .07 |
| 276 | Angels Leaders: Ken Forsch, Rod Carew | .20 |
| 277 | Terry Puhl | .07 |
| 278 | John Littlefield | .07 |
| 279 | Bill Russell | .07 |
| 280 | Ben Oglivie | .10 |
| 281 | John Verhoeven | .07 |
| 282 | Ken Macha | .07 |
| 283 | Brian Allard | .07 |
| 284 | Bob Grich | .10 |
| 285 | Sparky Lyle | .10 |
| 286 | Bill Fahey | .07 |
| 287 | Alan Bannister | .07 |
| 288 | Garry Templeton | .15 |
| 289 | Bob Stanley | .07 |
| 290 | Ken Singleton | .15 |
| 291 | Pirates Rookies: Vance Law, Bob Long, Johnny Ray | .85 |
| 292 | David Palmer | .07 |
| 293 | Rob Picciolo | .07 |
| 294 | Mike LaCoss | .07 |
| 295 | Jason Thompson | .10 |
| 296 | Bob Walk | .07 |
| 297 | Clint Hurdle | .07 |
| 298 | Danny Darwin | .07 |
| 299 | Steve Trout | .07 |
| 300 | Reggie Jackson | 1.00 |
| 301 | Jackson (Action) | .40 |
| 302 | Doug Flynn | .07 |
| 303 | Bill Caudill | .10 |
| 304 | Johnnie LeMaster | .07 |
| 305 | Don Sutton | .40 |
| 306 | Sutton (Action) | .10 |
| 307 | Randy Bass | .07 |
| 308 | Charlie Moore | .07 |
| 309 | Pete Redfern | .07 |
| 310 | Mike Hargrove | .10 |
| 311 | Dodgers Leaders: Dusty Baker, Burt Hooton | .20 |
| 312 | Lenny Randle | .07 |
| 313 | John Harris | .07 |
| 314 | Buck Martinez | .07 |
| 315 | Burt Hooton | .07 |
| 316 | Steve Braun | .07 |
| 317 | Dick Ruthven | .07 |
| 318 | Mike Heath | .07 |
| 319 | Dave Rozema | .07 |
| 320 | Chris Chambliss | .10 |
| 321 | Chambliss (Action) | .07 |
| 322 | Garry Hancock | .07 |
| 323 | Bill Lee | .07 |
| 324 | Steve Dillard | .07 |
| 325 | Jose Cruz | .15 |
| 326 | Pete Falcone | .07 |
| 327 | Joe Nolan | .07 |
| 328 | Ed Farmer | .07 |
| 329 | U.L. Washington | .07 |
| 330 | Rick Wise | .07 |
| 331 | Benny Ayala | .07 |
| 332 | Don Robinson | .07 |
| 333 | Brewers Rookies: Frank DiPino, M. Edwards, Chuck Porter | .20 |
| 334 | Aurelio Rodriguez | .07 |
| 335 | Jim Sundberg | .07 |
| 336 | Mariners Leaders: G. Abbott, T. Paciorek | .15 |
| 337 | Pete Rose (AS) | .75 |
| 338 | Dave Lopes (AS) | .10 |
| 339 | Mike Schmidt (AS) | .45 |
| 340 | Dave Concepcion (AS) | .15 |
| 341 | Andre Dawson (AS) | .20 |
| 342 | George Foster (AS) | .25 |
| 342 | George Foster (autograph deleted) | 3.00 |
| 343 | Dave Parker (AS) | .25 |
| 344 | Gary Carter (AS) | .25 |
| 345 | F. Valenzuela (AS) | .25 |
| 346 | Tom Seaver (AS) | .25 |
| 347 | Bruce Sutter (AS) | .15 |
| 348 | Derrel Thomas | .07 |
| 349 | George Frazier | .07 |
| 350 | Thad Bosley | .07 |
| 351 | Reds Rookies: Geoff Coumbe, Scott Brown, P. Householder | .15 |
| 352 | Dick Davis | .07 |
| 353 | Jack O'Connor | .07 |
| 354 | Roberto Ramos | .07 |
| 355 | Dwight Evans | .15 |
| 356 | Denny Lewallyn | .07 |
| 357 | Butch Hobson | .07 |
| 358 | Mike Parrott | .07 |
| 359 | Jim Dwyer | .07 |
| 360 | Len Barker | .07 |
| 361 | Rafael Landestoy | .07 |
| 362 | Jim Wright (wrong autograph) | .07 |
| 363 | Bob Molinaro | .07 |
| 364 | Doyle Alexander | .07 |
| 365 | Bill Madlock | .25 |
| 366 | Padres Leaders: L. Salazar, J. Eichelberger | .15 |
| 367 | Jim Kaat | .15 |
| 368 | Alex Trevino | .07 |
| 369 | Champ Summers | .07 |
| 370 | Mike Norris | .07 |
| 371 | Jerry Don Gleaton | .07 |
| 372 | Luis Gomez | .07 |
| 373 | Gene Nelson | .10 |
| 374 | Tim Blackwell | .07 |
| 375 | Dusty Baker | .12 |
| 376 | Chris Welsh | .10 |
| 377 | Kiko Garcia | .07 |
| 378 | Mike Caldwell | .07 |
| 379 | Rob Wilfong | .07 |
| 380 | Dave Stieb | .20 |
| 381 | Red Sox Rookies: D. Schmidt, Julio Valdez, Bruce Hurst | .40 |
| 382 | Joe Simpson | .07 |
| 383 | P. Perez (error) No position on front | 30.00 |
| 384 | Keith Moreland | .07 |
| 385 | Ken Forsch | .07 |
| 386 | Jerry White | .07 |
| 387 | Tom Veryzer | .07 |
| 388 | Joe Rudi | .07 |
| 389 | George Vukovich | .07 |
| 390 | Eddie Murray | 1.00 |
| 391 | Dave Tobik | .07 |
| 392 | Rick Bosetti | .07 |
| 393 | Al Hrabosky | .07 |
| 394 | Checklist No. 3 | .12 |
| 395 | Omar Moreno | .10 |
| 396 | Twins Leaders: John Castino, F. Arroyo | .15 |
| 397 | Ken Brett | .07 |
| 398 | Mike Squires | .07 |
| 399 | Pat Zachry | .07 |
| 400 | Johnny Bench | .75 |
| 401 | Bench (Action) | .35 |
| 402 | Bill Stein | .07 |
| 403 | Jim Tracy | .07 |
| 404 | Dickie Thon | .10 |
| 405 | Rick Reuschel | .07 |
| 406 | Al Holland | .07 |
| 407 | Danny Boone | .07 |
| 408 | Ed Romero | .07 |
| 409 | Don Cooper | .07 |
| 410 | Ron Cey | .15 |
| 411 | Cey (Action) | .10 |
| 412 | Luis Leal | .07 |
| 413 | Dan Meyer | .07 |
| 414 | Elias Sosa | .07 |
| 415 | Don Baylor | .15 |

| NO. PLAYER | MINT |
|---|---|
| 416 Marty Bystrom | .07 |
| 417 Pat Kelly | .07 |
| 418 Rangers Rookies: | .25 |
| John Butcher, B. Johnson, Dave Schmidt | |
| 419 Steve Stone | .10 |
| 420 George Hendrick | .10 |
| 421 Mark Clear | .07 |
| 422 Cliff Johnson | .07 |
| 423 Stan Papi | .07 |
| 424 Bruce Benedict | .07 |
| 425 John Candelaria | .10 |
| 426 Orioles Leaders: | .15 |
| Eddie Murray, S. Stewart | |
| 427 Ron Oester | .07 |
| 428 LaMarr Hoyt | .15 |
| 429 John Wathan | .07 |
| 430 Vida Blue | .10 |
| 431 Blue (Action) | .07 |
| 432 Mike Scott | .50 |
| 433 Alan Ashby | .07 |
| 434 Joe LeFebvre | .07 |
| 435 Robin Yount | .60 |
| 436 Joe Strain | .07 |
| 437 Juan Berenguer | .07 |
| 438 Pete Mackanin | .07 |
| 439 Dave Righetti (R) | 2.00 |
| 440 Jeff Burroughs | .07 |
| 441 Astros Rookies: | .15 |
| Danny Heep, Billy Smith, Bobby Sprowl | |
| 442 Bruce Kison | .07 |
| 443 Mark Wagner | .07 |
| 444 Terry Forster | .10 |
| 445 Larry Parrish | .10 |
| 446 Wayne Garland | .07 |
| 447 Darrell Porter | .12 |
| 448 Porter (Action) | .07 |
| 449 Luis Aguayo | .07 |
| 450 Jack Morris | .50 |
| 451 Ed Miller | .07 |
| 452 Lee Smith (R) | 1.00 |
| 453 Art Howe | .07 |
| 454 Rick Langford | .07 |
| 455 Tom Burgmeier | .07 |
| 456 Cubs Leaders: | .15 |
| R. Martz, Bill Buckner | |
| 457 Tim Stoddard | .07 |
| 458 Willie Montanez | .07 |
| 459 Bruce Berenyi | .07 |
| 460 Jack Clark | .50 |
| 461 Rich Dotson | .10 |
| 462 Dave Chalk | .07 |
| 463 Jim Kern | .07 |
| 464 Juan Bonilla | .10 |
| 465 Lee Mazzilli | .07 |
| 466 Randy Lerch | .07 |
| 467 Mickey Hatcher | .07 |
| 468 Floyd Bannister | .10 |
| 469 Ed Ott | .07 |
| 470 John Mayberry | .07 |
| 471 Royals Rookies: | .30 |
| Mike Jones, Atlee Hammaker, Darryl Motley | |
| 472 Oscar Gamble | .07 |
| 473 Mike Stanton | .07 |
| 474 Ken Oberkfell | .07 |
| 475 Alan Trammell | .50 |
| 476 Brian Kingman | .07 |
| 477 Steve Yeager | .10 |
| 478 Ray Searage | .10 |
| 479 Rowland Office | .07 |
| 480 Steve Carlton | .75 |
| 481 Carlton (Action) | .30 |
| 482 Glenn Hubbard | .07 |
| 483 Gary Woods | .07 |
| 484 Ivan DeJesus | .07 |
| 485 Kent Tekulve | .10 |
| 486 Yankees Leaders: | .20 |
| J. Mumphrey, Tommy John | |
| 487 Bob McClure | .07 |
| 488 Ron Jackson | .07 |
| 489 Rick Dempsey | .07 |
| 490 Dennis Eckersley | .75 |
| 491 Checklist No. 4 | .15 |

| NO. PLAYER | MINT |
|---|---|
| 492 Joe Price | .07 |
| 493 Chet Lemon | .10 |
| 494 Hubie Brooks | .25 |
| 495 Dennis Leonard | .07 |
| 496 Johnny Grubb | .07 |
| 497 Jim Anderson | .07 |
| 498 Dave Bergman | .07 |
| 499 Paul Mirabella | .07 |
| 500 Rod Carew | .75 |
| 501 Carew (Action) | .30 |
| 502 Braves Rookies: | 1.25 |
| Steve Bedrosian, B. Butler, Larry Owen | |
| 503 Julio Gonzalez | .07 |
| 504 Rick Peters | .07 |
| 505 Graig Nettles | .20 |
| 506 Nettles (Action) | .15 |
| 507 Terry Harper | .07 |
| 508 Jody Davis (R) | .50 |
| 509 Harry Spilman | .07 |
| 510 Fernando Valenzuela | 1.00 |
| 511 Ruppert Jones | .07 |
| 512 Jerry Dybzinski | .07 |
| 513 Rick Rhoden | .07 |
| 514 Joe Ferguson | .07 |
| 515 Larry Bowa | .10 |
| 516 Bowa (Action) | .07 |
| 517 Mark Brouhard | .10 |
| 518 Garth Iorg | .07 |
| 519 Glenn Adams | .07 |
| 520 Mike Flanagan | .10 |
| 521 Billy Almon | .07 |
| 522 Chuck Rainey | .07 |
| 523 Gary Gray | .07 |
| 524 Tom Hausman | .07 |
| 525 Ray Knight | .10 |
| 526 Expos Leaders: | .15 |
| W. Cromartie, Bill Gullickson | |
| 527 John Henry Johnson | .07 |
| 528 Matt Alexander | .07 |
| 529 Allen Ripley | .07 |
| 530 Dickie Noles | .07 |
| 531 A's Rookies: | .12 |
| Rich Bordi, M. Budaska, Kelvin Moore | |
| 532 Toby Harrah | .07 |
| 533 Joaquin Andujar | .15 |
| 534 Dave McKay | .07 |
| 535 Lance Parrish | .40 |
| 536 Rafael Ramirez | .07 |
| 537 Doug Capilla | .07 |
| 538 Lou Piniella | .15 |
| 539 Vern Ruhle | .07 |
| 540 Andre Dawson | .50 |
| 541 Barry Evans | .07 |
| 542 Ned Yost | .07 |
| 543 Bill Robinson | .07 |
| 544 Larry Christenson | .07 |
| 545 Reggie Smith | .10 |
| 546 Smith (Action) | .07 |
| 547 Rod Carew (AS) | .25 |
| 548 Willie Randolph (AS) | .12 |
| 549 George Brett (AS) | .40 |
| 550 Bucky Dent (AS) | .12 |
| 551 Reggie Jackson (AS) | .40 |
| 552 Ken Singleton (AS) | .12 |
| 553 Dave Winfield (AS) | .35 |
| 554 Carlton Fisk (AS) | .20 |
| 555 Scott McGregor (AS) | .12 |
| 556 Jack Morris (AS) | .15 |
| 557 Rich Gossage (AS) | .20 |
| 558 Jim Tudor | .25 |
| 559 Indians Leaders: | .15 |
| M. Hargrove, B. Blyleven | |
| 560 Doug Corbett | .07 |
| 561 Cardinals Rookies: | .20 |
| Glenn Brummer, Luis DeLeon, Gene Roof | |
| 562 Mike O'Berry | .07 |
| 563 Ross Baumgarten | .07 |
| 564 Doug DeCinces | .15 |
| 565 Jackson Todd | .07 |
| 566 Mike Jorgensen | .07 |
| 567 Bob Babcock | .07 |

| NO. PLAYER | MINT |
|---|---|
| 568 Joe Pettini | .07 |
| 569 Willie Randolph | .10 |
| 570 Randolph (Action) | .07 |
| 571 Glenn Abbott | .07 |
| 572 Juan Beniquez | .07 |
| 573 Rick Waits | .07 |
| 574 Mike Ramsey | .07 |
| 575 Al Cowens | .07 |
| 576 Giants Leaders: | .12 |
| Milt May, Vida Blue | |
| 577 Rick Monday | .07 |
| 578 Shooty Babitt | .07 |
| 579 Rick Mahler (R) | .35 |
| 580 Bobby Bonds | .10 |
| 581 Ron Reed | .07 |
| 582 Luis Pujols | .07 |
| 583 Tippy Martinez | .07 |
| 584 Hosken Powell | .07 |
| 585 Rollie Fingers | .25 |
| 586 Fingers (Action) | .15 |
| 587 Tim Lollar | .07 |
| 588 Dale Berra | .07 |
| 589 Dave Stapleton | .07 |
| 590 Al Oliver | .25 |
| 591 Oliver (Action) | .15 |
| 592 Craig Swan | .07 |
| 593 Billy Smith | .07 |
| 594 Renie Martin | .07 |
| 595 Dave Collins | .07 |
| 596 Damaso Garcia | .12 |
| 597 Wayne Nordhagen | .07 |
| 598 Bob Galasso | .07 |
| 599 White Sox Rookies: | .12 |
| Jay Loviglio, R. Patterson, Leo Sutherland | |
| 600 Dave Winfield | .75 |
| 601 Sid Monge | .07 |
| 602 Freddie Patek | .07 |
| 603 Rich Hebner | .07 |
| 604 Orlando Sanchez | .10 |
| 605 Steve Rogers | .10 |
| 606 Blue Jays Leaders: | .10 |
| John Mayberry, Dave Stieb | |
| 607 Leon Durham | .30 |
| 608 Jerry Royster | .07 |
| 609 Rick Sutcliffe | .20 |
| 610 Rickey Henderson | 1.50 |
| 611 Joe Niekro | .12 |
| 612 Gary Ward | .07 |
| 613 Jim Gantner | .07 |
| 614 Juan Eichelberger | .07 |
| 615 Bob Boone | .07 |
| 616 Boone (Action) | .07 |
| 617 Scott McGregor | .10 |
| 618 Tim Foli | .07 |
| 619 Bill Campbell | .07 |
| 620 Ken Griffey | .12 |
| 621 Griffey (Action) | .07 |
| 622 Dennis Lamp | .07 |
| 623 Mets Rookies: | .75 |
| Ron Gardenhire, T. Leach, Tim Leary | |
| 624 Fergie Jenkins | .15 |
| 625 Hal McRae | .10 |
| 626 Randy Jones | .07 |
| 627 Enos Cabell | .07 |
| 628 Bill Travers | .07 |
| 629 Johnny Wockenfuss | .07 |
| 630 Joe Charboneau | .07 |
| 631 Gene Tenace | .07 |
| 632 Bryan Clark | .10 |
| 633 Mitchell Page | .07 |
| 634 Checklist No. 5 | .15 |
| 635 Ron Davis | .07 |
| 636 Phillies Leaders: | .25 |
| Pete Rose, Steve Carlton | |
| 637 Rick Camp | .07 |
| 638 John Milner | .07 |
| 639 Ken Kravec | .07 |
| 640 Cesar Cedeno | .10 |
| 641 Steve Mura | .07 |
| 642 Mike Scioscia | .07 |
| 643 Pete Vuckovich | .12 |
| 644 John Castino | .07 |
| 645 Frank White | .10 |

| NO. PLAYER | MINT |
|---|---|
| 646 White (Action) | .07 |
| 647 Warren Brusstar | .07 |
| 648 Jose Morales | .07 |
| 649 Ken Clay | .07 |
| 650 Carl Yastrzemski | 1.00 |
| 651 Yastrzemski (Action) | .50 |
| 652 Steve Nicosia | .07 |
| 653 Angels Rookies: | 2.50 |
| Luis Sanchez, Tom Brunansky, Daryl Sconiers | |
| 654 Jim Morrison | .07 |
| 655 Joel Youngblood | .07 |
| 656 Eddie Whitson | .10 |
| 657 Tom Poquette | .07 |
| 658 Tito Landrum | .07 |
| 659 Fred Martinez | .07 |
| 660 Dave Concepcion | .12 |
| 661 Concepcion (Action) | .07 |
| 662 Luis Salazar | .07 |
| 663 Hector Cruz | .07 |
| 664 Dan Spillner | .07 |
| 665 Jim Clancy | .07 |
| 666 Tigers Leaders: | .20 |
| Steve Kemp, Dan Petry | |
| 667 Jeff Reardon | .10 |
| 668 Dale Murphy | 2.00 |
| 669 Larry Milbourne | .07 |
| 670 Steve Kemp | .10 |
| 671 Mike Davis | .15 |
| 672 Bob Knepper | .07 |
| 673 Keith Drumright | .07 |
| 674 Dave Goltz | .07 |
| 675 Cecil Cooper | .25 |
| 676 Sal Butera | .07 |
| 677 Alfredo Griffin | .10 |
| 678 Tom Paciorek | .07 |
| 679 Sammy Stewart | .07 |
| 680 Gary Matthews | .10 |
| 681 Dodgers Rookies: | 2.50 |
| Steve Sax, Mike Marshall, Ron Roenicke | |
| 682 Jesse Jefferson | .07 |
| 683 Phil Garner | .07 |
| 684 Harold Baines | .75 |
| 685 Bert Blyleven | .15 |
| 686 Gary Allenson | .07 |
| 687 Greg Minton | .07 |
| 688 Leon Roberts | .07 |
| 689 Larry Sorensen | .07 |
| 690 Dave Kingman | .20 |
| 691 Dan Schatzeder | .07 |
| 692 Wayne Gross | .07 |
| 693 Cesar Geronimo | .07 |
| 694 Dave Wehrmeister | .07 |
| 695 Warren Cromartie | .07 |
| 696 Pirates Leaders: | .15 |
| Bill Madlock, B. Solomon | |
| 697 John Montefusco | .07 |
| 698 Tony Scott | .07 |
| 699 Dick Tidrow | .07 |
| 700 George Foster | .25 |
| 701 Foster (Action) | .15 |
| 702 Steve Renko | .07 |
| 703 Brewers Leaders: | .15 |
| Cecil Cooper, P. Vuckovich | |
| 704 Mickey Rivers | .07 |
| 705 Rivers (Action) | .07 |
| 706 Barry Foote | .07 |
| 707 Mark Bomback | .07 |
| 708 Gene Richards | .07 |
| 709 Don Money | .07 |
| 710 Jerry Reuss | .10 |
| 711 Mariners Rookies: | .50 |
| Dave Edler, Reggie Walton, Dave Henderson | |
| 712 Denny Martinez | .07 |
| 713 Del Unser | .07 |
| 714 Jerry Koosman | .10 |
| 715 Willie Stargell | .50 |
| 716 Stargell (Action) | .20 |
| 717 Rick Miller | .07 |
| 718 Charlie Hough | .07 |
| 719 Jerry Narron | .07 |
| 720 Greg Luzinski | .15 |
| 721 Luzinski (Action) | .10 |

| NO. PLAYER | MINT |
|---|---|
| 722 Jerry Martin | .07 |
| 723 Junior Kennedy | .07 |
| 724 Dave Rosello | .07 |
| 725 Amos Otis | .10 |
| 726 Otis (Action) | .07 |
| 727 Sixto Lezcano | .07 |
| 728 Aurelio Lopez | .07 |
| 729 Jim Spencer | .07 |
| 730 Gary Carter | .75 |
| 731 Padres Rookies: | .15 |
|     Doug Gwosdz, Mike | |
|     Armstrong, Fred Kuhaulua | |
| 732 Mike Lum | .07 |
| 733 Larry McWilliams | .10 |
| 734 Mike Ivie | .07 |
| 735 Rudy May | .07 |
| 736 Jerry Turner | .07 |
| 737 Reggie Cleveland | .07 |
| 738 Dave Engle | .07 |
| 739 Joey McLaughlin | .07 |

| NO. PLAYER | MINT |
|---|---|
| 740 Dave Lopes | .10 |
| 741 Lopes (Action) | .07 |
| 742 Dick Drago | .07 |
| 743 John Stearns | .07 |
| 744 Mike Witt (R) | 1.00 |
| 745 Bake McBride | .07 |
| 746 Andre Thornton | .12 |
| 747 John Lowenstein | .07 |
| 748 Marc Hill | .07 |
| 749 Bob Shirley | .07 |
| 750 Jim Rice | .75 |
| 751 Rick Honeycutt | .07 |
| 752 Lee Lacy | .07 |
| 753 Tom Brookens | .07 |
| 754 Joe Morgan | .50 |
| 755 Morgan (Action) | .20 |
| 756 Reds Leaders: | .20 |
|     Ken Griffey, Tom Seaver | |
| 757 Tom Underwood | .07 |

| NO. PLAYER | MINT |
|---|---|
| 758 Claudell Washington | .12 |
| 759 Paul Splittorff | .07 |
| 760 Bill Buckner | .15 |
| 761 Dave Smith | .07 |
| 762 Mike Phillips | .07 |
| 763 Tom Hume | .07 |
| 764 Steve Swisher | .07 |
| 765 Gorman Thomas | .12 |
| 766 Twins Rookies: | 4.00 |
|     Lenny Faedo, Kent Hrbek, | |
|     Tim Laudner | |
| 767 Roy Smalley | .07 |
| 768 Jerry Garvin | .07 |
| 769 Richie Zisk | .07 |
| 770 Rich Gossage | .25 |
| 771 Gossage (Action) | .15 |
| 772 Bert Campaneris | .07 |
| 773 John Denny | .10 |
| 774 Jay Johnstone | .07 |

| NO. PLAYER | MINT |
|---|---|
| 775 Bob Forsch | .07 |
| 776 Mark Belanger | .07 |
| 777 Tom Griffin | .07 |
| 778 Kevin Hickey | .07 |
| 779 Grant Jackson | .07 |
| 780 Pete Rose | 2.50 |
| 781 Rose (Action) | .85 |
| 782 Frank Taveras | .07 |
| 783 Greg Harris | .20 |
| 784 Milt Wilcox | .07 |
| 785 Dan Driessen | .07 |
| 786 Red Sox Leaders: | .20 |
|     C. Lansford, M. Torrez | |
| 787 Fred Stanley | .07 |
| 788 Woodie Fryman | .07 |
| 789 Checklist No. 6 | .15 |
| 790 Larry Gura | .07 |
| 791 Bobby Brown | .07 |
| 792 Frank Tanana | .15 |

## 1982 Topps Traded....Complete Set of 132 Cards—Value $25.00

Updates the main 1982 card set with players who changed teams during the season and rookies. Unlike the 1981 Traded set, the cards are numbered from 1T to 132T. The complete set was packaged in a printed box and only distributed through card hobby dealers.

| NO. PLAYER | MINT |
|---|---|
| 1 T Doyle Alexander | .15 |
| 2 T Jesse Barfield | 3.00 |
| 3 T Ross Baumgarten | .10 |
| 4 T Steve Bedrosian | .75 |
| 5 T Mark Belanger | .10 |
| 6 T Kurt Bevacqua | .10 |
| 7 T Tim Blackwell | .10 |
| 8 T Vida Blue | .15 |
| 9 T Bob Boone | .10 |
| 10 T Larry Bowa | .20 |
| 11 T Dan Briggs | .10 |
| 12 T Bobby Brown | .10 |
| 13 T Tom Brunansky | 1.50 |
| 14 T Jeff Burroughs | .12 |
| 15 T Enos Cabell | .10 |
| 16 T Bill Campbell | .10 |
| 17 T Bobby Castillo | .10 |
| 18 T Bill Caudill | .15 |
| 19 T Cesar Cedeno | .15 |
| 20 T Dave Collins | .12 |
| 21 T Doug Corbett | .10 |
| 22 T Al Cowens | .15 |
| 23 T Chili Davis | 1.25 |
| 24 T Dick Davis | .10 |
| 25 T Ron Davis | .10 |
| 26 T Doug DeCince | .25 |
| 27 T Ivan DeJesus | .12 |
| 28 T Bob Dernier | .20 |
| 29 T Bo Diaz | .10 |
| 30 T Roger Erickson | .10 |
| 31 T Jim Essian | .10 |
| 32 T Ed Farmer | .10 |
| 33 T Doug Flynn | .10 |

| NO. PLAYER | MINT |
|---|---|
| 34 T Tim Foli | .10 |
| 35 T Dan Ford | .10 |
| 36 T George Foster | .35 |
| 37 T Dave Frost | .10 |
| 38 T Rich Gale | .10 |
| 39 T Ron Gardenhire | .10 |
| 40 T Ken Griffey | .15 |
| 41 T Greg Harris | .10 |
| 42 T Von Hayes | 1.25 |
| 43 T Larry Herndon | .10 |
| 44 T Kent Hrbek | 4.00 |
| 45 T Mike Ivie | .10 |
| 46 T Grant Jackson | .10 |
| 47 T Reggie Jackson | 2.00 |
| 48 T Ron Jackson | .10 |
| 49 T Fergie Jenkins | .40 |
| 50 T Lamar Johnson | .10 |
| 51 T Ray Johnson | .10 |
| 52 T Jay Johnstone | .10 |
| 53 T Mick Kelleher | .10 |
| 54 T Steve Kemp | .12 |
| 55 T Junior Kennedy | .10 |
| 56 T Jim Kern | .10 |
| 57 T Ray Knight | .20 |
| 58 T Wayne Krenchicki | .10 |
| 59 T Mike Krukow | .10 |
| 60 T Duane Kuiper | .10 |
| 61 T Mike LaCoss | .10 |
| 62 T Chet Lemon | .15 |
| 63 T Sixto Lezcano | .10 |
| 64 T Dave Lopes | .15 |
| 65 T Jerry Martin | .10 |
| 66 T Renie Martin | .10 |

| NO. PLAYER | MINT |
|---|---|
| 67 T John Mayberry | .10 |
| 68 T Lee Mazzilli | .10 |
| 69 T Bake McBride | .15 |
| 70 T Dan Meyer | .10 |
| 71 T Larry Milbourne | .10 |
| 72 T Eddie Milner | .25 |
| 73 T Sid Monge | .10 |
| 74 T John Montefusco | .10 |
| 75 T Jose Morales | .10 |
| 76 T Keith Moreland | .15 |
| 77 T Jim Morrison | .10 |
| 78 T Rance Mulliniks | .10 |
| 79 T Steve Mura | .10 |
| 80 T Gene Nelson | .10 |
| 81 T Joe Nolan | .10 |
| 82 T Dickie Noles | .10 |
| 83 T Al Oliver | .35 |
| 84 T Jorge Orta | .10 |
| 85 T Tom Paciorek | .10 |
| 86 T Larry Parrish | .20 |
| 87 T Jack Perconte | .10 |
| 88 T Gaylord Perry | 1.00 |
| 89 T Rob Picciolo | .10 |
| 90 T Joe Pittman | .10 |
| 91 T Hosken Powell | .10 |
| 92 T Mike Proly | .10 |
| 93 T Greg Pryor | .10 |
| 94 T Charlie Puleo | .10 |
| 95 T Shane Rawley | .12 |
| 96 T Johnny Ray | .75 |
| 97 T Dave Revering | .10 |
| 98 T Cal Ripken | 10.00 |
| 99 T Allen Ripley | .10 |

| NO. PLAYER | MINT |
|---|---|
| 100 T Bill Robinson | .10 |
| 101 T Aurelio Rodriquez | .10 |
| 102 T Joe Rudi | .10 |
| 103 T Steve Sax | 2.00 |
| 104 T Dan Schatzeder | .10 |
| 105 T Bob Shirley | .10 |
| 106 T Eric Show (RR) | .60 |
| 107 T Roy Smalley | .10 |
| 108 T Lonnie Smith | .15 |
| 109 T Ozzie Smith | 2.50 |
| 110 T Reggie Smith | .20 |
| 111 T Lary Sorensen | .10 |
| 112 T Elias Sosa | .10 |
| 113 T Mike Stanton | .10 |
| 114 T Steve Stroughter | .10 |
| 115 T Champ Summers | .10 |
| 116 T Rick Sutcliffe | .50 |
| 117 T Frank Tanana | .10 |
| 118 T Frank Taveras | .10 |
| 119 T Garry Templeton | .20 |
| 120 T Alex Trevino | .10 |
| 121 T Jerry Turner | .10 |
| 122 T Ed VandeBerg (RR) | .25 |
| 123 T Tom Veryzer | .10 |
| 124 T Ron Washington | .10 |
| 125 T Bob Watson | .10 |
| 126 T Dennis Werth | .10 |
| 127 T Eddie Whitson | .10 |
| 128 T Rob Wilfong | .10 |
| 129 T Bump Wills | .10 |
| 130 T Gary Woods | .10 |
| 131 T Butch Wynegar | .10 |
| 132 T Traded Checklist | .25 |

# 1983 Topps....Complete Set of 792 Cards—Value $100.00

Features the rookie cards of Willie McGee, Ryne Sandberg, Wade Boggs, and Tony Gwynn.

| NO. | PLAYER | MINT |
|---|---|---|
| 1 | Record—T. Armas | .20 |
| | 11 Rightfield Putouts | |
| 2 | Record—R. Henderson | .30 |
| | Stolen Base Record | |
| 3 | Record—G. Minton | .08 |
| | No HR's in 269⅓ Innings | |
| 4 | Record—L. Parrish | .15 |
| | Threw Out 3 in AS Game | |
| 5 | Record—Trillo | .08 |
| | 479 Errorless Chances | |
| 6 | Record—J. Wathan | .08 |
| | 31st Stolen Base, Catcher | |
| 7 | Gene Richards | .06 |
| 8 | Steve Balboni | .10 |
| 9 | Joey McLaughlin | .06 |
| 10 | Gorman Thomas | .15 |
| 11 | Billy Gardner (Mgr.) | .06 |
| 12 | Paul Mirabella | .06 |
| 13 | Larry Herndon | .08 |
| 14 | Frank LaCorte | .06 |
| 15 | Ron Cey | .15 |
| 16 | George Vukovich | .06 |
| 17 | Kent Tekulve | .06 |
| 18 | Tekulve (Veteran) | .06 |
| 19 | Oscar Gamble | .08 |
| 20 | Carlton Fisk | .20 |
| 21 | Orioles Leaders: | .20 |
| | Eddie Murray, Jim Palmer | |
| 22 | Randy Martz | .06 |
| 23 | Mike Heath | .06 |
| 24 | Steve Mura | .06 |
| 25 | Hal McRae | .06 |
| 26 | Jerry Roystar | .06 |
| 27 | Doug Corbett | .06 |
| 28 | Bruce Bochte | .06 |
| 29 | Randy Jones | .06 |
| 30 | Jim Rice | .50 |
| 31 | Bill Gullickson | .08 |
| 32 | Dave Bergman | .06 |
| 33 | Jack O'Connor | .06 |
| 34 | Paul Householder | .06 |
| 35 | Rollie Fingers | .25 |
| 36 | Fingers (Veteran) | .15 |
| 37 | Darrell Johnson (Mgr.) | .06 |
| 38 | Tim Flannery | .06 |
| 39 | Terry Puhl | .06 |
| 40 | Fernando Valenzuela | .40 |
| 41 | Jerry Turner | .06 |
| 42 | Dale Murray | .06 |
| 43 | Bob Dernier | .08 |
| 44 | Don Robinson | .06 |
| 45 | John Mayberry | .06 |
| 46 | Richard Dotson | .08 |
| 47 | Dave McKay | .06 |
| 48 | Lary Sorensen | .06 |
| 49 | Willie McGee (R) | 3.00 |
| 50 | Bob Horner | .25 |
| 51 | Cubs Leaders: | .20 |
| | Leon Durham, F. Jenkens | |
| 52 | Onix Concepcion | .15 |
| 53 | Mike Witt | .20 |
| 54 | Jim Maler | .10 |
| 55 | Mookie Wilson | .08 |
| 56 | Chuck Rainey | .06 |
| 57 | Tim Blackwell | .06 |
| 58 | Al Holland | .06 |

| NO. | PLAYER | MINT |
|---|---|---|
| 59 | Benny Ayala | .06 |
| 60 | Johnny Bench | .75 |
| 61 | Bench (Veteran) | .30 |
| 62 | Bob McClure | .06 |
| 63 | Rick Monday | .08 |
| 64 | Bill Stein | .06 |
| 65 | Jack Morris | .35 |
| 66 | Bob Lillis (Mgr.) | .06 |
| 67 | Sal Butera | .06 |
| 68 | Eric Show (R) | .30 |
| 69 | Lee Lacy | .08 |
| 70 | Steve Carlton | .50 |
| 71 | Carlton (Veteran) | .25 |
| 72 | Tom Paciorek | .06 |
| 73 | Allen Ripley | .06 |
| 74 | Julio Gonzalez | .06 |
| 75 | Amos Otis | .06 |
| 76 | Rick Mahler | .06 |
| 77 | Hosken Powell | .06 |
| 78 | Bill Caudill | .08 |
| 79 | Mick Kelleher | .06 |
| 80 | George Foster | .25 |
| 81 | Yankees Leaders: | .20 |
| | J. Mumphrey, D. Righetti | |
| 82 | Bruce Hurst | .06 |
| 83 | Ryne Sandberg (R) | 5.50 |
| 84 | Milt May | .06 |
| 85 | Ken Singleton | .08 |
| 86 | Tom Hume | .06 |
| 87 | Joe Rudi | .06 |
| 88 | Jim Gantner | .06 |
| 89 | Leon Roberts | .06 |
| 90 | Jerry Reuss | .08 |
| 91 | Larry Milbourne | .06 |
| 92 | Mike LaCoss | .06 |
| 93 | John Castino | .06 |
| 94 | Dave Edwards | .06 |
| 95 | Alan Trammell | .35 |
| 96 | Dick Howser (Mgr.) | .06 |
| 97 | Ross Baumgarten | .06 |
| 98 | Vance Law | .06 |
| 99 | Dickie Noles | .06 |
| 100 | Pete Rose | 2.00 |
| 101 | Rose (Veteran) | .60 |
| 102 | Dave Beard | .06 |
| 103 | Darrell Porter | .08 |
| 104 | Bob Walk | .06 |
| 105 | Don Baylor | .20 |
| 106 | Gene Nelson | .06 |
| 107 | Mike Jorgensen | .06 |
| 108 | Glenn Hoffman | .06 |
| 109 | Luis Leal | .06 |
| 110 | Ken Griffey | .15 |
| 111 | Expos Leaders: | .15 |
| | Al Oliver, Steve Rogers | |
| 112 | Bob Shirley | .06 |
| 113 | Ron Roenicke | .06 |
| 114 | Jim Slaton | .06 |
| 115 | Chili Davis | .15 |
| 116 | Dave Schmidt | .06 |
| 117 | Alan Knicely | .06 |
| 118 | Chris Welsh | .06 |
| 119 | Tom Brookens | .06 |
| 120 | Len Barker | .06 |
| 121 | Mickey Hatcher | .06 |
| 122 | Jimmy Smith | .10 |

| NO. | PLAYER | MINT |
|---|---|---|
| 123 | George Frazier | .06 |
| 124 | Marc Hill | .06 |
| 125 | Leon Durham | .25 |
| 126 | Joe Torre (Mgr.) | .08 |
| 127 | Preston Hanna | .06 |
| 128 | Mike Ramsey | .06 |
| 129 | Checklist No. 1 | .12 |
| 130 | Dave Stieb | .25 |
| 131 | Ed Ott | .06 |
| 132 | Todd Cruz | .06 |
| 133 | Jim Barr | .06 |
| 134 | Hubie Brooks | .10 |
| 135 | Dwight Evans | .15 |
| 136 | Willie Aikens | .06 |
| 137 | Woodie Fryman | .06 |
| 138 | Rick Dempsey | .08 |
| 139 | Bruce Berenyi | .06 |
| 140 | Willie Randolph | .10 |
| 141 | Indians Leaders: | .12 |
| | Toby Harrah, Rick Sutcliffe | |
| 142 | Mike Caldwell | .06 |
| 143 | Joe Pettini | .06 |
| 144 | Mark Wagner | .06 |
| 145 | Don Sutton | .35 |
| 146 | Don Sutton (Veteran) | .15 |
| 147 | Rick Leach | .06 |
| 148 | Dave Roberts | .06 |
| 149 | Johnny Ray | .15 |
| 150 | Bruce Sutter | .20 |
| 151 | B. Sutter (Veteran) | .15 |
| 152 | Jay Johnstone | .06 |
| 153 | Jerry Koosman | .06 |
| 154 | Johnnie LeMaster | .06 |
| 155 | Dan Quisenberry | .25 |
| 156 | Billy Martin (Mgr.) | .15 |
| 157 | Steve Bedrosian | .12 |
| 158 | Rob Wilfong | .06 |
| 159 | Mike Stanton | .06 |
| 160 | Dave Kingman | .15 |
| 161 | D. Kingman (Veteran) | .10 |
| 162 | Mark Clear | .06 |
| 163 | Cal Ripken | 2.00 |
| 164 | David Palmer | .06 |
| 165 | Dan Driessen | .06 |
| 166 | John Pacella | .06 |
| 167 | Mark Brouhard | .06 |
| 168 | Juan Eichelberger | .06 |
| 169 | Doug Flynn | .06 |
| 170 | Steve Howe | .06 |
| 171 | Giants Leaders: | .12 |
| | Bill Laskey, Joe Morgan | |
| 172 | Vern Ruhle | .06 |
| 173 | Jim Morrison | .06 |
| 174 | Jerry Ujdur | .06 |
| 175 | Bo Diaz | .06 |
| 176 | Dave Righetti | .35 |
| 177 | Harold Baines | .30 |
| 178 | Luis Tiant | .08 |
| 179 | Luis Tiant (Veteran) | .06 |
| 180 | Rickey Henderson | 1.00 |
| 181 | Terry Felton | .12 |
| 182 | Mike Fischlin | .06 |
| 183 | Ed VandeBerg (R) | .25 |
| 184 | Bob Clark | .06 |
| 185 | Tim Lollar | .06 |
| 186 | Whitey Herzog (Mgr.) | .06 |

| NO. | PLAYER | MINT |
|---|---|---|
| 187 | Terry Leach | .06 |
| 188 | Rick Miller | .06 |
| 189 | Dan Schatzeder | .06 |
| 190 | Cecil Cooper | .25 |
| 191 | Joe Price | .06 |
| 192 | Floyd Rayford | .06 |
| 193 | Harry Spilman | .06 |
| 194 | Cesar Geronimo | .06 |
| 195 | Bob Stoddard | .10 |
| 196 | Bill Fahey | .06 |
| 197 | Jim Eisenreich | .20 |
| 198 | Kiko Garcia | .06 |
| 199 | Marty Bystrom | .06 |
| 200 | Rod Carew | .50 |
| 201 | Rod Carew (Veteran) | .25 |
| 202 | Blue Jays Leaders: | .12 |
| | Damaso Garcia, Dave Stieb | |
| 203 | Mike Morgan | .06 |
| 204 | Junior Kennedy | .06 |
| 205 | Dave Parker | .35 |
| 206 | Ken Oberkfell | .06 |
| 207 | Rick Camp | .06 |
| 208 | Dan Meyer | .06 |
| 209 | Mike Moore (R) | .30 |
| 210 | Jack Clark | .40 |
| 211 | John Denny | .15 |
| 212 | John Stearns | .06 |
| 213 | Tom Burgmeier | .06 |
| 214 | Jerry White | .06 |
| 215 | Mario Soto | .10 |
| 216 | Tony LaRussa (Mgr.) | .08 |
| 217 | Tim Stoddard | .06 |
| 218 | Roy Howell | .06 |
| 219 | Mike Armstrong | .06 |
| 220 | Dusty Baker | .12 |
| 221 | Joe Niekro | .08 |
| 222 | Damaso Garcia | .15 |
| 223 | John Montefusco | .06 |
| 224 | Mickey Rivers | .06 |
| 225 | Enos Cabell | .06 |
| 226 | Enrique Romo | .06 |
| 227 | Chris Bando | .06 |
| 228 | Joaquin Andujar | .12 |
| 229 | Phillies Leaders: | .12 |
| | Bo Diaz, Steve Carlton | |
| 230 | Fergie Jenkins | .12 |
| 231 | F. Jenkins (Veteran) | .08 |
| 232 | Tom Brunansky | .25 |
| 233 | Wayne Gross | .06 |
| 234 | Larry Andersen | .06 |
| 235 | Claudell Washington | .15 |
| 236 | Steve Renko | .06 |
| 237 | Dan Norman | .06 |
| 238 | Bud Black (R) | .30 |
| 239 | Dave Stapleton | .06 |
| 240 | Rich Gossage | .25 |
| 241 | Gossage (Veteran) | .15 |
| 242 | Joe Nolan | .06 |
| 243 | Duane Walker | .12 |
| 244 | Dwight Bernard | .06 |
| 245 | Steve Sax | .30 |
| 246 | G. Bamberger (Mgr.) | .06 |
| 247 | Dave Smith | .06 |
| 248 | Bake McBride | .06 |
| 249 | Checklist No. 2 | .12 |
| 250 | Bill Buckner | .15 |

| NO. PLAYER | MINT |
|---|---|
| 251 Alan Wiggins (R) | .25 |
| 252 Luis Aguayo | .06 |
| 253 Larry McWilliams | .06 |
| 254 Rick Cerone | .06 |
| 255 Gene Garber | .06 |
| 256 G. Garber (Veteran) | .06 |
| 257 Jesse Barfield | .70 |
| 258 Manny Castillo | .06 |
| 259 Jeff Jones | .06 |
| 260 Steve Kemp | .08 |
| 261 Tigers Leaders: | .12 |
| L. Herndon, Dan Petry | |
| 262 Ron Jackson | .06 |
| 263 Renie Martin | .06 |
| 264 Jamie Quirk | .06 |
| 265 Joel Youngblood | .06 |
| 266 Paul Boris | .08 |
| 267 Terry Francona | .06 |
| 268 Storm Davis (R) | .45 |
| 269 Ron Oester | .06 |
| 270 Dennis Eckersley | .06 |
| 271 Ed Romero | .06 |
| 272 Frank Tanana | .06 |
| 273 Mark Belanger | .06 |
| 274 Terry Kennedy | .10 |
| 275 Ray Knight | .06 |
| 276 Gene Mauch (Mgr.) | .06 |
| 277 Rance Mulliniks | .06 |
| 278 Kevin Hickey | .06 |
| 279 Greg Gross | .06 |
| 280 Bert Blyleven | .15 |
| 281 Andre Robertson | .06 |
| 282 Reggie Smith | .10 |
| 283 R. Smith (Veteran) | .08 |
| 284 Jeff Lahti | .15 |
| 285 Lance Parrish | .35 |
| 286 Rick Langford | .06 |
| 287 Bobby Brown | .06 |
| 288 Joe Cowley (R) | .30 |
| 289 Jerry Dybzinski | .06 |
| 290 Jeff Reardon | .08 |
| 291 Pirates Leaders: | .12 |
| B. Madlock, J. Candelaria | |
| 292 Craig Swan | .06 |
| 293 Glen Gulliver | .08 |
| 294 Dave Engle | .06 |
| 295 Jerry Remy | .06 |
| 296 Greg Harris | .06 |
| 297 Ned Yost | .06 |
| 298 Floyd Chiffer | .10 |
| 299 George Wright | .20 |
| 300 Mike Schmidt | 1.00 |
| 301 M. Schmidt (Veteran) | .25 |
| 302 Ernie Whitt | .06 |
| 303 Miguel Dilone | .06 |
| 304 Dave Rucker | .06 |
| 305 Larry Bowa | .10 |
| 306 Tom Lasorda (Mgr.) | .10 |
| 307 Lou Piniella | .12 |
| 308 Jesus Vega | .08 |
| 309 Jeff Leonard | .15 |
| 310 Greg Luzinski | .15 |
| 311 Glenn Brummer | .06 |
| 312 Brian Kingman | .06 |
| 313 Gary Gray | .06 |
| 314 Ken Dayley | .06 |
| 315 Rick Burleson | .06 |
| 316 Paul Splittorff | .06 |
| 317 Gary Rajsich | .10 |
| 318 John Tudor | .30 |
| 319 Lenn Sakata | .06 |
| 320 Steve Rogers | .08 |
| 321 Brewers Leaders: | .15 |
| P. Vuckovich, R. Yount | |
| 322 Dave Van Gorder | .10 |
| 323 Luis DeLeon | .06 |
| 324 Mike Marshall | .25 |
| 325 Von Hayes | .20 |
| 326 Garth Iorg | .06 |
| 327 Bobby Castillo | .06 |
| 328 Craig Reynolds | .06 |
| 329 Randy Niemann | .06 |
| 330 Buddy Bell | .15 |
| 331 Mike Krukow | .06 |
| 332 Glenn Wilson (R) | .75 |

| NO. PLAYER | MINT |
|---|---|
| 333 Dave LaRoche | .06 |
| 334 D. LaRoche (Veteran) | .06 |
| 335 Steve Henderson | .06 |
| 336 R. Lachemann (Mgr.) | .06 |
| 337 Tito Landrum | .06 |
| 338 Bob Owchinko | .06 |
| 339 Terry Harper | .06 |
| 340 Larry Gura | .06 |
| 341 Doug DeCinces | .15 |
| 342 Atlee Hammaker | .08 |
| 343 Bob Bailor | .06 |
| 344 Roger LaFrancois | .08 |
| 345 Jim Clancy | .06 |
| 346 Joe Pittman | .06 |
| 347 Sammy Stewart | .06 |
| 348 Alan Bannister | .06 |
| 349 Checklist No. 3 | .12 |
| 350 Robin Yount | .30 |
| 351 Reds Leaders: | .12 |
| Cesar Cedeno, Mario Soto | |
| 352 Mike Scioscia | .06 |
| 353 Steve Comer | .06 |
| 354 Randy Johnson | .06 |
| 355 Jim Bibby | .06 |
| 356 Gary Woods | .06 |
| 357 Len Matuszek | .15 |
| 358 Jerry Garvin | .06 |
| 359 Dave Collins | .08 |
| 360 Nolan Ryan | .50 |
| 361 N. Ryan (Veteran) | .20 |
| 362 Bill Almon | .06 |
| 363 John Stuper | .15 |
| 364 Bret Butler | .15 |
| 365 Dave Lopes | .07 |
| 366 Dick Williams (Mgr.) | .06 |
| 367 Bud Anderson | .06 |
| 368 Richie Zisk | .06 |
| 369 Jesse Orosco | .10 |
| 370 Gary Carter | .50 |
| 371 Mike Richardt | .08 |
| 372 Terry Crowley | .06 |
| 373 Kevin Saucier | .06 |
| 374 Wayne Krenchicki | .06 |
| 375 Pete Vuckovich | .06 |
| 376 Ken Landreaux | .06 |
| 377 Lee May | .06 |
| 378 Lee May (Veteran) | .06 |
| 379 Guy Sularz | .10 |
| 380 Ron Davis | .06 |
| 381 Red Sox Leaders: | .15 |
| Bob Stanley, Jim Rice | |
| 382 Bob Knepper | .06 |
| 383 Ozzie Virgil | .06 |
| 384 Dave Dravecky (R) | .50 |
| 385 Mike Easler | .06 |
| 386 Rod Carew (AS) | .25 |
| 387 Bob Grich (AS) | .08 |
| 388 George Brett (AS) | .40 |
| 389 Robin Yount (AS) | .25 |
| 390 Reggie Jackson (AS) | .30 |
| 391 Rickey Henderson (AS) | .35 |
| 392 Fred Lynn (AS) | .15 |
| 393 Carlton Fisk (AS) | .15 |
| 394 Pete Vuckovich (AS) | .08 |
| 395 Larry Gura (AS) | .08 |
| 396 Dan Quisenberry (AS) | .12 |
| 397 Pete Rose (AS) | .60 |
| 398 Manny Trillo (AS) | .08 |
| 399 Mike Schmidt (AS) | .35 |
| 400 Dave Concepcion (AS) | .10 |
| 401 Dale Murphy (AS) | .50 |
| 402 Andre Dawson (AS) | .20 |
| 403 Tim Raines (AS) | .18 |
| 404 Gary Carter (AS) | .25 |
| 405 Steve Rogers (AS) | .08 |
| 406 Steve Carlton (AS) | .25 |
| 407 Bruce Sutter (AS) | .20 |
| 408 Rudy May | .06 |
| 409 Marvis Foley | .06 |
| 410 Phil Niekro | .25 |
| 411 P. Niekro (Veteran) | .12 |
| 412 Rangers Leaders: | .12 |
| Buddy Bell, Charlie Hough | |
| 413 Matt Keough | .06 |
| 414 Julio Cruz | .06 |

| NO. PLAYER | MINT |
|---|---|
| 415 Bob Forsch | .06 |
| 416 Joe Ferguson | .06 |
| 417 Tom Hausman | .06 |
| 418 Greg Pryor | .06 |
| 419 Steve Crawford | .06 |
| 420 Al Oliver | .15 |
| 421 Al Oliver (Veteran) | .08 |
| 422 George Cappuzzello | .06 |
| 423 Tom Lawless | .08 |
| 424 Jerry Augustine | .06 |
| 425 Pedro Guerrero | .50 |
| 426 Earl Weaver (Mgr.) | .12 |
| 427 Roy Lee Jackson | .06 |
| 428 Champ Summers | .06 |
| 429 Eddie Whitson | .08 |
| 430 Kirk Gibson | .30 |
| 431 Gary Gaetti (R) | 2.50 |
| 432 Porfirio Altamirano | .10 |
| 433 Dale Berra | .06 |
| 434 Dennis Lamp | .06 |
| 435 Tony Armas | .15 |
| 436 Bill Campbell | .06 |
| 437 Rick Sweet | .06 |
| 438 Dave LaPoint (R) | .25 |
| 439 Rafael Ramirez | .06 |
| 440 Ron Guidry | .25 |
| 441 Astros Leaders: | .12 |
| Joe Niekro, Ray Knight | |
| 442 Brian Downing | .06 |
| 443 Don Hood | .06 |
| 444 Wally Backman | .20 |
| 445 Mike Flanagan | .08 |
| 446 Reid Nichols | .06 |
| 447 Bryn Smith | .06 |
| 448 Darrell Evans | .12 |
| 449 Eddie Milner | .12 |
| 450 Ted Simmons | .15 |
| 451 Ted Simmons (Veteran) | .10 |
| 452 Lloyd Moseby | .15 |
| 453 Lamar Johnson | .06 |
| 454 Bob Welch | .06 |
| 455 Sixto Lezcano | .06 |
| 456 Lee Elia (Mgr.) | .06 |
| 457 Milt Wilcox | .06 |
| 458 Ron Washington | .08 |
| 459 Ed Farmer | .06 |
| 460 Roy Smalley | .06 |
| 461 Steve Trout | .06 |
| 462 Steve Nicosia | .06 |
| 463 Gaylord Perry | .25 |
| 464 G. Perry (Veteran) | .12 |
| 465 Lonnie Smith | .12 |
| 466 Tom Underwood | .06 |
| 467 Rufino Linares | .06 |
| 468 Dave Goltz | .06 |
| 469 Ron Gardenhire | .06 |
| 470 Greg Minton | .06 |
| 471 Royals Leaders: | .12 |
| Willie Wilson, Vida Blue | |
| 472 Gary Allenson | .06 |
| 473 John Lowenstein | .06 |
| 474 Ray Burris | .06 |
| 475 Cesar Cedeno | .12 |
| 476 Rob Picciolo | .06 |
| 477 Tom Niedenfuer | .12 |
| 478 Phil Garner | .06 |
| 479 Charlie Hough | .06 |
| 480 Toby Harrah | .06 |
| 481 Scot Thompson | .06 |
| 482 Tony Gwynn (R) | 16.00 |
| 483 Lynn Jones | .06 |
| 484 Dick Ruthven | .06 |
| 485 Omar Moreno | .06 |
| 486 Clyde King (Mgr.) | .06 |
| 487 Jerry Hairston | .06 |
| 488 Alfredo Griffin | .06 |
| 489 Tom Herr | .20 |
| 490 Jim Palmer | .25 |
| 491 Jim Palmer (Veteran) | .15 |
| 492 Paul Serna | .06 |
| 493 Steve McCatty | .06 |
| 494 Bob Brenly | .08 |
| 495 Warren Cromartie | .06 |
| 496 Tom Veryzer | .06 |
| 497 Rick Sutcliffe | .20 |

| NO. PLAYER | MINT |
|---|---|
| 498 Wade Boggs (R) | 32.00 |
| 499 Jeff Little | .10 |
| 500 Reggie Jackson | .75 |
| 501 R. Jackson (Veteran) | .25 |
| 502 Braves Leaders: | .15 |
| Dale Murphy, Phil Niekro | |
| 503 Moose Haas | .06 |
| 504 Don Werner | .06 |
| 505 Garry Templeton | .15 |
| 506 Jim Gott | .20 |
| 507 Tony Scott | .06 |
| 508 Tom Filer (R) | .20 |
| 509 Lou Whitaker | .25 |
| 510 Tug McGraw | .08 |
| 511 Tug McGraw (Veteran) | .06 |
| 512 Doyle Alexander | .06 |
| 513 Fred Stanley | .06 |
| 514 Rudy Law | .06 |
| 515 Gene Tenace | .06 |
| 516 Bill Virdon (Mgr.) | .06 |
| 517 Gary Ward | .06 |
| 518 Bill Laskey (R) | .25 |
| 519 Terry Bulling | .06 |
| 520 Fred Lynn | .25 |
| 521 Bruce Benedict | .06 |
| 522 Pat Zachry | .06 |
| 523 Carney Lansford | .15 |
| 524 Tom Brennan | .06 |
| 525 Frank White | .06 |
| 526 Checklist No. 4 | .12 |
| 527 Larry Biittner | .06 |
| 528 Jamie Easterly | .06 |
| 529 Tim Laudner | .06 |
| 530 Eddie Murray | .60 |
| 531 A's Leaders: | .12 |
| R. Henderson, R. Langford | |
| 532 Dave Stewart | .06 |
| 533 Luis Salazar | .06 |
| 534 John Butcher | .06 |
| 535 Manny Trillo | .08 |
| 536 Johnny Wockenfuss | .06 |
| 537 Rod Scurry | .06 |
| 538 Danny Heep | .06 |
| 539 Roger Erickson | .06 |
| 540 Ozzie Smith | .30 |
| 541 Britt Burns | .08 |
| 542 Jody Davis | .10 |
| 543 Alan Fowlkes | .10 |
| 544 Larry Whisenton | .06 |
| 545 Floyd Bannister | .06 |
| 546 Dave Garcia (Mgr.) | .06 |
| 547 Geoff Zahn | .06 |
| 548 Brian Giles | .08 |
| 549 Charlie Puleo | .09 |
| 550 Carl Yastrzemski | .75 |
| 551 Yastrzemski (Veteran) | .30 |
| 552 Tim Wallach | .30 |
| 553 Denny Martinez | .06 |
| 554 Mike Vail | .06 |
| 555 Steve Yeager | .06 |
| 556 Willie Upshaw | .15 |
| 557 Rick Honeycutt | .06 |
| 558 Dickie Thon | .08 |
| 559 Peter Redfern | .06 |
| 560 Ron LeFlore | .08 |
| 561 Cardinals Leaders: | .12 |
| L. Smith, J. Andujar | |
| 562 Dave Rozema | .06 |
| 563 Juan Bonilla | .06 |
| 564 Sid Monge | .06 |
| 565 Bucky Dent | .06 |
| 566 Manny Sarmiento | .06 |
| 567 Joe Simpson | .06 |
| 568 Willie Hernandez | .20 |
| 569 Jack Perconte | .06 |
| 570 Vida Blue | .08 |
| 571 Mickey Klutts | .06 |
| 572 Bob Watson | .06 |
| 573 Andy Hassler | .06 |
| 574 Glenn Adams | .06 |
| 575 Neil Allen | .06 |
| 576 Frank Robinson (Mgr.) | .15 |
| 577 Luis Aponte | .08 |
| 578 David Green | .15 |
| 579 Rich Dauer | .06 |

| NO. PLAYER | MINT |
|---|---|
| 580 Tom Seaver | .75 |
| 581 T. Seaver (Veteran) | .25 |
| 582 Marshall Edwards | .06 |
| 583 Terry Forster | .08 |
| 584 Dave Hostetler | .12 |
| 585 Jose Cruz | .12 |
| 586 Frank Viola (R) | 3.50 |
| 587 Ivan DeJesus | .06 |
| 588 Pat Underwood | .06 |
| 589 Alvis Woods | .06 |
| 590 Tony Pena | .15 |
| 591 White Sox Leaders: | .12 |
| Greg Luzinski, LaMarr Hoyt | |
| 592 Shane Rawley | .06 |
| 593 Broderick Perkins | .06 |
| 594 Eric Rasmussen | .06 |
| 595 Tim Raines | .75 |
| 596 Randy Johnson | .10 |
| 597 Mike Proly | .06 |
| 598 Dwayne Murphy | .06 |
| 599 Don Aase | .06 |
| 600 George Brett | .85 |
| 601 Ed Lynch | .06 |
| 602 Rich Gedman | .15 |
| 603 Joe Morgan | .35 |
| 604 Joe Morgan (Veteran) | .15 |
| 605 Gary Roenicke | .06 |
| 606 Bobby Cox (Mgr.) | .06 |
| 607 Charlie Leibrandt | .08 |
| 608 Don Money | .06 |
| 609 Danny Darwin | .06 |
| 610 Steve Garvey | .60 |
| 611 Bert Roberge | .06 |
| 612 Steve Swisher | .06 |
| 613 Mike Ivie | .06 |
| 614 Ed Glynn | .08 |
| 615 Garry Maddox | .06 |
| 616 Bill Nahorodny | .06 |
| 617 Butch Wynegar | .06 |
| 618 LaMarr Hoyt | .15 |
| 619 Keith Moreland | .08 |
| 620 Mike Norris | .06 |
| 621 Mets Leaders: | .12 |
| Mookie Wilson, Craig Swan | |
| 622 Dave Edler | .06 |
| 623 Luis Sanchez | .06 |
| 624 Glenn Hubbard | .06 |
| 625 Ken Forsch | .06 |
| 626 Jerry Martin | .06 |
| 627 Doug Bair | .06 |
| 628 Julio Valdez | .06 |
| 629 Charlie Lea | .06 |
| 630 Paul Molitor | .30 |
| 631 Tippy Martinez | .06 |
| 632 Alex Trevino | .06 |
| 633 Vicente Romo | .06 |
| 634 Max Venable | .06 |
| 635 Graig Nettles | .15 |

| NO. PLAYER | MINT |
|---|---|
| 636 G. Nettles (Veteran) | .10 |
| 637 Pat Corrales (Mgr.) | .06 |
| 638 Dan Petry | .15 |
| 639 Art Howe | .06 |
| 640 Andre Thornton | .10 |
| 641 Billy Sample | .06 |
| 642 Checklist: No. 5 | .12 |
| 643 Bump Wills | .06 |
| 644 Joe LeFebvre | .06 |
| 645 Bill Madlock | .15 |
| 646 Jim Essian | .06 |
| 647 Bobby Mitchell | .06 |
| 648 Jeff Burroughs | .06 |
| 649 Tommy Boggs | .06 |
| 650 George Hendrick | .10 |
| 651 Angels Leaders: | .20 |
| Rod Carew, Mike Witt | |
| 652 Butch Hobson | .06 |
| 653 Ellis Valentine | .06 |
| 654 Bob Ojeda | .12 |
| 655 Al Bumbry | .06 |
| 656 Dave Frost | .06 |
| 657 Mike Gates | .08 |
| 658 Frank Pastore | .06 |
| 659 Charlie Moore | .06 |
| 660 Mike Hargrove | .06 |
| 661 Bill Russell | .06 |
| 662 Joe Sambito | .06 |
| 663 Tom O'Malley (R) | .12 |
| 664 Bob Molinaro | .06 |
| 665 Jim Sundberg | .06 |
| 666 Sparky Anderson (Mgr.) | .06 |
| 667 Dick Davis | .06 |
| 668 Larry Christenson | .06 |
| 669 Mike Squires | .06 |
| 670 Jerry Mumphrey | .06 |
| 671 Lenny Faedo | .06 |
| 672 Jim Kaat | .10 |
| 673 Jim Kaat (Veteran) | .06 |
| 674 Kurt Bevacqua | .06 |
| 675 Jim Beattie | .06 |
| 676 Biff Pocoroba | .06 |
| 677 Dave Revering | .06 |
| 678 Juan Beniquez | .06 |
| 679 Mike Scott | .40 |
| 680 Andre Dawson | .30 |
| 681 Dodgers Leaders: | .15 |
| Fernando Valenzuela, | |
| Pedro Guerrero | |
| 682 Bob Stanley | .06 |
| 683 Dan Ford | .06 |
| 684 Rafael Landestoy | .06 |
| 685 Lee Mazzilli | .06 |
| 686 Randy Lerch | .06 |
| 687 U.L. Washington | .06 |
| 688 Jim Wohlford | .06 |
| 689 Ron Hassey | .06 |
| 690 Kent Hrbek | .60 |

| NO. PLAYER | MINT |
|---|---|
| 691 Dave Tobik | .06 |
| 692 Denny Walling | .06 |
| 693 Sparky Lyle | .08 |
| 694 S. Lyle (Veteran) | .06 |
| 695 Ruppert Jones | .06 |
| 696 Chuck Tanner (Mgr.) | .06 |
| 697 Barry Foote | .06 |
| 698 Tony Bernazard | .06 |
| 699 Lee Smith | .10 |
| 700 Keith Hernandez | .40 |
| 701 Batting Leaders: | .15 |
| Willie Wilson, Al Oliver | |
| 702 Home Run Leaders: | .15 |
| Gorman Thomas, Reggie | |
| Jackson, Dave Kingman | |
| 703 RBI Leaders: | .15 |
| Hal McRae, Al Oliver | |
| Dale Murphy | |
| 704 Stolen Base Leaders: | .25 |
| R. Henderson, T. Raines | |
| 705 Victory Leaders: | .15 |
| LaMarr Hoyt, Steve Carlton | |
| 706 Strikeout Leaders: | .15 |
| F. Bannister, Steve Carlton | |
| 707 ERA Leaders: | .12 |
| Rick Sutcliffe, Steve Rogers | |
| 708 Leading Firemen: | .12 |
| D. Quisenberry, B. Sutter | |
| 709 Jimmy Sexton | .06 |
| 710 Willie Wilson | .20 |
| 711 Mariners Leaders: | .10 |
| Bruce Bochte, Jim Beattie | |
| 712 Bruce Kison | .06 |
| 713 Ron Hodges | .06 |
| 714 Wayne Nordhagen | .06 |
| 715 Tony Perez | .15 |
| 716 T. Perez (Veteran) | .10 |
| 717 Scott Sanderson | .06 |
| 718 Jim Dwyer | .06 |
| 719 Rich Gale | .06 |
| 720 Dave Concepcion | .12 |
| 721 John Martin | .06 |
| 722 Jorge Orta | .06 |
| 723 Randy Moffitt | .06 |
| 724 Johnny Grubb | .06 |
| 725 Dan Spillner | .06 |
| 726 Harvey Kuenn (Mgr.) | .06 |
| 727 Chet Lemon | .10 |
| 728 Ron Reed | .06 |
| 729 Jerry Morales | .06 |
| 730 Jason Thompson | .12 |
| 731 Al Williams | .06 |
| 732 Dave Henderson | .06 |
| 733 Buck Martinez | .06 |
| 734 Steve Braun | .06 |
| 735 Tommy John | .15 |
| 736 T. John (Veteran) | .08 |
| 737 Mitchell Page | .06 |

| NO. PLAYER | MINT |
|---|---|
| 738 Tim Foli | .06 |
| 739 Rick Ownbey | .08 |
| 740 Rusty Staub | .12 |
| 741 R. Staub (Veteran) | .08 |
| 742 Padres Leaders: | .10 |
| Terry Kennedy, Tim Lollar | |
| 743 Mike Torrez | .06 |
| 744 Brad Mills | .06 |
| 745 Scott McGregor | .18 |
| 746 John Wathan | .06 |
| 747 Fred Breining | .06 |
| 748 Derrel Thomas | .06 |
| 749 Jon Matlack | .06 |
| 750 Ben Oglivie | .10 |
| 751 Brad Havens | .06 |
| 752 Luis Pujols | .06 |
| 753 Elias Sosa | .06 |
| 754 Bill Robinson | .06 |
| 755 John Candelaria | .06 |
| 756 Russ Nixon (Mgr.) | .06 |
| 757 Rick Manning | .06 |
| 758 Aurelio Rodriguez | .06 |
| 759 Doug Bird | .06 |
| 760 Dale Murphy | 1.50 |
| 761 Gary Lucas | .06 |
| 762 Cliff Johnson | .06 |
| 763 Al Cowens | .06 |
| 764 Pete Falcone | .06 |
| 765 Bob Boone | .06 |
| 766 Barry Bonnell | .06 |
| 767 Duane Kuiper | .06 |
| 768 Chris Speier | .06 |
| 769 Checklist No. 6 | .12 |
| 770 Dave Winfield | .50 |
| 771 Twins Leaders: | .10 |
| Kent Hrbek, Bobby Castillo | |
| 772 Jim Kern | .06 |
| 773 Larry Hisle | .06 |
| 774 Alan Ashby | .06 |
| 775 Burt Hooton | .06 |
| 776 Larry Parrish | .06 |
| 777 John Curtis | .06 |
| 778 Rich Hebner | .06 |
| 779 Rick Waits | .06 |
| 780 Gary Matthews | .10 |
| 781 Rick Rhoden | .06 |
| 782 Bobby Murcer | .08 |
| 783 B. Murcer (Veteran) | .06 |
| 784 Jeff Newman | .06 |
| 785 Dennis Leonard | .06 |
| 786 Ralph Houk (Mgr.) | .06 |
| 787 Dick Tidrow | .06 |
| 788 Dane Iorg | .06 |
| 789 Bryan Clark | .06 |
| 790 Bob Grich | .06 |
| 791 Gary Lavelle | .06 |
| 792 Chris Chambliss | .15 |

## 1983 Topps Traded. . . .Complete Set of 132 Cards—Value $50.00

Updates the main 1983 card set with players who changed teams during the season, and rookies. Features the first Topps card of Darryl Strawberry. The complete set was packaged in a printed box and only distributed through card hobby dealers.

# 1983 Topps Traded (Continued)

| NO. | PLAYER | MINT |
|---|---|---|
| 1 T | Neil Allen | .12 |
| 2 T | Bill Almon | .09 |
| 3 T | Joe Altobelli (Mgr.) | .09 |
| 4 T | Tony Armas | .25 |
| 5 T | Doug Bair | .09 |
| 6 T | Steve Baker | .09 |
| 7 T | Floyd Bannister | .12 |
| 8 T | Don Baylor | .25 |
| 9 T | Tony Bernazard | .09 |
| 10 T | Larry Biittner | .09 |
| 11 T | Dann Bilardello | .09 |
| 12 T | Doug Bird | .09 |
| 13 T | Steve Boros (Mgr.) | .09 |
| 14 T | Greg Brock (RR) | .50 |
| 15 T | Mike Brown | .12 |
| 16 T | Tom Burgmeier | .09 |
| 17 T | Randy Bush | .09 |
| 18 T | Bert Campaneris | .20 |
| 19 T | Ron Cey | .25 |
| 20 T | Chris Codiroli | .12 |
| 21 T | Dave Collins | .15 |
| 22 T | Terry Crowley | .09 |
| 23 T | Julio Cruz | .09 |
| 24 T | Mike Davis | .15 |
| 25 T | Frank DiPino | .12 |
| 26 T | Bill Doron (RR) | 1.00 |
| 27 T | Jerry Dybzinski | .09 |
| 28 T | Jamie Easterly | .09 |
| 29 T | Juan Eichelberger | .09 |
| 30 T | Jim Essian | .09 |
| 31 T | Pete Falcone | .09 |
| 32 T | Mike Ferraro (Mgr.) | .09 |
| 33 T | Terry Forster | .12 |
| 34 T | Julio Franco (RR) | 1.25 |
| 35 T | Rich Gale | .09 |
| 36 T | Kiko Garcia | .09 |
| 37 T | Steve Garvey | 1.25 |
| 38 T | Johnny Grubb | .09 |
| 39 T | Mel Hall | .75 |
| 40 T | Von Hayes | .50 |
| 41 T | Danny Heep | .09 |
| 42 T | Steve Henderson | .09 |
| 43 T | Keith Hernandez | .75 |
| 44 T | Leo Hernandez | .20 |
| 45 T | Willie Hernandez | .40 |
| 46 T | Al Holland | .12 |
| 47 T | F. Howard (Mgr.) | .09 |
| 48 T | Bobby Johnson | .09 |
| 49 T | Cliff Johnson | .09 |
| 50 T | Odell Jones | .09 |
| 51 T | Mike Jorgenson | .09 |
| 52 T | Bob Kearney | .09 |
| 53 T | Steve Kemp | .12 |
| 54 T | Matt Keough | .09 |
| 55 T | Ron Kittle (RR) | .75 |
| 56 T | Mickey Klutts | .09 |
| 57 T | Alan Knicely | .09 |
| 58 T | Mike Krukow | .09 |
| 59 T | Rafael Landestoy | .09 |
| 60 T | Carney Lansford | .20 |
| 61 T | Joe Lefebvre | .09 |
| 62 T | Bryan Little | .12 |
| 63 T | Aurelio Lopez | .15 |
| 64 T | Mike Madden | .25 |
| 65 T | Rick Manning | .09 |
| 66 T | Billy Martin (Mgr.) | .15 |
| 67 T | Lee Mazzilli | .12 |
| 68 T | Andy McGaffigan | .09 |
| 69 T | Craig McMurtry | .25 |
| 70 T | J. McNamara (Mgr.) | .09 |
| 71 T | Orlando Mercado | .09 |
| 72 T | Larry Milbourne | .09 |
| 73 T | Randy Moffitt | .09 |
| 74 T | Sid Monge | .09 |
| 75 T | Jose Morales | .09 |
| 76 T | Omar Moreno | .12 |
| 77 T | Joe Morgan | .75 |
| 78 T | Mike Morgan | .09 |
| 79 T | Dale Murray | .09 |
| 80 T | Jeff Newman | .09 |
| 81 T | Pete O'Brien (RR) | 1.50 |
| 82 T | Jorge Orta | .09 |
| 83 T | Alejandro Pena (RR) | .50 |
| 84 T | Pascual Perez | .12 |
| 85 T | Tony Perez | .50 |
| 86 T | Broderick Perkins | .09 |
| 87 T | Tony Phillips | .09 |
| 88 T | Charlie Puleo | .09 |
| 89 T | Pat Putnam | .09 |
| 90 T | Jamie Quirk | .09 |
| 91 T | Doug Rader (Mgr.) | .12 |
| 92 T | Chuck Rainey | .09 |
| 93 T | Bobby Ramos | .09 |
| 94 T | Gary Redus (RR) | .50 |
| 95 T | Steve Renko | .09 |
| 96 T | Leon Roberts | .09 |
| 97 T | Aurelio Rodriguez | .09 |
| 98 T | Dick Ruthven | .09 |
| 99 T | Daryl Sconiers | .09 |
| 100 T | Mike Scott | .75 |
| 101 T | Tom Seaver | 1.25 |
| 102 T | John Shelby (RR) | .40 |
| 103 T | Bob Shirley | .08 |
| 104 T | Joe Simpson | .08 |
| 105 T | Doug Sisk | .15 |
| 106 T | Mike Smithson (RR) | .25 |
| 107 T | Elias Sosa | .06 |
| 108 T | D. Strawberry (RR) | 35.00 |
| 109 T | Tom Tellmann | .08 |
| 110 T | Gene Tenace | .08 |
| 111 T | Gorman Thomas | .25 |
| 112 T | Dick Tidrow | .08 |
| 113 T | Dave Tobik | .08 |
| 114 T | Wayne Tolleson | .12 |
| 115 T | Mike Torrez | .10 |
| 116 T | Manny Trillo | .12 |
| 117 T | Steve Trout | .10 |
| 118 T | Lee Tunnell | .12 |
| 119 T | Mike Vail | .08 |
| 120 T | Ellis Valentine | .15 |
| 121 T | Tom Veryzer | .08 |
| 122 T | George Vukovich | .08 |
| 123 T | Rick Waits | .08 |
| 124 T | Greg Walker (RR) | 1.50 |
| 125 T | Chris Welsh | .08 |
| 126 T | Len Whitehouse | .08 |
| 127 T | Eddie Whitson | .10 |
| 128 T | Jim Wohlford | .08 |
| 129 T | Matt Young (RR) | .20 |
| 130 T | Joel Youngblood | .08 |
| 131 T | Pat Zachry | .08 |
| 132 T | Traded Checklist | .25 |

## 1984 Topps....Complete Set of 792 Cards—Value $100.00

Features the rookie cards of Don Mattingly and Darryl Strawberry.

| NO. | PLAYER | MINT |
|---|---|---|
| 1 | Highlight—S. Carlton 300th Win and SO King | .25 |
| 2 | Highlight—Henderson 100 SB's, 3 Seasons | .30 |
| 3 | Highlight—Quisenberry Save Record | .15 |
| 4 | Highlight—N. Ryan, G. Perry, S. Carlton—Surpass Walter Johnson | .25 |
| 5 | Highlight—D. Righetti, B. Forsch, B. Warren—No Hitters | .15 |
| 6 | Highlight—Bench, Yaz, Perry,—All Retire | .35 |
| 7 | Gary Lucas | .06 |
| 8 | Don Mattingly (R) | 30.00 |
| 9 | Jim Gott | .06 |
| 10 | Robin Yount | .35 |
| 11 | Twins Leaders: Kent Hrbek, Ken Schrom | .10 |
| 12 | Billy Sample | .06 |
| 13 | Scott Holman | .06 |
| 14 | Tom Brookens | .06 |
| 15 | Burt Hooton | .06 |
| 16 | Omar Moreno | .08 |
| 17 | John Denny | .08 |
| 18 | Dale Berra | .06 |
| 19 | Ray Fontenot | .15 |
| 20 | Greg Luzinski | .12 |
| 21 | Joe Altobelli (Mgr.) | .06 |
| 22 | Bryan Clark | .06 |
| 23 | Keith Moreland | .08 |
| 24 | John Martin | .06 |
| 25 | Glenn Hubbard | .08 |
| 26 | Bill Black | .06 |
| 27 | Daryl Sconiers | .06 |
| 28 | Frank Viola | .30 |
| 29 | Danny Heep | .06 |
| 30 | Wade Boggs | 6.00 |
| 31 | Andy McGaffigan | .06 |
| 32 | Bobby Ramos | .06 |
| 33 | Tom Burgmeier | .06 |
| 34 | Eddie Milner | .06 |
| 35 | Don Sutton | .25 |
| 36 | Denny Walling | .06 |
| 37 | Rangers Leaders: Buddy Bell, Rick Honeycutt | .10 |
| 38 | Luis DeLeon | .06 |
| 39 | Garth Iorg | .06 |
| 40 | Dusty Baker | .10 |
| 41 | Tony Bernazard | .06 |
| 42 | Johnny Grubb | .06 |
| 43 | Ron Reed | .06 |
| 44 | Jim Morrison | .06 |
| 45 | Jerry Mumphrey | .06 |
| 46 | Ray Smith | .08 |
| 47 | Rudy Law | .06 |
| 48 | Julio Franco | .40 |
| 49 | John Stuper | .06 |
| 50 | Chris Chambliss | .08 |
| 51 | Jim Fray (Mgr.) | .06 |
| 52 | Paul Splittorff | .06 |
| 53 | Juan Beniquez | .08 |
| 54 | Jesse Orosco | .10 |
| 55 | Dave Concepcion | .15 |
| 56 | Gary Allenson | .06 |
| 57 | Dan Schatzeder | .06 |
| 58 | Max Venable | .06 |
| 59 | Sammy Stewart | .06 |
| 60 | Paul Molitor | .15 |
| 61 | Chris Codiroli (R) | .15 |
| 62 | Dave Hostetler | .06 |
| 63 | Ed VandeBerg | .08 |
| 64 | Mike Scioscia | .06 |
| 65 | Kirk Gibson | .40 |
| 66 | Astros Leaders: Nolan Ryan, Jose Cruz | .10 |
| 67 | Gary Ward | .06 |
| 68 | Luis Salazar | .06 |
| 69 | Rod Scurry | .06 |
| 70 | Gary Matthews | .08 |
| 71 | Leo Hernandez | .15 |
| 72 | Mike Squires | .06 |
| 73 | Jody Davis | .10 |
| 74 | Jerry Martin | .06 |
| 75 | Bob Forsch | .06 |
| 76 | Alfredo Griffin | .06 |
| 77 | Brett Butler | .08 |
| 78 | Mike Torrez | .06 |
| 79 | Rob Wilfong | .06 |
| 80 | Steve Rogers | .08 |
| 81 | Billy Martin (Mgr.) | .15 |
| 82 | Doug Bird | .06 |
| 83 | Richie Zisk | .08 |
| 84 | Lenny Faedo | .06 |
| 85 | Atlee Hammaker | .06 |
| 86 | John Shelby | .30 |
| 87 | Frank Pastore | .06 |
| 88 | Rob Picciolo | .06 |
| 89 | Mike Smithson | .15 |
| 90 | Pedro Guerrero | .40 |
| 91 | Dan Spillner | .06 |
| 92 | Lloyd Moseby | .20 |
| 93 | Bob Knepper | .06 |

| NO. PLAYER | MINT |
|---|---|
| 94 Mario Ramirez | .08 |
| 95 Aurelio Lopez | .06 |
| 96 Royals Leaders: | .10 |
| Hal McRae, Larry Gura | |
| 97 LaMarr Hoyt | .15 |
| 98 Steve Nicosia | .06 |
| 99 Criag Lefferts (R) | .15 |
| 100 Reggie Jackson | .50 |
| 101 Porfirio Altamirano | .06 |
| 102 Ken Oberkfell | .06 |
| 103 Dwayne Murphy | .08 |
| 104 Ken Dayley | .06 |
| 105 Tony Armas | .15 |
| 106 Tim Stoddard | .06 |
| 107 Ned Yost | .06 |
| 108 Randy Moffitt | .06 |
| 109 Brad Wellman | .08 |
| 110 Ron Guidry | .20 |
| 111 Bill Virdon (Mgr.) | .06 |
| 112 Tom Niedenfuer | .08 |
| 113 Kelly Paris | .12 |
| 114 Checklist No. 1 | .08 |
| 115 Andre Thornton | .08 |
| 116 George Bjorkman | .08 |
| 117 Tom Veryzer | .06 |
| 118 Charlie Hough | .06 |
| 119 Johnny Wockenfuss | .06 |
| 120 Keith Hernandez | .35 |
| 121 Pat Sheridan | .15 |
| 122 Cecilio Guante | .06 |
| 123 Butch Wynegar | .06 |
| 124 Damaso Garcia | .10 |
| 125 Britt Burns | .08 |
| 126 Braves Leaders: | .10 |
| Dale Murphy, C. McMurtry | |
| 127 Mike Madden | .15 |
| 128 Rick Manning | .06 |
| 129 Bill Laskey | .06 |
| 130 Ozzie Smith | .25 |
| 131 Batting Leaders: | .35 |
| Bill Madlock, Wade Boggs | |
| 132 Home Run Leaders: | .30 |
| Mike Schmidt, Jim Rice | |
| 133 RBI Leaders: | .25 |
| Dale Murphy, C. Cooper, | |
| Jim Rice | |
| 134 Stolen Base Leaders: | .25 |
| T. Raines, R. Henderson | |
| 135 Victory Leaders: | .15 |
| John Denny, LaMarr Hoyt | |
| 136 Stikeout Leaders: | .15 |
| Steve Carlton, Jack Morris | |
| 137 ERA Leaders: | .08 |
| A. Hammaker, R. Honeycutt | |
| 138 Leading Firemen: | .10 |
| A. Holland, D. Quisenberry | |
| 139 Bert Campaneris | .06 |
| 140 Storm Davis | .12 |
| 141 Pat Corrales (Mgr.) | .06 |
| 142 Rich Gale | .06 |
| 143 Jose Morales | .06 |
| 144 Brian Harper | .15 |
| 145 Gary Lavelle | .06 |
| 146 Ed Romero | .06 |
| 147 Dan Petry | .15 |
| 148 Joe Lefebvre | .06 |
| 149 Jon Matlack | .06 |
| 150 Dale Murphy | 1.00 |
| 151 Steve Trout | .06 |
| 152 Glenn Brummer | .06 |
| 153 Dick Tidrow | .06 |
| 154 Dave Henderson | .06 |
| 155 Frank White | .10 |
| 156 A's Leaders: | .10 |
| R. Henderson, T. Conroy | |
| 157 Gary Gaetti | .50 |
| 158 John Curtis | .06 |
| 159 Darryl Cias | .08 |
| 160 Mario Soto | .08 |
| 161 Junior Ortiz | .10 |
| 162 Bob Ojeda | .06 |
| 163 Lorenzo Gray | .08 |
| 164 Scott Sanderson | .06 |
| 165 Ken Singleton | .08 |
| 166 Jamie Nelson | .12 |

| NO. PLAYER | MINT |
|---|---|
| 167 Marshall Edwards | .06 |
| 168 Juan Bonilla | .06 |
| 169 Larry Parrish | .06 |
| 170 Jerry Reuss | .08 |
| 171 Frank Robinson (Mgr.) | .12 |
| 172 Frank DiPino | .06 |
| 173 Marvell Wynne | .15 |
| 174 Juan Berenguer | .06 |
| 175 Graig Nettles | .15 |
| 176 Lee Smith | .10 |
| 177 Jerry Hairston | .06 |
| 178 Bill Krueger | .12 |
| 179 Buck Martinez | .06 |
| 180 Manny Trillo | .08 |
| 181 Roy Thomas | .06 |
| 182 Darryl Strawberry (R) | 13.00 |
| 183 Al Williams | .06 |
| 184 Mike O'Berry | .06 |
| 185 Sixto Lezcano | .06 |
| 186 Cardinal Leaders: | .10 |
| Lonnie Smith, John Stuper | |
| 187 Luis Aponte | .06 |
| 188 Bryan Little | .08 |
| 189 Tim Conroy | .12 |
| 190 Ben Oglivie | .08 |
| 191 Mike Boddicker | .15 |
| 192 Nick Esasky (R) | .35 |
| 193 Darrell Brown | .08 |
| 194 Domingo Ramos | .08 |
| 195 Jack Morris | .20 |
| 196 Don Slaught | .06 |
| 197 Garry Hancock | .06 |
| 198 Bill Doran (R) | .75 |
| 199 Willie Hernandez | .30 |
| 200 Andre Dawson | .25 |
| 201 Bruce Kison | .06 |
| 202 Bobby Cox (Mgr.) | .06 |
| 203 Matt Keough | .06 |
| 204 Bobby Meacham (R) | .25 |
| 205 Greg Minton | .06 |
| 206 Andy Van Slyke (R) | 1.00 |
| 207 Donnie Moore | .08 |
| 208 Jose Oquendo (R) | .40 |
| 209 Manny Sarmiento | .06 |
| 210 Joe Morgan | .20 |
| 211 Rick Sweet | .06 |
| 212 Broderick Perkins | .06 |
| 213 Bruce Hurst | .06 |
| 214 Paul Householder | .06 |
| 215 Tippy Martinez | .06 |
| 216 White Sox Leaders: | .10 |
| C. Fisk, R. Dotson | |
| 217 Alan Ashby | .06 |
| 218 Rick Waits | .06 |
| 219 Joe Simpson | .06 |
| 220 Fernando Valenzuela | .40 |
| 221 Cliff Johnson | .06 |
| 222 Rick Honeycutt | .08 |
| 223 Wayne Krenchicki | .06 |
| 224 Sid Monge | .06 |
| 225 Lee Mazzilli | .06 |
| 226 Juan Eichelberger | .06 |
| 227 Steve Braun | .06 |
| 228 John Rabb | .15 |
| 229 Paul Owens (Mgr.) | .06 |
| 230 Rickey Henderson | .60 |
| 231 Gary Woods | .06 |
| 232 Tim Wallach | .10 |
| 233 Checklist No. 2 | .08 |
| 234 Rafael Ramirez | .06 |
| 235 Matt Young | .20 |
| 236 Ellis Valentine | .06 |
| 237 John Castino | .06 |
| 238 Reid Nichols | .06 |
| 239 Jay Howell | .06 |
| 240 Eddie Murray | .50 |
| 241 Billy Almon | .06 |
| 242 Alex Trevino | .06 |
| 243 Pete Ladd | .06 |
| 244 Candy Maldonado | .40 |
| 245 Rick Sutcliffe | .25 |
| 246 Mets Leaders: | .12 |
| M. Wilson, Tom Seaver | |
| 247 Onix Concepcion | .06 |
| 248 Bill Dawley (R) | .20 |

| NO. PLAYER | MINT |
|---|---|
| 249 Jay Johnstone | .06 |
| 250 Bill Madlock | .15 |
| 251 Tony Gwynn | 2.00 |
| 252 Larry Christenson | .06 |
| 253 Jim Wohlford | .06 |
| 254 Shane Rawley | .06 |
| 255 Bruce Benedict | .06 |
| 256 Dave Geisel | .06 |
| 257 Julio Cruz | .06 |
| 258 Luis Sanchez | .06 |
| 259 Sparky Anderson (Mgr.) | .08 |
| 260 Scott McGregor | .08 |
| 261 Bobby Brown | .06 |
| 262 Tom Candiotti | .15 |
| 263 Jack Fimple | .08 |
| 264 Doug Frobel | .12 |
| 265 Donnie Hill (R) | .15 |
| 266 Steve Lubratich | .08 |
| 267 Carmelo Martinez (R) | .25 |
| 268 Jack O'Connor | .06 |
| 269 Aurelio Rodriquez | .06 |
| 270 Jeff Russell | .20 |
| 271 Moose Haas | .06 |
| 272 Rick Dempsey | .06 |
| 273 Charlie Puleo | .06 |
| 274 Rick Monday | .06 |
| 275 Len Matuszek | .06 |
| 276 Angels Leaders: | .10 |
| Rod Carew, Geoff Zahn | |
| 277 Eddie Whitson | .06 |
| 278 Jorge Bell | 1.00 |
| 279 Ivan DeJesus | .06 |
| 280 Floyd Bannister | .10 |
| 281 Larry Milbourne | .06 |
| 282 Jim Barr | .06 |
| 283 Larry Biittner | .06 |
| 284 Howard Bailey | .06 |
| 285 Darrell Porter | .06 |
| 286 Lary Sorensen | .06 |
| 287 Warren Cromartie | .06 |
| 288 Jim Beattie | .06 |
| 289 Randy Johnson | .06 |
| 290 Dave Dravecky | .08 |
| 291 Chuck Tanner (Mgr.) | .06 |
| 292 Tony Scott | .06 |
| 293 Ed Lynch | .06 |
| 294 U.L. Washington | .06 |
| 295 Mike Flanagan | .08 |
| 296 Jeff Newman | .06 |
| 297 Bruce Berenyi | .06 |
| 298 Jim Gantner | .06 |
| 299 John Butcher | .06 |
| 300 Pete Rose | 1.25 |
| 301 Frank LaCorte | .06 |
| 302 Barry Bonnell | .06 |
| 303 Marty Castillo | .06 |
| 304 Warren Brusstar | .06 |
| 305 Roy Smalley | .06 |
| 306 Dodgers Leaders: | .12 |
| Pedro Guerrero, Bob Welch | |
| 307 Bobby Mitchell | .06 |
| 308 Ron Hassey | .06 |
| 309 Tony Phillips | .08 |
| 310 Willie McGee | .40 |
| 311 Jerry Koosman | .06 |
| 312 Jorge Orta | .06 |
| 313 Mike Jorgensen | .06 |
| 314 Orlando Mercado | .08 |
| 315 Bob Grich | .06 |
| 316 Mark Bradley | .08 |
| 317 Greg Pryor | .06 |
| 318 Bill Gullickson | .08 |
| 319 Al Bumbry | .06 |
| 320 Bob Stanley | .06 |
| 321 Harvey Kuenn (Mgr.) | .06 |
| 322 Ken Schrom | .06 |
| 323 Alan Knicely | .06 |
| 324 Alejandro Pena (R) | .30 |
| 325 Darrell Evans | .12 |
| 326 Bob Kearney | .06 |
| 327 Ruppert Jones | .06 |
| 328 Vern Ruhle | .06 |
| 329 Pat Tabler | .20 |
| 330 John Candelaria | .06 |
| 331 Bucky Dent | .06 |

| NO. PLAYER | MINT |
|---|---|
| 332 Kevin Gross (R) | .30 |
| 333 Larry Herndon | .06 |
| 334 Chuck Rainey | .06 |
| 335 Don Baylor | .12 |
| 336 Mariners Leaders: | .10 |
| Pat Putnam, M. Young | |
| 337 Kevin Hagen | .08 |
| 338 Mike Warren | .12 |
| 339 Roy Lee Jackson | .06 |
| 340 Hal McRae | .06 |
| 341 Dave Tobik | .06 |
| 342 Tim Foli | .06 |
| 343 Mark Davis | .06 |
| 344 Rick Miller | .06 |
| 345 Kent Hrbek | .30 |
| 346 Kurt Bevacqua | .06 |
| 347 Allan Ramirez | .08 |
| 348 Toby Harrah | .06 |
| 349 Bob Gibson | .12 |
| 350 George Foster | .20 |
| 351 Russ Nixon (Mgr.) | .06 |
| 352 Dave Stewart | .06 |
| 353 Jim Anderson | .06 |
| 354 Jeff Burroughs | .06 |
| 355 Jason Thompson | .08 |
| 356 Glenn Abbott | .06 |
| 357 Ron Cey | .15 |
| 358 Bob Dernier | .08 |
| 359 Jim Acker (R) | .15 |
| 360 Willie Randolph | .08 |
| 361 Dave Smith | .06 |
| 362 David Green | .06 |
| 363 Tim Laudner | .06 |
| 364 Scott Fletcher | .12 |
| 365 Steve Bedrosian | .08 |
| 366 Padres Leaders: | .10 |
| T. Kennedy, D. Dravecky | |
| 367 Jamie Easterly | .06 |
| 368 Hubie Brooks | .10 |
| 369 Steve McCatty | .06 |
| 370 Tim Raines | .50 |
| 371 Dave Gumpert | .08 |
| 372 Gary Roenicke | .06 |
| 373 Bill Scherrer | .08 |
| 374 Don Money | .06 |
| 375 Dennis Leonard | .06 |
| 376 Dave Anderson | .15 |
| 377 Danny Darwin | .06 |
| 378 Bob Brenly | .06 |
| 379 Checklist No.3 | .08 |
| 380 Steve Garvey | .40 |
| 381 Ralph Houk (Mgr.) | .06 |
| 382 Chris Nyman | .08 |
| 383 Terry Puhl | .06 |
| 384 Lee Tunnell | .12 |
| 385 Tony Perez | .15 |
| 386 George Hendrick (AS) | .10 |
| 387 Johnny Ray (AS) | .10 |
| 388 Mike Schmidt (AS) | .30 |
| 389 Ozzie Smith (AS) | .12 |
| 390 Tim Raines (AS) | .20 |
| 391 Dale Murphy (AS) | .40 |
| 392 Andre Dawson (AS) | .25 |
| 393 Gary Carter (AS) | .30 |
| 394 Steve Rogers (AS) | .12 |
| 395 Steve Carlton (AS) | .30 |
| 396 Jesse Orosco (AS) | .08 |
| 397 Eddie Murray (AS) | .35 |
| 398 Lou Whitaker (AS) | .12 |
| 399 George Brett (AS) | .40 |
| 400 Cal Ripken (AS) | .30 |
| 401 Jim Rice (AS) | .25 |
| 402 Dave Winfield (AS) | .25 |
| 403 Lloyd Moseby (AS) | .12 |
| 404 Ted Simmons (AS) | .12 |
| 405 LaMarr Hoyt (AS) | .12 |
| 406 Ron Guidry (AS) | .15 |
| 407 Dan Quisenberry (AS) | .15 |
| 408 Lou Piniella | .10 |
| 409 Juan Agosto | .15 |
| 410 Claudell Washington | .08 |
| 411 Houston Jimenez | .08 |
| 412 Doug Rader (Mgr.) | .06 |
| 413 Spike Owen (R) | .20 |
| 414 Mitchell Page | .06 |

| NO. | PLAYER | MINT |
|---|---|---|
| 415 | Tommy John | .15 |
| 416 | Dane Iorg | .06 |
| 417 | Mike Armstrong | .06 |
| 418 | Ron Hodges | .06 |
| 419 | John Johnson | .06 |
| 420 | Cecil Cooper | .20 |
| 421 | Charlie Lea | .06 |
| 422 | Jose Cruz | .12 |
| 423 | Mike Morgan | .06 |
| 424 | Dann Bilardello | .08 |
| 425 | Steve Howe | .06 |
| 426 | Orioles Leaders: | .12 |
| | M. Boddicker, C. Ripken | |
| 427 | Rick Leach | .06 |
| 428 | Fred Breining | .06 |
| 429 | Randy Bush | .09 |
| 430 | Rusty Staub | .10 |
| 431 | Chris Bando | .06 |
| 432 | Charlie Hudson (R) | .20 |
| 433 | Rich Hebner | .06 |
| 434 | Harold Baines | .20 |
| 435 | Neil Allen | .06 |
| 436 | Rick Peters | .06 |
| 437 | Mike Proly | .06 |
| 438 | Biff Pocoroba | .06 |
| 439 | Bob Stoddard | .06 |
| 440 | Steve Kemp | .06 |
| 441 | Bob Lillis (Mgr.) | .06 |
| 442 | Byron McLaughlin | .06 |
| 443 | Benny Ayala | .06 |
| 444 | Steve Renko | .06 |
| 445 | Jerry Remy | .06 |
| 446 | Luis Pujols | .06 |
| 447 | Tom Brunansky | .20 |
| 448 | Ben Hayes | .06 |
| 449 | Joe Pettini | .06 |
| 450 | Gary Carter | .45 |
| 451 | Bob Jones | .06 |
| 452 | Chuck Porter | .06 |
| 453 | Willie Upshaw | .15 |
| 454 | Joe Beckwith | .06 |
| 455 | Terry Kennedy | .10 |
| 456 | Cubs Leaders: | .12 |
| | F. Jenkins, K. Moreland | |
| 457 | Dave Rozema | .06 |
| 458 | Kiko Garcia | .06 |
| 459 | Kevin Hickey | .06 |
| 460 | Dave Winfield | .40 |
| 461 | Jim Maler | .06 |
| 462 | Lee Lacy | .06 |
| 463 | Dave Engle | .06 |
| 464 | Jeff Jones | .06 |
| 465 | Mookie Wilson | .08 |
| 466 | Gene Garber | .06 |
| 467 | Mike Ramsey | .06 |
| 468 | Geoff Zahn | .06 |
| 469 | Tom O'Malley | .06 |
| 470 | Nolan Ryan | .40 |
| 471 | Dick Howser (Mgr.) | .06 |
| 472 | Mike Brown | .08 |
| 473 | Jim Dwyer | .06 |
| 474 | Greg Bargar | .09 |
| 475 | Gary Redus (R) | .30 |
| 476 | Tom Tellmann | .06 |
| 477 | Rafael Landestoy | .06 |
| 478 | Alan Bannister | .06 |
| 479 | Frank Tanana | .06 |
| 480 | Ron Kittle | .25 |
| 481 | Mark Thurmond (R) | .20 |
| 482 | Enos Cabell | .06 |
| 483 | Fergie Jenkins | .15 |
| 484 | Ozzie Virgil | .06 |
| 485 | Rick Rhoden | .06 |
| 486 | Yankees Leaders: | .12 |
| | Don Baylor, Ron Guidry | |
| 487 | Ricky Adams | .08 |
| 488 | Jesse Barfield | .30 |
| 489 | Dave Von Ohlen | .09 |
| 490 | Cal Ripken | .75 |
| 491 | Bobby Castillo | .06 |
| 492 | Tucker Ashford | .06 |
| 493 | Mike Norris | .06 |
| 494 | Chili Davis | .15 |
| 495 | Rollie Fingers | .15 |
| 496 | Terry Francona | .06 |

| NO. | PLAYER | MINT |
|---|---|---|
| 497 | Bud Anderson | .06 |
| 498 | Rich Gedman | .06 |
| 499 | Mike Witt | .20 |
| 500 | George Brett | .80 |
| 501 | Steve Henderson | .06 |
| 502 | Joe Torre (Mgr.) | .08 |
| 503 | Elias Sosa | .06 |
| 504 | Mickey Rivers | .08 |
| 505 | Pete Vuckovich | .08 |
| 506 | Ernie Whitt | .06 |
| 507 | Mike LaCoss | .06 |
| 508 | Mel Hall | .30 |
| 509 | Brad Havens | .06 |
| 510 | Alan Trammell | .30 |
| 511 | Marty Bystrom | .06 |
| 512 | Oscar Gamble | .08 |
| 513 | Dave Beard | .06 |
| 514 | Floyd Rayford | .06 |
| 515 | Gorman Thomas | .15 |
| 516 | Expos Leaders: | .10 |
| | Al Oliver, Charlie Lea | |
| 517 | John Moses | .08 |
| 518 | Greg Walker (R) | .75 |
| 519 | Ron Davis | .06 |
| 520 | Bob Boone | .06 |
| 521 | Pete Falcone | .06 |
| 522 | Dave Bergman | .06 |
| 523 | Glenn Hoffman | .06 |
| 524 | Carlos Diaz | .06 |
| 525 | Willie Wilson | .20 |
| 526 | Ron Oester | .06 |
| 527 | Checklist No. 4 | .08 |
| 528 | Mark Brouhard | .06 |
| 529 | Keith Atherton | .08 |
| 530 | Dan Ford | .06 |
| 531 | Steve Boros (Mgr.) | .06 |
| 532 | Eric Show | .06 |
| 533 | Ken Landreaux | .06 |
| 534 | Pete O'Brien (R) | 1.00 |
| 535 | Bo Diaz | .06 |
| 536 | Doug Bair | .06 |
| 537 | Johnny Ray | .12 |
| 538 | Kevin Bass | .06 |
| 539 | George Frazier | .06 |
| 540 | George Hendrick | .08 |
| 541 | Dennis Lamp | .06 |
| 542 | Duane Kuiper | .06 |
| 543 | Craig McMurtry (R) | .15 |
| 544 | Cesar Geronimo | .06 |
| 545 | Bill Buckner | .10 |
| 546 | Indians Leaders: | .08 |
| | Mike Hargrove, L. Sorensen | |
| 547 | Mike Moore | .06 |
| 548 | Ron Jackson | .06 |
| 549 | Walt Terrell (R) | .35 |
| 550 | Jim Rice | .40 |
| 551 | Scott Ullger | .08 |
| 552 | Ray Burris | .06 |
| 553 | Joe Nolan | .06 |
| 554 | Ted Power | .06 |
| 555 | Greg Brock | .10 |
| 556 | Joey McLaughlin | .06 |
| 557 | Wayne Tolleson | .10 |
| 558 | Mike Davis | .08 |
| 559 | Mike Scott | .35 |
| 560 | Carlton Fisk | .20 |
| 561 | Whitey Herzog (Mgr.) | .08 |
| 562 | Manny Castillo | .06 |
| 563 | Glenn Wilson | .12 |
| 564 | Al Holland | .06 |
| 565 | Leon Durham | .20 |
| 566 | Jim Bibby | .06 |
| 567 | Mike Heath | .06 |
| 568 | Pete Filson | .10 |
| 569 | Bake McBride | .06 |
| 570 | Dan Quisenberry | .20 |
| 571 | Bruce Bochy | .06 |
| 572 | Jerry Royster | .06 |
| 573 | Dave Kingman | .10 |
| 574 | Brian Downing | .06 |
| 575 | Jim Clancy | .06 |
| 576 | Giants Leaders: | .07 |
| | J. Leonard, A. Hammaker | |
| 577 | Mark Clear | .06 |
| 578 | Lenn Sakata | .06 |

| NO. | PLAYER | MINT |
|---|---|---|
| 579 | Bob James (R) | .30 |
| 580 | Lonnie Smith | .08 |
| 581 | Jose DeLeon (R) | .25 |
| 582 | Bob McClure | .06 |
| 583 | Derrel Thomas | .06 |
| 584 | Dave Schmidt | .06 |
| 585 | Dan Driessen | .06 |
| 586 | Joe Niekro | .08 |
| 587 | Von Hayes | .20 |
| 588 | Milt Wilcox | .06 |
| 589 | Mike Easler | .08 |
| 590 | Dave Stieb | .20 |
| 591 | Tony LaRussa (Mgr.) | .06 |
| 592 | Andre Robertson | .06 |
| 593 | Jeff Lahti | .06 |
| 594 | Gene Richards | .06 |
| 595 | Jeff Reardon | .08 |
| 596 | Ryne Sandberg | 1.00 |
| 597 | Rick Camp | .06 |
| 598 | Rusty Kuntz | .06 |
| 599 | Doug Sisk (R) | .15 |
| 600 | Rod Carew | .50 |
| 601 | John Tudor | .15 |
| 602 | John Wathan | .06 |
| 603 | Renie Martin | .06 |
| 604 | John Lowenstein | .06 |
| 605 | Mike Caldwell | .06 |
| 606 | Blue Jays Leaders: | .10 |
| | Lloyd Moseby, Dave Stieb | |
| 607 | Tom Hume | .06 |
| 608 | Bobby Johnson | .06 |
| 609 | Dan Meyer | .06 |
| 610 | Steve Sax | .25 |
| 611 | Chet Lemon | .08 |
| 612 | Harry Spilman | .06 |
| 613 | Greg Gross | .06 |
| 614 | Len Barker | .06 |
| 615 | Garry Templeton | .12 |
| 616 | Don Robinson | .06 |
| 617 | Rick Cerone | .06 |
| 618 | Dickie Noles | .06 |
| 619 | Jerry Dybzinski | .06 |
| 620 | Al Oliver | .15 |
| 621 | Frank Howard (Mgr.) | .06 |
| 622 | Al Cowens | .06 |
| 623 | Ron Washington | .06 |
| 624 | Terry Harper | .06 |
| 625 | Larry Gura | .06 |
| 626 | Bob Clark | .06 |
| 627 | Dave LaPoint | .06 |
| 628 | Ed Jurak | .08 |
| 629 | Rick Langford | .06 |
| 630 | Ted Simmons | .12 |
| 631 | Denny Martinez | .06 |
| 632 | Tom Foley | .12 |
| 633 | Mike Krukow | .06 |
| 634 | Mike Marshall | .15 |
| 635 | Dave Righetti | .20 |
| 636 | Pat Putnam | .06 |
| 637 | Phillies Leaders: | .10 |
| | G. Matthews, J. Denny | |
| 638 | George Vuckovich | .06 |
| 639 | Rick Lysander | .08 |
| 640 | Lance Parrish | .25 |
| 641 | Mike Richardt | .06 |
| 642 | Tom Underwood | .06 |
| 643 | Mike Brown (R) | .15 |
| 644 | Tim Lollar | .06 |
| 645 | Tony Pena | .12 |
| 646 | Checklist No.5 | .08 |
| 647 | Ron Roenicke | .06 |
| 648 | Len Whitehouse | .08 |
| 649 | Tom Herr | .12 |
| 650 | Phil Niekro | .25 |
| 651 | J. McNamara (Mgr.) | .06 |
| 652 | Rudy May | .06 |
| 653 | Dave Stapleton | .06 |
| 654 | Bob Bailor | .06 |
| 655 | Amos Otis | .06 |
| 656 | Bryn Smith | .06 |
| 657 | Thad Bosley | .06 |
| 658 | Jerry Augustine | .06 |
| 659 | Duane Walker | .06 |
| 660 | Ray Knight | .06 |
| 661 | Steve Yeager | .06 |

| NO. | PLAYER | MINT |
|---|---|---|
| 662 | Tom Brennan | .06 |
| 663 | Johnnie LeMaster | .06 |
| 664 | Dave Stegman | .06 |
| 665 | Buddy Bell | .15 |
| 666 | Tigers Leaders: | .12 |
| | Lou Whitaker, J. Morris | |
| 667 | Vance Law | .06 |
| 668 | Larry McWilliams | .06 |
| 669 | Dave Lopes | .08 |
| 670 | Rich Gossage | .20 |
| 671 | Jamie Quirk | .06 |
| 672 | Ricky Nelson | .12 |
| 673 | Mike Walters | .12 |
| 674 | Tim Flannery | .06 |
| 675 | Pascual Perez | .08 |
| 676 | Brian Giles | .06 |
| 677 | Doyle Alexander | .06 |
| 678 | Chris Speier | .06 |
| 679 | Art Howe | .06 |
| 680 | Fred Lynn | .20 |
| 681 | Tom Lasorda (Mgr.) | .08 |
| 682 | Dan Morogiello | .08 |
| 683 | Marty Barrett (R) | 2.00 |
| 684 | Bob Shirley | .06 |
| 685 | Willie Aikens | .06 |
| 686 | Joe Price | .06 |
| 687 | Roy Howell | .06 |
| 688 | George Wright | .06 |
| 689 | Mike Fischlin | .06 |
| 690 | Jack Clark | .35 |
| 691 | Steve Lake | .08 |
| 692 | Dickie Thon | .06 |
| 693 | Alan Wiggins | .08 |
| 694 | Mike Stanton | .06 |
| 695 | Lou Whitaker | .20 |
| 696 | Pirates Leaders: | .08 |
| | Bill Madlock, Rick Rhoden | |
| 697 | Dale Murray | .06 |
| 698 | Marc Hill | .06 |
| 699 | Dave Rucker | .06 |
| 700 | Mike Schmidt | .60 |
| 701 | Batting Leaders: | .30 |
| | Bill Madlock, Dave Parker, Pete Rose | |
| 702 | Hit Leaders: | .30 |
| | Pete Rose, Rusty Staub, Tony Perez | |
| 703 | Home Run Leaders: | .25 |
| | Mike Schmidt, Tony Perez, D. Kingman | |
| 704 | RBI Leaders: | .15 |
| | Rusty Staub, Tony Perez, Al Oliver | |
| 705 | Stolen Bases Leaders: | .12 |
| | Larry Bowa, Joe Morgan, Cesar Cedeno | |
| 706 | Victory Leaders: | .15 |
| | Steve Carlton, F. Jenkins, Tom Seaver | |
| 707 | Strikeout Leaders: | .20 |
| | Tom Seaver, Steve Carlton, Nolan Ryan | |
| 708 | ERA Leaders: | .15 |
| | Tom Seaver, Steve Rogers, Steve Carlton | |
| 709 | Save Leaders: | .12 |
| | Bruce Sutter, Tug McGraw, G. Garber | |
| 710 | Batting Leaders: | .25 |
| | Rod Carew, Cecil Cooper, George Brett | |
| 711 | Hit Leaders: | .20 |
| | Reggie Jackson, Rod Carew, Bert Campaneris | |
| 712 | Home Run Leaders: | .20 |
| | Graig Nettles, Reggie Jackson, Greg Luzinski | |
| 713 | RBI Leaders: | .20 |
| | Reggie Jackson, Ted Simmons, Graig Nettles | |
| 714 | Stolen Bases Leaders: | .12 |
| | Bert Campaneris, D. Lopes, Omar Moreno | |
| 715 | Victory Leaders: | .15 |
| | Jim Palmer, Don Sutton, Tommy John | |

| NO. | PLAYER | MINT |
|---|---|---|
| 716 | Strikeouts Leaders: | 12 |
| | Don Sutton, Jerry | |
| | Koosman, Bert Blyleven | |
| 717 | ERA Leaders: | 15 |
| | Jim Palmer, R. Fingers, | |
| | Ron Guidry | |
| 718 | Save Leaders: | 15 |
| | Rollie Fingers, R. Gossage, | |
| | Dan Quisenberry | |
| 719 | Andy Hassler | 06 |
| 720 | Dwight Evans | 15 |
| 721 | Del Crandall (Mgr.) | 06 |
| 722 | Bob Welch | 06 |
| 723 | Rich Dauer | 06 |
| 724 | Eric Rasmussen | 06 |
| 725 | Cesar Cedeno | 08 |
| 726 | Brewers Leaders: | 10 |
| | Ted Simmons, Moose Haas | |
| 727 | Joel Youngblood | 06 |
| 728 | Tug McGraw | 08 |
| 729 | Gene Tenace | 06 |
| 730 | Bruce Sutter | 20 |

| NO. | PLAYER | MINT |
|---|---|---|
| 731 | Lynn Jones | 06 |
| 732 | Terry Crowley | 06 |
| 733 | Dave Collins | 06 |
| 734 | Odell Jones | 06 |
| 735 | Rick Burleson | 06 |
| 736 | Dick Ruthven | 06 |
| 737 | Jim Essian | 06 |
| 738 | Bill Schroeder (R) | 20 |
| 739 | Bob Watson | 06 |
| 740 | Tom Seaver | 35 |
| 741 | Wayne Gross | 06 |
| 742 | Dick Williams (Mgr.) | 06 |
| 743 | Don Hood | 06 |
| 744 | Jamie Allen | 12 |
| 745 | Dennis Eckersley | 06 |
| 746 | Mickey Hatcher | 06 |
| 747 | Pat Zachry | 06 |
| 748 | Jeff Leonard | 06 |
| 749 | Doug Flynn | 06 |
| 750 | Jim Palmer | 40 |
| 751 | Charlie Moore | 06 |

| NO. | PLAYER | MINT |
|---|---|---|
| 752 | Phil Garner | 06 |
| 753 | Doug Gwosdz | 06 |
| 754 | Kent Tekulve | 06 |
| 755 | Garry Maddox | 06 |
| 756 | Reds Leaders: | 08 |
| | Ron Oester, Mario Soto | |
| 757 | Larry Bowa | 08 |
| 758 | Bill Stein | 06 |
| 759 | Richard Dotson | 08 |
| 760 | Bob Horner | 25 |
| 761 | John Montefusco | 06 |
| 762 | Rance Mulliniks | 06 |
| 763 | Craig Swan | 06 |
| 764 | Mike Hargrove | 06 |
| 765 | Ken Forsch | 06 |
| 766 | Mike Vail | 06 |
| 767 | Carney Lansford | 08 |
| 768 | Champ Summers | 06 |
| 769 | Bill Caudill | 08 |
| 770 | Ken Griffey | 08 |
| 771 | Billy Gardner (Mgr.) | 06 |

| NO. | PLAYER | MINT |
|---|---|---|
| 772 | Jim Slaton | 06 |
| 773 | Todd Cruz | 06 |
| 774 | Tom Gorman | 12 |
| 775 | Dave Parker | 25 |
| 776 | Craig Reynolds | 06 |
| 777 | Tom Paciorek | 06 |
| 778 | Andy Hawkins (R) | 20 |
| 779 | Jim Sundberg | 06 |
| 780 | Steve Carlton | 35 |
| 781 | Checklist No. 6 | 08 |
| 782 | Steve Balboni | 06 |
| 783 | Luis Leal | 06 |
| 784 | Leon Roberts | 06 |
| 785 | Joaquin Andujar | 12 |
| 786 | Red Sox Leaders: | 20 |
| | Bob Ojeda, Wade Boggs | |
| 787 | Bill Campbell | 06 |
| 788 | Milt May | 06 |
| 789 | Bert Blyleven | 08 |
| 790 | Doug DeCinces | 08 |
| 791 | Terry Forster | 06 |
| 792 | Bill Russell | 12 |

## 1984 Topps Traded...Complete Set of 132 Cards—Value $85.00

Updates the main 1984 card set with players who changed teams during the season and rookies. Features the first Topps card for Dwight Gooden and Bret Saberhagen. The complete set was packaged in a printed box and only distributed through card hobby dealers.

| NO. | | PLAYER | MINT |
|---|---|---|---|
| 1 | T | Willie Aikens | 15 |
| 2 | T | Luis Aponte | 10 |
| 3 | T | Mike Armstrong | 10 |
| 4 | T | Bob Bailor | 10 |
| 5 | T | Dusty Baker | 12 |
| 6 | T | Steve Balboni | 15 |
| 7 | T | Alan Bannister | 10 |
| 8 | T | Dave Beard | 10 |
| 9 | T | Joe Beckwith | 10 |
| 10 | T | Bruce Berenyi | 10 |
| 11 | T | Dave Bergman | 10 |
| 12 | T | Tony Bernazard | 10 |
| 13 | T | Yogi Berra (Mgr.) | 50 |
| 14 | T | Barry Bonnell | 10 |
| 15 | T | Phil Bradley (RR) | 2.50 |
| 16 | T | Fred Breining | 10 |
| 17 | T | Bill Buckner | 25 |
| 18 | T | Ray Burris | 10 |
| 19 | T | John Butcher | 10 |
| 20 | T | Brett Butler | 35 |
| 21 | T | Enos Cabell | 10 |
| 22 | T | Bill Campbell | 10 |
| 23 | T | Bill Caudill | 15 |
| 24 | T | Bob Clark | 10 |
| 25 | T | Bryan Clark | 10 |
| 26 | T | Jaimes Cocanower | 20 |
| 27 | T | Ron Darling (RR) | 6.00 |
| 28 | T | Alvin Davis (RR) | 4.50 |
| 29 | T | Ken Dayley | 12 |
| 30 | T | Jeff Dedmon | 20 |
| 31 | T | Bob Dernier | 10 |
| 32 | T | Carlos Diaz | 10 |
| 33 | T | Mike Easler | 12 |

| NO. | | PLAYER | MINT |
|---|---|---|---|
| 34 | T | Dennis Eckersley | 12 |
| 35 | T | Jim Essian | 08 |
| 36 | T | Darrell Evans | 25 |
| 37 | T | Mike Fitzgerald | 15 |
| 38 | T | Tim Foli | 10 |
| 39 | T | George Frazier | 10 |
| 40 | T | Rich Gale | 10 |
| 41 | T | Barbaro Garbey | 20 |
| 42 | T | D. Gooden (RR) | 40.00 |
| 43 | T | Rich Gossage | 30 |
| 44 | T | Wayne Gross | 10 |
| 45 | T | Mark Gubicza (RR) | 1.50 |
| 46 | T | Jackie Gutierrez | 15 |
| 47 | T | Mel Hall | 20 |
| 48 | T | Toby Harrah | 12 |
| 49 | T | Ron Hassey | 10 |
| 50 | T | Rich Hebner | 10 |
| 51 | T | Willie Hernandez | 40 |
| 52 | T | Ricky Horton (RR) | 35 |
| 53 | T | Art Howe | 10 |
| 54 | T | Dane Iorg | 10 |
| 55 | T | Brook Jacoby (RR) | 1.50 |
| 56 | T | Mike Jeffcoat | 15 |
| 57 | T | D. Johnson (Mgr.) | 25 |
| 58 | T | Lynn Jones | 10 |
| 59 | T | Ruppert Jones | 10 |
| 60 | T | Mike Jorgensen | 10 |
| 61 | T | Bob Kearney | 10 |
| 62 | T | Jimmy Key (RR) | 3.00 |
| 63 | T | Dave Hassey | 25 |
| 64 | T | Jerry Koosman | 40 |
| 65 | T | Wayne Krenchicki | 10 |
| 66 | T | Rusty Kuntz | 10 |

| NO. | | PLAYER | MINT |
|---|---|---|---|
| 67 | T | R. Lachemann (Mgr.) | 10 |
| 68 | T | Frank LaCorte | 10 |
| 69 | T | Dennis Lamp | 10 |
| 70 | T | Mark Langston (RR) | 2.50 |
| 71 | T | Rich Leach | 10 |
| 72 | T | Craig Lefferts | 10 |
| 73 | T | Gary Lucas | 10 |
| 74 | T | Jerry Martin | 10 |
| 75 | T | Carmelo Martinez | 25 |
| 76 | T | Mike Mason | 20 |
| 77 | T | Gary Matthews | 15 |
| 78 | T | Andy McGaffigan | 10 |
| 79 | T | Larry Milbourne | 10 |
| 80 | T | Sid Monge | 10 |
| 81 | T | Jackie Moore (Mgr.) | 10 |
| 82 | T | Joe Morgan | 1.25 |
| 83 | T | Graig Nettles | 50 |
| 84 | T | Phil Niekro | 75 |
| 85 | T | Ken Oberkfell | 12 |
| 86 | T | Mike O'Berry | 10 |
| 87 | T | Al Oliver | 20 |
| 88 | T | Jorge Orta | 10 |
| 89 | T | Amos Otis | 15 |
| 90 | T | Dave Parker | 75 |
| 91 | T | Tony Perez | 50 |
| 92 | T | Gerald Perry | 1.25 |
| 93 | T | Gary Pettis (RR) | 35 |
| 94 | T | Rob Picciolo | 08 |
| 95 | T | Vern Rapp (Mgr.) | 08 |
| 96 | T | Floyd Rayford | 08 |
| 97 | T | Randy Ready (RR) | 35 |
| 98 | T | Ron Reed | 10 |
| 99 | T | Gene Richards | 10 |

| NO. | | PLAYER | MINT |
|---|---|---|---|
| 100 | T | Jose Rijo (RR) | 75 |
| 101 | T | Jeff Robinson | 25 |
| 102 | T | Ron Romanick (RR) | 25 |
| 103 | T | Pete Rose | 7.00 |
| 104 | T | B. Saberhagen (RR) | 12.00 |
| 105 | T | Juan Samuel (RR) | 3.00 |
| 106 | T | Scott Sanderson | 12 |
| 107 | T | Dick Schofield | 50 |
| 108 | T | Tom Seaver | 3.00 |
| 109 | T | Jim Slaton | 08 |
| 110 | T | Mike Smithson | 08 |
| 111 | T | Lary Sorensen | 08 |
| 112 | T | Tim Stoddard | 08 |
| 113 | T | Champ Summers | 08 |
| 114 | T | Jim Sundberg | 08 |
| 115 | T | Rick Sutcliffe | 50 |
| 116 | T | Craig Swan | 10 |
| 117 | T | Tim Teufel (RR) | 40 |
| 118 | T | Derrel Thomas | 10 |
| 119 | T | Gorman Thomas | 15 |
| 120 | T | Alex Trevino | 08 |
| 121 | T | Manny Trillo | 12 |
| 122 | T | John Tudor | 30 |
| 123 | T | Tom Underwood | 10 |
| 124 | T | Mike Vail | 10 |
| 125 | T | Tom Waddell | 20 |
| 126 | T | Gary Ward | 20 |
| 127 | T | Curt Wilkerson | 25 |
| 128 | T | Frank Williams | 20 |
| 129 | T | Glenn Wilson | 25 |
| 130 | T | Johnny Wockenfuss | 10 |
| 131 | T | Ned Yost | 10 |
| 132 | T | Traded Checklist | 15 |

# 1985 Topps....Complete Set of 792 Cards—Value $105.00

Features the rookie cards of Dwight Gooden, Roger Clemens, Eric Davis, Bert Saberhagen, Orel Hershiser, and Kirby Puckett. Includes players and coaches of the 1984 USA Olympic Baseball Team.

| NO. PLAYER | MINT | NO. PLAYER | MINT | NO. PLAYER | MINT | NO. PLAYER | MINT |
|---|---|---|---|---|---|---|---|
| 1 Record—C. Fisk | .15 | 57 Pat Zachry | .05 | 123 Dave Smith | .05 | 176 Bill Schroeder | .05 |
|    Longest Game, Catcher | | 58 Orlando Mercado | .05 | 124 Rich Hebner | .05 | 177 Dave Von Ohlen | .05 |
| 2 Record—S. Garvey | .20 | 59 Rick Waits | .05 | 125 Ken Tekulve | .05 | 178 Miguel Dilone | .05 |
|    Errorless Games, 18 | | 60 George Hendrick | .08 | 126 Ruppert Jones | .05 | 179 Tommy John | .15 |
| 3 Record—D. Gooden | 1.00 | 61 Curt Kaufman (R) | .15 | 127 Mark Gubicza (R) | .40 | 180 Dave Winfield | .40 |
|    Most Strikeouts, Rookie | | 62 Mike Ramsey | .05 | 128 Ernie Whitt | .05 | 181 Roger Clemens (R) | 10.00 |
| 4 Record—C. Johnson | .08 | 63 Steve McCatty | .05 | 129 Gene Garber | .05 | 182 Tim Flannery | .05 |
|    Most Pinch Homers | | 64 Mark Bailey (R) | .15 | 130 Al Oliver | .10 | 183 Larry McWilliams | .05 |
| 5 Record—J. Morgan | .15 | 65 Bill Buckner | .10 | 131 Father & Son: | .07 | 184 Carmen Castillo | .05 |
|    Most Homers, 2B | | 66 Dick Williams (Mgr.) | .05 |    Gus and Buddy Bell | | 185 Al Holland | .05 |
| 6 Record—P. Rose | .50 | 67 Rafael Santana (R) | .20 | 132 Father & Son: | .07 | 186 Bob Lillis (Mgr.) | .05 |
|    Most Singles, Career | | 68 Von Hayes | .15 |    Yogi and Dale Berra | | 187 Mike Walters | .05 |
| 7 Record—N. Ryan | .20 | 69 Jim Winn | .12 | 133 Father & Son: | .07 | 188 Greg Pryor | .05 |
|    Most Strikeouts, Career | | 70 Don Baylor | .10 |    Ray and Bob Boone | | 189 Warren Brusstar | .05 |
| 8 Record—J. Samuel | .15 | 71 Tim Laudner | .05 | 134 Father & Son: | .07 | 190 Rusty Staub | .12 |
|    Stolen Bases, Rookie | | 72 Rick Sutcliffe | .15 |    Tito and Terry Francona | | 191 Steve Nicosia | .05 |
| 9 Record—B. Sutter | .12 | 73 Rusty Kuntz | .05 | 135 Father & Son: | .07 | 192 Howard Johnson | 2.00 |
|    Most Saves, Season | | 74 Mike Krukow | .05 |    Bob and Terry Kennedy | | 193 Jimmy Key (R) | 1.00 |
| 10 Record—D. Sutton | .12 | 75 Willie Upshaw | .10 | 136 Father & Son: | .07 | 194 Dave Stegman | .05 |
|    100 Strikeout Seasons | | 76 Alan Bannister | .05 |    Jim and Jeff Kunkel | | 195 Glenn Hubbard | .05 |
| 11 Ralph Houk (Mgr.) | .05 | 77 Joe Beckwith | .05 | 137 Father & Son: | .07 | 196 Pete O'Brien | .10 |
| 12 Dave Lopes | .08 | 78 Scott Fletcher | .05 |    Vern and Vance Law | | 197 Mike Warren | .05 |
| 13 Tim Lollar | .05 | 79 Rick Mahler | .05 | 138 Father & Son: | .07 | 198 Eddie Milner | .05 |
| 14 Chris Bando | .05 | 80 Keith Hernandez | .30 |    Dick and Dick Schofield | | 199 Denny Martinez | .05 |
| 15 Jerry Koosman | .15 | 81 Lenn Sakata | .05 | 139 Father & Son: | .07 | 200 Reggie Jackson | .40 |
| 16 Bobby Meacham | .05 | 82 Joe Price | .05 |    Bob and Joel Skinner | | 201 Burt Hooton | .05 |
| 17 Mike Scott | .30 | 83 Charlie Moore | .05 | 140 Father & Son: | .07 | 202 Gorman Thomas | .08 |
| 18 Mickey Hatcher | .05 | 84 Spike Owen | .05 |    Roy and Roy Smalley | | 203 Bob McClure | .05 |
| 19 Geroge Frazier | .05 | 85 Mike Marshall | .12 | 141 Father & Son: | .07 | 204 Art Howe | .05 |
| 20 Chet Lemon | .08 | 86 Don Aase | .05 |    Dave and Mike Stenhouse | | 205 Steve Rogers | .05 |
| 21 Lee Tunnell | .05 | 87 David Green | .05 | 142 Father & Son: | .07 | 206 Phil Garner | .05 |
| 22 Duane Kuiper | .05 | 88 Bryn Smith | .05 |    Dizzy and Steve Trout | | 207 Mark Clear | .05 |
| 23 Bret Saberhagen (R) | 4.00 | 89 Jackie Gutierrez | .12 | 143 Father & Son: | .07 | 208 Champ Summers | .05 |
| 24 Jesse Barfield | .35 | 90 Rich Gossage | .15 |    Ossie and Ozzie Virgil | | 209 Bill Campbell | .05 |
| 25 Steve Bedrosian | .15 | 91 Jeff Burroughs | .05 | 144 Ron Gardenhire | .05 | 210 Gary Matthews | .08 |
| 26 Ray Smalley | .05 | 92 Paul Owens (Mgr.) | .05 | 145 Alvin Davis (R) | 1.50 | 211 Clay Christiansen | .15 |
| 27 Bruce Berenyi | .05 | 93 Don Schulze | .10 | 146 Gary Redus | .08 | 212 George Vukovich | .05 |
| 28 Dann Bilardello | .05 | 94 Toby Harrah | .05 | 147 Bill Swaggerty | .12 | 213 Billy Gardner (Mgr.) | .05 |
| 29 Odell Jones | .05 | 95 Jose Cruz | .08 | 148 Steve Yeager | .05 | 214 John Tudor | .15 |
| 30 Cal Ripken | .50 | 96 Johnny Ray | .12 | 149 Dickie Noles | .05 | 215 Bob Brenly | .08 |
| 31 Terry Whitfield | .05 | 97 Pete Filson | .05 | 150 Jim Rice | .30 | 216 Jerry Don Gleaton | .05 |
| 32 Chuck Porter | .05 | 98 Steve Lake | .05 | 151 Moose Haas | .05 | 217 Leon Roberts | .05 |
| 33 Tito Landrum | .05 | 99 Milt Wilcox | .05 | 152 Steve Braun | .05 | 218 Doyle Alexander | .05 |
| 34 Ed Nunez | .10 | 100 George Brett | .50 | 153 Frank LaCorte | .05 | 219 Gerald Perry | .50 |
| 35 Graig Nettles | .12 | 101 Jim Acker | .05 | 154 Argenis Salazar (R) | .12 | 220 Fred Lynn | .15 |
| 36 Fred Breining | .05 | 102 Tommy Dunbar | .08 | 155 Yogi Berra (Mgr.) | .12 | 221 Ron Reed | .05 |
| 37 Reid Nichols | .05 | 103 Randy Lerch | .05 | 156 Craig Reynolds | .05 | 222 Hubie Brooks | .08 |
| 38 Jackie Moore (Mgr.) | .05 | 104 Mike Fitzgerald | .07 | 157 Tug McGraw | .08 | 223 Tom Hume | .05 |
| 39 Johnny Wockenfuss | .05 | 105 Ron Kittle | .15 | 158 Pat Tabler | .05 | 224 Al Cowens | .05 |
| 40 Phil Niekro | .20 | 106 Pascual Perez | .05 | 159 Carlos Diaz | .05 | 225 Mike Boddicker | .10 |
| 41 Mike Fischlin | .05 | 107 Tom Foley | .05 | 160 Lance Parrish | .25 | 226 Juan Beniquez | .05 |
| 42 Luis Sanchez | .05 | 108 Darnell Coles | .15 | 161 Ken Schrom | .05 | 227 Danny Darwin | .05 |
| 43 Andre David | .12 | 109 Gary Roenicke | .05 | 162 Benny Distefano | .15 | 228 Dion James | .20 |
| 44 Dickie Thon | .07 | 110 Alejandro Pena | .05 | 163 Dennis Eckersley | .05 | 229 Dave LaPoint | .05 |
| 45 Greg Minton | .05 | 111 Doug DeCinces | .10 | 164 Jorge Orta | .05 | 230 Gary Carter | .45 |
| 46 Gary Woods | .05 | 112 Tom Tellmann | .05 | 165 Dusty Baker | .08 | 231 Dwayne Murphy | .08 |
| 47 Dave Rozema | .05 | 113 Tom Herr | .15 | 166 Keith Atherton | .05 | 232 Dave Beard | .05 |
| 48 Tony Fernandez | 1.25 | 114 Bob James | .05 | 167 Rufino Linares | .05 | 233 Ed Jurak | .05 |
| 49 Butch Davis | .05 | 115 Rickey Henderson | .45 | 168 Garth Iorg | .05 | 234 Jerry Narron | .05 |
| 50 John Candelaria | .08 | 116 Dennis Boyd | .25 | 169 Dan Spillner | .05 | 235 Garry Maddox | .05 |
| 51 Rob Watson | .05 | 117 Greg Gross | .05 | 170 George Foster | .15 | 236 Mark Thurmond | .08 |
| 52 Jerry Dybzinski | .05 | 118 Eric Show | .08 | 171 Bill Stein | .05 | 237 Julio Franco | .15 |
| 53 Tom Gorman | .07 | 119 Pat Corrales (Mgr.) | .05 | 172 Jack Perconte | .05 | 238 Jose Rijo (R) | .35 |
| 54 Cesar Cedeno | .08 | 120 Steve Kemp | .05 | 173 Mike Young | .10 | 239 Tim Teufel | .20 |
| 55 Frank Tanana | .05 | 121 Checklist No. 1 | .08 | 174 Rick Honeycutt | .05 | 240 Dave Stieb | .15 |
| 56 Jim Dwyer | .05 | 122 Tom Brunansky | .30 | 175 Dave Parker | .25 | 241 Jim Frey (Mgr.) | .05 |

Card values from this set fluctuate considerably.

| NO. PLAYER | MINT |
| --- | --- |
| 242 Greg Harris | .05 |
| 243 Barbaro Garbey | .12 |
| 244 Mike Jones | .05 |
| 245 Chili Davis | .08 |
| 246 Mike Norris | .05 |
| 247 Wayne Tolleston | .05 |
| 248 Terry Forster | .05 |
| 249 Harold Baines | .20 |
| 250 Jesse Orosco | .05 |
| 251 Brad Gulden | .05 |
| 252 Dan Ford | .05 |
| 253 Sid Bream (R) | .35 |
| 254 Pete Vuckovich | .08 |
| 255 Lonnie Smith | .08 |
| 256 Mike Stanton | .05 |
| 257 Bryan Little | .05 |
| 258 Mike Brown | .05 |
| 259 Gary Allenson | .05 |
| 260 Dave Righetti | .12 |
| 261 Checklist No. 2 | .08 |
| 262 Greg Booker | .12 |
| 263 Mel Hall | .10 |
| 264 Joe Sambito | .05 |
| 265 Juan Samuel | .75 |
| 266 Frank Viola | .30 |
| 267 Henry Cotto | .20 |
| 268 Chuck Tanner (Mgr.) | .05 |
| 269 Doug Baker | .12 |
| 270 Dan Quisenberry | .15 |
| **No. 271 to 282 (# 1 Draft Picks)** | |
| 271 Tim Foli (1968) | .07 |
| 272 Jeff Burroughs (1969) | .07 |
| 273 Bill Almon (1974) | .07 |
| 274 Floyd Bannister (1976) | .07 |
| 275 Harold Baines (1977) | .12 |
| 276 Bob Horner (1978) | .12 |
| 277 Al Chambers (1979) | .07 |
| 278 D. Strawberry (1980) | .75 |
| 279 Mike Moore (1981) | .07 |
| 280 S. Dunston (R) (1982) | .75 |
| 281 Tim Belcher (R) (1983) | .30 |
| 282 S. Abner (R) (1984) | .60 |
| 283 Fran Mullins | .05 |
| 284 Marty Bystrom | .05 |
| 285 Dan Driessen | .05 |
| 286 Rudy Law | .05 |
| 287 Walt Terrell | .05 |
| 288 Jeff Kunkel | .12 |
| 289 Tom Underwood | .05 |
| 290 Cecil Cooper | .15 |
| 291 Bob Welch | .05 |
| 292 Brad Komminsk | .10 |
| 293 Curt Young (R) | .50 |
| 294 Tom Nieto | .12 |
| 295 Joe Niekro | .12 |
| 296 Ricky Nelson | .05 |
| 297 Gary Lucas | .05 |
| 298 Marty Barrett | .12 |
| 299 Andy Hawkins | .08 |
| 300 Rod Carew | .35 |
| 301 John Montefusco | .05 |
| 302 Tim Corcoran | .05 |
| 303 Mike Jeffcoat | .05 |
| 304 Gary Gaetti | .20 |
| 305 Dale Berra | .05 |
| 306 Rick Reuschel | .10 |
| 307 Sparky Anderson (Mgr.) | .05 |
| 308 John Wathan | .05 |
| 309 Mike Witt | .10 |
| 310 Manny Trillo | .05 |
| 311 Jim Gott | .05 |
| 312 Marc Hill | .05 |
| 313 Dave Schmidt | .05 |
| 314 Ron Oester | .05 |
| 315 Doug Sisk | .05 |
| 316 John Lowenstein | .05 |
| 317 Jack Lazorko | .12 |
| 318 Ted Simmons | .10 |
| 319 Jeff Jones | .05 |
| 320 Dale Murphy | .75 |
| 321 Ricky Horton (R) | .25 |
| 322 Dave Stapleton | .05 |
| 323 Andy McGaffigan | .05 |
| 324 Bruce Bochy | .05 |
| 325 John Denny | .05 |

| NO. PLAYER | MINT |
| --- | --- |
| 326 Kevin Bass | .15 |
| 327 Brook Jacoby | .40 |
| 328 Bob Shirley | .05 |
| 329 Ron Washington | .05 |
| 330 Leon Durham | .15 |
| 331 Bill Laskey | .05 |
| 332 Brian Harper | .05 |
| 333 Willie Hernandez | .15 |
| 334 Dick Howser (Mgr.) | .05 |
| 335 Bruce Benedict | .05 |
| 336 Rance Mulliniks | .05 |
| 337 Billy Sample | .05 |
| 338 Britt Burns | .05 |
| 339 Danny Heep | .05 |
| 340 Robin Yount | .40 |
| 341 Floyd Rayford | .05 |
| 342 Ted Power | .05 |
| 343 Bill Russell | .05 |
| 344 Dave Henderson | .05 |
| 345 Charlie Lea | .05 |
| 346 Terry Pendleton (R) | .60 |
| 347 Rick Langford | .05 |
| 348 Bob Boone | .05 |
| 349 Domingo Ramos | .05 |
| 350 Wade Boggs | 4.00 |
| 351 Juan Agosto | .05 |
| 352 Joe Morgan | .25 |
| 353 Julio Solano | .12 |
| 354 Andre Robertson | .05 |
| 355 Bert Blyleven | .10 |
| 356 Dave Meier | .12 |
| 357 Rich Bordi | .05 |
| 358 Tony Pena | .12 |
| 359 Pat Sheridan | .05 |
| 360 Steve Carlton | .30 |
| 361 Alfredo Griffin | .05 |
| 362 Craig McMurtry | .05 |
| 363 Ron Hodges | .05 |
| 364 Richard Dotson | .05 |
| 365 Danny Ozark (Mgr.) | .05 |
| 366 Todd Cruz | .05 |
| 367 Keefe Cato | .12 |
| 368 Dave Bergman | .05 |
| 369 R.J. Reynolds (R) | .25 |
| 370 Bruce Sutter | .15 |
| 371 Mickey Rivers | .05 |
| 372 Roy Howell | .05 |
| 373 Mike Moore | .07 |
| 374 Brian Downing | .05 |
| 375 Jeff Reardon | .15 |
| 376 Jeff Newman | .05 |
| 377 Checklist No.3 | .08 |
| 378 Alan Wiggins | .08 |
| 379 Charles Hudson | .05 |
| 380 Ken Griffey | .08 |
| 381 Roy Smith | .12 |
| 382 Denny Walling | .05 |
| 383 Rick Lysander | .05 |
| 384 Jody Davis | .10 |
| 385 Jose DeLeon | .05 |
| 386 Dan Gladden (R) | .30 |
| 387 Buddy Biancalana | .12 |
| 388 Bert Roberge | .05 |
| **No. 389 to 404 (U.S. Olympic Team)** | |
| 389 Rod Dedeaux (Coach) | .10 |
| 390 Sid Akins | .10 |
| 391 Flavio Alfaro | .10 |
| 392 Don August | .25 |
| 393 Scott Bankhead | .40 |
| 394 Bob Caffrey | .10 |
| 395 Mike Dunne (R) | 1.25 |
| 396 Gary Green | .10 |
| 397 John Hoover | .10 |
| 398 Shane Mack (R) | .50 |
| 399 John Marzano (R) | .50 |
| 400 Oddibe McDowell (R) | .75 |
| 401 Mark McGwire (R) | 20.00 |
| 402 Pat Pacillo (R) | .25 |
| 403 Cory Snyder (R) | 8.00 |
| 404 Billy Swift | .20 |
| 405 Tom Veryzer | .05 |
| 406 Len Whitehouse | .05 |
| 407 Bobby Ramos | .05 |
| 408 Sid Monge | .05 |
| 409 Brad Wellman | .05 |

| NO. PLAYER | MINT |
| --- | --- |
| 410 Bob Horner | .20 |
| 411 Bobby Cox (Mgr.) | .05 |
| 412 Bud Black | .05 |
| 413 Vance Law | .05 |
| 414 Gary Ward | .05 |
| 415 Ron Darling | 1.75 |
| 416 Wayne Gross | .05 |
| 417 John Franco (R) | .80 |
| 418 Ken Landreaux | .05 |
| 419 Mike Caldwell | .05 |
| 420 Andre Dawson | .35 |
| 421 Dave Rucker | .05 |
| 422 Carney Lansford | .10 |
| 423 Barry Bonnell | .05 |
| 424 Al Nipper (R) | .25 |
| 425 Mike Hargrove | .05 |
| 426 Vern Ruhle | .05 |
| 427 Mario Ramirez | .05 |
| 428 Larry Andersen | .05 |
| 429 Rick Cerone | .05 |
| 430 Ron Davis | .05 |
| 431 U.L. Washington | .05 |
| 432 Thad Bosley | .05 |
| 433 Jim Morrison | .05 |
| 434 Gene Richards | .05 |
| 435 Dan Petry | .12 |
| 436 Willie Aikens | .05 |
| 437 Al Jones | .12 |
| 438 Joe Torre (Mgr.) | .07 |
| 439 Junior Ortiz | .05 |
| 440 Fernando Valenzuela | .30 |
| 441 Duane Walker | .05 |
| 442 Ken Forsch | .05 |
| 443 George Wright | .05 |
| 444 Tony Phillips | .05 |
| 445 Tippy Martinez | .05 |
| 446 Jim Sundberg | .05 |
| 447 Jeff Lahti | .05 |
| 448 Derrel Thomas | .05 |
| 449 Phil Bradley (R) | 1.00 |
| 450 Steve Garvey | .40 |
| 451 Bruce Hurst | .05 |
| 452 John Castino | .05 |
| 453 Tom Waddell | .12 |
| 454 Glenn Wilson | .10 |
| 455 Bob Knepper | .05 |
| 456 Tim Foli | .05 |
| 457 Cecillio Guante | .05 |
| 458 Randy Johnson | .05 |
| 459 Charlie Leibrandt | .05 |
| 460 Ryne Sandberg | .40 |
| 461 Marty Castillo | .05 |
| 462 Gary Lavelle | .05 |
| 463 Dave Collins | .05 |
| 464 Mike Mason | .12 |
| 465 Bob Grich | .07 |
| 466 Tony LaRussa (Mgr.) | .05 |
| 467 Ed Lynch | .05 |
| 468 Wayne Krenchicki | .05 |
| 469 Sammy Stewart | .05 |
| 470 Steve Sax | .30 |
| 471 Pete Ladd | .05 |
| 472 Jim Essian | .05 |
| 473 Tim Wallach | .12 |
| 474 Kurt Kepshire | .12 |
| 475 Andre Thornton | .08 |
| 476 Jeff Stone (R) | .30 |
| 477 Bob Ojeda | .05 |
| 478 Kurt Bevacqua | .05 |
| 479 Mike Madden | .05 |
| 480 Lou Whitaker | .15 |
| 481 Dale Murray | .05 |
| 482 Harry Spilman | .05 |
| 483 Mike Smithson | .05 |
| 484 Larry Bowa | .05 |
| 485 Matt Young | .06 |
| 486 Steve Balboni | .06 |
| 487 Frank Williams | .12 |
| 488 Joel Skinner | .12 |
| 489 Bryan Clark | .05 |
| 490 Jason Thompson | .08 |
| 491 Rick Camp | .05 |
| 492 Dave Johnson (Mgr.) | .20 |
| 493 Orel Hershiser (R) | 5.00 |
| 494 Rich Dauer | .05 |

| NO. PLAYER | MINT |
| --- | --- |
| 495 Mario Soto | .08 |
| 496 Donnie Scott | .12 |
| 497 Gary Pettis | .40 |
| (wrong photo—It's his brother—Lynn) | |
| 498 Ed Romero | .05 |
| 499 Danny Cox | .25 |
| 500 Mike Schmidt | .50 |
| 501 Dan Schatzeder | .05 |
| 502 Rick Miller | .05 |
| 503 Tim Conroy | .05 |
| 504 Jerry Willard | .08 |
| 505 Jim Beattie | .05 |
| 506 Franklin Stubbs (R) | .50 |
| 507 Ray Fontenot | .05 |
| 508 John Shelby | .05 |
| 509 Milt May | .05 |
| 510 Kent Hrbek | .30 |
| 511 Lee Smith | .08 |
| 512 Tom Brookens | .05 |
| 513 Lynn Jones | .05 |
| 514 Jeff Cornell | .12 |
| 515 Dave Concepcion | .08 |
| 516 Roy Lee Jackson | .05 |
| 517 Jerry Martin | .05 |
| 518 Chris Chambliss | .05 |
| 519 Doug Rader (Mgr.) | .05 |
| 520 LaMarr Hoyt | .08 |
| 521 Rick Dempsey | .05 |
| 522 Paul Molitor | .20 |
| 523 Candy Maldonado | .15 |
| 524 Rob Wilfong | .05 |
| 525 Darrell Porter | .05 |
| 526 Dave Palmer | .05 |
| 527 Checklist No. 4 | .08 |
| 528 Bill Krueger | .05 |
| 529 Rich Gedman | .08 |
| 530 Dave Dravecky | .08 |
| 531 Joe Lefebvre | .25 |
| 532 Frank DiPino | .05 |
| 533 Tony Bernazard | .05 |
| 534 Brian Dayett | .08 |
| 535 Pat Putnam | .05 |
| 536 Kirby Puckett (R) | 9.00 |
| 537 Don Robinson | .05 |
| 538 Keith Moreland | .05 |
| 539 Aurelio Lopez | .05 |
| 540 Claudell Washington | .08 |
| 541 Mark Davis | .05 |
| 542 Don Slaught | .05 |
| 543 Mike Squires | .05 |
| 544 Bruce Kison | .05 |
| 545 Lloyd Moseby | .15 |
| 546 Brent Gaff | .05 |
| 547 Pete Rose (Mgr.) | .50 |
| 548 Larry Parrish | .07 |
| 549 Mike Scioscia | .05 |
| 550 Scott McGregor | .07 |
| 551 Andy Van Slyke | .25 |
| 552 Chris Codiroli | .05 |
| 553 Bob Clark | .05 |
| 554 Doug Flynn | .05 |
| 555 Bob Stanley | .05 |
| 556 Sixto Lezcano | .05 |
| 557 Len Barker | .05 |
| 558 Carmelo Martinez | .05 |
| 559 Jay Howell | .05 |
| 560 Bill Madlock | .15 |
| 561 Darryl Motley | .05 |
| 562 Houston Jimenez | .05 |
| 563 Dick Ruthven | .05 |
| 564 Alan Ashby | .05 |
| 565 Kirk Gibson | .35 |
| 566 Ed Vande Berg | .05 |
| 567 Joel Youngblood | .05 |
| 568 Cliff Johnson | .05 |
| 569 Ken Oberkfell | .05 |
| 570 Darryl Strawberry | 3.00 |
| 571 Charlie Hough | .05 |
| 572 Tom Paciorek | .05 |
| 573 Jay Tibbs (R) | .30 |
| 574 Joe Altobelli (Mgr.) | .05 |
| 575 Pedro Guerrero | .25 |
| 576 Jaime Cocanower | .12 |
| 577 Chris Speier | .05 |

| NO. PLAYER | MINT | NO. PLAYER | MINT | NO. PLAYER | MINT | NO. PLAYER | MINT |
|---|---|---|---|---|---|---|---|
| 578 Terry Francona | .05 | 632 Bruce Bochte | .05 | 686 Mike Easler | .05 | 740 Jack Clark | .30 |
| 579 Ron Romanick (R) | .15 | 633 Glenn Hoffman | .05 | 687 Bill Gullickson | .05 | 741 John Butcher | .05 |
| 580 Dwight Evans | .12 | 634 Bill Dawley | .05 | 688 Len Matuszek | .05 | 742 Ron Hassey | .05 |
| 581 Mark Wagner | .05 | 635 Terry Kennedy | .08 | 689 Luis DeLeon | .05 | 743 Frank White | .05 |
| 582 Ken Phelps | .35 | 636 Shane Rawley | .05 | 690 Alan Trammell | .35 | 744 Doug Bair | .05 |
| 583 Bobby Brown | .05 | 637 Brett Butler | .08 | 691 Dennis Rasmussen | .25 | 745 Buddy Bell | .10 |
| 584 Kevin Gross | .05 | 638 Mike Pagliarulo (R) | 2.00 | 692 Randy Bush | .05 | 746 Jim Clancy | .05 |
| 585 Butch Wynegar | .05 | 639 Ed Hodge | .10 | 693 Tim Stoddard | .05 | 747 Alex Trevino | .05 |
| 586 Bill Scherrer | .05 | 640 Steve Henderson | .05 | 694 Joe Carter | 1.50 | 748 Lee Mazzilli | .05 |
| 587 Doug Frobel | .05 | 641 Rod Scurry | .05 | 695 Rick Rhoden | .05 | 749 Julio Cruz | .05 |
| 588 Bobby Castillo | .05 | 642 Dave Owen | .10 | 696 John Rabb | .05 | 750 Rollie Fingers | .15 |
| 589 Bob Dernier | .05 | 643 Johnny Grubb | .05 | 697 Onix Concepcion | .05 | 751 Kelvin Chapman | .12 |
| 590 Ray Knight | .05 | 644 Mark Huismann | .10 | 698 Jorge Bell | .60 | 752 Bob Owchinko | .05 |
| 591 Larry Herndon | .05 | 645 Damaso Garcia | .08 | 699 Donnie Moore | .08 | 753 Greg Brock | .08 |
| 592 Jeff Robinson | .30 | 646 Scot Thompson | .05 | 700 Eddie Murray | .45 | 754 Larry Milbourne | .05 |
| 593 Rick Leach | .05 | 647 Rafael Ramierz | .05 | 701 Eddie Murray (AS) | .25 | 755 Ken Singleton | .08 |
| 594 Curt Wilkerson | .08 | 648 Bob Jones | .05 | 702 Damaso Garcia (AS) | .08 | 756 Rob Picciolo | .05 |
| 595 Larry Gura | .05 | 649 Sid Fernandez | 1.25 | 703 George Brett (AS) | .30 | 757 Willie McGee | .35 |
| 596 Jerry Hairston | .05 | 650 Greg Luzinski | .08 | 704 Cal Ripken (AS) | .25 | 758 Ray Burris | .05 |
| 597 Brad Lesley | .05 | 651 Jeff Russell | .05 | 705 Dave Winfield (AS) | .20 | 759 Jim Fanning (Mgr.) | .05 |
| 598 Jose Oquendo | .05 | 652 Joe Nolan | .05 | 706 Rickey Henderson (AS) | .30 | 760 Nolan Ryan | .35 |
| 599 Storm Davis | .08 | 653 Mark Brouhard | .05 | 707 Tony Armas (AS) | .08 | 761 Jerry Remy | .05 |
| 600 Pete Rose | 1.25 | 654 Dave Anderson | .05 | 708 Lance Parrish (AS) | .15 | 762 Eddie Whitson | .05 |
| 601 Tom Lasorda (Mgr.) | .08 | 655 Joaquin Andujar | .08 | 709 Mike Boddicker (AS) | .08 | 763 Kiko Garcia | .05 |
| 602 Jeff Dedmon | .12 | 656 Chuck Cottier (Mgr.) | .05 | 710 Frank Viola (AS) | .08 | 764 Jamie Easterly | .05 |
| 603 Rick Manning | .05 | 657 Jim Slaton | .05 | 711 Dan Quisenberry (AS) | .15 | 765 Willie Randolph | .05 |
| 604 Daryl Sconiers | .05 | 658 Mike Stenhouse | .05 | 712 Keith Hernandez (AS) | .20 | 766 Paul Mirabella | .05 |
| 605 Ozzie Smith | .30 | 659 Checklist No. 5 | .08 | 713 Ryne Sandberg (AS) | .25 | 767 Darrell Brown | .05 |
| 606 Rich Gale | .05 | 660 Tony Gwynn | 1.25 | 714 Mike Schmidt (AS) | .25 | 768 Ron Cey | .10 |
| 607 Bill Almon | .05 | 661 Steve Crawford | .05 | 715 Ozzie Smith (AS) | .08 | 769 Joe Cowley | .05 |
| 608 Craig Lefferts | .05 | 662 Mike Heath | .05 | 716 Dale Murphy (AS) | .30 | 770 Carlton Fisk | .15 |
| 609 Broderick Perkins | .05 | 663 Luis Aguayo | .05 | 717 Tony Gwynn (AS) | .25 | 771 Geoff Zahn | .05 |
| 610 Jack Morris | .25 | 664 Steve Farr | .12 | 718 Jeff Leonard (AS) | .08 | 772 Johnnie LeMaster | .05 |
| 611 Ozzie Virgil | .05 | 665 Don Mattingly | 10.00 | 719 Gary Carter (AS) | .20 | 773 Hal McRae | .05 |
| 612 Mike Armstrong | .05 | 666 Mike LaCoss | .05 | 720 Rick Sutcliffe (AS) | .15 | 774 Dennis Lamp | .05 |
| 613 Terry Puhl | .05 | 667 Dave Engle | .05 | 721 Bob Knepper (AS) | .08 | 775 Mookie Wilson | .08 |
| 614 Al Williams | .05 | 668 Steve Trout | .05 | 722 Bruce Sutter (AS) | .15 | 776 Jerry Royster | .05 |
| 615 Marvell Wynne | .05 | 669 Lee Lacy | .05 | 723 Dave Stewart | .05 | 777 Ned Yost | .05 |
| 616 Scott Sanderson | .05 | 670 Tom Seaver | .35 | 724 Oscar Gamble | .05 | 778 Mike Davis | .08 |
| 617 Willie Wilson | .15 | 671 Dane Iorg | .05 | 725 Floyd Bannister | .05 | 779 Nick Esasky | .05 |
| 618 Pete Falcone | .05 | 672 Juan Berenguer | .05 | 726 Al Bumbry | .05 | 780 Mike Flanagan | .05 |
| 619 Jeff Leonard | .05 | 673 Buck Martinez | .05 | 727 Frank Pastore | .05 | 781 Jim Gantner | .05 |
| 620 Dwight Gooden (R) | 9.00 | 674 Atlee Hammaker | .05 | 728 Bob Bailor | .05 | 782 Tom Niedenfuer | .05 |
| 621 Marvis Foley | .05 | 675 Tony Perez | .15 | 729 Don Sutton | .20 | 783 Mike Jorgensen | .05 |
| 622 Luis Leal | .05 | 676 Albert Hall | .12 | 730 Dave Kingman | .10 | 784 Checklist No. 6 | .08 |
| 623 Greg Walker | .12 | 677 Wally Backman | .05 | 731 Neil Allen | .05 | 785 Tony Armas | .12 |
| 624 Benny Ayala | .05 | 678 Joey McLaughlin | .05 | 732 John McNamara (Mgr.) | .05 | 786 Enos Cabell | .05 |
| 625 Mark Langston (R) | 1.00 | 679 Bob Kearney | .05 | 733 Tony Scott | .05 | 787 Jim Wohlford | .05 |
| 626 German Rivera | .15 | 680 Jerry Reuss | .05 | 734 John Henry Johnson | .05 | 788 Steve Comer | .05 |
| 627 Eric Davis (R) | 17.50 | 681 Ben Oglivie | .05 | 735 Garry Templeton | .10 | 789 Luis Salazar | .05 |
| 628 R. Lachemann (Mgr.) | .05 | 682 Doug Corbett | .05 | 736 Jerry Mumphrey | .05 | 790 Ron Guidry | .20 |
| 629 Dick Schofield | .12 | 683 Whitey Herzog (Mgr.) | .05 | 737 Bo Diaz | .05 | 791 Ivan DeJesus | .05 |
| 630 Tim Raines | .40 | 684 Bill Doran | .10 | 738 Omar Moreno | .05 | 792 Darrell Evans | .12 |
| 631 Bob Forsch | .05 | 685 Bill Caudill | .08 | 739 Ernie Camacho | .05 | | |

## 1985 Topps Traded....Complete Set of 132 Cards—Value $16.00

Updates the main 1985 card set with players who changed teams during the season and rookies who joined their teams early in the season. Features the first Topps card of Vince Coleman, Chris Brown, and Jim Presley. The complete set was packaged in a printed box and only distributed through card hobby dealers. Topps tested a small quantity of wax packs.

CHRIS BROWN

TOM BROWNING

VINCE COLEMAN

MARIANO DUNCAN

JIM PRESLEY

| NO. PLAYER | MINT | NO. PLAYER | MINT | NO. PLAYER | MINT | NO. PLAYER | MINT |
|---|---|---|---|---|---|---|---|
| 1 T Don Aase | .08 | 5 T G. Bamberger (Mgr.) | .06 | 9 T Hubie Brooks | .12 | 13 T Ray Burris | .06 |
| 2 T Bill Almon | .06 | 6 T Dale Berra | .10 | 10 T Chris Brown (RR) | 1.00 | 14 T Jeff Burroughs | .06 |
| 3 T Benny Ayala | .06 | 7 T Rich Bordi | .06 | 11 T T. Browning (RR) | .50 | 15 T Bill Campbell | .06 |
| 4 T Dusty Baker | .12 | 8 T Daryl Boston (RR) | .20 | 12 T Al Bumbry | .06 | 16 T Don Carman | .25 |

| NO. PLAYER | MINT | NO. PLAYER | MINT | NO. PLAYER | MINT | NO. PLAYER | MINT |
|---|---|---|---|---|---|---|---|
| 17 T Gary Carter | .75 | 46 T Toby Harrah | .08 | 75 T Sixto Lezcano | .06 | 104 T Rick Schu | .25 |
| 18 T Bobby Castillo | .06 | 47 T Greg Harris | .06 | 76 T Tim Lollar | .06 | 105 T Donnie Scott | .06 |
| 19 T Bill Caudill | .10 | 48 T Ron Hassey | .06 | 77 T Fred Lynn | .20 | 106 T Larry Sheets | .75 |
| 20 T Rick Cerone | .08 | 49 T Rickey Henderson | 1.25 | 78 T Billy Martin (Mgr.) | .15 | 107 T Don Slaught | .06 |
| 21 T Bryan Clark | .06 | 50 T Steve Henderson | .06 | 79 T Ron Mathis | .15 | 108 T Roy Smalley | .08 |
| 22 T Jack Clark | .40 | 51 T George Hendrik | .12 | 80 T Len Matuszek | .06 | 109 T Lonnie Smith | .12 |
| 23 T Pat Clements | .25 | 52 T Joe Hesketh (RR) | .35 | 81 T Gene Mauch (Mgr.) | .06 | 110 T Nate Snell | .20 |
| 24 T V. Coleman (RR) | 6.00 | 53 T T. Higuera (RR) | 2.00 | 82 T Oddibe McDowell | .75 | 111 T Chris Speier | .06 |
| 25 T Dave Collins | .08 | 54 T Donnie Hill | .06 | 83 T R. McDowell (RR) | 1.00 | 112 T Mike Stenhouse | .06 |
| 26 T Dave Darwin | .06 | 55 T Al Holland | .08 | 84 T J. McNamara (Mgr.) | .06 | 113 T Tim Stoddard | .06 |
| 27 T J. Davenport (Mgr.) | .06 | 56 T Burt Hooton | .06 | 85 T Donnie Moore | .08 | 114 T Jim Sundberg | .08 |
| 28 T Jerry Davis | .12 | 57 T Jay Howell | .08 | 86 T Gene Nelson | .06 | 115 T Bruce Sutter | .25 |
| 29 T Brian Dayett | .06 | 58 T Ken Howell | .20 | 87 T Steve Nicosia | .06 | 116 T Don Sutton | .50 |
| 30 T Ivan DeJesus | .06 | 59 T LaMarr Hoyt | .12 | 88 T Al Oliver | .12 | 117 T Kent Tekulve | .08 |
| 31 T Ken Dixon | .25 | 60 T Tim Hulett | .20 | 89 T Joe Orsulak | .25 | 118 T Tom Tellmann | .06 |
| 32 T M. Duncan (RR) | .30 | 61 T Bob James | .06 | 90 T Rob Picciolo | .06 | 119 T Walt Terrell | .15 |
| 33 T John Felske (Mgr.) | .06 | 62 T Steve Jeltz (RR) | .25 | 91 T Chris Pittaro | .15 | 120 T Mickey Tettleton | .12 |
| 34 T Mike Fitzgerald | .06 | 63 T Cliff Johnson | .06 | 92 T Jim Presley (RR) | 1.50 | 121 T Derrel Thomas | .06 |
| 35 T Ray Fontenot | .06 | 64 T Howard Johnson | 1.25 | 93 T Rick Reuschel | .15 | 122 T Rich Thompson | .15 |
| 36 T Greg Gagne | .40 | 65 T Ruppert Jones | .08 | 94 T Bert Roberge | .06 | 123 T Alex Trevino | .06 |
| 37 T Oscar Gamble | .10 | 66 T Steve Kemp | .06 | 95 T Bob Rodgers (Mgr.) | .06 | 124 T John Tudor | .20 |
| 38 T Scott Garrelts (RR) | .40 | 67 T Bruce Kison | .06 | 96 T Jerry Royster | .06 | 125 T Jose Uribe | .25 |
| 39 T Bob Gibson | .06 | 68 T Alan Knicely | .06 | 97 T Dave Rozema | .06 | 126 T B. Valentine (Mgr.) | .10 |
| 40 T Jim Gott | .06 | 69 T Mike LaCoss | .06 | 98 T Dave Rucker | .06 | 127 T Dave Von Ohlen | .06 |
| 41 T David Green | .12 | 70 T Lee Lacy | .08 | 99 T Vern Ruhle | .06 | 128 T U.L. Washington | .06 |
| 42 T Alfredo Griffin | .12 | 71 T Dave LaPoint | .06 | 100 T Paul Runge | .15 | 129 T Earl Weaver (Mgr.) | .12 |
| 43 T Ozzie Guillen (RR) | .75 | 72 T Gary Lavelle | .06 | 101 T Mark Salas (R) | .30 | 130 T Eddie Whitson | .08 |
| 44 T Eddie Haas (Mgr.) | .06 | 73 T Vance Law | .06 | 102 T Luis Salazar | .06 | 131 T Herm Winningham | .20 |
| 45 T Terry Harper | .06 | 74 T Johnnie LeMaster | .06 | 103 T Joe Sambito | .08 | 132 T Traded Checklist | .10 |

## 1986 Topps....Complete Set of 792 Cards—Value $35.00

Features the rookie cards of Vince Coleman, Chris Brown and Len Dykstra. Topps printed 16 cards on the bottom of gum pack display boxes (not part of the set). There are four cards on each box—four different boxes. These 16 cards are identified by a letter code—A through P.

VINCE COLEMAN

CHRIS BROWN

ROGER McDOWELL

LEN DYKSTRA

FLOYD YOUMANS

| NO. PLAYER | MINT | NO. PLAYER | MINT | NO. PLAYER | MINT | NO. PLAYER | MINT |
|---|---|---|---|---|---|---|---|
| 1 Pete Rose | 1.25 | 28 Eric Davis | 3.00 | 53 Len Dykstra (R) | 1.00 | 80 Darryl Strawberry | .75 |
| 2 Rose (Years 1963-66) | .40 | 29 Tony Phillips | .04 | 54 John Franco | .08 | 81 Gene Mauch (Mgr.) | .08 |
| 3 Rose (Years 1967-70) | .40 | 30 Eddie Murray | .40 | 55 Fred Lynn | .20 | Angels Checklist | |
| 4 Rose (Years 1971-74) | .40 | 31 Jamie Easterly | .04 | 56 Tom Niedenfuer | .08 | 82 Tippy Martinez | .04 |
| 5 Rose (Years 1975-78) | .40 | 32 Steve Yeager | .06 | 57 Bill Doran | .08 | 83 Phil Garner | .04 |
| 6 Rose (Years 1979-82) | .40 | 33 Jeff Lahti | .04 | 58 Bill Krueger | .04 | 84 Curt Young | .04 |
| 7 Rose (Years 1983-85) | .40 | 34 Ken Phelps | .04 | 59 Andre Thornton | .08 | 85 Tony Perez | .30 |
| 8 Dwayne Murphy | .08 | 35 Jeff Reardon | .12 | 60 Dwight Evans | .12 | 86 Tom Waddell | .04 |
| 9 Roy Smith | .04 | 36 Tigers Leaders: | .15 | 61 Karl Best | .12 | 87 Candy Maldonado | .04 |
| 10 Tony Gwynn | .50 | Lance Parrish | | 62 Bob Boone | .04 | 88 Tom Nieto | .04 |
| 11 Bob Ojeda | .05 | 37 Mark Thurmond | .04 | 63 Ron Roenicke | .04 | 89 Randy St. Claire | .08 |
| 12 Jose Uribe (R) | .30 | 38 Glenn Hoffman | .04 | 64 Floyd Bannister | .04 | 90 Garry Templeton | .15 |
| 13 Bob Kearney | .04 | 39 Dave Rucker | .04 | 65 Dan Driessen | .04 | 91 Steve Crawford | .04 |
| 14 Julio Cruz | .04 | 40 Ken Griffey | .10 | 66 Cardinals Leaders: | .08 | 92 Al Cowens | .04 |
| 15 Eddie Whitson | .06 | 41 Brad Wellman | .04 | Bob Forsch | | 93 Scot Thompson | .04 |
| 16 Rick Schu | .10 | 42 Geoff Zahn | .04 | 67 Carmelo Martinez | .04 | 94 Rich Bordi | .04 |
| 17 Mike Stenhouse | .04 | 43 Dave Engle | .04 | 68 Ed Lynch | .04 | 95 Ozzie Virgil | .04 |
| 18 Brent Gaff | .04 | 44 Lance McCullers (R) | .30 | 69 Luis Aguayo | .04 | 96 Blue Jays Leaders: | .06 |
| 19 Rich Hebner | .04 | 45 Damaso Garcia | .12 | 70 Dave Winfield | .30 | Jim Clancy | |
| 20 Lou Whitaker | .15 | 46 Billy Hatcher | .35 | 71 Ken Schrom | .04 | 97 Gary Gaetti | .20 |
| 21 G. Bamberger (Mgr.) | .04 | 47 Juan Berenguer | .04 | 72 Shawon Dunston | .06 | 98 Dick Ruthven | .04 |
| Brewers Checklist | | 48 Bill Almon | .04 | 73 Randy O'Neal | .08 | 99 Buddy Biancalana | .04 |
| 22 Duane Walker | .08 | 49 Rick Manning | .04 | 74 Rance Mulliniks | .04 | 100 Nolan Ryan | .30 |
| 23 Manny Lee | .15 | 50 Dan Quisenberry | .15 | 75 Jose DeLeon | .04 | 101 Dave Bergman | .04 |
| 24 Len Barker | .06 | 51 Rob Wine (Mgr.) | .08 | 76 Dion James | .04 | 102 Joe Orsulak (R) | .20 |
| 25 Willie Wilson | .20 | Braves Checklist | | 77 Charlie Leibrandt | .06 | 103 Luis Salazar | .04 |
| 26 Frank DePino | .04 | Error-reads card no. 57 | | 78 Bruce Benedict | .04 | 104 Sid Fernandez | .15 |
| 27 Ray Knight | .06 | 52 Chris Welsh | .04 | 79 Dave Schmidt | .04 | 105 Gary Ward | .04 |

| NO. PLAYER | MINT | NO. PLAYER | MINT | NO. PLAYER | MINT | NO. PLAYER | MINT |
|---|---|---|---|---|---|---|---|
| 106 Ray Burris | .04 | 184 Tim Laudner | .04 | 254 Ozzie Guillen (R) | .50 | 334 Ken Oberkfell | .04 |
| 107 Rafael Ramirez | .04 | 185 Rollie Fingers | .15 | 255 Tony Armas | .10 | 335 Don Sutton | .20 |
| 108 Ted Power | .04 | 186 Astros Leaders: | .08 | 256 Kurt Kepshire | .04 | 336 Indians Leaders: | .08 |
| 109 Len Matuszek | .04 | Jose Cruz | | 257 Doug DeCinces | .08 | Andre Thornton | |
| 110 Scott McGregor | .06 | 187 Scott Fletcher | .04 | 258 Tim Burke (R) | .25 | 337 Darnell Coles | .04 |
| 111 Roger Craig (Mgr.) | .08 | 188 Bob Dernier | .04 | 259 Dan Pasqua | .30 | 338 Jorge Bell | .35 |
| Giants Checklist | | 189 Mike Mason | .04 | 260 Tony Pena | .10 | 339 Bruce Berenyi | .04 |
| 112 Bill Campbell | .04 | 190 George Hendrick | .08 | 261 Bobby Valentine (Mgr.) | .08 | 340 Cal Ripken | .40 |
| 113 U.L. Washington | .04 | 191 Wally Backman | .04 | Rangers Checklist | | 341 Frank Williams | .04 |
| 114 Mike Brown | .04 | 192 Milt Wilcox | .04 | 262 Mario Ramirez | .04 | 342 Gary Redus | .04 |
| 115 Jay Howell | .04 | 193 Daryl Sconiers | .04 | 263 Checklist No. 2 | .08 | 343 Carlos Diaz | .04 |
| 116 Brook Jacoby | .10 | 194 Craig McMurtry | .04 | 264 Darren Daulton (R) | .20 | 344 Jim Wohlford | .04 |
| 117 Bruce Kison | .04 | 195 Dave Concepcion | .08 | 265 Ron Davis | .04 | 345 Donnie Moore | .04 |
| 118 Jerry Royster | .04 | 196 Doyle Alexander | .04 | 266 Keith Moreland | .04 | 346 Bryan Little | .04 |
| 119 Barry Bonnell | .04 | 197 Enos Cabell | .04 | 267 Paul Molitor | .20 | 347 Teddy Higuera (R) | 1.00 |
| 120 Steve Carlton | .30 | 198 Ken Dixon | .08 | 268 Mike Scott | .30 | 348 Cliff Johnson | .04 |
| 121 Nelson Simmons | .20 | 199 Dick Howser (Mgr.) | .08 | 269 Dane Iorg | .04 | 349 Mark Clear | .04 |
| 122 Pete Filson | .04 | (Royals Checklist) | | 270 Jack Morris | .15 | 350 Jack Clark | .30 |
| 123 Greg Walker | .10 | 200 Mike Schmidt | .40 | 271 Dave Collins | .04 | 351 Chuck Tanner (Mgr.) | .08 |
| 124 Luis Sanchez | .04 | 201 Record—V. Coleman | .30 | 272 Tim Tolman | .15 | Pirates Checklist | |
| 125 Dave Lopes | .06 | Most Stolen Bases— | | 273 Jerry Willard | .04 | 352 Harry Spilman | .04 |
| 126 Mets Leaders: | .08 | Season, Rookie | | 274 Ron Gardenhire | .04 | 353 Keith Atherton | .04 |
| Mookie Wilson | | 202 Record—D. Gooden | .40 | 275 Charlie Hough | .04 | 354 Tony Bernazard | .04 |
| 127 Jack Howell (R) | .30 | Youngest 20-Game Winner | | 276 Yankees Leaders: | .10 | 355 Lee Smith | .06 |
| 128 John Wathan | .04 | 203 Rec.—K. Hernandez | .20 | Willie Randolph | | 356 Mickey Hatcher | .04 |
| 129 Jeff Dedmon | .04 | Most Game Winning RBI, | | 277 Jaime Cocanower | .04 | 357 Ed VandeBerg | .04 |
| 130 Alan Trammell | .20 | Season | | 278 Sixto Lezcano | .04 | 358 Rick Dempsey | .04 |
| 131 Checklist No. 1 | .08 | 204 Record—Phil Niekro | .15 | 279 Al Pardo | .15 | 359 Mike LaCoss | .04 |
| 132 Razor Shines | .08 | Oldest Shutout Pitcher | | 280 Tim Raines | .25 | 360 Lloyd Moseby | .15 |
| 133 Andy McGaffigan | .04 | 205 Record—Tony Perez | .12 | 281 Steve Mura | .04 | 361 Shane Rawley | .04 |
| 134 Carney Lansford | .08 | Oldest to Hit Grand Slam | | 282 Jerry Mumphrey | .04 | 362 Tom Paciorek | .04 |
| 135 Joe Niekro | .04 | 206 Record—Pete Rose | .40 | 283 Mike Fischlin | .04 | 363 Terry Forster | .06 |
| 136 Mike Hargrove | .04 | Most Hits, Career | | 284 Brian Dayett | .04 | 364 Reid Nichols | .04 |
| 137 Charlie Moore | .04 | 207 Record—F. Valenzuela | .15 | 285 Buddy Bell | .10 | 365 Mike Flanagan | .06 |
| 138 Mark Davis | .04 | Most Consecutive Innings, | | 286 Luis DeLeon | .04 | 366 Reds Leaders: | .10 |
| 139 Daryl Boston | .10 | No Earned Runs | | 287 John Christensen | .15 | Dave Concepcion | |
| 140 John Candelaria | .08 | 208 Ramon Romero | .15 | 288 Don Aase | .04 | 367 Aurelio Lopez | .04 |
| 141 Chuck Cottier (Mgr.) | .08 | 209 Randy Ready | .10 | 289 Johnnie LeMaster | .04 | 368 Greg Brock | .06 |
| Mariners Checklist | | 210 Calvin Schiraldi | .10 | 290 Carlton Fisk | .15 | 369 Al Holland | .04 |
| see card 171 | | 211 Ed Wojna | .15 | 291 Tom Lasorda (Mgr.) | .12 | 370 Vince Coleman (R) | 2.00 |
| 142 Bob Jones | .04 | 212 Chris Speier | .04 | Dodgers Checklist | | 371 Bill Stein | .04 |
| 143 Dave Van Gorder | .04 | 213 Bob Shirley | .04 | 292 Chuck Porter | .04 | 372 Ben Ogilvie | .06 |
| 144 Doug Sisk | .04 | 214 Randy Bush | .04 | 293 Chris Chambliss | .06 | 373 Urbano Lugo | .15 |
| 145 Pedro Guerrero | .25 | 215 Frank White | .04 | 294 Danny Cox | .10 | 374 Terry Francona | .06 |
| 146 Jack Perconte | .04 | 216 A's Leaders: | .08 | 295 Kirk Gibson | .30 | 375 Rich Gedman | .06 |
| 147 Larry Sheets | .40 | Dwayne Murphy | | 296 Geno Petralli | .04 | 376 Bill Dawley | .04 |
| 148 Mike Heath | .04 | 217 Bill Scherrer | .04 | 297 Tim Lollar | .04 | 377 Joe Carter | .20 |
| 149 Brett Butler | .10 | 218 Randy Hunt | .12 | 298 Craig Reynolds | .04 | 378 Bruce Bochte | .04 |
| 150 Joaquin Andujar | .08 | 219 Dennis Lamp | .04 | 299 Bryn Smith | .04 | 379 Bobby Meacham | .04 |
| 151 Dave Stapleton | .04 | 220 Bob Horner | .15 | 300 George Brett | .50 | 380 LaMarr Hoyt | .10 |
| 152 Mike Morgan | .04 | 221 Dave Henderson | .04 | 301 Dennis Rasmussen | .04 | 381 Ray Miller (Mgr.) | .08 |
| 153 Ricky Adams | .04 | 222 Craig Gerber | .15 | 302 Greg Gross | .04 | Twins Checklist | |
| 154 Bert Roberge | .04 | 223 Atlee Hammaker | .06 | 303 Curt Wardle | .15 | 382 Ivan Calderon (R) | .80 |
| 155 Bob Grich | .06 | 224 Cesar Cedeno | .08 | 304 Mike Gallego | .15 | 383 Chris Brown (R) | .60 |
| 156 White Sox Leaders: | .08 | 225 Ron Darling | .20 | 305 Phil Bradley | .20 | 384 Steve Trout | .04 |
| Richard Dotson | | 226 Lee Lacy | .04 | 306 Padres Leaders: | .08 | 385 Cecil Cooper | .15 |
| 157 Ron Hassey | .04 | 227 Al Jones | .04 | Terry Kennedy | | 386 Cecil Fielder (R) | .25 |
| 158 Derrel Thomas | .04 | 228 Tom Lawless | .04 | 307 Dave Sax | .04 | 387 Steve Kemp | .06 |
| 159 Orel Hershiser | .50 | 229 Bill Gullickson | .04 | 308 Ray Fontenot | .04 | 388 Dickie Noles | .04 |
| 160 Chet Lemon | .06 | 230 Terry Kennedy | .06 | 309 John Shelby | .04 | 389 Glenn Davis | 1.00 |
| 161 Lee Tunnell | .04 | 231 Jim Frey (Mgr.) | .08 | 310 Greg Minton | .04 | 390 Tom Seaver | .25 |
| 162 Greg Gagne | .12 | Cubs Checklist | | 311 Dick Schofield | .04 | 391 Julio Franco | .10 |
| 163 Pete Ladd | .04 | 232 Rick Rhoden | .04 | 312 Tom Filer | .04 | 392 John Russell | .08 |
| 164 Steve Balboni | .08 | 233 Steve Lyons | .10 | 313 Joe De Sa | .15 | 393 Chris Pittaro | .15 |
| 165 Mike Davis | .06 | 234 Doug Corbett | .04 | 314 Frank Pastore | .04 | 394 Checklist No. 3 | .08 |
| 166 Dickie Thon | .04 | 235 Butch Wynegar | .06 | 315 Mookie Wilson | .06 | 395 Scott Garrelts | .10 |
| 167 Zane Smith | .15 | 236 Frank Eufemia | .15 | 316 Sammy Khalifa | .15 | 396 Red Sox Leaders: | .08 |
| 168 Jeff Burroughs | .04 | 237 Ted Simmons | .15 | 317 Ed Romero | .04 | Dwight Evans | |
| 169 George Wright | .04 | 238 Larry Parrish | .06 | 318 Terry Whitfield | .04 | 397 Steve Buechele (R) | .20 |
| 170 Gary Carter | .30 | 239 Joel Skinner | .04 | 319 Rick Camp | .04 | 398 Earnie Riles (R) | .25 |
| 171 Bob Rodgers (Mgr.) | .08 | 240 Tommy John | .15 | 320 Jim Rice | .25 | 399 Bill Swift | .04 |
| Expo Checklist | | 241 Tony Fernandez | .20 | 321 Earl Weaver (Mgr.) | .12 | 400 Rod Carew | .30 |
| error—reads #141 | | 242 Rich Thompson | .12 | Orioles Checklist | | 401 Turn Back the Clock: | .15 |
| 172 Jerry Reed | .15 | 243 Johnny Grubb | .04 | 322 Bob Forsch | .04 | F. Valenzuela (1981) | |
| 173 Wayne Gross | .04 | 244 Craig Lefferts | .04 | 323 Jerry Davis | .08 | 402 Turn Back the Clock: | .15 |
| 174 Brian Snyder | .15 | 245 Jim Sundberg | .04 | 324 Dan Schatzeder | .04 | Tom Seaver (1976) | |
| 175 Steve Sax | .15 | 246 Phillies Leaders: | .15 | 325 Juan Beniquez | .04 | 403 Turn Back the Clock: | .15 |
| 176 Jay Tibbs | .04 | Steve Carlton | | 326 Kent Tekulve | .04 | Willie Mays (1971) | |
| 177 Joel Youngblood | .04 | 247 Terry Harper | .04 | 327 Mike Pagliarulo | .12 | 404 Turn Back the Clock: | .15 |
| 178 Ivan DeJesus | .04 | 248 Spike Owen | .04 | 328 Pete O'Brien | .12 | Frank Robinson (1966) | |
| 179 Stu Cliburn | .20 | 249 Rob Deer | .40 | 329 Kirby Puckett | 1.25 | 405 Turn Back the Clock: | .15 |
| 180 Don Mattingly | 4.00 | 250 Dwight Gooden | 1.50 | 330 Rick Sutcliffe | .12 | Roger Maris (1961) | |
| 181 Al Nipper | .04 | 251 Rich Dauer | .04 | 331 Alan Ashby | .04 | 406 Scott Sanderson | .04 |
| 182 Bobby Brown | .04 | 252 Bobby Castillo | .04 | 332 Darryl Motley | .04 | 407 Sal Butera | .04 |
| 183 Larry Andersen | .04 | 253 Dann Bilardello | .04 | 333 Tom Henke | .25 | 408 Dave Smith | .04 |

| NO. PLAYER | MINT | NO. PLAYER | MINT | NO. PLAYER | MINT | NO. PLAYER | MINT |
|---|---|---|---|---|---|---|---|
| 409 Paul Runge (R) | .15 | 488 Lou Thornton | .12 | 568 Donnie Scott | .04 | 648 Steve Bedrosian | .10 |
| 410 Dave Kingman | .10 | 489 Jim Winn | .04 | 569 Jim Acker | .04 | 649 Ronn Reynolds | .10 |
| 411 Sparky Anderson (Mgr.) | .10 | 490 Jeff Leonard | .04 | 570 Rusty Staub | .08 | 650 Dave Stieb | .15 |
| Tigers Checklist | | 491 Pascual Perez | .04 | 571 Mike Jeffcoat | .04 | 651 Billy Martin (Mgr.) | .10 |
| 412 Jim Clancy | .04 | 492 Kelvin Chapman | .04 | 572 Paul Zuvella | .08 | Yankees Checklist | |
| 413 Tim Flannery | .04 | 493 Gene Nelson | .04 | 573 Tom Hume | .04 | 652 Tom Browning | .15 |
| 414 Tom Gorman | .04 | 494 Garry Roenicke | .04 | 574 Ron Kittle | .10 | 653 Jim Dwyer | .04 |
| 415 Hal McRae | .04 | 495 Mark Langston | .12 | 575 Mike Boddicker | .10 | 654 Ken Howell | .10 |
| 416 Denny Martinez | .04 | 496 Jay Johnstone | .04 | 576 Expos Leaders: | .12 | 655 Manny Trillo | .04 |
| 417 R.J. Reynolds | .04 | 497 John Stuper | .04 | Andre Dawson | | 656 Brian Harper | .04 |
| 418 Alan Knicely | .04 | 498 Tito Landrum | .04 | 577 Jerry Reuss | .06 | 657 Juan Agosto | .04 |
| 419 Frank Wills | .15 | 499 Bob Gibson | .04 | 578 Lee Mazzilli | .04 | 658 Rob Wilfong | .04 |
| 420 Von Hayes | .15 | 500 Rickey Henderson | .45 | 579 Jim Slaton | .04 | 659 Checklist No. 5 | .08 |
| 421 Dave Palmer | .04 | 501 Dave Johnson (Mgr.) | .12 | 580 Willie McGee | .25 | 660 Steve Garvey | .30 |
| 422 Mike Jorgensen | .04 | Mets Checklist | | 581 Bruce Hurst | .10 | 661 Roger Clemens | 2.00 |
| 423 Dan Spillner | .04 | 502 Glen Cook | .12 | 582 Jim Gantner | .04 | 662 Bill Schroeder | .04 |
| 424 Rick Miller | .04 | 503 Mike Fitzgerald | .04 | 583 Al Bumbry | .04 | 663 Neil Allen | .04 |
| 425 Larry McWilliams | .04 | 504 Denny Walling | .04 | 584 Brian Fisher (R) | .30 | 664 Tim Corcoran | .04 |
| 426 Brewers Leaders: | .04 | 505 Jerry Koosman | .08 | 585 Garry Maddox | .04 | 665 Alejandro Pena | .06 |
| Charlie Moore | | 506 Bill Russell | .04 | 586 Greg Harris | .04 | 666 Rangers Leaders: | .06 |
| 427 Joe Cowley | .04 | 507 Steve Ontiveros (R) | .20 | 587 Rafael Santana | .04 | Charlie Hough | |
| 428 Max Venable | .04 | 508 Alan Wiggins | .08 | 588 Steve Lake | .04 | 667 Tim Tuefel | .08 |
| 429 Greg Booker | .04 | 509 Ernie Camacho | .04 | 589 Sid Bream | .04 | 668 Cecilio Guante | .04 |
| 430 Kent Hrbek | .25 | 510 Wade Boggs | 2.00 | 590 Bob Knepper | .04 | 669 Ron Cey | .10 |
| 431 George Frazier | .04 | 511 Ed Nunez | .04 | 591 Jackie Moore (Mgr.) | .08 | 670 Willie Hernandez | .12 |
| 432 Mark Bailey | .04 | 512 Thad Bosley | .04 | A's Checklist | | 671 Lynn Jones | .04 |
| 433 Chirs Codiroli | .04 | 513 Ron Washington | .04 | 592 Frank Tanana | .06 | 672 Rob Picciolo | .04 |
| 434 Curt Wilkerson | .04 | 514 Mike Jones | .04 | 593 Jesse Barfield | .25 | 673 Ernie Whitt | .04 |
| 435 Bill Caudill | .04 | 515 Darrell Evans | .08 | 594 Chris Bando | .04 | 674 Pat Tabler | .04 |
| 436 Doug Flynn | .04 | 516 Giants Leaders: | .08 | 595 Dave Parker | .25 | 675 Claudell Washington | .06 |
| 437 Rick Mahler | .04 | Greg Minton | | 596 Onix Concepcion | .04 | 676 Matt Young | .04 |
| 438 Clint Hurdle | .04 | 517 Milt Thompson (R) | .40 | 597 Sammy Stewart | .04 | 677 Nick Esasky | .06 |
| 439 Rick Honeycutt | .04 | 518 Buck Martinez | .04 | 598 Jim Presley | .30 | 678 Dan Gladden | .06 |
| 440 Alvin Davis | .20 | 519 Danny Darwin | .04 | 599 Rick Aguilera (R) | .40 | 679 Britt Burns | .06 |
| 441 Whitey Herzog (Mgr.) | .10 | 520 Keith Hernandez | .25 | 600 Dale Murphy | .40 | 680 George Foster | .15 |
| Cardinals Checklist | | 521 Nate Snell | .12 | 601 Gary Lucas | .04 | 681 Dick Williams (Mgr.) | .08 |
| 442 Ron Robinson | .08 | 522 Bob Bailor | .04 | 602 Mariano Duncan (R) | .25 | Padres Checklist | |
| 443 Bill Buckner | .08 | 523 Joe Price | .04 | 603 Bill Laskey | .04 | 682 Junior Ortiz | .04 |
| 444 Alex Trevino | .04 | 524 Darrell Miller | .08 | 604 Gary Pettis | .08 | 683 Andy Van Slyke | .15 |
| 445 Bert Blyleven | .10 | 525 Marvel Wynne | .04 | 605 Dennis Boyd | .06 | 684 Bob McClure | .04 |
| 446 Lenn Sakata | .04 | 526 Charlie Lea | .04 | 606 Royals Leaders: | .10 | 685 Tim Wallach | .08 |
| 447 Jerry Don Gleaton | .04 | 527 Checklist No. 4 | .08 | Hal McRae | | 686 Jeff Stone | .06 |
| 448 Herm Winningham | .15 | 528 Terry Pendleton | .08 | 607 Ken Dayley | .04 | 687 Mike Trujillo | .12 |
| 449 Rod Scurry | .04 | 529 Marc Sullivan | .12 | 608 Bruce Bochy | .04 | 688 Larry Herndon | .04 |
| 450 Graig Nettles | .15 | 530 Rich Gossage | .15 | 609 Barbaro Garbey | .04 | 689 Dave Stewart | .04 |
| 451 Mark Brown | .15 | 531 Tony LaRussa (Mgr.) | .08 | 610 Ron Guidry | .15 | 690 Ryne Sandberg | .30 |
| 452 Bob Clark | .04 | White Sox Checklist | | 611 Gary Woods | .04 | 691 Mike Madden | .04 |
| 453 Steve Jeltz | .10 | 532 Don Carman (R) | .25 | 612 Richard Dotson | .06 | 692 Dale Berra | .04 |
| 454 Burt Hooton | .04 | 533 Billy Sample | .04 | 613 Roy Smalley | .04 | 693 Tom Tellmann | .04 |
| 455 Willie Randolph | .08 | 534 Jeff Calhoun | .12 | 614 Rick Waits | .04 | 694 Garth Iorg | .04 |
| 456 Braves Leaders: | .20 | 535 Toby Harrah | .04 | 615 Johnny Ray | .08 | 695 Mike Smithson | .04 |
| Dale Murphy | | 536 Jose Rijo | .04 | 616 Glenn Brummer | .04 | 696 Dodgers Leaders: | .10 |
| 457 Mickey Tettleton | .12 | 537 Mark Salas | .15 | 617 Lonnie Smith | .08 | Bill Russell | |
| 458 Kevin Bass | .04 | 538 Dennis Eckersley | .08 | 618 Jim Pankovits | .06 | 697 Bud Black | .04 |
| 459 Luis Leal | .04 | 539 Glenn Hubbard | .04 | 619 Danny Heep | .04 | 698 Brad Komminsk | .06 |
| 460 Leon Durham | .15 | 540 Dan Petry | .15 | 620 Bruce Sutter | .15 | 699 Pat Corrales (Mgr.) | .08 |
| 461 Walt Terrell | .04 | 541 Jorge Orta | .04 | 621 John Felske (Mgr.) | .08 | Indians Checklist | |
| 462 Domingo Ramos | .04 | 542 Don Schulze | .04 | Phillies Checklist | | 700 Reggie Jackson | .40 |
| 463 Jim Gott | .04 | 543 Jerry Narron | .04 | 622 Gary Lavelle | .04 | 701 Keith Hernandez (AS) | .15 |
| 464 Ruppert Jones | .04 | 544 Eddie Milner | .04 | 623 Floyd Rayford | .04 | 702 Tom Herr (AS) | .08 |
| 465 Jesse Orosco | .04 | 545 Jimmy Key | .12 | 624 Steve McCatty | .04 | 703 Tim Wallach (AS) | .08 |
| 466 Tom Foley | .04 | 546 Mariners Leaders: | .06 | 625 Bob Brenly | .04 | 704 Ozzie Smith (AS) | .08 |
| 467 Bob James | .04 | Dave Henderson | | 626 Roy Thomas | .04 | 705 Dale Murphy (AS) | .30 |
| 468 Mike Scioscia | .04 | 547 Roger McDowell (R) | .45 | 627 Ron Oester | .04 | 706 Pedro Guerrero (AS) | .20 |
| 469 Storm Davis | .08 | 548 Mike Young | .20 | 628 Kirk McCaskill (R) | .40 | 707 Willie McGee (AS) | .20 |
| 470 Bill Madlock | .15 | 549 Bob Welch | .06 | 629 Mitch Webster (R) | .40 | 708 Gary Carter (AS) | .20 |
| 471 Bobby Cox (Mgr.) | .08 | 550 Tom Herr | .10 | 630 Fernando Valenzuela | .25 | 709 Dwight Gooden (AS) | .45 |
| Blue Jays Checklist | | 551 Dave LaPoint | .04 | 631 Steve Braun | .04 | 710 John Tudor (AS) | .08 |
| 472 Joe Hesketh | .15 | 552 Marc Hill | .04 | 632 Dave Von Ohlen | .04 | 711 Jeff Reardon (AS) | .08 |
| 473 Mark Brouhard | .04 | 553 Jim Morrison | .04 | 633 Jackie Gutierrez | .04 | 712 Don Mattingly (AS) | .70 |
| 474 John Tudor | .15 | 554 Paul Householder | .04 | 634 Roy Lee Jackson | .04 | 713 Damaso Garcia (AS) | .08 |
| 475 Juan Samuel | .15 | 555 Hubie Brooks | .08 | 635 Jason Thompson | .06 | 714 George Brett (AS) | .35 |
| 476 Ron Mathis | .12 | 556 John Denny | .06 | 636 Cubs Leaders: | .10 | 715 Cal Ripken (AS) | .30 |
| 477 Mike Easler | .04 | 557 Gerald Perry | .20 | Lee Smith | | 716 Rickey Henderson (AS) | .30 |
| 478 Andy Hawkins | .08 | 558 Tim Stoddard | .04 | 637 Rudy Law | .04 | 717 Dave Winfield (AS) | .25 |
| 479 Bob Melvin | .12 | 559 Tommy Dunbar | .04 | 638 John Butcher | .04 | 718 Jorge Bell (AS) | .08 |
| 480 Oddibe McDowell | .25 | 560 Dave Righetti | .10 | 639 Bo Diaz | .04 | 719 Carlton Fisk (AS) | .10 |
| 481 Scott Bradley | .10 | 561 Bob Lillis (Mgr.) | .06 | 640 Jose Cruz | .08 | 720 Bret Saberhagen (AS) | .25 |
| 482 Rick Lysander | .04 | Astros Checklist | | 641 Wayne Tolleson | .04 | 721 Ron Guidry (AS) | .10 |
| 483 George Vukovich | .04 | 562 Joe Beckwith | .04 | 642 Ray Searage | .04 | 722 Dan Quisenberry (AS) | .10 |
| 484 Donnie Hill | .04 | 563 Alejandro Sanchez | .08 | 643 Tom Brookens | .04 | 723 Marty Bystrom | .04 |
| 485 Gary Matthews | .06 | 564 Warren Brusstar | .04 | 644 Mark Gubicza | .06 | 724 Tim Hulett | .08 |
| 486 Angels Leaders: | .08 | 565 Tom Brunansky | .12 | 645 Dusty Baker | .06 | 725 Mario Soto | .08 |
| Bob Grich | | 566 Alfredo Griffin | .04 | 646 Mike Moore | .04 | 726 Orioles Leaders: | .08 |
| 487 Bret Saberhagen | .50 | 567 Jeff Barkley | .12 | 647 Mel Hall | .06 | Rick Dempsey | |

| NO. PLAYER | MINT | NO. PLAYER | MINT | NO. PLAYER | MINT | NO. PLAYER | MINT |
|---|---|---|---|---|---|---|---|
| 727 David Green | .04 | 748 Steve Henderson | .04 | 769 Harold Reynolds (R) | .40 | 789 Kurt Bevacqua | .04 |
| 728 Mike Marshall | .15 | 749 Ed Jurak | .04 | 770 Vida Blue | .08 | 790 Phil Niekro | .15 |
| 729 Jim Beattie | .04 | 750 Gorman Thomas | .08 | 771 John McNamara (Mgr.) | .08 | 791 Checklist No. 6 | .08 |
| 730 Ozzie Smith | .20 | 751 Howard Johnson | .20 | Red Sox Checklist | | 792 Charles Hudson | .06 |
| 731 Don Robinson | .04 | 752 Mike Krukow | .04 | 772 Brian Downing | .04 | | |
| 732 Floyd Youmans (R) | .40 | 753 Dan Ford | .04 | 773 Greg Pryor | .04 | **Cards Printed on Gum Boxes** | |
| 733 Ron Romanick | .06 | 754 Pat Clements (R) | .20 | 774 Terry Leach | .04 | A Jorge Bell | .25 |
| 734 Marty Barrett | .15 | 755 Harold Baines | .20 | 775 Al Oliver | .10 | B Wade Boggs | .75 |
| 735 Dave Dravecky | .04 | 756 Pirates Leaders: | .06 | 776 Gene Garber | .04 | C George Brett | .40 |
| 736 Glenn Wilson | .08 | Rick Rhoden | | 777 Wayne Krenchicki | .04 | D Vince Coleman | .60 |
| 737 Pete Vuckovich | .04 | 757 Darrell Porter | .04 | 778 Jerry Hairston | .04 | E Carlton Fisk | .20 |
| 738 Andre Robertson | .04 | 758 Dave Anderson | .04 | 779 Rick Reuschel | .04 | F Dwight Gooden | .75 |
| 739 Dave Rozema | .04 | 759 Moose Haas | .04 | 780 Robin Yount | .20 | G Pedro Guerrero | .20 |
| 740 Lance Parrish | .20 | 760 Andre Dawson | .25 | 781 Joe Nolan | .04 | H Ron Guidry | .25 |
| 741 Pete Rose (Mgr.) | .40 | 761 Don Slaught | .04 | 782 Ken Landreaux | .04 | I Reggie Jackson | .50 |
| Reds Checklist | | 762 Eric Show | .04 | 783 Ricky Horton | .04 | J Don Mattingly | 1.00 |
| 742 Frank Viola | .25 | 763 Terry Puhl | .04 | 784 Alan Bannister | .04 | K Oddibe McDowell | .25 |
| 743 Pat Sheridan | .04 | 764 Kevin Gross | .04 | 785 Bob Stanley | .04 | L Willie McGee | .25 |
| 744 Lary Sorensen | .04 | 765 Don Baylor | .15 | 786 Twins Leaders: | .06 | M Dale Murphy | .50 |
| 745 Willie Upshaw | .08 | 766 Rick Langford | .04 | Mickey Hatcher | | N Pete Rose | .75 |
| 746 Denny Gonzalez | .08 | 767 Jody Davis | .08 | 787 Vance Law | .04 | O Bret Saberhagen | .20 |
| 747 Rick Cerone | .04 | 768 Vern Ruhle | .04 | 788 Marty Castillo | .04 | P Fernando Valenzuela | .20 |

# 1986 Topps Traded....Complete Set of 132 Cards—Value $20.00

Updates the main 1986 card set with players who changed teams during the season, and rookies. Features the first Topps card of Wally Joyner, Kevin Mitchell, Pete Incaviglia, and Andres Galarraga. The set was packaged in a printed box and distributed exclusively through card hobby dealers.

JOSE CANSECO

WILL CLARK

PETE INCAVIGLIA

BO JACKSON

WALLY JOYNER

| NO. PLAYER | MINT | NO. PLAYER | MINT | NO. PLAYER | MINT | NO. PLAYER | MINT |
|---|---|---|---|---|---|---|---|
| 1T Andy Allanson | .15 | 34T Mark Eichhorn (RR) | .30 | 67T Steve Lyons | .06 | 100T Ken Schrom | .06 |
| 2T Neil Allen | .06 | 35T Steve Farr | .06 | 68T Mickey Mahler | .06 | 101T Tom Seaver | .60 |
| 3T Joaquin Andujar | .06 | 36T Scott Fletcher | .06 | 69T Candy Maldonado | .25 | 102T Ted Simmons | .06 |
| 4T Paul Assenmacher | .15 | 37T Terry Forster | .06 | 70T Roger Mason | .10 | 103T Sammy Stewart | .06 |
| 5T Scott Bailes | .15 | 38T Terry Francona | .06 | 71T Bob McClure | .06 | 104T Kurt Stillwell | .50 |
| 6T Don Baylor | .20 | 39T Jim Fregosi | .06 | 72T Andy McGaffigan | .06 | 105T Franklin Stubbs | .30 |
| 7T Steve Bedrosian | .10 | 40T Andres Galarraga (RR) | 2.00 | 73T Gene Michael | .06 | 106T Dale Sveum | .30 |
| 8T Juan Beniquez | .06 | 41T Ken Griffey | .06 | 74T Kevin Mitchell (RR) | .50 | 107T Chuck Tanner | .06 |
| 9T Juan Berenguer | .06 | 42T Bill Gullickson | .06 | 75T Omar Moreno | .06 | 108T Danny Tartabull | .90 |
| 10T Mike Bielecki | .12 | 43T Jose Guzman | .25 | 76T Jerry Mumphrey | .06 | 109T Tim Teufel | .06 |
| 11T Barry Bonds (RR) | 1.00 | 44T Moose Haas | .06 | 77T Phil Niekro | .30 | 110T Bob Tewksbury | .30 |
| 12T Bobby Bonilla (RR) | 1.00 | 45T Billy Hatcher | .20 | 78T Randy Nieman | .06 | 111T Andres Thomas | .25 |
| 13T Juan Bonilla | .06 | 46T Mike Heath | .06 | 79T Juan Nieves | .25 | 112T Milt Thomson | .06 |
| 14T Rich Bordi | .06 | 47T Tom Hume | .06 | 80T Otis Nixon | .15 | 113T Robby Thompson | .50 |
| 15T Steve Boros | .06 | 48T Pete Incaviglia (RR) | 1.50 | 81T Bob Ojeda | .08 | 114T Jay Tibbs | .06 |
| 16T Rick Burleson | .06 | 49T Dane Iorg | .06 | 82T Jose Oquendo | .10 | 115T Wayne Tolleson | .06 |
| 17T Bill Campbell | .06 | 50T Bo Jackson (RR) | 2.00 | 83T Tom Paciorek | .06 | 116T Alex Trevino | .06 |
| 18T Tom Candiotti | .06 | 51T Wa. Joyner (RR) | 2.50 | 84T Dave Palmer | .06 | 117T Manny Trillo | .06 |
| 19T John Cangelosi | .30 | 52T Charlie Kerfeld | .30 | 85T Frank Pastore | .06 | 118T Ed VandeBerg | .06 |
| 20T Jose Canseco (RR) | 7.00 | 53T Eric King | .30 | 86T Lou Piniella | .08 | 119T Ozzie Virgil | .06 |
| 21T Carmen Castillo | .10 | 54T Bob Kipper | .06 | 87T Dan Plesac | .30 | 120T Bob Walk | .06 |
| 22T Rick Cerone | .06 | 55T Wayne Krenchicki | .06 | 88T Darrell Porter | .06 | 121T Gene Walter | .10 |
| 23T John Cerutti | .30 | 56T John Kruk. (RR) | 1.00 | 89T Rey Quinones | .20 | 122T C. Washington | .06 |
| 24T Will Clark (RR) | 3.00 | 57T Mike LaCoss | .06 | 90T Gary Redus | .06 | 123T Bill Wegman | .25 |
| 25T Mark Clear | .06 | 58T Pete Ladd | .06 | 91T Bip Roberts | .20 | 124T Dick Williams | .06 |
| 26T Darrell Coles | .15 | 59T Mike Laga | .06 | 92T Billy Jo Robidoux | .30 | 125T Mitch Williams | .20 |
| 27T Dave Collins | .06 | 60T Hal Lanier | .06 | 93T Jeff Robinson | .06 | 126T Bobby Witt (RR) | .35 |
| 28T Tim Conroy | .06 | 61T Dave LaPoint | .06 | 94T Gary Roenicke | .06 | 127T Todd Worrell (RR) | .75 |
| 29T Joe Cowley | .10 | 62T Rudy Law | .06 | 95T Ed Romero | .06 | 128T George Wright | .06 |
| 30T Joel Davis | .15 | 63T Rick Leach | .06 | 96T Argenis Salazar | .06 | 129T Ricky Wright | .06 |
| 31T Rob Deer | .30 | 64T Tim Leary | .06 | 97T Joe Sambito | .06 | 130T Steve Yeager | .06 |
| 32T John Denny | .06 | 65T Dennis Leonard | .06 | 98T Billy Sample | .06 | 131T Paul Zuvella | .06 |
| 33T Mike Easler | .06 | 66T Jim Leyland | .06 | 99T Dave Schmidt | .06 | 132T Checklist | .06 |

# 1987 Topps....Complete Set of 792 Cards—Value $25.00

Features the rookie cards of Wally Joyner, Bo Jackson, Ruben Sierra and Pete Incaviglia. Topps printed 8 cards on the bottom of gum pack display boxes (not part of the set). There are two cards on each box—four different boxes. These 8 cards are identified by a letter code—A through H. Card numbers 92, 603 and 606 exist with the trademark deleted and are worth a premium.

| NO. PLAYER | MINT | NO. PLAYER | MINT | NO. PLAYER | MINT | NO. PLAYER | MINT |
|---|---|---|---|---|---|---|---|
| 1 '86 Record: Clemens | .45 | 67 Bill Swift | .04 | 133 Jose Oquendo | .04 | 199 Mariano Duncan | .10 |
| 2 '86 Record: Deshaies | .08 | 68 Tony LaRussa (Mgr.) | .04 | 134 Rich Yett (R) | .15 | 200 Pete Rose | .60 |
| 3 '86 Record: Evans | .10 | 69 Lonnie Smith | .04 | 135 Mike Easler | .04 | 201 John Cangelosi (R) | .25 |
| 4 '86 Record: Lopes | .10 | 70 Charlie Hough | .04 | 136 Ron Romanick | .04 | 202 Ricky Wright | .04 |
| 5 '86 Record: Righetti | .08 | 71 Mike Aldrete (R) | .35 | 137 Jerry Willard | .04 | 203 Mike Kingery (R) | .25 |
| 6 '86 Record: Sierra | .15 | 72 Walt Terrell | .04 | 138 Roy Lee Jackson | .04 | 204 Sammy Stewart | .04 |
| 7 '86 Record: Worrell | .15 | 73 Dave Anderson | .04 | 139 Devon White (R) | 1.00 | 205 Graig Nettles | .08 |
| 8 Terry Pendleton | .04 | 74 Dan Pasqua | .15 | 140 Bret Saberhagen | .25 | 206 Twins Leaders | .06 |
| 9 Jay Tibbs | .04 | 75 Ron Darling | .20 | 141 Herm Winningham | .04 | 207 George Frazier | .04 |
| 10 Cecil Cooper | .08 | 76 Rafael Ramirez | .04 | 142 Rick Sutcliffe | .12 | 208 John Shelby | .04 |
| 11 Indians Leaders | .06 | 77 Bryan Oelkers | .04 | 143 Steve Boros (Mgr.) | .04 | 209 Rick Schu | .04 |
| 12 Jeff Sellers (R) | .15 | 78 Tom Foley | .04 | 144 Mike Scioscia | .04 | 210 Lloyd Moseby | .12 |
| 13 Nick Esasky | .04 | 79 Juan Nieves | .15 | 145 Charlie Kerfeld | .15 | 211 John Morris | .04 |
| 14 Dave Stewart | .04 | 80 Wally Joyner (R) | 1.50 | 146 Tracy Jones (R) | .45 | 212 Mike Fitzgerald | .04 |
| 15 Claudell Washington | .04 | 81 Padres Leaders | .06 | 147 Randy Niemann | .04 | 213 Randy Myers (R) | .50 |
| 16 Pat Clements | .04 | 82 Rob Murphy (R) | .20 | 148 Dave Collins | .04 | 214 Omar Moreno | .04 |
| 17 Pete O'Brien | .10 | 83 Mike Davis | .04 | 149 Ray Searage | .04 | 215 Mark Langston | .15 |
| 18 Dick Howser (Mgr.) | .04 | 84 Steve Lake | .04 | 150 Wade Boggs | 1.25 | 216 B.J. Surhoff (R) | .65 |
| 19 Matt Young | .04 | 85 Kevin Bass | .04 | 151 Mike LaCoss | .04 | 217 Chris Codiroli | .04 |
| 20 Gary Carter | .35 | 86 Nate Snell | .04 | 152 Toby Harrah | .04 | 218 S. Anderson (Mgr.) | .04 |
| 21 Mark Davis | .04 | 87 Mark Salas | .04 | 153 Duane Ward (R) | .20 | 219 Cecilio Guante | .04 |
| 22 Doug DeCinces | .06 | 88 Ed Wojna | .04 | 154 Tom O'Malley | .04 | 220 Joe Carter | .25 |
| 23 Lee Smith | .04 | 89 Ozzie Guillen | .08 | 155 Eddie Whitson | .04 | 221 Vern Ruhle | .04 |
| 24 Tony Walker (R) | .15 | 90 Dave Stieb | .10 | 156 Mariners Leaders | .06 | 222 Denny Walling | .04 |
| 25 Bert Blyleven | .08 | 91 Harold Reynolds | .08 | 157 Danny Darwin | .04 | 223 Charlie Leibrandt | .04 |
| 26 C. Brock | .04 | 92 U. Lugo (no t.m.) | .30 | 158 Tim Teufel | .04 | 224 Wayne Tolleson | .04 |
| 27 Joe Cowley | .04 | 93 Jim Leyland (Mgr.) | .04 | 159 Ed Olwine (R) | .15 | 225 Mike Smithson | .04 |
| 28 Rick Dempsey | .04 | 94 Calvin Schiraldi | .08 | 160 Julio Franco | .10 | 226 Max Venable | .04 |
| 29 Jimmy Key | .15 | 95 Oddibe McDowell | .15 | 161 Steve Ontiveros | .04 | 227 Jamie Moyer (R) | .20 |
| 30 Tim Raines | .30 | 96 Frank Williams | .04 | 162 Mike LaValliere (R) | .20 | 228 Curt Wilkerson | .04 |
| 31 Braves Leaders | .06 | 97 Glenn Wilson | .08 | 163 Kevin Gross | .04 | 229 Mike Birkbeck (R) | .15 |
| 32 Tim Leary | .04 | 98 Bill Scherrer | .04 | 164 Sammy Khalifa | .04 | 230 Don Baylor | .12 |
| 33 Andy Van Slyke | .12 | 99 Darryl Motley | .04 | 165 Jeff Reardon | .08 | 231 Giants Leaders | .06 |
| 34 Jose Rijo | .04 | 100 Steve Garvey | .25 | 166 Bob Boone | .04 | 232 Reggie Williams (R) | .20 |
| 35 Sid Bream | .04 | 101 Carl Willis (R) | .15 | 167 Jim Deshaies (R) | .30 | 233 Russ Morman (R) | .20 |
| 36 Eric King (R) | .20 | 102 Paul Zuvella | .04 | 168 Lou Piniella (Mgr.) | .06 | 234 Pat Sheridan | .04 |
| 37 Marvell Wynne | .04 | 103 Rick Aguilera | .04 | 169 Ron Washington | .04 | 235 Alvin Davis | .12 |
| 38 Dennis Leonard | .04 | 104 Billy Sample | .04 | 170 Bo Jackson | 1.00 | 236 Tommy John | .12 |
| 39 Marty Barrett | .06 | 105 Floyd Youmans | .15 | 171 Chuck Cary (R) | .15 | 237 Jim Morrison | .04 |
| 40 Dave Righetti | .10 | 106 Blue Jays Leaders | .06 | 172 Ron Oester | .04 | 238 Bill Krueger | .04 |
| 41 Bo Diaz | .04 | 107 John Butcher | .04 | 173 Alex Trevino | .04 | 239 Juan Espino | .04 |
| 42 Gary Redus | .04 | 108 Jim Gantner | .04 | 174 Henry Cotto | .04 | 240 Steve Balboni | .08 |
| 43 Gene Michael (Mgr.) | .04 | 109 R. J. Reynolds | .04 | 175 Bob Stanley | .04 | 241 Danny Heep | .04 |
| 44 Greg Harris | .04 | 110 John Tudor | .12 | 176 Steve Buechele | .04 | 242 Rick Mahler | .04 |
| 45 Jim Presley | .15 | 111 Alfredo Griffin | .04 | 177 Keith Moreland | .04 | 243 Whitey Herzog (Mgr.) | .04 |
| 46 Danny Gladden | .04 | 112 Alan Ashby | .04 | 178 Cecil Fielder | .08 | 244 Dickie Noles | .04 |
| 47 Dennis Powell | .12 | 113 Neil Allen | .04 | 179 Bill Wegman | .04 | 245 Willie Upshaw | .04 |
| 48 Wally Backman | .04 | 114 Billy Beane | .08 | 180 Chris Brown | .10 | 246 Jim Dwyer | .04 |
| 49 Terry Harper | .04 | 115 Donnie Moore | .04 | 181 Cardinals Leaders | .06 | 247 Jeff Reed | .04 |
| 50 Dave Smith | .04 | 116 Bill Russell | .04 | 182 Lee Lacy | .04 | 248 Gene Walter | .10 |
| 51 M. Hall | .04 | 117 Jim Beattie | .04 | 183 Andy Hawkins | .04 | 249 Jim Pankovits | .04 |
| 52 Keith Atherton | .04 | 118 Bobby Valentine (Mgr.) | .04 | 184 Bobby Bonilla (R) | .80 | 250 Teddy Higuera | .20 |
| 53 Ruppert Jones | .04 | 119 Ron Robinson | .04 | 185 Roger McDowell | .10 | 251 Rob Wilfong | .04 |
| 54 Bill Dawley | .04 | 120 Eddie Murray | .30 | 186 Bruce Benedict | .04 | 252 Denny Martinez | .04 |
| 55 Tim Wallach | .08 | 121 Kevin Romine (R) | .15 | 187 Mark Huismann | .04 | 253 Eddie Milner | .04 |
| 56 Brewers Leaders | .06 | 122 Jim Clancy | .04 | 188 Tony Phillips | .04 | 254 Bob Tewksbury (R) | .25 |
| 57 Scott Nielsen (R) | .20 | 123 John Kruk (R) | .60 | 189 Joe Hesketh | .04 | 255 Juan Samuel | .15 |
| 58 Thad Bosley | .04 | 124 Ray Fontenot | .04 | 190 Jim Sundberg | .04 | 256 Royals Leaders | .06 |
| 59 Ken Dayley | .04 | 125 Bob Brenly | .04 | 191 Charles Hudson | .04 | 257 Bob Forsch | .04 |
| 60 Tony Pena | .10 | 126 Mike Loynd (R) | .15 | 192 Cory Snyder | .75 | 258 Steve Yeager | .04 |
| 61 Bobby Thigpen (R) | .25 | 127 Vance Law | .04 | 193 Roger Craig (Mgr.) | .04 | 259 Mike Greenwell (R) | 4.00 |
| 62 Bobby Meacham | .04 | 128 Checklist: 1-132 | .06 | 194 Kirk McCaskill | .10 | 260 Vida Blue | .06 |
| 63 Fred Toliver | .12 | 129 Rick Cerone | .04 | 195 Mike Pagliarulo | .20 | 261 Ruben Sierra (R) | 1.25 |
| 64 Harry Spilman | .04 | 130 Dwight Gooden | .75 | 196 Randy O'Neal | .04 | 262 Jim Winn | .04 |
| 65 Tom Browning | .10 | 131 Pirates Leaders | .06 | 197 Mark Bailey | .04 | 263 Stan Javier | .08 |
| 66 Marc Sullivan | .04 | 132 P. Assenmacher (R) | .15 | 198 Lee Mazzilli | .08 | 264 Checklist: 133-264 | .04 |

Card values from this set fluctuate considerably.

| NO. | PLAYER | MINT |
|-----|--------|------|
| 265 | Darrell Evans | .10 |
| 266 | Jeff Hamilton (R) | .15 |
| 267 | Howard Johnson | .15 |
| 268 | Pat Corrales (Mgr.) | .04 |
| 269 | Cliff Speck (R) | .15 |
| 270 | Jody Davis | .04 |
| 271 | Mike Brown | .04 |
| 272 | Andres Galarraga | 1.25 |
| 273 | Gene Nelson | .04 |
| 274 | Jeff Hearron (R) | .15 |
| 275 | LaMarr Hoyt | .04 |
| 276 | Jackie Gutierrez | .04 |
| 277 | Juan Agosto | .04 |
| 278 | Gary Pettis | .04 |
| 279 | Dan Plesac (R) | .35 |
| 280 | Jeffrey Leonard | .04 |
| 281 | Reds Leaders | .12 |
| 282 | Jeff Calhoun | .04 |
| 283 | Doug Drabek (R) | .20 |
| 284 | John Moses | .10 |
| 285 | Dennis Boyd | .12 |
| 286 | Mike Woodard | .10 |
| 287 | Dave Von Ohlen | .04 |
| 288 | Tito Landrum | .04 |
| 289 | Bob Kipper | .04 |
| 290 | Leon Durham | .10 |
| 291 | Mitch Williams (R) | .30 |
| 292 | Franklin Stubbs | .12 |
| 293 | Bob Rodgers (Mgr.) | .04 |
| 294 | Steve Jeltz | .04 |
| 295 | Len Dykstra | .15 |
| 296 | Andres Thomas (R) | .20 |
| 297 | Don Schulze | .04 |
| 298 | Larry Herndon | .04 |
| 299 | Joel Davis | .10 |
| 300 | Reggie Jackson | .30 |
| 301 | Luis Aquino | .15 |
| 302 | Bill Schroeder | .04 |
| 303 | Juan Berenguer | .04 |
| 304 | Phil Garner | .04 |
| 305 | John Franco | .10 |
| 306 | Red Sox Leaders | .10 |
| 307 | Lee Guetterman (R) | .15 |
| 308 | Don Slaught | .04 |
| 309 | Mike Young | .04 |
| 310 | Frank Viola | .20 |
| 311 | Turn Back—1982 | .15 |
| 312 | Turn Back-1977 | .15 |
| 313 | Turn Back—1972 | .15 |
| 314 | Turn Back—1967 | .15 |
| 315 | Turn Back—1962 | .15 |
| 316 | Brian Fisher | .04 |
| 317 | Clint Hurdle | .04 |
| 318 | Jim Fregosi (Mgr.) | .04 |
| 319 | Greg Swindell (R) | .60 |
| 320 | Barry Bonds (R) | .75 |
| 321 | Mike Laga | .04 |
| 322 | Chris Bando | .04 |
| 323 | Al Newman (R) | .15 |
| 324 | Dave Palmer | .04 |
| 325 | Garry Templeton | .04 |
| 326 | Mark Gubicza | .04 |
| 327 | Dale Sveum (R) | .35 |
| 328 | Bob Welch | .04 |
| 329 | Ron Roenicke | .04 |
| 330 | Mike Scott | .25 |
| 331 | Mets Leaders | .25 |
| 332 | Joe Price | .04 |
| 333 | Ken Phelps | .04 |
| 334 | Ed Correa (R) | .25 |
| 335 | Candy Maldonado | .06 |
| 336 | Allan Anderson (R) | .30 |
| 337 | Darrell Miller | .04 |
| 338 | Tim Conroy | .04 |
| 339 | Donnie Hill | .04 |
| 340 | Roger Clemens | 1.00 |
| 341 | Mike Brown | .04 |
| 342 | Bob James | .04 |
| 343 | Hal Lanier (Mgr.) | .04 |
| 344 | Joe Niekro | .06 |
| 345 | Andre Dawson | .25 |
| 346 | Shawon Dunston | .15 |
| 347 | Mickey Brantley | .15 |
| 348 | Carmelo Martinez | .04 |
| 349 | Storm Davis | .06 |
| 350 | Keith Hernandez | .25 |
| 351 | Gene Garber | .04 |
| 352 | Mike Felder | .12 |
| 353 | Ernie Camacho | .04 |
| 354 | Jamie Quick | .04 |
| 355 | Don Carman | .04 |
| 356 | White Sox Leaders | .06 |
| 357 | Steve Fireovid (R) | .15 |
| 358 | Sal Butera | .04 |
| 359 | Doug Corbett | .04 |
| 360 | Pedro Guerrero | .20 |
| 361 | Mark Thurmond | .04 |
| 362 | Luis Quinones (R) | .15 |
| 363 | Jose Guzman | .15 |
| 364 | Randy Bush | .04 |
| 365 | Rick Rhoden | .04 |
| 366 | Mark McGwire | 3.00 |
| 367 | Jeff Lahti | .04 |
| 368 | J. McNamara (Mgr.) | .04 |
| 369 | Brian Dayett | .04 |
| 370 | Fred Lynn | .15 |
| 371 | Mark Eichhorn (R) | .25 |
| 372 | Jerry Mumphrey | .04 |
| 373 | Jeff Dedmon | .04 |
| 374 | Glenn Hoffman | .04 |
| 375 | Ron Guidry | .15 |
| 376 | Scott Bradley | .04 |
| 377 | John Henry Johnson | .04 |
| 378 | Rafael Santana | .04 |
| 379 | John Russell | .04 |
| 380 | Rich Gossage | .12 |
| 381 | Expos Leaders | .06 |
| 382 | Rudy Law | .04 |
| 383 | Ron Davis | .04 |
| 384 | Johnny Grubb | .04 |
| 385 | Orel Hershiser | .30 |
| 386 | Dickie Thon | .04 |
| 387 | T. R. Bryden (R) | .20 |
| 388 | Geno Petralli | .04 |
| 389 | Jeff Robinson | .04 |
| 390 | Gary Matthews | .04 |
| 391 | Jay Howell | .04 |
| 392 | Checklist: 265-396 | .06 |
| 393 | Pete Rose (Mgr.) | .40 |
| 394 | Mike Bielecki | .04 |
| 395 | Damaso Garcia | .04 |
| 396 | Tim Lollar | .04 |
| 397 | Greg Walker | .08 |
| 398 | Brad Havens | .04 |
| 399 | Curt Ford | .12 |
| 400 | George Brett | .35 |
| 401 | Billy Jo Robidoux | .15 |
| 402 | Mike Trujillo | .04 |
| 403 | Jerry Royster | .04 |
| 404 | Doug Sisk | .04 |
| 405 | Brook Jacoby | .10 |
| 406 | Yankees Leaders | .25 |
| 407 | Jim Acker | .04 |
| 408 | John Mizerock | .04 |
| 409 | Milt Thompson | .04 |
| 410 | Fernando Valenzuela | .20 |
| 411 | Darnell Coles | .04 |
| 412 | Eric Davis | 1.00 |
| 413 | Moose Haas | .04 |
| 414 | Joe Orsulak | .04 |
| 415 | Bobby Witt (R) | .35 |
| 416 | Tom Nieto | .04 |
| 417 | Pat Perry | .08 |
| 418 | Dick Williams (Mgr.) | .04 |
| 419 | Mark Portugal (R) | .15 |
| 420 | Will Clark (R) | 1.50 |
| 421 | Jose DeLeon | .04 |
| 422 | Jack Howell | .04 |
| 423 | Jaime Cocanower | .04 |
| 424 | Chris Speier | .04 |
| 425 | Tom Seaver | .30 |
| 426 | Floyd Rayford | .04 |
| 427 | Ed Nunez | .04 |
| 428 | Bruce Bochy | .04 |
| 429 | Tim Pyznarski (R) | .20 |
| 430 | Mike Schmidt | .30 |
| 431 | Dodgers Leaders | .15 |
| 432 | Jim Slaton | .04 |
| 433 | Ed Hearn (R) | .12 |
| 434 | Mike Fischlin | .04 |
| 435 | Bruce Sutter | .10 |
| 436 | Andy Allanson (R) | .15 |
| 437 | Ted Power | .04 |
| 438 | Kelly Downs (R) | .25 |
| 439 | Karl Best | .04 |
| 440 | Willie McGee | .15 |
| 441 | Dave Leiper | .15 |
| 442 | Mitch Webster | .04 |
| 443 | John Felske (Mgr.) | .04 |
| 444 | Jeff Russell | .04 |
| 445 | Dave Lopes | .08 |
| 446 | Chuck Finley (R) | .15 |
| 447 | Bill Almon | .04 |
| 448 | Chris Bosio (R) | .15 |
| 449 | Pat Dodson (R) | .20 |
| 450 | Kirby Puckett | .60 |
| 451 | Joe Sambito | .04 |
| 452 | Dave Henderson | .04 |
| 453 | Scott Terry (R) | .15 |
| 454 | Luis Salazar | .04 |
| 455 | Mike Boddicker | .04 |
| 456 | A's Leaders | .06 |
| 457 | Len Matuszek | .04 |
| 458 | Kelly Gruber | .08 |
| 459 | Dennis Eckersley | .06 |
| 460 | Darryl Strawberry | .50 |
| 461 | Craig McMurtry | .04 |
| 462 | Scott Fletcher | .04 |
| 463 | Tom Candiotti | .04 |
| 464 | Butch Wynegar | .04 |
| 465 | Todd Worrell | .40 |
| 466 | Kal Daniels | 1.50 |
| 467 | Randy St. Claire | .04 |
| 468 | G. Bamberger (Mgr.) | .04 |
| 469 | Mike Diaz (R) | .20 |
| 470 | Dave Dravecky | .04 |
| 471 | Ronn Reynolds | .04 |
| 472 | Bill Doran | .08 |
| 473 | Steve Farr | .04 |
| 474 | Jerry Narron | .04 |
| 475 | Scott Garrelts | .04 |
| 476 | Danny Tartabull | 1.00 |
| 477 | Ken Howell | .04 |
| 478 | Tim Laudner | .04 |
| 479 | Bob Sebra (R) | .15 |
| 480 | Jim Rice | .25 |
| 481 | Phillies Leaders | .06 |
| 482 | Daryl Boston | .04 |
| 483 | Dwight Lowry (R) | .15 |
| 484 | Jim Traber | .10 |
| 485 | Tony Fernandez | .12 |
| 486 | Otis Nixon | .08 |
| 487 | Dave Gumpert | .04 |
| 488 | Ray Knight | .04 |
| 489 | Bill Gullickson | .04 |
| 490 | Dale Murphy | .40 |
| 491 | Ron Karkovice (R) | .15 |
| 492 | Mike Heath | .04 |
| 493 | Tom Lasorda | .04 |
| 494 | Barry Jones (R) | .15 |
| 495 | Gorman Thomas | .10 |
| 496 | Bruce Bochte | .04 |
| 497 | Dale Mohorcic (R) | .15 |
| 498 | Bob Kearney | .04 |
| 499 | Bruce Ruffin (R) | .25 |
| 500 | Don Mattingly | 2.00 |
| 501 | Craig Lefferts | .04 |
| 502 | Dick Schofield | .04 |
| 503 | Larry Andersen | .04 |
| 504 | Mickey Hatcher | .04 |
| 505 | Bryn Smith | .04 |
| 506 | Orioles Leaders | .08 |
| 507 | Dave Stapleton | .04 |
| 508 | Scott Bankhead | .15 |
| 509 | Enos Cabell | .04 |
| 510 | Tom Henke | .10 |
| 511 | Steve Lyons | .04 |
| 512 | Dave Magadan (R) | .50 |
| 513 | Carmen Castillo | .04 |
| 514 | Orlando Mercado | .04 |
| 515 | Willie Hernandez | .10 |
| 516 | Ted Simmons | .10 |
| 517 | Mario Soto | .04 |
| 518 | Gene Mauch (Mgr.) | .04 |
| 519 | Curt Young | .04 |
| 520 | Jack Clark | .25 |
| 521 | Rick Reuschel | .04 |
| 522 | Checklist: 397-528 | .06 |
| 523 | Earnie Riles | .04 |
| 524 | Bob Shirley | .04 |
| 525 | Phil Bradley | .12 |
| 526 | Roger Mason | .08 |
| 527 | Jim Wohlford | .04 |
| 528 | Ken Dixon | .04 |
| 529 | Alvaro Espinoza (R) | .10 |
| 530 | Tony Gwynn | .45 |
| 531 | Astros Leaders | .06 |
| 532 | Jeff Stone | .04 |
| 533 | Argenis Salazar | .04 |
| 534 | Scott Sanderson | .04 |
| 535 | Tony Armas | .06 |
| 536 | Terry Mulholland (R) | .15 |
| 537 | Rance Mulliniks | .04 |
| 538 | Tom Niedenfuer | .04 |
| 539 | Reid Nichols | .04 |
| 540 | Terry Kennedy | .04 |
| 541 | Rafael Belliard (R) | .12 |
| 542 | Ricky Horton | .04 |
| 543 | Dave Johnson (Mgr.) | .04 |
| 544 | Zane Smith | .04 |
| 545 | Buddy Bell | .10 |
| 546 | Mike Morgan | .04 |
| 547 | Rob Deer | .20 |
| 548 | Bill Mooneyham (R) | .15 |
| 549 | Bob Melvin | .04 |
| 550 | Pete Incaviglia (R) | .75 |
| 551 | Frank Wills | .04 |
| 552 | Larry Sheets | .15 |
| 553 | Mike Maddux (R) | .15 |
| 554 | Buddy Biancalana | .04 |
| 555 | Dennis Rasmussen | .10 |
| 556 | Angels Leaders | .06 |
| 557 | John Cerutti (R) | .20 |
| 558 | Greg Gagne | .04 |
| 559 | Lance McCullers | .04 |
| 560 | Glenn Davis | .30 |
| 561 | Rey Quinones (R) | .20 |
| 562 | B. Clutterbuck (R) | .15 |
| 563 | John Stefero | .04 |
| 564 | Larry McWilliams | .04 |
| 565 | Dusty Baker | .04 |
| 566 | Tim Hulett | .04 |
| 567 | Greg Mathews (R) | .25 |
| 568 | Earl Weaver (Mgr.) | .04 |
| 569 | Wade Rowdon | .15 |
| 570 | Sid Fernandez | .20 |
| 571 | Ozzie Virgil | .04 |
| 572 | Pete Ladd | .04 |
| 573 | Hal McRae | .04 |
| 574 | Manny Lee | .04 |
| 575 | Pat Tabler | .04 |
| 576 | Frank Pastore | .04 |
| 577 | Dann Bilardello | .04 |
| 578 | Billy Hatcher | .08 |
| 579 | Rick Burleson | .04 |
| 580 | Mike Krukow | .04 |
| 581 | Cubs Leaders | .08 |
| 582 | Bruce Berenyi | .04 |
| 583 | Junior Ortiz | .04 |
| 584 | Ron Kittle | .08 |
| 585 | Scott Bailes (R) | .15 |
| 586 | Ben Oglivie | .04 |
| 587 | Eric Plunk | .10 |
| 588 | Wallace Johnson | .04 |
| 589 | Steve Crawford | .04 |
| 590 | Vince Coleman | .30 |
| 591 | Spike Owen | .04 |
| 592 | Chris Welsh | .04 |
| 593 | Chuck Tanner (Mgr.) | .08 |
| 594 | Rick Anderson (R) | .15 |
| 595 | Keith Hernandez (AS) | .15 |
| 596 | Steve Sax (AS) | .10 |
| 597 | Mike Schmidt (AS) | .25 |
| 598 | Ozzie Smith (AS) | .10 |
| 599 | Tony Gwynn (AS) | .25 |
| 600 | Dave Parker (AS) | .15 |
| 601 | Darryl Strawberry (AS) | .25 |
| 602 | Gary Carter (AS) | .20 |
| 603 | Dwight Gooden (AS) | .35 |
| 603 | D. Gooden (no t.m.) | 1.00 |

Card values from this set fluctuate considerably.

| NO. PLAYER | MINT | NO. PLAYER | MINT | NO. PLAYER | MINT | NO. PLAYER | MINT |
|---|---|---|---|---|---|---|---|
| 604 F. Valenzuela (AS) | .15 | 654 Checklist: 529-660 | .06 | 704 Jesse Orosco | .06 | 754 Dave LaPoint | .04 |
| 605 Todd Worrell (AS) | .15 | 655 Jesse Barfield | .25 | 705 Bruce Hurst | .12 | 755 Luis Aguayo | .04 |
| 606 Don Mattingly (AS) | .65 | 656 Rangers Leaders | .06 | 706 Rick Manning | .04 | 756 Carlton Fisk | .15 |
| 606 D. Matt (no t.m.) | 2.00 | 657 Tom Waddell | .04 | 707 Bob McClure | .04 | 757 Nolan Ryan | .25 |
| 607 Tony Bernazard (AS) | .08 | 658 Robby Thompson (R) | .35 | 708 Scott McGregr | .04 | 758 Tony Bernazard | .04 |
| 608 Wade Boggs (AS) | .40 | 659 Aurelio Lopez | .04 | 709 Dave Kingman | .10 | 759 Joel Youngblood | .04 |
| 609 Cal Ripken (AS) | .15 | 660 Bob Horner | .10 | 710 Gary Gaetti | .10 | 760 Mike Witt | .10 |
| 610 Jim Rice (AS) | .15 | 661 Lou Whitaker | .10 | 711 Ken Griffey | .08 | 761 Greg Pryor | .04 |
| 611 Kirby Puckett (AS) | .25 | 662 Frank DiPino | .04 | 712 Don Robinson | .04 | 762 Gary Ward | .04 |
| 612 George Bell (AS) | .15 | 663 Cliff Johnson | .04 | 713 Tom Brookens | .04 | 763 Tim Flannery | .04 |
| 613 Lance Parrish (AS) | .10 | 664 Mike Marshall | .12 | 714 Don Quisenberry | .12 | 764 Bill Buckner | .04 |
| 614 Roger Clemens (AS) | .35 | 665 Rod Scurry | .04 | 715 Bob Dernier | .04 | 765 Kirk Gibson | .20 |
| 615 Teddy Higuera (AS) | .10 | 666 Von Hayes | .10 | 716 Rick Leach | .04 | 766 Don Aase | .04 |
| 616 Dave Righetti (AS) | .10 | 667 Ron Hassey | .04 | 717 Ed Vande Berg | .04 | 767 Ron Cey | .04 |
| 617 Al Nipper | .04 | 668 Juan Bonilla | .04 | 718 Steve Carlton | .25 | 768 Dennis Lamp | .04 |
| 618 Tom Kelly (Mgr.) | .04 | 669 Bud Black | .04 | 719 Tom Hume | .04 | 769 Steve Sax | .15 |
| 619 Jerry Reed | .04 | 670 Jose Cruz | .08 | 720 Richard Dotson | .04 | 770 Dave Winfield | .25 |
| 620 Jose Canseco | 4.00 | 671 Ray Soff (R) | .12 | 721 Tom Herr | .04 | 771 Shane Rawley | .04 |
| 621 Danny Cox | .08 | 672 Chili Davis | .10 | 722 Bob Knepper | .08 | 772 Harold Baines | .15 |
| 622 Glenn Braggs (R) | .50 | 673 Don Sutton | .10 | 723 Brett Butler | .04 | 773 Robin Yount | .25 |
| 623 Kurt Stillwell (R) | .35 | 674 Bill Campbell | .04 | 724 Greg Minton | .04 | 774 Wayne Krenchicki | .04 |
| 624 Tim Burke | .04 | 675 Ed Romero | .04 | 725 George Hendrick | .04 | 775 Joaquin Andujar | .04 |
| 625 Mookie Wilson | .04 | 676 Charlie Moore | .04 | 726 Frank Tanana | .04 | 776 Tom Brunansky | .12 |
| 626 Joel Skinner | .04 | 677 Bob Grich | .04 | 727 Mike Moore | .04 | 777 Chris Chambliss | .04 |
| 627 Ken Oberkfell | .04 | 678 Carney Lansford | .10 | 728 Tippy Martinez | .04 | 778 Jack Morris | .15 |
| 628 Bob Walk | .04 | 679 Kent Hrbek | .15 | 729 Tom Paciorek | .04 | 779 Craig Reynolds | .04 |
| 629 Larry Parrish | .04 | 680 Ryne Sandberg | .20 | 730 Eric Show | .06 | 780 Andre Thornton | .04 |
| 630 John Candelaria | .04 | 681 George Bell | .30 | 731 Dave Concepcion | .08 | 781 Atlee Hammaker | .04 |
| 631 Tigers Leaders | .15 | 682 Jerry Reuss | .04 | 732 Manny Trillo | .04 | 782 Brian Downing | .04 |
| 632 Rob Woodward | .08 | 683 Gary Roenicke | .04 | 733 Bill Caudill | .04 | 783 Willie Wilson | .10 |
| 633 Jose Uribe | .04 | 684 Kent Tekulve | .04 | 734 Bill Madlock | .12 | 784 Cal Ripken | .25 |
| 634 Rafael Palmeiro (R) | .75 | 685 Jerry Hairston | .04 | 735 Rickey Henderson | .35 | 785 Terry Francona | .04 |
| 635 Ken Schrom | .04 | 686 Doyle Alexander | .04 | 736 Steve Bedrosian | .10 | 786 Jimy Williams (Mgr.) | .04 |
| 636 Darren Daulton | .04 | 687 Alan Trammell | .15 | 737 Floyd Bannister | .04 | 787 Alejandro Pena | .04 |
| 637 Bip Roberts (R) | .15 | 688 Juan Beniquez | .04 | 738 Jorge Orta | .04 | 788 Tim Stoddard | .04 |
| 638 Rich Bordi | .04 | 689 Darrell Porter | .04 | 739 Chet Lemon | .06 | 789 Dan Schatzeder | .04 |
| 639 Gerald Perry | .20 | 690 Dane Iorg | .04 | 740 Rich Gedman | .04 | 790 Julio Cruz | .04 |
| 640 Mark Clear | .04 | 691 Dave Parker | .20 | 741 Paul Molitor | .15 | 791 Lance Parris | .15 |
| 641 Domino Ramos | .04 | 692 Frank White | .04 | 742 Andy McGaffigan | .04 | 792 Checklist: 661-792 | .06 |
| 642 Al Pulido | .04 | 693 Terry Puhl | .04 | 743 Dwayne Murphy | .04 | | |
| 643 Ron Shepherd | .15 | 694 Phil Niekro | .15 | 744 Roy Smalley | .04 | | |
| 644 John Denny | .04 | 695 Chico Walker (R) | .20 | 745 Glenn Hubbard | .04 | **Cards Printed on Gum Boxes** | |
| 645 Dwight Evans | .12 | 696 Gary Lucas | .04 | 746 Bob Ojeda | .12 | | |
| 646 Mike Mason | .04 | 697 Ed Lynch | .04 | 747 Johnny Ray | .04 | A Don Baylor | .15 |
| 647 Tom Lawless | .04 | 698 Ernie Whitt | .04 | 748 Mike Flanagan | .06 | B Steve Carlton | .20 |
| 648 Barry Larkin (R) | 1.00 | 699 Ken Landreaux | .04 | 749 Ozzie Smith | .15 | C Ron Cey | .15 |
| 649 Mickey Tettleton | .04 | 700 Dave Bergman | .04 | 750 Steve Trout | .04 | D Cecil Cooper | .15 |
| 650 Hubie Brooks | .10 | 701 Willie Randolph | .08 | 751 Garth Iorg | .04 | E Rickey Henderson | .40 |
| 651 Benny Distefano | .04 | 702 Greg Gross | .04 | 752 Dan Petry | .04 | F Jim Rice | .20 |
| 652 Terry Forster | .04 | 703 Dave Schmidt | .04 | 753 Rick Honeycutt | .04 | G Don Sutton | .15 |
| 653 Kevin Mitchell (R) | .35 | | | | | H Dave Winfield | .20 |

Card values from this set fluctuate considerably.

## 1987 Topps Traded. . . .Complete Set of 132 Cards—Value $13.00

Updates the main 1987 card set with players who changed teams during the season and rookies who joined their teams early in the season. Features the first Topps card of Ellis Burks, Matt Nokes, Benito Santiago and Kevin Seitzer. The complete set was packaged in a printed box and primarily distributed through card hobby dealers.

| NO. PLAYER | MINT | NO. PLAYER | MINT | NO. PLAYER | MINT | NO. PLAYER | MINT |
|---|---|---|---|---|---|---|---|
| 1T Bill Almon | .06 | 8T Larry Bowa | .08 | 15T Ivan Calderon | .25 | 22T Ron Cey | .12 |
| 2T Scott Bankhead | .10 | 9T Greg Brock | .10 | 16T Jeff Calhoun | .06 | 23T John Christensen | .06 |
| 3T Eric Bell | .15 | 10T Bob Brower | .15 | 17T Casey Candaele | .15 | 24T Dave Cone | 1.00 |
| 4T Juan Beniquez | .06 | 11T Jerry Browne | .12 | 18T John Cangelosi | .10 | 25T Chuck Grim | .20 |
| 5T Juan Berenguer | .06 | 12T Ralph Bryant | .15 | 19T Steve Carlton | .25 | 26T Storm Daviss | .06 |
| 6T Greg Booker | .06 | 13T DeWayne Buice | .20 | 20T Juan Castillo | .10 | 27T Andre Dawson | .45 |
| 7T Thad Bosley | .06 | 14T Ellis Burks (RR) | 1.50 | 21T Rick Cerone | .06 | 28T Rick Dempsey | .10 |

# 1987 Topps Traded (Continued)

| NO. PLAYER | MINT | NO. PLAYER | MINT | NO. PLAYER | MINT | NO. PLAYER | MINT |
|---|---|---|---|---|---|---|---|
| 29T Doug Drabek | .12 | 55T Stan Jefferson | .25 | 81T Kevin Mitchell | .15 | 107T Mark Salas | .06 |
| 30T Mike Dunne | .45 | 56T Joe Johnson | .06 | 82T Charlie Moore | .06 | 108T Luis Salazar | .06 |
| 31T Dennis Eckersley | .15 | 57T Terry Kennedy | .08 | 83T Jeff Musselman | .20 | 109T Benny Santiago (RR) | .75 |
| 32T Lee Ella | .06 | 58T Mike Kingery | .10 | 84T Gene Nelson | .06 | 110T Dave Schmidt | .06 |
| 33T Brian Fisher | .10 | 59T Ray Knight | .08 | 85T Graig Nettles | .15 | 111T Kevin Seitzer (RR) | 2.00 |
| 34T Terry Francona | .06 | 60T Gene Larkin | .25 | 86T Al Newman | .06 | 112T John Shelby | .06 |
| 35T Willie Fraser | .25 | 61T Mike LaValliere | .10 | 87T Reid Nichols | .06 | 113T Steve Shields | .25 |
| 36T Billy Gardner | .06 | 62T Jack Lazorko | .06 | 88T Tom Niedenfuer | .06 | 114T John Smiley | .45 |
| 37T Ken Gerhart | .25 | 63T Terry Leach | .15 | 89T Joe Niekro | .15 | 115T Chris Speier | .06 |
| 38T Danny Gladden | .10 | 64T Tim Leary | .06 | 90T Tom Nieto | .06 | 116T Mike Stanley (RR) | .30 |
| 39T Jim Gott | .12 | 65T Jim Lindeman (RR) | .35 | 91T Matt Nokes (RR) | 1.00 | 117T Terry Steinbach (RR) | .40 |
| 40T Cecilio Guante | .06 | 66T Steve Lombardozzi | .15 | 92T Dickie Noles | .06 | 118T Les Straker | .20 |
| 41T Albert Hall | .08 | 67T Bill Long | .20 | 93T Pat Pacillo | .20 | 119T Jim Sundberg | .06 |
| 42T Terry Harper | .06 | 68T Barry Lyons | .25 | 94T Lance Parrish | .20 | 120T Danny Tartabull | .40 |
| 43T Mickey Hatcher | .06 | 69T Shane Mack | .25 | 95T Tony Pena | .15 | 121T Tom Trebelhorn | .06 |
| 44T Brad Havens | .06 | 70T Greg Maddux | .60 | 96T Luis Polonia | .30 | 122T Dave Valle | .06 |
| 45T Neal Heaton | .10 | 71T Bill Madlock | .15 | 97T Randy Ready | .08 | 123T Ed VandeBerg | .06 |
| 46T Mike Henneman | .45 | 72T Joe Magrane (RR) | .60 | 98T Jeff Reardon | .12 | 124T Andy Van Slyke | .35 |
| 47T Donnie Hill | .06 | 73T Dave Martinez | .25 | 99T Gary Redus | .08 | 125T Gary Ward | .06 |
| 48T Guy Hoffman | .06 | 74T Fred McGriff (RR) | .80 | 100T Jeff Reed | .06 | 126T Alan Wiggins | .06 |
| 49T Brian Holton | .30 | 75T Mark McLemore | .12 | 101T Rick Rhoden | .10 | 127T Bill Wilkinson | .10 |
| 50T Charles Hudson | .06 | 76T Kevin McReynolds | .30 | 102T Cal Ripken, Sr. | .06 | 128T Frank Williams | .06 |
| 51T Dany Jackson | .35 | 77T Dave Meads | .25 | 103T Wally Ritchie | .15 | 129T Matt Williams (RR) | .50 |
| 52T Reggie Jackson | .60 | 78T Eddie Milner | .06 | 104T Jeff Robinson (RR) | .60 | 130T Jim Winn | .06 |
| 53T Chris James (RR) | .45 | 79T Greg Minton | .06 | 105T Gary Roenicke | .06 | 131T Matt Young | .06 |
| 54T Dion James | .12 | 80T John Mitchell | .15 | 106T Jerry Royster | .06 | 132T Checklist | .06 |

Card values shown here fluctuate considerably.

# 1988 Topps.... Complete Set of 792 Cards—Value $20.00

Features the rookie cards of Ellis Burks, Matt Nokes, Sam Horn, and Al Leiter. A new feature of this year's set was "This Way to the Clubhouse" which explained how a player joined his current team.

| NO. PLAYER | MINT | NO. PLAYER | MINT | NO. PLAYER | MINT | NO. PLAYER | MINT |
|---|---|---|---|---|---|---|---|
| 1 '87 Record: Coleman | .20 | 29 Argenis Salazar | .04 | 57 Tim Crews (R) | .15 | 85 Howard Johnson | .10 |
| 2 '87 Record: Mattingly | .50 | 30 Sid Fernandez | .10 | 58 Dave Magadan | .08 | 86 Ron Karkovice | .04 |
| 3 '87 Record: McGwire | .40 | 31 Bruce Bochy | .04 | 59 Danny Cox | .04 | 87 Mike Mason | .04 |
| 4 '87 Record: Murray | .12 | 32 Mike Morgan | .04 | 60 Rickey Henderson | .30 | 88 Earnie Riles | .04 |
| 4 Murray (error) | 1.50 | 33 Rob Deer | .15 | 61 Mark Knudson (R) | .15 | 89 Gary Thurman (R) | .35 |
| 5 '87 Record: Niekro Bros. | .10 | 34 Rickey Horton | .04 | 62 Jeff Hamilton | .04 | 90 Dale Murphy | .30 |
| 6 '87 Record: Ryan | .12 | 35 Harold Baines | .10 | 63 Jimmy Jones | .10 | 91 Joey Cora (R) | .15 |
| 7 '87 Record: Santiago | .20 | 36 Jamie Moyer | .04 | 64 Ken Caminiti (R) | .20 | 92 Len Matuszek | .04 |
| 8 Kevin Elster | .30 | 37 Ed Romero | .04 | 65 Leon Durham | .06 | 93 Bob Sebra | .04 |
| 9 Andy Hawkins | .04 | 38 Jeff Calhoun | .04 | 66 Shane Rawley | .04 | 94 Chuck Johnson (R) | .15 |
| 10 Ryne Sandberg | .12 | 39 Gerald Perry | .08 | 67 Ken Oberkfell | .04 | 95 Lance Parrish | .08 |
| 11 Mike Young | .04 | 40 Orel Hershiser | .20 | 68 Dave Dravecky | .06 | 96 Todd Benzinger (R) | .35 |
| 12 Bill Schroeder | .04 | 41 Bob Melvin | .04 | 69 Mike Hart (R) | .12 | 97 Scott Garrelts | .04 |
| 13 Andres Thomas | .04 | 42 Bill Landrum (R) | .10 | 70 Roger Clemens | .60 | 98 Rene Gonzales (R) | .15 |
| 14 Sparky Anderson | .04 | 43 Dick Schofield | .04 | 71 Gary Pettis | .04 | 99 Chuck Finley | .04 |
| 15 Chili Davis | .08 | 44 Lou Piniella | .06 | 72 Dennis Eckersley | .06 | 100 Jack Clark | .15 |
| 16 Kirk McCaskill | .06 | 45 Kent Hrbek | .10 | 73 Randy Bush | .04 | 101 Allan Anderson | .04 |
| 17 Ron Oester | .04 | 46 Darnell Coles | .04 | 74 Tom Lasorda (Mgr.) | .04 | 102 Barry Larkin | .10 |
| 18 Al Leiter (error-R) | 1.50 | 47 Joaquin Andujar | .04 | 75 Joe Carter | .12 | 103 Curt Young | .04 |
| 18 Al Leiter (correct-R) | 1.00 | 48 Alan Ashby | .04 | 76 Denny Martinez | .04 | 104 Dick Williams | .04 |
| 19 Mark Davidson (R) | .15 | 49 Dave Clark | .12 | 77 Tom O'Malley | .04 | 105 Jesse Orosco | .06 |
| 20 Kevin Gross | .04 | 50 Hubie Brooks | .04 | 78 Dan Petry | .06 | 106 Jim Walewander (R) | .15 |
| 21 Red Sox Team | .08 | 51 Oriole Team | .10 | 79 Ernie Whitt | .04 | 107 Scott Bailes | .04 |
| 22 Greg Swindell | .12 | 52 Don Robinson | .04 | 80 Mark Langston | .10 | 108 Steve Lyons | .04 |
| 23 Ken Landreaux | .04 | 53 Curt Wilkerson | .04 | 81 Reds Team | .06 | 109 Joel Skinner | .04 |
| 24 Jim Deshaies | .04 | 54 Jim Clancy | .04 | 82 Darrel Akerfelds (R) | .20 | 110 Teddy Higuera | .12 |
| 25 Andres Galarraga | .25 | 55 Phil Bradley | .10 | 83 Jose Oquendo | .06 | 111 Expos Team | .06 |
| 26 Mitch William | .04 | 56 Ed Hearn | .04 | 84 Cecilio Guante | .04 | 112 Les Lancaster (R) | .15 |
| 27 R.J. Reynolds | .04 | | | | | | |
| 28 Jose Nunez (R) | .15 | | | | | | |

Card values shown here fluctuate considerably.

| NO. PLAYER | MINT | NO. PLAYER | MINT | NO. PLAYER | MINT | NO. PLAYER | MINT |
|---|---|---|---|---|---|---|---|
| 113 Kelly Gruber | .04 | 198 Franklin Stubbs | .06 | 283 Phil Lombardi | .08 | 368 Gerald Young (R) | .25 |
| 114 Jeff Russell | .04 | 199 Dave Meads (R) | .12 | 284 Larry Bowa | .04 | 369 Greg Harris | .04 |
| 115 Johnny Ray | .04 | 200 Wade Boggs | .75 | 285 Jim Presley | .08 | 370 Jose Canseco | 1.00 |
| 116 J.D. Gleaton | .04 | 201 Rangers Team | .06 | 286 Chuck Grim (R) | .12 | 371 Joe Hesketh | .04 |
| 117 James Steels (R) | .10 | 202 Glenn Hoffman | .04 | 287 Manny Trillo | .04 | 372 Matt Williams (R) | .30 |
| 118 Bob Welch | .04 | 203 Fred Toliver | .04 | 288 Pat Pacillo | .12 | 373 Checklist: 265-396 | .06 |
| 119 Robbie Wine (R) | .15 | 204 Paul O'Neill | .08 | 289 Dave Bergman | .04 | 374 Doc Edwards | .04 |
| 120 Kirby Puckett | .25 | 205 Nelson Liriano (R) | .20 | 290 Tony Fernandez | .12 | 375 Tom Brunansky | .08 |
| 121 Checklist: 1-132 | .06 | 206 Domingo Ramos | .04 | 291 Astros Team | .06 | 376 Bill Wilkinson (R) | .12 |
| 122 Tony Bernazard | .04 | 207 John Mitchell (R) | .15 | 292 Carney Lansford | .04 | 377 Sam Horn (R) | .50 |
| 123 Tom Candiotti | .06 | 208 Steve Lake | .04 | 293 Doug Jones (R) | .20 | 378 Todd Frohwirth (R) | .15 |
| 124 Ray Knight | .04 | 209 Richard Dotson | .04 | 294 Al Pedrique (R) | .12 | 379 Rafael Ramirez | .04 |
| 125 Bruce Hurst | .08 | 210 Willie Randolph | .10 | 295 Bert Blyleven | .06 | 380 Joe Magrane (R) | .30 |
| 126 Steve Jeltz | .04 | 211 Frank Dipino | .04 | 296 Floyd Rayford | .04 | 381 Angels Team | .06 |
| 127 Jim Gott | .04 | 212 Greg Brock | .04 | 297 Zane Smith | .04 | 382 Keith Miller (R) | .20 |
| 128 Johnny Grubb | .04 | 213 Albert Hall | .04 | 298 Milt Thompson | .04 | 383 Eric Bell (R) | .12 |
| 129 Greg Minton | .04 | 214 Dave Schmidt | .04 | 299 Steve Crawford | .04 | 384 Neil Allen | .04 |
| 130 Buddy Bell | .15 | 215 Von Hayes | .08 | 300 Don Mattingly | 1.25 | 385 Carlton Fisk | .10 |
| 131 Don Schulze | .04 | 216 Jerry Reuss | .04 | 301 Bud Black | .06 | 386 Don Mattingly (AS) | .60 |
| 132 Donnie Hill | .04 | 217 Harry Spillman | .04 | 302 Jose Uribe | .04 | 387 Willie Randolph (AS) | .08 |
| 133 Greg Mathews | .04 | 218 Dan Schatzeder | .04 | 303 Eric Show | .06 | 388 Wade Boggs (AS) | .40 |
| 134 Chuck Tanner (mgr.) | .04 | 219 Mike Stanley | .12 | 304 George Hendrick | .06 | 389 Alan Trammell (AS) | .08 |
| 135 Dennis Rasmussen | .06 | 220 Tom Henke | .04 | 305 Steve Sax | .10 | 390 George Bell (AS) | .15 |
| 136 Brian Dayett | .04 | 221 Rafael Belliard | .04 | 306 Billy Hatcher | .10 | 391 Kirby Puckett (AS) | .15 |
| 137 Chris Bosio | .04 | 222 Steve Farr | .04 | 307 Mike Trujillo | .04 | 392 Dave Winfield (AS) | .12 |
| 138 Mitch Webster | .06 | 223 Stan Jefferson | .12 | 308 Lee Mazzilli | .06 | 393 Matt Nokes (AS) | .25 |
| 139 Jerry Browne | .08 | 224 Tom Trebelhorn (R) | .12 | 309 Bill Long (R) | .15 | 394 Roger Clemens (AS) | .30 |
| 140 Jesse Barfield | .15 | 225 Mike Scioscia | .04 | 310 Tom Herr | .04 | 395 Jimmy Key (AS) | .15 |
| 141 Royals Team | .10 | 226 Dave Lopes | .06 | 311 Scott Sanderson | .04 | 396 Tom Henke (AS) | .04 |
| 142 Andy Van Slyke | .08 | 227 Ed Correa | .04 | 312 Joey Meyer | .25 | 397 Jack Clark (AS) | .15 |
| 143 Mickey Tettleton | .04 | 228 Wallace Johnson | .04 | 313 Bob McClure | .04 | 398 Juan Samuel (AS) | .08 |
| 144 Don Gordon (R) | .10 | 229 Jeff Musselman | .12 | 314 Jimy Williams (R) | .12 | 399 Tim Wallach (AS) | .06 |
| 145 Bill Madlock | .08 | 230 Pat Tabler | .04 | 315 Dave Parker | .15 | 400 Ozzie Smith (AS) | .08 |
| 146 Donnell Nixon (R) | .12 | 231 Pirates Team | .06 | 316 Jose Rijo | .04 | 401 Andre Dawson (AS) | .12 |
| 147 Bill Buckner | .04 | 232 Bob James | .04 | 317 Tom Nieto | .04 | 402 Tony Gwynn (AS) | .15 |
| 148 Carmelo Martinez | .04 | 233 Rafael Santana | .04 | 318 Mel Hall | .04 | 403 Tim Raines (AS) | .10 |
| 149 Ken Howell | .04 | 234 Ken Dayley | .04 | 319 Mike Loynd | .04 | 404 Benny Santiago (AS) | .15 |
| 150 Eric Davis | .75 | 235 Gary Ward | .04 | 320 Alan Trammell | .15 | 405 Dwight Gooden (AS) | .20 |
| 151 Bob Knepper | .04 | 236 Ted Power | .04 | 321 White Sox Team | .06 | 406 Shane Rawley (AS) | .06 |
| 152 Jody Reed (R) | .20 | 237 Mike Heath | .04 | 322 Vincente Palacios (R) | .20 | 407 Steve Bedrosian (AS) | .08 |
| 153 John Habyan | .08 | 238 Luis Polonia (R) | .20 | 323 Rick Leach | .04 | 408 Dion James | .04 |
| 154 Jeff Stone | .04 | 239 Roy Smalley | .04 | 324 Danny Jackson | .15 | 409 Joel McKeon | .04 |
| 155 Bruce Sutter | .08 | 240 Lee Smith | .08 | 325 Glenn Hubbard | .04 | 410 Tony Pena | .04 |
| 156 Gary Mathews | .04 | 241 Damaso Garcia | .06 | 326 Al Nipper | .04 | 411 Wayne Tolleson | .04 |
| 157 Atlee Hammaker | .04 | 242 Tom Niedenfuer | .04 | 327 Larry Sheets | .12 | 412 Randy Myers | .12 |
| 158 Tim Hulett | .04 | 243 Mark Ryal | .12 | 328 Greg Cadaret (R) | .15 | 413 John Christensen | .04 |
| 159 Brad Arnsberg (R) | .20 | 244 Jeff D. Robinson | .04 | 329 Chris Speier | .04 | 414 John McNamara | .04 |
| 160 Willie McGee | .10 | 245 Rich Gedman | .04 | 330 Eddie Whitson | .04 | 415 Don Carman | .04 |
| 161 Bryn Smith | .04 | 246 Mike Campbell (R) | .20 | 331 Brian Downing | .04 | 416 Keith Moreland | .04 |
| 162 Mark McLemore | .08 | 247 Thad Bosley | .04 | 332 Jerry Reed | .04 | 417 Mark Ciardi (R) | .12 |
| 163 Dale Mahorcic | .04 | 248 Storm Davis | .04 | 333 Wally Backman | .04 | 418 Joel Youngblood | .04 |
| 164 Dave Johnson | .04 | 249 Mike Marshall | .08 | 334 Dave LaPoint | .04 | 419 Scott McGregor | .04 |
| 165 Robin Yount | .15 | 250 Nolan Ryan | .20 | 335 C. Washington | .04 | 420 Wally Joyner | .50 |
| 166 Rick Rodriguez (R) | .12 | 251 Tom Foley | .04 | 336 Ed Lynch | .04 | 421 Ed VandeBerg | .04 |
| 167 Rance Mulliniks | .04 | 252 Bob Brower | .08 | 337 Jim Gantner | .04 | 422 Dave Concepcion | .04 |
| 168 Barry Jones | .04 | 253 Checklist: 133-264 | .06 | 338 Brian Holton | .08 | 423 John Smiley (R) | .20 |
| 169 Ross Jones (R) | .15 | 254 Lee Elia | .04 | 339 Kurt Stillwell | .08 | 424 Dwayne Murphy | .04 |
| 170 Rich Gossage | .08 | 255 Mookie Wilson | .06 | 340 Jack Morris | .12 | 425 Jeff Reardon | .04 |
| 171 Cubs Team | .06 | 256 Ken Schrom | .04 | 341 Carmen Castillo | .04 | 426 Randy Ready | .04 |
| 172 Lloyd McClendon (R) | .15 | 257 Jerry Royster | .04 | 342 Larry Andersen | .04 | 427 Paul Kilgus (R) | .12 |
| 173 Eric Plunk | .04 | 258 Ed Nunez | .04 | 343 Greg Gagne | .04 | 428 John Shelby | .04 |
| 174 Phil Garner | .04 | 259 Ron Kittle | .06 | 344 Tony LaRussa | .04 | 429 Tigers Team | .08 |
| 175 Kevin Bass | .15 | 260 Vince Coleman | .20 | 345 Scott Fletcher | .04 | 430 Glenn Davis | .12 |
| 176 Jeff Reed | .04 | 261 Giants Team | .06 | 346 Vance Law | .04 | 431 Casey Candaele | .08 |
| 177 Frank Tanana | .08 | 262 Drew Hall | .12 | 347 Joe Johnson | .06 | 432 Mike Moore | .04 |
| 178 Dwayne Henry | .08 | 263 Glenn Braggs | .12 | 348 Jim Eisenreich | .04 | 433 Bill Pecota (R) | .15 |
| 179 Charlie Puleo | .04 | 264 Les Straker (R) | .15 | 349 Bob Walk | .04 | 434 Rick Aguilera | .04 |
| 180 Terry Kennedy | .04 | 265 Bo Diaz | .04 | 350 Will Clark | .65 | 435 Mike Pagliarulo | .06 |
| 181 Dave Cone | .35 | 266 Paul Assenmacher | .04 | 351 Cardinals Team | .06 | 436 Mike Bielecki | .04 |
| 182 Ken Phelps | .04 | 267 Billy Bean (R) | .15 | 352 Billy Ripken (R) | .30 | 437 Fred Manrique (R) | .15 |
| 183 Tom Lawless | .04 | 268 Bruce Ruffin | .04 | 353 Ed Olwine | .04 | 438 Rob Ducey (R) | .12 |
| 184 Ivan Calderon | .15 | 269 Ellis Burks (R) | 1.00 | 354 Marc Sullivan | .04 | 439 Dave Martinez | .15 |
| 185 Rick Rhoden | .04 | 270 Mike Witt | .06 | 355 Roger McDowell | .04 | 440 Steve Bedrosian | .10 |
| 186 Rafael Palmeiro | .25 | 271 Ken Gerhart | .10 | 356 Luis Aguayo | .04 | 441 Rick Manning | .04 |
| 187 Steve Kiefer | .12 | 272 Steve Ontiveros | .04 | 357 Floyd Bannister | .04 | 442 Tom Bolton (R) | .12 |
| 188 John Russell | .04 | 273 Garth Iorg | .04 | 358 Rey Quinones | .04 | 443 Ken Griffey | .04 |
| 189 Wes Gardner (R) | .15 | 274 Junior Ortiz | .04 | 359 Tim Stoddard | .04 | 444 Cal Ripken, Sr. | .04 |
| 190 Candy Maldonado | .10 | 275 Kevin Seitzer | 1.25 | 360 Tony Gwynn | .35 | 445 Mike Krukow | .04 |
| 191 John Cerutti | .04 | 276 Luis Salazar | .04 | 361 Greg Maddux | .20 | 446 Doug DeCinces | .04 |
| 192 Devon White | .20 | 277 Alejandro Pena | .04 | 362 Juan Castillo | .10 | 447 Jeff Montgomery (R) | .20 |
| 193 Brian Fisher | .06 | 278 Jose Cruz | .04 | 363 Willie Fraser | .10 | 448 Mike Davis | .04 |
| 194 Tom Kelly | .04 | 279 Randy St. Claire | .04 | 364 Nick Esasky | .04 | 449 Jeff M. Robinson (R) | .25 |
| 195 Dan Quisenberry | .08 | 280 Pete Incaviglia | .20 | 365 Floyd Youmans | .04 | 450 Barry Bonds | .15 |
| 196 Dave Engle | .04 | 281 Jerry Hairston | .04 | 366 Chet Lemon | .04 | 451 Keith Atherton | .04 |
| 197 Lance McCullers | .04 | 282 Pat Perry | .04 | 367 Tim Leary | .04 | 452 Willie Wilson | .08 |

Card values shown here fluctuate considerably.

| NO. | PLAYER | MINT |
|---|---|---|
| 453 | Dennis Powell | .04 |
| 454 | Marvell Wynne | .04 |
| 455 | Shawn Hillegas (R) | .30 |
| 456 | Dave Anderson | .04 |
| 457 | Terry Leach | .04 |
| 458 | Ron Hassey | .04 |
| 459 | Yankees Team | .08 |
| 460 | Ozzie Smith | .12 |
| 461 | Danny Darwin | .04 |
| 462 | Don Slaught | .04 |
| 463 | Fred McGriff | .25 |
| 464 | Jay Tibbs | .04 |
| 465 | Paul Molitor | .08 |
| 466 | Jerry Mumphrey | .04 |
| 467 | Don Aase | .04 |
| 468 | Darren Daulton | .04 |
| 469 | Jeff Dedmon | .04 |
| 470 | Dwight Evans | .08 |
| 471 | Donnie Moore | .04 |
| 472 | Robby Thompson | .04 |
| 473 | Joe Niekro | .06 |
| 474 | Tom Brookens | .04 |
| 475 | Pete Rose (mgr.) | .30 |
| 476 | Dave Stewart | .04 |
| 477 | Jamie Quirk | .04 |
| 478 | Sid Bream | .04 |
| 479 | Brett Butler | .04 |
| 480 | Dwight Gooden | .40 |
| 481 | Mariano Duncan | .06 |
| 482 | Mark Davis | .04 |
| 483 | Rod Booker (R) | .15 |
| 484 | Pat Clements | .04 |
| 485 | Harold Reynolds | .04 |
| 486 | Pat Keedy (R) | .12 |
| 487 | Jim Pankovits | .04 |
| 488 | Andy McGaffigan | .04 |
| 489 | Dodgers Team | .10 |
| 490 | Larry Parrish | .04 |
| 491 | B.J. Surhoff | .15 |
| 492 | Doyle Alexander | .04 |
| 493 | Mike Greenwell | .75 |
| 494 | Wally Ritchie (R) | .12 |
| 495 | Eddie Murray | .25 |
| 496 | Guy Hoffman | .04 |
| 497 | Kevin Mitchell | .06 |
| 498 | Bob Boone | .04 |
| 499 | Eric King | .04 |
| 500 | Andre Dawson | .20 |
| 501 | Tim Birtsas | .04 |
| 502 | Danny Gladden | .04 |
| 503 | Junior Noboa (R) | .12 |
| 504 | Bob Rodgers | .04 |
| 505 | Willie Upshaw | .06 |
| 506 | John Cangelosi | .04 |
| 507 | Mark Gubicza | .04 |
| 508 | Tim Teufel | .04 |
| 509 | Bill Dawley | .04 |
| 510 | Dave Winfield | .25 |
| 511 | Joel Davis | .04 |
| 512 | Alex Trevino | .04 |
| 513 | Tim Flannery | .04 |
| 514 | Pat Sheridan | .04 |
| 515 | Juan Nieves | .04 |
| 516 | Jim Sundberg | .04 |
| 517 | Ron Robinson | .04 |
| 518 | Greg Gross | .04 |
| 519 | Mariners Team | .04 |
| 520 | Dave Smith | .04 |
| 521 | Jim Dwyer | .04 |
| 522 | Bob Patterson (R) | .12 |
| 523 | Gary Roenicke | .04 |
| 524 | Gary Lucas | .04 |
| 525 | Marty Barrett | .06 |
| 526 | Juan Berenguer | .04 |
| 527 | Steve Henderson | .04 |
| 528 | Checklist: 397-528 | .12 |
| 529 | Tim Burke | .04 |
| 530 | Gary Carter | .20 |
| 531 | Rich Yett | .04 |
| 532 | Mike Kingery | .04 |
| 533 | John Farrell (R) | .20 |
| 534 | John Wathan | .04 |
| 535 | Ron Guidry | .10 |
| 536 | John Morris | .04 |
| 537 | Steve Buechele | .04 |
| 538 | Bill Wegman | .04 |
| 539 | Mike LaValliere | .04 |
| 540 | Bret Saberhagen | .12 |
| 541 | Juan Beniquez | .04 |
| 542 | Paul Noce (R) | .12 |
| 543 | Kent Tekulve | .04 |
| 544 | Jim Traber | .04 |
| 545 | Don Baylor | .08 |
| 546 | John Candelaria | .06 |
| 547 | Felix Fermin (R) | .10 |
| 548 | Shane Mack | .15 |
| 549 | Braves Team | .06 |
| 550 | Pedro Guerrero | .20 |
| 551 | Terry Steinbach | .15 |
| 552 | Mark Thurmond | .04 |
| 553 | Tracy Jones | .10 |
| 554 | Mike Smithson | .04 |
| 555 | Brook Jacoby | .08 |
| 556 | Stan Clarke (R) | .10 |
| 557 | Craig Reynolds | .04 |
| 558 | Bob Ojeda | .04 |
| 559 | Ken Williams (R) | .25 |
| 560 | Tim Wallach | .08 |
| 561 | Rick Cerone | .04 |
| 562 | Jim Lindeman | .15 |
| 563 | Jose Guzman | .04 |
| 564 | Frank Lucchesi | .04 |
| 565 | Lloyd Moseby | .15 |
| 566 | Charlie O'Brien (R) | .10 |
| 567 | Mike Diaz | .04 |
| 568 | Chris Brown | .10 |
| 569 | C. Liebrandt | .06 |
| 570 | Jeffrey Leonard | .04 |
| 571 | Mark Williamson (R) | .15 |
| 572 | Chris James | .20 |
| 573 | Bob Stanley | .04 |
| 574 | Graig Nettles | .10 |
| 575 | Don Sutton | .15 |
| 576 | Tommy Hinzo (R) | .12 |
| 577 | Tom Browning | .06 |
| 578 | Gary Gaetti | .12 |
| 579 | Mets Team | .15 |
| 580 | Mark McGwire | 1.00 |
| 581 | Tito Landrum | .04 |
| 582 | Mike Henneman (R) | .15 |
| 583 | Dave Valle | .08 |
| 584 | Steve Trout | .04 |
| 585 | Ozzie Guillen | .04 |
| 586 | Bob Forsch | .04 |
| 587 | Terry Puhl | .04 |
| 588 | Jeff Parrett (R) | .15 |
| 589 | Geno Petralli | .04 |
| 590 | George Bell | .20 |
| 591 | Doug Drabek | .04 |
| 592 | Dale Sveum | .06 |
| 593 | Bob Tewksbury | .15 |
| 594 | Bobby Valentine | .04 |
| 595 | Frank White | .04 |
| 596 | John Kruk | .20 |
| 597 | Gene Garber | .04 |
| 598 | Lee Lacy | .04 |
| 599 | Calvin Schiraldi | .04 |
| 600 | Mike Schmidt | .35 |
| 601 | Jack Lazorko | .04 |
| 602 | Mike Aldrete | .04 |
| 603 | Rob Murphy | .04 |
| 604 | Chris Bando | .04 |
| 605 | Kirk Gibson | .15 |
| 606 | Moose Haas | .04 |
| 607 | Mickey Hatcher | .04 |
| 608 | Charlie Kerfeld | .06 |
| 609 | Twins Team | .08 |
| 610 | Keith Hernandez | .15 |
| 611 | Tommy John | .08 |
| 612 | Curt Ford | .04 |
| 613 | Bobby Thigpen | .15 |
| 614 | Herm Winningham | .04 |
| 615 | Jody Davis | .04 |
| 616 | Jay Aldrich (R) | .12 |
| 617 | Oddibe McDowell | .10 |
| 618 | Cecil Fielder | .04 |
| 619 | Mike Dunne | .30 |
| 620 | Cory Snyder | .35 |
| 621 | Gene Nelson | .04 |
| 622 | Kal Daniels | .35 |
| 623 | Mike Flanagan | .04 |
| 624 | Jim Leyland | .04 |
| 625 | Frank Viola | .15 |
| 626 | Glenn Wilson | .04 |
| 627 | Joe Boever (R) | .12 |
| 628 | Dave Henderson | .04 |
| 629 | Kelly Downs | .04 |
| 630 | Darrell Evans | .12 |
| 631 | Jack Howell | .04 |
| 632 | Steve Shields | .10 |
| 633 | Barry Lyons (R) | .20 |
| 634 | Jose DeLeon | .06 |
| 635 | Terry Pendleton | .06 |
| 636 | Charles Hudson | .04 |
| 637 | Jay Bell (R) | .20 |
| 638 | Steve Balboni | .04 |
| 639 | Brewers Team | .06 |
| 640 | Garry Templeton | .06 |
| 641 | Rick Honeycutt | .06 |
| 642 | Bob Dernier | .04 |
| 643 | Rocky Childress (R) | .12 |
| 644 | Terry McGriff | .15 |
| 645 | Matt Nokes (R) | 1.00 |
| 646 | Checklist: 529-660 | .06 |
| 647 | Pascual Perez | .04 |
| 648 | Al Newman | .04 |
| 649 | DeWayne Buice (R) | .15 |
| 650 | Cal Ripken | .20 |
| 651 | Mike Jackson | .25 |
| 652 | Bruce Benedict | .04 |
| 653 | Jeff Sellers | .04 |
| 654 | Roger Craig | .04 |
| 655 | Len Dykstra | .15 |
| 656 | Lee Guetterman | .04 |
| 657 | Gary Redus | .04 |
| 658 | Tim Conroy | .04 |
| 659 | Bobby Meacham | .04 |
| 660 | Rick Reuschel | .04 |
| 661 | Turn Back—1983 | .08 |
| 662 | Turn Back—1978 | .08 |
| 663 | Turn Back—1973 | .08 |
| 664 | Turn Back—1968 | .08 |
| 665 | Turn Back—1963 | .10 |
| 666 | Mario Soto | .04 |
| 667 | Luis Quinones | .04 |
| 668 | Walt Terrell | .04 |
| 669 | Phillies Team | .06 |
| 670 | Dan Plesac | .04 |
| 671 | Tim Laudner | .04 |
| 672 | John Davis (R) | .20 |
| 673 | Tony Phillips | .04 |
| 674 | Mike Fitzgerald | .04 |
| 675 | Jim Rice | .15 |
| 676 | Ken Dixon | .04 |
| 677 | Eddie Milner | .04 |
| 678 | Jim Acker | .04 |
| 679 | Darrell Miller | .04 |
| 680 | Charlie Hough | .06 |
| 681 | Bobby Bonilla | .15 |
| 682 | Jimmy Key | .12 |
| 683 | Julio Franco | .04 |
| 684 | Hal Lanier | .04 |
| 685 | Ron Darling | .15 |
| 686 | Terry Francona | .04 |
| 687 | Mickey Brantley | .08 |
| 688 | Jim Winn | .04 |
| 689 | Tom Pagnozzi (R) | .20 |
| 690 | Jay Howell | .04 |
| 691 | Dan Pasqua | .10 |
| 692 | Mike Birkbeck | .04 |
| 693 | Benny Santiago | .75 |
| 694 | Eric Nolte | .12 |
| 695 | Shawon Dunston | .04 |
| 696 | Duane Ward | .04 |
| 697 | S. Lombardozzi | .10 |
| 698 | Brad Havens | .04 |
| 699 | Padres Team | .15 |
| 700 | George Brett | .25 |
| 701 | Sammy Stewart | .04 |
| 702 | Mike Gallego | .04 |
| 703 | Bob Brenly | .04 |
| 704 | Dennis Boyd | .04 |
| 705 | Juan Samuel | .15 |
| 706 | Rick Mahler | .04 |
| 707 | Fred Lynn | .10 |
| 708 | Gus Polidor | .08 |
| 709 | George Frazier | .04 |
| 710 | D. Strawberry | .40 |
| 711 | Bill Gullickson | .04 |
| 712 | John Moses | .04 |
| 713 | Willie Hernandez | .08 |
| 714 | Jim Fregosi | .04 |
| 715 | Todd Worrell | .10 |
| 716 | Lenn Sakata | .04 |
| 717 | Jay Baller | .08 |
| 718 | Mike Felder | .04 |
| 719 | Denny Walling | .04 |
| 720 | Tim Raines | .20 |
| 721 | Pete O'Brien | .10 |
| 722 | Manny Lee | .04 |
| 723 | Bob Kipper | .04 |
| 724 | Danny Tartabull | .25 |
| 725 | Mike Boddicker | .04 |
| 726 | Alfredo Griffin | .04 |
| 727 | Greg Booker | .04 |
| 728 | Andy Allanson | .04 |
| 729 | Blue Jays Team | .06 |
| 730 | John Franco | .06 |
| 731 | Rick Schu | .04 |
| 732 | Dave Palmer | .04 |
| 733 | Spike Owen | .04 |
| 734 | Craig Lefferts | .04 |
| 735 | Kevin McReynolds | .15 |
| 736 | Matt Young | .04 |
| 737 | Butch Wynegar | .04 |
| 738 | Scott Bankhead | .04 |
| 739 | Daryl Boston | .04 |
| 740 | Rick Sutcliffe | .15 |
| 741 | Mike Easler | .04 |
| 742 | Mark Clear | .04 |
| 743 | Larry Herndon | .04 |
| 744 | Whitey Herzog (mgr.) | .04 |
| 745 | Bill Doran | .10 |
| 746 | Gene Larkin (R) | .25 |
| 747 | Bobby Witt | .04 |
| 748 | Reid Nichols | .04 |
| 749 | Mark Eichhorn | .04 |
| 750 | Bo Jackson | .30 |
| 751 | Jim Morrison | .04 |
| 752 | Mark Grant | .08 |
| 753 | Danny Heep | .04 |
| 754 | Mike LaCoss | .04 |
| 755 | Ozzie Virgil | .06 |
| 756 | Mike Maddux | .04 |
| 757 | John Marzano | .15 |
| 758 | Eddie Williams (R) | .25 |
| 759 | A's Team | .30 |
| 760 | Mike Scott | .15 |
| 761 | Tony Armas | .06 |
| 762 | Scott Bradley | .04 |
| 763 | Doug Sisk | .04 |
| 764 | Greg Walker | .08 |
| 765 | Neal Heaton | .10 |
| 766 | Henry Cotto | .04 |
| 767 | Jose Lind (R) | .25 |
| 768 | Dickie Noles | .04 |
| 769 | Cecil Cooper | .06 |
| 770 | Lou Whitaker | .15 |
| 771 | Ruben Sierra | .30 |
| 772 | Sal Butera | .04 |
| 773 | Frank Williams | .04 |
| 774 | Gene Mauch | .04 |
| 775 | Dave Stieb | .06 |
| 776 | Checklist: 661-792 | .06 |
| 777 | Lonnie Smith | .04 |
| 778 | K. Comstock (R)(error) | 4.00 |
| 778 | K. Comstock (R)(correct) | .35 |
| 779 | Tom Glavine (R) | .25 |
| 780 | F. Valenzuela | .15 |
| 781 | Keith Hughes (R) | .20 |
| 782 | Jeff Ballard (R) | .20 |
| 783 | Ron Roenicke | .04 |
| 784 | Joe Sambito | .04 |
| 785 | Alvin Davis | .08 |
| 786 | Joe Price | .04 |
| 787 | Bill Almon | .04 |
| 788 | Ray Searage | .04 |
| 789 | Indians Team | .08 |
| 790 | Dave Righetti | .10 |
| 791 | Ted Simmons | .08 |
| 792 | John Tudor | .08 |

Card values shown here fluctuate considerably.

# 1988 Topps Traded . . . Complete Set of 132 Cards—Value $12.00

Updates the main 1988 card set with players who changed teams during the season and rookies. Features the first Topps card for Mark Grace, Chris Sabo, and the USA Olympic Team. The complete set was packaged in a printed box and distributed primarily through card hobby dealers.

| NO. | PLAYER | MINT |
|---|---|---|
| 1 T | Jim Abbott (OLY) | .75 |
| 2 T | Juan Agosto | .06 |
| 3 T | Luis Alicea | .15 |
| 4 T | Roberto Alomar | .40 |
| 5 T | Brady Anderson | .35 |
| 6 T | Jack Armstrong | .25 |
| 7 T | Don August | .12 |
| 8 T | Floyd Bannister | .06 |
| 9 T | Bret Barberie (OLY) | .20 |
| 10 T | Jose Bautista | .15 |
| 11 T | Don Baylor | .06 |
| 12 T | Tim Belcher | .06 |
| 13 T | Buddy Bell | .06 |
| 14 T | Andy Benes (OLY) | .60 |
| 15 T | Damon Berryhill | .30 |
| 16 T | Bud Black | .06 |
| 17 T | Pat Borders | .25 |
| 18 T | Phil Bradley | .06 |
| 19 T | Jeff Branson (OLY) | .20 |
| 20 T | Tom Brunansky | .15 |
| 21 T | Jay Buhner | .30 |
| 22 T | Brett Butler | .06 |
| 23 T | Jim Campanis (OLY) | .25 |
| 24 T | Sil Campusano | .25 |
| 25 T | John Candelaria | .06 |
| 26 T | Jose Cecana | .20 |
| 27 T | Rick Cerone | .06 |
| 28 T | Jack Clark | .15 |
| 29 T | Kevin Coffman | .15 |
| 30 T | Pat Combs (OLY) | .20 |
| 31 T | Henry Cotto | .06 |
| 32 T | Chill Davis | .06 |
| 33 T | Mike Davis | .06 |

| NO. | PLAYER | MINT |
|---|---|---|
| 34 T | Jose DeLeon | .06 |
| 35 T | Richard Dotson | .06 |
| 36 T | Cecil Espy | .10 |
| 37 T | Tom Filer | .06 |
| 38 T | Mike Fiore (OLY) | .25 |
| 39 T | Ron Gant | .45 |
| 40 T | Kirk Gibson | .20 |
| 41 T | Rich Gossage | .06 |
| 42 T | Mark Grace (RR) | 2.00 |
| 43 T | Alfredo Griffin | .06 |
| 44 T | Ty Griffin (OLY) | .90 |
| 45 T | Bryan Harvey | .30 |
| 46 T | Ron Hassey | .06 |
| 47 T | Ray Hayward | .15 |
| 48 T | Dave Henderson | .06 |
| 49 T | Tom Herr | .06 |
| 50 T | Bob Horner | .06 |
| 51 T | Rickey Horton | .06 |
| 52 T | Jay Howell | .06 |
| 53 T | Glenn Hubbard | .06 |
| 54 T | Jeff Innis | .06 |
| 55 T | Danny Jackson | .20 |
| 56 T | Darrin Jackson | .20 |
| 57 T | Roberto Kelly | .25 |
| 58 T | Ron Kittle | .06 |
| 59 T | Ray Knight | .06 |
| 60 T | Vance Law | .06 |
| 61 T | Jeffrey Leonard | .06 |
| 62 T | Mike Macfarlane | .15 |
| 63 T | Scott Madison | .15 |
| 64 T | Kirt Manwaring | .15 |
| 65 T | Mark Marquess | .06 |
| 66 T | Tino Martinez (OLY) | .75 |

| NO. | PLAYER | MINT |
|---|---|---|
| 67 T | Billy Masse (OLY) | .25 |
| 68 T | Jack McDowell | .15 |
| 69 T | Jack McKeon | .06 |
| 70 T | Larry McWilliams | .06 |
| 71 T | M. Morandini (OLY) | .30 |
| 72 T | Keith Moreland | .06 |
| 73 T | Mike Morgan | .06 |
| 74 T | Charles Nagy (OLY) | .25 |
| 75 T | Al Nipper | .06 |
| 76 T | Russ Nixon | .06 |
| 77 T | Jesse Orosco | .06 |
| 78 T | Joe Orsulak | .06 |
| 79 T | Dave Palmer | .06 |
| 80 T | Mark Parent | .20 |
| 81 T | Dave Parker | .15 |
| 82 T | Dan Pasqua | .06 |
| 83 T | Melido Perez | .20 |
| 84 T | Steve Peters | .20 |
| 85 T | Dan Petry | .06 |
| 86 T | Gary Pettis | .06 |
| 87 T | Jeff Pico | .15 |
| 88 T | Jim Poole (OLY) | .20 |
| 89 T | Ted Power | .06 |
| 90 T | Rafael Ramirez | .06 |
| 91 T | Dennis Rasmussen | .06 |
| 92 T | Jose Rijo | .06 |
| 93 T | Ernie Riles | .06 |
| 94 T | Luis Rivera | .15 |
| 95 T | Doug Robbins | .06 |
| 96 T | Frank Robinson | .15 |
| 97 T | Cookie Rojas | .06 |
| 98 T | Chris Sabo (RR) | 2.00 |
| 99 T | Mark Salas | .06 |

| NO. | PLAYER | MINT |
|---|---|---|
| 100 T | Luis Salazar | .06 |
| 101 T | Rafael Santana | .06 |
| 102 T | Nelson Santovenia | .15 |
| 103 T | Mackey Sasser | .30 |
| 104 T | Calvin Schiraldi | .06 |
| 105 T | Mike Schooler | .15 |
| 106 T | Scott Servais (OLY) | .20 |
| 107 T | Dave Silvestri (OLY) | .20 |
| 108 T | Don Slaught | .06 |
| 109 T | Joe Slusarski (OLY) | .20 |
| 110 T | Lee Smith | .06 |
| 111 T | Pete Smith | .20 |
| 112 T | Jim Snyder | .06 |
| 113 T | Ed Sprague (OLY) | .20 |
| 114 T | Pete Stanicek | .15 |
| 115 T | Kurt Stillwell | .06 |
| 116 T | Todd Stottlemyre | .15 |
| 117 T | Bill Swift | .06 |
| 118 T | Pat Tabler | .06 |
| 119 T | Scott Terry | .06 |
| 120 T | Mickey Tettleton | .06 |
| 121 T | Dickie Thon | .06 |
| 122 T | Jeff Treadway | .20 |
| 123 T | Willie Upshaw | .06 |
| 124 T | Robin Ventura (OLY) | .75 |
| 125 T | Ron Washington | .06 |
| 126 T | Walt Weiss (RR) | .60 |
| 127 T | Bob Welch | .06 |
| 128 T | David Wells | .15 |
| 129 T | Glenn Wilson | .06 |
| 130 T | Ted Wood (OLY) | .20 |
| 131 T | Don Zimmer | .06 |
| 132 T | Checklist | .06 |

Card values shown here fluctuate considerably.

# 1989 Topps. . . . Complete Set of 792 Cards—Value $20.00

Features the rookie cards of Sandy Alomar, Jr., Chris Sabo and Gary Sheffield. New features this year are "#1 Draft Picks," and 1988 "Monthly Scoreboard."

| NO. | PLAYER | MINT |
|---|---|---|
| 1 | '88 Record: G. Bell | .15 |
| 2 | '88 Record: Boggs | .25 |
| 3 | '88 Record: G. Carter | .10 |

| NO. | PLAYER | MINT |
|---|---|---|
| 4 | '88 Record: Dawson | .10 |
| 5 | '88 Rec.: Hershiser | .10 |
| 6 | '88 Record: D. Jones | .05 |

| NO. | PLAYER | MINT |
|---|---|---|
| 7 | '88 Rec.: McReynolds | .10 |
| 8 | Dave Eiland (R) | .25 |
| 9 | Tim Teufel | .05 |

| NO. | PLAYER | MINT |
|---|---|---|
| 10 | Andre Dawson | .15 |
| 11 | Bruce Sutter | .08 |
| 12 | Dale Sveum | .08 |

| NO. | PLAYER | MINT |
|----|--------|------|
| 13 | Doug Sisk | .05 |
| 14 | Tom Kelly | .05 |
| 15 | Robby Thompson | .05 |
| 16 | Ron Robinson | .08 |
| 17 | Brian Downing | .08 |
| 18 | Rick Rhoden | .05 |
| 19 | Greg Gagne | .05 |
| 20 | Steve Bedrosian | .08 |
| 21 | Walker: *Bonus* | .05 |
| 22 | Tim Crews | .05 |
| 23 | Mike Fitzgerald | .05 |
| 24 | Larry Andersen | .05 |
| 25 | Frank White | .05 |
| 26 | Dale Mohorcac | .05 |
| 27 | Orestes Destrade (R) | .25 |
| 28 | Mike Moore | .05 |
| 29 | Kelly Gruber | .05 |
| 30 | Doc Gooden | .40 |
| 31 | Terry Francona | .10 |
| 32 | Dennis Rasmussen | .05 |
| 33 | B.J. Surhoff | .08 |
| 34 | Ken Williams | .05 |
| 35 | John Tudor | .05 |
| 36 | Mitch Webster | .05 |
| 37 | Bob Stanley | .05 |
| 38 | Paul Runge | .05 |
| 39 | Mike Maddux | .05 |
| 40 | Steve Sax | .08 |
| 41 | Terry Mulholland | .05 |
| 42 | Jim Eppard | .10 |
| 43 | Guillermo Hernandez | .05 |
| 44 | Jim Snyder | .15 |
| 45 | Kal Daniels | .25 |
| 46 | Mark Portugal | .05 |
| 47 | Carney Lansford | .08 |
| 48 | Tim Burke | .05 |
| 49 | Craig Biggio (R) | .25 |
| 50 | George Bell | .15 |
| 51 | McLemore: *Bonus* | .05 |
| 52 | Bob Brenly | .05 |
| 53 | Ruben Sierra | .20 |
| 54 | Steve Trout | .05 |
| 55 | Julio Franco | .08 |
| 56 | Pat Tabler | .08 |
| 57 | Alejandro Pena | .08 |
| 58 | Lee Mazzilli | .05 |
| 59 | Mark Davis | .05 |
| 60 | Tom Brunansky | .08 |
| 61 | Neil Allen | .05 |
| 62 | Alfredo Griffin | .05 |
| 63 | Mark Clear | .05 |
| 64 | Alex Trevino | .05 |
| 65 | Rick Reuschel | .05 |
| 66 | Manny Trillo | .05 |
| 67 | Dave Palmer | .05 |
| 68 | Darrell Miller | .05 |
| 69 | Jeff Ballard | .05 |
| 70 | Mark McGwire | 1.00 |
| 71 | Mike Boddicker | .08 |
| 72 | John Moses | .05 |
| 73 | Pascual Perez | .05 |
| 74 | Nick Leyva | .05 |
| 75 | Tom Henke | .05 |
| 76 | Terry Blocker (R) | .15 |
| 77 | Doyle Alexander | .05 |
| 78 | Jim Sundberg | .05 |
| 79 | Scott Bankhead | .05 |
| 80 | Cory Snyder | .15 |
| 81 | Raines: *Bonus* | .08 |
| 82 | Dave Leiper | .05 |
| 83 | Jeff Blauser | .10 |
| 84 | Bill Bene (R) | .35 |
| 85 | Kevin McReynolds | .15 |
| 86 | Al Nipper | .05 |
| 87 | Larry Owen | .05 |
| 88 | Darryl Hamilton (R) | .20 |
| 89 | Dave LaPoint | .05 |
| 90 | Vince Coleman | .15 |
| 91 | Floyd Youmans | .05 |
| 92 | Jeff Kunkel | .05 |
| 93 | Ken Howell | .05 |
| 94 | Chris Speier | .05 |
| 95 | Gerald Young | .08 |
| 96 | Rick Cerone | .05 |
| 97 | Greg Mathews | .05 |
| 98 | Larry Sheets | .05 |
| 99 | Sherman Corbett (R) | .15 |
| 100 | Mike Schmidt | .30 |
| 101 | Les Straker | .05 |
| 102 | Mike Gallego | .05 |
| 103 | Tim Birtsas | .05 |
| 104 | Dallas Green | .05 |
| 105 | Ron Darling | .10 |
| 106 | Willie Upshaw | .05 |
| 107 | Jose DeLeon | .05 |
| 108 | Fred Manrique | .05 |
| 109 | Hipolito Pena (R) | .15 |
| 110 | Paul Molitor | .08 |
| 111 | Davis: *Bonus* | .25 |
| 112 | Jim Presley | .05 |
| 113 | Lloyd Moseby | .12 |
| 114 | Bob Kipper | .05 |
| 115 | Jody Davis | .05 |
| 116 | Jeff Montgomery | .05 |
| 117 | Dave Anderson | .05 |
| 118 | Checklist: 1-132 | .08 |
| 119 | Terry Puhl | .05 |
| 120 | Frank Viola | .15 |
| 121 | Garry Templeton | .05 |
| 122 | Lance Johnson | .10 |
| 123 | Spike Owen | .05 |
| 124 | Jim Traber | .05 |
| 125 | Mike Krukow | .05 |
| 126 | Sid Bream | .05 |
| 127 | Walt Terrell | .05 |
| 128 | Milt Thompson | .05 |
| 129 | Terry Clark (R) | .20 |
| 130 | Gerald Perry | .10 |
| 131 | Dave Otto | .15 |
| 132 | Curt Ford | .05 |
| 133 | Bill Long | .05 |
| 134 | Don Zimmer | .05 |
| 135 | Jose Rijo | .08 |
| 136 | Joey Meyer | .05 |
| 137 | Geno Petralli | .05 |
| 138 | Wallace Johnson | .05 |
| 139 | Mike Flanagan | .05 |
| 140 | Shawon Dunston (R) | .10 |
| 141 | Jacoby: *Bonus* | .05 |
| 142 | Mike Diaz | .05 |
| 143 | Mike Campbell | .05 |
| 144 | Jay Bell | .05 |
| 145 | Dave Stewart | .10 |
| 146 | Gary Pettis | .05 |
| 147 | DeWayne Buice | .05 |
| 148 | Bill Pecota | .05 |
| 149 | Doug Dascenzo (R) | .20 |
| 150 | Fernando Valenzuela | .10 |
| 151 | Terry McGriff | .05 |
| 152 | Mark Thurmond | .05 |
| 153 | Jim Pankovits | .05 |
| 154 | Don Carman | .05 |
| 155 | Marty Barrett | .05 |
| 156 | Dave Gallagher (R) | .25 |
| 157 | Tom Glavine | .30 |
| 158 | Mike Aldrete | .05 |
| 159 | Pat Clements | .05 |
| 160 | Jeffrey Leonard | .05 |
| 161 | Gregg Olson (R) | .50 |
| 162 | John Davis | .05 |
| 163 | Bob Forsch | .05 |
| 164 | Hal Lanier | .05 |
| 165 | Mike Dunne | .05 |
| 166 | Doug Jennings (R) | .35 |
| 167 | Steve Searcy (R) | .20 |
| 168 | Willie Wilson | .08 |
| 169 | Mike Jackson | .05 |
| 170 | Tony Fernandez | .10 |
| 171 | Thomas: *Bonus* | .05 |
| 172 | Frank Williams | .05 |
| 173 | Mel Hall | .05 |
| 174 | Todd Burns (R) | .25 |
| 175 | John Shelby | .05 |
| 176 | Jeff Parrett | .08 |
| 177 | Monty Fariss (R) | .35 |
| 178 | Mark Grant | .05 |
| 179 | Ozzie Virgil | .05 |
| 180 | Mike Scott | .15 |
| 181 | Craig Worthington (R) | .30 |
| 182 | Bob McClure | .05 |
| 183 | Oddibe McDowell | .08 |
| 184 | John Costello (R) | .15 |
| 185 | Claudell Washington | .05 |
| 186 | Pat Perry | .05 |
| 187 | Darren Daulton | .05 |
| 188 | Dennis Lamp | .05 |
| 189 | Kevin Mitchell | .08 |
| 190 | Mike Witt | .08 |
| 191 | Sil Campusano (R) | .20 |
| 192 | Paul Mirabella | .05 |
| 193 | Sparky Anderson | .05 |
| 194 | Greg Harris (R) | .20 |
| 195 | Ozzie Guillen | .08 |
| 196 | Denny Walling | .05 |
| 197 | Neal Heaton | .05 |
| 198 | Danny Heep | .05 |
| 199 | Mike Schooler (R) | .15 |
| 200 | George Brett | .25 |
| 201 | Gruber: *Bonus* | .05 |
| 202 | Brad Moore (R) | .15 |
| 203 | Rob Ducey | .05 |
| 204 | Brad Havens | .05 |
| 205 | Dweight Evans | .15 |
| 206 | Roberto Alomar | .20 |
| 207 | Terry Leach | .05 |
| 208 | Tom Pagnozzi | .05 |
| 209 | Jeff Bittiger (R) | .15 |
| 210 | Dale Murphy | .25 |
| 211 | Mike Pagliarulo | .10 |
| 212 | Scott Sanderson | .05 |
| 213 | Rene Gonzales | .05 |
| 214 | Charlie O'Brien | .05 |
| 215 | Kevin Gross | .05 |
| 216 | Jack Howell | .08 |
| 217 | Joe Price | .05 |
| 218 | Mike LaValliere | .05 |
| 219 | Jim Clancy | .05 |
| 220 | Gary Gaetti | .10 |
| 221 | Cecil Espy | .10 |
| 222 | Mark Lewis | .25 |
| 223 | Jay Buhner | .25 |
| 224 | Tony LaRussa | .05 |
| 225 | Ramon Martinez (R) | .50 |
| 226 | Bill Doran | .08 |
| 227 | John Farrell | .10 |
| 228 | Nelson Santovenia (R) | .15 |
| 229 | Jimmy Key | .12 |
| 230 | Ozzie Smith | .08 |
| 231 | R. Alomar: *Bonus* | .10 |
| 232 | Ricky Horton | .05 |
| 233 | Gregg Jefferies | 2.75 |
| 234 | Tom Browning | .08 |
| 235 | John Kruk | .15 |
| 236 | Charles Hudson | .08 |
| 237 | Glenn Hubbard | .05 |
| 238 | Eric King | .05 |
| 239 | Tim Laudner | .05 |
| 240 | Greg Maddux | .20 |
| 241 | Brett Butler | .05 |
| 242 | Ed VandeBerg | .05 |
| 243 | Bob Boone | .05 |
| 244 | Jim Acker | .05 |
| 245 | Jim Rice | .12 |
| 246 | Rey Quinones | .05 |
| 247 | Shawn Hillegas | .05 |
| 248 | Tony Phillips | .05 |
| 249 | Tim Leary | .10 |
| 250 | Cal Ripken | .20 |
| 251 | John Dopson (R) | .25 |
| 252 | Billy Hatcher | .05 |
| 253 | Jose Alvarez (R) | .15 |
| 254 | Tom Lasorda | .05 |
| 255 | Ron Guidry | .08 |
| 256 | Benny Santiago | .10 |
| 257 | Rick Aguilera | .05 |
| 258 | Checklist: 133-264 | .08 |
| 259 | Larry McWilliams | .05 |
| 260 | Dave Winfield | .15 |
| 261 | Brunansky *Bonus* | .08 |
| 262 | Jeff Pico (R) | .25 |
| 263 | Mike Felder | .05 |
| 264 | Rob Dibble (R) | .15 |
| 265 | Kent Hrbek | .10 |
| 266 | Luis Aquino | .05 |
| 267 | Jeff Robinson | .05 |
| 268 | Keith Miller | .05 |
| 269 | Tom Bolton | .05 |
| 270 | Wally Joyner | .15 |
| 271 | Jay Tibbs | .05 |
| 272 | Ron Hassey | .05 |
| 273 | Jose Lind | .05 |
| 274 | Mark Eichhorn | .05 |
| 275 | Danny Tartabull | .20 |
| 276 | Paul Kilgus | .05 |
| 277 | Mike Davis | .05 |
| 278 | Andy McGaffigan | .05 |
| 279 | Scott Bradley | .05 |
| 280 | Bob Knepper | .05 |
| 281 | Gary Redus | .05 |
| 282 | Cris Carpenter (R) | .20 |
| 283 | Andy Allanson | .05 |
| 284 | Jim Leyland | .05 |
| 285 | John Candelaria | .08 |
| 286 | Darrin Jackson | .12 |
| 287 | Juan Nieves | .05 |
| 288 | Pat Sheridan | .05 |
| 289 | Ernie Whitt | .05 |
| 290 | John Franco | .08 |
| 291 | Strawberry: *Bonus* | .25 |
| 292 | Jim Corsi (R) | .20 |
| 293 | Glenn Wilson | .05 |
| 294 | Juan Berenguer | .05 |
| 295 | Scott Fletcher | .05 |
| 296 | Ron Gant | .40 |
| 297 | Oswald Peraza (R) | .15 |
| 298 | Chris James | .08 |
| 299 | Steve Ellsworth (R) | .15 |
| 300 | Darryl Strawberry | .45 |
| 301 | Charlie Leibrandt | .08 |
| 302 | Gary Ward | .05 |
| 303 | Felix Fermin | .05 |
| 304 | Joel Youngblood | .05 |
| 305 | Dave Smith | .05 |
| 306 | Tracy Woodson | .10 |
| 307 | Lance McCullers | .08 |
| 308 | Ron Karkovice | .05 |
| 309 | Mario Diaz | .05 |
| 310 | Rafael Palmeiro | .15 |
| 311 | Chris Bosio | .05 |
| 312 | Tom Lawless | .05 |
| 313 | Denny Martinez | .05 |
| 314 | Bobby Valentine | .05 |
| 315 | Greg Swindell | .10 |
| 316 | Walt Weiss | 1.25 |
| 317 | Jack Armstrong (R) | .20 |
| 318 | Gene Larkin | .05 |
| 319 | Greg Booker | .05 |
| 320 | Lou Whitaker | .08 |
| 321 | Reed: *Bonus* | .10 |
| 322 | John Smiley | .08 |
| 323 | Gary Thurman | .05 |
| 324 | Bob Milacki (R) | .20 |
| 325 | Jesse Barfield | .12 |
| 326 | Dennis Boyd | .08 |
| 327 | Mark Lemke (R) | .30 |
| 328 | Rick Honeycutt | .05 |
| 329 | Bob Melvin | .05 |
| 330 | Eric Davis | .65 |
| 331 | Curt Wilkerson | .05 |
| 332 | Tony Armas | .05 |
| 333 | Bob Ojeda | .08 |
| 334 | Steve Lyons | .05 |
| 335 | Dave Righetti | .10 |
| 336 | Steve Balboni | .05 |
| 337 | Calvin Schiraldi | .05 |
| 338 | Jim Adduci | .08 |
| 339 | Scott Bailes | .05 |
| 340 | Kirk Gibson | .20 |
| 341 | Jim Deshaies | .05 |
| 342 | Tom Brookens | .05 |
| 343 | Gary Sheffield (R) | 1.50 |
| 344 | Tom Trebelhorn | .05 |
| 345 | Charlie Hough | .08 |
| 346 | Rex Hudler | .10 |
| 347 | John Cerutti | .05 |
| 348 | Ed Hearn | .05 |
| 349 | Ron Jones (R) | .75 |
| 350 | Andy Van Slyke | .15 |
| 351 | Melvin: *Bonus* | .05 |
| 352 | Rick Schu | .05 |

Card values shown here fluctuate considerably.

| NO. | PLAYER | MINT | NO. | PLAYER | MINT | NO. | PLAYER | MINT | NO. | PLAYER | MINT |
|---|---|---|---|---|---|---|---|---|---|---|---|
| 353 | Marvell Wynne | .05 | 438 | Greg Gross | .05 | 523 | Andres Thomas | .05 | 608 | Phil Bradley | .08 |
| 354 | Larry Parrish | .05 | 439 | Frank Dipino | .05 | 524 | Checklist: 397-528 | .08 | 609 | Tanana: Bonus | .08 |
| 355 | Mark Langston | .10 | 440 | Bobby Bonilla | .20 | 525 | Chili Davis | .08 | 610 | Randy Myers | .08 |
| 356 | Kevin Elster | .08 | 441 | Jerry Reed | .05 | 526 | Wes Gardner | .05 | 611 | Don Slaught | .05 |
| 357 | Jerry Reuss | .05 | 442 | Jose Oquendo | .05 | 527 | Dave Henderson | .05 | 612 | Dan Quisenberry | .08 |
| 358 | Ricky Jordan (R) | 2.25 | 443 | Rod Nichols (R) | .25 | 528 | Luis Medina (R) | .60 | 613 | Gary Varsho (R) | .20 |
| 359 | Tommy John | .10 | 444 | Moose Stubing | .05 | 529 | Tom Foley | .05 | 614 | Joe Hesketh | .05 |
| 360 | Ryne Sandberg | .12 | 445 | Matt Nokes | .10 | 530 | Nolan Ryan | .20 | 615 | Robin Yount | .15 |
| 361 | Kelly Downs | .05 | 446 | Rob Murphy | .05 | 531 | Dave Hengel | .10 | 616 | Steve Rosenberg (R) | .15 |
| 362 | Jack Lazorko | .05 | 447 | Donell Nixon | .05 | 532 | Jerry Browne | .05 | 617 | Mark Parent (R) | .15 |
| 363 | Rich Yett | .05 | 448 | Eric Plunk | .05 | 533 | Andy Hawkins | .05 | 618 | Rance Mulliniks | .05 |
| 364 | Rob Deer | .08 | 449 | Carmelo Martinez | .05 | 534 | Doc Edwards | .05 | 619 | Checklist: 529-660 | .08 |
| 365 | Mike Henneman | .05 | 450 | Roger Clemens | .50 | 535 | Todd Worrell | .08 | 620 | Barry Bonds | .20 |
| 366 | Herm Winningham | .05 | 451 | Mark Davidson | .05 | 536 | Joel Skinner | .05 | 621 | Rick Mahler | .05 |
| 367 | Johnny Paredes (R) | .20 | 452 | Israel Sanchez (R) | .15 | 537 | Pete Smith | .12 | 622 | Stan Javier | .05 |
| 368 | Brian Holton | .05 | 453 | Tom Prince | .10 | 538 | Juan Castillo | .05 | 623 | Fred Toliver | .05 |
| 369 | Ken Caminiti | .05 | 454 | Paul Assenmacher | .05 | 539 | Barry Jones | .05 | 624 | Jack McKeon | .05 |
| 370 | Dennis Eckersley | .10 | 455 | Johnny Ray | .10 | 540 | Bo Jackson | .25 | 625 | Eddie Murray | .30 |
| 371 | Manny Lee | .05 | 456 | Tim Belcher | .15 | 541 | Cecil Fielder | .05 | 626 | Jeff Reed | .05 |
| 372 | Craig Lefferts | .05 | 457 | Mackey Sasser | .15 | 542 | Todd Frohwirth | .05 | 627 | Greg Harris | .20 |
| 373 | Tracy Jones | .05 | 458 | Donn Pall (R) | .15 | 543 | Damon Berryhill | .25 | 628 | Matt Williams | .08 |
| 374 | John Wathan | .05 | 459 | Valle: Bonus | .05 | 544 | Jeff Sellers | .05 | 629 | Pete O'Brien | .10 |
| 375 | Terry Pendleton | .08 | 460 | Dave Stieb | .08 | 545 | Mookie Wilson | .08 | 630 | Mike Greenwell | 1.25 |
| 376 | Steve Lombardozzi | .05 | 461 | Buddy Bell | .08 | 546 | Mark Williamson | .05 | 631 | Dave Bergman | .05 |
| 377 | Mike Smithson | .05 | 462 | Jose Guzman | .05 | 547 | Mark McLemore | .05 | 632 | Bryan Harvey (R) | .25 |
| 378 | Checklist: 265-396 | .08 | 463 | Steve Lake | .05 | 548 | Bobby Witt | .05 | 633 | Daryl Boston | .05 |
| 379 | Tim Flannery | .05 | 464 | Bryn Smith | .05 | 549 | Moyer: Bonus | .05 | 634 | Marvin Freeman | .10 |
| 380 | Rickey Henderson | .30 | 465 | Mark Grace | 1.25 | 550 | Orel Hershiser | .25 | 635 | Willie Randolph | .08 |
| 381 | Sheets: Bonus | .05 | 466 | Chuck Crim | .05 | 551 | Randy Ready | .05 | 636 | Bill Wilkinson | .05 |
| 382 | John Smoltz (R) | .30 | 467 | Jim Walewander | .05 | 552 | Greg Cadaret | .05 | 637 | Carmen Castillo | .05 |
| 383 | Howard Johnson | .10 | 468 | Henry Cotto | .05 | 553 | Luis Salazar | .05 | 638 | Floyd Bannister | .05 |
| 384 | Mark Salas | .05 | 469 | Jose Bautista (R) | .20 | 554 | Nick Esasky | .10 | 639 | Weiss: Bonus | .50 |
| 385 | Von Hayes | .08 | 470 | Lance Parrish | .10 | 555 | Bert Blyleven | .15 | 640 | Willie McGee | .08 |
| 386 | Andres Galarraga | .10 | 471 | Steve Curry (R) | .15 | 556 | Bruce Fields | .10 | 641 | Curt Young | .05 |
| 387 | Ryne Sandberg | .10 | 472 | Brian Harper | .05 | 557 | Keith Miller | .05 | 642 | Argenis Salazar | .05 |
| 388 | Bobby Bonilla | .10 | 473 | Don Robinson | .05 | 558 | Dan Pasqua | .08 | 643 | Louie Meadows (R) | .15 |
| 389 | Ozzie Smith | .08 | 474 | Bob Rodgers | .05 | 559 | Juan Agosto | .05 | 644 | Lloyd McClendon | .05 |
| 390 | Darryl Strawberry | .20 | 475 | Dave Parker | .10 | 560 | Tim Raines | .15 | 645 | Jack Morris | .10 |
| 391 | Andre Dawson | .10 | 476 | Jon Perlman | .05 | 561 | Luis Aguayo | .05 | 646 | Kevin Bass | .08 |
| 392 | Andy Van Slyke | .10 | 477 | Dick Schofield | .05 | 562 | Danny Cox | .05 | 647 | Randy Johnson (R) | .25 |
| 393 | Gary Carter | .10 | 478 | Doug Drabek | .10 | 563 | Bill Schroeder | .05 | 648 | Sandy Alomar (R) | 1.25 |
| 394 | Orel Hershiser | .10 | 479 | Mike Macfarlane (R) | .20 | 564 | Russ Nixon | .05 | 649 | Stewart Cliburn | .05 |
| 395 | Danny Jackson | .08 | 480 | Keith Hernandez | .15 | 565 | Jeff Russell | .05 | 650 | Kirby Puckett | .25 |
| 396 | Kirk Gibson | .10 | 481 | Chris Brown | .08 | 566 | Al Pedrique | .05 | 651 | Tom Niedenfuer | .05 |
| 397 | Don Mattingly | .75 | 482 | Steve Peters (R) | .15 | 567 | David Wells | .10 | 652 | Rich Gedman | .05 |
| 398 | Julio Franco | .08 | 483 | Mickey Hatcher | .05 | 568 | Mickey Brantley | .08 | 653 | Tommy Barrett (R) | .15 |
| 399 | Wade Boggs | .25 | 484 | Steve Shields | .05 | 569 | German Jimenez (R) | .15 | 654 | Whitey Herzog | .05 |
| 400 | Alan Trammell | .08 | 485 | Hubie Brooks | .05 | 570 | Tony Gwynn | .35 | 655 | Dave Magadan | .10 |
| 401 | Jose Canseco | .25 | 486 | Jack McDowell | .20 | 571 | Billy Ripken | .05 | 656 | Ivan Calderon | .10 |
| 402 | Mike Greenwell | .65 | 487 | Scott Lusader | .10 | 572 | Atlee Hammaker | .05 | 657 | Joe Magrane | .10 |
| 403 | Kirby Puckett | .15 | 488 | Kevin Coffman | .10 | 573 | Jim Abbott (R) | .75 | 658 | R.J. Reynolds | .05 |
| 404 | Bob Boone | .05 | 489 | Schmidt: Bonus | .15 | 574 | Dave Clark | .05 | 659 | Al Leiter | .10 |
| 405 | Roger Clemens | .20 | 490 | Chris Sabo (R) | 1.25 | 575 | Juan Samuel | .10 | 660 | Will Clark | .50 |
| 406 | Frank Viola | .10 | 491 | Mike Birkbeck | .05 | 576 | Greg Minton | .05 | 661 | Turn Back—1984 | .15 |
| 407 | Dave Winfield | .08 | 492 | Alan Ashby | .05 | 577 | Randy Bush | .05 | 662 | Turn Back—1979 | .15 |
| 408 | Greg Walker | .05 | 493 | Todd Benzinger | .15 | 578 | John Morris | .05 | 663 | Turn Back—1974 | .15 |
| 409 | Ken Dayley | .05 | 494 | Shane Rawley | .05 | 579 | G. Davis: Bonus | .08 | 664 | Turn Back—1969 | .15 |
| 410 | Jack Clark | .10 | 495 | Candy Maldonado | .10 | 580 | Harold Reynolds | .08 | 665 | Turn Back—1964 | .15 |
| 411 | Mitch Williams | .05 | 496 | Dwayne Henry | .05 | 581 | Gene Nelson | .05 | 666 | Randy St. Claire | .15 |
| 412 | Barry Lyons | .05 | 497 | Pete Stanicek | .08 | 582 | Mike Marshall | .08 | 667 | Dwayne Murphy | .05 |
| 413 | Mike Kingery | .05 | 498 | Dave Valle | .05 | 583 | Paul Gibson (R) | .15 | 668 | Mike Bielecki | .05 |
| 414 | Jim Fregosi | .05 | 499 | Don Heinkel (R) | .15 | 584 | Randy Velarde | .05 | 669 | Hershiser: Bonus | .15 |
| 415 | Rich Gossage | .08 | 500 | Jose Canseco | 1.25 | 585 | Harold Baines | .10 | 670 | Kevin Seitzer | .35 |
| 416 | Fred Lynn | .08 | 501 | Vance Law | .05 | 586 | Joe Boever | .05 | 671 | Jim Gantner | .05 |
| 417 | Mike LaCoss | .05 | 502 | Duane Ward | .05 | 587 | Mike Stanley | .05 | 672 | Allan Anderson | .08 |
| 418 | Bob Dernier | .05 | 503 | Al Newman | .05 | 588 | Luis Alicea (R) | .15 | 673 | Don Baylor | .08 |
| 419 | Tom Filer | .05 | 504 | Bob Walk | .05 | 589 | Dave Meads | .05 | 674 | Otis Nixon | .05 |
| 420 | Joe Carter | .15 | 505 | Pete Rose | .20 | 590 | Andres Galarraga | .25 | 675 | Bruce Hurst | .15 |
| 421 | Kirk McCaskill | .05 | 506 | Kirt Manwaring | .15 | 591 | Jeff Musselman | .05 | 676 | Ernie Riles | .05 |
| 422 | Bo Diaz | .05 | 507 | Steve Farr | .05 | 592 | John Cangelosi | .05 | 677 | Dave Schmidt | .05 |
| 423 | Brian Fisher | .05 | 508 | Wally Backman | .05 | 593 | Drew Hall | .05 | 678 | Dion James | .05 |
| 424 | Luis Polonia | .05 | 509 | Bud Black | .05 | 594 | Jimy Williams | .05 | 679 | Willie Fraser | .05 |
| 425 | Jay Howell | .08 | 510 | Bob Horner | .05 | 595 | Teddy Higuera | .10 | 680 | Gary Carter | .20 |
| 426 | Danny Gladden | .05 | 511 | Richard Dotson | .08 | 596 | Kurt Stillwell | .05 | 681 | Jeff Robinson | .15 |
| 427 | Eric Show | .05 | 512 | Donnie Hill | .05 | 597 | Terry Taylor (R) | .20 | 682 | Rick Leach | .05 |
| 428 | Craig Reynolds | .05 | 513 | Jesse Orosco | .05 | 598 | Ken Gerhart | .05 | 683 | Jose Cecena (R) | .15 |
| 429 | Gagne: Bonus | .05 | 514 | Chet Lemon | .05 | 599 | Tom Candiotti | .08 | 684 | Dave Johnson | .05 |
| 430 | Mark Gubicza | .10 | 515 | Barry Larkin | .10 | 600 | Wade Boggs | .75 | 685 | Jeff Treadway | .15 |
| 431 | Luis Rivera | .15 | 516 | Eddie Whitson | .05 | 601 | Dave Dravecky | .05 | 686 | Scott Terry | .08 |
| 432 | Chad Kreuter (R) | .20 | 517 | Greg Brock | .05 | 602 | Devon White | .08 | 687 | Alvin Davis | .08 |
| 433 | Albert Hall | .05 | 518 | Bruce Ruffin | .05 | 603 | Frank Tanana | .08 | 688 | Zane Smith | .05 |
| 434 | Ken Patterson (R) | .15 | 519 | Randolph: Bonus | .08 | 604 | Paul O'Neill | .05 | 689 | Stan Jefferson | .08 |
| 435 | Len Dykstra | .15 | 520 | Rick Sutcliffe | .10 | 605 | Bob Welch | .08 | 690 | Doug Jones | .05 |
| 436 | Bobby Meacham | .05 | 521 | Mickey Tettleton | .05 | 606 | Rick Dempsey | .05 | 691 | Roberto Kelly | .15 |
| 437 | Andy Benes (R) | .50 | 522 | Randy Kramer (R) | .15 | 607 | Willie Ansley (R) | .40 | 692 | Steve Ontiveros | .05 |

Card values shown here fluctuate considerably.

| NO. | PLAYER | MINT |
|-----|--------|------|
| 693 | Pat Borders (R) | .25 |
| 694 | Les Lancaster | .05 |
| 695 | Carlton Fisk | .10 |
| 696 | Don August | .10 |
| 697 | Franklin Stubbs | .05 |
| 698 | Keith Atherton | .05 |
| 699 | Pedrique: Bonus | .05 |
| 700 | Don Mattingly | 1.50 |
| 701 | Storm Davis | .05 |
| 702 | Jamie Quirk | .05 |
| 703 | Scott Garrelts | .05 |
| 704 | Carlos Quintana (R) | .35 |
| 705 | Terry Kennedy | .05 |
| 706 | Pete Incaviglia | .10 |
| 707 | Steve Jeltz | .05 |
| 708 | Chuck Finley | .05 |
| 709 | Tom Herr | .05 |
| 710 | Dave Cone | .35 |
| 711 | Candy Sierra (R) | .15 |
| 712 | Bill Swift | .05 |
| 713 | Ty Griffin (R) | .75 |
| 714 | Joe Morgan | .05 |
| 715 | Tony Pena | .08 |
| 716 | Wayne Tolleson | .05 |
| 717 | Jamie Moyer | .05 |

| NO. | PLAYER | MINT |
|-----|--------|------|
| 718 | Glenn Braggs | .05 |
| 719 | Danny Darwin | .05 |
| 720 | Tim Wallach | .08 |
| 721 | Ron Tingley | .05 |
| 722 | Todd Stottlemyre | .12 |
| 723 | Rafael Belliard | .05 |
| 724 | Jerry Don Gleaton | .05 |
| 725 | Terry Steinbach | .12 |
| 726 | Dickie Thon | .05 |
| 727 | Joe Orsulak | .05 |
| 728 | Charlie Puleo | .05 |
| 729 | Buechele: Bonus | .05 |
| 730 | Danny Jackson | .10 |
| 731 | Mike Young | .05 |
| 732 | Steve Buechele | .05 |
| 733 | Randy Bockus (R) | .15 |
| 734 | Jody Reed | .15 |
| 735 | Roger McDowell | .05 |
| 736 | Jeff Hamilton | .05 |
| 737 | Norm Charlton (R) | .20 |
| 738 | Darnell Coles | .05 |
| 739 | Brook Jacoby | .05 |
| 740 | Dan Plesac | .05 |
| 741 | Ken Phelps | .05 |
| 742 | Mike Harkey (R) | .75 |

| NO. | PLAYER | MINT |
|-----|--------|------|
| 743 | Mike Heath | .05 |
| 744 | Roger Craig | .05 |
| 745 | Fred McGriff | .40 |
| 746 | German Gonzalez (R) | .20 |
| 747 | Wil Tejada | .10 |
| 748 | Jimmy Jones | .05 |
| 749 | Rafael Ramirez | .05 |
| 750 | Bret Saberhagen | .10 |
| 751 | Ken Oberkfell | .05 |
| 752 | Jim Gott | .05 |
| 753 | Jose Uribe | .05 |
| 754 | Bob Brower | .05 |
| 755 | Mike Scioscia | .05 |
| 756 | Scott Medvin (R) | .15 |
| 757 | Brady Anderson (R) | .30 |
| 758 | Gene Walter | .05 |
| 759 | Deer: Bonus | .05 |
| 760 | Lee Smith | .08 |
| 761 | Dante Bichette (R) | .20 |
| 762 | Bobby Thigpen | .05 |
| 763 | Dave Martinez | .05 |
| 764 | Robin Ventura (R) | 1.50 |
| 765 | Glenn Davis | .10 |
| 766 | Cecilio Guante | .05 |
| 767 | Mike Capel (R) | .15 |

| NO. | PLAYER | MINT |
|-----|--------|------|
| 768 | Bill Wegman | .05 |
| 769 | Junior Ortiz | .05 |
| 770 | Alan Trammell | .10 |
| 771 | Ron Kittle | .08 |
| 772 | Ron Oester | .05 |
| 773 | Keith Moreland | .05 |
| 774 | Frank Robinson | .08 |
| 775 | Jeff Reardon | .08 |
| 776 | Nelson Liriano | .05 |
| 777 | Ted Power | .05 |
| 778 | Bruce Benedict | .05 |
| 779 | Craig McMurtry | .05 |
| 780 | Pedro Guerrero | .15 |
| 781 | Greg Briley (R) | .20 |
| 782 | Checklist: 681-792 | .08 |
| 783 | Trevor Wilson (R) | .25 |
| 784 | Steve Avery (R) | .40 |
| 785 | Ellis Burks | .35 |
| 786 | Melido Perez | .15 |
| 787 | Dave West (R) | .75 |
| 788 | Mike Morgan | .05 |
| 789 | Jackson: Bonus | .08 |
| 790 | Sid Fernandez | .10 |
| 791 | Jim Lindeman | .05 |
| 792 | Rafael Santana | .05 |

Card values shown here fluctuate considerably.

# 1981 Donruss....Complete Set of 605 Cards (1st printing)—Value $25.00; Complete Set of 605 Cards (2nd printing)—Value $20.00

This was Donruss' *first* baseball card set. Over 35 cards contained *errors;* they were corrected in the 2nd printing run. There is very little interest by collectors in the *variety* (error) cards; none are scarce or worth much more than ordinary cards. If a *variety* (error) is significant, it is listed and explained; if it is *minor*, it is noted by an *asterisk*. This set features the rookie cards of Tim Raines and Leon Durham. The 2½"x3½" cards were printed on thinner than usual paper stock. The checklist *cards* are *not* numbered.

LAMARR HOYT PITCHER
White Sox

CHARLIE LEIBRANDT PITCHER
Reds

LEON DURHAM INFIELD OF
Cardinals

JOHN TUDOR PITCHER
Red Sox

TIM RAINES SECOND BASE
Expos

| NO. PLAYER | MINT | NO. PLAYER | MINT | NO. PLAYER | MINT | NO. PLAYER | MINT |
|---|---|---|---|---|---|---|---|
| 1 Ozzie Smith | .40 | 65 George Foster | .25 | 131 Pete Rose* | 1.50 | 197 Rick Camp | .05 |
| 2 Rollie Fingers | .30 | 66 Jeff Burroughs | .05 | 132 Willie Stargell | .30 | 198 Andre Thornton | .10 |
| 3 Rick Wise | .05 | 67 Keith Hernandez | .40 | 133 Ed Ott | .05 | 199 Tom Veryzer | .05 |
| 4 Gene Richards | .05 | 68 Tommy Herr | .15 | 134 Jim Bibby | .05 | 200 Gary Alexander | .05 |
| 5 Alan Trammell | .35 | 69 Bob Forsch | .05 | 135 Bert Blyleven | .10 | 201 Rick Waits | .05 |
| 6 Tom Brookens | .05 | 70 John Fulgham | .05 | 136 Dave Parker | .40 | 202 Rick Manning | .05 |
| 7 Duffy Dyer* | .05 | 71 Bobby Bonds* | .12 | 137 Bill Robinson | .05 | 203 Paul Molitor | .25 |
| 8 Mark Fidrych* | .08 | 72 Rennie Stennett* | .10 | 138 Enos Cabell | .05 | 204 Jim Gantner | .05 |
| 9 Dave Rozema | .05 | 73 Joe Strain | .05 | 139 Dave Bergman | .05 | 205 Paul Mitchell | .05 |
| 10 Ricky Peters | .05 | 74 Ed Whitson | .10 | 140 J.R. Richard | .05 | 206 Reggie Cleveland | .05 |
| 11 Mike Schmidt | .90 | 75 Tom Griffin | .05 | 141 Ken Forsch | .05 | 207 Sixto Lezcano | .05 |
| 12 Willie Stargell | .40 | 76 Bill North | .05 | 142 Larry Bowa | .05 | 208 Bruce Benedict | .05 |
| 13 Tim Foli | .05 | 77 Gene Garber | .05 | 143 Frank LaCorte | .05 | 209 Rodney Scott | .05 |
| 14 Manny Sanguillen | .05 | 78 Mike Hargrove | .05 | 144 Dennis Walling | .05 | 210 John Tamargo | .05 |
| 15 Grant Jackson | .05 | 79 Dave Rosello | .05 | 145 Buddy Bell | .10 | 211 Bill Lee | .05 |
| 16 Eddie Solomon | .05 | 80 Ron Hassey | .05 | 146 Ferguson Jenkins | .10 | 212 Andre Dawson | .40 |
| 17 Omar Moreno | .05 | 81 Sid Monge | .05 | 147 Danny Darwin | .05 | 213 Rowland Office | .05 |
| 18 Joe Morgan | .35 | 82 Joe Charboneau* | .10 | 148 Johnny Grubb | .05 | 214 Carl Yastrzemski | .75 |
| 19 Rafael Landestoy | .05 | 83 Cecil Cooper | .25 | 149 Alfredo Griffin | .05 | 215 Jerry Remy | .05 |
| 20 Bruce Bochy | .05 | 84 Sal Bando | .05 | 150 Jerry Garvin | .05 | 216 Mike Torrez | .05 |
| 21 Joe Sambito | .05 | 85 Moose Haas | .05 | 151 Paul Mirabella | .05 | 217 Skip Lockwood | .05 |
| 22 Manny Trillo | .05 | 86 Mike Caldwell | .05 | 152 Rick Bosetti | .05 | 218 Fred Lynn | .25 |
| 23 Dave Smith* (R) | .25 | 87 Larry Hisle* | .10 | 153 Dick Ruthven | .05 | 219 Chris Chambliss | .08 |
| 24 Terry Puhl | .05 | 88 Luis Gomez | .05 | 154 Frank Taveras | .05 | 220 Willie Aikens | .05 |
| 25 Bump Wills | .05 | 89 Larry Parrish | .10 | 155 Craig Swan | .05 | 221 John Wathan | .05 |
| 26 John Ellis (error) | .40 | 90 Gary Carter | .50 | 156 Jeff Reardon (R) | .40 | 222 Dan Quisenberry | .30 |
| (photo of Danny Walten) | | 91 Bill Gullickson (R) | .35 | 157 Steve Henderson | .05 | 223 Willie Wilson | .15 |
| 26 John Ellis (correct) | .10 | 92 Fred Norman | .05 | 158 Jim Morrison | .05 | 224 Clint Hurdle | .05 |
| 27 Jim Kern | .05 | 93 Tom Hutton | .05 | 159 Glenn Borgmann | .05 | 225 Bob Watson | .05 |
| 28 Richie Zisk | .05 | 94 Carl Yastrzemski | .75 | 160 LaMarr Hoyt | .30 | 226 Jim Spencer | .05 |
| 29 John Mayberry | .05 | 95 Glenn Hoffman | .08 | 161 Rich Wortham | .05 | 227 Ron Guidry | .25 |
| 30 Bob Davis | .05 | 96 Dennis Eckersley | .05 | 162 Thad Bosley | .05 | 228 Reggie Jackson | .75 |
| 31 Jackson Todd | .05 | 97 Tom Burgmeier* | .10 | 163 Julio Cruz | .05 | 229 Oscar Gamble | .05 |
| 32 Al Woods | .05 | 98 Win Remmerswaal | .05 | 164 Del Unser* | .05 | 230 Jeff Cox | .05 |
| 33 Steve Carlton | .60 | 99 Bob Horner | .25 | 165 Jim Anderson | .05 | 231 Luis Tiant | .05 |
| 34 Lee Mazzilli | .05 | 100 George Brett | 1.00 | 166 Jim Beattie | .05 | 232 Rich Dauer | .05 |
| 35 John Stearns | .05 | 101 Dave Chalk | .05 | 167 Shane Rawley | .05 | 233 Dan Graham | .05 |
| 36 Roy Jackson | .08 | 102 Dennis Leonard | .05 | 168 Joe Simpson | .05 | 234 Mike Flanagan | .05 |
| 37 Mike Scott | .50 | 103 Renie Martin | .05 | 169 Rod Carew | .50 | 235 John Lowenstein | .05 |
| 38 Lamar Johnson | .05 | 104 Amos Otis | .05 | 170 Freddie Patek | .05 | 236 Benny Ayala | .05 |
| 39 Kevin Bell | .05 | 105 Graig Nettles | .15 | 171 Frank Tanana | .05 | 237 Wayne Gross | .05 |
| 40 Ed Farmer | .05 | 106 Eric Soderholm | .05 | 172 Alfredo Martinez | .05 | 238 Rick Langford | .05 |
| 41 Ross Baumgarten | .05 | 107 Tommy John | .20 | 173 Chris Knapp | .05 | 239 Tony Armas | .20 |
| 42 Leo Sutherland | .05 | 108 Tom Underwood | .05 | 174 Joe Rudi | .05 | 240 Bob Lacey* | .10 |
| 43 Danny Meyer | .05 | 109 Lou Piniella | .15 | 175 Greg Luzinski | .10 | 241 Gene Tenace | .05 |
| 44 Ron Reed | .05 | 110 Mickey Klutts | .05 | 176 Steve Garvey | .50 | 242 Bob Shirley | .05 |
| 45 Mario Mendoza | .05 | 111 Bobby Murcer | .10 | 177 Joe Ferguson | .05 | 243 Gary Lucas | .05 |
| 46 Rick Honeycutt | .05 | 112 Eddie Murray | .75 | 178 Bob Welch | .05 | 244 Jerry Turner | .05 |
| 47 Glenn Abbott | .05 | 113 Rick Dempsey | .05 | 179 Dusty Baker | .10 | 245 John Wockenfuss | .05 |
| 48 Leon Roberts | .05 | 114 Scott McGregor | .05 | 180 Rudy Law | .05 | 246 Stan Papi | .05 |
| 49 Rod Carew | .50 | 115 Ken Singleton | .05 | 181 Dave Concepcion | .15 | 247 Milt Wilcox | .05 |
| 50 Bert Campaneris | .05 | 116 Gary Roenicke | .05 | 182 Johnny Bench | .50 | 248 Dan Schatzeder | .05 |
| 51 Tom Donahue | .10 | 117 Dave Revering | .05 | 183 Mike LaCoss | .05 | 249 Steve Kemp | .08 |
| 52 Dave Frost | .05 | 118 Mike Norris | .05 | 184 Ken Griffey | .10 | 250 Jim Lentine | .05 |
| 53 Ed Halicki | .05 | 119 Rickey Henderson | .75 | 185 Dave Collins | .05 | 251 Pete Rose | 1.25 |
| 54 Dan Ford | .05 | 120 Mike Heath | .05 | 186 Brian Asselstine | .05 | 252 Bill Madlock | .25 |
| 55 Garry Maddox | .05 | 121 Dave Cash | .05 | 187 Garry Templeton | .10 | 253 Dale Berra | .05 |
| 56 Steve Garvey* | .65 | 122 Randy Jones | .05 | 188 Mike Phillips | .05 | 254 Kent Tekulve | .05 |
| 57 Bill Russell | .05 | 123 Eric Rasmussen | .05 | 189 Pete Vuckovich | .08 | 255 Enrique Romo | .05 |
| 58 Don Sutton | .20 | 124 Jerry Mumphrey | .05 | 190 John Urrea | .05 | 256 Mike Easler | .05 |
| 59 Reggie Smith | .10 | 125 Richie Hebner | .05 | 191 Tony Scott | .05 | 257 Chuck Tanner (Mgr.) | .05 |
| 60 Rick Monday | .05 | 126 Mark Wagner | .05 | 192 Darrell Evans | .10 | 258 Art Howe | .05 |
| 61 Ray Knight | .05 | 127 Jack Morris | .30 | 193 Milt May | .05 | 259 Alan Ashby | .05 |
| 62 Johnny Bench | .50 | 128 Dan Petry | .25 | 194 Bob Knepper | .05 | 260 Nolan Ryan | .50 |
| 63 Mario Soto | .15 | 129 Bruce Robbins | .05 | 195 Randy Moffitt | .05 | 261 Vern Ruhle (error) | .40 |
| 64 Doug Bair | .05 | 130 Champ Summers | .05 | 196 Larry Herndon | .05 | (Photo of Ken Forsch) | |

| NO. PLAYER | MINT |
|---|---|
| 261 Vern Ruhle (correct) | .10 |
| 262 Bob Boone | .08 |
| 263 Cesar Cedeno | .08 |
| 264 Jeff Leonard | .15 |
| 265 Pat Putnam | .05 |
| 266 John Matlack | .05 |
| 267 Dave Rajsich | .05 |
| 268 Billy Sample | .05 |
| 269 Damaso Garcia (R) | .30 |
| 270 Tom Buskey | .05 |
| 271 Joey McLaughlin | .05 |
| 272 Barry Bonnell | .05 |
| 273 Tug McGraw | .08 |
| 274 Mike Jorgensen | .05 |
| 275 Pat Zachry | .05 |
| 276 Neil Allen | .05 |
| 277 Joel Youngblood | .05 |
| 278 Greg Pryor | .05 |
| 279 Britt Burns (R) | .25 |
| 280 Rich Dotson (R) | .40 |
| 281 Chet Lemon | .10 |
| 282 Rusty Kuntz | .05 |
| 283 Ted Cox | .05 |
| 284 Sparky Lyle | .08 |
| 285 Larry Cox | .05 |
| 286 Floyd Bannister | .05 |
| 287 Byron McLaughlin | .05 |
| 288 Rodney Craig | .05 |
| 289 Bob Grich | .08 |
| 290 Dickie Thon | .10 |
| 291 Mark Clear | .05 |
| 292 Dave Lemanczyk | .05 |
| 293 Jason Thompson | .05 |
| 294 Rick Miller | .05 |
| 295 Lonnie Smith | .08 |
| 296 Ron Cey | .15 |
| 297 Steve Yeager | .05 |
| 298 Bobby Castillo | .05 |
| 299 Manny Mota | .05 |
| 300 Jay Johnstone | .05 |
| 301 Dan Driessen | .05 |
| 302 Joe Nolan | .05 |
| 303 Paul Householder | .08 |
| 304 Harry Spilman | .05 |
| 305 Cesar Geronimo | .05 |
| 306 Gary Matthews* | .10 |
| 307 Ken Reitz | .05 |
| 308 Ted Simmons | .10 |
| 309 John Littlefield | .05 |
| 310 George Frazier | .05 |
| 311 Dane Iorg | .05 |
| 312 Mike Ivie | .05 |
| 313 Dennis Littlejohn | .05 |
| 314 Gary LaVelle | .05 |
| 315 Jack Clark | .40 |
| 316 Jim Wohlford | .05 |
| 317 Rick Matula | .05 |
| 318 Toby Harrah | .05 |
| 319 Duane Kuiper* | .10 |
| 320 Len Barker | .05 |
| 321 Victor Cruz | .05 |
| 322 Dell Alston | .05 |
| 323 Robin Yount | .50 |
| 324 Charlie Moore | .05 |
| 325 Lary Sorensen | .05 |
| 326 Gorman Thomas* | .15 |
| 327 Bob Rodgers | .05 |
| 328 Phil Niekro | .30 |
| 329 Chris Speier | .05 |
| 330 Steve Rogers* | .10 |
| 331 Woodie Fryman | .05 |
| 332 Warren Cromartie | .05 |
| 333 Jerry White | .05 |
| 334 Tony Perez | .20 |
| 335 Carlton Fisk | .30 |
| 336 Dick Drago | .05 |
| 337 Steve Renko | .05 |
| 338 Jim Rice | .40 |
| 339 Jerry Royster | .05 |
| 340 Frank White | .05 |
| 341 Jamie Quirk | .05 |
| 342 Paul Splittorff* | .05 |
| 343 Marty Pattin | .05 |
| 344 Pete LaCock | .05 |
| 345 Willie Randolph | .10 |
| 346 Rick Cerone | .05 |
| 347 Rich Gossage | .25 |

| NO. PLAYER | MINT |
|---|---|
| 348 Reggie Jackson | .75 |
| 349 Ruppert Jones | .05 |
| 350 Dave McKay | .05 |
| 351 Yogi Berra | .20 |
| 352 Doug DeCinces | .15 |
| 353 Jim Palmer | .30 |
| 354 Tippy Martinez | .05 |
| 355 Al Bumbry | .05 |
| 356 Earl Weaver (Mgr.) | .10 |
| 357 Rob Picciolo* | .10 |
| 358 Matt Keough | .05 |
| 359 Dwayne Murphy | .05 |
| 360 Brian Kingman | .05 |
| 361 Bill Fahey | .05 |
| 362 Steve Mura | .05 |
| 363 Dennis Kinney | .05 |
| 364 Dave Winfield | .60 |
| 365 Lou Whitaker | .30 |
| 366 Lance Parrish | .40 |
| 367 Tim Corcoran | .05 |
| 368 Pat Underwood | .05 |
| 369 Al Cowens | .05 |
| 370 Sparky Anderson (Mgr.) | .05 |
| 371 Pete Rose | 1.25 |
| 372 Phil Garner | .05 |
| 373 Steve Nicosia | .05 |
| 374 John Candelaria | .05 |
| 375 Don Robinson | .05 |
| 376 Lee Lacy | .05 |
| 377 John Milner | .05 |
| 378 Craig Reynolds | .05 |
| 379 Luis Pujols* | .10 |
| 380 Joe Niekro | .10 |
| 381 Joaquin Andujar | .25 |
| 382 Keith Moreland (R) | .40 |
| 383 Jose Cruz | .15 |
| 384 Bill Virdon (Mgr.) | .05 |
| 385 Jim Sundberg | .05 |
| 386 Doc Medich | .05 |
| 387 Al Oliver | .20 |
| 388 Jim Norris | .05 |
| 389 Bob Bailor | .05 |
| 390 Ernie Whitt | .05 |
| 391 Otto Velez | .05 |
| 392 Roy Howell | .05 |
| 393 Bob Walk | .15 |
| 394 Doug Flynn | .05 |
| 395 Pete Falcone | .05 |
| 396 Tom Hausman | .05 |
| 397 Elliott Maddox | .05 |
| 398 Mike Squires | .05 |
| 399 Marvis Foley | .05 |
| 400 Steve Trout | .05 |
| 401 Wayne Nordhagen | .05 |
| 402 Tony LaRussa (Mgr.) | .05 |
| 403 Bruce Bochte | .05 |
| 404 Bake McBride | .05 |
| 405 Jerry Narron | .05 |
| 406 Rob Dressler | .05 |
| 407 Dave Heaverlo | .05 |
| 408 Tom Paciorek | .05 |
| 409 Carney Lansford | .15 |
| 410 Brian Downing | .05 |
| 411 Don Aase | .05 |
| 412 Jim Barr | .05 |
| 413 Don Baylor | .25 |
| 414 Jim Fregosi (Mgr.) | .05 |
| 415 Dallas Green (Mgr.) | .05 |
| 416 Dave Lopes | .10 |
| 417 Jerry Reuss | .05 |
| 418 Rick Sutcliffe | .40 |
| 419 Derrel Thomas | .05 |
| 420 Tommy Lasorda (Mgr.) | .15 |
| 421 Charlie Leibrandt (R) | .40 |
| 422 Tom Seaver | .40 |
| 423 Ron Oester | .05 |
| 424 Junior Kennedy | .05 |
| 425 Tom Seaver | .40 |
| 426 Bobby Cox (Mgr.) | .05 |
| 427 Leon Durham (R) | .60 |
| 428 Terry Kennedy | .10 |
| 429 Silvio Martinez | .05 |
| 430 George Hendrick | .05 |
| 431 R. Schoendienst (Mgr.) | .05 |
| 432 John LeMaster | .05 |
| 433 Vida Blue | .05 |

| NO. PLAYER | MINT |
|---|---|
| 434 John Montefusco | .05 |
| 435 Terry Whitfield | .05 |
| 436 Dave Bristol (Mgr.) | .05 |
| 437 Dale Murphy | 1.25 |
| 438 Jerry Dybzinski | .05 |
| 439 Jorge Orta | .05 |
| 440 Wayne Garland | .05 |
| 441 Miguel Dilone | .05 |
| 442 Dave Garcia (Mgr.) | .05 |
| 443 Don Money | .05 |
| 444 Buck Martinez* | .10 |
| 445 Jerry Augustine | .05 |
| 446 Ben Oglivie | .10 |
| 447 Jim Slaton | .05 |
| 448 Doyle Alexander | .05 |
| 449 Tony Bernazard | .05 |
| 450 Scott Sanderson | .05 |
| 451 Dave Palmer | .05 |
| 452 Stan Bahnsen | .05 |
| 453 Dick Williams (Mgr.) | .05 |
| 454 Rick Burleson | .05 |
| 455 Gary Allenson | .05 |
| 456 Bob Stanley | .05 |
| 457 John Tudor (R) | 1.25 |
| 458 Dwight Evans | .15 |
| 459 Glenn Hubbard | .05 |
| 460 U.L. Washington | .05 |
| 461 Larry Gura | .05 |
| 462 Rich Gale | .05 |
| 463 Hal McRae | .05 |
| 464 Jim Frey (Mgr.) | .05 |
| 465 Bucky Dent | .05 |
| 466 Dennis Werth | .05 |
| 467 Ron Davis | .05 |
| 468 Reggie Jackson | .75 |
| 469 Bobby Brown | .05 |
| 470 Mike Davis (R) | .30 |
| 471 Gaylord Perry | .30 |
| 472 Mark Belanger | .05 |
| 473 Jim Palmer | .30 |
| 474 Sammy Stewart | .05 |
| 475 Tim Stoddard | .05 |
| 476 Steve Stone | .05 |
| 477 Jeff Newman | .05 |
| 478 Steve McCatty | .05 |
| 479 Billy Martin (Mgr.) | .15 |
| 480 Mitchell Page | .05 |
| 481 S. Carlton (Cy Young) | .40 |
| 482 Bill Buckner | .15 |
| 483 Ivan DeJesus* | .10 |
| 484 Cliff Johnson | .05 |
| 485 Lenny Randle | .05 |
| 486 Larry Milbourne | .05 |
| 487 Roy Smalley | .05 |
| 488 John Castino | .05 |
| 489 Ron Jackson | .05 |
| 490 Dave Roberts* | .05 |
| 491 George Brett (MVP) | .60 |
| 492 Mike Cubbage | .05 |
| 493 Rob Wilfong | .05 |
| 494 Danny Goodwin | .05 |
| 495 Jose Morales | .05 |
| 496 Mickey Rivers | .05 |
| 497 Mike Edwards | .05 |
| 498 Mike Sadek | .05 |
| 499 Lenn Sakata | .05 |
| 500 Gene Michael (Mgr.) | .05 |
| 501 Dave Roberts | .05 |
| 502 Steve Dillard | .05 |
| 503 Jim Essian | .05 |
| 504 Rance Mulliniks | .05 |
| 505 Darrell Porter | .10 |
| 506 Joe Torre (Mgr.) | .05 |
| 507 Terry Crowley | .05 |
| 508 Bill Travers | .05 |
| 509 Nelson Norman | .05 |
| 510 Bob McClure | .05 |
| 511 Steve Howe (R) | .20 |
| 512 Dave Rader | .05 |
| 513 Mick Kelleher | .05 |
| 514 Kiko Garcia | .05 |
| 515 Larry Biittner | .05 |
| 516 Willie Norwood* | .05 |
| 517 Bo Diaz | .10 |
| 518 Juan Beniqez | .05 |
| 519 Scot Thompson | .05 |

| NO. PLAYER | MINT |
|---|---|
| 520 Jim Tracy | .05 |
| 521 Carlos Lezcano | .05 |
| 522 Joe Amalfitano | .05 |
| 523 Preston Hanna | .05 |
| 524 Ray Burris* | .10 |
| 525 Broderick Perkins | .05 |
| 526 Mickey Hatcher | .05 |
| 527 John Goryl (Mgr.) | .05 |
| 528 Dick Davis | .05 |
| 529 Butch Wynegar | .05 |
| 530 Sal Butera | .05 |
| 531 Jerry Koosman | .05 |
| 532 Jeff Zahn* | .10 |
| 533 Dennis Martinez | .05 |
| 534 Gary Thomasson | .05 |
| 535 Steve Macko | .05 |
| 536 Jim Kaat | .15 |
| 537 Best Hitters: | 1.00 |
| George Brett, Rod Carew | |
| 538 Tim Raines (R) | 5.00 |
| 539 Keith Smith | .05 |
| 540 Ken Macha | .05 |
| 541 Burt Hooton | .05 |
| 542 Butch Hobson | .05 |
| 543 Bill Stein | .05 |
| 544 Dave Stapleton (R) | .15 |
| 545 Bob Pate | .05 |
| 546 Doug Corbett | .08 |
| 547 Darrell Jackson | .05 |
| 548 Pete Redfern | .05 |
| 549 Roger Erickson | .05 |
| 550 Al Hrabosky | .05 |
| 551 Dick Tidrow | .05 |
| 552 Dave Ford | .05 |
| 553 Dave Kingman | .15 |
| 554 Mike Vail* | .10 |
| 555 Jerry Martin* | .10 |
| 556 Jesus Figueroa* | .10 |
| 557 Don Stanhouse | .05 |
| 558 Barry Foote | .05 |
| 559 Tim Blackwell | .05 |
| 560 Bruce Sutter | .25 |
| 561 Rick Reuschel | .05 |
| 562 Lynn McGlothen | .05 |
| 563 Bob Owchinko* | .10 |
| 564 John Verhoeven | .05 |
| 565 Ken Landreaux | .05 |
| 566 Glenn Adams* | .10 |
| 567 Hosken Powell | .05 |
| 568 Dick Noles | .05 |
| 569 Danny Ainge (R) | .30 |
| 570 Bobby Mattick (Mgr.) | .05 |
| 571 Joe LeFebvre (R) | .15 |
| 572 Bobby Clark | .05 |
| 573 Dennis Lamp | .05 |
| 574 Randy Lerch | .05 |
| 575 Mookie Wilson (R) | .35 |
| 576 Ron LeFlore | .05 |
| 577 Jim Dwyer | .05 |
| 578 Bill Castro | .05 |
| 579 Greg Minton | .05 |
| 580 Mark Littell | .05 |
| 581 Andy Hassler | .05 |
| 582 Dave Stieb | .25 |
| 583 Ken Oberkfell | .05 |
| 584 Larry Bradford | .05 |
| 585 Fred Stanley | .05 |
| 586 Bill Caudill | .10 |
| 587 Doug Capilla | .05 |
| 588 George Riley | .05 |
| 589 Willie Hernandez | .25 |
| 590 Mike Schmidt (MVP) | .50 |
| 591 Steve Stone (Cy Young) | .10 |
| 592 Rick Sofield | .05 |
| 593 Bombo Rivera | .05 |
| 594 Gary Ward | .05 |
| 595 Dave Edwards* | .10 |
| 596 Mike Proly | .05 |
| 597 Tommy Boggs | .05 |
| 598 Greg Gross | .05 |
| 599 Elias Sosa | .05 |
| 600 Pat Kelly | .05 |
| — Checklist No. 1* | .10 |
| — Checklist No. 2 | .10 |
| — Checklist No. 3* | .10 |
| — Checklist No. 4* | .10 |
| — Checklist No. 5* | .10 |

# 1982 Donruss....Complete Set of 660 Cards—Value $30.00

Features the rookie cards of Cal Ripken and Kent Hrbek. Several errors were corrected; none are scarce or worth much more than ordinary cards. If a *variety* (error) is significant, it is listed and explained; if it is minor, it is noted by an *asterisk*. The *checklist* cards are *not* numbered.

| NO. | PLAYER | MINT |
|---|---|---|
| **No. 1 to 26—Diamond Kings** | | |
| 1 | Pete Rose (DK) | 1.25 |
| 2 | Gary Carter (DK) | .50 |
| 3 | Steve Garvey (DK) | .50 |
| 4 | Vida Blue (DK) | .10 |
| 5 | Alan Trammell* (DK) | .30 |
| 6 | Len Barker (DK) | .10 |
| 7 | Dwight Evans (DK) | .15 |
| 8 | Rod Carew (DK) | .40 |
| 9 | George Hendrick (DK) | .10 |
| 10 | Phil Niekro (DK) | .25 |
| 11 | Richie Zisk (DK) | .10 |
| 12 | Dave Parker (DK) | .30 |
| 13 | Nolan Ryan (DK) | .40 |
| 14 | Ivan DeJesus (DK) | .10 |
| 15 | George Brett (DK) | .75 |
| 16 | Tom Seaver (DK) | .50 |
| 17 | Dave Kingman (DK) | .10 |
| 18 | Dave Winfield (DK) | .50 |
| 19 | Mike Norris (DK) | .10 |
| 20 | Carlton Fisk (DK) | .30 |
| 21 | Ozzie Smith (DK) | .15 |
| 22 | Roy Smalley (DK) | .10 |
| 23 | Buddy Bell (DK) | .10 |
| 24 | Ken Singleton (DK) | .10 |
| 25 | John Mayberry (DK) | .10 |
| 26 | Garmon Thomas (DK) | .10 |
| 27 | Earl Weaver (Mgr.) | .10 |
| 28 | Rollie Fingers | .20 |
| 29 | Sparky Anderson (Mgr.) | .10 |
| 30 | Dennis Eckersley | .05 |
| 31 | Dave Winfield | .50 |
| 32 | Burt Hooton | .05 |
| 33 | Rick Waits | .05 |
| 34 | George Brett | .75 |
| 35 | Steve McCatty | .05 |
| 36 | Steve Rogers | .05 |
| 37 | Bill Stein | .05 |
| 38 | Steve Renko | .05 |
| 39 | Mike Squires | .05 |
| 40 | George Hendrick | .08 |
| 41 | Bob Knepper | .12 |
| 42 | Steve Carlton | .50 |
| 43 | Larry Biittner | .05 |
| 44 | Chris Welsh | .07 |
| 45 | Steve Nicosia | .05 |
| 46 | Jack Clark | .35 |
| 47 | Chris Chambliss | .05 |
| 48 | Ivan DeJesus | .05 |
| 49 | Lee Mazzilli | .05 |
| 50 | Julio Cruz | .05 |
| 51 | Pete Redfern | .05 |
| 52 | Dave Stieb | .25 |
| 53 | Doug Corbett | .05 |
| 54 | Jorge Bell (R) | 6.00 |
| 55 | Joe Simpson | .05 |
| 56 | Rusty Staub | .10 |
| 57 | Hector Cruz | .05 |
| 58 | Claudell Washington | .10 |
| 59 | Enrique Romo | .05 |
| 60 | Gary Lavelle | .05 |
| 61 | Tim Flannery | .05 |
| 62 | Joe Nolan | .05 |
| 63 | Larry Bowa | .05 |
| 64 | Sixto Lezcano | .05 |
| 65 | Joe Sambito | .05 |

| NO. | PLAYER | MINT |
|---|---|---|
| 66 | Bruce Kison | .05 |
| 67 | Wayne Nordhagen | .05 |
| 68 | Woodie Fryman | .05 |
| 69 | Billy Sample | .05 |
| 70 | Amos Otis | .10 |
| 71 | Matt Keough | .05 |
| 72 | Toby Harrah | .05 |
| 73 | Dave Righetti (R) | 1.50 |
| 74 | Carl Yastrzemski | .75 |
| 75 | Bob Welch | .10 |
| 76 | Alan Trammell* | .35 |
| 77 | Rick Dempsey | .05 |
| 78 | Paul Molitor | .30 |
| 79 | Dennis Martinez | .05 |
| 80 | Jim Slaton | .05 |
| 81 | Champ Summers | .05 |
| 82 | Carney Lansford | .10 |
| 83 | Barry Foote | .05 |
| 84 | Steve Garvey | .50 |
| 85 | Rick Manning | .05 |
| 86 | John Wathan | .05 |
| 87 | Brian Kingman | .05 |
| 88 | Andre Dawson | .40 |
| 89 | Jim Kern | .05 |
| 90 | Bobby Grich | .05 |
| 91 | Bob Forsch | .05 |
| 92 | Art Howe | .05 |
| 93 | Marty Bystrom | .05 |
| 94 | Ozzie Smith | .25 |
| 95 | Dave Parker | .30 |
| 96 | Doyle Alexander | .05 |
| 97 | Al Hrabosky | .05 |
| 98 | Frank Taveras | .05 |
| 99 | Tim Blackwell | .05 |
| 100 | Floyd Bannister | .05 |
| 101 | Alfredo Griffin | .05 |
| 102 | Dave Engle | .05 |
| 103 | Mario Soto | .15 |
| 104 | Ross Baumgarten | .05 |
| 105 | Ken Singleton | .10 |
| 106 | Ted Simmons | .15 |
| 107 | Jack Morris | .25 |
| 108 | Bob Watson | .05 |
| 109 | Dwight Evans | .15 |
| 110 | Tommy LaSorda (Mgr.) | .10 |
| 111 | Bert Blyleven | .15 |
| 112 | Dan Quisenberry | .25 |
| 113 | Rickey Henderson | .75 |
| 114 | Gary Carter | .50 |
| 115 | Brian Downing | .05 |
| 116 | Al Oliver | .15 |
| 117 | LaMarr Hoyt | .15 |
| 118 | Cesar Cedeno | .10 |
| 119 | Keith Moreland | .05 |
| 120 | Bob Shirley | .05 |
| 121 | Terry Kennedy | .10 |
| 122 | Frank Pastore | .05 |
| 123 | Gene Garber | .05 |
| 124 | Tony Pena | .25 |
| 125 | Allen Ripley | .05 |
| 126 | Randy Martz | .05 |
| 127 | Richie Zisk | .05 |
| 128 | Mike Scott | .35 |
| 129 | Lloyd Moseby | .15 |
| 130 | Rob Wilfong | .05 |
| 131 | Tim Stoddard | .05 |

| NO. | PLAYER | MINT |
|---|---|---|
| 132 | Gorman Thomas | .15 |
| 133 | Dan Petry | .15 |
| 134 | Bob Stanley | .05 |
| 135 | Lou Piniella | .10 |
| 136 | Pedro Guerrero | .35 |
| 137 | Len Barker | .05 |
| 138 | Richard Gale | .05 |
| 139 | Wayne Gross | .05 |
| 140 | Tim Wallach (R) | 1.00 |
| 141 | Gene Mauch | .05 |
| 142 | Doc Medich | .05 |
| 143 | Tony Bernazard | .05 |
| 144 | Bill Virdon (Mgr.) | .05 |
| 145 | John Littlefield | .05 |
| 146 | Dave Bergman | .05 |
| 147 | Dick Davis | .05 |
| 148 | Tom Seaver | .50 |
| 149 | Matt Sinatro | .07 |
| 150 | Chuck Tanner (Mgr.) | .05 |
| 151 | Leon Durham | .25 |
| 152 | Gene Tenace | .05 |
| 153 | Al Bumbry | .05 |
| 154 | Mark Brouhard | .05 |
| 155 | Rick Peters | .05 |
| 156 | Jerry Remy | .05 |
| 157 | Rick Reuschel | .10 |
| 158 | Steve Howe | .05 |
| 159 | Alan Bannister | .05 |
| 160 | U.L. Wasington | .05 |
| 161 | Rick Langford | .05 |
| 162 | Bill Gullickson | .05 |
| 163 | Mark Wagner | .05 |
| 164 | Geoff Zahn | .05 |
| 165 | Ron LeFlore | .05 |
| 166 | Dane Iorg | .05 |
| 167 | Joe Niekro | .10 |
| 168 | Pete Rose | 1.00 |
| 169 | Dave Collins | .05 |
| 170 | Rick Wise | .05 |
| 171 | Jim Bibby | .05 |
| 172 | Larry Herndon | .05 |
| 173 | Bob Horner | .25 |
| 174 | Steve Dillard | .05 |
| 175 | Mookie Wilson | .10 |
| 176 | Danny Meyer | .05 |
| 177 | Fernando Arroyo | .05 |
| 178 | Jackson Todd | .05 |
| 179 | Darrell Jackson | .05 |
| 180 | Al Woods | .05 |
| 181 | Jim Anderson | .05 |
| 182 | Dave Kingman | .15 |
| 183 | Steve Henderson | .05 |
| 184 | Brian Asselstine | .05 |
| 185 | Rod Scurry | .05 |
| 186 | Fred Breining | .08 |
| 187 | Danny Boone | .05 |
| 188 | Junior Kennedy | .05 |
| 189 | Sparky Lyle | .05 |
| 190 | Whitey Herzog (Mgr.) | .05 |
| 191 | Dave Smith | .05 |
| 192 | Ed Ott | .05 |
| 193 | Greg Luzinski | .10 |
| 194 | Bill Lee | .05 |
| 195 | Don Zimmer (Mgr.) | .05 |
| 196 | Hal McRae | .05 |
| 197 | Mike Norris | .05 |

| NO. | PLAYER | MINT |
|---|---|---|
| 198 | Duane Kuiper | .05 |
| 199 | Rick Cerone | .05 |
| 200 | Jim Rice | .40 |
| 201 | Steve Yeager | .05 |
| 202 | Tom Brookens | .05 |
| 203 | Jose Morales | .05 |
| 204 | Roy Howell | .05 |
| 205 | Tippy Martinez | .05 |
| 206 | Moose Haas | .05 |
| 207 | Al Cowens | .05 |
| 208 | Dave Stapleton | .05 |
| 209 | Bucky Dent | .05 |
| 210 | Ron Cey | .15 |
| 211 | Jorge Orta | .05 |
| 212 | Jamie Quirk | .05 |
| 213 | Jeff Jones | .05 |
| 214 | Tim Raines | .75 |
| 215 | Jon Matlack | .05 |
| 216 | Rod Carew | .45 |
| 217 | Jim Kaat | .10 |
| 218 | Joe Pittman | .05 |
| 219 | Larry Christenson | .05 |
| 220 | Juan Bonilla | .07 |
| 221 | Mike Easler | .05 |
| 222 | Vida Blue | .05 |
| 223 | Rick Camp | .05 |
| 224 | Mike Jorgensen | .05 |
| 225 | Jody Davis (R) | .40 |
| 226 | Mike Parrott | .05 |
| 227 | Jim Clancy | .05 |
| 228 | Hosken Powell | .05 |
| 229 | Tom Hume | .05 |
| 230 | Britt Burns | .05 |
| 231 | Jim Palmer | .30 |
| 232 | Bob Rodgers (Mgr.) | .05 |
| 233 | Milt Wilcox | .05 |
| 234 | Dave Revering | .05 |
| 235 | Mike Torrez | .05 |
| 236 | Bobby Castillo | .05 |
| 237 | Von Hayes (R) | .75 |
| 238 | Renie Martin | .05 |
| 239 | Dwayne Murphy | .05 |
| 240 | Rodney Scott | .05 |
| 241 | Freddie Patek | .05 |
| 242 | Mickey Rivers | .05 |
| 243 | Steve Trout | .05 |
| 244 | Jose Cruz | .10 |
| 245 | Manny Trillo | .05 |
| 246 | Lary Sorensen | .05 |
| 247 | Dave Edwards | .05 |
| 248 | Dan Driessen | .05 |
| 249 | Tommy Boggs | .05 |
| 250 | Dale Berra | .05 |
| 251 | Ed Whitson | .05 |
| 252 | Lee Smith (R) | .50 |
| 253 | Tom Paciorek | .05 |
| 254 | Pat Zachry | .05 |
| 255 | Luis Leal | .05 |
| 256 | John Castino | .05 |
| 257 | Rich Dauer | .05 |
| 258 | Cecil Cooper | .20 |
| 259 | Dave Rozema | .05 |
| 260 | John Tudor | .10 |
| 261 | Jerry Mumphrey | .05 |
| 262 | Jay Johnstone | .05 |
| 263 | Bo Diaz | .05 |

| NO. | PLAYER | MINT |
|---|---|---|
| 264 | Dennis Leonard | .05 |
| 265 | Jim Spencer | .05 |
| 266 | Jim Milner | .05 |
| 267 | Don Aase | .05 |
| 268 | Jim Sundberg | .05 |
| 269 | Lamar Johnson | .05 |
| 270 | Frank LaCorte | .05 |
| 271 | Barry Evans | .05 |
| 272 | Enos Cabell | .05 |
| 273 | Del Unser | .05 |
| 274 | George Foster | .20 |
| 275 | Brett Butler (R) | .50 |
| 276 | Lee Lacy | .05 |
| 277 | Ken Reitz | .05 |
| 278 | Keith Hernandez | .40 |
| 279 | Doug DeCinces | .10 |
| 280 | Charlie Moore | .05 |
| 281 | Lance Parrish | .30 |
| 282 | Ralph Houk (Mgr.) | .05 |
| 283 | Rich Gossage | .20 |
| 284 | Jerry Reuss | .05 |
| 285 | Mike Stanton | .05 |
| 286 | Frank White | .05 |
| 287 | Bob Owchinko | .05 |
| 288 | Scott Sanderson | .05 |
| 289 | Bump Wills | .05 |
| 290 | Dave Frost | .05 |
| 291 | Chet Lemon | .05 |
| 292 | Tito Landrum | .05 |
| 293 | Vern Ruhle | .05 |
| 294 | Mike Schmidt | .75 |
| 295 | San Mejias | .05 |
| 296 | Gary Lucas | .05 |
| 297 | John Candelaria | .05 |
| 298 | Jerry Martin | .05 |
| 299 | Dale Murphy | 1.00 |
| 300 | Mike Lum | .05 |
| 301 | Tom Hausman | .05 |
| 302 | Glenn Abbott | .05 |
| 303 | Roger Erickson | .05 |
| 304 | Otto Velez | .05 |
| 305 | Danny Goodwin | .05 |
| 306 | John Mayberry | .05 |
| 307 | Lenny Randle | .05 |
| 308 | Bob Bailor | .05 |
| 309 | Jerry Morales | .05 |
| 310 | Rufino Linares | .05 |
| 311 | Kent Tekulve | .05 |
| 312 | Joe Morgan | .30 |
| 313 | John Urrea | .05 |
| 314 | Paul Householder | .05 |
| 315 | Garry Maddox | .05 |
| 316 | Mike Ramsey | .05 |
| 317 | Alan Ashby | .05 |
| 318 | Bob Clark | .05 |
| 319 | Tony LaRussa (Mgr.) | .05 |
| 320 | Charlie Lea | .05 |
| 321 | Danny Darwin | .05 |
| 322 | Cesar Geronimo | .05 |
| 323 | Tom Underwood | .05 |
| 324 | Andre Thornton | .10 |
| 325 | Rudy May | .05 |
| 326 | Frank Tanana | .05 |
| 327 | Davey Lopes | .05 |
| 328 | Richie Hebner | .05 |
| 329 | Mike Flanagan | .08 |
| 330 | Mike Caldwell | .05 |
| 331 | Scott McGregor | .05 |
| 332 | Jerry Augustine | .05 |
| 333 | Stan Papi | .05 |
| 334 | Rick Miller | .05 |
| 335 | Graig Nettles | .15 |
| 336 | Dusty Baker | .10 |
| 337 | Dave Garcia (Mgr.) | .05 |
| 338 | Larry Gura | .05 |
| 339 | Cliff Johnson | .05 |
| 340 | Warren Cromartie | .05 |
| 341 | Steve Comer | .05 |
| 342 | Rick Burleson | .05 |
| 343 | John Martin | .05 |
| 344 | Craig Reynolds | .05 |
| 345 | Mike Proly | .05 |
| 346 | Ruppert Jones | .05 |
| 347 | Omar Moreno | .05 |
| 348 | Greg Minton | .05 |
| 349 | Rick Mahler (R) | .25 |
| 350 | Alex Trevino | .05 |
| 351 | Mike Krukow | .05 |
| 352 | Shane Rawley | .50 |
| | (photo of Jim Anderson) | |
| 352 | Shane Rawley (correct) | .10 |
| 353 | Garth Iorg | .05 |
| 354 | Pete Mackanin | .05 |
| 355 | Paul Moskau | .05 |
| 356 | Rich Dotson | .05 |
| 357 | Steve Stone | .05 |
| 358 | Larry Hisle | .05 |
| 359 | Aurelio Lopez | .05 |
| 360 | Oscar Gamble | .05 |
| 361 | Tom Burgmeier | .05 |
| 362 | Terry Forster | .08 |
| 363 | Joe Charboneau | .05 |
| 364 | Ken Brett | .05 |
| 365 | Tony Armas | .15 |
| 366 | Chris Speier | .05 |
| 367 | Fred Lynn | .20 |
| 368 | Buddy Bell | .10 |
| 369 | Jim Essian | .05 |
| 370 | Terry Puhl | .05 |
| 371 | Greg Gross | .05 |
| 372 | Bruce Sutter | .25 |
| 373 | Joe LeFebvre | .05 |
| 374 | Ray Knight | .05 |
| 375 | Bruce Benedict | .05 |
| 376 | Tim Foli | .05 |
| 377 | Al Holland | .05 |
| 378 | Ken Kravec | .05 |
| 379 | Jeff Burroughs | .05 |
| 380 | Pete Falcone | .05 |
| 381 | Ernie Whitt | .05 |
| 382 | Brad Havens | .05 |
| 383 | Terry Crowley | .05 |
| 384 | Don Money | .05 |
| 385 | Dan Schatzeder | .05 |
| 386 | Gary Allenson | .05 |
| 387 | Yogi Berra | .15 |
| 388 | Ken Landreaux | .05 |
| 389 | Mike Hargrove | .05 |
| 390 | Darryl Motley | .20 |
| 391 | Dave McKay | .05 |
| 392 | Stan Bahnsen | .05 |
| 393 | Ken Forsch | .05 |
| 394 | Mario Mendoza | .05 |
| 395 | Jim Morrison | .05 |
| 396 | Mike Ivie | .05 |
| 397 | Broderick Perkins | .05 |
| 398 | Darrell Evans | .10 |
| 399 | Ron Reed | .05 |
| 400 | Johnny Bench | .60 |
| 401 | Steve Bedrosian (R) | .75 |
| 402 | Bill Robinson | .05 |
| 403 | Bill Buckner | .15 |
| 404 | Ken Oberkfell | .05 |
| 405 | Cal Ripken Jr. (R) | 8.00 |
| 406 | Jim Gantner | .05 |
| 407 | Kirk Gibson | 1.25 |
| 408 | Tony Perez | .15 |
| 409 | Tommy John | .15 |
| 410 | Dave Stewart (R) | 1.00 |
| 411 | Dan Spillner | .05 |
| 412 | Willie Aikens | .05 |
| 413 | Mike Heath | .05 |
| 414 | Ray Burris | .05 |
| 415 | Leon Roberts | .05 |
| 416 | Mike Witt (R) | .75 |
| 417 | Bobby Molinaro | .05 |
| 418 | Steve Braun | .05 |
| 419 | Nolan Ryan | .50 |
| 420 | Tug McGraw | .05 |
| 421 | Dave Concepcion | .10 |
| 422 | Juan Eichelberger | .45 |
| | (photo of Gary Lucas) | |
| 422 | J. Eichelberger (correct) | .05 |
| 423 | Rick Rhoden | .05 |
| 424 | Frank Robinson (Mgr.) | .15 |
| 425 | Eddie Miller | .05 |
| 426 | Bill Caudill | .05 |
| 427 | Doug Flynn | .05 |
| 428 | Larry Andersen | .05 |
| 429 | Al Williams | .05 |
| 430 | Jerry Garvin | .05 |
| 431 | Glenn Adams | .05 |
| 432 | Barry Bonnell | .05 |
| 433 | Jerry Narron | .05 |
| 434 | John Stearns | .05 |
| 435 | Mike Tyson | .05 |
| 436 | Glenn Hubbard | .05 |
| 437 | Eddie Solomon | .05 |
| 438 | Jeff Leonard | .05 |
| 439 | Randy Bass | .05 |
| 440 | Mike LaCoss | .05 |
| 441 | Gary Matthews | .10 |
| 442 | Mark Littell | .05 |
| 443 | Don Sutton | .35 |
| 444 | John Harris | .05 |
| 445 | Vada Pinson | .05 |
| 446 | Elias Sosa | .05 |
| 447 | Charlie Hough | .05 |
| 448 | Willie Wilson | .20 |
| 449 | Fred Stanley | .05 |
| 450 | Tommy Veryzer | .05 |
| 451 | Ron Davis | .05 |
| 452 | Mark Clear | .05 |
| 453 | Bill Russell | .05 |
| 454 | Lou Whitaker | .20 |
| 455 | Dan Graham | .05 |
| 456 | Reggie Cleveland | .05 |
| 457 | Sammy Stewart | .05 |
| 458 | Pete Vuckovich | .10 |
| 459 | John Wockenfuss | .05 |
| 460 | Glenn Hoffman | .05 |
| 461 | Willie Randolph | .05 |
| 462 | Fernando Valenzuela | .60 |
| 463 | Ron Hassey | .05 |
| 464 | Paul Splittorff | .05 |
| 465 | Rob Picciolo | .05 |
| 466 | Larry Parrish | .05 |
| 467 | John Grubb | .05 |
| 468 | Dan Ford | .05 |
| 469 | Silvio Martinez | .05 |
| 470 | Kiko Garcia | .05 |
| 471 | Bob Boone | .05 |
| 472 | Luis Salazar | .15 |
| 473 | Randy Niemann | .05 |
| 474 | Tom Griffin | .05 |
| 475 | Phil Niekro | .20 |
| 476 | Hubie Brooks | .25 |
| 477 | Dick Tidrow | .05 |
| 478 | Jim Beattie | .05 |
| 479 | Damaso Garcia | .10 |
| 480 | Mickey Hatcher | .05 |
| 481 | Joe Price | .05 |
| 482 | Ed Farmer | .05 |
| 483 | Eddie Murray | .75 |
| 484 | Ben Oglivie | .10 |
| 485 | Kevin Saucier | .05 |
| 486 | Bobby Murcer | .10 |
| 487 | Bill Campbell | .05 |
| 488 | Reggie Smith | .10 |
| 489 | Wayne Garland | .05 |
| 490 | Jim Wright | .05 |
| 491 | Billy Martin (Mgr.) | .20 |
| 492 | Jim Fanning (Mgr.) | .05 |
| 493 | Don Baylor | .15 |
| 494 | Rick Honeycutt | .05 |
| 495 | Carlton Fisk | .20 |
| 496 | Denny Walling | .05 |
| 497 | Bake McBride | .05 |
| 498 | Darrell Porter | .05 |
| 499 | Gene Richards | .05 |
| 500 | Ron Oester | .05 |
| 501 | Ken Dayley (R) | .25 |
| 502 | Jason Thompson | .10 |
| 503 | Milt May | .05 |
| 504 | Doug Bird | .05 |
| 505 | Bruce Bochte | .05 |
| 506 | Neil Allen | .05 |
| 507 | Joey McLaughlin | .05 |
| 508 | Butch Wynegar | .06 |
| 509 | Gary Roenicke | .05 |
| 510 | Robin Yount | .50 |
| 511 | Dave Tobik | .05 |
| 512 | Rich Gedman (R) | .50 |
| 513 | Gene Nelson | .08 |
| 514 | Rick Monday | .05 |
| 515 | Miguel Dilone | .05 |
| 516 | Clint Hurdle | .05 |
| 517 | Jeff Newman | .05 |
| 518 | Grant Jackson | .05 |
| 519 | Andy Hassler | .05 |
| 520 | Pat Putnam | .05 |
| 521 | Greg Pryor | .05 |
| 522 | Tony Scott | .05 |
| 523 | Steve Mura | .05 |
| 524 | John LeMaster | .05 |
| 525 | Dick Ruthven | .05 |
| 526 | John McNamara (Mgr.) | .05 |
| 527 | Larry McWilliams | .05 |
| 528 | Johnny Ray (R) | .50 |
| 529 | Pat Tabler (R) | .60 |
| 530 | Tom Herr | .10 |
| 531 | San Diego Chicken* | 1.00 |
| 532 | Sal Butera | .05 |
| 533 | Mike Griffin | .05 |
| 534 | Kelvin Moore | .05 |
| 535 | Reggie Jackson | .50 |
| 536 | Ed Romero | .05 |
| 537 | Derrel Thomas | .05 |
| 538 | Mike O'Berry | .05 |
| 539 | Jack O'Connor | .05 |
| 540 | Bob Ojeda (R) | .75 |
| 541 | Roy Lee Jackson | .05 |
| 542 | Lynn Jones | .05 |
| 543 | Gaylord Perry | .25 |
| 544 | Phil Garner* | .10 |
| 545 | Garry Templeton | .10 |
| 546 | Rafael Ramirez | .05 |
| 547 | Jeff Reardon | .05 |
| 548 | Ron Guidry | .20 |
| 549 | Tim Laudner | .15 |
| 550 | John Henry Johnson | .05 |
| 551 | Chris Bando | .05 |
| 552 | Bobby Brown | .05 |
| 553 | Larry Bradford | .05 |
| 554 | Scott Fletcher (R) | .35 |
| 555 | Jerry Royster | .05 |
| 556 | Shooty Babbitt | .05 |
| 557 | Kent Hrbek (R) | 3.50 |
| 558 | Yankee Winners: | .15 |
| | Ron Guidry, Tommy John | |
| 559 | Mark Bomback | .05 |
| 560 | Julio Valdez | .08 |
| 561 | Buck Martinez | .05 |
| 562 | Mike Marshall (R) | 1.00 |
| 563 | Rennie Stennett | .05 |
| 564 | Steve Crawford | .07 |
| 565 | Bob Babcock | .05 |
| 566 | Johnny Podres | .05 |
| 567 | Paul Serna | .07 |
| 568 | Harold Baines | .40 |
| 569 | Dave LaRoche | .05 |
| 570 | Lee May | .05 |
| 571 | Gary Ward | .05 |
| 572 | John Denny | .05 |
| 573 | Roy Smalley | .05 |
| 574 | Bob Brenly (R) | .30 |
| 575 | Bronx Bombers: | .45 |
| | R. Jackson, D. Winfield | |
| 576 | Luis Pujols | .05 |
| 577 | Butch Hobson | .05 |
| 578 | Harvey Kuenn (Mgr.) | .05 |
| 579 | Cal Ripken, Sr. | .05 |
| 580 | Juan Berenguer | .05 |
| 581 | Benny Ayala | .05 |
| 582 | Vance Law | .15 |
| 583 | Rick Leach | .08 |
| 584 | George Frazier | .05 |
| 585 | Phillies Finest: | |
| | Pete Rose, Mike Schmidt | |
| 586 | Joe Rudi | .05 |
| 587 | Juan Beniquez | .05 |
| 588 | Luis DeLeon (R) | .15 |
| 589 | Craig Swan | .05 |
| 590 | Dave Chalk | .05 |
| 591 | Billy Gardner (Mgr.) | .05 |
| 592 | Sal Bando | .05 |
| 593 | Bert Campaneris | .05 |
| 594 | Steve Kemp | .05 |
| 595 | Randy Lerch' (Braves) | .35 |
| 595 | Randy Lerch (Brewers) | .08 |

| NO. | PLAYER | MINT |
|---|---|---|
| 596 | Bryan Clark | .08 |
| 597 | Dave Ford | .05 |
| 598 | Mike Scioscia | .05 |
| 599 | John Lowenstein | .05 |
| 600 | Rene Lachmann (Mgr.) | .05 |
| 601 | Mick Kelleher | .05 |
| 602 | Ron Jackson | .05 |
| 603 | Jerry Koosman | .15 |
| 604 | Dave Goltz | .05 |
| 605 | Ellis Valentine | .05 |
| 606 | Lonnie Smith | .10 |
| 607 | Joaquin Andujar | .15 |
| 608 | Garry Hancock | .05 |
| 609 | Jerry Turner | .05 |
| 610 | Bob Bonner | .05 |
| 611 | Jim Dwyer | .05 |
| 612 | Terry Bulling | .05 |

| NO. | PLAYER | MINT |
|---|---|---|
| 613 | Joel Youngblood | .05 |
| 614 | Larry Milbourne | .05 |
| 615 | Phil Roof | .07 |
| 616 | Keith Drumright | .05 |
| 617 | Dave Rosello | .05 |
| 618 | Rickey Keeton | .05 |
| 619 | Dennis Lamp | .05 |
| 620 | Sid Monge | .05 |
| 621 | Jerry White | .05 |
| 622 | Luis Aguayo | .05 |
| 623 | Jamie Easterly | .05 |
| 624 | Steve Sax (R) | 1.50 |
| 625 | Dave Roberts | .05 |
| 626 | Rick Bosetti | .05 |
| 627 | Terry Francona (R) | .20 |
| 628 | Pride of Reds: | .35 |
|  | Tom Seaver, Johnny Bench | |

| NO. | PLAYER | MINT |
|---|---|---|
| 629 | Paul Mirabella | .05 |
| 630 | Rance Mulliniks | .05 |
| 631 | Kevin Hickey | .05 |
| 632 | Reid Nichols | .05 |
| 633 | Dave Geisel | .05 |
| 634 | Ken Griffey | .10 |
| 635 | Bob Lemon (Mgr.) | .10 |
| 636 | Orlando Sanchez | .08 |
| 637 | Bill Almon | .05 |
| 638 | Danny Ainge | .05 |
| 639 | Willie Stargell | .40 |
| 640 | Bob Sykes | .05 |
| 641 | Ed Lynch (R) | .10 |
| 642 | John Ellis | .05 |
| 643 | Fergie Jenkins | .10 |
| 644 | Lenn Sakata | .05 |
| 645 | Julio Gonzalez | .05 |

| NO. | PLAYER | MINT |
|---|---|---|
| 646 | Jesse Orosco | .10 |
| 647 | Jerry Dybzinski | .05 |
| 648 | Tommy Davis | .05 |
| 649 | Ron Gardenhire | .10 |
| 650 | Felipe Alou | .05 |
| 651 | Harvey Haddix | .05 |
| 652 | Willie Upshaw | .10 |
| 653 | Bill Madlock | .15 |
|  | DK Checklist* | .10 |
| — | Checklist No. 1 | .08 |
| — | Checklist No. 2 | .08 |
| — | Checklist No. 3 | .08 |
| — | Checklist No. 4 | .08 |
| — | Checklist No. 5 | .08 |
| — | Checklist No. 6 | .08 |

## 1983 Donruss....Complete Set of 660 Cards—Value $45.00  (Factory-Sealed set—Value $60.00)

Features the rookie cards of Wade Boggs, Ryne Sandberg, Willie McGee and Tony Gwynn. There were a few errors, but unlike previous years they were not corrected. The *checklist* cards are *not* numbered.

**No. 1 to 26—Diamond Kings**

| NO. | PLAYER | MINT |
|---|---|---|
| 1 | F. Valenzuela (DK) | .50 |
| 2 | Rollie Fingers (DK) | .25 |
| 3 | Reggie Jackson (DK) | .50 |
| 4 | Jim Palmer (DK) | .30 |
| 5 | Jack Morris (DK) | .30 |
| 6 | George Foster (DK) | .20 |
| 7 | Jim Sundberg (DK) | .10 |
| 8 | Willie Stargell (DK) | .35 |
| 9 | Dave Stieb (DK) | .30 |
| 10 | Joe Niekro (DK) | .10 |
| 11 | Rickey Henderson (DK) | .60 |
| 12 | Dale Murphy (DK) | .75 |
| 13 | Toby Harrah (DK) | .10 |
| 14 | Bill Buckner (DK) | .15 |
| 15 | Willie Wilson (DK) | .25 |
| 16 | Steve Carlton (DK) | .40 |
| 17 | Ron Guidry (DK) | .30 |
| 18 | Steve Rogers (DK) | .10 |
| 19 | Kent Hrbek (DK) | .35 |
| 20 | Keith Hernandez (DK) | .35 |
| 21 | Floyd Bannister (DK) | .10 |
| 22 | Johnny Bench (DK) | .40 |
| 23 | Britt Burns (DK) | .10 |
| 24 | Joe Morgan (DK) | .25 |
| 25 | Carl Yastrzemski (DK) | .60 |
| 26 | Jerry Kennedy (DK) | .10 |
| 27 | Gary Roenicke | .05 |
| 28 | Dwight Bernard | .05 |
| 29 | Pat Underwood | .05 |
| 30 | Gary Allenson | .05 |
| 31 | Ron Guidry | .20 |
| 32 | Burt Hooton | .05 |
| 33 | Chris Bando | .05 |
| 34 | Vida Blue | .05 |
| 35 | Rickey Henderson | .50 |
| 36 | Ray Burris | .05 |
| 37 | John Butcher | .05 |
| 38 | Don Aase | .05 |
| 39 | Jerry Koosman | .05 |
| 40 | Bruce Sutter | .20 |

| NO. | PLAYER | MINT |
|---|---|---|
| 41 | Jose Cruz | .10 |
| 42 | Pete Rose | 1.00 |
| 43 | Cesar Cedeno | .10 |
| 44 | Floyd Chiffer | .07 |
| 45 | Larry McWilliams | .05 |
| 46 | Alan Fowlkes | .07 |
| 47 | Dale Murphy | .75 |
| 48 | Doug Bird | .05 |
| 49 | Hubie Brooks | .08 |
| 50 | Floyd Bannister | .05 |
| 51 | Joe O'Connor | .05 |
| 52 | Steve Senteney | .07 |
| 53 | Gary Gaetti (R) | 2.50 |
| 54 | Damaso Garcia | .10 |
| 55 | Gene Nelson | .05 |
| 56 | Mookie Wilson | .08 |
| 57 | Allen Ripley | .05 |
| 58 | Bob Horner | .25 |
| 59 | Tony Pena | .15 |
| 60 | Gary Lavelle | .05 |
| 61 | Tim Lollar | .05 |
| 62 | Frank Pastore | .05 |
| 63 | Garry Maddox | .05 |
| 64 | Bob Forsch | .05 |
| 65 | Harry Spilman | .05 |
| 66 | Geoff Zahn | .05 |
| 67 | Salome Barojas | .07 |
| 68 | David Palmer | .05 |
| 69 | Charlie Hough | .05 |
| 70 | Dan Quisenberry | .20 |
| 71 | Tony Armas | .15 |
| 72 | Rick Sutcliffe | .20 |
| 73 | Steve Balboni | .10 |
| 74 | Jerry Remy | .05 |
| 75 | Mike Scioscia | .05 |
| 76 | John Wockenfuss | .05 |
| 77 | Jim Palmer | .25 |
| 78 | Rollie Fingers | .25 |
| 79 | Joe Nolan | .05 |
| 80 | Pete Vuckovich | .05 |
| 81 | Rick Leach | .05 |

| NO. | PLAYER | MINT |
|---|---|---|
| 82 | Rick Miller | .05 |
| 83 | Graig Nettles | .10 |
| 84 | Ron Cey | .15 |
| 85 | Miguel Dilone | .05 |
| 86 | John Wathan | .05 |
| 87 | Kelvin Moore | .05 |
| 88 | Bryn Smith | .05 |
| 89 | Dave Hostetler | .08 |
| 90 | Rod Carew | .40 |
| 91 | Lonnie Smith | .07 |
| 92 | Bob Knepper | .05 |
| 93 | Marty Bystrom | .05 |
| 94 | Chris Welsh | .05 |
| 95 | Jason Thompson | .07 |
| 96 | Tom O'Malley | .08 |
| 97 | Phil Niekro | .20 |
| 98 | Neil Allen | .05 |
| 99 | Bill Buckner | .10 |
| 100 | Ed VandeBerg | .10 |
| 101 | Jim Clancy | .05 |
| 102 | Robert Castillo | .05 |
| 103 | Bruce Berenyi | .05 |
| 104 | Carlton Fisk | .20 |
| 105 | Mike Flanagan | .10 |
| 106 | Cecil Cooper | .15 |
| 107 | Jack Morris | .20 |
| 108 | Mike Morgan | .05 |
| 109 | Luis Aponte | .05 |
| 110 | Pedro Guerrero | .30 |
| 111 | Len Barker | .05 |
| 112 | Willie Wilson | .20 |
| 113 | Dave Beard | .05 |
| 114 | Mike Gates | .07 |
| 115 | Reggie Jackson | .45 |
| 116 | George Wright | .15 |
| 117 | Vance Law | .05 |
| 118 | Nolan Ryan | .30 |
| 119 | Mike Krukow | .05 |
| 120 | Ozzie Smith | .25 |
| 121 | Broderick Perkins | .05 |
| 122 | Tom Seaver | .35 |

| NO. | PLAYER | MINT |
|---|---|---|
| 123 | Chris Chambliss | .05 |
| 124 | Chuck Tanner (Mgr.) | .05 |
| 125 | Johnnie LeMaster | .05 |
| 126 | Mel Hall (R) | .50 |
| 127 | Bruce Bochte | .05 |
| 128 | Charlie Puleo | .07 |
| 129 | Luis Leal | .05 |
| 130 | John Pacella | .05 |
| 131 | Glenn Gulliver | .07 |
| 132 | Don Money | .05 |
| 133 | Dave Rozema | .05 |
| 134 | Bruce Hurst | .15 |
| 135 | Rudy May | .05 |
| 136 | Tom LaSorda (Mgr.) | .10 |
| 137 | Dan Spillner | .10 |
|  | (photo of Ed Whitson) | |
| 138 | Jerry Martin | .05 |
| 139 | Mike Norris | .05 |
| 140 | Al Oliver | .10 |
| 141 | Daryl Sconiers | .05 |
| 142 | Lamar Johnson | .05 |
| 143 | Harold Baines | .20 |
| 144 | Alan Ashby | .05 |
| 145 | Garry Templeton | .10 |
| 146 | Al Holland | .05 |
| 147 | Bo Diaz | .05 |
| 148 | Dave Concepcion | .10 |
| 149 | Rick Camp | .05 |
| 150 | Jim Morrison | .05 |
| 151 | Randy Martz | .05 |
| 152 | Keith Hernandez | .30 |
| 153 | John Lowenstein | .05 |
| 154 | Mike Caldwell | .05 |
| 155 | Milt Wilcox | .05 |
| 156 | Rich Gedman | .05 |
| 157 | Rich Gossage | .20 |
| 158 | Jerry Reuss | .05 |
| 159 | Ron Hassey | .05 |
| 160 | Larry Gura | .05 |
| 161 | Dwayne Murphy | .05 |
| 162 | Woodie Fryman | .05 |

| NO. PLAYER | MINT | NO. PLAYER | MINT | NO. PLAYER | MINT | NO. PLAYER | MINT |
|---|---|---|---|---|---|---|---|
| 163 Steve Comer | .05 | 247 Joe Pittman | .10 | 330 Jim Slaton | .05 | 414 Charlie Lea | .05 |
| 164 Ken Forsch | .05 | (photo of Juan Eichelberger) | | 331 Benny Ayala | .05 | 415 Rick Honeycutt | .05 |
| 165 Dennis Lamp | .05 | 248 Mario Soto | .10 | 332 Ted Simmons | .10 | 416 Mike Witt | .25 |
| 166 David Green (R) | .20 | 249 Claudell Washington | .10 | 333 Lou Whitaker | .20 | 417 Steve Trout | .05 |
| 167 Terry Puhl | .05 | 250 Rick Rhoden | .05 | 334 Chuck Rainey | .05 | 418 Glenn Brummer | .05 |
| 168 Mike Schmidt | .50 | 251 Darrell Evans | .10 | 335 Lou Piniella | .10 | 419 Denny Walling | .05 |
| 169 Eddie Milner (R) | .15 | 252 Steve Henderson | .05 | 336 Steve Sax | .20 | 420 Gary Matthews | .10 |
| 170 John Curtis | .05 | 253 Manny Castillo | .05 | 337 Toby Harrah | .05 | 421 Charlie Leibrandt | .05 |
| 171 Don Robinson | .05 | 254 Craig Swan | .05 | 338 George Brett | .50 | 422 Juan Eichelberger | .05 |
| 172 Richard Gale | .05 | 255 Joey McLaughlin | .05 | 339 Davey Lopes | .05 | 423 Matt Guante | .07 |
| 173 Steve Bedrosian | .20 | 256 Pete Redfern | .05 | 340 Gary Carter | .40 | 424 Bill Laskey (R) | .15 |
| 174 Willie Hernandez | .20 | 257 Ken Singleton | .08 | 341 John Grubb | .05 | 425 Jerry Royster | .05 |
| 175 Ron Gardenhire | .05 | 258 Robin Yount | .30 | 342 Tim Foli | .05 | 426 Dickie Noles | .05 |
| 176 Jim Beattie | .05 | 259 Elias Sosa | .05 | 343 Jim Kaat | .05 | 427 George Foster | .20 |
| 177 Tim Laudner | .05 | 260 Bob Ojeda | .08 | 344 Mike LaCoss | .05 | 428 Mike Moore (R) | .25 |
| 178 Buck Martinez | .05 | 261 Bobby Murcer | .10 | 345 Larry Christenson | .05 | 429 Gary Ward | .05 |
| 179 Kent Hrbek | .40 | 262 Candy Maldonado (R) | .75 | 346 Juan Bonilla | .05 | 430 Barry Bonnell | .05 |
| 180 Alfredo Griffin | .05 | 263 Rick Waits | .05 | 347 Omar Moreno | .05 | 431 Ron Washington | .08 |
| 181 Larry Andersen | .05 | 264 Greg Pryor | .05 | 348 Chili Davis | .30 | 432 Rance Mulliniks | .05 |
| 182 Pete Falcone | .05 | 265 Bob Owchinko | .05 | 349 Tommy Boggs | .05 | 433 Mike Stanton | .05 |
| 183 Jody Davis | .12 | 266 Chris Speier | .05 | 350 Rusty Staub | .10 | 434 Jesse Orosco | .10 |
| 184 Glenn Hubbard | .05 | 267 Bruce Kison | .05 | 351 Bump Wills | .05 | 435 Larry Bowa | .08 |
| 185 Dale Berra | .05 | 268 Mark Wagner | .05 | 352 Rick Sweet | .05 | 436 Biff Pocoroba | .05 |
| 186 Greg Minton | .05 | 269 Steve Kemp | .05 | 353 Jim Gott | .25 | 437 Johnny Ray | .12 |
| 187 Gary Lucas | .05 | 270 Phil Garner | .05 | 354 Terry Felton | .05 | 438 Joe Morgan | .30 |
| 188 Dave Van Gorder | .08 | 271 Gene Richards | .05 | 355 Jim Kern | .05 | 439 Eric Show (R) | .30 |
| 189 Bob Dernier | .05 | 272 Renie Martin | .05 | 356 Bill Almon | .05 | 440 Larry Biittner | .05 |
| 190 Willie McGee (R) | 2.00 | 273 Dave Roberts | .05 | 357 Tippy Martinez | .05 | 441 Greg Gross | .05 |
| 191 Dickie Thon | .07 | 274 Dan Driessen | .05 | 358 Roy Howell | .05 | 442 Gene Tenace | .05 |
| 192 Bob Boone | .05 | 275 Rufino Linares | .05 | 359 Dan Petry | .20 | 443 Danny Heep | .05 |
| 193 Britt Burns | .05 | 276 Lee Lacy | .05 | 360 Jerry Mumphrey | .05 | 444 Bobby Clark | .05 |
| 194 Jeff Reardon | .10 | 277 Ryne Sandberg (R) | 4.00 | 361 Mark Clear | .05 | 445 Kevin Hickey | .05 |
| 195 Jon Matlack | .05 | 278 Darrell Porter | .05 | 362 Mike Marshall | .20 | 446 Scott Sanderson | .05 |
| 196 Don Slaught (R) | .25 | 279 Cal Ripken | 1.00 | 363 Lary Sorensen | .05 | 447 Frank Tanana | .10 |
| 197 Fred Stanley | .05 | 280 Jamie Easterly | .05 | 364 Amos Otis | .08 | 448 Cesar Geronimo | .05 |
| 198 Rick Manning | .05 | 281 Bill Fahey | .05 | 365 Rick Langford | .05 | 449 Jimmy Sexton | .05 |
| 199 Dave Righetti | .25 | 282 Glenn Hoffman | .05 | 366 Brad Mills | .05 | 450 Mike Hargrove | .05 |
| 200 Dave Stapleton | .05 | 283 Willie Randolph | .10 | 367 Brian Downing | .05 | 451 Doyle Alexander | .05 |
| 201 Steve Yeager | .05 | 284 Fernando Valenzuela | .30 | 368 Mike Richardt | .07 | 452 Dwight Evans | .20 |
| 202 Enos Cabell | .05 | 285 Alan Bannister | .05 | 369 Aurelio Rodriguez | .05 | 453 Terry Forster | .05 |
| 203 Sammy Stewart | .05 | 286 Paul Splittorff | .05 | 370 Dave Smith | .05 | 454 Tom Brookens | .05 |
| 204 Moose Haas | .05 | 287 Joe Rudi | .05 | 371 Tug McGraw | .08 | 455 Rich Dauer | .05 |
| 205 Lenn Sakata | .05 | 288 Bill Gullickson | .05 | 372 Doug Bair | .10 | 456 Rob Picciolo | .05 |
| 206 Charlie Moore | .05 | 289 Danny Darwin | .05 | 373 Ruppert Jones | .05 | 457 Terry Crowley | .05 |
| 207 Alan Trammell | .25 | 290 Andy Hassler | .05 | 374 Alex Trevino | .05 | 458 Ned Yost | .05 |
| 208 Jim Rice | .30 | 291 Ernesto Escarrega | .07 | 375 Ken Dayley | .05 | 459 Kirk Gibson | .40 |
| 209 Roy Smalley | .05 | 292 Steve Mura | .05 | 376 Rod Scurry | .05 | 460 Reid Nichols | .05 |
| 210 Bill Russell | .05 | 293 Tony Scott | .05 | 377 Bob Brenly | .05 | 461 Oscar Gamble | .05 |
| 211 Andre Thornton | .07 | 294 Manny Trillo | .05 | 378 Scot Thompson | .05 | 462 Dusty Baker | .10 |
| 212 Willie Aikens | .05 | 295 Greg Harris | .05 | 379 Julio Cruz | .05 | 463 Jack Perconte | .05 |
| 213 Dave McKay | .05 | 296 Luis DeLeon | .05 | 380 John Stearns | .05 | 464 Frank White | .05 |
| 214 Tim Blackwell | .05 | 297 Kent Tekulve | .05 | 381 Dale Murray | .05 | 465 Mickey Klutts | .05 |
| 215 Buddy Bell | .10 | 298 Atlee Hammaker | .05 | 382 Frank Viola (R) | 2.50 | 466 Warren Cromartie | .05 |
| 216 Doug DeCinces | .15 | 299 Bruce Benedict | .05 | 383 Al Bumbry | .05 | 467 Larry Parrish | .05 |
| 217 Tom Herr | .10 | 300 Fergie Jenkins | .10 | 384 Ben Oglivie | .10 | 468 Bobby Grich | .08 |
| 218 Frank LaCorte | .05 | 301 Dave Kingman | .10 | 385 Dave Tobik | .05 | 469 Dane Iorg | .05 |
| 219 Steve Carlton | .30 | 302 Bill Caudill | .05 | 386 Bob Stanley | .05 | 470 Joe Niekro | .10 |
| 220 Terry Kennedy | .10 | 303 John Castino | .05 | 387 Andre Robertson | .05 | 471 Ed Farmer | .05 |
| 221 Mike Easler | .05 | 304 Ernie Whitt | .05 | 388 Jorge Orta | .05 | 472 Tim Flannery | .05 |
| 222 Jack Clark | .30 | 305 Randy Johnson | .05 | 389 Ed Whitson | .05 | 473 Dave Parker | .30 |
| 223 Gene Garber | .05 | 306 Garth Iorg | .05 | 390 Don Hood | .05 | 474 Jeff Leonard | .05 |
| 224 Scott Holman | .07 | 307 Gaylord Perry | .20 | 391 Tom Underwood | .05 | 475 Al Hrabosky | .05 |
| 225 Mike Proly | .05 | 308 Ed Lynch | .05 | 392 Tim Wallach | .15 | 476 Ron Hodges | .05 |
| 226 Terry Bulling | .05 | 309 Keith Moreland | .10 | 393 Steve Renko | .05 | 477 Leon Durham | .20 |
| 227 Jerry Garvin | .05 | 310 Rafael Ramirez | .05 | 394 Mickey Rivers | .05 | 478 Jim Essian | .05 |
| 228 Ron Davis | .05 | 311 Bill Madlock | .15 | 395 Greg Luzinski | .10 | 479 Roy Lee Jackson | .05 |
| 229 Tom Hume | .05 | 312 Milt May | .05 | 396 Art Howe | .05 | 480 Brad Havens | .05 |
| 230 Marc Hill | .05 | 313 John Montefusco | .05 | 397 Alan Wiggins (R) | .20 | 481 Joe Price | .05 |
| 231 Dennis Martinez | .05 | 314 Wayne Krenchicki | .05 | 398 Jim Barr | .05 | 482 Tony Bernazard | .05 |
| 232 Jim Gantner | .05 | 315 George Vukovich | .05 | 399 Ivan DeJesus | .05 | 483 Scott McGregor | .08 |
| 233 Larry Pashnick | .07 | 316 Joaquin Andujar | .10 | 400 Tom Lawless | .08 | 484 Paul Molitor | .20 |
| 234 Dave Collins | .05 | 317 Craig Reynolds | .05 | 401 Bob Walk | .05 | 485 Mike Ivie | .05 |
| 235 Tom Burgmeier | .05 | 318 Rick Burleson | .05 | 402 Jimmy Smith | .07 | 486 Ken Griffey | .10 |
| 236 Ken Landreaux | .05 | 319 Richard Dotson | .05 | 403 Lee Smith | .10 | 487 Dennis Eckersley | .08 |
| 237 John Denny | .10 | 320 Steve Rogers | .05 | 404 George Hendrick | .10 | 488 Steve Garvey | .40 |
| 238 Hal McRae | .05 | 321 Dave Schmidt | .10 | 405 Eddie Murray | .50 | 489 Mike Fischlin | .05 |
| 239 Matt Keough | .05 | 322 Bud Black (R) | .25 | 406 Marshall Edwards | .05 | 490 U.L. Washington | .05 |
| 240 Doug Flynn | .05 | 323 Jeff Burroughs | .05 | 407 Lance Parrish | .30 | 491 Steve McCatty | .05 |
| 241 Fred Lynn | .20 | 324 Von Hayes | .25 | 408 Carney Lansford | .10 | 492 Roy Johnson | .07 |
| 242 Billy Sample | .05 | 325 Butch Wynegar | .05 | 409 Dave Winfield | .40 | 493 Don Baylor | .10 |
| 243 Tom Paciorek | .05 | 326 Carl Yastrzemski | .60 | 410 Bob Welch | .05 | 494 Bobby Johnson | .05 |
| 244 Joe Sambito | .05 | 327 Ron Roenicke | .05 | 411 Larry Milbourne | .05 | 495 Mike Squires | .05 |
| 245 Sid Monge | .05 | 328 Howard Johnson (R) | 2.50 | 412 Dennis Leonard | .05 | 496 Bert Roberge | .05 |
| 246 Ken Oberkfell | .05 | 329 Rick Dempsey | .05 | 413 Dan Meyer | .05 | 497 Dick Ruthven | .05 |

| NO. | PLAYER | MINT |
|---|---|---|
| 498 | Tito Landrum | .05 |
| 499 | Sixto Lezcano | .05 |
| 500 | Johnny Bench | .45 |
| 501 | Larry Whisenton | .05 |
| 502 | Manny Sarmiento | .05 |
| 503 | Fred Breining | .05 |
| 504 | Bill Campbell | .05 |
| 505 | Todd Cruz | .05 |
| 506 | Bob Bailor | .05 |
| 507 | Dave Stieb | .20 |
| 508 | Al Williams | .05 |
| 509 | Dan Ford | .05 |
| 510 | Gorman Thomas | .10 |
| 511 | Chet Lemon | .10 |
| 512 | Mike Torrez | .05 |
| 513 | Shane Rawley | .05 |
| 514 | Mark Belanger | .05 |
| 515 | Rodney Craig | .05 |
| 516 | Onix Concepcion (R) | .10 |
| 517 | Mike Heath | .05 |
| 518 | Andre Dawson | .35 |
| 519 | Luis Sanchez | .05 |
| 520 | Terry Bogener | .07 |
| 521 | Rudy Law | .05 |
| 522 | Ray Knight | .05 |
| 523 | Joe LeFebvre | .05 |
| 524 | Jim Wohlford | .05 |
| 525 | Julio Franco (R) | 1.75 |
| 526 | Ron Oester | .05 |
| 527 | Rick Mahler | .05 |
| 528 | Steve Nicosia | .05 |
| 529 | Junior Kennedy | .05 |
| 530 | Whitey Herzog (Mgr.) | .05 |
| 531 | Don Sutton | .35 |
| 532 | Mark Brouhard | .05 |
| 533 | Sparky Anderson (Mgr.) | .05 |
| 534 | Roger LaFrancois | .05 |
| 535 | George Frazier | .05 |
| 536 | Tom Niedenfuer | .07 |
| 537 | Ed Glynn | .05 |
| 538 | Lee May | .05 |
| 539 | Bob Kearney | .10 |

| NO. | PLAYER | MINT |
|---|---|---|
| 540 | Tim Raines | .40 |
| 541 | Paul Mirabella | .05 |
| 542 | Luis Tiant | .10 |
| 543 | Ron LeFlore | .05 |
| 544 | Dave LaPoint (R) | .25 |
| 545 | Randy Moffitt | .05 |
| 546 | Luis Aguayo | .05 |
| 547 | Brad Lesley | .10 |
| 548 | Luis Salazar | .05 |
| 549 | John Candelaria | .05 |
| 550 | Dave Bergman | .05 |
| 551 | Bob Watson | .05 |
| 552 | Pat Tabler | .05 |
| 553 | Brent Gaff | .08 |
| 554 | Al Cowens | .05 |
| 555 | Tom Brunansky | .50 |
| 556 | Lloyd Moseby | .15 |
| 557 | Pascual Perez | .05 |
| 558 | Willie Upshaw | .10 |
| 559 | Richie Zisk | .05 |
| 560 | Pat Zachry | .05 |
| 561 | Jay Johnstone | .05 |
| 562 | Carlos Diaz | .10 |
| 563 | John Tudor | .10 |
| 564 | Frank Robinson (Mgr.) | .15 |
| 565 | Dave Edwards | .05 |
| 566 | Paul Householder | .05 |
| 567 | Ron Reed | .05 |
| 568 | Mike Ramsey | .05 |
| 569 | Kiko Garcia | .05 |
| 570 | Tommy John | .20 |
| 571 | Tony LaRussa (Mgr.) | .05 |
| 572 | Joel Youngblood | .05 |
| 573 | Wayne Tolleson | .20 |
| 574 | Keith Creel | .07 |
| 575 | Billy Martin (Mgr.) | .15 |
| 576 | Jerry Dybzinski | .05 |
| 577 | Rick Cerone | .05 |
| 578 | Tony Perez | .15 |
| 579 | Greg Brock (R) | .35 |
| 580 | Glen Wilson (R) | .45 |

| NO. | PLAYER | MINT |
|---|---|---|
| 581 | Tim Stoddard | .05 |
| 582 | Bob McClure | .05 |
| 583 | Jim Dwyer | .05 |
| 584 | Ed Romero | .05 |
| 585 | Larry Herndon | .05 |
| 586 | Wade Boggs (R) | 15.00 |
| 587 | Jay Howell | .05 |
| 588 | Dave Stewart | .12 |
| 589 | Bert Blyleven | .12 |
| 590 | Dick Howser (Mgr.) | .08 |
| 591 | Wayne Gross | .05 |
| 592 | Terry Francona | .08 |
| 593 | Don Werner | .05 |
| 594 | Bill Stein | .05 |
| 595 | Jesse Barfield | .60 |
| 596 | Bobby Molinaro | .05 |
| 597 | Mike Vail | .05 |
| 598 | Tony Gwynn (R) | 9.00 |
| 599 | Gary Rajsich | .08 |
| 600 | Jerry Ujdur | .05 |
| 601 | Cliff Johnson | .05 |
| 602 | Jerry White | .05 |
| 603 | Bryan Clark | .05 |
| 604 | Joe Ferguson | .05 |
| 605 | Guy Sularz | .07 |
| 606 | Ozzie Virgil | .10 |
| 607 | Terry Harper | .05 |
| 608 | Harvey Kuenn (Mgr.) | .05 |
| 609 | Jim Sundberg | .05 |
| 610 | Willie Stargell | .30 |
| 611 | Reggie Smith | .10 |
| 612 | Rob Wilfong | .05 |
| 613 | Niekro Brothers | .15 |
| | Joe and Phil | |
| 614 | Lee Elia (Mgr.) | .05 |
| 615 | Mickey Hatcher | .05 |
| 616 | Jerry Hairston | .05 |
| 617 | John Martin | .05 |
| 618 | Wally Backman | .20 |
| 619 | Storm Davis (R) | .40 |
| 620 | Alan Knicely | .05 |

| NO. | PLAYER | MINT |
|---|---|---|
| 621 | John Stuper | .10 |
| 622 | Matt Sinatro | .05 |
| 623 | Gene Petralli | .07 |
| 624 | Duane Walker (R) | .15 |
| 625 | Dick Williams (Mgr.) | .05 |
| 626 | Pat Corrales (Mgr.) | .05 |
| 627 | Vern Ruhle | .05 |
| 628 | Joe Torre (Mgr.) | .05 |
| 629 | Anthony Johnson | .08 |
| 630 | Steve Howe | .05 |
| 631 | Gary Woods | .05 |
| 632 | LaMarr Hoyt | .15 |
| 633 | Steve Swisher | .05 |
| 634 | Terry Leach | .15 |
| 635 | Jeff Newman | .05 |
| 636 | Brett Butler | .10 |
| 637 | Gary Gray | .05 |
| 638 | Lee Mazzilli | .05 |
| 639 | Ron Jackson | .05 |
| 640 | Juan Beniquez | .05 |
| 641 | Dave Rucker | .05 |
| 642 | Luis Pujols | .05 |
| 643 | Rick Monday | .05 |
| 644 | Hosken Powell | .05 |
| 645 | The Chicken | .30 |
| 646 | Dave Engle | .05 |
| 647 | Dick Davis | .05 |
| 648 | MVP's: Frank Robinson, | .15 |
| | Vida Blue, Joe Morgan | |
| 649 | Al Chambers | .10 |
| 650 | Jesus Vega | .07 |
| 651 | Jeff Jones | .05 |
| 652 | Marvis Foley | .05 |
| 653 | Ty Cobb Puzzle | .20 |
| — | Checklist (DK) | .08 |
| — | Checklist No. 1 | .08 |
| — | Checklist No. 2 | .08 |
| — | Checklist No. 3 | .08 |
| — | Checklist No. 4 | .08 |
| — | Checklist No. 5 | .08 |
| — | Checklist No. 6 | .08 |

## 1984 Donruss....Complete Set of 658 Cards—Value $200.00

**(Factory-Sealed set which includes corrected cards no. 29 and 30—Value $250.00)**

Features the rookie cards of Don Mattingly and Darryl Strawberry. For the first time Donruss limited production of its main card set, creating a serious shortage. *Living Legends* cards "A" and "B" could only be found in wax packs, and are not considered to be part of the set. The checklist cards are *not* numbered. Cards 29 and 30 exist with the numbers deleted. Values for card no's. 1 to 26 are for the error cards (Perez "Steel") on the back. The corrected cards (Perez "Steele") are worth double the value.

| NO. | PLAYER | MINT |
|---|---|---|
| **No. 1 to 26—Diamond Kings** | | |
| 1 | Robin Yount (DK) | .75 |
| 2 | Dave Concepcion (DK) | .20 |
| 3 | Dwayne Murphy (DK) | .15 |
| 4 | John Castino (DK) | .15 |
| 5 | Leon Durham (DK) | .30 |
| 6 | Rusty Staub (DK) | .15 |
| 7 | Jack Clark (DK) | .30 |
| 8 | Dave Dravecky (DK) | .15 |
| 9 | Al Oliver (DK) | .20 |
| 10 | Dave Righetti (DK) | .25 |
| 11 | Hal McRae (DK) | .15 |
| 12 | Ray Knight (DK) | .15 |
| 13 | Bruce Sutter (DK) | .25 |
| 14 | Bob Horner (DK) | .25 |
| 15 | Lance Parrish (DK) | .30 |
| 16 | Matt Young (DK) | .15 |
| 17 | Fred Lynn (DK) | .25 |

| NO. | PLAYER | MINT |
|---|---|---|
| 18 | Ron Kittle (DK) | .25 |
| 19 | Jim Clancy (DK) | .15 |
| 20 | Bill Madlock (DK) | .20 |
| 21 | Larry Parrish (DK) | .20 |
| 22 | Eddie Murray (DK) | .75 |
| 23 | Mike Schmidt (DK) | 1.00 |
| 24 | Pedro Guerrero (DK) | .40 |
| 25 | Andre Thornton (DK) | .15 |
| 26 | Wade Bogg (DK) | 3.50 |
| **No. 27 to 46—(Rated Rookies)** | | |
| 27 | Joel Skinner (R) | .30 |
| 28 | Tommy Dunbar (R) | .15 |
| 29 | Mike Stenhouse (R) | .25 |
| | (no number on back) | |
| 29 | Mike Stenhouse (R) | 2.00 |
| 30 | Ron Darling (R) | 5.00 |
| | (no number on back) | |
| 30 | Ron Darling (R) | 10.00 |

| NO. | PLAYER | MINT |
|---|---|---|
| 31 | Dion James (R) | 1.00 |
| 32 | Tony Fernandez (R) | 7.50 |
| 33 | Angel Salazar (R) | .15 |
| 34 | Kevin McReynolds (R) | 7.50 |
| 35 | Dick Schofield (R) | .75 |
| 36 | Brad Komminsk (R) | .30 |
| 37 | Tim Teufel (R) | .45 |
| 38 | Doug Frobel (R) | .15 |
| 39 | Greg Gagne (R) | .50 |
| 40 | Mike Fuentes (R) | .15 |
| 41 | Joe Carter (R) | 11.00 |
| 42 | Mike Brown (R) | .25 |
| 43 | Mike Jeffcoat (R) | .15 |
| 44 | Sid Fernandez (R) | 6.00 |
| 45 | Brian Dayett (R) | .20 |
| 46 | Chris Smith (R) | .15 |
| 47 | Eddie Murray | .75 |
| 48 | Robin Yount | .50 |

| NO. | PLAYER | MINT |
|---|---|---|
| 49 | Lance Parrish | .40 |
| 50 | Jim Rice | .50 |
| 51 | Dav Winfeld | .50 |
| 52 | Fernando Valenzuela | .50 |
| 53 | George Brett | 1.00 |
| 54 | Rickey Henderson | 1.00 |
| 55 | Gary Carter | .60 |
| 56 | Buddy Bell | .15 |
| 57 | Reggie Jackson | 1.25 |
| 58 | Harold Baines | .25 |
| 59 | Ozzie Smith | .40 |
| 60 | Nolan Ryan | .60 |
| 61 | Pete Rose | 2.00 |
| 62 | Ron Oester | .10 |
| 63 | Steve Garvey | .75 |
| 64 | Jason Thompson | .15 |
| 65 | Jack Clark | .35 |
| 66 | Dale Murphy | 1.35 |

| NO. | PLAYER | MINT | NO. | PLAYER | MINT | NO. | PLAYER | MINT | NO. | PLAYER | MINT |
|---|---|---|---|---|---|---|---|---|---|---|---|
| 67 | Leon Durham | .30 | 152 | Don Baylor | .20 | 237 | Mike Caldwell | .08 | 322 | Jim Morrison | .08 |
| 68 | Darryl Strawberry (R) | 22.00 | 153 | Bob Welch | .15 | 238 | Keith Hernandez | .60 | 323 | Max Venable | .08 |
| 69 | Richie Zisk | .08 | 154 | Alan Bannister | .08 | 239 | Larry Bowa | .10 | 324 | Tony Gwynn | 4.00 |
| 70 | Kent Hrbek | .40 | 155 | Willie Aikens | .08 | 240 | Tony Bernazard | .08 | 325 | Duane Walker | .08 |
| 71 | Dave Stieb | .25 | 156 | Jeff Burroughs | .08 | 241 | Damaso Garcia | .15 | 326 | Ozzie Virgil | .08 |
| 72 | Ken Schrom | .08 | 157 | Bryan Little | .15 | 242 | Tom Brunansky | .40 | 327 | Jeff Lahti | .08 |
| 73 | George Bell | 1.75 | 158 | Bob Boone | .08 | 243 | Dan Driessen | .15 | 328 | Bill Dawley | .25 |
| 74 | Jon Moses | .15 | 159 | Dave Hostetler | .08 | 244 | Ron Kittle | .25 | 329 | Rob Wilfong | .08 |
| 75 | Ed Lynch | .08 | 160 | Jerry Dybzinski | .08 | 245 | Tim Stoddard | .08 | 330 | Marc Hill | .08 |
| 76 | Chuck Rainey | .08 | 161 | Mike Madden | .15 | 246 | Bob Gibson | .10 | 331 | Ray Burris | .08 |
| 77 | Biff Pocoroba | .08 | 162 | Luis DeLeon | .08 | 247 | Marty Castillo | .08 | 332 | Allan Ramirez | .12 |
| 78 | Cecilio Guante | .08 | 163 | Willie Hernandez | .25 | 248 | Don Mattingly (R) | 65.00 | 333 | Chuck Porter | .08 |
| 79 | Jim Barr | .08 | 164 | Frank Pastore | .08 | 249 | Jeff Newman | .08 | 334 | Wayne Krenchicki | .08 |
| 80 | Kurt Bevacqua | .08 | 165 | Rick Camp | .08 | 250 | Alejandro Pena | .35 | 335 | Gary Allenson | .08 |
| 81 | Tom Foley | .15 | 166 | Lee Mazzilli | .12 | 251 | Toby Harrah | .12 | 336 | Bob Meacham | .25 |
| 82 | Joe LeFebvre | .08 | 167 | Scot Thompson | .08 | 252 | Cesar Geronimo | .08 | 337 | Joe Beckwith | .08 |
| 83 | Andy Van Slyke (R) | 3.00 | 168 | Bob Forsch | .12 | 253 | Tom Underwood | .08 | 338 | Rick Sutcliffe | .25 |
| 84 | Bob Lillis (Mgr.) | .08 | 169 | Mike Flanagan | .08 | 254 | Doug Flynn | .08 | 339 | Mark Huismann | .15 |
| 85 | Rick Adams | .15 | 170 | Rick Manning | .08 | 255 | Andy Hassler | .08 | 340 | Tim Conroy | .15 |
| 86 | Jerry Hairston | .08 | 171 | Chet Lemon | .15 | 256 | Odell Jones | .08 | 341 | Scott Sanderson | .08 |
| 87 | Bob James | .25 | 172 | Jerry Remy | .08 | 257 | Rudy Law | .08 | 342 | Larry Biittner | .08 |
| 88 | Joe Altobelli (Mgr.) | .08 | 173 | Ron Guidry | .30 | 258 | Harry Spilman | .08 | 343 | Dave Stewart | .20 |
| 89 | Ed Romero | .08 | 174 | Pedro Guerrero | .40 | 259 | Marty Bystrom | .08 | 344 | Darryl Motley | .08 |
| 90 | John Grubb | .08 | 175 | Willie Wilson | .25 | 260 | Dave Rucker | .08 | 345 | Chris Codiroli | .12 |
| 91 | John H. Johnson | .08 | 176 | Carney Lansford | .15 | 261 | Ruppert Jones | .08 | 346 | Rich Behenna | .12 |
| 92 | Juan Espino | .12 | 177 | Al Oliver | .15 | 262 | Jeff Jones | .15 | 347 | Andre Robertson | .08 |
| 93 | Candy Maldonado | .20 | 178 | Jim Sundberg | .08 | 263 | Gerald Perry | 2.25 | 348 | Mike Marshall | .20 |
| 94 | Andre Thornton | .15 | 179 | Bobby Grich | .08 | 264 | Gene Tenace | .08 | 349 | Larry Herndon | .08 |
| 95 | Onix Concepcion | .08 | 180 | Richard Dotson | .08 | 265 | Brad Wellman | .12 | 350 | Rich Dauer | .08 |
| 96 | Don Hill | .12 | 181 | Joaquin Andujar | .15 | 266 | Dickie Noles | .08 | 351 | Cecil Cooper | .15 |
| 97 | Andre Dawson | .50 | 182 | Jose Cruz | .10 | 267 | Jamie Allen | .12 | 352 | Rod Carew | .50 |
| 98 | Frank Tanana | .15 | 183 | Mike Schmidt | 1.50 | 268 | Jim Gott | .12 | 353 | Willie McGee | .50 |
| 99 | Curt Wilkerson | .15 | 184 | Gary Redus (R) | .40 | 269 | Ron Davis | .08 | 354 | Phil Garner | .08 |
| 100 | Larry Gura | .08 | 185 | Garry Templeton | .15 | 270 | Benny Ayala | .08 | 355 | Joe Morgan | .40 |
| 101 | Dwayne Murphy | .15 | 186 | Tony Pena | .15 | 271 | Ned Yost | .08 | 356 | Luis Salazar | .08 |
| 102 | Tom Brennan | .08 | 187 | Greg Minton | .08 | 272 | Dave Rozema | .08 | 357 | John Candelaria | .15 |
| 103 | Dave Righetti | .30 | 188 | Phil Niekro | .35 | 273 | Dave Stapleton | .08 | 358 | Bill Laskey | .08 |
| 104 | Steve Sax | .30 | 189 | Ferguson Jenkins | .15 | 274 | Lou Piniella | .10 | 359 | Bob McClure | .08 |
| 105 | Dan Petry | .20 | 190 | Mookie Wilson | .15 | 275 | Jose Morales | .08 | 360 | Dave Kingman | .15 |
| 106 | Cal Ripken | 1.00 | 191 | Jim Beattie | .08 | 276 | Brod Perkins | .08 | 361 | Ron Cey | .15 |
| 107 | Paul Molitor | .30 | 192 | Gary Ward | .08 | 277 | Butch Davis | .15 | 362 | Matt Young (R) | .20 |
| 108 | Fred Lynn | .25 | 193 | Jesse Barfield | .35 | 278 | Tony Phillips | .12 | 363 | Lloyd Moseby | .20 |
| 109 | Neil Allen | .15 | 194 | Pete Filson | .15 | 279 | Jeff Reardon | .15 | 364 | Frank Viola | .75 |
| 110 | Joe Niekro | .15 | 195 | Roy Lee Jackson | .08 | 280 | Ken Forsch | .08 | 365 | Eddie Milner | .08 |
| 111 | Steve Carlton | .50 | 196 | Rick Sweet | .08 | 281 | Pete O'Brien (R) | 1.50 | 366 | Floyd Bannister | .12 |
| 112 | Terry Kennedy | .15 | 197 | Jesse Orosco | .15 | 282 | Tom Paciorek | .08 | 367 | Dan Ford | .12 |
| 113 | Bill Madlock | .20 | 198 | Steve Lake | .12 | 283 | Frank LaCorte | .08 | 368 | Moose Haas | .08 |
| 114 | Chili Davis | .15 | 199 | Ken Dayley | .08 | 284 | Tim Lollar | .08 | 369 | Doug Bair | .08 |
| 115 | Jim Gantner | .08 | 200 | Manny Sarmiento | .08 | 285 | Greg Gross | .08 | 370 | Ray Fontenot (R) | .15 |
| 116 | Tom Seaver | .70 | 201 | Mark Davis | .08 | 286 | Alex Trevino | .08 | 371 | Luis Aponte | .08 |
| 117 | Bill Buckner | .15 | 202 | Tim Flannery | .08 | 287 | Gene Garber | .08 | 372 | Jack Fimple | .08 |
| 118 | Bill Caudill | .08 | 203 | Bill Scherrer | .12 | 288 | Dave Parker | .40 | 373 | Neal Heaton | .20 |
| 119 | Jim Clancy | .08 | 204 | Al Holland | .08 | 289 | Lee Smith | .15 | 374 | Greg Pryor | .08 |
| 120 | John Castino | .08 | 205 | Dave Von Ohlen | .15 | 290 | Dave LaPoint | .08 | 375 | Wayne Gross | .08 |
| 121 | Dave Concepcion | .15 | 206 | Mike LaCoss | .08 | 291 | John Shelby | .75 | 376 | Charlie Lea | .08 |
| 122 | Greg Luzinski | .15 | 207 | Juan Beniquez | .08 | 292 | Charlie Moore | .08 | 377 | Steve Lubratich | .12 |
| 123 | Mike Boddicker | .15 | 208 | Juan Agosto | .25 | 293 | Alan Trammell | .40 | 378 | Jon Matlack | .12 |
| 124 | Pete Ladd | .08 | 209 | Bobby Ramos | .08 | 294 | Tony Armas | .15 | 379 | Julio Cruz | .08 |
| 125 | Juan Berenguer | .08 | 210 | Al Bumbry | .08 | 295 | Shane Rawley | .12 | 380 | John Mizerock | .12 |
| 126 | John Montefusco | .08 | 211 | Mark Brouhard | .08 | 296 | Greg Brock | .15 | 381 | Kevin Gross (R) | .40 |
| 127 | Ed Jurak | .12 | 212 | Howard Bailey | .08 | 297 | Hal McRae | .12 | 382 | Mike Ramsey | .08 |
| 128 | Tom Niedenfuer | .08 | 213 | Bruce Hurst | .15 | 298 | Mike Davis | .10 | 383 | Doug Gwosdz | .08 |
| 129 | Bert Blyleven | .15 | 214 | Bob Shirley | .08 | 299 | Tim Raines | .60 | 384 | Kelly Paris | .15 |
| 130 | Bud Black | .08 | 215 | Pat Zachry | .08 | 300 | Bucky Dent | .12 | 385 | Pete Falcone | .08 |
| 131 | Gorman Heimueller | .15 | 216 | Julio Franco | .35 | 301 | Tommy John | .30 | 386 | Milt May | .08 |
| 132 | Dan Schatzeder | .08 | 217 | Mike Armstrong | .08 | 302 | Carlton Fisk | .25 | 387 | Fred Breining | .08 |
| 133 | Ron Jackson | .08 | 218 | Dave Beard | .08 | 303 | Darrell Porter | .08 | 388 | Craig Lefferts (R) | .15 |
| 134 | Tom Henke (R) | .75 | 219 | Steve Rogers | .08 | 304 | Dickie Thon | .08 | 389 | Steve Henderson | .08 |
| 135 | Kevin Hickey | .08 | 220 | John Butcher | .08 | 305 | Garry Maddox | .08 | 390 | Randy Moffitt | .08 |
| 136 | Mike Scott | .30 | 221 | Mike Smithson | .15 | 306 | Cesar Cedeno | .15 | 391 | Ron Washington | .08 |
| 137 | Bo Diaz | .08 | 222 | Frank White | .12 | 307 | Gary Lucas | .08 | 392 | Gary Roenicke | .08 |
| 138 | Glenn Brummer | .08 | 223 | Mike Heath | .08 | 308 | Johnny Ray | .20 | 393 | Tom Candiotti (R) | .40 |
| 139 | Sid Monge | .08 | 224 | Chris Bando | .08 | 309 | Andy McGaffigan | .08 | 394 | Larry Pashnick | .08 |
| 140 | Rich Gale | .08 | 225 | Roy Smalley | .08 | 310 | Claudell Washington | .15 | 395 | Dwight Evans | .20 |
| 141 | Brett Butler | .15 | 226 | Dusty Baker | .10 | 311 | Ryne Sandberg | 2.00 | 396 | Goose Gossage | .20 |
| 142 | Brian Harper | .12 | 227 | Lou Whitaker | .25 | 312 | George Foster | .20 | 397 | Derrel Thomas | .08 |
| 143 | John Rabb | .12 | 228 | John Lowenstein | .08 | 313 | Spike Owen (R) | .40 | 398 | Juan Eichelberger | .08 |
| 144 | Gary Woods | .08 | 229 | Ben Ogilvie | .08 | 314 | Gary Gaetti | .75 | 399 | Leon Roberts | .08 |
| 145 | Pat Putnam | .08 | 230 | Doug DeCinces | .15 | 315 | Willie Upshaw | .15 | 400 | Davey Lopes | .15 |
| 146 | Jim Acker | .15 | 231 | Lonnie Smith | .15 | 316 | Al Williams | .08 | 401 | Bill Gullickson | .12 |
| 147 | Mickey Hatcher | .08 | 232 | Ray Knight | .15 | 317 | Jorge Orta | .08 | 402 | Geoff Zahn | .08 |
| 148 | Todd Cruz | .08 | 233 | Gary Matthews | .15 | 318 | Orlando Mercado | .12 | 403 | Billy Sample | .08 |
| 149 | Tom Tellmann | .08 | 234 | Juan Bonilla | .08 | 319 | Junior Ortiz | .12 | 404 | Mike Squires | .08 |
| 150 | John Wockenfuss | .08 | 235 | Rod Scurry | .08 | 320 | Mike Proly | .08 | 405 | Craig Reynolds | .08 |
| 151 | Wade Boggs | 10.00 | 236 | Atlee Hammaker | .08 | 321 | Randy Johnson | .08 | 406 | Eric Show | .08 |

| NO. PLAYER | MINT |
|---|---|
| 407 John Denny | .20 |
| 408 Dann Bilardello | .12 |
| 409 Bruce Benedict | .08 |
| 410 Kent Tekulve | .12 |
| 411 Mel Hall | .15 |
| 412 John Stuper | .08 |
| 413 Rick Dempsey | .12 |
| 414 Don Sutton | .40 |
| 415 Jack Morris | .30 |
| 416 John Tudor | .30 |
| 417 Willie Randolph | .15 |
| 418 Jerry Reuss | .12 |
| 419 Don Slaught | .12 |
| 420 Steve McCatty | .08 |
| 421 Tim Wallach | .20 |
| 422 Larry Parrish | .15 |
| 423 Brian Downing | .15 |
| 424 Britt Burns | .15 |
| 425 David Green | .15 |
| 426 Jerry Mumphrey | .08 |
| 427 Ivn DeJesus | .08 |
| 428 Mario Soto | .12 |
| 429 Gene Richards | .08 |
| 430 Dale Berra | .08 |
| 431 Darrell Evans | .15 |
| 432 Glenn Hubbard | .08 |
| 433 Jody Davis | .12 |
| 434 Danny Heep | .08 |
| 435 Ed Nunez | .30 |
| 436 Bobby Castillo | .08 |
| 437 Ernie Whitt | .08 |
| 438 Scott Ullger | .15 |
| 439 Doyle Alexander | .15 |
| 440 Domingo Ramos | .12 |
| 441 Craig Swan | .08 |
| 442 Warren Brusstar | .08 |
| 443 Len Barker | .10 |
| 444 Mike Easler | .10 |
| 445 Renie Martin | .08 |
| 446 Dennis Rasmussen (R) | .75 |
| 447 Ted Power | .15 |
| 448 Charlie Hudson (R) | .40 |
| 449 Danny Cox (R) | .75 |
| 450 Kevin Bass | .35 |
| 451 Daryl Sconiers | .08 |
| 452 Scott Fletcher | .12 |
| 453 Bryn Smith | .12 |
| 454 Jim Dwyer | .08 |
| 455 Rob Picciolo | .08 |
| 456 Enos Cabell | .08 |
| 457 "Oil Can" Boyd (R) | .75 |
| 458 Butch Wynegar | .08 |
| 459 Burt Hooton | .08 |
| 460 Ron Hassey | .08 |
| 461 Danny Jackson (R) | 3.50 |
| 462 Bob Kearney | .08 |
| 463 Terry Francona | .08 |
| 464 Wayne Tolleson | .08 |
| 465 Mickey Rivers | .15 |
| 466 John Wathan | .08 |
| 467 Bill Almon | .08 |
| 468 George Vukovich | .08 |
| 469 Steve Kemp | .12 |
| 470 Ken Landreaux | .08 |
| 471 Milt Wilcox | .08 |

| NO. PLAYER | MINT |
|---|---|
| 472 Tippy Martinez | .08 |
| 473 Ted Simmons | .15 |
| 474 Tim Foli | .08 |
| 475 George Hendrick | .10 |
| 476 Terry Puhl | .15 |
| 477 Von Hayes | .20 |
| 478 Bobby Brown | .08 |
| 479 Lee Lacy | .08 |
| 480 Joel Youngblood | .08 |
| 481 Jim Slaton | .08 |
| 482 Mike Fitzgerald | .10 |
| 483 Keith Moreland | .08 |
| 484 Ron Roenicke | .08 |
| 485 Luis Leal | .08 |
| 486 Bryan Oelkers | .12 |
| 487 Bruce Berenyi | .08 |
| 488 LaMarr Hoyt | .15 |
| 489 Joe Nolan | .08 |
| 490 Marshall Edwards | .08 |
| 491 Mike Laga | .12 |
| 492 Rick Cerone | .08 |
| 493 Rick Miller | .08 |
| 494 Rick Honeycutt | .12 |
| 495 Mike Hargrove | .12 |
| 496 Joe Simpson | .08 |
| 497 Keith Atherton | .12 |
| 498 Chris Welsh | .08 |
| 499 Bruce Kison | .08 |
| 500 Bobby Johnson | .08 |
| 501 Jerry Koosman | .20 |
| 502 Frank DiPino | .08 |
| 503 Tony Perez | .20 |
| 504 Ken Oberkfell | .08 |
| 505 Mark Thurmond (R) | .25 |
| 506 Joe Price | .08 |
| 507 Pascual Perez | .08 |
| 508 Marvell Wynne | .20 |
| 509 Mike Krukow | .15 |
| 510 Dick Ruthven | .08 |
| 511 Al Cowens | .08 |
| 512 Cliff Johnson | .08 |
| 513 Randy Bush | .08 |
| 514 Sammy Stewart | .08 |
| 515 Bill Schroeder (R) | .20 |
| 516 Aurelio Lopez | .08 |
| 517 Mike Brown | .15 |
| 518 Graig Nettles | .20 |
| 519 Dave Sax | .12 |
| 520 Gerry Willard | .15 |
| 521 Paul Splittorff | .12 |
| 522 Tom Burgmeier | .08 |
| 523 Chris Speier | .08 |
| 524 Bobby Clark | .08 |
| 525 George Wright | .08 |
| 526 Dennis Lamp | .08 |
| 527 Tony Scott | .08 |
| 528 Ed Whitson | .12 |
| 529 Ron Reed | .08 |
| 530 Charlie Puleo | .08 |
| 531 Jerry Royster | .08 |
| 532 Don Robinson | .08 |
| 533 Steve Trout | .08 |
| 534 Bruce Sutter | .20 |
| 535 Bob Horner | .20 |
| 536 Pat Tabler | .15 |

| NO. PLAYER | MINT |
|---|---|
| 537 Chris Chambliss | .15 |
| 538 Bob Ojeda | .20 |
| 539 Alan Ashby | .08 |
| 540 Jay Johnstone | .12 |
| 541 Bob Dernier | .08 |
| 542 Brook Jacoby (R) | 1.50 |
| 543 U.L. Washington | .08 |
| 544 Danny Darwin | .08 |
| 545 Kiko Garcia | .08 |
| 546 Vance Law | .08 |
| 547 Tug McGraw | .15 |
| 548 Dave Smith | .08 |
| 549 Len Matuszek | .08 |
| 550 Tom Hume | .08 |
| 551 Dave Dravecky | .12 |
| 552 Rick Rhoden | .15 |
| 553 Duane Kuiper | .08 |
| 554 Rusty Staub | .15 |
| 555 Bill Campbell | .08 |
| 556 Mike Torrez | .08 |
| 557 Dave Henderson | .08 |
| 558 Len Whitehouse | .12 |
| 559 Barry Bonnell | .08 |
| 560 Rick Lysander | .12 |
| 561 Garth Iorg | .08 |
| 562 Bryan Clark | .08 |
| 563 Brian Giles | .08 |
| 564 Vern Ruhle | .08 |
| 565 Steve Bedrosian | .25 |
| 566 Larry McWilliams | .08 |
| 567 Jeff Leonard | .15 |
| 568 Alan Wiggins | .12 |
| 569 Jeff Russell | .20 |
| 570 Salome Barojas | .08 |
| 571 Dane Iorg | .08 |
| 572 Bob Knepper | .15 |
| 573 Gary Lavelle | .08 |
| 574 Gorman Thomas | .15 |
| 575 Manny Trillo | .08 |
| 576 Jim Palmer | .50 |
| 577 Dale Murray | .08 |
| 578 Tom Brookens | .08 |
| 579 Rich Gedman | .12 |
| 580 Bill Doran (R) | 1.50 |
| 581 Steve Yeager | .08 |
| 582 Dan Spillner | .08 |
| 583 Dan Quisenberry | .25 |
| 584 Rance Mulliniks | .08 |
| 585 Storm Davis | .15 |
| 586 Dave Schmidt | .08 |
| 587 Bill Russell | .08 |
| 588 Pat Sheridan | .30 |
| 589 Rafael Ramirez | .12 |
| 590 Bud Anderson | .08 |
| 591 George Frazier | .08 |
| 592 Lee Tunnell | .15 |
| 593 Kirk Gibson | .50 |
| 594 Scott McGregor | .08 |
| 595 Bob Bailor | .08 |
| 596 Tom Herr | .15 |
| 597 Luis Sanchez | .08 |
| 598 Dave Engle | .08 |
| 599 Craig McMurtry (R) | .15 |
| 600 Carlos Diaz | .08 |
| 601 Tom O'Malley | .08 |

| NO. PLAYER | MINT |
|---|---|
| 602 Nick Esasky (R) | .35 |
| 603 Ron Hodges | .08 |
| 604 Ed Vande Berg | .08 |
| 605 Alfredo Griffin | .15 |
| 606 Glenn Hoffman | .08 |
| 607 Hubie Brooks | .20 |
| 608 Richard Barnes | .12 |
| 609 Greg Walker (R) | .50 |
| 610 Ken Singleton | .15 |
| 611 Mark Clear | .08 |
| 612 Buck Martinez | .08 |
| 613 Ken Griffey | .15 |
| 614 Reid Nichols | .08 |
| 615 Doug Sisk (R) | .15 |
| 616 Bob Brenly | .10 |
| 617 Joey McLaughlin | .08 |
| 618 Glenn Wilson | .15 |
| 619 Bob Stoddard | .08 |
| 620 Len Sakata | .08 |
| 621 Mike Young (R) | .50 |
| 622 John Stefero | .12 |
| 623 Carmelo Martinez (R) | .30 |
| 624 Dave Bergman | .08 |
| 625 Runnin' Redbirds: | .25 |
| David Green, Willie McGee, Lonnie Smith, Ozzie Smith | |
| 626 Rudy May | .08 |
| 627 Matt Keough | .08 |
| 628 Jose DeLeon (R) | .50 |
| 629 Jim Essian | .08 |
| 630 Darnell Coles (R) | .35 |
| 631 Mike Warren | .15 |
| 632 Del Crandall (Mgr.) | .08 |
| 633 Dennis Martinez | .12 |
| 634 Mike Moore | .08 |
| 635 Lary Sorensen | .08 |
| 636 Ricky Nelson | .15 |
| 637 Omar Moreno | .08 |
| 638 Charlie Hough | .08 |
| 639 Dennis Eckersley | .15 |
| 640 Walt Terrell (R) | .35 |
| 641 Denny Walling | .08 |
| 642 Dave Anderson | .25 |
| 643 Jose Oquendo (R) | .35 |
| 644 Bob Stanley | .08 |
| 645 Dave Geisel | .08 |
| 646 Scott Garrelts (R) | .40 |
| 647 Gary Pettis (R) | .35 |
| 648 Duke Snider Puzzle | .15 |
| 649 Johnnie LeMaster | .08 |
| 650 Dave Collins | .12 |
| 651 The Chicken | .25 |
| — Checklist (DK) | .12 |
| — Checklist No. 1 | .10 |
| — Checklist No. 2 | .10 |
| — Checklist No. 3 | .10 |
| — Checklist No. 4 | .10 |
| — Checklist No. 5 | .10 |
| — Checklist No. 6 | .10 |

**Cards From Wax Packs**

| | |
|---|---|
| A Living Legends: | 2.00 |
| G. Perry, R. Fingers | |
| B Living Legends: | 3.00 |
| C. Yastrzemski, J. Bench | |

## 1985 Donruss....Complete Set of 660 Cards—Value $150.00

(Factory-Sealed set which includes corrected cards no. 424 and 534—Value $175.00)

Features the rookie cards of Dwight Gooden, Roger Clemens, Alvin Davis, Orel Hershiser, Bret Saberhagen and Kirby Puckett. As in 1984, Donruss limited the quantity of cards printed. The *checklist* cards are *not* numbered. Four cards are printed on the bottom of gum pack display boxes; they are not part of the set. Errors found on cards 424 and 534 were corrected.

| NO. PLAYER | MINT | NO. PLAYER | MINT | NO. PLAYER | MINT | NO. PLAYER | MINT |
|---|---|---|---|---|---|---|---|
| **No. 1 to 26 (Diamond Kings)** | | 84 Bill Doran | .15 | 169 Cal Ripken, Jr. | .45 | 254 Pete Rose | 1.25 |
| 1 Ryne Sandberg (DK) | .50 | 85 Rod Carew | .50 | 170 Cecil Cooper | .15 | 255 Don Aase | .10 |
| 2 Doug DeCinces (DK) | .10 | 86 LaMarr Hoyt | .10 | 171 Alan Trammell | .25 | 256 George Wright | .05 |
| 3 Rich Dotson (DK) | .10 | 87 Tim Wallach | .10 | 172 Wade Boggs | 5.00 | 257 Britt Burns | .05 |
| 4 Bert Blyleven (DK) | .10 | 88 Mike Flanagan | .05 | 173 Don Baylor | .15 | 258 Mike Scott | .30 |
| 5 Lou Whitaker (DK) | .20 | 89 Jim Sundberg | .05 | 174 Pedro Guerrero | .25 | 259 Len Matuszek | .05 |
| 6 Dan Quisenberry (DK) | .10 | 90 Chet Lemon | .05 | 175 Frank White | .05 | 260 Dave Rucker | .05 |
| 7 Don Mattingly (DK) | 6.00 | 91 Bob Stanley | .05 | 176 Rickey Henderson | .50 | 261 Craig Lefferts | .05 |
| 8 Carney Lansford (DK) | .10 | 92 Willie Randolph | .05 | 177 Charlie Lea | .05 | 262 Jay Tibbs | .25 |
| 9 Frank Tanana (DK) | .10 | 93 Bill Russell | .05 | 178 Pete O'Brien | .10 | 263 Bruce Benedict | .05 |
| 10 Willie Upshaw (DK) | .10 | 94 Julio Franco | .15 | 179 Doug DeCinces | .10 | 264 Don Robinson | .05 |
| 11 C. Washington (DK) | .10 | 95 Dan Quisenberry | .20 | 180 Ron Kittle | .15 | 265 Gary Lavelle | .05 |
| 12 Mike Marshall (DK) | .15 | 96 Bill Claudill | .05 | 181 George Hendrick | .05 | 266 Scott Sanderson | .05 |
| 13 Joaquin Andujar (DK) | .10 | 97 Bill Gullickson | .05 | 182 Joe Niekro | .08 | 267 Matt Young | .05 |
| 14 Cal Ripken (DK) | .50 | 98 Danny Darwin | .05 | 183 Juan Samuel | 1.00 | 268 Ernie Whitt | .05 |
| 15 Jim Rice (DK) | .35 | 99 Curt Wilkerson | .05 | 184 Mario Soto | .10 | 269 Houston Jimenez | .05 |
| 16 Don Sutton (DK) | .25 | 100 Bud Black | .05 | 185 Goose Gossage | .15 | 270 Ken Dixon | .20 |
| 17 Frank Viola (DK) | .35 | 101 Tony Phillips | .05 | 186 Johnny Ray | .10 | 271 Peter Ladd | .05 |
| 18 Alvin Davis (DK) | .40 | 102 Tony Bernazard | .05 | 187 Bob Brenly | .05 | 272 Juan Berenguer | .05 |
| 19 Mario Soto (DK) | .10 | 103 Jay Howell | .05 | 188 Craig McMurtey | .05 | 273 Roger Clemens (R) | 13.50 |
| 20 Jose Cruz (DK) | .10 | 104 Burt Hooton | .05 | 189 Leon Durham | .15 | 274 Rick Cerone | .05 |
| 21 Charlie Lea (DK) | .10 | 105 Milt Wilcox | .05 | 190 Dwight Gooden (R) | 11.00 | 275 Dave Anderson | .05 |
| 22 Jesse Orosco (DK) | .10 | 106 Rich Dauer | .05 | 191 Barry Bonnell | .05 | 276 George Vukovich | .05 |
| 23 Juan Samuel (DK) | .30 | 107 Don Sutton | .20 | 192 Tim Teufel | .05 | 277 Greg Pryor | .05 |
| 24 Tony Pena (DK) | .10 | 108 Mike Witt | .10 | 193 Dave Stieb | .25 | 278 Mike Warren | .05 |
| 25 Tony Gwynn (DK) | .75 | 109 Bruce Sutter | .15 | 194 Mickey Hatcher | .05 | 279 Bob James | .05 |
| 26 Bob Brenly (DK) | .10 | 110 Enos Cabell | .05 | 195 Jesse Barfield | .30 | 280 Bobby Grich | .07 |
| **No. 27 to 46 (Rated Rookies)** | | 111 John Denny | .10 | 196 Al Cowens | .05 | 281 Mike Mason | .10 |
| 27 Danny Tartabull (R) | 6.00 | 112 Dave Dravecky | .10 | 197 Hubie Brooks | .15 | 282 Ron Reed | .05 |
| 28 Mike Bielecki (R) | .15 | 113 Marvell Wynne | .05 | 198 Steve Trout | .05 | 283 Alan Ashby | .05 |
| 29 Steve Lyons (R) | .20 | 114 John LeMaster | .05 | 199 Glenn Hubbard | .05 | 284 Mark Thurmond | .05 |
| 30 Jeff Reed (R) | .15 | 115 Chuck Porter | .05 | 200 Bill Madlock | .10 | 285 Joe Lefebvre | .05 |
| 31 Tony Brewer (R) | .15 | 116 John Gibbons | .10 | 201 Jeff Robinson (R) | .35 | 286 Ted Power | .05 |
| 32 John Morris (R) | .15 | 117 Keith Moreland | .05 | 202 Eric Show | .15 | 287 Chris Chambliss | .05 |
| 33 Daryl Boston (R) | .35 | 118 Darnell Coles | .05 | 203 Dave Concepcion | .10 | 288 Lee Tunnell | .05 |
| 34 Alfonso Pulido (R) | .15 | 119 Dennis Lamp | .05 | 204 Ivan DeJesus | .05 | 289 Rich Bordi | .05 |
| 35 Steve Kiefer (R) | .15 | 120 Ron Davis | .05 | 205 Neil Allen | .10 | 290 Glenn Brummer | .05 |
| 36 Larry Sheets (R) | 1.25 | 121 Nick Esasky | .05 | 206 Jerry Mumphrey | .05 | 291 Mike Boddicker | .10 |
| 37 Scott Bradley (R) | .35 | 122 Vance Law | .05 | 207 Mike Brown | .05 | 292 Rollie Fingers | .15 |
| 38 Calvin Schiraldi (R) | .40 | 123 Gary Roenicke | .05 | 208 Carlton Fisk | .15 | 293 Lou Whitaker | .15 |
| 39 Shawon Dunston (R) | 1.25 | 124 Bill Schroeder | .05 | 209 Bryn Smith | .05 | 294 Dwight Evans | .15 |
| 40 Charlie Mitchell (R) | .15 | 125 Dave Rozema | .05 | 210 Tippy Martinez | .05 | 295 Don Mattingly | 15.00 |
| 41 Billy Hatcher (R) | 1.00 | 126 Bobby Meacham | .05 | 211 Dion James | .05 | 296 Mike Marshall | .15 |
| 42 Russ Stephans (R) | .15 | 127 Marty Barrett | .25 | 212 Willie Hernandez | .15 | 297 Willie Wilson | .12 |
| 43 Alejandro Sanchez (R) | .15 | 128 R.J. Reynolds (R) | .40 | 213 Mike Easler | .05 | 298 Mike Heath | .05 |
| 44 Steve Jeltz (R) | .20 | 129 Ernie Camacho | .05 | 214 Ron Guidry | .20 | 299 Tim Raines | .40 |
| 45 Jim Traber (R) | .50 | 130 Jorge Orta | .05 | 215 Rick Honeycutt | .05 | 300 Larry Parrish | .05 |
| 46 Doug Loman (R) | .25 | 131 Lary Sorensen | .05 | 216 Brett Butler | .08 | 301 Geoff Zahn | .05 |
| 47 Eddie Murray | .50 | 132 Terry Francona | .05 | 217 Larry Gura | .05 | 302 Rich Dotson | .05 |
| 48 Robin Yount | .30 | 133 Fred Lynn | .20 | 218 Ray Burris | .05 | 303 David Green | .05 |
| 49 Lance Parrish | .20 | 134 Bobby Jones | .05 | 219 Steve Rogers | .05 | 304 Jose Cruz | .10 |
| 50 Jim Rice | .35 | 135 Jerry Hairston | .05 | 220 Frank Tanana | .05 | 305 Steve Carlton | .30 |
| 51 Dave Winfield | .35 | 136 Kevin Bass | .15 | 221 Ned Yost | .05 | 306 Gary Redus | .05 |
| 52 Fernando Valenzuela | .25 | 137 Garry Maddox | .05 | 222 Bret Saberhagen (R) | 5.00 | 307 Steve Garvey | .35 |
| 53 George Brett | .60 | 138 Dave LaPoint | .05 | 223 Mike Davis | .05 | 308 Jose DeLeon | .05 |
| 54 Dave Kingman | .10 | 139 Kevin McReynolds | .60 | 224 Bert Blyleven | .10 | 309 Randy Lerch | .05 |
| 55 Gary Carter | .30 | 140 Wayne Krenchicki | .05 | 225 Steve Kemp | .05 | 310 Claudell Washington | .10 |
| 56 Buddy Bell | .10 | 141 Rafael Ramirez | .05 | 226 Jerry Reuss | .05 | 311 Lee Smith | .10 |
| 57 Reggie Jackson | .40 | 142 Rod Scurry | .05 | 227 Darrell Evans | .15 | 312 Darryl Strawberry | 4.00 |
| 58 Harold Baines | .20 | 143 Greg Minton | .05 | 228 Wayne Gross | .05 | 313 Jim Beattie | .05 |
| 59 Ozzie Smith | .30 | 144 Tim Stoddard | .05 | 229 Jim Gantner | .05 | 314 John Butcher | .05 |
| 60 Nolan Ryan | .35 | 145 Steve Henderson | .05 | 230 Bob Boone | .05 | 315 Damaso Garcia | .07 |
| 61 Mike Schmidt | .65 | 146 George Bell | .60 | 231 Lonnie Smith | .05 | 316 Mike Smithson | .05 |
| 62 Dave Parker | .20 | 147 Dave Meier | .10 | 232 Frank DiPino | .05 | 317 Luis Leal | .05 |
| 63 Tony Gwynn | 1.00 | 148 Sammy Stewart | .05 | 233 Jerry Koosman | .05 | 318 Ken Phelps | .25 |
| 64 Tony Pena | .15 | 149 Mark Brouhard | .05 | 234 Graig Nettles | .15 | 319 Wally Backman | .05 |
| 65 Jack Clark | .30 | 150 Larry Herndon | .05 | 235 John Tudor | .15 | 320 Ron Cey | .10 |
| 66 Dale Murphy | .75 | 151 Oil Can Boyd | .10 | 236 John Rabb | .05 | 321 Brad Komminsk | .10 |
| 67 Ryne Sandberg | .50 | 152 Brian Dayett | .05 | 237 Rick Manning | .05 | 322 Jason Thompson | .08 |
| 68 Keith Hernandez | .30 | 153 Tom Niedenfuer | .05 | 238 Mike Fitzgerald | .05 | 323 Frank Williams | .10 |
| 69 Alvin Davis (R) | 2.00 | 154 Brook Jacoby | .10 | 239 Gary Matthews | .05 | 324 Tim Lollar | .05 |
| 70 Kent Hrbek | .40 | 155 Onix Concepcion | .05 | 240 Jim Presley (R) | 1.00 | 325 Eric Davis (R) | 16.00 |
| 71 Willie Upshaw | .10 | 156 Tim Conroy | .05 | 241 Dave Collins | .05 | 326 Von Hayes | .15 |
| 72 Dave Engle | .05 | 157 Joe Hesketh (R) | .20 | 242 Gary Gaetti | .35 | 327 Andy Van Slyke | .35 |
| 73 Alfredo Griffin | .05 | 158 Brian Downing | .15 | 243 Dann Bilardello | .05 | 328 Craig Reynolds | .05 |
| 74 Jack Perconte | .05 | 159 Tom Dunbar | .05 | 244 Rudy Law | .05 | 329 Dick Schofield | .10 |
| 75 Jesse Orosco | .10 | 160 Marc Hill | .05 | 245 John Lowenstein | .05 | 330 Scott Fletcher | .10 |
| 76 Jody Davis | .10 | 161 Phil Garner | .05 | 246 Tom Tellman | .05 | 331 Jeff Reardon | .10 |
| 77 Bob Horner | .15 | 162 Jerry Davis | .10 | 247 Howard Johnson | .75 | 332 Rick Dempsey | .10 |
| 78 Larry McWilliams | .05 | 163 Bill Campbell | .05 | 248 Ray Fontenot | .05 | 333 Ben Oglivie | .15 |
| 79 Joel Youngblood | .05 | 164 John Franco (R) | 1.25 | 249 Tony Armas | .10 | 334 Dan Petry | .15 |
| 80 Alan Wiggins | .10 | 165 Len Barker | .05 | 250 Candy Maldonado | .15 | 335 Jackie Gutierrez | .10 |
| 81 Ron Oester | .05 | 166 Benny Distefano | .10 | 251 Mike Jeffcoat | .05 | 336 Dave Righetti | .15 |
| 82 Ozzie Virgil | .05 | 167 George Frazier | .05 | 252 Dane Iorg | .05 | 337 Alejandro Pena | .05 |
| 83 Ricky Horton (R) | .25 | 168 Tito Landrum | .05 | 253 Bruce Bochte | .05 | 338 Mel Hall | .05 |

Card values from this set fluctuate considerably.

| NO. PLAYER | MINT |
|---|---|
| 339 Pat Sheridan | .05 |
| 340 Keith Atherton | .05 |
| 341 David Palmer | .05 |
| 342 Gary Ward | .05 |
| 343 Dave Stewart | .15 |
| 344 Mark Gubicza (R) | .75 |
| 345 Carney Lansford | .10 |
| 346 Jerry Willard | .05 |
| 347 Ken Griffey | .05 |
| 348 Franklin Stubbs (R) | .50 |
| 349 Aurelio Lopez | .05 |
| 350 Al Bumbry | .05 |
| 351 Charlie Moore | .05 |
| 352 Luis Sanchez | .05 |
| 353 Darrell Porter | .05 |
| 354 Bill Dawley | .05 |
| 355 Charlie Hudson | .05 |
| 356 Garry Templeton | .10 |
| 357 Cecilio Guante | .05 |
| 358 Jeff Leonard | .10 |
| 359 Paul Molitor | .25 |
| 360 Ron Gardenhire | .05 |
| 361 Larry Bowa | .05 |
| 362 Bob Kearney | .05 |
| 363 Garth Iorg | .05 |
| 364 Tom Brunansky | .30 |
| 365 Brad Gulden | .05 |
| 366 Greg Walker | .10 |
| 367 Mike Young | .15 |
| 368 Rick Waits | .05 |
| 369 Doug Bair | .05 |
| 370 Bob Shirley | .05 |
| 371 Bob Ojeda | .05 |
| 372 Bob Welch | .05 |
| 373 Neal Heaton | .05 |
| 374 Dan Jackson | .50 |
| 375 Donnie Hill | .05 |
| 376 Mike Stenhouse | .05 |
| 377 Bruce Kison | .05 |
| 378 Wayne Tolleson | .05 |
| 379 Floyd Bannister | .05 |
| 380 Vern Ruhle | .05 |
| 381 Tim Corcoran | .05 |
| 382 Kurt Kepshire (R) | .15 |
| 383 Bobby Brown | .05 |
| 384 Dave Van Gorder | .05 |
| 385 Rick Mahler | .05 |
| 386 Lee Mazzilli | .05 |
| 387 Bill Laskey | .05 |
| 388 Thad Bosley | .05 |
| 389 Al Chambers | .05 |
| 390 Tony Fernandez | .40 |
| 391 Ron Washington | .05 |
| 392 Bill Swaggerty (R) | .15 |
| 393 Bob L. Gibson | .05 |
| 394 Marty Castillo | .05 |
| 395 Steve Crawford | .05 |
| 396 Clay Christiansen (R) | .15 |
| 397 Bob Bailor | .05 |
| 398 Mike Hargrove | .05 |
| 399 Charlie Leibrandt | .05 |
| 400 Tom Burgmeier | .05 |
| 401 Razor Shines (R) | .15 |
| 402 Rob Wilfong | .05 |
| 403 Tom Henke | .15 |
| 404 Al Jones (R) | .15 |
| 405 Mike LaCoss | .05 |
| 406 Luis DeLeon | .05 |
| 407 Greg Gross | .05 |
| 408 Tom Hume | .05 |
| 409 Rick Camp | .05 |
| 410 Milt May | .05 |
| 411 Henry Cotto (R) | .20 |
| 412 David Von Ohlen | .05 |
| 413 Scott McGregor | .10 |
| 414 Ted Simmons | .10 |
| 415 Jack Morris | .20 |
| 416 Bill Buckner | .10 |
| 417 Butch Wynegar | .05 |
| 418 Steve Sax | .20 |
| 419 Steve Balboni | .05 |
| 420 Dwayne Murphy | .05 |
| 421 Andre Dawson | .25 |

| NO. PLAYER | MINT |
|---|---|
| 422 Charlie Hough | .05 |
| 423 Tommy John | .15 |
| 424 Tom Seaver | 1.00 |
| (photo of Floyd Bannister) | |
| 424 Tom Seaver | 5.00 |
| 425 Tom Herr | .10 |
| 426 Terry Puhl | .05 |
| 427 Al Holland | .05 |
| 428 Eddie Milner | .05 |
| 429 Terry Kennedy | .05 |
| 430 John Candelaria | .05 |
| 431 Manny Trillo | .05 |
| 432 Ken Oberkfell | .05 |
| 433 Rick Sutcliffe | .15 |
| 434 Ron Darling | 1.25 |
| 435 Spike Owen | .05 |
| 436 Frank Viola | .40 |
| 437 Lloyd Moseby | .20 |
| 438 Kirby Puckett (R) | 12.00 |
| 439 Jim Clancy | .05 |
| 440 Mike Moore | .05 |
| 441 Doug Sisk | .05 |
| 442 Dennis Eckersley | .05 |
| 443 Gerald Perry | .25 |
| 444 Dale Berra | .05 |
| 445 Dusty Baker | .05 |
| 446 Ed Whitson | .05 |
| 447 Cesar Cedeno | .08 |
| 448 Rick Schu (R) | .25 |
| 449 Joaquin Andujar | .10 |
| 450 Mark Bailey | .15 |
| 451 Ron Romanick (R) | .30 |
| 452 Julio Cruz | .05 |
| 453 Miguel Dilone | .05 |
| 454 Storm Davis | .05 |
| 455 Jaime Cocanower (R) | .15 |
| 456 Barbaro Garbey (R) | .15 |
| 457 Rich Gedman | .05 |
| 458 Phil Niekro | .15 |
| 459 Mike Scioscia | .05 |
| 460 Pat Tabler | .10 |
| 461 Darryl Motley | .05 |
| 462 Chris Codoroli | .05 |
| 463 Doug Flynn | .05 |
| 464 Billy Sample | .05 |
| 465 Mickey Rivers | .05 |
| 466 John Wathan | .05 |
| 467 Bill Krueger | .05 |
| 468 Andre Thornton | .10 |
| 469 Rex Hudler (R) | .15 |
| 470 Sid Bream (R) | .35 |
| 471 Kirk Gibson | .30 |
| 472 John Shelby | .05 |
| 473 Moose Haas | .05 |
| 474 Doug Corbett | .05 |
| 475 Willie McGee | .30 |
| 476 Bob Knepper | .10 |
| 477 Kevin Gross | .05 |
| 478 Carmelo Martinez | .10 |
| 479 Kent Tekulve | .05 |
| 480 Chili Davis | .10 |
| 481 Bobby Clark | .05 |
| 482 Mookie Wilson | .05 |
| 483 Dave Owen (R) | .15 |
| 484 Ed Nunez | .05 |
| 485 Rance Mulliniks | .05 |
| 486 Ken Schrom | .05 |
| 487 Jeff Russell | .05 |
| 488 Tom Paciorek | .05 |
| 489 Dan Ford | .05 |
| 490 Mike Caldwell | .05 |
| 491 Scottie Earl (R) | .15 |
| 492 Jose Rijo (R) | .35 |
| 493 Bruce Hurst | .05 |
| 494 Ken Landreaux | .05 |
| 495 Mike Fischlin | .05 |
| 496 Don Slaught | .05 |
| 497 Steve McCatty | .05 |
| 498 Gary Lucas | .05 |
| 499 Gary Pettis | .10 |
| 500 Marvis Foley | .05 |
| 501 Mike Squires | .05 |
| 502 Jim Pankovits | .10 |

| NO. PLAYER | MINT |
|---|---|
| 503 Luis Aguayo | .05 |
| 504 Ralph Citarella | .10 |
| 505 Bruce Bochy | .05 |
| 506 Bob Owchinko | .05 |
| 507 Pascual Perez | .05 |
| 508 Lee Lacy | .05 |
| 509 Atlee Hammaker | .05 |
| 510 Bob Dernier | .05 |
| 511 Ed Vande Berg | .05 |
| 512 Cliff Johnson | .05 |
| 513 Len Whitehouse | .05 |
| 514 Dennis Martinez | .10 |
| 515 Ed Romero | .05 |
| 516 Rusty Kuntz | .05 |
| 517 Rick Miller | .05 |
| 518 Dennis Rasmussen | .10 |
| 519 Steve Yeager | .05 |
| 520 Chris Bando | .05 |
| 521 U.L. Washington | .05 |
| 522 Curt Young (R) | .50 |
| 523 Angel Salazar | .05 |
| 524 Curt Kaufman (R) | .15 |
| 525 Odell Jones | .05 |
| 526 Juan Agosto | .05 |
| 527 Denny Walling | .05 |
| 528 Andy Hawkins | .05 |
| 529 Sixto Lezcano | .05 |
| 530 Skeeter Barnes | .10 |
| 531 Randy Johnson | .05 |
| 532 Jim Morrison | .05 |
| 533 Warren Brusstar | .05 |
| 534 Jeff Pendleton | .75 |
| (incorrect first name) | |
| 534 Terry Pendleton | 2.00 |
| 535 Vic Rodriguez (R) | .15 |
| 536 Bob McClure | .05 |
| 537 Dave Bergman | .05 |
| 538 Mark Clear | .05 |
| 539 Mike Pagliarulo (R) | 2.00 |
| 540 Terry Whitfield | .05 |
| 541 Joe Beckwith | .05 |
| 542 Jeff Burroughs | .05 |
| 543 Dan Schatzeder | .05 |
| 544 Donnie Scott | .10 |
| 545 Jim Slaton | .05 |
| 546 Greg Luzinski | .10 |
| 547 Mark Salas (R) | .25 |
| 548 Dave Smith | .05 |
| 549 John Wockenfuss | .05 |
| 550 Frank Pastore | .05 |
| 551 Tim Flannery | .05 |
| 552 Rick Rhoden | .10 |
| 553 Mark Davis | .05 |
| 554 Jeff Dedmon (R) | .10 |
| 555 Gary Woods | .05 |
| 556 Danny Heep | .05 |
| 557 Mark Langston (R) | 1.50 |
| 558 Darrell Brown | .05 |
| 559 Jimmy Key (R) | 1.75 |
| 560 Rick Lysander | .05 |
| 561 Doyle Alexander | .05 |
| 562 Mike Stanton | .05 |
| 563 Sid Fernandez | .75 |
| 564 Richie Hebner | .05 |
| 565 Alex Trevino | .05 |
| 566 Brian Harper | .05 |
| 567 Dan Gladden (R) | .40 |
| 568 Luis Salazar | .05 |
| 569 Tom Foley | .05 |
| 570 Larry Andersen | .05 |
| 571 Danny Cox | .10 |
| 572 Joe Sambito | .05 |
| 573 Juan Beniquez | .05 |
| 574 Joel Skinner | .05 |
| 575 Randy St. Claire | .10 |
| 576 Floyd Rayford | .05 |
| 577 Roy Howell | .05 |
| 578 John Grubb | .05 |
| 579 Ed Jurak | .05 |
| 580 John Montefusco | .05 |
| 581 Orel Hershiser (R) | 7.00 |
| 582 Tom Waddell (R) | .15 |
| 583 Mark Huismann | .05 |

| NO. PLAYER | MINT |
|---|---|
| 584 Joe Morgan | .30 |
| 585 Jim Wohlford | .05 |
| 586 Dave Schmidt | .05 |
| 587 Jeff Kunkel | .15 |
| 588 Hal McRae | .05 |
| 589 Bill Almon | .05 |
| 590 Carmen Castillo | .05 |
| 591 Omar Moreno | .05 |
| 592 Ken Howell (R) | .20 |
| 593 Tom Brookens | .05 |
| 594 Joe Nolan | .05 |
| 595 Willie Lozado | .10 |
| 596 Tom Nieto | .10 |
| 597 Walt Terrell | .05 |
| 598 Al Oliver | .10 |
| 599 Shane Rawley | .05 |
| 600 Denny Gonzalez | .10 |
| 601 Mark Grant | .10 |
| 602 Mike Armstrong | .05 |
| 603 George Foster | .15 |
| 604 Davey Lopes | .10 |
| 605 Salome Barojas | .05 |
| 606 Roy Lee Jackson | .05 |
| 607 Pete Filson | .05 |
| 608 Duane Walker | .05 |
| 609 Glenn Wilson | .10 |
| 610 Rafael Santana (R) | .25 |
| 611 Roy Smith | .15 |
| 612 Ruppert Jones | .05 |
| 613 Joe Cowley | .05 |
| 614 Al Nipper (R) | .20 |
| 615 Gene Nelson | .05 |
| 616 Joe Carter | 1.25 |
| 617 Ray Knight | .10 |
| 618 Chuck Rainey | .05 |
| 619 Dan Driessen | .05 |
| 620 Daryl Sconiers | .05 |
| 621 Bill Stein | .05 |
| 622 Roy Smalley | .05 |
| 623 Ed Lynch | .05 |
| 624 Jeff Stone (R) | .30 |
| 625 Bruce Berenyi | .05 |
| 626 Kelvin Chapman (R) | .15 |
| 627 Joe Price | .05 |
| 628 Steve Bedrosian | .12 |
| 629 Vic Mata | .15 |
| 630 Mike Krukow | .10 |
| 631 Phil Bradley (R) | 1.25 |
| 632 Jim Gott | .05 |
| 633 Randy Bush | .05 |
| 634 Tom Browning (R) | 1.50 |
| 635 Lou Gehrig Puzzle | .10 |
| 636 Reid Nichols | .05 |
| 637 Dan Pasqua (R) | .75 |
| 638 German Rivera | .10 |
| 639 Don Schulze | .05 |
| 640 Mike Jones | .10 |
| 641 Pete Rose (Mgr.) | 1.00 |
| 642 Wade Rowdon | .10 |
| 643 Jerry Narron | .05 |
| 644 Darrell Miller | .15 |
| 645 Tim Hulett (R) | .20 |
| 646 Andy McGaffigan | .05 |
| 647 Kurt Bevacqua | .05 |
| 648 John Russell (R) | .20 |
| 649 Ron Robinson | .20 |
| 650 Donnie Moore | .05 |
| 651 Two For the Title: | 3.50 |
| D. Winfield, D. Mattingly | |
| 652 Tim Laudner | .05 |
| 653 Steve Farr | .25 |
| — Checklist (DK) | .10 |
| — Checklist No. 1 | .08 |
| — Checklist No. 2 | .08 |
| — Checklist No. 3 | .08 |
| — Checklist No. 4 | .08 |
| — Checklist No. 5 | .08 |
| — Checklist No. 6 | .08 |
| **Gum Pack "Display Box" Cards** | |
| PC1 Dwight Gooden | 3.00 |
| PC2 Ryne Sandberg | .30 |
| PC3 Ron Kittle | .12 |
| — Lou Gehrig Puzzle | .15 |

Card values from this set fluctuate considerably.

Features the rookie cards of Jose Canseco and Vince Coleman. Donruss limited production. Three cards (PC-4 to PC-6) and an Aaron puzzle card were printed on the bottom of gum pack display boxes. Three other cards (PC-7 to PC-9) and the Aaron puzzle card were printed on the bottom of display boxes of 1986 All-Star cards. These cards are not part of the set. The *checklist* cards are *not* numbered.

| NO. PLAYER | MINT |
|---|---|
| **No. 1 to 26—Diamond Kings** | |
| 1 Kirk Gibson (DK) | .25 |
| 2 Goose Gossage (DK) | .15 |
| 3 Willie McGee (DK) | .30 |
| 4 George Bell (DK) | .30 |
| 5 Tony Armas (DK) | .10 |
| 6 Chili Davis (DK) | .10 |
| 7 Cecil Cooper (DK) | .15 |
| 8 Mike Boddicker (DK) | .10 |
| 9 Davey Lopes (DK) | .10 |
| 10 Bill Doran (DK) | .10 |
| 11 Bret Saberhagen (DK) | .25 |
| 12 Brett Butler (DK) | .10 |
| 13 Harold Baines (DK) | .20 |
| 14 Mike Davis (DK) | .10 |
| 15 Tony Perez (DK) | .15 |
| 16 Willie Randolph (DK) | .10 |
| 17 Bob Boone (DK) | .10 |
| 18 Orel Hershiser (DK) | .60 |
| 19 Johnny Ray (DK) | .10 |
| 20 Gary Ward (DK) | .10 |
| 21 Rick Mahler (DK) | .10 |
| 22 Phil Bradley (DK) | .20 |
| 23 Jerry Koosman (DK) | .10 |
| 24 Tom Brunansky (DK) | .10 |
| 25 Andre Dawson (DK) | .20 |
| 26 Dwigt Gooden (DK) | 1.00 |
| **No. 27 to 46 (Rated Rookies)** | |
| 27 Kal Daniels (R) | 6.00 |
| 28 Fred McGriff (R) | 4.00 |
| 29 Cory Snyder (R) | 3.00 |
| 30 Jose Guzman (R) | .40 |
| 31 Ty Gainey (R) | .20 |
| 32 Johnny Abrego (R) | .15 |
| 33 Andres Galarraga (R) | 5.00 |
| 34 Dave Shipanoff (R) | .15 |
| 35 Mark McLemore (R) | .20 |
| 36 Marty Clary (R) | .15 |
| 37 Paul O'Neill (R) | .30 |
| 38 Danny Tartabull | 1.50 |
| 39 Jose Canseco (R) | 50.00 |
| 40 Juan Nieves (R) | .30 |
| 41 Lance McCullers (R) | .35 |
| 42 Rick Surhoff (R) | .15 |
| 43 Todd Worrell (R) | .75 |
| 44 Bob Kipper (R) | .20 |
| 45 John Habyan (R) | .15 |
| 46 Mike Woodard (R) | .15 |
| 47 Mike Boddicker | .10 |
| 48 Robin Yount | .30 |
| 49 Lou Whitaker | .15 |
| 50 Oil Can Boyd | .05 |
| 51 Ricky Henderson | .35 |
| 52 Mike Marshall | .10 |
| 53 George Brett | .50 |
| 54 Dave Kingman | .10 |
| 55 Hubie Brooks | .10 |
| 56 Oddibe McDowell | .30 |
| 57 Doug DeCinces | .10 |
| 58 Britt Burns | .05 |
| 59 Ozzie Smith | .25 |
| 60 Jose Cruz | .10 |
| 61 Mike Schmidt | .50 |
| 62 Pete Rose | .75 |
| 63 Steve Garvey | .35 |
| 64 Tony Pena | .10 |

| NO. PLAYER | MINT |
|---|---|
| 65 Chili Davis | .10 |
| 66 Dale Murphy | .50 |
| 67 Ryne Sandberg | .30 |
| 68 Gary Carter | .30 |
| 69 Alvin Davis | .15 |
| 70 Kent Hrbek | .15 |
| 71 George Bell | .30 |
| 72 Kirby Puckett | 1.50 |
| 73 Lloyd Moseby | .10 |
| 74 Bob Kearney | .05 |
| 75 Dwight Gooden | 2.00 |
| 76 Gary Matthews | .05 |
| 77 Rick Mahler | .05 |
| 78 Benny Distefano | .05 |
| 79 Jeff Leonard | .05 |
| 80 Kevin McReynolds | .30 |
| 81 Ron Oester | .05 |
| 82 John Russell | .05 |
| 83 Tommy Herr | .10 |
| 84 Jerry Mumphrey | .05 |
| 85 Ron Romanick | .05 |
| 86 Daryl Boston | .05 |
| 87 Andre Dawson | .25 |
| 88 Eddie Murray | .40 |
| 89 Dion James | .05 |
| 90 Chet Lemon | .05 |
| 91 Bob Stanley | .05 |
| 92 Willie Randolph | .05 |
| 93 Mike Scioscia | .05 |
| 94 Tom Waddell | .05 |
| 95 Danny Jackson | .30 |
| 96 Mike Davis | .05 |
| 97 Mike Fitzgerald | .05 |
| 98 Gary Ward | .05 |
| 99 Pete O'Brien | .05 |
| 100 Bret Saberhagen | .40 |
| 101 Alfredo Griffin | .05 |
| 102 Brett Butler | .05 |
| 103 Ron Guidry | .15 |
| 104 Jerry Reuss | .05 |
| 105 Jack Morris | .15 |
| 106 Rick Dempsey | .05 |
| 107 Ray Burris | .05 |
| 108 Brian Downing | .05 |
| 109 Willie McGee | .20 |
| 110 Bill Doran | .05 |
| 111 Kent Tekulve | .05 |
| 112 Tony Gwynn | .75 |
| 113 Marvell Wynne | .05 |
| 114 David Green | .05 |
| 115 Jim Gantner | .05 |
| 116 George Foster | .15 |
| 117 Steve Trout | .05 |
| 118 Mark Langston | .12 |
| 119 Tony Fernandez | .15 |
| 120 John Butcher | .05 |
| 121 Ron Robinson | .05 |
| 122 Dan Spillner | .05 |
| 123 Mike Young | .15 |
| 124 Paul Molitor | .20 |
| 125 Kirk Gibson | .30 |
| 126 Ken Griffey | .05 |
| 127 Tony Armas | .05 |
| 128 Mariano Duncan (R) | .25 |
| 129 Pat Tabler | .05 |
| 130 Frank White | .05 |

| NO. PLAYER | MINT |
|---|---|
| 131 Carney Lansford | .10 |
| 132 Vance Law | .05 |
| 133 Dick Schofield | .05 |
| 134 Wayne Tolleson | .05 |
| 135 Greg Walker | .10 |
| 136 Denny Walling | .05 |
| 137 Ozzie Virgil | .05 |
| 138 Ricky Horton | .05 |
| 139 LaMarr Hoyt | .10 |
| 140 Wayne Krenchicki | .05 |
| 141 Glenn Hubbard | .05 |
| 142 Cecilio Guante | .05 |
| 143 Mike Krukow | .05 |
| 144 Lee Smith | .05 |
| 145 Ed Nunez | .05 |
| 146 Dave Stieb | .15 |
| 147 Mike Smithson | .05 |
| 148 Ken Dixon | .05 |
| 149 Danny Darwin | .05 |
| 150 Chris Pittaro | .15 |
| 151 Bill Buckner | .10 |
| 152 Mike Pagliarulo | .25 |
| 153 Bill Russell | .05 |
| 154 Brook Jacoby | .10 |
| 155 Pat Sheridan | .05 |
| 156 Mike Gallego | .10 |
| 157 Jim Wohlford | .05 |
| 158 Gary Pettis | .10 |
| 159 Toby Harrah | .05 |
| 160 Rich Dotson | .05 |
| 161 Bob Knepper | .05 |
| 162 Dave Dravecky | .05 |
| 163 Greg Gross | .05 |
| 164 Eric Davis | 3.00 |
| 165 Gerald Perry | .25 |
| 166 Rick Rhoden | .05 |
| 167 Keith Moreland | .05 |
| 168 Jack Clark | .25 |
| 169 Storm Davis | .05 |
| 170 Cecil Cooper | .15 |
| 171 Alan Trammell | .25 |
| 172 Roger Clemens | 3.50 |
| 173 Don Mattingly | 5.00 |
| 174 Pedro Guerrero | .25 |
| 175 Willie Wilson | .15 |
| 176 Dwayne Murphy | .05 |
| 177 Tim Raines | .25 |
| 178 Larry Parrish | .05 |
| 179 Mike Witt | .10 |
| 180 Harold Baines | .20 |
| 181 Vince Coleman (R) | 2.00 |
| 182 Jeff Heathcock (R) | .15 |
| 183 Steve Carlton | .30 |
| 184 Mario Soto | .10 |
| 185 Goose Gossage | .15 |
| 186 Johnny Ray | .10 |
| 187 Dan Gladden | .05 |
| 188 Bob Horner | .15 |
| 189 Rick Sutcliffe | .15 |
| 190 Keith Hernandez | .25 |
| 191 Phil Bradley | .20 |
| 192 Tom Brunansky | .25 |
| 193 Jesse Barfield | .25 |
| 194 Frank Viola | .75 |
| 195 Willie Upshaw | .10 |
| 196 Jim Beattie | .05 |

| NO. PLAYER | MINT |
|---|---|
| 197 Darryl Strawberry | 1.50 |
| 198 Ron Cey | .10 |
| 199 Steve Bedrosian | .15 |
| 200 Steve Kemp | .05 |
| 201 Manny Trillo | .05 |
| 202 Garry Templeton | .05 |
| 203 Dave Parker | .20 |
| 204 John Denny | .05 |
| 205 Terry Pendleton | .05 |
| 206 Terry Puhl | .05 |
| 207 Bobby Grich | .05 |
| 208 Ozzie Guillen (R) | .50 |
| 209 Jeff Reardon | .10 |
| 210 Cal Ripken, Jr. | .40 |
| 211 Bill Schroeder | .05 |
| 212 Dan Petry | .15 |
| 213 Jim Rice | .25 |
| 214 Dave Righetti | .10 |
| 215 Fernando Valenzuela | .25 |
| 216 Julio Franco | .15 |
| 217 Darryl Motley | .05 |
| 218 Dave Collins | .05 |
| 219 Tim Wallach | .10 |
| 220 George Wright | .05 |
| 221 Tommy Dunbar | .05 |
| 222 Steve Balboni | .05 |
| 223 Jay Howell | .05 |
| 224 Joe Carter | .30 |
| 225 Ed Whitson | .05 |
| 226 Orel Hershiser | .60 |
| 227 Willie Hernandez | .15 |
| 228 Lee Lacy | .05 |
| 229 Rollie Fingers | .10 |
| 230 Bob Boone | .05 |
| 231 Joaquin Andujar | .10 |
| 232 Craig Reynolds | .05 |
| 233 Shane Rawley | .05 |
| 234 Eric Show | .05 |
| 235 Jose DeLeon | .05 |
| 236 Jose Uribe (R) | .15 |
| 237 Moose Haas | .05 |
| 238 Wally Backman | .05 |
| 239 Dennis Eckersley | .05 |
| 240 Mike Moore | .05 |
| 241 Damaso Garcia | .05 |
| 242 Tim Teufel | .05 |
| 243 Dave Concepcion | .05 |
| 244 Floyd Bannister | .05 |
| 245 Fred Lynn | .15 |
| 246 Charlie Moore | .05 |
| 247 Walt Terrell | .05 |
| 248 Dave Winfield | .30 |
| 249 Dwight Evans | .10 |
| 250 Dennis Powell | .10 |
| 251 Andre Thornton | .05 |
| 252 Onix Concepcion | .05 |
| 253 Mike Heath | .05 |
| 254 David Palmer | .05 |
| 255 Donnie Moore | .05 |
| 256 Curtis Wilkerson | .05 |
| 257 Julio Cruz | .05 |
| 258 Nolan Ryan | .30 |
| 259 Jeff Stone | .05 |
| 260 John Tudor | .15 |
| 261 Mark Thurmond | .05 |
| 262 Jay Tibbs | .05 |

Card values from this set fluctuate considerably.

| NO. | PLAYER | MINT |
|-----|--------|------|
| 263 | Rafael Ramirez | .05 |
| 264 | Larry McWilliams | .05 |
| 265 | Mark Davis | .05 |
| 266 | Bob Dernier | .05 |
| 267 | Matt Young | .05 |
| 268 | Jim Clancy | .05 |
| 269 | Mickey Hatcher | .05 |
| 270 | Sammy Stewart | .05 |
| 271 | Bob Gibson | .05 |
| 272 | Nelson Simmons (R) | .15 |
| 273 | Rich Gedman | .05 |
| 274 | Butch Wynegar | .05 |
| 275 | Ken Howell | .05 |
| 276 | Mel Hall | .05 |
| 277 | Jim Sundberg | .05 |
| 278 | Chris Codiroli | .05 |
| 279 | H. Winningham (R) | .15 |
| 280 | Rod Carew | .30 |
| 281 | Don Slaught | .05 |
| 282 | Scott Fletcher | .05 |
| 283 | Bill Dawley | .05 |
| 284 | Andy Hawkins | .05 |
| 285 | Glenn Wilson | .10 |
| 286 | Nick Esasky | .05 |
| 287 | Claudell Washington | .05 |
| 288 | Lee Mazzilli | .05 |
| 289 | Jody Davis | .05 |
| 290 | Darrell Porter | .05 |
| 291 | Scott McGregor | .05 |
| 292 | Ted Simmons | .10 |
| 293 | Aurelio Lopez | .05 |
| 294 | Marty Barrett | .05 |
| 295 | Dale Berra | .05 |
| 296 | Greg Brock | .05 |
| 297 | Charlie Leibrandt | .05 |
| 298 | Bill Krueger | .05 |
| 299 | Bryn Smith | .05 |
| 300 | Burt Hooton | .05 |
| 301 | Stu Cliburn (R) | .20 |
| 302 | Luis Salazar | .05 |
| 303 | Ken Dayley | .05 |
| 304 | Frank DiPino | .05 |
| 305 | Von Hayes | .15 |
| 306 | Gary Redus | .05 |
| 307 | Craig Lefferts | .05 |
| 308 | Sam Khalifa | .15 |
| 309 | Scott Garrelts | .05 |
| 310 | Rick Cerone | .05 |
| 311 | Shawon Dunston | .05 |
| 312 | Howard Johnson | .25 |
| 313 | Jim Presley | .20 |
| 314 | Gary Gaetti | .30 |
| 315 | Luis Leal | .05 |
| 316 | Mark Salas | .05 |
| 317 | Bill Caudill | .05 |
| 318 | Dave Henderson | .05 |
| 319 | Rafael Santana | .05 |
| 320 | Leon Durham | .15 |
| 321 | Bruce Sutter | .15 |
| 322 | Jason Thompson | .05 |
| 323 | Bob Brenly | .05 |
| 324 | Carmelo Martinez | .05 |
| 325 | Eddie Milner | .05 |
| 326 | Juan Samuel | .15 |
| 327 | Tom Nieto | .05 |
| 328 | Dave Smith | .05 |
| 329 | Urbano Lugo (R) | .15 |
| 330 | Joel Skinner | .05 |
| 331 | Bill Gullickson | .05 |
| 332 | Floyd Rayford | .05 |
| 333 | Ben Oglivie | .05 |
| 334 | Lance Parrish | .15 |
| 335 | Jackie Gutierrez | .05 |
| 336 | Dennis Rasmussen | .05 |
| 337 | Terry Whitfield | .05 |
| 338 | Neal Heaton | .05 |
| 339 | Jorge Orta | .05 |
| 340 | Donnie Hill | .05 |
| 341 | Joe Hesketh | .10 |
| 342 | Charlie Hough | .05 |
| 343 | Dave Rozema | .05 |
| 344 | Greg Pryor | .05 |
| 345 | Mickey Tettleton (R) | .10 |
| 346 | George Vukovich | .05 |
| 347 | Don Baylor | .10 |

| NO. | PLAYER | MINT |
|-----|--------|------|
| 348 | Carlos Diaz | .05 |
| 349 | Barbaro Garbey | .05 |
| 350 | Larry Sheets | .15 |
| 351 | Teddy Higuera (R) | 1.25 |
| 352 | Juan Beniquez | .05 |
| 353 | Bob Forsch | .05 |
| 354 | Mark Bailey | .05 |
| 355 | Larry Andersen | .05 |
| 356 | Terry Kennedy | .05 |
| 357 | Don Robinson | .05 |
| 358 | Jim Gott | .05 |
| 359 | Earnest Riles (R) | .30 |
| 360 | John Christensen | .15 |
| 361 | Ray Fontenot | .05 |
| 362 | Spike Owen | .05 |
| 363 | Jim Acker | .05 |
| 364 | Ron Davis | .05 |
| 365 | Tom Hume | .05 |
| 366 | Carlton Fisk | .15 |
| 367 | Nate Snell (R) | .15 |
| 368 | Rick Manning | .05 |
| 369 | Darrell Evans | .10 |
| 370 | Ron Hassey | .05 |
| 371 | Wade Boggs | 2.50 |
| 372 | Rick Honeycutt | .05 |
| 373 | Chris Bando | .05 |
| 374 | Bud Black | .05 |
| 375 | Steve Henderson | .05 |
| 376 | Charlie Lea | .05 |
| 377 | Reggie Jackson | .40 |
| 378 | Dave Schmidt | .05 |
| 379 | Bob James | .05 |
| 380 | Glenn Davis | 2.00 |
| 381 | Tim Corcoran | .05 |
| 382 | Danny Cox | .10 |
| 383 | Tim Flannery | .05 |
| 384 | Tom Browning | .15 |
| 385 | Rick Camp | .05 |
| 386 | Jim Morrison | .05 |
| 387 | Dave LaPoint | .05 |
| 388 | Davey Lopes | .05 |
| 389 | Al Cowens | .05 |
| 390 | Doyle Alexander | .05 |
| 391 | Tim Laudner | .05 |
| 392 | Don Aase | .05 |
| 393 | Jaime Cocanower | .05 |
| 394 | Randy O'Neal | .05 |
| 395 | Mike Easler | .05 |
| 396 | Scott Bradley | .05 |
| 397 | Tom Niedenfuer | .05 |
| 398 | Jerry Willard | .05 |
| 399 | Lonnie Smith | .07 |
| 400 | Bruce Bochte | .05 |
| 401 | Terry Francona | .05 |
| 402 | Jim Slaton | .05 |
| 403 | Bill Stein | .05 |
| 404 | Timmy Hulett | .05 |
| 405 | Alan Ashby | .05 |
| 406 | Tim Stoddard | .05 |
| 407 | Garry Maddox | .05 |
| 408 | Ted Power | .05 |
| 409 | Len Barker | .05 |
| 410 | Denny Gonzalez | .05 |
| 411 | George Frazier | .05 |
| 412 | Andy Van Slyke | .30 |
| 413 | Jim Dwyer | .05 |
| 414 | Paul Householder | .05 |
| 415 | Alejandro Sanchez | .05 |
| 416 | Steve Crawford | .05 |
| 417 | Dan Pasqua | .15 |
| 418 | Enos Cabell | .05 |
| 419 | Mike Jones | .05 |
| 420 | Steve Kiefer | .05 |
| 421 | Tim Burke (R) | .25 |
| 422 | Mike Mason | .05 |
| 423 | Ruppert Jones | .05 |
| 424 | Jerry Hairston | .05 |
| 425 | Tito Landrum | .05 |
| 426 | Jeff Calhoun (R) | .10 |
| 427 | Don Carman (R) | .25 |
| 428 | Tony Perez | .15 |
| 429 | Jerry Davis | .05 |
| 430 | Bob Walk | .05 |
| 431 | Brad Wellman | .05 |
| 432 | Terry Forster | .05 |

| NO. | PLAYER | MINT |
|-----|--------|------|
| 433 | Billy Hatcher | .10 |
| 434 | Clint Hurdle | .05 |
| 435 | Ivan Calderon (R) | 1.00 |
| 436 | Pete Filson | .05 |
| 437 | Tom Henke | .10 |
| 438 | Dave Engle | .05 |
| 439 | Tom Filer | .05 |
| 440 | Gorman Thomas | .10 |
| 441 | Rick Aguilera (R) | .25 |
| 442 | Scott Sanderson | .05 |
| 443 | Jeff Dedmon | .05 |
| 444 | Joe Orsulak (R) | .20 |
| 445 | Atlee Hammaker | .05 |
| 446 | Jerry Royster | .05 |
| 447 | Buddy Bell | .10 |
| 448 | Dave Rucker | .05 |
| 449 | Ivan DeJesus | .05 |
| 450 | Jim Pankovits | .05 |
| 451 | Jerry Narron | .05 |
| 452 | Bryan Little | .05 |
| 453 | Gary Lucas | .05 |
| 454 | Dennis Martinez | .05 |
| 455 | Ed Romero | .05 |
| 456 | Bob Melvin (R) | .10 |
| 457 | Glenn Hoffman | .05 |
| 458 | Bob Shirley | .05 |
| 459 | Bob Welch | .05 |
| 460 | Carmen Castillo | .05 |
| 461 | Dave Leeper (R) | .10 |
| 462 | Tim Birtsas (R) | .15 |
| 463 | Randy St. Claire | .05 |
| 464 | Chris Welsh | .05 |
| 465 | Greg Harris | .05 |
| 466 | Lynn Jones | .05 |
| 467 | Dusty Baker | .05 |
| 468 | Roy Smith | .05 |
| 469 | Andre Robertson | .05 |
| 470 | Ken Landreaux | .05 |
| 471 | Dave Bergman | .05 |
| 472 | Gary Roenicke | .05 |
| 473 | Pete Vuckovich | .05 |
| 474 | Kirk McCaskill (R) | .35 |
| 475 | Jeff Lahti | .05 |
| 476 | Mike Scott | .35 |
| 477 | Darren Daulton (R) | .25 |
| 478 | Graig Nettles | .10 |
| 479 | Bill Almon | .05 |
| 480 | Greg Minton | .05 |
| 481 | Randy Ready | .05 |
| 482 | Len Dykstra (R) | .90 |
| 483 | Thad Bosley | .05 |
| 484 | Harold Reynolds (R) | .40 |
| 485 | Al Oliver | .10 |
| 486 | Roy Smalley | .05 |
| 487 | John Franco | .10 |
| 488 | Juan Agosto | .05 |
| 489 | Al Pardo | .15 |
| 490 | Bill Wegman (R) | .15 |
| 491 | Frank Tanana | .05 |
| 492 | Brian Fisher (R) | .30 |
| 493 | Mark Clear | .05 |
| 494 | Len Matuszek | .05 |
| 495 | Ramon Romero (R) | .10 |
| 496 | John Wathan | .05 |
| 497 | Rob Picciolo | .05 |
| 498 | U.L. Washington | .05 |
| 499 | John Candelaria | .05 |
| 500 | Duane Walker | .05 |
| 501 | Gene Nelson | .05 |
| 502 | John Mizerock | .05 |
| 503 | Luis Aguayo | .05 |
| 504 | Kurt Kepshire | .05 |
| 505 | Ed Wojna (R) | .15 |
| 506 | Joe Price | .05 |
| 507 | Milt Thompson (R) | .45 |
| 508 | Junior Ortiz | .05 |
| 509 | Vida Blue | .05 |
| 510 | Steve Engel (R) | .10 |
| 511 | Karl Best (R) | .10 |
| 512 | Cecil Fielder (R) | .25 |
| 513 | Frank Eufemia (R) | .15 |
| 514 | Tippy Martinez | .05 |
| 515 | Billy Robidoux (R) | .25 |
| 516 | Bill Scherrer | .05 |
| 517 | Bruce Hurst | .10 |

| NO. | PLAYER | MINT |
|-----|--------|------|
| 518 | Rich Bordi | .05 |
| 519 | Steve Yeager | .05 |
| 520 | Tony Bernazard | .05 |
| 521 | Hal McRae | .05 |
| 522 | Jose Rijo | .05 |
| 523 | Mitch Webster (R) | .40 |
| 524 | Jack Howell (R) | .50 |
| 525 | Alan Bannister | .05 |
| 526 | Ron Kittle | .10 |
| 527 | Phil Garner | .05 |
| 528 | Kurt Bevacqua | .05 |
| 529 | Kevin Gross | .05 |
| 530 | Bo Diaz | .05 |
| 531 | Ken Oberkfell | .05 |
| 532 | Rick Reuschel | .05 |
| 533 | Ron Meridith (R) | .10 |
| 534 | Steve Braun | .05 |
| 535 | Wayne Gross | .05 |
| 536 | Ray Searage | .05 |
| 537 | Tom Brookens | .05 |
| 538 | Al Nipper | .05 |
| 539 | Billy Sample | .05 |
| 540 | Steve Sax | .20 |
| 541 | Dan Quisenberry | .15 |
| 542 | Tony Phillips | .05 |
| 543 | Floyd Youmans (R) | .50 |
| 544 | Steve Buechele (R) | .25 |
| 545 | Craig Gerber (R) | .10 |
| 546 | Joe DeSa (R) | .15 |
| 547 | Brian Harper | .05 |
| 548 | Kevin Bass | .05 |
| 549 | Tom Foley | .05 |
| 550 | Dave Van Gorder | .05 |
| 551 | Bruce Bochy | .05 |
| 552 | R.J. Reynolds | .05 |
| 553 | Chris Brown (R) | .50 |
| 554 | Bruce Benedict | .05 |
| 555 | Warren Brusstar | .05 |
| 556 | Danny Heep | .05 |
| 557 | Darnell Coles | .05 |
| 558 | Greg Gagne | .05 |
| 559 | Ernie Whitt | .05 |
| 560 | Ron Washington | .05 |
| 561 | Jimmy Key | .15 |
| 562 | Billy Swift | .05 |
| 563 | Ron Darling | .25 |
| 564 | Dick Ruthven | .05 |
| 565 | Zane Smith | .25 |
| 566 | Sid Bream | .05 |
| 567 | Joel Youngblood | .05 |
| 568 | Mario Ramirez | .05 |
| 569 | Tom Runnells (R) | .10 |
| 570 | Rick Schu | .05 |
| 571 | Bill Campbell | .05 |
| 572 | Dickie Thon | .05 |
| 573 | Al Holland | .05 |
| 574 | Reid Nichols | .05 |
| 575 | Bert Roberge | .05 |
| 576 | Mike Flanagan | .05 |
| 577 | Tim Leary | .30 |
| 578 | Mike Laga | .05 |
| 579 | Steve Lyons | .05 |
| 580 | Phil Niekro | .15 |
| 581 | Gilberto Reyes (R) | .15 |
| 582 | Jamie Easterly | .05 |
| 583 | Mark Gubicza | .05 |
| 584 | Stan Javier (R) | .20 |
| 585 | Bill Laskey | .05 |
| 586 | Jeff Russell | .05 |
| 587 | Dickie Noles | .05 |
| 588 | Steve Farr | .05 |
| 589 | Steve Ontiveros (R) | .20 |
| 590 | Mike Hargrove | .05 |
| 591 | Marty Bystrom | .05 |
| 592 | Franklin Stubbs | .10 |
| 593 | Larry Herndon | .05 |
| 594 | Bill Swaggerty | .05 |
| 595 | Carlos Ponce (R) | .10 |
| 596 | Pat Perry (R) | .10 |
| 597 | Ray Knight | .05 |
| 598 | Steve Lombardozzi (R) | .20 |
| 599 | Brad Havens | .05 |
| 600 | Pat Clements (R) | .20 |
| 601 | Joe Niekro | .10 |
| 602 | Hank Aaron Puzzle | .15 |

Card values from this set fluctuate considerably.

| NO. | PLAYER | MINT |
|---|---|---|
| 603 | Dwayne Henry (R) | .10 |
| 604 | Mookie Wilson | .05 |
| 605 | Buddy Biancalana | .05 |
| 606 | Rance Mulliniks | .05 |
| 607 | Alan Wiggins | .07 |
| 608 | Joe Cowley | .05 |
| 609 | Tom Seaver | .35 |
| 610 | Neil Allen | .05 |
| 611 | Don Sutton | .20 |
| 612 | Fred Toliver (R) | .15 |
| 613 | Jay Baller (R) | .15 |
| 614 | Marc Sullivan (R) | .10 |
| 615 | John Grubb | .05 |
| 616 | Bruce Kison | .05 |
| 617 | Bill Madlock | .10 |
| 618 | Chris Chambliss | .05 |
| 619 | Dave Stewart | .10 |
| 620 | Tim Lollar | .05 |
| 621 | Gary Lavelle | .05 |

| NO. | PLAYER | MINT |
|---|---|---|
| 622 | Charles Hudson | .05 |
| 623 | Joel Davis (R) | .20 |
| 624 | Joe Johnson (R) | .20 |
| 625 | Sid Fernandez | .15 |
| 626 | Dennis Lamp | .05 |
| 627 | Terry Harper | .05 |
| 628 | Jack Lazorko | .05 |
| 629 | Roger McDowell (R) | .50 |
| 630 | Mark Funderburk (R) | .25 |
| 631 | Ed Lynch | .05 |
| 632 | Rudy Law | .05 |
| 633 | Roger Mason (R) | .15 |
| 634 | Mike Felder (R) | .15 |
| 635 | Ken Schrom | .05 |
| 636 | Bob Ojeda | .05 |
| 637 | Ed Vande Berg | .05 |
| 638 | Bobby Meacham | .05 |
| 639 | Cliff Johnson | .05 |

| NO. | PLAYER | MINT |
|---|---|---|
| 640 | Garth Iorg | .05 |
| 641 | Dan Driessen | .05 |
| 642 | Mike Brown | .05 |
| 643 | John Shelby | .05 |
| 644 | Pete Rose Ty-Breaking Hit #4192: | .30 |
| 645 | Knuckle Brothers: Phil and Joe Niekro | .10 |
| 646 | Jesse Orosco | .05 |
| 647 | Billy Beane (R) | .25 |
| 648 | Cesar Cedeno | .05 |
| 649 | Bert Blyleven | .10 |
| 650 | Max Venable | .05 |
| 651 | Fleet Feet: W. McGee, V. Coleman | .30 |
| 652 | Calvin Schiraldi | .05 |
| 653 | King of Kings: Pete Rose | .75 |

| NO. | PLAYER | MINT |
|---|---|---|
| — | Checklist (DK) | .08 |
| — | Checklist No. 1 | .08 |
| — | Checklist No. 2 | .08 |
| — | Checklist No. 3 | .08 |
| — | Checklist No. 4 | .08 |
| — | Checklist No. 5 | .08 |
| — | Checklist No. 6 | .08 |

**Gum Pack Display Box Cards**
| NO. | PLAYER | MINT |
|---|---|---|
| PC4 | Kirk Gibson | .35 |
| PC5 | Willie Hernandez | .20 |
| PC6 | Doug DeCinces | .15 |
| — | Aaron Puzzle | .15 |

**All-Star Display Box Cards**
| NO. | PLAYER | MINT |
|---|---|---|
| PC7 | Wade Boggs | 1.00 |
| PC8 | Lee Smith | .15 |
| PC9 | Cecil Cooper | .15 |
| — | Aaron Puzzle | .15 |

# 1986 Donruss Rookies....Complete Set of 56 Cards—Value $20.00

Features the outstanding rookies of the 1986 season. The cards are coated with a glossy finish. The entire set was packaged in a printed box, and distributed exclusively through card hobby dealers.

| NO. | PLAYER | MINT |
|---|---|---|
| 1 | Wally Joyner (RR) | 5.00 |
| 2 | Tracy Jones | .50 |
| 3 | Allan Anderson | .15 |
| 4 | Ed Correa | .30 |
| 5 | Reggie Williams | .25 |
| 6 | Charlie Kerfeld | .30 |
| 7 | Andres Galarraga | 1.00 |
| 8 | Bob Tewksbury | .25 |
| 9 | Al Newman | .20 |
| 10 | Andres Thomas | .25 |
| 11 | Barry Bonds (RR) | 1.00 |
| 12 | Juan Nieves | .20 |
| 13 | Mark Eichhorn | .75 |
| 14 | Dan Plesac | .30 |

| NO. | PLAYER | MINT |
|---|---|---|
| 15 | Cory Snyder | 1.50 |
| 16 | Kelly Gruber | .20 |
| 17 | Kevin Mitchell (RR) | .50 |
| 18 | Steve Lombardozzi | .20 |
| 19 | Mitch Williams | .20 |
| 20 | John Cerutti | .25 |
| 21 | Todd Worrell | .45 |
| 22 | Jose Canseco | 8.00 |
| 23 | Pete Incaviglia (RR) | 1.25 |
| 24 | Jose Guzman | .25 |
| 25 | Scott Bailes | .20 |
| 26 | Greg Matthews | .30 |
| 27 | Eric King | .25 |
| 28 | Paul Assenmacher | .25 |

| NO. | PLAYER | MINT |
|---|---|---|
| 29 | Jeff Sellers | .20 |
| 30 | Bobby Bonilla | 1.25 |
| 31 | Doug Drabek | .35 |
| 32 | Will Clark (RR) | 3.00 |
| 33 | Leon "Bip" Roberts | .30 |
| 34 | Jim Deshaies | .35 |
| 35 | Mike Lavalliere | .30 |
| 36 | Scott Bankhead | .30 |
| 37 | Dale Sveum | .35 |
| 38 | Bo Jackson (RR) | 2.00 |
| 39 | Rob Thompson | .35 |
| 40 | Eric Plunk | .25 |
| 41 | Bill Bathe | .25 |
| 42 | John Kruk..(RR) | .75 |

| NO. | PLAYER | MINT |
|---|---|---|
| 43 | Andy Allanson | .20 |
| 44 | Mark Portugal | .20 |
| 45 | Danny Tartabull | 1.00 |
| 46 | Bob Kpper | .20 |
| 47 | Gene Walter | .25 |
| 48 | Rey Quinonez | .25 |
| 49 | Bobby Witt | .40 |
| 50 | Bill Mooneyham | .30 |
| 51 | John Cangelos | .35 |
| 52 | Ruben Sierra (RR) | 2.00 |
| 53 | Rob Woodward | .20 |
| 54 | Ed Hearn | .20 |
| 55 | Joel McKeon | .20 |
| 56 | Checklist | .20 |

# 1987 Donruss....Complete Set of 660 Cards—Value $40.00 (Factory-Sealed set—Value $50.00)

Features the rookie cards of Bo Jackson, Wally Joyner, Ruben Sierra and Pete Incaviglia. Donruss limited production. Six cards (PC10 to PC15) and a Clemente puzzle card were printed on the bottom of gum display boxes. These cards are not part of the set. Cards 14, 22 and 25 exist with the "yellow" strip missing on back—worth triple the value of the corrected cards.

| NO. PLAYER | MINT | NO. PLAYER | MINT | NO. PLAYER | MINT | NO. PLAYER | MINT |
|---|---|---|---|---|---|---|---|
| **No. 1 to 26—Diamond Kings** | | 65 R.J. Reynolds | .05 | 131 Julio Franco | .12 | 197 Tom Henke | .10 |
| 1 Wally Joyner (DK) | 1.50 | 66 Will Clark (R) | 2.25 | 132 Bret Saberhagen | .20 | 198 Karl Best | .05 |
| 2 Roger Clemens (DK) | .75 | 67 Ozzie Virgil | .05 | 133 Mike Davis | .05 | 199 Dwight Gooden | .75 |
| 3 Dale Murphy (DK) | .40 | 68 Rick Sutcliffe | .10 | 134 Joe Hesketh | .05 | 200 Checklist: 134-209 | .08 |
| 4 Darryl Strawberry (DK) | .60 | 69 Gary Carter | .30 | 135 Wally Joyner (R) | 2.00 | 201 Steve Trout | .05 |
| 5 Ozzie Smith (DK) | .10 | 70 Mike Moore | .05 | 136 Don Slaught | .05 | 202 Rafael Ramirez | .05 |
| 6 Jose Canseco (DK) | 1.25 | 71 Bert Blyleven | .05 | 137 Daryl Boston | .05 | 203 Bob Walk | .05 |
| 7 Charlie Hough (DK) | .10 | 72 Tony Fernandez | .20 | 138 Nolan Ryan | .30 | 204 Roger Mason | .05 |
| 8 Brook Jacoby (DK) | .10 | 73 Kent Hrbek | .15 | 139 Mike Schmidt | .45 | 205 Terry Kennedy | .05 |
| 9 Fred Lynn (DK) | .15 | 74 Lloyd Moseby | .05 | 140 Tommy Herr | .05 | 206 Ron Oester | .05 |
| 10 Rick Rhoden (DK) | .10 | 75 Alvin Davis | .10 | 141 Garry Templeton | .05 | 207 John Russell | .05 |
| 11 Chris Brown (DK) | .15 | 76 Keith Hernandez | .25 | 142 Kal Daniels | 1.00 | 208 Greg Mathews (R) | .25 |
| 12 Von Hayes (DK) | .10 | 77 Ryne Sandberg | .20 | 143 Billy Sample | .05 | 209 Charlie Kerfeld | .15 |
| 13 Jack Morris (DK) | .20 | 78 Dale Murphy | .40 | 144 Johnny Ray | .12 | 210 Reggie Jackson | .35 |
| 14 K. McReynolds (DK) | .35 | 79 Sid Bream | .05 | 145 Rob Thompson (R) | .30 | 211 Floyd Bannister | .05 |
| 15 George Brett (DK) | .35 | 80 Chris Brown | .20 | 146 Bob Dernier | .05 | 212 Vance Law | .05 |
| 16 Ted Higuera (DK) | .20 | 81 Steve Garvey | .30 | 147 Danny Tartabull | .40 | 213 Rich Bordi | .05 |
| 17 Hubie Brooks (DK) | .10 | 82 Mario Soto | .05 | 148 Ernie Whitt | .05 | 214 Dan Plesac (R) | .30 |
| 18 Mike Scott (DK) | .20 | 83 Shane Rawley | .05 | 149 Kirby Puckett | .60 | 215 Dave Collins | .05 |
| 19 Kirby Puckett (DK) | .45 | 84 Willie McGee | .20 | 150 Mike Young | .05 | 216 Bob Stanley | .05 |
| 20 Dave Winfield (DK) | .25 | 85 Jose Cruz | .12 | 151 Ernest Riles | .15 | 217 Joe Niekro | .10 |
| 21 Lloyd Moseby (DK) | .10 | 86 Brian Downing | .05 | 152 Frank Tanana | .05 | 218 Tom Niedenfuer | .05 |
| 22 Eric Davis (DK) | .80 | 87 Ozzie Guillen | .10 | 153 Rich Gedman | .05 | 219 Brett Butler | .05 |
| 23 Jim Presley (DK) | .20 | 88 Hubie Brooks | .12 | 154 Willie Randolph | .08 | 220 Charlie Leibrandt | .05 |
| 24 Keith Moreland (DK) | .10 | 89 Cal Ripken | .30 | 155 Bill Madlock | .15 | 221 Steve Ontiveros | .05 |
| 25 Greg Walker (DK) | .20 | 90 Juan Nieves | .10 | 156 Joe Carter | .20 | 222 Tim Burke | .05 |
| 26 St. Sax (DK) | .15 | 91 Lance Parrish | .20 | 157 Danny Jackson | .25 | 223 Curtis Wilkerson | .05 |
| 27 Checklist (DK) | .10 | 92 Jim Rice | .25 | 158 Carney Lansford | .05 | 224 Pete Incaviglia (R) | 1.25 |
| **No. 28 to 47—Rated Rookies** | | 93 Ron Guidry | .15 | 159 Bryn Smith | .05 | 225 Lonnie Smith | .05 |
| 28 B.J. Surhoff (R) | .60 | 94 Fernando Valenzuela | .25 | 160 Gary Pettis | .05 | 226 Chris Codiroli | .05 |
| 29 Randy Myers (R) | .50 | 95 Andy Allanson (R) | .20 | 161 Oddibe McDowell | .20 | 227 Scott Bailes (R) | .15 |
| 30 Ken Gerhart (R) | .30 | 96 Willie Wilson | .15 | 162 John Cangelosi (R) | .20 | 228 Rickey Henderson | .40 |
| 31 Benito Santiago | 1.50 | 97 Jose Canseco | 5.00 | 163 Mike Scott | .20 | 229 Ken Howell | .05 |
| 32 Greg Swindell (R) | .75 | 98 Jeff Reardon | .05 | 164 Eric Show | .05 | 230 Darnell Coles | .08 |
| 33 Mike Birkbeck (R) | .20 | 99 Bobby Witt (R) | .40 | 165 Juan Samuel | .12 | 231 Don Aase | .05 |
| 34 Terry Steinbach (R) | .50 | 100 Checklist: 28 to 133 | .10 | 166 Nick Esasky | .05 | 232 Tim Leary | .05 |
| 35 Bo Jackson (R) | 1.50 | 101 Jose Guzman | .20 | 167 Zane Smith | .05 | 233 Bob Boone | .05 |
| 36 Greg Maddux (R) | 1.25 | 102 Steve Balboni | .10 | 168 Mike Brown | .05 | 234 Ricky Horton | .05 |
| 37 Jim Lindeman (R) | .35 | 103 Tony Phillips | .05 | 169 Keith Moreland | .05 | 235 Mark Bailey | .05 |
| 38 Devon White (R) | 1.00 | 104 Brook Jacoby | .10 | 170 John Tudor | .10 | 236 Kevin Gross | .05 |
| 39 Eric Bell (R) | .20 | 105 Dave Winfield | .25 | 171 Ken Dixon | .05 | 237 Lance McCullers | .10 |
| 40 Will Fraser (R) | .25 | 106 Orel Hershiser | .40 | 172 Jim Gantner | .05 | 238 Cecilio Guante | .05 |
| 41 Jerry Browne (R) | .20 | 107 Lou Whitaker | .15 | 173 Jack Morris | .15 | 239 Bob Melvin | .05 |
| 42 Chris James (R) | .75 | 108 Fred Lynn | .15 | 174 Bruce Hurst | .10 | 240 Billy Jo Robidoux | .12 |
| 43 Rafael Palmeiro (R) | 1.50 | 109 Bill Wegman | .05 | 175 Dennis Rasmussen | .12 | 241 Roger McDowell | .15 |
| 44 Pat Dodson (R) | .20 | 110 Donnie Moore | .05 | 176 Mike Marshall | .10 | 242 Leon Durham | .10 |
| 45 Duane Ward (R) | .30 | 111 Jack Clark | .20 | 177 Dan Quisenberry | .12 | 243 Ed Nunez | .05 |
| 46 Mark McGwire | 8.00 | 112 Bob Knepper | .05 | 178 Eric Plunk | .10 | 244 Jimmy Key | .10 |
| 47 Bruce Fields (R) | .15 | 113 Von Hayes | .10 | 179 Tim Wallach | .05 | 245 Mike Smithson | .05 |
| 48 Eddie Murray | .30 | 114 "Bip" Roberts (R) | .15 | 180 Steve Buechele | .05 | 246 Bo Diaz | .05 |
| 49 Ted Higuera | .15 | 115 Tony Pena | .12 | 181 Don Sutton | .15 | 247 Carlton Fisk | .15 |
| 50 Kirk Gibson | .30 | 116 Scott Garrelts | .05 | 182 Dave Schmidt | .05 | 248 Larry Sheets | .15 |
| 51 Oil Can Boid | .10 | 117 Paul Molitor | .15 | 183 Terry Pendleton | .05 | 249 Juan Castillo | .05 |
| 52 Don Mattingly | 2.50 | 118 Darryl Strawberry | .90 | 184 Jim Deshaies (R) | .25 | 250 Eric King (R) | .15 |
| 53 Pedro Guerrero | .20 | 119 Shawon Dunston | .10 | 185 Steve Bedrosian | .15 | 251 Doug Drabek (R) | .30 |
| 54 George Brett | .40 | 120 Jim Presley | .20 | 186 Pete Rose (Mgr.) | .50 | 252 Wade Boggs | 1.50 |
| 55 Jose Rijo | .05 | 121 Jesse Barfield | .25 | 187 Dave Dravecky | .05 | 253 Mariano Duncan | .10 |
| 56 Tim Raines | .25 | 122 Gary Gaetti | .20 | 188 Rick Reuschel | .05 | 254 Pat Tabler | .05 |
| 57 Ed Correa (R) | .30 | 123 Kurt Stillwell (R) | .30 | 189 Dan Gladden | .05 | 255 Frank White | .05 |
| 58 Mike Witt | .10 | 124 Joel Davis | .05 | 190 Rick Mahler | .05 | 256 Alfredo Griffin | .05 |
| 59 Greg Walker | .05 | 125 Mike Boddicker | .05 | 191 Thad Bosley | .05 | 257 Floyd Youmans | .15 |
| 60 Ozzie Smith | .25 | 126 Robin Yount | .25 | 192 Ron Darling | .20 | 258 Rob Wilfong | .05 |
| 61 Glenn Davis | .35 | 127 Alan Trammell | .20 | 193 Matt Young | .05 | 259 Pete O'Brien | .08 |
| 62 Glenn Wilson | .10 | 128 Dave Righetti | .15 | 194 Tom Brunansky | .20 | 260 Tim Hulett | .05 |
| 63 Tom Browning | .05 | 129 Dwight Evans | .10 | 195 Dave Stieb | .15 | 261 Dickie Thon | .05 |
| 64 Tony Gwynn | .50 | 130 Mike Scioscia | .05 | 196 Frank Viola | .25 | 262 Darren Daulton | .05 |

Card values from this set fluctuate considerably.

| NO. | PLAYER | MINT |
|-----|--------|------|
| 263 | Vince Coleman | .40 |
| 264 | Andy Hawkins | .05 |
| 265 | Eric Davis | 1.50 |
| 266 | Andres Thomas (R) | .25 |
| 267 | Mike Diaz (R) | .15 |
| 268 | Chili Davis | .10 |
| 269 | Jody Davis | .05 |
| 270 | Phil Bradley | .10 |
| 271 | George Bell | .25 |
| 272 | Keith Atherton | .05 |
| 273 | Storm Davis | .08 |
| 274 | Rob Deer | .20 |
| 275 | Walt Terrell | .05 |
| 276 | Roger Clemens | 1.25 |
| 277 | Mike Easler | .05 |
| 278 | Steve Sax | .15 |
| 279 | Andre Thornton | .05 |
| 280 | Jim Sundberg | .05 |
| 281 | Bill Bathe (R) | .15 |
| 282 | Jay Tibbs | .05 |
| 283 | Dick Schofield | .05 |
| 284 | Mike Mason | .05 |
| 285 | Jerry Hairston | .05 |
| 286 | Bill Doran | .05 |
| 287 | Tim Flannery | .05 |
| 288 | Gary Redus | .05 |
| 289 | John Franco | .05 |
| 290 | P. Assenmacher (R) | .15 |
| 291 | Joe Orsulak | .05 |
| 292 | Lee Smith | .05 |
| 293 | Mike Laga | .05 |
| 294 | Rick Dempsey | .05 |
| 295 | Mike Felder | .05 |
| 296 | Tom Brookens | .05 |
| 297 | Al Nipper | .05 |
| 298 | Mike Pagliarulo | .20 |
| 299 | Franklin Stubbs | .15 |
| 300 | Checklist: 240-345 | .08 |
| 301 | Steve Farr | .05 |
| 302 | Bill Mooneyham (R) | .15 |
| 303 | Andres Galarraga | .35 |
| 304 | Scott Fletcher | .05 |
| 305 | Jack Howell | .05 |
| 306 | Russ Morman (R) | .20 |
| 307 | Todd Worrell | .25 |
| 308 | Dave Smith | .05 |
| 309 | Jeff Stone | .05 |
| 310 | Ron Robinson | .05 |
| 311 | Bruce Bochy | .05 |
| 312 | Jim Winn | .05 |
| 313 | Mark Davis | .05 |
| 314 | Jeff Dedmon | .05 |
| 315 | Jamie Moyer (R) | .25 |
| 316 | Wally Backman | .05 |
| 317 | Ken Phelps | .05 |
| 318 | Steve Lombardozzi | .12 |
| 319 | Rance Mulliniks | .05 |
| 320 | Tim Laudner | .05 |
| 321 | Mark Eichhorn | .30 |
| 322 | Lee Guetterman (R) | .25 |
| 323 | Sid Fernandez | .20 |
| 324 | Jerry Mumphrey | .05 |
| 325 | David Palmer | .05 |
| 326 | Bill Almon | .05 |
| 327 | Candy Maldonado | .10 |
| 328 | Joe Kruk (R) | .50 |
| 329 | John Denny | .05 |
| 330 | Milt Thompson | .05 |
| 331 | Mike LaValliere (R) | .25 |
| 332 | Alan Ashby | .05 |
| 333 | Doug Corbett | .05 |
| 334 | Ron Karkovice (R) | .15 |
| 335 | Mitch Webster | .05 |
| 336 | Lee Lacy | .05 |
| 337 | Glenn Braggs (R) | .50 |
| 338 | Dwight Lowry (R) | .15 |
| 339 | Don Baylor | .15 |
| 340 | Brian Fisher | .05 |
| 341 | Reggie Williams (R) | .20 |
| 342 | Tom Candiotti | .05 |
| 343 | Rudy Law | .05 |
| 344 | Curt Young | .05 |
| 345 | Mike Fitzgerald | .05 |
| 346 | Ruben Sierra (R) | 1.25 |
| 347 | Mitch Williams (R) | .25 |
| 348 | Jorge Orta | .05 |
| 349 | Mickey Tettleton | .05 |
| 350 | Ernie Camacho | .05 |
| 351 | Ron Kittle | .10 |
| 352 | Ken Landreaux | .05 |
| 353 | Chet Lemon | .08 |
| 354 | John Shelby | .05 |
| 355 | Mark Clear | .05 |
| 356 | Doug DeCinces | .08 |
| 357 | Ken Kayley | .05 |
| 358 | Phil Garner | .05 |
| 359 | Steve Jeltz | .05 |
| 360 | Ed Whitson | .05 |
| 361 | Barry Bonds (R) | .85 |
| 362 | Vida Blue | .08 |
| 363 | Cecil Cooper | .10 |
| 364 | Bob Ojeda | .15 |
| 365 | Dennis Eckersley | .08 |
| 366 | Mike Morgan | .05 |
| 367 | Willie Upshaw | .05 |
| 368 | Allan Anderson (R) | .30 |
| 369 | Bill Gullickson | .05 |
| 370 | Bobby Thigpen (R) | .25 |
| 371 | Juan Beniquez | .05 |
| 372 | Charlie Moore | .05 |
| 373 | Dan Petry | .08 |
| 374 | Rod Scurry | .05 |
| 375 | Tom Seaver | .35 |
| 376 | Ed Vande Berg | .05 |
| 377 | Tony Bernazard | .05 |
| 378 | Greg Pryor | .05 |
| 379 | Dwayne Murphy | .05 |
| 380 | Andy McGaffigan | .05 |
| 381 | Kirk McCaskill | .10 |
| 382 | Greg Harris | .05 |
| 383 | Rich Dotson | .05 |
| 384 | Craig Reynolds | .05 |
| 385 | Greg Gross | .05 |
| 386 | Tito Landrum | .05 |
| 387 | Craig Lefferts | .05 |
| 388 | Dave Parker | .20 |
| 389 | Bob Horner | .15 |
| 390 | Pat Clements | .05 |
| 391 | Jeff Leonard | .10 |
| 392 | Chris Speier | .05 |
| 393 | John Moses | .15 |
| 394 | Garth Iorg | .05 |
| 395 | Greg Gagne | .05 |
| 396 | Nate Snell | .05 |
| 397 | Bryan Clutterbuck (R) | .15 |
| 398 | Darrell Evans | .12 |
| 399 | Steve Crawford | .05 |
| 400 | Checklist: 346-451 | .08 |
| 401 | Phil Lombardi (R) | .20 |
| 402 | Rick Honeycutt | .05 |
| 403 | Ken Schrom | .05 |
| 404 | Bud Black | .05 |
| 405 | Donnie Hill | .05 |
| 406 | Wayne Krenchicki | .05 |
| 407 | Chuck Finley (R) | .15 |
| 408 | Toby Harrah | .05 |
| 409 | Steve Lyons | .05 |
| 410 | Kevin Bass | .10 |
| 411 | Marvell Wynne | .05 |
| 412 | Ron Roenicke | .05 |
| 413 | Tracy Jones (R) | .35 |
| 414 | Gene Garber | .05 |
| 415 | Mike Bielecki | .05 |
| 416 | Frank DiPino | .05 |
| 417 | Andy Van Slyke | .15 |
| 418 | Jim Dwyer | .05 |
| 419 | Ben Oglivie | .05 |
| 420 | Dave Bergman | .05 |
| 421 | Joe Sambito | .05 |
| 422 | Bob Tewksbury (R) | .20 |
| 423 | Len Matuszek | .05 |
| 424 | Mike Kingery (R) | .15 |
| 425 | Dave Kingman | .10 |
| 426 | Al Newman (R) | .15 |
| 427 | Gary Ward | .05 |
| 428 | Ruppert Jones | .05 |
| 429 | Harold Baines | .12 |
| 430 | Pat Perry | .05 |
| 431 | Terry Puhl | .05 |
| 432 | Don Carman | .05 |
| 433 | Eddie Milner | .05 |
| 434 | LaMarr Hoyt | .05 |
| 435 | Rick Rhoden | .05 |
| 436 | Jose Uribe | .05 |
| 437 | Ken Oberkfell | .05 |
| 438 | Ron Davis | .05 |
| 439 | Jesse Orosco | .08 |
| 440 | Scott Bradley | .05 |
| 441 | Randy Bush | .05 |
| 442 | John Cerutti (R) | .20 |
| 443 | Roy Smalley | .05 |
| 444 | Kelly Gruber | .10 |
| 445 | Bob Kearney | .05 |
| 446 | Ed Hearn (R) | .15 |
| 447 | Scott Sanderson | .05 |
| 448 | Bruce Benedict | .05 |
| 449 | Junior Ortiz | .05 |
| 450 | Mike Aldrete (R) | .40 |
| 451 | Kevin McReynolds | .30 |
| 452 | Rob Murphy | .25 |
| 453 | Kent Tekulve | .05 |
| 454 | Curt Ford | .15 |
| 455 | Davey Lopes | .08 |
| 456 | Bobby Grich | .05 |
| 457 | Jose DeLeon | .05 |
| 458 | Andre Dawson | .25 |
| 459 | Mike Flanagan | .05 |
| 460 | Joey Meyer (R) | .70 |
| 461 | Chuck Cary (R) | .15 |
| 462 | Bill Buckner | .08 |
| 463 | Bob Shirley | .05 |
| 464 | Jeff Hamilton (R) | .25 |
| 465 | Phil Niekro | .12 |
| 466 | Mark Gubicza | .05 |
| 467 | Jerry Willard | .05 |
| 468 | Bob Sebra (R) | .15 |
| 469 | Larry Parrish | .05 |
| 470 | Charlie Hough | .05 |
| 471 | Hal McRae | .05 |
| 472 | Dave Leiper | .05 |
| 473 | Mel Hall | .05 |
| 474 | Dan Pasqua | .15 |
| 475 | Bob Welch | .05 |
| 476 | Johnny Grubb | .05 |
| 477 | Jim Traber | .12 |
| 478 | Chris Bosio (R) | .20 |
| 479 | Mark McLemore | .08 |
| 480 | John Morris | .05 |
| 481 | Billy Hatcher | .05 |
| 482 | Dan Schatzeder | .05 |
| 483 | Rich Gossage | .12 |
| 484 | Jim Morrison | .05 |
| 485 | Bob Brenly | .05 |
| 486 | Bill Schroeder | .05 |
| 487 | Mookie Wilson | .05 |
| 488 | Dave Martinez | .25 |
| 489 | Harold Reynolds | .05 |
| 490 | Jeff Hearron | .15 |
| 491 | Mickey Hatcher | .05 |
| 492 | Barry Larkin (R) | 1.40 |
| 493 | Bob James | .05 |
| 494 | John Habyan | .05 |
| 495 | Jim Adduci (R) | .15 |
| 496 | Mike Heath | .05 |
| 497 | Tim Stoddard | .05 |
| 498 | Tony Armas | .08 |
| 499 | Dennis Powell | .05 |
| 500 | Checklist: 452-557 | .08 |
| 501 | Chris Bando | .05 |
| 502 | David Cone (R) | 4.00 |
| 503 | Jay Howell | .05 |
| 504 | Tom Foley | .05 |
| 505 | Ray Chadwick (R) | .15 |
| 506 | Mike Loynd (R) | .15 |
| 507 | Neil Allen | .05 |
| 508 | Danny Darwin | .05 |
| 509 | Rick Schu | .05 |
| 510 | Jose Oquendo | .05 |
| 511 | Gene Walter | .10 |
| 512 | Terry McGriff (R) | .15 |
| 513 | Ken Griffey | .08 |
| 514 | Benny Distefano | .05 |
| 515 | Terry Mulholland (R) | .15 |
| 516 | Ed Lynch | .05 |
| 517 | Bill Swift | .05 |
| 518 | Manny Lee | .05 |
| 519 | Andre David | .05 |
| 520 | Scott McGregor | .05 |
| 521 | Rick Manning | .05 |
| 522 | Willie Hernandez | .05 |
| 523 | Marty Barrett | .10 |
| 524 | Wayne Tolleson | .05 |
| 525 | Jose Gonzalez (R) | .20 |
| 526 | Cory Snyder | .75 |
| 527 | Buddy Biancalana | .05 |
| 528 | Moose Haas | .05 |
| 529 | Wilfredo Tejada (R) | .15 |
| 530 | Stu Cliburn | .05 |
| 531 | Dale Mohorcic (R) | .15 |
| 532 | Ron Hassey | .05 |
| 533 | Ty Gainey | .05 |
| 534 | Jerry Royster | .05 |
| 535 | Mike Maddux (R) | .25 |
| 536 | Ted Power | .05 |
| 537 | Ted Simmons | .08 |
| 538 | Rafael Belliard (R) | .15 |
| 539 | Chico Walker (R) | .15 |
| 540 | Bob Forsch | .05 |
| 541 | John Stefero | .05 |
| 542 | Dale Sveum (R) | .30 |
| 543 | Mark Thurmond | .05 |
| 544 | Jeff Sellers (R) | .15 |
| 545 | Joel Skinner | .05 |
| 546 | Alex Trevino | .05 |
| 547 | Randy Kutcher (R) | .15 |
| 548 | Joaquin Andujar | .05 |
| 549 | Casey Candaele (R) | .15 |
| 550 | Jeff Russell | .05 |
| 551 | John Candelaria | .08 |
| 552 | Joe Cowley | .05 |
| 553 | Danny Cox | .05 |
| 554 | Denny Walling | .05 |
| 555 | Bruce Ruffin (R) | .30 |
| 556 | Buddy Bell | .10 |
| 557 | Jimmy Jones (R) | .20 |
| 558 | Bobby Bonilla (R) | 1.25 |
| 559 | Jeff Robinson | .05 |
| 560 | Ed Olwine (R) | .15 |
| 561 | Glenallen Hill (R) | .15 |
| 562 | Lee Mazzilli | .08 |
| 563 | Mike Brown | .05 |
| 564 | George Frazier | .05 |
| 565 | Mike Sharperson (R) | .15 |
| 566 | Mark Portugal (R) | .15 |
| 567 | Rick Leach | .05 |
| 568 | Mark Langston | .15 |
| 569 | Rafael Santana | .05 |
| 570 | Manny Trillo | .05 |
| 571 | Cliff Speck (R) | .15 |
| 572 | Bob Kipper | .05 |
| 573 | Kelly Downs (R) | .40 |
| 574 | Randy Asadoor (R) | .15 |
| 575 | Dave Magadan (R) | .60 |
| 576 | Marvin Freeman (R) | .15 |
| 577 | Jeff Lahti | .05 |
| 578 | Jeff Calhoun | .05 |
| 579 | Gus Polidor | .05 |
| 580 | Gene Nelson | .05 |
| 581 | Tim Teufel | .05 |
| 582 | Odell Jones | .05 |
| 583 | Mark Ryal (R) | .15 |
| 584 | Randy O'Neal | .05 |
| 585 | Mike Greenwell | 8.00 |
| 586 | Ray Knight | .10 |
| 587 | Ralph Bryant (R) | .25 |
| 588 | Carmen Castillo | .05 |
| 589 | Ed Wojna | .05 |
| 590 | Stan Javier | .05 |
| 591 | Jeff Musselman (R) | .25 |
| 592 | Mike Stanley (R) | .30 |
| 593 | Darrell Porter | .05 |
| 594 | Drew Hall (R) | .15 |
| 595 | Rob Nelson (R) | .15 |
| 596 | Bryan Oelkers | .05 |
| 597 | Scott Nielsen (R) | .15 |
| 598 | Brian Holton (R) | .20 |

Card values from this set fluctuate considerably.

# 1987 Donruss (Continued)

| NO. | PLAYER | MINT |
|---|---|---|
| 599 | Kevin Mitchell (R) | .35 |
| 600 | Checklist: 558-660 | .08 |
| 601 | Jackie Gutierrez | .05 |
| 602 | Barry Jones (R) | .15 |
| 603 | Jerry Narron | .05 |
| 604 | Steve Lake | .05 |
| 605 | Jim Pankovits | .05 |
| 606 | Ed Romero | .05 |
| 607 | Dave LaPoint | .05 |
| 608 | Don Robinson | .05 |
| 609 | Mike Krukow | .05 |
| 610 | Dave Valle | .05 |
| 611 | Len Dykstra | .20 |
| 612 | "Puzzle"—Clemente | .08 |
| 613 | Mike Trujillo | .05 |
| 614 | Damaso Garcia | .05 |
| 615 | Neal Heaton | .05 |
| 616 | Juan Berenguer | .05 |

| NO. | PLAYER | MINT |
|---|---|---|
| 617 | Steve Carlton | .25 |
| 618 | Gary Lucas | .05 |
| 619 | Geno Petralli | .05 |
| 620 | Rick Aguilera | .08 |
| 621 | Fred McGriff | .60 |
| 622 | Dave Henderson | .05 |
| 623 | Dave Clark (R) | .30 |
| 624 | Angel Salazar | .05 |
| 625 | Randy Hunt | .05 |
| 626 | John Gibbons | .05 |
| 627 | Kevin Brown (R) | .15 |
| 628 | Bill Dawley | .05 |
| 629 | Aurelio Lopez | .05 |
| 630 | Charlie Hudson | .05 |
| 631 | Ray Soff (R) | .15 |
| 632 | Ray Hayward (R) | .15 |
| 633 | Spike Owen | .05 |
| 634 | Glenn Hubbard | .05 |

| NO. | PLAYER | MINT |
|---|---|---|
| 635 | Kevin Elster (R) | .75 |
| 636 | Mike LaCoss | .05 |
| 637 | Dwayne Henry | .05 |
| 638 | Rey Quinones (R) | .25 |
| 639 | Jim Clancy | .05 |
| 640 | Larry Anderson | .05 |
| 641 | Calvin Schiraldi | .08 |
| 642 | Stan Jefferson (R) | .30 |
| 643 | Marc Sullivan | .05 |
| 644 | Mark Grant (R) | .15 |
| 645 | Cliff Johnson | .05 |
| 646 | Howard Johnson | .20 |
| 647 | Dave Sax | .05 |
| 648 | Dave Stewart | .05 |
| 649 | Danny Heep | .05 |
| 650 | Joe Johnson | .05 |
| 651 | Bob Brower (R) | .15 |
| 652 | Rob Woodward | .05 |

| NO. | PLAYER | MINT |
|---|---|---|
| 653 | John Mizerock | .05 |
| 654 | Tim Pyznarski (R) | .15 |
| 655 | Luis Aquino | .10 |
| 656 | Mickey Brantley | .20 |
| 657 | Doyle Alexander | .05 |
| 658 | Sammy Stewart | .05 |
| 659 | Jim Acker | .05 |
| 660 | Pete Ladd | .05 |

**Cards Printed on Gum Boxes**

| NO. | PLAYER | MINT |
|---|---|---|
| PC10 | Dale Murphy | .30 |
| PC11 | Jeff Reardon | .15 |
| PC12 | Jose Canseco | .75 |
| — | Clemente Puzzle | .10 |
| PC13 | Mike Scott | .20 |
| PC14 | Roger Clemens | .75 |
| PC15 | Mike Krukow | .15 |

Card values from this set fluctuate considerably.

## 1987 Donruss Rookies. . . .Complete Set of 56 Cards—Value $15.00

Features the outstanding rookies of the 1987 season. The cards are coated with a glossy finish. The entire set was packaged in a printed box, and distributed exclusively through card hobby dealers. Features Donruss' first card of Ellis Burks, Matt Nokes and Kevin Seitzer.

| NO. | PLAYER | MINT |
|---|---|---|
| 1 | Mark McGwire | 2.50 |
| 2 | Eric Bell | .10 |
| 3 | Mark Williamson | .20 |
| 4 | Mike Greenwell | 3.00 |
| 5 | Ellis Burks (RR) | 1.25 |
| 6 | DeWayne Buice | .15 |
| 7 | Mark McLemore | .10 |
| 8 | Devon White | .50 |
| 9 | Willie Fraser | .10 |
| 10 | Les Lancaster | .15 |
| 11 | Ken Williams | .25 |
| 12 | Matt Nokes (RR) | .60 |
| 13 | Jeff Robinson | .40 |
| 14 | Bo Jackson | .50 |

| NO. | PLAYER | MINT |
|---|---|---|
| 15 | Kevin Seitzer (RR) | 1.50 |
| 16 | Billy Ripken (RR) | .35 |
| 17 | B.J. Surhoff | .25 |
| 18 | Chuck Crim | .20 |
| 19 | Mike Birkbeck | .10 |
| 20 | Chris Bosio | .10 |
| 21 | Les Straker | .20 |
| 22 | Mark Davidson | .15 |
| 23 | Gene Larkin | .35 |
| 24 | Ken Gerhart | .20 |
| 25 | Luis Polonia | .40 |
| 26 | Jerry Steinbach | .25 |
| 27 | Mickey Brantley | .25 |
| 28 | Mike Stanley | .15 |

| NO. | PLAYER | MINT |
|---|---|---|
| 29 | Jerry Browne | .10 |
| 30 | Todd Benzinger (RR) | .50 |
| 31 | Fred McGriff | .75 |
| 32 | Mike Henneman | .35 |
| 33 | Casey Candaele | .10 |
| 34 | Dave Magadan | .25 |
| 35 | David Cone | 1.50 |
| 36 | Mike Jackson | .30 |
| 37 | John Mitchell | .20 |
| 38 | Mike Dunne (RR) | .30 |
| 39 | John Smiley | .30 |
| 40 | Joe Magrane (RR) | .50 |
| 41 | Jim Lindeman | .20 |
| 42 | Shane Mack (RR) | .40 |

| NO. | PLAYER | MINT |
|---|---|---|
| 43 | Stanley Jefferson | .15 |
| 44 | Benito Santiago | .50 |
| 45 | Matt Williams (RR) | .40 |
| 46 | Dave Meads | .15 |
| 47 | Rafael Palmeiro | .60 |
| 48 | Bill Long | .15 |
| 49 | Bob Brower | .10 |
| 50 | James Steels | .15 |
| 51 | Paul Noci | .15 |
| 52 | Greg Maddux | .30 |
| 53 | Jeff Musselman | .10 |
| 54 | Brian Holton | .10 |
| 55 | Chuck Jackson | .25 |
| 56 | Checklist | .15 |

## 1988 Donruss. . . .Complete Set of 660 Cards—Value $35.00 (Factory-Sealed Set—Value $40.00)

Features the rookie cards of Matt Nokes, Ellis Burks, Sam Horn and Gregg Jefferies. Donruss limited production. 26 Bonus Cards featuring major stars are randomly distributed in wax and rack packs. These cards are numbered BC-1 to BC-26, and are not part of the set. 26 cards were issued in much smaller quantities than other cards in the set (see asterisk) and are worth a premium.

**No. 1 to 26—Diamond Kings**

| NO. | PLAYER | MINT |
|---|---|---|
| 1 | Mark McGwire (DK) | 1.00 |
| 2 | Tim Raines (DK) | .25 |
| 3 | Benito Santiago (DK) | .35 |
| 4 | Alan Trammell (DK) | .20 |
| 5 | Danny Tartabull (DK) | .20 |
| 6 | Ron Darling (DK) | .15 |
| 7 | Paul Molitor (DK) | .15 |
| 8 | Devon White (DK) | .20 |
| 9 | Andre Dawson (DK) | .15 |
| 10 | Julio Franco (DK) | .10 |
| 11 | Scott Fletcher (DK) | .10 |
| 12 | Tony Fernandez (DK) | .15 |
| 13 | Shane Rawley (DK) | .10 |
| 14 | Kal Daniels (DK) | .25 |
| 15 | Jack Clark (DK) | .15 |
| 16 | Dwight Evans (DK) | .10 |
| 17 | Tommy John (DK) | .10 |
| 18 | Andy Van Slyke (DK) | .15 |
| 19 | Gary Gaetti (DK) | .10 |
| 20 | Mark Langston (DK) | .10 |
| 21 | Will Clark (DK) | .50 |
| 22 | Glenn Hubbard (DK) | .10 |
| 23 | Billy Hatcher (DK) | .15 |
| 24 | Bob Welch (DK) | .10 |
| 25 | Ivan Calderon. (DK) | .10 |
| 26 | Cal Ripkin, Jr., (DK) | .25 |
| 27 | Checklist | .15 |

**No. 28 to 47—Rated Rookies**

| NO. | PLAYER | MINT |
|---|---|---|
| 28 | Mackey Sasser (R) | .35 |
| 29 | Jeff Treadway (R) | .45 |
| 30 | Mike Campbell (R) | .30 |
| 31 | Lance Johnson (R) | .20 |
| 32 | Nelson Liriano (R) | .25 |
| 33 | Shawn Abner | .35 |
| 34 | Roberto Alomar (R) | .40 |
| 35 | Shawn Hillegas (R) | .30 |
| 36 | Joey Meyer | .25 |
| 37 | Kevin Elster | .20 |
| 38 | Jose Lind (R) | .35 |
| 39 | Kirt Manwaring (R) | .40 |
| 40 | Mark Grace (R) | 2.50 |
| 41 | Jody Reed (R) | .40 |
| 42 | John Farrell (R) | .40 |
| 43 | Al Leiter (R) | 1.00 |
| 44 | Gary Thurman (R) | .50 |
| 45 | Vincente Palacios (R) | .25 |
| 46 | Eddie Williams (R) | .25 |
| 47 | Jack McDowell (R) | .40 |
| 48 | Ken Dixon | .05 |
| 49 | Mike Birkbeck | .05 |
| 50 | Eric King | .05 |
| 51 | Roger Clemen | .50 |
| 52 | Pat Clements | .05 |
| 53 | Fernando Valenzuela | .20 |
| 54 | Mark Gubicza | .05 |
| 55 | Jay Howell | .05 |
| 56 | Floyd Youmans | .12 |
| 57 | Ed Correa | .10 |
| 58 | DeWayne Buice (R) | .15 |
| 59 | Jose DeLeon | .05 |
| 60 | Danny Cox | .08 |
| 61 | Nolan Ryan | .30 |
| 62 | Steve Bedrosian | .10 |
| 63 | Tom Browning | .08 |
| 64 | Mark Davis | .05 |
| 65 | R.J. Reynolds | .08 |
| 66 | Kevin Mitchell | .10 |
| 67 | Ken Oberkfell | .05 |
| 68 | Rick Sutcliffe | .12 |
| 69 | Dwight Gooden | .50 |
| 70 | Scott Bankhead | .12 |
| 71 | Bert Blyleven | .15 |
| 72 | Jimmy Key | .12 |
| 73 | Les Straker (R) | .15 |
| 74 | Jim Clancy | .08 |
| 75 | Mike Moore | .08 |
| 76 | Ron Darling | .15 |
| 77 | Ed Lynch | .08 |
| 78 | Dale Murphy | .35 |
| 79 | Doug Drabek | .05 |
| 80 | Scott Garrelts | .05 |
| 81 | Ed Whitson | .05 |
| 82 | Rob Murphy | .05 |
| 83 | Shane Rawley | .05 |
| 84 | Greg Mathews | .08 |

| NO. | PLAYER | MINT |
|---|---|---|
| 85 | Jim Deshaies | .10 |
| 86 | Mike Witt | .12 |
| 87 | Donnie Hill | .08 |
| 88 | Jeff Reed | .08 |
| 89 | Mike Boddicker | .12 |
| 90 | Ted Higuera | .15 |
| 91 | Walt Terrell | .08 |
| 92 | Bob Stanley | .05 |
| 93 | Dave Righetti | .15 |
| 94 | Orel Hershiser | .15 |
| 95 | Chris Bando | .05 |
| 96 | Bret Saberhagen | .15 |
| 97 | Curt Young | .05 |
| 98 | Tim Burke | .05 |
| 99 | Charlie Hough | .05 |
| 100 | Checklist | .05 |
| 101 | Bobby Witt | .10 |
| 102 | George Brett | .35 |
| 103 | Mickey Tettleton | .05 |
| 104 | Scott Bailes | .05 |
| 105 | Mike Pagliarulo | .10 |
| 106 | Mike Scioscia | .05 |
| 107 | Tom Brookens | .05 |
| 108 | Ray Knight | .10 |
| 109 | Dan Plesac | .12 |
| 110 | Wally Joyner | .60 |
| 111 | Bob Forsch | .08 |
| 112 | Mike Scott | .15 |
| 113 | Kevin Gross | .08 |
| 114 | Benito Santiago | .50 |
| 115 | Bob Kipper | .05 |
| 116 | Mike Krukow | .05 |
| 117 | Chris Bosio | .05 |
| 118 | Sid Fernandez | .12 |
| 119 | Jody Davis | .05 |
| 120 | Mike Morgan | .05 |
| 121 | Mark Eichhorn | .05 |
| 122 | Jeff Reardon | .10 |
| 123 | John Franco | .08 |
| 124 | Richard Dotson | .05 |
| 125 | Eric Bell | .05 |
| 126 | Juan Nieves | .10 |
| 127 | Jack Morris | .15 |
| 128 | Rick Rhoden | .08 |
| 129 | Rich Gedman | .05 |
| 130 | Ken Howell | .05 |
| 131 | Brook Jacoby | .08 |
| 132 | Danny Jackson | .05 |
| 133 | Gene Nelson | .05 |
| 134 | Neal Heaton | .05 |
| 135 | Willie Fraser | .05 |
| 136 | Jose Guzman | .05 |
| 137 | Ozzie Guillen | .10 |
| 138 | Bob Knepper | .08 |
| 139 | Mike Jackson (R) | .15 |
| 140 | Joe Magrane (R) | .40 |
| 141 | Jimmy Jones | .05 |
| 142 | Ted Power | .05 |
| 143 | Ozzie Virgil | .05 |
| 144 | Felix Fermin (R) | .15 |
| 145 | Kelly Downs | .08 |
| 146 | Shawon Dunston | .08 |
| 147 | Scott Bradley | .05 |
| 148 | Dave Stieb | .12 |
| 149 | Frank Viola | .08 |
| 150 | Terry Kennedy | .05 |
| 151 | Bill Wegman | .05 |
| 152 | Matt Nokes (R) | .75 |
| 153 | Wade Boggs | 1.00 |
| 154 | Wayne Tolleson | .05 |
| 155 | Mariano Duncan | .05 |
| 156 | Julio Franco | .12 |
| 157 | Charlie Leibrandt | .08 |
| 158 | Terry Steinbach | .12 |
| 159 | Mike Fitzgerald | .05 |
| 160 | Jack Lazorko | .05 |
| 161 | Mitch Williams | .05 |
| 162 | Greg Walker | .05 |
| 163 | Alan Ashby | .05 |
| 164 | Tony Gwynn | .30 |
| 165 | Bruce Ruffin | .08 |
| 166 | Ron Robinson | .05 |
| 167 | Zane Smith | .08 |
| 168 | Junior Ortiz | .05 |
| 169 | Jamie Moyer | .05 |
| 170 | Tony Pena | .08 |

| NO. | PLAYER | MINT |
|---|---|---|
| 171 | Cal Ripken | .25 |
| 172 | B.J. Surhoff | .20 |
| 173 | Lou Whitaker | .15 |
| 174 | Ellis Burks (R) | 1.50 |
| 175 | Ron Guidry | .15 |
| 176 | Steve Sax | .15 |
| 177 | Danny Tartabull | .20 |
| 178 | Carney Lansford | .05 |
| 179 | Casey Candaele | .05 |
| 180 | Scott Fletcher | .05 |
| 181 | Mark McLemore | .05 |
| 182 | Ivan Calderon | .15 |
| 183 | Jack Clark | .20 |
| 184 | Glenn Davis | .15 |
| 185 | Luis Aguayo | .05 |
| 186 | Bo Diaz | .05 |
| 187 | Stan Jefferson | .08 |
| 188 | Sid Bream | .05 |
| 189 | Bob Brenly | .05 |
| 190 | Dion James | .05 |
| 191 | Leon Durham | .10 |
| 192 | Jesse Orosco | .05 |
| 193 | Alvin Davis | .10 |
| 194 | Gary Gaetti | .12 |
| 195 | Fred McGriff | .15 |
| 196 | Steve Lombardozzi | .08 |
| 197 | Rance Mulliniks | .05 |
| 198 | Rey Quinones | .05 |
| 199 | Gary Carter | .25 |
| 200 | Checklist | .08 |
| 201 | Keith Moreland | .05 |
| 202 | Ken Griffey | .05 |
| 203 | Tommy Gregg (R) | .25 |
| 204 | Will Clark | .75 |
| 205 | John Kruk | .35 |
| 206 | Buddy Bell | .15 |
| 207 | Von Hayes | .10 |
| 208 | Tommy Herr | .05 |
| 209 | Craig Reynolds | .05 |
| 210 | Gary Pettis | .05 |
| 211 | Harold Baines | .15 |
| 212 | Vance Law | .05 |
| 213 | Ken Gerhart | .08 |
| 214 | Jim Gantner | .05 |
| 215 | Chet Lemon | .08 |
| 216 | Dwight Evans | .10 |
| 217 | Don Mattingly | 1.50 |
| 218 | Franklin Stubbs | .08 |
| 219 | Pat Tabler | .05 |
| 220 | Bo Jackson | .50 |
| 221 | Tony Phillips | .05 |
| 222 | Tim Wallach | .08 |
| 223 | Ruben Sierra | .30 |
| 224 | Steve Buechele | .05 |
| 225 | Frank White | .05 |
| 226 | Alfredo Griffin | .05 |
| 227 | Greg Swindell | .20 |
| 228 | Willie Randolph | .05 |
| 229 | Mike Marshall | .10 |
| 230 | Alan Trammell | .15 |
| 231 | Eddie Murray | .25 |
| 232 | Dale Sveum | .08 |
| 233 | Dick Schofield | .05 |
| 234 | Jose Oquendo | .05 |
| 235 | Bill Doran | .05 |
| 236 | Milt Thompson | .05 |
| 237 | Marvell Wynne | .05 |
| 238 | Bobby Bonilla | .15 |
| 239 | Chris Speier | .05 |
| 240 | Glenn Braggs | .10 |
| 241 | Wally Backman | .05 |
| 242 | Ryne Sandberg | .20 |
| 243 | Phil Bradley | .12 |
| 244 | Kelly Gruber | .05 |
| 245 | Tom Brunansky | .10 |
| 246 | Ron Oester | .05 |
| 247 | Bobby Thigpen | .05 |
| 248 | Fred Lynn | .15 |
| 249 | Paul Molitor | .15 |
| 250 | Darrell Evans | .10 |
| 251 | Gary Ward | .08 |
| 252 | Bruce Hurst | .08 |
| 253 | Bob Welch | .05 |
| 254 | Joe Carter | .12 |
| 255 | Willie Wilson | .12 |
| 256 | Mark McGwire | 1.25 |

| NO. | PLAYER | MINT |
|---|---|---|
| 257 | Mitch Webster | .05 |
| 258 | Brian Downing | .05 |
| 259 | Mike Stanley | .05 |
| 260 | Carlton Fisk | .15 |
| 261 | Billy Hatcher | .10 |
| 262 | Glenn Wilson | .05 |
| 263 | Ozzie Smith | .15 |
| 264 | Randy Ready | .05 |
| 265 | Kurt Stillwell | .10 |
| 266 | David Palmer | .05 |
| 267 | Mike Diaz | .05 |
| 268 | Rob Thompson | .08 |
| 269 | Andre Dawson | .20 |
| 270 | Lee Guetterman | .05 |
| 271 | Willie Upshaw | .05 |
| 272 | Randy Bush | .05 |
| 273 | Larry Sheets | .12 |
| 274 | Rob Deer | .10 |
| 275 | Kirk Gibson | .20 |
| 276 | Marty Barrett | .10 |
| 277 | Rickey Henderson | .35 |
| 278 | Pedro Guerrero | .20 |
| 279 | Brett Butler | .05 |
| 280 | Kevin Seitzer | 1.25 |
| 281 | Mike Davis | .05 |
| 282 | Andres Galarraga | .20 |
| 283 | Devon White | .20 |
| 284 | Pete O'Brien | .10 |
| 285 | Jerry Hairston | .05 |
| 286 | Kevin Bass | .08 |
| 287 | Carmelo Martinez | .05 |
| 288 | Juan Samuel | .10 |
| 289 | Kal Daniels | .35 |
| 290 | Albert Hall | .05 |
| 291 | Andy Van Slyke | .12 |
| 292 | Lee Smith | .10 |
| 293 | Vince Coleman | .20 |
| 294 | Tom Niedenfuer | .05 |
| 295 | Robin Yount | .20 |
| 296 | Jeff Robinson (R) | .30 |
| 297 | Todd Benzinger (R) | .50 |
| 298 | Dave Winfield | .25 |
| 299 | Mickey Hatcher | .05 |
| 300 | Checklist | .08 |
| 301 | Bud Black | .05 |
| 302 | Jose Canseco | 1.50 |
| 303 | Tom Foley | .05 |
| 304 | Pete Incaviglia | .30 |
| 305 | Bob Boone | .05 |
| 306 | Bill Long (R) | .20 |
| 307 | Willie McGee | .15 |
| 308 | Ken Caminiti (R) | .25 |
| 309 | Darren Daulton | .05 |
| 310 | Tracy Jones | .10 |
| 311 | Greg Booker | .05 |
| 312 | Mike LaValliere | .05 |
| 313 | Chili Davis | .10 |
| 314 | Glenn Hubbard | .05 |
| 315 | Paul Noce | .15 |
| 316 | Keith Hernandez | .20 |
| 317 | Mark Langston | .10 |
| 318 | Keith Atherton | .05 |
| 319 | Tony Fernandez | .08 |
| 320 | Kent Hrbek | .15 |
| 321 | John Cerutti | .05 |
| 322 | Mike Kingery | .05 |
| 323 | Dave Magadan | .15 |
| 324 | Rafael Palmeiro | .30 |
| 325 | Jeff Dedmon | .05 |
| 326 | Barry Bonds | .20 |
| 327 | Jeffrey Leonard | .05 |
| 328 | Tim Flannery | .05 |
| 329 | Dave Concepcion | .05 |
| 330 | Mike Schmidt | .30 |
| 331 | Bill Dawley | .05 |
| 332 | Larry Anderson | .05 |
| 333 | Jack Howell | .05 |
| 334 | Ken Williams (R) | .25 |
| 335 | Bryn Smith | .05 |
| 336 | Billy Ripken (R) | .35 |
| 337 | Greg Brock | .05 |
| 338 | Mike Heath | .05 |
| 339 | Mike Greenwell | 1.00 |
| 340 | Claudell Washington | .05 |
| 341 | Jose Gonzalez | .05 |
| 342 | Mel Hall | .05 |

Card values shown here fluctuate considerably.

| NO. | PLAYER | MINT | NO. | PLAYER | MINT | NO. | PLAYER | MINT | NO. | PLAYER | MINT |
|---|---|---|---|---|---|---|---|---|---|---|---|
| 343 | Jim Eisenreich | .08 | 430 | Ricky Horton | .05 | 516 | Manny Trillo | .05 | 602 | Don August | .20 |
| 344 | Tony Bernazard | .05 | 431 | Gerald Young (R) | .40 | 517 | Jerry Reed | .05 | *603 | Terry Leach | .08 |
| 345 | Tim Raines | .25 | 432 | Rick Schu | .05 | 518 | Rick Leach | .05 | 604 | Tom Newell (R) | .25 |
| 346 | Bob Brower | .05 | 433 | Paul O'Neill | .05 | 519 | Mark Davidson (R) | .15 | *605 | Randall Byers (R) | .35 |
| 347 | Larry Parrish | .05 | 434 | Rich Gossage | .15 | 520 | Jeff Ballard (R) | .15 | 606 | Jim Gott | .05 |
| 348 | Thad Bosley | .05 | 435 | John Cangelosi | .05 | 521 | Dave Stapleton | .20 | 607 | Harry Spilman | .05 |
| 349 | Dennis Eckersley | .05 | 436 | Mike LaCoss | .05 | 522 | Pat Sheridan | .05 | 608 | John Candelaria | .05 |
| 350 | Cory Snyder | .25 | 437 | Gerald Perry | .10 | 523 | Al Nipper | .05 | 609 | Mike Brumley (R) | .20 |
| 351 | Rick Cerone | .05 | 438 | Dave Martinez | .05 | 524 | Steve Trout | .05 | 610 | Mickey Brantley | .15 |
| 352 | John Shelby | .05 | 439 | Darryl Strawberry | .50 | 525 | Jeff Hamilton | .05 | *611 | Jose Nunez (R) | .30 |
| 353 | Larry Herndon | .05 | 440 | John Moses | .05 | 526 | Tommy Hinzo (R) | .15 | 612 | Tom Nieto | .05 |
| 354 | John Habyan | .05 | 441 | Greg Gagne | .05 | 527 | Lonnie Smith | .08 | 613 | Rick Reuschel | .05 |
| 355 | Chuck Crim (R) | .15 | 442 | Jesse Barfield | .15 | 528 | Greg Cadaret (R) | .15 | *614 | Lee Mazzilli | .10 |
| 356 | Gus Polidor | .05 | 443 | George Frazier | .05 | 529 | Rob McClure | .05 | 615 | Scott Lusader (R) | .25 |
| 357 | Ken Dayley | .05 | 444 | Garth Iorg | .05 | 530 | Chuck Finley | .05 | 616 | Bobby Meacham | .05 |
| 358 | Danny Darwin | .05 | 445 | Ed Nunez | .05 | 531 | Jeff Russell | .05 | *617 | Kevin McReynolds | .15 |
| 359 | Lance Parrish | .15 | 446 | Rick Aguilera | .05 | 532 | Steve Lyons | .05 | 618 | Gene Garber | .05 |
| 360 | James Steels (R) | .15 | 447 | Jerry Mumphrey | .05 | 533 | Terry Puhl | .05 | *619 | Barry Lyons | .25 |
| 361 | Al Pedrique (R) | .15 | 448 | Rafael Ramirez | .05 | 534 | Eric Nolte (R) | .20 | 620 | Randy Myers | .15 |
| 362 | Mike Aldrete | .05 | 449 | John Smiley (R) | .25 | 535 | Kent Tekulve | .05 | 621 | Donnie Moore | .05 |
| 363 | Juan Castillo | .05 | 450 | Atlee Hammaker | .05 | 536 | Pat Pacillo | .15 | 622 | Domingo Ramos | .05 |
| 364 | Len Dykstra | .15 | 451 | Lance McCullers | .08 | 537 | Charlie Puleo | .05 | 623 | Ed Romero | .05 |
| 365 | Luis Quinones | .05 | 452 | Guy Hoffman | .05 | 538 | Tom Prince (R) | .15 | 624 | Greg Myers (R) | .15 |
| 366 | Jim Presley | .10 | 453 | Chris James | .10 | 539 | Greg Maddux | .15 | 625 | Ripken Family | .25 |
| 367 | Lloyd Moseby | .10 | 454 | Terry Pendleton | .05 | 540 | Jim Lindeman | .10 | *626 | Pat Perry | .15 |
| 368 | Kirby Puckett | .40 | 455 | Dave Meads (R) | .15 | 541 | Pete Stanicek (R) | .25 | *627 | Andres Thomas | .15 |
| 369 | Eric Davis | .75 | 456 | Bill Buckner | .05 | 542 | Steve Kiefer | .05 | *628 | Matt Williams (R) | .40 |
| 370 | Gary Redus | .05 | 457 | John Pawlowski (R) | .15 | 543 | Jim Morrison | .05 | 629 | Dave Hengel (R) | .25 |
| 371 | Dave Schmidt | .05 | 458 | Bob Sebra | .05 | 544 | Spike Owen | .05 | *630 | Jeff Musselman | .15 |
| 372 | Mark Clear | .05 | 459 | Jim Dwyer | .05 | 545 | Jay Buhner (R) | .35 | 631 | Tim Laudner | .05 |
| 373 | Dave Bergman | .05 | 460 | Jay Aldrich (R) | .15 | 546 | Mike Devereaux (R) | .30 | *632 | Bob Ojeda | .05 |
| 374 | Charles Hudson | .05 | 461 | Frank Tanana | .05 | 547 | Jerry Don Gleaton | .05 | 633 | Rafael Santana | .05 |
| 375 | Calvin Schiraldi | .05 | 462 | Oil Can Boyd | .05 | 548 | Jose Rijo | .05 | 634 | Wes Gardner | .25 |
| 376 | Alex Trevino | .05 | 463 | Dan Pasqua | .08 | 549 | Dennis Martinez | .05 | *635 | Roberto Kelly (R) | .50 |
| 377 | Tom Candiotti | .05 | 464 | Tim Crews (R) | .20 | 550 | Mike Loynd | .05 | *636 | Mike Flanagan | .15 |
| 378 | Steve Farr | .05 | 465 | Andy Allanson | .05 | 551 | Darrell Miller | .05 | 637 | Jay Bell | .25 |
| 379 | Mike Gallego | .05 | 466 | Bill Pecota (R) | .15 | 552 | Dave LaPoint | .05 | 638 | Bob Melvin | .05 |
| 380 | Andy McGaffigan | .05 | 467 | Steve Ontiveros | .05 | 553 | John Tudor | .10 | 639 | Damon Berryhill (R) | .25 |
| 381 | Kirk McCaskill | .05 | 468 | Hubie Brooks | .05 | 554 | Rocky Childress (R) | .15 | *640 | David Wells (R) | .25 |
| 382 | Oddibe McDowell | .08 | 469 | Paul Kilgus (R) | .20 | 555 | Wally Ritchie (R) | .15 | 641 | Puzzle Card | .05 |
| 383 | Floyd Bannister | .08 | 470 | Dale Mohorcic | .05 | 556 | Terry McGriff | .05 | 642 | Doug Sisk | .05 |
| 384 | Denny Walling | .05 | 471 | Dan Quisenberry | .10 | 557 | Dave Leiper | .05 | 643 | Keith Hughes (R) | .25 |
| 385 | Don Carman | .05 | 472 | Dave Stewart | .08 | 558 | Jeff Robinson | .05 | 644 | Tom Glavine (R) | .30 |
| 386 | Todd Worrell | .15 | 473 | Dave Clark | .05 | 559 | Jose Uribe | .05 | 645 | Al Newman | .15 |
| 387 | Eric Show | .05 | 474 | Joel Skinner | .05 | 560 | Ted Simmons | .05 | 646 | Scott Sanderson | .05 |
| 388 | Dave Parker | .20 | 475 | Dave Anderson | .05 | 561 | Lester Lancaster (R) | .20 | 647 | Scott Terry | .10 |
| 389 | Rick Mahler | .05 | 476 | Dan Petry | .05 | 562 | Keith Miller (R) | .25 | *648 | Tim Teufel | .15 |
| 390 | Mike Dunne | .40 | 477 | Carl Nichols (R) | .15 | 563 | Harold Reynolds | .05 | *649 | Garry Templeton | .15 |
| 391 | Candy Maldonado | .08 | 478 | Ernest Riles | .05 | 564 | Gene Larkin (R) | .25 | *650 | Manny Lee | .15 |
| 392 | Bob Dernier | .05 | 479 | George Hendrick | .05 | 565 | Cecil Fielder | .05 | *651 | Roger McDowell | .15 |
| 393 | Dave Valle | .05 | 480 | John Morris | .05 | 566 | Roy Smalley | .05 | *652 | Mookie Wilson | .15 |
| 394 | Ernie Whitt | .08 | 481 | Manny Hernandez (R) | .15 | 567 | Duane Ward | .05 | *653 | David Cone | .35 |
| 395 | Juan Berenguer | .05 | 482 | Jeff Stone | .05 | 568 | Bill Wilkinson (R) | .15 | *654 | Ron Gant (R) | .60 |
| 396 | Mike Young | .08 | 483 | Chris Brown | .10 | 569 | Howard Johnson | .10 | *655 | Joe Price | .15 |
| 397 | Mike Felder | .05 | 484 | Mike Bielecki | .05 | 570 | Frank DiPino | .05 | *656 | George Bell | .25 |
| 398 | Willie Hernandez | .08 | 485 | Dave Dravecky | .05 | 571 | Pete Smith (R) | .15 | *657 | Gregg Jefferies (R) | 7.00 |
| 399 | Jim Rice | .25 | 486 | Rick Manning | .05 | 572 | Darnell Coles | .05 | *658 | Todd Stottlemyre | .40 |
| 400 | Checklist | .08 | 487 | Bill Almon | .05 | 573 | Don Robinson | .05 | *659 | Geronimo Berroa (R) | .40 |
| 401 | Tommy John | .12 | 488 | Jim Sundberg | .05 | 574 | Rob Nelson | .05 | *660 | Jerry Royster | .15 |
| 402 | Brian Holton | .05 | 489 | Ken Phelps | .05 | 575 | Dennis Rasmussen | .05 | | | |
| 403 | Carmen Castillo | .05 | 490 | Tom Henke | .05 | 576 | Steve Jeltz | .05 | | **Bonus Cards (Rack and Wax)** | |
| 404 | Jamie Quirk | .05 | 491 | Dan Gladden | .05 | 577 | Tom Pagnozzi (R) | .15 | BC 1 | Cal Ripken | .30 |
| 405 | Dwayne Murphy | .05 | 492 | Barry Larkin | .15 | 578 | Ty Gainey | .05 | BC 2 | Eric Davis | .75 |
| 406 | Jeff Parrett (R) | .15 | 493 | Fred Manrique (R) | .20 | 579 | Gary Lucas | .05 | BC 3 | Paul Molitor | .25 |
| 407 | Don Sutton | .15 | 494 | Mike Griffin | .05 | 580 | Ron Hassey | .05 | BC 4 | Mike Schmidt | .30 |
| 408 | Jerry Browne | .05 | 495 | Mark Knudson (R) | .12 | 581 | Herm Winningham | .05 | BC 5 | Ivan Calderon | .10 |
| 409 | Jim Winn | .05 | 496 | Bill Madlock | .12 | 582 | Rene Gonzales (R) | .15 | BC 6 | Tony Gwynn | .50 |
| 410 | Dave Smith | .05 | 497 | Tim Stoddard | .05 | 583 | Brad Komminsk | .05 | BC 7 | Wade Boggs | .75 |
| 411 | Shane Mack | .25 | 498 | Sam Horn (R) | .75 | 584 | Doyle Alexander | .05 | BC 8 | Andy Van Slyke | .10 |
| 412 | Greg Gross | .05 | 499 | Tracy Woodson (R) | .20 | 585 | Jeff Sellers | .05 | BC 9 | Joe Carter | .15 |
| 413 | Nick Esasky | .05 | 500 | Checklist | .08 | 586 | Bill Gullickson | .05 | BC10 | Andre Dawson | .30 |
| 414 | Damaso Garcia | .05 | 501 | Ken Schrom | .05 | 587 | Tim Belcher | .10 | BC11 | Alan Trammell | .20 |
| 415 | Brian Fisher | .05 | 502 | Angel Salazar | .05 | 588 | Doug Jones (R) | .25 | BC12 | Mike Scott | .20 |
| 416 | Brian Dayett | .05 | 503 | Eric Plunk | .05 | 589 | Melido Perez (R) | .20 | BC13 | Wally Joyner | .75 |
| 417 | Curt Ford | .05 | 504 | Joe Hesketh | .05 | 590 | Rick Honeycutt | .05 | BC14 | Dale Murphy | .40 |
| 418 | Mark Williamson (R) | .15 | 505 | Greg Minton | .05 | 591 | Pascual Perez | .05 | BC15 | Kirby Puckett | .50 |
| 419 | Bill Schroeder | .05 | 506 | Geno Petralli | .05 | 592 | Curt Wilkerson | .05 | BC16 | Pedro Guerrero | .15 |
| 420 | Mike Henneman (R) | .25 | 507 | Bob James | .05 | 593 | Steve Howe | .05 | BC17 | Kevin Seitzer | 1.00 |
| 421 | John Marzano | .20 | 508 | Robbie Wine (R) | .15 | 594 | John Davis (R) | .20 | BC18 | Tim Raines | .25 |
| 422 | Ron Kittle | .08 | 509 | Jeff Calhoun | .05 | 595 | Storm Davis | .05 | BC19 | George Bell | .25 |
| 423 | Matt Young | .05 | 510 | Steve Lake | .05 | 596 | Sammy Stewart | .05 | BC20 | Darryl Strawberry | 1.00 |
| 424 | Steve Balboni | .05 | 511 | Mark Grant | .05 | 597 | Neil Allen | .05 | BC21 | Don Mattingly | 1.50 |
| 425 | Luis Polonia (R) | .25 | 512 | Frank Williams | .05 | 598 | Alejandro Pena | .05 | BC22 | Ozzie Smith | .15 |
| 426 | Randy St. Claire | .05 | 513 | Jeff Blauser (R) | .20 | 599 | Mark Thurmond | .05 | BC23 | Mark McGwire | 1.25 |
| 427 | Greg Harris | .05 | 514 | Bob Walk | .05 | 600 | Checklist | .08 | BC24 | Will Clark | .75 |
| 428 | Johnny Ray | .05 | 515 | Craig Lefferts | .05 | 601 | Jose Mesa (R) | .15 | BC25 | Alvin Davis | .20 |
| 429 | Ray Searage | .05 | | | | | | | BC26 | Ruben Sierra | .30 |

Card values shown here fluctuate considerably.

## 1988 Donruss Rookies. . . . Complete Set of 56 Cards—Value $12.00

Features the outstanding rookies of the 1988 season. The cards are coated with a glossy finish. The entire set was packaged in a printed box, and distributed primarily through card hobby dealers. Features Donruss' first card of Chris Sabo and Mark Grace.

| NO. | PLAYER | MINT | NO. | PLAYER | MINT | NO. | PLAYER | MINT | NO. | PLAYER | MINT |
|-----|--------|------|-----|--------|------|-----|--------|------|-----|--------|------|
| 1 | Mark Grace | 2.00 | 15 | Pete Stanicek | 15 | 29 | Johnny Paredes | 15 | 43 | John Dopson | 25 |
| 2 | Mike Campbell | 10 | 16 | Roberto Kelly | 15 | 30 | Chris Sabo (RR) | 2.00 | 44 | Jody Reed | 20 |
| 3 | Todd Frohwirth | 10 | 17 | Jeff Treadway | 15 | 31 | Dannon Berryhill | 15 | 45 | Darrin Jackson | 20 |
| 4 | Dave Stapleton | 10 | 18 | Walt Weiss (RR) | 65 | 32 | Randy Miligan | 15 | 46 | Mike Capel | 10 |
| 5 | Shawn Abner | 15 | 19 | Paul Gibson | 25 | 33 | Gary Thurman | 15 | 47 | Ron Gant | 35 |
| 6 | Jose Cecenazi | 10 | 20 | Tim Crews | 10 | 34 | Kevin Elster | 30 | 48 | John Davis | 10 |
| 7 | Dave Gallagher | 15 | 21 | Melido Perez | 10 | 35 | Roberto Alomar | 25 | 49 | Kevin Coffman | 15 |
| 8 | Mark Parent | 15 | 22 | Steve Peters | 15 | 36 | Edgar Martinez | 25 | 50 | Cris Carpenter (RR) | 35 |
| 9 | Cecil Espy | 15 | 23 | Craig Worthington | 35 | 37 | Todd Stottlemyre | 15 | 51 | Mick Sasser | 20 |
| 10 | Pete Smith | 10 | 24 | John Trautwein | 25 | 38 | Joey Meyer | 30 | 52 | Luis Alicea | 15 |
| 11 | Jay Buhner | 25 | 25 | DeWayne Vaughn | 15 | 39 | Carl Nichols | 10 | 53 | Bryan Harvey (RR) | 40 |
| 12 | Pat Borders | 25 | 26 | David Well | 15 | 40 | Jack McDowell | 15 | 54 | Steve Ellsworth | 20 |
| 13 | Doug Jennings | 20 | 27 | Al Leiter | 20 | 41 | Jose Bautista | 20 | 55 | Mike Macfarlane | 20 |
| 14 | Brady Anderson | 30 | 28 | Tim Belcher | 15 | 42 | Sil Campusano | 25 | 56 | Checklist | 10 |

## 1989 Donruss. . . . Complete Set of 660 Cards—Value $30.00

Features the rookie cards of Sandy Alomar, Jr., Gary Sheffield, and Rickey Jordan. 26 Bonus Cards featuring major stars are randomly distributed in wax and rack packs. These cards are numbered BC-1 to BC-26.

| NO. | PLAYER | MINT | NO. | PLAYER | MINT | NO. | PLAYER | MINT | NO. | PLAYER | MINT |
|-----|--------|------|-----|--------|------|-----|--------|------|-----|--------|------|
| | **No. 1 to 26—Diamond Kings** | | 7 | Carlton Fisk (DK) | .08 | 14 | Andres Galarraga (DK) | .15 | 21 | Harold Reynolds (DK) | .10 |
| 1 | Mike Greenwell (DK) | .75 | 8 | Cory Snyder (DK) | .10 | 15 | Kirk Gibson (DK) | .10 | 22 | Gerald Perry (DK) | .10 |
| 2 | Bobby Bonilla (DK) | .15 | 9 | David Cone (DK) | .25 | 16 | Fred McGriff (DK) | .25 | 23 | Frank Viola (DK) | .10 |
| 3 | Pete Incaviglia (DK) | .10 | 10 | Kevin Seitzer (DK) | .20 | 17 | Mark Grace (DK) | .35 | 24 | Steve Bedrosian (DK) | .08 |
| 4 | Chris Sabo (DK) | .50 | 11 | Rick Rueschel (DK) | .08 | 18 | Jeff Robinson (DK) | .10 | 25 | Glenn Davis (DK) | .10 |
| 5 | Robin Yount (DK) | .10 | 12 | Johnny Ray (DK) | .08 | 19 | Vince Coleman (DK) | .10 | 26 | Don Mattingly (DK) | .75 |
| 6 | Tony Gwynn (DK) | .15 | 13 | Dave Schmidt (DK) | .08 | 20 | Dave Henderson (DK) | .10 | 27 | Diamond King Checklist | .08 |

Card values shown here fluctuate considerably.

| NO. | PLAYER | MINT |
|---|---|---|
| **No. 28 to 47—Rated Rookies** | | |
| 28 | Sandy Alomar, Jr. (R) | 1.25 |
| 29 | Steve Searcy (R) | .20 |
| 30 | Cameron Drew (R) | .35 |
| 31 | Gary Sheffield (R) | 1.50 |
| 32 | Erik Hanson (R) | .20 |
| 33 | Ken Griffey, Jr. (R) | 2.75 |
| 34 | Greg Harris (R) | .20 |
| 35 | Gregg Jefferies | 1.75 |
| 36 | Luis Medina (R) | .60 |
| 37 | Carlos Quintana (R) | .35 |
| 38 | Felix Jose (R) | .25 |
| 39 | Cris Carpenter (R) | .20 |
| 40 | Ron Jones (R) | .75 |
| 41 | Dave West (R) | .75 |
| 42 | Randy Johnson (R) | .25 |
| 43 | Mike Harkey (R) | .75 |
| 44 | Pete Harnisch (R) | .20 |
| 45 | Tom Gordon (R) | .25 |
| 46 | Gregg Olson (R) | .60 |
| 47 | Alex Sanchez (R) | .25 |
| 48 | Ruben Sierra | .20 |
| 49 | Rafael Palmeiro | .15 |
| 50 | Ron Gant | .30 |
| 51 | Cal Ripken, Jr. | .20 |
| 52 | Wally Joyner | .15 |
| 53 | Gary Carter | .20 |
| 54 | Andy Van Slyke | .15 |
| 55 | Robin Yount | .15 |
| 56 | Pete Incaviglia | .10 |
| 57 | Greg Brock | .05 |
| 58 | Melido Perez | .10 |
| 59 | Craig Lefferts | .05 |
| 60 | Gary Pettis | .05 |
| 61 | Danny Tartabull | .20 |
| 62 | Guillermo Hernandez | .05 |
| 63 | Ozzie Smith | .08 |
| 64 | Gary Gaetti | .10 |
| 65 | Mark Davis | .05 |
| 66 | Lee Smith | .08 |
| 67 | Dennis Eckersley | .10 |
| 68 | Wade Boggs | .75 |
| 69 | Mike Scott | .15 |
| 70 | Fred McGriff | .40 |
| 71 | Tom Browning | .08 |
| 72 | Claudell Washington | .05 |
| 73 | Mel Hall | .05 |
| 74 | Don Mattingly | 1.50 |
| 75 | Steve Bedrosian | .08 |
| 76 | Juan Samuel | .10 |
| 77 | Mike Scioscia | .05 |
| 78 | Dave Righetti | .10 |
| 79 | Alfredo Griffin | .05 |
| 80 | Eric Davis | .65 |
| 81 | Juan Berenquer | .05 |
| 82 | Todd Worrell | .05 |
| 83 | Joe Carter | .15 |
| 84 | Steve Sax | .08 |
| 85 | Frank White | .05 |
| 86 | John Kruk | .15 |
| 87 | Rance Mulliniks | .05 |
| 88 | Alan Ashby | .05 |
| 89 | Charlie Leibrandt | .08 |
| 90 | Frank Tanana | .08 |
| 91 | Jose Canseco | 1.25 |
| 92 | Barry Bonds | .20 |
| 93 | Harold Reynolds | .08 |
| 94 | Mark McLemore | .05 |
| 95 | Mark McGwire | 1.00 |
| 96 | Eddie Murray | .30 |
| 97 | Tim Raines | .15 |
| 98 | Rob Thompsomn | .05 |
| 99 | Kevin McReynolds | .15 |
| 100 | Checklist | .08 |
| 101 | Carlton Fisk | .10 |
| 102 | Dave Martinez | .05 |
| 103 | Glenn Braggs | .05 |
| 104 | Dale Murphy | .25 |
| 105 | Ryne Sandberg | .12 |
| 106 | Dennis Martinez | .05 |
| 107 | Pete O'Brien | .10 |
| 108 | Dick Schofield | .05 |
| 109 | Henry Cotto | .05 |
| 110 | Mike Marshall | .08 |
| 111 | Keith Moreland | .08 |
| 112 | Tom Brunansky | .08 |
| 113 | Kelly Gruber | .05 |
| 114 | Brook Jacoby | .05 |
| 115 | Keith Brown (R) | .20 |
| 116 | Matt Nokes | .10 |
| 117 | Keith Hernandez | .15 |
| 118 | Bob Forsch | .05 |
| 119 | Bert Blyleven | .15 |
| 120 | Willie Wilson | .08 |
| 121 | Tommy Gregg | .05 |
| 122 | Jim Rice | .12 |
| 123 | Bob Knepper | .05 |
| 124 | Danny Jackson | .10 |
| 125 | Eric Plunk | .05 |
| 126 | Brian Fisher | .05 |
| 127 | Mike Pagliarulo | .10 |
| 128 | Tony Gwynn | .35 |
| 129 | Lance McCullers | .08 |
| 130 | Andres Galarraga | .25 |
| 131 | Jose Uribe | .05 |
| 132 | Kirk Gibson | .20 |
| 133 | David Palmer | .05 |
| 134 | R. J. Reynolds | .05 |
| 135 | Greg Walker | .05 |
| 136 | Kirk McCaskill | .05 |
| 137 | Shawon Dunston | .10 |
| 138 | Andy Allanson | .05 |
| 139 | Rob Murphy | .05 |
| 140 | Mike Aldrete | .05 |
| 141 | Terry Kennedy | .05 |
| 142 | Scott Fletcher | .05 |
| 143 | Steve Balboni | .05 |
| 144 | Bret Saberhagen | .10 |
| 145 | Ozzie Virgil | .05 |
| 146 | Dale Sveum | .08 |
| 147 | Darryl Strawberry | .45 |
| 148 | Harold Baines | .10 |
| 149 | George Bell | .15 |
| 150 | Dave Parker | .10 |
| 151 | Bobby Bonilla | .20 |
| 152 | Mookie Wilson | .08 |
| 153 | Tod Power | .05 |
| 154 | Nolan Ryan | .20 |
| 155 | Jeff Reardon | .08 |
| 156 | Tim Wallach | .08 |
| 157 | Jamie Moyer | .05 |
| 158 | Rich Gossage | .08 |
| 159 | Dave Winfield | .15 |
| 160 | Von Hayes | .08 |
| 161 | Willie McGee | .08 |
| 162 | Rich Gedman | .05 |
| 163 | Tony Pena | .08 |
| 164 | Mike Morgan | .05 |
| 165 | Charlie Hough | .08 |
| 166 | Mike Stanley | .05 |
| 167 | Andre Dawson | .15 |
| 168 | Joe Boever | .05 |
| 169 | Pete Stanicek | .05 |
| 170 | Bob Boone | .05 |
| 171 | Ron Darling | .10 |
| 172 | Bob Walk | .05 |
| 173 | Rob Deer | .08 |
| 174 | Steve Buechele | .05 |
| 175 | Ted Higuera | .10 |
| 176 | Ozzie Guillen | .08 |
| 177 | Candy Maldonado | .10 |
| 178 | Doyle Alexander | .05 |
| 179 | Mark Gubicza | .10 |
| 180 | Alan Trammell | .10 |
| 181 | Vince Coleman | .15 |
| 182 | Kirby Puckett | .25 |
| 183 | Chris Brown | .08 |
| 184 | Marty Barrett | .05 |
| 185 | Stan Javier | .05 |
| 186 | Mike Greenwell | 1.25 |
| 187 | Billy Hatcher | .05 |
| 188 | Jimmy Key | .12 |
| 189 | Nick Esasky | .10 |
| 190 | Don Slaught | .05 |
| 191 | Cory Snyder | .15 |
| 192 | John Candelaria | .08 |
| 193 | Mike Schmidt | .30 |
| 194 | Kevin Gross | .05 |
| 195 | John Tudor | .05 |
| 196 | Neil Allen | .05 |
| 197 | Orel Hershiser | .25 |
| 198 | Kal Daniels | .25 |
| 199 | Kent Hrbek | .10 |
| 200 | Checklist | .08 |
| 201 | Joe Magrane | .10 |
| 202 | Scott Bailes | .05 |
| 203 | Tim Belcher | .15 |
| 204 | George Brett | .25 |
| 205 | Benito Santiago | .10 |
| 206 | Tony Fernandez | .10 |
| 207 | Gerald Young | .08 |
| 208 | Bo Jackson | .25 |
| 209 | Chet Lemon | .05 |
| 210 | Storm Davis | .05 |
| 211 | Doug Drabek | .10 |
| 212 | Mickey Brantley | .08 |
| 213 | Devon White | .08 |
| 214 | Dave Stewart | .10 |
| 215 | Dave Schmidt | .05 |
| 216 | Bryn Smith | .05 |
| 217 | Brett Butler | .05 |
| 218 | Bob Ojeda | .08 |
| 219 | Steve Rosenberg (R) | .15 |
| 220 | Hubie Brooks | .05 |
| 221 | B.J. Surhoff | .08 |
| 222 | Rick Mahler | .05 |
| 223 | Rick Sutcliffe | .10 |
| 224 | Neal Heaton | .05 |
| 225 | Mitch Williams | .05 |
| 226 | Chuck Finley | .05 |
| 227 | Mark Langston | .10 |
| 228 | Jesse Orosco | .05 |
| 229 | Ed Whitson | .05 |
| 230 | Terry Pendelton | .08 |
| 231 | Lloyd Moseby | .15 |
| 232 | Greg Swindell | .10 |
| 233 | John Franco | .08 |
| 234 | Jack Morris | .10 |
| 235 | Howard Johnson | .10 |
| 236 | Glenn Davis | .10 |
| 237 | Frank Viola | .15 |
| 238 | Kevin Seitzer | .35 |
| 239 | Gerald Perry | .10 |
| 240 | Dwight Evans | .15 |
| 241 | Jim Deshaies | .05 |
| 242 | Bo Diaz | .05 |
| 243 | Carney Lansford | .08 |
| 244 | Mike Lavalliere | .05 |
| 245 | Rickey Henderson | .30 |
| 246 | Roberto Alomar | .15 |
| 247 | Jimmy Jones | .05 |
| 248 | Pascual Perez | .05 |
| 249 | Will Clark | .50 |
| 250 | Fernando Valenzuela | .10 |
| 251 | Shane Rawley | .05 |
| 252 | Sid Bream | .05 |
| 253 | Steve Lyons | .05 |
| 254 | Brian Downing | .08 |
| 255 | Mark Grace | .75 |
| 256 | Tom Candiotti | .08 |
| 257 | Barry Larkin | .10 |
| 258 | Mike Krukow | .08 |
| 259 | Billy Ripken | .05 |
| 260 | Cecilio Guante | .05 |
| 261 | Scott Bradley | .05 |
| 262 | Floyd Bannister | .05 |
| 263 | Pete Smith | .08 |
| 264 | Jim Gantner | .05 |
| 265 | Roger McDowell | .05 |
| 266 | Bobby Thigpen | .05 |
| 267 | Jim Clancy | .05 |
| 268 | Terry Steinbach | .12 |
| 269 | Mike Dunne | .05 |
| 270 | Dwight Gooden | .40 |
| 271 | Mike Heath | .05 |
| 272 | Dave Smith | .05 |
| 273 | Keith Atherton | .05 |
| 274 | Tim Burke | .05 |
| 275 | Damon Beryhill | .15 |
| 276 | Vance Law | .05 |
| 277 | Rich Dotson | .08 |
| 278 | Lance Parrish | .10 |
| 279 | Denny Walling | .05 |
| 280 | Roger Clemens | .50 |
| 281 | Greg Mathews | .05 |
| 282 | Tom Niedenfuer | .05 |
| 283 | Paul Kilgus | .05 |
| 284 | Jose Guzman | .05 |
| 285 | Calvin Schiraldi | .05 |
| 286 | Charlie Puleo | .05 |
| 287 | Joe Orsulak | .05 |
| 288 | Jack Howell | .08 |
| 289 | Kevin Elster | .08 |
| 290 | Jose Lind | .05 |
| 291 | Paul Molitor | .08 |
| 292 | Cecil Espy | .10 |
| 293 | Bill Wegman | .05 |
| 294 | Dan Pasqua | .08 |
| 295 | Scott Garrelts | .05 |
| 296 | Walt Terrell | .05 |
| 297 | Ed Hearn | .05 |
| 298 | Lou Whitaker | .08 |
| 299 | Ken Dayley | .05 |
| 300 | Checklist | .08 |
| 301 | Tommy Herr | .05 |
| 302 | Mike Brumley | .05 |
| 303 | Ellis Burks | .35 |
| 304 | Curt Young | .05 |
| 305 | Jody Reed | .15 |
| 306 | Bill Doran | .08 |
| 307 | David Wells | .05 |
| 308 | Ron Robinson | .08 |
| 309 | Rafael Santana | .05 |
| 310 | Julio Franco | .08 |
| 311 | Jack Clark | .10 |
| 312 | Chris James | .08 |
| 313 | Milt Thompson | .05 |
| 314 | John Shelby | .05 |
| 315 | Al Leiter | .10 |
| 316 | Mike Davis | .05 |
| 317 | Chris Sabo (R) | 1.25 |
| 318 | Greg Gagne | .05 |
| 319 | Jose Oquendo | .05 |
| 320 | John Farrell | .10 |
| 321 | Franklin Stubbs | .05 |
| 322 | Kurt Stillwell | .05 |
| 323 | Shawn Abner | .05 |
| 324 | Mike Flanagan | .05 |
| 325 | Kevin Bass | .08 |
| 326 | Pat Tabler | .08 |
| 327 | Mike Henneman | .05 |
| 328 | Rick Honeycutt | .05 |
| 329 | John Smiley | .08 |
| 330 | Rey Quinones | .05 |
| 331 | Johnny Ray | .10 |
| 332 | Bob Welch | .08 |
| 333 | Larry Sheets | .05 |
| 334 | Jeff Parrett | .08 |
| 335 | Rick Rueschel | .05 |
| 336 | Randy Myers | .08 |
| 337 | Ken Williams | .05 |
| 338 | Andy McGaffigan | .05 |
| 339 | Joey Meyer | .05 |
| 340 | Dion James | .05 |
| 341 | Les Lancaster | .05 |
| 342 | Tom Foley | .05 |
| 343 | Geno Petralli | .05 |
| 344 | Dan Petry | .05 |
| 345 | Alvin Davis | .08 |
| 346 | Mickey Hatcher | .05 |
| 347 | Marvelle Wynn | .05 |
| 348 | Danny Cox | .05 |
| 349 | Dave Stieb | .08 |
| 350 | Jay Bell | .05 |
| 351 | Jeff Treadway | .05 |
| 352 | Luis Salazar | .05 |
| 353 | Lenny Dykstra | .15 |
| 354 | Juan Agosto | .05 |
| 355 | Gene Larkin | .05 |
| 356 | Steve Farr | .05 |
| 357 | Paul Assenmacher | .05 |
| 358 | Todd Benzinger | .15 |
| 359 | Larry Andersen | .05 |
| 360 | Paul O'Neill | .05 |
| 361 | Ron Hassey | .05 |
| 362 | Jim Gott | .05 |

Card values shown here fluctuate considerably.

| NO. | PLAYER | MINT | NO. | PLAYER | MINT | NO. | PLAYER | MINT | NO. | PLAYER | MINT |
|---|---|---|---|---|---|---|---|---|---|---|---|
| 363 | Ken Phelps | .05 | 444 | Jerry Don Gleaton | .05 | 525 | Bryan Harvey (R) | .25 | 606 | Lance Johnson | .05 |
| 364 | Tim Flannery | .05 | 445 | Paul Gibson (R) | .15 | 526 | Rick Aguilera | .05 | 607 | Terry Clark (R) | .25 |
| 365 | Randy Ready | .05 | 446 | Walt Weiss | 1.25 | 527 | Tom Prince | .05 | 608 | Manny Trillo | .05 |
| 366 | Nelson Santovenia (R) | .15 | 447 | Glenn Wilson | .05 | 528 | Mark Clear | .05 | 609 | Scott Jordan (R) | .25 |
| 367 | Kelly Downs | .05 | 448 | Mike Moore | .05 | 529 | Jerry Browne | .05 | 610 | Jay Howell | .08 |
| 368 | Danny Heep | .05 | 449 | Chili Davis | .08 | 530 | Juan Castillo | .05 | 611 | Francisco Melendez (R) | .25 |
| 369 | Phil Bradley | .08 | 450 | Dave Henderson | .05 | 531 | Jack McDowell | .10 | 612 | Mike Boddicker | .08 |
| 370 | Jeff Robinson | .05 | 451 | Jose Bautista (R) | .20 | 532 | Chris Speier | .05 | 613 | Kevin Brown (R) | .25 |
| 371 | Ivan Calderon | .10 | 452 | Rex Hudler | .10 | 533 | Darrell Evans | .05 | 614 | Dave Valle | .05 |
| 372 | Mike Witt | .08 | 453 | Bob Brenly | .05 | 534 | Luis Aquino | .05 | 615 | Tim Laudner | .05 |
| 373 | Greg Maddux | .20 | 454 | Mackey Sasser | .08 | 535 | Eric King | .05 | 616 | Andy Nezelek (R) | .25 |
| 374 | Carmen Castillo | .05 | 455 | Daryl Boston | .05 | 536 | Ken Hill (R) | .20 | 617 | Chuck Crim | .05 |
| 375 | Jose Rijo | .08 | 456 | Mike Fitzgerald | .05 | 537 | Randy Bush | .05 | 618 | Jack Savage | .15 |
| 376 | Joe Price | .05 | 457 | Jefferey Leonard | .05 | 538 | Shane Mack | .05 | 619 | Adam Peterson | .20 |
| 377 | R.C. Gonzalez | .05 | 458 | Bruce Sutter | .08 | 539 | Tom Bolton | .05 | 620 | Todd Stottlemyre | .08 |
| 378 | Oddibe McDowell | .08 | 459 | Mitch Webster | .05 | 540 | Gene Nelson | .05 | 621 | Lance Blankenship (R) | .25 |
| 379 | Jim Presley | .05 | 460 | Joe Hesketh | .05 | 541 | Wes Gardner | .05 | 622 | Miquel Garcia (R) | .30 |
| 380 | Brad Wellman | .05 | 461 | Bobby Witt | .05 | 542 | Ken Caminiti | .05 | 623 | Keith Miller | .05 |
| 381 | Tom Glavine | .05 | 462 | Stew Cliburn | .05 | 543 | Duane Ward | .05 | 624 | Ricky Jordan (R) | 2.75 |
| 382 | Dan Plesac | .05 | 463 | Scott Bankhead | .05 | 544 | Norm Charlton (R) | .20 | 625 | Ernest Riles | .05 |
| 383 | Wally Backman | .05 | 464 | Ramon Martinez (R) | .50 | 545 | Hal Morris (R) | .25 | 626 | John Moses | .05 |
| 384 | Dave Gallagher (R) | .25 | 465 | Dave Leiper | .05 | 546 | Rich Yett | .05 | 627 | Nelson Liriano | .05 |
| 385 | Tom Henke | .05 | 466 | Luis Alicea (R) | .15 | 547 | Hensley Meulens (R) | 1.25 | 628 | Mike Smithson | .05 |
| 386 | Luis Polonia | .05 | 467 | John Cerutti | .05 | 548 | Greg Harris | .20 | 629 | Scott Sanderson | .05 |
| 387 | Junior Ortiz | .05 | 468 | Ron Washington | .05 | 549 | Darren Daulton | .05 | 630 | Dale Mohorcic | .05 |
| 388 | David Cone | .35 | 469 | Jeff Reed | .05 | 550 | Jeff Hamilton | .05 | 631 | Marvin Freeman | .05 |
| 389 | Dave Bergman | .05 | 470 | Jeff Robinson | .10 | 551 | Luis Aguayo | .05 | 632 | Mike Young | .05 |
| 390 | Danny Darwin | .05 | 471 | Sid Fernandez | .10 | 552 | Tim Leary | .10 | 633 | Dennis Lamp | .05 |
| 391 | Dan Gladden | .05 | 472 | Terry Puhl | .05 | 553 | Ron Oester | .05 | 634 | Dante Bichette (R) | .25 |
| 392 | John Dopson (R) | .25 | 473 | Charlie Lea | .05 | 554 | Steve Lombardozzi | .05 | 635 | Curt Schilling (R) | .25 |
| 393 | Frank DiPino | .05 | 474 | Israel Sanchez (R) | .15 | 555 | Tim Jones (R) | .20 | 636 | Scott May (R) | .25 |
| 394 | Al Nipper | .05 | 475 | Bruce Benedict | .05 | 556 | Bud Black | .05 | 637 | Mike Schooler (R) | .25 |
| 395 | Willie Randolph | .08 | 476 | Oil Can Boyd | .08 | 557 | Alejandro Pena | .08 | 638 | Rick Leach | .05 |
| 396 | Don Carman | .05 | 477 | Craig Reynolds | .05 | 558 | Jose DeJesus (R) | .15 | 639 | Tom Lampkin (R) | .25 |
| 397 | Scott Terry | .05 | 478 | Frank Williams | .05 | 559 | Dennis Rasmussen | .05 | 640 | Brian Meyer (R) | .25 |
| 398 | Rick Cerone | .05 | 479 | Greg Cadaret | .05 | 560 | Pat Borders (R) | .25 | 641 | Brian Harper | .05 |
| 399 | Tom Pagnozzi | .05 | 480 | Randy Kramer (R) | .15 | 561 | Craig Biggio (R) | .25 | 642 | John Smoltz (R) | .35 |
| 400 | Checklist | .08 | 481 | Dave Eiland (R) | .25 | 562 | Luis de los Santos (R) | .20 | 643 | Jose—40/40 Club | .35 |
| 401 | Mickey Tettleton | .05 | 482 | Eric Show | .05 | 563 | Fred Lynn | .08 | 644 | Bill Schroeder | .05 |
| 402 | Curtis Wilkerson | .05 | 483 | Garry Templeton | .05 | 564 | Todd Burns (R) | .25 | 645 | Edgar Martinez | .05 |
| 403 | Jeff Russel | .05 | 484 | Wallace Johnson | .05 | 565 | Felix Fermin | .05 | 646 | Dennis Cook (R) | .25 |
| 404 | Pat Perry | .05 | 485 | Kevin Mitchell | .08 | 566 | Darnell Coles | .05 | 647 | Barry Jones | .05 |
| 405 | Jose Alvarez (R) | .15 | 486 | Tim Crews | .05 | 567 | Willie Fraser | .05 | 648 | Orel—59 and Counting | .10 |
| 406 | Rick Schu | .05 | 487 | Mike Maddux | .05 | 568 | Glenn Hubbard | .05 | 649 | Rod Nichols | .25 |
| 407 | Sherman Corbett (R) | .15 | 488 | Dave LaPoint | .05 | 569 | Craig Worthington (R) | .30 | 650 | Jody Davis | .05 |
| 408 | Dave Magadan | .10 | 489 | Fred Manrique | .05 | 570 | Johnny Paredes (R) | .20 | 651 | Bob Milacki (R) | .25 |
| 409 | Bob Kipper | .05 | 490 | Greg Minton | .05 | 571 | Don Robinson | .05 | 652 | Mike Jackson | .05 |
| 410 | Don August | .10 | 491 | Doug Dascenzo (R) | .20 | 572 | Barry Lyons | .05 | 653 | Derek Lilliquist (R) | .30 |
| 411 | Bob Brower | .05 | 492 | Willie Upshaw | .05 | 573 | Bill Long | .05 | 654 | Paul Mirabella | .05 |
| 412 | Chris Bosio | .05 | 493 | Jack Armstrong (R) | .20 | 574 | Tracy Jones | .05 | 655 | Mike Diaz | .05 |
| 413 | Jerry Reuss | .05 | 494 | Kirt Manwaring | .05 | 575 | Juan Nieves | .05 | 656 | Jeff Musselman | .05 |
| 414 | Atlee Hammaker | .05 | 495 | Jeff Ballard | .05 | 576 | Andres Thomas | .05 | 657 | Jerry Reed | .05 |
| 415 | Jim Walewander | .10 | 496 | Jeff Kunkel | .05 | 577 | Rolando Roomes (R) | .25 | 658 | Kevin Blankenship (R) | .25 |
| 416 | Mike Macfarlane (R) | .20 | 497 | Mike Campbell | .05 | 578 | Luis Rivera | .15 | 659 | Wayne Tolleson | .05 |
| 417 | Pat Sheridan | .05 | 498 | Gary Thurman | .05 | 579 | Chad Kreuter (R) | .20 | 660 | Eric Hetzel (R) | .25 |
| 418 | Pedro Guerrero | .15 | 499 | Zane Smith | .05 | 580 | Tony Armas | .05 | | **Bonus Cards (Rack and Wax)** | |
| 419 | Allan Anderson | .08 | 500 | Checklist | .08 | 581 | Jay Buhner | .15 | BC1 | Kirby Puckett | .25 |
| 420 | Mark Parent (R) | .15 | 501 | Mike Birkbeck | .05 | 582 | Ricky Horton | .05 | BC2 | Mike Scott | .15 |
| 421 | Bob Stanley | .05 | 502 | Terry Leach | .05 | 583 | Andy Hawkins | .05 | BC3 | Joe Carter | .15 |
| 422 | Mike Gallego | .05 | 503 | Shawn Hillegas | .05 | 584 | Sil Campusano (R) | .20 | BC4 | Orel Hershiser | .25 |
| 423 | Bruce Hurst | .15 | 504 | Manny Lee | .05 | 585 | Dave Clark | .05 | BC5 | Jose Canseco | 1.00 |
| 424 | Dave Meads | .05 | 505 | Doug Jennings (R) | .35 | 586 | Van Snider (R) | .30 | BC6 | Darryl Strawberry | .45 |
| 425 | Jesse Barfield | .12 | 506 | Ken Oberkfell | .05 | 587 | Todd Frohwirth | .05 | BC7 | George Brett | .25 |
| 426 | Rob Dibble (R) | .15 | 507 | Tim Tuefel | .05 | 588 | Puzzle Card | .08 | BC8 | Andre Dawson | .20 |
| 427 | Joel Skinner | .05 | 508 | Tom Brookens | .05 | 589 | William Brennan (R) | .25 | BC9 | Paul Molitor | .15 |
| 428 | Ron Kittle | .08 | 509 | Rafael Ramirez | .05 | 590 | German Gonzalez (R) | .20 | BC10 | Andy Van Slyke | .15 |
| 429 | Rick Rhoden | .05 | 510 | Fred Toliver | .05 | 591 | Ernie Whitt | .05 | BC11 | Dave Winfield | .15 |
| 430 | Bob Dernier | .05 | 511 | Brian Holman (R) | .25 | 592 | Jeff Blauser | .05 | BC12 | Kevin Gross | .10 |
| 431 | Steve Jeltz | .05 | 512 | Mike Bielecki | .05 | 593 | Spike Owen | .05 | BC13 | Mike Greenwell | .75 |
| 432 | Rick Dempsey | .05 | 513 | Jeff Pico (R) | .25 | 594 | Matt Williams | .08 | BC14 | Ozzie Smith | .15 |
| 433 | Roberto Kelly | .10 | 514 | Charles Hudson | .08 | 595 | Lloyd McClendon | .05 | BC15 | Cal Ripken | .20 |
| 434 | Dave Anderson | .05 | 515 | Bruce Ruffin | .05 | 596 | Steve Ontiveros | .05 | BC16 | Andres Galarraga | .15 |
| 435 | Herm Winningham | .05 | 516 | Larry McWilliams | .05 | 597 | Scott Medvin (R) | .15 | BC17 | Alan Trammell | .15 |
| 436 | Al Newman | .05 | 517 | Jeff Sellers | .05 | 598 | Hipolito Pena (R) | .15 | BC18 | Kal Daniels | .25 |
| 437 | Jose Deleon | .05 | 518 | John Costello (R) | .15 | 599 | Jerald Clark (R) | .15 | BC19 | Fred McGriff | .40 |
| 438 | Doug Jones | .05 | 519 | Brady Anderson (R) | .30 | 600 | Checklist | .08 | BC20 | Tony Gwynn | .35 |
| 439 | Brian Holton | .05 | 520 | Craig McMurtry | .05 | 601 | Carmelo Martinez | .05 | BC21 | Wally Joyner | .15 |
| 440 | Jeff Montgomery | .05 | 521 | Ray Hayward | .05 | 602 | Mike LaCoss | .05 | BC22 | Will Clark | .50 |
| 441 | Dickie Thon | .05 | 522 | Drew Hall | .10 | 603 | Mike Devereaux | .05 | BC23 | Ozzie Guillen | .10 |
| 442 | Cecil Fielder | .05 | 523 | Mark Lemke (R) | .30 | 604 | Alex Madrid (R) | .25 | BC24 | Gerald Perry | .10 |
| 443 | John Fishel (R) | .25 | 524 | Oswald Peraza (R) | .15 | 605 | Gary Redus | .05 | BC25 | Alvin Davis | .10 |
| | | | | | | | | | BC26 | Ruben Sierra | .20 |

Card values shown here fluctuate considerably.

## 1981 Fleer.... Complete Set of 660 Cards (1st printing, with corrected "Graig" Nettles)—Value $25.00; Complete Set of 660 Cards (1st printing, with error "Craig" Nettles)—Value $30.00; Complete Set of 660 Cards (2nd printing)—Value $22.00; Complete Set of 660 Cards (3rd printing)—Value $25.00

This was Fleer's first baseball card set since 1963. Over 30 cards contained errors; they were corrected in the 2nd and 3rd printing runs. The "Craig" Nettles error was corrected during the first printing. There is very little interest by collectors in the *variety* (error) cards; none are scarce or worth much more than ordinary cards, except card 87, "Craig" Nettles. If a *variety* (error) is significant, it is listed and explained; if it is *minor*, it is noted by an *asterisk*. This set features the rookie cards of Fernando Valenzuela, Kirk Gibson and Harold Baines.

  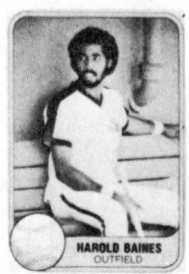  

| NO. | PLAYER | MINT |
|---|---|---|
| **PHILADELPHIA PHILLIES** | | |
| 1 | Pete Rose | 1.50 |
| 2 | Larry Bowa | .12 |
| 3 | Manny Trillo | .05 |
| 4 | Bob Boone | .05 |
| 5 | Mike Schmidt | .75 |
| | (MVP) Third Base | |
| | See No. 640 | |
| 6 | Steve Carlton | .50 |
| | (Pitcher of Year) | |
| | See No. 660 | |
| | Error—"1066" | |
| | Cardinals" on Back | |
| 6 | Steve Carlton | 2.00 |
| | Corrected "1966" Cardinals | |
| 7 | Tug McGraw | .07 |
| | See No. 657 | |
| 8 | Larry Christenson | .05 |
| 9 | Bake McBride | .05 |
| 10 | Greg Luzinski | .10 |
| 11 | Ron Reed | .05 |
| 12 | Dickie Noles | .05 |
| 13 | Keith Moreland (R) | .40 |
| 14 | Bob Walk | .30 |
| 15 | Lonnie Smith | .08 |
| 16 | Dick Ruthven | .05 |
| 17 | Sparky Lyle | .07 |
| 18 | Greg Gross | .05 |
| 19 | Garry Maddox | .05 |
| 20 | Nino Espinosa | .05 |
| 21 | George Vukovich | .05 |
| 22 | John Vukovich | .05 |
| 23 | Ramon Aviles | .05 |
| 24 | Ken Saucier* | .08 |
| 25 | Randy Lerch | .05 |
| 26 | Del Uncer | .05 |
| 27 | Tim McCarver | .08 |
| **KANSAS CITY ROYALS** | | |
| 28 | George Brett—MVP | .75 |
| | See No. 655 | |
| 29 | Willie Wilson | .20 |
| | See No. 653 | |
| 30 | Paul Splittorff | .05 |
| 31 | Dan Quisenberry | .20 |
| 32 | Amos Otis* | .10 |
| 33 | Steve Busby | .05 |
| 34 | U.L. Washington | .05 |
| 35 | Dave Chalk | .05 |
| 36 | Darrell Porter | .08 |
| 37 | Marty Pattin | .05 |
| 38 | Larry Gura | .05 |
| 39 | Renie Martin | .05 |
| 40 | Rich Gale | .05 |
| 41 | Hal McRae* | .40 |
| 42 | Dennis Leonard | .05 |
| 43 | Willie Aikens | .05 |
| 44 | Frank White | .08 |
| 45 | Clint Hurdle | .05 |
| 46 | John Wathan | .05 |
| 47 | Pete LaCock | .05 |
| 48 | Rance Mulliniks | .05 |

| NO. | PLAYER | MINT |
|---|---|---|
| 49 | Jeff Twitty | .05 |
| 50 | Jamie Quirk | .05 |
| **HOUSTON ASTROS** | | |
| 51 | Art How | .05 |
| 52 | Ken Forsch | .05 |
| 53 | Vern Ruhle | .05 |
| 54 | Joe Niekro | .08 |
| 55 | Frank LaCorte | .05 |
| 56 | J.R. Richard | .08 |
| 57 | Nolan Ryan | .60 |
| 58 | Enos Cabell | .05 |
| 59 | Cesar Cedeno | .08 |
| 60 | Jose Cruz | .15 |
| 61 | Bill Virdon (Mgr.) | .05 |
| 62 | Terry Puhl | .05 |
| 63 | Joaquin Andujar | .10 |
| 64 | Alan Ashby | .05 |
| 65 | Joe Sambito | .05 |
| 66 | Denny Walling | .05 |
| 67 | Jeff Leonard | .05 |
| 68 | Luis Pujols | .05 |
| 69 | Bruce Bochy | .05 |
| 70 | Rafael Landestoy | .05 |
| 71 | Dave Smith (R) | .30 |
| 72 | Danny Heep | .20 |
| 73 | Julio Gonzalez | .05 |
| 74 | Craig Reynolds | .05 |
| 75 | Gary Woods | .05 |
| 76 | Dave Bergman | .05 |
| 77 | Randy Niemann | .05 |
| 78 | Joe Morgan | .30 |
| **NEW YORK YANKEES** | | |
| 79 | Reggie Jackson | .75 |
| | See No. 650 | |
| 80 | Bucky Dent | .07 |
| 81 | Tommy John | .15 |
| 82 | Luis Tiant | .05 |
| 83 | Rick Cerone | .05 |
| 84 | Dick Howser (Mgr.) | .05 |
| 85 | Lou Piniella | .10 |
| 86 | Ron Davis | .05 |
| 87 | Graig Nettles | 11.00 |
| | Error—"Craig" on Back | |
| 87 | Graig Nettles | .30 |
| | Corrected—"Graig" | |
| 88 | Ron Guidry | .25 |
| 89 | Rich Gossage | .20 |
| 90 | Rudy May | .05 |
| 91 | Gaylord Perry | .30 |
| 92 | Eric Soderholm | .05 |
| 93 | Bob Watson | .05 |
| 94 | Bobby Murcer | .08 |
| 95 | Bobby Brown | .05 |
| 96 | Jim Spencer | .05 |
| 97 | Tom Underwood | .05 |
| 98 | Oscar Gamble | .05 |
| 99 | Johnny Oates | .05 |
| 100 | Fred Stanley | .05 |
| 101 | Ruppert Jones | .05 |
| 102 | Dennis Werth | .05 |
| 103 | Joe LeFebvre | .12 |

| NO. | PLAYER | MINT |
|---|---|---|
| 104 | Brian Doyle | .05 |
| 105 | Aurelio Rodriguez | .05 |
| 106 | Doug Bird | .05 |
| 107 | Mike Griffin | .05 |
| 108 | Tim Lollar (R) | .20 |
| 109 | Willie Randolph | .12 |
| **LOS ANGELES DODGERS** | | |
| 110 | Steve Garvey | .50 |
| 111 | Reggie Smith | .08 |
| 112 | Don Sutton | .25 |
| 113 | Burt Hooton | .05 |
| 114 | Dave Lopes* | .08 |
| 115 | Dusty Baker | .10 |
| 116 | Tom Lasorda (Mgr.) | .08 |
| 117 | Bill Russell | .05 |
| 118 | Jerry Reuss | .08 |
| 119 | Terry Forster | .05 |
| 120 | Robert Welch* | .15 |
| 121 | Don Stanhouse | .05 |
| 122 | Rick Monday | .08 |
| 123 | Derrel Thomas | .05 |
| 124 | Joe Ferguson | .05 |
| 125 | Rick Sutcliffe | .30 |
| 126 | Ron Cey* | .15 |
| 127 | Dave Goltz | .05 |
| 128 | Jay Johnstone | .05 |
| 129 | Steve Yeager | .05 |
| 130 | Gary Weiss | .05 |
| 131 | Mike Scioscia (R) | .40 |
| 132 | Vic Davalillo | .05 |
| 133 | Doug Rau | .05 |
| 134 | Pepe Frias | .05 |
| 135 | Mickey Hatcher | .05 |
| 136 | Steve Howe (R) | .20 |
| 137 | Robert Castillo | .05 |
| 138 | Gary Thomasson | .05 |
| 139 | Rudy Law | .05 |
| 140 | F. Valenzuela (R) | 4.00 |
| 141 | Manny Mota | .08 |
| **MONTREAL EXPOS** | | |
| 142 | Gary Carter | .40 |
| 143 | Steve Rogers | .08 |
| 144 | Warren Cromartie | .05 |
| 145 | Andre Dawson | .30 |
| 146 | Larry Parrish | .05 |
| 147 | Rowland Office | .05 |
| 148 | Ellis Valentine | .05 |
| 149 | Dick Williams (Mgr.) | .05 |
| 150 | Bill Gullickson (R) | .25 |
| 151 | Elias Sosa | .05 |
| 152 | John Tamargo | .05 |
| 153 | Chris Speier | .05 |
| 154 | Ron LeFlore | .05 |
| 155 | Rodney Scott | .05 |
| 156 | Stan Bahnsen | .05 |
| 157 | Bill Lee | .05 |
| 158 | Fred Norman | .05 |
| 159 | Woodie Fryman | .05 |
| 160 | Dave Palmer | .05 |
| 161 | Jerry White | .05 |
| 162 | Roberto Ramos | .05 |

| NO. | PLAYER | MINT |
|---|---|---|
| 163 | John D'Acquisto | .05 |
| 164 | Tommy Hutton | .05 |
| 165 | Charlie Lea (R) | .25 |
| 166 | Scott Sanderson | .05 |
| 167 | Ken Macha | .05 |
| 168 | Tony Bernazard | .05 |
| **BALTIMORE ORIOLES** | | |
| 169 | Jim Palmer | .35 |
| 170 | Steve Stone | .05 |
| 171 | Mike Flanagan | .08 |
| 172 | Al Bumbry | .05 |
| 173 | Doug DeCinces | .12 |
| 174 | Scott McGregor | .08 |
| 175 | Mark Belanger | .05 |
| 176 | Tim Stoddard | .05 |
| 177 | Rick Dempsey* | .10 |
| 178 | Earl Weaver (Mgr.) | .10 |
| 179 | Tippy Martinez | .05 |
| 180 | Dennis Martinez | .05 |
| 181 | Sammy Stewart | .05 |
| 182 | Rich Dauer | .05 |
| 183 | Lee May | .05 |
| 184 | Eddie Murray | .60 |
| 185 | Benny Ayala | .05 |
| 186 | John Lowenstein | .05 |
| 187 | Gary Roenicke | .05 |
| 188 | Ken Singleton | .08 |
| 189 | Dan Graham | .05 |
| 190 | Terry Crowley | .05 |
| 191 | Kiko Garcia | .05 |
| 192 | Dave Ford | .05 |
| 193 | Mark Corey | .05 |
| 194 | Lenn Sakata | .05 |
| 195 | Doug DeCinces | .08 |
| **CINCINNATI REDS** | | |
| 196 | Johnny Bench | .50 |
| 197 | Dave Concepcion | .15 |
| 198 | Ray Knight | .08 |
| 199 | Ken Griffey | .08 |
| 200 | Tom Seaver | .40 |
| 201 | Dave Collins | .07 |
| 202 | George Foster | .25 |
| | (Slugger) Error—No. 216 | |
| 202 | George Foster | .25 |
| | (Slugger) Correct No. 202 | |
| 203 | Junior Kennedy | .05 |
| 204 | Frank Pastore | .05 |
| 205 | Dan Driessen | .05 |
| 206 | Hector Cruz | .05 |
| 207 | Paul Moskau | .05 |
| 208 | Charlie Leibrandt (R) | .40 |
| 209 | Harry Spilman | .05 |
| 210 | Joe Price | .05 |
| 211 | Tom Hume | .05 |
| 212 | Joe Nolan | .05 |
| 213 | Doug Bair | .05 |
| 214 | Mario Soto | .08 |
| 215 | Bill Bonham* | .08 |
| 216 | George Foster | .20 |
| | See No. 202 | |
| 217 | Paul Householder | .05 |

| NO. PLAYER | MINT |
|---|---|
| 218 Ron Oester | .05 |
| 219 Sam Mejias | .05 |
| 220 Sheldon Burnside | .05 |
| **BOSTON RED SOX** | |
| 221 Carl Yastrzemski | .75 |
| 222 Jim Rice | .30 |
| 223 Fred Lynn | .25 |
| 224 Carlton Fisk | .25 |
| 225 Rick Burleson | .05 |
| 226 Dennis Eckersley | .10 |
| 227 Butch Hobson | .05 |
| 228 Tom Burgmeier | .05 |
| 229 Garry Hancock | .05 |
| 230 Don Zimmer (Mgr.) | .05 |
| 231 Steve Renko | .05 |
| 232 Dwight Evans | .20 |
| 233 Mike Torrez | .05 |
| 234 Bob Stanley | .08 |
| 235 Jim Dwyer | .05 |
| 236 Dave Stapleton | .14 |
| 237 Glenn Hoffman | .12 |
| 238 Jerry Remy | .05 |
| 239 Dick Drago | .05 |
| 240 Bill Campbell | .05 |
| 241 Tony Perez | .15 |
| **ATLANTA BRAVES** | |
| 242 Phil Niekro | .25 |
| 243 Dale Murphy | 1.00 |
| 244 Bob Horner | .20 |
| 245 Jeff Burroughs | .05 |
| 246 Rick Camp | .05 |
| 247 Bob Cox (Mgr.) | .05 |
| 248 Bruce Benedict | .05 |
| 249 Gene Garber | .05 |
| 250 Jerry Royster | .05 |
| 251 Gary Matthews* | .10 |
| 252 Chris Chambliss | .08 |
| 253 Luis Gomez | .05 |
| 254 Bill Nahorodny | .05 |
| 255 Doyle Alexander | .10 |
| 256 Brian Asselstine | .05 |
| 257 Biff Pocoroba | .05 |
| 258 Mike Lum | .05 |
| 259 Charlie Spikes | .05 |
| 260 Glenn Hubbard | .05 |
| 261 Tommy Boggs | .05 |
| 262 Al Hrabosky | .05 |
| 263 Rick Matula | .05 |
| 264 Preston Hanna | .05 |
| 265 Larry Bradford | .05 |
| 266 Rafael Ramirez | .20 |
| 267 Larry McWilliams | .05 |
| **CALIFORNIA ANGELS** | |
| 268 Rod Carew | .40 |
| 269 Bobby Grich | .08 |
| 270 Carney Lansford | .10 |
| 271 Don Baylor | .20 |
| 272 Joe Rudi | .05 |
| 273 Dan Ford | .05 |
| 274 Jim Fregosi | .05 |
| 275 Dave Frost | .05 |
| 276 Frank Tanana | .10 |
| 277 Dickie Thon | .07 |
| 278 Jason Thompson | .08 |
| 279 Rick Miller | .05 |
| 280 Bert Campaneris | .10 |
| 281 Tom Donohue | .05 |
| 282 Brian Downing | .05 |
| 283 Fred Patek | .05 |
| 284 Bruce Kison | .05 |
| 285 Dave LaRoche | .05 |
| 286 Don Aase | .05 |
| 287 Jim Barr | .05 |
| 288 Alfredo Martinez | .05 |
| 289 Larry Harlow | .05 |
| 290 Andy Hassler | .05 |
| **CHICAGO CUBS** | |
| 291 Dave Kingman | .12 |
| 292 Bill Buckner | .10 |
| 293 Rick Reuschel | .10 |
| 294 Bruce Sutter | .20 |
| 295 Jerry Martin | .05 |
| 296 Scot Thompson | .05 |
| 297 Ivan DeJesus | .05 |
| 298 Steve Dillard | .05 |

| NO. PLAYER | MINT |
|---|---|
| 299 Dick Tidrow | .05 |
| 300 Randy Martz | .05 |
| 301 Lenny Randle | .05 |
| 302 Lynn McGlothen | .05 |
| 303 Cliff Johnson | .05 |
| 304 Tim Blackwell | .05 |
| 305 Dennis Lamp | .05 |
| 306 Bill Caudill | .08 |
| 307 Carlos Lezcano | .05 |
| 308 Jim Tracy | .05 |
| 309 Doug Capilla | .05 |
| 310 Willie Hernandez | .20 |
| 311 Mike Vail | .05 |
| 312 Mike Krukow | .05 |
| 313 Barry Foote | .05 |
| 314 Larry Biittner | .05 |
| 315 Mike Tyson | .05 |
| **NEW YORK METS** | |
| 316 Lee Mazzilli | .05 |
| 317 John Stearns | .05 |
| 318 Alex Trevino | .05 |
| 319 Craig Swan | .05 |
| 320 Frank Taveras | .05 |
| 321 Steve Henderson | .05 |
| 322 Neil Allen | .05 |
| 323 Mark Bomback | .05 |
| 324 Mike Jorgensen | .05 |
| 325 Joe Torre | .07 |
| 326 Elliott Maddox | .05 |
| 327 Pete Falcone | .05 |
| 328 Ray Burris | .05 |
| 329 Claudell Washington | .08 |
| 330 Doug Flynn | .05 |
| 331 Joel Youngblood | .05 |
| 332 Bill Almon | .05 |
| 333 Tom Hausman | .05 |
| 334 Pat Zachry | .05 |
| 335 Jeff Reardon (R) | .50 |
| 336 Wally Backman (R) | .40 |
| 337 Dan Norman | .05 |
| 338 Jerry Morales | .05 |
| **CHICAGO WHITE SOX (Except 351)** | |
| 339 Ed Farmer | .05 |
| 340 Bob Molinaro | .05 |
| 341 Todd Cruz | .05 |
| 342 Britt Burns* | .35 |
| 343 Kevin Bell | .05 |
| 344 Tony LaRussa (Mgr.) | .05 |
| 345 Steve Trout | .05 |
| 346 Harold Baines (R) | 1.50 |
| 347 Richard Wortham | .05 |
| 348 Wayne Nordhagen | .05 |
| 349 Mike Squires | .05 |
| 350 Lamar Johnson | .05 |
| 351 Rickey Henderson | 1.25 |
| Most Stolen Bases, AL | |
| 352 Francisco Barrios | .05 |
| 353 Thad Bosley | .05 |
| 354 Chet Lemon | .08 |
| 355 Bruce Kimm | .05 |
| 356 Richard Dotson (R) | .45 |
| 357 Jim Morrison | .05 |
| 358 Mike Proly | .05 |
| 359 Greg Pryor | .05 |
| **PITTSBURGH PIRATES** | |
| 360 Dave Parker | .30 |
| 361 Omar Moreno | .05 |
| 362 Kent Tekulve* | .10 |
| 363 Willie Stargell | .30 |
| 364 Phil Garner | .05 |
| 365 Ed Ott | .05 |
| 366 Don Robinson | .05 |
| 367 Chuck Tanner (Mgr.) | .05 |
| 368 Jim Rooker | .05 |
| 369 Dale Berra | .05 |
| 370 Jim Bibby | .05 |
| 371 Steve Nicosia | .05 |
| 372 Mike Easler | .10 |
| 373 Bill Robinson | .05 |
| 374 Lee Lacy | .05 |
| 375 John Candelaria | .10 |
| 376 Manny Sanguillen | .05 |
| 377 Rick Rhoden | .12 |
| 378 Grant Jackson | .05 |
| 379 Tim Foli | .05 |

| NO. PLAYER | MINT |
|---|---|
| 380 Rod Scurry | .05 |
| 381 Bill Madlock | .15 |
| 382 Kurt Bevacqua* | .08 |
| 383 Bert Blyleven | .12 |
| 384 Eddie Solomon | .05 |
| 385 Enrique Romo | .05 |
| 386 John Milner | .05 |
| **CLEVELAND INDIANS** | |
| 387 Mike Hargrove | .05 |
| 388 Jorge Orta | .05 |
| 389 Toby Harrah | .05 |
| 390 Tom Veryzer | .05 |
| 391 Miguel Dilone | .05 |
| 392 Dan Spillner | .05 |
| 393 Jack Brohamer | .05 |
| 394 Wayne Garland | .05 |
| 395 Sid Monge | .05 |
| 396 Rick Waits | .05 |
| 397 Joe Charboneau | .12 |
| 398 Gary Alexander | .05 |
| 399 Jerry Dybzinski | .05 |
| 400 Mike Stanton | .05 |
| 401 Mike Paxton | .05 |
| 402 Gary Gray | .05 |
| 403 Rick Manning | .05 |
| 404 Bo Diaz | .08 |
| 405 Ron Hassey | .05 |
| 406 Ross Grimsley | .05 |
| 407 Victor Cruz | .05 |
| 408 Len Barker | .08 |
| **TORONTO BLUE JAYS** | |
| 409 Bob Bailor | .05 |
| 410 Otto Velez | .05 |
| 411 Ernie Whitt | .05 |
| 412 Jim Clancy | .05 |
| 413 Barry Bonnell | .05 |
| 414 Dave Stieb | .30 |
| 415 Damaso Garcia (R) | .30 |
| 416 John Mayberry | .05 |
| 417 Roy Howell | .05 |
| 418 Dan Ainge | .25 |
| 419 Jesse Jefferson* | .08 |
| 420 Joey McLaughlin | .05 |
| 421 Lloyd Moseby (R) | 1.25 |
| 422 Al Woods | .05 |
| 423 Garth Iorg | .05 |
| 424 Doug Ault | .05 |
| 425 Ken Schrom | .15 |
| 426 Mike Willis | .05 |
| 427 Steve Braun | .05 |
| 428 Bob Davis | .05 |
| 429 Jerry Garvin | .05 |
| 430 Alfredo Griffin | .08 |
| 431 Bob Mattick (Mgr.) | .05 |
| **SAN FRANCISCO GIANTS** | |
| 432 Vida Blue | .08 |
| 433 Jack Clark | .30 |
| 434 Willie McCovey | .35 |
| 435 Mike Ivie | .05 |
| 436 Darrell Evans* | .15 |
| 437 Terry Whitfield | .05 |
| 438 Rennie Stennett | .05 |
| 439 John Montefusco | .05 |
| 440 Jim Wohlford | .05 |
| 441 Bill North | .05 |
| 442 Milt May | .05 |
| 443 Max Venable | .05 |
| 444 Ed Whitson | .05 |
| 445 Al Holland | .20 |
| 446 Randy Moffitt | .05 |
| 447 Bob Knepper | .05 |
| 448 Gary Lavelle | .05 |
| 449 Greg Minton | .05 |
| 450 Johnnie LeMaster | .05 |
| 451 Larry Herndon | .05 |
| 452 Rich Murray | .05 |
| 453 Joe Pettini | .05 |
| 454 Allen Ripley | .05 |
| 455 Dennis Littlejohn | .05 |
| 456 Tom Griffin | .05 |
| 457 Alan Hargesheimer | .05 |
| 458 Joe Strain | .05 |
| **DETROIT TIGERS** | |
| 459 Steve Kemp | .08 |
| 460 Sparky Anderson (Mgr.) | .08 |

| NO. PLAYER | MINT |
|---|---|
| 461 Alan Trammell | .30 |
| 462 Mark Fidrych | .08 |
| 463 Lou Whitaker | .25 |
| 464 Dave Rozema | .05 |
| 465 Milt Wilcox | .05 |
| 466 Champ Summers | .05 |
| 467 Lance Parrish | .30 |
| 468 Dan Petry | .15 |
| 469 Pat Underwood | .05 |
| 470 Rick Peters | .10 |
| 471 Al Cowens | .05 |
| 472 John Wockenfuss | .05 |
| 473 Tom Brookens | .05 |
| 474 Richie Hebner | .05 |
| 475 Jack Morris | .35 |
| 476 Jim Lentine | .05 |
| 477 Bruce Robbins | .05 |
| 478 Mark Wagner | .05 |
| 479 Tim Corcoran | .05 |
| 480 Stan Papi* | .08 |
| 481 Kirk Gibson (R) | 4.00 |
| 482 Dan Schatzeder | .05 |
| 483 Amos Otis | .60 |
| See card No. 32 | |
| **SAN DIEGO PADRES** | |
| 484 Dave Winfield | .50 |
| 485 Rollie Fingers | .30 |
| 486 Gene Richards | .05 |
| 487 Randy Jones | .05 |
| 488 Ozzie Smith | .35 |
| 489 Gene Tenace | .05 |
| 490 Bill Fahey | .05 |
| 491 John Curtis | .05 |
| 492 Dave Cash | .05 |
| 493 Tim Flannery* | .12 |
| 494 Jerry Mumphrey | .05 |
| 495 Bob Shirley | .05 |
| 496 Steve Mura | .05 |
| 497 Eric Rasmussen | .05 |
| 498 Broderick Perkins | .05 |
| 499 Barry Evans | .05 |
| 500 Chuck Baker | .05 |
| 501 Luis Salazar | .05 |
| 502 Gary Lucas | .10 |
| 503 Mike Armstrong | .05 |
| 504 Jerry Turner | .05 |
| 505 Dennis Kinney | .05 |
| 506 Willie Montanez | .05 |
| **MILWAUKEE BREWERS** | |
| 507 Gorman Thomas | .15 |
| 508 Ben Oglivie | .08 |
| 509 Larry Hisle | .05 |
| 510 Sal Bando | .70 |
| 511 Robin Yount | .45 |
| 512 Mike Caldwell | .05 |
| 513 Sixto Lezcano | .05 |
| 514 Bill Travers | .15 |
| Error—Jerry Augustine photo and back | |
| 514 Bill Travers | .08 |
| 515 Paul Molitor | .30 |
| 516 Moose Haas | .05 |
| 517 Bill Castro | .05 |
| 518 Jim Slaton | .05 |
| 519 Lary Sorensen | .05 |
| 520 Bob McClure | .05 |
| 521 Charlie Moore | .05 |
| 522 Jim Gantner | .05 |
| 523 Reggie Cleveland | .05 |
| 524 Don Money | .05 |
| 525 Bill Travers | .05 |
| 526 Buck Martinez | .05 |
| 527 Dick Davis | .05 |
| **ST. LOUIS CARDINALS** | |
| 528 Ted Simmons | .12 |
| 529 Garry Templeton | .12 |
| 530 Ken Reitz | .05 |
| 531 Tony Scott | .05 |
| 532 Ken Oberkfell | .05 |
| 533 Bob Sykes | .05 |
| 534 Keith Smith | .05 |
| 535 John Littlefield | .05 |
| 536 Jim Kaat | .10 |
| 537 Bob Forsch | .05 |
| 538 Mike Phillips | .05 |

| NO. PLAYER | MINT |
|---|---|
| 539 Terry Landrum | .08 |
| 540 Leon Durham (R) | .75 |
| 541 Terry Kennedy | .08 |
| 542 George Hendrick | .08 |
| 543 Dane Iorg | .05 |
| 544 Mark Littell | .05 |
| 545 Keith Hernandez | .30 |
| 546 Silvio Martinez | .05 |
| 547 Don Hood | .25 |
| Error—Pete Vuckovich photo and back | |
| 547 Don Hood | .10 |
| 548 Bobby Bonds | .08 |
| 549 Mike Ramsey | .05 |
| 550 Tom Herr | .15 |
| **MINNESOTA TWINS** | |
| 551 Roy Smalley | .05 |
| 552 Jerry Koosman | .15 |
| 553 Ken Landreaux | .05 |
| 554 John Castino | .05 |
| 555 Doug Corbett | .12 |
| 556 Bombo Rivera | .05 |
| 557 Ron Jackson | .05 |
| 558 Butch Wynegar | .05 |
| 559 Hosken Powell | .05 |
| 560 Pete Redfern | .05 |
| 561 Roger Erickson | .05 |
| 562 Glenn Adams | .08 |
| 563 Rick Sofield | .05 |
| 564 Geoff Zahn | .05 |
| 565 Pete Mackanin | .05 |
| 566 Mike Cubbage | .05 |
| 567 Darrell Jackson | .05 |
| 568 Dave Edwards | .05 |
| 569 Rob Wilfong | .05 |
| 570 Sal Butera | .05 |
| 571 Jose Morales | .05 |
| **OAKLAND A'S** | |
| 572 Rick Langford | .05 |
| 573 Mike Norris | .05 |

| NO. PLAYER | MINT |
|---|---|
| 574 Rickey Henderson | 1.00 |
| 575 Tony Armas | .15 |
| 576 Dave Revering | .05 |
| 577 Jeff Newman | .05 |
| 578 Bob Lacey | .05 |
| 579 Brian Kingman | .05 |
| 580 Mitchell Page | .05 |
| 581 Billy Martin (Mgr.) | .12 |
| 582 Rob Picciolo | .05 |
| 583 Mike Heath | .05 |
| 584 Mickey Klutts | .05 |
| 585 Orlando Gonzalez | .05 |
| 586 Mike Davis (R) | .40 |
| 587 Wayne Gross | .05 |
| 588 Matt Keough | .05 |
| 589 Steve McCatty | .05 |
| 590 Dwayne Murphy | .08 |
| 591 Mario Guerrero | .05 |
| 592 Dave McKay | .05 |
| 593 Jim Essian | .05 |
| 594 Dave Heaverlo | .05 |
| **SEATTLE MARINERS (Except 606)** | |
| 595 Maury Wills (Mgr.) | .10 |
| 596 Juan Beniquez | .05 |
| 597 Rodney Craig | .05 |
| 598 Jim Anderson | .05 |
| 599 Floyd Bannister | .08 |
| 600 Bruce Bochte | .05 |
| 601 Julio Cruz | .05 |
| 602 Ted Cox | .05 |
| 603 Dan Meyer | .05 |
| 604 Larry Cox | .05 |
| 605 Bill Stein | .05 |
| 606 Steve Garvey | .50 |
| Most Hits, NL | |
| 607 Dave Roberts | .05 |
| 608 Leon Roberts | .05 |
| 609 Reggie Walton | .05 |
| 610 Dave Edler | .05 |

| NO. PLAYER | MINT |
|---|---|
| 611 Larry Milbourne | .05 |
| 612 Kim Allen | .05 |
| 613 Mario Mendoza | .05 |
| 614 Tom Paciorek | .05 |
| 615 Glenn Abbott | .05 |
| 616 Joe Simpson | .05 |
| **TEXAS RANGERS** | |
| 617 Mickey Rivers | .08 |
| 618 Jim Kern | .05 |
| 619 Jim Sundberg | .05 |
| 620 Richie Zisk | .05 |
| 621 Jon Matlack | .05 |
| 622 Ferguson Jenkins | .12 |
| 623 Pat Corrales (Mgr.) | .05 |
| 624 Ed Figueroa | .05 |
| 625 Buddy Bell | .15 |
| 626 Al Oliver | .20 |
| 627 Doc Medich | .05 |
| 628 Bump Wills | .05 |
| 629 Rusty Staub | .12 |
| 630 Pat Putnam | .05 |
| 631 John Grubb | .05 |
| 632 Danny Darwin | .05 |
| 633 Ken Clay | .05 |
| 634 Jim Norris | .05 |
| 635 John Butcher | .20 |
| 636 Dave Roberts | .05 |
| 637 Billy Sample | .05 |
| **SPECIAL CARDS** | |
| 638 Carl Yastrzemski | .75 |
| 400 Home Run Club | |
| 639 Cecil Cooper | .20 |
| 640 Mike Schmidt | 1.00 |
| (Third Base) Error—No. 5 | |
| 640 Mike Schmidt | 1.00 |
| (Home Run King) | |
| 641 Checklist (1 to 50)* | .08 |
| 642 Checklist (51 to 109) | .08 |
| 643 Checklist (110 to 168) | .08 |

| NO. PLAYER | MINT |
|---|---|
| 644 Checklist (169 to 220)* | .08 |
| 645 Triple Threat:* | 1.75 |
| Schmidt, Rose, Bowa | |
| 646 Checklist (221 to 267) | .08 |
| 647 Checklist (268 to 315) | .08 |
| 648 Checklist (316 to 359) | .08 |
| 649 Checklist (360 to 408) | .08 |
| 650 Reggie Jackson | 1.00 |
| Mr. Baseball Error—No. 79 | |
| 650 Reggie Jackson | .75 |
| Mr. Baseball | |
| 651 Checklist (409 to 458) | .08 |
| 652 Checklist (459 to 506)* | .08 |
| 653 Willie Wilson | .25 |
| Most Hits, Most Runs Error—No. 29 | |
| 653 Willie Wilson | .25 |
| Most Hits, Most Runs | |
| 654 Checklist (507 to 550)* | .08 |
| 655 G. Brett (.390 Avg.) | .75 |
| Error—No. 28* | |
| 656 Checklist (551 to 593) | .08 |
| 657 Tug McGraw | .08 |
| Game Saver, Error—No. 7 | |
| 657 Tug McGraw | .08 |
| Game Saver | |
| 658 Checklist (594 to 637) | .08 |
| 659 Checklist (Specials)* | .08 |
| 660 Steve Carlton | .50 |
| "Lefty"—The Golden Arm Errors—Card No.6 and "1066" Cardinals | |
| 660 Steve Carlton | .50 |
| "Lefty"—The Golden Arm Error—"1066" Cardinals | |
| 660 Steve Carlton | 1.50 |
| "Lefty"—The Golden Arm Corrected—"1966" Cardinals | |

## 1982 Fleer....Complete Set of 660 Cards—Value $30.00

Features the rookie card of Cal Ripken. Several errors were corrected; none are scarce or worth much more than ordinary cards, except cards 438 and 576. If a *variety* (error) is significant, it is listed and explained; if it is minor it is noted by an *asterisk*.

| NO. PLAYER | MINT |
|---|---|
| **LOS ANGELES DODGERS** | |
| 1 Dusty Baker | .10 |
| 2 Robert Castillo | .05 |
| 3 Roy Cey | .15 |
| 4 Terry Forster | .05 |
| 5 Steve Garvey | .40 |
| 6 Dave Goltz | .05 |
| 7 Pedro Guerrero | .30 |
| 8 Burt Hooton | .05 |
| 9 Steve Howe | .05 |
| 10 Jay Johnstone | .05 |
| 11 Ken Landreaux | .05 |
| 12 Davey Lopes | .05 |
| 13 Mike Marshall (R) | 1.25 |
| 14 Bobby Mitchell | .09 |
| 15 Rick Monday | .10 |
| 16 Tom Niedenfuer (R) | .30 |
| 17 Ted Power (R) | .25 |

| NO. PLAYER | MINT |
|---|---|
| 18 Jerry Reuss | .10 |
| 19 Ron Roenicke | .05 |
| 20 Bill Russell | .05 |
| 21 Steve Sax (R) | 1.75 |
| 22 Mike Scioscia | .05 |
| 23 Reggie Smith | .10 |
| 24 Dave Stewart (R) | .50 |
| 25 Rick Sutcliffe | .25 |
| 26 Darrell Thomas | .05 |
| 27 Fernando Valenzuela | .40 |
| 28 Bob Welch | .12 |
| 29 Steve Yeager | .05 |
| **NEW YORK YANKEES** | |
| 30 Bobby Brown | .05 |
| 31 Rick Cerone | .05 |
| 32 Ron Davis | .05 |
| 33 Bucky Dent | .08 |
| 34 Barry Foote | .05 |

| NO. PLAYER | MINT |
|---|---|
| 35 George Frazier | .05 |
| 36 Oscar Gamble | .05 |
| 37 Rich Gossage | .20 |
| 38 Ron Guidry | .20 |
| 39 Reggie Jackson | .50 |
| 40 Tommy John | .15 |
| 41 Rudy May | .05 |
| 42 Larry Milbourne | .05 |
| 43 Jerry Mumphrey | .05 |
| 44 Bobby Murcer | .10 |
| 45 Gene Nelson (R) | .15 |
| 46 Graig Nettles | .15 |
| 47 Johnny Oates | .05 |
| 48 Lou Piniella | .10 |
| 49 Willie Randolph | .12 |
| 50 Rick Reuschel | .12 |
| 51 Dave Reverink | .05 |
| 52 Dave Righetti (R) | 1.25 |

| NO. PLAYER | MINT |
|---|---|
| 53 Aurelio Rodriguez | .05 |
| 54 Bob Watson | .05 |
| 55 Dennis Werth | .05 |
| 56 Dave Winfield | .50 |
| **CINCINNATI REDS** | |
| 57 Johnny Bench | .45 |
| 58 Bruce Berenyi | .05 |
| 59 Larry Biittner | .05 |
| 60 Scott Brown | .09 |
| 61 Dave Collins | .05 |
| 62 Geoff Combe | .05 |
| 63 Dave Concepcion | .10 |
| 64 Dan Driessen | .05 |
| 65 Joe Edelen | .05 |
| 66 George Foster | .20 |
| 67 Ken Griffey | .10 |
| 68 Paul Householder | .05 |
| 69 Tom Hume | .05 |

| NO. PLAYER | MINT |
|---|---|
| 70 Junior Kennedy | .05 |
| 71 Ray Knight | .10 |
| 72 Mike LaCoss | .05 |
| 73 Rafael Landestoy | .05 |
| 74 Charlie Leibrandt | .05 |
| 75 Sam Mejias | .05 |
| 76 Paul Moskau | .05 |
| 77 Joe Nolan | .05 |
| 78 Mike O'Berry | .05 |
| 79 Ron Oester | .05 |
| 80 Frank Pastore | .05 |
| 81 Joe Price | .05 |
| 82 Tom Seaver | .45 |
| 83 Mario Soto | .10 |
| 84 Mike Vail | .05 |

**OAKLAND A'S**

| NO. PLAYER | MINT |
|---|---|
| 85 Tony Armas | .10 |
| 86 Shooty Babitt | .05 |
| 87 Dave Beard | .05 |
| 88 Rick Bosetti | .05 |
| 89 Keith Drumright | .05 |
| 90 Wayne Gross | .05 |
| 91 Mike Heath | .05 |
| 92 Rickey Henderson | .60 |
| 93 Cliff Johnson | .05 |
| 94 Jeff Jones | .05 |
| 95 Matt Keough | .05 |
| 96 Brian Kingman | .05 |
| 97 Mickey Klutts | .05 |
| 98 Rick Langford | .05 |
| 99 Steve McCatty | .05 |
| 100 Dave McKay | .05 |
| 101 Dwayne Murphy | .07 |
| 102 Jeff Newman | .05 |
| 103 Mike Norris | .05 |
| 104 Bob Owchinko | .05 |
| 105 Mitchell Page | .05 |
| 106 Rob Picciolo | .05 |
| 107 Jim Spencer | .05 |
| 108 Fred Stanley | .05 |
| 109 Tom Underwood | .05 |

**ST. LOUIS CARDINALS**

| NO. PLAYER | MINT |
|---|---|
| 110 Joaquin Andujar | .15 |
| 111 Steve Braun | .05 |
| 112 Bob Forsch | .05 |
| 113 George Hendrick | .08 |
| 114 Keith Hernandez | .30 |
| 115 Tom Herr | .15 |
| 116 Dane Iorg | .05 |
| 117 Jim Kaat | .10 |
| 118 Tito Landrum | .05 |
| 119 Sixto Lezcano | .05 |
| 120 Mark Littell | .05 |
| 121 John Martin | .05 |
| 122 Silvio Martinez | .05 |
| 123 Ken Oberkfell | .05 |
| 124 Darrell Porter | .05 |
| 125 Mike Ramsey | .05 |
| 126 Orlando Sanchez | .08 |
| 127 Bob Shirley | .05 |
| 128 Lary Sorensen | .05 |
| 129 Bruce Sutter | .25 |
| 130 Bob Sykes | .05 |
| 131 Garry Templeton | .15 |
| 132 Gene Tenace | .05 |

**MILWAUKEE BREWERS**

| NO. PLAYER | MINT |
|---|---|
| 133 Jerry Augustine | .05 |
| 134 Sal Bando | .05 |
| 135 Mark Brouhard | .08 |
| 136 Mike Caldwell | .05 |
| 137 Reggie Cleveland | .05 |
| 138 Cecil Cooper | .20 |
| 139 Jamie Easterly | .05 |
| 140 Marshall Edwards | .05 |
| 141 Rollie Fingers | .20 |
| 142 Jim Gantner | .05 |
| 143 Moose Haas | .05 |
| 144 Larry Hisle | .05 |
| 145 Roy Howell | .05 |
| 146 Rickey Keeton | .05 |
| 147 Randy Lerch | .05 |
| 148 Paul Molitor | .25 |
| 149 Don Money | .05 |
| 150 Charlie Moore | .05 |
| 151 Ben Oglivie | .10 |

| NO. PLAYER | MINT |
|---|---|
| 152 Ted Simmons | .10 |
| 153 Jim Slaton | .05 |
| 154 Gorman Thomas | .10 |
| 155 Robin Yount | .45 |
| 156 Pete Vuckovich | .10 |

**BALTIMORE ORIOLES**

| NO. PLAYER | MINT |
|---|---|
| 157 Benny Ayala | .05 |
| 158 Mark Belanger | .05 |
| 159 Al Bumbry | .05 |
| 160 Terry Crowley | .05 |
| 161 Rich Dauer | .05 |
| 162 Doug DeCinces | .10 |
| 163 Rick Dempsey | .05 |
| 164 Jim Dwyer | .05 |
| 165 Mike Flanagan | .10 |
| 166 Dave Ford | .05 |
| 167 Dan Graham | .05 |
| 168 Wayne Krenchicki | .05 |
| 169 John Lowenstein | .05 |
| 170 Dennis Martinez | .05 |
| 171 Tippy Martinez | .05 |
| 172 Scott McGregor | .10 |
| 173 Jose Morales | .05 |
| 174 Eddie Murray | .60 |
| 175 Jim Palmer | .30 |
| 176 Cal Ripken, Jr. (R) | 7.50 |
| 177 Gary Roenicke | .05 |
| 178 Lenn Sakata | .05 |
| 179 Ken Singleton | .10 |
| 180 Sammy Stewart | .05 |
| 181 Tim Stoddard | .05 |
| 182 Steve Stone | .05 |

**MONTREAL EXPOS**

| NO. PLAYER | MINT |
|---|---|
| 183 Stan Bahnsen | .05 |
| 184 Ray Burris | .05 |
| 185 Gary Carter | .50 |
| 186 Warren Cromartie | .05 |
| 187 Andre Dawson | .35 |
| 188 Terry Francona (R) | .20 |
| 189 Woodie Fryman | .05 |
| 190 Bill Gullickson | .05 |
| 191 Grant Jackson | .05 |
| 192 Wallace Johnson | .05 |
| 193 Charlie Lea | .05 |
| 194 Bill Lee | .05 |
| 195 Jerry Manuel | .05 |
| 196 Brad Mills | .07 |
| 197 John Milner | .05 |
| 198 Rowland Office | .05 |
| 199 David Palmer | .05 |
| 200 Larry Parrish | .05 |
| 201 Mike Phillips | .05 |
| 202 Tim Raines | 1.25 |
| 203 Bobby Ramos | .05 |
| 204 Jeff Reardon | .12 |
| 205 Steve Rogers | .10 |
| 206 Scott Sanderson | .05 |
| 207 Rodney Scott | .10 |
| 208 Elias Sosa | .05 |
| 209 Chris Speier | .05 |
| 210 Tim Wallach (R) | .75 |
| 211 Jerry White | .05 |

**HOUSTON ASTROS**

| NO. PLAYER | MINT |
|---|---|
| 212 Alan Ashby | .05 |
| 213 Cesar Cedeno | .10 |
| 214 Jose Cruz | .15 |
| 215 Kiko Garcia | .05 |
| 216 Phil Garner | .05 |
| 217 Danny Heep | .05 |
| 218 Art Howe | .05 |
| 219 Bob Knepper | .05 |
| 220 Frank LaCorte | .05 |
| 221 Joe Niekro | .10 |
| 222 Joe Pittman | .05 |
| 223 Terry Puhl | .05 |
| 224 Luis Pujols | .05 |
| 225 Craig Reynolds | .05 |
| 226 J.R. Richard | .10 |
| 227 Dave Roberts | .05 |
| 228 Vern Ruhle | .05 |
| 229 Nolan Ryan | .40 |
| 230 Joe Sambito | .05 |
| 231 Tony Scott | .05 |
| 232 Dave Smith | .05 |
| 233 Harry Spilman | .05 |

| NO. PLAYER | MINT |
|---|---|
| 234 Don Sutton | .25 |
| 235 Dickie Thon | .10 |
| 236 Denny Walling | .05 |
| 237 Gary Woods | .05 |

**PHILADELPHIA PHILLIES**

| NO. PLAYER | MINT |
|---|---|
| 238 Luis Aguayo | .05 |
| 239 Ramon Aviles | .05 |
| 240 Bob Boone | .05 |
| 241 Larry Bowa | .10 |
| 242 Warren Brusstar | .05 |
| 243 Steve Carlton | .50 |
| 244 Larry Christenson | .05 |
| 245 Dick Davis | .05 |
| 246 Greg Gross | .05 |
| 247 Sparky Lyle | .08 |
| 248 Garry Maddox | .10 |
| 249 Gary Matthews | .10 |
| 250 Bake McBride | .05 |
| 251 Tug McGraw | .10 |
| 252 Keith Moreland | .08 |
| 253 Dickie Noles | .05 |
| 254 Mike Proly | .05 |
| 255 Ron Reed | .05 |
| 256 Pete Rose | 1.00 |
| 257 Dick Ruthven | .05 |
| 258 Mike Schmidt | .75 |
| 259 Lonnie Smith | .10 |
| 260 Manny Trillo | .05 |
| 261 Del Unser | .05 |
| 262 George Vukovich | .05 |

**DETROIT TIGERS**

| NO. PLAYER | MINT |
|---|---|
| 263 Tom Brookens | .05 |
| 264 George Cappuzzello | .05 |
| 265 Marty Castillo | .05 |
| 266 Al Cowens | .05 |
| 267 Kirk Gibson | .75 |
| 268 Richie Hebner | .05 |
| 269 Ron Jackson | .05 |
| 270 Lynn Jones | .05 |
| 271 Steve Kemp | .10 |
| 272 Rick Leach | .08 |
| 273 Aurelio Lopez | .05 |
| 274 Jack Morris | .30 |
| 275 Kevin Saucier | .05 |
| 276 Lance Parrish | .25 |
| 277 Rick Peters | .05 |
| 278 Dan Petry | .15 |
| 279 David Rozema | .05 |
| 280 Stan Papi | .05 |
| 281 Dan Schatzeder | .05 |
| 282 Champ Summers | .05 |
| 283 Alan Trammell | .30 |
| 284 Lou Whitaker | .20 |
| 285 Milt Wilcox | .05 |
| 286 John Wockenfuss | .05 |

**BOSTON RED SOX**

| NO. PLAYER | MINT |
|---|---|
| 287 Gary Allenson | .05 |
| 288 Tom Burgmeier | .05 |
| 289 Bill Campbell | .05 |
| 290 Mark Clear | .05 |
| 291 Steve Crawford | .05 |
| 292 Dennis Eckersley | .15 |
| 293 Dwight Evans | .15 |
| 294 Rich Gedman (R) | .40 |
| 295 Garry Hancock | .05 |
| 296 Glenn Hoffman | .05 |
| 297 Bruce Hurst | .50 |
| 298 Carney Lansford | .20 |
| 299 Rick Miller | .05 |
| 300 Reid Nichols | .05 |
| 301 Bob Ojeda (R) | .45 |
| 302 Tony Perez | .15 |
| 303 Chuck Rainey | .05 |
| 304 Jerry Remy | .05 |
| 305 Jim Rice | .35 |
| 306 Joe Rudi | .05 |
| 307 Bob Stanley | .05 |
| 308 Dave Stapleton | .05 |
| 309 Frank Tanana | .15 |
| 310 Mike Torrez | .05 |
| 311 John Tudor | .15 |
| 312 Carl Yastrzemski | .70 |

**TEXAS RANGERS**

| NO. PLAYER | MINT |
|---|---|
| 313 Buddy Bell | .15 |
| 314 Steve Comer | .05 |

| NO. PLAYER | MINT |
|---|---|
| 315 Danny Darwin | .05 |
| 316 John Ellis | .05 |
| 317 John Grubb | .05 |
| 318 Rick Honeycutt | .05 |
| 319 Charlie Hough | .05 |
| 320 Ferguson Jenkins | .15 |
| 321 John Henry Johnson | .05 |
| 322 Jim Kern | .05 |
| 323 Jon Matlack | .05 |
| 324 Doc Medich | .05 |
| 325 Mario Mendoza | .05 |
| 326 Al Oliver | .15 |
| 327 Pat Putnam | .05 |
| 328 Mickey Rivers | .05 |
| 329 Leon Roberts | .05 |
| 330 Billy Sample | .05 |
| 331 Bill Stein | .05 |
| 332 Jim Sundberg | .05 |
| 333 Mark Wagner | .05 |
| 334 Bump Wills | .05 |

**CHICAGO WHITE SOX**

| NO. PLAYER | MINT |
|---|---|
| 335 Bill Almon | .05 |
| 336 Harold Baines | .30 |
| 337 Ross Baumgarten | .05 |
| 338 Tony Bernazard | .05 |
| 339 Britt Burns | .10 |
| 340 Richard Dotson | .10 |
| 341 Jim Essian | .05 |
| 342 Ed Farmer | .05 |
| 343 Carlton Fisk | .20 |
| 344 Kevin Hickey | .05 |
| 345 LaMarr Hoyt | .10 |
| 346 Lamar Johnson | .05 |
| 347 Jerry Koosman | .05 |
| 348 Rusty Kuntz | .05 |
| 349 Dennis Lamp | .05 |
| 350 Ron LeFlore | .05 |
| 351 Chet Lemon | .08 |
| 352 Greg Luzinski | .10 |
| 353 Bob Molinaro | .05 |
| 354 Jim Morrison | .05 |
| 355 Wayne Nordhagen | .05 |
| 356 Greg Pryor | .05 |
| 357 Mike Squires | .05 |
| 358 Steve Trout | .05 |

**CLEVELAND INDIANS**

| NO. PLAYER | MINT |
|---|---|
| 359 Alan Bannister | .05 |
| 360 Len Barker | .05 |
| 361 Bert Blyleven | .15 |
| 362 Joe Charboneau | .05 |
| 363 John Denny | .10 |
| 364 Bo Diaz | .05 |
| 365 Miguel Dilone | .05 |
| 366 Jerry Dybzinski | .05 |
| 367 Wayne Garland | .05 |
| 368 Mike Hargrove | .05 |
| 369 Toby Harrah | .05 |
| 370 Ron Hassey | .05 |
| 371 Von Hayes (R) | .90 |
| 372 Pat Kelly | .05 |
| 373 Duane Kuiper | .05 |
| 374 Rick Manning | .05 |
| 375 Sid Monge | .05 |
| 376 Jorge Orta | .05 |
| 377 Dave Rosello | .05 |
| 378 Dan Spillner | .05 |
| 379 Mike Stanton | .05 |
| 380 Andre Thornton | .10 |
| 381 Tom Veryzer | .05 |
| 382 Rick Waits | .05 |

**SAN FRANCISCO GIANTS**

| NO. PLAYER | MINT |
|---|---|
| 383 Doyle Alexander | .05 |
| 384 Vida Blue | .05 |
| 385 Fred Breining | .07 |
| 386 Enos Cabell | .05 |
| 387 Jack Clark | .25 |
| 388 Darrell Evans | .10 |
| 389 Tom Griffin | .05 |
| 390 Larry Herndon | .05 |
| 391 Al Holland | .05 |
| 392 Gary Lavelle | .05 |
| 393 Johnnie LeMaster | .05 |
| 394 Jerry Martin | .05 |
| 395 Milt May | .05 |
| 396 Greg Minton | .05 |

| NO. | PLAYER | MINT |
|---|---|---|
| 397 | Joe Morgan | .25 |
| 398 | Joe Pettini | .05 |
| 399 | Alan Ripley | .05 |
| 400 | Billy Smith | .05 |
| 401 | Rennie Stennett | .05 |
| 402 | Ed Whitson | .05 |
| 403 | Jim Wohlford | .05 |

**KANSAS CITY ROYALS**

| NO. | PLAYER | MINT |
|---|---|---|
| 404 | Willie Aikens | .05 |
| 405 | George Brett | .75 |
| 406 | Ken Brett | .05 |
| 407 | Dave Chalk | .05 |
| 408 | Rich Gale | .05 |
| 409 | Cesar Geronimo | .05 |
| 410 | Larry Gura | .05 |
| 411 | Clint Hurdle | .05 |
| 412 | Mike Jones | .05 |
| 413 | Dennis Leonard | .05 |
| 414 | Renie Martin | .05 |
| 415 | Lee May | .05 |
| 416 | Hal McRae | .05 |
| 417 | Darryl Motley (R) | .15 |
| 418 | Rance Mulliniks | .05 |
| 419 | Amos Otis | .05 |
| 420 | Ken Phelps (R) | .60 |
| 421 | Jamie Quirk | .05 |
| 422 | Dan Quisenberry | .20 |
| 423 | Paul Splittorff | .05 |
| 424 | U.L. Washington | .05 |
| 425 | John Wathan | .05 |
| 426 | Frank White | .05 |
| 427 | Willie Wilson | .20 |

**ATLANTA BRAVES**

| NO. | PLAYER | MINT |
|---|---|---|
| 428 | Brian Asselstine | .05 |
| 429 | Bruce Benedict | .05 |
| 430 | Tom Boggs | .05 |
| 431 | Larry Bradford | .05 |
| 432 | Rick Camp | .05 |
| 433 | Chris Chambliss | .05 |
| 434 | Gene Garber | .05 |
| 435 | Preston Hanna | .05 |
| 436 | Bob Horner | .25 |
| 437 | Glenn Hubbard | .05 |
| 438 | "All" Hrabosky (error) | 16.00 |
| | "Al" misspelled | |
| 438 | Al Hrabosky | 1.00 |
| | (height 5'1"—error) | |
| 438 | Al Hrabosky | .12 |
| | (height 5'10" correct) | |
| 439 | Rufino Linares | .05 |
| 440 | Rick Mahler (R) | .25 |
| 441 | Ed Miller | .05 |
| 442 | John Montefusco | .05 |
| 443 | Dale Murphy | 1.00 |
| 444 | Phil Niekro | .25 |
| 445 | Gaylord Perry | .30 |
| 446 | Biff Pocoroba | .05 |
| 447 | Rafael Ramirez | .05 |
| 448 | Jerry Royster | .05 |
| 449 | Claudell Washington | .08 |

**CALIFORNIA ANGELS**

| NO. | PLAYER | MINT |
|---|---|---|
| 450 | Don Aase | .05 |
| 451 | Don Baylor | .15 |
| 452 | Juan Beniquez | .05 |
| 453 | Rick Burleson | .05 |
| 454 | Bert Campaneris | .05 |
| 455 | Rod Carew | .50 |
| 456 | Bob Clark | .05 |
| 457 | Brian Downing | .05 |
| 458 | Dan Ford | .05 |
| 459 | Ken Forsch | .05 |
| 460 | Dave Frost* | .05 |
| 461 | Bobby Grich | .10 |
| 462 | Larry Harlow | .05 |
| 463 | John Harris | .05 |
| 464 | Andy Hassler | .05 |

| NO. | PLAYER | MINT |
|---|---|---|
| 465 | Butch Hobson | .05 |
| 466 | Jesse Jefferson | .05 |
| 467 | Bruce Kison | .05 |
| 468 | Fred Lynn | .25 |
| 469 | Angel Moreno | .05 |
| 470 | Ed Ott | .05 |
| 471 | Fred Patek | .05 |
| 472 | Steve Renko | .05 |
| 473 | Mike Witt (R) | .75 |
| 474 | Geoff Zahn | .05 |

**PITTSBURGH PIRATES**

| NO. | PLAYER | MINT |
|---|---|---|
| 475 | Gary Alexander | .05 |
| 476 | Dale Berra | .05 |
| 477 | Kurt Bevacqua | .05 |
| 478 | Jim Bibby | .05 |
| 479 | John Candelaria | .05 |
| 480 | Victor Cruz | .05 |
| 481 | Mike Easler | .05 |
| 482 | Tim Foli | .05 |
| 483 | Lee Lacy | .05 |
| 484 | Vance Law | .12 |
| 485 | Bill Madlock | .15 |
| 486 | Willie Montanez | .05 |
| 487 | Omar Moreno | .05 |
| 488 | Steve Nicosia | .05 |
| 489 | Dave Parker | .25 |
| 490 | Tony Pena | .20 |
| 491 | Pascual Perez | .05 |
| 492 | Johnny Ray (R) | .60 |
| 493 | Rick Rhoden | .05 |
| 494 | Bill Robinson | .05 |
| 495 | Don Robinson | .05 |
| 496 | Enrique Romo | .05 |
| 497 | Rod Scurry | .05 |
| 498 | Eddie Solomon | .05 |
| 499 | Willie Stargell | .40 |
| 500 | Kent Tekulve | .05 |
| 501 | Jason Thompson | .05 |

**SEATTLE MARINERS**

| NO. | PLAYER | MINT |
|---|---|---|
| 502 | Glenn Abbott | .05 |
| 503 | Jim Anderson | .05 |
| 504 | Floyd Bannister | .05 |
| 505 | Bruce Bochte | .05 |
| 506 | Jeff Burroughs | .05 |
| 507 | Bryan Clark | .07 |
| 508 | Ken Clay | .05 |
| 509 | Julio Cruz | .05 |
| 510 | Dick Drago | .05 |
| 511 | Gary Gray | .05 |
| 512 | Dan Meyer | .05 |
| 513 | Jerry Narron | .05 |
| 514 | Tom Paciorek | .05 |
| 515 | Casey Parsons | .05 |
| 516 | Lenny Randle | .05 |
| 517 | Shane Rawley | .05 |
| 518 | Joe Simpson | .05 |
| 519 | Richie Zisk | .05 |

**NEW YORK METS**

| NO. | PLAYER | MINT |
|---|---|---|
| 520 | Neil Allen | .05 |
| 521 | Bob Bailor | .05 |
| 522 | Hubie Brooks | .35 |
| 523 | Mike Cubbage | .05 |
| 524 | Pete Falcone | .05 |
| 525 | Doug Flynn | .05 |
| 526 | Tom Hausman | .05 |
| 527 | Ron Hodges | .05 |
| 528 | Randy Jones | .05 |
| 529 | Mike Jorgensen | .05 |
| 530 | Dave Kingman | .15 |
| 531 | Ed Lynch | .10 |
| 532 | Mike Marshall | .05 |
| 533 | Lee Mazzilli | .05 |
| 534 | Dyar Miller | .05 |
| 535 | Mike Scott | .25 |
| 536 | Rusty Staub | .10 |
| 537 | John Stearns | .05 |

| NO. | PLAYER | MINT |
|---|---|---|
| 538 | Craig Swan | .05 |
| 539 | Frank Taveras | .05 |
| 540 | Alex Trevino | .05 |
| 541 | Ellis Valentine | .05 |
| 542 | Mookie Wilson | .05 |
| 543 | Joel Youngblood | .05 |
| 544 | Pat Zachry | .05 |

**MINNESOTA TWINS**

| NO. | PLAYER | MINT |
|---|---|---|
| 545 | Glenn Adams | .05 |
| 546 | Fernando Arroyo | .05 |
| 547 | John Verhoeven | .05 |
| 548 | Sal Butera | .05 |
| 549 | John Castino | .05 |
| 550 | Don Cooper | .05 |
| 551 | Doug Corbett | .05 |
| 552 | Dave Engle | .05 |
| 553 | Roger Erickson | .05 |
| 554 | Danny Goodwin | .05 |
| 555 | Darrell Jackson | 1.25 |
| | (error—black hat) | |
| 555 | Darrell Jackson | .10 |
| | (correct—red hat) | |
| 556 | Pete Mackanin | .05 |
| 557 | Jack O'Connor | .05 |
| 558 | Hosken Powell | .05 |
| 559 | Pete Redfern | .05 |
| 560 | Roy Smalley | .05 |
| 561 | Chuck Baker | .05 |
| 562 | Gary Ward | .05 |
| 563 | Rob Wilfong | .05 |
| 564 | Al Williams | .05 |
| 565 | Butch Wynegar | .05 |

**SAN DIEGO PADRES**

| NO. | PLAYER | MINT |
|---|---|---|
| 566 | Randy Bass | .05 |
| 567 | Juan Bonilla | .07 |
| 568 | Danny Boone | .05 |
| 569 | John Curtis | .05 |
| 570 | Juan Eichelberger | .05 |
| 571 | Barry Evans | .05 |
| 572 | Tim Flannery | .05 |
| 573 | Ruppert Jones | .05 |
| 574 | Terry Kennedy | .10 |
| 575 | Joe LeFebvre | .05 |
| 576 | John Littlefield | 70.00 |
| | (left handed—error) | |
| 576 | John Littlefield | .10 |
| | (right handed—corrected) | |
| 577 | Gary Lucas | .05 |
| 578 | Steve Mura | .05 |
| 579 | Broderick Perkins | .05 |
| 580 | Gene Richards | .05 |
| 581 | Luis Salazar | .05 |
| 582 | Ozzie Smith | .30 |
| 583 | John Urrea | .05 |
| 584 | Chris Welsh | .07 |
| 585 | Rick Wise | .05 |

**CHICAGO CUBS**

| NO. | PLAYER | MINT |
|---|---|---|
| 586 | Doug Bird | .05 |
| 587 | Tim Blackwell | .05 |
| 588 | Bobby Bonds | .10 |
| 589 | Bill Buckner | .10 |
| 590 | Bill Caudill | .05 |
| 591 | Hector Cruz | .05 |
| 592 | Jody Davis (R) | .40 |
| 593 | Ivan DeJesus | .05 |
| 594 | Steve Dillard | .05 |
| 595 | Leon Durham | .15 |
| 596 | Rawly Eastwick | .05 |
| 597 | Steve Henderson | .05 |
| 598 | Mike Krukow | .05 |
| 599 | Mike Lum | .05 |
| 600 | Randy Martz | .05 |
| 601 | Jerry Morales | .05 |
| 602 | Ken Reitz | .05 |
| 603 | Lee Smith (R)* | .75 |
| 604 | Dick Tidrow | .05 |

| NO. | PLAYER | MINT |
|---|---|---|
| 605 | Jim Tracy | .05 |
| 606 | Mike Tyson | .05 |
| 607 | Ty Waller | .08 |

**TORONTO BLUE JAYS**

| NO. | PLAYER | MINT |
|---|---|---|
| 608 | Danny Ainge | .10 |
| 609 | Jorge Bell (R) | 7.00 |
| 610 | Mark Bomback | .05 |
| 611 | Barry Bonnell | .05 |
| 612 | Jim Clancy | .05 |
| 613 | Damaso Garcia | .10 |
| 614 | Jerry Garvin | .05 |
| 615 | Alfredo Griffin | .10 |
| 616 | Garth Iorg | .05 |
| 617 | Luis Leal | .05 |
| 618 | Ken Macha | .05 |
| 619 | John Mayberry | .05 |
| 620 | Joey McLaughlin | .05 |
| 621 | Lloyd Moseby | .15 |
| 622 | Dave Stieb | .20 |
| 623 | Jackson Todd | .05 |
| 624 | Willie Upshaw | .15 |
| 625 | Otto Velez | .05 |
| 626 | Ernie Whitt | .05 |
| 627 | Al Woods | .05 |

**SPECIAL CARDS**

| NO. | PLAYER | MINT |
|---|---|---|
| 628 | All-Star Game | .05 |
| 629 | All-Star Infielders: | .05 |
| | Frank White, Bucky Dent | |
| 630 | Big Red Machine: | .10 |
| | Driessen, Concepcion, Foster | |
| 631 | Bruce Sutter | .10 |
| | "Top NL Relief Pitcher" | |
| 632 | "Steve and Carlton" | .20 |
| | Steve Carlton, Carlton Fisk | |
| 633 | Carl Yastrzemski | .30 |
| | "3000th Game" | |
| 634 | "Dynamic Duo" | .25 |
| | Johnny Bench, Tom Seaver | |
| 635 | "West Meets East" | .25 |
| | Valenzuela, Carter | |
| 636 | Fernando Valenzuela:* | .30 |
| | "NL Strikeout King" | |
| 637 | Mike Schmidt | .30 |
| | "Home Run King" | |
| 638 | "NL All Stars" | .20 |
| | Gary Carter, Dave Parker | |
| 639 | "Perfect Game" | .10 |
| | Len Barker, Bo Diaz | |
| 640 | "Pete & Re-Pete" | 1.00 |
| | Pete Rose and Son | |
| 641 | "Phillies' Finest" | .30 |
| | Carlton, Smith, Schmidt | |
| 642 | "Red Sox Reunion" | .10 |
| | Fred Lynn, Dwight Evans | |
| 643 | Rickey Henderson | .30 |
| | "Most Hits, Most Runs" | |
| 644 | Rollie Fingers | .10 |
| | "Most 'Saves AL" | |
| 645 | Tom Seaver | .20 |
| | "Most 1981 Wins" | |
| 646 | "Yankee Powerhouse"* | .50 |
| | R. Jackson, D. Winfield | |
| 647 | Checklist No. 1 | .08 |
| 648 | Checklist No. 2 | .08 |
| 649 | Checklist No. 3 | .08 |
| 650 | Checklist No. 4 | .08 |
| 651 | Checklist No. 5 | .08 |
| 652 | Checklist No. 6 | .08 |
| 653 | Checklist No. 7 | .08 |
| 654 | Checklist No. 8 | .08 |
| 655 | Checklist No. 9 | .08 |
| 656 | Checklist No. 10 | .08 |
| 657 | Checklist No. 11 | .08 |
| 658 | Checklist No. 12 | .08 |
| 659 | Checklist No. 13 | .08 |
| 660 | Checklist No. 14 | .08 |

# 1983 Fleer....Complete Set of 660 Cards—Value $45.00

Features the rookie cards of Wade Boggs, Tony Gwynn, Willie McGee and Ryne Sandberg.

**Willie McGee**

**Storm Davis**

**Wade Boggs**

**Tony Gwynn**

**Ryne Sandberg**

| NO. PLAYER | MINT |
|---|---|
| **ST. LOUIS CARDINALS** | |
| 1 Joaquin Andujar | .15 |
| 2 Doug Bair | .05 |
| 3 Steve Braun | .05 |
| 4 Glenn Brummer | .05 |
| 5 Bob Forsch | .05 |
| 6 David Green (R) | .20 |
| 7 George Hendrick | .10 |
| 8 Keith Hernandez | .30 |
| 9 Tom Herr | .15 |
| 10 Dane Iorg | .05 |
| 11 Jim Kaat | .10 |
| 12 Jeff Lahti | .12 |
| 13 Tito Landrum | .05 |
| 14 Dave LaPoint (R) | .25 |
| 15 Willie McGee (R) | 2.50 |
| 16 Steve Mura | .05 |
| 17 Ken Oberkfell | .05 |
| 18 Darrell Porter | .05 |
| 19 Mike Ramsey | .05 |
| 20 Gene Roof | .05 |
| 21 Lonnie Smith | .10 |
| 22 Ozzie Smith | .30 |
| 23 John Stuper | .12 |
| 24 Bruce Sutter | .15 |
| 25 Gene Tenace | .05 |
| **MILWAUKEE BREWERS** | |
| 26 Jerry Augustin | .05 |
| 27 Dwight Bernard | .05 |
| 28 Mark Brouhard | .05 |
| 29 Mike Caldwell | .05 |
| 30 Cecil Cooper | .15 |
| 31 Jamie Easterly | .05 |
| 32 Marshall Edwards | .05 |
| 33 Rollie Fingers | .20 |
| 34 Jim Gantner | .05 |
| 35 Moose Haas | .05 |
| 36 Roy Howell | .05 |
| 37 Peter Ladd | .05 |
| 38 Bob McClure | .05 |
| 39 Doc Medich | .05 |
| 40 Paul Molitor | .20 |
| 41 Don Money | .05 |
| 42 Charlie Moore | .05 |
| 43 Ben Oglivie | .07 |
| 44 Ed Romero | .05 |
| 45 Ted Simmons | .10 |
| 46 Jim Slaton | .05 |
| 47 Don Sutton | .25 |
| 48 Gorman Thomas | .10 |
| 49 Pete Vuckovich | .05 |
| 50 Ned Yost | .05 |
| 51 Robin Yount | .30 |
| **BALTIMORE ORIOLES** | |
| 52 Benny Ayala | .05 |
| 53 Bob Bonner | .05 |
| 54 Al Bumbry | .05 |
| 55 Terry Crowley | .05 |
| 56 Storm Davis (R) | .40 |
| 57 Rich Dauer | .05 |
| 58 Rick Dempsey | .05 |
| 59 Jim Dwyer | .05 |
| 60 Mike Flanagan | .10 |
| 61 Dan Ford | .05 |
| 62 Glenn Gulliver | .12 |
| 63 John Lowenstein | .05 |

| NO. PLAYER | MINT |
|---|---|
| 64 Dennis Martinez | .05 |
| 65 Tippy Martinez | .05 |
| 66 Scott McGregor | .10 |
| 67 Eddie Murray | .50 |
| 68 Joe Nolan | .05 |
| 69 Jim Palmer | .25 |
| 70 Cal Ripken Jr. | 1.00 |
| 71 Gary Roenicke | .05 |
| 72 Lenn Sakata | .05 |
| 73 Ken Singleton | .05 |
| 74 Sammy Stewart | .05 |
| 75 Tim Stoddard | .05 |
| **CALIFORNIA ANGELS** | |
| 76 Don Aase | .05 |
| 77 Don Baylor | .10 |
| 78 Juan Beniquez | .05 |
| 79 Bob Boone | .05 |
| 80 Rick Burleson | .05 |
| 81 Rod Carew | .40 |
| 82 Bobby Clark | .05 |
| 83 Doug Corbett | .05 |
| 84 John Curtis | .05 |
| 85 Doug DeCinces | .10 |
| 86 Brian Downing | .05 |
| 87 Joe Ferguson | .05 |
| 88 Tim Foli | .05 |
| 89 Ken Forsch | .05 |
| 90 Dave Goltz | .05 |
| 91 Bobby Grich | .05 |
| 92 Andy Hassler | .05 |
| 93 Reggie Jackson | .45 |
| 94 Ron Jackson | .05 |
| 95 Tommy John | .15 |
| 96 Bruce Kison | .05 |
| 97 Fred Lynn | .20 |
| 98 Ed Ott | .05 |
| 99 Steve Renko | .05 |
| 100 Luis Sanchez | .05 |
| 101 Rob Wilfong | .05 |
| 102 Mike Witt | .10 |
| 103 Geoff Zahn | .05 |
| **KANSAS CITY ROYALS** | |
| 104 Willie Aikens | .05 |
| 105 Mike Armstrong | .05 |
| 106 Vida Blue | .10 |
| 107 Bud Black (R) | .25 |
| 108 George Brett | .50 |
| 109 Bill Castro | .05 |
| 110 Onix Concepcion | .12 |
| 111 Dave Frost | .05 |
| 112 Cesar Geronimo | .05 |
| 113 Larry Gura | .05 |
| 114 Steve Hammond | .12 |
| 115 Don Hood | .05 |
| 116 Dennis Leonard | .05 |
| 117 Jerry Martin | .05 |
| 118 Lee May | .05 |
| 119 Hal McRae | .05 |
| 120 Amos Otis | .05 |
| 121 Greg Pryor | .05 |
| 122 Dan Quisenberry | .20 |
| 123 Don Slaught (R) | .25 |
| 124 Paul Splittorff | .05 |
| 125 U.L. Washington | .05 |
| 126 John Wathan | .05 |
| 127 Frank White | .07 |

| NO. PLAYER | MINT |
|---|---|
| 128 Willie Wilson | .20 |
| **ATLANTA BRAVES** | |
| 129 Steve Bedrosian | .30 |
| 130 Bruce Benedict | .05 |
| 131 Tommy Boggs | .05 |
| 132 Brett Butler | .05 |
| 133 Rick Camp | .05 |
| 134 Chris Chambliss | .05 |
| 135 Ken Dayley | .05 |
| 136 Gene Garber | .05 |
| 137 Terry Harper | .05 |
| 138 Bob Horner | .20 |
| 139 Glenn Hubbard | .05 |
| 140 Rufino Linares | .05 |
| 141 Rick Mahler | .05 |
| 142 Dale Murphy | .75 |
| 143 Phil Niekro | .20 |
| 144 Pascual Perez | .10 |
| 145 Biff Pocoroba | .05 |
| 146 Rafael Ramirez | .05 |
| 147 Jerry Royster | .05 |
| 148 Ken Smith | .12 |
| 149 Bob Walk | .05 |
| 150 Claudell Washington | .10 |
| 151 Bob Watson | .05 |
| 152 Larry Whisenton | .05 |
| **PHILADELPHIA PHILLIES** | |
| 153 Porfirio Altamirano | .12 |
| 154 Marty Bystrom | .05 |
| 155 Steve Carlton | .40 |
| 156 Larry Christenson | .05 |
| 157 Ivan DeJesus | .05 |
| 158 John Denny | .10 |
| 159 Bob Dernier | .05 |
| 160 Bo Diaz | .05 |
| 161 Ed Farmer | .05 |
| 162 Greg Gross | .05 |
| 163 Mike Krukow | .05 |
| 164 Garry Maddox | .05 |
| 165 Gary Matthews | .10 |
| 166 Tug McGraw | .08 |
| 167 Bob Molinaro | .05 |
| 168 Sid Monge | .05 |
| 169 Ron Reed | .05 |
| 170 Bill Robinson | .05 |
| 171 Pete Rose | 1.00 |
| 172 Dick Ruthven | .05 |
| 173 Mike Schmidt | .50 |
| 174 Manny Trillo | .05 |
| 175 Ozzie Virgil | .05 |
| 176 George Vuckovich | .05 |
| **BOSTON RED SOX** | |
| 177 Gary Allenson | .05 |
| 178 Luis Aponte | .12 |
| 179 Wade Boggs (R) | 17.50 |
| 180 Tom Burgmeier | .05 |
| 181 Mark Clear | .05 |
| 182 Dennis Eckersley | .10 |
| 183 Dwight Evans | .15 |
| 184 Rich Gedman | .05 |
| 185 Glenn Hoffman | .05 |
| 186 Bruce Hurst | .10 |
| 187 Carney Lansford | .10 |
| 188 Rick Miller | .05 |
| 189 Reid Nichols | .05 |
| 190 Bob Ojeda | .10 |

| NO. PLAYER | MINT |
|---|---|
| 191 Tony Perez | .15 |
| 192 Chuck Rainey | .05 |
| 193 Jerry Remy | .05 |
| 194 Jim Rice | .35 |
| 195 Bob Stanley | .05 |
| 196 Dave Stapleton | .05 |
| 197 Mike Torrez | .05 |
| 198 John Tudor | .15 |
| 199 Julio Valdez | .05 |
| 200 Carl Yastrzemski | .60 |
| **LOS ANGELES DODGERS** | |
| 201 Dusty Baker | .10 |
| 202 Joe Beckwith | .05 |
| 203 Greg Brock (R) | .50 |
| 204 Roy Cey | .15 |
| 205 Terry Forster | .05 |
| 206 Steve Garvey | .40 |
| 207 Pedro Guerrero | .30 |
| 208 Burt Hooton | .05 |
| 209 Steve Howe | .05 |
| 210 Ken Landreaux | .05 |
| 211 Mike Marshall | .20 |
| 212 Candy Maldonado (R) | .75 |
| 213 Rick Monday | .05 |
| 214 Tom Niedenfuer | .05 |
| 215 Jorge Orta | .05 |
| 216 Jerry Reuss | .05 |
| 217 Ron Roenicke | .05 |
| 218 Vicente Romo | .05 |
| 219 Bill Russell | .05 |
| 220 Steve Sax | .15 |
| 221 Mike Scioscia | .05 |
| 222 Dave Stewart | .05 |
| 223 Derrel Thomas | .05 |
| 224 Fernando Valenzuela | .30 |
| 225 Bob Welch | .05 |
| 226 Ricky Wright | .12 |
| 227 Steve Yeager | .05 |
| **CHICAGO WHITE SOX** | |
| 228 Bill Almon | .05 |
| 229 Harold Baines | .25 |
| 230 Salome Barojas | .12 |
| 231 Tony Bernazard | .05 |
| 232 Britt Burns | .05 |
| 233 Richard Dotson | .05 |
| 234 Ernesto Escarrega | .12 |
| 235 Carlton Fisk | .20 |
| 236 Jerry Hairston | .05 |
| 237 Kevin Hickey | .05 |
| 238 LaMarr Hoyt | .15 |
| 239 Steve Kemp | .05 |
| 240 Jim Kern | .05 |
| 241 Ron Kittle (R) | .60 |
| 242 Jerry Koosman | .15 |
| 243 Dennis Lamp | .05 |
| 244 Rudy Law | .05 |
| 245 Vance Law | .05 |
| 246 Ron LeFlore | .05 |
| 247 Greg Luzinski | .10 |
| 248 Tom Paciorek | .05 |
| 249 Aurelio Rodriguez | .05 |
| 250 Mike Squires | .05 |
| 251 Steve Trout | .05 |
| **SAN FRANCISCO GIANTS** | |
| 252 Jim Barr | .05 |
| 253 Dave Bergman | .05 |

| NO. | PLAYER | MINT |
|-----|--------|------|
| 254 | Fred Breining | .05 |
| 255 | Bob Brenly | .05 |
| 256 | Jack Clark | .30 |
| 257 | Chili Davis | .20 |
| 258 | Darrell Evans | .10 |
| 259 | Alan Fowlkes | .12 |
| 260 | Rich Gale | .05 |
| 261 | Atlee Hammaker | .05 |
| 262 | Al Holland | .05 |
| 263 | Duane Kuiper | .05 |
| 264 | Bill Laskey (R) | .15 |
| 265 | Gary Lavelle | .05 |
| 266 | Johnnie LeMaster | .05 |
| 267 | Renie Martin | .05 |
| 268 | Milt May | .05 |
| 269 | Greg Minton | .05 |
| 270 | Joe Morgan | .20 |
| 271 | Tom O'Malley | .12 |
| 272 | Reggie Smith | .10 |
| 273 | Guy Sularz | .12 |
| 274 | Champ Summers | .05 |
| 275 | Max Venable | .05 |
| 276 | Jim Wohlford | .05 |

**MONTREAL EXPOS**

| NO. | PLAYER | MINT |
|-----|--------|------|
| 277 | Ray Burris | .05 |
| 278 | Gary Carter | .35 |
| 279 | Warren Cromartie | .05 |
| 280 | Andre Dawson | .40 |
| 281 | Terry Francona | .05 |
| 282 | Doug Flynn | .05 |
| 283 | Woody Fryman | .05 |
| 284 | Bill Gullickson | .05 |
| 285 | Wallace Johnson | .05 |
| 286 | Charlie Lea | .05 |
| 287 | Randy Lerch | .05 |
| 288 | Brad Mills | .05 |
| 289 | Dan Norman | .05 |
| 290 | Al Oliver | .20 |
| 291 | David Palmer | .05 |
| 292 | Tim Raines | .40 |
| 293 | Jeff Reardon | .10 |
| 294 | Steve Rogers | .10 |
| 295 | Scott Sanderson | .05 |
| 296 | Dan Schatzeder | .05 |
| 297 | Bryn Smith | .05 |
| 298 | Chris Speier | .05 |
| 299 | Tim Wallach | .15 |
| 300 | Jerry White | .05 |
| 301 | Joel Youngblood | .05 |

**PITTSBURGH PIRATES**

| NO. | PLAYER | MINT |
|-----|--------|------|
| 302 | Ross Baumgarten | .05 |
| 303 | Dale Berra | .05 |
| 304 | John Candelaria | .05 |
| 305 | Dick Davis | .05 |
| 306 | Mike Easler | .05 |
| 307 | Richie Hebner | .05 |
| 308 | Lee Lacy | .05 |
| 309 | Bill Madlock | .15 |
| 310 | Larry McWilliams | .05 |
| 311 | John Milner | .05 |
| 312 | Omar Moreno | .05 |
| 313 | Jim Morrison | .05 |
| 314 | Steve Nicosia | .05 |
| 315 | Dave Parker | .25 |
| 316 | Tony Pena | .15 |
| 317 | Johnny Ray | .15 |
| 318 | Rick Rhoden | .05 |
| 319 | Don Robinson | .05 |
| 320 | Enrique Romo | .05 |
| 321 | Manny Sarmiento | .05 |
| 322 | Rod Scurry | .05 |
| 323 | Jim Smith | .12 |
| 324 | Willie Stargell | .30 |
| 325 | Jason Thompson | .10 |
| 326 | Kent Tekulve | .05 |

**DETROIT TIGERS**

| NO. | PLAYER | MINT |
|-----|--------|------|
| 327 | Tom Brookens | .05 |
| 328 | Enos Cabell | .05 |
| 329 | Kirk Gibson | .40 |
| 330 | Larry Herndon | .05 |
| 331 | Mike Ivie | .05 |
| 332 | Howard Johnson (R) | 3.00 |
| 333 | Lynn Jones | .05 |
| 334 | Rick Leach | .05 |
| 335 | Chet Lemon | .07 |

| NO. | PLAYER | MINT |
|-----|--------|------|
| 336 | Jack Morris | .20 |
| 337 | Lance Parrish | .25 |
| 338 | Larry Pashnick | .12 |
| 339 | Dan Petry | .15 |
| 340 | Dave Rozema | .05 |
| 341 | Dave Rucker | .05 |
| 342 | Elias Sosa | .05 |
| 343 | Dave Tobik | .05 |
| 344 | Alan Trammell | .25 |
| 345 | Jerry Turner | .05 |
| 346 | Jerry Ujdur | .05 |
| 347 | Pat Underwood | .05 |
| 348 | Lou Whitaker | .20 |
| 349 | Milt Wilcox | .05 |
| 350 | Glenn Wilson (R) | .40 |
| 351 | John Wockenfuss | .05 |

**SAN DIEGO PADRES**

| NO. | PLAYER | MINT |
|-----|--------|------|
| 352 | Kurt Bevacqua | .05 |
| 353 | Juan Bonilla | .05 |
| 354 | Floyd Chiffer | .12 |
| 355 | Luis DeLeon | .05 |
| 356 | Dave Dravecky (R) | .40 |
| 357 | Dave Edwards | .05 |
| 358 | Juan Eichelberger | .05 |
| 359 | Tim Flannery | .05 |
| 360 | Tony Gwynn (R) | 8.00 |
| 361 | Ruppert Jones | .05 |
| 362 | Terry Kennedy | .10 |
| 363 | Joe Lefebvre | .05 |
| 364 | Sixto Lezcano | .05 |
| 365 | Tim Lollar | .05 |
| 366 | Gary Lucas | .05 |
| 367 | John Montefusco | .05 |
| 368 | Broderick Perkins | .05 |
| 369 | Joe Pittman | .05 |
| 370 | Gene Richards | .05 |
| 371 | Luis Salazar | .05 |
| 372 | Eric Show (R) | .30 |
| 373 | Garry Templeton | .10 |
| 374 | Chris Welsh | .05 |
| 375 | Alan Wiggins (R) | .25 |

**NEW YORK YANKEES**

| NO. | PLAYER | MINT |
|-----|--------|------|
| 376 | Rick Cerone | .05 |
| 377 | Dave Collins | .05 |
| 378 | Roger Erickson | .05 |
| 379 | George Frazier | .05 |
| 380 | Oscar Gamble | .05 |
| 381 | Goose Gossage | .20 |
| 382 | Ken Griffey | .10 |
| 383 | Ron Guidry | .20 |
| 384 | Dave LaRoche | .05 |
| 385 | Rudy May | .05 |
| 386 | John Mayberry | .05 |
| 387 | Lee Mazzilli | .05 |
| 388 | Mike Morgan | .05 |
| 389 | Jerry Mumphrey | .05 |
| 390 | Bobby Murcer | .10 |
| 391 | Graig Nettles | .15 |
| 392 | Lou Piniella | .10 |
| 393 | Willie Randolph | .05 |
| 394 | Shane Rawley | .05 |
| 395 | Dave Righetti | .15 |
| 396 | Andre Robertson | .05 |
| 397 | Roy Smalley | .05 |
| 398 | Dave Winfield | .40 |
| 399 | Butch Wynegar | .05 |

**CLEVELAND INDIANS**

| NO. | PLAYER | MINT |
|-----|--------|------|
| 400 | Chris Bando | .05 |
| 401 | Alan Bannister | .05 |
| 402 | Len Barker | .05 |
| 403 | Tom Brennan | .05 |
| 404 | Carmelo Castillo (R) | .10 |
| 405 | Miguel Dilone | .05 |
| 406 | Jerry Dybzinski | .05 |
| 407 | Mike Fischlin | .05 |
| 408 | Ed Glynn | .05 |
| 409 | Mike Hargrove | .05 |
| 410 | Toby Harrah | .05 |
| 411 | Ron Hassey | .05 |
| 412 | Von Hayes | .15 |
| 413 | Rick Manning | .05 |
| 414 | Bake McBride | .05 |
| 415 | Larry Milbourne | .05 |
| 416 | Bill Nahorodny | .05 |
| 417 | Jack Perconte | .05 |

| NO. | PLAYER | MINT |
|-----|--------|------|
| 418 | Lary Sorensen | .05 |
| 419 | Dan Spillner | .05 |
| 420 | Rick Sutcliffe | .20 |
| 421 | Andre Thornton | .10 |
| 422 | Rick Waits | .05 |
| 423 | Eddie Whitson | .05 |

**TORONTO BLUE JAYS**

| NO. | PLAYER | MINT |
|-----|--------|------|
| 424 | Jesse Barfield | .50 |
| 425 | Barry Bonnell | .05 |
| 426 | Jim Clancy | .05 |
| 427 | Damaso Garcia | .10 |
| 428 | Jerry Garvin | .05 |
| 429 | Alfredo Griffin | .05 |
| 430 | Garth Iorg | .05 |
| 431 | Roy Lee Jackson | .05 |
| 432 | Luis Leal | .05 |
| 433 | Buck Martinez | .05 |
| 434 | Joey McLaughlin | .05 |
| 435 | Lloyd Moseby | .15 |
| 436 | Rance Mulliniks | .05 |
| 437 | Dale Murray | .05 |
| 438 | Wayne Nordhagen | .05 |
| 439 | Gene Petralli | .12 |
| 440 | Hosken Powell | .05 |
| 441 | Dave Stieb | .20 |
| 442 | Willie Upshaw | .10 |
| 443 | Ernie Whitt | .05 |
| 444 | Al Woods | .05 |

**HOUSTON ASTROS**

| NO. | PLAYER | MINT |
|-----|--------|------|
| 445 | Alan Ashby | .05 |
| 446 | Jose Cruz | .15 |
| 447 | Kiko Garcia | .05 |
| 448 | Phil Garner | .05 |
| 449 | Danny Heep | .05 |
| 450 | Art Howe | .05 |
| 451 | Bob Knepper | .05 |
| 452 | Alan Knicely | .05 |
| 453 | Ray Knight | .05 |
| 454 | Frank LaCorte | .05 |
| 455 | Mike LaCoss | .05 |
| 456 | Randy Moffitt | .05 |
| 457 | Joe Niekro | .05 |
| 458 | Terry Puhl | .05 |
| 459 | Luis Pujols | .05 |
| 460 | Craig Reynolds | .05 |
| 461 | Bert Roberge | .05 |
| 462 | Vern Ruhle | .05 |
| 463 | Nolan Ryan | .35 |
| 464 | Joe Sambito | .05 |
| 465 | Tony Scott | .05 |
| 466 | Dave Smith | .05 |
| 467 | Harry Spilman | .05 |
| 468 | Dickie Thon | .05 |
| 469 | Denny Walling | .05 |

**SEATTLE MARINERS**

| NO. | PLAYER | MINT |
|-----|--------|------|
| 470 | Larry Andersen | .05 |
| 471 | Floyd Bannister | .08 |
| 472 | Jim Beattie | .05 |
| 473 | Bruce Bochte | .05 |
| 474 | Manny Castillo | .05 |
| 475 | Bill Caudill | .05 |
| 476 | Bryan Clark | .05 |
| 477 | Al Cowens | .05 |
| 478 | Julio Cruz | .05 |
| 479 | Todd Cruz | .05 |
| 480 | Gary Gray | .05 |
| 481 | Dave Henderson | .05 |
| 482 | Mike Moore (R) | .25 |
| 483 | Gaylord Perry | .30 |
| 484 | Dave Revering | .05 |
| 485 | Joe Simpson | .05 |
| 486 | Mike Stanton | .05 |
| 487 | Rick Sweet | .05 |
| 488 | Ed VandeBerg (R) | .15 |
| 489 | Richie Zisk | .05 |

**CHICAGO CUBS**

| NO. | PLAYER | MINT |
|-----|--------|------|
| 490 | Doug Bird | .05 |
| 491 | Larry Bowa | .10 |
| 492 | Bill Buckner | .10 |
| 493 | Bill Campbell | .05 |
| 494 | Jody Davis | .10 |
| 495 | Leon Durham | .15 |
| 496 | Steve Henderson | .05 |
| 497 | Willie Hernandez | .20 |
| 498 | Ferguson Jenkins | .15 |

| NO. | PLAYER | MINT |
|-----|--------|------|
| 499 | Jay Johnstone | .05 |
| 500 | Junior Kennedy | .05 |
| 501 | Randy Martz | .05 |
| 502 | Jerry Morales | .05 |
| 503 | Keith Moreland | .05 |
| 504 | Dickie Noles | .05 |
| 505 | Mike Proly | .05 |
| 506 | Allen Ripley | .05 |
| 507 | Ryne Sandberg | 4.00 |
| 508 | Lee Smith | .10 |
| 509 | Pat Tabler | .20 |
| 510 | Dick Tidrow | .05 |
| 511 | Bump Wills | .05 |
| 512 | Gary Woods | .05 |

**OAKLAND A'S**

| NO. | PLAYER | MINT |
|-----|--------|------|
| 513 | Tony Armas | .15 |
| 514 | Dave Beard | .05 |
| 515 | Jeff Burroughs | .05 |
| 516 | John D'Acquisto | .05 |
| 517 | Wayne Gross | .05 |
| 518 | Mike Heath | .05 |
| 519 | Rickey Henderson | .60 |
| 520 | Cliff Johnson | .05 |
| 521 | Matt Keough | .05 |
| 522 | Brian Kingman | .05 |
| 523 | Rick Langford | .05 |
| 524 | Davey Lopes | .05 |
| 525 | Steve McCatty | .05 |
| 526 | Dave McKay | .05 |
| 527 | Dan Meyer | .05 |
| 528 | Dwayne Murphy | .05 |
| 529 | Jeff Newman | .05 |
| 530 | Mike Norris | .05 |
| 531 | Bob Owchinko | .05 |
| 532 | Joe Rudi | .05 |
| 533 | Jimmy Sexton | .05 |
| 534 | Fred Stanley | .05 |
| 535 | Tom Underwood | .05 |

**NEW YORK METS**

| NO. | PLAYER | MINT |
|-----|--------|------|
| 536 | Neil Allen | .05 |
| 537 | Wally Backman | .05 |
| 538 | Bob Bailor | .05 |
| 539 | Hubie Brooks | .15 |
| 540 | Carlos Diaz (R) | .15 |
| 541 | Pete Falcone | .05 |
| 542 | George Foster | .15 |
| 543 | Ron Gardenhire | .05 |
| 544 | Brian Giles | .12 |
| 545 | Ron Hodges | .05 |
| 546 | Randy Jones | .05 |
| 547 | Mike Jorgensen | .05 |
| 548 | Dave Kingman | .15 |
| 549 | Ed Lynch | .05 |
| 550 | Jesse Orosco | .10 |
| 551 | Rick Ownbey | .12 |
| 552 | Charlie Puleo | .05 |
| 553 | Gary Rajsich | .12 |
| 554 | Mike Scott | .30 |
| 555 | Rusty Staub | .10 |
| 556 | John Stearns | .05 |
| 557 | Craig Swan | .05 |
| 558 | Ellis Valentine | .05 |
| 559 | Tom Veryzer | .05 |
| 560 | Mookie Wilson | .10 |
| 561 | Pat Zachry | .05 |

**TEXAS RANGERS**

| NO. | PLAYER | MINT |
|-----|--------|------|
| 562 | Buddy Bell | .15 |
| 563 | John Butcher | .05 |
| 564 | Steve Comer | .05 |
| 565 | Danny Darwin | .05 |
| 566 | Bucky Dent | .05 |
| 567 | John Grubb | .05 |
| 568 | Rick Honeycutt | .05 |
| 569 | Dave Hostetler | .12 |
| 570 | Charlie Hough | .05 |
| 571 | Lamar Johnson | .05 |
| 572 | Jon Matlack | .05 |
| 573 | Paul Mirabella | .05 |
| 574 | Larry Parrish | .05 |
| 575 | Mike Richardt | .12 |
| 576 | Mickey Rivers | .05 |
| 577 | Billy Sample | .05 |
| 578 | Dave Schmidt | .10 |
| 579 | Bill Stein | .05 |
| 580 | Jim Sundberg | .05 |

| NO. PLAYER | MINT |
|---|---|
| 581 Frank Tanana | .10 |
| 582 Mark Wagner | .05 |
| 583 George Wright (R) | .15 |
| **CINCINNATI REDS** | |
| 584 Johnny Bench | .40 |
| 585 Bruce Berenyi | .05 |
| 586 Larry Biittner | .05 |
| 587 Cesar Cedeno | .10 |
| 588 Dave Concepcion | .10 |
| 589 Dan Driessen | .05 |
| 590 Greg Harris | .05 |
| 591 Ben Hayes | .12 |
| 592 Paul Householder | .05 |
| 593 Tom Hume | .05 |
| 594 Wayne Krenchicki | .05 |
| 595 Rafael Landestoy | .05 |
| 596 Charlie Leibrandt | .05 |
| 597 Eddie Milner | .10 |
| 598 Ron Oester | .05 |
| 599 Frank Pastore | .05 |
| 600 Joe Price | .05 |
| 601 Tom Seaver | .35 |
| 602 Bob Shirley | .05 |
| 603 Mario Soto | .10 |
| 604 Alex Trevino | .05 |
| 605 Mike Vail | .05 |

| NO. PLAYER | MINT |
|---|---|
| 606 Duane Walker (R) | .15 |
| **MINNESOTA TWINS** | |
| 607 Tom Brunansky | .40 |
| 608 Bobby Castillo | .05 |
| 609 John Castino | .05 |
| 610 Ron Davis | .05 |
| 611 Lenny Gaetti | .05 |
| 612 Terry Felton | .12 |
| 613 Gary Gaetti (R) | 2.50 |
| 614 Mickey Hatcher | .05 |
| 615 Brad Havens | .05 |
| 616 Kent Hrbek | .75 |
| 617 Randy Johnson | .05 |
| 618 Tim Laudner | .05 |
| 619 Jeff Little | .12 |
| 620 Bob Mitchell | .05 |
| 621 Jack O'Connor | .05 |
| 622 John Pacella | .05 |
| 623 Pete Redfern | .05 |
| 624 Jesus Vega | .12 |
| 625 Frank Viola (R) | 3.00 |
| 626 Ron Washington | .12 |
| 627 Gary Ward | .05 |
| 628 Al Williams | .05 |
| **SPECIAL CARDS** | |
| 629 Red Sox All-Stars: | .20 |
| Eckersley, Yaz, Clear | |

| NO. PLAYER | MINT |
|---|---|
| 630 "300 Career Wins" | .15 |
| Perry and Bulling | |
| 631 Pride of Venezuela: | .10 |
| Concepcion, Trillo | |
| 632 All-Star Infielders: | .15 |
| Yount and Bell | |
| 633 Mr. Vet & Mr. Rookie: | .25 |
| Winfield, Hrbek | |
| 634 Fountain of Youth: | .60 |
| Stargell, Rose | |
| 635 Big Chiefs: | .10 |
| Harrah, Thornton | |
| 636 Smith Brothers: | .10 |
| Ozzie and Lonnie | |
| 637 Base Stealers' Threat: | .10 |
| Diaz and Carter | |
| 638 All-Star Catchers: | .15 |
| Fisk, Carter | |
| 639 The Silver Shoe: | .35 |
| Rickey Henderson | |
| 640 Home Run Threats: | .15 |
| Oglivie, Jackson | |
| 641 Two Teams on the | |
| Same Day: | .08 |
| Joel Youngblood 8/4/82 | |

| NO. PLAYER | MINT |
|---|---|
| 642 Last Perfect Game: | .08 |
| Hassey, Barker | |
| 643 Black and Blue: | .08 |
| Vida Blue | |
| 644 Black and Blue: | .08 |
| Bud Black | |
| 645 Speed and Power: | .35 |
| Reggie Jackson | |
| 646 Speed and Power: | .35 |
| Rickey Henderson | |
| 647 Checklist No. 1 | .08 |
| 648 Checklist No. 2 | .08 |
| 649 Checklist No. 3 | .08 |
| 650 Checklist No. 4 | .08 |
| 651 Checklist No. 5 | .08 |
| 652 Checklist No. 6 | .08 |
| 653 Checklist No. 7 | .08 |
| 654 Checklist No. 8 | .08 |
| 655 Checklist No. 9 | .08 |
| 656 Checklist No. 10 | .08 |
| 657 Checklist No. 11 | .08 |
| 658 Checklist No. 12 | .08 |
| 659 Checklist No. 13 | .08 |
| 660 Checklist No. 14 | .08 |

## 1984 Fleer....Complete Set of 660 Cards—Value $110.00

Features the rookie cards of Don Mattingly and Darryl Strawberry. For the first time a traded update set was issued later in the year.

| NO. PLAYER | MINT |
|---|---|
| **BALTIMORE ORIOLES** | |
| 1 Mike Boddicker | .20 |
| 2 Al Bumbry | .05 |
| 3 Todd Cruz | .05 |
| 4 Rich Dauer | .05 |
| 5 Storm Davis | .10 |
| 6 Rick Dempsey | .05 |
| 7 Jim Dwyer | .05 |
| 8 Mike Flanagan | .10 |
| 9 Dan Ford | .05 |
| 10 John Lowenstein | .05 |
| 11 Dennis Martinez | .10 |
| 12 Tippy Martinez | .05 |
| 13 Scott McGregor | .10 |
| 14 Eddie Murray | .50 |
| 15 Joe Nolan | .05 |
| 16 Jim Palmer | .30 |
| 17 Cal Ripken, Jr. | .60 |
| 18 Gary Roenicke | .05 |
| 19 Lenn Sakata | .05 |
| 20 John Shelby (R) | .35 |
| 21 Ken Singleton | .10 |
| 22 Sammy Stewart | .05 |
| 23 Tim Stoddard | .05 |
| **PHILADELPHIA PHILLIES** | |
| 24 Marty Bystrom | .05 |
| 25 Steve Carlton | .35 |
| 26 Ivon DeJesus | .05 |
| 27 John Denny | .10 |
| 28 Bob Dernier | .05 |
| 29 Bo Diaz | .05 |
| 30 Kiko Garcia | .05 |
| 31 Greg Gross | .05 |
| 32 Kevin Gross (R) | .30 |

| NO. PLAYER | MINT |
|---|---|
| 33 Von Hayes | .15 |
| 34 Willie Hernandez | .20 |
| 35 Al Holland | .05 |
| 36 Charles Hudson (R) | .35 |
| 37 Joe Lefebvre | .05 |
| 38 Sixto Lezcano | .05 |
| 39 Garry Maddox | .05 |
| 40 Gary Matthews | .10 |
| 41 Len Matuszek | .05 |
| 42 Tug McGraw | .10 |
| 43 Joe Morgan | .25 |
| 44 Tony Perez | .15 |
| 45 Ron Reed | .05 |
| 46 Pete Rose | 1.00 |
| 47 Juan Samuel (R) | 4.00 |
| 48 Mike Schmidt | .60 |
| 49 Ozzie Virgil | .05 |
| **CHICAGO WHITE SOX** | |
| 50 Juan Agosto | .20 |
| 51 Howard Baines | .20 |
| 52 Floyd Bannister | .10 |
| 53 Salome Barojas | .05 |
| 54 Britt Burns | .05 |
| 55 Julio Cruz | .05 |
| 56 Richard Dotson | .10 |
| 57 Jerry Dybzinski | .05 |
| 58 Carlton Fisk | .15 |
| 59 Scott Fletcher | .20 |
| 60 Jerry Hairston | .05 |
| 61 Kevin Hickey | .05 |
| 62 Marc Hill | .05 |
| 63 LaMarr Hoyt | .10 |
| 64 Ron Kittle | .15 |
| 65 Jerry Koosman | .15 |

| NO. PLAYER | MINT |
|---|---|
| 66 Dennis Lamp | .05 |
| 67 Rudy Law | .05 |
| 68 Vance Law | .05 |
| 69 Greg Luzinski | .10 |
| 70 Tom Paciorek | .05 |
| 71 Mike Squires | .05 |
| 72 Dick Tidrow | .05 |
| 73 Greg Walker (R) | .45 |
| **DETROIT TIGERS** | |
| 74 Glenn Abbott | .05 |
| 75 Howard Bailey | .05 |
| 76 Doug Bair | .05 |
| 77 Juan Berenguer | .05 |
| 78 Tom Brookens | .05 |
| 79 Enos Cabell | .05 |
| 80 Kirk Gibson | .35 |
| 81 John Grubb | .05 |
| 82 Larry Herndon | .05 |
| 83 Wayne Krenchicki | .05 |
| 84 Rick Leach | .05 |
| 85 Chet Lemon | .10 |
| 86 Aurelio Lopez | .05 |
| 87 Jack Morris | .25 |
| 88 Lance Parrish | .25 |
| 89 Dan Petry | .15 |
| 90 Dave Rozema | .05 |
| 91 Alan Trammell | .30 |
| 92 Lou Whitaker | .20 |
| 93 Milt Wilcox | .05 |
| 94 Glenn Wilson | .10 |
| 95 John Wockenfuss | .05 |
| **LOS ANGELES DODGERS** | |
| 96 Dusty Baker | .10 |
| 97 Joe Beckwith | .05 |

| NO. PLAYER | MINT |
|---|---|
| 98 Greg Brock | .10 |
| 99 Jack Fimple | .12 |
| 100 Pedro Guerrero | .25 |
| 101 Rick Honeycutt | .05 |
| 102 Burt Hooton | .05 |
| 103 Steve Howe | .05 |
| 104 Ken Landreaux | .05 |
| 105 Mike Marshall | .15 |
| 106 Rick Monday | .05 |
| 107 Jose Morales | .05 |
| 108 Tom Niedenfuer | .05 |
| 109 Alejandro Pena (R) | .25 |
| 110 Jerry Reuss | .05 |
| 111 Bill Russell | .05 |
| 112 Steve Sax | .15 |
| 113 Mike Scioscia | .05 |
| 114 Derrel Thomas | .05 |
| 115 Fernando Valenzuela | .30 |
| 116 Bob Welch | .10 |
| 117 Steve Yeager | .05 |
| 118 Pat Zachry | .05 |
| **NEW YORK YANKEES** | |
| 119 Don Baylor | .10 |
| 120 Bert Campaneris | .05 |
| 121 Rick Cerone | .05 |
| 122 Ray Fontenot (R) | .15 |
| 123 George Frazier | .05 |
| 124 Oscar Gamble | .05 |
| 125 Goose Gossage | .15 |
| 126 Ken Griffey | .10 |
| 127 Ron Guidry | .15 |
| 128 Jay Howell | .15 |
| 129 Steve Kemp | .05 |
| 130 Matt Keough | .05 |

| NO. | PLAYER | MINT |
|---|---|---|
| 131 | Don Mattingly (R) | 30.00 |
| 132 | John Montefusco | .05 |
| 133 | Omar Moreno | .05 |
| 134 | Dale Murray | .05 |
| 135 | Graig Nettles | .10 |
| 136 | Lou Piniella | .10 |
| 137 | Willie Randolph | .10 |
| 138 | Shane Rawley | .05 |
| 139 | Dave Righetti | .15 |
| 140 | Andre Robertson | .05 |
| 141 | Bob Shirley | .05 |
| 142 | Roy Smalley | .05 |
| 143 | Dave Winfield | .35 |
| 144 | Butch Wynegar | .05 |

**TORONTO BLUE JAYS**

| NO. | PLAYER | MINT |
|---|---|---|
| 145 | Jim Acker (R) | .15 |
| 146 | Doyle Alexander | .10 |
| 147 | Jesse Barfield | .25 |
| 148 | Jorge Bell | 1.00 |
| 149 | Barry Bonnell | .05 |
| 150 | Jim Clancy | .05 |
| 151 | Dave Collins | .05 |
| 152 | Tony Fernandez (R) | 3.75 |
| 153 | Damaso Garcia | .10 |
| 154 | Dave Geisel | .05 |
| 155 | Jim Gott | .15 |
| 156 | Alfredo Griffin | .05 |
| 157 | Garth Iorg | .05 |
| 158 | Roy Lee Jackson | .05 |
| 159 | Cliff Johnson | .05 |
| 160 | Luis Leal | .05 |
| 161 | Buck Martinez | .05 |
| 162 | Joey McLaughlin | .05 |
| 163 | Randy Moffitt | .05 |
| 164 | Lloyd Moseby | .15 |
| 165 | Rance Mulliniks | .05 |
| 166 | Jorge Orta | .05 |
| 167 | Dave Stieb | .20 |
| 168 | Willie Upshaw | .15 |
| 169 | Ernie Whitt | .05 |

**ATLANTA BRAVES**

| NO. | PLAYER | MINT |
|---|---|---|
| 170 | Len Barker | .05 |
| 171 | Steve Bedrosian | .10 |
| 172 | Bruce Benedict | .05 |
| 173 | Brett Butler | .10 |
| 174 | Rick Camp | .05 |
| 175 | Chris Chambliss | .05 |
| 176 | Ken Dayley | .05 |
| 177 | Pete Falcone | .05 |
| 178 | Terry Forster | .05 |
| 179 | Gene Garber | .05 |
| 180 | Terry Harper | .05 |
| 181 | Bob Horner | .20 |
| 182 | Glenn Hubbard | .05 |
| 183 | Randy Johnson | .05 |
| 184 | Craig McMurtry | .10 |
| 185 | Donnie Moore | .05 |
| 186 | Dale Murphy | .75 |
| 187 | Phil Niekro | .15 |
| 188 | Pascual Perez | .05 |
| 189 | Biff Pocoroba | .05 |
| 190 | Rafael Ramirez | .05 |
| 191 | Jerry Royster | .05 |
| 192 | Claudell Washington | .10 |
| 193 | Bob Watson | .05 |

**MILWAUKEE BREWERS**

| NO. | PLAYER | MINT |
|---|---|---|
| 194 | Jerry Augustine | .05 |
| 195 | Mark Brouhard | .05 |
| 196 | Mike Caldwell | .05 |
| 197 | Tom Candiotti (R) | .35 |
| 198 | Cecil Cooper | .15 |
| 199 | Rollie Fingers | .15 |
| 200 | Jim Gantner | .05 |
| 201 | Bob Gibson | .12 |
| 202 | Moose Haas | .05 |
| 203 | Roy Howell | .05 |
| 204 | Pete Ladd | .05 |
| 205 | Rick Manning | .05 |
| 206 | Bob McClure | .05 |
| 207 | Paul Molitor | .20 |
| 208 | Don Money | .05 |
| 209 | Charlie Moore | .05 |
| 210 | Ben Oglivie | .10 |
| 211 | Chuck Porter | .05 |
| 212 | Ed Romero | .05 |

| NO. | PLAYER | MINT |
|---|---|---|
| 213 | Ted Simmons | .10 |
| 214 | Jim Slaton | .05 |
| 215 | Don Sutton | .10 |
| 216 | Tom Tellmann | .05 |
| 217 | Pete Vuckovich | .05 |
| 218 | Ned Yost | .05 |
| 219 | Robin Yount | .30 |

**HOSTON ASTROS**

| NO. | PLAYER | MINT |
|---|---|---|
| 220 | Alan Ashby | .05 |
| 221 | Kevin Bass | .25 |
| 222 | Jose Cruz | .10 |
| 223 | Bill Dawley (R) | .20 |
| 224 | Frank DiPino | .05 |
| 225 | Bill Doran (R) | .70 |
| 226 | Phil Garner | .05 |
| 227 | Art Howe | .05 |
| 228 | Bob Knepper | .05 |
| 229 | Ray Knight | .10 |
| 230 | Frank LaCorte | .05 |
| 231 | Mike LaCoss | .05 |
| 232 | Mike Madden (R) | .15 |
| 233 | Jerry Mumphrey | .05 |
| 234 | Joe Niekro | .10 |
| 235 | Terry Puhl | .05 |
| 236 | Luis Pujols | .05 |
| 237 | Craig Reynolds | .05 |
| 238 | Vern Ruhle | .05 |
| 239 | Nolan Ryan | .35 |
| 240 | Mike Scott | .25 |
| 241 | Tony Scott | .05 |
| 242 | Dave Smith | .05 |
| 243 | Dickie Thon | .08 |
| 244 | Denny Walling | .05 |

**PITTSBURGH PIRATES**

| NO. | PLAYER | MINT |
|---|---|---|
| 245 | Dale Berra | .05 |
| 246 | Jim Bibby | .05 |
| 247 | John Candelaria | .05 |
| 248 | Jose DeLeon (R) | .25 |
| 249 | Mike Easler | .08 |
| 250 | Cecilio Guante | .05 |
| 251 | Richie Hebner | .05 |
| 252 | Lee Lacy | .05 |
| 253 | Bill Madlock | .15 |
| 254 | Milt May | .05 |
| 255 | Lee Mazzilli | .05 |
| 256 | Larry McWilliams | .05 |
| 257 | Jim Morrison | .05 |
| 258 | Dave Parker | .25 |
| 259 | Tony Pena | .15 |
| 260 | Johnny Ray | .15 |
| 261 | Rick Rhoden | .05 |
| 262 | Don Robinson | .05 |
| 263 | Manny Sarmiento | .05 |
| 264 | Rod Scurry | .05 |
| 265 | Kent Tekulve | .05 |
| 266 | Gene Tenace | .05 |
| 267 | Jason Thompson | .10 |
| 268 | Lee Tunnell (R) | .15 |
| 269 | Marvell Wynne (R) | .15 |

**MONTREAL EXPOS**

| NO. | PLAYER | MINT |
|---|---|---|
| 270 | Ray Burris | .05 |
| 271 | Gary Carter | .35 |
| 272 | Warren Cromartie | .05 |
| 273 | Andre Dawson | .30 |
| 274 | Doug Flynn | .05 |
| 275 | Terry Francona | .05 |
| 276 | Bill Gullickson | .05 |
| 277 | Bob James (R) | .25 |
| 278 | Charlie Lea | .05 |
| 279 | Bryan Little | .05 |
| 280 | Al Oliver | .15 |
| 281 | Tim Raines | .35 |
| 282 | Bobby Ramos | .05 |
| 283 | Jeff Reardon | .10 |
| 284 | Steve Rogers | .05 |
| 285 | Scott Sanderson | .05 |
| 286 | Dan Schatzeder | .05 |
| 287 | Bryn Smith | .05 |
| 288 | Chris Speier | .05 |
| 289 | Manny Trillo | .05 |
| 290 | Mike Vail | .05 |
| 291 | Tim Wallach | .10 |
| 292 | Chris Welsh | .05 |
| 293 | Jim Wohlford | .05 |

**SAN DIEGO PADRES**

| NO. | PLAYER | MINT |
|---|---|---|
| 294 | Kurt Bevacqua | .05 |
| 295 | Juan Bonilla | .05 |
| 296 | Bobby Brown | .05 |
| 297 | Luis DeLeon | .05 |
| 298 | Dave Dravecky | .10 |
| 299 | Tim Flannery | .05 |
| 300 | Steve Garvey | .40 |
| 301 | Tony Gwynn | 2.00 |
| 302 | Andy Hawkins (R) | .30 |
| 303 | Ruppert Jones | .05 |
| 304 | Terry Kennedy | .10 |
| 305 | Tim Lollar | .05 |
| 306 | Gary Lucas | .05 |
| 307 | Kevin McReynolds (R) | 5.50 |
| 308 | Sid Monge | .05 |
| 309 | Mario Ramirez | .05 |
| 310 | Gene Richards | .12 |
| 311 | Luis Salazar | .05 |
| 312 | Eric Show | .05 |
| 313 | Elias Sosa | .05 |
| 314 | Garry Templeton | .10 |
| 315 | Mark Thurmond (R) | .20 |
| 316 | Ed Whitson | .05 |
| 317 | Alan Wiggins | .10 |

**ST. LOUIS CARDINALS**

| NO. | PLAYER | MINT |
|---|---|---|
| 318 | Neil Allen | .05 |
| 319 | Joaquin Andujar | .10 |
| 320 | Steve Braun | .05 |
| 321 | Glenn Brummer | .05 |
| 322 | Bob Forsch | .10 |
| 323 | David Green | .05 |
| 324 | George Hendrick | .08 |
| 325 | Tom Herr | .10 |
| 326 | Dane Iorg | .05 |
| 327 | Jeff Lahti | .05 |
| 328 | Dave LaPoint | .05 |
| 329 | Willie McGee | .40 |
| 330 | Ken Oberkfell | .05 |
| 331 | Darrell Porter | .05 |
| 332 | Jamie Quirk | .05 |
| 333 | Mike Ramsey | .05 |
| 334 | Floyd Rayford | .05 |
| 335 | Lonnie Smith | .10 |
| 336 | Ozzie Smith | .30 |
| 337 | John Stuper | .05 |
| 338 | Bruce Sutter | .15 |
| 339 | Andy Van Slyke (R) | 2.25 |
| 340 | Dave Von Ohlen | .12 |

**KANSAS CITY ROYALS**

| NO. | PLAYER | MINT |
|---|---|---|
| 341 | Willie Aikens | .05 |
| 342 | Mike Armstrong | .05 |
| 343 | Bud Black | .05 |
| 344 | George Brett | .50 |
| 345 | Onix Concepcion | .05 |
| 346 | Keith Creel | .05 |
| 347 | Larry Gura | .05 |
| 348 | Don Hood | .05 |
| 349 | Dennis Leonard | .05 |
| 350 | Hal McRae | .05 |
| 351 | Amos Otis | .05 |
| 352 | Gaylord Perry | .15 |
| 353 | Greg Pryor | .05 |
| 354 | Dan Quisenberry | .20 |
| 355 | Steve Renko | .05 |
| 356 | Leon Roberts | .05 |
| 357 | Pat Sheridan (R) | .35 |
| 358 | Joe Simpson | .05 |
| 359 | Don Slaught | .05 |
| 360 | Paul Splittorff | .05 |
| 361 | U.L. Washington | .05 |
| 362 | John Wathan | .05 |
| 363 | Frank White | .05 |
| 364 | Willie Wilson | .15 |

**SAN FRANCISCO GIANTS**

| NO. | PLAYER | MINT |
|---|---|---|
| 365 | Jim Barr | .05 |
| 366 | Dave Bergman | .05 |
| 367 | Fred Breining | .05 |
| 368 | Bob Brenly | .05 |
| 369 | Jack Clark | .30 |
| 370 | Chili Davis | .15 |
| 371 | Mark Davis | .05 |
| 372 | Darrell Evans | .10 |
| 373 | Atlee Hammaker | .05 |
| 374 | Mike Krukow | .05 |

| NO. | PLAYER | MINT |
|---|---|---|
| 375 | Duane Kuiper | .05 |
| 376 | Bill Laskey | .05 |
| 377 | Gary Lavelle | .05 |
| 378 | Johnnie LeMaster | .05 |
| 379 | Jeff Leonard | .05 |
| 380 | Randy Lerch | .05 |
| 381 | Renie Martin | .05 |
| 382 | Andy McGaffigan | .05 |
| 383 | Greg Minton | .05 |
| 384 | Tom O'Malley | .05 |
| 385 | Max Venable | .05 |
| 386 | Brad Wellman | .05 |
| 387 | Joel Youngblood | .12 |

**BOSTON RED SOX**

| NO. | PLAYER | MINT |
|---|---|---|
| 388 | Gary Allenson | .05 |
| 389 | Luis Aponte | .05 |
| 390 | Tony Armas | .15 |
| 391 | Doug Bird | .05 |
| 392 | Wade Boggs | 6.50 |
| 393 | Dennis Boyd (R) | .40 |
| 394 | Mike Brown | .12 |
| 395 | Mark Clear | .05 |
| 396 | Dennis Eckersley | .05 |
| 397 | Dwight Evans | .15 |
| 398 | Rich Gedman | .10 |
| 399 | Glenn Hoffman | .05 |
| 400 | Bruce Hurst | .15 |
| 401 | John Henry Johnson | .05 |
| 402 | Ed Jurak | .12 |
| 403 | Rick Miller | .05 |
| 404 | Jeff Newman | .05 |
| 405 | Reid Nichols | .05 |
| 406 | Bob Ojeda | .10 |
| 407 | Jerry Remy | .05 |
| 408 | Jim Rice | .30 |
| 409 | Bob Stanley | .05 |
| 410 | Dave Stapleton | .05 |
| 411 | John Tudor | .15 |
| 412 | Carl Yastrzemski | .50 |

**TEXAS RANGERS**

| NO. | PLAYER | MINT |
|---|---|---|
| 413 | Buddy Bell | .15 |
| 414 | Larry Biittner | .05 |
| 415 | John Butcher | .05 |
| 416 | Danny Darwin | .05 |
| 417 | Bucky Dent | .05 |
| 418 | Dave Hostetler | .05 |
| 419 | Charlie Hough | .05 |
| 420 | Bobby Johnson | .05 |
| 421 | Odell Jones | .05 |
| 422 | Jon Matlack | .05 |
| 423 | Pete O'Brien (R) | .75 |
| 424 | Larry Parrish | .05 |
| 425 | Mickey Rivers | .10 |
| 426 | Billy Sample | .05 |
| 427 | Dave Schmidt | .05 |
| 428 | Mike Smithson (R) | .15 |
| 429 | Bill Stein | .05 |
| 430 | Dave Stewart | .05 |
| 431 | Jim Sundberg | .05 |
| 432 | Frank Tanana | .10 |
| 433 | Dave Tobik | .05 |
| 434 | Wayne Tolleson | .05 |
| 435 | George Wright | .05 |

**OAKLAND A'S**

| NO. | PLAYER | MINT |
|---|---|---|
| 436 | Bill Almon | .05 |
| 437 | Keith Atherton | .12 |
| 438 | Dave Beard | .05 |
| 439 | Tom Burgmeier | .05 |
| 440 | Jeff Burroughs | .05 |
| 441 | Chris Codiroli | .10 |
| 442 | Tim Conroy | .12 |
| 443 | Mike Davis | .10 |
| 444 | Wayne Gross | .05 |
| 445 | Garry Hancock | .05 |
| 446 | Mike Heath | .05 |
| 447 | Rickey Henderson | .50 |
| 448 | Don Hill | .12 |
| 449 | Bob Kearney | .05 |
| 450 | Bill Krueger | .12 |
| 451 | Rick Langford | .05 |
| 452 | Carney Lansford | .10 |
| 453 | Davey Lopes | .10 |
| 454 | Steve McCatty | .05 |
| 455 | Dan Meyer | .05 |
| 456 | Dwayne Murphy | .05 |

| NO. PLAYER | MINT |
|---|---|
| 457 Mike Norris | .05 |
| 458 Ricky Peters | .05 |
| 459 Tony Phillips | .12 |
| 460 Tom Underwood | .05 |
| 461 Mike Warren (R) | .15 |

**CINCINNATI REDS**

| NO. PLAYER | MINT |
|---|---|
| 462 Johnny Bench | .40 |
| 463 Bruce Berenyi | .05 |
| 464 Dann Bilardello | .05 |
| 465 Cesar Cedeno | .05 |
| 466 Dave Concepcion | .10 |
| 467 Dan Driessen | .05 |
| 468 Nick Esasky (R) | .30 |
| 469 Rich Gale | .05 |
| 470 Ben Hayes | .05 |
| 471 Paul Householder | .05 |
| 472 Tom Hume | .05 |
| 473 Alan Knicely | .05 |
| 474 Eddie Milner | .05 |
| 475 Ron Oester | .05 |
| 476 Kelly Paris | .10 |
| 477 Frank Pastore | .05 |
| 478 Ted Power | .05 |
| 479 Joe Price | .05 |
| 480 Charlie Puleo | .05 |
| 481 Gary Redus (R) | .25 |
| 482 Bill Scherrer | .12 |
| 483 Mario Soto | .10 |
| 484 Alex Trevino | .05 |
| 485 Duane Walker | .05 |

**CHICAGO CUBS**

| NO. PLAYER | MINT |
|---|---|
| 486 Larry Bowa | .05 |
| 487 Warren Brusstar | .05 |
| 488 Bill Buckner | .10 |
| 489 Bill Campbell | .05 |
| 490 Ron Cey | .15 |
| 491 Jody Davis | .05 |
| 492 Leon Durham | .15 |
| 493 Mel Hall | .25 |
| 494 Ferguson Jenkins | .15 |
| 495 Jay Johnstone | .05 |
| 496 Craig Lefferts (R) | .15 |
| 497 Carmelo Martinez (R) | .30 |
| 498 Jerry Morales | .05 |
| 499 Keith Moreland | .05 |
| 500 Dickie Noles | .05 |
| 501 Mike Proly | .05 |
| 502 Chuck Rainey | .05 |
| 503 Dick Ruthven | .05 |
| 504 Ryne Sandberg | 1.00 |
| 505 Lee Smith | .12 |
| 506 Steve Trout | .05 |
| 507 Gary Woods | .05 |

**CALIFORNIA ANGELS**

| NO. PLAYER | MINT |
|---|---|
| 508 Juan Beniquez | .05 |
| 509 Bob Boone | .05 |
| 510 Rick Burleson | .10 |
| 511 Rod Carew | .40 |
| 512 Bobby Clark | .05 |
| 513 John Curtis | .05 |
| 514 Doug DeCinces | .10 |
| 515 Brian Downing | .05 |
| 516 Tim Foli | .05 |
| 517 Ken Forsch | .05 |
| 518 Bobby Grich | .05 |
| 519 Andy Hassler | .05 |
| 520 Reggie Jackson | .50 |
| 521 Ron Jackson | .05 |
| 522 Tommy John | .10 |
| 523 Bruce Kison | .05 |
| 524 Steve Lubratich | .12 |
| 525 Fred Lynn | .15 |
| 526 Gary Pettis (R) | .40 |
| 527 Luis Sanchez | .05 |
| 528 Daryl Sconiers | .05 |
| 529 Ellis Valentine | .05 |
| 530 Rob Wilfong | .05 |
| 531 Mike Witt | .10 |
| 532 Geoff Zahn | .05 |

**CLEVELAND INDIANS**

| NO. PLAYER | MINT |
|---|---|
| 533 Bud Anderson | .05 |
| 534 Chris Bando | .05 |
| 535 Alan Bannister | .05 |
| 536 Bert Blyleven | .10 |
| 537 Tom Brennan | .05 |
| 538 Jamie Easterly | .05 |
| 539 Juan Eichelberger | .05 |
| 540 Jim Essian | .05 |
| 541 Mike Fischlin | .05 |
| 542 Julio Franco | .50 |
| 543 Mike Hargrove | .05 |
| 544 Toby Harrah | .05 |
| 545 Ron Hassey | .05 |
| 546 Neal Heaton (R) | .15 |
| 547 Bake McBride | .05 |
| 548 Broderick Perkins | .12 |
| 549 Lary Sorensen | .05 |
| 550 Dan Spillner | .05 |
| 551 Rick Sutcliffe | .20 |
| 552 Pat Tabler | .10 |
| 553 Gorman Thomas | .10 |
| 554 Andre Thornton | .10 |
| 555 George Vukovich | .05 |

**MINNESOTA TWINS**

| NO. PLAYER | MINT |
|---|---|
| 556 Darrell Brown | .05 |
| 557 Tom Brunansky | .25 |
| 558 Randy Bush | .05 |
| 559 Bobby Castillo | .05 |
| 560 John Castino | .05 |
| 561 Ron Davis | .05 |
| 562 Dave Engle | .05 |
| 563 Lenny Faedo | .05 |
| 564 Pete Filson | .12 |
| 565 Gary Gaetti | .75 |
| 566 Mickey Hatcher | .05 |
| 567 Kent Hrbek | .40 |
| 568 Rusty Kuntz | .05 |
| 569 Tim Laudner | .05 |
| 570 Rick Lysander | .12 |
| 571 Bobby Mitchell | .05 |
| 572 Ken Schrom | .05 |
| 573 Ray Smith | .12 |
| 574 Tim Teufel (R) | .30 |
| 575 Frank Viola | .50 |
| 576 Gary Ward | .05 |
| 577 Ron Washington | .05 |
| 578 Len Whitehouse | .05 |
| 579 Al Williams | .05 |

**NEW YORK METS**

| NO. PLAYER | MINT |
|---|---|
| 580 Bob Bailor | .05 |
| 581 Mark Bradley | .10 |
| 582 Hubie Brooks | .15 |
| 583 Carlos Diaz | .05 |
| 584 George Foster | .15 |
| 585 Brian Giles | .05 |
| 586 Danny Heep | .05 |
| 587 Keith Hernandez | .30 |
| 588 Ron Hodges | .05 |
| 589 Scott Holman | .05 |
| 590 Dave Kingman | .15 |
| 591 Ed Lynch | .05 |
| 592 Jose Oquendo | .30 |
| 593 Jesse Orosco | .10 |
| 594 Junior Ortiz | .12 |
| 595 Tom Seaver | .35 |
| 596 Doug Sisk | .15 |
| 597 Rusty Staub | .10 |
| 598 John Stearns | .05 |
| 599 Darryl Strawberry (R) | 17.50 |
| 600 Craig Swan | .05 |
| 601 Walt Terrell (R) | .35 |
| 602 Mike Torrez | .05 |
| 603 Mookie Wilson | .10 |

**SEATTLE MARINERS**

| NO. PLAYER | MINT |
|---|---|
| 604 Jamie Allen | .12 |
| 605 Jim Beattie | .05 |
| 606 Tony Bernazard | .05 |
| 607 Manny Castillo | .05 |
| 608 Bill Caudill | .05 |
| 609 Bryan Clark | .05 |
| 610 Al Cowens | .05 |
| 611 Dave Henderson | .05 |
| 612 Steve Henderson | .05 |
| 613 Orlando Mercado | .12 |
| 614 Mike Moore | .05 |
| 615 Ricky Nelson | .12 |
| 616 Spike Owen (R) | .20 |
| 617 Pat Putnam | .05 |
| 618 Ron Roenicke | .05 |
| 619 Mike Stanton | .05 |
| 620 Bob Stoddard | .05 |
| 621 Rick Sweet | .05 |
| 622 Roy Thomas | .05 |
| 623 Ed Vande Berg | .05 |
| 624 Matt Young (R) | .15 |

| NO. PLAYER | MINT |
|---|---|
| 625 Richie Zisk | .05 |

**SPECIAL CARDS**

| NO. PLAYER | MINT |
|---|---|
| 626 Fred Lynn: "All-Star Record Breaker" | .15 |
| 627 Manny Trillo: "All-Star Record Breaker" | .05 |
| 628 Steve Garvey: "NL Iron Man" | .25 |
| 629 Rod Carew: "AL Batting Runner-Up" | .20 |
| 630 Wade Boggs: "AL Batting Champion" | .50 |
| 631 Tim Raines: "Letting Go Of The Raines" | .15 |
| 632 Al Oliver: "Double Trouble" | .15 |
| 633 Steve Sax: "All-Star Second Base" | .10 |
| 634 Dickie Thon: "All-Star Shortstop" | .10 |
| 635 Quisenberry & Martinez "Ace Fireman" | .10 |
| 636 Perez, Rose, & Morgan "Reds Reunited" | .40 |
| 637 Parrish & Boone: "Backstop Stars" | .10 |
| 638 Brett & Perry: "Pine Tar Incident" | .25 |
| 639 Forsch, Warren & Righetti: "1983 No-Hitters" | .10 |
| 640 Bench and Yaz: "Retiring Superstars" | .25 |
| 641 Gaylord Perry: "Going Out In Style" | .15 |
| 642 Steve Carlton: 300 Club and Strikeout Record | .20 |
| 643 Altobelli and Owens: "World Series Managers" | .05 |
| 644 Rick Dempsey: "World Series MVP" | .05 |
| 645 Mike Boddicker: "Rookie Winner" | .10 |
| 646 Scott McGregor: "The Clincher" | .10 |
| 647 Checklist No. 1 | .08 |
| 648 Checklist No. 2 | .08 |
| 649 Checklist No. 3 | .08 |
| 650 Checklist No. 4 | .08 |
| 651 Checklist No. 5 | .08 |
| 652 Checklist No. 6 | .08 |
| 653 Checklist No. 7 | .08 |
| 654 Checklist No. 8 | .08 |
| 655 Checklist No. 9 | .08 |
| 656 Checklist No. 10 | .08 |
| 657 Checklist No. 11 | .08 |
| 658 Checklist No. 12 | .08 |
| 659 Checklist No 13 | .08 |
| 660 Checklist No. 14 | .08 |

# 1984 Fleer Traded Update....Complete Set of 132 Cards—Value $275.00

This was Fleer's first traded update set. It updates the main 1984 card set with players who had changed teams during the season and rookies. This set features Fleer's first card of Dwight Gooden, Roger Clemens, Bret Saberhagen and Kirby Puckett. Production was extremely limited. The complete set was packaged in its own printed box and distributed exclusively through card hobby dealers.

Card values shown here fluctuate considerably.

| NO. PLAYER | MINT | NO. PLAYER | MINT | NO. PLAYER | MINT | NO. PLAYER | MINT |
|---|---|---|---|---|---|---|---|
| U1 Willie Aikens | .25 | U34 Dennis Eckersley | .20 | U67 Frank LaCorte | .20 | U100 Jeff Robinson | .40 |
| U2 Luis Aponte | .20 | U35 Jim Essian | .20 | U68 Dennis Lamp | .20 | U101 R. Romanick (RR) | 1.00 |
| U3 Mark Bailey | .35 | U36 Darrell Evans | .35 | U69 Tito Landrum | .20 | U102 Pete Rose | 24.00 |
| U4 Bob Bailor | .20 | U37 Mike Fitzgerald | .35 | U70 Mark Langston (RR) | 6.00 | U103 B. Saberhagen (RR) | 16.00 |
| U5 Dusty Baker | .25 | U38 Tim Foli | .20 | U71 Rick Leach | .20 | U104 Scott Sanderson | .25 |
| U6 Steve Balboni | .40 | U39 John Franco (RR) | 5.00 | U72 Craig Lefferts | .20 | U105 Dick Schofield | .75 |
| U7 Alan Bannister | .20 | U40 George Frazier | .20 | U73 Gary Lucas | .20 | U106 Tom Seaver | 10.00 |
| U8 Marty Barrett (RR) | 3.50 | U41 Rich Gale | .20 | U74 Jerry Martin | .20 | U107 Jim Slaton | .20 |
| U9 Dave Beard | .20 | U42 Barbaro Garbey | .40 | U75 Carmelo Martinez | .25 | U108 Mike Smithson | .20 |
| U10 Joe Beckwith | .20 | U43 Dwight Gooden (RR) | .65.00 | U76 Mike Mason | .40 | U109 Lary Sorensen | .20 |
| U11 Dave Bergman | .20 | U44 Goose Gossage | .50 | U77 Gary Matthews | .20 | U110 Tim Stoddard | .20 |
| U12 Tony Bernazard | .20 | U45 Wayne Gross | .20 | U78 Andy McGaffigan | .20 | U111 Jeff Stone (RR) | .75 |
| U13 Bruce Bochte | .20 | U46 Mark Gubicza | 3.00 | U79 Joey McLaughlin | .20 | U112 Champ Summers | .20 |
| U14 Barry Bonnell | .20 | U47 Jackie Gutierrez | .40 | U80 Joe Morgan | 2.50 | U113 Jim Sundberg | .20 |
| U15 Phil Bradley (RR) | 4.00 | U48 Toby Harrah | .20 | U81 Darryl Motley | .25 | U114 Rick Sutcliffe | .75 |
| U16 Fred Breining | .20 | U49 Ron Hassey | .20 | U82 Graig Nettles | .75 | U115 Craig Swan | .20 |
| U17 Mike Brown | .35 | U50 Richie Hebner | .20 | U83 Phil Niekro | 2.00 | U116 Derrel Thomas | .20 |
| U18 Bill Buckner | .30 | U51 Willie Hernandes | .60 | U84 Ken Oberkfell | .20 | U117 Gorman Thomas | .25 |
| U19 Ray Burris | .20 | U52 Ed Hodge | .35 | U85 Al Oliver | .60 | U118 Alex Trevino | .20 |
| U20 John Butcher | .20 | U53 Ricky Horton | .60 | U86 Jorge Orta | .20 | U119 Manny Trillo | .20 |
| U21 Brett Butler | .40 | U54 Art Howe | 1.25 | U87 Amos Otis | .35 | U120 John Tudor | .60 |
| U22 Enos Cabell | .20 | U55 Dane Iorg | .20 | U88 Bob Owchinko | .20 | U121 Tom Underwood | .20 |
| U23 Bill Campbell | .20 | U56 Brook Jacoby (RR) | 3.00 | U89 Dave Parker | 2.25 | U122 Mike Vail | .20 |
| U24 Bill Caudill | .20 | U57 Dion James | 1.25 | U90 Jack Perconte | .20 | U123 Tom Waddell | .35 |
| U25 Bobby Clark | .20 | U58 Mike Jeffcoat | .40 | U91 Tony Perez | 1.50 | U124 Gary Ward | .20 |
| U26 Brian Clark | .20 | U59 Ruppert Jones | .20 | U92 Gerald Perry | 3.00 | U125 Terry Whitfield | .20 |
| U27 R. Clemens (RR) | 80.00 | U60 Bob Kearney | .20 | U93 Kirby Puckett (RR) | 70.00 | U126 Curtis Wilkerson | .35 |
| U28 Jaime Cocanower | .40 | U61 Jimmy Key (RR) | 7.00 | U94 Shane Rawley | .30 | U127 Frank Williams | .40 |
| U29 Ron Darling (RR) | 10.00 | U62 Dave Kingman | .35 | U95 Floyd Rayford | .20 | U128 Glenn Wilson | .30 |
| U30 Alvin Davis (RR) | 6.00 | U63 B. Komminsk (RR) | .45 | U96 Ron Reed | .20 | U129 John Wockenfuss | .20 |
| U31 Bob Dernier | .25 | U64 Jerry Koosman | .50 | U97 R.J. Reynolds (RR) | 1.25 | U130 Ned Yost | .20 |
| U32 Carlos Diaz | .20 | U65 Wayne Krenchicki | .20 | U98 Gene Richards | .20 | U131 Mike Young (RR) | .75 |
| U33 Mike Easler | .20 | U66 Rusty Kuntz | .20 | U99 Jose Rijo | 1.25 | U132 Checklist | .75 |

# 1985 Fleer....Complete Set of 660 Cards—Value $110.00

Features the rookie cards of Dwight Gooden, Roger Clemens, Bret Saberhagen, Eric Davis, Orel Hershiser and Kirby Puckett.

| NO. PLAYER | MINT | NO. PLAYER | MINT | NO. PLAYER | MINT | NO. PLAYER | MINT |
|---|---|---|---|---|---|---|---|
| **DETROIT TIGERS** | | 7 Barbaro Garbey (R) | .20 | 14 Rusty Kuntz | .05 | 21 Dave Rozema | .05 |
| 1 Doug Bair | .10 | 8 Kirk Gibson | .40 | 15 Chet Lemon | .05 | 22 Bill Scherrer | .05 |
| 2 Juan Berenguer | .05 | 9 John Grubb | .05 | 16 Aurelio Lopez | .05 | 23 Alan Trammell | .20 |
| 3 Dave Bergman | .05 | 10 Willie Hernandez | .15 | 17 Sid Monge | .05 | 24 Lou Whitaker | .20 |
| 4 Tom Brookens | .05 | 11 Larry Herndon | .05 | 18 Jack Morris | .20 | 25 Milt Wilcox | .05 |
| 5 Marty Castillo | .05 | 12 Howard Johnson | .50 | 19 Lance Parrish | .20 | **SAN DIEGO PADRES** | |
| 6 Darrell Evans | .10 | 13 Ruppert Jones | .05 | 20 Dan Petry | .15 | 26 Curt Bevacqua | .05 |

Card values shown here fluctuate considerably.

| NO. PLAYER | MINT |
|---|---|
| 27 Greg Booker (R) | .10 |
| 28 Bobby Brown | .05 |
| 29 Luis DeLeon | .05 |
| 30 Dave Dravecky | .05 |
| 31 Tim Flannery | .05 |
| 32 Steve Garvey | .40 |
| 33 Goose Gossage | .15 |
| 34 Tony Gwynn | 1.25 |
| 35 Greg Harris | .05 |
| 36 Andy Hawkins | .05 |
| 37 Terry Kennedy | .05 |
| 38 Craig Lefferts | .05 |
| 39 Tim Lollar | .05 |
| 40 Carmelo Martinez | .05 |
| 41 Kevin McReynolds | .60 |
| 42 Graig Nettles | .10 |
| 43 Luis Salazar | .05 |
| 44 Eric Show | .05 |
| 45 Garry Templeton | .12 |
| 46 Mark Thurmond | .05 |
| 47 Ed Whitson | .05 |
| 48 Alan Wiggins | .10 |
| **CHICAGO CUBS** | |
| 49 Rich Bordi | .05 |
| 50 Larry Bowa | .10 |
| 51 Warren Brusster | .05 |
| 52 Ron Cey | .15 |
| 53 Henry Cotto (R) | .15 |
| 54 Jody Davis | .10 |
| 55 Bob Dernier | .05 |
| 56 Leon Durham | .15 |
| 57 Dennis Eckersley | .10 |
| 58 George Frazier | .05 |
| 59 Richie Hebner | .05 |
| 60 Dave Lopes | .10 |
| 61 Gary Matthews | .10 |
| 62 Keith Moreland | .05 |
| 63 Rick Reuschel | .10 |
| 64 Dick Ruthven | .05 |
| 65 Ryne Sandberg | .40 |
| 66 Scott Sanderson | .05 |
| 67 Lee Smith | .10 |
| 68 Tim Stoddard | .05 |
| 69 Rick Sutcliffe | .20 |
| 70 Steve Trout | .05 |
| 71 Gary Woods | .05 |
| **NEW YORK METS** | |
| 72 Wally Backman | .05 |
| 73 Bruce Berenyi | .05 |
| 74 Hubie Brooks | .10 |
| 75 Kelvin Chapman (R) | .15 |
| 76 Ron Darling | 1.00 |
| 77 Sid Fernandez | .75 |
| 78 Mike Fitzgerald | .05 |
| 79 George Foster | .15 |
| 80 Brent Gaff | .05 |
| 81 Ron Gardenhire | .05 |
| 82 Dwight Gooden (R) | 9.00 |
| 83 Tom Gorman | .05 |
| 84 Danny Heep | .05 |
| 85 Keith Hernandez | .30 |
| 86 Ray Knight | .10 |
| 87 Ed Lynch | .05 |
| 88 Jose Oquendo | .12 |
| 89 Jesse Orosco | .10 |
| 90 Rafael Santana (R) | .35 |
| 91 Doug Sisk | .05 |
| 92 Rusty Staub | .10 |
| 93 Darryl Strawberry | 4.00 |
| 94 Walt Terrell | .05 |
| 95 Mookie Wilson | .05 |
| **TORONTO BLUE JAYS** | |
| 96 Jim Acker | .05 |
| 97 Willie Aikens | .05 |
| 98 Doyle Alexander | .05 |
| 99 Jesse Barfield | .35 |
| 100 George Bell | .50 |
| 101 Jim Clancy | .05 |
| 102 Dave Collins | .05 |
| 103 Tony Fernandez | .20 |
| 104 Damaso Garcia | .10 |
| 105 Jim Gott | .05 |
| 106 Alfredo Griffin | .05 |
| 107 Garth Iorg | .05 |
| 108 Roy Lee Jackson | .05 |
| 109 Cliff Johnson | .05 |

| NO. PLAYER | MINT |
|---|---|
| 110 Jimmy Key (R) | 1.00 |
| 111 Dennis Lamp | .05 |
| 112 Rick Leach | .05 |
| 113 Luis Leal | .05 |
| 114 Buck Martinez | .05 |
| 115 Lloyd Moseby | .15 |
| 116 Rance Mulliniks | .05 |
| 117 Dave Stieb | .15 |
| 118 Willie Upshaw | .10 |
| 119 Ernie Whitt | .05 |
| **NEW YORK YANKEES** | |
| 120 Mike Armstrong | .05 |
| 121 Don Baylor | .10 |
| 122 Marty Bystrom | .05 |
| 123 Rick Cerone | .05 |
| 124 Joe Cowley | .05 |
| 125 Brian Dayett | .05 |
| 126 Tim Foli | .05 |
| 127 Ray Fontenot | .05 |
| 128 Ken Griffey | .10 |
| 129 Ron Guidry | .15 |
| 130 Toby Harrah | .05 |
| 131 Jay Howell | .05 |
| 132 Steve Kemp | .05 |
| 133 Don Mattingly | 12.00 |
| 134 Bobby Meacham | .05 |
| 135 John Montefusco | .05 |
| 136 Omar Moreno | .05 |
| 137 Dale Murray | .05 |
| 138 Phil Niekro | .20 |
| 139 Mike Pagliarulo (R) | 1.50 |
| 140 Willie Randolph | .05 |
| 141 Dennis Rasmussen | .25 |
| 142 Dave Righetti | .10 |
| 143 Jose Rijo (R) | .40 |
| 144 Andre Robertson | .05 |
| 145 Bob Shirley | .05 |
| 146 Dave Winfield | .35 |
| 147 Butch Wynegar | .05 |
| **BOSTON RED SOX** | |
| 148 Gary Allenson | .05 |
| 149 Tony Armas | .10 |
| 150 Marty Barrett | .35 |
| 151 Wade Boggs | 3.50 |
| 152 Dennis Boyd | .10 |
| 153 Bill Buckner | .10 |
| 154 Mark Clear | .05 |
| 155 Roger Clemens (R) | 11.00 |
| 156 Steve Crawford | .05 |
| 157 Mike Easler | .05 |
| 158 Dwight Evans | .20 |
| 159 Rich Gedman | .10 |
| 160 Jackie Gutierrez (R) | .15 |
| 161 Bruce Hurst | .15 |
| 162 John H. Johnson | .05 |
| 163 Rick Miller | .05 |
| 164 Reid Nichols | .05 |
| 165 Al Nipper (R) | .20 |
| 166 Bob Ojeda | .10 |
| 167 Jerry Remy | .05 |
| 168 Jim Rice | .35 |
| 169 Bob Stanley | .05 |
| **BALTIMORE ORIOLES** | |
| 170 Mike Boddicker | .10 |
| 171 Al Bumbry | .05 |
| 172 Todd Cruz | .05 |
| 173 Rich Dauer | .05 |
| 174 Storm Davis | .05 |
| 175 Rick Dempsey | .05 |
| 176 Jim Dwyer | .05 |
| 177 Mike Flanagan | .05 |
| 178 Dan Ford | .05 |
| 179 Wayne Gross | .05 |
| 180 John Lowenstein | .05 |
| 181 Dennis Martinez | .10 |
| 182 Tippy Martinez | .05 |
| 183 Scott McGregor | .05 |
| 184 Eddie Murray | .50 |
| 185 Joe Nolan | .05 |
| 186 Floyd Rayford | .05 |
| 187 Cal Ripken, Jr. | .50 |
| 188 Gary Roenicke | .05 |
| 189 Lenn Sakata | .05 |
| 190 John Shelby | .05 |
| 191 Ken Singleton | .05 |

| NO. PLAYER | MINT |
|---|---|
| 192 Sammy Stewart | .05 |
| 193 Bill Swaggerty (R) | .15 |
| 194 Tom Underwood | .05 |
| 195 Mike Young | .10 |
| **KANSAS CITY ROYALS** | |
| 196 Steve Balboni | .10 |
| 197 Joe Beckwith | .05 |
| 198 Bud Black | .05 |
| 199 George Brett | .50 |
| 200 Onix Concepcion | .05 |
| 201 Mark Gubicza (R) | 1.00 |
| 202 Larry Gura | .05 |
| 203 Mark Huismann | .05 |
| 204 Dane Iorg | .05 |
| 205 Danny Jackson | 1.25 |
| 206 Charlie Leibrandt | .05 |
| 207 Hal McRae | .05 |
| 208 Darryl Motley | .05 |
| 209 Jorge Orta | .05 |
| 210 Greg Pryor | .05 |
| 211 Dan Quisenberry | .15 |
| 212 Bret Saberhagen (R) | 3.00 |
| 213 Pat Sheridan | .05 |
| 214 Don Slaught | .05 |
| 215 U.L. Washington | .05 |
| 216 John Wathan | .05 |
| 217 Frank White | .05 |
| 218 Willie Wilson | .15 |
| **ST. LOUIS CARDINALS** | |
| 219 Neil Allen | .05 |
| 220 Joaquin Andujar | .10 |
| 221 Steve Braun | .05 |
| 222 Danny Cox | .05 |
| 223 Bob Forsch | .10 |
| 224 David Green | .05 |
| 225 George Hendrick | .08 |
| 226 Tom Herr | .10 |
| 227 Ricky Horton (R) | .25 |
| 228 Art Howe | .05 |
| 229 Mike Jorgensen | .05 |
| 230 Kurt Kepshire (R) | .15 |
| 231 Jeff Lahti | .05 |
| 232 Tito Landrum | .05 |
| 233 Dave LaPoint | .05 |
| 234 Willie McGee | .30 |
| 235 Tom Nieto (R) | .15 |
| 236 Terry Pendleton (R) | .50 |
| 237 Darrell Porter | .05 |
| 238 Dave Rucker | .05 |
| 239 Lonnie Smith | .12 |
| 240 Ozzie Smith | .30 |
| 241 Bruce Sutter | .15 |
| 242 Andy Van Slyke | .40 |
| 243 Dave Von Ohlen | .05 |
| **PHILADELPHIA PHILLIES** | |
| 244 Larry Andersen | .05 |
| 245 Bill Campbell | .05 |
| 246 Steve Carlton | .30 |
| 247 Tim Corcoran | .05 |
| 248 Ivan DeJesus | .05 |
| 249 John Denny | .05 |
| 250 Bo Diaz | .05 |
| 251 Greg Gross | .05 |
| 252 Kevin Gross | .05 |
| 253 Von Hayes | .15 |
| 254 Al Holland | .05 |
| 255 Charles Hudson | .05 |
| 256 Jerry Koosman | .10 |
| 257 Joe Lefebvre | .05 |
| 258 Sixto Lezcano | .05 |
| 259 Garry Maddox | .05 |
| 260 Len Matuszek | .05 |
| 261 Tug McGraw | .10 |
| 262 Al Oliver | .10 |
| 263 Shane Rawley | .05 |
| 264 Juan Samuel | .30 |
| 265 Mike Schmidt | .45 |
| 266 Jeff Stone (R) | .30 |
| 267 Ozzie Virgil | .05 |
| 268 Glenn Wilson | .10 |
| 269 John Wockenfuss | .05 |
| **MINNESOTA TWINS** | |
| 270 Darrell Brown | .05 |
| 271 Tom Brunansky | .30 |
| 272 Randy Bush | .05 |

| NO. PLAYER | MINT |
|---|---|
| 273 John Butcher | .05 |
| 274 Bobby Castillo | .05 |
| 275 Ron Davis | .05 |
| 276 Dave Engle | .05 |
| 277 Pete Filson | .05 |
| 278 Gary Gaetti | .40 |
| 279 Mickey Hatcher | .05 |
| 280 Ed Hodge (R) | .15 |
| 281 Kent Hrbek | .35 |
| 282 Houston Jimenez | .05 |
| 283 Tim Laudner | .05 |
| 284 Rick Lysander | .05 |
| 285 Dave Meier (R) | .15 |
| 286 Kirby Puckett (R) | 10.00 |
| 287 Pat Putnam | .05 |
| 288 Ken Schrom | .05 |
| 289 Mike Smithson | .05 |
| 290 Tim Teufel | .05 |
| 291 Frank Viola | .45 |
| 292 Ron Washington | .05 |
| **CALIFORNIA ANGELS** | |
| 293 Don Aase | .05 |
| 294 Juan Beniquez | .05 |
| 295 Bob Boone | .05 |
| 296 Mike Brown | .05 |
| 297 Rod Carew | .35 |
| 298 Doug Corbett | .05 |
| 299 Doug DeCinces | .05 |
| 300 Brian Downing | .10 |
| 301 Ken Forsch | .05 |
| 302 Bobby Grich | .05 |
| 303 Reggie Jackson | .40 |
| 304 Tommy John | .15 |
| 305 Curt Kaufman (R) | .15 |
| 306 Bruce Kison | .05 |
| 307 Fred Lynn | .15 |
| 308 Gary Pettis | .10 |
| 309 Ron Romanick (R) | .30 |
| 310 Luis Sanchez | .05 |
| 311 Dick Schofield | .05 |
| 312 Daryl Sconiers | .05 |
| 313 Jim Slaton | .05 |
| 314 Derrel Thomas | .05 |
| 315 Rob Wilfong | .05 |
| 316 Mike Witt | .10 |
| 317 Geoff Zahn | .05 |
| **ATLANTA BRAVES** | |
| 318 Len Barker | .05 |
| 319 Steve Bedrosian | .10 |
| 320 Bruce Benedict | .05 |
| 321 Rick Camp | .05 |
| 322 Chris Chambliss | .10 |
| 323 Jeff Dedmon (R) | .10 |
| 324 Terry Forster | .05 |
| 325 Gene Garber | .05 |
| 326 Albert Hall (R) | .15 |
| 327 Terry Harper | .05 |
| 328 Bob Horner | .15 |
| 329 Glenn Hubbard | .05 |
| 330 Randy Johnson | .05 |
| 331 Brad Komminsk | .05 |
| 332 Rick Mahler | .05 |
| 333 Craig McMurtry | .05 |
| 334 Donnie Moore | .05 |
| 335 Dale Murphy | .60 |
| 336 Ken Oberkfell | .05 |
| 337 Pascual Perez | .05 |
| 338 Gerald Perry | .50 |
| 339 Rafael Ramirez | .05 |
| 340 Jerry Royster | .05 |
| 341 Alex Trevino | .05 |
| 342 Claudell Washington | .08 |
| **HOUSTON ASTROS** | |
| 343 Alan Ashby | .05 |
| 344 Mark Bailey | .05 |
| 345 Kevin Bass | .10 |
| 346 Enos Cabell | .05 |
| 347 Jose Cruz | .10 |
| 348 Bill Dawley | .05 |
| 349 Frank DiPino | .05 |
| 350 Bill Doran | .05 |
| 351 Phil Garner | .05 |
| 352 Bob Knepper | .10 |
| 353 Mike LaCoss | .05 |
| 354 Jerry Mumphrey | .05 |
| 355 Joe Niekro | .10 |

Card values shown here fluctuate considerably.

| NO. PLAYER | MINT |
|---|---|
| 356 Terry Puhl | .05 |
| 357 Craig Reynolds | .05 |
| 358 Vern Ruhle | .05 |
| 359 Nolan Ryan | .35 |
| 360 Joe Sambito | .05 |
| 361 Mike Scott | .25 |
| 362 Dave Smith | .05 |
| 363 Julio Solano (R) | .10 |
| 364 Dickie Thon | .05 |
| 365 Denny Walling | .05 |

**LOS ANGELES DODGERS**

| NO. PLAYER | MINT |
|---|---|
| 366 Dave Anderson | .05 |
| 367 Bob Bailor | .05 |
| 368 Greg Brock | .05 |
| 369 Carlos Diaz | .05 |
| 370 Pedro Guerrero | .25 |
| 371 Orel Hershiser (R) | 6.00 |
| 372 Rick Honeycutt | .05 |
| 373 Burt Hooton | .05 |
| 374 Ken Howell (R) | .20 |
| 375 Ken Landreaux | .05 |
| 376 Candy Maldonado | .15 |
| 377 Mike Marshall | .10 |
| 378 Tom Niedenfuer | .05 |
| 379 Alejandro Pena | .05 |
| 380 Jerry Reuss | .10 |
| 381 R.J. Reynolds (R) | .30 |
| 382 German Rivera (R) | .15 |
| 383 Bill Russell | .05 |
| 384 Steve Sax | .20 |
| 385 Mike Scioscia | .05 |
| 386 Franklin Stubbs (R) | .40 |
| 387 Fernando Valenzuela | .30 |
| 388 Bob Welch | .10 |
| 389 Terry Whitfield | .05 |
| 390 Steve Yeager | .05 |
| 391 Pat Zachry | .05 |

**MONTREAL EXPOS**

| NO. PLAYER | MINT |
|---|---|
| 392 Fred Breining | .05 |
| 393 Gary Carter | .30 |
| 394 Andre Dawson | .30 |
| 395 Miguel Dilone | .05 |
| 396 Dan Driessen | .05 |
| 397 Doug Flynn | .05 |
| 398 Terry Francona | .05 |
| 399 Bill Gullickson | .05 |
| 400 Bob James | .05 |
| 401 Chrlie Lea | .05 |
| 402 Bryan Little | .05 |
| 403 Gary Lucas | .05 |
| 404 David Palmer | .05 |
| 405 Tim Raines | .30 |
| 406 Mike Ramsey | .05 |
| 407 Jeff Reardon | .10 |
| 408 Steve Rogers | .05 |
| 409 Dan Schatzeder | .05 |
| 410 Bryn Smith | .05 |
| 411 Mike Stenhouse | .05 |
| 412 Tim Wallach | .12 |
| 413 Jim Wohlford | .05 |

**OAKLAND A'S**

| NO. PLAYER | MINT |
|---|---|
| 414 Bill Almon | .05 |
| 415 Keith Atherton | .05 |
| 416 Bruce Bochte | .05 |
| 417 Tom Burgmeier | .05 |
| 418 Ray Burris | .05 |
| 419 Bill Caudill | .05 |
| 420 Chris Codiroli | .05 |
| 421 Tim Conroy | .05 |
| 422 Mike Davis | .05 |
| 423 Jim Essian | .05 |
| 424 Mike Heath | .05 |
| 425 Rickey Henderson | .50 |
| 426 Donnie Hill | .05 |
| 427 Davè Kingman | .10 |
| 428 Bill Krueger | .05 |
| 429 Carney Lansford | .10 |
| 430 Steve McCatty | .05 |
| 431 Joe Morgan | .15 |
| 432 Dwayne Murphy | .05 |
| 433 Tony Phillips | .05 |
| 434 Lary Sorensen | .05 |
| 435 Mike Warren | .05 |
| 436 Curt Young (R) | .35 |

**CLEVELAND INDIANS**

| NO. PLAYER | MINT |
|---|---|
| 437 Luis Aponte | .05 |
| 438 Chris Bando | .05 |
| 439 Tony Bernazard | .05 |
| 440 Bert Blyleven | .10 |
| 441 Brett Butler | .05 |
| 442 Ernie Camacho | .05 |
| 443 Joe Carter | 1.50 |
| 444 Carmelo Castillo | .05 |
| 445 Jamie Easterly | .05 |
| 446 Steve Farr (R) | .25 |
| 447 Mike Fischlin | .05 |
| 448 Julio Franco | .20 |
| 449 Mel Hall | .10 |
| 450 Mike Hargrove | .05 |
| 451 Neal Heaton | .05 |
| 452 Brook Jacoby | .10 |
| 453 Mike Jeffcoat | .05 |
| 454 Don Schulze (R) | .15 |
| 455 Roy Smith (R) | .15 |
| 456 Pat Tabler | .05 |
| 457 Andre Thornton | .05 |
| 458 George Vukovich | .05 |
| 459 Tom Waddell (R) | .15 |
| 460 Jerry Willard | .05 |

**PITTSBURGH PIRATES**

| NO. PLAYER | MINT |
|---|---|
| 461 Dale Berra | .05 |
| 462 John Candelaria | .10 |
| 463 Jose DeLeon | .05 |
| 464 Doug Frobel | .05 |
| 465 Cecilio Guante | .05 |
| 466 Brian Harper | .05 |
| 467 Lee Lacy | .05 |
| 468 Bill Madlock | .10 |
| 469 Lee Mazzilli | .05 |
| 470 Larry McWilliams | .05 |
| 471 Jim Morrison | .05 |
| 472 Tony Pena | .10 |
| 473 Johnny Ray | .10 |
| 474 Rick Rhoden | .10 |
| 475 Don Robinson | .05 |
| 476 Rod Scurry | .05 |
| 477 Kent Tekulve | .05 |
| 478 Jason Thompson | .05 |
| 479 John Tudor | .10 |
| 480 Lee Tunnell | .05 |
| 481 Marvell Wynne | .05 |

**SEATTLE MARINERS**

| NO. PLAYER | MINT |
|---|---|
| 482 Salome Barojas | .05 |
| 483 Dave Beard | .05 |
| 484 Jim Beattie | .05 |
| 485 Barry Bonnell | .05 |
| 486 Phil Bradley (R) | 1.00 |
| 487 Al Cowens | .05 |
| 488 Alvin Davis (R) | 1.50 |
| 489 Dave Henderson | .05 |
| 490 Steve Henderson | .05 |
| 491 Bob Kearney | .05 |
| 492 Mark Langston (R) | 1.50 |
| 493 Larry Milbourne | .05 |
| 494 Paul Mirabella | .05 |
| 495 Mike Moore | .05 |
| 496 Edwin Nunez | .05 |
| 497 Spike Owen | .05 |
| 498 Jack Perconte | .05 |
| 499 Ken Phelps | .05 |
| 500 Jim Presley (R) | .90 |
| 501 Mike Stanton | .05 |
| 502 Bob Stoddard | .05 |
| 503 Gorman Thomas | .10 |
| 504 Ed VandeBerg | .05 |
| 505 Matt Young | .05 |

**CHICAGO WHITE SOX**

| NO. PLAYER | MINT |
|---|---|
| 506 Juan Agosto | .05 |
| 507 Harold Baines | .20 |
| 508 Floyd Bannister | .10 |
| 509 Britt Burns | .05 |
| 510 Julio Cruz | .05 |
| 511 Richard Dotson | .05 |
| 512 Jerry Dybzinski | .05 |
| 513 Carlton Fisk | .15 |
| 514 Scott Fletcher | .05 |
| 515 Jerry Hairston | .05 |
| 516 Marc Hill | .05 |
| 517 LaMarr Hoyt | .10 |
| 518 Ron Kittle | .15 |

| NO. PLAYER | MINT |
|---|---|
| 519 Rudy Law | .05 |
| 520 Vance Law | .05 |
| 521 Greg Luzinski | .10 |
| 522 Gene Nelson | .05 |
| 523 Tom Paciorek | .05 |
| 524 Ron Reed | .05 |
| 525 Bert Roberge | .05 |
| 526 Tom Seaver | .35 |
| 527 Roy Smalley | .05 |
| 528 Dan Spillner | .05 |
| 529 Mike Squires | .05 |
| 530 Greg Walker | .10 |

**CINCINNATI REDS**

| NO. PLAYER | MINT |
|---|---|
| 531 Cesar Cedeno | .10 |
| 532 Dave Concepcion | .10 |
| 533 Eric Davis (R) | 16.00 |
| 534 Nick Esasky | .05 |
| 535 Tom Foley | .05 |
| 536 John Franco (R) | 1.00 |
| 537 Brad Guden | .05 |
| 538 Tom Hume | .05 |
| 539 Wayne Krenchicki | .05 |
| 540 Andy McGaffigan | .05 |
| 541 Eddie Milner | .05 |
| 542 Ron Oester | .05 |
| 543 Bob Owchinko | .05 |
| 544 Dave Parker | .15 |
| 545 Frank Pastore | .05 |
| 546 Tony Perez | .15 |
| 547 Ted Power | .05 |
| 548 Joe Price | .05 |
| 549 Gary Redus | .05 |
| 550 Pete Rose | .75 |
| 551 Jeff Russell | .10 |
| 552 Mario Soto | .10 |
| 553 Jay Tibbs (R) | .20 |
| 554 Duane Walker | .05 |

**TEXAS RANGERS**

| NO. PLAYER | MINT |
|---|---|
| 555 Alan Bannister | .05 |
| 556 Buddy Bell | .10 |
| 557 Danny Darwin | .05 |
| 558 Charlie Hough | .05 |
| 559 Bobby Jones | .05 |
| 560 Odell Jones | .05 |
| 561 Jeff Kunkel (R) | .15 |
| 562 Mike Mason (R) | .15 |
| 563 Pete O'Brien | .10 |
| 564 Larry Parrish | .05 |
| 565 Mickey Rivers | .10 |
| 566 Billy Sample | .05 |
| 567 Dave Schmidt | .05 |
| 568 Donnie Scott (R) | .15 |
| 569 Dave Stewart | .12 |
| 570 Frank Tanana | .10 |
| 571 Wayne Tolleson | .05 |
| 572 Gary Ward | .05 |
| 573 Curtis Wilkerson | .05 |
| 574 George Wright | .05 |
| 575 Ned Yost | .05 |

**MILWAUKEE BREWERS**

| NO. PLAYER | MINT |
|---|---|
| 576 Mark Brouhard | .05 |
| 577 Mike Caldwell | .05 |
| 578 Bobby Clark | .05 |
| 579 Jaime Cocanower (R) | .15 |
| 580 Cecil Cooper | .10 |
| 581 Rollie Fingers | .15 |
| 582 Jim Gantner | .05 |
| 583 Moose Haas | .05 |
| 584 Dion James | .20 |
| 585 Pete Ladd | .05 |
| 586 Rick Manning | .05 |
| 587 Bob McClure | .05 |
| 588 Paul Molitor | .20 |
| 589 Charlie Moore | .05 |
| 590 Ben Oglivie | .05 |
| 591 Chuck Porter | .05 |
| 592 Randy Ready (R) | .25 |
| 593 Ed Romero | .05 |
| 594 Bill Schroeder | .05 |
| 595 Ray Searage | .05 |
| 596 Ted Simmons | .10 |
| 597 Jim Sundberg | .05 |
| 598 Don Sutton | .20 |
| 599 Tom Tellmann | .05 |
| 600 Rick Waits | .05 |

| NO. PLAYER | MINT |
|---|---|
| 601 Robin Yount | .30 |

**SAN FRANCISCO GIANTS**

| NO. PLAYER | MINT |
|---|---|
| 602 Dusty Baker | .05 |
| 603 Bob Brenly | .05 |
| 604 Jack Clark | .25 |
| 605 Chili Davis | .10 |
| 607 Dan Gladden (R) | .50 |
| 608 Atlee Hammaker | .05 |
| 609 Mike Krukow | .05 |
| 610 Duane Kuiper | .05 |
| 611 Bob Lacey | .05 |
| 612 Bill Laskey | .05 |
| 613 Gary Lavelle | .05 |
| 614 Johnnie LeMaster | .05 |
| 615 Jeff Leonard | .15 |
| 616 Randy Lerch | .05 |
| 617 Greg Minton | .05 |
| 618 Steve Nicosia | .05 |
| 619 Gene Richards | .05 |
| 620 Jeff Robinson (R) | .35 |
| 621 Scot Thompson | .05 |
| 622 Manny Trillo | .05 |
| 623 Brad Wellman | .05 |
| 624 Frank Williams (R) | .15 |
| 625 Joel Youngblood | .05 |

**SPECIAL CARDS**

| NO. PLAYER | MINT |
|---|---|
| 626 Ripken-In-Action | .25 |
| 627 Schmidt-In-Action | .25 |
| 628 Giving The Signs: | .05 |
| Sparky Anderson | |
| 629 AL Pitcher's Nightmare: | .25 |
| Henderson & Winfield | |
| 630 NL Pitcher's Nightmare: | .25 |
| Schmidt & Sandberg | |
| 631 NL All-Stars: | .25 |
| Strawberry, Carter, | |
| Garvey, Smith | |
| 632 All-Star Game | |
| Winning Battery: | .10 |
| Carter, Lea | |
| 633 NL Pennant Clinchers: | .15 |
| Garvey, Gossage | |
| 634 NL Rookie Phenoms: | .75 |
| Samuel, Gooden | |
| 635 Toronto's Big Guns: | .10 |
| Willie Upshaw | |
| 636 Toronto's Big Guns: | .10 |
| Lloyd Moseby | |
| 637 Al Holland | .05 |
| 638 Lee Tunnell | .05 |
| 639 500th Homer: | .25 |
| Reggie Jackson | |
| 640 4,000th Hit: Pete Rose | .50 |
| 641 Father and Son: | .25 |
| Cal Ripken & Cal, Jr. | |
| 642 Cubs: Division Champs | .05 |
| 643 Two Perfect Games and | .10 |
| One No-Hitter: | |
| Witt, Palmer, Morris | |
| 644 Willie Lozado (R), | .15 |
| Vic Mata (R) | |
| 645 Kelly Gruber (R), | .35 |
| Randy O'Neal (R) | |
| 646 Jose Roman (R), | .20 |
| Joel Skinner (R) | |
| 647 Steve Kiefer (R), | 5.00 |
| Danny Tartabull (R) | |
| 648 Rob Deer (R), | 1.00 |
| Alejandro Sanchez (R) | |
| 649 Bill Hatcher (R), | 1.00 |
| Shawon Dunston (R) | |
| 650 Ron Robinson (R), | .25 |
| Mike Bielecki (R) | |
| 651 Zane Smith (R), | .50 |
| Paul Zuvella (R) | |
| 652 Joe Hesketh (R), | 5.00 |
| Glenn Davis (R) | |
| 653 John Russell (R), | .25 |
| Steve Jeltz (R) | |
| 654 Checklist No. 1 | .08 |
| 655 Checklist No. 2 | .08 |
| 656 Checklist No. 3 | .08 |
| 657 Checklist No. 4 | .08 |
| 658 Checklist No. 5 | .08 |
| 659 Checklist No. 6 | .08 |
| 660 Checklist No. 7 | .08 |

Card values shown here fluctuate considerably.

## 1985 Fleer Traded Update....Complete Set of 132 Cards—Value $20.00

This set updates the main 1985 card set with players who had changed teams during the season, and rookies. This set features Fleer's first card of Vince Coleman, Chris Brown and Oddibe McDowell. The set was packaged in a printed box and distributed exclusively through card hobby dealers.

| NO. | PLAYER | MINT | NO. | PLAYER | MINT | NO. | PLAYER | MINT | NO. | PLAYER | MINT |
|---|---|---|---|---|---|---|---|---|---|---|---|
| U1 | Don Aase | .15 | U34 | Jerry Davis | .15 | U67 | Lee Lacy | .07 | U100 | Rick Schu | .25 |
| U2 | Bill Almon | .07 | U35 | Brian Dayett | .15 | U68 | Dave LaPoint | .07 | U101 | Larry Sheets | .50 |
| U3 | Dusty Baker | .10 | U36 | Ken Dixon (RR) | .35 | U69 | Gary Lavelle | .07 | U102 | Ron Shephard | .15 |
| U4 | Dale Berra | .07 | U37 | Tommy Dunbar | .20 | U70 | Vance Law | .07 | U103 | Nelson Simmons | .15 |
| U5 | Karl Best | .20 | U38 | M. Duncan (RR) | .30 | U71 | Manny Lee | .15 | U104 | Don Slaught | .10 |
| U6 | Tim Birtsas | .25 | U39 | Bob Fallon | .15 | U72 | Sixto Lezcano | .07 | U105 | Roy Smalley | .10 |
| U7 | Vida Blue | .07 | U40 | Brian Fisher (RR) | .35 | U73 | Tim Lollar | .07 | U106 | Lonnie Smith | .10 |
| U8 | Rich Bordi | .07 | U41 | Mike Fitzgerald | .07 | U74 | Urbano Lugo | .12 | U107 | Nate Snell | .10 |
| U9 | Daryl Boston | .20 | U42 | Ray Fontenot | .07 | U75 | Fred Lynn | .20 | U108 | Lary Sorensen | .07 |
| U10 | Hubie Brooks | .25 | U43 | Greg Gagne | .35 | U76 | Steve Lyons | .30 | U109 | Chris Speier | .07 |
| U11 | Chris Brown (RR) | .75 | U44 | Oscar Gamble | .07 | U77 | Mickey Mahler | .07 | U110 | Mike Stenhouse | .07 |
| U12 | T. Browning | 1.00 | U45 | Jim Gott | .07 | U78 | Ron Mathis | .15 | U111 | Tim Stoddard | .07 |
| U13 | Al Bumbry | .07 | U46 | David Green | .07 | U79 | Len Matuszek | .10 | U112 | John Stuper | .07 |
| U14 | Tim Burke | .35 | U47 | Alfredo Griffin | .07 | U80 | O. McDowell (RR) | .75 | U113 | Jim Sundberg | .07 |
| U15 | Ray Burris | .07 | U48 | Ozzie Guillen (RR) | .75 | U81 | R. McDowell (RR) | .90 | U114 | Bruce Sutter | .25 |
| U16 | Jeff Burroughs | .07 | U49 | Toby Harrah | .07 | U82 | Donnie Moore | .10 | U115 | Don Sutton | .50 |
| U17 | Ivan Calderon | 1.00 | U50 | Ron Hassey | .07 | U83 | Ron Musselman | .12 | U116 | Bruce Tanner | .15 |
| U18 | Jeff Calhoun | .20 | U51 | Rickey Hendersen | .75 | U84 | Al Oliver | .15 | U117 | Kent Tekulve | .10 |
| U19 | Bill Campbell | .07 | U52 | Steve Henderson | .07 | U85 | Joe Orsulak | .20 | U118 | Walt Terrell | .10 |
| U20 | Don Carman | .30 | U53 | George Hendrick | .07 | U86 | Dan Pasqua | .60 | U119 | Mickey Tettleton | .12 |
| U21 | Gary Carter | .60 | U54 | Teddy Higuera (RR) | 2.00 | U87 | Chris Pittaro | .15 | U120 | Rich Thompson | .10 |
| U22 | Bobby Castillo | .07 | U55 | Al Holland | .07 | U88 | Rick Reuschel | .12 | U121 | Louis Thornton | .10 |
| U23 | Bill Caudill | .07 | U56 | Burt Hooton | .07 | U89 | Earnie Riles (RR) | .35 | U122 | Alex Trevino | .07 |
| U24 | Rick Cerone | .07 | U57 | Jay Howell | .15 | U90 | Jerry Royster | .07 | U123 | John Tudor | .20 |
| U25 | Jack Clark | .40 | U58 | LaMarr Hoyt | .12 | U91 | Dave Rozema | .07 | U124 | Jose Uribe | .25 |
| U26 | Pat Clement | .25 | U59 | Tim Hulett | .15 | U92 | Dave Rucker | .07 | U125 | Dave Valle | .12 |
| U27 | Stewart Cliburn | .20 | U60 | Bob James | .07 | U93 | Vern Ruhle | .07 | U126 | Dave Von Ohlen | .07 |
| U28 | V. Coleman (RR) | 4.00 | U61 | Cliff Johnson | .05 | U94 | Mark Salas | .20 | U127 | Curt Wardle | .07 |
| U29 | Dave Collins | .07 | U62 | Howard Johnson | .75 | U95 | Luis Salazar | .07 | U128 | U.L. Washington | .07 |
| U30 | Fritz Connally | .20 | U63 | Ruppert Jones | .07 | U96 | Joe Sambito | .07 | U129 | Ed Whitson | .07 |
| U31 | Henry Cotto | .07 | U64 | Steve Kemp | .07 | U97 | Billy Sample | .07 | U130 | Herm Winningham | .20 |
| U32 | Danny Darwin | .07 | U65 | Bruce Kison | .07 | U98 | Alex Sanchez | .07 | U131 | Rich Yett | .12 |
| U33 | Darren Daulton | .25 | U66 | Mike LaCoss | .07 | U99 | Calvin Schiraldi | .30 | U132 | Update Checklist | .20 |

## 1986 Fleer....Complete Set of 660 Cards—Value $75.00

Features the rookie cards of Vince Coleman, Jose Canseco, Andres Galarraga and Cory Snyder. Eight different cards (C1 to C8) were printed on the bottom of gum pack display boxes or cello pack display boxes; each box contained four cards, either C1 to C4 or C5 to C8. These cards are not part of the set. *Future Hall of Famer* cards and *All-Star* cards were used as *inserts* inside gum packs and cello packs.

| NO. | PLAYER | MINT | NO. | PLAYER | MINT | NO. | PLAYER | MINT | NO. | PLAYER | MINT |
|---|---|---|---|---|---|---|---|---|---|---|---|
| | **KANSAS CITY ROYALS** | | 8 | Mark Gubicza | .05 | 16 | Darryl Motley | .05 | 24 | Frank White | .05 |
| 1 | Steve Balboni | .10 | 9 | Dane Iorg | .05 | 17 | Jorge Orta | .05 | 25 | Willie Wilson | .15 |
| 2 | Joe Beckwith | .05 | 10 | Danny Jackson | .30 | 18 | Dan Quisenberry | .15 | | **ST. LOUIS CARDINALS** | |
| 3 | Buddy Biancalana | .05 | 11 | Lynn Jones | .05 | 19 | Bret Saberhagen | .45 | 26 | Joaquin Andejar | .10 |
| 4 | Bud Black | .05 | 12 | Mike Jones | .05 | 20 | Pat Sheridan | .05 | 27 | Steve Braun | .05 |
| 5 | George Brett | .45 | 13 | Charlie Leibrandt | .05 | 21 | Lonnie Smith | .05 | 28 | Bill Campbell | .05 |
| 6 | Onix Concepcion | .05 | 14 | Hal McRae | .05 | 22 | Jim Sundberg | .05 | 29 | Cesar Cedeno | .05 |
| 7 | Steve Farr | .05 | 15 | Omar Moreno | .05 | 23 | John Wathan | .05 | 30 | Jack Clark | .25 |

Card values from this set fluctuate considerably.

| NO. | PLAYER | MINT |
|---|---|---|
| 31 | Vince Coleman (R) | 2.00 |
| 32 | Danny Cox | .10 |
| 33 | Ken Dayley | .05 |
| 34 | Ivan DeJesus | .05 |
| 35 | Bob Forsch | .05 |
| 36 | Brian Harper | .05 |
| 37 | Tom Herr | .10 |
| 38 | Ricky Horton | .05 |
| 39 | Kurt Kepshire | .05 |
| 40 | Jeff Lahti | .05 |
| 41 | Tito Landrum | .05 |
| 42 | Willie McGee | .20 |
| 43 | Tom Nieto | .05 |
| 44 | Terry Pendleton | .05 |
| 45 | Darrell Porter | .05 |
| 46 | Ozzie Smith | .20 |
| 47 | John Tudor | .15 |
| 48 | Andy Van Slyke | .30 |
| 49 | Todd Worrell (R) | .75 |

**TORONTO BLUE JAYS**

| NO. | PLAYER | MINT |
|---|---|---|
| 50 | Jim Acker | .05 |
| 51 | Doyl Alexander | .05 |
| 52 | Jesse Barfield | .20 |
| 53 | George Bell | .25 |
| 54 | Jeff Burroughs | .05 |
| 55 | Bill Caudill | .05 |
| 56 | Jim Clancy | .05 |
| 57 | Tony Fernandez | .15 |
| 58 | Tom Filer | .05 |
| 59 | Damaso Garcia | .10 |
| 60 | Tom Henke | .10 |
| 61 | Garth Iorg | .05 |
| 62 | Cliff Johnson | .05 |
| 63 | Jimmy Key | .10 |
| 64 | Dennis Lamp | .05 |
| 65 | Gary Lavelle | .05 |
| 66 | Buck Martinez | .05 |
| 67 | Lloyd Moseby | .10 |
| 68 | Rance Mulliniks | .05 |
| 69 | Al Oliver | .10 |
| 70 | Dave Stieb | .15 |
| 71 | Louis Thornton | .15 |
| 72 | Willie Upshaw | .10 |
| 73 | Ernie Whitt | .05 |

**NEW YORK METS**

| NO. | PLAYER | MINT |
|---|---|---|
| 74 | Rick Aguilera (R) | .30 |
| 75 | Wally Backman | .05 |
| 76 | Gary Carter | .30 |
| 77 | Ron Darling | .30 |
| 78 | Len Dykstra (R) | 1.00 |
| 79 | Sid Fernandez | .10 |
| 80 | George Foster | .05 |
| 81 | Dwight Gooden | 1.75 |
| 82 | Tom Gorman | .05 |
| 83 | Danny Heep | .05 |
| 84 | Keith Hernandez | .25 |
| 85 | Howard Johnson | .30 |
| 86 | Ray Knight | .05 |
| 87 | Terry Leach | .05 |
| 88 | Ed Lynch | .05 |
| 89 | Roger McDowell (R) | .45 |
| 90 | Jesse Orosco | .05 |
| 91 | Tom Paciorek | .05 |
| 92 | Ronn Reynolds | .15 |
| 93 | Rafael Santana | .05 |
| 94 | Doug Sisk | .05 |
| 95 | Rusty Staub | .10 |
| 96 | Darryl Strawberry | 1.50 |
| 97 | Mookie Wilson | .05 |

**NEW YORK YANKEES**

| NO. | PLAYER | MINT |
|---|---|---|
| 98 | Neil Allen | .05 |
| 99 | Don Baylor | .10 |
| 100 | Dale Berra | .05 |
| 101 | Rich Bordi | .05 |
| 102 | Marty Bystrom | .05 |
| 103 | Joe Cowley | .05 |
| 104 | Brian Fisher (R) | .25 |
| 105 | Ken Griffey | .05 |
| 106 | Ron Guidry | .15 |
| 107 | Ron Hassey | .05 |
| 108 | Rickey Henderson | .45 |
| 109 | Dan Mattingly | 4.00 |
| 110 | Bobby Meacham | .05 |
| 111 | John Montefusco | .05 |
| 112 | Phil Niekro | .15 |
| 113 | Mike Pagliarulo | .10 |
| 114 | Dan Pasqua | .15 |
| 115 | Willie Randolph | .05 |
| 116 | Dave Righetti | .10 |
| 117 | Andre Robertson | .05 |
| 118 | Billy Sample | .05 |
| 119 | Bob Shirley | .05 |
| 120 | Ed Whitson | .05 |
| 121 | Dave Winfield | .30 |
| 122 | Butch Wynegar | .05 |

**LOS ANGELES DODGERS**

| NO. | PLAYER | MINT |
|---|---|---|
| 123 | Dave Anderson | .05 |
| 124 | Bob Bailor | .05 |
| 125 | Greg Brock | .05 |
| 126 | Enos Cabell | .05 |
| 127 | Bobby Castillo | .05 |
| 128 | Carlos Diaz | .05 |
| 129 | Mariano Duncan (R) | .25 |
| 130 | Pedro Guerrero | .25 |
| 131 | Orel Hershiser | .60 |
| 132 | Rick Honeycutt | .05 |
| 133 | Ken Howell | .05 |
| 134 | Ken Landreaux | .05 |
| 135 | Bill Madlock | .10 |
| 136 | Candy Maldonado | .10 |
| 137 | Mike Marshall | .10 |
| 138 | Len Matuszek | .05 |
| 139 | Tom Niedenfuer | .05 |
| 140 | Alejandro Pena | .05 |
| 141 | Jerry Reuss | .05 |
| 142 | Bill Russell | .05 |
| 143 | Steve Sax | .15 |
| 144 | Mike Scioscia | .05 |
| 145 | Fernando Valenzuela | .30 |
| 146 | Bob Welch | .05 |
| 147 | Terry Whitfield | .05 |

**CALIFORNIA ANGELS**

| NO. | PLAYER | MINT |
|---|---|---|
| 148 | Juan Beniquez | .05 |
| 149 | Bob Boone | .05 |
| 150 | John Candelaria | .05 |
| 151 | Rod Carew | .30 |
| 152 | Stewart Cliburn (R) | .25 |
| 153 | Doug DeCinces | .10 |
| 154 | Brian Downing | .05 |
| 155 | Ken Forsch | .05 |
| 156 | Craig Gerber (R) | .15 |
| 157 | Bobby Grich | .10 |
| 158 | George Hendrick | .05 |
| 159 | Al Holland | .05 |
| 160 | Reggie Jackson | .30 |
| 161 | Ruppert Jones | .05 |
| 162 | Urbano Lugo (R) | .15 |
| 163 | Kirk McCaskill (R) | .35 |
| 164 | Donnie Moore | .05 |
| 165 | Gary Pettis | .05 |
| 166 | Ron Romanick | .05 |
| 167 | Dick Schofield | .05 |
| 168 | Darly Sconiers | .05 |
| 169 | Jim Slaton | .05 |
| 170 | Don Sutton | .20 |
| 171 | Mike Witt | .10 |

**CINCINNATI REDS**

| NO. | PLAYER | MINT |
|---|---|---|
| 172 | Buddy Bell | .10 |
| 173 | Tom Browning | .15 |
| 174 | Dave Concepcion | .10 |
| 175 | Eric Davis | 3.00 |
| 176 | Bo Diaz | .05 |
| 177 | Nick Esasky | .05 |
| 178 | John Franco | .10 |
| 179 | Tom Hume | .05 |
| 180 | Wayne Krenchicki | .05 |
| 181 | Andy McGaffigan | .05 |
| 182 | Eddie Milner | .05 |
| 183 | Ron Oester | .05 |
| 184 | Dave Parker | .15 |
| 185 | Frank Pastore | .05 |
| 186 | Tony Perez | .10 |
| 187 | Ted Power | .05 |
| 188 | Joe Price | .05 |
| 189 | Gary Redus | .05 |
| 190 | Ron Robinson | .05 |
| 191 | Pete Rose | .60 |
| 192 | Mario Soto | .10 |
| 193 | John Stuper | .05 |
| 194 | Jay Tibbs | .05 |
| 195 | Dave Van Gorder | .05 |
| 196 | Max Venable | .05 |

**CHICAGO WHITE SOX**

| NO. | PLAYER | MINT |
|---|---|---|
| 197 | Juan Agosto | .05 |
| 198 | Harold Baines | .15 |
| 199 | Floyd Bannister | .05 |
| 200 | Britt Burns | .05 |
| 201 | Julio Cruz | .05 |
| 202 | Joel Davis (R) | .20 |
| 203 | Richard Dotson | .05 |
| 204 | Carlton Fisk | .15 |
| 205 | Scott Fletcher | .05 |
| 206 | Ozzie Guillen (R) | .50 |
| 207 | Jerry Hairston | .05 |
| 208 | Tim Hulett | .05 |
| 209 | Bob James | .05 |
| 210 | Ron Kittle | .10 |
| 211 | Rudy Law | .05 |
| 212 | Bryan Little | .05 |
| 213 | Gene Nelson | .05 |
| 214 | Reid Nichols | .05 |
| 215 | Luis Salazar | .05 |
| 216 | Tom Seaver | .35 |
| 217 | Dan Spillner | .05 |
| 218 | Bruce Tanner (R) | .15 |
| 219 | Greg Walker | .10 |
| 220 | Dave Wehrmeister | .05 |

**DETROIT TIGERS**

| NO. | PLAYER | MINT |
|---|---|---|
| 221 | Juan Berenguer | .05 |
| 222 | Dave Bergman | .05 |
| 223 | Tom Brookens | .05 |
| 224 | Darrell Evans | .10 |
| 225 | Barbaro Garbey | .05 |
| 226 | Kirk Gibson | .30 |
| 227 | John Grubb | .05 |
| 228 | Willie Hernandez | .15 |
| 229 | Larry Herndon | .05 |
| 230 | Chet Lemon | .05 |
| 231 | Aurelio Lopez | .05 |
| 232 | Jack Morris | .20 |
| 233 | Randy O'Neal | .05 |
| 234 | Lance Parrish | .15 |
| 235 | Dan Petry | .15 |
| 236 | Alex Sanchez | .05 |
| 237 | Bill Scherrer | .05 |
| 238 | Nelson Simmons (R) | .10 |
| 239 | Frank Tanana | .05 |
| 240 | Walt Terrell | .05 |
| 241 | Alan Trammell | .20 |
| 242 | Lou Whitaker | .15 |
| 243 | Milt Wilcox | .05 |

**MONTREAL EXPOS**

| NO. | PLAYER | MINT |
|---|---|---|
| 244 | Hubie Brooks | .10 |
| 245 | Tim Burke (R) | .25 |
| 246 | Andre Dawson | .25 |
| 247 | Mike Fitzgerald | .05 |
| 248 | Terry Francona | .05 |
| 249 | Bill Gullickson | .05 |
| 250 | Joe Hesketh | .10 |
| 251 | Bill Laskey | .05 |
| 252 | Vance Law | .05 |
| 253 | Charlie Lea | .05 |
| 254 | Gary Lucas | .05 |
| 255 | David Palmer | .05 |
| 256 | Tim Raines | .25 |
| 257 | Jeff Reardon | .10 |
| 258 | Bert Roberge | .05 |
| 259 | Dan Schatzeder | .05 |
| 260 | Bryn Smith | .05 |
| 261 | Randy St. Claire | .05 |
| 262 | Scot Thompson | .05 |
| 263 | Tim Wallach | .10 |
| 264 | U.L. Washington | .05 |
| 265 | Mitch Webster (R) | .35 |
| 266 | Herm Winningham (R) | .15 |
| 267 | Floyd Youmans (R) | .50 |

**BALTIMORE ORIOLES**

| NO. | PLAYER | MINT |
|---|---|---|
| 268 | Don Aase | .05 |
| 269 | Mike Boddicker | .10 |
| 270 | Rich Dauer | .05 |
| 271 | Storm Davis | .05 |
| 272 | Rick Dempsey | .05 |
| 273 | Ken Dixon | .05 |
| 274 | Jim Dwyer | .05 |
| 275 | Mike Flanagan | .05 |
| 276 | Wayne Gross | .05 |
| 277 | Lee Lacy | .05 |
| 278 | Fred Lynn | .15 |
| 279 | Tippy Martinez | .05 |
| 280 | Dennis Martinez | .05 |
| 281 | Scott McGregor | .05 |
| 282 | Eddie Murray | .30 |
| 283 | Floyd Rayford | .05 |
| 284 | Cal Ripken, Jr. | .35 |
| 285 | Gary Roenicke | .05 |
| 286 | Larry Sheets | .35 |
| 287 | John Shelby | .05 |
| 288 | Nate Snell (R) | .15 |
| 289 | Sammy Stewart | .05 |
| 290 | Alan Wiggins | .05 |
| 291 | Mike Young | .10 |

**HOUSTON ASTROS**

| NO. | PLAYER | MINT |
|---|---|---|
| 292 | Alan Ashby | .05 |
| 293 | Mark Bailey | .05 |
| 294 | Kevin Bass | .05 |
| 295 | Jeff Calhoun (R) | .15 |
| 296 | Jose Cruz | .10 |
| 297 | Glenn Davis | .60 |
| 298 | Bill Dawley | .05 |
| 299 | Frank DiPino | .05 |
| 300 | Bill Doran | .05 |
| 301 | Phil Garner | .05 |
| 302 | Jeff Heathcock (R) | .15 |
| 303 | Charlie Kerfeld (R) | .20 |
| 304 | Bob Knepper | .05 |
| 305 | Ron Mathis (R) | .15 |
| 306 | Jerry Mumphrey | .05 |
| 307 | Jim Pankovits | .05 |
| 308 | Terry Puhl | .05 |
| 309 | Craig Reynolds | .05 |
| 310 | Nolan Ryan | .25 |
| 311 | Mike Scott | .25 |
| 312 | Dave Smith | .05 |
| 313 | Dickie Thon | .05 |
| 314 | Denny Walling | .05 |

**SAN DIEGO PADRES**

| NO. | PLAYER | MINT |
|---|---|---|
| 315 | Kurt Bevacqua | .05 |
| 316 | Al Bumbry | .05 |
| 317 | Jerry Davis | .05 |
| 318 | Luis DeLeon | .05 |
| 319 | Dave Dravecky | .05 |
| 320 | Tim Flannery | .05 |
| 321 | Steve Garvey | .35 |
| 322 | Goose Gossage | .15 |
| 323 | Tony Gwynn | .60 |
| 324 | Andy Hawkins | .05 |
| 325 | LaMarr Hoyt | .05 |
| 326 | Roy Lee Jackson | .05 |
| 327 | Terry Kennedy | .05 |
| 328 | Craig Lefferts | .05 |
| 329 | Carmelo Martinez | .05 |
| 330 | Lance McCullers (R) | .30 |
| 331 | Kevin McReynolds | .20 |
| 332 | Graig Nettles | .10 |
| 333 | Jerry Royster | .05 |
| 334 | Eric Show | .05 |
| 335 | Tim Stoddard | .05 |
| 336 | Garry Templeton | .08 |
| 337 | Mark Thurmond | .05 |
| 338 | Ed Wojna (R) | .15 |

**BOSTON RED SOX**

| NO. | PLAYER | MINT |
|---|---|---|
| 339 | Tony Armas | .10 |
| 340 | Marty Barrett | .05 |
| 341 | Wade Boggs | 2.50 |
| 342 | Dennis Boyd | .10 |
| 343 | Bill Buckner | .10 |
| 344 | Mark Clear | .05 |
| 345 | Roger Clemens | 2.50 |
| 346 | Steve Crawford | .05 |
| 347 | Mike Easler | .05 |
| 348 | Dwight Evans | .12 |
| 349 | Rich Gedman | .08 |
| 350 | Jackie Gutierrez | .05 |
| 351 | Glenn Hoffman | .05 |
| 352 | Bruce Hurst | .10 |
| 353 | Bruce Kison | .05 |
| 354 | Tim Lollar | .05 |
| 355 | Steve Lyons | .05 |
| 356 | Al Nipper | .05 |
| 357 | Bob Ojeda | .05 |
| 358 | Jim Rice | .25 |
| 359 | Bob Stanley | .05 |
| 360 | Mike Trujillo (R) | .10 |

Card values from this set fluctuate considerably.

| NO. PLAYER | MINT |
|---|---|

**CHICAGO CUBS**
| 361 | Thad Bosley | .05 |
| 362 | Warren Brusstar | .05 |
| 363 | Ron Cey | .10 |
| 364 | Jody Davis | .07 |
| 365 | Bob Dernier | .05 |
| 366 | Shawon Dunston | .05 |
| 367 | Leon Durham | .15 |
| 368 | Dennis Eckersley | .05 |
| 369 | Ray Fontenot | .05 |
| 370 | George Frazier | .05 |
| 371 | Bill Hatcher | .15 |
| 372 | Dave Lopes | .05 |
| 373 | Gary Matthews | .05 |
| 374 | Ron Meredith (R) | .15 |
| 375 | Keith Moreland | .05 |
| 376 | Reggie Patterson | .05 |
| 377 | Dick Ruthven | .05 |
| 378 | Ryne Sandberg | .20 |
| 379 | Scott Sanderson | .05 |
| 380 | Lee Smith | .10 |
| 381 | Lary Sorensen | .05 |
| 382 | Chris Speier | .05 |
| 383 | Rick Sutcliffe | .15 |
| 384 | Steve Trout | .05 |
| 385 | Gary Woods | .05 |

**MINNESOTA TWINS**
| 386 | Bert Blyleven | .10 |
| 387 | Tom Brunansky | .15 |
| 388 | Randy Bush | .05 |
| 389 | John Butcher | .05 |
| 390 | Ron Davis | .05 |
| 391 | Dave Engle | .05 |
| 392 | Frank Eufemia | .15 |
| 393 | Pete Filson | .05 |
| 394 | Gary Gaetti | .20 |
| 395 | Greg Gagne | .05 |
| 396 | Mickey Hatcher | .05 |
| 397 | Kent Hrbek | .20 |
| 398 | Tim Laudner | .05 |
| 399 | Rick Lysander | .05 |
| 400 | Dave Meier | .05 |
| 401 | Kirby Puckett | 1.50 |
| 402 | Mark Salas | .05 |
| 403 | Ken Schrom | .05 |
| 404 | Roy Smalley | .05 |
| 405 | Mike Smithson | .05 |
| 406 | Mike Stenhouse | .05 |
| 407 | Tim Teufel | .05 |
| 408 | Frank Viola | .30 |
| 409 | Ron Washington | .05 |

**OAKLAND A'S**
| 410 | Keith Atherton | .05 |
| 411 | Dusty Baker | .05 |
| 412 | Tim Birtsas (R) | .15 |
| 413 | Bruce Bochte | .05 |
| 414 | Chris Codiroli | .05 |
| 415 | Dave Collins | .05 |
| 416 | Mike Davis | .05 |
| 417 | Alfredo Griffin | .05 |
| 418 | Mike Heath | .05 |
| 419 | Steve Henderson | .05 |
| 420 | Donnie Hill | .05 |
| 421 | Jay Howell | .10 |
| 422 | Tommy John | .10 |
| 423 | Dave Kingman | .10 |
| 424 | Bill Krueger | .05 |
| 425 | Rick Langford | .05 |
| 426 | Carney Lansford | .10 |
| 427 | Steve McCatty | .05 |
| 428 | Dwayne Murphy | .05 |
| 429 | Steve Ontiveros (R) | .15 |
| 430 | Tony Phillips | .05 |
| 431 | Jose Rijo | .05 |
| 432 | Mickey Tettleton (R) | .15 |

**PHILADELPHIA PHILLIES**
| 433 | Luis Aguayo | .05 |
| 434 | Larry Andersen | .05 |
| 435 | Steve Carlton | .30 |
| 436 | Don Carman (R) | .25 |
| 437 | Tim Corcoran | .05 |
| 438 | Darren Daulton (R) | .15 |
| 439 | John Denny | .08 |
| 440 | Tom Foley | .05 |
| 441 | Greg Gross | .05 |
| 442 | Kevin Gross | .05 |
| 443 | Von Hayes | .15 |

| 444 | Charles Hudson | .05 |
| 445 | Garry Maddox | .05 |
| 446 | Shane Rawley | .05 |
| 447 | Dave Rucker | .05 |
| 448 | John Russell | .05 |
| 449 | Juan Samuel | .10 |
| 450 | Mike Schmidt | .40 |
| 451 | Rick Schu | .05 |
| 452 | Dave Shipanoff (R) | .15 |
| 453 | Dave Stewart | .05 |
| 454 | Jeff Stone | .05 |
| 455 | Kent Tekulve | .05 |
| 456 | Ozzie Virgil | .05 |
| 457 | Glenn Wilson | .10 |

**SEATTLE MARINERS**
| 458 | Jim Beattie | .05 |
| 459 | Karl Best | .10 |
| 460 | Barry Bonnell | .05 |
| 461 | Phil Bradley | .20 |
| 462 | Ivan Calderon (R) | 1.00 |
| 463 | Al Cowens | .05 |
| 464 | Alvin Davis | .20 |
| 465 | Dave Henderson | .05 |
| 466 | Bob Kearney | .05 |
| 467 | Mark Langston | .15 |
| 468 | Bob Long | .05 |
| 469 | Mike Moore | .05 |
| 470 | Edwin Nunez | .05 |
| 471 | Spike Owen | .05 |
| 472 | Jack Perconte | .05 |
| 473 | Jim Presley | .25 |
| 474 | Donnie Scott | .05 |
| 475 | Bill Swift | .05 |
| 476 | Danny Tartabull | .65 |
| 477 | Gorman Thomas | .10 |
| 478 | Roy Thomas | .05 |
| 479 | Ed VandeBerg | .05 |
| 480 | Frank Wills (R) | .15 |
| 481 | Matt Young | .05 |

**MILWAUKEE BREWERS**
| 482 | Ray Burris | .05 |
| 483 | Jaime Cocanower | .05 |
| 484 | Cecil Cooper | .15 |
| 485 | Danny Darwin | .05 |
| 486 | Rollie Fingers | .15 |
| 487 | Jim Gantner | .05 |
| 488 | Bob Gibson | .05 |
| 489 | Moose Haas | .05 |
| 490 | Teddy Higuera (R) | 1.00 |
| 491 | Paul Householder | .05 |
| 492 | Pete Ladd | .05 |
| 493 | Rick Manning | .05 |
| 494 | Bob McClure | .05 |
| 495 | Paul Molitor | .20 |
| 496 | Charlie Moore | .05 |
| 497 | Ben Oglivie | .05 |
| 498 | Randy Ready | .05 |
| 499 | Earnie Riles (R) | .30 |
| 500 | Ed Romero | .05 |
| 501 | Bill Schroeder | .05 |
| 502 | Ray Searage | .05 |
| 503 | Ted Simmons | .10 |
| 504 | Pete Vuckovich | .05 |
| 505 | Rick Waits | .05 |
| 506 | Robin Yount | .25 |

**ATLANTA BRAVES**
| 507 | Len Barker | .05 |
| 508 | Steve Bedrosian | .15 |
| 509 | Bruce Benedict | .05 |
| 510 | Rick Camp | .05 |
| 511 | Rick Cerone | .05 |
| 512 | Chris Chambliss | .05 |
| 513 | Jeff Dedmon | .05 |
| 514 | Terry Forster | .05 |
| 515 | Gene Garber | .05 |
| 516 | Terry Harper | .05 |
| 517 | Bob Horner | .15 |
| 518 | Glenn Hubbard | .05 |
| 519 | Joe Johnson (R) | .20 |
| 520 | Brad Komminsk | .05 |
| 521 | Rick Mahler | .05 |
| 522 | Dale Murphy | .50 |
| 523 | Ken Oberkfell | .05 |
| 524 | Pascual Perez | .05 |
| 525 | Gerald Perry | .20 |
| 526 | Rafael Ramirez | .05 |

| 527 | Steve Shields (R) | .15 |
| 528 | Zane Smith | .10 |
| 529 | Bruce Sutter | .15 |
| 530 | Milt Thompson (R) | .50 |
| 531 | Claudell Washington | .05 |
| 532 | Paul Zuvella | .05 |

**S.F. GIANTS**
| 533 | Vida Blue | .05 |
| 534 | Bob Brenly | .05 |
| 535 | Chris Brown (R) | .50 |
| 536 | Chili Davis | .10 |
| 537 | Mark Davis | .05 |
| 538 | Rob Deer | .15 |
| 539 | Dan Driessen | .05 |
| 540 | Scott Garrelts | .05 |
| 541 | Dan Gladden | .05 |
| 542 | Jim Gott | .05 |
| 543 | David Green | .05 |
| 544 | Atlee Hammaker | .05 |
| 545 | Mike Jeffcoat | .05 |
| 546 | Mike Krukow | .05 |
| 547 | Dave LaPoint | .05 |
| 548 | Jeff Leonard | .05 |
| 549 | Greg Minton | .05 |
| 550 | Alex Trevino | .05 |
| 551 | Manny Trillo | .05 |
| 552 | Jose Uribe (R) | .35 |
| 553 | Brad Wellman | .05 |
| 554 | Frank Williams | .05 |
| 555 | Joel Youngblood | .05 |

**TEXAS RANGERS**
| 556 | Alan Bannister | .05 |
| 557 | Glenn Brummer | .05 |
| 558 | Steve Buechele (R) | .25 |
| 559 | Jose Guzman | .35 |
| 560 | Toby Harrah | .05 |
| 561 | Greg Harris | .05 |
| 562 | Dwayne Henry (R) | .15 |
| 563 | Burt Hooton | .05 |
| 564 | Charlie Hough | .05 |
| 565 | Mike Mason | .05 |
| 566 | Oddibe McDowell | .30 |
| 567 | Dickie Noles | .05 |
| 568 | Pete O'Brien | .15 |
| 569 | Larry Parrish | .05 |
| 570 | Dave Rozema | .05 |
| 571 | Dave Schmidt | .05 |
| 572 | Don Slaught | .05 |
| 573 | Wayne Tolleson | .05 |
| 574 | Duane Walker | .05 |
| 575 | Gary Ward | .05 |
| 576 | Chris Welsh | .05 |
| 577 | Curtis Wilkerson | .05 |
| 578 | George Wright | .05 |

**CLEVELAND INDIANS**
| 579 | Chris Bando | .05 |
| 580 | Tony Bernazard | .05 |
| 581 | Brett Butler | .10 |
| 582 | Ernie Camacho | .05 |
| 583 | Joe Carter | .30 |
| 584 | Carmello Castillo | .05 |
| 585 | Jamie Easterly | .05 |
| 586 | Julio Franco | .10 |
| 587 | Mel Hall | .05 |
| 588 | Mike Hargrove | .05 |
| 589 | Neal Heaton | .05 |
| 590 | Brook Jacoby | .10 |
| 591 | Otis Nixon (R) | .20 |
| 592 | Jerry Reed (R) | .15 |
| 593 | Vern Ruhle | .05 |
| 594 | Pat Tabler | .05 |
| 595 | Rich Thompson (R) | .15 |
| 596 | Andre Thornton | .05 |
| 597 | Dave Von Ohlen | .05 |
| 598 | George Vuckovich | .05 |
| 599 | Tom Waddell | .05 |
| 600 | Curt Wardle (R) | .15 |
| 601 | Jerry Willard | .05 |

**PITTSBURGH PIRATES**
| 602 | Bill Almon | .05 |
| 603 | Mike Bielecki | .05 |
| 604 | Sid Bream | .05 |
| 605 | Mike Brown | .05 |
| 606 | Pat Clements (R) | .25 |
| 607 | Jose DeLeon | .05 |
| 608 | Denny Gonzalez | .05 |

| 609 | Cecilio Guante | .05 |
| 610 | Steve Kemp | .05 |
| 611 | Sam Khalifa (R) | .15 |
| 612 | Lee Mazzilli | .05 |
| 613 | Larry McWilliams | .05 |
| 614 | Jim Morrison | .05 |
| 615 | Joe Orsulak (R) | .20 |
| 616 | Tony Pena | .10 |
| 617 | Johnny Ray | .10 |
| 618 | Rick Reuschel | .05 |
| 619 | R.J. Reynolds | .05 |
| 620 | Rick Rhoden | .05 |
| 621 | Don Robinson | .05 |
| 622 | Jason Thompson | .05 |
| 623 | Lee Tunnell | .05 |
| 624 | Jim Winn | .05 |
| 625 | Marvell Wynne | .05 |

**SPECIAL CARDS**
| 626 | Gooden in Action | .50 |
| 627 | Mattingly in Action | 1.25 |
| 628 | Pete Rose—4,192 | .50 |
| 629 | 3,000 Career Hits: Rod Carew | .25 |
| 630 | 300 Career Wins: Tom Seaver, Phil Niekro | .20 |
| 631 | Ouch: Don Baylor | .15 |
| 632 | Instant Offense: Raines and Strawberry | .30 |
| 633 | Shortstops Supreme: Trammell & Ripken | .25 |
| 634 | Boggs and "Hero" Wade Boggs, George Brett | .50 |
| 635 | Braves Dynamic Duo: Horner and Murphy | .30 |
| 636 | Cardinal Ignitors: Coleman and McGee | .35 |
| 637 | Terror on Basepaths: Vince Coleman | .35 |
| 638 | Charlie Hustle and Dr. K: Rose and Gooden | .75 |
| 639 | 1984 and 1985 AL Batting Champs: Mattingly and Boggs | 1.50 |
| 640 | NL West Sluggers: Murphy, Garvey, Parker | .30 |
| 641 | Staff Aces: Valenzuela & Gooden | .35 |
| 642 | Blue Jay Stoppers: Key and Stieb | .10 |
| 643 | AL All-Star Backstops: Fisk & Gedman | .10 |
| 644 | Benito Santiago (R) and Gene Walter (R) | 4.50 |
| 645 | Mike Woodard (R) and Colin Ward (R) | .15 |
| 646 | Kal Daniels (R) and Paul O'Neill (R) | 5.00 |
| 647 | Fred Toliver (R) and Andres Galarraga (R) | 4.50 |
| 648 | Bob Kipper (R) and Curt Ford (R) | .25 |
| 649 | Eric Plunk (R) and Jose Canseco (R) | 30.00 |
| 650 | Gus Polidor (R) and Mark McLemore (R) | .20 |
| 651 | Rob Woodward (R) and Mickey Brantley (R) | 1.25 |
| 652 | Billy Joe Robidoux (R) and Mark Funderburk (R) | .25 |
| 653 | Cecil Fielder (R) and Cory Snyder | 4.00 |
| 654 | Checklist No. 1 | .08 |
| 655 | Checklist No. 2 | .08 |
| 656 | Checklist No. 3 | .08 |
| 657 | Checklist No. 4 | .08 |
| 658 | Checklist No. 5 | .08 |
| 659 | Checklist No. 6 | .08 |
| 660 | Checklist No. 7 | .08 |

**Cards Printed on Gum Boxes**
| C1 | K.C. Royals Logo | .12 |
| C2 | George Brett | .50 |
| C3 | Ozzie Guillen | .30 |
| C4 | Dale Murphy | .75 |
| C5 | St. L. Cardinals Logo | .12 |
| C6 | Tom Browning | .25 |
| C7 | Gary Carter | .30 |
| C8 | Carlton Fisk | .20 |

Card values shown here fluctuate considerably.

# 1986 Fleer Traded Update... Complete Set of 132 Cards—Value $22.00

This set updates the main 1986 card set with players who had changed teams during the season, and rookies. This set features Fleer's first card of Wally Joyner, Ruben Sierra, and Will Clark. The set was packaged in a printed box and distributed exclusively through card hobby dealers.

| NO. PLAYER | MINT | NO. PLAYER | MINT | NO. PLAYER | MINT | NO. PLAYER | MINT |
|---|---|---|---|---|---|---|---|
| U1 Mike Aldrete (RR) | .60 | U34 John Denny | .07 | U67 Dennis Leonard | .07 | U100 Angel Salazar | .07 |
| U2 Andy Allanson | .20 | U35 Jim DeShaies | .40 | U68 Steve Lombardozzi | .20 | U101 Joe Sambito | .07 |
| U3 Nell Allen | .07 | U36 Doug Drabek | .35 | U69 Aurelio Lopez | .07 | U102 Billy Sample | .07 |
| U4 Joaquin Andujar | .07 | U37 Mike Easler | .07 | U70 Miceky Mahler | .07 | U103 Dave Schmidt | .07 |
| U5 Paul Assenmacher | .25 | U38 Mark Eichhorn | .25 | U71 Candy Maldonado | .25 | U104 Ken Schrom | .07 |
| U6 Scott Bailes | .15 | U39 Dave Engle | .07 | U72 Roger Mason | .15 | U105 Ruben Sierra (RR) | 2.00 |
| U7 Jay Baller | .15 | U40 Mike Fischlin | .07 | U73 Greg Mathews | .30 | U106 Ted Simmons | .10 |
| U8 Scott Bankhead | .15 | U41 Scott Fletcher | .07 | U74 Andy McGaffigan | .10 | U107 Sammy Stewart | .07 |
| U9 Bill Bathe | .15 | U42 Terry Forster | .07 | U75 Joel McKeon | .15 | U108 Kurt Stillwell (RR) | .40 |
| U10 Don Baylor | .12 | U43 Terry Francona | .07 | U76 Kevin Mitchell (RR) | .50 | U109 Dale Sveum | .35 |
| U11 Billy Beane | .15 | U44 Andres Galarraga | 1.00 | U77 Bill Mooneyham | .12 | U110 Tim Teufel | .07 |
| U12 Steve Bedrosian | .15 | U45 Lee Guetterman | .25 | U78 Omar Moreno | .07 | U111 Bob Tewksbury | .30 |
| U13 Juan Beniquez | .10 | U46 Bill Gullickson | .07 | U79 Jerry Mumphrey | .07 | U112 Andres Thomas | .20 |
| U14 Barry Bonds (RR) | 1.25 | U47 Jackie Gutierrez | .07 | U80 Al Newman | .12 | U113 Jason Thompson | .12 |
| U15 Bobby Bonilla (RR) | 1.50 | U48 Moose Haas | .07 | U81 Phil Niekro | .35 | U114 Milt Thompson | .07 |
| U16 Rich Bordi | .07 | U49 Bily Hatcher | .25 | U82 Randy Niemann | .07 | U115 Rob Thompson | .40 |
| U17 Bill Campbell | .07 | U50 Mike Heath | .10 | U83 Juan Nieves | .25 | U116 Jay Tibbs | .07 |
| U18 Tom Candiotti | .10 | U51 Guy Hofman | .07 | U84 Bob Ojeda | .20 | U117 Fred Toliver | .07 |
| U19 John Cangelosi | .25 | U52 Tom Hume | .07 | U85 Rick Ownbey | .07 | U118 Wayne Tolleson | .07 |
| U20 Jose Canseco (RR) | 8.00 | U53 Pete Incaviglia (RR) | 1.00 | U86 Tom Paciorek | .07 | U119 Alex Trevino | .07 |
| U21 Chuck Cary | .15 | U54 Dane Iorg | .07 | U87 David Palmer | .07 | U120 Manny Trillo | .07 |
| U22 Juan Castillo | .15 | U55 Chris James (RR) | 1.00 | U88 Jeff Parrett | .35 | U121 Ed Vande Berg | .07 |
| U23 Rick Cerone | .07 | U56 Stan Javier | .35 | U89 Pat Perry | .25 | U122 Ozzie Virgil | .07 |
| U24 John Cerutti | .15 | U57 Tommy John | .15 | U90 Dan Plesac | .35 | U123 Tony Walker | .20 |
| U25 Will Clark (RR) | 3.00 | U58 Tracy Jones | .60 | U91 Darrell Porter | .07 | U124 Gene Walter | .15 |
| U26 Marc Clear | .07 | U59 Wally Joyner | 3.00 | U92 Luis Quinones | .15 | U125 Duane Ward | .25 |
| U27 Darnell Coles | .15 | U60 Wayne Krenchicki | .07 | U93 Rey Quinonez | .40 | U126 Jerry Willard | .07 |
| U28 Dave Collins | .07 | U61 John Kruk (RR) | .50 | U94 Gary Redus | .12 | U127 Mitch Williams | .20 |
| U29 Tim Conroy | .07 | U62 Mike LaCoss | .07 | U95 Jeff Reed | .12 | U128 Reggie Williams | .25 |
| U30 Ed Correa | .25 | U63 Pete Ladd | .07 | U96 Bip Roberts | .20 | U129 Bobby Witt (RR) | .40 |
| U31 Joe Cowley | .07 | U64 Dave LaPoint | .07 | U97 Billy Joe Robidoux | .25 | U130 Marvell Wynne | .07 |
| U32 Bill Dawley | .07 | U65 Mike LaValliere | .25 | U98 Gary Roenicke | .07 | U131 Steve Yeager | .10 |
| U33 Rob Deer | .25 | U66 Rudy Law | .07 | U99 Ron Roenicke | .07 | U132 Checklist | .15 |

# 1987 Fleer....Complete Set of 660 Cards—Value $50.00

Features the rookie cards of Kevin Seitzer, Will Clark, Wally Joyner, Ruben Sierra and Pete Incaviglia. The back of each card features a *scouting report*. Sixteen different cards (C1 to C16) were printed on the bottom of gum boxes. These cards are not part of the set. Factory sealed 660-card vending sets included a 12-card World Series set as a bonus. Each gum and cello pack included a randomly distributed card from a 12-card All-Star set.

| NO. PLAYER | MINT | NO. PLAYER | MINT | NO. PLAYER | MINT | NO. PLAYER | MINT |
|---|---|---|---|---|---|---|---|
| **NEW YORK METS** | | 10 Ed Hearn (R) | .15 | 20 Jesse Orosco | .07 | 29 Wade Boggs | 1.50 |
| 1 Rick Aguilera | .15 | 11 Danny Heep | .05 | 21 Rafael Santana | .07 | 30 Oil Can Boyd | .12 |
| 2 R. Anderson (R) | .15 | 12 Keith Hernandez | .25 | 22 Doug Sisk | .07 | 31 Bill Buckner | .08 |
| 3 Wally Backman | .07 | 13 Howard Johnson | .20 | 23 Darryl Strawberry | 1.00 | 32 Roger Clemens | 1.25 |
| 4 Gary Carter | .25 | 14 Ray Knight | .07 | 24 Tim Teufel | .07 | 33 Steve Crawford | .07 |
| 5 Ron Darling | .20 | 15 Lee Mazzilli | .07 | 25 Mookie Wilson | .07 | 34 Dwight Evans | .10 |
| 6 Len Dykstra | .20 | 16 Roger McDowell | .15 | **BOSTON RED SOX** | | 35 Rich Gedman | .07 |
| 7 Kevin Elster (R) | .75 | 17 Kevin Mitchell (R) | .35 | 26 Toni Armas | .07 | 36 Dave Henderson | .07 |
| 8 Sid Fernandez | .20 | 18 Randy Niemann | .05 | 27 Marty Barrett | .12 | 37 Bruce Hurst | .10 |
| 9 Dwight Gooden | 1.00 | 19 Bob Ojeda | .15 | 28 Don Baylor | .12 | 38 Tim Lollar | .07 |

Card values from this set fluctuate considerably.

| NO. | PLAYER | MINT |
|---|---|---|
| 39 | Al Nipper | .07 |
| 40 | Spike Owen | .07 |
| 41 | Jim Rice | .30 |
| 42 | Ed Romero | .07 |
| 43 | Joe Sambito | .07 |
| 44 | Calvin Schiraldi | .15 |
| 45 | Tom Seaver | .30 |
| 46 | Jeff Sellers (R) | .15 |
| 47 | Bob Stanley | .07 |
| 48 | Sammy Stewart | .07 |
| **HOUSTON ASTROS** | | |
| 49 | Larry Andersen | .05 |
| 50 | Alan Ashby | .05 |
| 51 | Keven Bass | .05 |
| 52 | Jeff Calhoun | .05 |
| 53 | Jose Cruz | .10 |
| 54 | Danny Darwin | .05 |
| 55 | Glenn Davis | .35 |
| 56 | Jim Deshaies (R) | .35 |
| 57 | Bill Doran | .05 |
| 58 | Phil Garner | .05 |
| 59 | Billy Hatcher | .10 |
| 60 | Charlie Kerfeld | .12 |
| 61 | Bob Knepper | .08 |
| 62 | Dave Lopes | .08 |
| 63 | Aurelio Lopez | .05 |
| 64 | Jim Pankovits | .05 |
| 65 | Terry Puhl | .08 |
| 66 | Craig Reynolds | .08 |
| 67 | Nolan Ryan | .30 |
| 68 | Mike Scott | .20 |
| 69 | Dave Smith | .05 |
| 70 | Dickie Thon | .05 |
| 71 | Tony Walker (R) | .15 |
| 72 | Denny Walling | .05 |
| **CALIFORNIA ANGELS** | | |
| 73 | Bob Boone | .05 |
| 74 | Rick Burleson | .05 |
| 75 | John Candelaria | .08 |
| 76 | Doug Corbett | .05 |
| 77 | Doug DeCinces | .08 |
| 78 | Brian Downing | .05 |
| 79 | Chuck Finley (R) | .15 |
| 80 | Terry Forster | .05 |
| 81 | Bobby Grich | .05 |
| 82 | George Hendrick | .05 |
| 83 | Jack Howell | .05 |
| 84 | Reggie Jackson | .35 |
| 85 | Ruppert Jones | .05 |
| 86 | Wally Joyner (R) | 2.00 |
| 87 | Gary Lucas | .05 |
| 88 | Kirk McCaskill | .12 |
| 89 | Donnie Moore | .05 |
| 90 | Gary Pettis | .05 |
| 91 | Vern Ruhle | .05 |
| 92 | Dick Schofield | .05 |
| 93 | Don Sutton | .12 |
| 94 | Rob Wilfong | .05 |
| 95 | Mike Witt | .12 |
| **NEW YORK YANKEES** | | |
| 96 | Doug Drabek (R) | .40 |
| 97 | Mike Easler | .07 |
| 98 | Mike Fischlin | .07 |
| 99 | Brian Fisher | .07 |
| 100 | Ron Guidry | .15 |
| 101 | Rickey Henderson | .35 |
| 102 | Tommy John | .15 |
| 103 | Ron Kittle | .10 |
| 104 | Don Mattingly | 2.25 |
| 105 | Bobby Meacham | .07 |
| 106 | Joe Niekro | .12 |
| 107 | Mike Pagliarulo | .20 |
| 108 | Dan Pasqua | .15 |
| 109 | Willie Randolph | .10 |
| 110 | Dennis Rasmussen | .10 |
| 111 | Dave Righetti | .15 |
| 112 | Gary Roenicke | .07 |
| 113 | Rod Scurry | .07 |
| 114 | Bob Shirley | .07 |
| 115 | Joel Skinner | .07 |
| 116 | Tim Stoddard | .07 |
| 117 | Bob Tewksbury (R) | .25 |
| 118 | Wayne Tolleson | .07 |
| 119 | C. Washington | .07 |
| 120 | Dave Winfield | .30 |
| **TEXAS RANGERS** | | |
| 121 | Steve Buechele | .05 |

| NO. | PLAYER | MINT |
|---|---|---|
| 122 | Ed Correa (R) | .25 |
| 123 | Scott Fletcher | .05 |
| 124 | Joe Guzman | .15 |
| 125 | Toby Harrah | .05 |
| 126 | Greg Harris | .05 |
| 127 | Charlie Hough | .05 |
| 128 | Pete Incaviglia (R) | 1.25 |
| 129 | Mike Mason | .05 |
| 130 | Oddibe McDowell | .25 |
| 131 | Dale Mohorcic (R) | .15 |
| 132 | Pete O'Brien | .10 |
| 133 | Tom Paciorek | .05 |
| 134 | Larry Parrish | .05 |
| 135 | Geno Petralli | .05 |
| 136 | Darrell Porter | .05 |
| 137 | Jeff Russell | .05 |
| 138 | Ruben Sierra (R) | 1.25 |
| 139 | Don Slaught | .05 |
| 140 | Gary Ward | .05 |
| 141 | Curtis Wilkerson | .05 |
| 142 | Mitch Williams (R) | .25 |
| 143 | Bobby Witt (R) | .30 |
| **DETROIT TIGERS** | | |
| 144 | Dave Bergman | .05 |
| 145 | Tom Brookens | .05 |
| 146 | Bill Campbell | .05 |
| 147 | Chuck Cary (R) | .20 |
| 148 | Darnell Coles | .05 |
| 149 | Dave Collins | .05 |
| 150 | Darrell Evans | .12 |
| 151 | Kirk Gibson | .30 |
| 152 | John Grubb | .05 |
| 153 | Willie Hernandez | .05 |
| 154 | Larry Herndon | .05 |
| 155 | Eric King (R) | .15 |
| 156 | Chet Lemon | .07 |
| 157 | Dwight Lowry (R) | .20 |
| 158 | Jack Morris | .15 |
| 159 | Randy O'Neal | .05 |
| 160 | Lance Parrish | .20 |
| 161 | Dan Petry | .10 |
| 162 | Pat Sheridan | .05 |
| 163 | Jim Slaton | .05 |
| 164 | Frank Tanana | .05 |
| 165 | Walt Terrell | .05 |
| 166 | Mark Thurmond | .05 |
| 167 | Alan Trammell | .20 |
| 168 | Lou Whitaker | .12 |
| **PHILADELPHIA PHILLIES** | | |
| 169 | Luis Aguayo | .05 |
| 170 | Steve Bedrosian | .15 |
| 171 | Don Carman | .05 |
| 172 | Darren Daulton | .05 |
| 173 | Greg Gross | .05 |
| 175 | Von Hayes | .12 |
| 176 | Charles Hudson | .05 |
| 177 | Tom Hume | .05 |
| 178 | Steve Jeltz | .05 |
| 179 | Mike Maddux (R) | .30 |
| 180 | Shane Rawley | .05 |
| 181 | Gary Redus | .05 |
| 182 | Ron Roenicke | .05 |
| 183 | Bruce Ruffin (R) | .25 |
| 184 | John Russell | .05 |
| 185 | Juan Samuel | .15 |
| 186 | Dan Schatzeder | .05 |
| 187 | Mike Schmidt | .35 |
| 188 | Rick Schu | .05 |
| 189 | Jeff Stone | .05 |
| 190 | Kent Tekulve | .05 |
| 191 | Milt Thompson | .05 |
| 192 | Glenn Wilson | .05 |
| **CINCINNATI REDS** | | |
| 193 | Buddy Bell | .10 |
| 194 | Tom Browning | .07 |
| 195 | Sal Butera | .05 |
| 196 | Dave Concepcion | .07 |
| 197 | Kal Daniels | 1.00 |
| 198 | Eric Davis | 1.50 |
| 199 | John Denny | .05 |
| 200 | Bo Diaz | .05 |
| 201 | Nick Esasky | .05 |
| 202 | John Franco | .10 |
| 203 | Bill Gullickson | .05 |
| 204 | Barry Larkin (R) | 1.25 |
| 205 | Eddie Milner | .05 |
| 206 | Rob Murphy (R) | .20 |

| NO. | PLAYER | MINT |
|---|---|---|
| 207 | Ron Oester | .05 |
| 208 | Dave Parker | .15 |
| 209 | Tony Perez | .12 |
| 210 | Ted Power | .05 |
| 211 | Joe Price | .05 |
| 212 | Ron Robinson | .05 |
| 213 | Pete Rose (Mgr.) | .50 |
| 214 | Mario Soto | .05 |
| 215 | Kurt Stillwell (R) | .30 |
| 216 | Max Venable | .05 |
| 217 | Chris Welsh | .05 |
| 218 | Carl Willis (R) | .15 |
| **TORONTO BLUE JAYS** | | |
| 219 | Jesse Barfield | .15 |
| 220 | George Bell | .30 |
| 221 | Bill Caudill | .05 |
| 222 | John Cerutti (R) | .25 |
| 223 | Jim Clancy | .05 |
| 224 | Mark Eichhorn (R) | .25 |
| 225 | Tony Fernandez | .15 |
| 226 | Damaso Garcia | .07 |
| 227 | Kelly Gruber | .05 |
| 228 | Tom Henke | .10 |
| 229 | Garth Iorg | .05 |
| 230 | Joe Johnson | .07 |
| 231 | Cliff Johnson | .05 |
| 232 | Jimmy Key | .10 |
| 233 | Dennis Lamp | .05 |
| 234 | Rick Leach | .05 |
| 235 | Buck Martinez | .05 |
| 236 | Lloyd Moseby | .07 |
| 237 | Rance Mulliniks | .05 |
| 238 | Dave Stieb | .10 |
| 239 | Willie Upshaw | .05 |
| 240 | Ernie Whitt | .05 |
| **CLEVELAND INDIANS** | | |
| 241 | Andy Allanson (R) | .15 |
| 242 | Scott Bailes (R) | .15 |
| 243 | Chris Bando | .05 |
| 244 | Tony Bernazard | .05 |
| 245 | John Butcher | .05 |
| 246 | Brett Butler | .05 |
| 247 | Ernie Camacho | .05 |
| 248 | Tom Candiotti | .05 |
| 249 | Joe Carter | .20 |
| 250 | Carmen Castillo | .05 |
| 251 | Julio Franco | .10 |
| 252 | Mel Hall | .05 |
| 253 | Brook Jacoby | .05 |
| 254 | Phil Niekro | .15 |
| 255 | Otis Nixon | .05 |
| 256 | Dickie Noles | .05 |
| 257 | Bryan Oelkers | .05 |
| 258 | Ken Schrom | .05 |
| 259 | Don Schulze | .05 |
| 260 | Cory Snyder | .75 |
| 261 | Pat Tabler | .10 |
| 262 | Andre Thornton | .05 |
| 263 | Rich Yett (R) | .10 |
| **SAN FRANCISCO GIANTS** | | |
| 264 | Mike Aldrete (R) | .50 |
| 265 | Juan Berenguer | .05 |
| 266 | Vida Blue | .05 |
| 267 | Bob Brenly | .05 |
| 268 | Chris Brown | .05 |
| 269 | Will Clark (R) | 2.00 |
| 270 | Chili Davis | .10 |
| 271 | Mark Davis | .05 |
| 272 | Kelly Downs (R) | .30 |
| 273 | Scott Garrelts | .05 |
| 274 | Dan Gladden | .05 |
| 275 | Mike Krukow | .05 |
| 276 | Randy Kutcher (R) | .15 |
| 277 | Mike LaCoss | .05 |
| 278 | Jeff Leonard | .05 |
| 279 | Candy Maldonado | .15 |
| 280 | Roger Mason | .05 |
| 281 | Bob Melvin | .05 |
| 282 | Greg Minton | .05 |
| 283 | Jeff Robinson | .05 |
| 284 | Harry Spilman | .05 |
| 285 | Rob Thompson (R) | .30 |
| 286 | Jose Uribe | .05 |
| 287 | Frank Williams | .05 |
| 288 | Joel Youngblood | .05 |
| **ST. LOUIS CARDINALS** | | |
| 289 | Jack Clark | .20 |

| NO. | PLAYER | MINT |
|---|---|---|
| 290 | Vince Coleman | .40 |
| 291 | Tim Conroy | .05 |
| 292 | Danny Cox | .05 |
| 293 | Ken Dayley | .05 |
| 294 | Curt Ford | .08 |
| 295 | Bob Forsch | .05 |
| 296 | Tom Herr | .05 |
| 297 | Ricky Horton | .05 |
| 298 | Clint Hurdle | .05 |
| 299 | Jeff Lahti | .05 |
| 300 | Steve Lake | .05 |
| 301 | Tito Landrum | .05 |
| 302 | Mike LaValliere (R) | .25 |
| 303 | Greg Mathews (R) | .25 |
| 304 | Willie McGee | .15 |
| 305 | Jose Oquendo | .05 |
| 306 | Terry Pendleton | .05 |
| 307 | Pat Perry | .10 |
| 308 | Ozzie Smith | .20 |
| 309 | Ray Soff (R) | .15 |
| 310 | John Tudor | .10 |
| 311 | Andy Van Slyke | .20 |
| 312 | Todd Worrell | .25 |
| **MONTREAL EXPOS** | | |
| 313 | Dann Bilardello | .05 |
| 314 | Hubie Brooks | .10 |
| 315 | Tim Burke | .05 |
| 316 | Andre Dawson | .25 |
| 317 | Mike Fitzgerald | .05 |
| 318 | Tom Foley | .05 |
| 319 | Andres Galarraga | .35 |
| 320 | Joe Hesketh | .05 |
| 321 | Wallace Johnson | .05 |
| 322 | Wayne Krenchicki | .05 |
| 323 | Vance Law | .05 |
| 324 | Dennis Martinez | .05 |
| 325 | Bob McClure | .05 |
| 326 | Andy McGaffigan | .05 |
| 327 | Al Newman (R) | .15 |
| 328 | Tim Raines | .30 |
| 329 | Jeff Reardon | .10 |
| 330 | Luis Rivera (R) | .15 |
| 331 | Bob Sebra (R) | .15 |
| 332 | Bryn Smith | .05 |
| 333 | Jay Tibbs | .05 |
| 334 | Tim Wallach | .05 |
| 335 | Mitch Webster | .12 |
| 336 | John Wohlford | .05 |
| 337 | Floyd Youmans | .15 |
| **MILWAUKEE BREWERS** | | |
| 338 | Chris Bosio (R) | .15 |
| 339 | Glenn Braggs (R) | .35 |
| 340 | Rick Cerone | .05 |
| 341 | Mark Clear | .05 |
| 342 | B. Clutterbuck (R) | .15 |
| 343 | Cecil Cooper | .15 |
| 344 | Rob Deer | .20 |
| 345 | Jim Gantner | .05 |
| 346 | Ted Higuera | .20 |
| 347 | J.H. Johnson | .05 |
| 348 | Tim Leary | .25 |
| 349 | Rick Manning | .05 |
| 350 | Paul Molitor | .15 |
| 351 | Charlie Moore | .05 |
| 352 | Juan Nieves | .15 |
| 353 | Ben Oglivie | .05 |
| 354 | Dan Plesac (R) | .25 |
| 355 | Ernest Riles | .05 |
| 356 | Billy Joe Robidoux | .10 |
| 357 | Bill Schroeder | .05 |
| 358 | Dale Sveum (R) | .20 |
| 359 | Gorman Thomas | .10 |
| 360 | Bill Wegman | .05 |
| 361 | Robin Yount | .25 |
| **KC ROYALS** | | |
| 362 | Steve Balboni | .07 |
| 363 | Scott Bankhead | .20 |
| 364 | Buddy Biancalana | .05 |
| 365 | Bud Black | .05 |
| 366 | George Brett | .40 |
| 367 | Steve Farr | .05 |
| 368 | Mark Gubicza | .05 |
| 369 | Bo Jackson (R) | 1.50 |
| 370 | Danny Jackson | .05 |
| 371 | Mike Kingery (R) | .20 |
| 372 | Rudy Law | .05 |
| 373 | Charlie Leibrandt | .05 |

Card values from this set fluctuate considerably.

| NO. PLAYER | MINT |
|---|---|
| 374 Dennis Leonard | .05 |
| 375 Hal McRae | .05 |
| 376 Jorge Orta | .05 |
| 377 Jamie Quirk | .05 |
| 378 Dan Quisenberry | .10 |
| 379 Bret Saberhagen | .20 |
| 380 Angel Salazar | .05 |
| 381 Lonnie Smith | .05 |
| 382 Jim Sundberg | .05 |
| 383 Frank White | .05 |
| 384 Willie Wilson | .12 |
| **OAKLAND A's** | |
| 385 Joaquin Andujar | .05 |
| 386 Doug Bair | .05 |
| 387 Dusty Baker | .05 |
| 388 Bruce Bochte | .05 |
| 389 Jose Canseco | 5.00 |
| 390 Chris Codiroli | .05 |
| 391 Mike Davis | .05 |
| 392 Alfredo Griffin | .05 |
| 393 Moose Haas | .05 |
| 394 Donnie Hill | .05 |
| 395 Jay Howell | .05 |
| 396 Dave Kingman | .12 |
| 397 Carney Lansford | .05 |
| 398 David Leiper | .12 |
| 399 B. Mooneyham (R) | .15 |
| 400 Dwayne Murphy | .05 |
| 401 Steve Ontiveros | .05 |
| 402 Tony Phillips | .05 |
| 403 Eric Plunk | .05 |
| 404 Jose Rijo | .05 |
| 405 Terry Steinbach (R) | .50 |
| 406 Dave Stewart | .05 |
| 407 Mickey Tettleton | .05 |
| 408 Dave Von Ohlen | .05 |
| 409 Jerry Willard | .05 |
| 410 Curt Young | .05 |
| **SAN DIEGO PADRES** | |
| 411 Bruce Bochy | .05 |
| 412 Dave Dravecky | .05 |
| 413 Tim Flannery | .05 |
| 414 Steve Garvey | .30 |
| 415 Goose Gossage | .12 |
| 416 Tony Gwynn | .50 |
| 417 Andy Hawkins | .05 |
| 418 LaMarr Hoyt | .05 |
| 419 Terry Kennedy | .05 |
| 420 John Kruk (R) | .50 |
| 421 Dave LaPoint | .05 |
| 422 Craig Letters | .05 |
| 423 Carmelo Martinez | .05 |
| 424 Lance McCullers | .12 |
| 425 Kevin McReynolds | .30 |
| 426 Graig Nettles | .10 |
| 427 Bip Roberts (R) | .15 |
| 428 Jerry Royster | .05 |
| 429 Benito Santiago | .75 |
| 430 Eric Show | .07 |
| 431 Bob Stoddard | .05 |
| 432 Garry Templeton | .05 |
| 433 Gene Walter | .10 |
| 434 Ed Whitson | .05 |
| 435 Marvell Wynne | .05 |
| **LA DODGERS** | |
| 436 Dave Anderson | .05 |
| 437 Greg Brock | .05 |
| 438 Enos Cabell | .05 |
| 439 Mariano Duncan | .12 |
| 440 Pedro Guerrero | .20 |
| 441 Orel Hershiser | .40 |
| 442 Rick Honeycutt | .05 |
| 443 Ken Howell | .05 |
| 444 Ken Landreaux | .05 |
| 445 Bill Madlock | .08 |
| 446 Mike Marshall | .08 |
| 447 Len Matuszek | .05 |
| 448 Tom Niedenfuer | .05 |
| 449 Alejandro Pena | .05 |
| 450 Dennis Powell | .05 |
| 451 Jerry Reuss | .05 |
| 452 Bill Russell | .05 |
| 453 Steve Sax | .12 |
| 454 Mike Scioscia | .05 |
| 455 Franklin Stubbs | .05 |
| 456 Alex Trevino | .05 |
| 457 F. Valenzuela | .25 |
| 458 Ed Vande Berg | .05 |

| NO. PLAYER | MINT |
|---|---|
| 459 Bob Welch | .05 |
| 460 Reggie Williams (R) | .20 |
| **BALTIMORE ORIOLES** | |
| 461 Don Aase | .05 |
| 462 Juan Beniquez | .05 |
| 463 Mike Boddicker | .05 |
| 464 Juan Bonilla | .05 |
| 465 Rich Bordi | .05 |
| 466 Storm Davis | .05 |
| 467 Rick Dempsey | .05 |
| 468 Ken Dixon | .05 |
| 469 Jim Dwyer | .05 |
| 470 Mike Flanagan | .05 |
| 471 Jackie Gutierrez | .05 |
| 472 Brad Havens | .05 |
| 473 Lee Lacy | .05 |
| 474 Fred Lynn | .15 |
| 475 Scott McGregor | .08 |
| 476 Eddie Murray | .30 |
| 477 Tom O'Malley | .05 |
| 478 Cal Ripken, Jr. | .30 |
| 479 Larry Sheets | .10 |
| 480 John Shelby | .05 |
| 481 Nate Snell | .05 |
| 482 Jim Traber | .10 |
| 483 Mike Young | .05 |
| **CHICAGO WHITE SOX** | |
| 484 Neil Allen | .05 |
| 485 Harold Baines | .15 |
| 486 Floyd Bannister | .05 |
| 487 Daryl Boston | .05 |
| 488 Ivan Calderon | .20 |
| 489 John Cangelosi (R) | .25 |
| 490 Steve Carlton | .25 |
| 491 Joe Cowley | .05 |
| 492 Julio Cruz | .05 |
| 493 Bill Dawley | .05 |
| 494 Jose DeLeon | .05 |
| 495 Richard Dotson | .05 |
| 496 Carlton Fisk | .10 |
| 497 Ozzie Guillen | .12 |
| 498 Jerry Hairston | .05 |
| 499 Ron Hassey | .05 |
| 500 Tim Hulett | .05 |
| 501 Bob James | .05 |
| 502 Steve Lyons | .05 |
| 503 Joel McKeon (R) | .15 |
| 504 Gene Nelson | .05 |
| 505 Dave Schmidt | .05 |
| 506 Ray Searage | .05 |
| 507 Bobby Thigpen (R) | .25 |
| 508 Greg Walker | .05 |
| **ATLANTA BRAVES** | |
| 509 Jim Acker | .05 |
| 510 Doyle Alexander | .05 |
| 511 P. Assenmacher (R) | .15 |
| 512 Bruce Benedict | .05 |
| 513 Chris Chambliss | .08 |
| 514 Jeff Dedmon | .05 |
| 515 Gene Garber | .05 |
| 516 Ken Griffey | .08 |
| 517 Terry Harper | .05 |
| 518 Bob Horner | .15 |
| 519 Glenn Hubbard | .05 |
| 520 Rick Mahler | .05 |
| 521 Omar Moreno | .05 |
| 522 Dale Murphy | .40 |
| 523 Ken Oberkfell | .05 |
| 524 Ed Olwine (R) | .15 |
| 525 David Palmer | .05 |
| 526 Rafael Ramirez | .05 |
| 527 Billy Sample | .05 |
| 528 Ted Simmons | .05 |
| 529 Zane Smith | .05 |
| 530 Bruce Sutter | .12 |
| 531 Andres Thomas (R) | .25 |
| 532 Ozzie Virgil | .05 |
| **MINNESOTA TWINS** | |
| 533 A. Anderson (R) | .30 |
| 534 Keith Atherton | .05 |
| 535 Billy Beane | .05 |
| 536 Bert Blyleven | .05 |
| 537 Tom Brunansky | .20 |
| 538 Randy Bush | .05 |
| 539 George Frazier | .05 |
| 540 Gary Gaetti | .25 |
| 541 Greg Gagne | .05 |
| 542 Mickey Hatcher | .05 |

| NO. PLAYER | MINT |
|---|---|
| 543 Neal Heaton | .05 |
| 544 Kent Hrbek | .15 |
| 545 Roy Lee Jackson | .05 |
| 546 Tim Laudner | .05 |
| 547 Steve Lombardozzi | .05 |
| 548 Mark Portugal (R) | .15 |
| 549 Kirby Puckett | .50 |
| 550 Jeff Reed | .05 |
| 551 Mark Salas | .05 |
| 552 Roy Smalley | .05 |
| 553 Mike Smithson | .05 |
| 554 Frank Viola | .15 |
| **CHICAGO CUBS** | |
| 555 Thad Bosley | .05 |
| 556 Ron Cey | .05 |
| 557 Jody Davis | .10 |
| 558 Ron Davis | .05 |
| 559 Bob Dernier | .05 |
| 560 Frank DiPino | .05 |
| 561 Shawon Dunston | .07 |
| 562 Leon Durham | .10 |
| 563 Dennis Eckersley | .05 |
| 564 Terry Francona | .05 |
| 565 Dave Gumpert | .05 |
| 566 Guy Hoffman | .05 |
| 567 Ed Lynch | .05 |
| 568 Gary Matthews | .05 |
| 569 Keith Moreland | .05 |
| 570 Jamie Moyer (R) | .20 |
| 571 Jerry Mumphrey | .05 |
| 572 Ryne Sandberg | .20 |
| 573 Scott Sanderson | .05 |
| 574 Lee Smith | .05 |
| 575 Chris Speier | .05 |
| 576 Rick Sutcliffe | .07 |
| 577 Manny Trillo | .05 |
| 578 Steve Trout | .05 |
| **SEATTLE MARINERS** | |
| 579 Karl Best | .05 |
| 580 Scott Bradley | .10 |
| 581 Phil Bradley | .05 |
| 582 Mickey Brantley | .05 |
| 583 Mike Brown | .05 |
| 584 Alvin Davis | .10 |
| 585 L. Guetterman (R) | .15 |
| 586 Mark Huismann | .05 |
| 587 Bob Kearney | .05 |
| 588 Pete Ladd | .05 |
| 589 Mark Langston | .10 |
| 590 Mike Moore | .05 |
| 591 Mike Morgan | .05 |
| 592 John Moses | .05 |
| 593 Ken Phelps | .05 |
| 594 Jim Presley | .20 |
| 595 Rey Quinonez (R) | .20 |
| 596 Harold Reynolds | .05 |
| 597 Billy Swift | .05 |
| 598 Danny Tartabull | .50 |
| 599 Steve Yeager | .05 |
| 600 Matt Young | .05 |
| **PITTSBURGH PIRATES** | |
| 601 Bill Almon | .05 |
| 602 Rafael Belliard (R) | .15 |
| 603 Mike Bielecki (R) | .05 |
| 604 Barry Bonds (R) | 1.00 |
| 605 Bobby Bonilla (R) | 1.25 |
| 606 Sid Bream | .05 |
| 607 Mike Brown | .05 |
| 608 Pat Clements | .05 |
| 609 Mike Diaz (R) | .20 |
| 610 Cecilio Guante | .05 |
| 611 Barry Jones (R) | .15 |
| 612 Bob Kipper | .05 |
| 613 Larry McWilliams | .05 |
| 614 Jim Morrison | .05 |
| 615 Joe Orsulak | .05 |
| 616 Junior Ortiz | .05 |
| 617 Tony Pena | .05 |
| 618 Johnny Ray | .05 |
| 619 Rick Reuschel | .05 |
| 620 R.J. Reynolds | .05 |
| 621 Rick Rhoden | .05 |
| 622 Don Robinson | .05 |
| 623 Bob Walk | .05 |
| 624 Jim Winn | .05 |
| **SPECIAL CARDS** | |
| 625 Youthful Power: | .60 |
| P. Incaviglia, J. Canseco | |

| NO. PLAYER | MINT |
|---|---|
| 626 300 Game Winners: | .15 |
| D. Sutton, P. Niekro | |
| 627 A.L. Firemen: | .15 |
| D. Righetti, D. Asse | |
| 628 Rookie All-Stars: | 1.25 |
| W. Joyner, J. Canseco | |
| 629 Magic Mets: | .75 |
| G. Carter, S. Fernandez, | |
| D. Gooden, K. Hernandez, | |
| D. Strawberry | |
| 630 N.L. Best Righties: | .15 |
| M. Scott, M. Krukow | |
| 631 Sensational Southpaws: | .15 |
| F. Venezuela, J. Franco | |
| 632 4 HR's in Game: | .15 |
| Bob Horner | |
| 633 Pitcher's Nightmare: | .60 |
| J. Canseco, J. Rice, | |
| K. Puckett | |
| 634 All-Star Battery: | .50 |
| G. Carter, R. Clemens | |
| 635 4,000 Strikeouts: | .20 |
| S. Carlton | |
| 636 Big Bats at First Sack: | .20 |
| G. Davis, E. Murray | |
| 637 On Base: | .10 |
| W. Boggs, K. Hernandez | |
| 638 Sluggers from Left Side: | 1.00 |
| D. Mattingly, | |
| D. Strawberry | |
| 639 Former MVP's: | .20 |
| D. Parker, R. Sandberg | |
| 640 Dr. K. & Super K: | .75 |
| D. Gooden, R. Clemens | |
| 641 A.L. West Stoppers: | .15 |
| M. Witt, C. Hough | |
| 642 Doubles & Triples: | .15 |
| J. Samuel, T. Raines | |
| 643 Outfielders with Punch: | .15 |
| H. Baines, J. Barfield | |
| **No. 644 to 653—Major** | |
| **League Prospects** | |
| 644 D. Clark (R) and | |
| G. Swindell (R) | 1.00 |
| 645 Ron Karkovice (R) and | |
| Russ Morman (R) | .25 |
| 646 Devon White (R) and | |
| Willie Fraser (R) | 1.25 |
| 647 Mike Stanley (R) and | |
| Jerry Browne (R) | .30 |
| 648 Dave Magadan (R) and | |
| Phil Lombardi (R) | .60 |
| 649 Jose Gonzalez (R) and | |
| Ralph Bryant (R) | .30 |
| 650 Jimmy Jones (R) and | |
| Randy Asadoor (R) | .25 |
| 651 Tracy Jones (R) and | |
| Marvin Freeman (R) | .60 |
| 652 John Stefero (R) and | |
| Kevin Seitzer (R) | 9.00 |
| 653 Rob Nelson (R) and | |
| Steve Fireovid (R) | .30 |
| 654 Checklist No. 1 | .08 |
| 655 Checklist No. 2 | .08 |
| 656 Checklist No. 3 | .08 |
| 657 Checklist No. 4 | .08 |
| 658 Checklist No. 5 | .08 |
| 659 Checklist No. 6 | .08 |
| 660 Checklist No. 7 | .08 |
| | |
| **Cards Printed on Gum Boxes** | |
| C 1 Mets logo | .10 |
| C 2 Jesse Barfield | .15 |
| C 3 George Brett | .40 |
| C 4 Dwight Gooden | .50 |
| C 5 Red Sox logo | .10 |
| C 6 Keith Hernandez | .15 |
| C 7 Wally Joyner | .50 |
| C 8 Dale Murphy | .40 |
| C 9 Astros logo | .10 |
| C10 Dave Parker | .15 |
| C11 Kirby Puckett | .35 |
| C12 Dave Righetti | .15 |
| C13 Angels logo | .15 |
| C14 Ryne Sandberg | .15 |
| C15 Mike Schmidt | .35 |
| C16 Robin Yount | .20 |

Card values from this set fluctuate considerably.

# 1987 Fleer Traded Update. . . .Complete Set of 132 Cards—Value $13.00

This set updates the main 1987 card set with players who had changed teams during the season, and rookies. This set features Fleer's first card of Ellis Burks, Mike Greenwell, Mark McGwire, and Matt Nokes. The set was packaged in a printed box and distributed exclusively through card dealers.

| NO. PLAYER | MINT |
|---|---|
| U1 Scott Bankhead | .07 |
| U2 Eric Bell | .15 |
| U3 Juan Beniquez | .07 |
| U4 Juan Berenguer | .07 |
| U5 Mike Birkbeck | .10 |
| U6 Randy Bockus | .12 |
| U7 Rod Booker | .07 |
| U8 Thad Bosley | .07 |
| U9 Greg Brock | .10 |
| U10 Bob Brower | .12 |
| U11 Chris Brown | .10 |
| U12 Jerry Browne | .07 |
| U13 Ralph Bryant | .07 |
| U14 De Wayne Buice | .10 |
| U15 Ellis Burks (RR) | 1.50 |
| U16 Casey Candaele | .20 |
| U17 Steve Carlton | .15 |
| U18 Juan Castillo | .07 |
| U19 Chuck Crim | .15 |
| U20 Mark Davidson | .15 |
| U21 Mark Davis | .07 |
| U22 Storm Davis | .15 |
| U23 Bill Dawley | .07 |
| U24 Andre Dawson | .35 |
| U25 Brian Dayett | .07 |
| U26 Rick Dempsay | .07 |
| U27 Ken Dowell | .12 |
| U28 Dave Dravecky | .07 |
| U29 Mike Dunne (RR) | .30 |
| U30 Dennis Eckersley | .15 |
| U31 Cecil Fielder | .07 |
| U32 Brian Fisher | .07 |
| U33 Willie Fraser | .07 |

| NO. PLAYER | MINT |
|---|---|
| U34 Ken Gerhart | .25 |
| U35 Jim Gott | .07 |
| U36 Dan Gladden | .07 |
| U37 Mike Greenwell (RR) | 3.00 |
| U38 Cecilio Guante | .07 |
| U39 Albert Hall | .07 |
| U40 Atlee Hammaker | .07 |
| U41 Mickey Hatcher | .07 |
| U42 Mike Heath | .07 |
| U43 Neal Heaton | .07 |
| U44 Mike Henneman | .30 |
| U45 Guy Hoffman | .07 |
| U46 Charlie Hudson | .07 |
| U47 Chuck Jackson | .15 |
| U48 Mike Jackson | .30 |
| U49 Reggie Jackson | .35 |
| U50 Chris James | .30 |
| U51 Dian James | .15 |
| U52 Stan Javier | .07 |
| U53 Stan Jefferson | .25 |
| U54 Jimmy Jones | .10 |
| U55 Tracy Jones | .20 |
| U56 Terry Kennedy | .07 |
| U57 Mike Kingery | .07 |
| U58 Ray Knight | .07 |
| U59 Gene Larkin | .30 |
| U60 Mike La Valliere | .07 |
| U61 Jack Lazorko | .12 |
| U62 Terry Leach | .12 |
| U63 Rick Leach | .07 |
| U64 Craig Lefferts | .07 |
| U65 Jim Lindeman (RR) | .35 |
| U66 Bill Long | .20 |

| NO. PLAYER | MINT |
|---|---|
| U67 Mike Loynd | .15 |
| U68 Greg Maddux (RR) | .65 |
| U69 Bill Madlock | .07 |
| U70 Dave Magadan | .20 |
| U71 Joe Magrane (RR) | .60 |
| U72 Fred Manrique | .15 |
| U73 Mike Mason | .07 |
| U74 Lloyd McClendon | .20 |
| U75 Fred McGriff (RR) | 1.50 |
| U76 Mark McGwire (RR) | 2.50 |
| U77 Mark McLemore | .07 |
| U78 Kevin McReynolds | .30 |
| U79 Dave Meads | .15 |
| U80 Greg Minton | .12 |
| U81 John Mitchell | .12 |
| U82 Kevin Mitchell | .12 |
| U83 John Morris | .07 |
| U84 Jeff Musselman | .20 |
| U85 Randy Myers (RR) | .50 |
| U86 Gene Nelson | .07 |
| U87 Joe Niekro | .15 |
| U88 Tom Nieto | .07 |
| U89 Reid Nichols | .07 |
| U90 Matt Nokes (RR) | 1.00 |
| U91 Dickie Noles | .07 |
| U92 Edwin Nunez | .07 |
| U93 Jose Nunez | .15 |
| U94 Paul O'Neill | .12 |
| U95 Jim Paciorek | .15 |
| U96 Lance Parrish | .20 |
| U97 Bill Pecota | .15 |
| U98 Tony Pena | .07 |
| U99 Luis Polonia | .25 |

| NO. PLAYER | MINT |
|---|---|
| U100 Randy Ready | .07 |
| U101 Jeff Reardon | .15 |
| U102 Gary Redus | .07 |
| U103 Rick Rhoden | .15 |
| U104 Wally Ritchie | .12 |
| U105 Jeff Robinson (RR) | .50 |
| U106 Mark Salas | .07 |
| U107 Dave Schmidt | .07 |
| U108 Kevin Seitzer | 2.00 |
| U109 John Shelby | .07 |
| U110 John Smiley (RR) | .35 |
| U111 Lary Sorensen | .07 |
| U112 Chris Speier | .07 |
| U113 Randy St. Claire | .07 |
| U114 Jim Sundberg | .07 |
| U115 B.J. Surhoff (RR) | .40 |
| U116 Greg Swindell | .35 |
| U117 Danny Tartabull | .35 |
| U118 Dorn Taylor | .07 |
| U119 Lee Tunnell | .07 |
| U120 Ed Vande Berg | .07 |
| U121 Andy Van Slyke | .25 |
| U122 Gary Ward | .07 |
| U123 Devon White | .50 |
| U124 Alan Wiggins | .07 |
| U125 Bill Wilkinson | .07 |
| U126 Jim Winn | .07 |
| U127 Frank Williams | .07 |
| U128 Kenny Williams (RR) | .25 |
| U129 Matt Williams (RR) | .50 |
| U130 Herm Winningham | .07 |
| U131 Matt Young | .07 |
| U132 Checklist | .08 |

# 1988 Fleer. . . .Complete Set of 660 Cards—Value $40.00

Features the rookie cards of Matt Nokes, Gregg Jefferies, Ellis Burks and Sam Horn. A 12-card World Series set was included as a bonus with the 660 card factory-sealed set. Each wax and cello pack included a randomly distributed card from a 12-card All-Star set. Sixteen different cards (12 players and four team logos) were printed on the bottom of gum and cello display boxes. A new feature in 1988 is photos and statistics of every ballpark printed on the back of the team logo stickers.

| NO. PLAYER | MINT |
|---|---|
| **MINNESOTA TWINS** | |
| 1 Keith Atherton | .05 |
| 2 Don Baylor | .08 |
| 3 Juan Berenguer | .05 |
| 4 Bert Blyleven | .10 |
| 5 Tom Brunansky | .15 |
| 6 Randy Bush | .05 |
| 7 Steve Carlton | .12 |

| NO. PLAYER | MINT |
|---|---|
| 8 Mark Davidson (R) | .25 |
| 9 George Frazier | .05 |
| 10 Gary Gaetti | .15 |
| 11 Greg Gagne | .05 |
| 12 Dan Gladden | .05 |
| 13 Kent Hrbek | .15 |
| 14 Gene Larkin (R) | .30 |
| 15 Tim Laudner | .05 |

| NO. PLAYER | MINT |
|---|---|
| 16 Steve Lombardozzi | .05 |
| 17 Al Newman | .05 |
| 18 Joe Niekro | .08 |
| 19 Kirby Puckett | .30 |
| 20 Jeff Reardon | .05 |
| 21 Dan Schatzader | .05 |
| 22 Roy Smalley | .05 |
| 23 Mike Smithson | .05 |

| NO. PLAYER | MINT |
|---|---|
| 24 Les Straker (R) | .20 |
| 25 Frank Viola | .15 |
| **ST. LOUIS CARDINALS** | |
| 26 Jk. Clark | .25 |
| 27 Vince Coleman | .20 |
| 28 Danny Cox | .05 |
| 29 Bill Dawley | .05 |
| 30 Ken Dayley | .05 |

Card values shown here fluctuate considerably.

| NO. | PLAYER | MINT |
|---|---|---|
| 31 | Doug DeCinces | .05 |
| 32 | Curt Ford | .05 |
| 33 | Bob Forsch | .05 |
| 34 | David Green | .05 |
| 35 | Tom Herr | .05 |
| 36 | Ricky Horton | .05 |
| 37 | Lance Johnson (R) | .25 |
| 38 | Steve Lake | .05 |
| 39 | Jim Lindeman | .12 |
| 40 | Joe Magrane (R) | .40 |
| 41 | Greg Mathews | .05 |
| 42 | Willie McGee | .15 |
| 43 | John Morris | .12 |
| 44 | Jose Oquendo | .05 |
| 45 | Tony Pena | .05 |
| 46 | Terry Pendleton | .05 |
| 47 | Ozzie Smith | .15 |
| 48 | John Tudor | .10 |
| 49 | Lee Tunnell | .05 |
| 50 | Todd Worrell | .10 |

**DETROIT TIGERS**

| NO. | PLAYER | MINT |
|---|---|---|
| 51 | Doyle Alexander | .05 |
| 52 | Dave Bergman | .05 |
| 53 | Tom Brookens | .05 |
| 54 | Darrell Evans | .05 |
| 55 | Kirk Gibson | .20 |
| 56 | Mike Heath | .05 |
| 57 | Mike Henneman (R) | .25 |
| 58 | Willie Hernandez | .10 |
| 59 | Larry Herndon | .05 |
| 60 | Eric King | .05 |
| 61 | Chet Lemon | .05 |
| 62 | Scott Lusader (R) | .25 |
| 63 | Bill Madlock | .15 |
| 64 | Jack Morris | .15 |
| 65 | Jim Morrison | .05 |
| 66 | Matt Nokes (R) | 1.00 |
| 67 | Dan Petry | .05 |
| 68 | Jeff Robinson (R) | .40 |
| 69 | Pat Sheridan | .05 |
| 70 | Nate Snell | .05 |
| 71 | Frank Tanana | .05 |
| 72 | Walt Terrell | .05 |
| 73 | Mark Thurmond | .05 |
| 74 | Alan Trammell | .15 |
| 75 | Lou Whitaker | .20 |

**SAN FRANCISCO GIANTS**

| NO. | PLAYER | MINT |
|---|---|---|
| 76 | Mike Aldrete | .05 |
| 77 | Bob Brenly | .05 |
| 78 | Will Clark | .60 |
| 79 | Chili Davis | .10 |
| 80 | Kelly Downs | .05 |
| 81 | Dave Dravecky | .05 |
| 82 | Scott Garrelts | .05 |
| 83 | Atlee Hammaker | .05 |
| 84 | Dave Henderson | .05 |
| 85 | Mike Krukow | .05 |
| 86 | Mike LaCoss | .05 |
| 87 | Craig Lefferts | .05 |
| 88 | Jeff Leonard | .10 |
| 89 | Candy Maldonado | .10 |
| 90 | Bob Melvin | .05 |
| 91 | Ed Milner | .05 |
| 92 | Kevin Mitchell | .05 |
| 93 | Jon Perlman (R) | .12 |
| 94 | Rick Reuschel | .05 |
| 95 | Don Robinson | .05 |
| 96 | Chris Speier | .05 |
| 97 | Harry Spilman | .05 |
| 98 | Robbie Thompson | .05 |
| 99 | Jose Uribe | .05 |
| 100 | Mark Wasinger (R) | .25 |
| 101 | Matt Williams (R) | .30 |

**TORONTO BLUE JAYS**

| NO. | PLAYER | MINT |
|---|---|---|
| 102 | Jesse Barfield | .15 |
| 103 | George Bell | .25 |
| 104 | Juan Beniquez | .05 |
| 105 | John Cerutti | .05 |
| 106 | Jim Clancy | .05 |
| 107 | Rob Ducey (R) | .20 |
| 108 | Mark Eichhorn | .05 |
| 109 | Tony Fernandez | .12 |
| 110 | Cecil Fielder | .05 |
| 111 | Kelly Gruber | .05 |
| 112 | Tom Henke | .05 |
| 113 | Garth Iorg | .05 |
| 114 | Jimmy Key | .10 |

| NO. | PLAYER | MINT |
|---|---|---|
| 115 | Rick Leach | .05 |
| 116 | Manny Lee | .08 |
| 117 | Nelson Liriano (R) | .20 |
| 118 | Fred McGriff | .85 |
| 119 | Lloyd Moseby | .10 |
| 120 | Rance Mulliniks | .05 |
| 121 | Jeff Musselman | .12 |
| 122 | Jose Nunez | .25 |
| 123 | Dave Stieb | .05 |
| 124 | Willie Upshaw | .05 |
| 125 | Duane Ward | .08 |
| 126 | Ernie Whitt | .05 |

**NEW YORK METS**

| NO. | PLAYER | MINT |
|---|---|---|
| 127 | Rick Aguilera | .05 |
| 128 | Wally Backman | .05 |
| 129 | Mark Carreon (R) | .20 |
| 130 | Gary Carter | .20 |
| 131 | David Cone | 1.25 |
| 132 | Ron Darling | .15 |
| 133 | Len Dykstra | .15 |
| 134 | Sid Fernandez | .08 |
| 135 | Dwight Gooden | .60 |
| 136 | Keith Hernandez | .20 |
| 137 | Gregg Jefferies (R) | 8.00 |
| 138 | Howard Johnson | .15 |
| 139 | Terry Leach | .05 |
| 140 | Barry Lyons (R) | .20 |
| 141 | Dave Magadan | .15 |
| 142 | Roger McDowell | .05 |
| 143 | Kevin McReynolds | .15 |
| 144 | Keith Miller (R) | .25 |
| 145 | John Mitchell (R) | .20 |
| 146 | Randy Myers | .25 |
| 147 | Bob Ojeda | .10 |
| 148 | Jesse Orosco | .05 |
| 149 | Rafael Santana | .05 |
| 150 | Doug Sisk | .05 |
| 151 | Darryl Strawberry | .60 |
| 152 | Tim Teufel | .05 |
| 153 | Gene Walter | .05 |
| 154 | Mookie Wilson | .08 |

**MILWAUKEE BREWERS**

| NO. | PLAYER | MINT |
|---|---|---|
| 155 | Jay Aldrich (R) | .15 |
| 156 | Chris Bosio | .05 |
| 157 | Glenn Braggs | .10 |
| 158 | Greg Brock | .05 |
| 159 | Juan Castillo | .08 |
| 160 | Mark Clear | .05 |
| 161 | Cecil Cooper | .08 |
| 162 | Chuck Crim (R) | .15 |
| 163 | Rob Deer | .10 |
| 164 | Mike Felder | .05 |
| 165 | Jim Gantner | .05 |
| 166 | Ted Higuera | .12 |
| 167 | Steve Kiefer | .05 |
| 168 | Rick Manning | .05 |
| 169 | Paul Molitor | .15 |
| 170 | Juan Nieves | .10 |
| 171 | Dan Plesac | .05 |
| 172 | Earnest Riles | .05 |
| 173 | Bill Schroeder | .05 |
| 174 | Steve Stanicek (R) | .20 |
| 175 | B.J. Surhoff | .20 |
| 176 | Dale Sveum | .08 |
| 177 | Bill Wegman | .05 |
| 178 | Robin Yount | .20 |

**MONTREAL EXPOS**

| NO. | PLAYER | MINT |
|---|---|---|
| 179 | Hubie Brooks | .10 |
| 180 | Tim Burke | .05 |
| 181 | Casey Candaele | .10 |
| 182 | Mike Fitzgerald | .05 |
| 183 | Tom Foley | .05 |
| 184 | Andres Galarraga | .30 |
| 185 | Neal Heaton | .05 |
| 186 | Wallace Johnson | .05 |
| 187 | Vance Law | .05 |
| 188 | Dennis Martinez | .08 |
| 189 | Bob McClure | .05 |
| 190 | Andy McGaffigan | .05 |
| 191 | Reid Nichols | .05 |
| 192 | Pascual Perez | .05 |
| 193 | Tim Raines | .20 |
| 194 | Jeff Reed | .05 |
| 195 | Bob Sebra | .05 |
| 196 | Bryn Smith | .05 |
| 197 | Randy St. Claire | .05 |
| 198 | Tim Wallach | .10 |

| NO. | PLAYER | MINT |
|---|---|---|
| 199 | Mitch Webster | .05 |
| 200 | Herm Winningham | .05 |
| 201 | Floyd Youmans | .08 |

**N.Y. YANKEES**

| NO. | PLAYER | MINT |
|---|---|---|
| 202 | Brad Arnsberg (R) | .15 |
| 203 | Rick Cerone | .05 |
| 204 | Pat Clements | .05 |
| 205 | Henry Cotto | .05 |
| 206 | Mike Easler | .05 |
| 207 | Ron Guidry | .10 |
| 208 | Bill Gullickson | .05 |
| 209 | Rickey Henderson | .35 |
| 210 | Charles Hudson | .05 |
| 211 | Tommy John | .10 |
| 212 | Roberto Kelly (R) | .35 |
| 213 | Ron Kittle | .08 |
| 214 | Don Mattingly | 1.50 |
| 215 | Bobby Meacham | .05 |
| 216 | Mike Pagliarulo | .15 |
| 217 | Dan Pasqua | .10 |
| 218 | Willie Randolph | .12 |
| 219 | Rick Rhoden | .05 |
| 220 | Dave Righetti | .10 |
| 221 | Jerry Royster | .05 |
| 222 | Tim Stoddard | .05 |
| 223 | Wayne Tolleson | .05 |
| 224 | Gary Ward | .05 |
| 225 | Claudell Washington | .05 |
| 226 | Dave Winfield | .20 |

**CINCINNATI REDS**

| NO. | PLAYER | MINT |
|---|---|---|
| 227 | Buddy Bell | .15 |
| 228 | Tom Browning | .05 |
| 229 | Dave Concepcion | .05 |
| 230 | Kal Daniels | .30 |
| 231 | Eric Davis | 1.00 |
| 232 | Bo Diaz | .05 |
| 233 | Nick Esasky | .05 |
| 234 | John Franco | .08 |
| 235 | Guy Hoffman | .05 |
| 236 | Tom Hume | .05 |
| 237 | Tracy Jones | .10 |
| 238 | Bill Landrum (R) | .12 |
| 239 | Barry Larkin | .15 |
| 240 | Terry McGriff | .12 |
| 241 | Rob Murphy | .05 |
| 242 | Ron Oester | .05 |
| 243 | Dave Parker | .15 |
| 244 | Pat Perry | .05 |
| 245 | Ted Power | .05 |
| 246 | Dennis Rasmussen | .05 |
| 247 | Ron Robinson | .05 |
| 248 | Kurt Stillwell | .08 |
| 249 | Jeff Treadway (R) | .40 |
| 250 | Frank Williams | .05 |

**K.C. ROYALS**

| NO. | PLAYER | MINT |
|---|---|---|
| 251 | Steve Balboni | .05 |
| 252 | Bud Black | .05 |
| 253 | Thad Bosley | .05 |
| 254 | George Brett | .35 |
| 255 | John Davis (R) | .25 |
| 256 | Steve Farr | .05 |
| 257 | Gene Garber | .05 |
| 258 | Jerry Gleaton | .05 |
| 259 | Mark Gubicza | .05 |
| 260 | Bo Jackson | .50 |
| 261 | Danny Jackson | .05 |
| 262 | Ross Jones (R) | .12 |
| 263 | Charlie Leibrandt | .05 |
| 264 | Bill Pecota (R) | .20 |
| 265 | Melido Perez (R) | .25 |
| 266 | Jamie Quirk | .05 |
| 267 | Dan Quisenberry | .10 |
| 268 | Bret Saberhagen | .15 |
| 269 | Angel Salazar | .05 |
| 270 | Kevin Seitzer | 1.00 |
| 271 | Danny Tartabull | .25 |
| 272 | Gary Thurman (R) | .50 |
| 273 | Frank White | .05 |
| 274 | Willie Wilson | .10 |

**OAKLAND A'S**

| NO. | PLAYER | MINT |
|---|---|---|
| 275 | Tony Bernazard | .05 |
| 276 | Jose Canseco | 2.00 |
| 277 | Mike Davis | .05 |
| 278 | Storm Davis | .05 |
| 279 | Dennis Eckersley | .05 |
| 280 | Alfredo Griffin | .05 |
| 281 | Rick Honeycutt | .05 |

| NO. | PLAYER | MINT |
|---|---|---|
| 282 | Jay Howell | .05 |
| 283 | Reggie Jackson | .30 |
| 284 | Dennis Lamp | .05 |
| 285 | Carney Lansford | .05 |
| 286 | Mark McGwire | 1.50 |
| 287 | Dwayne Murphy | .05 |
| 288 | Gene Nelson | .05 |
| 289 | Steve Ontiveros | .05 |
| 290 | Tony Philips | .05 |
| 291 | Eric Plunk | .05 |
| 292 | Luis Polonia (R) | .20 |
| 293 | Rick Rodriguez (R) | .15 |
| 294 | Terry Steinbach | .10 |
| 295 | Dave Stewart | .05 |
| 296 | Curt Young | .05 |

**PHILADELPHIA PHILLIES**

| NO. | PLAYER | MINT |
|---|---|---|
| 297 | Luis Aguayo | .05 |
| 298 | Steve Bedrosian | .05 |
| 299 | Jeff Calhoun | .05 |
| 300 | Don Carman | .05 |
| 301 | Todd Frohwirth (R) | .25 |
| 302 | Greg Gross | .05 |
| 303 | Kevin Gross | .05 |
| 304 | Von Hayes | .05 |
| 305 | Keith Hughes (R) | .20 |
| 306 | Mike Jackson (R) | .15 |
| 307 | Chris James | .15 |
| 308 | Steve Jeltz | .05 |
| 309 | Mike Maddux | .05 |
| 310 | Lance Parrish | .12 |
| 311 | Shane Rawley | .05 |
| 312 | Wally Ritchie (R) | .15 |
| 313 | Bruce Ruffin | .05 |
| 314 | Juan Samuel | .10 |
| 315 | Mike Schmidt | .35 |
| 316 | Rick Schu | .05 |
| 317 | Jeff Stone | .05 |
| 318 | Kent Tekulve | .05 |
| 319 | Milt Thompson | .05 |
| 320 | Glenn Wilson | .08 |

**PITTSBURGH PIRATES**

| NO. | PLAYER | MINT |
|---|---|---|
| 321 | Rafael Belliard | .05 |
| 322 | Barry Bonds | .30 |
| 323 | Bobby Bonilla | .30 |
| 324 | Sid Bream | .05 |
| 325 | John Cangelosi | .05 |
| 326 | Mike Diaz | .05 |
| 327 | Doug Drabek | .05 |
| 328 | Mike Dunne | .30 |
| 329 | Brian Fisher | .05 |
| 330 | Brett Gideon (R) | .15 |
| 331 | Terry Harper | .05 |
| 332 | Bob Kipper | .05 |
| 333 | Mike LaValliere | .05 |
| 334 | Jose Lind (R) | .25 |
| 335 | Junior Ortiz | .05 |
| 336 | Vincente Palacios (R) | .20 |
| 337 | Bob Patterson (R) | .15 |
| 338 | Al Pedrique (R) | .15 |
| 339 | R.J. Reynolds | .05 |
| 340 | John Smiley (R) | .35 |
| 341 | Andy Van Slyke | .15 |
| 342 | Bob Walk | .05 |

**BOSTON RED SOX**

| NO. | PLAYER | MINT |
|---|---|---|
| 343 | Marty Barrett | .10 |
| 344 | Todd Benzinger (R) | .60 |
| 345 | Wade Boggs | 1.00 |
| 346 | Tom Bolton (R) | .15 |
| 347 | Oil Can Boyd | .05 |
| 348 | Ellis Burks (R) | 1.00 |
| 349 | Roger Clemens | .75 |
| 350 | Steve Crawford | .15 |
| 351 | Dwight Evans | .05 |
| 352 | Wes Gardner (R) | .25 |
| 353 | Rich Gedman | .05 |
| 354 | Mike Greenwell | 2.50 |
| 355 | Sam Horn (R) | .75 |
| 356 | Bruce Hurst | .10 |
| 357 | John Marzano | .20 |
| 358 | Al Nipper | .05 |
| 359 | Spike Owen | .05 |
| 360 | Jody Reed (R) | .30 |
| 361 | Jim Rice | .20 |
| 362 | Ed Romero | .05 |
| 363 | Kevin Romine | .10 |
| 364 | Joe Sambito | .05 |
| 365 | Calvin Schiraldi | .05 |

Card values shown here fluctuate considerably.

| NO. PLAYER | MINT |
|---|---|
| 366 Jeff Sellers | .05 |
| 367 Bob Stanley | .05 |
| **SEATTLE MARINERS** | |
| 368 Scott Bankhead | .05 |
| 369 Phil Bradley | .08 |
| 370 Scott Bradley | .05 |
| 371 Mickey Brantley | .10 |
| 372 Mike Campbell (R) | .25 |
| 373 Alvin Davis | .08 |
| 374 Lee Guetterman | .05 |
| 375 Dave Hengel (R) | .20 |
| 376 Mike Kingery | .05 |
| 377 Mark Langston | .08 |
| 378 Edgar Martinez (R) | .15 |
| 379 Mike Moore | .05 |
| 380 Mike Morgan | .05 |
| 381 John Moses | .05 |
| 382 Donnell Nixon (R) | .15 |
| 383 Edwin Nunez | .05 |
| 384 Ken Phelps | .05 |
| 385 Jim Presley | .05 |
| 386 Rey Quinones | .05 |
| 387 Jerry Reed | .05 |
| 388 Harold Reynolds | .05 |
| 389 Dave Valle | .08 |
| 390 Bill Wilkinson (R) | .15 |
| **CHICAGO WHITE SOX** | |
| 391 Harold Baines | .10 |
| 392 Floyd Bannister | .05 |
| 393 Daryl Boston | .05 |
| 394 Ivan Calderon | .05 |
| 395 Jose DeLeon | .05 |
| 396 Richard Dotson | .05 |
| 397 Carlton Fisk | .15 |
| 398 Ozzie Guillen | .05 |
| 399 Ron Hassey | .05 |
| 400 Donnie Hill | .05 |
| 401 Bob James | .05 |
| 402 Dave LaPoint | .05 |
| 403 Bill Lindsey (R) | .15 |
| 404 Bill Long (R) | .20 |
| 405 Steve Lyons | .05 |
| 406 Fred Manrique (R) | .20 |
| 407 Jack McDowell (R) | .35 |
| 408 Gary Redus | .05 |
| 409 Ray Searage | .05 |
| 410 Bobby Thigpen | .05 |
| 411 Greg Walker | .05 |
| 412 Kenny Williams (R) | .25 |
| 413 Jim Winn | .05 |
| **CHICAGO CUBS** | |
| 414 Jody Davis | .05 |
| 415 Andre Dawson | .25 |
| 416 Brian Dayett | .05 |
| 417 Bob Dernier | .05 |
| 418 Frank DiPino | .05 |
| 419 Shawon Dunston | .05 |
| 420 Leon Durham | .10 |
| 421 Les Lancaster (R) | .20 |
| 422 Ed Lynch | .05 |
| 423 Greg Maddux | .60 |
| 424 Dave Martinez | .20 |
| 425 K. Moreland (error) | 4.50 |
| (photo of Jody Davis) | |
| 425 K. Moreland (correct) | .25 |
| 426 Jamie Moyer | .05 |
| 427 Jerry Mumphrey | .05 |
| 428 Paul Noce (R) | .20 |
| 429 Rafael Palmeiro | .75 |
| 430 Wade Rowdon | .10 |
| 431 Ryne Sandberg | .20 |
| 432 Scott Sanderson | .05 |
| 433 Lee Smith | .10 |
| 434 Jim Sundberg | .05 |
| 435 Rick Sutcliffe | .10 |
| 436 Manny Trillo | .05 |
| **HOUSTON ASTROS** | |
| 437 Juan Agosto | .05 |
| 438 Larry Andersen | .05 |
| 439 Alan Ashby | .05 |
| 440 Kevin Bass | .05 |
| 441 Ken Caminiti (R) | .25 |
| 442 Rocky Childress (R) | .20 |
| 443 Jose Cruz | .05 |
| 444 Danny Darwin | .05 |
| 445 Glenn Davis | .15 |
| 446 Jim Deshaies | .05 |

| NO. PLAYER | MINT |
|---|---|
| 447 Bill Doran | .05 |
| 448 Ty Gainey | .05 |
| 449 Billy Hatcher | .10 |
| 450 Jeff Heathcock | .05 |
| 451 Bob Knepper | .05 |
| 452 Rob Mallicoat (R) | .15 |
| 453 Dave Meads (R) | .15 |
| 454 Craig Reynolds | .05 |
| 455 Nolan Ryan | .25 |
| 456 Mike Scott | .05 |
| 457 Dave Smith | .05 |
| 458 Denny Walling | .05 |
| 459 Robbie Wine (R) | .20 |
| 460 Gerald Young (R) | .50 |
| **TEXAS RANGERS** | |
| 461 Bob Brower | .10 |
| 462 J. Browne (error) | 4.50 |
| (photo of Bob Brower) | |
| 462 J. Browne (correct) | .25 |
| 463 Steve Buechele | .05 |
| 464 Edwin Correa | .05 |
| 465 Cecil Espy (R) | .15 |
| 466 Scott Fletcher | .05 |
| 467 Jose Guzman | .05 |
| 468 Greg Harris | .05 |
| 469 Charlie Hough | .05 |
| 470 Pete Incaviglia | .25 |
| 471 Paul Kilgus (R) | .20 |
| 472 Mike Loynd | .08 |
| 473 Oddibe McDowell | .10 |
| 474 Dale Mohorcic | .05 |
| 475 Pete O'Brien | .10 |
| 476 Larry Parrish | .05 |
| 477 Geno Petralli | .05 |
| 478 Jeff Russell | .05 |
| 479 Ruben Sierra | .25 |
| 480 Mike Stanley | .05 |
| 481 Curtis Wilkerson | .05 |
| 482 Mitch Williams | .05 |
| 483 Bobby Witt | .05 |
| **CALIFORNIA ANGELS** | |
| 484 Tony Armas | .05 |
| 485 Bob Boone | .05 |
| 486 Bill Buckner | .05 |
| 487 DeWayne Buice (R) | .15 |
| 488 Brian Downing | .05 |
| 489 Chuck Finley | .05 |
| 490 Willie Fraser | .05 |
| 491 Jack Howell | .05 |
| 492 Ruppert Jones | .05 |
| 493 Wally Joyner | .60 |
| 494 Jack Lazorko | .10 |
| 495 Gary Lucas | .05 |
| 496 Kirk McCaskill | .05 |
| 497 Mark McLemore | .05 |
| 498 Darrell Miller | .05 |
| 499 Greg Minton | .05 |
| 500 Donnie Moore | .05 |
| 501 Gus Polidor | .05 |
| 502 Johnny Ray | .05 |
| 503 Mark Ryal | .05 |
| 504 Dick Schofield | .05 |
| 505 Don Sutton | .15 |
| 506 Devon White | .25 |
| 507 Mike Witt | .10 |
| **LOS ANGELES DODGERS** | |
| 508 Dave Anderson | .05 |
| 509 Tim Belcher | .15 |
| 510 Ralph Bryant | .05 |
| 511 Tim Crews (R) | .20 |
| 512 Mike Devereaux (R) | .30 |
| 513 Mariano Duncan | .05 |
| 514 Pedro Guerrero | .20 |
| 515 Jeff Hamilton | .15 |
| 516 Mickey Hatcher | .05 |
| 517 Brad Havens | .05 |
| 518 Orel Hershiser | .30 |
| 519 Shawn Hillegas (R) | .20 |
| 520 Ken Howell | .05 |
| 521 Tim Leary | .05 |
| 522 Mike Marshall | .10 |
| 523 Steve Sax | .15 |
| 524 Mike Scioscia | .05 |
| 525 Mike Sharperson | .05 |
| 526 John Shelby | .05 |
| 527 Franklin Stubbs | .05 |

| NO. PLAYER | MINT |
|---|---|
| 528 Fernando Valenzuela | .20 |
| 529 Bob Welch | .05 |
| 530 Matt Young | .05 |
| **ATLANTA BRAVES** | |
| 531 Jim Acker | .05 |
| 532 Paul Assenmacher | .05 |
| 533 Jeff Blauser (R) | .30 |
| 534 Joe Boever (R) | .15 |
| 535 Martin Clary | .05 |
| 536 Kevin Coffman | .15 |
| 537 Jeff Dedmon | .05 |
| 538 Ron Gant (R) | .50 |
| 539 Tom Glavine (R) | .25 |
| 540 Ken Griffey | .05 |
| 541 Al Hall | .05 |
| 542 Glenn Hubbard | .05 |
| 543 Dion James | .05 |
| 544 Dale Murphy | .35 |
| 545 Ken Oberkfell | .05 |
| 546 David Palmer | .05 |
| 547 Gerald Perry | .15 |
| 548 Charlie Puleo | .05 |
| 549 Ted Simmons | .05 |
| 550 Zane Smith | .05 |
| 551 Andres Thomas | .05 |
| 552 Ozzie Virgil | .05 |
| **BALTIMORE ORIOLES** | |
| 553 Don Aase | .05 |
| 554 Jeff Ballard (R) | .25 |
| 555 Eric Bell | .05 |
| 556 Mike Boddicker | .05 |
| 557 Ken Dixon | .05 |
| 558 Jim Dwyer | .05 |
| 559 Ken Gehart | .05 |
| 560 Rene Gonzales (R) | .15 |
| 561 Mike Griffin | .05 |
| 562 John Hayban | .10 |
| 563 Terry Kennedy | .05 |
| 564 Ray Knight | .05 |
| 565 Lee Lacy | .05 |
| 566 Fred Lynn | .15 |
| 567 Eddie Murray | .25 |
| 568 Tom Niedenfuer | .05 |
| 569 Bill Ripken (R) | .25 |
| 570 Cal Ripken, Jr. | .25 |
| 571 Dave Schmidt | .05 |
| 572 Larry Sheets | .10 |
| 573 Pete Stanicek (R) | .25 |
| 574 Mark Williamson (R) | .15 |
| 575 Mike Young | .05 |
| **SAN DIEGO PADRES** | |
| 576 Shawn Abner | .25 |
| 577 Greg Booker | .05 |
| 578 Chris Brown | .10 |
| 579 Keith Comstock (R) | .20 |
| 580 Joey Cora (R) | .15 |
| 581 Mark Davis | .05 |
| 582 Tim Flannery | .05 |
| 583 Goose Gossage | .10 |
| 584 Mark Grant | .05 |
| 585 Tony Gwynn | .30 |
| 586 Andy Hawkins | .05 |
| 587 Stan Jefferson | .15 |
| 588 Jimmy Jones | .05 |
| 589 John Kruk | .20 |
| 590 Shane Mack | .25 |
| 591 Carmelo Martinez | .05 |
| 592 Lance McCullers | .05 |
| 593 Eric Nolte (R) | .15 |
| 594 Randy Ready | .05 |
| 595 Luis Salazar | .05 |
| 596 Benito Santiago | .40 |
| 597 Eric Show | .05 |
| 598 Garry Templeton | .05 |
| 599 Ed Whitson | .05 |
| **CLEVELAND INDIANS** | |
| 600 Scott Bailes | .05 |
| 601 Chris Bando | .05 |
| 602 Jay Bell (R) | .20 |
| 603 Brett Butler | .05 |
| 604 Tom Candiotti | .10 |
| 605 Joe Carter | .15 |
| 606 Carmen Castillo | .05 |
| 607 Brian Dorsett (R) | .15 |
| 608 John Farrell (R) | .25 |
| 609 Julio Franco | .10 |

| NO. PLAYER | MINT |
|---|---|
| 610 Mel Hall | .05 |
| 611 Tommy Hinzo (R) | .15 |
| 612 Brook Jacoby | .10 |
| 613 Doug Jones (R) | .35 |
| 614 Ken Schrom | .05 |
| 615 Cory Snyder | .20 |
| 616 Sammy Stewart | .05 |
| 617 Greg Swindell | .10 |
| 618 Pat Tabler | .05 |
| 619 Ed Vande Berg | .05 |
| 620 Eddie Williams (R) | .15 |
| 621 Rich Yett | .05 |
| **SPECIAL CARDS** | |
| 622 Slugging Sophomores | .25 |
| 623 Dominican Dynamite | .10 |
| 624 Oakland's Power Team | .75 |
| 625 Classic Relief | .10 |
| 626 All Star Righties | .10 |
| 627 Game Closers | .10 |
| 628 Masters of Double Play | .10 |
| 629 Rookie Record Setter | .50 |
| 630 Changing the Guard | 1.00 |
| 631 N.L. Batting Champs | .25 |
| 632 Pitching Magic | .10 |
| 633 Big Bats At First | .40 |
| 634 Hitting King and Thief | .20 |
| 635 Slugging Shortstop | .10 |
| 636 Tried and True Sluggers | .20 |
| 637 Crunch Time | .30 |
| 638 A.L. All Stars | .25 |
| 639 N.L. All-Stars | .15 |
| 640 The "O's" Brothers | .10 |
| **No. 641 to 653—** | |
| **Major League Prospects** | |
| 641 Mark Grace (R) and Darrin Jackson (R) | 4.00 |
| 642 Damon Berryhill (R) and Jeff Montgomery (R) | .60 |
| 643 Felix Fermin (R) and Jessie Reid (R) | .25 |
| 644 Greg Myers (R) and Greg Tabor (R) | .30 |
| 645 Joey Meyer and Jim Eppard (R) | .35 |
| 646 Adam Peterson (R) and Randy Velarde (R) | .35 |
| 647 Peter Smith (R) and Chris Gwynn (R) | .40 |
| 648 Tom Newell (R) and Greg Jelks (R) | .30 |
| 649 Mario Diaz (R) and Clay Parker (R) | .30 |
| 650 Jack Savage (R) and Todd Simmons (R) | .30 |
| 651 John Burkett (R) and Kirt Manwaring (R) | .35 |
| 652 Dave Otto (R) and Walt Weiss (R) | 1.50 |
| 653 Jeff King (R) and Randell Byers (R) | .30 |
| 654 Checklist No. 1 | .08 |
| 655 Checklist No. 2 | .08 |
| 656 Checklist No. 3 | .08 |
| 657 Checklist No. 4 | .08 |
| 658 Checklist No. 5 | .08 |
| 659 Checklist No. 6 | .08 |
| 660 Checklist No. 7 | .08 |
| **Cards Printed on Gum Boxes** | |
| C 1 Cardinals Logo | .10 |
| C 2 Dwight Evans | .15 |
| C 3 Andres Galarraga | .20 |
| C 4 Wally Joyner | .35 |
| C 5 Twins Logo | .10 |
| C 6 Dale Murphy | .30 |
| C 7 Kirby Puckett | .35 |
| C 8 Shane Rawley | .15 |
| C 9 Giants Logo | .10 |
| C10 Ryne Sandberg | .20 |
| C11 Mike Schmidt | .30 |
| C12 Kevin Seitzer | .50 |
| C13 Tigers Logo | .10 |
| C14 Dave Stewart | .20 |
| C15 Tim Wallach | .15 |
| C16 Todd Worrell | .15 |

# 1988 Fleer Traded Update.... Complete Set of 132 Cards—Value $12.00

This set updates the main 1988 card set with players who had changed teams during the season, and rookies. This set features Fleer's first card of Chris Sabo and Ricky Jordan. This set was packaged in a printed box and distributed primarily through card dealers.

| NO. PLAYER | MINT | NO. PLAYER | MINT | NO. PLAYER | MINT | NO. PLAYER | MINT |
|---|---|---|---|---|---|---|---|
| U1 Jose Bautista | .12 | U34 Israel Sanchez | .12 | U67 Mike Flanagan | .07 | U100 Brian Holman | .15 |
| U2 Jose Orsulak | .10 | U35 Kurt Stillwelll | .07 | U68 Todd Stottlemyre | .20 | U101 Rex Hudler | .15 |
| U3 Doug Sisk | .07 | U36 Pat Tabler | .07 | U69 David Wells | .15 | U102 Jeff Parrett | .07 |
| U4 Craig Worthington | .15 | U37 Don August | .15 | U70 Jose Alvarez | .20 | U103 Nelson Santovenia | .20 |
| U5 Mike Boddiker | .07 | U38 Darryl Hamilton | .20 | U71 Paul Runge | .07 | U104 Kevin Elster | .15 |
| U6 Rick Cerone | .07 | U39 Jeff Leonard | .07 | U72 Cesar Jimenez | .12 | U105 Jeff Innis | .15 |
| U7 Larry Parrish | .07 | U40 Joey Meyer | .30 | U73 Pete Smith | .20 | U106 Mackey Sasser | .30 |
| U8 Lee Smith | .07 | U41 Allan Anderson | .07 | U74 John Smoltz | .20 | U107 Phil Bradley | .07 |
| U9 Mike Smithson | .07 | U42 Brian Harper | .07 | U75 Damon Berryhill | .25 | U108 Danny Clay | .07 |
| U10 John Trautwein | .12 | U43 Tom Herr | .07 | U76 Goose Gossage | .07 | U109 Greg Harris | .07 |
| U11 Sherman Corbett | .25 | U44 Charlie Lea | .07 | U77 Mark Grace | 1.75 | U110 Ricky Jordan (RR) | 1.00 |
| U12 Chili Davis | .10 | U45 John Moses | .07 | U78 Darrin Jackson | .25 | U111 David Palmer | .07 |
| U13 Jim Eppard | .15 | U46 John Candelaria | .10 | U79 Vance Law | .07 | U112 Jim Gott | .07 |
| U14 Bryan Harvey | .35 | U47 Jack Clark | .12 | U80 Jeff Pico | .15 | U113 Tommy Gregg | .25 |
| U15 John Davis | .07 | U48 Richard Dotson | .07 | U81 Gary Varsho | .20 | U114 Barry Jones | .07 |
| U16 Dave Gallagher | .15 | U49 Al Leiter | .40 | U82 Tim Birtsas | .07 | U115 Randy Miligan | .25 |
| U17 Ricky Horton | .07 | U50 Rafael Santana | .07 | U83 Rob Dibble | .25 | U116 Luis Alicea | .15 |
| U18 Dan Pasqua | .07 | U51 Dons Slaught | .07 | U84 Danny Jackson | .25 | U117 Tom Brunansky | .15 |
| U19 Melido Perez | .07 | U52 Todd Burns | .25 | U85 Paul O'Neill | .07 | U118 John Costello | .20 |
| U20 Jose Segura | .12 | U53 Dave Henderson | .07 | U86 Jose Rijo | .07 | U119 Jose DeLeon | .07 |
| U21 Andy Allanson | .07 | U54 Doug Jennings | .30 | U87 Chris Sabo (RR) | 2.25 | U120 Bob Horner | .07 |
| U22 John Perlman | .07 | U55 Dave Parker | .25 | U88 John Fishel | .25 | U121 Scott Terry | .20 |
| U23 Domingo Ramos | .07 | U56 Walt Weiss | .40 | U89 Craig Biggio | .20 | U122 Roberto Alomar (RR) | .35 |
| U24 Rick Rodriquez | .07 | U57 Bob Welch | .07 | U90 Terry Puhl | .07 | U123 Dave Leiper | .07 |
| U25 Willie Upshaw | .10 | U58 Henry Cotto | .07 | U91 Rafael Ramirez | .07 | U124 Keith Moreland | .07 |
| U26 Phil Gibson | .12 | U59 Mario Diaz | .07 | U92 Louie Meadows | .15 | U125 Mark Parent | .20 |
| U27 Don Heinkel | .20 | U60 Mike Jackson | .07 | U93 Kirk Gibson | .25 | U126 Dennis Rasmussen | .07 |
| U28 Ray Knight | .07 | U61 Bill Swift | .07 | U94 Alfredo Griffin | .07 | U127 Randy Bockus | .07 |
| U29 Gary Pettis | .07 | U62 Jose Cecena | .12 | U95 Jay Howell | .12 | U128 Brett Butler | .07 |
| U30 Luis Salazar | .07 | U63 Ray Haywad | .15 | U96 Jesse Orosco | .07 | U129 Donnell Nixon | .07 |
| U31 Mike MacFarlane | .15 | U64 Jim Steels | .12 | U97 Alejandro Pena | .07 | U130 Ernest Riles | .07 |
| U32 Jeff Montgomery | .15 | U65 Pat Borders | .15 | U98 Tracy Woodson | .25 | U131 Roger Samuels | .15 |
| U33 Ted Power | .07 | U66 Sil Campusano | .25 | U99 John Dopson | .15 | U132 Checklist | .07 |

# 1989 Fleer.... Complete Set of 660 Cards—Value $35.00

A 12-card World Series set was included as a bonus with the 660 card factory sealed set. Each wax pack and cello pack included a randomly distributed card from a 12 card All-Star set. A new feature on the back is a comparison of each player's stat before and after the All-Star break.

| NO. PLAYER | MINT | NO. PLAYER | MINT | NO. PLAYER | MINT | NO. PLAYER | MINT |
|---|---|---|---|---|---|---|---|
| **OAKLAND A'S** | | 8 Mike Gallego | .05 | 16 Carney Lansford | .08 | 24 Walt Weiss | .50 |
| 1 Don Baylor | .08 | 9 Ron Hassey | .05 | 17 Mark McGwire | 1.15 | 25 Bob Welch | .08 |
| 2 Lance Blankenship (R) | .25 | 10 Dave Henderson | .05 | 18 Gene Nelson | .05 | 26 Curt Young | .05 |
| 3 Todd Burns (R) | .25 | 11 Rick Honeycutt | .05 | 19 Dave Parker | .10 | **NEW YORK METS** | |
| 4 Greg Cadaret | .05 | 12 Glenn Hubbard | .05 | 20 Eric Plunk | .05 | 27 Rick Aguilera | .05 |
| 5 Jose Canseco | 1.50 | 13 Stan Javier | .05 | 21 Luis Polonia | .05 | 28 Wally Backman | .05 |
| 6 Storm Davis | .05 | 14 Doug Jennings (R) | .40 | 22 Terry Steinbach | .15 | 29 Mark Carreon | .05 |
| 7 Dennis Eckersley | .12 | 15 Felix Jose (R) | .30 | 23 Dave Stewart | .10 | 30 Gary Carter | .25 |

Card values shown here fluctuate considerably.

| NO. | PLAYER | MINT |
|---|---|---|
| 31 | Dave Cone | .40 |
| 32 | Ron Darling | .10 |
| 33 | Len Dykstra | .20 |
| 34 | Kevin Elster | .08 |
| 35 | Sid Fernandez | .10 |
| 36 | Dwight Gooden | .45 |
| 37 | Keith Hernandez | .20 |
| 38 | Gregg Jefferies | 2.00 |
| 39 | Howard Johnson | .10 |
| 40 | Terry Leach | .05 |
| 41 | Dave Magadan | .10 |
| 42 | Bob McClure | .05 |
| 43 | Roger McDowell | .05 |
| 44 | Kevin McReynolds | .20 |
| 45 | Keith Miller | .05 |
| 46 | Randy Myers | .08 |
| 47 | Bob Ojeda | .08 |
| 48 | Mackey Sasser | .05 |
| 49 | Darryl Strawberry | .50 |
| 50 | Tim Teufel | .05 |
| 51 | Dave West (R) | .85 |
| 52 | Mookie Wilson | .08 |

**LOS ANGELES DODGERS**

| NO. | PLAYER | MINT |
|---|---|---|
| 53 | Dave Anderson | .05 |
| 54 | Tim Belcher | .15 |
| 55 | Mike Davis | .05 |
| 56 | Mike Devereaux | .05 |
| 57 | Kirk Gibson | .25 |
| 58 | Alfredo Griffin | .05 |
| 59 | Chris Gwynn | .10 |
| 60 | Jeff Hamilton | .05 |
| 61 | Danny Heep | .05 |
| 62 | Orel Hershiser | .30 |
| 63 | Brian Holton | .05 |
| 64 | Jay Howell | .08 |
| 65 | Tim Leary | .10 |
| 66 | Mike Marshall | .08 |
| 67 | Ramon Martinez (R) | .65 |
| 68 | Jesse Orosco | .05 |
| 69 | Alejandro Pena | .08 |
| 70 | Steve Sax | .08 |
| 71 | Mike Scioscia | .05 |
| 72 | Mike Sharperson | .05 |
| 73 | John Shelby | .05 |
| 74 | Franklin Stubbs | .05 |
| 75 | John Tudor | .05 |
| 76 | Fernando Velenzuela | .12 |
| 77 | Tracy Woodson | .10 |

**BOSTON RED SOX**

| NO. | PLAYER | MINT |
|---|---|---|
| 78 | Marty Barrett | .05 |
| 79 | Todd Benzinger | .15 |
| 80 | Mike Boddicker | .08 |
| 81 | Wade Boggs | .85 |
| 82 | "Oil Can" Boyd | .08 |
| 83 | Ellis Burks | .40 |
| 84 | Rick Cerone | .05 |
| 85 | Roger Clemens | .60 |
| 86 | Steve Curry (R) | .05 |
| 87 | Dwight Evans | .15 |
| 88 | Wes Gardner | .05 |
| 89 | Rich Gedman | .05 |
| 90 | Mike Greenwell | 1.35 |
| 91 | Bruce Hurst | .15 |
| 92 | Dennis Lamp | .05 |
| 93 | Spike Owen | .05 |
| 94 | Larry Parrish | .10 |
| 95 | Carlos Quintana (R) | .40 |
| 96 | Jody Reed | .15 |
| 97 | Jim Rice | .15 |
| 98 | Kevin Romine | .05 |
| 99 | Lee Smith | .08 |
| 100 | Mike Smithson | .05 |
| 101 | Bob Stanley | .05 |

**MINNESOTA TWINS**

| NO. | PLAYER | MINT |
|---|---|---|
| 102 | Allan Anderson | .08 |
| 103 | Keith Atherton | .05 |
| 104 | Juan Berenguer | .05 |
| 105 | Bert Blyleven | .15 |
| 106 | Eric Bullock | .15 |
| 107 | Randy Bush | .05 |
| 108 | John Christensen | .05 |
| 109 | Mark Davidson | .05 |
| 110 | Gary Gaetti | .10 |
| 111 | Greg Gagne | .05 |
| 112 | Dan Gladden | .05 |
| 113 | German Gonzalez (R) | .25 |
| 114 | Brian Harper | .05 |
| 115 | Tom Herr | .05 |
| 116 | Kent Hrbek | .15 |
| 117 | Gene Larken | .05 |
| 118 | Tim Laudner | .05 |
| 119 | Charlie Lea | .05 |
| 120 | Steve Lombardozzi | .05 |
| 121 | John Moses | .05 |
| 122 | Al Newman | .05 |
| 123 | Mark Portugal | .05 |
| 124 | Kirby Puckett | .30 |
| 125 | Jeff Reardon | .08 |
| 126 | Fred Toliver | .05 |
| 127 | Frank Viola | .15 |

**DETROIT TIGERS**

| NO. | PLAYER | MINT |
|---|---|---|
| 128 | Doyle Alexander | .05 |
| 129 | Dave Bergman | .05 |
| 130 | Tom Brookens | .05 |
| 131 | Paul Gibson (R) | .15 |
| 132 | Mike Heath | .05 |
| 133 | Don Heinkel (R) | .15 |
| 134 | Mike Henneman | .05 |
| 135 | Guillermo Hernandez | .05 |
| 136 | Eric King | .05 |
| 137 | Chet Lemon | .05 |
| 138 | Fred Lynn | .08 |
| 139 | Jack Morris | .10 |
| 140 | Matt Nokes | .10 |
| 141 | Gary Pettis | .05 |
| 142 | Ted Power | .05 |
| 143 | Jeff M. Robinson | .20 |
| 144 | Luis Salazar | .05 |
| 145 | Steve Searcy (R) | .25 |
| 146 | Pat Sheridan | .05 |
| 147 | Frank Tanana | .08 |
| 148 | Alan Trammell | .12 |
| 150 | Jim Walewander | .10 |
| 151 | Lou Whitaker | .08 |

**CINCINNATI REDS**

| NO. | PLAYER | MINT |
|---|---|---|
| 152 | Tim Birtsas | .05 |
| 153 | Tom Browning | .08 |
| 154 | Keith Brown (R) | .25 |
| 155 | Norm Charlton (R) | .20 |
| 156 | Dave Concepcion | .05 |
| 157 | Kal Daniels | .30 |
| 158 | Eric Davis | .75 |
| 159 | Bo Diaz | .05 |
| 160 | Rob Dibble | .15 |
| 161 | Nick Esasky | .10 |
| 162 | John Franco | .08 |
| 163 | Danny Jackson | .12 |
| 164 | Barry Larkin | .10 |
| 165 | Rob Murphy | .05 |
| 166 | Paul O'Neil | .05 |
| 167 | Jeff Reed | .10 |
| 168 | Jose Rijo | .08 |
| 169 | Ron Robinson | .08 |
| 170 | Chris Sabo (R) | 1.50 |
| 171 | Candy Sierra (R) | .25 |
| 172 | Van Snider (R) | .35 |
| 173 | Jeff Treadway | .08 |
| 174 | Frank Williams | .05 |
| 175 | Herm Winningham | .05 |

**MILWAUKEE BREWERS**

| NO. | PLAYER | MINT |
|---|---|---|
| 176 | Jim Adduci | .08 |
| 177 | Don August | .15 |
| 178 | Mike Birkbeck | .05 |
| 179 | Chris Bosio | .05 |
| 180 | Glenn Braggs | .05 |
| 181 | Greg Brock | .05 |
| 182 | Mark Clear | .05 |
| 183 | Chuck Crim | .05 |
| 184 | Rob Deer | .08 |
| 185 | Tom Filer | .05 |
| 186 | Jim Gantner | .05 |
| 187 | Darryl Hamilton (R) | .25 |
| 188 | Ted Higuera | .10 |
| 189 | Odell Jones | .05 |
| 190 | Jeffrey Leonard | .05 |
| 191 | Joey Meyer | .05 |
| 192 | Paul Mirabella | .05 |
| 193 | Paul Molitor | .08 |
| 194 | Charlie O'Brien | .05 |
| 195 | Dan Plesac | .05 |
| 196 | Gary Sheffield (R) | 1.75 |
| 197 | B.J. Surhoff | .08 |
| 198 | Dale Sveum | .08 |
| 199 | Bill Wegman | .05 |
| 200 | Robin Yount | .15 |

**PITTSBURGH PIRATES**

| NO. | PLAYER | MINT |
|---|---|---|
| 201 | Rafael Belliard | .05 |
| 202 | Barry Bonds | .20 |
| 203 | Bobby Bonilla | .25 |
| 204 | Sid Bream | .05 |
| 205 | Benny Distefano | .10 |
| 206 | Doug Drabek | .10 |
| 207 | Mike Dunne | .05 |
| 208 | Felix Fermin | .05 |
| 209 | Brian Fisher | .05 |
| 210 | Jim Gott | .05 |
| 211 | Bob Kipper | .05 |
| 212 | Dave LaPoint | .05 |
| 213 | Mike LaValliere | .05 |
| 214 | Jose Lind | .05 |
| 215 | Junior Ortiz | .05 |
| 216 | Vincente Palacios | .05 |
| 217 | Tom Prince | .10 |
| 218 | Gary Redus | .05 |
| 219 | R.J. Reynolds | .05 |
| 220 | Jeff Robinson | .05 |
| 221 | John Smiley | .08 |
| 222 | Andy Van Slyke | .20 |
| 223 | Bob Walk | .05 |
| 224 | Glenn Wilson | .05 |

**TORONTO BLUE JAYS**

| NO. | PLAYER | MINT |
|---|---|---|
| 225 | Jesse Barfield | .12 |
| 226 | George Bell | .15 |
| 227 | Pat Borders (R) | .30 |
| 228 | John Cerutti | .05 |
| 229 | Jim Clancy | .05 |
| 230 | Mark Eichhorn | .05 |
| 231 | Tony Fernandez | .10 |
| 232 | Cecil Fielder | .05 |
| 233 | Mike Flanagan | .05 |
| 234 | Kelly Gruber | .05 |
| 235 | Tom Henke | .05 |
| 236 | Jimmy Key | .15 |
| 237 | Rick Leach | .05 |
| 238 | Manny Lee | .05 |
| 239 | Nelson Liriano | .05 |
| 240 | Fred McGriff | .45 |
| 241 | Lloyd Moseby | .12 |
| 242 | Rance Mulliniks | .05 |
| 243 | Jeff Musselman | .05 |
| 244 | Dave Stieb | .08 |
| 245 | Todd Stottlemyre | .15 |
| 246 | Duane Ward | .05 |
| 247 | David Wells | .10 |
| 248 | Ernie Whitt | .05 |

**NEW YORK YANKEES**

| NO. | PLAYER | MINT |
|---|---|---|
| 249 | Luis Aguayo | .05 |
| 250 | Neil Allen | .05 |
| 251 | John Candelaria | .08 |
| 252 | Jack Clark | .10 |
| 253 | Richard Dotson | .08 |
| 254 | Rickey Henderson | .35 |
| 255 | Tommy John | .10 |
| 256 | Roberto Kelly | .10 |
| 257 | Al Leiter | .20 |
| 258 | Don Mattingly | 1.75 |
| 259 | Dale Mohorcic | .05 |
| 260 | Hal Morris | .25 |
| 261 | Scott Nielsen | .05 |
| 262 | Mike Pagliarulo | .10 |
| 263 | Hipolito Peno (R) | .15 |
| 264 | Ken Phelps | .05 |
| 265 | Willie Randolph | .08 |
| 266 | Rick Rhoden | .05 |
| 267 | Dave Righetti | .10 |
| 268 | Rafael Santana | .05 |
| 269 | Steve Shields | .05 |
| 270 | Joel Skinner | .05 |
| 271 | Don Slaught | .05 |
| 272 | Claudell Washington | .05 |
| 273 | Gary Ward | .05 |
| 274 | Dave Winfield | .15 |

**KC ROYALS**

| NO. | PLAYER | MINT |
|---|---|---|
| 275 | Luis Aquino | .05 |
| 276 | Floyd Bannister | .05 |
| 277 | George Brett | .30 |
| 278 | Bill Buckner | .08 |
| 279 | Nick Capra (R) | .15 |
| 280 | Jose DeJesus (R) | .15 |
| 281 | Steve Farr | .05 |
| 282 | Jerry Don Gleaton | .05 |
| 283 | Mark Gubicza | .10 |
| 284 | Tom Gordon (R) | .30 |
| 285 | Bo Jackson | .30 |
| 286 | Charlie Leibrandt | .08 |
| 287 | Mike MacFarlane (R) | .25 |
| 288 | Jeff Montgomery | .05 |
| 289 | Bill Pecota | .05 |
| 290 | Jamie Quirk | .05 |
| 291 | Bret Saberhagen | .12 |
| 292 | Kevin Seitzer | .40 |
| 293 | Kurt Stillwell | .05 |
| 294 | Pat Tabler | .08 |
| 295 | Danny Tartabull | .25 |
| 296 | Gary Thurman | .05 |
| 297 | Frank White | .05 |
| 298 | Willie Wilson | .08 |

**SAN DIEGO PADRES**

| NO. | PLAYER | MINT |
|---|---|---|
| 299 | Roberto Alomar | .20 |
| 300 | Sandy Alomar Jr. (R) | 1.50 |
| 301 | Chris Brown | .08 |
| 302 | Mike Brumley | .10 |
| 303 | Mark Davis | .05 |
| 304 | Mark Grant | .05 |
| 305 | Tony Gwynn | .40 |
| 306 | Greg W. Harris (R) | .20 |
| 307 | Andy Hawkins | .05 |
| 308 | Jimmy Jones | .05 |
| 309 | John Kruk | .20 |
| 310 | Dave Leiper | .05 |
| 311 | Carmelo Martinez | .05 |
| 312 | Lance McCullers | .08 |
| 313 | Keith Moreland | .05 |
| 314 | Dennis Rasmussen | .05 |
| 315 | Randy Ready | .05 |
| 316 | Benito Santiago | .10 |
| 317 | Eric Show | .05 |
| 318 | Todd Simmons | .05 |
| 319 | Garry Templeton | .05 |
| 320 | Dickie Thon | .05 |
| 321 | Ed Whitson | .05 |
| 322 | Marvell Wynne | .05 |

**SF GIANTS**

| NO. | PLAYER | MINT |
|---|---|---|
| 323 | Mike Aldrete | .05 |
| 324 | Bret Butler | .05 |
| 325 | Will Clark | .60 |
| 326 | Kelly Downs | .05 |
| 327 | Dave Dravecky | .05 |
| 328 | Scott Garrelts | .05 |
| 329 | Atlee Hammaker | .05 |
| 330 | Charlie Hayes (R) | .35 |
| 331 | Mike Krukow | .08 |
| 332 | Craig Lefferts | .05 |
| 333 | Candy Maldonado | .10 |
| 334 | Kirt Manwaring | .05 |
| 335 | Bob Melvin | .05 |
| 336 | Kevin Mitchell | .08 |
| 337 | Donell Nixon | .05 |
| 338 | Tony Perezchica (R) | .30 |
| 339 | Joe Price | .05 |
| 340 | Rick Reuschel | .05 |
| 341 | Ernest Riles | .05 |
| 342 | Don Robinson | .05 |
| 343 | Chris Speier | .05 |
| 344 | Robby Thompson | .05 |
| 345 | Jose Uribe | .08 |
| 346 | Matt Williams | .08 |
| 347 | Trevor Wilson (R) | .30 |

**HOUSTON ASTROS**

| NO. | PLAYER | MINT |
|---|---|---|
| 348 | Juan Agosto | .05 |
| 349 | Larry Anderson | .15 |
| 350 | Alan Ashby | .05 |
| 351 | Kevin Bass | .08 |
| 352 | Buddy Bell | .08 |
| 353 | Craig Biggio (R) | .30 |
| 354 | Danny Darwin | .05 |
| 355 | Glenn Davis | .10 |
| 356 | Jim Deshaies | .08 |
| 357 | Bill Doran | .08 |
| 358 | John Fisher (R) | .30 |
| 359 | Billy Hatcher | .05 |
| 360 | Bob Knepper | .05 |
| 361 | Louie Meadows (R) | .15 |
| 362 | Dave Meads | .05 |
| 363 | Jim Pankovits | .05 |
| 364 | Terry Puhl | .05 |
| 365 | Rafael Ramirez | .05 |

Card values shown here fluctuate considerably.

| NO. | PLAYER | MINT |
|-----|--------|------|
| 366 | Craig Reynolds | .05 |
| 367 | Nolan Ryan | .25 |
| 368 | Mike Scott | .20 |
| 369 | Dave Smith | .05 |
| 370 | Gerald Young | .08 |

**MONTREAL EXPOS**

| NO. | PLAYER | MINT |
|-----|--------|------|
| 371 | Hubie Brooks | .05 |
| 372 | Tim Burke | .05 |
| 373 | John Dopson (R) | .30 |
| 374 | Mike Fitzgerald | .05 |
| 375 | Tom Foley | .05 |
| 376 | Andres Galarraga | .30 |
| 377 | Neal Heaton | .05 |
| 378 | Joe Hesketh | .05 |
| 379 | Brian Holman (R) | .30 |
| 380 | Rex Hudler | .10 |
| 381 | Randy Johnson (R) | .30 |
| 382 | Wallace Johnson | .05 |
| 383 | Tracy Jones | .05 |
| 384 | Dave Martinez | .05 |
| 385 | Dennis Martinez | .05 |
| 386 | Andy McGaffigan | .05 |
| 387 | Otis Nixon | .05 |
| 388 | Johnny Padres (R) | .25 |
| 389 | Jeff Parrett | .08 |
| 390 | Pascual Perez | .05 |
| 391 | Tim Raines | .20 |
| 392 | Luis Rivera | .05 |
| 393 | Nelson Santovenia (R) | .15 |
| 394 | Bryn Smith | .05 |
| 395 | Tim Wallach | .08 |

**CLEVELAND INDIANS**

| NO. | PLAYER | MINT |
|-----|--------|------|
| 396 | Andy Allanson | .05 |
| 397 | Rod Allen (R) | .15 |
| 398 | Scott Bailes | .05 |
| 399 | Tom Candiotti | .08 |
| 400 | Joe Carter | .20 |
| 401 | Carmen Castillo | .05 |
| 402 | Dave Clark | .05 |
| 403 | John Farrell | .10 |
| 404 | Julio Franco | .08 |
| 405 | Don Gordon | .10 |
| 406 | Mel Hall | .05 |
| 407 | Brad Havens | .05 |
| 408 | Brook Jacoby | .05 |
| 409 | Doug Jones | .05 |
| 410 | Jeff Kaiser (R) | .25 |
| 411 | Luis Medina (R) | .75 |
| 412 | Cory Snyder | .20 |
| 413 | Greg Swindell | .10 |
| 414 | Ron Tingley | .15 |
| 415 | Willie Upshaw | .05 |
| 416 | Ron Washington | .05 |
| 417 | Rich Yett | .05 |

**CHICAGO CUBS**

| NO. | PLAYER | MINT |
|-----|--------|------|
| 418 | Damon Berryhill | .15 |
| 419 | Mike Bielecki | .05 |
| 420 | Doug Dascenzo (R) | .25 |
| 421 | Jody Davis | .05 |
| 422 | Andre Dawson | .20 |
| 423 | Frank Dipino | .05 |
| 424 | Shawon Dunston | .10 |
| 425 | "Goose" Gossage | .08 |
| 426 | Mark Grace | .85 |
| 427 | Mike Harkey (R) | .85 |
| 428 | Darrin Jackson | .08 |
| 429 | Les Lancaster | .05 |
| 430 | Vance Law | .05 |
| 431 | Greg Maddux | .25 |
| 432 | Jamie Moyer | .05 |
| 433 | Al Nipper | .05 |
| 434 | Rafael Palmeiro | .20 |
| 435 | Pat Perry | .05 |
| 436 | Jeff Pico (R) | .30 |
| 437 | Ryne Sandberg | .15 |
| 438 | Calvin Schiraldi | .05 |
| 439 | Rick Sutcliffe | .10 |
| 440 | Manny Trillo | .05 |
| 441 | Gary Varsho (R) | .25 |
| 442 | Mitch Webster | .05 |

**ST. LOUIS CARDINALS**

| NO. | PLAYER | MINT |
|-----|--------|------|
| 443 | Luis Alicea (R) | .15 |
| 444 | Tom Brunansky | .08 |
| 445 | Vince Coleman | .20 |
| 446 | John Costello (R) | .15 |
| 447 | Danny Cox | .05 |
| 448 | Ken Dayley | .05 |
| 449 | Jose Deleon | .05 |
| 450 | Curt Ford | .05 |
| 451 | Pedro Guerrero | .15 |
| 452 | Bob Horner | .05 |
| 453 | Tim Jones (R) | .25 |
| 454 | Steve Lake | .05 |
| 455 | Joe Magrane | .10 |
| 456 | Greg Mathews | .05 |
| 457 | Willie McGee | .08 |
| 458 | Larry McWilliams | .05 |
| 459 | Jose Oquendo | .05 |
| 460 | Tony Pena | .08 |
| 461 | Terry Pendleton | .08 |
| 462 | Steve Peters (R) | .15 |
| 463 | Ozzie Smith | .08 |
| 464 | Scott Terry | .05 |
| 465 | Denny Walling | .05 |
| 466 | Todd Worrell | .08 |

**CALIFORNIA ANGELS**

| NO. | PLAYER | MINT |
|-----|--------|------|
| 467 | Tony Armas | .05 |
| 468 | Dante Bichette (R) | .25 |
| 469 | Bob Boone | .05 |
| 470 | Terry Clark (R) | .25 |
| 471 | Stew Cliburn | .05 |
| 472 | Mike Cook (R) | .25 |
| 473 | Sherman Corbett (R) | .15 |
| 474 | Chili Davis | .08 |
| 475 | Brian Downing | .08 |
| 476 | Jim Eppard | .05 |
| 477 | Chuck Finley | .05 |
| 478 | Willie Fraser | .05 |
| 479 | Bryan Harvey (R) | .30 |
| 480 | Jack Howell | .08 |
| 481 | Wally Joyner | .20 |
| 482 | Jack Lazorko | .05 |
| 483 | Kirk McCaskill | .05 |
| 484 | Mark McLemore | .05 |
| 485 | Greg Minton | .05 |
| 486 | Dan Petry | .05 |
| 487 | Johnny Ray | .10 |
| 488 | Dick Schofield | .05 |
| 489 | Devon White | .08 |
| 490 | Mike Witt | .08 |

**CHICAGO WHITE SOX**

| NO. | PLAYER | MINT |
|-----|--------|------|
| 491 | Harold Baines | .10 |
| 492 | Daryl Boston | .05 |
| 493 | Ivan Calderon | .10 |
| 494 | Mike Diaz | .05 |
| 495 | Carlton Fisk | .10 |
| 496 | Dave Gallagher (R) | .30 |
| 497 | Ozzie Guillen | .08 |
| 498 | Shawn Hillegas | .05 |
| 499 | Lance Johnson | .05 |
| 500 | Barry Jones | .05 |
| 501 | Bill Long | .05 |
| 502 | Steve Lyons | .05 |
| 503 | Fred Manrique | .05 |
| 504 | Jack McDowell | .10 |
| 505 | Donn Pall | .15 |
| 506 | Kelly Paris | .05 |
| 507 | Dan Pasqua | .08 |
| 508 | Ken Patterson (R) | .15 |
| 509 | Melido Perez | .10 |
| 510 | Jerry Reuss | .05 |
| 511 | Mark Salas | .05 |
| 512 | Bobby Thigpen | .05 |
| 513 | Mike Woodard | .05 |

**TEXAS RANGERS**

| NO. | PLAYER | MINT |
|-----|--------|------|
| 514 | Bob Brower | .05 |
| 515 | Steve Buechele | .05 |
| 516 | Jose Cecena (R) | .15 |
| 517 | Cecil Espy | .05 |
| 518 | Scott Fletcher | .05 |
| 519 | Cecilio Guante | .05 |
| 520 | Jose Guman | .05 |
| 521 | Ray Hayward | .05 |
| 522 | Charlie Hough | .08 |
| 523 | Pete Incaviglia | .10 |
| 524 | Mike Jeffcoat | .05 |
| 525 | Paul Kilgus | .05 |
| 526 | Chad Kreuter (R) | .25 |
| 527 | Jeff Kunkel | .05 |
| 528 | Oddibe McDowell | .08 |
| 529 | Pete O'Brien | .10 |
| 530 | Geno Petralli | .05 |

| NO. | PLAYER | MINT |
|-----|--------|------|
| 531 | Jeff Russell | .05 |
| 532 | Ruben Sierra | .25 |
| 533 | Mike Stanley | .05 |
| 534 | Ed VandeBerg | .05 |
| 535 | Curtis Wilkerson | .05 |
| 536 | Mitch Williams | .05 |
| 537 | Bobby Witt | .05 |

**SEATTLE MARINERS**

| NO. | PLAYER | MINT |
|-----|--------|------|
| 538 | Steve Balboni | .05 |
| 539 | Scott Bankhead | .05 |
| 540 | Scott Bradley | .05 |
| 541 | Mickey Brantley | .08 |
| 542 | Jay Buhner | .25 |
| 543 | Mike Campbell | .05 |
| 544 | Darnell Coles | .05 |
| 545 | Henry Cotto | .05 |
| 546 | Alvin Davis | .08 |
| 547 | Mario Diaz | .05 |
| 548 | Ken Griffey Jr. (R) | 3.00 |
| 549 | Erik Hanson (R) | .25 |
| 550 | Mike Jackson | .05 |
| 551 | Mark Langston | .12 |
| 552 | Edgar Martinez | .15 |
| 553 | Bill McGuire (R) | .25 |
| 554 | Mike Moore | .05 |
| 555 | Jim Presley | .05 |
| 556 | Rey Quinones | .05 |
| 557 | Jerry Reed | .05 |
| 558 | Harold Reynolds | .08 |
| 559 | Mike Schooler (R) | .20 |
| 560 | Bill Swift | .05 |
| 561 | Dave Valle | .05 |

**PHILADELPHIA PHILLIES**

| NO. | PLAYER | MINT |
|-----|--------|------|
| 562 | Steve Bedrosian | .08 |
| 563 | Phil Bradley | .08 |
| 564 | Don Carman | .05 |
| 565 | Bob Dernier | .05 |
| 566 | Marvin Freeman | .05 |
| 567 | Todd Frohwirth | .05 |
| 568 | Greg Gross | .05 |
| 569 | Kevin Gross | .05 |
| 570 | Greg Harris | .25 |
| 571 | Von Hayes | .08 |
| 572 | Chris James | .08 |
| 573 | Steve Jeltz | .05 |
| 574 | Ron Jones | .85 |
| 575 | Ricky Jordan (R) | 2.50 |
| 576 | Mike Maddux | .05 |
| 577 | David Palmer | .05 |
| 578 | Lance Parrish | .10 |
| 579 | Shane Rawley | .05 |
| 580 | Bruce Ruffin | .05 |
| 581 | Juan Samuel | .10 |
| 582 | Mike Schmidt | .35 |
| 583 | Kent Tekulve | .05 |
| 584 | Milt Thompson | .05 |

**ATLANTA BRAVES**

| NO. | PLAYER | MINT |
|-----|--------|------|
| 585 | Jose Alvarez (R) | .15 |
| 586 | Paul Assenmacher | .05 |
| 587 | Bruce Benedict | .05 |
| 588 | Jeff Blauser | .05 |
| 589 | Terry Blockner (R) | .15 |
| 590 | Ron Gant | .35 |
| 591 | Tom Glavine | .05 |
| 592 | Tommy Gregg | .15 |
| 593 | Albert Hall | .05 |
| 594 | Dion James | .05 |
| 595 | Rich Mahler | .05 |
| 596 | Dale Murphy | .30 |
| 597 | Gerald Perry | .12 |
| 598 | Charlie Puleo | .05 |
| 599 | Ted Simmons | .05 |
| 600 | Pete Smith | .08 |
| 601 | Zane Smith | .05 |
| 602 | John Smoltz (R) | .35 |
| 603 | Bruce Sutter | .08 |
| 604 | Andres Thomas | .05 |
| 605 | Ozzie Virgil | .05 |

**BALTIMORE ORIOLES**

| NO. | PLAYER | MINT |
|-----|--------|------|
| 606 | Brady Anderson (R) | .35 |
| 607 | Jeff Ballard | .05 |
| 608 | Jose Bautista (R) | .25 |
| 609 | Ken Gerhart | .05 |
| 610 | Terry Kennedy | .05 |
| 611 | Eddie Murray | .35 |

| NO. | PLAYER | MINT |
|-----|--------|------|
| 612 | Carl Nichols | .15 |
| 613 | Tom Niedenfuer | .05 |
| 614 | Joe Orsulak | .05 |
| 615 | Oswaldo Perraza (R) | .15 |
| 616 | Bill Ripken | .05 |
| 617 | Cal Ripken Jr. | .25 |
| 618 | Dave Schmidt | .35 |
| 619 | Rich Schu | .05 |
| 620 | Larry Sheets | .05 |
| 621 | Doug Sisk | .05 |
| 622 | Pete Stanicek | .05 |
| 623 | Mickey Tettleton | .05 |
| 624 | Jay Tibbs | .05 |
| 625 | Jim Traber | .05 |
| 626 | Mark Williamson | .05 |
| 627 | Craig Worthington (R) | .35 |

**SPECIAL CARDS**

| NO. | PLAYER | MINT |
|-----|--------|------|
| 628 | Speed/Power | .50 |
| 629 | Pitcher Perfect | .08 |
| 630 | Like Father-Like Son | .50 |
| 631 | N.L. All Stars | .25 |
| 632 | Homeruns-Coast to Coast | .25 |
| 633 | Hot Corners-Hot Hitters | .25 |
| 634 | Triple A's | .75 |
| 635 | Dual Heat | .25 |
| 636 | N.L. Pitching Power | .20 |
| 637 | Cannon Arms | .60 |
| 638 | Double Trouble | .15 |
| 639 | Power Center | .35 |

**No. 640 to 643—**
**Major League Prospects**

| NO. | PLAYER | MINT |
|-----|--------|------|
| 640 | S. Wilson (R)/C. Drew (R) | .40 |
| 641 | K.Brown (R)/K. Reimer (R) | .25 |
| 642 | B.Pounders (R)/J.Clark (R) | .25 |
| 643 | M. Capel (R)/D. Hall | .15 |
| 644 | J.Girardi (R)/R. Roomes (R) | .30 |
| 645 | L. Harris (R)/M. Brown (R) | .25 |
| 646 | L.Santos (R)/J.Campbell(R) | .25 |
| 647 | R.Kramer (R)/M.Garcia (R) | .30 |
| 648 | T.Lovullo (R)/R.Palacios(R) | .25 |
| 649 | J. Corsi (R)/B. Milacki (R) | .25 |
| 650 | G.Hall (R)/M.Rochford (R) | .25 |
| 651 | T.Taylor(R)/V.Lovelace(R) | .25 |
| 652 | K. Hill (R)/D. Cook (R) | .25 |
| 653 | S. Service (R)/S.Turner (R) | .30 |
| 654 | Checklist No. 1 | .08 |
| 655 | Checklist No. 2 | .08 |
| 656 | Checklist No. 3 | .08 |
| 657 | Checklist No. 4 | .08 |
| 658 | Checklist No. 5 | .08 |
| 659 | Checklist No. 6 | .08 |
| 660 | Checklist No. 7 | .08 |

Card values shown here fluctuate considerably.

# 1988 Score....Complete Set of 660 Cards—Value $25.00

This was Score's *first* baseball card set. It was issued by the same company that produced the Sportsflic card sets. Features the rookie cards of Matt Nokes, Ellis Burks and Sam Horn. A 24-card All-Star set was printed on the bottom of display boxes. Three different player cards and one trivia card were printed on six different boxes.

| NO. PLAYER | MINT | NO. PLAYER | MINT | NO. PLAYER | MINT | NO. PLAYER | MINT |
|---|---|---|---|---|---|---|---|
| 1 Don Mattingly | 1.25 | 67 Mike Boddicker | .05 | 133 Larry Andersen | .05 | 199 John Grubb | .05 |
| 2 Wade Boggs | .65 | 68 Vince Coleman | .20 | 134 Bob Brenley | .08 | 200 Bill Ripken (R) | .25 |
| 3 Tim Raines | .20 | 69 Howard Johnson | .15 | 135 Mike Marshall | .10 | 201 Sam Horn (R) | .45 |
| 4 Andre Dawson | .20 | 70 Tim Wallach | .08 | 136 Gerald Perry | .15 | 202 Todd Worrell | .10 |
| 5 Mark McGwire | 1.00 | 71 Keith Moreland | .05 | 137 Bobby Meacham | .05 | 203 Terry Leach | .05 |
| 6 Kevin Seitzer | 1.00 | 72 Barry Larkin | .12 | 138 Larry Herndon | .05 | 204 Garth Iorg | .05 |
| 7 Wally Joyner | .50 | 73 Alan Ashby | .05 | 139 Fred Manrique (R) | .15 | 205 Brian Dayett | .05 |
| 8 Jesse Barfield | .20 | 74 Rick Rhoden | .05 | 140 Charlie Hough | .05 | 206 Bo Diaz | .05 |
| 9 Pedro Guerrero | .15 | 75 Darrell Evans | .08 | 141 Ron Darling | .10 | 207 Craig Reynolds | .05 |
| 10 Eric Davis | .75 | 76 Dave Stieb | .08 | 142 Herm Winningham | .05 | 208 Brian Holton | .15 |
| 11 George Brett | .30 | 77 Dan Plesac | .08 | 143 Mike Diaz | .05 | 209 Marvelle Wynne | .05 |
| 12 Ozzie Smith | .15 | 78 Will Clark | .50 | 144 Mike Jackson (R) | .10 | 210 Dave Concepcion | .10 |
| 13 Rickey Henderson | .30 | 79 Frank White | .05 | 145 Denny Walling | .05 | 211 Mike Davis | .05 |
| 14 Jim Rice | .20 | 80 Joe Carter | .15 | 146 Rob Thompson | .05 | 212 Devon White | .20 |
| 15 Matt Nokes (R) | .60 | 81 Mike Witt | .08 | 147 Franklin Stubbs | .05 | 213 Mickey Brantley | .08 |
| 16 Mike Schmidt | .30 | 82 Terry Steinbach | .20 | 148 Albert Hall | .05 | 214 Greg Gagne | .05 |
| 17 Dave Parker | .15 | 83 Alvin Davis | .08 | 149 Bobby Witt | .05 | 215 Oddibe McDowell | .08 |
| 18 Eddie Murray | .20 | 84 Tom Herr | .05 | 150 Lance McCullers | .08 | 216 Jimmy Key | .10 |
| 19 Andres Galarraga | .25 | 85 Vance Law | .05 | 151 Scott Bradley | .05 | 217 Dave Bergman | .05 |
| 20 Tony Fernandez | .08 | 86 Kal Daniels | .25 | 152 Mark McLemore | .08 | 218 Calvin Schiraldi | .05 |
| 21 Kevin McReynolds | .12 | 87 Rick Honeycutt | .05 | 153 Tim Laudner | .05 | 219 Larry Sheets | .10 |
| 22 B.J. Surhoff | .15 | 88 Alfredo Griffin | .05 | 154 Greg Swindell | .10 | 220 Mike Easler | .05 |
| 23 Pat Tabler | .05 | 89 Bret Saberhagen | .15 | 155 Marty Barrett | .10 | 221 Kurt Stillwell | .05 |
| 24 Kirby Puckett | .35 | 90 Bert Blyleven | .08 | 156 Mike Heath | .05 | 222 Chuck Jackson (R) | .15 |
| 25 Benito Santiago | .40 | 91 Jeff Reardon | .05 | 157 Gary Ward | .05 | 223 Dave Martinez | .05 |
| 26 Ryn Sandberg | .15 | 92 Cory Snyder | .20 | 158 Lee Mazzilli | .10 | 224 Tim Leary | .05 |
| 27 Kelly Downs | .05 | 93 Greg Walker | .08 | 159 Tom Foley | .05 | 225 Steve Garvey | .20 |
| 28 Jose Cruz | .05 | 94 Joe Magrane (R) | .35 | 160 Robin Yount | .15 | 226 Greg Mathews | .05 |
| 29 Pete O'Brien | .08 | 95 Rob Deer | .10 | 161 Steve Bedrosian | .08 | 227 Doug Sisk | .05 |
| 30 Mark Langston | .08 | 96 Ray Knight | .05 | 162 Bob Walk | .05 | 228 Dave Henderson | .05 |
| 31 Lee Smith | .08 | 97 Casey Candaele | .05 | 163 Nick Esasky | .05 | 229 Jimmy Dwyer | .05 |
| 32 Juan Samuel | .10 | 98 John Cerutti | .05 | 164 Ken Caminiti (R) | .25 | 230 Larry Owen | .05 |
| 33 Kevin Bass | .08 | 99 Buddy Bell | .10 | 165 Jose Uribe | .05 | 231 Andre Thornton | .05 |
| 34 R.J. Reynolds | .08 | 100 Jack Clark | .25 | 166 Dave Anderson | .05 | 232 Mark Salas | .05 |
| 35 Steve Sax | .10 | 101 Eric Bell (R) | .05 | 167 Ed Whitson | .05 | 233 Tom Brookens | .05 |
| 36 John Kruk | .20 | 102 Willie Wilson | .10 | 168 Ernie Whitt | .05 | 234 Greg Brock | .05 |
| 37 Alan Trammell | .15 | 103 Dave Schmidt | .05 | 169 Cecil Cooper | .10 | 235 Rance Mulliniks | .05 |
| 38 Chris Bosio | .05 | 104 Dennis Eckersley | .10 | 170 Mike Pagliarulo | .10 | 236 Bob Brower | .08 |
| 39 Brook Jacoby | .08 | 105 Don Sutton | .10 | 171 Pat Sheridan | .05 | 237 Joe Niekro | .10 |
| 40 Willie McGee | .10 | 106 Danny Tartabull | .20 | 172 Chris Bando | .05 | 238 Scott Bankhead | .05 |
| 41 Dave Magadan | .15 | 107 Fred McGriff | .75 | 173 Lee Lacy | .05 | 239 Doug DeCinces | .05 |
| 42 Fred Lynn | .10 | 108 Les Straker (R) | .15 | 174 Steve Lombardozzi | .05 | 240 Tommy John | .10 |
| 43 Kent Hrbek | .15 | 109 Lloyd Moseby | .15 | 175 Mike Greenwell | 1.75 | 241 Rich Gedman | .05 |
| 44 Brian Downing | .05 | 110 Roger Clemens | .50 | 176 Greg Minton | .05 | 242 Ted Power | .05 |
| 45 Jose Canseco | 1.25 | 111 Glenn Hubbard | .05 | 177 Moose Haas | .05 | 243 Dave Meads (R) | .15 |
| 46 Jim Presley | .05 | 112 Ken Williams (R) | .25 | 178 Mike Kingery | .05 | 244 Jim Sundberg | .05 |
| 47 Mike Stanley | .10 | 113 Ruben Sierra | .30 | 179 Greg Harris | .05 | 245 Ken Oberkfell | .05 |
| 48 Tony Pena | .05 | 114 Stan Jefferson | .15 | 180 Bo Jackson | .35 | 246 Jimmy Jones | .10 |
| 49 David Cone | .75 | 115 Milt Thompson | .05 | 181 Carmelo Martinez | .05 | 247 Ken Landreaux | .05 |
| 50 Rick Sutcliffe | .10 | 116 Bobby Bonilla | .20 | 182 Alex Trevino | .05 | 248 Jose Oquendo | .05 |
| 51 Doug Drabek | .05 | 117 Wayne Tolleson | .05 | 183 Ron Oester | .05 | 249 John Mitchell (R) | .15 |
| 52 Bill Doran | .05 | 118 Matt Williams (R) | .30 | 184 Danny Darwin | .05 | 250 Don Baylor | .05 |
| 53 Mike Scioscia | .05 | 119 Chet Lemon | .05 | 185 Mike Krukow | .05 | 251 Scott Fletcher | .05 |
| 54 Candy Maldonado | .08 | 120 Dale Sveum | .05 | 186 Rafael Palmeiro | .50 | 252 Al Newman | .05 |
| 55 Dave Winfield | .20 | 121 Dennis Boyd | .05 | 187 Tim Burke | .05 | 253 Carney Lansford | .05 |
| 56 Lou Whitaker | .10 | 122 Brett Butler | .05 | 188 Roger McDowell | .05 | 254 Johnny Ray | .08 |
| 57 Tom Henke | .05 | 123 Terry Kennedy | .05 | 189 Garry Templeton | .05 | 255 Gary Pettis | .05 |
| 58 Ken Gerhardt | .08 | 124 Jack Howell | .05 | 190 Terry Pendleton | .05 | 256 Ken Phelps | .05 |
| 59 Glenn Braggs | .08 | 125 Curt Young | .05 | 191 Larry Parrish | .05 | 257 Tim Stoddard | .05 |
| 60 Julio Franco | .08 | 126 Dale Valle | .08 | 192 Rey Quinones | .05 | 258 Rick Leach | .05 |
| 61 Charlie Leibrandt | .05 | 127 Curt Wilkerson | .05 | 193 Joaquin Andujar | .05 | 259 Ed Romero | .05 |
| 62 Gary Gaetti | .15 | 128 Tim Teufel | .05 | 194 Tom Brunansky | .10 | 260 Sid Bream | .05 |
| 63 Bob Boone | .05 | 129 Ozzie Virgil | .05 | 195 Donnie Moore | .05 | 261 Tom Niedenfuer | .05 |
| 64 Luis Polonia (R) | .20 | 130 Brian Fisher | .05 | 196 Dan Pasqual | .10 | 262 Rick Dempsey | .05 |
| 65 Dwight Evans | .10 | 131 Lance Parrish | .10 | 197 Jim Gantner | .05 | 263 Lonnie Smith | .05 |
| 66 Phil Bradley | .08 | 132 Tom Browning | .05 | 198 Mark Eichhorn | .05 | 264 Bob Forsch | .05 |

151

| NO. | PLAYER | MINT | NO. | PLAYER | MINT | NO. | PLAYER | MINT | NO. | PLAYER | MINT |
|---|---|---|---|---|---|---|---|---|---|---|---|
| 265 | Barry Bonds | .20 | 349 | Ernest Riles | .05 | 433 | Wallace Johnson | .05 | 517 | Ken Dayley | .05 |
| 266 | Willie Randolph | .10 | 350 | Dwight Gooden | .60 | 434 | Jack O'Connor | .05 | 518 | Don Aase | .05 |
| 267 | Mike Ramsey | .10 | 351 | Dave Righetti | .10 | 435 | Steve Jeltz | .05 | 519 | Rick Reuschel | .05 |
| 268 | Don Slaught | .05 | 352 | Pat Dodson | .12 | 436 | Donnell Nixon (R) | .15 | 520 | Mike Henneman (R) | .20 |
| 269 | Mickey Tettleton | .05 | 353 | John Habyan | .08 | 437 | Jack Lazorko | .05 | 521 | Rick Aguilera | .05 |
| 270 | Jerry Reuss | .05 | 354 | Jim Deshaies | .05 | 438 | Keith Comstock (R) | .12 | 522 | Jay Howell | .05 |
| 271 | Marc Sullivan | .05 | 355 | Butch Wynegar | .05 | 439 | Jeff Robinson | .05 | 523 | Ed Correa | .05 |
| 272 | Jim Morrison | .05 | 356 | Bryn Smith | .05 | 440 | Graig Nettles | .10 | 524 | Manny Trillo | .05 |
| 273 | Steve Balboni | .05 | 357 | Matt Young | .05 | 441 | Mel Hall | .05 | 525 | Kirk Gibson | .25 |
| 274 | Dick Schofield | .05 | 358 | Tom Pagnozzi (R) | .15 | 442 | Gerald Young (R) | .25 | 526 | Wally Ritchie (R) | .15 |
| 275 | John Tudor | .10 | 359 | Floyd Rayford | .05 | 443 | Gary Redus | .05 | 527 | Al Nipper | .05 |
| 276 | Gene Larkin (R) | .30 | 360 | Darryl Strawberry | .60 | 444 | Charlie Moore | .05 | 528 | Atlee Hammaker | .05 |
| 277 | Harold Reynolds | .05 | 361 | Sal Butera | .05 | 445 | Bill Madlock | .08 | 529 | Shawon Dunston | .05 |
| 278 | Jerry Browne | .05 | 362 | Domingo Ramos | .05 | 446 | Mark Clear | .05 | 530 | Jim Clancy | .05 |
| 279 | Willie Upshaw | .05 | 363 | Chris Brown | .10 | 447 | Greg Booker | .05 | 531 | Tom Paciorek | .05 |
| 280 | Ted Higuera | .15 | 364 | Jose Gonzalez | .10 | 448 | Rick Schu | .05 | 532 | Joel Skinner | .05 |
| 281 | Terry McGriff | .20 | 365 | Dave Smith | .05 | 449 | Ron Kittle | .10 | 533 | Scott Garrelts | .05 |
| 282 | Terry Puhl | .05 | 366 | Andy McGaffigan | .05 | 450 | Dale Murphy | .30 | 534 | Tom O'Malley | .05 |
| 283 | Mark Wasinger (R) | .20 | 367 | Stan Javier | .05 | 451 | Bob Dernier | .05 | 535 | John Franco | .10 |
| 284 | Luis Salazar | .05 | 368 | Henry Cotto | .05 | 452 | Dale Mohorcic | .05 | 536 | Paul Kilgus (R) | .20 |
| 285 | Ted Simmons | .08 | 369 | Mike Birkbeck | .05 | 453 | Rafael Belliard | .05 | 537 | Darrell Porter | .05 |
| 286 | John Shelby | .05 | 370 | Len Dykstra | .15 | 454 | Charlie Puleo | .05 | 538 | Walt Terrell | .05 |
| 287 | John Smiley (R) | .20 | 371 | Dave Collins | .05 | 455 | Dwayne Murphy | .05 | 539 | Bill Long (R) | .12 |
| 288 | Curt Ford | .05 | 372 | Spike Owen | .05 | 456 | Jim Eisenreich | .05 | 540 | George Bell | .15 |
| 289 | Steve Crawford | .05 | 373 | Geno Petralli | .05 | 457 | David Palmer | .05 | 541 | Jeff Sellers | .05 |
| 290 | Dan Quisenberry | .08 | 374 | Ron Karkovice | .05 | 458 | Dave Stewart | .15 | 542 | Joe Boever (R) | .15 |
| 291 | Alan Wiggins | .05 | 375 | Shane Rawley | .05 | 459 | Pasqual Perez | .05 | 543 | Steve Howe | .05 |
| 292 | Randy Bush | .05 | 376 | Dewayne Buice (R) | .15 | 460 | Glenn Davis | .12 | 544 | Scott Sanderson | .05 |
| 293 | John Candelaria | .08 | 377 | Bill Pecota (R) | .15 | 461 | Dan Petry | .05 | 545 | Jack Morris | .10 |
| 294 | Tony Phillips | .05 | 378 | Leon Durham | .05 | 462 | Jim Winn | .05 | 546 | Todd Benzinger (R) | .40 |
| 295 | Mike Morgan | .05 | 379 | Ed Olwine | .05 | 463 | Darrell Miller | .05 | 547 | Steve Henderson | .05 |
| 296 | Bill Wegman | .05 | 380 | Bruce Hurst | .10 | 464 | Mike Moore | .05 | 548 | Eddie Milner | .05 |
| 297 | Terry Francona | .05 | 381 | Bob McClure | .05 | 465 | Mike LaCoss | .05 | 549 | Jeff Robinson (R) | .50 |
| 298 | Mickey Hatcher | .05 | 382 | Mark Thurmond | .05 | 466 | Steve Farr | .05 | 550 | Cal Ripken, Jr. | .20 |
| 299 | Andres Thomas | .05 | 383 | Buddy Biancalana | .05 | 467 | Jerry Mumphrey | .05 | 551 | Jody Davis | .08 |
| 300 | Bob Stanley | .05 | 384 | Tim Conroy | .05 | 468 | Kevin Gross | .05 | 552 | Kirk McCaskill | .05 |
| 301 | Alfredo Pedrique (R) | .12 | 385 | Tony Gwynn | .40 | 469 | Bruce Bochy | .05 | 553 | Craig Lefferts | .05 |
| 302 | Jim Lindeman | .10 | 386 | Greg Gross | .05 | 470 | Orel Hershiser | .15 | 554 | Darnell Coles | .05 |
| 303 | Wally Backman | .05 | 387 | Barry Lyons (R) | .20 | 471 | Eric King | .05 | 555 | Phil Niekro | .15 |
| 304 | Paul O'Neill | .10 | 388 | Mike Felder | .05 | 472 | Ellis Burks (R) | 1.00 | 556 | Mike Aldrete | .05 |
| 305 | Hubie Brooks | .08 | 389 | Pat Clements | .05 | 473 | Darren Daulton | .05 | 557 | Pat Perry | .05 |
| 306 | Steve Buechele | .05 | 390 | Ken Griffey | .08 | 474 | Mookie Wilson | .05 | 558 | Juan Agosto | .05 |
| 307 | Bobby Thigpen | .05 | 391 | Mark Davis | .05 | 475 | Frank Viola | .15 | 559 | Rob Murphy | .05 |
| 308 | George Hendrick | .05 | 392 | Jose Rijo | .05 | 476 | Ron Robinson | .05 | 560 | Dennis Rasmussen | .05 |
| 309 | John Moses | .05 | 393 | Mike Young | .05 | 477 | Bob Melvin | .05 | 561 | Manny Lee | .05 |
| 310 | Ron Guidry | .08 | 394 | Willie Fraser | .10 | 478 | Jeff Musselman | .12 | 562 | Jeff Blauser (R) | .20 |
| 311 | Bill Schroeder | .05 | 395 | Dion James | .05 | 479 | Charlie Kerfeld | .05 | 563 | Bob Ojeda | .05 |
| 312 | Jose Nunez (R) | .20 | 396 | Steve Shields | .12 | 480 | Richard Dotson | .05 | 564 | Dave Dravecky | .05 |
| 313 | Bud Black | .05 | 397 | Randy St. Claire | .05 | 481 | Kevin Mitchell | .05 | 565 | Gene Garber | .05 |
| 314 | Joe Sambito | .05 | 398 | Danny Jackson | .20 | 482 | Gary Roenicke | .05 | 566 | Ron Roenicke | .05 |
| 315 | Scott McGregor | .05 | 399 | Cecil Fielder | .05 | 483 | Tim Flannery | .05 | 567 | Tommy Hinzo (R) | .15 |
| 316 | Rafael Santana | .05 | 400 | Keith Hernandez | .25 | 484 | Rich Yett | .05 | 568 | Eric Nolte (R) | .12 |
| 317 | Frank Williams | .05 | 401 | Don Carman | .05 | 485 | Pete Incaviglia | .20 | 569 | Ed Hearn | .05 |
| 318 | Mike Fitzgerald | .05 | 402 | Chuck Crim (R) | .15 | 486 | Rick Cerone | .05 | 570 | Mark Davidson (R) | .20 |
| 319 | Rick Mahler | .05 | 403 | Rob Woodward | .05 | 487 | Tony Armas | .05 | 571 | Jim Walewander (R) | .20 |
| 320 | Jim Gott | .05 | 404 | Junior Ortiz | .05 | 488 | Jerry Reed | .05 | 572 | Donnie Hill | .05 |
| 321 | Marinao Duncan | .05 | 405 | Glenn Wilson | .05 | 489 | Davey Lopes | .05 | 573 | Jamie Moyer | .05 |
| 322 | Jose Guzman | .05 | 406 | Ken Howell | .05 | 490 | Frank Tanana | .05 | 574 | Ken Schrom | .05 |
| 323 | Lee Guetterman | .05 | 407 | Jeff Kunkel | .05 | 491 | Mike Loynd | .10 | 575 | Nolan Ryan | .20 |
| 324 | Dan Gladden | .05 | 408 | Jeff Reed | .05 | 492 | Bruce Ruffin | .05 | 576 | Jim Acker | .05 |
| 325 | Gary Carter | .20 | 409 | Chris James | .15 | 493 | Chris Speier | .05 | 577 | Jamie Quirk | .05 |
| 326 | Tracy Jones | .08 | 410 | Zane Smith | .05 | 494 | Tom Hume | .05 | 578 | Jay Alrich (R) | .12 |
| 327 | Floyd Youmans | .05 | 411 | Ken Dixon | .05 | 495 | Jesse Orosco | .05 | 579 | Claudell Washington | .05 |
| 328 | Bill Dawley | .05 | 412 | Rickey Horton | .05 | 496 | Robbie Wine, Jr. (R) | .20 | 580 | Jeff Leonard | .08 |
| 329 | Paul Noce (R) | .15 | 413 | Frank Dipino | .05 | 497 | Jeff Montgomery (R) | .20 | 581 | Carmen Castillo | .05 |
| 330 | Angel Salazar | .05 | 414 | Shane Mack | .20 | 498 | Jeff Dedmon | .05 | 582 | Darryl Boston | .05 |
| 331 | Goose Gossage | .10 | 415 | Danny Cox | .05 | 499 | Luis Aguayo | .05 | 583 | Jeff DeWillis (R) | .20 |
| 332 | George Frazier | .05 | 416 | Andy Van Slyke | .20 | 500 | Reggie Jackson #1 | .20 | 584 | John Marzano (R) | .20 |
| 333 | Ruppert Jones | .05 | 417 | Danny Heep | .05 | 501 | Reggie Jackson #2 | .20 | 585 | Bill Gullickson | .05 |
| 334 | Billy Jo Robidoux | .05 | 418 | John Cangelosi | .05 | 502 | Reggie Jackson #3 | .20 | 586 | Andy Allanson | .05 |
| 335 | Mike Scott | .10 | 419 | John Christensen | .05 | 503 | Reggie Jackson #4 | .20 | 587 | Lee Tunnell | .05 |
| 336 | Randy Myers | .25 | 420 | Joey Cora (R) | .15 | 504 | Reggie Jackson #5 | .20 | 588 | Gene Nelson | .05 |
| 337 | Bob Sebra | .05 | 421 | Mike Lavalliere | .05 | 505 | Billy Hatcher | .10 | 589 | Dave LaPoint | .05 |
| 338 | Eric Show | .05 | 422 | Kelly Gruber | .05 | 506 | Ed Lynch | .05 | 590 | Harold Baines | .10 |
| 339 | Mitch Williams | .05 | 423 | Bruce Benedict | .05 | 507 | Willie Hernandez | .05 | 591 | Bill Buckner | .05 |
| 340 | Paul Molitor | .15 | 424 | Len Matuszek | .05 | 508 | Jose DeLeon | .05 | 592 | Carlton Fisk | .10 |
| 341 | Gus Polidor | .05 | 425 | Kent Tekulve | .05 | 509 | Joel Youngblood | .05 | 593 | Rick Manning | .05 |
| 342 | Steve Trout | .05 | 426 | Rafael Ramirez | .05 | 510 | Bob Welch | .05 | 594 | Doug Jones (R) | .25 |
| 343 | Jerry Don Gleaton | .05 | 427 | Mike Flanagan | .05 | 511 | Steve Ontiveros | .05 | 595 | Tom Candiotti | .08 |
| 344 | Bob Knepper | .05 | 428 | Mike Gallego | .05 | 512 | Randy Ready | .05 | 596 | Steve Lake | .05 |
| 345 | Mitch Webster | .05 | 429 | Juan Castillo | .05 | 513 | Juan Nieves | .05 | 597 | Jose Lind (R) | .20 |
| 346 | John Morris | .05 | 430 | Neal Heaton | .05 | 514 | Jeff Russell | .05 | 598 | Ross Jones (R) | .15 |
| 347 | Andy Hawkins | .05 | 431 | Phil Garner | .05 | 515 | Von Hayes | .10 | 599 | Gary Matthews | .05 |
| 348 | Dave Leiper | .05 | 432 | Mike Dunne (R) | .20 | 516 | Mark Gubicza | .05 | 600 | Fernando Valenzuela | .20 |

# 1988 Score (Continued)

| NO. | PLAYER | MINT |
|---|---|---|
| 601 | Dennis Martinez | .05 |
| 602 | Les Lancaster (R) | .12 |
| 603 | Ozzie Guillen | .05 |
| 604 | Tony Bernazard | .05 |
| 605 | Chili Davis | .05 |
| 606 | Roy Smalley | .05 |
| 607 | Ivan Calderon | .15 |
| 608 | Jay Tibbs | .05 |
| 609 | Guy Hoffman | .05 |
| 610 | Doyle Alexander | .05 |
| 611 | Mike Bielecki | .05 |
| 612 | Shawn Hillegas (R) | .15 |
| 613 | Keith Atherton | .05 |
| 614 | Eric Plunk | .05 |
| 615 | Sid Fernandez | .10 |
| 616 | Dennis Lamp | .05 |
| 617 | Dave Engle | .05 |
| 618 | Harry Spilman | .05 |

| NO. | PLAYER | MINT |
|---|---|---|
| 619 | Don Robinson | .05 |
| 620 | John Farrell (R) | .30 |
| 621 | Nelson Liriano (R) | .20 |
| 622 | Floyd Bannister | .05 |
| 623 | Randy Milligan (R) | .40 |
| 624 | Kevin Elster | .25 |
| 625 | Jody Reed (R) | .30 |
| 626 | Shawn Abner | .25 |
| 627 | Kurt Manwaring (R) | .25 |
| 628 | Pete Stanicek (R) | .25 |
| 629 | Rob Ducey (R) | .30 |
| 630 | Steve Kiefer | .10 |
| 631 | Gary Thurman (R) | .35 |
| 632 | Darrel Akerfelds (R) | .20 |
| 633 | Dave Clark | .15 |
| 634 | Roberto Kelly (R) | .40 |
| 635 | Keith Hughes (R) | .25 |

| NO. | PLAYER | MINT |
|---|---|---|
| 636 | John Davis (R) | .20 |
| 637 | Mike Devereaux (R) | .25 |
| 638 | Tom Glavine (R) | .25 |
| 639 | Keith Miller (R) | .25 |
| 640 | Chris Gwynn (R) | .40 |
| 641 | Tim Crews (R) | .20 |
| 642 | Mackey Sasser (R) | .30 |
| 643 | Vincente Palacios (R) | .20 |
| 644 | Kevin Romine (R) | .15 |
| 645 | Gregg Jefferies (R) | 4.00 |
| 646 | Jeff Treadway (R) | .35 |
| 647 | Ronnie Gant (R) | .45 |
| 648 | M. McGwire/M. Nokes | .50 |
| 649 | E. Davis/T. Raines | .25 |
| 650 | D. Mattingly/J. Clark | .50 |
| 651 | A. Trammell/T. Fernandez/ C. Ripken | .15 |

| NO. | PLAYER | MINT |
|---|---|---|
| 652 | Highlights: Coleman 100 SB | .15 |
| 653 | Highlights: Puckett 10 Hits | .25 |
| 654 | Highlights: Santiago Hit Streak | .20 |
| 655 | Highlights: Nieves No-Hitter | .10 |
| 656 | Highlights: Bedrosian Saves | .10 |
| 657 | Highlights: Schmidt 500 HR's | .25 |
| 658 | Highlights: Mattingly HR's | .50 |
| 659 | Highlights: McGwire HR's | .50 |
| 660 | Highlights: Molitor Hit Streak | .20 |

## 1988 Score Traded & Rookie. . . . Complete Set of 110 Cards—Value $10.00

Updates the main 1988 card set with players who changed teams during the season, and rookies. Features the first Score card of Mark Grace, Chris Sabo, Robert Alomar and Jim Belcher. The set was packaged in a printed box and distributed primarily through card hobby dealers.

| NO. | PLAYER | MINT |
|---|---|---|
| 1 | Jack Clark | .12 |
| 2 | Danny Jackson | .15 |
| 3 | Brett Butler | .06 |
| 4 | Kurt Stillwell | .06 |
| 5 | Tom Brunansky | .10 |
| 6 | Dennis Lamp | .06 |
| 7 | Jose DeLeon | .06 |
| 8 | Tom Herr | .06 |
| 9 | Keith Moreland | .06 |
| 10 | Kirk Gibson | .12 |
| 11 | Bud Black | .06 |
| 12 | Rafael Ramirez | .06 |
| 13 | Luis Salazar | .06 |
| 14 | Goose Gossage | .06 |
| 15 | Bob Welch | .06 |
| 16 | Vance Law | .06 |
| 17 | Ray Knight | .06 |
| 18 | Dan Quisenberry | .06 |
| 19 | Don Slaught | .06 |
| 20 | Lee Smith | .06 |
| 21 | Rick Cerone | .06 |
| 22 | Pat Tabler | .06 |
| 23 | Larry McWilliams | .06 |
| 24 | Rick Horton | .06 |
| 25 | Graig Nettles | .06 |
| 26 | Dan Petry | .06 |
| 27 | Jose Rijo | .06 |
| 28 | Chili Davis | .06 |

| NO. | PLAYER | MINT |
|---|---|---|
| 29 | Dickie Thon | .06 |
| 30 | Mackey Sasser | .12 |
| 31 | Mickey Tettleton | .06 |
| 32 | Rick Dempsey | .06 |
| 33 | Ron Hassey | .06 |
| 34 | Phil Bradley | .06 |
| 35 | Jay Howell | .06 |
| 36 | Bill Buckner | .06 |
| 37 | Alfredo Griffin | .06 |
| 38 | Gary Pettis | .06 |
| 39 | Calvin Schiraldi | .06 |
| 40 | John Candelaria | .06 |
| 41 | Joe Orsulak | .06 |
| 42 | Willie Upshaw | .06 |
| 43 | Herm Winningham | .06 |
| 44 | Ron Kittle | .06 |
| 45 | Bob Dernier | .06 |
| 46 | Steve Balboni | .06 |
| 47 | Steve Shields | .06 |
| 48 | Henry Cotto | .06 |
| 49 | Dave Henderson | .06 |
| 50 | Dave Parker | .12 |
| 51 | Mike Young | .06 |
| 52 | Mark Salas | .06 |
| 53 | Mike Davis | .06 |
| 54 | Rafael Santana | .06 |
| 55 | Don Baylor | .06 |

| NO. | PLAYER | MINT |
|---|---|---|
| 56 | Dan Pasqua | .06 |
| 57 | Ernest Riles | .06 |
| 58 | Glenn Hubbard | .06 |
| 59 | Mike Smithson | .06 |
| 60 | Richard Dotson | .06 |
| 61 | Jerry Reuss | .06 |
| 62 | Mike Jackson | .06 |
| 63 | Floyd Bannister | .06 |
| 64 | Jesse Orosco | .06 |
| 65 | Larry Parrish | .06 |
| 66 | Jeff Bittiger | .06 |
| 67 | Ray Hayward | .06 |
| 68 | Ricky Jordan (RR) | .90 |
| 69 | Tommy Gregg | .15 |
| 70 | Brady Anderson | .40 |
| 71 | Jeff Montgomery | .06 |
| 72 | Darryl Hamilton | .20 |
| 73 | Cecil Espy | .15 |
| 74 | Greg Briley | .15 |
| 75 | Joey Meyer (RR) | .35 |
| 76 | Mike Macfarlane | .15 |
| 77 | Oswald Peraza | .15 |
| 78 | Jack Armstrong | .20 |
| 79 | Don Heinkel | .15 |
| 80 | Mark Grace (RR) | 1.50 |
| 81 | Steve Curry | .25 |
| 82 | Damon Barryhill (RR) | .40 |

| NO. | PLAYER | MINT |
|---|---|---|
| 83 | Steve Ellsworth | .15 |
| 84 | Pete Smith | .15 |
| 85 | Jack McDowell | .25 |
| 86 | Rob Dibble | .20 |
| 87 | Bryan Harvey (RR) | .35 |
| 88 | John Dopson | .15 |
| 89 | Dave Gallagher | .20 |
| 90 | Todd Stottlemyre | .30 |
| 91 | Mike Schooler | .15 |
| 92 | Don Gordon | .15 |
| 93 | Sil Campusano | .30 |
| 94 | Jeff Pico | .15 |
| 95 | Jay Buhner | .30 |
| 96 | Nelson Santovenia | .15 |
| 97 | Al Leiter (RR) | .40 |
| 98 | Luis Alicea | .20 |
| 99 | Pat Borders | .20 |
| 100 | Chris Sabo (RR) | 2.00 |
| 101 | Tim Belcher | .25 |
| 102 | Walt Weiss | .45 |
| 103 | Craig Biggio | .15 |
| 104 | Don August | .20 |
| 105 | Roberto Alomar (RR) | .40 |
| 106 | Todd Burns | .25 |
| 107 | John Costello | .15 |
| 108 | Melodo Perez | .35 |
| 109 | Darrin Jackson | .35 |
| 110 | Orestes Destrade | .25 |

## 1989 Score. . . . Complete Set of 660 Cards—Value $20.00

Features the rookie cards of Sandy Alomar, Jr., Mike Harkey and Gary Sheffield. The set includes 9 Highlight cards and 31 Rookie Prospect cards.

| NO. | PLAYER | MINT |
|---|---|---|
| 1 | Jose Canseco | 1.25 |
| 2 | Andre Dawson | .15 |
| 3 | Mark McGwire | 1.00 |
| 4 | Benny Santiago | .10 |
| 5 | Rick Reuschel | .05 |
| 6 | Fred McGriff | .40 |
| 7 | Kal Daniels | .25 |
| 8 | Gary Gaetti | .10 |
| 9 | Ellis Burks | .35 |
| 10 | Darryl Strawberry | .45 |
| 11 | Julio Franco | .08 |
| 12 | Lloyd Moseby | .12 |
| 13 | Jeff Pico (R) | .25 |
| 14 | Johnny Ray | .10 |
| 15 | Cal Ripken, Jr. | .20 |
| 16 | Dick Schofield | .05 |
| 17 | Mel Hall | .05 |
| 18 | Bill Ripken | .05 |
| 19 | Brook Jacoby | .05 |
| 20 | Kirby Puckett | .25 |
| 21 | Bill Doran | .08 |
| 22 | Pete O'Brien | .10 |
| 23 | Matt Nokes | .10 |
| 24 | Brian Fisher | .05 |
| 25 | Jack Clark | .10 |
| 26 | Gary Petis | .05 |
| 27 | Dave Valle | .05 |
| 28 | Willie Wilson | .08 |
| 29 | Curt Young | .05 |
| 30 | Dale Murphy | .25 |
| 31 | Barry Larkin | .10 |
| 32 | Dave Stewart | .10 |
| 33 | Mike LaValliere | .05 |
| 34 | Glen Hubbard | .05 |
| 35 | Ryne Sandberg | .12 |
| 36 | Tony Pena | .08 |
| 37 | Greg Walker | .05 |
| 38 | Von Hayes | .08 |
| 39 | Kevin Mitchell | .08 |
| 40 | Tim Raines | .15 |
| 41 | Keith Hernandez | .15 |
| 42 | Keith Moreland | .05 |
| 43 | Ruben Sierra | .20 |
| 44 | Chet Lemon | .05 |
| 45 | Willie Randolph | .08 |
| 46 | Andy Allanson | .05 |
| 47 | Candy Maldonado | .10 |
| 48 | Sid Bream | .05 |
| 49 | Denny Walling | .05 |
| 50 | Dave Winfield | .15 |
| 51 | Alvin Davis | .08 |
| 52 | Cory Snyder | .15 |
| 53 | Hubie Brooks | .05 |
| 54 | Chili Davis | .08 |
| 55 | Kevin Seitzer | .35 |
| 56 | Jose Uribe | .05 |
| 57 | Tony Fernandez | .10 |
| 58 | Tim Teufel | .05 |
| 59 | Oddibe McDowell | .08 |
| 60 | Les Lancaster | .05 |
| 61 | Billy Hatcher | .05 |
| 62 | Dan Gladden | .05 |
| 63 | Marty Barrett | .05 |
| 64 | Nick Esasky | .10 |
| 65 | Wally Joyner | .15 |
| 66 | Mike Greenwell | 1.25 |
| 67 | Ken Williams | .05 |
| 68 | Bob Horner | .05 |
| 69 | Steve Sax | .08 |
| 70 | Rickey Henderson | .30 |
| 71 | Mitch Webster | .05 |
| 72 | Rob Deer | .08 |
| 73 | Jim Presley | .05 |
| 74 | Albert Hall | .05 |
| 75 | George Brett | .25 |
| 76 | Brian Downing | .08 |
| 77 | Dave Martinez | .05 |
| 78 | Scott Fletcher | .05 |
| 79 | Phil Bradley | .08 |
| 80 | Ozzie Smith | .08 |
| 81 | Larry Sheets | .05 |
| 82 | Mike Aldrete | .05 |
| 83 | Darnell Coles | .05 |
| 84 | Len Dykstra | .15 |

| NO. | PLAYER | MINT |
|---|---|---|
| 85 | Jim Rice | .12 |
| 86 | Jeff Treadway | .05 |
| 87 | Jose Lind | .05 |
| 88 | Willie McGee | .08 |
| 89 | Mickey Brantley | .08 |
| 90 | Tony Gwynn | .35 |
| 91 | R.J. Reynolds | .05 |
| 92 | Milt Thompson | .05 |
| 93 | Kevin McReynolds | .15 |
| 94 | Eddie Murray | .30 |
| 95 | Lance Parrish | .10 |
| 96 | Ron Kittle | .08 |
| 97 | Gerald Young | .08 |
| 98 | Ernie Whitt | .05 |
| 99 | Jeff Reed | .05 |
| 100 | Don Mattingly | 1.50 |
| 101 | Gerald Perry | .10 |
| 102 | Vance Law | .05 |
| 103 | John Shelby | .05 |
| 104 | Chris Sabo (R) | 1.25 |
| 105 | Danny Tartabull | .20 |
| 106 | Glenn Wilson | .05 |
| 107 | Mark Davidson | .05 |
| 108 | Dave Parker | .10 |
| 109 | Eric Davis | .65 |
| 110 | Alan Trammell | .10 |
| 111 | Ozzie Virgil | .05 |
| 112 | Frank Tanana | .08 |
| 113 | Rafael Ramirez | .05 |
| 114 | Dennis Martinez | .05 |
| 115 | Jose DeLeon | .05 |
| 116 | Bob Ojeda | .08 |
| 117 | Doug Drabek | .10 |
| 118 | Andy Hawkins | .05 |
| 119 | Greg Maddux | .20 |
| 120 | Cecil Fielder | .05 |
| 121 | Mike Scioscia | .05 |
| 122 | Dan Petry | .05 |
| 123 | Terry Kennedy | .05 |
| 124 | Kelly Downs | .05 |
| 125 | Greg Gross | .05 |
| 126 | Fred Lynn | .08 |
| 127 | Barry Bonds | .20 |
| 128 | Harold Baines | .10 |
| 129 | Doyle Alexander | .05 |
| 130 | Kevin Elster | .08 |
| 131 | Mike Heath | .05 |
| 132 | Teddy Higuera | .10 |
| 133 | Charlie Leibrandt | .08 |
| 134 | Tim Laudner | .05 |
| 135 | Ray Knight | .05 |
| 136 | Howard Johnson | .10 |
| 137 | Terry Pendleton | .08 |
| 138 | Andy McGaffigan | .05 |
| 139 | Ken Oberkfell | .05 |
| 140 | Butch Wynegar | .05 |
| 141 | Rob Murphy | .05 |
| 142 | Rich Renteria | .10 |
| 143 | Jose Guzman | .05 |
| 144 | Andres Galarraga | .25 |
| 145 | Rick Horton | .05 |
| 146 | Frank DiPino | .05 |
| 147 | Glenn Braggs | .05 |
| 148 | John Kruk | .15 |
| 149 | Mike Schmidt | .30 |
| 150 | Lee Smith | .08 |
| 151 | Robin Yount | .15 |
| 152 | Mark Eichhorn | .05 |
| 153 | DeWayne Buice | .05 |
| 154 | B.J. Surhoff | .08 |
| 155 | Vince Coleman | .15 |
| 156 | Tony Phillips | .05 |
| 157 | Willie Fraser | .05 |
| 158 | Lance McCullers | .08 |
| 159 | Greg Gagne | .05 |
| 160 | Jesse Barfield | .12 |
| 161 | Mark Langston | .10 |
| 162 | Kurt Stillwell | .05 |
| 163 | Dion James | .05 |
| 164 | Glenn Davis | .10 |
| 165 | Walt Weiss | 1.25 |
| 166 | Dave Concepcion | .05 |
| 167 | Alfredo Griffin | .05 |
| 168 | Don Heinkel (R) | .15 |

| NO. | PLAYER | MINT |
|---|---|---|
| 169 | Luis Rivera | .15 |
| 170 | Shane Rawley | .05 |
| 171 | Darrell Evans | .05 |
| 172 | Robby Thompson | .05 |
| 173 | Jody Davis | .05 |
| 174 | Andy Van Slyke | .15 |
| 175 | Wade Boggs | .75 |
| 176 | Garry Templeton | .05 |
| 177 | Gary Redus | .05 |
| 178 | Craig Lefferts | .05 |
| 179 | Carney Lansford | .08 |
| 180 | Ron Darling | .10 |
| 181 | Kirk McCaskill | .05 |
| 182 | Tony Armas | .05 |
| 183 | Steve Farr | .05 |
| 184 | Tom Brunansky | .08 |
| 185 | Bryan Harvey (R) | .25 |
| 186 | Mike Marshall | .08 |
| 187 | Bo Diaz | .05 |
| 188 | Willie Upshaw | .05 |
| 189 | Mike Pagliarulo | .10 |
| 190 | Mike Krukow | .08 |
| 191 | Tommy Herr | .05 |
| 192 | Jim Pankovits | .05 |
| 193 | Dwight Evans | .15 |
| 194 | Kelly Gruber | .05 |
| 195 | Bobby Bonilla | .10 |
| 196 | Wallace Johnson | .05 |
| 197 | Dave Stieb | .08 |
| 198 | Pat Borders (R) | .25 |
| 199 | Rafael Palmeiro | .15 |
| 200 | Doc Gooden | .40 |
| 201 | Pete Incaviglia | .10 |
| 202 | Chris James | .08 |
| 203 | Marvell Wynne | .05 |
| 204 | Pat Sheridan | .05 |
| 205 | Don Baylor | .08 |
| 206 | Paul O'Neill | .05 |
| 207 | Pete Smith | .12 |
| 208 | Mark McLemore | .05 |
| 209 | Henry Cotto | .05 |
| 210 | Kirk Gibson | .20 |
| 211 | Claudell Washington | .05 |
| 212 | Randy Bush | .05 |
| 213 | Joe Carter | .15 |
| 214 | Bill Buckner | .08 |
| 215 | Bert Blyleven | .15 |
| 216 | Brett Butler | .05 |
| 217 | Lee Mazzilli | .05 |
| 218 | Spike Owen | .05 |
| 219 | Bill Swift | .05 |
| 220 | Tim Wallach | .08 |
| 221 | David Cone | .35 |
| 222 | Don Carman | .05 |
| 223 | Rich Gossage | .08 |
| 224 | Bob Walk | .05 |
| 225 | Dave Righetti | .10 |
| 226 | Kevin Bass | .08 |
| 227 | Kevin Gross | .05 |
| 228 | Tim Burke | .05 |
| 229 | Rick Mahler | .05 |
| 230 | Lou Whitaker | .08 |
| 231 | Luis Alicea (R) | .15 |
| 232 | Roberto Alomar | .20 |
| 233 | Bob Boone | .05 |
| 234 | Dickie Thon | .05 |
| 235 | Shawon Dunston | .10 |
| 236 | Pete Stanicek | .05 |
| 237 | Craig Biggio (R) | .25 |
| 238 | Dennis Boyd | .08 |
| 239 | Tom Candiotti | .08 |
| 240 | Gary Carter | .20 |
| 241 | Mike Stanley | .05 |
| 242 | Ken Phelps | .05 |
| 243 | Chris Bosio | .05 |
| 244 | Les Straker | .05 |
| 245 | Dave Smith | .05 |
| 246 | John Candelaria | .05 |
| 247 | Joe Orsulak | .05 |
| 248 | Storm Davis | .05 |
| 249 | Floyd Bannister | .05 |
| 250 | Jack Morris | .10 |
| 251 | Bret Saberhagen | .10 |
| 252 | Tom Niedenfuer | .05 |

| NO. | PLAYER | MINT |
|---|---|---|
| 253 | Neal Heaton | .05 |
| 254 | Eric Show | .05 |
| 255 | Juan Samuel | .10 |
| 256 | Dale Sveum | .08 |
| 257 | Jim Gott | .05 |
| 258 | Scott Garrelts | .05 |
| 259 | Larry McWilliams | .05 |
| 260 | Steve Bedrosian | .08 |
| 261 | Jack Howell | .08 |
| 262 | Jay Tibbs | .05 |
| 263 | Jamie Moyer | .05 |
| 264 | Doug Sisk | .05 |
| 265 | Todd Worrell | .08 |
| 266 | John Farrell | .10 |
| 267 | Dave Collins | .05 |
| 268 | Sid Fernandez | .10 |
| 269 | Tom Brookens | .05 |
| 270 | Shane Mack | .05 |
| 271 | Paul Kilgus | .05 |
| 272 | Chuck Crim | .05 |
| 273 | Bob Knepper | .05 |
| 274 | Mike Moore | .05 |
| 275 | Guillermo Hernandez | .05 |
| 276 | Dennis Eckersley | .10 |
| 277 | Craig Nettles | .10 |
| 278 | Rich Dotson | .08 |
| 279 | Larry Herndon | .05 |
| 280 | Gene Larkin | .05 |
| 281 | Roger McDowell | .05 |
| 282 | Greg Swindell | .10 |
| 283 | Juan Agosto | .05 |
| 284 | Jeff Robinson | .15 |
| 285 | Mike Dunne | .05 |
| 286 | Greg Mathews | .05 |
| 287 | Kent Tekulve | .05 |
| 288 | Jerry Mumphrey | .05 |
| 289 | Jack McDowell | .20 |
| 290 | Frank Viola | .15 |
| 291 | Mark Gubicza | .10 |
| 292 | Dave Schmidt | .05 |
| 293 | Mike Henneman | .05 |
| 294 | Jimmy Jones | .05 |
| 295 | Charlie Hough | .08 |
| 296 | Rafael Santana | .05 |
| 297 | Chris Speier | .05 |
| 298 | Mike Witt | .08 |
| 299 | Pascual Perez | .05 |
| 300 | Nolan Ryan | .20 |
| 301 | Mitch Williams | .05 |
| 302 | Mookie Wilson | .08 |
| 303 | Mackey Sasser | .08 |
| 304 | John Cerutti | .05 |
| 305 | Jeff Reardon | .08 |
| 306 | Randy Myers | .08 |
| 307 | Greg Brock | .05 |
| 308 | Bob Welch | .08 |
| 309 | Jeff Robinson | .05 |
| 310 | Harold Reynolds | .05 |
| 311 | Jim Walewander | .05 |
| 312 | Dave Magadan | .10 |
| 313 | Jim Gantner | .05 |
| 314 | Walt Terrell | .05 |
| 315 | Wally Backman | .05 |
| 316 | Luis Salazar | .05 |
| 317 | Rick Rhoden | .05 |
| 318 | Tom Henke | .05 |
| 319 | Mike Macfarlane (R) | .20 |
| 320 | Dan Plesac | .05 |
| 321 | Calvin Schiraldi | .05 |
| 322 | Stan Javier | .05 |
| 323 | Devon White | .08 |
| 324 | Scott Bradley | .05 |
| 325 | Bruce Hurst | .15 |
| 326 | Manny Lee | .05 |
| 327 | Rick Aguilera | .05 |
| 328 | Bruce Ruffin | .05 |
| 329 | Ed Whitson | .05 |
| 330 | Bo Jackson | .25 |
| 331 | Ivan Calderon | .10 |
| 332 | Mickey Hatcher | .05 |
| 333 | Barry Jones | .05 |
| 334 | Ron Hassey | .05 |
| 335 | Bill Wegman | .05 |
| 336 | Damon Berryhill | .05 |

Card values shown here fluctuate considerably.

| NO. | PLAYER | MINT |
|---|---|---|
| 337 | Steve Ontiveros | .05 |
| 338 | Dan Pasqua | .08 |
| 339 | Bill Pecota | .05 |
| 340 | Greg Cadaret | .05 |
| 341 | Scott Bankhead | .05 |
| 342 | Ron Guidry | .08 |
| 343 | Danny Heep | .05 |
| 344 | Bob Brower | .05 |
| 345 | Rich Gedman | .05 |
| 346 | Nelson Santovenia (R) | .15 |
| 347 | George Bell | .15 |
| 348 | Ted Power | .05 |
| 349 | Mark Grant | .05 |
| 350 | Roger Clemens | .50 |
| 351 | Bill Long | .05 |
| 352 | Jay Bell | .05 |
| 353 | Steve Balboni | .05 |
| 354 | Bob Kipper | .05 |
| 355 | Steve Jeltz | .05 |
| 356 | Jesse Orosco | .05 |
| 357 | Bob Dernier | .05 |
| 358 | Mickey Tettleton | .05 |
| 359 | Duane Ward | .05 |
| 360 | Darrin Jackson | .12 |
| 361 | Rey Quinones | .05 |
| 362 | Mark Grace | 1.25 |
| 363 | Steve Lake | .05 |
| 364 | Pat Perry | .05 |
| 365 | Terry Steinbach | .12 |
| 366 | Alan Ashby | .05 |
| 367 | Jeff Montgomery | .05 |
| 368 | Steve Buechele | .05 |
| 369 | Chris Brown | .08 |
| 370 | Orel Hershiser | .25 |
| 371 | Todd Benzinger | .15 |
| 372 | Ron Gant | .30 |
| 373 | Paul Assenmacher | .05 |
| 374 | Joey Meyer | .05 |
| 375 | Neil Allen | .05 |
| 376 | Mike Davis | .05 |
| 377 | Jeff Parrett | .08 |
| 378 | Jay Howell | .08 |
| 379 | Rafael Belliard | .05 |
| 380 | Luis Polonia | .05 |
| 381 | Keith Atherton | .05 |
| 382 | Kent Hrbek | .10 |
| 383 | Bob Stanley | .05 |
| 384 | Dave LaPoint | .05 |
| 385 | Rance Mulliniks | .05 |
| 386 | Melido Perez | .10 |
| 387 | Doug Jones | .05 |
| 388 | Steve Lyons | .05 |
| 389 | Alejandro Pena | .08 |
| 390 | Frank White | .05 |
| 391 | Pat Tabler | .08 |
| 392 | Eric Plunk | .05 |
| 393 | Mike Maddux | .05 |
| 394 | Allan Anderson | .08 |
| 395 | Bob Brenly | .05 |
| 396 | Rick Cerone | .05 |
| 397 | Scott Terry | .05 |
| 398 | Mike Jackson | .05 |
| 399 | Bobby Thigpen | .05 |
| 400 | Don Sutton | .10 |
| 401 | Cecil Espy | .10 |
| 402 | Junior Ortiz | .05 |
| 403 | Mike Smithson | .05 |
| 404 | Bud Black | .05 |
| 405 | Tom Foley | .05 |
| 406 | Andres Thomas | .05 |
| 407 | Rick Sutcliffe | .10 |
| 408 | Brian Harper | .05 |
| 409 | John Smoley | .08 |
| 410 | Juan Nieves | .05 |
| 411 | Shawn Abner | .05 |
| 412 | Wes Gardner | .05 |
| 413 | Darren Daulton | .05 |
| 414 | Juan Berenguer | .05 |
| 415 | Charles Hudson | .08 |
| 416 | Rick Honeycutt | .05 |
| 417 | Greg Booker | .05 |
| 418 | Tim Belcher | .15 |
| 419 | Don August | .15 |
| 420 | Dale Mohorcic | .05 |
| 421 | Steve Lombardozzi | .05 |
| 422 | Atlee Hammaker | .05 |
| 423 | Jerry Don Gleaton | .05 |
| 424 | Scott Bailes | .05 |
| 425 | Bruce Sutter | .08 |
| 426 | Randy Ready | .05 |
| 427 | Jerry Reed | .05 |
| 428 | Bryn Smith | .05 |
| 429 | Tim Leary | .10 |
| 430 | Mark Clear | .05 |
| 431 | Terry Leach | .05 |
| 432 | John Moses | .05 |
| 433 | Ozzie Guillen | .08 |
| 434 | Gene Nelson | .05 |
| 435 | Gary Ward | .05 |
| 436 | Luis Aguayo | .05 |
| 437 | Fernando Valenzuela | .10 |
| 438 | Jeff Russell | .05 |
| 439 | Cecilio Guante | .05 |
| 440 | Don Robinson | .05 |
| 441 | Rick Anderson | .05 |
| 442 | Tom Glavine | .05 |
| 443 | Daryl Boston | .05 |
| 444 | Joe Price | .05 |
| 445 | Stewart Cliburn | .05 |
| 446 | Manny Trillo | .05 |
| 447 | Joel Skinner | .05 |
| 448 | Charlie Puleo | .05 |
| 449 | Carlton Fisk | .10 |
| 450 | Will Clark | .50 |
| 451 | Otis Nixon | .05 |
| 452 | Rick Schu | .05 |
| 453 | Todd Stottlemyre | .12 |
| 454 | Tim Birtsas | .05 |
| 455 | Dave Gallagher (R) | .25 |
| 456 | Barry Lyons | .05 |
| 457 | Fred Manrique | .05 |
| 458 | Ernest Riles | .05 |
| 459 | Doug Jennings (R) | .35 |
| 460 | Joe Magrane | .10 |
| 461 | Jamie Quirk | .05 |
| 462 | Jack Armstrong (R) | .20 |
| 463 | Bobby Witt | .05 |
| 464 | Keith Miller | .05 |
| 465 | Todd Burns (R) | .25 |
| 466 | John Dopson (R) | .25 |
| 467 | Rich Yett | .05 |
| 468 | Craig Reynolds | .05 |
| 469 | Dave Bergman | .05 |
| 470 | Rex Hudler | .10 |
| 471 | Eric King | .05 |
| 472 | Joaquin Andujar | .05 |
| 473 | Sil Campusano (R) | .20 |
| 474 | Terry Mulholland | .05 |
| 475 | Mike Flanagan | .05 |
| 476 | Greg Harris | .20 |
| 477 | Tommy John | .10 |
| 478 | Dave Anderson | .05 |
| 479 | Fred Toliver | .05 |
| 480 | Jimmy Key | .12 |
| 481 | Donell Nixon | .05 |
| 482 | Mark Portugal | .05 |
| 483 | Tom Pagnozzi | .05 |
| 484 | Jeff Kunkel | .05 |
| 485 | Frank Williams | .05 |
| 486 | Jody Reed | .15 |
| 487 | Roberto Kelly | .10 |
| 488 | Shawn Hillegas | .05 |
| 489 | Jerry Reuss | .05 |
| 490 | Mark Davis | .05 |
| 491 | Jeff Sellers | .05 |
| 492 | Zane Smith | .05 |
| 493 | Al Newman | .05 |
| 494 | Mike Young | .05 |
| 495 | Larry Parrish | .05 |
| 496 | Herm Winningham | .05 |
| 497 | Carmen Castillo | .05 |
| 498 | Joe Hesketh | .05 |
| 499 | Darrell Miller | .05 |
| 500 | Mike LaCoss | .05 |
| 501 | Charlie Lea | .05 |
| 502 | Bruce Benedict | .05 |
| 503 | Chuck Finley | .05 |
| 504 | Brad Wellman | .05 |
| 505 | Tim Crews | .05 |
| 506 | Ken Gerhart | .05 |
| 507 | Brian Holton | .05 |
| 508 | Dennis Lamp | .05 |
| 509 | Bobby Meacham | .05 |
| 510 | Tracy Jones | .05 |
| 511 | Mike Fitzgerald | .05 |
| 512 | Jeff Bittiger (R) | .15 |
| 513 | Tim Flannery | .05 |
| 514 | Ray Hayward | .05 |
| 515 | Dave Leiper | .05 |
| 516 | Rod Scurry | .05 |
| 517 | Carmelo Martinez | .05 |
| 518 | Curtis Wilkerson | .05 |
| 519 | Stan Jefferson | .08 |
| 520 | Dan Quisenberry | .08 |
| 521 | Lloyd McClendon | .05 |
| 522 | Steve Trout | .05 |
| 523 | Larry Andersen | .05 |
| 524 | Don Aase | .05 |
| 525 | Bob Forsch | .05 |
| 526 | Geno Petralli | .05 |
| 527 | Angel Salazar | .05 |
| 528 | Mike Schooler (R) | .15 |
| 529 | Jose Oquendo | .05 |
| 530 | Jay Buhner | .25 |
| 531 | Tom Bolton | .05 |
| 532 | Al Nipper | .05 |
| 533 | Dave Henderson | .05 |
| 534 | John Costello (R) | .15 |
| 535 | Donnie Moore | .05 |
| 536 | Mike Laga | .05 |
| 537 | Mike Gallego | .05 |
| 538 | Jim Clancy | .05 |
| 539 | Joel Youngblood | .05 |
| 540 | Rick Leach | .05 |
| 541 | Kevin Romine | .05 |
| 542 | Mark Salas | .05 |
| 543 | Greg Minton | .05 |
| 544 | Dave Palmer | .05 |
| 545 | Dwayne Murphy | .05 |
| 546 | Jim Deshaies | .05 |
| 547 | Don Gordon | .10 |
| 548 | Ricky Jordan (R) | 2.25 |
| 549 | Mike Boddicker | .08 |
| 550 | Mike Scott | .15 |
| 551 | Jeff Ballard | .05 |
| 552 | Jose Rijo | .08 |
| 553 | Danny Darwin | .05 |
| 554 | Tom Browning | .08 |
| 555 | Danny Jackson | .10 |
| 556 | Rick Dempsey | .05 |
| 557 | Jeffrey Leonard | .05 |
| 558 | Jeff Musselman | .05 |
| 559 | Ron Robinson | .08 |
| 560 | John Tudor | .05 |
| 561 | Don Slaught | .05 |
| 562 | Dennis Rasmussen | .05 |
| 563 | Brady Anderson (R) | .30 |
| 564 | Pedro Guerrero | .15 |
| 565 | Paul Molitor | .08 |
| 566 | Terry Clark (R) | .20 |
| 567 | Terry Puhl | .05 |
| 568 | Mike Campbell | .05 |
| 569 | Paul Mirabella | .05 |
| 570 | Jeff Hamilton | .05 |
| 571 | Oswald Peraza (R) | .15 |
| 572 | Bob McClure | .05 |
| 573 | Jose Bautista (R) | .20 |
| 574 | Alex Trevino | .05 |
| 575 | John Franco | .08 |
| 576 | Mark Parent (R) | .15 |
| 577 | Nelson Liriano | .05 |
| 578 | Steve Shields | .05 |
| 579 | Odell Jones | .05 |
| 580 | Al Leiter | .15 |
| 581 | Dave Stapleton | .05 |
| 582 | Wayne Tolleson | .05 |
| 583 | Donnie Hill | .05 |
| 584 | Chuck Jackson | .05 |
| 585 | Rene Gonzales | .05 |
| 586 | Tracy Woodson | .10 |
| 587 | Jim Adduci | .08 |
| 588 | Mario Soto | .05 |
| 589 | Jeff Blauser | .05 |
| 590 | Jim Traber | .05 |
| 591 | Jon Perlman | .05 |
| 592 | Mark Williamson | .05 |
| 593 | Dave Meads | .05 |
| 594 | Jim Eisenreich | .05 |
| 595 | Paul Gibson (R) | .15 |
| 596 | Mike Birkbeck | .05 |
| 597 | Terry Francona | .05 |
| 598 | Paul Zuvella | .05 |
| 599 | Franklin Stubbs | .05 |
| 600 | Gregg Jefferies | 1.50 |
| 601 | John Cangelosi | .05 |
| 602 | Mike Sharperson | .05 |
| 603 | Mike Diaz | .05 |
| 604 | Gary Varsho (R) | .20 |
| 605 | Terry Blocker (R) | .15 |
| 606 | Charlie O'Brien | .05 |
| 607 | Jim Eppard | .10 |
| 608 | John Davis | .05 |
| 609 | Ken Griffey, Sr. (R) | 2.75 |
| 610 | Buddy Bell | .05 |
| 611 | Ted Simmons | .05 |
| 612 | Matt Williams | .08 |
| 613 | Danny Cox | .05 |
| 614 | Al Pedrique | .05 |
| 615 | Ron Oester | .05 |
| 616 | John Smoltz (R) | .30 |
| 617 | Bob Melvin | .05 |
| 618 | Rob Dibble (R) | .15 |
| 619 | Kirt Manwaring | .05 |

**No. 620 to 651 (Rookie Prospects)**

| NO. | PLAYER | MINT |
|---|---|---|
| 620 | Felix Fermin | .10 |
| 621 | Doug Dascenzo (R) | .20 |
| 622 | Bill Brennan (R) | .25 |
| 623 | Carlos Quintana (R) | .35 |
| 624 | Mike Harkey (R) | .75 |
| 625 | Gary Sheffield (R) | 1.50 |
| 626 | Tom Prince | .10 |
| 627 | Steve Searcy (R) | .20 |
| 628 | Charlie Hayes (R) | .30 |
| 629 | Felix Jose (R) | .25 |
| 630 | Sandy Alomar (R) | 1.25 |
| 631 | Derek Lilliquist (R) | .30 |
| 632 | Geronimo Berroa | .20 |
| 633 | Luis Medina | .60 |
| 634 | Tom Gordon (R) | .25 |
| 635 | Ramon Martinez (R) | .50 |
| 636 | Craig Worthington (R) | .30 |
| 637 | Edgar Martinez | .25 |
| 638 | Chad Krueter (R) | .20 |
| 639 | Ron Jones (R) | .75 |
| 640 | Van Snider (R) | .30 |
| 641 | Lance Blankenship (R) | .20 |
| 642 | Dwight Smith (R) | .30 |
| 643 | Cameron Drew (R) | .35 |
| 644 | Jerald Clark (R) | .15 |
| 645 | Randy Johnson (R) | .25 |
| 646 | Norm Charlton (R) | .20 |
| 647 | Todd Frohwirth | .05 |
| 648 | Luis De los Santos (R) | .20 |
| 649 | Tim Jones (R) | .20 |
| 650 | Dave West (R) | .75 |
| 651 | Bob Milacki (R) | .20 |
| 652 | Highlight—Wrigley Field— night opener | .15 |
| 653 | Highlight—Hershiser— scoreless inning record | .10 |
| 654 | Highlight—Boggs—6 yrs. consecutive 200 hits | .25 |
| 655 | Highlight—Canseco—40 home runs—40 stolen bases | .50 |
| 656 | Highlight—Jones—saves | .05 |
| 657 | Highlight—Henderson— lead off homers | .15 |
| 658 | Highlight—Browning— perfect game | .10 |
| 659 | Highlight—Greenwell—A.L. game-winning record | .50 |
| 660 | Highlight—Red Sox—24 home game-winning streak | .15 |

Card values shown here fluctuate considerably.

# 1986 Sportflics.... Complete Set of 200 Cards —Value $40.00

Sportflics entered the baseball card market in 1986. Each 2½"x3½" card could be tilted to show three different photos. The set included 139 cards, each featuring three poses of the same player; 50 "Tri-Stars"—each card featuring three players; 10 "Big Six" cards—each featuring six players; 1 World Series card—featuring 12 players. 133 question and answer trivia cards were also issued. The complete set was packaged in a printed box for distribution through card hobby dealers. Wax packs were sold through mass market outlets. In addition to its main card set, Sportflics issued two other sets in 1986—50-card set of "Rookies" and 75-card set of "Decade Greats."

Dwight Gooden—Phase 1

Dwight Gooden—Phase 2

Dwight Gooden—Phase 3

| NO. PLAYER | MINT |
|---|---|
| 1 George Brett | 1.25 |
| 2 Don Mattingly | 4.00 |
| 3 Wade Boggs | 2.50 |
| 4 Eddie Murray | 1.00 |
| 5 Dale Murphy | 1.50 |
| 6 Rickey Henderson | 1.00 |
| 7 Harold Baines | .40 |
| 8 Cal Ripken, Jr. | .75 |
| 9 Orel Hershiser | .60 |
| 10 Bret Saberhagen | .50 |
| 11 Tim Raines | .50 |
| 12 Fernando Valenzuela | .50 |
| 13 Tony Gwynn | .75 |
| 14 Pedro Guerrero | .45 |
| 15 Keith Hernandez | .45 |
| 16 Ernest Riles | .25 |
| 17 Jim Rice | .50 |
| 18 Ron Guidry | .45 |
| 19 Willie McGee | .50 |
| 20 Ryne Sandberg | .75 |
| 21 Kirk Gibson | .50 |
| 22 Ozzie Guillen (R) | .40 |
| 23 Dave Parker | .50 |
| 24 Vince Coleman (R) | 2.00 |
| 25 Tom Seaver | .75 |
| 26 Bret Butler | .25 |
| 27 Steve Carlton | .60 |
| 28 Gary Carter | .60 |
| 29 Cecil Cooper | .35 |
| 30 Jose Cruz | .25 |
| 31 Alvin Davis | .30 |
| 32 Dwight Evans | .25 |
| 33 Julio Franco | .30 |
| 34 Damaso Garcia | .25 |
| 35 Steve Garvey | .75 |
| 36 Kent Hrbek | .40 |
| 37 Reggie Jackson | .75 |
| 38 Fred Lynn | .40 |
| 39 Paul Molitor | .50 |
| 40 Jim Presley | .30 |
| 41 Dave Righetti | .25 |
| 42 Robin Yount | .45 |
| 43 Nolan Ryan | .60 |
| 44 Mike Schmidt | 1.00 |
| 45 Lee Smith | .25 |
| 46 Rick Sutcliffe | .25 |
| 47 Bruce Sutter | .40 |
| 48 Lou Whitaker | .30 |
| 49 Dave Winfield | .75 |
| 50 Pete Rose | 2.00 |

**No. 51 to 75—TRI-STARS**

| NO. PLAYER | MINT |
|---|---|
| 51 Nat'l. League MVPs: | 1.00 |
| Ryn Sandberg, Steve Garvey, Pete Rose | |
| 52 Slugging Stars: | .75 |
| Harold Baines, George Brett, Jim Rice | |
| 53 No-Hitters: | .30 |
| Mike Witt, Phil Niekro, Jerry Reuss | |
| 54 Big Hitters: | 1.25 |
| Robin Yount, Don Mattingly, Cal Ripken, Jr. | |
| 55 Bullpen Aces: | .35 |
| Dan Quisenberry, Lee Smith, Goose Gossage | |
| 56 Rookies of The Year: | 1.25 |
| Pete Rose, Steve Sax, Darryl Strawberry | |
| 57 Am. League MVP's: | .75 |
| Cal Ripken, Jr., Don Baylor, Reggie Jackson | |
| 58 Batting Champs: | .75 |
| Bill Madlock, Pete Rose, Dave Parker | |
| 59 Cy Young Winners: | .30 |
| LaMarr Hoyt, Mike Flanagan, Ron Guidry | |
| 60 Double Award Winners: | .40 |
| Fernando Valenzuela, Rick Sutcliffe, Tom Seaver | |
| 61 Home Run Champs: | .75 |
| Tony Armas, Reggie Jackson, Jim Rice | |
| 62 Nat'l League MVP's: | 1.00 |
| Keith Hernandez, Mike Schmidt, Dale Murphy | |
| 63 Am. League MVP's | .75 |
| George Brett, Robin Yount, Fred Lynn | |
| 64 Comeback Players: | .25 |
| Bert Blyleven, Jerry Koosman, John Denny | |
| 65 Cy Young Relievers: | .25 |
| Willie Hernandez, Rollie Fingers, Bruce Sutter | |
| 66 Rookies of The Year: | .25 |
| Bob Horner, Andre Dawson, G. Matthews | |
| 67 Rookies of The Year: | .35 |
| Ron Kittle, Carlton Fisk, Tom Seaver | |
| 68 Home Run Champs: | .40 |
| Dave Kingman, Mike Schmidt, George Foster | |
| 69 Dbl. Award Winners: | 1.00 |
| Cal Ripken, Jr., Pete Rose, Rod Carew | |
| 70 Cy Young Winners: | .40 |
| Rick Sutcliffe, Steve Carlton, Tom Seaver | |
| 71 Top Sluggers: | .50 |
| Reggie Jackson, Fred Lynn, Robin Yount | |
| 72 Rookies of The Year: | .30 |
| Rick Sutcliffe, Dave Righetti, F. Valenzuela | |
| 73 Rookies of The Year: | .75 |
| Fred Lynn, Eddie Murray, Cal Ripken, Jr. | |
| 74 Rookies of The Year: | .40 |
| Alvin Davis, Lou Whitaker, Rod Carew | |
| 75 Batting Champs: | 1.50 |
| Don Mattingly, Carney Lansford, Wade Boggs | |

| NO. PLAYER | MINT |
|---|---|
| 76 Jesse Barfield | .35 |
| 77 Phil Bradley | .40 |
| 78 Chris Brown (R) | .50 |
| 79 Tom Browning | .40 |
| 80 Tom Brunansky | .25 |
| 81 Bill Buckner | .25 |
| 82 Chili Davis | .25 |
| 83 Mike Davis | .25 |
| 84 Rich Gedman | .25 |
| 85 Willie Hernandez | .25 |
| 86 Ron Kittle | .25 |
| 87 Lee Lacy | .20 |
| 88 Bill Madlock | .25 |
| 89 Mike Marshall | .25 |
| 90 Keith Moreland | .15 |
| 91 Graig Nettles | .25 |
| 92 Lance Parrish | .35 |
| 93 Kirby Puckett | 1.00 |
| 94 Juan Samuel | .25 |
| 95 Steve Sax | .25 |
| 96 Dave Stieb | .35 |
| 97 Darryl Strawberry | 1.50 |
| 98 Willie Upshaw | .25 |
| 99 Frank Viola | .25 |
| 100 Dwight Gooden | 1.25 |
| 101 Joaquin Andujar | .25 |
| 102 George Bell | .45 |
| 103 Bert Blyleven | .25 |
| 104 Mike Boddicker | .25 |
| 105 Britt Burns | .25 |
| 106 Rod Carew | .75 |
| 107 Jack Clark | .40 |
| 108 Danny Cox | .25 |
| 109 Ron Darling | .40 |
| 110 Andre Dawson | .45 |
| 111 Leon Durham | .25 |
| 112 Tony Fernandez | .25 |
| 113 Tom Herr | .20 |
| 114 Teddy Higuera (R) | .70 |
| 115 Bob Horner | .35 |
| 116 Dave Kingman | .25 |
| 117 Jack Morris | .35 |
| 118 Dan Quisenberry | .30 |
| 119 Jeff Reardon | .25 |
| 120 Bryn Smith | .25 |
| 121 Ozzie Smith | .35 |
| 122 John Tudor | .25 |
| 123 Tim Wallach | .25 |
| 124 Willie Wilson | .35 |
| 125 Carlton Fisk | .35 |

**No. 126 to 150—TRI-STARS**

| NO. PLAYER | MINT |
|---|---|
| 126 RBI Sluggers: | .35 |
| George Foster, Gary Carter, Al Oliver | |
| 127 Run Scorers: | .50 |
| Keith Hernandez, Tim Raines, Ryne Sandberg | |
| 128 Run Scorers: | .50 |
| Willie Wilson, Paul Molitor, Cal Ripken, Jr. | |
| 129 No-Hitters: | .25 |
| J. Candelaria, B. Forsch, D. Eckersley | |

| NO. PLAYER | MINT |
|---|---|
| 130 World Series MVP's: | .75 |
| Rollie Fingers, Pete Rose, Ron Cey | |
| 131 All-Star Game MVP's: | .25 |
| George Foster, Dave Concepcion, Bill Madlock | |
| 132 Cy Young Winners: | .30 |
| Vida Blue, John Denny, Fernando Valenzuela | |
| 133 Comeback Players: | .25 |
| Richard Dotson, Joaquin Andujar, Doyle Alexander | |
| 134 Big Winners: | .40 |
| Rick Sutcliffe, Tom Seaver, John Denny | |
| 135 Veteran Pitchers: | .40 |
| Tom Seaver, Phil Niekro, Don Sutton | |
| 136 Rookies of The Year: | 1.00 |
| Dwight Gooden, Vince Coleman, Alfredo Griffin | |
| 137 All-Star Game MVP's | .50 |
| Steve Garvey, Gary Carter, Fred Lynn | |
| 138 Veteran Hitters: | .75 |
| Tony Perez, Pete Rose, Rusty Staub | |
| 139 Power Hitters: | .50 |
| Mike Schmidt, Jim Rice, George Foster | |
| 140 Batting Champs: | .35 |
| Tony Gwynn, Al Oliver, Bill Buckner | |
| 141 No-Hitters: | .30 |
| Jack Morris, Dave Righetti, Nolan Ryan | |
| 142 No-Hitters: | .30 |
| Tom Seaver, Bert Blyleven, Vida Blue | |
| 143 Strikeout Kings: | 1.00 |
| Nolan Ryan, Fernando Valenzuela, Dwight Gooden | |
| 144 Base Stealers: | .40 |
| Willie Wilson, Tim Raines, Davey Lopes | |
| 145 RBI Sluggers: | .50 |
| Tony Armas, Cecil Cooper, Eddie Murray | |
| 146 Am. League MVP's: | .40 |
| Rod Carew, Jim Rice, Rollie Fingers | |
| 147 World Series MVP's: | .40 |
| Alan Trammell, Rick Dempsey, Reggie Jackson | |
| 148 World Series MVP's: | .40 |
| Darrell Porter, Mike Schmidt, Pedro Guerrero | |
| 149 ERA Leaders: | .30 |
| Mike Boddicker, Rick Sutcliffe, Ron Guidry | |
| 150 Comeback Players: | .50 |
| Reggie Jackson, Dave Kingman, Fred Lynn | |

| NO. PLAYER | MINT |
|---|---|
| 151 Buddy Bell | .25 |
| 152 Dennis Boyd | .25 |
| 153 Dave Concepcion | .25 |
| 154 Brian Downing | .25 |
| 155 Shawon Dunston | .25 |
| 156 John Franco | .25 |
| 157 Scott Garrelts | .25 |
| 158 Bob James | .25 |
| 159 Charlie Leibrandt | .25 |
| 160 Oddibe McDowell | .45 |
| 161 Roger McDowell (R) | .45 |
| 162 Mike Moore | .25 |
| 163 Phil Niekro | .45 |
| 164 Al Oliver | .25 |
| 165 Tony Pena | .25 |
| 166 Ted Power | .25 |
| 167 Mike Scioscia | .20 |
| 168 Mario Soto | .25 |
| 169 Bob Stanley | .25 |
| 170 Gary Templeton | .25 |
| 171 Andre Thornton | .25 |
| 172 Alan Trammell | .40 |
| 173 Doug DeCinces | .25 |
| 174 Greg Walker | .25 |
| 175 Don Sutton | .40 |

| NO. PLAYER | MINT |
|---|---|
| **No. 176 to 185—THE BIG SIX** | |
| 176 1985 Award Winners: | 1.50 |
| Vince Coleman, Ozzie | |
| Guillen, Bret Saberhagen, | |
| Don Mattingly, Dwight | |
| Gooden, Willie McGee | |
| 177 1985 Hot Rookies: | .90 |
| Mark Salas, Stew Cliburn, | |
| Brian Fisher, Joe Hesketh, | |
| Joe Orsulak, Larry Sheets | |
| 178 Future Stars: | 10.00 |
| Steve Lombardozzi, Jose | |
| Canseco, Mark Funderburk, | |
| Mike Greenwell, Billy Joe | |
| Robidoux, Dan Tartabull | |
| 179 1985 Gold Glovers: | 1.00 |
| George Brett, Don | |
| Mattingly, Ron Guidry, | |
| Keith Hernandez, Willie | |
| McGee, Dale Murphy | |
| 180 Active .300 Hitters | 1.00 |
| Wade Boggs, George Brett, | |
| Rod Carew, Cecil Cooper, | |
| Don Mattingly, W. Wilson | |

| NO. PLAYER | MINT |
|---|---|
| 181 Active .300 Hitters | 1.00 |
| Tony Gwynn, Bill Madlock, | |
| Pedro Guerrero, | |
| Dave Parker, Pete Rose, | |
| Keith Hernandez | |
| 182 1985 Milestones: | 1.00 |
| Rod Carew, Phil Niekro, | |
| Pete Rose, Tom Seaver, | |
| Nolan Ryan, Matt Tallman | |
| 183 1985 Triple Crown: | 1.00 |
| Willie McGee, Dave Parker, | |
| Wade Boggs, Darrell Evans, | |
| D. Mattingly, D. Murphy | |
| 184 1985 Highlights: | 1.25 |
| Wade Boggs, Rickey | |
| Henderson, Don Mattingly, | |
| Willie McGee, Dwight | |
| Gooden, John Tudor | |
| 185 20 Game Winners: | 1.25 |
| Dwight Gooden, | |
| Ron Guidry, John Tudor, | |
| Joaquin Andujar, | |
| Bret Saberhagen, | |
| Tom Browning | |

| NO. PLAYER | MINT |
|---|---|
| 186 W. Series Champions: | .50 |
| D. Iorg, W. Wilson, | |
| C. Leibrandt, L. Smith, | |
| G. Brett, B. Saberhagen, | |
| D. Motley, D. Quisenberry, | |
| J. Sundberg, S. Balboni, | |
| F. White, D. Jackson | |
| 187 Hubie Brooks | .25 |
| 188 Glenn Davis | .50 |
| 189 Darrell Evans | .25 |
| 190 Rich Gossage | .25 |
| 191 Andy Hawkins | .25 |
| 192 Jay Howell | .25 |
| 193 LaMarr Hoyt | .25 |
| 194 Davey Lopes | .25 |
| 195 Mike Scott | .40 |
| 196 Ted Simmons | .25 |
| 197 Gary Ward | .15 |
| 198 Bob Welch | .25 |
| 199 Mike Young | .25 |
| 200 Buddy Blancalana | .15 |

# 1987 Sportflics....Complete Set of 200 Cards—Value $40.00

Features the rookie cards of Bo Jackson, Wally Joyner, Will Clark and Pete Incaviglia.

| NO. PLAYER | MINT |
|---|---|
| 1 Don Mattingly | 2.50 |
| 2 Wade Boggs | 1.75 |
| 3 Dale Murphy | .75 |
| 4 Rickey Henderson | .60 |
| 5 George Brett | .60 |
| 6 Eddie Murray | .50 |
| 7 Kirby Puckett | .75 |
| 8 Ryne Sandberg | .35 |
| 9 Cal Ripken Jr. | .40 |
| 10 Roger Clemens | 1.25 |
| 11 Teddy Higuera | .25 |
| 12 Steve Sax | .25 |
| 13 Chris Brown | .25 |
| 14 Jesse Barfield | .25 |
| 15 Kent Hrbek | .20 |
| 16 Robin Yount | .35 |
| 17 Glenn Davis | .45 |
| 18 Hubie Brooks | .20 |
| 19 Mike Scott | .25 |
| 20 Darryl Strawberry | 1.00 |
| 21 Alvin Davis | .20 |
| 22 Eric Davis | 1.00 |
| 23 Danny Tartabull | .50 |
| 24 Cory Snyder (correct) | 1.50 |
| 24 C. Snyder (error) | 2.50 |
| (photo of Pat Tabler) | |
| 25 Pete Rose | 1.00 |
| 26 Wally Joiner (R) | 2.00 |
| 27 Pedro Guerrero | .25 |
| 28 Tom Seaver | .50 |
| 29 Bob Knepper | .20 |
| 30 Mike Schmidt | .75 |
| 31 Tony Gwynn | .75 |
| 32 Don Slaught | .15 |
| 33 Todd Worrell | .35 |
| 34 Tim Raines | .35 |
| 35 Dave Parker | .25 |
| 36 Bob Ojeda | .20 |
| 37 Pete Incaviglia (R) | .90 |
| 38 Bruce Hurst | .20 |
| 39 Bobby Witt (R) | .35 |
| 40 Steve Garvey | .50 |
| 41 Dave Winfield | .50 |
| 42 Jose Cruz | .15 |
| 43 Orel Hershiser | .35 |
| 44 Reggie Jackson | .75 |
| 45 Chili Davis | .20 |

| NO. PLAYER | MINT |
|---|---|
| 46 Robby Thompson | .30 |
| 47 Dennis Boyd | .15 |
| 48 Kirk Gibson | .50 |
| 49 Fred Lynn | .30 |
| 50 Gary Carter | .50 |
| 51 George Bell | .50 |
| 52 Pete O'Brien | .20 |
| 53 Ron Darling | .30 |
| 54 Paul Molitor | .25 |
| 55 Mike Pagliarulo | .30 |
| 56 Mike Boddicker | .15 |
| 57 Dave Righetti | .20 |
| 58 Len Dykstra | .30 |
| 59 Mike Witt | .15 |
| 60 Tony Bernazard | .15 |
| 61 John Kruk | .45 |
| 62 Mike Krukow | .15 |
| 63 Sid Fernandez | .35 |
| 64 Gary Gaetti | .35 |
| 65 Vince Coleman | .50 |
| 66 Pat Tabler | .30 |
| 67 Mike Scioscia | .15 |
| 68 Scott Garrelts | .15 |
| 69 Brett Butler | .20 |
| 70 Bill Buckner | .15 |
| 71 Dennis Rasmussen | .15 |
| 72 Tim Wallach | .25 |
| 73 Bob Horner | .25 |
| 74 Willie McGee | .35 |
| 75 Tri-Stars: | 1.25 |
| Mattingly, Joyner, Murray | |
| 76 Jesse Orosco | .20 |
| 77 Tri-Stars: | .25 |
| Worrell, Reardon, Smith | |
| 78 Candy Maldonado | .30 |
| 79 Tri-Stars: | .25 |
| Smith, Brooks, Dunston | |
| 80 Tri-Stars: | 1.25 |
| Bell, Canseco, Rice | |
| 81 Bert Blyleven | .20 |
| 82 Mike Marshall | .20 |
| 83 Ron Guidry | .20 |
| 84 Julio Franco | .20 |
| 85 Willie Wilson | .20 |
| 86 Lee Lacy | .15 |

| NO. PLAYER | MINT |
|---|---|
| 87 Jack Morris | .25 |
| 88 Ray Knight | .20 |
| 89 Phil Bradley | .25 |
| 90 Jose Canseco | 2.50 |
| 91 Gary Ward | .15 |
| 92 Mike Easler | .15 |
| 93 Tony Pena | .20 |
| 94 Dave Smith | .15 |
| 95 Will Clark (R) | 1.25 |
| 96 Lloyd Moseby | .15 |
| 97 Jim Rice | .45 |
| 98 Shawon Dunston | .20 |
| 99 Don Sutton | .30 |
| 100 Dwight Gooden | 1.00 |
| 101 Lance Parrish | .30 |
| 102 Mark Langston | .25 |
| 103 Floyd Youmans | .20 |
| 104 Lee Smith | .20 |
| 105 Willie Hernandez | .20 |
| 106 Doug DeCinces | .15 |
| 107 Ken Schrom | .15 |
| 108 Don Carman | .15 |
| 109 Brook Jacoby | .15 |
| 110 Steve Bedrosian | .25 |
| 111 Tri-Stars: | .50 |
| Clemens, Morris, Higuer | |
| 112 Tri-Stars: | .20 |
| Barrett, Bernazard, Whitaker | |
| 113 Tri-Stars: | .25 |
| Ripken, Fletcher, Fernandez | |
| 114 Tri-Stars: | 1.00 |
| Boggs, Brett, Gaetti | |
| 115 Tri-Stars: | .50 |
| Schmidt, Brown, Wallach | |
| 116 Tri-Stars: | .25 |
| Sandberg, Ray, Doran | |
| 117 Tri-Stars: | .25 |
| Parker, Gwynn, Bass | |
| 118 Big 6 Rookies: | 2.50 |
| Ty Gainey, Terry Steinbach, | |
| David Clark, Pat Dodson, | |
| Phil Lombardi, B. Santiago | |
| 119 Hi-Lite Tri-Stars: | .35 |
| Righetti, Valenzuela, Scott | |

| NO. PLAYER | MINT |
|---|---|
| 120 Tri-Stars: | .75 |
| Valenzuela, Scott, Gooden | |
| 121 Johnny Ray | .15 |
| 122 Keith Moreland | .15 |
| 123 Juan Samuel | .25 |
| 124 Wally Backman | .15 |
| 125 Nolan Ryan | .60 |
| 126 Greg Harris | .15 |
| 127 Kirk McCaskill | .20 |
| 128 Dwight Evans | .25 |
| 129 Rick Rhoden | .15 |
| 130 Bill Madlock | .20 |
| 131 Oddibe McDowell | .25 |
| 132 Darrell Evans | .20 |
| 133 Keith Hernandez | .35 |
| 134 Tom Brunansky | .25 |
| 135 Kevin McReynolds | .30 |
| 136 Scott Fletcher | .15 |
| 137 Lou Whitaker | .20 |
| 138 Carney Lansford | .15 |
| 139 Andre Dawson | .35 |
| 140 Carlton Fisk | .25 |
| 141 Buddy Bell | .15 |
| 142 Ozzie Smith | .30 |
| 143 Dan Pasqua | .25 |
| 144 Kevin Mitchell (R) | .30 |
| 145 Bret Saberhagen | .30 |
| 146 Charlie Kerfeld | .15 |
| 147 Phil Niekro | .30 |
| 148 John Candelaria | .15 |
| 149 Rich Gedman | .15 |
| 150 Fernando Valenzuela | .35 |
| 151 Tri-Stars: | .25 |
| Carter, Scioscia, Pena | |
| 152 Tri-Stars: | .50 |
| Raines, Cruz, Coleman | |
| 153 Tri-Stars: | .25 |
| Barfield, Baines, Winfield | |
| 154 Tri-Stars: | .25 |
| Parrish, Slaught, Gedman | |
| 155 Tri-Stars: | .60 |
| Murphy, McReynolds, Davis | |
| 156 Hi-Lite Tri-Stars: | .45 |
| Sutton, Schmidt, Deshaies | |

| NO. | PLAYER | MINT |
|---|---|---|
| 157 | Speedburners: | .40 |
| | Henderson, Cangelosi, Pettis | |
| 158 | Big 6 Rookies: | 3.00 |
| | Randy Asadoor, C. Candaele, K. Seitzer, Rafael Palmeiro, Tim Pyznarski, D. Cochrane | |
| 159 | Big 6: | 2.25 |
| | Mattingly, Henderson, Clemens, Murphy, Murray, Gooden | |
| 160 | Roger McDowell | .25 |
| 161 | Brian Downing | .15 |
| 162 | Bill Doran | .20 |
| 163 | Don Baylor | .25 |
| 164 | Alfredo Griffin | .15 |
| 165 | Don Aase | .15 |
| 166 | Glenn Wilson | .15 |
| 167 | Dan Quisenberry | .20 |
| 168 | Frank White | .15 |
| 169 | Cecil Cooper | .20 |
| 170 | Jody Davis | .20 |
| 171 | Harold Baines | .25 |
| 172 | Rob Deer | .20 |
| 173 | John Tudor | .20 |
| 174 | Larry Parrish | .15 |
| 175 | Kevin Bass | .15 |
| 176 | Joe Carter | .30 |
| 177 | Mitch Webster | .20 |
| 178 | Dave Kingman | .25 |
| 179 | Jim Presley | .35 |
| 180 | Mel Hall | .20 |
| 181 | Shane Rawley | .15 |
| 182 | Marty Barrett | .30 |
| 183 | Damaso Garcia | .15 |
| 184 | Bobby Grich | .15 |
| 185 | Leon Durham | .15 |
| 186 | Ozzie Guillen | .15 |
| 187 | Tony Fernandez | .25 |
| 188 | Alan Trammell | .30 |
| 189 | Jim Clancy | .15 |
| 190 | Bo Jackson (R) | 1.50 |
| 191 | Bob Forsch | .15 |
| 192 | John Franco | .25 |
| 193 | Von Hayes | .30 |
| 194 | Tri-Stars: | .25 |
| | Aase, Righetti, Eichhorn | |
| 195 | Tri-Stars: | .35 |
| | Hernandez, Clark, Davis | |
| 196 | Hi-Lite Tri-Stars: | .50 |
| | Clemens, Cowley, Horner | |
| 197 | Big 6: | 1.00 |
| | Brett, Brooks, Gwynn, Sandberg, Raines, Boggs | |
| 198 | Tri-Stars: | .35 |
| | Puckett, Henderson, Lynn | |
| 199 | Speedburners: | .50 |
| | Raines, Coleman, Davis | |
| 200 | Steve Carlton | .35 |

## 1988 Sportflics. . . .Complete Set of 225 Cards—Value $35.00

Features the rookie cards of Matt Nokes, Ellis Burks and Sam Horn.

| NO. | PLAYER | MINT |
|---|---|---|
| 1 | Don Mattingly | 2.50 |
| 2 | Tim Raines | .40 |
| 3 | Andre Dawson | .40 |
| 4 | George Bell | .40 |
| 5 | Joe Carter | .35 |
| 6 | Matt Nokes (R) | .65 |
| 7 | Dave Winfield | .35 |
| 8 | Kirby Puckett | .60 |
| 9 | Will Clark | .75 |
| 10 | Eric Davis | 1.00 |
| 11 | Rickey Henderson | .50 |
| 12 | Ryne Sandberg | .30 |
| 13 | Jesse Barfield | .35 |
| 14 | Ozzie Guillen | .20 |
| 15 | Bret Saberhagen | .25 |
| 16 | Tony Gwynn | .50 |
| 17 | Kevin Seitzer | 1.00 |
| 18 | Jack Clark | .30 |
| 19 | Danny Tartabull | .45 |
| 20 | Ted Higuera | .30 |
| 21 | Charlie Liebrandt, Jr. | .12 |
| 22 | Benny Santiago | .75 |
| 23 | Fred Lynn | .20 |
| 24 | Rob Thompson | .15 |
| 25 | Alan Trammell | .35 |
| 26 | T. Fernandez | .35 |
| 27 | Rick Sutcliffe | .25 |
| 28 | Gary Carter | .35 |
| 29 | Cory Snyder | .50 |
| 30 | Lou Whitaker | .30 |
| 31 | Keith Hernandez | .35 |
| 32 | Mike Witt | .20 |
| 33 | Harold Baines | .25 |
| 34 | Robin Yount | .40 |
| 35 | Mike Schmidt | .75 |
| 36 | Dion James | .12 |
| 37 | Tom Candiotti | .12 |
| 38 | Tracy Jones | .25 |
| 39 | Nolan Ryan | .50 |
| 40 | Fernando Valenzuela | .40 |
| 41 | Vance Law | .12 |
| 42 | Roger McDowell | .12 |
| 43 | Carlton Fisk | .25 |
| 44 | Scott Garrelts | .15 |
| 45 | Lee Guetterman | .15 |
| 46 | Mark Langston | .30 |
| 47 | Willie Randolph | .20 |
| 48 | Bill Doran | .25 |
| 49 | Larry Parrish | .12 |
| 50 | Wade Boggs | 1.50 |
| 51 | Shan Rawley | .12 |
| 52 | Alvin Davis | .12 |
| 53 | Jeff Reardon | .15 |
| 54 | Jim Presley | .30 |
| 55 | Kevin Bass | .25 |
| 56 | Kevin McReynolds | .25 |
| 57 | B.J. Surhoff | .30 |
| 58 | Julio Franco | .20 |
| 59 | Eddie Murray | .50 |
| 60 | Jody Davis | .12 |
| 61 | Todd Worrell | .20 |
| 62 | Von Hayes | .25 |
| 63 | Billy Hatcher | .25 |
| 64 | John Kruk | .35 |
| 65 | Tom Henke | .12 |
| 66 | Mike Scott | .25 |
| 67 | Vince Coleman | .40 |
| 68 | Ozzie Smith | .45 |
| 69 | Ken Williams | .25 |
| 70 | Steve Bedrosian | .25 |
| 71 | Luis Polonia | .35 |
| 72 | Brook Jacoby | .20 |
| 73 | Ron Darling | .30 |
| 74 | Lloyd Moseby | .30 |
| 75 | Wally Joyner | .60 |
| 76 | Dan Quisenberry | .25 |
| 77 | Scott Fletcher | .12 |
| 78 | Kirk McKaskill | .12 |
| 79 | Paul Molitor | .35 |
| 80 | Mike Aldrete | .20 |
| 81 | Neal Heaton | .12 |
| 82 | Jeffrey Leonard | .25 |
| 83 | Dave Magadan | .20 |
| 84 | Danny Cox | .25 |
| 85 | Lance McCullers | .12 |
| 86 | Jay Howell | .12 |
| 87 | Charlie Hough | .12 |
| 88 | Gene Garber | .12 |
| 89 | Jesse Orosco | .12 |
| 90 | Don Robinson | .12 |
| 91 | Willie McGee | .25 |
| 92 | Bert Blyleven | .12 |
| 93 | Phil Bradley | .25 |
| 94 | Terry Kennedy | .12 |
| 95 | Kent Hrbek | .35 |
| 96 | Juan Samuel | .25 |
| 97 | Pedro Guerrero | .30 |
| 98 | Sid Bream | .12 |
| 99 | Devon White | .40 |
| 100 | Mark McGwire | 1.50 |
| 101 | Dave Parker | .35 |
| 102 | Glen Davis | .25 |
| 103 | Greg Walker | .20 |
| 104 | Rick Rhoden | .15 |
| 105 | Mitch Webster | .12 |
| 106 | Lenny Dykstra | .15 |
| 107 | Gene Larkin | .30 |
| 108 | Floyd Youmans | .15 |
| 109 | Andy Van Slyke | .40 |
| 110 | Mike Scioscia | .12 |
| 111 | Kirk Gibson | .50 |
| 112 | Kal Daniels | .40 |
| 113 | Ruben Sierra | .50 |
| 114 | Sam Horn (R) | .50 |
| 115 | Ray Knight | .25 |
| 116 | Jimmy Key | .15 |
| 117 | Bo Diaz | .12 |
| 118 | Mike Greenwell | 1.25 |
| 119 | Barry Bonds | .60 |
| 120 | Reggie Jackson | .50 |
| 121 | Mike Pagliarulo | .20 |
| 122 | Tommy John | .30 |
| 123 | Bill Madlock | .25 |
| 124 | Ken Caminiti | .40 |
| 125 | Gary Ward | .15 |
| 126 | Candy Maldonado | .30 |
| 127 | Harold Reynolds | .15 |
| 128 | Joe Magrane | .40 |
| 129 | Mike Henneman | .35 |
| 130 | Jim Gantner | .12 |
| 131 | Bobby Bonilla | .40 |
| 132 | John Farrell | .35 |
| 133 | Frank Tanana | .25 |
| 134 | Zane Smith | .20 |
| 135 | Dave Righetti | .30 |
| 136 | Rick Reuschel | .25 |
| 137 | Dwight Evans | .30 |
| 138 | Howard Johnson | .35 |
| 139 | Terry Leach | .20 |
| 140 | Casey Candaele | .20 |
| 141 | Tom Herr | .15 |
| 142 | Tony Pena | .15 |
| 143 | Lance Parrish | .25 |
| 144 | Ellis Burks (R) | 1.00 |
| 145 | Pete O'Brien | .20 |
| 146 | Mike Boddicker | .25 |
| 147 | Buddy Bell | .25 |
| 148 | Bo Jackson | .60 |
| 149 | Frank White | .15 |
| 150 | George Brett | .50 |
| 151 | Tim Wallach | .25 |
| 152 | Cal Ripken, Jr. | .45 |
| 153 | Brett Butler | .20 |
| 154 | Gary Gaetti | .35 |
| 155 | Darryl Strawberry | 1.00 |
| 156 | Alredo Griffin | .20 |
| 157 | Marty Barrett | .30 |
| 158 | Jim Rice | .40 |
| 159 | Terry Pendleton | .15 |
| 160 | Orel Hershiser | .60 |
| 161 | Larry Sheets | .25 |
| 162 | Dave Stewart | .25 |
| 163 | Shawon Dunston | .20 |
| 164 | Keith Moreland | .15 |
| 165 | Ken Oberkfell | .15 |
| 166 | Ivan Calderon | .30 |
| 167 | Bob Welch | .25 |
| 168 | Fred McGriff | .60 |
| 169 | Pete Incaviglia | .40 |
| 170 | Dale Murphy | .60 |
| 171 | Mike Dunne | .35 |
| 172 | Chili Davis | .20 |
| 173 | Milt Thompson | .20 |
| 174 | Terry Steinbach | .30 |
| 175 | Oddibe McDowell | .20 |
| 176 | Jack Morris | .35 |
| 177 | Sid Fernandez | .30 |
| 178 | Ken Griffey | .15 |
| 179 | Lee Smith | .15 |
| 180 | Hi-Lite Tri-Stars: | .30 |
| | Puckett, Nieves, Schmidt | |
| 181 | Brian Downing | .15 |
| 182 | Andres Galarraga | .40 |
| 183 | Rob Deer | .20 |
| 184 | Greg Brock | .12 |
| 185 | Doug DeCinces | .12 |
| 186 | Johnny Ray | .12 |
| 187 | Hubie Brooks | .12 |
| 188 | Darrell Evans | .20 |
| 189 | Mel Hall | .20 |
| 190 | Jim Deshaies | .12 |
| 191 | Dan Plesac | .20 |
| 192 | Willie Wilson | .12 |
| 193 | Mike LaValliere | .12 |
| 194 | Tom Brunansky | .25 |
| 195 | John Franco | .25 |
| 196 | Frank Viola | .35 |
| 197 | Bruce Hurst | .30 |
| 198 | John Tudor | .25 |
| 199 | Bob Forsch | .15 |
| 200 | Dwight Gooden | 1.00 |
| 201 | Jose Canseco | 2.00 |
| 202 | Carney Lansford | .15 |
| 203 | Kelly Downs | .15 |
| 204 | Glenn Wilson | .15 |
| 205 | Pat Tabler | .15 |
| 206 | Mike Davis | .15 |
| 207 | Roger Clemens | 1.00 |
| 208 | Dave Smith | .15 |
| 209 | Curt Young | .15 |
| 210 | Mark Eichhorn | .15 |
| 211 | Juan Nieves | .15 |
| 212 | Bob Boone | .15 |
| 213 | Don Sutton | .35 |
| 214 | Cecil Upshaw | .15 |
| 215 | Jim Clancy | .15 |
| 216 | Bill Ripken (R) | .35 |
| 217 | Ozzie Virgil | .15 |
| 218 | Dave Concepcion | .15 |
| 219 | Alan Ashby | .15 |
| 220 | Mike Marshall | .25 |
| 221 | Hi-Lite Tri-Stars: | .75 |
| | McGwire, Molitor, Coleman | |
| 222 | Hi-Lite Tri-Stars: | .75 |
| | Santiago, Bedrosian, Mattingly | |
| 223 | Rookies: | 1.00 |
| | Shawn Abner, Jay Buhner, Gary Thurman | |
| 224 | Rookies: | .50 |
| | Tim Crews, Vincente Palacios, John Davis | |
| 225 | Rookies: | .75 |
| | Jody Reed, Jeff Treadway, Keith Miller | |

# 1989 Sportflics.... Complete Set of 225 Cards—Value $35.00

Features the rookie cards of Mike Harkey, Gary Sheffield and Ron Jones.

| NO. | PLAYER | MINT | | NO. | PLAYER | MINT | | NO. | PLAYER | MINT | | NO. | PLAYER | MINT |
|---|---|---|---|---|---|---|---|---|---|---|---|---|---|---|
| 1 | Jose Canseco | 1.75 | | 58 | Steve Sax | .15 | | 114 | Tim Wallach | .15 | | 170 | Will Clark | .75 |
| 2 | Wally Joyner | .35 | | 59 | Lance Parrish | .15 | | 115 | Nolan Ryan | .20 | | 171 | Chet Lemon | .12 |
| 3 | Roger Clemens | .75 | | 60 | Keith Hernandez | .20 | | 116 | Walt Weiss | 1.00 | | 172 | Pat Tabler | .12 |
| 4 | Greg Swindell | .15 | | 61 | Jose Uribe | .12 | | 117 | Brian Downing | .12 | | 173 | Jim Rice | .20 |
| 5 | Jack Morris | .15 | | 62 | Jose Lind | .12 | | 118 | Melido Perez | .15 | | 174 | Billy Hatcher | .12 |
| 6 | Mickey Brantley | .12 | | 63 | Steve Bedrosian | .12 | | 119 | Terry Steinbach | .20 | | 175 | Bruce Hurst | .20 |
| 7 | Jim Presley | .12 | | 64 | George Brett | .40 | | 120 | Mike Scott | .20 | | 176 | John Franco | .15 |
| 8 | Pete O'Brien | .15 | | 65 | Kirk Gibson | .20 | | 121 | Tim Belcher | .15 | | 177 | Van Snider | .50 |
| 9 | Jesse Barfield | .15 | | 66 | Cal Ripken Jr. | .30 | | 122 | Mike Boddicker | .15 | | 178 | Ron Jones | 1.00 |
| 10 | Frank Viola | .20 | | 67 | Mitch Webster | .12 | | 123 | Len Dykstra | .20 | | 179 | Jerald Clark | .25 |
| 11 | Kevin Bass | .12 | | 68 | Fred Lynn | .15 | | 124 | Fernando Valenzuela | .20 | | 180 | Tom Browning | .15 |
| 12 | Glenn Wilson | .12 | | 69 | Eric Davis | .75 | | 125 | Gerald Young | .15 | | 181 | Von Hayes | .12 |
| 13 | Chris Sabo | 1.50 | | 70 | Bo Jackson | .35 | | 126 | Tom Henke | .12 | | 182 | Bobby Bonilla | .25 |
| 14 | Fred McGriff | .65 | | 71 | Kevin Elster | .15 | | 127 | Dave Henderson | .15 | | 183 | Todd Worrell | .12 |
| 15 | Mark Grace | 1.25 | | 72 | Rick Reuschel | .12 | | 128 | Dan Plesac | .12 | | 184 | John Kruk | .12 |
| 16 | Devon White | .12 | | 73 | Tim Burke | .12 | | 129 | Chili Davis | .12 | | 185 | Scott Fletcher | .12 |
| 17 | Juan Samuel | .15 | | 74 | Mark Davis | .12 | | 130 | Bryan Harvey | .45 | | 186 | Willie Wilson | .15 |
| 18 | Lou Whitaker | .15 | | 75 | Claudell Washington | .15 | | 131 | Don August | .20 | | 187 | Jody Davis | .12 |
| 19 | Greg Walker | .12 | | 76 | Lance McCullers | .15 | | 132 | Mike Harkey | 1.00 | | 188 | Kent Hrbek | .15 |
| 20 | Roberto Alomar | .30 | | 77 | Mike Moore | .12 | | 133 | Luis Polonia | .12 | | 189 | Ruben Sierra | .25 |
| 21 | Mike Schmidt | .35 | | 78 | Robby Thompson | .12 | | 134 | Craig Worthington | .35 | | 190 | Shawon Dunston | .15 |
| 22 | Benny Santiago | .20 | | 79 | Roger McDowell | .15 | | 135 | Joey Meyer | .12 | | 191 | Ellis Burks | .50 |
| 23 | Dave Stewart | .20 | | 80 | Danny Jackson | .20 | | 136 | Barry Larkin | .15 | | 192 | Brook Jacoby | .12 |
| 24 | Dave Winfield | .20 | | 81 | Tim Leary | .15 | | 137 | Glenn Davis | .20 | | 193 | Jeff Robinson | .25 |
| 25 | George Bell | .12 | | 82 | Bobby Witt | .15 | | 138 | Mike Scioscia | .12 | | 194 | Rich Dotson | .15 |
| 26 | J. Clark | .20 | | 83 | Jim Gott | .12 | | 139 | Andres Galarraga | .35 | | 195 | Johnny Ray | .15 |
| 27 | Doug Drabek | .15 | | 84 | Andy Hawkins | .12 | | 140 | Dwight Gooden | .50 | | 196 | Cory Snyder | .20 |
| 28 | Ron Gant | .45 | | 85 | Ozzie Guillen | .15 | | 141 | Keith Moreland | .12 | | 197 | Mike Witt | .12 |
| 29 | Glenn Braggs | .12 | | 86 | John Tudor | .12 | | 142 | Kevin Mitchell | .15 | | 198 | Marty Barrett | .12 |
| 30 | Rafael Palmeiro | .25 | | 87 | Todd Burns | .35 | | 143 | Mike Greenwell | 1.50 | | 199 | Robin Yount | .20 |
| 31 | Brett Butler | .12 | | 88 | Dave Gallagher | .20 | | 144 | Mel Hall | .12 | | 200 | Mark McGwire | 1.00 |
| 32 | Ron Darling | .20 | | 89 | Jay Buhner | .40 | | 145 | Rickey Henderson | .40 | | 201 | Ryne Sandberg | .20 |
| 33 | Alvin Davis | .20 | | 90 | Gregg Jefferies | 2.75 | | 146 | Barry Bonds | .30 | | 202 | John Candelaria | .15 |
| 34 | Bob Walk | .12 | | 91 | Bob Welch | .15 | | 147 | Eddie Murray | .35 | | 203 | Matt Nokes | .15 |
| 35 | Dave Stieb | .15 | | 92 | Charlie Hough | .15 | | 148 | Lee Smith | .15 | | 204 | Dwight Evans | .20 |
| 36 | Orel Hershiser | .35 | | 93 | Tony Fernandez | .20 | | 149 | Julio Franco | .15 | | 205 | Darryl Strawberry | .75 |
| 37 | John Farrell | .15 | | 94 | Ozzie Virgil | .12 | | 150 | Tim Raines | .20 | | 206 | Willie McGee | .15 |
| 38 | Doug Jones | .12 | | 95 | Andre Dawson | .25 | | 151 | Mitch Williams | .12 | | 207 | Bobby Thigpen | .12 |
| 39 | Kelly Downs | .12 | | 96 | Hubie Brooks | .12 | | 152 | Tim Laudner | .12 | | 208 | B.J. Surhoff | .12 |
| 40 | Bob Boone | .12 | | 97 | Kevin McReynolds | .20 | | 153 | Mike Pagliarulo | .15 | | 209 | Paul Molitor | .15 |
| 41 | Gary Sheffield | 2.00 | | 98 | Mike LaValliere | .12 | | 154 | Floyd Bannister | .12 | | 210 | Jody Reed | .20 |
| 42 | Doug Dascenzo | .30 | | 99 | Terry Pendleton | .12 | | 155 | Gary Carter | .25 | | 211 | Doyle Alexander | .15 |
| 43 | Chad Krueter | .25 | | 100 | Wade Boggs | 1.00 | | 156 | Kirby Puckett | .40 | | 212 | Dennis Rasmussen | .12 |
| 44 | Ricky Jordan | 2.75 | | 101 | Dennis Eckersley | .15 | | 157 | Harold Baines | .15 | | 213 | Kevin Gross | .12 |
| 45 | Dave West | 1.00 | | 102 | Mark Gubicza | .20 | | 158 | Dave Righetti | .20 | | 214 | Kirk McCaskill | .12 |
| 46 | Danny Tartabull | .15 | | 103 | Frank Tanana | .15 | | 159 | Mark Langston | .15 | | 215 | Alan Trammell | .20 |
| 47 | Teddy Higuera | .15 | | 104 | Joe Carter | .25 | | 160 | Tony Gwynn | .50 | | 216 | Damon Berryhill | .35 |
| 48 | Gary Gaetti | .15 | | 105 | Ozzie Smith | .20 | | 161 | Tom Brunansky | .15 | | 217 | Rick Sutcliffe | .15 |
| 49 | Dave Parker | .15 | | 106 | Dennis Martinez | .15 | | 162 | Vance Law | .15 | | 218 | Don Slaught | .12 |
| 50 | Don Mattingly | 1.75 | | 107 | Jeff Treadway | .20 | | 163 | Kelly Gruber | .12 | | 219 | Carlton Fisk | .20 |
| 51 | David Cone | .75 | | 108 | Greg Maddux | .25 | | 164 | Gerald Perry | .15 | | 220 | Allan Anderson | .20 |
| 52 | Kal Daniels | .20 | | 109 | Bret Saberhagen | .20 | | 165 | Harold Reynolds | .12 | | 221 | Boggs, Canseco, |  |
| 53 | Carney Lansford | .15 | | 110 | Dale Murphy | .35 | | 166 | Andy Van Slyke | .20 | |  | Greenwell | 1.25 |
| 54 | Mike Marshall | .12 | | 111 | Rob Deer | .15 | | 167 | Jimmy Key | .20 | | 222 | Hershiser, Eckersley, |  |
| 55 | Kevin Seitzer | .45 | | 112 | Pete Incaviglia | .15 | | 168 | Jeff Reardon | .15 | |  | Browning | .75 |
| 56 | Mike Henneman | .15 | | 113 | Vince Coleman | .20 | | 169 | Milt Thompson | .12 | | 223 | Sheffield, Jefferies, Alomar | 2.00 |
| 57 | Bill Doran | .12 | |  |  |  | |  |  |  | | 224 | Milacki, Johnson, Martinez | .75 |
|  |  |  | |  |  |  | |  |  |  | | 225 | Drew, Berroa, Jones | .75 |

Card values shown here fluctuate considerably.

# SPECIAL CARD SETS

## TOPPS®

| Year | Description | Cards in Set | Value Mint |
|------|-------------|:---:|---:|
| 1988 | Lim. Ed. Glossy ............. | 792 | $120.00 |
| 1988 | All-Star Glossy (insert) ...... | 22 | 4.00 |
| 1988 | All-Star Glossy (col. ed) ..... | 60 | 13.00 |
| 1988 | Rookies Glossy ............. | 22 | 8.00 |
| 1988 | League Leaders (mini) ....... | 77 | 6.00 |
| 1988 | Big Baseball (series 1) ....... | 88 | 12.00 |
| 1988 | Big Baseball (series 2) ....... | 88 | 12.00 |
| 1988 | Big Baseball (series 3) ....... | 88 | 12.00 |
| 1987 | Lim. Ed. Glossy & Update .... | 924 | 140.00 |
| 1987 | All-Star Glossy (insert) ...... | 22 | 4.00 |
| 1987 | All-Star Glossy (col. ed) ..... | 60 | 12.00 |
| 1987 | Rookies Glossy (insert) ...... | 22 | 8.00 |
| 1987 | Glossy ................... | 40 | 12.00 |
| 1987 | League Leaders (mini) ....... | 77 | 7.50 |
| 1987 | Coins ................... | 48 | 10.00 |
| 1986 | Lim. Ed. Glossy & Update .... | 924 | 250.00 |
| 1986 | All-Star Glossy (mail-in) ..... | 60 | 16.00 |
| 1986 | Mini ..................... | 66 | 8.00 |
| 1986 | Three Dimensional ......... | 30 | 12.00 |
| 1986 | All-Star-Glossy (insert) ...... | 22 | 4.00 |
| 1986 | Super ................... | 60 | 10.00 |
| 1985 | Lim. Ed. Glossy & Update .... | 924 | 500.00 |
| 1985 | Three-Dimensional ......... | 30 | 15.00 |
| 1985 | All-Star-Glossy (mail-in) ..... | 40 | 12.00 |
| 1985 | All-Star-Glossy (insert) ...... | 22 | 4.00 |
| 1985 | Super ................... | 60 | 14.00 |
| 1984 | Lim. Ed. Glossy & Update | 924 | $500.00 |
| 1984 | All-Star Glossy (mail-in).... | 40 | 12.00 |
| 1984 | All-Star-Glossy (insert)..... | 22 | 5.00 |
| 1984 | Super .................... | 30 | 9.00 |
| 1983 | All-Star-Glossy (mail-in) ... | 40 | 12.00 |
| 1981 | Star Photo ................ | 15 | 5.00 |
| 1981 | Team Photo .............. | 102 | 35.00 |
| 1980 | Star Photo ................ | 60 | 7.50 |
| 1977 | Cloth Stickers ............. | 73 | 50.00 |
| 1975 | Mini .................... | 660 | 750.00 |
| 1974 | Team Checklist............. | 24 | 8.00 |
| 1971 | Greatest Moments ......... | 55 | 1,000.00 |
| 1971 | Super .................... | 63 | 150.00 |
| 1970 | Super .................... | 42 | 150.00 |
| 1969 | Deckle Edge................ | 33 | 50.00 |
| 1969 | Super .................... | 66 | 3,000.00 |
| 1968 | Three Dimensional ......... | 12 | 5,000.00 |
| 1968 | Game Cards ............... | 33 | 45.00 |
| 1965 | Gold Foil Embossed ....... | 72 | 60.00 |
| 1964 | Die-Cut .................. | 77 | 1,250.00 |
| 1964 | Giant ................... | 60 | 60.00 |
| 1955 | Double Header ............ | 66 | 2,000.00 |
| 1951 | Connie Mack All-Stars ..... | 11 | 4,000.00 |
| 1951 | Team Cards .............. | 9 | 1,000.00 |
| 1951 | Major-League All-Stars..... | 11 | 17,000.00 |

## DONRUSS®

| Year | Description | Cards in Set | Value Mint |
|------|-------------|:---:|---:|
| 1988 | Super Diamond Kings ....... | 27 | $6.50 |
| 1988 | Rookies ................. | 56 | 11.00 |
| 1988 | Pop-Ups.................. | 20 | 5.00 |
| 1988 | Action All-Stars ............. | 64 | 6.00 |
| 1988 | Baseball's Best ........... | 336 | 20.00 |
| 1987 | Opening Day .............. | 272 | 20.00 |
| 1987 | Super Diamond Kings ....... | 28 | 9.00 |
| 1987 | Rookies ................. | 56 | 15.00 |
| 1987 | Pop-Ups.................. | 20 | 6.00 |
| 1987 | Action All-Stars ............. | 60 | 6.00 |
| 1987 | Highlights ................. | 56 | 8.00 |
| 1986 | Super Diamond Kings ....... | 28 | 9.00 |
| 1986 | Rookies ................. | 56 | 15.00 |
| 1986 | Pop-Ups.................. | 18 | 4.00 |
| 1986 | Action All-Stars ............. | 60 | 7.00 |
| 1986 | Highlights ................. | 56 | 6.00 |
| 1985 | Super Diamond Kings ....... | 28 | 9.00 |
| 1985 | Action All-Stars ............. | 60 | 7.00 |
| 1985 | Highlights ................. | 56 | 25.00 |
| 1984 | Champions ............... | 60 | 7.00 |
| 1984 | Action All-Stars ............. | 60 | 7.00 |
| 1983 | Hall of Fame Heroes........ | 44 | 4.00 |
| 1983 | Action All-Stars ............. | 60 | 7.00 |

## FLEER®

| Year | Description | Cards in Set | Value Mint |
|------|-------------|:---:|---:|
| 1988 | Glossy (tin) ................ | 660 | $45.00 |
| 1988 | Update Glossy (tin) ......... | 132 | 20.00 |
| 1988 | Classic-Mini ................ | 120 | 80.00 |
| 1988 | All-Star Team .............. | 12 | 15.00 |
| 1988 | World Series .............. | 12 | 3.00 |
| 1987 | Glossy (tin) ................ | 660 | 45.00 |
| 1987 | Update Glossy (tin) ......... | 132 | 15.00 |
| 1987 | Classic Mini ............... | 120 | 10.00 |
| 1987 | All-Star Team .............. | 12 | 15.00 |
| 1987 | World Series .............. | 12 | 4.00 |
| 1987 | Headliners.................. | 6 | 7.00 |
| 1986 | Classic Mini ............... | 120 | 10.00 |
| 1986 | All-Star Team .............. | 12 | 16.00 |
| 1986 | Future Hall of Famers ....... | 6 | 8.00 |

## SCORE

| Year | Description | Cards in Set | Value Mint |
|------|-------------|:---:|---:|
| 1988 | Young Superstars (1) ........ | 40 | $5.00 |
| 1988 | Young Superstars (2) ........ | 40 | 5.00 |
| 1988 | Rookie Traded ............. | 110 | 10.00 |

## SPORTFLICS

| Year | Description | Cards in Set | Value Mint |
|------|-------------|:---:|---:|
| 1988 | Rookies ................... | 25 | $7.00 |
| 1987 | Rookies (series 1) .......... | 25 | 10.00 |
| 1987 | Rookies (series 2) .......... | 25 | 8.00 |
| 1987 | Rookie Prospects .......... | 10 | 9.00 |
| 1987 | Team Preview.............. | 26 | 9.00 |
| 1986 | Rookies ................... | 50 | 15.00 |
| 1986 | Decade Greats ............. | 75 | 15.00 |